East Africa

Red Sea

ERITREA

YEMEN

□ ASMARA ○ Massawa

Gulf of Aden

○ Adowa

○ Gondar

DJIBOUTI
□ DJIBOUTI

Bure ○

○ Debre Markos

SOMALIA

ADDIS ABABA □ ✈ ○ Awash

○ Gambela ETHIOPIA

○ Jimma

Bonga ○ ○ Yirga' Alem ○ Goba ○ Danan

SUDAN

Lake Abaya

○ Moyale

Lake Turkana

○ Arua ○ Gulu

○ Soroti KENYA

UGANDA

Fort Portal ○ ○ Kitale

□ ✈ KAMPALA Tororo ○

Thika ○ 🏔 *Kenya (5,199m)* ○ Garissa

Lake Kivu ✈ □ NAIROBI

RWANDA *Lake Victoria* ○ Musoma

○ Mwanza Meru (4,556m) 🏔 🏔 *Kilimanjaro (5,896m)* ○ Malindi

BURUNDI Arusha ○

Kigoma ○ Nzega ○ Singida ○ ○ Kondoa ✈ ○ Mombasa

Ujiji ○ Tabora ○ Tanga ○

TANZANIA Manyoni ○ ○ Zanzibar

Dodoma ○

Lake Tanganyika Rungwa ○ Morogoro ○ □ ✈ DAR ES SALAAM

Sumbawanga ○ ○ Iringa

Kasanga ○ ○ Ifakara Indian Ocean

○ Mahenge

N

ZAMBIA ○ Lindi

○ Mtwara 0 km   200

Lake Nyasa

MOÇAMBIQUE

MALAWI

East Africa Handbook

Published by Footprint Handbooks
6 Riverside Court
Lower Bristol Road
Bath BA2 3DZ. England
T +44 (0)1225 469141
F +44 (0)1225 469461
Email info@footprintbooks.com
Web www.footprintbooks.com

ISBN 1 900949 42 3
ISSN 1352-7886
CIP DATA: A catalogue record for this
book is available from the British Library

In USA, published by
Passport Books, a division of
NTC/Contemporary Publishing Group
4255 West Touhy Avenue, Lincolnwood
(Chicago), Illinois 60712-1975, USA
T 847 679 5500 F 847 679 24941
Email NTCPUB2@AOL.COM

ISBN 0-8442-4630-1
Library of Congress Catalog Card
Number: 99-74366

© Footprint Handbooks Ltd 1999
Sixth edition

Credits

Series editor
Patrick Dawson
Editorial
Senior editor: Sarah Thorowgood
Editor: Jo Williams
Maps: Sarah Sorensen
Production
Pre-press Manager: Jo Morgan
Typesetting: Ann Griffiths, Emma Bryers,
Emily Stapleton and Bookcraft Ltd
Maps: Kevin Feeney, Richard Ponsford,
Robert Lunn, Claire Benison, Alasdair
Dawson, Angus Dawson and Map
Creation Ltd
Proof reading: Tim Heybyrne, Nikki Koek,
Emily Palmer and Caroline Dawson

Design
Mytton Williams

Photography
Front cover: Alex Webb, Magnum Photos
Back cover: Tony Stone ImagesI
Colour section: Impact Photos Pictures
Colour Library; Robert Harding Picture
Library; La Belle Aurore (Steve Davey);
Pineapple Makasero Market; Images of
Africa; Eye Ubiquitous; Tony Stone
Images

Printed and bound
in Italy by LEGOPRINT

Footprint

East Africa

Handbook

Michael Hodd

*You must know that the giraffe is short in the body
and slopes down towards the rear, because its
hind legs are short … It has a small head and does
not harm anyone. Its colour is dappled red and
white. And a very pretty sight it is.*

Marco Polo, *Description of the World* (1298)

Contents

Left: Tinga Tinga paintings from Tanzania.

Right: street on Lamu Island, off the coast of Kenya.

A foot in the door

Highlights

You will find many special people, animals and places throughout Africa, but it is only in the east of the continent that you will find great mountain gorillas, swathes of pink flamingoes, the snow-capped, tropical mountains of Kilimanjaro, Kenya and the Rwenzoris, views over the great Rift Valley, the Blue Nile Gorge and the Tissisat falls of Ethiopia; not to mention Indian Ocean islands with unique blends of African and Arabic cultures, the magnificent Masai people, and the legacies of Persian, Portuguese, Omani, German, British, French, Italian and Belgian settlements.

Wildlife There is nowhere better than the great National Parks of East Africa to see the 'big nine' – elephant, rhino, buffalo, lion, leopard, cheetah, hippo, zebra, and giraffe – all in their natural surroundings. The bird-life, although less celebrated, is also exceptional and you should not be surprised to see spectacular vultures, marabou storks, cranes, flamingoes and ostriches. Reptiles, including crocodiles, abound and even many of the insects have fascinating habits and life-cycles. Flowering trees such as jacarandas, flame trees, corals and flamboyants, colourful and heavy with the scents of the tropics, are everywhere. And then there are the crops: tea plantations, sweet-smelling coffee trees, purple-flowered banana trees, fields of pyrethrum and miles of spiky sisal.

Coast The Indian Ocean shore is one of East Africa's glories. The mainland has glittering palm-fringed beaches of fine white sand and the ancient towns of Malindi, Mombasa, Pangani and Bagamoyo. The coral reefs have brilliant marine life which can be viewed by snorkelling or diving. The wonderful islands of Lamu, Zanzibar, Pemba and Mafia each have their own special charms and culture.

People East Africa is made up of numerous different cultural groups. There are many opportunities to see traditional dances, rituals, festivals and celebrations performed in exotic costume: the magnificent warriors of the Masai, Kamba and Turkana in Kenya; the wood-carving Makonde in Tanzania; Uganda with its traditional Kingdoms; the unique style and customs of the peoples of Ethiopia and Eritrea.

City life The capital cities and the major towns are also worth spending time getting to know. There is the sophistication of Nairobi, with great hotels, exciting nightlife, a wide range of restaurants, museums and galleries. Kampala is judged by many as the most beautiful city in Africa, green and cool, surrounded by seven hills. Dar es Salaam is in a magnificent harbour setting. There are the wide boulevards of Addis Ababa. The charm of Asmara with its Mediterranean architecture spilling over with bougainvillea. Everywhere there are displays of brightly coloured cloth, vegetables, fruits, locally-crafted utensils and implements in local markets; the bustle of crowded buses, *dala dala*, *matatus* and *boda boda*; street kiosks with charcoal-grilled food; bands in bars and clubs playing thrilling *lingala* music; churches packed with singing worshippers.

Art African art is quite unique in its inspiration and in the imagination of its designs. This is particularly true of wood-carvings, with their exaggerated and fantastically conceived figures. Pottery is made with red clay, intricate patterning and fired in open pits. Cloth is woven from cotton and wool, sometimes with batik designs. Traditional leatherwork is sun-dried and cured with clotted milk and linseed oil and horn is carved and polished to make drinking vessels, boxes and ornaments. Jewellery is twisted from silver, copper, brass and amber and basketwork and woven mats are crafted from banana leaves, reeds and sisal.

Left: woman carrying firewood on North beach at Mombasa, Kenya. *Below*: Amboseli National Park and Mount Kilimanjaro, Kenya.

Bottom left: street musicians in Kampala, Uganda's capital. *Bottom right*: stall selling pineapples in Nakasero Market, Kampala, Uganda.

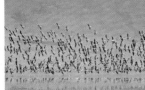

Top left: huge flock of Lesser Flamingoes flying over Lake Magadi, Ngorongoro Crater, Tanzania. *Top right*: hot air balloon landing amongst wildebeest herds, Masai Mara, Kenya. **Above**: large Baobab tree in Arusha National Park, Tanzania. **Right**: tree-climbing lion from the Ngorongoro crater.

Safari

Safari means "a journey" in Swahili (the language of the coastal people of East Africa), but for the visitor it has a special meaning – going up-country to see the most wondrous display of wildlife to be found anywhere on this earth. For most visitors, a trip to the great parks will be the highlight of their visit. It is a great adventure – in Nairobi and Arusha you can just feel the excitement of groups about to set off. If at all possible, visit the parks as part of a camping safari – or at the very least, stay in one of the tented camps. Such a safari is a unique experience, the atmosphere is very special and you will be well looked after by the staff.

Just close to Kenya's capital is the Nairobi National Park, and even if you are not able to travel up-country, visit this park in the early morning or at dusk and with a bit of luck, half-an-hour from the city, you will see lions, leopards, cheetahs, zebras, giraffes, buffaloes, hippos and antelopes. **Nairobi National Park**

The Masai Mara has a wealth of game that will take your breath away. It is an unforgettable experience to take off at dawn in a hot-air balloon and drift serenely over the landscape as the sun rises. There are many other fine parks in Kenya, including Lake Nakuru where millions of spectacular pink flamingoes wade on the lake shore. **Masai Mara, Lake Nakuru**

In Tanzania the Serengeti is very special, particularly at the beginning of the dry season (around the end of June), when a million-and-a-half wildebeest stampede north, plunging through rivers, struggling to keep up with the herd, whilst fighting off predatory lions and leopards. Nearby Ngorongoro is an extinct volcanic crater about 20 kilometres across. The rim, about half a kilometre above the crater floor, provides glorious views and all the big nine are there – even hippos in the small lake on the crater floor. Lake Manyara has a special charm – its abundant birdlife includes swathes of shimmering pink flamingoes and it is famous for its tree-climbing lions. **Serengeti, Ngorongoro, Lake Manyara**

Only a few hundred of Africa's mighty mountain gorillas survive. They can be seen close-up in the Virungu Mountains, bordered by Rwanda, R D Congo (formerly Zaire) and Uganda. Visits are once again possible to the colony in Rwanda pioneered by Dian Fossey and improved security has allowed gorilla visits to resume in Uganda's Bwindi Forest. Another unique experience is a close-up visit to the chimpanzees made famous by Jane Goodall, at Gombe Stream on the shore of Lake Tanganyika. **Gorillas & chimpanzees**

Mount Kilimanjaro (the highest peak in Africa) and Mount Kenya offer special challenges. They are both high enough to be topped by snow and ice all the year round, despite being close to the equator. Both can be climbed by the reasonably active, though it must be said that they can be demanding and the last section of Mount Kenya can only be managed by experienced climbers. A memorable adventure in Uganda is to go white-water rafting on the rapids of the Nile, on one of the well-organized trips from Kampala. **Mountains and rivers**

When you are on safari it can be tough: in the dry weather it is dusty, in the wet the roads can be difficult or impassable, the rain, when it arrives, is like standing under a waterfall and the tracks are rough and bumpy. There is a challenge and a sense of achievement in coming through it all. But having washed off the dust of the day and changed into fresh clothes, there is nothing quite like a sundowner in the cool of the evening by the campfire, with the aroma of an evening meal being prepared, a blood-red sunset, a velvety dusk and the exotic sounds and scents of the African night. **Sundown**

Swahili

Swahili is the language and culture of the people of the East African coast. A unique blend of Africa, Islam, the classical world and eastern civilisation, it has given rise to distinctive architecture, literature, culture and customs.

Lamu Lamu is a magical island off Kenya's Indian Ocean coast. Lamu Town is a maze of narrow streets with mosques and traditional, cool stone dwellings with carved, brass-studded doors. There are no vehicles. Donkeys from the island's sanctuary wander around the streets. The centre of town has a large fort dating from 1809, there is a fine collection of Swahili exhibits including the famous Siwa horns at Lamu museum, the old German Post Office has been reconstructed and the Swahili House Museum gives a fascinating insight into traditional family life. The quayside runs along the water's edge and restaurants and hotels look out over the harbour where dhows sail by. There are few more relaxing places on earth.

Zanzibar There can be few travellers who have not longed to visit Zanzibar, and indeed it is no disappointment. Arriving by sea there is a skyline of the old Customs House, the colonial Hotel d'Afrique Centrale, the former Sultan's Palace, the House of Wonders and the Portuguese Fort. The ancient Stone Town, now being restored, is a World Heritage site. The winding streets are mostly free of cars and there are fine buildings, museums, palaces, mosques, hotels in restored Swahili houses, relics of the slave trade, rooftop restaurants, gardens with alfresco eating, Persian bath houses. Every evening, from the verandah bar of the old English Club, you can watch a magnificent sunset. Beyond the town, Zanzibar island is strewn with the palaces of the former Sultans, the air is fragrant with the spices of the plantations and there are glorious beaches, such as Jambiani and Nungwe, where you can stay in simple accommodation for a song.

Bagamoyo Bagamoyo, just close to Dar es Salaam, is a small historic town that was the centre of the slave trade on the mainland. From here caravans set out by foot on their mighty journeys to the interior. Reminders of the slave trade are everywhere and as well as a Slave Museum, there are Livingstone's church, German colonial buildings, Shirazi ruins and the Holy Ghost Mission, the first Christian settlement on the mainland.

Beaches, fishing, diving All along the Indian Ocean Coast are splendid beaches and a fine range of places to stay. Perhaps the best beaches are Diani, south of Mombasa, and Jambiani in Zanzibar. You can surf at Malindi. The deep-sea fishing in the Pemba channel is rated among the best in the world. The crystal-clear water makes the marine parks at Watamu and Malindi magical places for snorkelling. Diving facilities are good and six sites in Kenya and another six off the islands of Zanzibar, Pemba and Mafia are among the best in the world. Dive training is offered at all the main sites and taking a PADI course is a popular part of a beach holiday.

Sea-going history Everywhere on the Indian Ocean Coast you are aware of the sea-going heritage that brought communities together to form the Swahili. Massive ocean-going dhows at the big ports, little coastal outriggers dipping through the shallows, boat-building yards, fishing villages and markets. The coast has always been seen as the place to rest and enjoy the pleasures of life. Weary caravan porters sang to keep up their spirits as they approached the end of their journey:

> "My spirits lift as the drum-beats roll
> Lay down my heart, and calm my soul
> At last I'm home, Bagamoyo."

Top left: Stone Town, now a World Heritage site, in Zanzibar. **Top right**: snorkelling amongst coral in the shallow, crystal waters off the coast at Mombasa, Kenya.

Above: men in traditional dhow in shallows near Malindi, Kenya. **Left**: Lamu Town's convoluted maze of streets and palm trees amongst old stone architecture.

Right: Gondar Royal enclosure, site of five of Gondar's many castles and palaces built by successive Ethiopian kings from the mid-seventeenth to the mid-nineteenth century. *Below*: Timkat, the colourful celebration of the Epiphany, in Lalibela, Ethiopia.

Bottom left: Kenya Railways, Atni Plains, Kenya. *Bottom right*: Murchison Falls seen from River Nile, Uganda. *Next page*: dawn mist in the foothills of the Rwenzori mountains near Fort Portal, Uganda.

Zamani

Zamani means "the past" in Swahili. Imagine viewing Africa through the eyes of the great explorers, scholars, writers and adventurers of bygone eras and seeing the great Dark Continent as they saw it.

Cradle of mankind

Charles Darwin was the first to express the view that human life originated in Africa and since then others, including the famous Leakey family, have made extraordinary discoveries which have established Africa as the 'cradle of mankind'. Olduvai Gorge in Tanzania is the site of many of their most famous finds and the museum there puts all the discoveries in the context of man's evolution. It sends a shiver down the spine to imagine the life of our ancestors: killing and skinning animals with sharp stone axes; battered by the tropical sun and rain and in constant fear of attack by wild animals.

The Mountain Kingdom

Ethiopia has a rich history that can be traced back to King Solomon. This long and illustrious past can be seen in the numerous artefacts that survive and in the unique style and manner of the Ethiopian people, sheltered from the world, as they have been through the centuries, by their mountainous homeland. The country's religion, literature, language, cuisine and spectacular festivals are quite unlike anywhere else in the continent.

Shiraz

All along the coast are the ruined cities and settlements of the Shirazi people, who migrated from Persia to Africa. Among these settlements those at Gedi, Tongoni and Kilwa were extensive and sophisticated. The remains of magnificent stone buildings at Kilwa reveal a once-prosperous 10th century settlement that grew rich providing an Indian Ocean terminus for the gold trade to the interior.

Vasco da Gama

Vasco de Gama rounded the Cape of Good Hope in 1498, and then voyaged north along the East African coast. The Portuguese left their mark with garrisons, settlements and great forts, most notably those still existing in Mombasa and Zanzibar. Their rule lasted until 1698 when they were vanquished by forces from Oman, heralding two centuries of Arab domination of the coast.

Explorers

Livingstone, Stanley, Burton, Speke, Grant and Thompson all made extraordinary journeys into the interior. It is difficult not to be inspired at the site in Uganda where Hannington Speke first glimpsed the source of the Nile – or Ujiji on the shore of Lake Tanganyika, 1500 kilometres from the coast, where Henry Morton Stanley finally found a sick and ailing David Livingstone – or Harar in Ethiopia where Sir Richard Burton was the first European to set foot in the Forbidden City.

Colonial railways

When Britains, Germans, Italians and French began their periods of rule at the end of the 19th century, they built railways. In Kenya, the British constructed a line that climbs a kilometre as it steadily winds its way from the coast to Kampala. The Germans built a line from Dar es Salaam to Lake Tanganyika and every railway town in Tanzania has a clutch of handsome buildings all constructed nearly a century ago. In Eritrea the Italians built a railway from the coast up to Asmara and beyond and the French laid down tracks for Emperor Menelik of Ethiopia from Djibouti to Addis Ababa. You can ride on all these railways, sometimes in restored, original steam engines and carriages.

Scribblers

Finally there are the great writers: Ernest Hemingway, Evelyn Waugh, Karen Blixen, Elspeth Huxley, Vidia Naipaul. We can retrace their journeys, visit their houses, see the great African continent anew through their eyes and as Winston Churchill observed in Uganda in 1898, "The more you study the past, the better you understand".

Essentials

2

Essentials

Planning your trip

Wildlife Quite superb natural attractions offer some very special experiences. In **Kenya** the Where to go
Parks have a range of spectacular lodges, tented camps and ballooning. The big game in the
Masai Mara and the flamingoes on the Rift Valley lakes are unforgettable. **Tanzania** has
perhaps the best wildlife in the region. The Serengetti, Ngorongoro Crater, Lake Manyara and
the Selous reserve are outstanding. The lodges are not as luxurious as in Kenya, but they are
improving, and there are some first-rate small establishments. Above all, the great game
areas of Tanzania are less crowded than those in Kenya. **Uganda** has two fine Parks in Queen
Elizabeth and Murchison Falls and, at the current time, the only viable prospect for viewing
mountain gorillas in the Virunga Mountains. Before its current problems, Rwanda offered
access to mountain gorillas, as did Eastern RD Congo (formerly Zaire).

Climbing and trekking Both **Kenya** and **Tanzania** have challenging peaks in Mount
Kenya and Mount Kilimanjaro. **Uganda** offers the prospect of the Ruwenzori Mountains and
the Virungas, as well as Mount Elgon, which can also be climbed from Kenya.

Beaches Kenya has an excellent range of beach hotels and some really fine places to stay.
Diani beach south of Mombasa is miles of white sand, blue seas and palm trees. **Tanzania's**
coast is less developed, but there are good beaches and simple, charming accommodation at
Pangani and Bagamoyo. The two most popular islands, Lamu in Kenya, and Zanzibar in
Tanzania, have good beaches.

Historical interest Olduvai Gorge in **Tanzania** has revealed the evolution of early man
from fossils going back three million years, and many discoveries there have led to the site
being called the 'Cradle of Mankind'.

    Ethiopia has a recorded past going back 2,000 years. There are the ancient cities of Axum,
Gondar, and Harar, as well as a wealth of monasteries and early Christian churches.

    Remnants of Shirazi settlements on the coast of mainland Africa are thought to date from
perhaps as early as the 10th century. The marvellous old town sections of Mogadishu,
Zanzibar, Mombasa, Bagamoyo and Lamu began to be developed somewhat later, from the
end of the 14th century. They contain fine houses with balconies and verandahs around
courtyards designed to stay cool by catching the ocean breezes, richly carved doors,
elaborately decorated mosques, narrow winding streets of cobblestones.

    The first European impact was with the arrival of the Portuguese in the 15th century. The
strategic forts they built to consolidate their trading presence remain, most notably in
Mombasa and Zanzibar.

    Of the eventual colonizers of the mainland, the Germans left by far the most impressive
architecture, a distinctive style adapting European technique to local materials and climatic
conditions, and examples are scattered throughout what is now mainland Tanzania, Rwanda
and Burundi. Railways were built by the British in Kenya and the Germans in Tanzania at the
beginning of the 20th century. The stations are still in use, and examples of the early rolling
stock and locomotives survive. In the Horn of Africa, Italy has left its mark, with a
Mediterranean style of architecture, which is most marked in Eritrea, but is also noticeable in
Somalia and Ethiopia.

Traditional life and culture Many of the mainland people have spectacular traditional
lifestyles. The dress, decoration and ceremonies of the Masai are perhaps best known.
However, on mainland East Africa over 300 distinct communities have their own traditional
dress, fables and stories, dances, ceremonies, customs and styles of dwelling.

Modern life Urban Africa has a style and excitement all its own: intricately laid-out goods at
markets; gaudily painted, sloganed and crowded minibuses with swashbuckling conductors;
churches packed to overflowing; weddings with exuberant processions; vibrant local bars,
dance halls and discos, with men in dress ranging from silk suits to baseball caps and lycra

cycling shorts; girls in second-hand wedding dresses, mini-skirts, designer jeans, wide-brimmed hats; hair natural, straightened, plaited; exciting music with sophisticated rhythms and delicate melodies.

Essentials

When to go
For very detailed local weather access the University of Michigan's Weather Net site on the World Wide Web (http://cirrus.sprlu.mich.edu/wxnet/). A brief five-day forecast is available.

Kenya There are two rainy seasons in the country, the long rains March-April and the short rains October-December. However, even during the rains there is invariably sunshine each day. January and February are the main months of the tourist season, as the weather is hot and dry, encouraging wild animals to the nearest water holes.

Tanzania March, April and May can be months of heavy rain making travel on unsealed roads difficult. Even in these months, however, there is an average of 4-6 hours of sunshine each day.

Uganda The heavy rainy season is March to May, and there are lighter rains in November and December. It is probably best to try to avoid March to May. Generally there is some sunshine each day, even in the rainy seasons.

Ethiopia It is best to avoid the rainy season from June to September. The hot and dry months are April and May. However, if you do` travel in the rainy season the countryside is very green, and the temperature is lower.

Geography
The geographical coordinates are given for several towns in the guide in degrees latitude (distance north or south of the Equator) and longitude (distance east or west of the prime meridian).

The countries in East Africa can be placed into four main groupings.

Firstly there are the great **Safarilands**, centred on the three former British territories of Kenya, Tanzania and Uganda. These countries have extensive spreads of grassland, dotted with thorn trees, home to much of the wildlife. They are bordered by the great lakes of the Rift Valley, and Kenya and Tanzania have long coastlines on the Indian Ocean. All the countries have highland areas, where the altitude makes for moderate temperatures, and peaks with glaciers and snow all the year round, despite the tropical location. Uganda and Kenya have extensive arid areas to the north.

The territories of the **Mountains**, clustering around the Rift Valley lakes in the centre of the continent, make up the second group. Comprising Burundi, Rwanda and the eastern part of RD Congo, they were all at one time administered by Belgium. The terrain is hilly, covered with dense vegetation and cultivation, and the peaks often wreathed in mist.

To the north are the countries of the **Horn** of Africa comprising Ethiopia, Eritrea, Djibouti and Somalia. Italian influence has been strong here in all the territiories except the port of Djibouti which was a French colony. Great areas of the countries of the Horn are arid. However, Ethiopia and Eritrea have extensive areas of highland with reasonable rainfall and vegetation and well able to support cultivation. Most of Somalia is desert, with some grassland dotted by scattered bushes and trees in the north and in the south, and mangroves along the coast.

Stability

The majority of territories (6) in the region can be visited with confidence, although there are areas in most of them where caution is required. Circumstances can change suddenly, however, and if you have any doubts, a source of reliable up-to-date information is to contact the appropriate country desk of your national External Affairs Ministry (for the UK call the Foreign and Commonwealth Office T0171-2701500 and ask for the appropriate country desk).

Safarilands: **Tanzania** has an enviable record of stability, and it has established a consensus among its many peoples that is allowing it to move peacefully toward a multi-party parliamentary democracy. The American Embassy in Dar es Salaam was bombed by external extremists in 1998, but this is regarded as an isolated incident, unlikely to be repeated.

Kenya had some disturbances following the introduction of a multi-party system in 1993, and there have been odd incidents involving tourists. With normal precautions, however, it is quite safe to visit. The American Embassy was bombed in 1998 by external extremists (the same outrage was perpetrated in Tanzania) – this is now seen as an isolated incident.

Uganda, since 1986, has made a remarkable recovery from the turmoil of the Amin period and its aftermath. It is not really safe to visit the north of the country, where there is still some unrest. The main tourist attractions are mostly in the other, quite secure, regions. The parks bordering RD Congo were subject to a horrific incident perpetrated by terrorists in March 1999 in which tourists were killed. The Ugandan authorities have improved security and insist that these parks are now safe to visit. Nevertheless, extreme caution is advised.

Horn: Ethiopia has made great strides since the fall of the Mengistu regime, and political accommodation has been made with the main rebel groups. There are some remote areas where there is danger, and it is important to take local advice on this. There has been an ongiong dispute with Eritrea over the border, and care needs to be exercised in the border zone.

Eritrea, having achieved effective independence from Ethiopia, is now largely peaceful for the first time in many years. However, the border dispute with Ethiopia has affected the area and some towns (including Asmara) have experienced sporadic air strikes.

Djibouti, bolstered by its links with France, and the commercial interests in the port, has always been very stable.

At the time of writing, four countries and parts of two others (Northern Ethiopia and Eritrea border zones) are effectively off limits to all but essential travel and will not therefore be covered in this edition of the handbook other than in this introduction. Circumstances can change, however, within a matter of months, and advice should be sought (see above). **Unsafe countries**

Rwanda, a beautiful country (the 'Switzerland of Africa') and for many years, well-organized and efficient, has plunged into chaos. The death of the president, shot down in a plane returning from peace talks early in 1994, sparked conflict and genocide between the country's two main groups, the Tutsi (15 percent) and the Hutu (80 percent). A massive exodus of over one million refugees to neighbouring countries, has taken place. Water and power are irregular, the police and judicial systems have not been restored, there are road blocks, and some unsealed roads are mined. Visas are not available at the point of entry.

Burundi, Rwanda's neighbour to the south, and with an identical ethnic mix of Tutsi and Hutu, has also descended into chaos. Rivalry between the Tutsi and Hutu has, in the past, been bitter and violent. The multi-party election of 1993 resulted in the first president from the Hutu, the overwhelming majority, coming to power. Efforts to form a broadly-based government were shattered when the president was assassinated by Tutsi army officers late in 1993. A new Hutu president was installed only for him to perish in the same plane as the Rwandan president. A coup has now installed a former president. There are regular episodes of violence between the two communities, and foreigners have been caught up in these incidents and killed.

Eastern RD Congo has been swamped by over a million Rwandan refugees, many still settling scores in the emergency camps. Preoccupation with these problems effectively rules out any tourism. Although it is undoubtedly beautiful, with mountains, lakes, colonial charm in the lake resorts, and the attraction of the mountain gorillas, even prior to the Rwandan crisis travel in Eastern RD Congo was problematical. The public sector in the east, cut off from the seat of government in the west of the country, has effectively collapsed. Public servants are not paid, petty corruption is rife, and there can be little confidence in the maintenance of law and order, particularly with armed groups of exiles forming up in the refugee camps.

Somalia has sunk into a desperate civil war between rival gangs of armed clans that has proved beyond the international community to resolve. In recent months the ferocity of the conflict has abated somewhat, and the northern part of the country (the former British Somaliland) is reported to be have established its own government, claimed *de facto* secession, and to be reasonably peaceful. Nevertheless, it will be some time before it is safe to travel there.

Travellers tend to take more than they need though requirements vary with the destination and the type of travel that is to be undertaken. Laundry services are generally cheap and speedy. A travelpack, a hybrid backpack/suitcase, rather than a rigid suitcase, covers most **What to take**

Essentials

☞ The history of East Africa

Archaeological sites at Olduvai Gorge in Tanzania and at Lower Awash River in Ethiopia suggest that man began to evolve in the Rift Valley more than three million years ago, and hunter-gatherer communities were established.

The area then experienced an influx of people from West Africa, which has become known as the Bantu Expansion, beginning around 500 BC. In the Horn it is thought that Cushitic immigrants came from Mesopotamia (now Iraq) around 300 BC. The newcomers were cultivators and pastoralists, and they began to change the pattern of subsistence away from hunting and gathering.

Contact with other areas began as sea-going traders arrived from the north, sailing down the east coast of Africa and coming from as far as India, China and South East Asia. A sprinkling of settlements by Islamic people from Shiraz in Persia (now Iran) were established along the coast from about 1000 AD.

European contact began with the arrival of the Portuguese who sailed round the southern tip of Africa and passed up the east coast from 1500 on. They set up fortified settlements to consolidate their trading presence, several of which remain, most notably Fort Jesus in Mombasa.

A struggle for dominance of these coastal strips began between Arab groups drawing support from the Persian Gulf and vying with the Portuguese for the trade in gold, ivory and slaves. By the end of the 17th century the Portuguese found themselves stretched to retain their hold in East Africa, and Fort Jesus fell to the Arabs in 1698. For most of the next two centuries Arab rule prevailed at the coast, and they began to penetrate the interior with caravans to capture slaves and ivory. These set out from Bagamoyo and Kilwa on the coast of present-day Tanzania, following routes that stretched over 1000 kilometres to the Great Lakes and beyond.

In the interior, meanwhile, pockets of centralized rule and formalized social structures emerged, particularly to the west of Lake Victoria. In the Horn of Africa, the dynasty that traces its origins to Biblical times was establishing cities at Axum, Gondar and Harar.

European exploration began in the 18th century. A Scot, James Bruce in 1768-73 travelled from Suskin on the Red Sea up the Abara River to join the Nile. Lacerda, a Portuguese explorer travelled up the Zambesi in 1798-9, and then headed north to reach Lake Tanganyika. Burckhardt in 1809-17 journeyed from Massawa to Lake Tana and down the Blue Nile to Khartoum. The brothers Antoine and Arnaud Abbadie in 1837-48 pressed further south from Gondar in Ethiopia. Kraf and Rebmann, two Germans, in 1848 travelled from the Kenya coast up through the highlands. Richard Burton in 1854-5 managed an excursion from Zaila on the Red Sea coast to Harar in Ethiopia.

The origins of the White Nile (which joins the Blue Nile at Khartoum) began to exercise the imagination in Europe, and the source was eventually traced to Lake Victoria by Burton and Speke in 1860. The two great journeys by David Livingstone in 1858-64 and 1866-73 reached to Lake Tanganyika and beyond, and were followed by Stanley's expedition in 1874-7 which crossed the continent from east to west.

The activities of the explorers were followed by missionary activity and a campaign to end the slave trade. Although

The Slave Trade

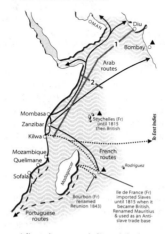

1 Slave trading east or south of line made illegal by Moresby Treaty, 1822

2 All northern slave trading made illegal by Hamerton Treaty, 1845

▲ British Anti-slave trade patrol bases

slavery was made illegal in 1873, it was some time before it was finally eliminated.

The European nations formalized their presence with the British occupying Kenya, Uganda and Zanzibar, and the Germans established themselves in what is now mainland Tanzania, Rwanda and Burundi. Eastern RD Congo was part of the Belgian Congo. Eritrea and southern Somalia were Italian, and northern Somalia was British. The French held the port of Djibouti. Only Ethiopia retained its independence, holding off the attentions of Italy.

Economic progress had taken place in the interior as iron implements replaced more primitive stone and wooden tools, and cultivators accumulated farming knowledge. However, droughts, locusts, rinderpest and local conflicts contrived to keep populations fairly stable. Progress accelerated with the advent of European occupation. Diseases were controlled, new crops introduced, roads and railways were built. Death rates fell, birth rates remained high and the population began a steady expansion. Living standards improved and significant sections of the population received basic education.

After the First World War the British took over the part of German East Africa that became Tanganyika, and Belgium absorbed Rwanda and Burundi. Italy occupied Ethiopia for a period from 1936-42. Settler presence increased, particularly in Kenya, and the Asian communities consolidated their positions in commerce and the skilled trades.

Nationalist movements began to emerge as significant political factors after the Second World War. Ethiopia federated with Eritrea in 1952. In Kenya, where there was by now a substantial settler population, there was an armed conflict in the 1950s (the Mau Mau uprising) over land grievances and generally in support of self-determination. Most countries obtained their independence in the early 1960s, although Djibouti did not break from France until 1977.

Tanzania was created when Tanganyika formed a union with Zanzibar in 1964. The immediate post-Independence period typically saw the establishment of single-party regimes, and in many cases government was unstable (although Tanzanian, Kenya and Djibouti have proved

exceptions). In Uganda, Somalia, Rwanda, Burundi, and Ethiopia there have been disastrous collapses of peace and security.

Economic development was pursued by the adoption of socialist development strategies with heavy reliance on the public sector. A deceleration of economic progress followed, and in the 1980s most countries reversed their economic policies and by 1994 had either undertaken, or were planning, multi-party elections.

In 1993, after a referendum, and with the approval of Ethiopia, Eritrea broke away to become an independent state.

The search for the source of the Nile

Essentials

☞ **The Forbidden Handbook**

Your Editor makes no apology for the high level of sophistication required to appreciate the following items.

On the pathway down to the shore next to Fort Jesus in Mombasa, Kenya is to be found a specialist photographic agency, **Willy Photos***. Muleba, Tanzania has a* **Willy Shop.**

For those with delicate alimentary canals, in the Ambal Building on Nkrumah Rd, Mombasa is **Bowel Insurance Agency***. In Zanzibar connoisseurs of modern religious art can add to their collections at* **Budda's Body Parts***.*

If you are bothered by pedestrians tossing litter into the open top of your saloon car, you might care to call in the **Sunroof Pest Control Unit***, PO Box 83011, T31360, Haile Selassie Rd in Mombasa.*

In an effort to reduce feeding costs, Mamba Village at Nyali, just N of Mombasa offers **Free Use of the Crocodile Pool***.*

For high-tech olfaction equipment, contact **Pong Electronics** *of Moi Ave, Mombasa.*

Specialized appliances can be obtained from **Phag Electronics** *near Utali House in Nairobi. Alas, they are not located in* **Butt Arcade***, which is in Malindi, nor in* **Rue du Bender***, a thoroughfare in Djibouti City or by Lake Naivasha in Kenya at the rather worrying* **Bottom Camp***.*

Doubtless many tourists are disappointed at their first sighting of **Somali Wild Ass***, especially if they have signed up with* **Dik Dik Safaris** *of Kenya.*

A brand of soap powder in Tanzania, **Toss** *is guaranteed to make your wash come out a brilliant – er, yellow.*

Experiences from 48 years of Rodwell's Column *is the alarming sub-title of Mombasa journalist Edward Rodwell's* **Coast Causerie I***.*

Sign in toilet of Bush Gardens Restaurant, Lamu is **Please Pull to Flash***.*

A clothes shop in Biharamulo offers **Nookie Fashions***.*

The advertising slogan for Gay Body Lotion in Kenya is **Gay Ladies Get Noticed***, and I bet they do, too.*

Sign in Emerson's House in Zanzibar – **The Rising Hope: a 1st Class Shag Guaranteed with this Signature***.*

Fans of Fawlty Towers should visit Axum in Ethiopia where they can see **King Basil's Tomb***.*

Full Dose *is a sign on the Bagamoyo Rd N of Dar es Salaam – it is not a house of ill-repute where an unpleasant social disease can be contracted, but a grocery.*

In Kitui in Kenya is the **TIT Joint***, actually the Talk in Town bar.*

I dare say Californians are a little wary of staying at **Manson's Hotel** *in Mombasa.*

It's wonderful what they can do with a pile of feathers and an oxy-acetylene welding torch at **Parrot Fabricators** *of Machakos, Kenya.*

Contract killing is available at Oscar Engineering Works of Machakos, Kenya, who offer **Bullet Service***.*

Those who wish to give pain to themselves and others should try **SM cigarettes** *on sale in Tanzania. Perhaps the most ominous health warning is the advertising slogan for Sportsman Cigarettes in Tanzania,* `**For Men Whose Decisions are Final***'.*

In Zanzibar, at the Seaview Restaurant in Zanzibar Stone Town, the food is truly orgasmic – as witnessed by the waiter collecting the plates and enquiring "And how was it for you, madam?"

Tourists visiting Gondar, Ethiopia, are advised to watch their backs since there is a **Tourist Trading Enterprise** *in town according to the sign next to the Quara Hotel.*

And finally, horny travellers to Lake Manyara NP are warned to "Take no liberties with game animals".

eventualities and survives the rigours of a variety of modes of travel well. Serious trekkers will need a framed backpack. A lock for your luggage is strongly advised – there are cases of pilfering by airport baggage handlers. In any case, take valuable items such as cameras, radios et cetera as hand baggage on airline flights for, even if locked, aluminium zip bags are easily broken. It is also sensible to take bottles of shampoo and so on, as hand baggage on aircraft – holds are not pressurized, and the air in a bottle expands forcing out the liquid, making a mess.

Clothing of light cotton or cotton/polyester with a woollen sweater for evenings. Alternatively a jacket with lots of pockets, although not essential, can be useful. Comfortable shoes with socks as feet may swell in hot weather. Modest dress for women including a sunhat and headscarf. Travelling Light, Morland, Penrith, Cumbria, CA10 3AZ, UK, T01931-714488 can supply specialized items by mail order.

Most important itemas are: air tickets; binoculars; camera; cash; chequebook; credit cards; passport including visa; passport photographs; photocopies of main documents (keep separate)and traveller's cheques.

Checklists

Apart from these everybody has their own list. Obviously what you take depends on where you are intending to go and also what your budget is. A selection of items most often recommended by travellers is listed here: **Toiletries** comb; concentrated detergent; contact lens cleaner; deodorant; elastoplasts; insect repellent; nailbrush; razor and blades; shampoo; sleeping tablets; soap; sun protection cream; talcum powder; tissues and toilet paper; toothbrush; toothpaste and vaseline/moisturiser. **Other**: ear plugs; electric insecticide vaporizer and tablets; electric plug adaptor; eye mask; folding umbrella; inflatable cushion; lock and chain (securing luggage at night); multiple outlet adaptor; plastic bags; sewing kit; short-wave radio and batteries; small torch plus batteries; sun-glasses; swiss army knife; traveller's heating jug; universal washbasin plug and water bottle.

Those intending to stay in budget accommodation might also include: cotton sheet sleeping bag; money belt; padlock (for hotel room and pack); soap; student card; towel; toilet paper and universal bath plug.

Before your travel

Traveller's cheques in US$ are a wise precaution. Almost every country (the exceptions are Somalia, Eritrea and Eastern RD Congo) has an American Express representative where US$500 of traveller's cheques can be bought against payment by personal cheque and production of an American Express card.

Money

Some cash is desirable, held in US dollars, with some in small denomination notes for requirements such as payment of airport departure taxes. It is advisable to take dollars issued after 1990 as there have been problems with forgeries of pre-1990 notes. You will get a better exchange rate on larger denomination US$ bills.

Exchange rates (September 1999)

	US$1	£1	DM1
Djibouti (Djib Fr)	172.00	276.09	93.22
Eritrea (Etritrean Nafca)*	7.30	11.72	4.02
Ethiopia (Ethiopia Birr)	8.00	12.85	4.34
Kenya (Kenya shilling)	75.75	121.59	41.05
Tanzania (Shilling)	792.25	1,271.72	429.38
Uganda (New Shilling)	1,470.00	2,359.64	796.70

*Based on 1998 rate

Insurance companies have tightened up considerably over recent years and it is now almost impossible to claim successfully if you have not followed procedures closely. The problem is that these often involve dealing with the country's red tape which can lead to some inconvenience at best and to some quite long delays at worst. There is no substitute for suitable precautions against petty crime.

Insurance tips

The level of insurance that you carry is often dictated by the sums of medical insurance which you carry. It is inevitably the highest if you go through the USA. Also don't forget to obtain sports extensions if you are going to go diving, rafting, climbing etc. Most policies do not cover very high levels of baggage/cash. Don't forget to check whether you can claim on your household insurance. They often have worldwide all risks extensions. Most policies exclude manual work whilst away although working in bars or restaurants is usually alright.

Here are our tips: they apply to most types of policies but always check the details of your own policy before you leave.

Essentials

Essentials

1 Take the policy with you (a photocopy will do but make sure it is a complete one).

2 Do not travel against medical advice. It will invalidate the medical insurance part of the cover.

3 There is a 24 hour medical emergency service helpline associated with your insurance. You need to contact them if you require in-patient hospital treatment or you need to return home early. The telephone number is printed on the policy. Make sure you note the time of the call, the person you were talking to and get a reference number. Even better get a receipt from the telephone company showing the number you called. Should you need to be airlifted home, this is always arranged through the insurance company's representative and the hospital authorities. Ironically this can lead to quite intense discussions which you will not be aware of: the local hospital is often quite keen to keep you!

4 If you have to cancel your trip for whatever reason, contact your travel agent, tour operator or airline without delay.

5 If your property is damage by an airline, report it immediately and always within 3 days and get a 'property irregularity report' from them.

6 Claims for baggage left unattended are very rarely settled unless they were left in a securely locked hotel room, apartment etc; locked in the boot of a car and there is evidence of a forced entry; cash is carried on your person or is in a locked safe or security box.

7 All loss must be reported to the police and/or hotel authorities within 24 hours of discovery and a written report obtained.

8 If medical attention is received for injury or sickness, a medical certificate showing its nature must be obtained, although some companies waive this if only out-patient treatment is required. Keep all receipts in a safe place as they will be needed to substantiate the claim.

9 Check your policy carefully to see if there is a date before which claims must be submitted. This is often within 30 days of returning home. It is now usual for companies to want your policy document, proof that you actually travelled (airline ticket or travel agent's confirmation of booking), receipts and written reports (in the event of loss). NB photocopies are not accepted.

Getting there

It is possible to fly directly to almost all the capitals in the region from Europe. The main exceptions are Somalia and Rwanda where international flights are currently suspended, and Eastern RD Congo, which can only be accessed from nearby countries.

However, many travellers will find it cheaper and often more convenient to fly to one of the well-serviced capitals, and connect from there.

Nairobi (Kenya) has many regular, cheap flights. There is little advantage in accessing Uganda or Tanzania from here unless you travel on by road or rail. There are good air connections from Nairobi to Rwanda and Burundi.

Addis Ababa (Ethiopia) is a natural centre for Eritrea and Djibouti (and for Somalia when access resumes). Ethiopian Airways run a frequent network of services. However, internal flights are cancelled without warning, and the fleet is too small to replace aircraft taken out of circulation for maintenance. Travellers have reported lengthy delays, with little information available.

Air
Further details on air links to and from each country, arrival and departure regulations, airport taxes, customs regulations and security arrangements for air travel are outlined in the relevant Essentials sections.

Essentials

Essentials

Discounts | **Specialist agents** will arrange economical fares from Europe, typically for fixed arrival and departure dates, and for stays of a week or longer. Among the specialist agencies offering discounted fares are:

Australia: *Africa Travel Centre*, 456 Kent St, Sydney, NSW 2000, T02-2673084; *STA Travel*, 222-224 Faraday St, Carlton, Melbourne 3053, T(03) 347-4711.

Canada: Travel Cuts, 187 College St, Toronto, ON M5T 1P7, T416-9792406.

New Zealand: *Africa Travel Centre*, 21 Remuera Rd, Newmarket, Auckland 3, T09-5245118. *STA Travel*, 10 High St Auckland T09-3099723.

UK: *Africa Travel Centre*, 21 Leigh St, London WC1H 9QV, T0171-3888878, www.africatravel.co.uk. *Key Travel*, 92-96 Eversholt St, London NW1 1BP, T0171-3874933, F0171-3871090 offer keen prices to and from major African cities from the UK but have no facilities for internal flights. *STA Travel*, 117 Euston Rd, London NW1, T0171-9379962, F0171-3379570. *RAJ Air*, 27 Central Chambers, The Broadway, Ealing, London W5 2NR T0181-8408881 offer competitive fares to East Africa.

USA: *Swan Travel*, 400 Madison Av, New York, NY, T212-42111010. *STA*, 48 East 11th St, New York, NY 10003, T212-4777166. *Around the World*, 2241 Polk St, San Fransisco, CA 94109, T415-6739950.

Jetlag & travel | Time differences, unsociable airline hours and touchdowns at intermediate points all serve to upset sleep patterns. Most doctors are happy to prescribe some sleeping tablets to help establish a sleep pattern at your destination and on your return. Inflatable pillows can be a great comfort on long journeys, especially by bus. Earplugs and eyemasks can also help with sleep on journeys.

Touching down

Rules, customs & etiquette | **Bargaining**   Bargaining is expected in the street markets. It is often the case that traders will attempt to overcharge tourists who are unaware of local prices. Start lower than you would expect to pay, be polite and good humoured, and if the final price doesn't suit – walk away. There are plenty more shops. Ask about the prices of taxis, excursions, souvenirs, and so on, at your hotel. Once you have gained confidence, try bargaining with taxi drivers and when negotiating a room.

Conduct   Great store is set everywhere by modesty and courtesy and an effort to dress smartly. Respect toward elderly people is particularly important. If you are making a formal visit to an official, for men a tie and neat dress (or safari suit) is a minimum; a jacket helps, and a suit is desirable. Women should dress soberly, modestly and smartly.

Mosques and temples   Make sure you follow observances as indicated by attendants. Shoes will normally need to be taken off, and there may be restriction on visits by women.

Tipping   In large establishments a service charge is invariably added. Elsewhere it is optional, but a modest tip for courteous and attentive service is greatly appreciated by hotel and restaurant staff, most of whom receive very low pay.

Safety | **Beggars**   A number of physically handicapped persons and destitute mothers with children are present in most large towns. Clearly many are genuine and heart-rending cases of need.

Street children, however, give pause for thought. In some places they request money to guard vehicles, in others they ask for money for food. Giving to one child usually leads the donor to be surrounded and harassed by a throng. A fight may arise as to who should guard a car. Giving a bank-note to one child with instructions that it should be shared will result in violence with the whole sum going to the strongest and most ruthless child. In some places street children are clearly organized by adults.

A constructive alternative is to make a donation to an organization such as *Save the Children Fund*, Mary Datchelor House, 17 Grove Lane, London, SE5 8RD, T0171-7035400,

People of East Africa

The population of the **Safarilands** is largely of Bantu origin, comprising several hundred identifiable communities. Most are settled cultivators, but there are many pastoralists, often nomadic. Kenya and Tanzania have Swahili people along the coast that are the product of intermarriage between Africans and Arabs. These two countries also have communities from the Indian sub-continent, mostly involved in commercial life and the professions. In Uganda, almost all Asians were expelled under Amin, and it is only now that they are beginning to return. Small communities of Europeans have remained in farming and business.

The **Mountain** countries of Rwanda and Burundi are riven by the division into the majority Hutu (80 percent) and the Tutsi 15 percent). The Tutsi are tall pastoralists from the north who traded cattle for land and established themselves as a land-owning class, dominating government, the armed forces and access to education. The Hutu are physically smaller, and engaged mostly in cultivation. Eastern RD Congo is a mixture of mostly Bantu people.

The inhabitants of the **Horn** have distinctive features with a more Arabic appearance and, except in Ethiopia, lighter skin colour. In Somalia there are many pastoralists, following Islam. The Ethiopians have a strong cultivating tradition and their own form of Christianity.

Essentials

F0171-703 2275 which provides subsistence and skill-training programmes in an attempt to provide a long-term solution. There are collection points in the departure lounges of some international airports. They are always very grateful for donations of loose coins or notes.

Confidence tricksters Particularly common in Kenya, but also found elsewhere. Be wary of anyone with a hard-luck story, soliciting sponsorship (particularly educational) or offering a deal to change money at favourable rates.

Drugs Illegal in all countries. There are considerable risks in using drugs even where a blind eye is turned to use by local people. In such circumstances you are extremely vulnerable to extortion.

Firearms Cannot be imported or carried, without special permission.

Personal security The overwhelming majority of countries in the region are safe, but sadly, it is no longer rare for a traveller to have a trip marred by theft or an unpleasant incident. Visitors in supervised parties, on excursions, or staying in large hotels are particularly safe.

Nevertheless, some countries have experienced collapse into chaos and turmoil. Somalia, Rwanda and Burundi are current examples; Uganda had severe breakdown prior to 1986. If there is any hint of serious instability, such as a coup attempt with armed supporters of rival factions on the streets, you should immediately leave the country. If necessary you should seek help from your national embassy, or any international agency.

Otherwise, it is sensible to take reasonable precautions by not walking in deserted, unlit areas at night, and by avoiding places of known risk during the day. Snatch thieves can be problem, particularly in Kenya, and risks can be minimised by not wearing jewellery, expensive watches, or carrying cameras in busy public places. Waist pouches are very vulnerable as the belt can be cut easily. Carry money and any valuables in a slim belt under clothing. Always lock room doors at night as noisy fans and air-conditioning can provide cover for sneak thieves. Be wary of leaving items by open windows in hotel rooms.

Photography in sensitive areas All countries have zones where there are military or communications installations which are off-limits. These are usually well sign-posted. You must avoid taking photographs, sketching or making notes, however innocent, in these areas. To take risks in this regard invites detention by the police and untold inconvenience. It may not be so obvious that an individual building belongs to the military: care should be taken

👉 **Four muggings and a funeral**

Africa is quite safe for travellers provided they are cautious and take care to avoid risky situations. This is a lesson quite lost on your Editor.

In Nairobi, during the rainy season, he was walking one evening from the Boulevard Hotel to a restaurant. The road was awash, and he went along the poorly lit, fairly unfrequented, Uhuru highway. Four guys grabbed him from behind, took his money (about US$30), his golf umbrella, his shoes – and legged it. Your Editor limped to the nearby police-station in his socks and was told to `wait in a rear room with the others' – three sorry-looking individuals without a pair of shoes between them.

In Dar es Salaam it can get hot, and you'd think that, even as dusk is falling, a beach, albeit deserted, but in front of a large hotel would be safe for a swim. Alas your Editor was surrounded by a gang. Their intention was clear, even though their English was limited to but one phrase – "Gimme the Reeboks, muthafucka".

North of Dar es Salaam the hotels have beaches patrolled by guards. At the end of one hotel beach is a large sign warning

against proceeding any further as muggers operate. Your Editor was not able to work out from this that if he went for a jog beyond the hotel limit he would actually get mugged. In any case, what could they take? This cost a pair of Nikes.

The dock area of Bujumbura in Burundi is fairly deserted, but a fatal attraction for an Editorial stroll. What a shock, then, when a chap jumped out from behind a tree brandishing a screwdriver. Your Editor had had enough of passive compliance by this time and set off, as briskly as he was able, up the road, toward a group of people in a petrol station, shouting for help. Unfortunately he tripped over a drain, his assailant snatched his wrist-watch, and having done so, departed in some haste. A triumph for your Editor, however, as he was able to saunter into the police station fully shod.

Back in Nairobi, a follow-up visit had to be made to the Police Station. The desk sergeant was looking fairly pleased with himself – `I've got some good news for you,' he said. `We had a decoy out on your Uhuru Highway last night and we shot a mugger dead'.

before photographing any official people or buildings. Some travellers attempt to circumvent this by photographing their travelling companion in front of the object desired, using a wide-angle lens. This tactic is not encouraged as travellers have been arrested.

Police If you have any items stolen, you must report the occurrence to the police, and keep a record of the incident number, the police station, and the name of the officer dealing with it. This is vital if you have lost official documents, or wish to make an insurance claim. The police will often insist that you report regularly to check on how the investigations are proceeding. These visits can be very time-consuming and tedious. Property is almost never recovered, and it is often possible to use your discretion as to whether it is worth following things up.

For petty offences (driving without lights switched on, for example) police will often try to solicit a bribe, masked as an 'on the spot' fine. Establish the amount being requested, and then offer to go to the police station to pay, at which point you will be released with a warning.

For any serious charges, immediately contact your embassy or consulate.

Where to stay

Hotels
See also inside front cover for a quick guide to hotel grade prices

Places to stay vary between those used by well-heeled tourists, which are expensive at around US$100 a day, self contained with air-conditioning, hot water and swimming pools, and those used by local people (and budget travellers) at under US$5 a day, which may comprise a simple bed, shared toilet and washing facilities, irregular water supply.

Some of the small beach hotels are in splendid locations and despite having only simple facilities are excellent value.

Hotel price categories

A+   Over US$150 a night. International standards and decor, air conditioning, self-contained rooms, swimming pool, restaurants, bars, business services.

A   US$100-150. First class standards, air-conditioning, attached bathrooms, restaurants and bars, swimming pool.

B   US$50-100. Tourist class, comfortable with air conditioning or fans, attached bathrooms, restaurant, bar, public rooms.

C   US$20-50. Budget, fans, shared bathroom facilities.

D   US$10-20. Guest house, no fan, shared bathroom, cold water.

E   Under US$10. Basic guest house, simple bed, no soap or towels, no wardrobe, shared bathroom facilities, erratic cold water supply, no fans or mosquito nets.

Restaurant price categories

Given the variations in price of food on any menu our restaurants are divided where possible into four simple grades:

4   Over US$10 for a meal. A three-course meal in a restaurant with pleasant decor. Beers, wines and spirits available.

3   US$5-10 for a meal. Two courses, not including alcohol, reasonable surroundings.

2   US$2-5 for a meal, probably only a single course, surroundings spartan but adequate.

1   Under US$2. Single course, often makeshift surroundings such as a street kiosk with simple benches and tables.

In the parks camping in either a tented camp or a campsite is often more atmospheric and cheaper than staying in one of the lodges.

Many hotels provide a high level of private security staff – often armed.

Insects Be prepared for mosquitoes, particularly, and other insects. Sleep under a net treated with insecticide where mosquitoes are a problem; smear exposed skin with repellent; use an electric heat-pad insecticide tablet vapouriser at night; buy a can of insecticide to spray your hotel room.

Food and drink

Bearing in mind the suggestions in the Health section (see page 38) on food best avoided in uncertain conditions, a great choice of African food still remains. For the less adventurous, Western style food is widely available.

The most common drink is tea. Coffee is generally available too. Bottled soft fizzy drinks are found even in small settlements and are safer than water. **Alcohol** is widely available. You will be expected to take your own supplies on camping safaris, however. **Bottled water** is an essential part of every traveller's baggage. However avoid buying the cheapest brand in supermarkets as, although it may be clean, it often doesn't taste so. A survey by the *Sunday Standard* in Nairobi in 1995 found that 75 out of 78 brands of bottled water sold were in fact Nairobi tap water. Safari companies usually stock bottled water for taking on camping safaris – take plenty with you.

Getting around

Air There are quite good regional airlines. However flights can be delayed and sometimes get overbooked. It is essential to reconfirm return flights 48 hours before departure. Allow plenty of time at departure. There is often a considerable amount of bureaucracy to go through involving lots of queuing. Make sure that you have hard currency (prefarably dollars) for departure taxes, as local currency, travellers' cheques and credit cards are not accepted. You will usually be able to change travellers cheques at the airport bank but beware of commission charges – you may have to change more than you thought. Beware of public holidays and the week before and after them. Flights are often hard to find during this period.

Rail Where rail systems exist, and haste is not of over-riding importance, this mode is thoroughly recommended. It is safe, cheap, and comfortable, albeit slow and often subject to delays.

Road Major road networks are serviceable almost everywhere, and improving all the time. However, rain can be torrential, and sealed roads are regularly washed away and unsealed roads rendered impassable. In the wet seasons road travel can be very difficult.

Bus and taxi For long journeys travellers should try to use big buses and coaches as first choice, on grounds of both comfort and safety. Peugeot taxis (station wagons with seats) are fast, comfortable and fairly safe. Small buses and minibuses have poor safety records, and are uncomfortable and usually overcrowded.

Own vehicle If you are arriving with your own vehicle, you will require a Carnet de Passage issued by a body in your own country (usually the Automobile Association) affiliated to the Alliance International de Tourisme in Geneva. An International Certificate for Motor Vehicles (ICVM) and an International Driving Permit (IDP), again from the appropriate national body, are useful additions to the documentation and can expedite clearance at borders.

You should check with the embassy of any country you are planning to visit. In some cases sureties need to be lodged with the authorities on entry, and there may be special regulations relating to insurance.

Car hire In most countries your national driving licence will allow you to drive for a period, usually 3 months. Nevertheless, it is a wise precaution to obtain an International Driving Permit (see above).

Driver For motoring in town, a driver is of limited advantage. However for touring or on long journeys a driver can be invaluable in terms of providing local knowledge, experience and resourcefulness. The cost of a driver is very modest, and when touring, the driver will lodge *Swahili* at night, that is, in simple local accommodation that he will find for himself.

Hitchhiking In the Western sense (standing beside the road and requesting a free ride) this is not an option. However, truck drivers and many private motorists will often carry you if you pay, and if you are stuck where there is no public transport you should not hesitate to approach likely vehicles on this basis.

Keeping in touch

English is widely used and understood. French is used in Rwanda, Burundi, Eastern RD Congo, Djibouti, and all the Indian Ocean countries. Swahili can be a help in Tanzania, Kenya and to a degree in Uganda. | **Language**

A variety of European and North American countries make short-wave radio broadcasts to East Africa. They are often a more reliable source of news on events in Africa than local radio stations – particularly on major sensitive political items such as coups and outbreaks of hostilities. There is also news of world events that may not be covered by local broadcasts. Finally, for many travellers they offer a welcome contact with home. | **International radio**

The following points are worth bearing in mind if you wish to listen to international services:

- Buy the best radio receiver you can afford – Sanyo receivers are well recommended. It must have **short waveband** reception, and a good radio with this facility will normally cost more than US$100. A radio with a digital display will enable you to key in the exact frequency you require without searching the dial to tune.

- Frequencies are measured in kilohertz (kHz) or Megahertz (MHz) – 1,000 kHz = 1 MHz. Some radios use metres (M) for frequency, rather than kilohertz. They are related by the formula M = 300,000/kHz.

- Reception on each frequency varies as the atmospheric conditions in the ionosphere alter – so if reception is poor on one frequency, try another. In general the shorter wavebands (lower kHz) are more effective during hours of darkness, while the longer wavebands (higher kHz) are better during the day.

- Using the radio by a window can improve reception as steel used in building construction can impair quality. An outside aerial – a length of insulated copper wire – allowed to hang out of the window, or tied up like a washing line, can sometimes improve reception quite a lot. Some radios include an outside aerial – if not, you can improvise one by using a length of insulated copper wire with the stripped wires of one end wrapped round the base of your telescopic aerial.

- Remember that a short-wave radio is a prime target for thieves. Do not leave it by an open hotel window at night. Keep it with you in hand baggage (with the batteries removed) when you fly – baggage handlers at airports have been known to pilfer luggage, breaking locks on bags to do so.

Frequencies for reception vary according to the time of day, as in the table (remember that local time is 1 hour earlier for Rwanda, Burundi and Eastern RD Congo). | **BBC World Service**

Highlights (local times) of the **BBC World Service (Africa)** transmissions are:
- **News Programmes** On the hour, every hour.
- **Sports Roundup** 0145 (not Sunday); 0615; 0915 (not Saturday, Sunday); 1245; 1545 (not Saturday); 2045.

Essentials

BBC World Service frequencies

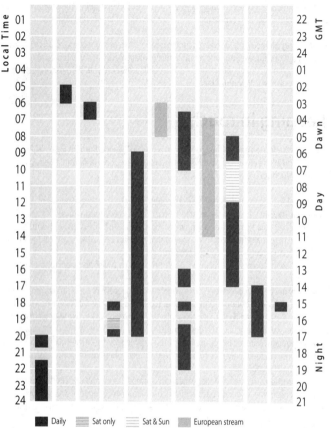

Kilohertz (kHz)

6005 9770 11730 11860 11940 12095 15420 17640 17885 21470 21490

Local Time		GMT

Daily   Sat only   Sat & Sun   European stream

- **African News and Features** 0630; 0830; 0930; 2030.
- **Letter from America** 1345 (Saturday); 0330 (Sunday); 0915 (Sunday); 0130 (Monday). Alastair Cook on affairs in the United States.
- **Sportsworld** 1700-2000 (Saturday) – emphasis on the weekend sport in the UK, usually with a live broadcast, but including good coverage of international events.

Full programme details can be obtained from the following sources:
UK, Bush House, London, WC2B 4PH, T+44-171-2403456, F +44-171-2578258, worldservice.letters@bbc.co.uk. **Ethiopia**, PO Box 12619, Addis Ababa; **Kenya**, PO Box 46682, Nairobi; **Tanzania**, PO Box 9100, Dar es Salaam; **Uganda**, PO Box 7620, Kampala; **RD Congo**, PO Box 10906, Kinshasha 1.

There are many frequencies in use for Africa, but experience indicates that the following frequencies (kHz) are the most reliable for East Africa: 6035 (mornings, 0600–0900 local time); 15410 (evenings and night, 1900–2400 local time).   **Voice of America**
    Highlights (local times) of the Voice of America transmissions are:
    Monday-Friday:
- **News** 0630; 0700; 0800; 1900; 2100; 2400.
- **Africa** 0600; 0730; 0900; 19.30; 2100; 2200; 2300.
Saturday:
- **News** 0600; 0700; 0800; 0900; 2000; 2100; 2200; 22.30; 2400.
- **Africa** 1900; 2300.

Health

It is essential you take every precaution to stay healthy. If you have never been to East Africa before, you should read through this Health Information section, as a matter of priority.
    With the following advice and precautions you should keep as healthy as you do at home. **Most visitors return home having experienced no problems at all apart from some travellers' diarrhoea.** In East Africa the health risks are different from those encountered in Europe or the USA. It also depends on where and how you travel. There are clear health differences between the countries of East Africa and in risks for the business traveller, who stays in international class hotels in large cities, the backpacker trekking from country to country and the tourist who heads for the beach or game parks. There is huge variation in climate, vegetation and wildlife from desert to tropical beaches, the mountains of Ethiopia to the rainforests of RD Congo and to the teeming capital cities. There are no hard and fast rules to follow; you will often have to make your own judgement on the healthiness or otherwise of your surroundings. There are English (or other foreign language) speaking doctors in most major cities who have particular experience in dealing with locally-occurring diseases. Your Embassy representative will often be able to give you the name of local reputable doctors and most of the better hotels have a doctor on standby.

Because much of the area is economically under-developed, infectious diseases still predominate in the same way as they did in the West some decades ago. Poor living conditions, malnutrition and inadequate medical facilities contribute to poor health in the local population in some of these countries.   **Local conditions & standards**
    Some diseases, however, are no respectors of persons and in some cases, malaria for example, local populations have a degree of immunity which is completely lacking in visitors. It is a myth to suppose that true tropical disease has been largely eradicated from East Africa: mosquito control is nowhere near as good as it used to be with a consequent increase in malaria. River blindness, schistosomiasis (bilharzia) are still common, specific African types of HIV infection are rampant and infections with leprosy and tuberculosis still widespread.
    Away from the main centres The quality and range of medical care is extremely variable from country to country and diminishes very rapidly as you move away from cities,

although some rural mission hospitals have been able to maintain good standards. It is generally recognized that standards of medical care are declining for a variety of reasons. In some of the countries there are systems and traditions of medicine rather different from the Western model and you may be confronted with unusual modes of treatment based on local beliefs. This is not a reference to witch doctors who certainly still exist but whose services you are unlikely to have to call upon. In general you can be reasonably sure that local medical practitioners have a lot of experience with the particular diseases of their region.

Before travelling

Take out medical insurance. Make sure it covers all eventualities especially evacuation to your home country by a medically equipped plane, if necessary. You should have a dental check up, obtain a spare glasses prescription, a spare oral contraceptive prescription (or enought pills to last) and, if you suffer from a chronic illness (such as diabetes, high blood pressure, ear or sinus troubles, cardio-pulmonary disease or nervous disorder) arrange for a check up with your doctor, who can at the same time provide you with a letter explaining the details of your disability in English and if possible French. Check the current practice in countries you are visiting for malaria prophylaxis (prevention). If you are on regular medication, make sure you have enough to cover the period of your travel.

Children More preparation is probably necessary for babies and children than for an adult and perhaps a little more care should be taken when travelling to remote areas where health services are primitive. This is because children can be become more rapidly ill than adults (on the other hand they often recover more quickly). Diarrhoea and vomiting are the most common problems, so take the usual precautions, but more intensively. Breastfeeding is best and most convenient for babies, but powdered milk is generally available and so are baby foods in most countries. Papaya, bananas and avocados are all nutritious and can be cleanly prepared. The treatment of diarrhoea is the same for adults, except that it should start earlier and be continued with more persistence. Children get dehydrated very quickly in hot countries and can become drowsy and uncooperative unless cajoled to drink water or juice plus salts. Upper respiratory infections, such as colds, catarrh and middle ear infections are also common and if your child suffers from these normally take some antibiotics against the possibility. Outer ear infections after swimming are also common and antibiotic eardrops will help. Wet wipes are always useful and sometimes difficult to find, as, in some places are disposable nappies.

Medicines & There is very little control on the sale of drugs and medicines. You will find that many of the
what to take drugs that are available have familiar names. This means you do not have to carry a whole chest of medicines with you, but remember that the shelf life of some items, especially vaccines and antibiotics, is markedly reduced in hot conditions. Unfortunately drugs are imported into Africa from many parts of the world where quality control is not good and there have been cases of drugs being supplied with the active principle substituted by inert materials. Buy your supplies at the better outlets where there are refrigerators, even though they are more expensive and check the expiry date of all preparations you buy.

    Self-medication may be forced on you by circumstances so the following text contains the names of drugs and medicines which you may find useful in an emergency or in out-of-the-way places. You may like to take some of the following items with you from home: **Sunglasses** ones designed for intense sunlight; **Earplugs** for sleeping on aeroplanes and in noisy hotels; **Suntan cream** with a high protection factor; **Insect repellent** containing DET for preference; **Mosquito net** lightweight, permethrin-impregnated for choice; **Tablets** for travel sickness; **Tampons** can be expensive in some countries; **Condoms; Contraceptives; Water sterilising tablets; Antimalarial tablets**; **Anti-infective ointment** for example Cetrimide; **Dusting powder** for feet et cetera containing fungicide; **Antacid tablets** for indigestion; **Sachets of rehydration salts** plus anti-diarrhoea preparations; **Painkillers** such as Paracetamol or Aspirin; **Antibiotics** for diarrhoea et cetera; **First Aid kit** Some may be reassured by carrying their own supplies – available from camping shops and airport shops. Get a small pack containing a few sterile syringes and needles and disposable gloves.

Smallpox vaccination is no longer required. Neither is cholera vaccination officially required, despite the fact that the disease is endemic in a number of East African counties. Only Rwanda requires a yellow fever vaccination certificate from all arriving travellers but Burundi, Djibouti, Ethiopia, Kenya, Madagascar, Mauritius, Réunion, Somalia, Tanzania, Uganda and Zaire may require yellow fever vaccination certificates from travellers who have entered from other, (especially Central and West) African, countries. Even though cholera vaccination is not officially required, nor recommended by the WHO because its effectiveness is limited, travellers are occasionally asked to produce vaccination certificates if they have been in cholera endemic areas such as parts of Asia or South America. If you are concerned this may be a problem but do not want to be given an ineffective vaccine, ask your own doctor for a cholera vaccination exemption certificate.

Vaccination & immunisation

Vaccination against the following diseases are recommended:

Yellow Fever This is a live vaccination not to be given to children under nine months of age or persons allergic to eggs. Immunity lasts for 10 years, an International Certificate of Yellow Fever Vaccination will be given and should be kept because it is sometimes asked for. The vaccination is practically without side effects and almost totally protective.

Typhoid A disease spread by the insanitary preparation of food. A number of new vaccines against this condition are now available; the older TAB and monovalent typhoid vaccines are being phased out. The newer, for example Typhim Vi, cause less side effects, but are more expensive. For those who do not like injections, there are now oral vaccines.

Poliomyelitis Despite its decline in the world this remains a serious disease if caught and is easy to protect against. There are live oral vaccines and in some countries injected inactivated or killed vaccines. Whichever one you choose it is a good idea to have booster every 5-10 years if visiting developing countries regularly.

Tetanus One dose should be given with a booster at six weeks and another at six months and 10 yearly boosters thereafter are recommended.

Children They should already be properly protected against diphtheria, poliomyelitis and pertussis (whooping cough), measles and HIB all of which can be more serious infections than at home. Measles, mumps and rubella vaccine is also given to children throughout the world, but those teenage girls who have not had rubella (german measles) should be tested and vaccinated. Hepatitis B vaccination for babies is now routine in some countries. Consult your doctor for advice on tuberculosis inoculation: the disease is still common in the region.

Infectious Hepatitis This is less of a problem for travellers than it used to be because of the development of two extremely effective vaccines against the A and B form of the disease. It remains common. A combined hepatitis A & B vaccine is now available – one jab covers both diseases.

Other vaccinations: Meningococcal meningitis occurs in epidemic form in a belt extending across Sub-Saharan Africa during most dry seasons. It may be worth being vaccinated against the A and C strains of this disease or indeed if there is an epidemic occurring locally in any of the countries. There is an effective vaccination against rabies which should be considered by all travellers, especially those going through remote areas or if there is a particular occupational risk, for example for zoologists or veterinarians.

Further information on health risks abroad, vaccinations et cetera may be available from a local travel clinic. If you wish to take specific drugs with you such as antibiotics these are best prescribed by your own doctor. Beware, however, that not all doctors can be experts on the health problems of remote countries. More detailed or more up-to-date information than local doctors can provide are available from various sources. In the UK there are hospital departments specialising in tropical diseases in London, Liverpool, Birmingham and Glasgow and the Malaria Reference Laboratory at the London School of Hygiene and Tropical Medicine provides free advice about malaria, T0891-600350. In the USA the local Public Health Services can give such information and information is available centrally from the Centre for Disease Control (CDC) in Atlanta, T404-3324559.

Further information

There are additional computerized databases which can be assessed for destination-specific up-to-the-minute information. In the UK there is MASTA (Medical Advisory Service to Travellers Abroad), T0171-6314408, F0171-4365389, Telex 8953473 and Travax (Glasgow,

T0141-9467120, ext 247). Other information on medical problems overseas can be obtained from the book by Dawood, Richard (Editor) (1999) *Travellers' Health: How to stay healthy abroad*, Oxford University Press 1992, £9.50. We strongly recommend this revised and updated edition, especially to the intrepid traveller heading for the more out of the way places. General advice is also available in the UK in *Health Information for Overseas Travel* published by the Department of Health and available from HMSO, and *International Travel and Health* published by WHO, Geneva. One of the better websites is Lonely Planet's www.lonelyplanet.com.au/health/predep.htm which offer good health advice and details about where to buy medical kits when travelling to Third World destinations.

Staying healthy

Intestinal upsets The thought of catching a stomach bug worries visitors but there have been great improvements in food hygiene and most such infections are preventable. Travellers' diarrhoea and vomiting is due, most of the time, to food poisoning, usually passed on by the insanitary habits of food handlers. As a general rule the cleaner your surroundings and the smarter the restaurant, the less likely you are to suffer.

Foods to avoid: uncooked, undercooked, partially cooked or reheated meat, fish, eggs, raw vegetables and salads, especially when they have been left out exposed to flies. Stick to fresh food that has been cooked from raw just before eating and make sure you peel fruit yourself. Wash and dry your hands before eating – disposable wet-wipe tissues are useful for this.

Pasteurised or heat treated milk is widely available in some of the countries as is ice cream or yoghurt produced by the same methods. Unpasteurised milk products, including cheese, are sources of tuberculosis, brucellosis, listeria and food poisoning germs. You can render fresh milk safe by heating it to 62°C for 30 minutes, followed by rapid cooling or by boiling it but this usually makes it taste horrible. Matured or processed cheeses are safer than the fresh varieties.

Tap water is generally held to be unsafe or at least unreliable throughout East Africa. Filtered or bottled water is usually available and safe, although you must make sure that somebody is not filling bottles from the tap and hammering on a new crown cap. Ice for drinks should be made from boiled water, but rarely is so stand your glass on the ice cubes, rather than putting them in the drink. The better hotels have water purifying systems.

Summary: Avoiding intestinal upsets

- Eat food that is freshly cooked and still hot
- Peel all fruit yourself
- Don't eat salads or raw vegetables
- Don't eat shellfish
- Don't eat ice cream
- Don't eat food that has been left uncovered – remember that flies can transmit faeces to food
- Don't drink tap water
- Don't put ice into drinks
- Don't drink unpasteurised milk
- Before drinking bottled water check the seal

Travellers' diarrhoea This is usually caused by eating food which has been contaminated by food poisoning germs. Drinking water is not always the culprit. Sea water or river water is more likely to be contaminated by sewage and so swimming in such dilute effluent can also be a cause.

Infection with various organisms can give rise to travellers' diarrhoea. They may be viruses, bacteria, for example Escherichia coli (probably the most common cause worldwide), protozoal (such as amoebas and giardia), salmonella and cholera. The diarrhoea may come on suddenly or rather slowly. It may or may not be accompanied by vomiting or by severe abdominal pain and the passage of blood or mucus when it is called dysentery.

Water purification

There are a number of ways of purifying water in order to make it safe to drink. Dirty water should first be strained through a filter bag (camping shops) and then boiled or treated. Bringing water to a rolling boil at sea level is sufficient to make the water safe for drinking, but at higher altitudes you have to boil the water for longer to ensure that all the microbes are killed.

There are sterilising methods that can be used and there are proprietary preparations containing chlorine (eg Puritabs) or iodine (eg Pota Aqua) compounds. Chlorine compounds generally do not kill protozoa (eg giardia).

There are a number of water filters now on the market available in personal and expedition size. They work either on mechanical or chemical principles, or may do both. Make sure you take the spare parts or spare chemicals with you and do not believe everything the manufacturers say.

How do you know which type you have caught and how to treat it?

If you can time the onset of the diarrhoea to the minute ('acute') then it is probably due to a virus or a bacterium and/or the onset of dysentery. The treatment in addition to rehydration is Ciprofloxacin 500 milligrams every 12 hours; the drug is now widely available and there are many similar ones.

The symptoms of **cholera** are passing profuse watery diarrhoea 1-5 days after infection which can lead to rapid dehydration. It may be accompanied by vomiting. More than half a litre of fluid may be lost every hour and must be replaced because the dehydration if untreated can be fatal. The cholera vaccine is largely ineffective. Cholera outbreaks were reported in East Africa after the heavy El Niño rains of 1997/8. Treatment of cholera is to replace lost fluids with water containing sugar/salt (see below for proportions). Tetracycline can shorten the period of diarrhoea and infectiousness.

If the diarrhoea comes on slowly or intermittently ('sub-acute') then it is more likely to be protozoal, that is caused by an amoeba or giardia. Antibiotics such a Ciprofloxacin will have little effect. These cases are best treated by a doctor as is any outbreak of diarrhoea continuing for more than three days. Sometimes blood is passed in ameobic dysentery and for this you should certainly seek medical help. If this is not available then the best treatment is probably Tinidazole (Fasigyn) one tablet four times a day for three days. If there are severe stomach cramps, the following drugs may help but are not very useful in the management of acute diarrhoea: Loperamide (Imodium) and Diphenoxylate with Atropine (Lomotil) They should not be given to children.

Any kind of diarrhoea, whether or not accompanied by vomiting, responds well to the replacement of water and salts, taken as frequent small sips, of some kind of rehydration solution. There are proprietary preparations consisting of sachets of powder which you dissolve in boiled water or you can make your own by adding half a teaspoonful of salt (three and a half grams) and four tablespoonsful of sugar (40 grams) to a litre of boiled water.

Thus the lynch pins of treatment for diarrhoea are rest, fluid and salt replacement, antibiotics such as Ciprofloxacin for the bacterial types and special diagnostic tests and medical treatment for the amoeba and giardia infections. Salmonella infections and cholera, although rare, can be devastating diseases and it would be wise to get to a hospital as soon as possible if these were suspected.

Fasting, peculiar diets and the consumption of large quantities of yoghurt have not been found useful in calming travellers' diarrhoea or in rehabilitating inflamed bowels. Oral rehydration has on the other hand, especially in children, been a life saving technique and should always be practised, whatever other treatment you use. As there is some evidence that alcohol and milk might prolong diarrhoea they should be avoided during and immediately after an attack.

Diarrhoea occurring day after day for long periods of time (chronic diarrhoea) is notoriously resistant to amateur attempts at treatment and again warrants proper diagnostic tests (most towns with reasonable sized hospitals have laboratories for stool samples). There are ways of preventing travellers' diarrhoea for short periods of time by taking antibiotics, but this is not a foolproof technique and should not be used other than in exceptional circumstances. Doxycycline is possibly the best drug. Some preventatives such as Enterovioform can have serious side effects if taken for long periods.

Paradoxically **constipation** is also common, probably induced by dietary change, inadequate fluid intake in hot places and long bus journeys. Simple laxatives are useful in the short-term and bulky foods such as maize, beans and plenty of fruit are also useful.

High altitude East Africa contains two well known mountains, Kilimanjaro and Mount Kenya both of which are over 5,000 metres in height. Addis Ababa in Ethiopia is about 2,400 metres. Spending time here is usually a pleasure – it is not so hot, there are no insects and the air is clear and spring like. Travelling to high altitudes, however, can cause medical problems, all of which can be prevented if care is taken.

On reaching heights above about 3,000 metres, heart pounding and shortness of breath, especially on exertion are a normal response to the lack of oxygen in the air. A condition called acute mountain sickness can also affect visitors. It is more likely to affect those who ascend rapidly, for example by plane and those who over-exert themselves (teenagers for example). Acute mountain sickness takes a few hours or days to come on and presents with a bad headache, extreme tiredness, sometimes dizziness, loss of appetite and frequently nausea and vomiting. Insomnia is common and is often associated with a suffocating feeling when lying in bed. Keen observers may note their breathing tends to wax and wane at night and their face tends to be puffy in the mornings – this is all part of the syndrome. Anyone can get this condition and past experience is not always a good guide: the author, having spent years in Peru travelling constantly between sea level and very high altitude never suffered symptoms, then was severely affected whilst climbing Kilimanjaro in Tanzania.

The treatment of acute mountain sickness is simple – rest, painkillers, (preferably not aspirin based) for the headache and anti sickness pills for vomiting. Oxygen is actually not much help, except at very high altitude.

To **prevent** the condition: on arrival at places over 3,000 metres have a few hours rest in a chair and avoid alcohol, cigarettes and heavy food. If the symptoms are severe and prolonged, it is best to descend to a lower altitude and to reascend slowly or in stages. If this is impossible because of shortage of time or if you are going so high that acute mountain sickness is very likely, then the drug Acetazolamide (Diamox) can be used as a preventative and continued during the ascent. There is good evidence of the value of this drug but some people do experience peculiar side effects. The usual dose is 500 milligrams of the slow release preparation each night, starting the night before ascending above 3,000 metres.

Watch out for **sunburn** at high altitude. The ultraviolet rays are extremely powerful. The air is also excessively dry at high altitude and you might find that your skin dries out and the inside of your nose becomes crusted. Use a moisturiser for the skin and some vaseline wiped into the nostrils. Some people find contact lenses irritate because of the dry air. It is unwise to ascend to high altitude if you are pregnant, especially in the first three months, or if you have a history of heart, lung or blood disease, including sickle cell.

A more unusual condition can affect mountaineers who ascend rapidly to high altitude – **acute pulmonary oedema**. Residents at altitude sometimes experience this when returning to the mountains from time spent at the coast. This condition is often preceded by acute mountain sickness and comes on quite rapidly with severe breathlessness, noisy breathing, cough, blueness of the lips and frothing at the mouth. Anybody who develops this must be brought down as soon as possible, given oxygen and taken to hospital.

A rapid descent from high places will make sinus problems and middle ear infections worse and might make your teeth ache. Lastly, don't fly to altitude within 24 hours of SCUBA diving. You might suffer from 'the bends'.

Heat & cold Full acclimatisation to high temperatures takes about two weeks. During this period it is normal to feel a bit apathetic, especially if the relative humidity is high. Drink plenty of water (up to 15 litres a day are required when working physically hard in the tropics), use salt on your food and avoid extreme exertion. Tepid showers are more cooling than hot or cold ones.

Large hats do not cool you down, but do prevent sunburn. Remember that, especially in the highlands, there can be a large and sudden drop in temperature between sun and shade and between night and day, so dress accordingly. Warm jackets or woollens are essential after dark at high altitude. Loose cotton is still the best material when the weather is hot.

Sunburn The burning power of the tropical sun, especially at high altitude, is phenomenal. Always wear a wide brimmed hat and use some form of suncream lotion on untanned skin. The sun can cause skin cancer and tanning ages the skin. If you insist on sunbathing then expose yourself gradually to sunlight and use a high factor sun-screen. Normal temperate zone suntan lotions (protection factor up to 7) are not much good; you need to use the types designed specifically for the tropics or for mountaineers or skiers with protection factors of 15 or above. Being in the water offers no protection from sunburn. Glare from the sun can cause conjunctivitis, so wear sunglasses especially on tropical beaches, where high protection factor sunscreen should also be used.

Heat stroke is a potentially life-threatening condition in which over-exposure to extreme heat causes causes the body's heat-regulating mechanisms to fail and the body temperature may reach 41.5°C (107°F). Without emergency treatment the person lapses into coma and may die.

Heat stroke is often preceded by **heat exhaustion**, the signs of which are profuse sweating, faintness, feeling weak and exhaustion. Over-strenuous activity, over-eating and drinking too much alcohol and wearing unsuitable clothing are all contributory factors. Older people in poor general health may be at greater risk of developing heat exhaustion which, if unrecognised and not treated, could proceed to heat stroke. Heat exhaustion can usually be avoided by gradual acclimatisation to hot conditions. If you get heat exhaustion, the most important thing is to avoid dehydration by taking frequent small amounts of non-alcoholic fluid, adding some salt, and staying in a cool environment.

Skin rashes & infections

Prickly heat A very common intensely itchy rash is avoided by frequent washing and by wearing loose clothing. Cured by allowing skin to dry off through use of powder and spending two nights in an air conditioned hotel!

Athletes foot This and other fungal skin infections are best treated with Tolnaftate or Clotrimazole.

Insects

These are mostly more of a nuisance than a serious hazard and if you try, you can prevent yourself entirely from being bitten. Some, such as mosquitos are, of course, carriers of potentially serious diseases, so it is sensible to avoid being bitten as much as possible. Sleep off the ground and use a mosquito net or some kind of insecticide. Preparations containing Pyrethrum or synthetic pyrethroids are safe. They are available as aerosols or pumps and the best way to use these is to spray the room thoroughly in all areas (follow the instructions rather than the insects) and then shut the door for a while, re-entering when the smell has dispersed. Mosquito coils release insecticide as they burn slowly. They are widely available and useful out of doors. Tablets of insecticide which are placed on a heated mat plugged into a wall socket are probably the most effective. They fill the room with insecticidal fumes in the same way as aerosols or coils.

You can also use insect repellents, most of which are effective against a wide range of pests. The most common and effective is diethyl metatoluamide (DEET). DEET liquid is best for arms and face (care around eyes and with spectacles – DEET dissolves plastic). Aerosol spray is good for clothes and ankles and liquid DEET can be dissolved in water and used to impregnate cotton clothes and mosquito nets. Some repellents now contain DEET and Permethrin, insecticide. Impregnated wrist and ankle bands can also be useful.

If you are bitten or stung, itching may be relieved by cool baths, antihistamine tablets (care with alcohol or driving) or mild corticosteroid creams, for example. hydrocortisone (great care: never use if any hint of infection). Careful scratching of all your bites once a day can be surprisingly effective. Calamine lotion and cream have limited effectiveness and antihistamine creams are not recommended – they can cause allergies themselves.

Bites which become infected should be treated with a local antiseptic or antibiotic cream such as Cetrimide, as should any infected sores or scratches. Minor scratches can become rapidly infected, so it is important to clean them scrupulously and take care of them.

Lice & scabies When living rough, skin infestations with body lice (crabs) and scabies are easy to pick up. Use whatever local commercial preparation is recommended for lice and scabies.

Crotamiton cream (Eurax) alleviates itching and also kills a number of skin parasites. Malathion lotion fivepercent (Prioderm) kills lice effectively, but avoid the use of the toxic agricultural preparation of Malathion, more often used to commit suicide.

Ticks They attach themselves usually to the lower parts of the body often after walking in areas where cattle have grazed. They take a while to attach themselves strongly, but swell up as they start to suck blood. The important thing is to remove them gently, so that they do not leave their head parts in your skin because this can cause a nasty allergic reaction some days later. Do not use petrol, vaseline, lighted cigarettes et cetera to remove the tick, but, with a pair of tweezers remove the beast gently by gripping it at the attached (head) end and rock it out in very much the same way that a tooth is extracted. Certain tropical flies which lay their eggs under the skin of sheep and cattle also occasionally do the same thing to humans with the unpleasant result that a maggot grows under the skin and pops up as a boil or pimple. The best way to remove these is to cover the boil with oil, vaseline or nail varnish so as to stop the maggot breathing, then to squeeze it out gently the next day.

In some parts of Africa the **jigger flea** commonly burrows its way into people's feet causing a painful itchy swelling which finally bursts in a rather disgusting fashion. Avoid these by not going barefoot or wearing sandals and if they do become established have someone experienced winkle them out with a sterile needle.

Snake bite This is a very rare event indeed for travellers. If you are unlucky (or careless) enough to be bitten by a venomous snake, spider, scorpion or sea creature, try to identify the creature, but do not put yourself in further danger. Snake bites in particular are very frightening, but in fact rarely poisonous – even venomous snakes bite without injecting venom. What you might expect if bitten are: fright, swelling, pain and bruising around the bite and soreness of the regional lymph glands, perhaps nausea, vomiting and a fever. Signs of serious poisoning would be the following symptoms: numbness and tingling of the face, muscular spasms, convulsions, shortness of breath and bleeding. Victims should be taken to a hospital or a doctor without delay. Commercial snake bite and scorpion kits are available, but usually only useful for the specific type of snake or scorpion for which they are designed. Most serum has to be given intravenously so it is not much good equipping yourself with it unless you are used to making injections into veins. It is best to rely on local practice in these cases, because the particular creatures will be known about locally and appropriate treatment can be given.

Treatment of snake bite Reassure and comfort the victim frequently. Immobilize the limb using a bandage or a splint or by getting the person to lie still. Do not slash the bite area and try to suck out the poison because this sort of heroism does more harm than good. If you know how to use a tourniquet in these circumstances, you will not need this advice. If you are not experienced do not apply a tourniquet.

Precautions Avoid walking in snake territory in bare feet or sandals – wear proper shoes or boots. If you encounter a snake stay put until it slithers away, and do not investigate a wounded snake. Spiders and scorpions may be found in the more basic hotels. If stung, rest and take plenty of fluids and call a doctor. The best precaution is to keep beds away from the walls and look inside your shoes and under the toilet seat every morning. Certain tropical sea fish when trodden upon inject venom into bathers' feet. This can be exceptionally painful. Wear plastic shoes when you go bathing if such creatures are reported. The pain can be relieved by immersing the foot in extremely hot water for as long as the pain persists.

AIDS This has had a devastating effect on the population of East Africa where it is mainly spread by heterosexual intercourse. Men and women are about equally affected. Some transmission occurs through infected blood transfusions. Screening for the HIV virus in blood for transfusion is not always accurately performed or even performed at all, so in some East African countries blood transfusion represents a real risk, not only of infection with HIV but with hepatitis, malaria and a few other infections. The main risk to travellers is from casual sex, heterosexual or homosexual. The same precautions should be taken as when encountering any sexually transmitted disease. Female prostitution is common throughout East Africa and an alarmingly high proportion of the prostitute population is HIV positive. There may in addition be transmission, especially in the big cities and holiday areas, via intravenous drug abuse. The AIDS virus (HIV) can be passed via unsterile needles which have been previously used to inject an HIV positive patient. Risks of acquiring blood-borne viruses need to be emphasised when considering having a tattoo, ear or body piercing. It would however be sensible to check that needles have been properly sterilised or disposable needles used. Hepatitis B is a much greater risk. Be wary of carrying disposable needles as Customs officials may find them suspicious, not so much in Africa but in Europe and North America. The risk of HIV transmission in a blood transfusion is greater than from dirty needles because of the amount of fluid exchanged.

Studies have shown that tourists most commonly contract HIV from local people or other travellers after having taken too much alcohol – as this impairs their judgement. Some countries require evidence of a negative HIV test before entry for certain categories of visitor. It is advisable to check with the embassy before travelling.

Immuno-compromised travellers should check the medical facilities in the country of destination before departure, and check that their medical insurance covers their requirements. Medication for their whole trip should be obtained before departure and should be clearly labelled.

Catching the AIDS virus (HIV) does not necessarily produce an illness in itself (although it may do). The only way to be sure if you feel you have been put at risk is to have a blood test for HIV antibodies on your return to a place where there are reliable laboratory facilities. The test does not become positive for many weeks and during those weeks the person who has caught the virus is likely to be extremely infectious.

Malaria

Malaria remains a serious disease and occurs with varying frequency throughout East Africa. Every year travellers die from malaria because they have not taken sufficient precautions. Malaria is a serious parasitic disease spread by the bites of the Anopheles mosquito. Malaria is the single most important disease hazard for travellers to warm climates. Mosquitoes have developed resistance to insecticides and in several areas to anti-malarial drugs. In some countries – Djibouti, Somalia, Tanzania, Uganda and Zaire it is very common indeed. Mosquitos do not thrive above 2,500 metres, so you are safe above that altitude. There are different varieties of malaria. The four species that cause disease in man are: *plasmodium falciparum, plasmodium vivax, plasmodium ovale* and *plasmodium malariaea*. Each species spends part of its life cycle in the Anopheles mosquito and part in humans. *Falciparum malaria* infections are most frequently contracted in Africa. The symptoms of malaria include shaking, fevers and chills. They appear when the red blood cells that are affected by the parasite rupture, releasing more parasites into the bloodstream. The period between being bitten by a mosquito and the appearance of symptoms is usually one to two weeks. However, it can be as long as a year if the person has been taking anti-malarial drugs, which may suppress rather than prevent the disease.

In classic malaria the main symptom is fever or malarial ague. This usually has three stages – a cold stage of uncontrollable shivering, a hot stage where the temperature may reach 40.5ºC (105ºF) and then a sweating stage which brings down the temperature and drenches the bedding. In addition the affected person may have a severe headache, feel generally very unwell and vomiting may accompany the attack. Following the malarial attack, the affected person is left feeling very weak and tired and may be extremely sleepy. The fever may develop in a cyclical pattern on alternate days.

Plasmodium falciparum is diffeerent from the other varieties of malaria because it affects all ages of red blood cells, whereas the other varieties attack only young or old red blood cells. As a result *falciparum* malaria affects a greater proportion of blood cells and is therefore more

Essentials

severe. This form of malaria can prove fatal within a few days of the appearance of symptoms. Fever may be prolonged and irregular and symptoms may resemble those of influenza. The severity of the disease may not be recognised at this stage. When red blood cells are infected with parasites they become sticky and cause blockages in small blood vessels in vital organs, like the kidneys, liver, spleen and the brain. Kidney failure and jaundice are common complications of *falciparum* malaria. Even if you have taken antimalarial drugs and precautions against bites it is possible to contract malaria. Anyone who develops fever and a headache after a trip to the tropics should see their doctor as soon as possible and mention the trip abroad to exclude malaria. Malaria is diagnosed by studying blood samples taken at 6-12 hour intervals. Parasites at differing developmental stages can be seen under a microscope.

Prophylaxis and treatment   It is important to take a prophylactic regime. Start taking the tablets a one to two weeks before exposure and continue to take them for four to six weeks after leaving the malarial zone as advised. Preventative antimalarial drugs should be taken by all visitors to the tropics: this includes pregnant women and children. Opinion varies on the precise drugs and dosage to be used for protection. All the drugs may have some side effects and it is important to balance the risk of catching the disease against the albeit rare side effects of the medication. If your itinerary takes you into a malarial area, seek expert advice before you go on a suitable prophylactic regime. Chloroquine is recommended for areas where there is no resistance to this drug. Proguanil may be preferred for longer term use because it has fewer side effects. Combinations of Chloroquine and Proguanil or Pyrimethamine and Dapsone may be prescribed. Mefloquine (Larium) is the most effective preventative drug against malaria but there are concerns about side-effects. Neuro-psychiatric side effects, such as depression and anxiety, can be quite severe in a small number of cases, estimated to be in the region of one in 200 cases. People with a history of depressive illnesses are advised not to take Mefloquine, but to take alternatives and be stringent in their avoidance of mosquito bite measures. Sub-Saharan Africa, where falciparum malaria is most prevalent is the zone where Mefloquine is the primary recommended anti-malarial medication. Mefloquine should be started two weeks before travelling to a malarial zone and continued for four weeks after leaving this zone.

The increasing complexity of the subject is such that, as the malarial parasite becomes immune to the new generation of drugs, the physical prevention of being bitten by mosquitos becomes all the more important. In addition to taking preventative medication, all travellers to the tropics should make every effort to avoid mosquito bites. The Anopheles mosquito is most active in the evening, emerging at dusk and hunting until dawn. It hunts at ground level and can bite through thin socks. Outdoor precautions include wearing long toursers and sturdy shoes in the evenings. Choose light coloured clothing. Apply an insect repellent containing DEET to exposed skin, but take care when applying it to your face. For longer-lasting protection, wear wrist and ankle bands soaked in DEET. Indoor precautions include choosing a room that has mosquito screens (intact) on all windows and doors. Using an intact mosquito net, preferably soaked in Permethrin, tucking the net under the mattress. Spray the room every evening with an insecticide spray, especially in dark recesses like the wardrobes or under the beds. Use a vaporizing mat for longer protection or mosquito smoke coils. Electric buzzers are ineffective.

It is important to complete the course of anti-malarial drugs when leaving the tropics. If you get any flu-like symptoms either during your stay or for three months after leaving a malarial zone, see a doctor immediately and have your blood tested for malaria. Certain people are at highter risk of contracting severe malaria and need to be forewarned. These include pregnant women, anyone who is immuno-compromised and anyone who has had their spleen removed.

Infectious hepatitis (jaundice)   The main symptoms are pains in the stomach, lack of appetite, lassitude and yellowness of the eyes and skin. Medically speaking there are two main types. The less serious, but more common is Hepatitis A for which the best protection is the careful preparation of food, the avoidance of contaminated drinking water and scrupulous attention to toilet hygiene. The other, more serious, version is Hepatitis B which is acquired usually as a sexually transmitted disease or by blood transfusions. It can less commonly be transmitted by injections with unclean needles and possibly by insect bites. The symptoms are the same as for Hepatitis A. The incubation period is much longer (up to six months compared with six weeks) and there are more likely to be complications.

Hepatitis A can be protected against with gamma globulin. It should be obtained from a reputable source and is certainly useful for travellers who intend to live rough. You should have a shot before leaving and have it repeated every six months. The dose of gamma globulin depends on the concentration of the particular preparation used, so the manufacturer's advice should be taken. The injection should be given as close as possible to your departure and as the dose depends on the likely time you are to spend in potentially affected areas, the manufacturer's instructions should be followed. Gamma globulin has really been superseded now by a proper vaccination against Hepatitis A (Havrix) which gives immunity lasting up to 10 years. After that boosters are required. Havrix monodose is now widely available as is Junior Havrix. The vaccination has negligible side effects and is extremely effective. Gamma globulin injections can be a bit painful, but it is much cheaper than Havrix and may be more available in some places.

Hepatitis B can be effectively prevented by a specific vaccine (Engerix) – three shots over six months before travelling. If you have had jaundice in the past it would be worthwhile having a blood test to see if you are immune to either of these two types, because this might avoid the necessity and costs of vaccination or gamma globulin. There are other kinds of viral hepatitis (C, E et cetera) which are fairly similar to A and B, but vaccines are not available as yet.

Other risks and serious diseases

Typhus Can still occur carried by ticks. There is usually a reaction at the site of the bite and a fever. Seek medical advice.

Intestinal worms These are common and the more serious ones such as hookworm can be contracted from walking barefoot on infested earth or beaches.

Filariasis This causes such diseases as elephantiasis occurs in many East African countries. It is also transmitted by mosquitoes.

Hydatid disease This is common in Ethiopia but can be avoided by keeping well clear of dogs which is good advice in any case.

Leishmaniasis This causes a skin ulcer which will not heal occurs in many East African countries. It is transmitted by sand flies. A more serious form, visceral leishmaniasis or kala-azar affects mainly children, rarely tourists but occurs all over East Africa.

Bilharzia (schistosomiasis) A parasitic disease caused by three species of flukes. It is caught by wading or bathing in infested waters, including lakes, rivers or irrigation systems. The fluke spends part of its life cycle inside freshwater snails which are found in slow-moving, well-oxygenated fresh water.

The first sign may be an itchy tingling patch where the fluke entered your skin, which may develop into a local rash. Some weeks later, when the adult starts producing eggs, the next symptom may be a flu-like illness with fevers, chills, and general malaise. Subsequent symptoms may include blood in the urine or faeces, abdominal or lower back pain and enlargement of the liver or spleen. Long-term complications may include liver cirrhosis and kidney failure.

There is no vaccine available against bilharzia. Prevention is the key. Avoid wading or swimming in rivers, lakes, and irrigation systems. Only swim in chlorinated swimming pools. Treatment is by a single dose of Praziquantel which kills the flukes and so limits the damage to internal organs.

Dengue fever This is a problem in some countries where it may be called Break Bone fever. It can be completely prevented by avoiding mosquito bites in the same way as malaria. No vaccine is available. Dengue is an unpleasant and painful acute viral infection, presenting with a high temperature and body pains, but at least visitors are spared the more serious forms (haemorrhagic types) which are more of a problem for local people who have been exposed to the disease more than once. There is no specific treatment for dengue – just pain killers and rest. Transmission is by day and evening – biting mosquitoes. Avoidance relies on the use of anti-mosquito measures as described in the section on malaria.

Trypanosomiasis This disease, essentially a brain infection causing drowsiness, is transmitted by a large, tenacious insect – the tsetse fly. This is a fly not always repelled by DET but very susceptible to Pyrethroid fly spray and Permethrin. The main risk is in game parks where these rather aggressive flies are common.

Rabies Remember that rabies is endemic throughout Africa, so avoid dogs that are behaving strangely. If you are bitten by a domestic or wild animal, do not leave things to chance: scrub the wound with soap and water and/or disinfectant, try to have the animal captured (within limits) or at least determine its ownership, where possible, and seek medical assistance at once. The course of treatment depends on whether you have already been satisfactorily vaccinated against rabies. If you have (this is worthwile if you are spending lengths of time in developing countries) then some further doses of vaccine are all that is required. Human diploid vaccine is the best, but expensive: other, older kinds of vaccine, such as that derived from duck embryos may be the only types available. These are effective, much cheaper and interchangeable generally with the human derived types. If not already vaccinated then anti rabies serum (immunoglobulin) may be required in addition. It is important to finish the course of treatment whether the animal survives or not.

Dangerous animals Apart from mosquitoes the most dangerous animals are men, be they bandits or behind steering wheels. Think carefully about violent confrontations and wear a seat belt if you are lucky enough to have one available to you.

When you return home

Remember to take your antimalarial tablets for four to six weeks after leaving the malarial area as advised. If you have had attacks of diarrhoea it is worth having a stool specimen tested in case you have picked up amoebas. If you have been living rough, blood tests may be worthwhile to detect worms and other parasites. If you have been exposed to bilharzia (*schistosomiasis*) by swimming in lakes et cetera, check by means of a blood test when you get home, but leave it for six weeks because the test is slow to become positive. Report any untowards symptoms to your doctor and tell the doctor exactly where you have been and, if you know, what the likelihood of disease is to which you were exposed.

Safaris

One of the main reasons for going to East Africa is the wonderful wildlife. Seeing the animals – going on Safari – can be a most rewarding experience at any time of year. However, for the vast majority of travellers it is something to be prepared for, as it will almost certainly involve a degree of discomfort and long journeys. The roads in East Africa can be very exhausting for travellers. The unsealed roads are bumpy and dusty, and it will be hot. It is also important to remember that despite the expert knowledge of the drivers, they cannot guarantee that you will see any animals. When they do spot one of the rarer animals – a leopard or rhinoceros perhaps – their pleasure is almost as enjoyable as seeing the animal. To get the best from your safari, approach it with humour, look after the driver as well as you are able (a disgruntled driver will quickly ruin your safari), and do your best to get on with, and be considerate to your fellow travellers.

Hotels and lodges These vary and may be either typical hotels with rooms and facilities in one building or individual bandas or rondavels (small huts) with a central dining area. Most have been built with great care and blend very well into the environment.

Sleeping

Tented camps A luxury tented camp is really the best of both worlds. They are usually built with a central dining area. Each tent will have a thatched roof to keep it cool inside, proper beds, and verandah and they will often have a small bathroom at the back with solar heated hot water. But at the same time you will have the feeling of being in the heart of Africa and at night you will hear animals surprisingly close by.

Campsites There are campsites in most national parks. They are extensively used by camping safari companies (although they often have their own 'permanent' campsites). They are often most attractively sited, perhaps in the elbow of a river course but always with plenty of shade. Birds are plentiful and several hours can be whiled away bird watching. Some campsites have attached to them a few bandas or huts run by the park where you may be able to shower. Toilet facilities can be primitive – the 'long drop', a basic hole in a concrete slab being very common. Away from the permanent sites, you will be expected to pitch your own tent. Sleeping mats are usually provided but you must bring your own sleeping bag and pillow. Sleeping bags can be hired from most companies for a modest amount. A deposit is required. Check on availability at the time of booking and reserve if necessary.

Most camps are guarded but despite this you should be careful to ensure that valuables are not left unattended. Be careful about leaving items outside your tent. Many campsites have troupes of baboons nearby. They can be a nuisance.

If you are camping on your own, you will almost always need to be totally self sufficient with all your own equipment. The campsites usually provide running water and firewood. The extent to which you will have to be self sufficient with food varies from park to park.

Safaris can be booked either at home or in the country concerned – if you go for the latter it may be possible to obtain substantial discounts. If you elect to book in the country avoid companies offering cheap deals on the street – they will almost always turn out to be a disaster and may appear cheap because they do not include National Park entrance fees.

Safaris do not run on every day of the week. Trips are often timed to end on a Thursday night. Thus a six-day safari will start on a Saturday, a four-day one on a Monday. In the low season you may also find that these will be combined. If you are on a four-day safari you can expect to join another party. This can be awkward as the 'six-dayers' will already have formed into a coherent group and you may feel that you are an outsider.

Booking Safaris
There are a huge number of companies offering safaris. These are noted under each country section.

Naming the animals

Several birds and animals in Africa are named after people, reflecting an era of African history when Europeans were exploring and travelling in Africa, and writing home to describe the wonders that were to be found in that continent. Most of African wildlife was not known to science in those days, and classifying and naming species became a preoccupation of these early writers.

Many of the early explorers and travellers are among those honoured in this way. Thomson's Gazelle and Grant's Gazelle are named after two early European travellers in Africa. Joseph Thomson (1858-95) was a young Scot who travelled widely in Masai land.

He and his companion Chuma, who is better known for having carried the body of David Livingstone to the coast in 1873, undertook many expeditions together in this part of Africa. James Grant (1827-92), another Scottish explorer, is particularly known for his travels in what is now Uganda. Kirk's Dikdik is named for Sir John Kirk a doctor and botanist, who started his African travels as a member of one of David Livingstone's expeditions in 1858 and later became British consul in Zanzibar. Jackson's Hartebeest is named for Sir Frederick Jackson (1860-1938) an amateur naturalist. As Governor of Uganda, he is particularly known for his work on the birds of the area.

Unfortunately, there are some "rogue" operators. At the tourist office in Arusha there is a 'black list' of unlicenced operators and people with convictions for cheating tourists.

Specialized safaris & tours
Details of specialized tours in individual countries are listed in the Essentials section of each country.

Almost any type of activity can be undertaken in the region. The majority concentrate on the wildlife but other specialized pasttimes can be organized for example walking and trekking, ballooning, bird watching, canoeing, cycling, and fishing. Truck safaris demand a little more fortitude and adventurous spirit from the traveller. The compensation is usually the camaraderie and life-long friendships that result from what is invariably a real adventure, going to places the more luxurious travellers will never visit. *Travel Africa*, 2 Potland Cottages, Toot Baldon, Oxford, OX44 9NH, T/F01865-434220, subs@travelafricamag.com, www.travelafricamag.com. This quarterly publication is a comprehensive source of information for all African travellers.

The following is a selection of some of the special tours available in East Africa.

Truck safaris
Acacia Expeditions, 5 Walm Lane, London, NW2 5SJ, UK, T0181-4513877, F0181-4514727. *Desert Rose Camels*, c/o Creo Safaris, PO Box 2406, Nairobi, Kenya, T884258, F884445. *Dragoman*, Camp Green, Keaton Rd, Debenham, Suffolk, IP14 6LA, UK, T01728-861133, F01728-861127. *Encounter Overland*, 267 Old Brompton Rd, London, SW5 9AJ, UK, T0171-3706845, F0171-9737, www.dragoman.co.uk. *Exodus*, 9 Weir Rd, London, SW12 0LT, UK, T0181-6755550, F0181-6730779, Tx0181-6730779. *Explore*, 1 Frederick St, Aldershot, Hants, GU11 1LQ, UK, T01252-39448, F01252-343170, Tx858954. *Gametrackers*, 1st Flr, Kenya Cinema Plaza, Moi Ave, Nairobi, Kenya, PO Box 62042, T338927/222703/212830. *Guerba*, 101 Eden Vale Rd, Westbury, Wiltshire, BA13 3QX, UK, T01373-826611/826689, F01373-838351, Tx449831. *Kumuka Expeditions*, 40 Earls Court Rd, London, W8 6EJ, UK, T0171-9378855, F0171-9376664, sales@kumuka.co.uk. *Top Deck Double Decker Bus Safaris*, 131-5 Earls Court Rd, London, SW5 9RH, UK, T0171-3704555, F0171-3736201, Tx8955339. *Tracks*, 12 Abingdon St, London, W8 6AF, UK. *Truck Africa*, 37 Ranelagh Mansions, London, SW6 3UQ, UK, T0171-7316142, F0171-3717445.

East Africa
Walking tours covering Mt Elgon and Mt Kenya; Mt Kilimanjaro and Kenya; Rwenzori Mts: *Sherpa Expeditions*, 131a Heston Rd, Hounslow, Middlesex, TW5 0RD, UK, T0181-5772717, F0181-5779788.

Old-style tented safaris; Walking; Climbing; Gorillas; Chimpanzees. Fishing on Rusinga Island, Lake Victoria, Kenya: *Safari Consultants*, Orchard House, Upper Rd, Little Cornan, Suffolk,

CO10, UK, T01787-228494, F0187-228949. *Jambo Tours*, Langscheider Str. 40C, D-59846 Sundern, Germany, T295-79191, F2935 79192, info@jambotours.de.

Wildlife; Walking; Trekking; with emphasis on the Environment, Conservation and Ecology: *Worldwide*, 8 Comeragh Rd, London, W14 9HP, UK, T0171-3818638, F0171-3810836

Hiking; Canoe Safaris; Gorillas: *Explore*, 1 Frederick St, Aldershot, Hants, GU11 1LQ, UK, T01252-39448, F01252-343170, Tx858954

Trekking; Whitewater Rafting: *Encounter Overland*, 267 Old Brompton Rd, London, SW5 9AJ, UK, T0171-3706845, F0171-9737

Cycling safaris in Kenya and Tanzania; Climbing Mt Kilimajaro: *Bike Tours*, PO Box 75, Bath, Avon, BA 1BX, UK, T01225-480130, F01225-480132

Cycling safaris through Rift Valley, Masai Mara, Coast, Mt Kilimanjaro: *Leisure Activity Safaris*, PO Box 10190, Mombasa, Kenya, T487326, F485454 or UK: T01626-775070

Bird watching; Trekking; Fishing; Mule trekking: *Yumo Tours, PO Box 5698, Addis Ababa, Ethiopia, T518-878/513783, F513451, Tx21313 or 4 Seymour House, 19 Hanson St, London, W1P 7IN, UK, T/F0171-6315337*

Ethiopia

Essentials

Historic routes; Rock-hewn churches; Bird watching; Trekking; Mountain climbing, Horse riding; Fishing: *Experience Ethiopia*, PO Box 9354, Addis Ababa, Ethiopia, T152336/519219, F519902 or 211 Clapham Rd, London, SW9 0QH, UK, T0171-7303197, F0171-7383067. Travel Ethiopia, PO Box 9438, Addis Ababa, T510168, f510200, Travelethiopia@telecom.net.et.

Expedition on the Nile: *Discovery Expeditions*, Motcombe, Dorset, SP7 9PB, UK, T01747-855050, F01747-855411

Kenya Bird watching; Climbing; Golf; Historical tours; Diving: *Twiga Tours*, Shina Towers, Meru Rd, PO Box 2288, Mombasa, Kenya, T228-134/222984, F222984. *East Africa Ornithological Safaris Ltd*,PO Box 48019, Nairobi, Kenya, T+254-2-331684/335935, F216528, eaos@africaonline.co.ke. *Acacia Expeditions*, 5 Walm Lane, London, NW2 5SJ, UK, T0181-4513877.

Balloon safaris; Camel safaris; Horseback safaris; Fishing; Gliding; Hang gliding; Para gliding; Golf; Walking, Trekking and climbing; Diving and watersports; Whitewater rafting: *Let's Go Travel*, Caxton House, Standard St, PO Box 60342, Nairobi, T340331/213033, F336890, info@letsgosafari.com

Trekking; Camel trekking; Mountain bike safaris; Canoe safaris; Climbing; Gorilla safaris: *Best Camping Tours and Safaris Ltd*, Nanak House 9, 2nd Flr, Room 212, corner of Kimath/Banda sts, Nairobi, T229675, F217923. *Gametrackers*, 1st Flr, Kenya Cinema Plaza, Moi Ave, PO Box 62042, Nairobi, Kenya, T338927/222703/12830. *Habib's Tours & Travel*, Agip House, Haile Selassie Ave, PO Box 48095, Nairobi, T220463/223816, F220985, habibtours@attmail.com. *Savage Camping Tours Ltd*, Soin Arcade, Westlands Rd, Westlands, c/o PO Box, Nairobi, T449467, F449469. *Sunny Safaris*, Portal Place, Banda St, PO Box 74495, Nairobi, T226587, F339809. *Vintage Safaris*, PO Box 59470, Kijabe St (T226547, F211660) and Shimmers Plaza (T742450, F742465), Nairobi. *Wanderlust Safaris Ltd*, 4th Flr, Gilfillan House, Kenyatta Ave, PO Box 42578, Nairobi, T212281, F212953. *Bush Homes of East Africa Ltd, PO Box 56923, Nairobi, Kenya, T+254-2-571647/571649/571661, F571665, Bush.homes@tt.gn.apc.org.*

Camel expedition to Lake Turkana: *Desert Rose Camels*, c/o Geo Safaris, PO Box 24696, Nairobi, T884258/59, F884445. *Discovery Expeditions*, Motcombe, Dorset, SP7 9PB, UK, T01747-855050, F01747-855411.

Lake and deep-sea fishing: *Finfoot*, PO Box 2434, Nairobi, Kenya, T891664, F884016 or Lucewater House, New Luce, Wigstownshire, DG8 0AW, UK, T01581-600271.

Deep Sea Fishing: *Howard Lawrence-Brown*, Hall Mark Charters, PO Box 10202, Bamburi Mombasa, T11-485680, T/F11-485808, F011-475217, Mobile 071-400095. (For other companies see page 176.)

Tanzania Balloon safaris:*Serengeti Balloon Safaris*, Unit 9D, Harleston Industrial Estate, Harleston, Norfolk IP20 9EB, UK, T01379-853129, F10379-853127 or through The Adventure Centre, PO Box 12116, Arusha, Tanzania, T578578, F578997, cost US$375 pp.

Wildlife exploration: *Afri Galaxy Tours & Travels Ltd*, CCM Building, Taifa Road, Moshi, T50268, F53666, Kit@form-nrt.com. *Classic Tours and Safaris*, PO Box 7302, Arusha T7197, F8220. *Hoopoe Adventure Tours*, India St, PO Box 2047, Arusha, T7011/7541, F8226, Hoopoesafari@cybernet.co.tz; UK Suite F1, Kebbell House, Carpenders Park, Watford WD1 5BE, UK, T0181-4288221, F0181-4211396, HoopoeUK@aol.com. *Let's Go Travel*, The Adventure Centre, PO Box 12799, Arusha, T2814/7111, F8997/4199. *Mashado*, Central Reservations: PO Box 14823, Arusha, T57-6585, F8020, E Mashado@ habari.co.tz, Mobitel: T+255-811510107 or 01/02, F+255-811-510104 or 03. Offer both safari and coastal

Papa's safaris

On 8 December 1933 Ernest Hemingway, then 34 and his second wife Pauline disembarked at Mombasa. They took the train up to Nairobi and stayed at the New Stanley Hotel. They engaged the foremost white hunter, Philip Percival, and stayed on the Percival farm near Machakos. Papa began hunting on the Kipiti Plains, shooting gazelles, kongoni impala and guineafowl. On 20 Dec the safari team motored to Arusha where they stayed at the Athenaeum Hotel (now the New Safari), before heading for the Serengeti where both Pauline and Ernest bagged lions and buffaloes. Ernest contracted amoebic dysentery, and was flown back to Nairobi to recuperate. On 23 Jan he rejoined the safari just S of Ngorongoro. As they proceeded S to Babati, he shot a rhinoceros and turning E to Kyungu he managed to fell a kudu and a sable. The party continued E to Tanga, then N to Malindi, staying in the Palm Beach Hotel for a few days of deep sea fishing, hooking kingfish, amberjacks, dolphin and sailfish. At the beginning of Mar they embarked at Mombasa for Europe.

It was another 20 years before Hemingway would visit Africa again, and this was to be an altogether more eventful trip. By now he was with his fourth wife, Mary. Aug 1953 saw them once again catching the train to stay on the Percival farm. The safari got underway at Kajiado, on the edge of what is now Amboseli National Park, where Ernest shot a big, black-maned lion, zebra and gerenuk. They then moved on to Fig Tree camp in the Masai Mara before returning to the Percivals'.

Here Ernest began getting into the spirit of Africa with some gusto. He shaved his head, dyed his suede jacket and two shirts with Masai red ochre and went leopard-hunting with a spear. He took a liking to an Akamba girl, Debba, purchased her and several friends dresses for Christmas and brought them back to the camp where the celebrations became so enthusiastic that they broke one of the beds. Some months later Ernest observed that he should now be a father in Africa.

On 21 Jan Ernest and Mary flew from Nairobi, piloted by Roy Marsh. They stopped at Fig Tree camp then headed for Mwanza where they refuelled, before staying over at Costermanville (now Bukavu). As they circled the glassy waters, dotted with islands and hemmed in by green hills, Mary thought Kivu was the most beautiful lake she had ever seen. They put down at Entebbe. The following day, circling Murchison Falls, the plane hit a telegraph wire and made an emergency landing. The three lit a fire and slept under coats. Next day a boat visiting the falls gave them a lift to Butiaba. They engaged a plane and a pilot to fly them from Butiaba airstrip to Entebbe, but taking off from the bumpy runway, the plane suddenly stopped, and burst into flames. Roy Marsh kicked out a window and managed to drag Mary through. Ernest butted the jammed door open and struggled out. A policeman drove them to Masindi, and they put up in the Railway Hotel before reaching Entebbe and Lake Victoria Hotel. A few days later they flew to Nairobi.

In the meantime, a civilian airliner had reported the plane wreck – the world thought Hemingway had died and newspapers published obituaries. Though alive, he was in poor shape with concussion, ruptured liver, spleen and kidney, a crushed vertebra and burns to his face and arms. There had been plans to conclude the safari with fishing off Mombasa. Although Ernest did fly down to the coast some time later he was not able to take any active part before they sailed from Mombasa.

In 1956 there were plans to make a third trip, but poor health meant that it never materialized. Hemingway's experiences on safari provided the material for many short stories, a fine collection of which are in The Green Hills of Africa.

experiences. UK agent: Jonathan Drew, East Whipley Farm, Shamley Green, Guildford GU5 0TE, T01483-276556, F01483 275670, Mobile: 0973-203203, DO189773@ infotrade.co.uk. **Easy Travel & Tours Ltd**, Avalon House, Sokoine Drive/Zanaki Street, Dar es Salaam, T123526, F113842, easytravel@raha.com; Joel Maeda Rd, Clock Tower, PO Box 1912, Arusha, T3929, F4110/7322, E easytravel@yako.habari.co.tz. **Savannah Tours Ltd**, PO Box 20517, Dar es Salaam, T115624, 113748, savtour@twiga.com. **Ostrich Tours & Safaris Ltd**, PO Box 12752, Arusha, T/F057 4140. Paradies Safaris Ltd, PO Box 2632, Arusha, T510334, F8002, paradies91@twiga.com. *The Safari Co*, PO Box 207, Arusha, T8424, F8272. *Sandgrouse Adventure Tours & Safaris Ltd*, PO Box 11661, Arusha, T3485/4065, F4095. *Sunny Safaris Ltd*, PO Box 7267, Arusha, T7145/8184, F8094, sunny@arusha.com. *Tanganyika Wildlife Safari*, PO Box 21880, Dar es Salaam, T051-865458, F051-866158 or PO Box 2231, Arusha, T057-8072/6021, UK representative Peter MacDougall, T01277-260280, F01277-260281. *United Touring Company*, PO Box 2221, Arusha, T8844/5, F8222. *Wildlife Explorer*, 'Manyara', Manpean, Riverside, St Austell, Cornwall, PL26, UK, T01726-824132, F01726-824399. *World Archipelago Ltd*, 6 Redgrave Rd, London, SW15 1PX, UK, T0181-7805838, F0181-7809482, E 100711.3161@compuserve.com.

Uganda *Abercrombie and Kent*, PO Box 7799, Tank Hill, T/F259181. Long established company offering upmarket tours to see Uganda's major tourist sights including the gorillas. *Adrift*, PO Box 8643, Kampala, T/F041-268670, cellphone 075-707668, E adrift@starcom.co.ug. UK representative: Safari Drive Ltd, Adrift UK, Wessex House, 127 High St, Hungerford, Berkshire RG17 0DL, T01488-684509, F01488-685055, Safari_Drive@compuserve.com/raft@adrift.co.uk, www.adrift.co.uk. *Volcanoes*, 27 Lumumba Avenue, Nakasero Hill, PO Box 22818, Kampala, T00256-41-346464/5, F341718, mobile 075-741718, volcanoes@infocom.co.ug, UK representative: PO Box 16345, London SW1 0ZD, T0171-2357897, F2351780, volcanoes@mailbox.co.uk, www.VolcanoesSafaris.com. Organise tours and run camps in the Ugandan hills.

White water rafting: *Adrift UK*, Wessex House, 127 High Street, Hungerford, RG17 0DL, T01488 684509, f01488 685055, raft@adrift.co.uk.

Food & drink Standards at lodges and tented sites are the same as at normal hotels. Camping safaris usually have a cook. Food is wholesome and surprisingly varied. You can expect eggs, bacon and sausages and toast for breakfast, salads at midday and meat/ pasta in the evening with perhaps a fruit salad for desert. Companies will cater for vegetarians. Tea and coffee are on hand at all times of the day.

Insects are a fact of life and despite valiant attempts by the cook it is virtually impossible to avoid flies (as well as moths at night) alighting on plates and uncovered food. Notwithstanding this, hygiene standards are high.

Game drives There are usually two game drives each day. The morning drive sets off at about 0700 and lasts until midday. The afternoon drive starts at about 1600 and lasts until the park closes (roughly 1830-1900). In addition you may have an early morning drive which will mean getting up well before dawn at about 0500.

If you have arrived at the park by public transport, the warden and guides will arrange drives for a moderate charge, in the park vehicles.

Transport It is worth emphasing that most parks are some way from departure points. Consequently if you go on a four-day safari, you will often find that two days are taken up with travelling to and from the park – leaving you with a limited amount of time in the park itself. You will be spending a lot of time in a vehicle. On a more upmarket safari these will almost certainly be of the Toyota mini van variety accommodating about eight people. Leg room can be very limited. They will have three viewing points through the roof (the really upmarket ones will also have a sun shade). In practice this means that only one or two people can view out through the roof at each point – those in the cab will therefore have problems viewing on the opposite side as the view is usually impeded by legs.

Camping safari companies tend to use converted 10-ton lorries. Although very basic, they are surprisingly comfortable being well sprung (essential on some roads), with good leg room and large windows which fully open. Views of the animals on both sides of the truck are therefore good. They can be a little cramped if there is a full party of about 20 people.

Tipping How much to tip the driver on safari is tricky. It is best to enquire from the company at the time of booking what the going rate is. However as a rough guide you should perhaps allow a sum of about US$5-7 per adult, per night (half this for a child). Always try to come to an agreement with

Rhino: now you see them

Two species of rhino are found in Africa, the **White Rhino** and the **Black Rhino**. These names have no bearing on the colour of the animals as they are both a rather nondescript dark grey. In some guide books the White Rhino is described as being paler in colour than the Black Rhino, but this by no means obvious in the field. The name White Rhino is derived from the Dutch word `weit' which means wide and refers to the shape of the animal's mouth. The White Rhino has a large square muzzle and this reflects the fact that it is a grazer and feeds by cropping grass. The Black Rhino, on the other hand, is a browser, usually feeding on shrubs and bushes. It achieves this by using its long, prehensile upper lip which is well adapted to the purpose. The horn of the rhino is not a true horn, but is made of a material called keratin, which is essentially the same as hair. If you see rhino with their young you will notice that the White Rhino tends to follow its young herding them from behind, whereas the Black Rhino usually leads its young from the front.

In E Africa the Black Rhino originally was found only to the E of the Nile, whereas the White Rhino was to be found only to the W of the river. However in 1961 some White Rhinos were introduced into Murchison Falls National Park in Uganda from their home in West Nile Province. This was an attempt to establish a breeding population and at one time it was possible to see them there. Unfortunately this fragile population did not survive the many civil wars that raged in Uganda in the 1970s and 80s. At the same time the original population in West Nile in Uganda was also poached to extinction. The White Rhino is now severely endangered in E Africa, and a small population has been introduced into Meru National Park in the hope of reversing this trend. The Black Rhino is also severely endangered due to poaching, and work continues to rescue both these species from extinction.

other members of the group and put the tip into a common kitty. Again remember that wages are low and there can be long lay-offs during the low season. If you are on a camping safari and have a cook, give all the money to the driver and leave him to sort out the split.

What to take Room is very limited in both mini vans and lorries. You will be asked to limit the amount you bring with you. There is very little point in taking too much clothing – expect to get dirty particularly during the dry season when dust can be a problem. Try to have a clean set of clothes to change into at night when it can also get quite cold. Comfortable, loose clothing and sensible footwear is best. Bear in mind that you may well travel through a variety of climates – it can be very cool at the top of the rift valley but very hot at the bottom. It is worth having warm clothing to hand in your transport as well as plenty of mineral water. Most safari companies do not provide drinking water and it is important to buy enough bottles to last your trip before you set off. It is surprising how much you get through and restocking is not easy.

The other important items are binoculars – preferably one pair for each member of your party, a camera with a telephoto lens (you will not get close enough to the animals for a compact version) and plenty of film. Take twice as much as you think you will need. Film can be purchased at the lodges but it will cost you three times as much.

The Wildlife section in this *Handbook* will enable you to identify most animals. However you may wish to take a more detailed Field Guide. The Collins series is particularly recommended. The drivers are usually a mine of information – bear in mind though that Africans have difficulty pronouncing Ls and Rs and often interchange the two. The Lilac-breasted Roller comes out as Rirac-bleasted Lorrer – and this can confuse. Take a notebook and pen as it is good fun to write down the number of species of animals and birds that you have spotted – anything over a 100 is thought to be pretty good.

Flora and fauna

Practically everyone travelling around East Africa will come into contact with animals during their stay. To this end you will find the more common animals, birds and reptiles featured in the Wildlife of Eastern and Southern Africa colour section in the middle of this book. On page 32 of the section is a chart showing where mammals are to be found and in which parks. The text is based on the one we have used in previous editions written by Margaret Carswell, an international expert on the subject. Of course there is much more than the big game to see. You will undoubtedly travel through different habitats from the coast to the the tropical rain forests. We hope that the following text about trees, flowers and flowering shrubs, insects and beachcombing, again written by Margaret Carswell, will help you to gain from the experience.

Trees

Visitors to Africa often comment on the numbers of flowering trees seen in all the major cities. Trees such as the Jacaranda and Flamboyant are very beautiful when in full flower. The **Jacaranda** (*Jacaranda mimosifolia*) is not in itself a beautiful tree being very straggly and rather tall, but when it bears its masses of beautiful mauvish blue tubular-shaped flowers it is very striking. It can be recognized when not in flower by the large divided leaves, each division of which carries very many small leaflets arranged along a central axis. The **Flamboyant Tree** (*Delonix rex*) has similar leaves. When not in flower it can be distinguished from the Jacaranda by its very different, and much more attractive, shape. It does not grow as tall, only up to about 7.5m and is spreading and more compact in shape. This makes it an ideal tree to sit under on a hot day. When seen in flower, it is obvious why it is called the Flamboyant Tree. It is covered in a mass of mainly scarlet flowers. Some of the flowers have yellow tips giving the tree a golden appearance. Both Jacaranda and Flamboyant trees are often planted in towns. Another tree with brilliant red flowers, and one which is often confused with the Flamboyant, is the indigenous **Flame Tree** (*Spathodea nilotica*). The two trees really look very different, except for the flowers. The Flame Tree is very tall, up to 18m with a straight smooth trunk, and in the wild is found on the forest edge. Particularly fine specimens can be seen in western Kenya. The rather shiny leaves are also divided, but into largish lobes, rather than the tiny leaflets of the Flamboyant Tree. The flowers are almost tulip shaped and bright scarlet in colour.

Other trees seen in towns and gardens include the **Bottle Brush** (*Callistemon*), a rather small and slender tree whose branches are thin and tend to droop downwards at the ends. Its flower is shaped just like a bottle brush and is usually red, though white ones occur. The leaf is long and narrow.

Yet another tree with scarlet flowers is the indigenous **Coral Tree** (*Erythrina*) which grows in rather scrubby land. This has a gnarled appearance with a rough corky bark, often armed with blunt spines. The leaves are rather leathery and divided into three sturdy leaflets. The scarlet flowers appear before the leaves. The seeds are interesting in that they are the familiar red and black 'lucky beans'. Often planted in or near towns and settlements is the **Gum** or **Eucalyptus Tree**. It was planted to drain swamps and also to provide firewood. This is readily recognized by its height, its characteristic long, thin leaves and the colourful peeling bark.

In the plains the most characteristic tree is no doubt the **Thorn Tree** (*Acacia*). There is more than one sort of Thorn Tree, and though they vary a lot in size and shape, they all have very divided, almost feathery leaves and long sharp thorns. Some have a noticeable yellow bark, and many are characteristically flat topped. Two other very noticeable trees are the **Baobab**

(*Adansonia digitata*) and the **Candelabra Tree** (*Euphorbia candelabrum*). The Baobab cannot be mistaken for anything else. It grows particularly on the coast and also inland for some miles. The trunk of a fully grown specimen is enormous in girth and the usually leafless branches stick out of the top of the tree for all the world as if they were roots and the tree was planted upside down. The Candelabra Tree is often mistaken for a large cactus, as it has succulent branches with ridges or 'wings' running up them. It is widespread in grasslands. These three trees are all indigenous to East Africa.

The **Sausage Tree** (*Kigelia aethiopica*), which grows on the African grasslands is a rather ordinary looking tree which has extraordinary looking fruit. The name given to it is understandable when you see the long sausage shaped fruit hanging down. These fruit can be nearly 1m in length and 15 cm wide. They hang down on long thin stalks, giving the tree a remarkable appearance.

Two fruits to be enjoyed are the **Mango** (*Mangerifera indica*) and the **Paw-paw** (*Carica papaya*), and both the trees are widely grown. The Mango Tree has very dense dark shiny foliage and grows in a round shape. It is a good shade tree, too. The Paw-Paw on the other hand has enormous hand-shaped leaves, which are almost invariably tattered in appearance. The trunk is thin and the leaves come off at the top. Only the female tree bears the fruit, which hang down close to the trunk just below the leaves.

Trees that grow in the coastal region include the well known **Coconut Palms** (*Cocos nucifera*) which are almost everywhere, both in commercial plantations and growing singly. Unlike the coconut with its familiar straight trunk, the trunk of the **Doum Palm** (*Hyphaene thebaica*) has branches. This palm grows well on abandoned cultivation. The young palm looks like a fan of palm leaves sticking up out of the soil. The **Screw Pine** (*Pandanus kirkii*), also known as Mangrove, whose fruits you will pick up on the beach, is common and noticeable. It grows just above the high water mark, and has remarkable roots. The feathery **Casaurina** tree is commonly seen. It has small spiky cones which fall and cover the ground beneath the tree.

Look out for the rounded, sturdy shape of the **Cashew Nut Tree** (*Anancardium occidentale*). This has bright green, shiny, rounded leaves and casts a very dense shade. It is, of course, cultivated and forms an important cash crop. The nuts grow on what are called cashew apples. Be careful of the juice of cashew apples - it makes a stain on clothing that cannot be removed.

Another tree which was introduced for its commercial value is the strange looking **Kapok Tree** (*Ceiba pentandra*). It is a very tall tree up to about 25m whose branches grow straight out horizontally, almost at right angles to the trunk. The seed pods produce the fluffy, white kapok which is used to stuff mattresses and pillows.

It is a curious fact that many of the familiar trees and shrubs, which are thought of as quintessentially African, are actually not indigenous at all, but were introduced into Africa by the early European settlers, many of whom were fanatical gardeners. For example the Jacaranda comes from Brazil, and the Flamboyant from Madagascar. The Frangipani (see under shrubs) was introduced from Mexico, both the Gum and the Bottle Brush are Australian in origin, the Mango and the Hibiscus come from Asia and the Pawpaw and the Purple Wreath (see under shrubs) from the Americas. Anyone interested in trees, both indigenous and introduced should make a point of visiting the Botanical Gardens in Entebbe. This is a beautiful spot on the shores of Lake Victoria.

Flowers and flowering shrubs

Flowers and flowering shrubs are everywhere in East Africa. They are planted in towns and cities and can be seen in the countryside too. One of the most colourful and widely planted in city flower beds is the **Canna Lily** *Canna indica*) with large leaves which are either green or bronze, and lots of large bright red or yellow flowers. It can be more than 1m high.

Flowering shrubs include the well-known **Frangipani** (*Plumeria rubra*), which often has a sweet scent. This is a shrub with fat rather stubby branches and long leaves. The flowers are about 3 cm across and usually pink or white in colour and of a waxy appearance. If the bark is cut the sticky sap which oozes out can be very irritating to the skin. The **Hibiscus** is another bushy shrub, which, like many other plants, is always known by its scientific name. This is cultivated in many forms, but is basically a trumpet shaped flower as much as 7 or 8 cm across, which has a very long 'tongue' growing out from the middle of the trumpet. The colours vary from scarlet to orange, yellow and white. The leaves are more or less heart shaped or oval with jagged edges.

One of the commonest cultivated flowering shrubs is the **Bougainvillea**. This is a dense bush, or sometimes a climber, with oval leaves and rather long thorns. The flowers often cover the whole bush and can be a wide variety of colours including pinkish-purple, orange, yellow and white. The brightly coloured part is not formed by the petals, which are quite small and undistinguished, but by the large bracts (modified leaves), which, at first glance may be mistaken for petals. Look out too for the **Purple Wreath** (*Petrea*) which is a semi-climber often used as a hedge. It has strange papery leaves, and the masses of small purple-blue flowers grow densely in long spikes. A plant which is both beautiful and interesting is a form of morning glory sometimes called the **Moon Flower** (*Ipomoea*). The Moon Flower is a creeper with large trumpet-shaped white flowers, very like a large version of the bindweed or convolvulus of Europe. The interesting thing about it is that it opens only after dark, and opens so quickly that you can watch it happening. This is a never-failing source of pleasure.

All the plants mentioned above are mainly to be seen in gardens and city parks, but there are also many interesting or beautiful flowering plants which grow wild. One of these, which is interesting rather than beautiful, is the **Touch-me-not** or **Sensitive Plant** (*Mimosa pudica*). The Touch-me-not is a prickly, woody, low growing plant only a few inches high which grows in poor soil. The leaves look like that of the mimosa and when touched they immediately fold up. As in the movement of the moonflower, you can see this happening. A very common flowering shrub in grassland and scrub is **Lantana**, which comes in various forms. It is rather straggly and has rough, toothed, oval leaves which grow in pairs up the square and prickly stem. The flowers grow together in a flattened head, the ones near the middle of the head being usually yellowish, while those at the rim are pink, pale purple or orange. The fruit is a black shiny berry.

In the mountains of East Africa there are many strange plants. They are the familiar types such as **Heather** (*Ericaceae*), **Groundsel** (*Senecio*) and **Red-hot Poker** (*Kniphofia*), but the strange thing about them is that they are giant sized.

Lastly mention must be made of a plant which is very common in all swamps, but does not have very distinguished looking flowers. This is the **Papyrus** (*Cyperus papyrus*). Its feathery topped stalks form huge swamps, especially in the region of the large lakes such as Lake Victoria.

Crops

Eastern Africa is very much an agricultural part of the world, and many different crops are grown here. Some of them will be very familiar to visitors from Europe and America, but others are quite different. Subsistence farming is still widespread, and most settlements have their small fields of crops planted nearby for the use of the inhabitants. These vary according to the part of the country. In the west of the area, in Uganda, small **banana** plantations surround almost every house. The very large, darkish green, shiny leaves are unlike any other, and the tree often has a tattered appearance. This banana is not the familiar sweet yellow one favoured in Europe, but a large green one which does not turn yellow and is more correctly called a **plantain,** known locally as **matooke.** Matooke is eaten as a staple rather in the way we eat potatoes. It is peeled and cooked by steaming. This is done by wrapping the raw plantain in its own leaves and steaming it, usually over an open fire out of doors, for several hours. It then becomes soft and a little like mashed potatoes in consistency. This matooke is quite local in its distribution being favoured by the Baganda and their neighbours around the shores of Lake Victoria.

Other crops are more widespread. In particular, **maize** (sweet corn) is eaten in many parts and as **posho**, is the staple food in large areas of Tanzania and Kenya. Mostly, but not exclusively, in the drier parts of the region **cassava** is grown. This is a rather straggly bush some 2m high. The leaves are dark green and divided into thin fingers. The part that is eaten is the root. Cassava is traditionally a famine, or reserve crop, because the root can stay in the ground for long periods without spoiling and be harvested when needed - a sort of living larder. In colonial times planting of cassava was compulsory as an insurance against famine. The plant is doubly useful as the leaves can be used to feed the Tilapia which are raised in fish farms. Cassava is better known in Europe as Tapioca.

Tea, coffee and sugar cane are all grown here in the wetter parts, and there are places where all three can be seen growing near each other, for example on the road from the Kenyan border to Kampala. If a herd of cows happens to be passing, you have all you need for a tea or coffee break. **Tea**, though, is mainly a highland crop, and the large tea gardens, with their flat topped, shiny leafed bushes can be seen in western Kenya and western Uganda. The tea gardens are almost all run by large, sometimes international companies. If left to itself tea will grow to a tree 10m tall. **Sugar cane** is a large grass-like crop standing nearly as high as a man, and is grown in many areas, but not the very dry parts. **Coffee** comes in two forms, **robusta** which used to grow wild in Uganda, and the more highly prized **arabica** which is native to Ethiopia, and is now grown in the highland regions. In East Africa coffee growing is a family enterprise and families grow and tend their own plots or plantations. They sell the coffee beans to the Government and it is East Africa's most important cash crop. When the flowers are in bloom, which is mainly in Jan and Feb, the sweet smell is quite overpowering and unforgettable. The unripe coffee berries, or cherries, can be seen as green, and later red, berries clustering along the length of the stems. These three crops are, of course, cash crops and need processing, but a stick of sugar cane is often chewed, especially by children, as a sweet.

Sisal which is grown in the hotter, drier areas of Kenya and Tanzania is another cash crop. It is planted in straight rows in large plantations, and looks rather like the familiar yucca seen growing in pots in Europe. The leaves are straight and have a very spiky tip. From the middle of the leaves grows a very tall stem on the top of which is the flower. The fibre, extracted from the leaves, was a very important cash crop for the making of rope and string, but the advent of synthetic fibres has affected the market. But it can still be seen especially in eastern Kenya and in northern Tanzania between Tanga and Moshi. Another cash crop subject to the whims of fashion is **cotton**. At one time it was the main export but now has been superseded by coffee. It can be seen by the roadside in the rather drier areas growing in rather nondescript knee high bushes. When the cotton is ready for picking the fluffy white bolls are unmistakable. It is processed in factories called ginneries.

Ground nuts are an inconspicuous crop which tend to lie close to the ground. The plant above ground has a leaf which is deeply divided into lobes. The nuts themselves are clustered on the roots and out of sight. Another low growing crop is the **sweet potato**Sweet Potato. This is invariably grown on mounds of soil scraped up with the local hoe or *jembe*. The plant is a straggly one with large flat leaves and a very pretty pale purple trumpet-shaped flower.

There are two flowers which are grown in parts of Kenya which are fairly recent cash crops. One of these is **pyrethrum**, which is grown in small plots near houses, especially in the highlands around Nairobi. It has a daisy-like flower and is harvested to make the natural insect killer, pyrethrum. The other flower which is being grown in the cooler parts of the region, especially near Hell's Gate in Kenya, is the **carnation**. This is grown for export and the square fields with the bright green foliage and almost constant irrigation, are conspicuous against the drier natural vegetation.

It may surprise you to know that apart from coffee and perhaps cotton, none of these crops is Origin of crops

Essentials

indigenous to Africa. The plantain probably originated in Asia, as did tea. Sugar cane is from the South Pacific. Cassava, sweet potato, ground nuts and maize are all from the Americas. They were all introduced by early settlers, mostly towards the end of the 19th century or the early part of this century.

Freshwater fish

The fish in this area are many and those who enjoy fishing can be sure of plenty of opportunity to practice their sport.

The king of the freshwater fish is without doubt the massive **Nile Perch** (*Lates albertianus*). This huge predator lives on other fish, and originally came from the Nile below Murchison Falls, but was introduced into Lake Kyoga and the Nile above the Falls in 1955 and 1956. It has now spread to Lake Victoria itself, which has proved to be very much a mixed blessing. Weights of 20 to 40 kilos are common and there are several records of over 100 kilos. The best place to catch them is in Murchison Falls Park in Uganda, although you can have luck on Lake Victoria. In eastern Zaire, where they are present in Lake Albert, they are known as 'Le Capitan'. Also caught commonly in fresh waters is the **Tilapia** (*Tilapia nilotica*), a much smaller, rather bony fish which makes good eating. Unlike the Nile Perch this much smaller fish is herbivorous, and is now being farmed in fish ponds, where it is fed largely on the green leaves of the cassava plant.

The beach, the reef and beachcombing

To most visitors the East African beaches mean the reef. The fish and coral here are indeed wonderful, and can be observed without having to dive to see them. This section concentrates on the many interesting creatures that can be seen by paddling and snorkelling. It is not necessary to be a strong swimmer to do this, nor is expensive equipment needed.

Many of the fish do not have universally recognized English names, but one that does is the very common **Scorpion** or **Lion Fish** (*Pterois*), which is probably the most spectacular fish to be seen without going out in a boat. It is likely to be wherever there is live coral, and sometimes it gets trapped in the deeper pools of the dead reef by the retreating tide. It can be up to 26 cm long and is easily recognized by its peculiar fins and zebra-like stripes. Although it has poisonous dorsal spines it will not attack if left alone.

While most visitors naturally want to spend time snorkelling on the live reef and watching the brilliant fish and many coloured living corals, do not bypass the smaller, humbler creatures which frequent dead as well as living coral. These can be seen on most of the beaches, but one of the best places is Tiwi beach by Twiga Lodge. Here a vast area of dead coral is partly exposed at low tide and you can safely paddle, which is especially good for children. Be sure to wear shoes though, because there are many sea urchins. These sea urchins (*Echinoidea*) are usually found further out towards the edge of the reef, but can be found anywhere. There are two forms, the more common **Short-needled Sea Urchin** and the much less common **Long-needled** variety. Their spines are very sharp and treading on them is extremely painful. A **Sea Urchin skeleton** which can be found lying on the sand makes a good souvenir to take home. These are fragile and beautiful spheres which can be up to the size of a small tangerine. They are sandy coloured with lines and dots running down the sides. Look out also for the common **Brittle Stars** (*Ophiuroidea*) which frequent sandy hollows. They vary considerably in size, but are usually 10 cm across. They are so called because the arms break off very readily, but they will grow again. These are not sea urchins, though they are related, and can safely be picked up for a closer look, but handle them carefully.

Other living creatures which can be seen crawling along in the shallows include the **Sea Slug** (*Nudibranchia*) and the **Snake Eel** (*Ophichthidae*). Both are quite common in sandy places. The Sea Slug is blackish brown and shaped a bit like the familiar garden slug, though much

Essentials

Dangers of the reef – watch your step

The reef and sea shore are very safe places, but there are a few things you should look out for. The Scorpion Fish has already been mentioned, but as long as you just look there is no danger. Stingrays are quite common too and lie buried in the sand: if you were to tread on one you could get quite a nasty wound. The most famous hazard of the reef is the dreaded Stonefish which looks exactly like a piece of old coral, and whose dorsal spines can inject a very painful venom. A sort of mythology has grown up around them but you are unlikely to see one, and even less likely to tread on one. You are much more likely to step on a Sea Urchin, which can be very painful. There are two poisonous shells: odd but true. They both have a conical shape, and are the Geography Cone and the Textile Cone. You quite often see dead ones washed up on the shore, but live ones keep buried in the sand. Should you see a live one, treat it with respect. Moray Eels are common on the reef, and though their bite is painful, it is not poisonous.

bigger. It often has grains of sand sticking to it. This is not a beautiful creature. Don't be put off by the name of the Snake Eel, it is quite harmless. It looks a bit like a snake and has alternating light and dark bands on its body. What are beautiful, without doubt, are the **Starfish**, (*Asteroidea*) which are best seen by going out in a boat, but some can be seen nearer in shore. *Please don't collect them.* The colours fade in a week or so, and they are far better left to themselves.

Small pieces of broken off coral can also be found on the reef. These can be safely collected, without doing any harm to the reef. In particular there is the **Mushroom Coral** (*Fungia*) which looks like the underside of a mushroom and can be up to 20 cm across, though it is usually less than that and the **Star Coral** (*Goniastraea*). The flat **Sand Dollar** (*Echinoidea*) can also be found lying on the sand. It is rather fragile and is the skeleton of a creature related to sea urchins.

Two rather hard objects which may be a puzzle are the seed of the **Mangrove** tree and small pieces of **pumice** which are still being washed up on this shore line, probably from the great explosion of Krakatoa, in Indonesia, in 1883.

The commonest shells are without doubt the **cowries**. Many dead ones can be found on the beach. *Please do not take live ones.* The two commonest cowries the **Ringed Cowrie** (*Cypraea annulus*) and the **Money Cowrie** (*Cypraea moneta*) are illustrated. Of these the Ringed is especially plentiful and is a pretty grey and white shell with a golden ring. The Money Cowrie was once used as money in Africa and varies in colour from greenish grey to pink according to its age. The big and beautiful **Tiger Cowrie** (*Cypraea tigris*) is also seen occasionally. This can be up to 8 cm in length. There is quite a lot of variation in colouring, but it is basically a very shiny shell with many dark round spots on, much more like a leopard than a tiger. There are many varied and beautiful sea creatures to be seen on the coast. The best way of doing this, especially if time is short, is to go to one of the Marine Parks, where you can go out in a glass bottomed boat with a guide.

Insects

There are probably 100,000 different species of insect in Africa, and certainly some not yet known to science. Even the casual visitor to Africa, who never leaves the urban areas and sees only the city streets and insides of houses, and whose only glimpse of animal life is urban dogs and cats, cannot fail to notice the insect life. Inside houses, especially in the kitchen, tiny brown **Sugar Ants** (*Camponotus maculatus*) can be seen following predetermined paths across the window sill and down the wall before disappearing into a tiny hole or crack in the plaster. They are harmless, but a bit of a nuisance in the kitchen. A good deal more unpleasant are the **cockroaches** which do not usually appear until after dark. The commonest household cockroach is known as the **American Cockroach** (*Periplaneta americana*). It is about 30mm in length, and a dark shiny reddish brown in colour, with long antennae which

The cicada: it's not a cricket

Cicadas have a very interesting life cycle. The African species have not been studied in quite such depth as have the American ones, but it is likely that they have similar life histories. The so-called periodical cicada lays its eggs in the bark of a tree. On hatching, the nymph drops to the ground and immediately burrows beneath the surface. It then spends its entire life tunnelling through the soil going from tree root to tree root. It feeds on these roots by sucking the sap from them. This nymph stage lasts in the African species probably two or three years. In some American species it lasts up to 17 years. When it is ready the nymph tunnels out of the soil and climbs up the bark of the nearest tree. At this stage you can see them. They are about 2.5 cm long and look like some monster from outer space with hard bodies and longish legs. They always emerge after dark and interestingly enough they will climb up the side of the tree away from any light. During the course of the night the hard skin splits down the back and a white soft floppy looking insect with crumpled wings emerges which gradually hardens and darkens into the familiar cicada. While they cling helplessly to their cast off 'skins' they are very vulnerable to ants. Eventually they fly off leaving the empty colourless skins still hanging on to the bark. You can see these quite often on trees.

are constantly waved about. Another smaller darker cockroach also occurs and is called the **German Cockroach** (*Blattella germanica*). The 'wild' cockroach which occurs in Africa, lives in the bark of trees and under fallen logs. Cockroaches are usually seen scuttling about the floor or up walls and furniture. They rarely fly, but when they do it is peculiarly disconcerting. Cockroaches do not bite or sting and their role in the spread of disease is debated, but nevertheless, they are associated in most people's mind with dirt.

On safari watch out for insects, and don't be tempted into ignoring everything less obviously impressive than a full grown lion. Termite mounds (or termataria) are a conspicuous feature of many parts of eastern Africa. **Ant hills** as they are also called, when freshly built, are the colour of the underlying soil and, therefore, often reddish. They can be 2m high or more, and old established ones acquire a covering of herbs and bushes and often small trees. The **Termites** (*Termitidae*) which live within these ant hills are commonly (though incorrectly) known as **White Ants**.

Stick Insects (*Phasmatodea*) and the **Praying Mantis** (*Mantodea*) are fairly common, but not easy to see. Both of them are masters of cryptic coloration, which means that they resemble their background in the most amazing ways. The incredibly thin, brown body of the stick insect, with its long legs, exactly resembles a piece of dry twig or grass. Similarly, some species of praying mantis grow the most extraordinary appendages on their bodies to mimic flowers and bark. The reproductive habits of some of these insects is rather strange, as it seems that male stick insects are very rare indeed, and, the female praying mantis devours her partner after mating. Neither praying mantises nor stick insects sting or bite, but both can hurt the fingers by the sharp spines on their legs. A praying mantis, so-called because it holds its front legs together in an attitude of prayer, is an attractive insect with an alert and seemingly intelligent way of moving its head from side to side.

Locusts (*Acrididae*) are probably the most famous members of the grasshopper group to be found in Africa. A classical swarm of the Desert Locust is unlikely to be seen, but occasional members of the group, which are recognizable as very large grasshoppers are quite common. When they fly, they reveal colourful wings. There are two important species of locust in Africa. The **Desert Locust** (*Schistocera gregaria*) which is the one mentioned in the Bible and which occurs mainly in northern Africa including Ethiopia, Somalia and northern Kenya, and the **Red Locust** (*Nomadacris septemfasciata*) which is found in southern Uganda and western Tanzania. While swarming, locusts fall prey to many birds such as Marabous, White Storks and various birds of prey which follow the swarms for the abundant food source they provide.

Another member of the grasshopper family very common in Uganda at certain times of the year, is the **Nsenene** or Edible Grasshopper. This is a mainly green or brown grasshopper about 6-8 cm long. It swarms at certain times of the year, and being attracted to light can be seen in hundreds, sometimes thousands around the lights of Kampala after dark. It is much prized as a delicacy and small boys risk death and injury from passing cars by running across the roads in attempts to catch the insects. They are eaten either raw or cooked and taste slightly sweet.

Out-of-doors in Africa the persistent high pitched whine of the **Cicada** (*Cicadidae*) is a characteristic sound. There are several species of cicada and they spend their time clinging to the bark of trees where their camouflage is so perfect that even guided by their song they are difficult to see. They are particularly irritating in that as soon as you get near enough to spot them they become silent and immediately invisible. They sing by day, especially in the heat of the day when their song is a quintessential part of the African noon, and also at nightfall.

Another noisy insect is the **Cricket** (*Gryllidae*). There are many species found in Africa, and many are nocturnal. If one gets into the room at night it is not possible to get any sleep until it has been captured and put out. Catch it in an upturned glass, then slide something like a postcard under the glass and shake it outside.

If you look on the dry ground under the eaves and overhangs of houses you will notice small smooth conical pits an inch or so wide and deep. These are seen in fine or sandy soil which remains dry all the time. These pits are made by the **Antlion** (*Myrmeleontidae*), a strange little creature which is the larval form of a dragonfly-like insect. Take a piece of grass and very gently scratch the side of the pit so that grains of sand tumble down into the bottom. If you do it right you will provoke the antlion, who lives in the pit, to attack. It builds these pits as traps for ants which tumble into the pit, and, because of the soft soil, are unable to climb out. The antlion promptly emerges and with its ferocious jaws, grabs the ant. Have a look at one of them. They are a brownish nondescript little insect perhaps 5-10mm long, with the most enormous jaws for the size of the animal. When let go it will burrow into the soil at great speed, going backwards. These quaint little creatures seem very different from the adult insect, which is rather like a dragonfly to look at, with large gauzy wings.

Ants seem to get everywhere in Africa and there are many different sorts. Everyone has heard of the so called **Driver Ants** (*Dorylinae*). They are more commonly known as **Safari Ants** or **Siafu** in this part of Africa. These are the ants of legend which supposedly can engulf whole households and devour every living thing. In reality it is not quite like that. For a start the column of ants moves quite slowly so most animals have plenty of time to get out of the way. Secondly the marching columns are not as big as the ones in story books. Still it is quite a sight to see these ants on the move. If you are unlucky enough to tread in the middle of a column, you will know all about it as their bite is ferocious. The adult breeding male of these ants is called a **Sausage Fly**. It is about 3.5 cm long and is a brown, slightly hairy looking insect which bumbles around the lights at night. Although it flies, it seems to spend a lot of its time crashing into objects in the room and falling to the floor where it wriggles about helplessly until it takes off again, only to crash into something else. It is difficult to associate its comic incompetence with the ruthless efficiency of the Safari Ants.

Perhaps the most photographed insects in Africa are the **Dung Beetles** (*Scarabaeidae*). Pictures of them rolling their balls of dung across the grasslands are often shown in natural history films. They collect the dung into balls, in which the female then lays her eggs and on which the young feed. They are related to the sacred scarab beetle, which was worshipped by the ancient Egyptians.

The **Mosquito** and the **Tsetse Fly** are two well-known insects in Africa. Not all mosquitoes are malarial, but only those belonging to the *Anopheline* group. These can be distinguished from the harmless *Culex* mosquitoes by the way they stand before biting. The malarial ones hold their body at an angle of 45° to the surface, whereas the body of the harmless ones is parallel to the surface. Only the female bites and she can be recognized by her thread-like antennae. The male has feathery antennae, and feeds only on the nectar of flowers. There is more than one species of **Tsetse Fly** (*Glossina*). They have a bite like a red hot needle and carry various diseases of animals, as well as sleeping sickness in humans. It is about 0mm long and holds its wings overlapping one on top of the other like the closed blades of a pair of scissors.

Mention must be made of a rather unpleasant insect. This is a *Staphylinid* beetle really called a rove beetle, but commonly known as **Nairobi Eye**, after the painful condition it inflicts if you crush it. It is a small, thin, red and black insect which on casual inspection does not appear to have wings. It has a way of wriggling its abdomen about. Typically, the insect alights on your neck, and you instinctively put up your hand to brush it away. In doing this you will crush the insect: its body juices are intensely irritating and cause very painful blistering of the skin. Should you then rub your eyes before washing your hands it will be extremely painful.

Be sure to look out for the beautiful **Firefly** (*Lampyridae*). The sight of dozens and dozens of these lovely insects flitting through the trees after dark is one of the sights of Africa never to be forgotten. They are rather local in their distribution, but are worth looking out for especially, but by no means only, in the higher areas.

Butterflies The butterflies of Africa are extremely numerous and in the whole of the continent there are more than 2,500 known species. Many, indeed most, of them, do not have an English name and are known only by their scientific Latin name. Because of this it is not possible to do more than mention a few of the more noticeable ones. However, even if the species cannot be identified, it is usually possible to recognize the family to which a butterfly belongs. In most cases this is not too difficult, but some species are extremely variable in appearance.

Sexual **dimorphism**, that is, when the males and the females of one species look quite different from each other, is very common in the animal kingdom. It is seen in birds, and most people are quite used to the idea. As well as exhibiting sexual dimorphism, butterflies freqently take this a step further, and individuals of the same species *and* the same sex often look quite different. This is known as polymorphism.

There is another interesting phenomenon, to be seen in certain species, known as **mimicry**. Generally speaking, brightly coloured butterflies, such as the Monarchs, are distasteful to birds and other predators who have learnt, over time, to avoid these insects. Certain other butterflies, which are not inedible, have learnt to mimic the inedible species to such an extent that they look extremely similar. This means that the predators are fooled into believing that they, too, are distasteful, and thus also leave them alone. This mimicry includes copying the way of flying, as well as the appearance.

The different species of butterfly vary in their habits, some being low level fliers and some high fliers. Some are weak fliers and some fast fliers, while some have a buoyant and sailing flight. Many of the more beautiful ones occur in the forests and the popular notion is that they are attracted to flowers. While this is true up to a point, unfortunately it is also true that many more are actually attracted to such things as rotting fruit and animal dung or urine deposited on mud. This does help the observer though, as it means that they can be seen on puddles and on muddy roadsides.

Although there are 10 families of African butterflies, the larger and more obvious ones belong to the following families: **Swallowtails** (*Papilionidae*) These are large and often colourful butterflies, many of which have an obvious 'tail' at the lower outer corner of the hind wing. They are all strong fliers, and some fly very low and readily settle on the ground. **Whites** (*Pieridae*) These are medium sized butterflies which have white or pale yellow as a background colour. **Monarchs** (*Danaidae*) These are large and spectacular butterflies with a characteristic slow and sailing flight. They are distasteful to predators, and thus are mimicked by others. **Browns** (*Satyridae*) This is a rather large family of sombre brown or greyish brown butterflies with a weak flight, often close to the ground. **Nymphalids** (*Nymphalidae*) This is a very large family of stout and colourful butterflies, which, with the Swallowtails are the most beautiful of all. They commonly exhibit the polymorphism described above.

63

Kenya

Kenya

Any visit to Kenya will be amply rewarded as there is such a diverse range of things to do and places to see. Kenya's coastline is beautiful, with miles of white sands, and a warm sea protected from sharks by a coral reef just off the coast. The Kenya Highlands are always popular with visitors interested in a more energetic holiday, particularly Mount Kenya. However, it is probably the wildlife for which Kenya is most famous, particularly the big 5 (lion, elephant, buffalo, leopard and rhino). Kenya is the most popular tourist vacation spot in East Africa and tourism has become Kenya's largest source of foreign exchange. Its long experience with visitors means the country has something to offer all types of travellers. The importance of tourism to the Kenyan economy is reflected in the quality of services: throughout the country there are first class hotels, and good quality western-style food is easy to find.

A recent spate of attacks on Europeans has caused worry in people's minds, but with common sense and sensible precautions travellers should be at no more risk than in their own countries. Those touring with the large safari companies are particularly well looked-after.

The heavy 'El Niño' rains of 1997/98 created havoc with farming, roads, rail lines, water supply and sewage systems, and it will be a while before things return completely to normal.

Exchange rate September 1999: Ksh 75.75 = US$1

Essentials

Before you travel

When to go   There are two rainy seasons in the country, the long rains March-April and the short rains October-December. However, even during the rains there is invariably sunshine each day. January and February are the main months of the tourist season, as the weather is hot and dry, encouraging wild animals to the nearest water holes.

Getting in   **Visas**   Visitors may or may not require visas depending on nationality. It is advisable to consult the relevent Embassy or High Commission in your area. British passport holders now require a visa.

Visa fees for UK passport holders single entry £35 valid for three months, multiple entry £70 valid for one year, multiple entry £120 valid for two years. Passports must be valid for 3 months or more at the time of arrival in Kenya.

If you do not need a visa, you will be issued with a visitor's pass on arrival which allows you to travel freely for up to three months. You will need to negotiate this with the official on arrival. If you want to get this extended, you can stay a maximum of six months in the country fairly easily but at extra cost. In Nairobi this can be done at Nyayo House, corner of Kenyatta Ave and Uhuru Highway (Monday-Friday 0830-1230 and 1400-1530); it can also be done at the Provincial Commissioner's Offices in Embu, Garissa, Kisumu, Mombasa and Nakuru. Do check your visitor's pass as it has been known for people who have overstayed their time in the country to be fined quite heavily.

For people who do need a visa, they can be obtained in advance from any Kenyan embassy, consulate or high commission or from a British embassy in any country with no Kenyan diplomatic representation. It normally takes 72 hours to be issued with your visa, you will need two passport photographs and either proof of financial status or a ticket out of the country. Visas are issued for six months, though this does not necessarily mean you can stay in the country for six months. The length of your stay is at the discretion of the immigration officer on entry, and usually depends on how much money you have and your appearance. You are asked how long you want to stay. You will then be issued with a visitors' pass, usually for three months. You can arrange visa extensions in Nairobi or any of the Provincial capitals: see above for visitor's pass extensions.

It is possible to get a visa on arrival, but this takes ages and if you arrive at night, you may have to wait until the next day.

Customs   You are expected to pay duty on items brought as gifts or for sale in Kenya, though not if they are for your personal use. You are more likely to be asked if you have anything to declare at airports than at the border crossings from neighbouring countries.

Vaccinations   None are required by law but if you are entering the country overland, you may be asked for a yellow fever and/or a cholera certificate. You should have these done before arrival as a sensible health precaution anyway. Seek advice from your local doctor about six weeks before your departure.

Money   **Currency**   The currency in Kenya is the Kenyan shilling (KSh). As it is not a hard currency, it cannot be brought into or out of the country. If you have any Kenyan shillings left when leaving the country, do not be tempted to destroy them – people have been arrested for doing this. There are banks and bureau de change at both Nairobi and Mombasa airports. There are inevitable queues but at Nairobi it is marginally quicker to change your money after you go through customs.

Kenya embeddings and consultates

Kenya embassies and consultates

Australia, PO Box 1990, 33 Ainslie Ave, GPO Canberra, T062-474788.

Austria, Rotenturmstrasse 22, 1010 Vienna, T01-633242.

Belgium, Av Joyeuse Entree 1-5, Brussels, T02-2303065.

Canada, Gillia Building, Suite 600, 415 Laurier Ave, West Ottawa, Ontario, T6135631773.

Egypt, PO Box 362, 20 Boulos Hanna St, Dokki, Cairo, T02-704455.

Ethiopia, PO Box 3301, Hiher 16, Kebelle 01, Fikre Mariam Rd, Addis Ababa, T180033.

France, 3 Rue Cimarosa, 75116 Paris, T1-4-553-3500.

Germany, Villichgasse 17, 5300 Bonn 2, T0228-356042.

India, 66 Vasant Marg, Vasant Vihar, New Delhi, T11-672280.

Italy, Consulate, CP 10755, 00144 Rome.

Japan, 24-20 Nishi-Azabu 3-Chome, Minato-Ku, Tokyo, T03-479-4006.

Netherlands, Nieuwe Parklaan 21, The Hague, T070-3504215.

Nigeria, PO Box 6464, 53 Queens Drive, Ikoyi, Lagos, T01-682768.

Russia, Bolshaya Ordinka, Dom 70, Moscow, T2374702.

Rwanda, Blvd de Nyabugogo, PO Box 1215, Kigali, T772774.

Saudi Arabia, PO Box 95458, Riyadh 11693, T01-4882484.

Sudan, Street 3, Amarat, PO Box 8242, Khartoum, T40386/43758.

Sweden, Birger Jarlsgatan 37, 2st 11145 Stockholm, T08-218300.

Tanzania, 4th Floor, NIC Investment House, Samora Ave, PO Box 5231, Dar-es-Salaam, T51-31502.

Uganda, 60 Kira Rd, PO Box 5220, Kampala, T41231861.

United Arab Emirates, PO Box 3854 Abu Dhabi.

United Kingdom, 45 Portland Place, London W1N 4AS, T0171-6362371.

USA, 2249 R St Northwest, Washington DC 20008, T2023876101; or 9100 Wilshire Blvd, Beverly Hills, CA 90212, T2132746635.

RD Congo, Plot 5002, ave de l'Ouganda, BP 9667 Zone Gombe, Kinshasa, T12-30117.

Zambia, 5207 United Nations Ave, PO Box 50298, Lusaka, T01-212531.

Zimbabwe, 95 Park Lane, PO Box 4069, Harare, T04792901.

Kenya

Credit cards Many are widely accepted around the country, particularly Diner's Club and American Express with Visa as a poor third. Access and Mastercard acceptability more limited.

Cost of living It is getting cheaper and cheaper for budget visitors as the Kenyan shilling devalues. It is quite possible for budget visitors to travel by public transport, eat and stay for US$20 a day. Services specifically designed for tourists, such as the safaris, car hire, access to national parks etc can be expensive, and prices are adjusted as the currency depreciates. Moderate hotel accommodation and meals can be had for US$40 a day.

Exchange rate The exchange rate floats and is likely to have changed from that quoted here. As of September 1999 the rate was: KSh 75.75 = US$1.

Travellers' cheques You should be able to change money or travellers' cheques throughout the country, particularly British pounds and American dollars. Most large hotels exchange money 24 hours a day, the rate usually less good than the rate in the banks.

Banking Hours are Monday to Friday 0830 -1300. Saturday 0830-1100. Foreign Exchange Bureau are usually open longer hours. There is a black market in Kenya but it seems hardly worth the effort. Not only is it risky (you may be treated unpleasantly and deported if caught), but the rate you will achieve is hardly more than bank rates.

Tourist information centre Located at the junction of Moi Ave and Mama Ngina St opposite the *Hilton* in Nairobi. There is also a free publication called *Tourist's Kenya* which is published fortnightly and which gives a run down on things going on. There is another publication called *What's On* which comes out monthly.

Finding out more

You should be able to buy most maps you need in Nairobi though you are quite likely to have a better choice of information and maps in your own country than in Kenya itself. A good source is *Stanford's Map and Travel Bookshop*, 12-14 Long Acre, London WC2E 9LP, T0171-8361321. The *Survey of Kenya* park maps are well worth getting and are inexpensive in Nairobi (they are double the price if you get them at the park gates). *The Nation*, located on Kenyatta Ave next to the *Thorn Tree Cafe* has a good selection of maps.

Tourist information overseas France 5 Rue Volnay, Paris 75002, T42606688. **Germany** Hochstrasse 53, 6000 Frankfurt 1, T69282551. **Hong Kong** 1309 Liu Chong Hing Bak Building, 24 Des Voeux Rd, Central GPO Box 5280, Hong Kong, T236053. **Japan** Room 216, Yurakucho Building, 1-10 Yurakucho, 1-Chome, Chiyoda-Ku, Tokyo, T2144595. **Sweden**, Birger Jarsgatan 37, 11145 Stockholm, T212300. **Switzerland**, Bleicherweg 30, CH-8039, Zurich T2022244. **United Kingdom**, 25 Brooks Mews, London W1Y 1LF, T0171-3553144. **USA** 424 Madison Ave, New York, NY 10017, T2124861300; 9100 Wilshire Blvd, Doheny Plaza Suite 111, Beverly Hills, CA 90121, T2132746634.

For a list of tour operators in Kenya, see Nairobi, page 105; Mombasa, page 176.

Getting there

Air Kenya is the cheapest country in East Africa to get to by air and consequently is a good place to start off a tour of the region.

London is by the far the cheapest place in the western world from which to get to Kenya and there are loads of discounted flights and package holidays. In the past, the only discounts were for unsold seats but now there is an enormous range of deals for students, academics or people under a certain age (usually either 26 or 32). Although not all the deals may mean cheaper flights, they usually do mean flexible flight arrangements and flight dates which is very helpful if you are planning a longish trip and do not know when you want to go back. A very good deal is to look for a package deal to Mombasa and travel on from there. All flights either go to Nairobi, the capital (about nine hours from London) or Mombasa on the Indian Ocean coast (about 11 hours).

The cheapest plane tickets are in the 'off-season' from February to June and again from October to early December. If you do have to go during peak times, book as far in advance as you can, particularly if you aim to get there in mid-December when flights get full very quickly. **Aeroflot** offers the cheapest deals, but the flight makes stops all over the place including a six-hour stop in Moscow. If you can afford slightly more, it is well worth it. **Balkan Bulgarian** or **EgyptAir** offer very good deals, the latter being the more reliable and offering a stop over in Cairo for as long as you like at no extra cost. **Air France**, **KLM**, **Kenya Airways**, **British Airways** all have surprisingly good deals as do **Saudia** and **Ethiopian Airlines**.

If you are short of time, a package holiday could well be a useful option particularly if you go out of the peak season when you can get excellent deals. Beach holidays are far cheaper than safaris. It is a good idea to find out as much as you can about the hotel in the package deal before going, though you can always stay elsewhere if necessary. It is sometimes the case that a package trip to the coast will be cheaper than a flight alone.

Specialist Agencies for discounted fares, see page 68.

From Europe Access by air to Kenya is from all over Europe.

From Africa There are a number of flights flying direct from around Africa: **Abidjan** (Ivory Coast). **Accra** (Ghana). **Addis Ababa** (Ethiopia). **Antananarivo** (Madagascar). **Bujumbura** (Burundi). **Cairo** (Egypt). **Dakar** (Senegal). **Dar-es-Salaam** (Tanzania). **Douala** (Cameroon). **Dzaoudzi** (Comoros). **Entebbe** (Uganda). **Gaborone** (Botswana). **Harare** (Zimbabwe). **Johannesburg** (South Africa). **Khartoum** (Sudan). **Kigali** (Rwanda). **Kinshasa** (RD Congo). **Lagos** (Nigeria). **Lome** (Togo). **Luanda** (Angola). **Lusaka** (Zambia). **Moroni** (Comoros). **Ouagadougou** (Burkina Faso). **Zanzibar** (Tanzania).

Kenya

Quite a popular option with travellers are the overland tours to Kenya from Europe. There are **Road** plenty on offer, though itineraries may change taking account of political and military events around Africa. A popular route is from Western Africa passing through RD Congo around Lake Victoria and cutting through Tanzania to get to Kenya. Another option would be to team up with other people and hire a vehicle or use public transport to cross Africa. This is perfectly feasible but does take some organizing and a lot of time.

Ethiopia   The crossing is at **Moyale**, between Marsabit and Addis Ababa. The restriction that only Kenyans and Ethiopians can make this crossing now apears to have been lifted. It is a matter of hiring lifts from truck drivers on the route.

Somalia   In more tranquil times it has been possible to take a bus from Kismayo to the border at **Liboi**, and then on to Garissa; or from Mogadishu to **Mandera**, and then on to Wajir. These crossings are currently not an option for travellers as a result of the civil war in Somalia.

Sudan   In principle it has in the past been possible to cross from Lodwar to Juba, although there was never any public transport on this route, and it was a matter of hiring rides from truck drivers. This is not currently an option for travellers as a result of civil war in the south of Sudan.

Tanzania   The main road crossing is at **Namanga** (see page 247) on the road between Arusha and Nairobi. This is reasonably quick and efficient and there are through buses and good roads all the way. Other crossings are at **Lunga Lunga** (see page 184) between Mombasa and Dar Es Salaam. The road on the Tanzanian side is less good, but there are overnight through buses between the two cities. There are also crossings at **Taveta** (see page 248) between Moshi and Voi; at **Isebania** (see page 301) between Kisumu, Tanzania section page 402) and Musoma; and across the border from Masai Mara Park into the Serengetti.

Uganda   There are buses that run from Nairobi to Kampala, crossing at **Malaba** and **Tororo**, taking about 15 hours and costing around US$15. There is a variety of standards of service. It is possible to do the journey in stages in minibuses or peugeot taxis, but buses are more comfortable and safer.

There are also border crossings at **Busia**, no through buses, but convenient for Kisumu; and at **Suam** to the north of Mount Elgon.

There have been boats (hydrofoils) from Mombasa to **Tanga**, **Zanzibar** and **Dar es Salaam**   **Boat** (see page 175). Although these have not been operating for a while partial resumption of the service has started. **Mega Speed Liners** now run a hydrofoil to **Pemba** US$30 and Zanzibar US$50 at 0900 Sunday. Book at *Kuldips Touring* on the south end of Mji Mpya Rd or when boarding boat leaves from Kilindini Harbour. The cost was about the same as the air fare from Mombasa (US$45).

It is possible to take a dhow from Mombasa to **Tanga** and **Dar es Salaam** (see page 338). However you must expect to wait around for a week or more for one to depart. It will take one or two days depending on the weather. Expect to pay about US$15, bring all your own food, and you will sit and sleep on the cargo. At one time it was also possible to get dhows to **Kismayo**, **Mogadishu**, **Berbera** and **Djibouti**. These are not currently an option with the civil war in Somalia.

There are a few companies which will take you by boat from Europe to Kenya, though this is certainly not a budget option. *Strand Cruise Centre*, Charing Cross Shopping Centre, The Strand, London T0171-8366363 specializes in cruises from England through the Mediterranean down the Suez Canal to Djibouti and on to Mombasa. It costs around US$3,000 one way and takes a month.

Kenya

Touching down

Business hours *Banks:* Monday to Friday 0830 to 1330 and from 0830 to 1100 on Saturday. *Embassies:* usually open in the mornings only. *Kiosks:* will often open all hours, as the owner frequently lives at the kiosk. *Post Offices:* Monday to Friday 0800 to 1300 and 1400 to 1630. Some are also open on Saturday. *Shops:* generally from 0800 to 1700 or 1800, and on Saturday.

IDD code *254*
Official time *Kenya is three hours ahead of GMT.*
Voltage *220-240 volts supply. Square three-pin plugs in modern buildings. Great variety in older places. An adapter is advised.*
Weights and measures *Metric. In country areas items are often sold by the piece.*

Touching down

Airport information

Departure tax You will need to pay a departure tax of US$20 when leaving the country by air. This has to be paid in a hard currency or Kenya Ksh.

Transport to town Nairobi, Jomo Kenyatta International Airport, located 15 kilometres from the centre to the south of the city. A taxi is roughly US$12. There are set rates to particular hotels – check with the dispatcher before entering taxi.

Mombasa, Moi International Airport is located on the mainland about 10 kilometres out of the centre of town. Kenya Airways operates a shuttle bus, about US$2. Taxi about US$9.

Rules, customs & etiquette

Beggars Most common in Nairobi and Mombasa. Many are clearly destitute and or disabled. Many Kenyans give money to beggars who in a country with no social welfare have few alternative means of livelihood. A fairly recent phenomena has been the rise of street children in Nairobi who swarm on tourists who give money. A more constructive approach is to make a donation to an organization rehabilitating street children (see page 29).

Conduct Stand for the national anthem and show respect if the national flag is being raised or lowered. Do not take photographs of military or official buildings or personnel, especially the President. Respect the national currency (do not tear it) and the currency laws of the country and if you have to have any dealings with the police be polite. Another useful thing to remember is to comply with the country's drug laws. There is an ambivalent attitude to both cannibis (*bhangi* – which is readily available) and *miraa* both of which are illegal, but appear to be tolerated by the authorities. However, if you are caught your embassy is unlikely to be sympathetic.

Safety A general rule to follow seems to be that the more prevalent tourists are, the greater the need to be on your guard. Nairobi and Mombasa seem to have the worst reputations, and the most popular National Parks have their fair share of robberies. In early 1998 there were three tourist fatalities, whilst robberies/muggings were in progress. Basically, you just have to be sensible and not carry expensive cameras, open bags or expensive jewellery and be careful about carrying large sums of money when you are rubbing shoulders with local people. Also, do not automatically expect your belongings to be safe in a tent. In built up areas, lock your car, and if there is a security guard (askari) nearby, pay him a small sum to watch over it. There is no need to pay street children (see page 29) to guard a vehicle. Avoid walking around after dusk, particularly in the more rundown urban areas – take a taxi. The majority of people you will meet are honest and ready to help you so there is no need to get paranoid about your safety. The British High Commission strongly advise against travel in Northeast Kenya (Moyale, Mandera, Wajit and Garissa), because of difficulties with the Somalian unrest. The road from Mombasa to Lamu has also been targeted by Somalian robbers, who have hi-jacked buses and robbed the passengers. Armed police escorts are now on buses to cope with this problem with the `Shiftas'. If possible leave valuables in Mombasa or Malindi.

Women Women do have to be more wary than men, though Kenya seems to be a more pleasant place for lone women travellers than many countries. If you are hassled, it is best to ignore the person totally whatever you feel, expressions of anger are often taken as acts of encouragement. Women in Kenya dress very decorously, and it is wise to follow suit particularly in small towns and rural areas. Kenyan women will generally be very supportive if they see you are being harassed and may well intervene if they think you need help, but the situation is very rarely anything more than a nuisance. You are more likely to be approached at the coast, as the number of women coming for sexual adventure has encouraged this type of pestering. The key is to keep patient and maintain a sense of humour.

Where to stay

Hotels Kenya has a huge range of hotels from the ultra-luxurious lodges and beach hotels to local board and lodgings. At the cheaper end of the market, a double room should cost you around US$3-5 going up slightly if it is with washing or toilet facilities.

Almost every town will have some form of accommodation even if it is a room hired in a local house, so you should rarely be stuck for somewhere to stay.

Prices of hotels are not always a good indication of their quality, and it is sensible to check what you will get before committing yourself to stay. You can expect to pay more in the high season particularly mid-December to mid-February and prices are often negotiable, even in large hotels. See hotel classifications, page 31.

Self-catering This is an increasingly popular option on the coast and is often surprisingly good value if you intend to stay for a while. For more information contact *Kenya Villas* Westminster House, PO Box 57046, Kenyatta Ave, Nairobi, T338072.

Hostels The youth hostel in Nairobi is not only an excellent place to stay, but also a good place to meet other travellers. Apart from this one, there are very few hostels around the country. There are a number of YMCAs and YWCAs, most of which are clean and safe and of course very cheap. The ones in Nairobi tend to cater for long-term residents and many people from the university stay at the YMCA, so it is a good place to meet Kenyans. The Naivasha YMCA has a deservedly good reputation.

Camping There are many campsites all over the country, they are usually very cheap with basic amenities and some are very good. Camping can be a very useful option as it allows you to stay wherever you want, and is an essential if you are on a tight budget but want to explore the national parks. You should always have your own tent and basic equipment as these cannot always be hired at the sites.

Work camps The Kenya Voluntary Development Association set these up in 1962. Their aim is to bring Kenyans and other nationals together to work on local projects such as irrigation ditches, building schools etc. The work is quite hard, but most people seem to enjoy them. The average length of stay is four weeks costing US$170. You will share local conditions implying pretty basic amenities. The average age is under 25. If you are interested contact *KVDA*, PO Box 48902, Nairobi, Kenya, T225379.

Getting around

Air Internal travel in Kenya is quite cheap and efficient. There are daily flights between Nairobi (the main international airport) and Mombasa and Kisumu on Kenya Airways. There are also several flights daily from Wilson Airport, Nairobi to Masai Mara, Malindi, Lamu and other upmarket destinations. There are daily scheduled flights along the coast between Mombasa, Malindi and Lamu. You may also be able to get onto private flights going up to the northeast of Kenya at very reasonable prices – these flights are primarily for carrying *miraa*, a popular herbal drug which is a mild stimulant.

···

Kenya Railways (Passenger Trains Schedule)

Nairobi-Voi – Mombasa Line
One service daily from:
Nairobi departing at 1900, arriving
Mombasa the following morning at 0817.
Mombasa departing at 1900, arriving
Nairobi the following morning at 0857.

Nairobi-Nakuru – Kisumu Line
One service daily from:
Nairobi departuring at 1800, arriving
Kisumu the following morning at 0710.
Kisumu departuring at 1800, arriving
Nairobi the following morning at 0620

Nairobi-Nakuru – Malaba Line
From Nairobi departing at 1500 on Friday
and Saturday, arriving Malaba the following
morning at 0845.

From Malaba departing at 1600, on
Saturday and Sunday, arriving Nairobi the
following morning at 0855.

Nairobi-Malaba – Kampala Line
From Nairobi departing at 1000 on Tuesday,
arriving Kampala the following morning
at 0910.
From Kampala departing at 1600, on
Wednesday, arriving Nairobi the following
afternoon at 1440.

Voi – Taveta Line
From Voi departing at 0500 on Tuesday,
Wednesday, Friday and Saturday, arriving
Taveta the same morning at 0950.
From Taveta departing at 1430 on Tuesday,
Wednesday, Friday and Saturday, arriving Voi
the same afternoon at 1912.

···

Above is the published timetable of Kenya Railways. However due to the effects of the El Niño rains in 1997/98 the service is greatly curtailed. At present (May 99) there are no train services running to the west of Nairobi. The daily Nairobi-Voi-Mombasa train and the twice weekly Voi-Taveta service on Friday and Saturday are the only operational services. Full restoration of all train services are planned, but there is no indication when the service will be re-established.

The Nairobi-Voi-Mombasa line. Taking the train is a splendid experience. They run overnight (it is said this is to avoid the heat of the day). There are plans, however, for a daytime departure to the coast, which will allow some sight-seeing through Tsavo National Park. Of the current rolling-stock, the first class carriages were built in the 1960s in the UK, the second class in the 1920s (UK), and the third class in 1980s Sweden. First class cabins are two-berth with wash basins. Second are four-berth, and the wash basins are pretty unreliable as the carriages are around 70 years old. Ear-plugs can be a boon. Bedding is provided in first and second class. Third class is seated, and can get very crowded. First class is recommended. First and second class should be booked in advance (or through an agent) – it is necessary to go down to the Railway Station to do this. Sexes are separated in first and second class sections, unless you book the whole compartment. The compartments cannot be locked from outside, so take your valuables and documents with you if you leave the carriage. Dinner can be taken on the train, and is reasonable. The fare includes dinner (but not drinks), breakfast and the provision of bedding. There is no reduction in cost if you choose not to use these services. Wines, beers and spirits available.

One train departs each way at 1900 and the journey takes about 13 hours. As it gets dark the train crosses the plains – looking out of the window you can get a real feeling of emptiness with just a glimpse of the occasional pair of glowing eyes. This is a narrow gauge railway, which enables the train to climb up the steep escarpments. However the narrow gauge makes this train more vulnerable to derailments, as happened near Voi in March 1999. It costs US$50 for first class, US$36 for second and US$9 for third.

Voi-Taveta Although the published timetable indicates that the service between Voi-Taveta runs four times weekly, this has been reduced to twice weekly running on Fridays and Saturdays. The service from Taveta on the Kenyan border to Moshi in Tanzania is not operational at present. The Nairobi train arrives at Voi at 0400 and the Taveta bound train departs at 0500. Journey time five to six hours. Cost approximately first US$8, second US$5, third US$2. Usually the cost to Taveta is included in the ticket issued from Nairobi or

....

Buses (schedule and fares)

Destination	From Nairobi		To Nairobi		Fare
	Dep	Arr	Dep	Arr	Kshs
Busia	2000	0630	2000	0600	430
Eldoret	0830	1430	1030	1630	290
	2200	0300	0900	1630	290
Homa Bay	0900	1800	0700	1630	390
	2030	0500	1930	0500	390
Isiolo	0930	1700	0730	1400	260
	2030	0300	2000	0100	260
Kisii	0900	1600	0900	1630	340
	2030	0430	2100	0500	340
Kisumu	1000	1600	1000	1600	320
	2200	0500	2030	0430	320
Kitau	0830	1700	0900	1630	360
	2200	0530	2100	1700	360
Magadi	1300	1630	0630	0930	130
	1500	1830	0730	1100	130
Malaba	2000	0530	2000	0630	410
Meru	1000	1500	0730	1300	230
	2100	0300	2000	0200	230
Mombasa	0900	1700	0900	1700	380
	2130	0500	2100	0530	380
Namanga	1330	1700	0730	1100	140
Kampala	0700	1930	0700	1830	750
	1900	1100	1500	0400	750
Arusha	0730	1230	1400	1930	400

	From Mombasa		To Mombasa		
Tanga	0830	1530	1930	0500	450
	1800	0200	1830	0400	450
Dar-es-Salaam	0830	1900	1600	0500	450
	1800	1500	1500	0400	450

....

Mombasa. Although Kenya Railways publish a timetable it must be borne in mind that there are frequent delays and disruptions to the service. Prices change and schedules are altered so you are advised to check locally before confirming your travel plans. Kenya Railways PO Box 30121 Nairobi, T02-221211, F340049, Tx22254. Reservations (Upper class bookings) Nairobi T335160, Mombasa PO Box 90674, T312221/3. The railway station is situated in Jomo Kenyatta Rd.

Bus There are lots of private bus companies operating in Kenya, and the system is very good on the whole, being reliable, running on time and cheap. Generally, you will be able to reserve a seat a day in advance and they are quite comfortable. If you have problems locating the bus station, or finding the right bus in the bus station just ask around. The government has recently started its own service called **Nyayo buses**. These are the cheapest buses around and very good.

Car hire Renting a car has certain advantages over public transport, particularly if you intend visiting any of the national parks or remoter regions of the country, or there are at least four of you to share the costs. One way of keeping the cost down is to link up with other people and share the expense. You should be able to rent either a fixed price per day or by mileage. Four-wheel drive Suzuki jeeps are a popular car if going on safari – they do not hold much petrol, so remember to carry a spare can.

Kenya

To hire a car you generally need to be over 23, have a full driving licence (it does not have to be an international licence, your home country one will do), and will be asked to leave a large deposit (or sign a blank American Express voucher). Always take out the collision damage waiver premium as even the smallest accident can be very expensive.

Driving in Kenya can be alarming. Although driving is on the left, actual practice is dictated by the state of the road to avoid potholes, debris or people and animals. Keeping to any formal `rules of the road' is further handicapped by many drivers ignoring traffic lights at night (they argue that this is to avoid being robbed while stationary) and the high speed of most motorists. The accident statistics in Kenya are very high, so be warned. If you break down, the common practice throughout Africa is to leave a bundle of leaves some 50 metres behind, and in front of, the vehicle.

Other land transport

Bicycle There are a number of specialist bicycle tours available. *Paradise Bicycle Tours* in the US (PO Box 1726, Evergreen, Colorado, 80439, USA) offers 12 day trips including a trip to the Masai Mara. *Leisure Activity Safaris* in the UK (164 Ellicks Close, Bradley Stoke North, Almondsbury, Bristol BS12 0EU) offers long or short safaris leaving from London.

Hitching Common in rural areas of Kenya as it is the easiest way for the majority of people to travel, making hitching a simple and safe method of travelling the country. If you intend to hitch, you will be expected to pay something to the driver though if you cannot afford to, and make this known at the outset, you will rarely be turned away. To gain a driver's attention, put out your arm, a thumb stuck in the air is unlikely to be noticed. On routes not served by much public transport it is invariably possible to hire a ride with truck drivers.

Matatus These are everywhere. Almost any vehicle will be used, but the most common is a pick-up van with wooden benches inside. They are the fastest and most prolific form of transport in the country. They are also the most dangerous, driving terrifyingly fast and often totally overloaded. The drivers often look about 13 years old and are chewing *miraa* to stay awake longer. However, as they are often the only means of travelling in remote areas, you may have to use them and they are the most convenient method of travelling around town because there are so many.

Peugeot taxis These are popular on long routes when you want to travel quickly. They are estate cars with an extra row of seats fitted in the back and are fast, comfortable and reliable. They are also quite expensive compared to matatus and buses. If you want to travel in the front by the driver, you will have to pay a premium.

Boat There is a ferry running between the islands of the Lamu archipelago. Motor ferries run between Kisumu and a number of lakeshore locations: Kendu Bay, Kuwur Bay, Homa Bay, Asembo Bay, Mbita, Mfangano. Tickets are very cheap and this is a nice way of seeing around Lake Victoria.

Keeping in touch

Language English is widely spoken throughout the country and is the language of all higher education. Swahili, however, is the official language and it is worth the effort to learn some basic phrases as a courtesy gesture. The more remote the area you visit, the less likely you are to find anyone who speaks anything but their tribal language.

Postal services Sending post out of the country is cheap and efficient, it generally takes a week to Europe and about 10 days to Australia and USA. Receiving post also is easy, though not parcels. All parcels need to be checked by officials for import duty also, it is not uncommon for them to go astray unless they have been sent by registered post or a similar scheme. If you are sending things out of the country they must be wrapped in brown paper with string. There is no point doing this before getting to the post office as you will be asked to undo it to be checked for export duty. The wrapping charge varies between US$1-1.50.

Area codes

0150 *Athi River*	**0125** *Kikambala*	**011** *Mombasa*	**0176** *Nanyuki*
0127 *Diani Beach*	**035** *Kisumu*	**0185** *Moyale*	**0171** *Nyeri*
0321 *Eldorat*	**0325** *Kitale*	**068** *Mwanza*	**0151** *Thika*
0161 *Embu*	**0121** *Lamu*	**0142** *Mwinge*	**0147** *Voi*
0385 *Homa Bay*	**0393** *Lodwar*	**02** *Nairobi*	**0122** *Watamu*
0331 *Kakamega*	**0123** *Malindi*	**0311** *Naivasha*	
0361 *Kericho*	**0164** *Meru*	**037** *Nakuru*	

Parcels must not weigh more than 20 kilograms seamail or 30 kilograms airmail or be more than 100 centimetres long.

The **poste restante** service, particularly in Nairobi, Mombasa, Malindi and Lamu, is reliable and free.

Telephone services

Generally speaking, the telephone system in Kenya is very good. You should be able to make international calls from public call boxes and the easiest way of doing this is if you get a phone card (available from most post offices). If this is not possible, you can book your call through post offices where you get your money back if you fail to get through. The rate is roughly US$4.50 per minute to Europe or North America and if you dial through the operator, there is a three minutes minimum. The number for the international operator is 0196.

Local calls are very easy, the main problem is finding a box. You can generally make phone calls from hotels, though they will usually charge you double the price for the privilege.

A new private phone company Unique Communications, Rattansi Educational Trust near the corner of Monrovia/Koinange St, T243302, offers phone/fax/email facilities.

Most parts of Kenya are covered by the ISD system. Telephone calls from Kenya to Tanzania and Uganda are charged at long distance tariffs rather than international. The public call boxes in Nairobi will only accept the new copper 1 or 5 Ksh coins.

Media

Cinemas There are cinemas in the larger towns throughout the country. Some show reasonably current films, but the most popular films appear to be action, martial arts or adventure movies.

Music and dance There are displays of dancing put on for the tourists all over the country including the Bomas of Kenya just outside Nairobi. The best known are the Masai and Samburu dances. Traditional Kenyan music is most likely to be performed by the drummers of Akamba and the Mijinkenda.

Congolese music (*Lingala*) is extremely popular and the type you are most likely to hear on matatus, in the streets, in bars and clubs, in fact anywhere and everywhere. Western music also has had its influence here. Many of the more upmarket discos and clubs play western music and there are a few reggae clubs in Nairobi.

Newspapers There is a range of locally produced papers and magazines. The best of the three English-language papers is the *Nation* which is the most daring in its editorial. The *Kenya Times* is the government-owned paper, and *The Standard* owned by Lonrho is dull. Of the magazines, *Law* is usually worth reading (if it has not been confiscated) and the *Weekly Review* carries very detailed reports on local political and social issues.

Of the international press, *Time* and *Newsweek* are regularly available, as is the *International Herald Tribune*. UK daily newspapers arrive a day or two late in larger towns.

Radio This is the most common method with which Kenyans keep informed. KBC broadcasts in Kiswahili, English and some local languages.

Kenya

Social events A major event in the social calendar is the Agriculture Society of Kenya's *Agricultural Shows* which are all over the country at different times of the year. They can be quite interesting, as well as the normal animal shows and beer tents there are women's groups, beekeeping, soil conservation booths and others.

Television There are two television channels: **Kenya Broadcasting Corporation** (KBC, which replaced Voice of Kenya), broadcasting in Swahili and English with a number considerable import of foreign programmes; and **Kenya Television News**, based on CNN material.

Food and drink

Food Market liberalization of the Kenyan economy and deregulation of price controls means the price of food has increased over recent years. This has caused hardship on many Kenyans but for tourists the prices are very low, mainly because devaluation of the Kenyan shilling means you get more shillings for your own currency than before. The quality of the food in Kenya is generally excellent. The fruit and vegetables taste very different, (invariably better) from produce you get at home (particularly avocados, mangos, pineapples and passion fruit). Kenya's meat is very good – you might get some tough cuts in the countryside at small restaurants. Kenyan buffets sometimes include some unusual meats such as zebra, crocodile, ostrich, wart-hog and giraffe. Salads tend to be fairly basic and are generally tomatoes, white cabbage and onions with no dressing.

Restaurant prices are low; it is quite possible to eat a meal in a basic restaurant for US$2 and even the most expensive places will often not be more than US$20 per person. The quality, standard and variety of food depends on where you are and what you intend to pay. However, even the smallest most remote *hoteli* meal will fill you up. Rice, potatoes, chapatis and ugali eaten with chicken, goat or beef are staple foods and in some restaurants you may be able to get spinach or *sukumawiki* (a type of green vegetable a bit like cabbage). Otherwise, vegetables and salads do not figure highly in cheaper restaurants where there is rarely much choice of dishes. Various western-style fried foods are becoming ever more popular such as chips, hamburgers, sausages and eggs. Roadside stalls selling *mandazi* (a kind of sweet or savoury donut), roasted maize, grilled skewered meat, or samosas are popular and very cheap.

There are a number of Kenyan dishes of note. Swahili cuisine is the most interesting in the country with coconut and tamarind figuring heavily in menus. In Kikuyu areas you will find *irio* of potatoes, peas and corn mashed together. A popular Luo dish is fried *tilapia* (fish) with a spicy tomato sauce and *ugali* (maize porridge). *Githeri* is a bean stew. Eating out is not common in Kenya (hardly surprisingly as most of the population are so poor), and if people do go out they want to eat something they would not normally have at home – which is meat. Consequently, the most popular places for Kenyans to eat out are *nyama choma* bars where you order your meat by the half kilo. They are popular places at weekends and very good value. The meat is usually goat or beef and you can choose what you want to eat before it is cooked.

Asian food is extremely good in Kenya and cheap, and an important option for vegetarians travelling in the country. Many Indian restaurants have a lunch time buffet where you can eat as much as you want for less than US$8 a head. Other cuisines include Italian, French, Chinese, Japanese and even Thai, though only in the larger towns. See restaurant classifications, page 31.

Drink Sodas (soft drinks) are available everywhere and are very cheap, bottles are refundable. The other common drink throughout the country is chai, milky sweet tea which is surprisingly refreshing. Fresh fruit juices when they are available are good as they really are freshly squeezed. Bottled water is expensive, costs around US$1 per 1.5 litres and is available in all but the smallest villages. However a survey in Nairobi in the Sunday Standard in 1995 found that 75 out of 78 bottled waters sold contained only Nairobi tap water. Tap water is reportedly safe in many parts of the country. However it is far more prudent to avoid drinking any tap water, or using it to brush your teeth without prior sterilisation. Place you glass on ice cubes to cool drinks unless the ice cubes are made of purified water. It is also best to avoid borehole or rainwater unless your stomach is quite hardy.

Kenyan beer is very good, *Tusker*, *White Cap* and *Pilsner* are the main brands sold in half-litre bottles. Fruit wines are also popular, they come in a variety of different flavours but tend to be sweet. Papaya wine is widely available, but is a little harsh.

Spirits tend to be extremely expensive and most local people will buy them in tiny sachets. Local alternatives are *Kenya Cane*, a type of rum, and the sweet *Kenya Gold* coffee liqueur.

Traditional Kenyan drinks include *chang'aa*, a fierce spirit made from maize and sugar and then distilled. Sentences for distilling and possessing *chang'aa* are severe and it is sometimes contaminated. It has been known to kill so think twice before tasting any. Far more pleasant and more common are *pombe* (beer) brewed from sugar and millet or banana depending on the region. It is quite legal, tastes a bit like flat cider and is far more potent than it appears at first. Palm wine is drunk at the coast.

Kenya

Shopping

Kenyan **baskets** are popular and cheap made from sisal and leather. They are particularly cheap around Kitui. **Soapstone** sculptures and objet-d'arts are good value (Kisumu) as are the wooden carvings which are for sale everywhere around the country. **Jewellery** is also popular with beaded necklaces and bracelets of turquoise and garnets or other semi-precious stones being good value.

See the essentials section in individual town listings for further information on local shopping

　　Many tribal people sell traditional objects including weapons, stools, jewellery and musical instruments. The authentic articles are considerably more expensive than items made for the tourist market. Antique masks are very rarely from Kenya, most have been imported from RD Congo or West Africa.

　　There are many different types of **cloth** peculiar to Kenya. **Kangas** are cotton wraps used by women, designed in hundreds of different styles, often with Kenyan proverbs printed onto them. **Kikois** are men's loincloths and are more sedate prints in wonderful reds, oranges and yellows. They are particularly good value along the coast.

There is an enormous difference between a `tourist' price and a local price. Until you get a feel for what the local prices might be it is hard to bargain effectively, but you will soon realize most prices are negotiable. As a general rule, you should be able to start by offering half of the price being asked.

Bargaining

Suspect anyone who has a hard-luck story. Do not change money on the black market, as this invites a confidence trick. Popular ploys are schoolboys with sponsorship forms, or being bumped into by some-one who drops something, you bend to pick it up for them – only to be taken by two men from behind who will relieve you of your possessions.

Tricksters

Sports

The biggest event in the year, for the international media at least, is the **Kenya Safari Rally** which normally takes place over the Easter weekend. It goes all over the country on some of the worst roads and often in appalling weather. The Asian community in particular comes out for this event, though it seems to attract large crowds everywhere.

Sport (spectator)

Football　A popular sport throughout the country and the quality is excellent, Kenya having some of the best teams in the continent. Matches are well attended and are great fun to go to even if you are not a keen football supporter just to soak up the friendly atmosphere.

Horse racing　Regular meetings in Nairobi.

Kenya

Golf, tennis and squash   Annual international tournaments at Nairobi Club.

Sport
(participant)

Riding   It is possible to hire horses in the Central Highlands and camels in northern Kenya.

Fishing   Not a particularly popular pastime in Kenya's rivers, though it is possible and an interesting trip is to go out with local fishermen, either on the coast or on Lake Victoria. Kenya has excellent deep-sea fishing. For further information, see page 173.

Climbing   Extremely popular among visitors, particularly up Mount Kenya where you will find many guides to help you. Other good climbing is possible in the Aberdares, Cheranganis Hills, Mathews Range, Hell's Gate and Rift Valley volcanoes. Each is described in the relevant section. The Mountain Club of Kenya (at Wilson Airport T02-501747) is a good source of advice and contacts.

Caving   Caving has been growing in popularity in Kenya and there is enormous potential for it in the country. Contact Kenya Caverns and Lodges, PO Box 47363, Nairobi if you want to know more about this.

Watersports   Widely available at the coast.

Running   Hash House Harriers meet regularly. Contact British Council in Nairobi.

Cricket, hockey and rugby   Played regularly by local clubs.

Holidays and festivals

New Year's Day   1 January
Good Friday and Easter Monday   March/April
International Labour Day   1 May
Madaraka Day, celebrates the granting of self-government   1 June
Moi Day   10 October
Kenyatta Day   20 October
Independence Day   12 December
Christmas Day   25 December
Boxing Day   26 December

All along the coast and in the northeast the Islamic calendar is followed, and festivals are celebrated. These include February (Beginning of Ramadan); March (End of Ramadan); June (Islamic New Year); August (Prophet's Birthday).

Health

**Staying
healthy**

On the whole, Kenya is a healthy country to visit but as with all tropical countries, it is best to take certain precautions. Firstly, malaria is a real problem in most areas of the country except way up in the highlands. Do not be fooled into thinking it is not very serious, it is one of the major killers in tropical Africa today. This means you will need to protect against it by taking tablets before, during and after your visit. Ask your doctor for advice on which anti-malaria tablets you should take as the parasite which passes on malaria becomes resistent to tablets from time to time.

Secondly, you should avoid the risk of contracting a sexually transmitted disease, Hepatitis B or HIV by not engaging in unprotected sex.

Water

To avoid Hepatitis A, it is best to be careful about water, particularly if you are travelling in areas where a lack of water is a common problem. This may sound easier said than done, but most places will have sodas to drink as an alternative to water. Bilharzia, which you usually get from being in stagnant waters, the home of freshwater snails which harbour the bug, is not a common problem with travellers. To avoid it, avoid stagnant waters.

The Sunday Standard, 28 May 1995, reported that 75 out of 78 brands of bottled water sold in Kenya are in fact Nairobi tap water.

It is important to get medical insurance whilst travelling as the only hospitals worth going to in Kenya are expensive. If you intend to spend any time in more remote areas, it may be worth subscribing to the flying doctor service at PO Box 30125, Nbi T02-501301/501280. They will fly you back to a medical centre if necessary. **Insurance**

To be on the safe side, you can get a travel pack from British Airways Travel Clinic and other places which includes syringes. You could also take pain killers, anti-diarrhoea pills, antiseptic cream and swabs, plasters and lipsalve all of which are very expensive in the country compared to Europe, North America or Australia. If you ever do have a bad stomach upset with diarrhoea and vomiting, weak black tea or water mixed with sugar and salt for 24 hours can help against dehydration. Also see Health Section, page 35. **Further health information**

Further reading

Miller C, *Lunatic Express*, highly readable history of East Africa, centring around the building of the railway. Hibbert C, 1984, *Africa Explored: Europeans in the Dark Continent 1769-1889*, London: Penguin, describes the exploits of the main explorers, including the search for the source of the Nile. Monbiot, G *No Man's Land*, published by Macmillan 1994, tells how the nomadic tribes in Kenya and Tanzanian were forced off their land. Murray Brown J, *Kenyatta*, biography of the man who became the first president of Kenya. Patterson J, *The Man-Eaters of Tsavo*, first-hand account of problems in building the railway. **History**

Blixen K, *Out of Africa*, wonderfully written, impressions of the author's life in Kenya. Huxley E, *Flame Trees of Thika*, stories of the lives of early pioneers. Markham B, *West with the Night*, marvellous autobiography of the woman who made the first solo east to west Atlantic flight. **Reminiscences**

Hemingway E, *Green Hills of Africa*, masterly short stories based on the author's African visits in 1933-4. Mwangi M, *Going Down River Road*, grim but entertaining story of African urban life. **Fiction**

Wielochowski A, *Mount Elgon Map and Guide*. Savage M and Wielochowski A, *Mount Kenya Map and Guide*, both obtainable in Nairobi at **The Nation** bookshop next to *Thorn Tree Café* on Kenyatta Ave; or from: 1 Meadow Close, Goring, Reading, Berks RG8 9AA, England. **Climbing guides**

The Lonely Planet Travel Atlas, scale 1:1,000,000 1997 is an excellent comprehensive atlas. Many of the larger maps have several inaccuracies, making driving in some of the more remote areas of Kenya a real adventure. Glenday B, *Kenya's Best: Hotels, Lodges and Homestays*, Nairobi: Kenway Publications, detailed descriptions of facilities available in over 200 up-market establishments, very nicely produced with line drawings. Oberlé P, 1991, *On Safari: 40 Circuits in Kenya*, very good for hikes and walking routes, with plenty of sketch-maps. Else D, *Mountain Walking in Kenya*, McCarta/Seven Hills Books, 1991. Else D, *The Camping Guide to Kenya*, Bradt Publications, 1990, comprehensive and useful guide if you intend to spend time under canvas during your visit. **Other guides**

Useful addresses

Abercrombie & Kent, Sloane Square House, Holbein Place, London SW1W 8NS, T0171-7309600. Range of packages.
Africa Travel Centre, 4 Medway Court, Leigh St, London WC1H 9QX, T0171-3871211, F0171-3837512. Inexpensive package trips.
Art of Travel, 286 Lavender Hill, London SW11 1LJ, T0171-7382038. Customized safaris.

Dragoman, Camp Green Kenton Rd, Debenham, Suffolk IP14 9LA, T01728-861133. Overland expedition specialist.

Exodus, 9 Weir Rd, London SW12 OLT, T0181-6757996. Overland expeditions.

Flamingo Tours, 167 Acton Lane, London W4 5HN, T0181-9953505. Inexpensive packages.

Guerba, 101 Eden Vale Rd, Westbury, Wiltshire BA13 3QX, T01373-827046, F01373-858351. Overland expedition specialist, range of packages.

Hayes & Jarvis, 152 Kings St, London W6 OQU, T0181-7485050. Inexpensive packages.

Kumuka Africa, 42 Westbourne Grove, London W2 5SH, T0171-2212348. Inexpensive packages.

Kuoni Travel, 33 Maddox St, London W1R 9LD, T0171-4998636. Range of packages.

Select Travel, 24 Culloden Rd, Enfield EN2 8QD, T0181-3638202.

Tracks Africa, 12 Abingdon Rd, London W8 6AF, T0171-9375964. Package and specialist safaris.

Twickers World, 22 Church St, Twickenham TW1 3NW, T0181-8927606. Special packages.

Kenya

Nairobi

Nairobi

Kenya

A lively, cosmopolitan and bustling city, the centre is modern and prosperous, and services are well-organized and efficient. Kenya's burgeoning population, however, combined with migration to the towns has resulted in the population of Nairobi increasing at an enormous rate. Housing and other facilities have failed to keep up and shanty towns in the outskirts are the inevitable result. The population is currently over two million and it is likely to exceed 3.5 million by the year 2000.

The city sits at 1,870 metres above sea level – from here it is a long and steady fall to the coast 500 kilometres away.

Ins and outs

Central Nairobi is bounded by Uhuru Highway to the west, Nairobi River to the north and east and the railway to the south. Across the Uhuru Highway is Uhuru Park and Central Park. In the southwest of this central triangle of about five square kilometres are most of the government buildings, offices, banks, hotels and shops. In the northern section the buildings are closer together and there are many less expensive shops and restaurants and to the east of the triangle is the poorer section where there are cheaper hotels and restaurants, shops and markets. This is the area around River Road, very lively, full of character and has the authentic atmosphere of the African section of a great city (although it is an area in which the visitor should take care over safety).

Getting around
1° 17' S, 36° 48' E
Population: 2 million
Altitude: 1,870m
Phone code: 02
Colour map 4, grid B3

The altitude makes for a marvellous climate with sunny days and cool nights. September to April are the hottest months, with maximum temperatures averaging 24°C, but falling at nights to around 13°C. May to August is cooler, with maximums averaging of 21°C, and minimums of 11°C at night. It can be quite chilly in the evenings. The heavy rains are in March-May, and smaller rains in November and December, although the timing of the rains has been less regular in recent years. Even on days of heavy rain there will invariably be some hours of sunshine.

Climate

History

The name Nairobi comes from the Masai words *enkare nyarobe* meaning sweet water for originally this was a watering hole for the Masai and their cattle. Just 100 years ago Nairobi hardly existed at all. It began life in 1896 as a railway camp during the building of the railway from the coast to the highlands. It grew steadily and by 1907 had become a town sufficient in size to take over from Mombasa as capital of British East Africa. Its climate was considered healthier than that of the coast and its position was ideal for developing into a trading centre for the settlers who farmed the White Highlands. Since then the city has continued to grow and is now the largest in East Africa.

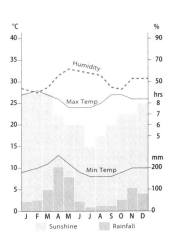

Climate: Nairobi

Early Nairobi

Dr Henry Boedeker became the first Medical Officer in Nairobi. He had walked with his wife from Mombasa to Fort Smith (now Kabete) in 1896, and thought the site 'the worst possible choice for any sort of urban centre by virtue of its swamps alone' which bred swarms of mosquitoes.

The town grew out of a camp at mile-post 327 on the rail track. Much of the soil was black cotton which didn't drain well in the rains and soon became a morass of mud. In the dry season it became very dusty and made the inhabitants susceptible to 'Nairobi throat'.

Sights

Kenya National Museum Located on Museum Hill this presents an overview of Kenya's history, culture and natural history. The section on Pre-history is particularly strong with exhibits of archaeological findings made so famous by the work of the Leakeys. The museum also has an excellent collection of butterfly and bird species found in Kenya. The Kenya Museum Society offers guided tours of certain exhibitions which are recommended. ■ *0930 - 1800, US$4.*

Snake Farm is found opposite the National Museum and houses examples of most of the snake species found in Kenya as well as crocodiles and tortoises. Some are in glass tanks and others in open pits. The opening hours and charge are the same as for the National Museum.

Nairobi city

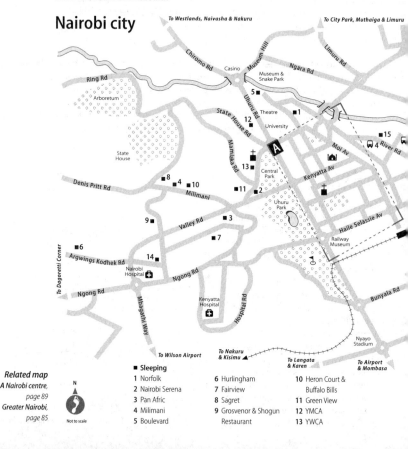

Related map
A Nairobi centre,
page 89
Greater Nairobi,
page 85

N

Not to scale

■ **Sleeping**
1 Norfolk
2 Nairobi Serena
3 Pan Afric
4 Milimani
5 Boulevard

6 Hurlingham
7 Fairview
8 Sagret
9 Grosvenor & Shogun
   Restaurant

10 Heron Court &
    Buffalo Bills
11 Green View
12 YMCA
13 YWCA

Railway Museum Located next to the railway station on Station Road. Visitors to the museum should approach it from Uhuru Highway, avoiding the two blocks of muddy footpath from the Post Office. Among the exhibits are a number of the old steam trains. Perhaps the most interesting is the carriage from which a man-eating lion dragged a victim as the line was being constructed through what is now Tsavo National Park. There is also a model of *MV Liemba*, the vessel built by the Germans and which still plies up and down Lake Tanganyika, see page 424. ■ *0800-1645.*

National Archives This is more interesting than it might sound to the non-historian. The building originally served as the Bank of India and is located on Moi Ave opposite the *Hilton Hotel*. It contains various exhibitions of arts and crafts as well as photographs and, of course, hundreds of thousands of documents. ■ *Weekdays 0800-1700. Entry is free.*

McMillan Memorial Library Located close to the Jamia Mosque and has an excellent collection of books, newspapers and parliamentary archives. The neo-classical building was built in 1928 and has huge lions on each side of the steps going up to the building. Books can be borrowed from here for a small charge. ■ *Monday-Friday 0900-1700, Saturday 0930-1300.* On the first floor is a collection of furniture from the house of Karen Blixen, several of the pieces can be recognized from descriptions in *Out of Africa*. Sadly many of these pieces are falling into disrepair. The library rooms housing this furniture collection have fallen into disarray.

Parliament House On Parliament Road and is recognisable by its clock tower. When Parliament is in session you can watch the proceedings from the public gallery, otherwise you can usually arrange to be shown around the building – ask at the main entrance.

Kenyatta Conference Centre This building is the tallest in the city with 28 floors and was built in 1972. At the top is the revolving restaurant which functions only periodically. However you can usually go up to the viewing level from where you can take photos – ask at the information desk on the ground floor. There can be stunning views of Mounts Kenya and Kilimanjaro on a clear day. It is free but it is usual to tip the guard.

Karen Blixen Museum The museum is found in the house of Karen Blixen (Isak Dinesen), in the suburb of Karen, and many people who have read her books or seen *Out of Africa* will want to savour the unique atmosphere. Most of the original furniture is housed in the McMillan Library. Sadly many of the pieces are falling into disrepair (see above). Exhibits include various agricultural implements. The house was bought by the Danish government in 1959 and presented to the Kenyan government at Independence, along with the nearby agricultural college. ■ *Open daily from 0930 to 1800 and entrance costs US$4. From Nairobi take the number 111 bus from the front of the Hilton. Journey time one hour, cost US$0.50. Change at Karen village to number 24 matatu or walk for half an hour (T882779).*

	Transport
14 Youth Hostel	**1** KBS Bus
15 New Kenya Lodge	**2** Country Bus
	3 Goldline Bus
	4 Akamba Bus
	5 Peugeot Taxis

Grogan: the flogging

In 1900 Grogan (see box, page 285) was moderately well-off. Gertrude, however, had inherited a considerable fortune. The Empire-builder, Cecil Rhodes, urged Grogan to 'give himself to Africa'. Grogan, Gertrude and their baby daughter, Dorothy, embarked for South Africa in 1902. A year later, they left for Mombasa and took the train to Nairobi. Grogan made huge land purchases: a forest concession of 64,000 acres in the Uasin Gishu Plateau to set up a saw mill; Mbaraki, a waterfront plot of 64 acres at Kilindi in Mombasa; and the area now called Westlands (but for many years was known as 'Groganville') to the northwest of the centre of Nairobi. Here he built a family home of grey volcanic rock which he named Chiromo after a pretty location he had admired in his Cape to Cairo journey. The house is now at the centre of Nairobi University Chiromo Campus and houses the East African Institute and administrative offices.

A second daughter, Joyce was born. Grogan prospered from the saw mill, and a deepwater pier at Mbaraki. He acquired more forest land and another huge tract in Nairobi from Ainsworth Bridge to Racecourse Road (now Tom Mboya Street). He was now Kenya's largest landowner with around 190,000 acres (Lord Delamere had 115,000), and was elected president of the Colonist Association which represented settlers.

There now occurred an incident that was to blight the memory of Grogan irrevocably. In 1911 Gertrude was ill with mastoids in her ears and went into hospital for an operation. Grogan's sister and a woman friend took a rickshaw to visit Gertrude in hospital. The three Kikuyu boys pulling the shafts had been drinking and they careered along, laughing, bouncing the passengers around, before they finally stopped, ran off, and the women were left to walk home. Grogan was incensed and the next day he rounded up the three boys, parading them through town to the Magistrates' Court on Government Avenue (now Moi Avenue). Despite being advised not to take the law into his own hands, Grogan stretched one of the lads on the ground and administered 25 lashes with a kiboko, a hippo-hide whip. Two cronies, Bowker and Grey flogged the other two. The three were arrested and tried. Bowker and Grey were were fined 450 Rupees each (about US$40) and sentenced to 14 days in jail. Grogan was fined 800 Rupees and sentenced to a month. Continued in box, page 249.

African Heritage Gallery (T333157) Now located on Banda Street. Arts and crafts are both exhibited and sold here.

Bomas of Kenya These are found in the Nairobi suburb of Langata. A Boma is a traditional homestead. Here programmes based on traditional dances of the different tribes of Kenya are presented. They are not in fact performed by people of the actual tribe but are a professional group of dancers. The dancers finish with a lively display of acrobatics and tumbling. There is also an open air museum showing the different life styles of each tribe. ■ *The shows begin at 1430 and costs US$2. If you are travelling independently you can get here on the matatu from outside Development House on Moi Ave which takes about 30 minutes.*

Langata Giraffe Centre Set in 15 acres of indigenous forest the Langata Giraffe Centre is located about 20 kilometres out of the city centre near the Hardy Estate Shopping Centre. If you do not have transport you can get there on the No 24 bus. The Centre is funded by the East African Fund for Endangered Wildlife and it houses a number of Rothschild's giraffes. There is information about them on display and it is designed to be interesting to children. You can watch and feed them from a raised wooden structure. The centre is also an excellent spot for bird-watching. ■ *During school and public holidays it is open from 1100 to 1730, and at other times it is only open 1400 to 1730 on weekdays and 1000 to 1730 on weekends. Admission is free for children, US$9 for adults and US$4.50 for students.*

Langata Bird Sanctuary This is a private sanctuary and has a splendid range of birds. You must book in advance and parties are accompanied by an ornithologist with a well-trained eye. Binoculars will add greatly to the pleasure of a visit. ■ *T225255. US$5.*

Nairobi National Park See Section on National Parks, page 274.

Animal Orphanage This is part of the Nairobi National Park and was opened in 1963 for orphaned or sick animals. Located close to the main entrance of the Nairobi National Park.

Excursions

Gikomba Village This village is well-known for wood carving and you can come here to see wood carvers learning their trade. It is found a few kilometres to the east of Nairobi toward Thika and is a popular stopping off point for tours.

Ngong Hills These hills are located about 25 kilometres to the southwest of Nairobi on the edge of the Great Rift Valley. Plan for at least half a day for the round trip. It is advisable to go in a group and to take care over security. Take the Langata Road out through the suburbs of Langata and Karen until you reach the town of Ngong. Just after this town turn right up the Panorama Road which should be well signposted. The road winds up fairly steeply in places. The route is about 100 kilometres in all and you climb up 1,000 metres. From the top you can look back from where you have come to see the skyline of Nairobi. The city centre with its sky scrapers is clearly visible and gradually peters out to the suburbs and farms. On a very clear day you can see Mount Kenya in the distance. Looking over in the other direction, towards the Great Rift Valley is a view of about 100 kilometres.

Lake Magadi is a lake on the base of the Rift Valley at 580 metres altitude which makes it the second lowest of the Rift Valley lakes. It is the most alkaline of all the Kenyan Rift Valley lakes. The high rate of evaporation is the only way by which water escapes from the lake. The highly alkaline water, with its accumulated minerals and salts makes the surrounding soils near the lakes alkaline, which has the knock on effect of turning ivory and bones into fossils. It is only 110 kilometres from Nairobi but the climate is very different to that of the capital – it is semi-desert and the temperatures are around 38°C. As with many of the other Rift Valley Lakes this is a soda lake and because of the high temperatures it is particularly rich in the mineral. A

Kenya

Greater Nairobi

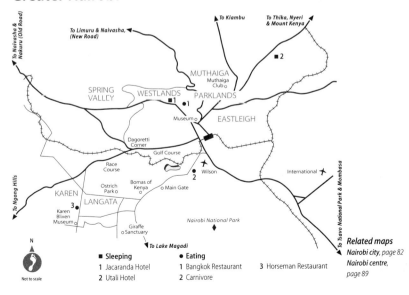

N
Not to scale

■ Sleeping
1 Jacaranda Hotel
2 Utali Hotel

● Eating
1 Bangkok Restaurant
2 Carnivore

3 Horseman Restaurant

Related maps
Nairobi city, page 82
Nairobi centre,
page 89

Early settlers

On 3 September 1896 a party of new arrivals set off from Mombasa to trek up-country with a view to settling in the Highlands around Nairobi. They were Henry Boedeker (a doctor), Jim McQueen, a blacksmith, and the two Wallace brothers, David, a doctor and George, a farmer and their respective wives.

There were porters to carry their belongings and a dozen or so donkeys – which the ladies would ride from time to time – Mary McQueen and Mary Wallace were both pregnant.

The route was through Machakos and then to Fort Smith (now Kabete). It took six weeks, sleeping in tents, and on average they covered about 10 miles each day they were on the trail.

The McQueens settled at Mbagahi about 12 miles west of Nairobi. They built their own house, roofed with makuti thatch, mud and wattle walls, windows without glass with wooden shutters. Lighting was by candle and paraffin hurricane lamps. Water was collected from the Magathi River in four gallon tins (debes), used to import paraffin. Cooking was done on a wood fire with pots balanced on three stones. A mud shell round a debe with a fire underneath served as an oven. Bird and game were plentiful, and were shot for meat.

The McQueens had six children who went barefoot. The children's clothes were sewn by hand from flour bags and Mary McQueen taught them to read, write and add up.

---

soda factory has been built on the lake shores. It is fairly remote and inaccessible for those without their own transport. There is no public transport at all and the railway line which serves the factory does not take passengers.

To get there take the Langata Road out past Wilson Airport and the National Park. Soon after the Park entrance there is a left fork. Take this road through the village of Kiserian and then climbs from where you will get some good views of the Rift. It then drops down into the Rift and as it does it gets hotter and drier. As you approach the views are splendid and you will probably see Masai grazing their cattle. There is an abundance of birdlife – in particular lesser flamingos, ibis and African spoonbills. At the southern end of the lake are hot springs.

Whistling Thorns, a property of approximately 20 acres, is an hours drive from Nairobi on good tarmac road, 13 kilometres from Kiserian, on the Kiserian-Isinya Pipeline road. Off the usual tourist track. Bus 111 to Kiserian, then matatu to Isinya and get off at Whistling Thorns.

Whistling Thorns is open daily for lunch/dinner. There is accommodation, twin room cottages and camping/hot showers. Other facilities include a swimming pool, horse riding, cycling and bush walks. Fabulous views of the Ngong Hills. Booking essential, T350720.

Olorgasailie Prehistoric Site A trip to this important prehistoric site can be combined with a visit to Lake Magadi. It is located 65 kilometres from Nairobi and is two kilometres off the road to Lake Magadi. It is well signposted. The National Museums of Kenya administer the site and arrange tours. At the site is a small museum with a number of exhibits including animal bones and hand axes believed to date from 700,000 years ago. The site was discovered in 1919 by a geologist JW Gregory and later in the 1940s excavated by Kenya's most famous archaeologists, Mary and Louis Leakey. In 1947 it was given National Park status. There is limited accommodation at the site. For further information of tours and also for details of accommodation contact the Nairobi Museum (T742161).

Muthaiga Club

Archie Morrison came to Kenya in 1912 to hunt, and was much taken with the country. He obtained a plot of land some five kilometres to the northeast of the Nairobi Centre to develop as a residential centre, and he planned a club for the settlers there, putting up the 60,000 required for the enterprise.

An English architect, HE Henderson was engaged, and he brought out craftsmen to undertake high-quality work. A mixture of of murram and lime was used for the stucco on the distinctive pink exterior walls.

The club opened for 14 exclusive guests on 31 December 1913, with dinner prepared by the chef from the Bombay Yacht Club, served by Goanese waiters, to the accompaniment of a band. Over the next half century, the Muthaiga Club was to become synonymous with the Bohemian high-life of the settlers.

Mathaiga is the Kikuyu name for the bark of the Greenheart tree. Appropriately it is the source of both an elixir and a poison. An extract can be used in moderate doses as a stimulant with curative powers. Concentrated, it makes a poison – which the Kikuyu use to tip their arrows.

Essentials

There is an enormous range of hotels from the most expensive to the most basic. Those at the top of the range have all the facilities that you would expect of 5-star hotels and are of an international standard.

Sleeping

■ on maps, pages 82 and 89
For price codes, see inside front cover

A+ *Grand Regency*, Loita St, PO Box 57549, T211199, F217120. Profusion of marble and gilt. **A+** *Hilton*, PO Box 30624, Watali St, just off Mama Ngina St, T334000, F339462/226477. It is rather like any other *Hilton* anywhere in the world although the large wildlife mural in the foyer does remind you that you're in Africa, it has over 300 rooms and facilities include a roof top swimming pool, shops, meeting rooms and a health club, it does an excellent buffet breakfast which is very good value and is open to non-residents. **A+** *Inter-Continental Nairobi*, PO Box 30353, City Hall Way and Uhuru Highway, T335550, F210675/214617, reservations Nairobi 240225, Nairobi@Interconti.com. Nairobi's largest hotel with over 400 rooms, facilities include a heated swimming pool, shops, casino and an excellent roof top restaurant *Le Chateau* that is popular in particular for its dinner dance evenings, this hotel welcomes children. **A+** *Landmark*, part of the Block Hotels chain, PO Box 14287, T448714/7, F448977, Waiyaki Way, Westlands, central bookings for Block Hotels PO Box 40075, Nairobi, T540780, F543810. Good quality hotel restaurant, balcony/garden pizza restaurant, comfortable rooms, swimming pool, bar, business facilities. **A+** *Nairobi Safari Club*, PO Box 43564, Lillian Towers, University Way at Koinage St, T251333, F224625. This is one of the newest of the Nairobi Hotels and probably the most expensive, it was originally known as the *Mount Kenya Safari Club* and is one of the few places where you are expected to wear a tie and jacket, it also does not welcome children under the age of 12, it has been described as palatial which is not far wrong – marble, fountains and lots of greenery, it has a swimming pool, sauna, health centre, hairdresser and meeting rooms, you will also have to pay temporary membership to stay. **A+** *Nairobi Serena*, PO Box 46302, Kenyatta Ave and Nyerere Rd close to All Saints Cathedral, T725111, F725184, central booking PO Box 48690 Nairobi, T710511/2, F718100/2/3, serenamk@africaonline.co.ke. Set in beautiful gardens it has plenty of parking space and runs a shuttle service into town, the *Serena* has a good reputation and is popular with business travellers and tourists, there are wonderful views of the city, especially at sunset, it has 192 rooms and facilities include a swimming pool, health club, meeting rooms, shops and an excellent restaurant. **A+** *Norfolk*, PO Box 40064, Harry Thuku Rd, T250900, F336742. Built in 1904 this is a world-famous hotel and as a result many people who cannot afford to actually stay, drop in for a drink, it suffered some damage in 1980 when a bomb, believed to be being carried by a terrorist in transit, went off in the hotel, however it was repaired and in 1991 it underwent extensive renovations, there are 129 rooms and 6 luxury

STAYING IN NAIROBI?

Try The Country Hotel In Town, Set Within 5 Acres of Luxuriant Tranquil Gardens. The Perfect Hotel for Business Travellers.

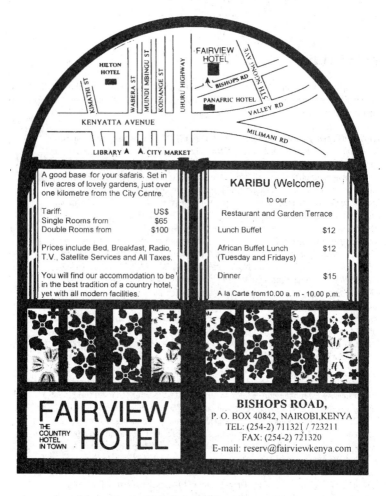

A good base for your safaris. Set in five acres of lovely gardens, just over one kilometre from the City Centre.

Tariff:	US$
Single Rooms from	$65
Double Rooms from	$100

Prices include Bed, Breakfast, Radio, T.V., Satellite Services and All Taxes.

You will find our accommodation to be in the best tradition of a country hotel, yet with all modern facilities.

KARIBU (Welcome)

to our

Restaurant and Garden Terrace

Lunch Buffet	$12
African Buffet Lunch (Tuesday and Fridays)	$12
Dinner	$15

A la Carte from 10.00 a. m - 10.00 p.m.

FAIRVIEW THE COUNTRY HOTEL IN TOWN **HOTEL**

BISHOPS ROAD,
P. O. BOX 40842, NAIROBI,KENYA
TEL: (254-2) 711321 / 723211
FAX: (254-2) 721320
E-mail: reserv@fairviewkenya.com

EFFECTIVE 1st JANUARY 2000

Nairobi Centre

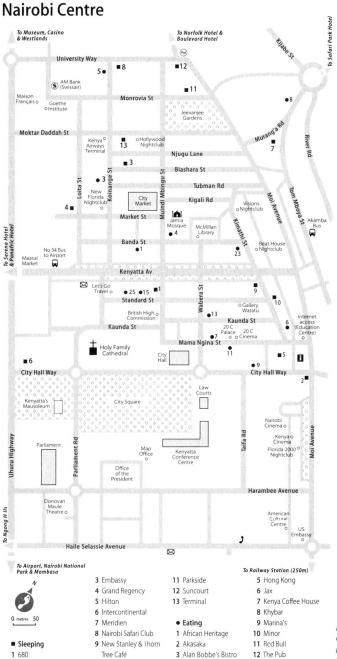

To Museum, Casino & Westlands

To Norfolk Hotel & Boulevard Hotel

To Safari Park Hotel

Kijabe St

University Way

5 ● ■ 8 ■ 12

Pol

AM Bank (Swissair)

Maison Français ○

Goethe Institute

Monrovia St ■ 11

Jeevanjee Gardens

● 8

Murang'a Rd

River Rd

Moktar Daddah St

Kenya Airways Terminal

■ 13 ○ Hollywood Nightclub

Njugu Lane

7

Loita St

Koinange St

■ 3

Biashara St

New Florida Nightclub

● 3

Tubman Rd

Muindi Mbingu St

Kigali Rd

Visions Nightclub

Moi Avenue

Tom Mboya St

Akamba Bus

4 ■

City Market

Market St

Jamia Mosque

● 4

McMillan Library

Kimathi St

Beat House ○ Nightclub

Banda St

● 1

23

Kenyatta Av

To Serena Hotel & Panafric Hotel

No 34 Bus to Airport

Maasai Market

Let's Go Travel

● 25 ● 15 ■ 1

9

Standard St

Wabera St

○ Gallery Watatu

10

British High Commission

■ 13

Kaunda St

6

Internet access (Education Centre)

Kaunda St

20 C Palace ○

20 C ○ Cinema

Mama Ngina St

● 7

5 ■

Holy Family Cathedral

11

City Hall

● 9

i

■ 6

City Hall Way

City Hall Way

2 ■

Uhuru Highway

Parliament Rd

Law Courts

Kenyatta's Mausoleum

City Square

Nairobi Cinema ○

Taifa Rd

Kenya ○ Cinema

Moi Avenue

Parliament

Map Office

Kenyatta Conference Centre

Florida 2000 Nightclub

Office of the President

Harambee Avenue

To Ngong H lls

Donovan Maule Theatre ○

American Cultural Centre ○

US Embassy

Haile Selassie Avenue

To Railway Station (250m)

To Airport, Nairobi National Park & Mombasa

N

0 metres 50

■ Sleeping
1 680
2 Ambassadeur

3 Embassy
4 Grand Regency
5 Hilton
6 Intercontinental
7 Meridien
8 Nairobi Safari Club
9 New Stanley & Ihorn Tree Café
10 Oakwood

11 Parkside
12 Suncourt
13 Terminal

● Eating
1 African Heritage
2 Akasaka
3 Alan Bobbe's Bistro
4 Blukat

5 Hong Kong
6 Jax
7 Kenya Coffee House
8 Khybar
9 Marina's
10 Minor
11 Rcd Bull
12 The Pub
13 Trattoria

Related maps
Greater Nairobi, page 85
Nairobi city, page 82

Kenya

cottages, the *Lord Delamare Bar* is a popular drinking spot and has a series of caricature cartoons of early settlers, you can also sit on the terrace or in the gardens near the aviary, other facilities include a swimming pool, shops, 2 restaurants and bars and a ballroom. **A+ *Safari Park***, c 13 kilometres, north of Nairobi on the Thika Rd, PO Box 45038, T802493/862222/222846, F802477/861584, safarih@arcc.or.ke. Completed in 1990, it has 125 rooms, 2 restaurants, 3 bars, a swimming pool, tennis and squash courts and meeting rooms, it has a few restaurants serving a very varied range of cuisines, all rooms have a balcony with a view, charges guests US$5 to use the gym. **A+ *Windsor Golf and Country Club***, north of Nairobi on Garden Estate Rd, T862300, F802322, windsor@users.africaonline.co.ke PO Box No 45587. Built in 1991 and is one of Nairobi's newer hotels, there are about 100 rooms and 15 luxury cottages modelled on a Victorian style English country hotel, it has extensive facilities including 2 restaurants, meeting rooms, a health club, an 18-hole golf course (located in forest), squash and tennis courts, and riding facilities. **A** *Fairview*, PO Box 40842, 2 kilometres from the centre on Bishops Rd, T711321/723211, F721320/711655, reserv@fairviewkenya.com. Very peaceful with well-kept and extensive tropical gardens, a wonderful hotel and extremely popular with overseas visitors and Kenyans, caters both for business people and families, Conference Rooms, an excellent Terrace Restaurant which is also a popular meeting place. New Conference Room, Swimming Pool and Health Club expected to be completed late 2000/early 2001. Highly recommended. **A** *Panafric*, PO Box 30486, Kenyatta Ave, T720822 (Sarova Group, central reservations, T717820, F721878/726356). It is a modern practical hotel of 200 rooms, but without an enormous amount of atmosphere, facilities include a swimming pool, shop, hairdressers and meeting rooms, there is a café by the pool and the *Simba Grill* is popular, with a live band most nights.

B *Boulevard*, Harry Thuku Rd, PO Box 42831, T227567/337221, F334071, hotelboulevard@form-net.com. 500 metres from city centre, good value, has 70 rooms, each with own balcony, facilities include a swimming pool, tennis courts, gardens and restaurant. **B** *Jacaranda*, PO Box 14287, T448713, about 5 kilometres out of town on Chiromo Rd close to the Westlands shopping centre this is a popular family hotel, it has about 135 rooms and facilities include a swimming pool, tennis court, and playground. **B** *Marble Arch*, PO Box 12224, T245720/245656, F245724. Newly opened hotel on the Lagos Rd off Tom Mboya St, smart, very modern, friendly and efficient businessman's hotel. Although central, it is unfortunately located between River Rd and Tom Mboya St, has an underground carpark but no garden or pool. **B** *Mayfair Court Hotel*, Parklands Rd, PO Box 66807, T740906/740920/750780, F748823. **B** *Milimani*, PO Box 30715, Milimani Rd, T720760. Large hotel popular with expatriates working in Kenya, prices include breakfast. **B** *New Stanley*, PO Box 30680, corner of Kenyatta Ave and Kimathi St, T333233/4/5/6, F229388 (Sarova Group, central reservations, T333248, F211472). It is actually the oldest hotel in Nairobi although joriginally it was not located here, the celebrated outdoor *Thorn Tree Café* is found here as well as the *Nation Bookshop*, the *Thorn Tree* is famous for its notice board where travellers leave messages for each other, the board can be used by anyone at no cost, but not for any advertisements, it has about 240 rooms and facilities include meeting rooms, shops and a moderate restaurant.

AM Jevanjee

AM Jevanjee was born in India in 1861 into a Parsee family with a ship-owning business. He came to British East Africa and quickly built up a powerful business in shipping, construction and trading. The first newspaper, The Africa Standard (later the East Africa Standard and now the Standard) was started by Jevanjee in Mombasa in 1899. Jevanjee owned the building in Victoria Street that was rented to Tommy Woods and turned into Wood's Hotel, opening in 1901. A racing enthusiast, his horse was the first ever winner when Nairobi Race Course was opened in 1903.

In 1906 Jevanjee acquired a plot of land between the Norfolk Hotel and the railway station, laid out lawns and flower beds, commissioned a statue of Queen Victoria and presented Jevanjee Gardens to Nairobi Council.

As the most prominent member of the Indian Community, Jevanjee was nominated to the Legislative Council (Legco) in 1908. Although this was welcomed by Winston Churchill at the Colonial office it received a hostile reception from the settlers, especially Grogan (see boxes, pages 285, 84, 249). The Europeans were aware that they were outnumbered by the Indian population and saw it as the thin end of a wedge that would lead to, if not loss of control, at least a situation where interests perhaps in conflict with their own were powerfully represented. The atmosphere was so sour for Jevanjee that he resigned. There was not another Indian on Legco until 1920.

Jevanjee was ever a stylish figure in Nairobi, dressed all in white, with a grey beard and gold turban. He died in 1923 aged 62.

C *Ambassadeur*, PO Box 30399, Moi Ave, T336803 (Sarova Group, central reservations, T333248, F211472). This has a good central location, it is fairly ordinary – nothing special and there are better value hotels in the same range. **C** *Hurlingham*, PO Box 43158, Argwings Kodhek Rd, T721920/723001. This is a small hotel with only 14 rooms, located in western Nairobi, it has a definite charm and is popular with local residents. **C** *Meridien Court Hotel*, T333675/333744/333846, Murang'a Rd. Good value. **C** *Six Eighty*, PO Box 43436, Muindi Mbingu St, T332680. Very central, it has 380 rooms and facilities include a Japanese restaurant, shops and a bar (currently being refurbished with a casino), staff helpful to visitors, clean rooms. **C** *Utalii*, PO Box 31067, located a bit out of town on the Thika Rd, T802540, F803094, Utali@Form-Net.com . *Utalii* is the Swahili word for tourism and this is the government-run training centre for hotel and catering students, as a result service is really very good, there are 50 rooms and facilities include swimming pool, lovely gardens, tennis courts and restaurant. **C** *Parkside*, PO Box 53104, T333329, F334681, reservations 333348/214154/5/6, Monrovia St. Rooms have bathrooms and hot water and the price includes breakfast, it is friendly and clean but relatively expensive and there is a restaurant attached.

In this price range it is particularly noticeable that for the same price the hotels out of town **D Central** tend to be of a higher standard than those in the centre. Those in the centre often suffer from the noise.

D *Africana*, Dubois Rd off Latema Rd, PO Box 47827, T220654. One of the best in this category, it is clean, safe and fairly quiet and rooms all have bathrooms with hot water. **D** *Embassy*, Biashara St/Tubman Rd, T224087/224533/4. Clean, safe and friendly and rooms have bathrooms with hot water. **D** *Grand Holiday Hotel*, Tsavo Rd, PO Box 69343, T243427/211372/224648/330704, F243851. Noisy but very clean, hot showers. **D** *Hermes*, PO Box 62997, T340066, a little way out on the corner of Tom Mboya St and Haile Selassie Ave. This is a good value hotel, it is clean and has a fairly good restaurant. **D** *Oakwood Hotel*, PO Box 40683, Kimathi St opposite the *New Stanley Hotel*, T220592/3, F332170. Good value, there are only 23 rooms and the price includes breakfast, facilities include a bar, restaurant and a roof terrace. **D** *Salama*, corner of Tom Mboya St and Luthuli Ave, PO Box 11386, T215338. Suffers from the noise, price includes breakfast but it is not terribly good value. **D** *Sirikwa Lodge*, corner of Accra Rd and Munyu St, T26089. Not too noisy, rooms have bathrooms with hot water and are clean, breakfast is included in the price. **D** *Solace Hotel*, PO

John Ainsworth

Three stations, at Kibwezi, Machakos and Fort Smith (now Kabote) were established by the British East Africa Company (BEAC) to serve as staging posts for the caravans from the coast to Uganda. Their role was to supply food and water, purchased in the local area. Machakos could service a caravan of 2,000 porters.

John Ainsworth came to Machakos in 1889 to work for the BEAC, and he threw himself into the life, extending the fort, establishing a modicum of law and order in the area and laying out a fruit garden around his house (now the District Commissioner's residence). When the BEAC decided in 1892 that it could no longer afford to keep the post going Ainsworth opted to carry on and a year later he was appointed Chief Native Commissioner for

the Akamba. He married Ina Scott, the sister of a missionary in 1897, and in 1909 he was relocated to Nairobi, occupying a house on the site of the present National Museum, and building the first bridge over the Nairobi River which still bears his name. In 1912 he started the Agricultural Show, introduced sisal from German East Africa (now Tanzania), and was a key influence in the resettlement of the Masai from Laikipia to the Mara.

A man with considerable physical presence, Ainsworth was the embodiment of the early colonial administrator, scrupulously fair, full of initiative, but with a yearning for the ways of home which saw him transplanting golf, horse racing, and flower shows to the tropics.

Box 48867, Tom Mboya St, T331277, F220129. Reasonable value, to be avoided if you can't sleep through noise. **D** *Terminal*, Moktar Daddah St in the northwest of town, T228817, located next door to the *Downtown Hotel*. Popular hotel although it has seen better days, it is however clean, safe and friendly, helpful staff, can be noisy early in the morning and at night. Rooms have bathrooms with hot water, breakfast is not included. Restaurant next door does good cheap food.

D Out of city centre **D** *Diplomat Hotel*, PO Box 30777, T246114/245948/332316, F220475, Tom Mboya St next to *Ambassadeur*. Extraordinary good value, pretty slick for the price, wall to wall carpeting, s/c modern rooms, colour TV, direct dial phones, breakfast included. **D** *Green View Hotel*, PO Box 42246, Minet ICDC Bldg, situated off Nyerere Rd, T729923. Nice surroundings, there are both private and shared bathrooms, there is a bar and restaurant and prices include breakfast. **D** *Hotel Greton*, Tsavo Rd. Good value, very secure, whether in room, safe or left luggage, clean, decent sized, furnished rooms, breakfast included, relaxed restaurant, better for drinks than food. **D** *Heron Court Apartment Hotel*, PO Box 41848, Milimani Rd, T720740/1/2/3. Popular, it is safe and has a guarded car park, rooms vary – all have bathrooms and hot water, and some are self contained with kitchens, facilities include swimming pool, sauna, shop and laundry service, some rooms can however be noisy as the celebrated *Buffalo Bill's* restaurant and bar is attached. **D** *Sagret Hotel Equatorial*, PO Box 18324, Corner of Milimani Rd and Ralph Bunche Rd, T720933/4/9. Not bad value, price includes breakfast and facilities include a bar and restaurant.

E Central **E** *Bujumbura Lodge*, Dubois Rd, just off Latema Rd, T221835, near *New Safe Lodging*, basic with shared bathrooms and unpredictable hot water supplies. **E** *Dolat*, Mfangano St, T222797/228663. Relatively quiet and friendly, very clean, secure and rooms all have bath and hot water. **E** *Evamay Hotel*, River Rd, excellent value, cosy s/c rooms with nets, phone and good furniture, very friendly staff, safe facilities, price includes breakfast. **E** *Gloria*, Ronald Ngala St, T228916. Rather noisy place to stay but as all rooms have bathrooms and hot water and the price includes breakfast it is really quite good value. **E** *Iqbal*, Latema Rd, T220914. One of the most popular places in central Nairobi, so if you want to stay you will have to arrive early, there is sometimes hot water in the mornings and although it's only basic it is friendly and you will meet lots of other travellers here, all rooms have shared bathrooms, it has baggage storage facilities and a notice board, reported to survive mostly on guide book history, rather than modern day service and comments. **E** *New Kenya Lodge and Annex*, River Rd by the junction of Latema St, T222202. The annex is just around the corner in Duruma Rd,

Settlers v Administrators

In 1907 a fancy dress football match was staged for charity in Nairobi before the Governor. The settlers found an imaginative way to highlight their grievances at administrative regulations. Dressed as officials, with huge medals made from lids *and red-tape ribbons, they pegged out areas of the pitch and marked them 'Quarantine Area', `Forest Reserve', 'Nature Reserve', 'Game Reserve' and so on until the whole playing area was marked as out of bounds.*

T338348. Another very popular budget hotel, again it is basic, bathrooms are shared and there is only hot water in the evenings, except in the Annex which only has cold water, however it is reasonably clean and friendly and has baggage storage facilities and a notice board, historically has been recommended in guide books, but tends to rest on its laurels. Travellers have reported that the associated Safari company called NEO-KL TOURS AND SAFARIS offers very poor service with badly organised tours and refuses to reimburse the costs of failed excursions. **E** *New Safe Life Lodging*, Dubois Rd just off Latema Rd. It is clean, basic with shared bathrooms but has the usual hot water problems, as with many of these places the single rooms are not very good value. **E** *Glory Palace Hotel*, Muranga Rd, northwest of centre, T744795/743826. Port of Glory chain based in Mombasa, basic facilities. **E** *Nyandarwa Lodging*, Dubois Rd, just off Latema Rd. Shared bathrooms and hot water, can be very noisy. **E** *Sunrise*, Latema Rd, T330362. Another basic but clean place with shared bathrooms which have hot water mornings and evenings, some of the rooms are rather noisy as it is next door to the *Modern 24 Hour Green Bar* which is, as its name implies, open all day and all night. **E** *Terrace*, Ronald Ngala St, T221636. This is close to the *Gloria* and is similar, it can be rather noisy, also the staff don't appear to make much of an effort. **E** *YMCA*, State House Rd, T724066. It is good value but caters for the long term visitor, many of the residents are Kenyan students who live there semi-permanently, swimming pool. **E** *YWCA*, Mamlaka Rd, off Nyerere Rd, T724699. Does take couples, good value.

E *Mrs Roche's*, it is a little way out, situated opposite the Aga Khan Hospital on Third Parklands Ave. This is a legend amongst travellers and remains popular, campers are also welcome and use the garden which can get rather crowded, if you get there late you will have to sleep on the floor until a bed is free. Security needs to be tightened up as recent travellers have reported thefts on site. Can be reached on matatu (which will say Aga Khan on the front) from outside the Odeon Cinema at the junction of Tom Mboya St and Latema Rd, ask the driver to tell you where to get off. **E** *Nairobi Park Services Campsite*, on Magadi Rd, off Langata Rd, PO Box 54867, T/F2-890325, shling@net2000ke.com or Allk@form-net.com. Opened in August 1997 this campsite offers good budget facilities, bars and restaurant. Tented accommodation, with 2-storeyed accommodation and bandas available soon. Hot showers, laundry facilities, western style toilets in a secure fenced compound. Vehicle parks, TV/Video US$3 per night. Can arrange game drives or camel safaris. **E** *Nairobi Youth Hostel*, about 2 kilometres out of town on Ralph Bunche Rd (which runs between Ngong Rd and Valley Rd), T723012. You must be a member of the International Youth Hostels Association to stay here but can join on the spot without any problem, bathrooms are shared but there is hot water all day, it is clean, friendly and safe, take the No 8 matatu from outside the *Hilton Hotel* or at the junction of Kenyatta Ave and Uhuru Highway down Ngong Rd and ask to be dropped off at Ralph Bunche Rd, do not walk back to the youth hostel at night – always take a taxi or matatu. **E** *Upper Hill Campsite Ltd*, Menengai Rd/Upper Hill, Nairobi, T720290, F723788. Site opened in 95 with 5 dorm beds, 2 double rooms and 1 single, tent space and tents for hire, good clean amenities, bar and restaurant, good security, reasonably central, 30 minutes walk from city centre, it's keen to attract visitors and risks being dominated by large overland trucks and their passengers. Food cheap but good. Staff friendly. The *Kenya Youth Hostels Association* is on Ralph Bunche Rd, T721765/723012.

E Out of city centre

Whistling Thorns, PO Box 51512, Nairobi, T/F350720, speccampsaf@thorntree.com, Website: ww.africaonline.co.ke/campingsafaris . Guest cottages and camping, food, organizes safaris (see also page 86).

Eating
● *on maps*
Price codes:
see inside front cover

There is a wide range of restaurants to suit all tastes and budgets. All the top hotels have good eating places. Take care, many brands of bottled water sold in Kenya are Nairobi tapwater (75 of 78 tested – Sunday Standard 28 May 1995).

4 *Alan Bobbe's Bistro*, this small restaurant is located on Koinange St, T224945. It is advisable to come here in something more than shorts and a T-shirt, it specializes in French cuisine and the food and atmosphere are both excellent, reservations are recommended. **4** *Café Maghreb*, T725111. *Serena Hotel*, another popular buffet place this is next to the swimming pool and is particularly busy on Friday evenings. **4** *Horseman*, in Karen and is highly recommended, T882033. You can also eat outside in the garden. **4** *Ibis Grill*, *Norfolk Hotel*, T335422. This specializes in nouvelle cuisine and is really excellent, the food is very good, it has a lovely setting and a good atmosphere, jacket and tie recommended, the *Norfolk* also does a wonderful buffet breakfast which is open to non-residents. **4** *Le Chateau*, *Intercontinental Hotel*. Rooftop restaurant is the only one of its kind in Nairobi and serves excellent food, dinner dancing at weekends. **4** *Red Bull*, located in Silopark House on Mama Ngina St, T224718. This has long been one of Nairobi's most popular restaurants – for residents, business people, and tourists alike, portions are generous and the food high quality. **4** *The Tamarind*, National Bank building on Harambee Ave, T338959/217990/220473. Probably Nairobi's finest seafood restaurant. Highly recommended, only open 1830-2130. **4** *The Tate Room*, *New Stanley Hotel*. Very plush and the food is good, Sunday buffet is very popular here.

3 *Carnivore*, Langata Rd about 20 minutes out of town past the airport, T501775/501709/501707. This was set up by the owners of the Tamarind. As is clear from the name it specializes in meat dishes including game (wart-hog, giraffe, zebra, gazelle, crocodile, wildebeest, etc) which are grilled over a huge charcoal fire, the waiters bring the skewer of meat to your table and carve until you say stop, it has become very popular with all types of travellers and is often included as part of tours, there is also a vegetarian menu, portions are huge and it works out as fairly good value.

2 *Buffalo Bill's*, *Heron Court Hotel* on Milimani Rd, T720740/712944. You can eat here although the main past time is drinking, lively atmosphere, the food is okay but not very good value. **2** *Hard Rock Café*, Barclays Plaza, Loita St, T220802/3. Lively in the evenings, live band on Thursday (usually). **2** *Jax*, Kimathi St, T228365. Popular with business people for quick cheap lunches, it is self-service and usually busy and includes a number of Indian dishes, closed Sunday. **2** *Thorn Tree Café*, *New Stanley Hotel*. Very popular place to meet people although the service is notoriously slow.

Cheap eating There are lots of cheap places in the River Rd area selling African and Indian food and snacks. The **1** *Iqbal* is particularly popular with travellers. The **1** *Jacaranda* is pleasant for a drink and snack and is a favourite with business people. **1** *The Coffee Bar* on Mama Ngina St is busy for lunches and does filling meals. Other places to try are the **1** *Beneve Coffee House* on the corner of Standard and Koinange Sts. **1** *Bull Café* on Ngariama Rd. Cheap and popular. **1** *Malindi Restaurant* on Gaborone Rd. Swahili dishes – tasty, and reasonable price.

African 3 *West African Paradise Restaurant*, T741396. If you fancy something a little different, open daily 0930-2130, in the Westlands district. **2** *African Heritage Café*, Banda St, T222010. African food, selection of dishes from a buffet, so it is possible to sample the various examples. Highly recommended. There is also a garden. **2** *A La Monde Restaurant* in an office building on Mamlaka just uphill from the *Nairobi Serena Hotel*, in the Utumishi Co-operative House, T721302. Run by a British educated Kenyan called Kui, serves a different African dish from one of the different ethnic groups each day, clientele is mostly office workers, prices very reasonable, food is good and the atmosphere is lively.

For good and cheap African local food the adventurous should try the Kariakor Market, turn right as you enter the main gate and at the first corner you come to a Nyama Choma wil be on your left, tables to the right. You eat with your hands. A specimen menu is goat's ribs, ugali, chopped spinach, irio made with peas, potatoes and sweetcorn, cost US$1.

Chinese 3 *China Plate*, Chancery Bldg, Valley Rd, T719194/727627. Expensive, but the food is very good, the decor authentic Chinese and the services attentive. **3** *Dragon Pearl*, Kenyatta Ave/Standard St, Ground Floor, in Bruce House, T338863/223194. Deservedly very popular. **3** *Great Chung Wa*, Mwindi Mbingu (opposite *Six Eighty Hotel*). Prominent location and recommended food. **3** *Hong Kong*, Koinange St, T228612. Specializes in Cantonese dishes and has a good reputation. Closed Monday. **3** *Mandarin*, Tom Mboya St, T20600. Reasonable standard. **3** *Pagoda*, T227036. Szechuan food. **3** *Panda*, located in Imenti House on Tom Mboya St, T331189. Good food and friendly staff. **3** *Rendezvous*, at Meridian Ct. Has a very good buffet of vegetarian, non-vegetarian and local dishes. **3** *Rickshaw*, in the Fehda Towers on Standard and Muindi Mbingu St, T223604. Extensive menu, highly rated.

Indian 4 *Haandi*, Westlands Mall, T448294/5/6. Very good standard. **4** *Minar*, there are 3 *Minar's*, one located on Banda St in the city centre, one in the Sarit Centre in Westlands, T229999/748340, and one in the Ya Ya Centre, Hurlingham, T561676. They are popular and reservations are recommended, they do a buffet lunch and the service is friendly, their tandoori dishes are especially good. **3** *Haveli Restaurant and Coffee House*, Dar es Salaam Rd, Industrial area, T531607/531693/532808. Excellent quality. **3** *Rasoi*, located on Parliament Rd, T25082/26049. Excellent standard. **3** *The Golden Candle*, Ralph Bunche Rd, T720480. Extensive menu, all of which is very good, closed on Monday. **2** *Al Mamin*, corner of Banda St and Kimathi. Open plan, airy and bustling, limited menu but cheap, filling and tasty biryanis, curry, nan and kebabs. **2** *Dhaba*, Tom Mboya St, T334862. Specializes in North Indian food, it is particularly popular with Nairobi Indians, their speciality is *taka taka* dishes, *taka taka* means rubbish in Swahili – although what that has to do with these delicious dishes is not totally clear – may be they were originally the left-overs. **2** *Durgar*, Ngara St, T742781. Although the decor is certainly not fancy this has good cheap food, with a good range of vegetarian dishes, also lots of Indian snacks which are very popular. **2** *Mayur*, T331586, corner of Tom Mboya St and Keekorok Rd. Specializes in vegetarian Indian food, has seen better days, but the food is still good. **2** *Satkar*, Moi Ave, T337197. Specializes in southern Indian food. **2** *Sunsweet Restaurant*, back of *New Kenya Lodge*. Serves excellent Indian Thali. **2** *Supreme*, located in the River Rd area, T25241. This Indian restaurant is excellent, it also does takeaways and has an extensive dessert menu. Others include **2** *Ambassadeur*, T336803, **2** *Nawab Tandoori*, T740209, **2** *New 3 Bells*, T220628, **2** *Safeer*, **2** *Zam Zam*, T212128, Keekorak Rd, near River Rd. Cheap and cheerful, large portions.

Kenya

Italian **4** *Foresta Magnetica*, Mama Ngina St, T728009. With a piano bar, the menu is probably better at lunchtime than in the evenings because the cafeteria does not operate in the evenings, but it has a very pleasant atmosphere in the evenings when the pianist is playing, closed Sunday. **2** *La Scala*, Phoenix House Arcade, Standard St, T332130. Trendy and friendly, good pizza, pasta, steaks and cakes, also capuccino, expresso and ice cold shakes. **3** *La Galleria* and **2** *The Toona Tree* are both in the International Casino, Westlands Rd, T742600/744477/4. *La Galleria* has good Italian food including some excellent seafood dishes, the *Toona Tree* is a cheaper outdoor restaurant which is especially good for drinks and snacks, it has live bands about 3 days a week, *Toona Tree* is closed on Monday and both close during the afternoon. **2** *Trattoria*, T340855/240205, situated on Kaunda St and Wabera St. Rather bustling if chaotic place, the food is fairly good which is more than can be said for the service, it does good cappuccinos and ice cream, reservations are recommended especially if you want one of the tables with a view, open until midnight. **2** *Twigs*, Nkrumah Rd, T335864/336308/335243. Menu is part Italian, part French as well as quite a lot of seafood, the food and service are both very good, downstairs is an ice-cream parlour. Others include **3** *Arturos*, T26940, **3** *Casino*, T742600.

Japanese **4** *Shogun*, located at the *Grosvener Hotel* on Ralph Bunche St, T720563/716080. This is one of Nairobi's two Japanese restaurants, they are fairly similar with comparable menus although the Shogun is not so good for lunches. **3** *Akaska Hotel*, 680 Hotel Ground Floor Muindi Mbingu St, T220299/219847. Open 1800-2100, very central, reasonable standard.

Mongolian *The Manchurian*, Brick Court, Mpaka Rd, Westlands, T444263. A rarity indeed.

Thai **3** *Bangkok*, located in Rank Xerox House, T751311/2. It is popular and deservedly so, open every day at lunchtime, and from 1800-2230.

Bars Eating, drinking and dancing are the most popular evening entertainments in Nairobi. There are a number of popular bars and clubs, and a number of casinos. For most of these clubs entrance for women is cheaper than for men. Single men should expect a lot of attention. As with most establishments in Kenya, dress is casual in all these clubs. The only exceptions to this rule are the *Nairobi Safari Club* and the *Windsor Golf and Country Club*.
Popular hotel bars include the *Norfolk*, *Fairview* and the *Grosvenor*. The *Thorn Tree* is a good meeting place but the service is notoriously slow. If you are there at lunchtime (1100 to 1400) or supper time (1700 to 1900) you will have to order food as well. *Buffalo Bill's* Bar in the *Heron Court Hotel* on Milimani Rd is popular and it is certainly one of the liveliest places in town. *The Pub* on Standard St is open from 1100 to 2300 and is also popular. *Shooters Cocktail Restaurant*, Murang'a Rd (opposite Meridian Ct), tastefully modern and spacious cocktail bar, open day and night, good food, drinks and music. If you want to drink all day and night and are not too fussy about your surroundings you can try the *Modern 24-Hour Green Bar* on Latema Rd. This is the authentic African city side of Nairobi.

Entertainment **Casinos** They are open until 0300 on weekdays and 0330 on weekends. The oldest is the *International Casino* which also houses the Bubbles nightclub. The others are found in the *Intercontinental*, located on Uhuru Highway, *Safari Park* located on Thika Rd. *Florida*, corner Uhuru Highway and University Way. *Mayfair*, Parklands Rd. *Esso Plaza*, Muthaiga. *680 Hotel*, when refurbished.

Children's entertainment *Carnivore Restaurant*, Langata Rd, puppet shows, acrobats, face painting and kids' TV every Saturday from 1300.

Cinemas There are a number of cinemas – including 2 drive-ins the *Fox* and *Belle-Vue*. Check the newspapers for programme details. If you have a vehicle an evening at the drive-in is well worth it. Other good cinemas are the *Nairobi* and *20th Century* on Mama Ngina St. There are other cheaper ones on Latema Rd but the quality of the films is less good. Films on show include British, American and Indian productions and there are often fairly recent releases.

Beryl Markham IV – Author and Champion Trainer

The Atlantic flight made Beryl (see box, page 102) a sensation in America – a crowd of 5,000 awaited her flight to New York – there were press conferences, radio interviews, banquets and guest spots on comedy shows. This was all cut short when she learned that Tom Campbell-Black, her flying instructor, had been killed in a flying accident. Beryl sailed back to England, attended the odd reception, but generally it was a rather muted welcome. She filled in time with an affair with Jack Doyle, the Irish heavyweight boxer, with dark good looks, a concert-standard tenor voice and a 'prick like a pony'.

In 1937 she returned to America to do some screen tests for a film of her epic flight – which were not a success. While in California she met Raoul Schumacher, five years younger than Beryl, tall, born in Minneapolis, comfortably off, good company, who was working as a writer in Hollywood. He and Beryl immediately hit it off.

Later in 1937 Beryl sailed to visit her father who was by now settled in Cape Town. By June 1939 she was back in California and living with Raoul in Orange Grove Boulevard, Los Angeles. They produced West with the Night, a memoir of Beryl's childhood and transatlantic flight. Although Beryl was credited as author it seems clear that Raoul provided the structure and style. It was published in 1942 to excellent reviews and was on the best seller lists. Ernest Hemingway judged it a 'bloody wonderful book'.

Raoul and Beryl married in 1942. They moved to Montecito a couple of years later to rent a large house The Monastery, high in the hills above Santa Barbara, from the Conductor Leopold Stokowski. They were not well off – Raoul's inheritance was spent and he only had a little income from his writing. Royalties from West with the Night had dried up, and, because of the war was hardly known in Europe. Beryl took a string of lovers and In 1946 Raoul moved out. Beryl continued to amuse herself in her accustomed manner, had a farewell fling with the singer Burl Ives, and in 1949 moved back to Kenya.

Beryl was not particularly well, suffering with anaemia and hormonal imbalance. In all the years of casual love affairs she had never used any contraception, yet had only conceived twice. Removal of ovarian cysts and a hysterectomy followed, and Beryl at last began to get back into form. She stayed in the guest cottage of Forest Farm near Nanyuki, owned by the Norman family. Forest Farm was managed by a Dane, Jorgen Thrane, who became Beryl's lover. Beryl bought a small farm nearby and Jorgen managed that as well.

A trip to see her father in South Africa got her in the mood for training horses again. Back in Kenya she set too with a purpose, and over the next 15 years she was outstandingly successful, training winners for all the Kenyan Classic Races, and winning the Derby four times.

In 1965, the relationship with Jorgen waning, Beryl found a property in South Africa going for a song and she re-located her training stables there, but the move was not a success. Returning to Kenya in 1970, Beryl managed to get her trainer's licence back and she had some triumphs including a fifth Derby win. She carried on training until 1983, although the latter part of this period was marred by continual squabbles with jockeys, owners and the stewards.

The Jockey Club made her an honorary member and allocated her a cottage on the Ngong course. Interest in her book was revived and a reissue in 1983 sold over a million copies. Beryl enjoyed a revival of her fame as a celebrity and she was the subject of considerable television and newspaper interest. Greeting well-wishers with a cigarette in one hand and a tumbler of vodka in the other, however, she could be less than gracious to visitors.

Beryl died in 1986 and her ashes were scattered at Cemetery Corner on Ngong Racecourse.

Music (classical) Choral concerts are held at All Saints Cathedral by the **Nairobi Music Society**, which also gives evening recitals at the British Council. There are occasional classical concerts held by the **Nairobi Orchestra**.

☞ Black men in white flannels: Kenyan cricket

In 1973 your Editor watched Kenya play against a touring MCC side at the Nairobi Club. The team comprised eight Asians and three Europeans. Cricket is an awkward game to learn – you need to start when you are young and there's really no scope for raw, untutored talent. Added to that, it's expensive. The cost of clothing, kit, match fees, meals, and travel is a formidable barrier to popular participation in a country where the average annual income per head is around US$270 (in the UK, by way of comparison, it is US$18,500). Cricket in Kenya seemed destined to remain the preserve of middle-class Asians and Europeans.

In 1994 Kenya qualified for the first time, through the ICC Trophy competition, as one of three Associate (that is non-Test Cricket playing) countries to participate in the 1996 World Cup. There was a triangular warm-up tournament in Kenya for the qualifiers, and in November 1994 your Editor went to see Kenya play the United Arab Emirates at the Aga Khan Club. He was astonished – three of the team were Asians, but the other eight, including the captain, were Africans. As the initial rounds of the 1996 World Cup got under-way, he sent a fax to the Independent newspaper suggesting that the emergence of the Kenya Africans was one of the more interesting features of the tournament, and perhaps worth a few lines. But he needn't have bothered – three days later Kenya beat the West Indies.

In Kenya, cricket has two main centres – around Mombasa, on the coast, where it is entirely an Asian pursuit, and Nairobi. In 1980, an Englishman, Robbie Armstrong and Bob Bresson, a West Indian stationed in Nairobi, encouraged a young African, Kenneth Odiambo to join in nets at their Wanderers ground, just beyond the famous Muthaiga

Club. They loaned kit and clothing and when he made the team, gave him lifts, paid for his lunch and waived his match fee. In a job-market where there are hundreds of qualified applicants for any post, Kenneth Odhiambo's cricket connections were crucial in getting him employment. Other members of his Luo community from western Kenya took notice. Young lads, all from poor homes, who up to then had earned a few shillings at the club as tennis ball-boys, began fielding for members as they practised in the nets. When the turnout for practice was low, they got a bowl and perhaps a bat. It became quite clear that they had a great flair for the game.

Cricket in Nairobi is based on the clubs that were formed by the various communities in the colonial period. Aga Khan is Ismaili; Premier the Patels; Nairobi Institute the Goans; Simba Union the Sikhs; Muthaiga the settlers; Nairobi the administrators; and so on. Rivalry between clubs – they all now have open membership – was such that in no time most of them had one or two African players. The clubs saw to it that their cricket cost them nothing: secondary school fees were paid, they were found jobs. Such was their progress that there were three Africans in the 1986 squad for the ICC Trophy, and, one, Tom Tikolo, was skipper. They were unplaced in 1986, but in 1990, when they had seven Africans in the squad and again Tom Tikolo was captain, they reached the semi-finals. In 1994 they were runners up. The managers of the Kenyan squad sensed they were onto something. They took a squad to Bangladesh to get experience of big crowds and wickets in the sub-continent where the final was to be played. They practised like demons and had dozens of warm-up matches. The world found out about them on 1 March 1996.

Music (popular) Can be heard at the *African Heritage Café* on Banda St who have live bands most weekends and *Jabali Africa* and guests on Saturday 1400-1700. *Simba Grill*, *Panafric Hotel*, Kenyatta Ave, has resident band playing Thursday, Friday and Saturday. *Carnivore*, Langata Rd, rock band every Wednesday. *Bombax Club* is located on Dagoretti Corner on the Ngong Rd. This has live bands from Thursday to Wednesday. It is a bit out of town so take a taxi, or else a minibus from outside Nyayo House on Kenyatta Ave. Quite a few of the hotels have bands from time to time – see the local press.

Nightclubs The *New Florida* and *Florida 2000* on Koinange St and Moi Ave respectively are both very popular. They have fairly good sound systems and lights and stay open until

0600. *Visions*, Kimathi St, is also popular. It is smaller but otherwise fairly similar and is open from 1200. Other places include *Beat House*, Kimathi St. *Bubbles*, Westlands Rd. *Hillock Inn*, Enterprise Rd. *Hollywood*, Moktar Daddah St. *JKA Resort Club*, located on Mombasa Rd just after the turn-off to the airport, which has an open air dance floor. *Kenya International* Murang'a Rd. *Milano Club*, Ronald Ngala Rd. There is a live band and disco at the *Carnivore* in Langata every night which is increasingly popular. For a very civilized dinner-dancing you cannot beat *Le Chateau* at the *Intercontinental*.

Sports (participant) Climbing: each Tuesday evening the *Kenya Mountaineering Club*, PO Box 45741, meets at its clubhouse at Wilson Airport to arrange expeditions and get high on Kendal Mint Cake, T501747. **Golf**: there are a number of very well kept golf courses in the suburbs of Nairobi. These include: *Karen Country Club*, Karen Rd, T882801. *Muthaiga Golf Club*, Muthaiga Rd, T762414. *Limuru Country Club*, Limuru, T0154-41351(Karuri). *Railway Golf Club*, Ngong Rd, T22116. *Windsor Golf and Country Club*, T862300. **Gym**: *Canyon Health Gymnasium*, R500, 5th Flr Uniafric House, Koinange St. Aerobics and weight training sessions available. Open 0900-1930 weekdays, 0900-1500 Saturdays. **Riding**: lessons and safaris can be arranged through the *Arifa Riding School*. Bookings T25255/21845/20365. **Running**: *Hash House Harriers*, meet regularly. See notices in British Council, or at British High Commission. **Sailing**: the *Nairobi Sailing Club*, sails on Nairobi Dam which is found off Langata Rd. Details T501250. **Swimming**: most of the big hotels have swimming pools which can also be used by non-residents for a daily fee of about US$2. The pool at YMCA is particularly good, or try the *Aga Khan's Sports Complex* (next to *Ma Roches* (US$3 for pool). There is a pool with diving board, and lots of other activities. **Tennis & squash**: many of the major hotels have courts. Other clubs include the *Karen Club*, Karen Rd, T882801 and *Limuru Country Club*, Limuru, T40033 (Karuri).

Sports (spectator) Cricket: main venues are Gymkhana, Premier Simba, Aga Khan, all in Parklands area just to the north of the centre, near City Park. Exciting league games played on Saturday and Sunday, with good crowds (see box). Take taxi from town centre, about US$4. **Horse racing**: the *Ngong Racecourse*, holds meetings most Sunday from January to June. It is a wonderful setting as well as being a great place to observe all sections of Nairobi society. **Polo**: this is played on Saturday and Sunday at *Jamhuri Club*, Ngong Rd, weather permitting.

Theatre There are 2 main theatres in Nairobi. *The Professional Centre* has performances at the Phoenix Theatre on Parliament Rd. Although a small group they are the most active and produce a range of drama of a very high standard. The other is the *Kenya National Theatre* located opposite the *Norfolk Hotel* on Harry Thuku Rd close to the University. Concerts are also held at the National Theatre. There are 2 high standard amateur groups, Lavington Players and Nairobi Players, who present a range of comedies, musicals and pantomimes, all of which are very popular. The local papers have notices of what's on.

Festivals The big event of the year is the annual *Safari Rally* which begins and ends in Nairobi. It is held around Easter time and is a great spectacle for local people. The route is over 4,000 kilometres – it used to be the East African Safari but now just covers Kenya. The *Nairobi International Show*, an agricultural fair, is held at the end of **September**.

Shopping There are a huge number of curio and souvenir shops in Nairobi. They vary enormously in terms of more price range and quality. At stalls you will be able bargain the prices down to between a third and a half of the original asking price, although not in the more formal shops which tend to be fixed price. Shops that are part of hotels are always much more expensive. The best prices on curios are at the *Zanzibar Curio Shop* on Moi Ave, marked prices and no haggling. *Rupas*, PO Box 43698, T224417/245555/333965, have an outstanding selection of gift purchases, good quality, courteous staff and competitve prices. Be sure to have a good look at any purchases – wood that may look like ebony may in fact just have been polished with black shoe polish – it is a popular trick. Also cracks may appear in the wood (particularly when it is placed in a centrally heated room) if it has not been properly seasoned.

Kenya

Bookshops *The Nation* is located on Kenyatta Ave next to the *Thorn Tree Café* and has a good selection of books (fiction and non-fiction) and maps. *Select* on Kimathi St is opposite the *New Stanley Hotel* and is larger although rather run down. There is a good but small antique East Africana section. Other bookshops which stock a fairly good Africana selection include the **Book Corner** and **Prestige** both located on Mama Ngina St, while the **Text Book Centre** on Kigabe St has text books as well as other Africana and fiction. There are a number of book stalls along Tom Mboya St and Latema Rd where you may be able to pick up a few bargain secondhand books. There is also a secondhand bookshop on Banda St.

The best maps of Nairobi are the *City of Nairobi: Map and Guide* published by the Survey of Kenya in English, German and French. If you want more detail or are staying a while it may be worth getting *A to Z Guide to Nairobi* by DT Dobie (Kenway Publications).

Clothing There is a cluster of shops selling material and cloth squares (kangas and kikois) on Biashara St quite close to the market. Here you can also watch tailors on their foot-propelled machines sewing clothes, cushions etc and stitching some of the most elaborate embroidery at amazing speed. *Lucky Wear* has a good range of clothes and fabric as does *Maridadi Fabrics* which is further out of town on Landies St. There are lots of places which will kit you out in safari gear. *Colpro* on Kimathi St is recommended as good quality and reliable.

Handicrafts and curios Perhaps the best place for baskets is the **Kariakor Market** located on the Ring Rd at Ngara. *Antique Gallery*, Kaunda St, T27759 and *Antique Auction*, Moktar Daddah St, T336383, have antique East African artefact collections. For paintings, batiks carvings and other higher quality crafts try: *African Heritage* on Kenyatta Ave. *Zanzibar Curio Shop*, Moi Ave, T222704. *Gallery Watatu* and *Roland Ward*, both on Standard St. *Spinners Web* located on Kijabe St close to the *Norfolk Hotel* is a good craft shop, in particular for fabrics and baskets. Its merchandise comes from various self-help groups around the country and the staff are very helpful. On Tuesday the *Masai Market* is held at the hillside site at Muranga Rd below Moi Ave. *Blue Market* opposite the city market between Tubman Rd and Kigah Rd, go in late afternoon, as prices are lowest just before they close. Bargain hard! Good for all wooden artefacts, soapstone, jewellery, etc.

Jewellery For jewellery and semi-precious stones try *Al-Safa Jewellers* at the *New Stanley Hotel* and *Treasures and Crafts* on Kaunda St.

Markets *City Market*, Muindi Mbingo St. Around the Market and the Jamia Mosque there are numerous stalls selling baskets, wooden and soapstone carvings, bracelets and lots of other souvenirs. Be prepared to look around and bargain.

Photography *Camera Maintenance Centre* located in the Hilton Arcade, Mama Ngina St, T26920 and *Camera Experts* on Mama Ngina St, T337750. Get a quote as repairs can be quite expensive. *Elite Camera House*, opposite *New Stanley Hotel* will hire out lenses (expensive). Only have bayonet fittings not screw fittings.

If you need passport size photos there are a few booths. One is on the corner of Tom Mboya St and Accra Rd, another is a few doors up from the *Thorn Tree Café* on the corner of Kenyatta Ave and Kimathi St. Several photoshops will do passport photographs. Cost US$2.50 for 4.

Supermarkets The Uchumi chain of supermarkets offer a reasonable product range. The branch at corner Loita/Monrovia St is very large and opens on Sundays. The Nakumatt chain of shops is a good source of household goods. There is one on Nanyuki Rd and Uhuru Highway.

Societies *Nairobi Photographic Club* Meet twice a month on Thursday evenings at the St Johns Ambulance Centre which is found behind the Donovan Maule Theatre off Parliament Rd. *Nairobi Chess Club* Meet weekly on Thursday evenings at the French Cultural Centre (PO

Box 50443, T25007). *East African Wildlife Society* PO Box 20110 (T27047). This society is worth joining if you are going to be in Kenya for a while. They produce a monthly newsletter. They are active in the struggle to save East Africa's wildlife.

Local There are plenty of buses, matatus and taxis, all of which are very cheap by Western standards. Buses and matatus are almost always very crowded and beware of pickpockets when travelling in them. **Bus**: the main city bus terminal is located at the end of River Rd and there are main bus stops outside the *Hilton Hotel* on Moi Ave, outside Nation House on Tom Mboya St and outside the General Post Office on Kenyatta Ave. **Car hire**: cars can be rented easily in Kenya, with or without a driver. You will usually need an international drivers' licence, and be required to be over 25 years of age. Companies include **Avis Rent a Car**, PO Box 49795, T336794; **Budget**, PO Box 59767, Parliament lane, Haile Selassie Ave, T337154; **Central Hire a Car**, PO Box 49439, Fehda Towers, Standard St, T222888/332296, good value with comprehensive insurance coverage; **Crossways**, on Banda St, T223949/220848, F214372, can arrange hire cars suitable for organizing your own safari; **Europ Car**, PO Box 49420; **Habib's Cars Ltd**, PO Box 48095, Agip House, Haile Se lassie Ave, T220463/223816, F220985; **Hertz**, PO Box 42196, T331960; *Let's Go Travel*, PO Box 60342, Caxton House, Standard St, T213033, F336890; as well as a number of other local companies. **Payless Car Hire and Tours Ltd**, *Hilton Hotel*, Shimba St, PO Box 49713, T223581/2, F223584; **Naz Car Hire**, Clyde House, Kimathi St, T246171, F221296. You can expect to pay between US$30 and US$40 per day plus a mileage charge of about US$0.20 per kilometre and rates are usually negotiable if for a longer period. It is worth asking around to compare prices. four-wheel drive hire will cost between US$30-45 per day plus insurance. Rates obviously vary, but try **Central Car Hire** for the best deal. Driving in Nairobi is a bit of an art and you will have to get used to a large number of roundabouts with rather bizarre lane systems. Be prepared for a lot of hooting, traffic light jumping and the odd potholes. Parking in Nairobi is a problem and you will be pestered by parking boys. Policies toward these vary although there is no evidence that it is necessary to pay them to ensure the safety of your vehicle. There is a multi-storey carpark at *Intercontinental Hotel*, at cost of around US$1 per hour. **Taxis**: taxis are available outside cinemas, restaurants, hotels and at official taxi stands. Your hotel will order one for you. They cannot be hailed in the street. It is recommended that you should always take a taxi if you want to get around at night. The cost of a taxi to the airport is approximately US$10, but you may be charged more on arrival.

Air The main airport is Jomo Kenyatta International Airport, located about 13 kilometres southeast of the city connected by a good dual carriageway, T822111. There is also Wilson Airport on Langata Rd from which smaller planes, including many internal charter flights, leave. If you are travelling on an arranged tour you will probably be met at the airport by your driver who will hold up a notice with your name or the name of the tour company on it. If you are travelling independently you can either take a taxi or bus into Nairobi. Be sure to agree on the price into town – it should be around US$12. You can find a taxi from the airport to town cheaper from outside the airport environs, because some taxis cannot find a return fare to town. US$9-11 bargaining required. The bus number 34 runs every 20 minutes from the airport into town. There is a stop opposite the new Post Office on Kenyatta Ave or at the *Ambassador Hotel*. The bus service runs from 0630 to 2030 hours. Journey time is half to 1 hour. Cost US$0.50. You can change money at the airport 24 hours a day. For international services into Nairobi see Essentials, page 68. **Kenya Airways** has daily flights to **Kisumu**, **Malindi** and **Mombasa** from Kenyatta Airport. Charter fly to Masai Mara, Malindi, Lamu and other destinations.

Train Please see page 72 for details of train services, timetables and fares.

Road Bus: the long distance bus station is on Landies Rd. There are at least daily departures to almost every destination. The timetable is fairly flexible. For a long journey you will be told to arrive at 0700 or earlier, but if the bus is not full it will usually not go until it is. For information and bookings there are a number of coach company offices along Accra Rd. There are

Transport

Kenya

Beryl Markham III – Against the Wind

In the London of 1929 flying became a very fashionable pastime. Both of Beryl's Royal lovers (see box, page 131) became aviators, and Denys Finch-Hatton had learnt to fly as a way to spot game. Beryl took some flying lessons before returning to Kenya in 1930, renting a cottage by the Golf course at the Muthaiga Club for the next five years. The Prince of Wales revisited. Karen Blixen's coffee farm was failing and about to be sold, and Denys Finch-Hatton, adored lover of both Karen Blixen and Beryl was killed when his plane crashed at Voi.

This tragedy did not deter Beryl, and under the tutelage of her instructor and lover, Tom Campbell-Black, she gained a pilot's licence in July 1931. The next year Beryl flew her Avro-Aviator solo from Nairobi to London – hopping through Uganda, the Sudan, Egypt, Libya, Italy and France – in seven days, and then back again. In 1933 she got her 'B' license which allowed her to work as a commercial pilot – the first woman in Kenya to do so – and began working as a professional flier, delivering mail, ferrying passengers and providing air ambulance services. Later Beryl was to pioneer scouting for game from the air – dropping notes in canvas pouches with trailing ribbons of yellow and blue, her racing colours. One client was Ernest Hemingway (see box, page 51) who observed 'I knew her fairly well in Africa' – implying they had been lovers.

One evening in the bar of the White Rhino in Nyeri a wealthy local flying enthusiast J.C. Carberry dared Beryl to fly solo across the Atlantic from east to west, 'against the wind'. Carberry offered to bankroll the flight. The feat had never been achieved in 39 previous attempts. Beryl ordered the recently designed Percival Vega Gull, a single engined monoplane, from De Havillands at Gravesend.

At the end of 1933 she flew to London in her Leopard Moth, hopping across Africa and Europe with Bror Blixen, a former lover and white hunter husband of Karen, as passenger.

Based at Claridges Hotel in Mayfair, Beryl began travelling down to Gravesend to work on the plane. It had a 200 horse-power Gipsy-Six engine. It could cruise at 160mph. To increase the range to 3,800 miles extra fuel tanks were installed in every vacant space, and the undercarriage reinforced to take the extra weight. There was no radio – once in the air Beryl would be very much alone. A larger runway was needed to get off the ground with three quarters of a ton of fuel and Beryl flew the plane, now named The Messenger to the RAF airfield at Abingdon in Oxfordshire.

The Daily Express bought exclusive rights to Beryl's story and the audacity of the attempt allied to Beryl's beauty created a fever of interest as she waited patiently for fair weather. On 4th September the winds had dropped. The Messenger was fuelled and rolled out. Beryl in a white leather flying suit and helmet squeezed into the cramped cockpit with 5 flasks of coffee, some cold meat, dried fruit, nuts and fruit pastilles and a hip flask of brandy. There was no room for a life jacket. Edgar Percival, the plane's designer, swung the propeller. With a wave, Beryl rumbled down the runway and climbed slowly into the air. It was close to twilight, just before 7pm. Edgar Percival shook his head and observed to onlookers, 'Well, that's the last we shall see of Beryl'.

It was touch-and-go. After a flight of over 21 hours Beryl saw land, but she was on the last tank of fuel, and the engine began to splutter. Beryl selected a landing field but ditched in a Nova Scotia bog.
Continued in box, page 131.

many companies to choose for buses between **Nairobi** and **Mombasa** and they go frequently taking 8 hours, costing around US$9. One shuttle service called 'The Connection' is operated by Inside Africa Safaris Ltd. They also operate a courier service. Depart from Jubilee House Bldg, Wabera St, Nairobi, T223304/225844, F215448, very comfortable service costing US$16. Sav-Line also offers air-conditioned 18 seater minibus shuttle services between Nairobi/Mombasa cost US$16. Sav-Line bookings c/o Savage Camping Tours, T228236. The Akamba Public Road Services, Kitui Rd off Kampala Rd, T555690/555637 is a bus company offering a good level of service. Buses go from Nairobi to a variety of destinations.

Since 1983 when the Kenya/Tanzania border was reopened there has been increasing traffic crossing to take advantage of the game parks in Tanzania – in particular the Serengeti and Ngorongoro Crater. There are a number of shuttle buses each day to and from **Arusha**, US$20-25, taking about 5 hours. There are 0800 and 1400 departures in both Nairobi and Arusha. With **Riverside Shuttle**, c/o Style Travel & Tours, Koinange St, Nairobi, T219020/214341. Or book through an agent such as *Let's Go*. To the Uganda border at **Busia** takes about 10 hours and costs about US$9. Not a journey for the faint-hearted. The buses frequently double-up as cargo carriers and are loaded to over-capacity. **Shared taxis and matatus**: shared taxis, usually Peugeot station wagons, are more expensive than matatus (mini-buses) but are quicker and safer. They generally take 7 people and leave when full, often early in the morning. Offices in Nairobi are around Accra Rd and River Rd. Some examples of fares and costs are Kisumu US$12, 4 hours; Nakuru US$6, 2 hours; and Tanzanian border US$6, 2 hours.

Airline offices International: *Aeroflot* Corner House, Mama Ngina St, T220746. *Air Canada*, Lonrho House, Standard St, 6th Flr, T218776. *Air France*, International House, Mama Ngina St, 2nd Flr, T217501/2. *Air India*, Jeevan Bharati Building, Harambee Ave, T334788. *Air Madagascar*, Hilton Hotel, 1st Flr, City Hall Way, T225286. *Air Malawi*, Hilton Hotel Arcade, City Hall Way, T333683/240965/340212. *Air Mauritius*, International House Mezz Flr Mama Ngina St, T229166/7/330315. *Air Seychelles*, Lonrho House, Standard St, 6th Flr, T229359. *Air Tanzania*, Chester House, Banda St, T336224. *Air Zaire*, Kimathi St, T230142. *Air Zimbabwe*, Chester House, Ground Flr, Koinanage St, T339524. *Alitalia*, Hilton Hotel, City Hall Way, T224361/3/4. *American Airlines*, 20th Century Plaza, 2nd Flr (Flying Rickshaw Ltd) Mama Ngina St, T242557. *British Airways*, 11th Flr, International House, Mama Ngina St, T334440. *Cameroon Airlines*, Rehani House 9th Flr, Kenyatta Ave, T224743/224827/337788. *EgyptAir*, Hilton Hotel Arcade, City Hall Way, T226821. *El Al*, Sweepstake House, Mama Ngina St, T228123/4. *Ethiopian Airlines*, Bruce House, Muindi Mbingu St, T330837. *Gulf Air*, Global Travel, International House, Mama Ngina St, T241123/4. *Iberia*, Hilton Hotel, Mama Ngina St, T331648/331658/338623. *Kenya Airways*, 6th Flr, Barclays Plaza, Loita St, T210771/229291. *KLM*, Fedha Towers, 12th Flr, Muindi Mbingu St, T332673. *Lufthansa*, A M Bank House 9th Flr, University Way, T226271/335819. *Olympic Airlines*, Hilton Hotel, City Hall Way, T338026. *Pakistan International Airlines*, ICEA Building, Banda St, T333901. *Qantas Airways*, Rehema House, Kaunda St, T213321. *Royal Swazi National Airlines*, KCS House 4th Flr, Mama Ngina St, T210670/216559. *Sabena*, A M Bank House 11th Flr, University Way, T241212/243964/251123. *Saudia Arabian Airlines*, Anniversary Towers, Mezz 11, University Way, T230337/240617. *Somali Airlines*, Bruce House, Muindi Mbingu St, T335409. *South African Airways*, Lonrho House 1st Flr, Kaunda St, T229663/227486, Standard St, 1st Flr, T245520/1. *Sudan Airways*, UTC House, Gen Kagao St, T822265. *Swissair*, 11th Flr A M Bank House, University Way, T250288/9, T250456/7, F331437. *Uganda Airlines*, Uganda House, Kenyatta Ave, 1st Flr, T221354. Domestic and charter: *Africair*, PO Box 45646, T501210. *Air Kenya Aviation*, Wilson Airport, T501421. *Eagle Aviation Ltd*, scheduled flights within Kenya, charter flights available, Nairobi T606015/6, F606017. *Equator Airlines*, Wilson Airport, T221177/501399/501360. *Kenya Airways*, Airways Terminal, Koinange St, T332750/229291.

Banks Hours are Mon to Fri 0830-1300. Sat 0830-1100. Bank Foreign Exchange Bureau are usually open longer hours. There is a black market in Kenya but it seems hardly worth the effort. Not only is it risky (you may be treated unpleasantly and deported if caught), but the rate you will achieve is hardly more than bank rates. Out of bank hours money can be exchanged at the large hotels, the airport and at some tourist shops.

Communications Post Office: Moi Ave, halfway between Kenyatta Ave and Tubman Rd on the east side, T227401. There is also a Post Office on Haile Selassie Ave, T228441, where you will find the fairly reliable, and free, Poste Restante. Post Offices are open from 0800 to 1230 and 1400 to 1700. **Telecommunications:** almost opposite the Post Office on Haile Selassie Ave is the Extelcoms office from which you can make international phone calls, minimal period of use is 3 mins, send faxes and telexes. You can also make calls from the Kenyatta Conference Centre – the telephone exchange is on the ground floor and it is usually much quieter than the Post Office. Alternatively go to the 1st Flr of the 20th Century Palace, Mama Ngina St, close to the cinema, US$3 per min. Other telephone services include *Danas Communications Centre*, Kaunda St, T223655, F243890, *Philmark Communications*, PO Box 60990, T217505, *Phone Home*, The Mall, Westlands, PO Box 34535, T443866. You can only buy phonecards from the Extelcoms Office.

Internet Services & Cyber Cafés: access the Internet at the *Education Centre*, 3rd Flr, Union Towers, Moi Ave, US$1.75 per 15 mins. *Unique Communications* is a new private phone, fax and email

Directory

Kenya

facility based at Rattansi Educational Trust near corner of Monrovia/Koinange St, T243302. *The Cyber Centre*, Norwich Union House 5th Flr, T217406/337714/243383, cybercentre@nbnet.co.ke, public access internet and email services. *Browse Internet Café*, Norwich Union House 4th Flr, T251947. *Cybersafaris* internet café is located in *Simmers Restaurant* on the corner of Kenyatta Ave and Muindi Mbinga Street, Internet and email services at less than US$6 per hr, ryansnider@hotmail.com. *Cybervore* at the Carnivore Restaurant, Langata Rd, T501775. *Hard Rock Café*, Barclays Plaza, Loita St, T220802/3. *Vyber Rap Bureau*, Embassy House, 2nd Flr, info@thorntree.com.

Cultural centres Other places that have films, concerts and talks include the *Alliance Francaise*, ICEA Building, Kenyatta Ave, T340054; *American Cultural Centre*, National Bank Building, Harambee Ave, T337877; *British Council*, ICEA Building, Kenyatta Ave, T334855; the *French Cultural Centre*, Maison Francaise, Loita St, T336263; *Goethe Institute*, Maendeleo House, Monrovia St, T224640; *Italian Cultural Institute*, Prudential Building, Wabera St, T220278; *Japan Information Centre*, Matungulu House, Mamlaka Rd, T340520; *Mzizi Cultural Centre*, Box 48955 Nairobi, T245364/6, F245366, 6th Flr Sonalux House, Moi Ave, very close to *Hilton Hotel*, and in same block of The Zanzibar Curio Shop. The centre has a gallery, housing works of Kenyan contemporary artists, it offers daily performances, story telling, poetry reading, and musical performances. They offer rare and reasonably priced souvenirs. At the centre, one can pick up the latest copy of their magazine, SANAA, (means Art in Kiswahili) which lists all activities in the city such as theatre performances, shows, film screenings and other activities. Enjoy the relaxed atmosphere, meet Kenyans in the arts, see some great performances for a very reasonable price, (shows cost about US$5) and get a real taste of what is going on in the forefront of the arts in the country. The people that run the place are very friendly, and will be delighted to show you around. Programmes are announced in the local press. If you want to see some newspapers from home they can be seen your particular cultural centre. All are free (except the American which is open to members only).

Embassies, High Commissions & Consulates *Algerian Embassy*, Comcraft House, Haile Selassie Ave, T213864/565173. *Argentina*, Town House 7th Flr, Kaunda St, PO Box 30283, T335242. *Australia*, PO Box 30360, ICIPE House, Riverside Drive, T445034/8. *Austria*, PO Box 30560, City House, Wabera St, T228281. *Bangladesh*, PO Box 41645, Lenana Rd, T728773/560268/583396. *Belgium*, PO Box 30461, Limuru Rd, T741565. *Brazil*, PO Box 30751, Jeevan Bharati Building, Harambee Ave, T337722. *British High Commission*, Upper Hill Rd, PO Box 30133, Nairobi, T714699, F719082. *Burundi*, PO Box 44439, Development House, Moi Ave, opposite the Milimani Police Station, T219005/729845. *Canada*, PO Box 30481, Comcraft House, Haile Selassie Ave, T214804. *Chile*, PO Box 45554, International House, Mama Ngina St, T331320/337987, James Gichuru Rd, T562956/562977. *China*, PO Box 30508, Woodlands Rd, T722559/726851. *Colombia*, PO Box 48494, Muthaiga Rd, T765927, International House, T246770/1. *Costa Rica*, PO Box 30750, T501501. *Cyprus*, PO Box 30739, Eagle House, Kimathi St, T220881, Karabarsiran Rd, T441954. *Denmark*, PO Box 40412, HFCK Building, Koinange St, T331088/89/90. *Djibouti*, PO Box 59528, T48089. *Egypt*, PO Box 30285, Harambee Plaza, 7th Flr, T250764, Fourways Towers 9th Flr, Muindi Mbingu St, T224709/337505. *Eritrea*, PO Box 38651, T443163. *Ethiopia*, PO Box 45198, State House Ave, T723027. *Finland*, PO Box 30379, International House, City Hall Way, T334777. *France*, PO Box 41784, Barclays Plaza, 9th Flr, Loita St, T339783, Issues Visas for Togo, Senegal, Burkina Faso, Mauritania and the Central African Republic. *Germany*, PO Box 30180, Williamson House, Ngong Ave, T712527. *Greece*, PO Box 30543. IPS Building, Kimathi St, T340722. *Holy See*, PO Box 14326, Apostolic Nunciature, Manyani Rd West, T442975. *Hungary*, PO Box 30523, Agip House, 2nd Flr, T560060. *Iceland* (consulate), Bendera Lane off Spring Valley Rd, T521487. *India*, PO Box 30074, Jeevan Bharati Building, Harambee Ave, T222556. *Indonesia*, PO Box 48868, Utalii House, Uhuru Highway, T215848/215874/219358. *Iran*, PO Box 49170, T720343. *Iraq*, PO Box 49213, Matungulu House, T580262. *Ireland* (consulate), Waumini House 5th Flr, Chiromo Rd, T444367/571635. *Israel*, PO Box 30354, T722182. *Italy*, PO Box 30107, International Life House, Mama Ngina St, T337356/337777/337017. *Japan*, PO Box 60202, Kenyatta Ave, T332955. *Korea*, PO Box 30455, Anniversary Towers, University Way, T333581. *Kuwait*, PO Box 42353, Muthaiga Rd, T761614/762837. *Lesotho*, PO Box 44096, International House, Mama Ngina St, T224876. *Luxembourg* Hon Con, International Life House, 8th Flr Mama Ngina St, T224318. *Malawi*, PO Box 30453, Standard St, T440569. *Mexico*, PO Box 14145, T582850. *Morocco*, PO Box 61098, T222264. *Mozambique*, PO Box 66923, T221979. *Netherlands*, PO Box 41537, Uchumi House, Nkrumah Av, T227111/332420/334093, Holland@Form-net.com . *Nigeria*, PO Box 30516, Hurlingham, T564116. *Norway*, Royal Norwegian Embassy, PO Box 46363, HFCK Bldg, Rehani House 8th Flr, Kenyatta Ave, T337121/2/4. *Pakistan*, PO Box 30045, St Michel Rd, Westlands, T443991. *Peru*, Lagutrop House, Enterprise Rd, T555744/555391. *Philippines*, State House Rd, T721791. *Poland*, PO Box 30086, Kabernet Rd, T566288. *Portugal*, PO Box

34020, T338990. *RD Congo*, PO Box 48106, Electricity House, Harambee Ave, T229771. *Romania*, PO Box 48412, T521357. *Russia*, PO Box 30049, Lenana Rd, T722559. *Rwanda*, PO Box 48579, International Life House, Mama Ngina St, T575977/240563/721146, Mon-Fri 0900-1630. *Saudi Arabia*, PO Box 58297, T762781. *Seychelles Consulate*, Agip House, Wayaki Way, 7th Flr, T441150. *Slovak Republic*, PO Box 30204, Milimani Rd, T721896. *South African High Comm*, PO Box 42441, Lonrho House, Standard St, 17th Flr, T215616/17/18/228469, F223687. *Spain*, PO Box 45503, Bruce House, Standard St, T335711. *Sri Lanka*, PO Box 48145, International Life House, Mama Ngina St, T227577. *Sudan*, PO Box 74059, Minet ICDC House, 7th Flr, T720853. *Swaziland*, PO Box 41887 Nbi, Silopark House, T339231. High Comm, Transnational Plaza, 3rd Flr, Mama Ngina St, T339232/33/31. *Sweden*, PO Box 30600, T229043/4/5, T334066/7/8, F218908. *Switzerland*, PO Box 30752, T228736. *Tanzania*, PO Box 47790, Continental House, T331056. *Thailand*, PO Box 58349, T715800. *Turkey*, PO Box 307853, Gigiri Rd, off Limuru Rd, T520404. *Uganda*, PO Box 60853, T330801. *USA*, PO Box 30137, Corner Moi and Haile Selassie Ave, T334141. *Venezuela*, PO Box 34477, International House, Mama Ngina St, T341078. *Yemen*, PO Box 44642, Ngong Rd, T574650/46/56. *Zambia*, PO Box 48741, Nyerere Rd, T724796. *Zimbabwe*, PO Box 30806, Minet ICDC House, Mamlaka Rd, T721045/49/71.

Hospitals & medical services Hospitals: there are 2 private hospitals which have good facilities and staff. The first is the *Nairobi Hospital* (T722160) located on Argwings Kodhek Rd and the other is the *Aga Khan Hospital* (T742531) located on Limuru Rd in Parklands. If you can help it, avoid the *Kenyatta Hospital*, although it is free it is not worth trying to save the money as the wait can be so long. For the more intrepid, moving in more isolated areas for a time, the *Flying Doctor* may be worth considering and is excellent value should an emergency arise. US$25 for 2 months membership within a 500 km radius of Wilson Airport, US$50 outside 500 km, T501301/500508, F502699, *Flying Doctors Society of Africa*, PO Box 30125, Nairobi. **Pharmacies:** these are found in all shopping centres but are generally expensive. Try *Jaga Chemists* on Koinange St, T215654, open Mon-Sat. If you know you will need anything then be sure to bring an adequate supply. The major hospitals (see above) have pharmacies which are open 24 hrs a day. Vaccinations are available from *City Hall Clinic* on Mama Ngina St, open only in the mornings.

Places of worship *All Saints Cathedral* is located on Kenyatta Ave close to Uhuru Park and the *Catholic Holy Family Minor Basilica* is situated on the corner of Parliament Ave and City Hall Way. Perhaps the most beautiful of all the places of worship is the *Jamia Mosque*, located near the City Market. This was built in 1925 in the Indian style and is set in a lively part of town close to the City Market.

Security There are increasing reports of muggings, snatchings and robberies in Nairobi. This can certainly be a problem if you are not sensible. If you walk around with a camera around your neck, an obviously expensive watch, jewellery or a money belt showing then you are vulnerable. If you are unsure take a taxi. Places to definitely avoid walking around at night include Uhuru Park, along Uhuru Highway and the road past the National Museum. Some thieves specialize in jostling, robbing and snatching from new arrivals on buses and matatus from the airport. On buses and matatus do not take items to eat offered by strangers: these have been known to have been drugged.

Tour companies & travel agents There are numerous tour operators based in Nairobi where you should be able to get fairly reliable information and book safaris etc. They include *Abercrombie and Kent*, Sixth Flr, Bruce House, Standard St, PO Box 59749, T334955/6/7, T228700, F215752, who arrange some of the most luxurious safaris in Kenya. *Acacia Trails Ltd*, PO Box 14249, Nairobi, T446261. *Bush Homes of East Africa Ltd*, PO Box 56923, Nairobi, T571647/49/61, F571665, Bush.homes@ tt.gn.apc.org. *Express Kenya Co (American Express Representative)*, PO Box 40433, Standard St, T334722. Others include *AA Travel*, Hurlingham Shopping Centre, PO Box 14982, T339700. *Africa Safaris Ltd*, Rehema House, 3rd Flr, Kaunda/Standard St, opposite *New Stanley Hotel*, PO Box 69513, Nairobi, T213186, 213254, 226189, F213254. *Best Camping Tours and Safaris Ltd*, Nanak House 9, 2nd Flr, Room 212, corner of Kimath/Banda Sts, PO Box 40223, T229675, F217923. *Bunson Travel Service*, PO Box 45456, Standard St, T21992. *Call of Africa Safaris*, Uganda House 3rd floor PO Box 27767, Nairobi, T02-229729/248469/248547, F604994, callafrica@africaonline.co.ke, after hours T604994/ 608994. Recommended for their quality of service. *Dallago Tours & Safaris*, Mercantile House, 1st Flr, Room 133, Koinance St, T331562, F245174, PO Box 66416. New and expanding company receiving good reviews. *Desert Rose Camels*, c/o Geo Safaris, PO Box 24969, Nairobi, T884258/9, F884445. Organize walking and camel safaris in the Northern Frontier District of Kenya. *East African Ornithological Safaris Ltd*, PO Box 48019, Nairobi, T331684/335935, F216528, eaos@africaonline.

co.ke. *Exotic Safaris*, described as being exceptionally helpful at the safari planning stage. *Flight Centre*, Lakhamshi House 2nd Flr, Biashara St, T210024/335974. Recommended travel agent. *Gametrackers*, 1st Flr, Kenya Cinema Plaza, Moi Ave, PO Box 62042, T338927/222703/212830/1/2, Tx22258, Tracker F330903. Camping safaris have been recommended. *Habib's Tours & Travel*, Agip House, Haile Selassie Ave, PO Box 48095, T220463/223816, F220985, habibtours@attmail.com. Good for car rental. *Hoopoe Adventure Tours*, off Enterprise Rd, PO Box 14662 (UK: Suite F1, Kebbell House, Carpenders Park, Watford, WD1 5BE, T0181-4288221, F0181-4211396, HoopoeUK@aol.com). *Kenia Tours & Safaris*, Jubilee Insurance Bldg, Kaunda/ Wabera St, T223699/217671, PO Box 19730, also have an office at *Iqbal Hotel*. Good, cheap camping tours. *Let's Go Travel*, Caxton House, Standard St, PO Box 60342, T340331/213033, F336890, info@letsgosafari.com, www.letsgosafari.com. Branch offices in Tanzania & Uganda. Well-run and efficient company. Recommended. *Lobelia Tours & Safaris Ltd*, Moi Ave/Moktar Daddah St, Jct Krisna Mansion, Room 59, PO Box 12459, T2-211426. Specialize in mountain safaris. Recommended. *Rajair Travel and Tours*, 27 Central Chambers, The Broadway, Ealing, London W5 2NR, T0181-8408881, F0181-8408882. Kenya specialist, a family-run firm who have been in Kenya for 100 years, include safaris, golf, diving, ballooning, fishing, tailor-made and groups catered for. *Savage Camping Tours Ltd*, Soin Arcade, Westlands Rd, Westlands, c/o PO Box 73193, T449467, F449469. *Savage Wilderness Safaris Ltd*, white water river rafting on several Kenyan rivers, PO Box 44827, Nairobi, Thigiri Rd, T/F521590, European Office: 22 Wilson Ave, Henley, Oxon RG9 1ET, UK, T01491-574752, USA Office: 925 31 St Ave, Seattle, WA 98122, T2063231220. *Savuka Tours & Safaris Ltd*, Pan Africa House, 4th floor, Kenyatta Ave, T215256. Good value for budget travellers, student card reduction. *Sights of Africa Safari Company*, Asili Co-operative Building 4th Flr, Moi Ave/Muranga Rd, PO Box 6251, T247439, F242415 (linked to Tanzannature, Arusha PO Box 13317). Highly recommended company. *Special Camping Safaris and Whistling Thorns*, PO Box 51512, Nairobi, T350720, speccampsaf@thorntree.com. Organizes safaris in the Ngong Hills, camping safaris to Lakes Baringo, Borofia, Nakura, plus the Masai Mara. *Sunny Safaris*, Portal Place, Banda St, PO Box 74495, T226587, F339809. *Travel Concepts Tours & Safaris Ltd*, Town House, 3rd Floor, Kaunda St, PO Box 52296, T2-230049, 2-241499, 2-252357. Offer Mount Kenya and Kilimanjaro treks and game

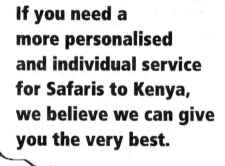

safaris. *United Touring International*, PO Box 42196, Muindi Mbingu St, T331960. *Vintage Safaris*, PO Box 59470, Kijabe St (T226547, F211660) and Shimmers Plaza (T742450, F742465). *Wanderlust Safaris Ltd*, 4th Flr, Gilfillan House, Kenyatta Ave, PO Box 42578, T212281, F212953. Most operators will be able to arrange a tour of Nairobi itself and this is a very useful way of familiarizing yourself with the layout of the city, as well as seeing some of the sites that are further out. The tours will usually include a trip to the City Market, which you may well want to return to later, the Parliament Buildings, and the National Museum. For a list of safari companies both in Kenya and overseas, see page 47.

Organizing your own safari: if you're on a tight budget it requires careful planning. A 4WD is essential, Land Rover, Pajero or Suzuki for **E** budget travellers. Minimum engine size should be 1300. Anything smaller cannot cope with the mud which forms on rainy days. Make sure that the car is not more than 2 years old. To do this you need to check the licence number plates of the car. The norm is K followed by 2 letters and then 3-4 digits. The sequence is then KAE, KA9, KAH which indicates a car first registered in Oct 1996. Travellers have reported that Crossways proved to be very helpful. *Tourist Consultant Kenya*, Beaver House, 1st Flr, Tom Mboya Rd. This agency is highly recommended because they tailor make the arrangements for the safari to fit your budget, and make the necessary calls to their recommended firms. This agency are helpful for other activities like mountaineering.

Tourist offices & information   Located at the junction of Moi Ave and Mama Ngina St opposite the Hilton. There is also a free publication called *Tourist's Kenya* which is published fortnightly and which gives a run down on things going on. There is another publication called *What's On* which comes out monthly.

Useful addresses   Police: Central Police Station is located on University Way, T22222. Always inform the police of any incidents – you will need a police form for any insurance claims. In emergencies dial 999.

Nairobi

Central Highlands: Mount Kenya

*The Central Highlands of Kenya is the area that was known as the 'White Highlands',
to the north of Nairobi. The area includes two national parks (Mount Kenya and the
Aberdares) and forms the eastern boundary to the Rift Valley. It is a very densely populated area, being fertile and well watered – for this reason it was here that many of the
White settlers chose for their farmland. This area is the heartland of the Kikuyu people
who make up the largest tribal group in Kenya.*

There is a railway going up into the highlands to Nyeri and on to Nanyuki and a
whole network of roads. There are a number of towns in the Central Highlands –
including Nyeri, Embu, Meru, Nanyuki and Isiolo. People come to the Central
Highlands to visit the Aberdare National Park (which is home to the famous hotels,
the *Ark* and *Treetops*), and also to climb Mount Kenya which is also part of a
National Park. (National Parks are dealt with separately in the National Park section, see page 251.)

    This area is very high – with peaks in the Aberdares of up to 4,000 metres, and
Mount Kenya which is 5,199 metres. You should therefore expect it to get fairly
chilly especially at night. The maximum temperatures range from 22-26°C, and the
minimum from 10-14°C. It is also very wet here with annual rainfall of up to 3,000
millimetres not unusual.

Mount Kenya region

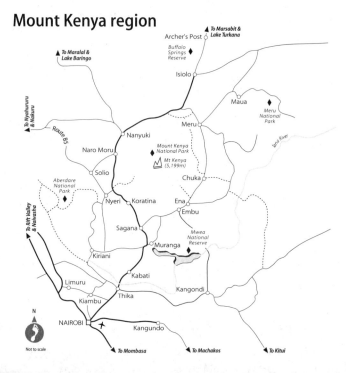

History

The first settlers to come to Kenya came in search of wealth and adventure and were **The settlers** encouraged by the Colonial Government, who were desperate to make the colony pay for itself. The White Highland Policy was established in the early 20th century. By 1915 there were 21,400 square kilometres set aside for about 1,000 settlers. This number was increased after the Second World War with the Soldier Settlement Scheme. Initially the settlers grew crops and raised animals basing their livelihood on wheat, wool, dairy and meat, but by 1914 it was clear that these had little potential as export goods so they changed to maize and coffee. Perhaps the most famous of the early settlers was Lord Delamere. He was important in early experimental agriculture and it was through his mistakes that many lessons were learnt about agriculture in the tropics. He experimented with wheat varieties until he developed a variety resistant to wheat rust. The 1920s saw the rapid expansion of settler agriculture – in particular coffee, sisal and maize and the prices for these commodities rose, giving the settlers reason to be optimistic about their future.

However, when the prices plummeted in the Depression of the 1930s the weaknesses of settler agriculture were revealed. By 1930 over 50 percent by value of settler export was accounted for by coffee alone, making them very vulnerable when prices fell. Many settlers were heavily mortgaged and could not service their debts. About 20 percent of the white farmers gave up their farms, while others left farming temporarily. Cultivated land on settler farms fell from 644,000 acres in 1930 to 502,000 acres in 1936, most of the loss being wheat and maize.

About one third of the colonial government's revenue was from duties on settlers' production and goods imported by the settlers. Therefore the government was also seriously affected by the fall in prices. In earlier years the government had shown its commitment to white agriculture by investment in infrastructure (for example railways and ports), and because of its dependence on custom duties for revenues it felt it could not simply abandon the settlers. Many were saved by the colonial government who pumped about £1mn into white agriculture with subsidies and rebates on exports and loans, and the formation of a Land Bank.

Following the Depression and the Second World War the numbers of settlers increased sharply so that by the 1950s the White population had reached about 80,000. The main crops that they grew were coffee, tea and maize as well as dairy farming. However discontent among the African population over the loss of their traditional land to the settlers was growing. The Africans had been confined to Native Reserves, and as their population grew, the pressure on these areas increased. Some of the Africans lived as squatters on White land, and many migrated and worked as wage labourers for the settlers.

Political demands by Kenyans accelerated throughout the late 1940s and 1950s and the issue of land was critical (see section on Colonial Period, page 285). Although there are still many White Kenyans in this area the size and number of their land holdings has been reduced considerably and land transferred to the Kikuyu. The allocation of land at and around the time of independence was a controversial issue – the aim was to distribute land bought by the British government from settlers as equitably as possible. However there is evidence that a few richer Kenyans managed to secure large areas. The issue of the polarisation and concentration of land ownership amongst a privileged few is one that continues today – it is not something that independence has solved.

Up until the 1930s African agriculture had been largely ignored by the Government. **Kikuyu in the** Africans were in fact banned from growing coffee, the most valuable crop. The rea- **Colonial-Period** son given for this was that production by thousands of small farmers would make it impossible to control coffee berry disease. It had the convenient side effect of ensuring a cheap labour supply for European farms as Africans could then only pay their hut and poll taxes by working as wage labourers.

Kenya

Kikuyu proverbs

Kikuyu proverbs are revealing about a number of elements of Kikuyu culture. In particular you will notice the position and influence of women; the status of the old; the strength of the more powerful against the weak; and the importance of children – something which helps explain the very high birth rate that is found here.

Brought up among boys, the young girl weakens
The weak cannot compete with the strong. Boys are better nourished than girls.
Women and the sky cannot be understood.
The man may be the head of the home; the wife is the heart.
Two wives, two pots of poison.
An old goat never sneezes for nothing.
The old do not speak without reason, they speak the truth.

A woman whose sons have died is richer than a barren woman.
Who will draw water for the childless old woman?
He who asks for mashed food has someone to mash it.
Only a married man can expect home comforts.
Women have only crooked words.
Women cannot keep secrets and seldom tell the truth.
Women's quarrels never end.
Women are relentless in their disputes.
A woman and an invalid man are the same thing.
The law of the fishes: the big ones eat the small ones.
Frowning frogs cannot stop the cows drinking from the pool.
They are friends when you have your beer party, they were not friends when your house had to be built.

When the effects of the Depression reached Kenya it became clear that African producers were more easily able to survive difficult years, and in particular were able to produce cereals more cheaply than the settlers. As European agriculture contracted, squatters on white land increased production of food crops and maize in particular, and found they could make a profit despite the low prices of the 1930s. The need to boost exports as prices fell undermined both official and settler opposition to African production, and the East African share of production increased from nine percent in 1931 to between 15 and 20 percent in 1933 as a result of increased maize production and the expansion of the cultivation of wattle by the Kikuyu.

Wattle production, encouraged by the Department of Agriculture, was expanded dramatically and earnings from wattle increased from £35,000 in 1929 to £79,500 in 1932. It was in many ways an ideal crop – it could be used or sold for fuel, or sold to expatriate firms for the extraction of tannin. It needed little attention after the initial planting, and so could be grown without interrupting the normal agricultural cycle. The areas most affected were Kiambu, Kikuyuland and Embu and many peasant producers made substantial profits.

Meanwhile, during the late 1920s and early 1930s there were a series of droughts which affected the lowland pastoral areas of the Rift Valley much more severely than Kikuyuland. Livestock prices fell dramatically as the pastoralists sold stock to buy food and Kikuyu agriculturalists took advantage. This was a structural change at the expense of the pastoralists from which they have never recovered. There is little doubt that the Kikuyu acted with great economic acumen. The situation also increased the inequalities within Kikuyu society as those with secure access to land not only made a comfortable living from maize and wattle, but were able to increase their wealth through acquiring more livestock, land and wives.

Observers have argued that the Kikuyu not only showed great resilience in the time of the Depression but (particularly those with assured access to land) managed to seize the opportunity given to them and benefit greatly. The decline of European production of maize, and the reassessment by the government of the importance of African agriculture, together with the favourable trading conditions with their neighbours, meant that the Kikuyu were given a real opportunity to increase their economic position, and ultimately their political power. The Depression can be seen therefore as a turning point in the fortunes of the Kikuyu – by stimulating production of both food and wattle.

People

Kikuyu, see page 104, are the largest tribal group in Kenya and make up an estimated 21 percent of the population, with a population of around 6mn. They are believed to have migrated into this area around the 16th century from the east and northeast of Africa as part of the Bantu expansion, and to have intermarried with the groups that occupied the area. These groups were largely hunter-gatherer peoples (unlike the Kikuyu who kept livestock and cultivated the land) and included the Athi and the Gumba.

The Kikuyu belong to age-sets and as they get older they advance in terms of status. One of the most important of the cultural aspects of the Kikuyu is circumcision which traditionally applied to both men and women. Circumcision of women, known as clitoridectomy, is now illegal (there was a campaign against the practice during the colonial period), but there is still evidence of some continuation of the practice. For men the ritual is still an important part of the transition from boyhood to manhood.

The Kikuyu are made up of clans, the two most important being based on Kiambu and Nyeri, and rivalry between the two is intense. In the 1992 multi-party elections, the Ford-Asili party, headed by Kenneth Matiba, effectively represented Kiambu interests, while the Democratic Party was led by Mwai Kibaki from Nyeri. Fragmentation of the opposition allowed the incumbent KANU party to retain power.

The **Embu** and the **Meru** are two groups, each with their own main town of the same name, which have strong affinities with the Kikuyu. In the 1970s a pressure group called the Gikuyu, Embu and Meru Association (GEMA) was active in advancing the interests of these three peoples.

Kiambu

Small town 16 kilometres north of Nairobi, set in an area of ridges formed by streams flowing southeast from Kinangop (3,900 metres). The soil and climate are ideal for coffee growing, which was introduced in 1902.

1° 8' S, 36° 50' E
Colour map 4, grid B3

Kiambu

It is also the centre of one of the main Kikuyu clans (the other is based on Nyeri). The Kiambu Kikuyu were particularly powerful during the Presidency of Jomo Kenyatta, who came from this clan. The **D** *Amani Hotel* near Barclays Bank has a bar, reasonable restaurant and simple accommodation.

Thika

From Muthaiga the road, which has four lanes and a good surface, continues up towards Thika which is actually off the main road north. This is the town which was made famous by the book (and later the television series) *The Flame Trees of Thika* by Elspeth Huxley. It is about her

1° 1' S, 37° 5' E
Phone code: 0151
Colour map 4, grid B4

childhood when her parents came out to Kenya as one of the first families, and their attempts to establish a farm. However, there is little special about Thika, not even many flame trees to brighten the place up apart from the **Blue Post Hotel**, a famous colonial landmark. A visit to the *Blue Post* is an absolute must if you're in Nairobi for any length of time, and are looking for a day out. It is nestled between Chania and Thika Falls. There are shaded tables within sight of the falls, where all you'll hear is the crashing waters, birdsong and the rustling of leaves. There are also easy trails around the base of the falls, thick with flowers and foliage, teeming with butterflies and dragon flies. Rare birds are occasionally sighted. Nearby is the **Ol Doinyo Sapuk National Park** which is located about 25 kilometres from Thika on the A3, the road leading east toward Garissa. In this area there are also the **Fourteen Falls** which are particularly splendid during the rainy season (see National Parks). Thika itself has a fair amount of manufacturing activity, particularly fruit canning for export.

Sleeping **C** *New Blue Posts*, PO Box 42, Thika, T21086. 30 minutes from Nairobi, just north of Thika, on the road to Murang'a, this has been renovated fairly recently and remains popular, it has a very good view over the Falls, and it is a good place to break a journey, and quite the nicest place to stay in the area, rustic sprawling safari style lodge, with large gardens and ostrich farm, busy at weekends. **D** *12th December*, PO Box 156, T22140. Good value, good size rooms, some with balconies, price includes breakfast. **D** *Sagret*, T21786. Behind Matatu area, fairly modern and clean. **D** *White Line*, this is located on the same road as the Post Office in the centre of Thika. It is not a bad place to stay, the rooms have bathrooms and there is sometimes hot water, usually in the evenings. Good value for the price, there is also a restaurant. **E** *New Fulilia Hotel*, Kwame, Nkrumah Rd. Good value, clean and basic rooms. **E** *Sky Motel*, Uhuru St. Very clean if a bit basic.

Eating **2** *Blue Post*, very good food and wide selection of dishes. **2** *Macvast Executive Restaurant*, good coffee. **1** *Prismos Hotel, 1st floor opposite New Fulilia* on Kwane Nkrumah. Large popular restaurant with covered balcony and some ambitious dishes.

Transport **Road** Murange Rd out of Nairobi for the well sign posted Blue Post. Frequent matatus from Racecourse Rd and Ronald Ngala Roundabout (45 minutes).

From Thika the road (A2) continues northwards through the green and verdant countryside. Almost every inch of ground is cultivated and you will see terraces on some of the steeper slopes. You will soon notice that this is pineapple country and many acres are taken up with plantations. They look similar to sisal plantations with spiky plants. There are a number of choices: you can go north to Nyeri and the Aberdare National Park; clockwise round the mountain via Naro Moru or anticlockwise via Embu. This section will cover the route clockwise around Mount Kenya, taking in Nyeri, Naro Moru, Nanyuki, Meru and then finally Embu.

Thika

Murang'a
0° 45' S, 37° 9' E
Colour map 4, grid B4

This is a small bustling town that is situated just off the main road north. At the turn of the century there was very little here – it was initially established as an administrative centre and as it was located in the Kikuyu Reserves rather than in the White Highlands it never became a settler town.

The town has become known as the Kikuyu Heartland because it is close to **Mugeka**, the *Mukuruwe wa Gathanga* (Garden of Eden of the Kikuyu) – which is an important place in Kikuyu mythology. The legend is that it was here that God found nine husbands under a fig tree for the nine Gikuyu and Mumbi daughters, who in mythology are the ancestors of all Kikuyu. These nine became the forefathers of the nine Kikuyu clans. At one time there was a museum at the site of the original fig tree.

In Murang'a is the **Church of St James and All Martyrs**, also known as CPK Cathedral. This is not particularly old but has some interesting decorations painted in 1955 by a Tanzanian artist named Elimo Njau. It shows various scenes from the bible with an African Christ and in African surroundings. The Church was founded in memory of the Kikuyu who died at the hands of the Mau Mau. **Sleeping & eating** E *Ngurunga Bar*, close to the bus station. Simple lodging. E *Rwathia Bar and Restaurant*, PO Box 243, located opposite the market, T22527. Reasonable meals.

From Murang'a the main road continues north towards Nyeri, Naro Moru and Nanyuki. It is possible to take a detour into the **Aberdare Forest**. To take the route into the Aberdare Range, follow one of the minor roads from Murang'a which eventually leads to Othaya and on to Nyeri – the turning for this is to the left just before you get to Murang'a.

Karatina

On the main road north this is the next town you will reach. There are baskets for sale from the Kikuyu women who sit on the road side. It is often the vendors themselves who make the baskets, and they are good value. Worth a visit on market days (Tuesday, Thursday and Saturday) one of the biggest fruit and vegetable markets in East Africa. Attracts buyers from as far as Mombasa. Also has a extensive market selling secondhand clothes and household goods either side of the railway line.

Karatina

Not to scale

Sleeping D *Tourist Lodge*, Private Bag Karatina, T71522. Reasonable restaurant and accommodation, used as a stop off point for tourist stop overs. **E** *Star Point Hotel*, Commercial St. Airy, basic but fine rooms. **E** *3 in 1*, near the bus stand.

Eating 2 *Tourist Lodge*. **1** *Three-in-one Hotel* and **1** *Mugi Motherland Hotel*, pleasant balcony overlooking street. **1** *Mokar Annex Restaurant*. **1** *Bethany Café*, behind the market.

Transport Regular Matatu to Nairobi, Nyeri and other central Province destinations.

Just beyond Karatina there is a track to the right which goes to the **Mountain Lodge** which is located in the foothills of Mount Kenya (See section on National Parks, page 271). About another 20 kilometres from Karatina is the turning off to Nyeri which is the largest town in the Province.

Nyeri

Nyeri is the administrative capital of the Central Province and is located about 120 kilometres from Nairobi. It is at the base of the Aberdares, close to the boundary of the Aberdare National Park. It is situated a few kilometres off the road that goes around Mount Kenya – the turning is signposted.

The surrounding area is fairly densely populated. On a clear morning you can see Mount Kenya in the distance. It is one of the wettest parts of Kenya and can be cold in the evenings.

0° 23' S, 36° 56' E
Phone code: 0171
Colour map 4, grid A3

Kenya

During the British colonial period Nyeri developed as an army base and then as an important trading centre for farmers in the surrounding countryside. The land is very fertile and as you drive into Nyeri you will see the many *shambas* (farms) growing maize, bananas and coffee as well as many varieties of vegetables.

Ins & outs The town has a main street, Kimathi Way on which you will find banks, the Post Office, the Clock Tower and several hotels. A little to the south of this cluster is the market and the bus stand. The Cemetery, just to the north of the Clock Tower, bears the grave of Robert Baden-Powell, founder of the international scout movement, who lived in Nyeri until his death.

Sights On the main road you can also see a memorial to those that died during the Mau Mau. It has the inscription: To the Memory of the Members of the Kikuyu Tribe Who Died in the Fight for Freedom 1951-57.

It is possible to visit Lord Baden-Powell's home, which contains a small museum with a display of memorabilia. The cottage 'Paxtu' lies in the grounds of the Outspan Hotel. Admission is free to Scouts in *uniform*, otherwise US$1.50. Pay at the hotel reception (and make the most of going inside Outspan to see the opulence of the public rooms!).

Sleeping **A+** *Aberdare Country Club*, PO Box 449, Nyeri, T17(Mweiga). This is located about 12 kilometres to the north of Nyeri itself and is now managed by the *Lonrho Group*, it is another old colonial type of country hotel, and is very luxurious with tennis courts and a 9-hole golf course, you can hire self-drive cars here, as well as arrange game drives into the National Park. **A+** *Outspan Hotel*, PO Box 24, Nyeri, T2424 – Booking c/o Block Hotels PO Box 40075, Nairobi, T02-540780, F543810. This hotel is located a little out of town (about 20 minutes walk or a taxi ride) opposite the golf course, built in the 1920s, it is set in some of the most beautiful gardens and has the full facilities of a country hotel, there are a range of rooms and prices depend on the season, the rooms are very spacious and the hotel has a wonderful atmosphere, if you are staying at *Treetops* you will come here to be picked up for the final drive, the *Outspan* is a good place to stop for breakfast or lunch – you can admire the gardens and, as long as the clouds are not down, you will get a good view of Mount Kenya and the Aberdare range behind, there is also a swimming pool, you can rent self-drive vehicles from the *Outspan*, and they also arrange game drives for the day into the Aberdare National Park which are good if you cannot afford the cost of accommodation in the Park itself.

Nyeri

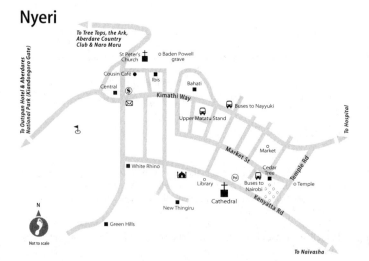

Baden-Powell

Lord Baden-Powell distinguished himself in the Boer War during the siege of Mafeking. At the time he was the youngest General in the British Army at 45 years old.

Baden-Powell is best known as the founder of the Boy Scout movement. Guides were soon to follow and, for younger children, Cubs and Brownies. The movement is immensely successful, and is popular around the world with millions of children.

Baden-Powell once visited a small boarding school in the Rift Valley which was popular amongst British settlers and missionaries. Some of the children there were as young as six, and considered to be too small to join the Brownies or the Cubs. Baden-Powell therefore decided to establish something for the youngest children - and so the "Chippets" were born. The Chippets have continued there to this day and the school (St Andrew's School, Turi, see page 115) remembers Lord Baden-Powell each year. They also have a flag mounted in one of the corridors which was presented to the school by Baden-Powell's wife after his death.

Nyeri was Baden-Powell's great love and he once wrote that "The nearer to Nyeri the nearer to bliss". In the grounds of the Outspan Hotel is the cottage, Paxtu, meaning "Just Peace", built with money collected by guides and scouts from around the world, where Baden Powell spent his final years. He died in 1941 and his obituary states: "No Chief, no Prince, no King, no Saint was ever mourned by so great a company of boys and girls, or men and women, in every land." He is buried in Nyeri cemetery, and his wife's ashes are buried beside him. Lady Baden-Powell was World Chief Guide until her death (in England) at the age of 88 on 25 June 1977.

C *Green Hills*, Mumbi Rd, PO Box 31326, Nyeri, T2017. This hotel is located close to the golf course on the top of a hill, it is spread over fairly extensive gardens and lawns and is large with over 100 rooms, it has excellent facilities including 2 restaurants, bar, swimming pool, and sauna.

D *Central*, Kanisa Rd, PO Box 1229, T4233. This is a modern hotel that is located close to the Post Office in the north of the town, it is good value and all the rooms have bathrooms with hot water, it has a bar and restaurant, and a disco at weekends. **D** *New Thingira Guest House*, PO Box 221, Nyeri, T4769. Another modern hotel, this is very good value, rooms have bathrooms with hot water, it is clean, friendly and secure, and there is a restaurant attached *Nyeri Star Restaurant and Hotel*, Market St, good value. **D** *White Rhino*, Kenyatta Rd, PO Box 30, T2189. This hotel is located fairly centrally in Nyeri and is one of the old colonial hotels that are found scattered all over the White Highlands, the facilities are not that extensive, but it has an atmosphere that makes it worth it, it has a bar, restaurant, and lounge.

There are a number of other cheap places but none particularly pleasant for more than the minimum stay. They include the **E** *Cedar Tree Board and Lodging* close to the southern Post Office which is not great. **F** *Green Leaf Restaurant and Hotel*, Kimathi Way. Very central, superb value, restaurant has a covered balcony, good s/c rooms. **E** *Ibis*, good value, clean, fairly large s/c rooms with nets.

Eating If you are staying in one of the top range hotels you will probably eat there. Otherwise the **2** *Central* and **2** *White Rhino* have restaurants which are both good value. For very basic, but cheap food, try the **1** *Cousin Café* which is located in the town centre just round the corner from Barclays Bank or the popular **1** *Uptown Café* nearby.

Shopping There are a number of good shops in Nyeri including bookshops, grocers, and hardware shops. There is also the market which is very good for fruit and vegetables.

Transport **Air** Nyeri is served by **Kenyan Airways** – flights to Nanyuki (10 minutes), Samburu (50 minutes) and Nairobi (about an hour) daily. It is not worth the bother of flying Nyeri-Nanyuki – by the time you have checked in and so on you could have driven there.

Train Although there is a railway line up to Nyeri, this no longer takes passengers, but is freight only.

Road Nyeri is located about 130 kilometres to the north of Nairobi and is on the very good A2 road. From here it is about 60 kilometres to Nanyuki. The bus and matatu stand is on Kimathi Way in the centre of town.

Directory **Tour companies & travel agents** Nyeri is the gateway to the Aberdare National Park and you will come here before you go to the Park. If you do not already have a trip arranged you can organize one through the *Outspan*. You will need a group of at least 3 people (the more people the cheaper it should work out) and they are just for the day. They are therefore ideal if you cannot afford the lodges in the Park itself. They are fairly good value and the price varies depending on where you want to go in the Park.

Mount Kenya

There are a number of towns located along the Kirinyaga Ring Road at the base of Mount Kenya which serve as starting points for the climb up the mountain. This section deals with these towns going clockwise – Naro Moru, Nanyuki, Meru and Embu. Details of the mountain and the actual routes up it, can be found in the Game Parks section (see page 271). The route is becoming increasingly popular as a tourist circuit which is not surprising for it is a beautiful part of the country, and the mountain and the game parks nearby are an added attraction. The base of the mountain is about 80 kilometres across making it one of the largest volcanic cones in the world. As you drive along this route you will spend much of the time looking towards the mountain – however, much of the time it is shrouded in cloud. There are some clear days – otherwise very early in the morning or just before nightfall the cloud will often lift suddenly revealing the two peaks for a few minutes.

Naro Moru

Colour map 4, grid A3 The road from Nyeri climbs gradually up to Naro Moru which is little more than a village located at the base of the mountain. It has a few shops, guesthouses and a post office and is clustered around the railway station which no longer functions as a passenger terminal. Bear in mind before you arrive here that there are no banks in the village. There are no restaurants apart from the one at the *Naro Moru River Lodge*, and if you are cooking your own food you would be advised to stock up before you get here. However, the village does receive quite a few visitors as it serves as the starting point of the Naro Moru Trail, one of the most popular routes up the mountain. Before you set off on this route you have to both book and pay for the mountain huts that you will stay in on the way up. This must be done through the *Naro Moru River Lodge*.

Sleeping **A** *The Naro Moru River Lodge*, PO Box 18, Naro Moru, T22018. This is located about 2 kilometres from the village itself off the main road. This hotel is the most popular place to stay as it organizes climbs up the mountain, the facilities are good including a swimming pool, charge for using pool is US$3.50 per person, restaurant, bar and roaring log fire which is perfect for the chilly evenings. **B/C** *Mountain Rock Hotel* formerly called Bantu Lodge PO Box 33 T62625/62098/62099, 8 kilometres north of Naro Moru lodge, Nanyuki, T22787, this is located on the road to Nanyuki – you will see a signpost off the main road. It is in lovely surroundings and has a range of self-catering cottages with full facilities, they even have fire places in each cottage which is very nice on a cold evening, the hotel also arranges a wide range of activities including riding, fishing, birdwatching and evening entertainment, the hotel is well known for its very well run treks up the mountain (taking the Naro Moru, Sirimon or Burguret routes), you can choose an itinerary to suit you – for more details see Mount Kenya section, page 271. **D** *Blueline Hotel*, Budget hotel about 3 kilometres off the main highway along a dirt road towards Mt. Kenya. Pleasant rooms with attached bathrooms. Good place to contact Naro Moru Porters and Guides Association direct, hire gear etc. Recommended. **E** *Mount Kenya Hostel*, this is located about 12 kilometres down the track towards the Park entrance off the main Nanyuki road, about 4 kilometres from the Park entrance gate. It is popular with budget travellers, hot showers and cooking facilities, construction work should be being undertaken for a more substantial building – the original building burnt down in 1988 and as they were not insured rebuilding has been delayed. **Camping** There is a site attached to *Naro Moru River Lodge*, **E**, and if you do not have the necessary equipment you can hire everything. You can use all the hotel facilities, and the campsite sometimes has hot showers. There are also bunk beds available in huts – but these are not very good value. Also at *Bantu's Mount Kenya Leisure*, good facilities available and *Mount Kenya Hostel*, where you can hire a tent.

Nanyuki

Nanyuki is a small up-country town located to the northwest of the mountain that dates back to about 1907 when it was established and used by white settlers as a trading centre and for socializing. The town today is home to the Kenyan air force as well as a British army base. Despite this it is a fairly sleepy kind of town and retains some of its colonial character. The town is visited by people planning to use the Sirimon or Buguret trails up the mountain. It has a good range of shops, banks including Barclays, Standard Chartered and Kenya Commercial Bank. The District Hospital is located about a kilometre out of town to the east.

0° 2′ N, 37° 4′ E
Phone code: 0176
Colour map 4, grid A3

On the main road to Nanyuki there are signposts marking the equator, and more than a few pushy souvenir sellers.

A+ *Mount Kenya Safari Club*, PO Box 35, Nanyuki, T2141/2142 or Nairobi 216940. This is Nanyuki's most exclusive hotel, one of the Lonrho chain and extremely luxurious.

Sleeping

C *New Silverbeck*, PO Box 79, T2740. This hotel is rather shabby, it offers a range of rooms but the facilities are poor and there are frequently problems with the water supply, however the cottages all have fireplaces and there is an Equator sign in the grounds, facilities include bar, restaurant and shops. **C** *Sportsman's Arms*, PO Box 3, Nanyuki, T32347, located across the river. Probably the best value hotel in Nanyuki, surrounded by gardens and in a lovely setting, rooms are s/c the price includes breakfast, it is clean and friendly.

D *Joskaki*, T22820, located close to the Park in the centre of town. Popular, all rooms have bathrooms and it has a bar and restaurant, and good views around, it has a disco and can be noisy. **D** *Landview Boarding and Lodging*, located on the north side of the park. All rooms have bathrooms and it has a bar and restaurant. **D** *Nanyuki River Lodge*, located near the Caltex petrol station near the park. Very good value. **D** *Nyakio Boarding and Lodging*, north side of the park. All rooms have bathrooms and a bar and restaurant. **D** *Riverside Hotel*, PO Box 101, T32523. A pleasant, smart hotel, attempting to rival the *Sportsman*, but without the grounds, set within its own compound with tour operators and curio shops, good value, has regular discos and a pool.

E *Juba Boarding and Lodging*, near Park. Very cheap. **E** *Jumbo Hotel*, located at west corner of the park. Hotel very popular with

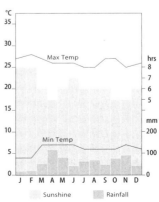

Climate: Nanyuki

Europeans, serve excellent samosas in the restaurants. **E** *Mutatnini*, cheap, basic but fine. **E** *Silent Guest House*, Market Rd. Simple but perfectly acceptable. **E** *Sirimon Guest House*, T22243. Situated facing the Park this hotel is very good value, it has a range of rooms with bathrooms – with hot water, it is secure and friendly and there is parking space available, laundry facilities available for an additional charge. **E** *Youth Hostel*, T22112, located on Market Rd. Very cheap, clean and friendly and has shared facilities, candle-light.

Camping **E** site at *Sportsman's Arms*.

Eating Apart from the restaurants attached to the hotels there are few places to eat in Nanyuki. **1** *Maridadi Café*, near bus stand. Good value. *Muneeras* formerly **1** *Marina Bar and Restaurant* (and advertised as both), opposite the Post Office. Convenient for a cold beer and a snack, good selection of deserts. **1** *Mid Pines Café*. **1** *Nanyuki Coffee House*, surprisingly modern interior, cheap local meals and snacks. **1** *Nanyuki River Lodge*. Highly recommended fresh food, enormous variety, excellent omelettes. **1** *Riverside Hotel*, wide ranging menu at low prices.

Shopping On main street there is **Settlers Stores** which is one of the oldest shops in town having been founded in 1938 and selling hardware and groceries. Other shops include the **United Stores** and **Modern Sanitary Stores** where you should be able to stock up on all your supplies. If you are interested in buying hand woven rugs and other items you may want to visit the **Nanyuki Spinners and Weavers Workshop**. This is run by a women's group who sell to the Spin and Weave Shop in Nairobi, but you will get a lower price here. Very interesting place to visit, pleased to give you a full guided tour.

Transport **Road** Nanyuki is located about 60 kilometres from **Nyeri** and 190 kilometres from **Nairobi** – a drive that will take you about 3 hours. **Bus** Buses leave from behind Ngumba House next to the Siriman. There are frequent buses and *matatus* running between Nanyuki and Nairobi. If you are heading north to Marsabit and Northern Kenya you can get buses and matatus from Nanyuki to **Isiolo** (which is the last town on the good road heading north) and from there continue north. The matatu station is located next to the Park.

Directory **Banks** On main street there are branches of *Barclays Bank*, *Kenya Commercial Bank* and *Standard Chartered Bank*. **Communications** Post Office: on the main street.

Nanyuki

■ Sleeping	3 Landview	6 Siriman
1 Josaki	4 Nyakio	7 Sportsman's Arms
2 Juba	5 Silent Night	8 Youth Hostel

Nanyuki to Nyahururu

From Nanyuki you can take the road west towards **Nyahururu**. This town is closer to Nakuru and more easily reached from there. The road between Nanyuki and Nyahururu is not good – particularly during the wet season. In the rainy season it is advisable to take the A2 road south towards Naro Moru. Then take the unmade gravel road to the right, which is a link road to the B5. This link road provides good opportunities to see a variety of wildlife. The B5 road towards Nyahururu is a sealed road which takes you through the thick green forests of the Aberdare. Later the land opens out into the great Golden Plains, reminiscent of the mid-West American Prairies. The attractions in this central Highlands region include a number of game ranches, some of which, including the **Laikipia Ranch**, have been important in the battle to save the rhino. The efforts have involved keeping the rhino as part of an integrated grazing system – they seem to do well and do not interfere with the cattle who graze using the same land. The **Ol Pejeta Game Reserve** which covers an area of about 400 kilometres is open to the public, but a stay in the original Ranch house costs upwards of US$300 – the facilities include a health spa. Ol Pejeta also has a luxury lodge called Sweetwaters Camp which is more reasonably priced but still in the **A+** category (located about 40 kilometres from Nanyuki) PO Box 585 81, Nairobi, T216940, F216796 and much of the Reserve is a rhino sanctuary. They organize night game viewing trips and you are likely to see rhino. Another ranch that is open to the public is the **D** El Karama Ranch (book through *Let's Go Travel*, PO Box 60342, Nairobi, T340331, F336890) located about 40 kilometres to the north of Nanyuki. They have a range of good value accommodation and also organize game viewing on horseback.

Nyahururu (Thomson's Falls)

Small town at high altitude (2,360 metres) with a splendid climate. Although only a few kilometres north of the equator, there are bracing nights with occasional frosts in the early months of the year. There is good rainfall, the surrounding area is well timbered, and a variety of vegetables and grains are grown. The town served settler farmers in the area during the colonial period, and was boosted when a branch line of the railway reached the town in 1929. It still runs, but only carries freight. In the postwar period the town was prosperous enough to boast a racecourse.

0° 2' N, 36° 27' E
Colour map 4, grid A3

Joseph Thomson, an explorer, came across the waterfall to the north of the town in 1883 which he named **Thomson's Falls** after his father. The cascade plunges 75 metres, and is a pretty area to walk around. It's more commonly known as 'T-falls'.

Sleeping

C *Baron Hotel*, Ol Kalou Rd, PO Box 423, T32056. Some rooms have bathrooms, bar-restaurant, more modern building, disco at weekends, a disadvantage is that it is very noisy from 0600 when the Matatus get going. **C** *Thomson's Falls Lodge*, PO Box 38, T0365-22006. The most popular choice, just off the road out of town toward Nyeri and Nanyuki, very charming colonial atmosphere, there is a choice of rooms in the main building, or cottages, built in 1931, and initially called *Barry's Hotel*, there's also a campsite on the grounds, with hot showers. There is free firewood at the campsite but you will need a machete or an axe. **D** *Kawa Falls Hotel*, PO Box 985, T32295, Ol Kalou Rd at edge of town.

E *Cyrus*, Ol Kalou Rd. Nothing elaborate, but sound, good restaurant (*Arafa*) attached. **E** *Good Shepherd Lodge*, just north of centre. Own bathrooms, good value. **E** *Manguo* (Stadium Lodging), next to open market. Simple, but clean and secure. **E** *New Murera*, Ol Kalou Rd. Basic, clean and functional. **E** *Nyahururu Lodging*, Ol Kalou Rd. Shared bathrooms, basic, but adequate. **E** *Nyaki Hotel*, T22313. Excellent value in quieter part of town, clean, s/c rooms with hot water, rooftop shaded tables and chairs.

Kenya

Eating   **2** *Baron Hotel*, good tasty food. **2** *Cyrus Bar and Restaurant*, Ol Kalou Rd. Attached to *Cyrus Hotel*, mainly Nyama Chana (barbecued meats). **2** *Thompsons Fall Lodge*, very good meals and snacks in attractive surroundings at inexpensive prices. Highly recommended, hot showers, lovely setting among tall trees. **1** *Ndururumo*, close to open market. Rough and ready, but reasonable value. **1** *Tropical Bar and Restaurant*, near the *Baron Hotel*.

Bars & nightlife   **Bars**   Lively atmosphere at *Muthengera Farmer's Lodge*, just east of Ol Kalou Rd. **Cinemas**   Just north of clocktower. **Discos**   At *Baron Hotel* at weekends.

Transport   **Road**   **Bus**: Regular buses and minibuses linking to **Nakuru** to the west and **Nyeri** to the east. 2-3 departures north each day for **Maralal**, leaving at 0700 and costing US$5.

Nanyuki to Meru

Northeast from Nanyuki the road continues around Mount Kenya. The next village that you will reach after Nanyuki is **Timau** – there is very little here. Another 35 odd kilometres down the road is the turning off to the left that goes on up to Marsabit and northern Kenya. The first town on this road is **Isiolo** which is located about 30 kilometres off the Nanyuki-Meru road and is where the good road ends. (See Nortern Kenya section, page 230).

    The Lewa Wildlife Conservancy is situated about 15 kilometres west of Isiola on the northern foothills of Mount Kenya approximately 65 kilometres northeast of Nanyuki. The land comprises savannah, wetland, grassland and indigenous forest. It was officially registered as a Non-Profit Organisation in 1995. Three quarters of Kenya's wildlife is found on private land outside the National Parks and reserves. The conservancy project aims to minimize the conflict between conservation and human settlement and protect and encourage the rhinoceros and other endangered species. The Lewa Downs and later the adjoining state owned Ngare Ndare Forest were fenced to reduce the human/wildlife conflict and loss of

Nyahururu (Thomson's Falls)

Nyahururu Lodging ■

Thomson's Falls

To Rumuruti & Maralal

To Lake Bogoria, Menengai Crater & Nakuru (61 km)

To Nyeri & Nanyuki

Catholic Church

Good Shepherd Lodge ■

Stadium

Cinema o

Covered Market

Manguo Lodging ■

Clocktower o

o Market

Muthangera Farmer's Bar ●

Buses to Maralal

Ndururumo ■ ●

Cyrus Lodge ■

Thomson's Falls Lodge ■

■ Baron

Bus Station

● Arafa

N

Not to scale

Ol Kalou Rd

To Equator & Gilgil (68 km)

Kenya

smallholders crops to elephants. It also incorporates the Ngare Sergoi Rhino Sanctuary, which no longer exists as a separate entity. Numbers of both black and white rhino have increased, with none lost to poachers. It is possible to see the 'Big Five' here, lion, leopard, rhinoceros, elephant and buffalo. Grevy's zebra numbers have risen from 81 to over 400.

Tourism is being expanded to help cover the cost on the conservancy, but will be kept within clear limits with a maximum of 60 tourist beds. The original homestead has been converted into a Conservation Centre. As it is a non-profit organisation all tourist generated income goes to pay for security and management of the wildlife.

There are two lodges on Lewa. *Lerai Tented Camp* is run by the Ngare Sergoi Ornithological Safaris Ltd, and *Wilderness Trails*, operated through Bush Homes of East Africa Ltd. Camping is available through *Abercrombie and Kent Ltd* and includes game drives, full board, laundry – maximum of 16 beds. Camel Safaris with a maximum of six people can be arranged through *Bush Homes of East Africa Ltd*. Details of these safari operators can be found under 'Tour companies and travel agents' in Nairobi. Tourist accommodation is now also available at two community wildlife schemes, supported by Lewa. *Il Ngwesi*, on Lewa's northwest boundary and *Namunyak Wildlife Conservation Trust* – about 90 kilometres north of Lewa in the Mathews Mountains. To visit the remote wilderness areas of *Il Ngwesi* and *Il Ngwesi Lodge* contact *Let's Go Travel* and for *Namunyak Wildlife Conservation Trust* and *Sarara Safari Camp* contact *Acacia Trails Ltd* – listed under Nairobi Tour companies. For further information contact Lewa Wildlife Conservancy, PO Box 49918, Nairobi, T607893, F607197, lewa@swiftkenya.com.

Continuing around the mountain about 30 kilometres on from the turning to Isiolo, you will reach the town of **Meru**, which is a thriving and bustling trading centre. The journey from Nanyuki to Meru is very beautiful – and shows the diversity of Kenya's landscape. To the south is Mount Kenya, to the north (on a clear, haze-free day) you can see miles and miles of the northern wilderness of Kenya.

Meru

Meru is located to the northeast of the Mountain and has a population of about 75,000. Although it serves as an important trading centre it is not visited by many tourists. It also does not have the advantage of proximity to any of the trails up the mountain and so has not been developed for this. It is however the base for visits to the **Meru National Park** the entrance of which is about 80 kilometres from the town (see Game Parks section, page 268). It is set at an altitude of about 3,000 metres and in the rainy season is cold and damp. If you are there on a clear day you may get good views around – it is heavily cultivated and forested.

0° 3' N, 37° 40' E
Phone code: 0164
Colour map 4, grid A4

The Meru National Museum. The most interesting section of the museum is that related to the customs and culture of the local Meru people: various ethnographic exhibits, examples of local timber and stone and tools from the prehistoric site at Lewa Downs. There is a Meru homestead which gives a good idea of how the Meru people live. Outside there is a display of various herbal and traditional medicinal plants – including an example of a miraa plant. There is also a display of stuffed birds and animals. The museum also has a snake pit. ■ *PO Box 592, T0164-20482. Entrance US$4. Located down the road roughly opposite the Meru County Hotel and in what is the oldest building in the town, originally the District Commissioner's office.*

The **Post Office** is on the main road on the left as you come in from Nanyuki. There are branches of **banks** situated just off the main road. There is an excellent well stocked supermarket on the road out towards Nanyuki called **Supermart**. There are two **markets** at Meru – one is situated on the main road towards Nanyuki and the other is the opposite side of town. The merchandise on sale is very cheap and

··

☞ Snow Mountain on the Equator: Halford Mackinder and the first ascent of Mount Kenya

Halford Mackinder was born in 1861 in Lincolnshire, where his father was a doctor. He attended school at Epsom College and then went to Christ Church College, Oxford, studying natural sciences and specializing in geology. On graduating he took up law and qualified as a barrister. However, his studies in geology had given him an enthusiasm for the new subject of geography, and in 1887 he was appointed the first teacher of geography at Oxford. In 1889 Mackinder married Bonnie Ginsburg. They had a son in 1891 who died in infancy.

When Mackinder learned of the railway under construction in British East Africa which would eliminate the 500 kilometre trek from the coast to Nairobi, he began to plan an expedition to climb Mount Kenya. He took courses in surveying, and in the summers of 1897 and 1898 went to the Swiss Alps to learn mountaineering.

A relative of Mackinder's wife, Campbell Hausburg; Edward Saunders, a biologist; Claude Camburn a taxidermist; César Ollier an Italian-Swiss mountain guide; and Joseph Brocheral, an Italian-Swiss porter, made up the core of the expedition. Mackinder and Hausburg contributed œ500 each to the cost, and the Royal Geographical Society chipped in £200.

The four Britons left London on 8 June 1899 and met up with the Swiss in Marseilles. The party sailed to Zanzibar, finalised arrangements with the British administration, and assembled their caravan. They took on 50 Swahili porters, eight Askaris (guards), two cooks, four tent-boys, an interpreter and a headman. The party sailed to Mombasa and entrained on 12 July for Nairobi, a three-day journey.

At camp in Nairobi they recruited another 46 Kikuyu porters before the caravan set out, trekking east along the Nairobi River, then north through Thika, Murango, and Kijango to Naro Moro. Headed by the Blue Ensign flag and winding back for over 200 metres down the trail, the whole party, with local guides and hangers-on, numbered about 170. Emergency rations were carried in 40 sealed tin boxes (iron-rations), but the main source of food was to be game shot along the route and local maize bartered for cloth

and beads. The whole of British East Africa was in the grip of a drought, however, and the procurement of food was everwhere problematical. Mackinder carried a knobkerry from Lenena, the Masai chief to ensure safe passage.

There were many difficulties. Two porters were killed on an expedition foraging for food. Porters deserted. Floggings were ordered for porters who threw away biological specimens. Rations were in desperately short supply all the time. A report by Hausburg remarks that eight Swahili porters were shot, presumably for indiscipline, but the event, if it did take place, was hushed-up. Mackinder kept up his spirits with the occasional bottle of champagne, and by reading Dickens' Old Curiosity Shop at night by candlelight.

On August 30, Mackinder and the two Swiss set off from the final base camp in the Teleki Valley for an attempt on the summit. After a bitterly cold sleepless night roped to rock pinnacles, they turned back.

They spent some days re-grouping and made another attempt on 12 September. After some stiff climbing, traversing glaciers and axing footholds in the ice, they reached the summit at noon. The peak was named Batian after the legendary heroic chief of the Masai, and the nearby lower peak, Nelion, after his son.

In the days following they made a circuit of the peaks and surveyed the glaciers. On 20 September they started back, trekking west to Nyahururu and then south to Niavasha. From Nairobi a telegram was sent to to the International Geographical Congress, then meeting in Berlin – "Reached Kenia summit. Mountain has fifteen glaciers. Mackinder." On October 5 they embarked at Mombasa, and Mackinder was back in Oxford to start his teaching on 30 October.

The next year Mackinder's marriage to Bonnie broke up. He channelled his energies into consolidating geography at Oxford, establishing the University College of Reading, and serving as Director of the London School of Economics. For services to academic life Mackinder was knighted, and his portrait hangs in the Mountain Club of Kenya (see page 99). He died in 1947 aged 86.

··

includes not just agricultural produce from the farms around Meru, but also baskets and household goods.

Sleeping

B *Forest Lodge*, about 10 kilometres out, to the north of the town. Has a range of comfortable cottages, facilities include bar, restaurant and swimming pool and it is set in fine gardens. **C** *Greenland Holiday Resort*, PO Box 2065, T0164-20409. Closer to town than the *Rocky Hill*, it also has a swimming pool. **C** *Rocky Hill Inn*, located 8 kilometres out of town in the same direction as the *Forest Lodge*. It has simple cottages for rent – unfortunately the water supply is not very reliable, there is a bar and they have a barbecue which is good value.

D *Meru County*, PO Box 1386, T0164-20427. This is situated on the main road and is probably the best hotel in the town itself, it is simple but clean, safe and friendly, it has a restaurant, bar and video lounge and there is plenty of parking space. **E** *Castella*, simple and good value. **E** *Continental*, fairly basic. **E** *New Milimani*, disco at weekends – plenty of parking space but often has water supply problems. **E** *Stansted*, PO Box 1337, T0164-20360. This is a very good value hotel – clean, comfortable and friendly.

Eating

2 *Canopy Restaurant*, main road near to *Castella Hotel*. Good standard and value. **2** *Meru County*, a very good restaurant, huge breakfast US$4, and dinner for US$6.50. **2** *New Milimani*, wide-ranging menu including curries. **2** *Professional Restaurant* (previously *Kenya Coffee Board*), serves a few snacks and drinks. **2** *Springboard Quality Café*, main road. Good for snacks. **1** *Conna's Hygienic Food Centre*, generous helpings of simple fare.

Transport

Air The airstrip serving Meru is in Mitunguru. The road from Mitunguru to Meru becomes very slippery in the wet season.

Road Bus: the main bus and matatu area is behind the Mosque, reached from the road going past Barclays. There are daily buses to Meru from **Nairobi** including the luxury service. The journey to Nairobi takes about 5 hours, to **Chogoria** about an hour and a half and to **Embu** about 2½ hours. The Kensilver Bus Service to Nairobi via Embu is cheap and reliable. You can even buy your ticket in advance and have a reserved seat. Matatus are not very safe as they are often involved in accidents on this route and the bus is definitely the better option. Meru is located about 70 kilometres from Nanyuki. Matatus north to Isiolo take about 45 minutes. The scenery quickly changes from healthy banana plantations to looming cacti and dry scrubland.

Meru

South from Meru the road to Embu is good. The scenery here is well worth spending the time to appreciate. If you can sit on the right you will be able to look out for glimpses of the mountain peaks. About five kilometres south of Meru you will again cross the equator.

Chogoria

Between Meru and Embu is the village of Chogoria which is the starting point for the **Chogoria trail**. This is the only eastern trail up the mountain and it is generally considered to be the most beautiful of the routes. It is also supposed to be the easiest as far as gradients are concerned (see Mount Kenya, page 271 for detail). The buses to Embu usually stop off at Chogoria (it takes about an hour and a half) so it is easily accessible.

Miraa

Miraa is also known as "qat" and "gatty" and is produced in large quantities around Meru. It is a leaf which is chewed and is a mild stimulant as well as acting as an appetite suppressant. You will see people all over Kenya (but particularly in the north and northeast) holding bunches of these leaves and twigs and chewing them. In the town centre there is a street corner that is devoted to the selling of miraa – in case you want to try some. It is a small tree that grows wild here and is also grown commercially. It is produced legally and it is also sold to the northeast of Kenya and exported to Somalia, Yemen and Djibouti.

Embu

0° 32' S, 37° 38' E
Phone code: 0161
Colour map 4, grid B4

This is the final town in the clockwise circuit around Mount Kenya, before rejoining the road south to Nairobi. The town is strung out along the main road. The town, named after the Embu people who live in this area, is the provincial headquarters of the Eastern Province. The surrounding area is densely populated and intensively cultivated. There's not a great deal to see here.

Sleeping **B** *Izaac Walton Inn*, PO Box 1, Embu, T0161-20128/9. This is the best hotel in Embu, situated about 2 kilometres out of town on the road that heads north towards Meru, it is an old colonial hotel apparently named after an English angler because of the proximity of good fishing spots in the mountain streams which surround, the inn is set in gardens with a comfortable lounge with a log-burning fire, rooms all have bathrooms with hot water and each room has a balcony, the price includes breakfast and there is a good bar and restaurant, it is very friendly and the staff helpful. **D** *Valley View Lodge*, PO Box 563, T0161-30369. Located away from the centre of town, it is quiet, clean and friendly, it has a range of rooms – all with hot water, and has a bar and good restaurant. **E** *Al-Aswad*, situated a little up the hill, it has a popular restaurant attached, serving simple fare. **E** *Kubua Kubua*, T0161-20191. Situated down the hill from the centre of town, reasonable – basic with small rooms but clean and simple. **E** *Al-Aswad*, situated a little up the hill, it has a popular restaurant attached, serving simple fare.

Eating **2** *Izaac Walton Inn*, good meals, and fine atmosphere. **1** *Arkland Hotel*, popular place for Indian snacks and other meals. **1** *New Beverley Castle*, next door to *Arklands* and equally popular. **1** *Rehana Café*, north part of town, off the main road, up the hill. Good spicy snacks.

Transport **Road** The road from Nairobi to Embu is a very good surface but is probably one of the most dangerous roads in Kenya and there are frequent accidents. Matatus are therefore not recommended for this journey. Instead take the Kensilver Bus (Nairobi to Meru, via Embu) bus, if possible, which goes everyday and is reasonably safe.

Embu

Directory **Banks** There is a branch of *Barclays Bank* located on the roundabout where the roads meet. **Communications** Post Office: is located on the Meru road that heads north. **Libraries** The town library is located on the Meru road that heads north.

The Rift Valley

The Great Rift Valley is one of the most dramatic features on earth, stretching some 6,000 kilometres from the Dead Sea in Jordan down to Mozambique in the south. In Kenya, the Rift Valley starts at Lake Turkana in the north, and runs right through the centre of the country to Lake Natron just across the southern border in Tanzania. It is up to 100 kilometres wide in places and a fascinating place of cliffs, escarpments, rivers and arid plains housing an enormous diversity of wildlife, and trees and plants. The valley floor rises from around 200 metres at Lake Turkana to about 1,900 metres above sea level at Lake Naivasha to the south. The walls rise where the valley floor is at its highest, and reach their peak in the Aberdares above Naivasha.

Kenya

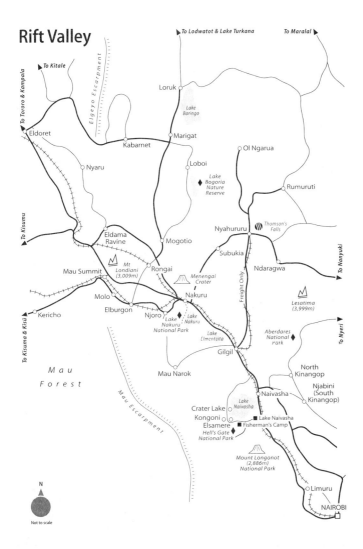

Bibi Kiboko

Mary O'Donnell was born in Ireland. At 17 she married and emigrated to Australia to a sheep farm. Before she was 30, her husband had died and her two children had gone to their graves, one dying from a snake-bite, the other by drowning. Leaving these tragic memories she went to Rhodesia where she met and married John Walsh and in 1886 they trekked north to try their luck in British East Africa. Walsh and a partner acquired mining rights for Lake Magadi and in 1902 sold their rights for £15,000. While her husband dealt in cattle around Nairobi, Mary variously traded in household goods and groceries, while running bars, bakeries, and donkey transport services, acquiring a reputation for toughness and ferocity. Her outfit included puttees (thick canvas leggings wound on spirally, like bandages from the ankle to the knee), a small revolver tucked into her waistband and a kiboko, a rhino-hide whip (from which she got her nickname from the locals) with which she was very free to anyone who annoyed her – or was unlucky enough to be around when she was blind drunk. She died at the age of 58, and the lasting monument to her eccentric and tough life is the house she built which later became the Bell Inn (now La Belle) in Naivasha.

There are some 30 active and semi-active volcanoes in the Rift Valley and countless springs bringing sodium carbonate up to the surface of the earth, forming the soda lakes. Soda lakes are a result of the poor drainage system in the valley resulting in a number of shallow lakes on the valley floor. Evaporation has left a high concentration of alkaline volcanic deposits in the remaining water. The algae and crustaceans which thrive in the soda lakes are ideal food for flamingos and there are many here, and they are quite spectacular.

The Rift Valley is one of the few ecosystems which has remained unchanged for centuries, holding a great array of Africa's wildlife. It is the site of two of the most significant digs in palaentological history, the **Koobi Fora** on the eastern shores of Lake Turkana and **Olduvai Gorge** in the Tanzania section of the Rift. No visit to Kenya is complete without spending some time in the Rift Valley.

Your first glimpse of it is likely to be from the viewpoints along the Nairobi-Naivasha new road just past Limuru, at the top of the escarpments of the Valley. Mount Longonot is directly in front, while the plains seem to sweep on for ever to the south. There are a number of tourist stalls along the route selling unremarkable curios. A reasonably good buy, however, are the sheepskins, though they are not particularly well cured.

Naivasha and environs

0° 40' S, 36° 30' E
Phone code: 0311
Colour map 4, grid B3

Naivasha is a small trading centre just off the main road from Nairobi to Nakuru. Most famous for its lake, Naivasha was traditionally used as grazing land by Masai, until they were displaced by European settlers at the turn of the 20th century. It used to be more popular with tourists as the old road passed through it, now the best reason to visit is for the excellent Belle Inn fruit juices and pastries. It is a stop on the way to **Lake Naivasha**, **Mount Longonot** and the **Hell's Gate National Park**. Naivasha is sufficiently close to Nairobi to be used as a weekend retreat for people working in the capital. There are still a number of White Kenyans farming the land around the lake.

Sights The most likely reason for stopping here is en route to either Lake Naivasha or Hell's Gate, see National Parks section, page 271. The lack of facilities for budget travellers around the lake makes staying in Naivasha a useful option. However, depending on your preference it can be more rewarding to camp down by the lake, as long as you take your own food and water. **Kamuta Ltd**, T0311-30091 is the base of Air

Naivasha which offers flights at US$150 an hour. Of particularly good value is the flight around Lake Naivasha and over Hell's Gate at US$25 each for two people for 30 minutes. It is on the same entrance as Lakeside House by Lake Naivasha.

Sleeping

There is plenty of accommodation in this popular and expanding weekend retreat for Nairobians, although there is little of attraction in the town itself except for *La Belle Inn*. For budget travellers, best to stock up in town and then head for the lake. Matatus to and from the lake are among the most packed you will find in Kenya – even the locals complain.

C *Ken-Vash Hotel*, just up from Moi Ave, T30049. Large new building, Naivasha's newest hotel. **C** *La Belle Inn*, Moi Ave, T20116. Popular place with a selection of rooms at different prices. **C** *Lakeside Tourist Lodge*, Moi Ave, T30268, 5 minutes walk, north along Moi Ave. Pleasant, large leafy verandah, good modern rooms in the quieter outskirts of town.

D *Four Seasons Naivasha*, Kariuki Chotara Rd, T20377. Very cheap rooms, clean. **D** *Heshima*, Kariuki Chotara Rd, T20361. Basic and cheap. **D** *Othaya Annexe*, Kariuki Chotara Rd, T20770. Very good value, bakery on premises, competes with *Heshima* for the best budget value in town. **D** *Wambuku Hotel*, Moi Ave, T30287. Very similar to *Ken-Vash* but much better value.

Eating

2 *Jim's Corner Dishes* (formerly *Brothers Café*), Station Lane. Relaxed place, good value, excellent local food. **2** *Ken-Vash Hotel*, good value restaurant, à la carte menu and regular buffets. **2** *Lakeside Tourist Lodge*, relaxed surroundings for a drink or reasonable meal. **2** *La Belle Inn*, Moi Ave. Has excellent fresh fruit juices served ice-cold, it also does very good (and huge) breakfasts including fruit juice, croissants, home made jam, butter, bacon, eggs and lots of coffee, also a good place to stop for a drink and a break from driving, it has a selection of pastries (many vegetarian which is unusual for Kenya) and meals for lunch or dinner, closed Tuesday, still the best place in town in which to eat. **2** *North Kinangop*, Moi Ave, a little further towards the Lake. Serves very good snacks and simple meals, good value.

Transport

Train Naivasha is on the main railway running from **Kisumu** on Lake Victoria in the west to **Mombasa** on the coast in the east. The train leaves Nairobi each evening at 1800 and arrives at 2100. From Naivasha West, the train leaves soon after it arrives 2100, gets to Nakuru at about 2300 and reaches Kisumu at 0800 the next morning. On the way back the Kisumu train to Nairobi leaves at 1830, reaches Nakuru at 0200, Naivasha at 0400, and Nairobi at about 0700.

Naivasha town

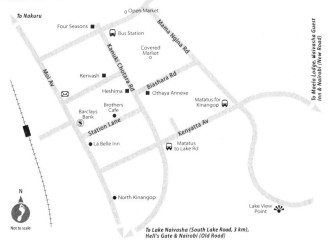

Trader Dick

Andrew Dick was born in Scotland and worked initially as an accountant for the Imperial British East Africa Company. He later set up as a trader with a concession of 11 plots between Mumias and Eldama Ravine which he farmed, supplying caravans on the Uganda road and organizing caravans of his own.

In 1895 a large caravan of over a thousand porters set off from Fort Smith (Kabete) for Eldama Ravine. A Swahili headman was in charge. On their return, passing through the Kedong Valley, a few of the porters took liberties with some Masai girls. A confrontation ensued which led to the Masai killing 1,038 of the porters.

Dick was on his way up country, when he met the fleeing handful of Kedong survivors.

He sent to Kikuyu for some reinforcements, then set off to take advantage of the mayhem to filch some Masai stock. They had rounded up a sizeable herd of cattle and donkeys, and were making their way back with the spoils when they were ambushed by the Masai and Dick was speared. John Ainsworth, the Chief Commissioner accepted that Dick had brought trouble on himself and sought to defuse the situation in negotiations with Lenana, the Masai Chief (Laibon).

The death of Dick was a nasty shock for the Europeans and they took to adding a stone each time they passed to the pile at the place where he fell. The cairn can still be seen today, by the old road from Kijabe to Naivasha, in the Kedong Valley.

Road If you are coming by road from Nairobi there are two routes. The first is along the old road which nowadays is the preserve of hundreds of lorries driving between Mombasa and Uganda. The road is poor, though the views are great and you are likely to see herds of zebra and other wildlife roaming the vast valley floors. The other route is along the new A104 road which does not come into Naivasha town itself. It is in good condition and has the added advantage of having the most wonderful views of the Rift Valley, particularly at the equator. **Bus**: you can also take many of the buses heading further west to Nakuru or Kisumu. Remember to ask the driver to let you off at the Naivasha turning, as he is unlikely to stop automatically. The road from the dropping off point to Naivasha town is a few kilometres to which you can either walk or flag down a matatu. **Taxi** Peugeot taxis run to Naivasha throughout the day taking about 1½ hours.

Directory **Useful addresses** The main street running through the town is Moi Ave and it is along here that you will find almost everything you need including the **Post Office** and a branch of *Barclays Bank* where you can change money. Moi Ave is also where you should stock up on groceries and bottled water if you intend to be self-catering while staying round Lake Naivasha. There is a **supermarket** called *Multiline* and there are some fruit stalls just opposite.

Lake Naivasha

Colour map 4, grid B3 Lake Naivasha, the 'Sunshine Lake' 170 square kilometres lying at about 1890 metres above sea level, is a lovely place to come for a weekend if you are staying in Nairobi as it is only an hour and a half's drive. The flying boats used to land here before Nairobi airport was built. It is a fresh water lake on the Rift Valley floor with no outlet, but is believed to be drained by underground seepage. The lake is dominated by the overshadowing of **Mount Longonot** (2,880 metres), a partially extinct volcano in the adjacent national park (52 square kilometres).

For a more interesting route to Naivasha, which need not add more than an hour to your overall journey time (if in your own car), Kiambu and Limuru could be used as transit points from Nairobi.

The drive to Kiambu is hilly, but smooth, through corridors of high trees and past the Windsor Golf and Country Club. The Kiambu-Limuru road provides a quite beautiful half hour drive through lush, fertile land full of rich tea and coffee plantations, and dotted with the elegant umbrella-like thorn trees.

Neither town itself is attractive, **Kiambu** is a one-way commuter town, lined with petrol stations and banks.

Limuru is a more lively market town, with many heavily laden folk bringing in their farm produce for local sale or transportation elsewhere. There is a good selection of shops, a dominant Barclays Bank building and a huge shoe factory. For refreshments in Limuru try the modern *Manga Corner Hotel* or else *Derby's Café*, 100 metres from Barclays.

Transport Road From Nairobi the A2 to Thika, which then has a sign-posted turning for Kiambu (20 minutes drive). Just before Kiambu town take a left turning for the Limuru Rd (sign-posted). Matatus go regularly to Kiambu and Limuru from the Tom Mboya end of River Rd. Matatus also go regularly between Kiambu and Limuru for the 1 hour drive from Limuru to Naivasha. The lower road to Naivasha is in a very poor state following the El Niño rains. If coming from Masai Mara it would be worth taking the longer route round and going back up to the top of the Rift first.

It is possible to come to spend a day at one of the Lakeside hotels without staying for the night – it may be free if you take meals or there may be a small charge. The lake itself is quite picturesque with a mountain in the background and floating islands of papyrus. The water level fluctuates as a result of underwater springs, although the actual mechanism is not clear. There are hippos in the lake which sometimes come out onto the shore at night, and there are many different types of water birds.

The lake is best explored by boat (a number of the hotels listed opposite rent vessels out for hire); or alternatively you could work your way around the shore by bicycle. There are a number of activities. A motorboat can be hired for US$20 per hour; a rowing boat for about US$7 an hour. There are fish eagle nests near the Yacht Club. The twin-hulled launch from the country club on its 'ornithological cruise' often tries to entice the birds with fish. The evening cruise at about 1800 is a good time to see them. Morning and evening birdwatching walks can be made to the **Crescent Island Game Sanctuary** via the Lake Naivasha Country Club, entrance costs US$8-10 plus boat across the lake.

Lake Naivasha

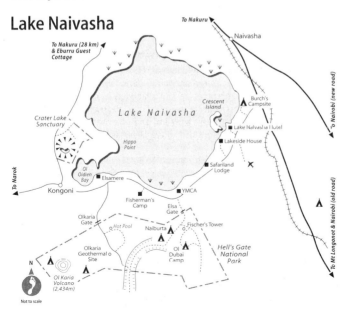

....

👉 **Loads of Fun**

At Limuru, just beyond Nairobi, Sam and Tom Morson from Wales bought 25 acres of forest and set up a saw-mill 'Romolo'. The rail line was nearby, and there was a big demand for sleepers and wood for fuel. The first task was levelling the site to set up the steam engine and lay out a yard. Workers and a foreman were recruited from Fort Hall (now Murang'a). The work progressed slowly and Sam Morson

went down to Nairobi and bought a dozen wheelbarrows which he sent up to Romolo on the train with instructions to start using them for shifting the soil. When he arrived back at Romolo a few days later, he saw that his instructions were being carried out to the letter. The barrows were being filled and then hoisted onto the heads of workers who staggered off to dump the soil in a gully.

....

On the way to Fisherman's Camp, the road goes through a major cut-flower growing area. Owned by Brooke Bond it is a major exporter and employs thousands of local people. The flowers are chilled and then airfreighted to Europe.

Just past Fisherman's Camp is **Elsamere**, the home of George and Joy Adamson. It is easy to miss – look out for the sign to Hell's Gate: it is a few hundred yards after it on the right-hand side. There is a small museum open between 1500-1800 daily (not as interesting as the display of her paintings in the National Museum) and the gardens are very pleasant with lots of birds flying amongst the trees. The entrance fee of US$3 includes a copious tea. A film shows the life (and death) of Joy. Beware though, it lasts well over one hour! You can stay here as well – book in advance as there's only capacity for about 15 guests. **B** *Elsamere Conservation Centre*, T0311-30079.

West of Lake Naivasha, one hour walk from Kongoni and approximately 17 kilometres past Fisherman's Camp is **Crater Lake**. Its jade-coloured waters are quite breathtaking. There is an animal sanctuary, but some of the tracks in this area are only manageable by foot or with four-wheel drive. Crater Lake has recently become a private game park, US$2 entry. You are allowed to walk around by yourself and it's easy to see the rare black and white Colombus monkey.

Sleeping **A** *Lake Naivasha Country Club*, T20013. The best lakeside option, with wonderful gardens which gently lead down to the lake, the rooms are quite good with all amenities including a swimming pool, this hotel welcomes children and has a small adventure playground for them, good food and does an excellent buffet lunch on Sunday (on lawns if good weather) which is very popular – eat as much as you like for around US$8, only drawback is it often gets crowded with tour groups from Nairobi. Run by Block Hotels PO Box 40075, Nairobi, T02-540780, F543810. **A** *Lakeside House*, T20908 or Nbi 567424. Package deal includes food and drink in the house of the Anglo-Kenyans who have lived here for many years, they also offer safaris at an extra cost, the prices are considerably less for residents. **A** *Safarilands Lodge*, T20241. Slightly further round the road beside the Lake, rambling colonial lodge of great charm, with log fires in the evening, splendid gardens, swimming pool, horse-riding, tennis and boat hire (US$30), excellent food with vegetables grown in the hotel gardens.

D *Eburru Guest Cottage*, North Lake Rd, Naivasha. Bookings through *Let's Go Travel*, Nairobi T340331/213033, F336890. Approximately 30 kilometres from Naivasha Town on Green Park development at an altitude of 7,000 feet up Eburru Hill. The cottage comprises 2 small buildings close to the main house, self-catering accommodates 4 adults, electricity. **D** *Fisherman's Camp*, T30276, bookings through *Let's Go Travel*, Caxton House, Standard St, PO Box 60342, Nairobi, T340331/213033, F336890/214713. Further along the lakeside road, this is set in beautiful surroundings, deeply shaded by huge trees, motor boat hire available, there are 2 types of accommodation, bandas are the most comfortable with reasonable facilities including showers and bedlinen, all the bandas have electricity. Cheaper is the spartan youth hostel of dormitory type bunks, now has a bar and restaurant, drinks and food available. **D** *Fish Eagle Inn*, T30306. Decent bandas available, as well as dormitories and camping facilities, not the best reputation for food and hospitality, but does have an excellent swimming

Beryl Markham II – Marriages and Royal Lovers

During the First World War, soldiers were billeted at Nakuru. One soldier recovering from dysentery was Jock Purves, a burly rugby-playing Scot serving with an Indian Army Regiment. He took a shine to Beryl (see box, page 141), and, in return for paying Beryl's school fees, Clutt agreed he could marry his daughter, an arrangement that Beryl went along with, albeit without immense enthusiasm. In 1919, at sixteen, Beryl married. After a honeymoon in India, Jock bought a farm next to Ndimu.

The marriage was a disaster. Jock liked a drink, and in his cups could become violent. Beryl found that Jock's drinking made him a woeful lover, and she saw no reason to abandon her practice of sleeping with anyone to whom she took a liking. Jock tried to make the best of an open secret. He installed a carved Lamu door at their farm and told visitors that the mass of brass studs had been accumulated by adding one each time Beryl took a new lover – among them Delamere's son Tom at home on vacation from school in England whom she welcomed to the adult world in the hayloft. Later she moved on to 'Boy' Long, Delamere's farm manager. More shocking for the settlers was the continuing liaison with Kibii, now entered into the ranks of adults and renamed Arap Ruta. Wearing a yellow warrior's shuka, colobus monkey skin anklets and a spear topped with black ostrich feather she was 'a piece of God'. Ruta went regularly with Beryl to take part in the frenzied and exciting Nandi ngomas (dances), coming home at dawn.

Now nineteen, Beryl began training horses, first for a neighbour, Ben Birkbeck, and then for Delamere at his nearby estate, Soysambu. Ruta worked for her. Denys Finch-Hatton, a tall charming and cultured white hunter and lover of Karen Blixen, began to engage Beryl's attention. Denys stayed at Karen's home Mbogani between safaris. As a friend of Karen Blixen, Beryl frequently stayed there as well.

Denys was more than a passing fancy and her interest did not end when he eventually became her lover. Learning that Denys was going to England in 1924, she followed, but Denys contrived to avoid her. Finding herself pregnant, Beryl thought it might be Denys' child – but she couldn't be sure and she had an abortion. She returned to Nairobi and lived for a while with Frank Greswolde-Williams, a rich and portly heavy drinker who supplied the fast set with cocaine.

A short engagement to wealthy Bobby Watson ended when Beryl sent his ring back, although she carried on seeing him. Despite still hankering after Denys, Beryl met and married Mansfield Markham, British, very well off, sophisticated, rather frail, and three years younger than his bride. Ruta accompanied them on their extravagant European honeymoon during which Beryl bought a stallion at Newmarket, and comprehensively failed to hit it off with the Markham family. They returned to Kenya and bought a farm at Elburgon.

Next year 1928, Kenyan society was in a frenzy of anticipation for the visit of Edward, Prince of Wales, and his younger brother Henry, Duke of Gloucester. Denys was engaged to organise their safaris. The Markhams took up residence for the duration at the Muthaiga Club. In next to no time Beryl had secured both Royal trophies.

When the Royal tour ended at the end of November, cut short by the illness of King George V, Beryl, although six months pregnant travelled to London where the Duke of Gloucester met her on the quay side and installed her in a suite at the Grosvenor Hotel, close to Buckingham Palace. When the Duke was out of town she would tryst with the Prince of Wales, usually at the Royal Aero Club in Piccadilly, and on one occasion in Buckingham Palace. Mansfield Markham came from Kenya for the birth of Gervaise Markham in February. As soon as was convenient, the child was looked after by a nanny and brought up at the Markham family home in Hurst Green, Sussex. When Mansfield's father, Sir Charles Markham learned of Beryl's protracted liaison with the Duke there were threats of a divorce action, citing Gloucester as co-respondent. In the event the Duke settled £15,000 on Beryl providing her with an income of £500 per annum.

pool (US$2 for visitors). Hippos come out of the water at night and graze within view a stones throw away from the *Fisherman's*. Recommended. Hot water available 24 hours, can get a bit crowded during holiday peak periods.

E *YMCA*, T30396. Cheapest place to stay, it is further along the road from *Fisherman's Camp*, unfortunately over time the *YMCA* has lost some of its land to farming, nowadays it is a good 15 minutes from the lakeside, though still set in beautiful gardens, it is sometimes possible to buy provisions, though these are not reliable.

Camping (**E**) at a site close to the water's edge at *Fisherman's camp* (need to bring provisions), next door at the *Fish Eagle Inn* or at *YMCA*. Several campsites have opened in Hells Gate National Park recently – see map for locations.

Eating   **2** *Geotherm Club*, half an hours walk from *Fisherman's Camp* towards Elsamere. Set in lovely gardens with pool at edge of lake, managed by *Belle Inn* so reliably good food. **2** *Yelogreen Bar and Restaurant*, 1st stop on South Lake Rd. Reasonable food but difficult to reach without own transport.

Transport   **Local Cycle hire**: there is cycle hire available (US$6 a day) at the entrance to *Fisherman's Camp*, greatly increasing your options for exploration, particularly to Hell's Gate National Park.

Hell's Gate is a major attraction (see National Parks section, page 260).

Mount Longonot
Colour map 4, grid B3

This can be climbed. Costs US$15 to do so (there are student reductions). You need to get to Longonot village along the old road, from there it is about six kilometres to the base of the mountain. You can be escorted up by Kenya Wildlife Service rangers and the fairly straightforward climb takes about an hour, but be prepared for the last section which is quite steep. A wander round the rim of the mountain takes a further two to three hours.

Mount Longonot is a dormant volcano standing at 2,886 metres. The mountain cone is made up of soft volcanic rock which has eroded into deep clefts and ridges. There are fine views over the Rift Valley on one side and into the enormous crater on the other.

The best places to stay are by the lakeside, there is nowhere in the immediate vicinity of Mount Longonot except the **A+** *Longonot Game Ranch* (book through Nairobi T332132). This caters for small groups of up to six people. If you want to see some wildlife on horseback, this would be a good option.

Travelling northwest along Naivasha Road towards Gilgil shortly after a signpost to *'Ilkek'* on your right there is a rough dirt road, which leads to *Ol'Morogi Ranch*, PO Box 791, Naivasha, T0311-21420. *Millaroutie Cottage*, set in its own garden, offers a peaceful setting, good fishing, easy access to Aberdare, Nakuru and Hell's Gate National Park. Tariff US$60, sleeps four.

Lake Elmenteita
Colour map 4, grid B3

This is a shallow soda lake, similar to Lake Nakuru though it does not attract the enormous numbers of flamingos. As it is not a national park, you can walk around it and you don't have to pay.

Now with Lake Nakuru's more seasonal status, Lake Elmenteita could be a more reliable source of flamingoes. It is between Naivasha and Nakuru, just off the main road, part of the Delamere Estate's Soysambu land. A luxury tented camp has recently opened here, but is expensive and somewhat impersonal. There are few facilities at the Lake or in Elmenteita town, but it is an easy day trip from Nakuru with direct matatus (one hour) or 30 minutes from Gilgil, which is on the Nairobi-Naivasha Road.

Gilgil has a bank, which doesn't change travellers' cheques and a Post Office. Otherwise it is best used as a transit point for matatus in all directions.

Kariandusi is a prehistoric site to the right of the Naivasha/Nakuru road discovered by Dr L Leakey in 1928 and excavated from 1929 to 1947. There is a small museum housing obsidian or black volcanic glass knives, Stone Age hand axes and a molar of the straight tusked elephant, a variety which roamed in Northern Europe before extinction. The nearby diatomite mine offers a fascinating visit.

An adventurous way back to Nairobi from Naivasha, which necessitates a very early start, and probably a night in Thika, would be to walk (or cycle) and hitch along the rough road between Njabini and Gatakaini, along the southern edges of the Aberdare mountain range. It is wild, noisy with bird and animal sounds (but safe) forest. Matatus leave early (0600) for the rural outpost of North Kinangop and the journey has dramatic views back to the lake and beyond. You could also go directly from Naivasha to Njadini (if time allows), or else it is another 17 kilometres from North Kingangop.

Njabini
(South Kinangop)

Njabini (South Kinangop) is a pleasant and friendly little agricultural community, framed by the Aberdares, existing in two parts either side of a small river. The Caltex and the recommended Japa Café are early sightings and then down and around the road is the town proper, with Post Office, bank and the excellent *Gimra Rest Lodge*.

It is 30 kilometres to paved road and *matatus* at Gatakaini. There are camping and hitching possibilities along the route, but bear in mind that after about 1500 it is difficult to hitch back.

Nakuru

Nakuru is the next major town along from Naivasha. It is Kenya's fourth largest town in the centre of some of the country's best farming land. It is a nice agricultural town with shops mostly selling farming equipment and supplies. The town itself came into existence in 1900 when the building of the railway opened up access to the surrounding lush countryside attracting hundreds of white settlers to the area. Lord Delamere, one of the most famous figures in colonial times, collected around 600 square kilometres of land here and developed wheat and dairy farming.

0° 23' S, 36° 5' E
Phone code: 037
Colour map 4, grid A3

An interesting structure is the **Eros Cinema** an example of functional post-war architecture, slender columns and glass walls. **Breaker's Music Centre** on the corner of Kenyatta and Club Road has an unusual cupola room on the corner. **Nyanger Park** is neat and central with a war memorial. **Nakuru Station** is another fine example of post-war architecture. The old station was opposite the Midland Hotel. The new station was built in 1957. A mural dominates the booking hall. The two artists, M Ginsburg and R McLellan-Sim depict settlers looking out over the Rift Valley showing the Masai, cattle and rolling wheatfields. A notable Hollywood film-star is said to have been the model for the male settler – he subsequently had a successful career in politics. In the restaurant there are photos of the railway. The station itself has a slender clock-tower which keeps still time, slim columns and delicate iron screens.

The other notable building is the **Rift Valley Sports Club**, PO Box 1, Nakuru, T212086/212085. This was formerly the Nakuru Club, and was first built in 1907, was burnt down in 1924 and then restored. A patio restaurant looks out over the cricket pitch. The cricket pavilion has photos of past teams and the ground prettily surrounded by jacarandas and mango trees. In the *Mens Bar* (ladies not allowed) there are sporting prints and etchings including one of the Sussex versus Kent match at Brighton in 1890 attended by Prince Albert. Tennis, squash, a small swimming pool, cricket nets on Tuesday and Thursday. It is possible to stay here – there are a variety of rooms, some with bathrooms. Non-members need to pay a Temporary Membership Fee, but even so it is excellent value, and the best place to stay in Nakuru.

Sights   **Menengai Crater** is on the northern side of Nakuru. Despite the fact that this extinct volcano is 2,490 metres high, it is not easy to see from the town itself. To get there you can walk (it takes a couple of hours but is pleasant enough). If walking leave from the Crater Climb Road, then Forest Road. However recent reports of robberies makes this a less safe option, although recent travellers have reported improved security in the area. Alternatively motor along Menengai Drive out through the suburbs. It is fairly well signposted. There is no public transport from the town to the Menengai Crater, and as few people visit it there is scant hope of hitching a lift. There are a number of kiosks en route to the top where you can get a drink and basic local foods. The views, as one ascends, are excellent over Lake Nakuru, although not visible from the top. No refreshments at the summit.

The views over Lake Nakuru are excellent (although the lake dried up completely in Spring 1994 but has now refilled) as are the views towards Lake Bogoria over the other side. The crater itself is enormous, about 12 kilometres across and 500 metres deep. Traditionally this was Masai land, and the site of some famous clan wars.

Hyrax Hill Prehistoric Site is a small settlement, first investigated by the Leakeys in the 1920s and work has been going on there, periodically, ever since. The excavations have found evidence of settlements from 3,000 years ago, and there are signs of habitation here up until about 300 years ago.

The northeast village has some enclosures where the digging was carried out though only one is not overgrown. It dates back about 400 years and the finds have been pieced together and are exhibited in the museum. There is no evidence of human dwellings suggesting this may have been used for livestock but not humans, though the evidence is not conclusive.

Up at the top of Hyrax Hill are the remains of the stone-walled fort and on the other side of the hill it is possible to see the position of two huts in a settlement which have been dated back to the Iron Age. A series of burial pits with 19 skeletons were found, most of them decapitated, dating back to the same time. The remains are all in a heap and all appear to be young men suggesting they were buried in a hurry – possibly the remains of the enemy after a battle.

On the path back to the museum, a bau board (a game using pebbles or beads) has been carved into the rock. One very curious find was six Indian coins dating back 500 years – no-one knows how they got here.

Underneath the Iron Age site, a neolithic site was found and the neolithic burial mound has been fenced off as a display, the stone slab which sealed the mound having been removed. The neolithic burial site has produced some very interesting things including nine female skeletons. Unlike the male remains, the females have been buried with grave goods including dishes, pestles and mortars. No-one can be sure why the women were buried with grave goods and not the men, but it could indicate that women were far more politically powerful in former times. Oral history in the region suggests this may have been the case. A further mystery is why the Iron Age burial site is directly on top of the neolithic one.

The site is open each day between 0930 and 1800 and there is a small entrance fee. It is just off the Nairobi road so it is easy to get to. Just take a matatu heading for Gilgil and ask them to drop you at the turning for Hyrax Hill. It is about one kilometre from here to the museum. You can camp here if you wish, though there are no facilities except those for the museum staff.

Lake Bogoria is a shallow soda lake 60 kilometres north of the Menengai Crater *Colour map 4, grid A3* (see National Parks, page 261). It is easy to get to along the B4 sealed road. The road is pleasant enough, passing sisal plantations as it goes deeper into the Valley. A sign marks the equator and you can be treated to a demonstration. 10 metres to the north of the line and water turns clockwise draining from a bowl; 10 metres to the south and it turns anti-clockwise; on the line it goes straight down.

It is a peaceful area with some wildlife, though most have migrated over recent years to the more fertile regions of Lake Nakuru. However as Lake Nakuru almost dried up in 1994, the lake was home to many thousands of flamingos. About three-quarters of the way down the lake there are a number of hot springs and geysers. This is a good place to watch the flamingos feed in the very hot water. But take care, you can get badly burnt. Along the eastern end of the lake you can see the northernmost part of the Aberdares. As this is a national park, there is an entrance fee of US$17 plus US$1.5 per vehicle and US$3.50 per person for camping. You can camp here by the northern entrance gate at a site with a shop selling basic foods, or there is a choice of two sites at the southern shore of the lake, though with no shop. Be prepared, it can get very hot at night.

Lake Baringo If you continue driving north past Lake Bogoria, you will come to *Colour map 4, grid A2* this peaceful and beautiful deeper fresh-water lake. There are said to be 450 species of birds at Lake Baringo (see National Parks, page 261). It is easy to get to from Nakuru. Buses leave twice daily to Kampi ya Samaki (*Fisherman's Camp*) on the lake and matatus go to the small town of Marigat. From either place you will be able to get a local matatu to the lake itself. The journey only takes a couple of hours on good roads. *Boat trips*, Boats take eight people. Allow for a two hour tour to see the lake, islands, crocodiles, hippos and birds. Cost: US$18 per hour. **A** *Lake Baringo Club*, well sited for viewing the birds and hippo. Run by Block Hotels, PO Box 40075, Nairobi, T02-540780, F543810. There is excellent accommodation at **D** *Mrs Roberts Campsite*, PO Box 1051, Nakuru, T3 (Kampi Ya Samaki). Camping is US$4 per person, bandas are US$25 for two persons. There is a general store for provisions and a bookshop and several cheap guesthouses. Boat hire is available, a thoroughly recommended place. Watch out for hippos in this area – although they seem docile they can be dangerous if startled by lights or noises, so don't approach them. There are many malaria bearing mosquitoes at the lake – use plenty of repellant.

Kenya

Nakuru

■ **Sleeping**	6 Midland	● **Eating**
1 Amigos &	7 Mukoh	1 Café Lemon Tart
Papa Rego's Café	8 Mt Sinai	2 Kabeer
2 Carnation	9 Seasons	3 Oyster Shell
3 Crater View	10 Shik Parkview	4 Red Sea
4 Gituamba Lodge	11 Shiriksho	5 Tipsy & Nakuru
5 Glory Guesthouse	12 Waterbuck	Sweetmart

N

Not to scale

Sleeping **A** *Lake Nakuru Lodge*, PO Box 561, Nakuru, T85446. Medium-sized lodge situated in the National Park near the Ndarit gate, with pleasant gardens and pool overlooking the park, sister lodges at Lake Elementaita and Lake Naivasha as well as *Sundowner Lodge* can be booked through the booking office in Nairobi (PO Box 70559, T224998, F230962). **B** *Kunste*, T212140, about 2 kilometres out on the Nairobi Rd. Newly opened. **B** *Midland*, on Kamati Rd, T43954. Long established hotel which used to be the most popular place in town for the more upmarket travellers, though it has been supplanted by the *Waterbuck* of recent years, the rooms have en suite bathrooms and breakfast is included in the price. **B** *Stem*, about 8 kilometres outside the town itself, close to Nakuru National Park, T85391. **C** *Rift Valley Sports Club*, PO Box 1, T212086/5, Club Rd, very central. You need to become a temporary member, best value in Nakuru. **C** *Waterbuck*, Government Ave, T214163/215622. Modern hotel offering some of the best facilities in town including a huge and reasonably priced buffet style lunch and an excellent breakfast.

D *Carnation*, Mosque Rd, T43522. Large hotel with own restaurant offering very good value in the centre of town. **D** *Mau View Lodge*, good cheap hotel, parking in an enclosed courtyard, on Oginga Odinga Ave, 1 kilometre out of town, well served by matatus, closure of the courtyard gates is noisy, own bar, simple meals. **D** *Mt Sinai Hotel*, Gusii Rd, PO Box 28238, T211779. Large building, very clean in fairly modern rooms, all s/c, restaurant. **D** *Mukoh*, corner of Mosque and Gusii Rd. Popular place offering clean, quiet and comfortable accommodation, it has some rooms with baths, breakfast is a bit overpriced. **D** *Seasons*, Government Ave, T45218. In part of a converted house, though the best rooms are the additional ones at the back, large s/c cosy rooms, quiet place except for disco night (Friday), excellent daily buffet lunch. **E** *Amigos*, above *Papa Rego's Café*. Basic. **E** *Carnation Hotel*, PO Box 1620, T43522, Mosque Rd. Good basic hotel. **E** *Crater View Hotel*, Mburu Gichua Rd, opposite the market. Cheap, clean s/c rooms, hot water. **E** *Gituamba Lodge*, PO Box 586, T4750. Clean, cheap, not s/c, hot water with breakfast, restaurant. **E** *Glory*, Mosque Rd. Small but perfectly acceptable for the token price, laundry facilities, no hot water but the best views in town from the open 6th floor roof, towards the lake and environs.

Eating **3** *Kabeer Restaurant*, on a par with the *Oyster Shell*, offers a choice of Indian or Chinese food, seafood or grills, open daily until 2200. **3** *Oyster Shell Restaurant*, T40946, Kenyatta Ave. Considered to be the best restaurant in town with an extensive menu for breakfast, lunch and dinner.

2 *Café Lemon Tart*, Moi Rd. Excellent breakfasts and light snacks. **2** *Mukoh*, best breakfast in town and is also good for snacks. **2** *Nakuru Sweet Mart*, vegetarian Indian food. **2** *Tipsy Restaurant*, Gusii Rd. Popular with local people and is good value, they have western dishes as well as good curries and tilapia (fish). **1** *Red Sea Restaurant*, Mosque Rd. Cannot miss it with its red painted decor, very good value, good biriyani, large portions, delicious filling yoghurt drinks. **1** *Mt Sinai*, ground floor restaurant has very tasty samosas and kebabs. *Waterbuck*, Kenyatta Ave. Has an outside restaurant with a barbecue bar at the back. *The Nakuru Coffeehouse*, Kenyatta Ave. Serves very good coffee. 2 kilometress outside Nakura on the road to Nairobi on the left hand side there is a shopping centre with good snacks for a short stop. 'Take a German one' sells grilled German sausages. Recommended.

Entertainment **Cinemas** There are 2 cinemas in Nakuru both on GK Kamau Highway, screenings are twice a night, usually. The better of the 2 is *Eros*. **Discos** *Illusions*, Kenyatta Ave. *Pivot* (weekends). *Oyster Shell Nightclub*, over the restaurant. MTV all day, young persons club with good sound and light systems. *Coco Savannah*, Club Rd, PO Box 664, T211426. Large, lively, US$2.

Shopping There is a branch of the food chain *Uchumi* on Kenyatta Lane which is open 7 days a week. There is also a supermarket at the *Sita Shopping Centre* to the east of the town centre.

Transport **Train** Please see page 72 for details of train services, timetables and fares.

Road There are regular matatus, buses and Peugeot taxis to Nakuru from Nairobi (3 hours), Nyahururu, Naivasha (1½ hours) and all points west including Kisumu (4½ hours), Eldoret (4 hours) and Busia (8 hours). The main bus station is on the eastern edge of town.

Banks *Barclays* and *Standard Chartered* on Kenyatta Ave. **Hospitals & medical services** Chemist: **Directory** *Fades*, Kenyatta Lane, T212627. **Tour companies & travel agents** It can be cheaper to book your safari in Nairobi. *Blackbird Tours*, T45383, at the *Carnation Hotel*. Very helpful and can help you with visits to nearby national parks and other safaris. *Crater Travel*, T45409, just off Kenyatta Ave. Can arrange air tickets. *Leisure Activity Safaris* (cycling), PO Box 7229, Nakuru, T/F37-210325. *Taylors Travel*, PO Box 527, Kenyatta Ave, near Standard Bank.

From Nakura southwards, there are regular matatus to **Njoro** (30 minutes) and **Mau Narok** (four hours). Driving to Mau Narok you pass through Njoro, which lies on a huge dry plain. It contains a Post Office, Police Station and basic shops. Onwards the land soon becomes hilly, cool and fertile, with potatoes, carrots and onions grown in abdundance. Mau Narok is a small village at the end of the road. There are no matatus but it is easy to walk to Elementeita and its lake from here, taking about two hours.

Rongai

Small, pretty village about 25 kilometres west of the Nakuru in the valley of the *Colour map 4, grid A2* Rongai River, which rises in the Elburgon Hills. Initially it was inhabited by the Tugen and Njembs tribes, before they were driven out by the Masai. However, the Masai never settled, and there is no record of of their ever constructing *manyatta* (Masai villages) in the valley.

The land was part of the great tract leased to Lord Delamere, who then rented it out to settlers. In the colonial period Rongai grew to prominence as a maize growing area. The crop was first introduced by the Portuguese, but it did not do well. Then an American variety was used to develop a hybrid known as Kenya White, which flourished. The land was tilled by teams of oxen, maize was being exported by 1910, and by 1917 there were 7,000 acres under maize around Rongai.

The railway arrived in 1926 as part of the line onward from Nairobi to Uganda. A branch line was built from Rongai northeast to Solai, now disused, althought you can still see the tracks. The branch went entirely through settler country, and, as there was no 'native land' along the route, it was much criticised as an example of the colonial adminstration favouring the interests of the settlers over those of the Africans.

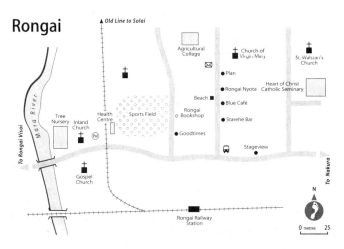

Rongai

A feature of Rongai is the number of churches. The **Africa Inland Church** has arched windows in pairs, glazed in yellow, green and orange, with sunrise airbricks above each pair. The walls are of grey volcanic stone, and it has a tin roof.

The **Catholic Church of St Mary** is a modern, neat, functional structure of grey stone with timber panelling. The **Heart of Christ Catholic Seminary** (PO Box 238, Rongai) is fairly new, dating from 1986, but is cloistered and quiet, with well-tended flower beds, run by Italian Fathers.

The prettiest, however, and a testament to the determination of the settlers to reproduce rural England on the Equator, is **St Walstan's Church**, built in 1960. It is an exact replica of an early English country church at Bawburgh, six kilometres east of Norwich in the UK, which dates from 1016. St Walstan is known as the 'Layman's Saint'. He came from a wealthy land-owning family, was fond of farm animals, and he insisted on toiling in the fields with the farm labourers. He collapsed and died while working one day, and on the spot a spring bubbled up.

The church building has a square tower with battlements, pointed windows, and a shingle (wooden tile) roof. In the vestibule is a piece of flint from the church in Bawburgh. Inside there is a tiny gallery with steps up to it cut into the wall. The Saints are depicted in orange, yellow and blue stained glass windows. The roof is is supported by timber beams and there is a small bell, about 30 centimetres across. The approach to the church is bordered by jacarandas which carpet the path with fallen blue blossoms when the trees are in flower.

Another rather charming building is the **Rongai Railway Station**. It has its name picked out in white cement on the ground. The platform has street lamps, glass panelled, lit by oil. The flower beds have frangipani and variegated sisal plants. The rods and wires of the signalling system and the points run over the ground. The station is of wooden weatherboarding in the cream and brick-red livery of Kenya Railways with a small verandah in front. Inside is the original control gear, now about seventy years old, with big brass keys for regulation of the traffic on the single line, and wicker hoops and pouches for collecting mail from non-stopping trains. The original telegraph system is still in place, now with the addition of some antique black bakelite telephones.

Sleeping As Rongai is only an hour from Nakuru, there is probably no need to stay. There is really only the **E** *Beach Hotel* but it is very simple. If you wished to stay for a while, it would be possible to stay at the **E** *Heart of Christ Catholic Seminary*.

Eating There are several eating places (*hotelis*) of which the **1** *Blue Café* is the best.

Transport **Road** 4 or 5 matatus leave each day, leaving when full. When departing Rongai it is best to take the first matatu leaving, as it is easy to pick up a matatu going in the direction you want when you reach the Nakuru-Eldoret road. Fare to Nakuru about US$0.50. **Train** In principle it should be possible to come by train from Nakuru – you will need to ask at one of the stations.

Northwards from Nakuru to Mogotio and Marigat

Buses leave up to midday and matatus all day from Barungo Ave to **Mogotio** (one hour) and **Marigat** (two hours). Mogotio is a very small place, of a few shops and local eateries at the junction to **Lake Bogoria** (see page 135). Lake Bogoria may also now be a good place to see the flamingoes that have migrated from Lake Nakuru.

Half an hour from Marigat you will start noticing large sawn off tree trunks lying horizontally in the higher branches of many of the trees. This odd sight, combined with the amazing effort to get these branches up there, is one of honey cultivation –

the trunks are hollowed out to the bee's taste. Delicious Asilah honey selling at the roadside is the result of these labours.

A friendly one street town, which is often extremely hot. Contains a few fruit and vegetable stalls and small general stores.

Marigat
Colour map 4, grid A2

Sleeping E *Marigat Inn*. Good value with a variety of rooms, all clean comfortable and with mosquito nets, well shaded surroundings. E *Salaam Lodge*. Fenced off compound behind the *Mtega Bar*. Friendly but tough looking hostess, very clean rooms with separate drop toilet and shower cubicle. Beware the rooms can get very hot.

Marigat

N

Not to scale

To the Lake & Loruk

Mtega Bar   Perkerra   Pol

Salaam Lodge

Marigat Inn

To Nakwell & Kabernet

Eating 1 *Kamco*, cheap good local food. **1** *Marigat Inn*, reasonable and cheap food. **1** *Mtega Bar*, has amiable staff, warm beer and soft drinks. **1** *Perkirra Hotel*, decent local food.

Transport Buses to Nakuru leave at around 0800 every morning. Matatus south to Nakuru, north to Loruk and west to Kabernet leave earlier in the morning.

Lake Baringo (see page 135) is about 20 kilometres further north from Marigat.

Loruk is of little interest, 25 kilometres east from Marigat past Lake Baringo. It is the last settlement before driving east then north to Maralal, a route popular among the Safari companies. Otherwise the road continues northwest to **Tot** but there is very little traffic. To get to Tot, you have to hitch or take infrequent matatu but because there is so little traffic, it is likely to involve a long wait, and it is extremely hot.

Colour map 4, grid A2

Northern Rift Valley

Much of the northern part of the Rift Valley is unexplored by travellers and facilities are few and far between. The landscape is quite different from the central and western parts of the Rift. It is hot and arid, and only sparsely inhabited, but it has a stark beauty and is the home of the spectacular **Cherangani Hills**.

Once past the lakes of Bogoria and Baringo which can easily be reached from Nakuru within a few hours, you are heading up into the less frequented regions of Kabarnet. **Kabarnet** is set on the Tugen Hills which are virtually impenetrable, and looks down into the **Kerio Valley**. The town itself is very unimposing despite the fact it is the capital of Baringo district.

Marigat to Kabernet is a torturously slow drive. The extremely steep climb and overloaded matatus make for a trotting pace in first gear. The advantage though is of lingering views back over the Rift Valley and the lakes below.

Kabernet

Isolated *shambas* (small farms) of the Kalenjin are dotted around the mountainous countryside. Kabernet is a quiet town, and the high altitude means it is cool, especially noticeable after the heat of Marigat. It has an Alpine summer feel and there are great views northwards over the Kerio Valley.

There is a good supermarket in the same building as the Sinkoro restaurant. It is a useful place to shop for food if you intend to go camping later in the Hills, and there are a few hotels which offer reasonable accommodation in the area including: **C** *Kabarnet*, T03282035. Has a pool, a fine modern hotel, five minutes walk from Post Office, set in well tended gardens, perched on top of a hill for fine views of the

Kenya

valley, it has a lovely cool pool (non-residents US$2), good set lunch US$6, and dinner US$8. **D** *Hotel Sinkoro*, PO Box 256, T22245. Located centrally, good value hotel, all rooms s/c with hot water and breakfast included. **E** *View Point Hotel*, excellent value, with a variety of good rooms. **Eating** *Hotel Sinkoro*, the restaurant here is really very good, for both snacks and meals regardless of budget. *Kabernet Hotel*, good food, at a price. **Transport Road** There are regular matatus to Eldoret, Nakuru and Marigat. Buses to Eldoret and Nakuru leave earlier in the morning. The journey to Eldoret, especially down to the valley floor is very beautiful. Journey times: two hours to Nakuru and three hours to Eldoret.

The Kerio Valley is home to many Kalenjin herders and their livestock, but little else. The unspoilt beauty and quiet of the place is hardly disturbed by vehicles, though this does make it hard to explore except by hiking. It is best to visit in June, July, August after the long rains when the land is at its greenest and the temperatures are comfortable.

The largest town in the valley is **Kimwarer,** a company town developed for the fluorspar mine at the head of the Kerio River. Fluorspar, used in the manufacture of steel, aluminium and cement, is an important industry here and the company which extracts it is evident everywhere with its own housing, schools, playgrounds and clinics.

Elgeyo Escarpment presents one of the most astonishing panoramic views in the Rift Valley. About 1,000 metres below the sheer cliff face south of the village of **Tot**, stretches the hazy scrublands extending as far as the eye can see to Turkana and Pokot. This region is not easy to access, nothing short of a four-wheel drive and calm nerves are needed to drive up the escarpment road. An easier approach is to walk from Tot (about 25 kilometres). If you intend to stay in the area, Tot offers a delightful peaceful atmosphere with small local hotels.

The Elgeyo Escarpment has been inhabited for centuries. The Marakwet who live here arrived around 1,000 years ago and claim they took over existing irrigation systems which zigzag all over the escarpment from the Cherangani Hills over 40 kilometres away. The waterways make this area a lush land of agriculture with back-to-back *shambas* (small farms) everywhere.

The Cherangani Hills These wild, thickly forested hills are miles away from the popular tourist circuit with fine mountain landscapes. The Cherangani range rises to 3,500 metres at the northern end of the Elgeyo Marakwet Escarpment and is Kenya's only range of fold mountains. The range offers some of the best walking in Kenya in a pleasant climate, the northern end being particularly attractive. But make sure you are equipped with a decent map.

You should be able to reach the Hills easily enough by public transport as there are a number of matatus running between Cheptongei and Chesoi. There are a

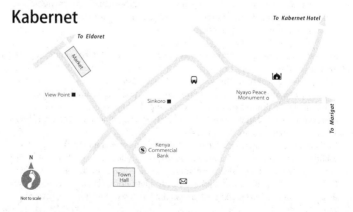

Kabernet

To Kabernet Hotel

To Eldoret

Market

View Point ■

Sinkoro ■

Nyayo Peace Monument ○

To Marigat

Kenya Commercial Bank ⑤

N

Town Hall

Not to scale

Beryl Markham I – Lakwet

Celebrated beauty, champion horse-trainer, record-breaking aviator, author, and with two members of the British Royal Family counted among her many lovers Beryl Markham was a glorious free spirit. Her style was formed by a unique childhood which embraced both traditional African and European ways of life.

Beryl was born at Ashwell in Leicestershire in 1902. Her older brother was born two years earlier. Her father, Charles Clutterbuck had been a lieutenant in the King's own Scottish Borders, but had fallen out with his regiment (he was 'removed from the service for absence without leave'), and he had taken up farming. Beryl's mother, the strikingly handsome Clara Alexander, was the daughter of an Indian Civil Servant with a passion for fox-hunting and steeple-chasing. She married Charles in 1898. When Beryl was two, the Clutterbucks underwent an estrangement, and Clara decamped for a while to run a tea-room in Melton Mowbury. The family sold up and sailed for East Africa in 1904.

Disembarking at Mombasa, the Clutterbucks took the train for Nairobi, put up at Woods Hotel, and after getting the lie of the land, Charles took a job as dairy manager for Lord Delamere at Equator Ranch near Njoro. Home was a rondavel, a mud hut with a thatched roof, and sacking covering the windows.

Beryl's brother, Dickie, was a sickly child and Clara had frequent visits to Nairobi. With her father, 'Clutt', working at the dairy, Beryl was left with local Nandi house servants and farm workers and their children with whom she formed an enduring bond, going barefoot, eating with her hand and wearing a shulen, an African shirt. Clutt then bought the nearby 500,000 acre Ndimu ('Lemon') Farm, and began establishing a flour mill and a timber mill and taking up horse breeding.

But Clara was ill-suited for pioneer life. She met Henry Kirkpatrick, a Major in the King's African Rifles and she left taking Beryl's older brother, Dickie, to meet up with Kirkpatrick in England. Clutt employed Emma Orchardson, herself separated with a young son, Arthur, as housekeeper, and they began living together in one of the rondavels. Arthur occupied a second rondavel and Beryl the third.

Beryl did not get on with Emma and resisted efforts to get her to wear shoes and dress in European clothes. Swahili was Beryl's first language. Despite being called Lakwet (very little girl), her situation was unique – as a European it was acceptable for her to play, wrestle and hunt with the Nandi boys. One of these African children, Kibii, became a favourite companion.

In the evenings there were folk tales from the Nandi grandmothers round the fire. Beryl wore a cowrie shell, the Nandi symbol of a vagina, on a leather thong as a necklace to ward off evil spirits. The arrangements at Ndimu farm, to say the least, drew disapproving comments from other settlers.

A strict governess, Miss Le May, was engaged when Beryl was seven. The rudiments of an education were administered along with liberal use of a ruler over the knuckles and whippings with a kiboko (a rhino hide whip), all of which Beryl accepted in the Nandi tradition of enduring pain without a murmur – in later life she would savour the excitement of ecstasy mingled with pain.

Beryl had her own pony, Wee Magregor, and greatly enjoyed helping her father with the work of the horses. She became particularly attached to Camciscan, a huge, fierce stallion.

At nine Beryl was sent to board at Nairobi European School, but she ran away after less than a year, returning to Njoro, the stables and her Kipsigis companions.

Nandi girls begin experimenting with boys around the age of ten or so. There are games in which the boys throw their clubs (nungu) in a pile and the girls choose one to spend the night with the owner. In this carefree atmosphere Kibii and Beryl became lovers.

There was another year of boarding at Mrs Seecombe's school when she was fourteen. By now Beryl was quite striking with long blonde hair, sky-blue eyes and a distinctive light-footed walk with an elegant sway of the hips and shoulders. The stage was now set for her to turn heads and break hearts across Africa and the world.

Continued in box, page 131

Kenya

> **St Andrew's School, Turi**
>
> The school has an interesting history. It was founded in 1932 and was, and still is, popular for children of farmers, missionaries, and aid workers of all nationalities from all over East Africa. It was home to Italian prisoners of war during the Second World War and their presence is still felt, for while they were there, they decorated many of the walls with paintings. The dining room, dormitories, bathrooms and corridors are covered in pictures of children's stories and fairytales such as Winnie the Pooh, the Pied Piper, and other such tales.

number of suitable campsites where you can stay. The town of **Kapenguira** is in these hills, the place where the colonial government held the trial of Jomo Kenyatta during the 1950s when he was convicted of being involved in Mau Mau activities.

Western Rift

The main road west (A104) taking you towards Kisumu is in good condition and is therefore quite fast. The more scenic route is the C56 which passes through the towns of Njoro, Elburgon and Molo over the Mau Escarpment, before joining the Kisumu Road. Few tourists travel this route mainly because there is little to visit, but the scenery is lovely, and quite varied.

The first town is **Njoro** by the Mau Escarpment about five kilometres west of Nakuru. It is home to **Egerton University** (about five kilometres out of town). The main street is an unpaved road lined with jacaranda and hotels serving basic Kenyan fare. You will find a post office, bank and petrol station here if you need them.

The road goes up into conifer country from here reaching the town of **Elburgon**. Elburgon is bigger than Njoro, and is quite a prosperous town owing its wealth to the logging industry. Evidence of logging is everywhere with most buildings being constructed of wood. The railway stops here between Nakuru and Kisumu. Again you will find a post office and bank in town as well as a number of small hotels offering extremely cheap accommodation. There is also a very good new hotel here called **C** *Eel*, T0363-3127. Set in a lovely garden. Apparently plans are underway to develop an adventure playground and disco here. If you are staying in the area it is worth knowing about the teacher's club at **St Andrew's School**, **Turi** which each Thursday night is open for meals and a drink. It is also sometimes open at weekends.

Just west of Elburgon, you will pass through the **Mau Forest**. This dense forest of huge gum trees has yet to be exploited for tourism, particularly by the Okiek people (hunter-gatherers) who have lived here for generations. The road emerges from the forest among fields of crops, primarily pyrethrum and cereals which border the town of **Molo**. There is a post office and bank along the main street, and plenty of places to stay including **D** *Molo Highlands Inn*, T0363-21036. Lovely wooden rooms with a log fire and a good restaurant. There is also the **D** *Green Garden Lodge* which is a nice enough place to stay, but very quiet. Just out of town heading south you will find **A** *Juani Farm*, a cosy establishment run by two white Kenyan farmers, with English-style gardens and food. Book through Kesana Ltd, Nairobi T749062.

West of Molo, between **Londiani** (a small town near the junction of the C56 with the B1 – the main road going into Kisumu) and **Kipkelion** is the **Cistercian Monastery**. This monastery, stuck in the middle of nowhere in the Kenyan countryside, is the only Cistercian monastery in Africa. It is a wonderful place to stay if you need a break from the outside world – donations for board and lodging are gratefully received. The monastery was founded in 1956 originally as a Trappist monastery but changed to being Cistercian. The monks still only talk when necessary, but are happy to receive guests and have rooms and dining facilities available. The monastery provides an important service for the local community through its hospital (the only one in the area) and its school. If you do wish to stay, you should write to them first to: Our Lady of Victoria, PO Box 40, Kipkelion. There is no phone to disturb the serenity.

The monastery is about 11 kilometres from **Baisheli** to the north of Londiani. If approaching from Kipkelion, you need to head off the main highway up the C35 unsurfaced road. Few matatus or cars go along this route, but you may be lucky. It is fairly well signposted, so you are unlikely to get lost.

Kenya

Nairobi

Western Kenya

Western Kenya is the most fertile and the most populous part of the country, teeming with market towns and busy fishing villages. For some reason it is not that popular with the big tour operators which is all to the benefit of the adventurous. In fact, conditions for independent budget travellers are perfect; over half the population of the whole country lives here so public transport is excellent (though slightly unpredictable) and the road surfaces tend to be above average; there are numerous cheap hotels and restaurants; people are generally helpful and friendly, not having become weary of tourists, and there is plenty to see and do. Facilities for tourists wanting slightly more upmarket services are less well catered for, their best bet being to stay in one of the better hotels in Kisumu and hire a car to explore other parts of the region.

There are a number of National Parks in this region. The Kakamega Forest is the only tract of equatorial rainforest in Kenya with many animals found nowhere else in the country; the Saiwa Swamp is near Kitale and worth a visit to see the rare sitatunga deer; Mount Elgon with good climbing accessed from Kitale; Ruma National Park in South Nyanza; and the northeastern section of Lake Victoria.

Lake region

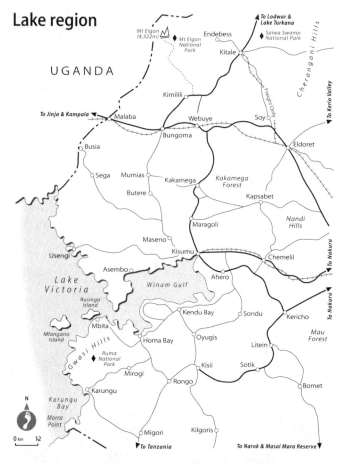

The climate is far warmer to the south, round Lake Victoria. This is traditionally Luoland and is quite a poor part of the country. The pace of life is slow and extremely friendly. The northern part of Western Kenya is lush and green and fertile, the climate is more temperate and there are more Europeans around.

Kisumu

Kisumu, on the shore of Lake Victoria, is the principal town in Western Kenya and the third largest in the country. It is a very pleasant place with a slow, gentle pace of life and a relaxed ambience, with the whole town coming to a standstill on Sunday. The sleepy atmosphere is as much due to lack of economic opportunities experienced here as to the extremely hot dry weather, which makes doing almost anything in the middle of the day quite hard work.

0° 35′, 34° 45′ E
Phone code: 035
Colour map 4, grid A1

Kenya

The town has been by- passed by post- independence development, and the signs are all too visible. Warehouses by the docks remain empty and the port does not have the bustling atmosphere you would expect in such an important town. Many of the wealthier people have moved out of Kisumu hence the number of large houses lying empty or rundown.

Kisumu developed during the colonial era into the principal port in the region. The railway line reached Lake Victoria in 1902 opening up trade opportunities. By the 1930s it had become the hub of administrative and military activities on the Lake. Kisumu was a difficult place at this time, bilharzia was endemic, malaria and sleeping sickness were common and the climate was sweltering. However, the area attracted investment from many different quarters, including Asians ending their contracts to work on the railway.

History

The Luo felt they were neglected immediately after independence, and that political life was dominated by Kikuyu who centred development on Central province. The breakdown of trade between Kenya, Uganda and Tanzania and the collapse of the East African Community in 1977 badly affected Kisumu and there has been no compensating expansion of manufacturing in the area.

The murder of Robert Ouko, a Luo, in 1990 led to riots where many people died and much property was destroyed. Later, in the build-up to multi-partyism in Kenya, the nearby area was the scene of outbreaks of ethnic violence and thousands of people fled their shambas, coming into Kisumu or heading up to Eldoret.

Kisumu Museum is to the east of the town's lively market. There are a number of stuffed birds, mammals, reptiles and fish. They include a lion bringing down a wildebeest. A 190 kilogram Nile perch is about to be added to these exhibits when the taxidermist has finished his work. The ethnographic exhibits centre on the customs and traditions of the tribal groups who lived in this area – the Luo, Masai, and Kalenjin (see page 288 and page 289). The curator is both imaginative and energetic, and intends to develop the scope and range of the museum including the traditional Luo homestead. ■ *Opening times are 0930-1800 and there is a nominal entrance fee of about US$4.*

Sights

Dunga is a small village just three kilometres outside Kisumu. It is a lovely

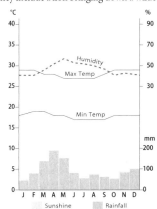

Climate: Kisumu

place to visit on the shores of Lake Victoria, peaceful and timeless. Avoid the temptation to swim in the lake here as bilharzia is rife, There are hippos here, but they are elusive. *Dunga Refreshments* has great views over the lake where you can get a cold soda and something to eat whilst watching fishermen bring their catch in. There is a **E** *Campsite* here, one of only a few in this area. Sadly it has become very rundown. Has a restaurant. Watching the sun set over the lake is a very pleasant way to end the day. It is possible to negotiate with the fishermen to join a night fishing trip. On the way up the dirt track to Dunga you pass the **Impala National Park** with a small herd of antelope.

Kisumu Bird Sanctuary is off the main A1 on the way to Ahero about eight kilometres out of Kisumu. You need to follow the track round the lake for the best sites. This is a nesting site for hundreds of birds including herons, ibises, cormorants, egrets and storks. The best time to visit is from April to May.

Sleeping   Kisumu is swarming with mosquitoes, so it is important to look for a room with mosquito nets if you don't have one with you. A fan is also a boon.

Kisumu

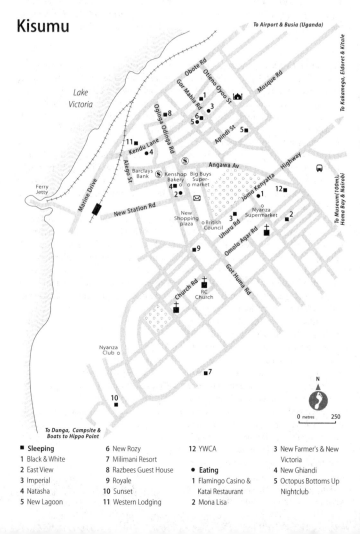

To Airport & Busia (Uganda)

To Kakamega, Eldoret & Kitale

Lake Victoria

To Museum (100m),
Homa Bay & Nairobi

To Dunga, Campsite &
Boats to Hippo Point

■ Sleeping	6 New Rozy	12 YWCA	3 New Farmer's & New Victoria
1 Black & White	7 Milimani Resort		
2 East View	8 Razbees Guest House	● Eating	4 New Ghiandi
3 Imperial	9 Royale	1 Flamingo Casino &	5 Octopus Bottoms Up
4 Natasha	10 Sunset	Katai Restaurant	Nightclub
5 New Lagoon	11 Western Lodging	2 Mona Lisa	

B *Imperial*, Jomo Kenyatta Ave, T035-41485. Probably the best value in this price range. **B** *Royale*, Jomo Kenyatta Ave, T035-44240. Average rooms, good Indian menu, swimming pool, clean, free for guests, non-residents US$1.50, temperamental hot water supply, upstairs rooms have netted windows, individual mosquito nets for each bed, although some have holes, casino open 1600-0500, no entry fee, no dress code, good restaurant on outside terrace, prices reasonable, slow service, Indian menu only available in the evenings, was the first hotel in Kisumu, has old polished wooden floors, spacious Old Colonial atmosphere, there is a nightclub at the back of the hotel, free to residents, otherwise entry fee US$2, sleepy receptionists. **B** *Sunset*, to the south of the town itself, T035-41100/42534. Has a verandah looking over beautiful lawns and a good swimming pool, all rooms have views of the lake and sunset, you can take a good photograph of the Lake from the Hotel roof. **B-C** *Milimani Resort Hotel*. New hotel. Quiet situation with car parking. Rooms have different prices. Breakfast included in the price.

C *Black & White*, Accra Rd. Has mosquito screens and hot water. **C** *East View*, Omolo Agar Rd, near the bus station. The hotel is reasonable and has a secure car park, price includes breakfast. **C** *New Victoria*, Gor Mahia Rd, T035-21067. Reasonable standard, price includes breakfast. **C** *Western Lodging*, Kendu Lane, T035-42586. New hotel with good rooms at cheap prices, there is good security in the hotel with a safe in each room.

D *Mona Lisa*, above the restaurant on Oginga Odinga Rd. **D** *New Lagoon Motel*, Otieno Oyoo St, T035-42118. Simple but reasonable. **D** *New Rozy Lodge*, Oganda St, T035-41990. Good value and clean. **D** *Safari*, Omino Crescent. Best value in this price category. **D** *YWCA*, off Ang'awa Ave, T035-43192. Reasonable, although there is not always water.

E *Black & Black Hotel*, a few yards from the *New Victoria Hotel*. Cheap, good place to stay, no mosquito nets, hot showers and toilets (shared), basins in rooms. **E** *Hotel Natasha*, Otuoma St, T43001. Hot water showers and toilet, s/c, very clean, friendly, quiet, no mosquito noets but has a fan, restaurant next door, phone booth outside. **E** *Razbees Guest House*. Clean, basic, friendly, has laundry facilities, communal shower, no fan or mosquito nets, like *Black & Black* but not too run down.

Campsite Near *Dunga Refreshments*. Best place to view the hippos. Once night has fallen they come out of the water to graze on land. You can also take a rowing boat, with guide, to nearby Hippo Point where one can see the hippos in the water. Cost of excursion US$2.

Eating

It is quite easy to get good cheap food in Kisumu, except on a Sunday, when most places are closed. Of particularly good value are the fish dishes. The large Asian community that has settled here means it is possible to get excellent Indian meals, including vegetarian, very cheaply. There are several very cheap kiosks near the bus station selling grilled meat on skewers or tilapia fish with ugali (maize dough).

3 *Bodega's*, just off Accra St. Good fresh fish, happy hour between 1900-2100. **3** *Dunga Refreshments*, on the lake shore to the south of town. A bit of a trek from the town centre, great buffet lunch on weekends with curries, the best time is to arrive at about 1700, amazing views. **3** *Sunset*, out of town to the south. Does a weekend buffet which is plentiful in slightly grand surroundings.

2 *New Farmers' Bar & Restaurant*. Has a good, if predictable, menu. **2** *New Ghiandi Paradise Bar & Restaurant*. A popular local hangout with a juke box. **2** *Katai Restaurant*, Chinese and Indian food, dark in daytime, pleasant at night, very good food, varied menu, on Thursday evenings there is an all-you-can-eat barbecue/buffet for US$6.50 per person recommended, starts at 1930.

1 *Kisumu Sweet Mart*, Oginga Odinga Rd. Sodas, bhajis and cheap Indian food. **1** *Mona Lisa*, Oginga Odinga Rd. Good breakfasts. **1** *New Victoria*, Gor Mahia Rd. Does a substantial breakfast from 0700 to 0900, good Indian menu, owned by a family from Yemem, very quick service and large portions, much quicker than the *Royale*!, can get quite busy, the menu states all food will be served within 15 minutes. **Kenshop Bakery**, next door to *Mona Lisa*. Very good pastries, bread, pizza and ice-cream, open 0900-1300, closed 1400-1500 and Sunday pm. **Wimpy**, fresh food, best pineapple milkshake ever.

Bars There are many African bars which play music, mainly Lingala, which are open till late. A particularly popular one is just outside Kisumu to the west near the molasses refinery. It is a bit rough and ready with only warm beers served from behind a metal grille, but the atmosphere on Friday nights is lively and it often has live bands. In town there is the far more sophisticated *Octopus* on Oganda St which plays western music. Good fun. It gets very crowded late in the evening, US$2 entry fee. The Octopus Restaurant is often empty, though the dancefloor is much more lively. Between the Restaurant and Disco, there are stairs leading up to the **Pirate's Den Rooftop Bar**, pleasant, has a dartboard and is a good place to have a drink as the sun goes down. **New Rozy**, 100 metres down the road to the right, lively, noisy. *Flamingo Casino*, located opposite the Nyanza Supermarket, PO Box 525, Kisumu, T43701.

Entertainment **Casinos** *Royale Hotel* on Jomo Kenyatta Ave. Open 1600-0500, no entry fee, no dress code.

Sports **Golf**: club just outside the town where you can hire equipment and a caddy. You need to pay a day's membership fee and the whole lot will come to around US$6. **Swimming** use pools rather than the lake as bilharzia is rife. There are 3, the best is at the *Sunset*, there are also pools at *Royale* and the *Imperial*.

Shopping **Handicrafts** For curios and crafts is quite good here as there are many artefacts from other parts of the country also available. Kisii stone is a particularly good buy as are kikois (woven cloth). The **Wananchi Crafts** shop is reasonable selling things made by local women. Street vendors are outside the post office and at stalls on the northern side of Oginga Odinga Rd.

Markets Kisumu's main fruit and vegetable market on Otieno Oyoo St is one of the largest in western Kenya, and worth a wander to soak up some of the atmosphere.

The market bustles every day, although Sunday tend to be quieter. You'll find that most things on offer tend to be quite similar. Look out for Kikois, some real gems are available if you look hard enough. Otherwise its the-run-of-the-mill-stuff – fruit and veg, childrens clothes, tools, flip-flops, radios, batteries, bags, sheets etc. The covered part of the market (like a large shed) is the best place to buy fruit, veg, pulses, herbs and rice very cheaply.

The main matatu/bus stopping point is just beyond the covered market.

Supermarkets Nyanza Supermarket at the new plaza on Oginga Odinga Rd. An ex-pat owned supermarket, slightly more expensive, but sells 'reassurables' for those feeling a little homesick! (Heinz beans/ ketchup/ marmite/ pringles/ Robertson's marmalade). Closes for lunch from 1245 to 1400.

The other good supermarket in Kisumu is 'Big Buys' on Oginga Odinga St. Slightly larger and cheaper than Nyanza, and has a wider array of goods. Good spice selection. Zahra House, PO Box 220, Kisumu. A new shopping arcade has opened off Oginga Odinga Rd. Apart from the well stocked supermarket, there is a bag shop, café bar with pool table and pet shop. There are still a number of empty shops in the complex.

Across the road from the *Royale Hotel* there are a number of stalls that sell Kisii stone (soapstone) and wooden ethnic artefacts. Excellent quality and good value. Advised to barter to improve the price. In Kisii stone there are chess boards, bowls, pots, candle holders and sculptures for sale. There are wooden animals, Masai warriors, drums, spoons/forks, masks and trinkets also available to purchase.

Transport **Local Car hire**: *Kisumu Travels*, T44122, only have a limited number of cars available and are more expensive than hiring a car from Nairobi; **Shiva Travels**, T43420.

Air Kenya Airways, T035-44055. There are daily flights from Nairobi taking 1 hour and costing US$54. There are also 5 flights a week from Mombasa (stopping at Nairobi) taking 2¾ hours and costing US$136.

Train Please see page 72 for details of train services, timetables and fares.

Road There are countless Peugeots, matatus and buses travelling between Kisumu and most major towns in Western Kenya leaving from the bus station. There are also many leaving for Nairobi passing through Nakuru, Kericho on the B1. Approximate times: **Nairobi** to Kisumu, express 6 hours or normal 8 hours. It takes approximately 2 hours to **Kericho**, 5 hours to **Nakuru**, 2 hours to **Eldoret**, 1 hour to **Kakamega**. The main matatu and bus stopping point is behind the covered section of the main market.

Boat Ferries: small motor ferries run between Kisumu and a number of lakeshore towns. Tickets can be bought from Kisumu wharf (it opens at 0800) and it is a good idea to board your boat as soon as possible as they are very popular and get full. Tickets are very cheap and this is a nice way of seeing around Lake Victoria. Outward: **Kisumu** 0900; **Kendu Bay** 1100; **Kuwur Bay** 1300; **Homa Bay** 1400; **Asembo Bay** 1700. Return: **Asembo Bay** 0800; **Kuwur Bay** 1000; **Homa Bay** 1040; **Kuwur Bay** 1150; **Kendu Bay** 1400; **Kisumu** 1600. There is also a ferry going from Kisumu to Mbita, Mfangano, Homa Bay and Kuwur Bay leaving Kisumu on Tuesday and returning on Sunday. Unfortunately there are no scheduled passenger ferries between Kenya, Uganda and Tanzania at present, though this situation is expected to change as relations between the three countries improve.

Banks *Barclays*, Kampala St or *Standard Chartered*, Oginga Odinga Rd are the most efficient for changing money. Banking hours are Mon to Fri 0900 to 1500 and Sat 0830 to 1100. Foreign exchange facilities. **Communications Post Office:** this is in the centre of town on Oginga Odinga Rd and has a reliable poste restante service. Hours are Mon to Fri 0800 to 1700 and Sat 0900 to 1200. **Telephone:** direct calls from the card phone outside the Post Office. **Internet** access available at Gener 8 near Razbees GH. Cost US$0.25 per min. **Libraries** *British Council* on Oginga Odinga Rd (T035-45004). Library open Mon to Fri from 0930 to 1700 with an hour for lunch and Sat from 0830 to 1245. Papers and magazines and occasional videos of BBC news. **Places of worship** Majority of people here are Christian (mainly Roman Catholics), but there are a significant number of Muslims. *Jamia Mosque* on Otieno Oyoo St is testament to the long tradition of Islam here, built in 1919 this green and white building has two imams and calls to prayer can be heard in much of the town. **Directory**

South Nyanza

This is an easy area to explore by public transport either by using the ferry from Kisumu, or the matatu services, which are excellent. There are also a few attractions for the more active tourist such as the **Lambwe Valley National Reserve**, **Ruma National Park** and **Thimlich Ohinga** archaeological site all near Homa Bay. Fishing (a male activity) and the smoking of fish (a female activity) are important occupations around here.

The biggest town in this area. Very busy at the end of the month when workers are paid and flock to town. No special reason to stay here unless you have to. **Sleeping B** *Homa Bay*, T0385-22070, on the lake shore. Rarely many guests here. **D** *Masawa*, simple but good value. **D** *New Brothers*, fairly basic, but has a few mosquito nets. **D** *Nyanza*, reasonable value.

Homa Bay
0° 50' S, 34° 30' E
Phone code: 0385
Colour map 4, grid B1

Quite near Homa Bay (60 kilometres) is one of the most significant archaeological sites in East Africa. The name means thick bush with stone enclosures in Luo and is an impressive example of a style of architecture whose remnants are all over the district. The main structure consists of a compound about 150 metres in diameter with

Thimlich Ohinga

five smaller enclosures in each and at least six house pits. The walls are about two and a half to three and a half metres high. Outside the compound, there is evidence of ironworks. They are similar to the stone ruins in Zimbabwe of the 17th century. It is believed the enclosure dates back to the 15th century, and the same style is used in some places by Luos today. There is no public transport to get here. You need to follow the Rongo-Homa Bay road as far as Rod Kopany then head southwest to Miranga. From Miranga there are sign posts to Thimlich Ohinga.

Homa Bay is the nearest town to **Lambwe Valley National Reserve** and **Ruma National Park** described in the section on National Parks (see page 275).

Rusinga Island
Colour map 4, grid B1

Access from Homa Bay is better by ferry than by road (it is now linked by causeway to the mainland) due to the poor state of the highway. The main town on Rusinga Island, Mbita, is unexceptional. Inland foreigners are rare and you are sure of a welcome. The traditional way of life is threatened here as drought coupled with environmental degradation (mainly tree clearance for fuel or land) has reduced agricultural productivity. This was the birthplace of Tom Mboya, an important Kenyan political figure during the fight for independence, who was assassinated in 1969 by a Kikuyu, sparking off ethnic violence. There is a school and a health centre named after him, and his mausoleum is at Kasawanga. On the shores of the island you may see the rare spotted-necked otter. If you do intend to walk around the island take plenty of water as it is hot here; there is little danger of getting lost.

Mfangano Island
Colour map 4, grid B1

Further along Lake Victoria, slightly bigger than Rusinga Island where hippos are very much in evidence as are monitor lizards basking in the sun. There are rock paintings here showing signs of centuries of habitation. The rock paintings are in a gently scooped cave on the north coast of the island and are reddish coloured shapes. It is not known who drew them, when or why. This is off the beaten track and there are few facilities for tourists apart from the **A+** *Island Camp* which will cost you over US$400 a night, and the newly-built luxurious **A** *Lake Victoria Game Safari*, PO Box 188, Kisumu (T035-43141), which mainly takes package tourists flying to Kisumu from the Masai Mara.

There are large wooden boats available to shuttle people between Mbita and surrounding places. It leaves Mbita at 0900 and takes about 90 minutes to Sena on the east of Mfangano. There is a government rest house (officially free though ask for permission to stay) and local people are usually willing to put up travellers. The island is completely free of vehicles, and has neither electricity nor piped water, so bear this in mind if you intend to stay.

Kendu Bay

Colour map 4, grid B1

Another stop on the ferry from Kisumu. The main reason for coming here is to visit the curious **Simbi Lake** which is bright green opaque water only a few kilometres from Lake Victoria. No-one knows what the source of the lake is and its size is constantly changing. Local people believe it to be unlucky and the surrounding area is certainly devoid of vegetation. It is not fished and the area is uninhabited. Legend has it the area was flooded by a woman who was ill-treated by villagers living there in the past.

Kendu Bay is a small town in South Nyanza, now Homa Bay District. It is an hours drive from Kisumu, on the Homa Bay – Katito Road, off the Ahero – Sondu-Kisii Road. It has become a fairly important lake port, receiving boats from Tanzania, and merchandise from the rich Kisii highlands, in the form of coffee and tea, although this has diminished in recent years. There has been a recent migration of 5,000 plus flamingoes and other waterfowl from Lake Nakuru and other Rift Valley Lakes to Lake Simbi, a crater lake, an upcoming tourist attraction. Take the road towards Homa Bay. It takes about two hours to walk around. There are no shops so take your own supplies of food and drink.

D *South Nyanza* is said to be the best and it has a disco each night. **E** *Kendu Country Hotel*,
hot water on request, mosquito nets, good view of lake, drinks/meals provided on request
but rather expensive. **E** *Hotel Big 5*, hot water and mosquito nets and coils on request, live
bands on Friday and weekends, African music, western music, weekend disco. African and
western food available reasonably priced, can be noisy, parking available.

Harbour/Pier Steamers dock here, arriving daily from Kisumu at 1100-1230. The service
also runs to Homa Bay.

For Ondago Flamingo site take the road for Homa Bay, past the Lake Simbi turning.
This is a seasonal mudflat frequented by both flamingoes and other birds each year.
Another Bird Sanctuary recently discovered on Rakewa off the Kisii road at Oyugis
23 kilometres on very rough road. Renowned as a pelican breeding site – both white
backed and pink backed. If you are in town, it is worth checking out the **Masjid
Tawakal Mosque**, a beautiful old building in town. If you are travelling by road, take
the newly tarred lakeshore road which meets the A1 Kisumu road going via Katito.
The drive is great through countryside which is just opening up.

  Migori The last town along this stretch, on the Tanzanian border. It is a transit
stop for people travelling to Musoma in Tanzania. The town has a rough reputation.
If you wish to get to Nairobi quickly, there are a number of buses going direct, one at
0600, one at 0700 and a few in the evening. If you have arrived here from Tanzania,
you will need to have a valid certificate to prove vaccination against yellow fever.

Busia and Siaya District

Northwest out of Kisumu towards the border town of Busia, is Siaya District, a
heavily-populated agricultural region. About 20 kilometres out of town is a small
hill, **Got Ramogi**. From the top of this are great views over the lake on one side and
of shambas on the other. The hill is significant to Luos as it is the site where Luos
fought for their right to settle here in the 15th century.

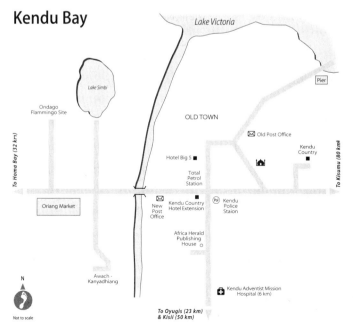

Kendu Bay

Busia
0° 25'N S, 34° 6' E
Colour map 4, grid A1

A small town on the border with Uganda. It primarily consists of one road lined with shops, kiosks and cafés. The border crossing itself is fairly straightforward, but quite thorough. The best hotel here is about one kilometre from the border, on the south side of the road slightly set back next to a small market. It costs around US$5 per night. The rooms are clean and have en suite bathrooms and there is a bar which is popular with local people. The restaurant is very good and cheap and serves mashed potatoes, a rarity in Kenya.

Kisii and Western Highlands

The Western Highlands are the agricultural heartland of Kenya separating Kisumu and environs from the rest of the country. They stretch from Kisii in the south up to the tea plantations around Kericho through to Kitale and Mount Elgon and Eldoret.

Kisii

0° 40' S, 34° 45' E
Colour map 4, grid B1

Set in picturesque undulating hills in some of the most fertile land of the country with abundant sunshine and rainfall. The town itself is growing fast and is very lively. As with so many other towns in agricultural areas, the market here is buzzing and has an excellent array of fresh fruit and vegetables. The town lies on a fault line, so earth tremors are not uncommon. This is the home of the Gusii people, and is famous for its *Kisii soapstone* though you may look to buy some in vain as most is bought up by traders to stock the tourist shops in Nairobi.

Sleeping **D** *Kisii*, north of town centre, T0381-20954. Own bathrooms, best of the slightly more expensive places, though the rooms are quite basic, comfortable colonial atmosphere. **D** *Safe Lodge*, just to the south of the market, T0381-21375. Own bathrooms, clean and friendly, though quite noisy. **D** *Sakawa Towers*, PO Box 541, by market, T0381-21218. Own bathrooms, newish high rise building with own bar and restaurant.

E *Capital Hotel*, clean s/c rooms, noisy. **E** *Highway Lodge*, T0381 21213. Cheapest in town and is clean but nothing special, try to get a room at the back – rooms at the front are very noisy as they are over the main road. **E** *Mount Everest Hotel*, basic facilities, communal showers, water supply irregular, noisy. **E** *Njau Guest House*, T0381-21375. Comfortable. **E** *Sabrina Lodge*, just around the corner from the matatu park. Friendly place with communal facilities, the hotel also has a bar and restaurant.

Eating **2** *Sakawa Towers*, close to market. Good restaurant, probably the best in town.

1 *Obomo*, popular, with good basic food and fresh fruit juices. **1** *Safe Lodge*, reasonable grilled meat skewers and a good breakfast.

Bars *Satellite Inn*, busy drinking den, though not very savoury.

Entertainment Centred around bars. There is a disco at *Mwalimu*, at the southern end of town. *Kisii*

Kisii

To Kisii Hotel & Kisumu

Njau Guest House
Supermarket
Highway Lodge

Matatus For Tabaka

Matatus for Kisumu
Market

Sabrina Lodge

Matatus for Kericho

Safe Lodge

Stadium

Capital

Sakawa Towers

Obomo

Mt Everest

Akamba Bus

Gusii Delux Bus

N
Not to scale

To Mwalimu Hotel & Kericho

Kenya

Sports Club, behind Barclays Bank on the main road, is worth joining if you are here for a few days. It has a friendly atmosphere and facilities for swimming, pool, tennis, squash, darts and bingo. There is a good bar to relax in afterwards. Kisii's football team, *Shabana FC*, is in the first division and the stadium is just to the west of the main road.

Road Matatus for Kisumu, takes 3 hours, leave in front of the market. All others leave from the station, the stand to the east of the main street. Nairobi is $8\frac{1}{2}$ hours away. **Transport**

About 25 kilometres from Kisii this village is the most important producer of soap-stone and the centre of carvings in the country. To visit the quarries or the carvers, you need to go past the Tabaka Mission Hospital to the Kisii Soapstone Carvers Co-operative. The children are happy to direct you. There are lots of local shops where you can buy soapstone artefacts. The stone comes in a variety of colours from orange (the softest) to deep red (the heaviest). Both *Standard Chartered*, near mar-ket, and *Barclays*, on main road, have branches here open Monday to Friday 0830 to 1300 and Saturday from 0830 to 1100. **Tabaka**

Kericho

Perched on the top of a hill, the tea plantations stretch for miles on either side of the road, their bushes neatly clipped to the same height with paths running in between, in straight lines, for the pickers to walk down. The predictable weather, (it rains each afternoon here) and the temperate climate makes this the most important tea-grow-ing region in Africa. This is an orderly part of Kenya, very different from the shambas further down the slopes, and very English exemplified by the *Tea Hotel* with its lovely gardens which used to be owned by Brooke Bond. The town's main purpose is to service the enormous tea plantations, so it has all basic amenities on the main road, Moi Highway; branches of the main banks, post office, market, library, English-style church, cemetery, Hindu Temple.

0° 30' S, 35° 15' E
Phone code: 0361
Colour map 4, grid A2

   Plantation tour The growing and picking procedures are explained, and there is a tour around the tea factory where the leaves are processed. To visit the plantation you need to apply the day before you wish to go. It is closed on Saturday afternoons and on Sundays.

Kericho

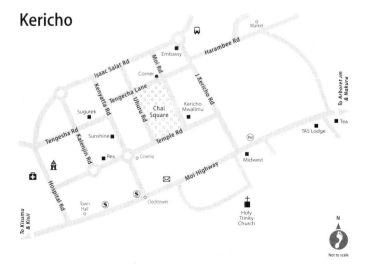

Chagaik Dam and Arboretum About eight kilometres to the northeast of Kericho off the road to Nakuru. Established after the Second World War by a Kericho teaplanter, John Grumbley, now retired to Malindi on the coast. Exceptionally attractive, well-tended, with lawns running down to the water's edge.

Trout fishing This is available in the Kiptariet River. The *Tea Hotel* will arrange for permissions and equipment hire. The river runs close-by the hotel.

Sleeping **B** *Tea*, PO Box 75, to northwest of town centre, on Moi Highway, on road to Nakuru, T0361-20280. Own bathrooms, comfortable and well-appointed, swimming pool. **C** *Midwest*, PO Box 1175, Moi Highway opposite Police Station, T20611. Own bathroom, modern, central, functional. **D** *Kericho Mwalimu*, PO Box 834, Temple Rd, just to north of Chai Square in the town centre, T20601. Own bathroom, restaurant and bar. **D** *TAS Lodge*, PO Box 304, to northwest of town centre, on Moi Highway, on road to Nakuru, close to *Tea Hotel*, T21112. Own bathroom, very good value, bar, restaurant, attractive garden setting. **E** *Embassy*, Isaac Salat Rd, close to bus stand, central. Reasonable value. **E** *Rex Inn Lodge* Temple Rd. Simple, but fairly central, no hot water, friendly, communal shower. **E** *Sugutek* Tengecha Rd. Shared bathroom, restaurant, fairly basic, but quite central. **Camping** At *TAS Lodge* on the road to Nakuru.

Eating **3** *Tea*, solid and dependable English-style menu, with some Indian dishes. **2** *Corner Restaurant*, cheap local food, recommended. **2** *Midwest*, good value set menu. **Sunshine Hotel*, Kenyatta Rd. Good value, closed Sunday.

Transport **Road** The matatu station, at the northern end of Isaac Salat Rd is well organized, and there is plenty of transport, both buses and matatus.

Maseno

Colour map 4, grid A1 Maseno is a growing university town, 26 kilometres northwest of Kisumu on the equator. It is a two-hour drive from the Kenya/Uganda border on the B1. It consists of a few hotels and restaurants, but it also has a Barclays Bank, a petrol station (Total), a Post Office with a public phonebox outside and a Mission Hospital. The University is the main focus of the town. The journey to Kisumu takes about 45 minutes by matatu.

Maseno

Kakamega Gold

During the 1930s, Kakamega was the centre of Kenya's gold-mining industry, and many coffee growers left their impoverished farms to become prospectors. Most gold was extracted by large South African-owned companies, mining the ore, crushing it, using steam-powered stampers, and sluicing out the gold.

The British mining engineers contrived to avoid the vulgarity associated with gold-rush towns and continued to dine in dinner-jackets at the Golf Hotel. When the Empire Airlines sea-plane service from London to Cape Town was introduced, hopping across Africa from lake to lake, one of the overnight stops was at Kisumu. The passengers were driven the 50 kilometres to Kakamega where they danced till dawn before returning to Kisumu to fly on the next leg down to Lake Naivasha.

Sleeping **E** *Land of Majitu Hotel*, basic with unreliable security, cheap, mosquito coil available on request, can get noisy at night. **E** *Maseno Inn*, offers restaurant, bar and lodging, cheap, very basic lax security, no hot water, jukebox downstairs accounts for the high noisy level. **E** *Maseno University College* has a small guesthouse, make enquiries T035-51011/08, phone for reservations.

Eating **1** *Maseno University College* guesthouse, enquire at University Gate or T51011. Generally good quality food, quick service. **1** *Sariba Campus*, situated 3 kilometres from B1 main road. No guesthouse but food quick and generally good quality, cost US$1.50 lunchtime only. **1** *Rock View Hotel* (has a chemist downstairs), the best restaurant in Maseno, deceptive menu as many items unavailable, clean, good view of Bunyore Hills from upstairs terrace, offers no accommodation although called a hotel. **1** *Equator Motel*, bar and restaurant, no accommodation, noisy. **1** *Ujamaa Bar*, noisy but good for an occasional drink. **1** *Maseno Club*, noisy but good for occassional drink. **1** *Maseno Inn*, basic restaurant, noisy.

Shopping *Maseno General Store*. Small range of basic items on offer, photocopying available here, also has a furniture shop adjacent. Other than the General Store there is a small market on Tuesday, which includes most things found in a typical African market: fruit (in season) woven baskets dried fish etc.

Directory **Banks** *Barclays Bank*, has only a minor branch (Agency) that does not handle foreign currency exchange, nor withdrawals exceeding 10,000 Ksh. Opening hours 0930-1330 Mon-Sat. **Communications** Opening hours 0800-1700, closes for lunch 1300-1400 and at weekends.

Two hours west of Maseno, along an unmade road, is the small village of **Kanbewa**. A further 45 minutes drive takes you to **Kit Mikayi Caves**. A guided tour through the caves costs US$4.

Kakamega

Pleasant lively place, and the main town of the Luhya people. A major attraction is the **Kakamega Forest** (see section on National Parks, page 260), and the town is the place to buy provisions for an excursion there. At the end of November is the **Kakamega Show**, with agricultural festival, at the showground just to the north of the town, on the Webuye Road. Most people head straight out to the Forest Reserve and stay there.

10° 20' N, 34° 46' E
Phone code: 0331
Colour map 4, grid A1

Sleeping **B** *Golf*, PO Box 118, just off main road, behind Sports Club, T0331-20460. Own bathrooms, swimming pool, facilities for golf, tennis and squash at the Sports Club, the bar is open to non-residents. **E** *Bendera*, just to the west of the main road. Good value and comfortable accommodation. **E** *Franca*, basic but clean. **E** *Kakamega Wayside House*, PO Box 900, close to Town Hall, T0331-20128. Central and inexpensive. **E** *New Garden House*, close to the main bus stand. Lively establishment, and reasonable standard and value.

Eating   **3** *Golf Hotel*, solid fare, English-style cooking with some Indian dishes. **1** *Dreamland Cafe*, good service, great-tasting food. **1** *New Garden House*, basic food, fairly busy atmosphere. **1** *Soweto*, close to main bus station and market. Mostly grilled skewered meats, simple and sound.

Transport   **Road**   The town is less than an hour from Kisumu (about 50 kilometres) along the excellent though very busy A1 and there are plenty of buses and matatus travelling this route. The main bus stand is close to the market. The Akamba bus service has its stand opposite the Hindu Temple, off the Mumias Rd.

Kericho to Eldoret

The journey from Kericho to Eldoret passes through the Nandi Hills, which provide some of the most spectacular scenery in this part of the country, and the Kano plains, bleak mountainous scrubland and ravines. The only town of note on this route is:

Kapsabet   Small town about 60 kilometres north of Kisumu. **Sleeping E** *Bogol Inn*, fairly
Colour map 4, grid A2   basic, reasonable restaurant. **E** *Kapsabet*, PO Box 449, T03231-2176. Inexpensive, restaurant and bar. **E** *Keben*, has a restaurant, bar and disco, rather lively.

Eldoret

0° 30' N, 35° 17' E   Pleasant, busy and fairly prosperous highland town surrounded by fertile country-
Phone code: 0321   side growing a mixture of food and cash crops. It is home to **Moi University** and this
Colour map 4, grid A2   appears to be benefiting the town and expanding its economic potential. Again, there's no special reason you should stay here, unless you're en route to the Cherangani Hills to the north.

Eldoret

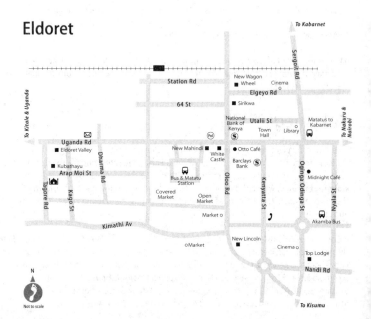

A snip at the price

Isaac Misigo, the chairman of Lukembe
Circumcisers of Kakamega, is dedicated to
improving the professional and ethical
standards of his members.
 In a statement to the Standard newspaper
in May 1996, Mr Misigo listed the new rules by
which his members will now be required to
abide:

- No circumcising dead people
- No circumciser to be drunk when operating
- No tools of the trade to be used to:
   threaten other people
   repair motor vehicles
   castrate dogs
Rate for job Ksh 3,000 (US$50) – although a
cow can be accepted in payment.

B *Sirikwa*, PO Box 3361, Elgeyo Rd, T0321-31655. Own bathrooms, swimming pool. **C** *New* **Sleeping**
Eldoret Wagon, Elgeyo Rd, PO Box 2408, T0321-32271. New and comfortable. **C** *White
Castle*, Uganda Rd, T0321-33095. Recently opened, with own bar and restaurant. **D** *Highlands Inn*, PO Box 2189, Elgeyo Rd, T0321-22092. Quiet place and good value. **D** *New Lin-
coln*, PO Box 551, Oloo Rd, T0321-22093. Own bathrooms with hot water, colonial-style
hotel, with some character. **E** *Eldoret Valley*, Uganda Rd, T0321-31488. Well-run and
quiet, but rather puritanical. **E** *Kubathayu Board & Lodging*, PO Box 832, Tagore Rd, to
west side of centre, T0321-22160. Comfortable, pleasant, inexpensive. **E** *Mountain View
Hotel*, on Uganda Rd opposite Post Office. Clean, own bathroom, restaurant, parking for
motorcycles. **E** *New Mahindi*, PO Box 1964, Uganda Rd, T0321-31520. Own bathrooms,
lively atmosphere. **E** *Top Lodge*, corner of Nandi and Oginga Odinga Rd. Is more used to
renting rooms by the hour, so not a great idea if you're a lone traveller, but has clean rooms
available for the night if you wish.

3 *Sirikwa*, on Elgeyo Rd. Has a buffet lunch at weekends including a barbecue. **2** *Eldoret* **Eating**
Valley, Uganda Rd. Mostly grills, skewered meat, good standard, Somali menu. **2** *New
Wagon*, Elgeyo Rd. Good value meals. **1** *Midnight Cave*, Oginga St. Cafeteria style. **1** *Otto
Cafe*, Uganda Rd. Simple, with good range of meat dishes.

Discos The best disco, and the newest, is *Sparkles Disco* on Kenyatta St. *Woodhouse Disco* **Entertainment**
on Oginga Odinga St is also popular and very lively.

Air There are 2 flights a week from **Nairobi** departing Wilson Airport Tuesday and Thursday **Transport**
at 0700 and 1545 respectively and returning at 2015 and 1700 on the same days.

Train Please refer to page 72 for details of train services, timetables and fares.

Road The matatu stand is in the centre of town just off Uganda Rd and there are a number
of Peugeots, matatus and buses throughout the day. The journey direct to Nairobi takes just
$3\frac{1}{2}$ hours.

Hospitals & medical services Dentist: Dr Wambugu has been recommended by travellers. Based at **Directory**
Batncetuny Plaza (shopping centre) on the Uganda Rd in the direction of Nakuro.

Eldoret to Malaba

From Eldoret the A104 passes through **Webuye** and **Bungoma** to reach **Malaba**,
the most common border crossing into Uganda. These are all geared toward the
transit traffic heading for Uganda. **Webuye Falls** are about five kilometres from the
road, and provide the water for **Panafric Paper Mills**. It is possible to visit the mills,
PO Box 535, T16 (Bungoma). **Chetambe's Fort** is a further eight kilometres from
the Webuye Falls, and is the site of the last stand of the Luhya against the British in
1896. **Sleeping** D *Hotel*, on the road from Eldoret to Malaba just before the bridge

👈 *Naipaul and Theroux II – Lions at Bay*

In the 1960s the Kaptagat Arms, near Eldoret in Kenya was run by an elderly retired English Major who had served in India. The Major's mission appeared to be to recreate, on the Equator, the way of life of English Home Counties. The hotel was an old farmhouse surrounded by lawns and flowerbeds stocked with spring snow-drops, daffodils crocuses and bluebells as well as summer roses, hollyhocks, lupins, forget-me-nots, snapdragons and geraniums, all surrounded by bouganvillea hedges – the only concession to the tropics. The English flowers apparently had some difficulty in deciding which of the African seasons was the appropriate time for them to bloom. The cuisine, likewise made little concession to the location – hot soups and roasts followed by steamed puddings with custard.

The Major had a reputation for eccentricity. A woman who had the nerve to ask for a Pimms had been flung out – 'we don't serve that muck here'. Local Europeans would bring their visiting friends to drink in the bar in the hope that the Major would be rude to them.

These stories filtered through to Uganda, and there was something in the demeanour of the Major that appealed to Naipaul (see box, page 265). He and his wife set out with Theroux to make a visit. As they checked in the opening exchanges were a little circumspect. Then the Major revealed that he knew of Naipaul and had read some of his books – and it was clear they were going to hit it off. The Naipauls took up residence and V. S. worked on his novel, The Mimic Men, tapping away on his portable typewriter in his room, while his wife Pat read outside on the lawn. They were the only guests. Theroux made visits from Uganda at weekends.

During their sojourn in Kaptagat the Naipauls made an excursion to Naorobi. Outside a cloth bazaar on Biashara Street they encountered a little Indian girl. Thirty years later she became Naipaul's second wife.

In Uganda there were political upheavals as President Obote ousted King Freddie of Bugand. A curfew was imposed and the feverish atmosphere in Kampala is vividly described by Theroux in one of his Collected Short Stories. Naipal finished his novel and with the curfew lifted and things settling down again in Uganda, Naipaul returned to Kampala in June 1966 and moved into Theroux's spare room.

at Malaba. Clean friendly. Safe parking for cars and motorcycles. Camping US$3, restaurant. Recommended.

Kitale

1° 0' N, 35° 0' E
Phone code 0325
Colour map 4, grid A1

Pleasant, small town in the middle of lush farmland between Mount Elgon and the Cherangani Hills. Originally this was Masai grazing land, but it was taken over by European settlers after the First World War. The town did not really develop until after 1925 and the arrival of a branch line of the railway. The region is known for its fruit and vegetables, including apples which are rare in East Africa. Kitale's main attraction for tourists is as a base from which to explore the **Cherangani Hills** (see section on Rift Valley, page 140 and information about guides later on in this section) or **Mount Elgon** and **Saiwa Swamp National Park** (see National Parks, page 269). It's also a stopping-off point on the route to Lake Turkana in the north.

Kitale Museum. Ethnographic displays of the life of the people of Western Kenya, butterfly and wildlife exhibits. Murals on local life in the Museum Hall. Excellent nature trail through local

°C / mm graph with Average Temp line and Rainfall bars across J F M A M J J A S O N D

Climate: Kitale
Rainfall

forest, with some pleasant picnic sites. ■ *Eldoret Road, just to the east of town centre. PO Box 1219 (T20690). 0930-1800 US$4.*

Kitale Show is at the beginning of November and is an agricultural festival.

B *Kitale Club*, PO Box 30, Eldoret Rd, just beyond the Kitale Museum, T0325-20030. Own bathroom, comfortable rooms with hot water, swimming pool, but a little overpriced. **C** *Alakara*, Kenyatta St, T0325-20395. Recommended. Has hot water all day. **D** *Bongo Hotel*, PO Box 530, Moi Ave, T0325-20593. Communal facilities, comfortable. **E** *Executive Lodge*, Kenyatta St. Communal facilities, good rooms, hot water. **E** *New Mbuni Lodge*, clean, hot water.

Sleeping

Camping There is a campsite about 20 kilometres north of Kitale, at **E** *Sirikwa Safaris*. This is a lovely site, with excellent facilities and good food. Highly recommended. Camping charges US$5 per person. To hire a tent costs US$15 per person, meals US$5. If you don't have a tent you can hire a room in the guesthouse fairly cheaply. A small, family-run place, you need to book through *Barnley's House*, PO Box 322, Kitale. *Sirikwa* is signposted on the right-hand side of the road a few kilometres past the entrance to Saiwa Swamp National Park. Alternatively you can camp in the Saiwa Swamp National Park. Camp charges are US$2 per person in addition to the NP entry fee.

Guides available from here for the Charangani Hills trekking. It can be difficult to obtain good local maps of the Hills. Guide charges from Sirikwa Safaris are US$5-US$7 per group, and the tour includes the villages of Kapsangar-Tapach and Tamcal. Allow 3-4 days for the trip.

3 *Kitale Club*, solid English fare, with some Indian dishes. **1** *Alakara*, Kenyatta St. Fairly simple food, but good value. **1** *Delicious Restaurant*, Kenyatta St. Mostly ice cream and snacks, but decent breakfasts too. **1** *Fun Rock Restaurant*, upstairs, cheap local food, good, friendly with live music daily.

Eating

Train See page 72 for details of passenger train services.

Transport

Road Various bus stands and matatu stops are at the western end of the road to Mount Elgon. Getting to and from Kitale is relatively easy as it is on the A1 heading for Kakamega and Kisumu in the south, and is the main route to Lake Turkana in the north. There are regular buses and matatus. The road north from Eldoret to Marich Pass/Lake Turkana is very good.

Kitale

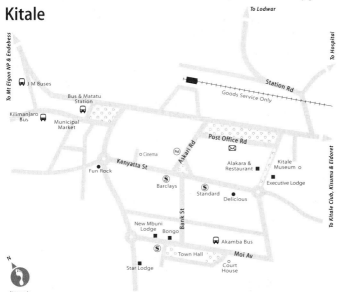

□ Nairobi

Kenya

Coast

Mombasa

4° 2' S, 39° 43' E
Colour map 3, grid A5

The town of Mombasa is situated on an island on the southern coast of Kenya. It is the oldest town in Kenya and is the most significant port in the country with a history going back 2,000 years. It owes its development to its location, for the island forms an ideal natural harbour.

Mombasa is Kenya's second largest town with a population of about 550,000 and has large communities of Indian and Arabic origin. It has the greatest concentration of Muslims in Kenya and their influence on the culture is strong. The town is centred on an island about four kilometres across and seven kilometres wide, but has now begun to sprawl onto the mainland. The island is now linked to the mainland at three points as well as by the Likoni Ferry.

Alas, the powers that be have seen fit in recent years to neglect or destroy the two best places to stay in Mombasa. The historic Castle Hotel has lain empty for several years, and in 1996 the exquisite Manor Hotel was demolished to build a shopping block. There is now no good reason to stay in Mombasa – much better to lodge at a beach hotel and visit Mombasa Old Town for the day – making sure you don't spend any money in the shops on the old Manor Hotel site.

The Coast

Hola

SOMALIA

Soni National Reserve

Tana Primate Reserve

Dodoni National Reserve

Tana River

Kiunga Marine Reserve

Mokowe

Pate Island

Garsen

Witu

Lamu Island

Tsavo East National Park

Formosa Bay

Galana River

Sabaki River

Malindi

Gedi Ruins

Malindi Marine National Park

Watamu Marine National Park

Kilifi

Kilifi Creek

Indian Ocean

To Voi & Nairobi

Mackinnon Rd

Mariakani

Mtwapa Creek

Kinango

MOMBASA

Shimba Hills NP

Diani Beach

TANZANIA

Lunga

Msambweni

N

Shimoni

Wasini Marine NP

Related maps
Mombasa North Coast, page 186
South Coast, page 177

0 km   50

To Tanga

What's in a name?

It was the practice of the earliest arrivals to name geographical features after themselves, their relatives or their friends.

In 1823 HMS Leven arrived at Mombasa and set about surveying the area and establishing a British presence. Port Owen Tudor was named after the ship's captain – and for good measure the main inlet was titled Tudor Creek. His crew were quick to take up on the practice – the River Nash was named after one of the lieutenants, River Barrett, after another lieutenant and the Williams River after a Midshipman.

Lieutenant John Reitz was shipped ashore to become the first British Governor of the Coastal region, and Port Reitz is a small ship dockyard on Mombasa Island. Having immortalized themselves, they began to think of others, and Flora Point was named after Owen Tudor's sweetheart back in England.

History

The earliest known reference to Mombasa dates from 150 AD when the Roman geographer Ptolemy placed the town on his map of the world. Roman, Arabic and Far Eastern seafarers took advantage of the port and were regular visitors. The port provided the town with the basis of economic development and it expanded steadily.

By the 16th century Mombasa was the most important town on the east coast of Africa with a population estimated at 10,000. By this time a wealthy settlement, it was captured by the Portuguese who were trying to break the Arab trading monopoly – particularly in the lucrative merchandising of spices. The town first fell to the Portuguese under the command of Dom Francisco in 1505. He ransacked the town and burnt it to the ground. It was rebuilt and returned to its former glory before it was sacked again in 1528. However, the Portuguese did not remain and having again looted and razed the town, they left.

Mombasa Island

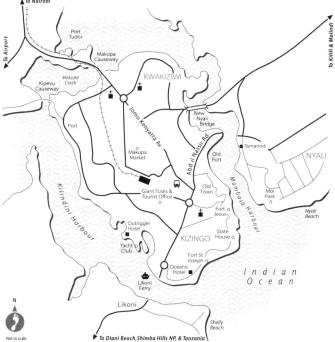

Related maps
Mombasa Old Town,
page 164
Central Mombasa,
page 169
*Central Mombasa
Detail*, page 170

👉 *Mombasa Cottage*

In 1823 the British Frigate HMS Leven put into Mombasa harbour. The French were casting an eye over the coast, and the Commander of the Leven, Captain Owen Tudor was asked by the Mazrui Sultan to take the coastal strip from Mombasa to Malindi under British protection. Lieutenant John Reitz, together with Midshipman Phillips, a Marine Corporal and three ratings were sent ashore. Their tasks were to maintain law and order, administer justice and wipe out the slave trade. Reitz immediately contracted a fever, as did one of the seamen, and in a matter of weeks both had died. Phillips took over as Governor. By this time the corporal and the remaining two seamen were in bad shape, and they were shipped out on a passing British warship.

When HMS Espiegle arrived, Phillips was transferred to customs, the 19-year-old Lieutenant James Emery disembarked to take over as Governor. Emery set about imposing strict observance to customs regulations, which brought him into continual conflict with the Sultan who was accustomed to ruling pretty much as he liked. Then Phillips died and Emery had to set about recruiting a

complement of staff under a Banyan, Lhadu, as Collector of Customs. This local crew were inducted with a supply of uniforms, a volley of musket fire, the presentation of a ceremonial shawl and turban, and rounded off with the launching of a couple of rockets and the firing of a canon. Alas, Lahdu was not completely intimidated by the display of Brittanic ceremonials and five months later he was dismissed for misappropriating US$200.

The British Government refused to ratify the conferment of Protectorate status, and Emery, the only survivor of the erstwhile administration resigned – but not before naming the ring ground at the head of the Barrett River, which runs west from Tudor Creek, the Emery Hills (see Box, page 163). It was not until 1886 and the advent of the Imperial British East Africa Company that Mombasa again came under British control.

After several other postings Emery retired to Surbiton in Surrey, England. The influence of East Africa lingered on, and he named his house in Adelaide Road Mombasa Cottage. He died there in 1899 at the age of 95 and is buried in nearby St Mark's churchyard.

The building of Fort Jesus in 1593, the stationing of a permanent garrison there, and the installation of their own nominee from Malindi as Sultan, represented the first major attempt to secure Mombasa permanently. However, an uprising by the towns people in 1631 led to the massacre of all the Portuguese. This led to yet another Portuguese fleet returning to try to recapture the town. In 1632 the leaders of the revolt retreated to the mainland leaving the island to the Europeans. Portuguese rule lasted less than 100 years and they were eventually expelled by the Omanis in 1698. The Omanis also held Zanzibar and were heavily involved in the slave trade. Their rule was in turn supplanted by the British in 1873.

The British efforts to stamp out the slave trade, and anxiety about German presence in what is now Tanzania, led, in 1896, to the beginning of the construction of the railway that was to link Uganda to the sea. One of the railway camps that was established before the construction of the line across the Rift Valley was at Nairobi. This town grew rapidly so that by 1907 it was large enough for the administrative quarters to move inland. The climate of Nairobi was considered to be healthier than the coast. Meanwhile, with the railway, the

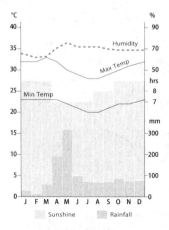

Climate: Mombasa

Bwana Martini

Antonio Martini was born in Malta in 1830. Having no schooling, he was apprenticed to a sailmaker and worked on ships repairing the canvases. While voyaging he picked up the rudiments of helmsmanship and navigation. On a voyage from Calcutta, with the Captain and the other officers below the worse for drink, he found himself at the wheel taking the vessel into Zanzibar, where he ran it aground. Coming ashore he began work as a builder and carpenter for the Central Missionary Society at Freretown (the old Mission Bell is just on the mainland side at Nyali), and changed his name to James Martin. His bad luck at sea continued, and he contrived to sink the Mission's steamer the Highland Lassie near Nyali Bridge.

On land he was more successful, and he quickly picked up a series of local languages. Joseph Thompson hired him to handle the porters for his expedition through Masailand.

Expanding his knowledge of the interior and its tongues he began leading regular caravans to Uganda, becoming known to local people along the route as 'Bwana Martini'. Although he could not read or write, Martin kept records with his own private code of symbols in his safari logs. He moved on to become deputy commander of the Sultan of Zanzibar's army, then a Magistrate and District Officer, trading in horses and ivory on the side. When his commercial activities met with official disapproval, he was sent to Buggala, one of the Sese Islands in Lake Victoria, to build a station to be named after Henry Morton Stanley.

In his latter years he lived in the Mombasa Club, and it was his practice to conceal his inability to write by asking a guest to sign his chits on his behalf – explaining that he had forgotten his spectacles. He died in 1925 at the age of 95.

importance of the port of Mombasa increased rapidly and it became known as the Gateway to East Africa, serving Kenya, Uganda, Rwanda and Burundi.

Sights

Mackinnon Market, Digo Road, named after Dr W Mackinnon, a colonial administrator, at the turn of the century, who was transport officer for the route between Mombasa and Uganda. Began the road to the interior that was also named after him. Lively, bustling and colourful. The main section of the market is situated in an enormous shed but numerous stalls have spilt out onto the streets. Obviously the number of tourists has affected the prices and the market is no longer the bargain that it used to be. However if you are prepared to haggle and bargain in a good-natured manner you can usually bring the price down quite considerably. Apart from fresh fruit and vegetables, you will be able to buy baskets, jewellery and other souvenirs. For kikois and kangas (brightly coloured cloth squares) the best place is Biashara Street. This is also the place to come if you want your clothes repaired quickly and cheaply.

Fort Jesus (T312839) Mombasa Old Town's major attraction. ■ *It is located on Nkrumah Road and the Fort and Museum are open every day from 0800 to 1800. Entrance is US$5 for non-residents. It is best to try and visit early in the morning.* **NB** *If you are not part of a tour, local guides will attempt to pick you up. They are very persistent and will expect payment.*

The Fort was designed in the 16th century by an Italian architect called Cairati who had also done some work for the Portuguese at Goa on the other side of the Indian Ocean. It dominates the entrance to the Old Harbour and is positioned so that even when it was under siege it was still possible to bring supplies in from the sea.

Despite this apparently secure position the Portuguese lost possession of the Fort in 1698 following an uprising by the towns people who had formed an alliance with the Omanis. The Fort had been under siege for 15 months before it finally fell. During the battle for the Fort a Portuguese ship named *Santo Antonio de Tanna* sank off the coast and the museum displays some of the relics that were recovered from the ship. The British took control of the Fort in 1825 and from then until 1958 the Fort served as a prison. In 1958 the money was raised to restore the Fort and convert it into a museum.

In the late 18th century the Omanis built a house in the northwest corner of the Fort in what is known as the San Felipe bastion. Since then this has served various purposes including being the prison warden's house. The Omanis also razed the walls of the Fort, built turrets and equipped the Fort with improved guns and other weaponry to increase its defensive capabilities. At the main gate are six cannons from the British ship the *Pegasus* and the German ship the *SS Konigsberg* (see page 365). The walls are particularly impressive being nearly 3 metres thick at the base.

Close to the Omani house one of the trolleys that used to be the mode of transport around town can be seen. There is also an excellent view over the Fort and Old Town from here.

The museum is situated in the southern part of the Fort and has an interesting collection. Exhibits include a fair amount of pottery as well as other archaeological finds from other digs on the coast. The diversity of the exhibits is a good illustration of the wide variety of influences that this coast was subject to over the centuries. Within the Fort are wall paintings and some of the oldest graffiti in Mombasa.

Old Town The best way to see Old Mombasa is by walking around, again early morning or late afternoon is preferable. You will pass women dressed in *bui buis* which cover them from head to toe, sometimes with just their eyes peeping through. The buildings in this part of town clearly reflect the Indian influences. Most of the buildings are not actually more than about 100 years old although there are some exceptions. The finer buildings may have a balcony and one of the elaborate doors which are now so prized. These were once much more numerous than they are now as they were a reflection of the wealth and status of the family.

One of the older buildings on the island is **Leven House** located just off the top end of Ndia Kuu. This was built around the beginning of the 19th century and has served many different purposes since then. It was originally occupied by a wealthy

Mombasa Old Town

Related map
Mombasa Island,
page 161

trading family and later was the head-quarters of the British East Africa Company. It also housed a German Diplomatic Mission and more recently has been used by the Customs Department. Among its most famous visitors were the explorers and missionaries Burton, Jackson and Ludwig Krapf. In front of Leven House are the Leven steps – here a tunnel has been carved through to the water edge where there is a fresh-water well. Burton actually mentions climbing up here through this tunnel but you do not need to follow his example – there are steps nearby. Photography in the area of the old harbour is forbidden for some reason, so take care.

The **Old Law Court** is located close to Fort Jesus on Nkrumah Road. The building dates from the beginning of this century. Near the Law Courts on Treasury Square is another building of approximately the same age. This was the District Administration headquarters. The roof is tiled and there is a first floor balcony.

The Ndia Kuu (Great Way) road which leads from Fort Jesus into the Old Town is one of the oldest roads in Mombasa. The road existed during the Portuguese period and formed the main street of their settlement. Mzizima Road was the main route between the Portugese town and the original Arab/Shirazi town. Mlango Wa Papa marks the wall of the Arab town – its name suggests gateway (Mlango) in the wall over Mzizima Road.

Mombasa Club

Bousted and Ridley began as suppliers in Zanzibar in 1874, providing goods for the fitting out of caravans to the interior. By 1892 Mombasa had become well established and Bousted and Ridley set up shop there. Dismayed at the dull social life, they acquired two rooms above the shop of R da Sousa in Ndia Kuu Street and opened the Mombasa Club. One room served as a mess and served food while the other had a bar and a billiard table.

By 1896, with the beginning of the construction of the railway, the two rooms were a bit cramped, and the present Mombasa Club was founded in 1897.

Mzizima

The Old Town is probably not the oldest part of Mombasa – the earliest settlement was probably around what is known as Mzizima to the north of the Old Town. The evidence for this is the discovery of pottery dating from the 11th to the 16th centuries. There is, however, very little left of this early settlement

Mbaraki Pillar

On the other side of the island at Mbaraki is the **Mbaraki Pillar** which is believed to have been built largely of coral as a tomb in the 14th century. There was also a mosque next to it which was used by a nearby village. Although this village has long since been abandoned, people still visit the pillar, pray to the spirits of the dead, burn incense and leave offerings.

Colonial Mombasa

The **Kizingo** area in the southern part of the island around the lighthouse has some very fine buildings, whose style has been called Coast Colonial. These buildings are spacious and airy and built to keep the occupants as cool as possible. There are wide balconies and shutters which ensure that the sun's rays do not enter, and the buildings are designed to take advantage of every breeze. Many of the building materials were imported from Europe and Asia and hardwoods were used. Unfortunately many of these buildings have now fallen into disrepair and you will have to look beyond the exterior to appreciate the architecture. Some are now used as public buildings such as the Aliens Office on State House Road.

Along Mama Ngina Drive at the south of the island it is possible to look over the cliffs that rise above Kilindini Channel and out towards the sea. Inland, at the Likoni end of Mama Ngina Drive close to the *Oceanic Hotel*, is the Golf Course. At the other end of the road is State House – this is a sensitive area so do not take photos or you risk being arrested. On the golf course is **Fort St Joseph** – this was also built by the Portuguese and can be reached by following the path from the lighthouse that runs between the Mombasa Golf Club and the Police Headquarters.

Kenya

Ludwig Krapf

Krapf was born in 1810 in the foot hills of the German Black Forest. He was the son of a prosperous farmer and during a period of convalescence he spent many hours reading the Bible. He also spent much of his childhood showing a keen interest in geography looking at maps of the world and reading travel books, and by the age of 14 had decided to become a sea captain in order to be able to see the countries that he had read about. His interest in the Church had not waned and he was soon to realise that joining the Church was the most feasible, and affordable, way to travel. He therefore set his mind on being a missionary and soon after his ordination he joined the Church Missionary Society (CMS).

He was appointed to a posting in Abyssinia but only stayed there two months. Krapf was married in 1842 to Rosine Dietrich – the couple had not met before they were married. The couple travelled down the coast and spent some time on Zanzibar. Krapf then set off alone to see some of the coast and during these travels he decided to work amongst the Wanyika people who were to be found inland from Mombasa. He returned to Zanzibar to collect his pregnant wife and they set off. However tragedy struck in Mombasa when both the Krapfs suffered from a severe fever, and Rosine died three days after giving birth and the child, a girl, lived for just a week. He was to write in his diary "I was obliged by the climate to conduct this second victim of the king of terrors to the grave of my beloved Rosine as soon as possible."

Having regained his health Krapf continued with his work translating the Bible into the Swahili and Wanyika languages. Two years later he was to be joined by Johann Rebmann and they set off inland and established themselves amongst the Wanyika peoples. Over the next few years the two made trips inland and it was in May 1848

that Rebmann became the first white man to set eyes on Mount Kilimanjaro. His reports of snow on the equator were greeted in Europe with disbelief.

Krapf's basic objective was to improve geographical knowledge of the "Dark Continent" which would in turn facilitate the stamping out of the slave trade, and allow the spread of Christianity. In 1849 Krapf set off on another journey inland; he went further than any white man before, crossing the Tsavo River and setting eyes on Mount Kenya in the distance. His next trip was along the coast as far south as Cape Delgado situated in the northeast of Mozambique.

After this he returned to Europe for about a year as his health had suffered from his time in the tropics. Whilst in Europe he persuaded the CMS that they should aim to set up a string of missions stretching from one side of Africa to the other. He returned to Africa with five volunteers but one absconded, one died of fever, two returned to Europe having been struck down by fever, and Krapf was left with just Brother Hagerman, a carpenter.

Krapf began what was to be his last expedition into the interior in 1851. It was to be a difficult journey. They were attacked by robbers, most of his porters deserted and he was held prisoner before he escaped and returned to the coast. Although only 43 years old his health was failing him, and in 1853 he was persuaded to return to Europe. He returned to Africa for a brief visit in 1861 but continued his work in Europe. His greatest contribution was perhaps in the field of linguistics – he translated the Scriptures into six vernacular languages, prepared a Swahili dictionary as well as the basic vocabulary of the Maasai, Galla, Pokomo and Ki-Nyika languages. He died at the age of 71 in Nov 1881.

At the western end of Nkrumah Road is the administrative centre of the British colonial period. The main buildings surround **Treasury Square**, with the handsome **Treasury** itself on the east side which has now been taken over by the City Council. On the southeast corner is another handsome building which currently houses the Kenya Commercial Bank. In the square is a bronze statue of **Allidina Visram**, born in 1851 in Cutch in India. In 1863, at the age of 12, he arrived in Mombasa and he became a prosperous merchant and planter, encouraging education and prominent in public life, dying in 1916. Also in the square is a miniature white gazebo, although what it commemorates is not clear.

On the south side of Nyerere Road, toward the Fort is the Old Law Court, now used as offices by the National Museums of Kenya. In the wall nearby is a **Wavell Memorial** commemorating Arthur John Byng Wavell, MC, who organized the local water carriers in Mombasa into the 'Arab Rifles' to defend the town during the First World War. From the same war came the cannons that can be seen, one of them from the Koenisberg, and it is daunting to think that it was hauled by hand over rough tracks the length and breadth of East Africa by von Lettow's forces after it was salvaged from a sunken battleship (see page 530).

Proceeding west from Treasury Gardens, on the left is the **Anglican Cathedral**, built in 1903 and with a plaque to mark 150 years of Christianity in Mombasa, celebrated in 1994. The Cathedral itself is a mixture of European and Mediterranean influences, whitewashed with Moorish arches, slender windows, a dome reminiscent of an Islamic mosque, with a cross, and two smaller towers topped by crosses.

On the right is the solid and imposing Barclay's Bank building, and on the same side, just behind the main road is the spectacular, modern, **Hindu Lord Shiva Temple**, dazzling white, and in the process of being completed.

Just before the intersection with Moi Ave is the **Holy Ghost Cathedral**, an elegant structure of concrete rendered in grey cement. It has a fine curved ceiling of three spans in cream and blue, *fleur de lis* designs, and stained glass windows. Cool and airy inside. The surrounding gardens are somewhat unkempt.

Going west on Haile Selassie Road, on the right-hand side is the **Ismaili Cemetery**, well tended, with frangipani trees and long green concrete benches. Adjacent is the **Islamic Cemetery**, with well-tended gardens, inscribed concrete benches and a small mosque. Finally, there is the **War Memorial** with bronze statues dedicated to the African and Arab soldiers who served with the East African Rifles in the First World War. At the westward end of Haile Selassie, in front of the Railway Station are the **Jubilee Gardens**, laid out to mark the sixtieth anniversary of Queen Victoria's reign in 1897. They are rather neglected, and the circular fountains no longer operate.

Near the Tusks are **Uhuru Gardens**. It is difficult to get in from Moi Ave as curio kiosks block most of the entrance. Inside are some handsome trees, a fountain (not working) a café, and a brass cannon worn smooth from serving as a makeshift seat.

At the eastern end of Moi Ave is **Coast House**, a good example of European architecture in the tropics, with a tin roof and two verandahs on the first floor to catch the breeze.

Datoo Auctioneers is located on Makadara Road and **Dodwell House** on Moi Ave was home to a shipping company. It has a splendid example of a Mangalore tiled roof which would have been imported from India. The large entrance hall has splendid columns and a fantastic hardwood counter. There are two hotels which date from the beginning of the century. The *Castle Hotel* is one of these located on Moi Ave. The *Manor Hotel* on Nyerere Ave, built in 1920s is similar with balconies, pillars and verandahs.

There are many mosques, over a hundred on the island, some of which date back over 150 years. On Mbarak Ali Hinawy Street, close to the Old Port is **Mandhry Mosque**, with a white minaret. Close to the Leven Steps and the Fish Market is **New Burhani Bohra Mosque** with a tall minaret, built in 1902, and is the third mosque to have been built on this site. On Kuze Road is the **Jamat-khana Mosque** of the Ismaili community. From the upstairs are good views over the Old Harbour where the dhows are docked. The **Bhadala Mosque** is on Samburu Road, with a fine dome and minaret. The Bhadala are a sea-faring people, and were among the first settlers. Near the Post Office on Digo Road is the **Baluchi Mosque**. The Baluchis were a fierce fighting people who served as mercenaries for various Sultans. The **Zenzi Mosque** is a small attractive building with a minaret on Digo Street at the intersection with Haile Selassie. The **Jundani Mosque** is on Gusii Street, and was rebuilt in 1958 on the site of a mosque that was established in 1870. Before you enter any of

Mosques & temples

Kenya

these mosques be sure you are appropriately dressed, ask for permission to enter, and remove your shoes. Women will probably not be allowed to enter. As well as mosques there are also a number of Hindu Temples.

On the corner of Haile Selassie and Aga Khan is the **Swaminaryan Temple** an exotic confection in powder blue and pink. **Siri Guru Singh Saba** on Haile Selassie is a cool, elegant and well-maintained Sikh temple built in 1837.

Moi Ave   This is Mombasa's main road and is about four kilometres long. Along Moi Ave there are many shops that the tourist will want to visit including souvenir shops, travel agencies and the tourist information office. The **Tusks** are found on Moi Ave and were were built in 1952 to commemorate the visit of Queen Elizabeth (Princess Elizabeth as she was then). They are actually rather disappointing close to. There are curio shops for about 50 yards in both directions – the goods are not very good quality and are rather expensive.

Nyali   One of the wealthier suburbs of Mombasa. There are a number of good restaurants here as well as the Ratna Shopping Centre. It was in this area that newly freed slaves settled, and a bell tower is erected in memory. Across the bridge there is a fork in the road. The right goes towards the village of **Kongowea** which is believed to date back to the 11th century. It is a fishing village and the influence of the missionaries in the 19th century remains strong. It is also near here that the graves of the wife and daughter of the missionary Ludwig Krapf are to be found (see box, page 166).

Essentials

Sleeping
■ on maps, pages 169 and 170
For price codes, see inside front cover

A *New Outrigger*, PO Box 82345, Ras Liwatoni, right on the beach, T20822. Excellent hotel run by Belgians, there are about 50 rooms all of which are a/c with a bathroom and balcony, other facilities include a swimming pool and the price includes breakfast. **A** *Oceanic*, PO Box 90371, Mama Ngina Drive, in the south of the island, T311191/311192. Large hotel that has been renovated fairly recently, facilities include 3 restaurants, swimming pool, health centre, meeting rooms and transport into town is provided.

C *Hotel Pollana*, PO Box 41983, Maungano St, T229171/92/94. Large modern hotel, 140 rooms, comfortable s/c, a/c, restaurant, good buffet lunch. **C** *Mombasa Club*, located close to Fort Jesus. It is possible to stay if you pay a temporary membership fee, variety of rooms, charming and comfortable, pool jutting into harbour, restaurant and bar. **C** *Royal Court Hotel*, Haile Selassie Rd, PO Box 41247, T223379/312389/312317, F312398. New hotel, central, a/c, hot water, s/c, balconies, good Indian restaurant, excellent curries , rooftop bar, well-run and good value. Recommended. **C** *Sapphire Hotel*, PO Box 1254, Mwembe Tanjire Rd, T491657/4952801/494841, F495280. Comfortable modern, marble decor, s/c, a/c, balconies, Mehfil restaurant, terrace barbecue, buffet lunch.

D *Casablanca*, just next to bar and disco on Mnazi Moja, PO Box 88098. Not s/c, noisy, but near the action, rather overpriced. **D** *Excellent Hotel*, Haile Selassie Rd, PO Box 90228, T227683. Popular hotel so arrive early on in the day, rooms have bathrooms and the price includes breakfast, it is clean and well run, restaurant, good for pastas. **D** *Glory Guest House*, PO Box 85527, Kwa Shibu Rd, T314557/228202/313204. All rooms in this hotel have bathrooms and some have a/c, a bit pokey, breakfast included, part of Glory chain. There has been an expansion of this chain of guesthouses with several in Mombasa alone. Others are situated on Haile Selaisse Ave and Digo Rd. Feedback recently has been very negative about cleanliness, safety and security. Recent travellers report thefts and poor security. Problems include possible inside involvement. **D** *Hermes*, PO Box 94819, Msanifu Kombo St, T313599. All rooms have bathrooms attached and there is very good restaurant, s/c, a/c, very good value. **D** *Lotus*, PO Box 90193, Mvita Rd, close to Fort Jesus, T313207. Quite new but recently renovated, it has a charming central courtyard and a lovely atmosphere, the rooms are all a/c, s/c, hot water and there is a good restaurant with buffet lunches. **D** *Manson Hotel*, Kisumu

Rd, PO Box 83565, T222365/222619/222420/222421. Fans, some a/c, restaurant, massage, fairly new, good value. **D** *New Carlton*, PO Box 86779, Moi Ave, T23776/315116. Comfortable, reasonably priced hotel, all rooms have bathrooms and there is a restaurant which is fairly good. **D** *New Palm Tree*, PO Box 90013, Nkrumah Rd, T311756/312169/312296. One of the best hotels in this price bracket, simple, quiet hotel, fans, s/c, no hot water, rather gloomy atmosphere, there is a restaurant which serves basic dishes. **D** *Splendid*, PO Box 90482, Msanifu Kombo St, T220967. Large modern hotel, it is clean but the rooms are rather small and dark, facilities include a roof top restaurant and bar, a/c, price includes breakfast. **D** *Unity*, off Msanifu Kombo St, T221298. Fairly good value. **D** *Visitors Inn*, corner of Haile Selassie Rd and Shibu Rd. Price includes bathrooms and breakfast, some rooms are noisy.

E *Al Nasser Lodgings*, Abdel Nasser Rd, T313032. Budget hotel, the rooms have their own bathrooms. **E** *Balgis*, Digo Rd, T313358. Very cheap, it has a range of rooms from dorms upwards, some of the rooms are hot and noisy but it is probably the cheapest place you will find, however, not recommended for lone female travellers, water supply – only rainwater. **E** *Bollos Hotel*, PO Box 88825, Nkrumah Ave, T313833. Fans, not s/c, rather univiting. **E** *Cosy Guest House*, Haile Selassie Rd, T313064. Popular with budget travellers and all rooms have fans with shared facilities, it is however a bit run down, no hot water. **E** *Down Town Lodge*, Hospital St. Range of rooms, very cheap but can be hot and noisy. **E** *Euas*, Abdul Nassir Rd, PO Box 82577. Fans, not s/c, convenient buses, cheap, small. **E** *Gathecha Guesthouse*, Kenya Rd, off Kisumu Rd, PO Box 98642, T224165. Fans, no hot water. **E** *Glory Bed & Breakfast*, just off Digo Rd, PO Box 85527, T228493. Fans, s/c, part of Glory chain, well-run, good value. **E** *Glory* (Haile Selassie), PO Box 85527, T220265. Fans, part of Glory chain, well-run, good value. **E** *Glory Annexe*, PO Box 85527, off Mnazi Moja, behind *Casablanca Club*, T220419. Includes breakfast, small patio bar and restaurant, some a/c, well-run, good value. **E** *Hotel Mir Mar*, Tagana Rd, next to station. Not s/c, fans, breakfast included, restaurant with Indian food. **E** *Hotel Relax*, PO Box 98235, Msanifu Kombo St, T311646. S/c, fans. **E** *Hydro*, PO Box

Central Mombasa

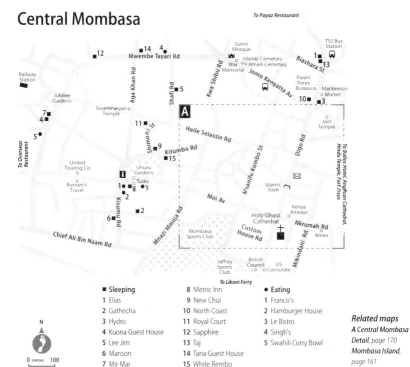

■ Sleeping	8 Metric Inn	● Eating
1 Elias	9 New Chui	1 Franco's
2 Gathecha	10 North Coast	2 Hamburger House
3 Hydro	11 Royal Court	3 Le Bistro
4 Kuona Guest House	12 Sapphire	4 Singh's
5 Lee Jim	13 Taj	5 Swahili Curry Bowl
6 Manson	14 Tana Guest House	
7 Mir Mar	15 White Rembo	

Related maps
A Central Mombasa
Detail, page 170
Mombasa Island,
page 161

N

0 metres 100

Kenya

85360 on Digo Rd at junction with Kenyatta Ave, T23784. Well located and inexpensive. **E** *Kivulini Lodge*, near Haile Selassie Rd and Digo Rd, PO Box 82192. Fans, first floor cafeteria, inexpensive and secure. **E** *Kuona Guesthouse*, PO Box 98756, Tagana Rd, near station, T220792/314341. Not s/c, fans. **E** *Lee Jim*, Dwana Rd, PO Box 80094, T222867/222868. Massage. **E** *Lee Jim*, Meru Rd, PO Box 60094, T228764. S/c, fans, includes breakfast. **E** *Lucky Hotel*, Shibu Rd, T220895. Fans, hot water, s/c, good value. **E** *Metric Inn*, PO Box 98658. In small alleyway behind *Franco's Restaurant*, near Tusks, not s/c, patio bar and restaurant, being improved, well located, good value. **E** *New Al Jazira*, Shibu St, just off Haile Selassie Rd, PO Box 40432, T222127. Double and triple rooms with shared bathrooms but no singles. **E** *New Chui Lodge*, Shimoni St. No hot water, not s/c, fairly basic. **E** *New Peoples Lodge*, PO Box 95342, Abdel Nasser Rd, T312831. Popular budget hotel, however, it has also seen better days and some rooms are rather noisy, there are a variety of rooms some with own bathrooms and some with shared bathrooms, it is generally safe, reasonably clean and is friendly, it has its own restaurant. **E** *North Coast Lodge*, on corner of Kenyatta Ave and Digo Rd. Variety of singles, doubles and domitory, "women not allowed" so it is appropriate to mention that thats fine as you are homosexual (*shoga* or *msenge*) and that, incidentally, you are anticipating indulging in some pretty unspeakable acts with your boyfriend. **E** *Tahfif Hotel*, Jomo Kenyatta Ave, entrance in side street behind cafe, convenient for buses. "Miraa, gambling, prostitutes and noise not allowed", tidy, bright and clean, balconies, good value. **E** *Taj*, Digo Rd, PO Box 82021, T223198. Some s/c rooms, well run and inexpensive. **E** *Tana Guesthouse*, PO Box 42200, Mwembe Tayori Rd, T490550. S/c, fans, well run. **E** *Unity Guesthouse*,

Central Mombasa Detail

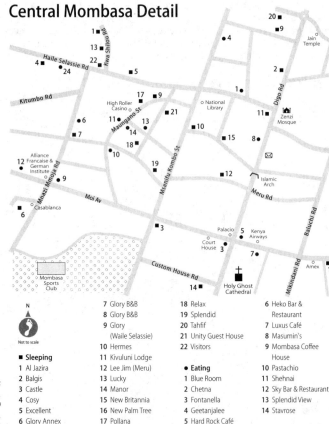

N
Not to scale

Related maps
Central Mombasa,
page 169
Mombasa Island,
page 161

■ Sleeping
1 Al Jazira
2 Balgis
3 Castle
4 Cosy
5 Excellent
6 Glory Annex
7 Glory B&B
8 Glory B&B
9 Glory
  (Waile Selassie)
10 Hermes
11 Kivulini Lodge
12 Lee Jim (Meru)
13 Lucky
14 Manor
15 New Britannia
16 New Palm Tree
17 Pollana
18 Relax
19 Splendid
20 Tahfif
21 Unity Guest House
22 Visitors

● Eating
1 Blue Room
2 Chetna
3 Fontanella
4 Geetanjalee
5 Hard Rock Café
6 Heko Bar &
  Restaurant
7 Luxus Café
8 Masumin's
9 Mombasa Coffee
  House
10 Pastachio
11 Shehnai
12 Sky Bar & Restaurant
13 Splendid View
14 Stavrose

Rahaleo St, off Digo Rd and Haile Selassie Rd, PO Box 90759, T311169. Fans, s/c, some a/c, nets, includes breakfast, very good value. **E** *Visitors Inn*, corner of Shibu Rd and Haile Selassie, PO Box 22971, T229971. Fans, hot water. **E** *White Rembo Lodge*, Kitumbo Rd, near Uhuru Gardens. Simple and small. **E** *YWCA*, corner Kaunda and Kiambu Ave, T220632. Accepts men as well as women. Reasonable option.

There are a number of eating places in Mombasa to choose from apart from hotel restaurants. With its large Indian population there is a lot of excellent Indian food as well as fresh fish and shellfish.

Eating
● *on maps*
Price codes:
see inside front cover

African **2** *Recoda*, Nyeri St in the Old Town. This serves Indian and African food and is popular with locals as well as budget travellers, the food is basic but cheap and you should try it if you can, it is only open in the evenings. **2** *Swahili Curry Bowl*, Tangana Rd off Moi Ave. Very good for traditional coastal African dishes, closed on Sunday, the ice cream is also very good.

Kenya

Chinese **3** *Overseas*, Moi Ave just north of the Tusks, T21585. Popular Chinese and Korean, it is family run, friendly and the food is pretty good. **3** *Galaxy Chinese Restaurant*, Archbishop Makarios St, T26132. Popular Chinese restaurant and is probably one of the best in town, it has especially good seafood dishes. **3** *Hong Kong*, Moi Ave, T26707. Another fairly good Chinese restaurant.

Indian **4** *Roshani Basserie*, in the *Royal Court Hotel*, Haile Selassie Rd, PO Box 41247, T223379/312389/312317, F312398. High quality food in balcony restaurant with pleasant decor with green plants. Also **4** *Tawa Terrace*, on rooftop with wicker furniture and fine views, cool breezes, specializes in tandoori dishes. Well recommended. **3** *Fayaz*, Abdul Nassir Rd, upstairs from café. High quality Moghul, North Indian cuisine, pleasant, bright decor. **3** *Hermes*, Msanifu Kombo Rd, T313599. A bit shabby and the surroundings are not anything special but it is a/c and the food is good. **3** *Nawab*, Moi Ave, T20754. A/c restaurant, good value, the staff are reasonably friendly but the service is slow. **3** *Singh*, Mwembe Tayari Rd, T493283. Good a/c restaurant, although the menu is not very extensive the food is freshly prepared and very tasty. **2** *New Chetna*, Haile Selassie Rd. South Indian, vegetarian, all you can eat for US$3, very good value. **2** *Indian Ocean* restaurant, (previously *Geetanjali*), Msanifu Kombo St. New name and owner. Recommended. **2** *Indo Africa*, Haile Selassie Rd, T21430. Reasonable value. **2** *Shehnai*, Fatemi House, Maungano St, T312492. Sound cuisine, pleasant decor.

International **4** *Tamarind*, Silo Rd at Nyali this is a 15 minute drive from central Mombasa, T471747. It is well worth the journey for it has marvellous views looking over a creek that flows into the ocean, the Moorish design of the building is well thought out – it has high arches and is cool and spacious, the food and service are both excellent – it specializes in seafood, if you can't choose between dishes try the seafood platter, be sure to phone and reserve a table. **3** *Hard Rock Cafe*, Ground Flr, Electricity House, next to Kenya Airways, Nkrumah Rd, PO Box 99458, Mombasa, T222221/222228. Lively atmosphere, good quality but rather expensive food, a/c, gilt and marble decor. **3** *Le Bistro*, on Moi Ave. Fairly new place, open all day, and serving a range of food from pizza to seafood, high quality, imaginative food, looking decidedly shabby now, tile topped tables, wicker lamps covered with red cloth, bar upstairs, tables on pavement. Well recommended. **3** *Splendid*, Msanifu Kombo St, rooftop restaurant of the *Hotel Splendid*. Pleasant and not too expensive. **2** *Blue Room Restaurant*, Haile Selassie Rd. Excellent bright, clean cafeteria style, tile floor and tables, it serves fish and chips, burgers, chicken and all the usual Indian snacks, popular with locals.

Italian **4** *Capri Restaurant*, Ambalal House, on Nkrumah Rd, T311156. This Italian restaurant is one of Mombasa's most sophisticated restaurants, it is well a/c, the food is superb – especially the seafood dishes – and it has a wonderful atmosphere, it is infamous for its slow service, closed Sunday. **3** *Cinabar*, located in Nyali close to the new Nyali Bridge, T472373. Italian cuisine, good value. **2** *Franco's*, Moi Ave, just west of Tusks. Rather gloomy inside, pizzas and grills.

Cafés **2** *Afro Take Away*, Moi Ave near Kenya Airways. Good cheap food, friendly staff. **2** *Arcade Café*, Ambalal House, Nkrumah Rd. Curries and burgers, cheerful modern decor. **2** *Blue Fin*, bit run down, mostly grills and fish, nothing special. **2** *Castle*, centrally located on Moi Ave. Mombasa's answer to the *Thorn Tree* in Nairobi, very popular and is ideal for a snack and cold drink. **2** *Fayaz*, Abdul Nassir Rd. Pastisserie and snacks, clean, bright and modern. **2** *Gemini*, Ambalal House, Nkrumah Rd, in Ambalal arcade. Fast food, ice cream, bright and smart. **2** *Ingo's Snack Bar*, in arcade on Moi Ave, west of Tusks. Plenty of mirrors, glass, pastas, grills, ice cream, bar, modern and pleasant decor. **2** *Luxus Café*, on Nkrumah Ave, just in front of Holy Ghost Cathedral. Grills, sound and sensible, comfortable and clean. **2** *Palacio*, corner of Digo St and Moi Ave. Snacks and ice cream, pleasant modern decor. **2** *Paradise*, at entrance to Fort Jesus, excellent cold juices and snacks. **2** *Pistacchio Ice Cream and Coffee Bar*, Msanifu Kombo St. Wonderful ice cream and fruit juices, it serves snacks and you can also have proper meals – including a buffet lunch, pleasant decor, well-run. Thoroughly recommended. **2** *Whimpey*, behind Tusks on Moi Ave. Hamburgers and ice cream. **1** *Anglo-Swiss Bakery*, on Chembe Rd. Delicious bread and pastries. **1** *Hamburger House*, Kisumu Rd, not far from Tusks. Rather dilapidated, nothing special. **1** *Hastee Tastee Ice Cream Parlour*, Nyerere Ave. Another favourite. **1** *Heko Bar and Restaurant*, Kwa Shibu Rd, near Meru Rd. Large lively bar with extensive courtyard area to the rear, charcoal grills. **1** *Mombasa Coffee House*, Moi Ave. The best in Kenyan coffee, cold juices.

Bars   *Lotus Hotel*, corner of Mvita, comfortable atmosphere. *Sky Bar and Restaurant*, bar and disco, large, central location, has become one of the main social centres of town since the demise of the *Castle Hotel* and its famous terrace, no entrance fee. *Casablanca Club*, bar and disco, not really a club, open courtyard bar on ground floor, disco and bar upstairs, fairly new, pleasant decor, very lively in evenings, no entrance fee. Well recommended.

Entertainment   **Cinemas**   *Lotus* and the *Kenya*, which are both located fairly centrally as well as the *Drive In*. See what's on in *Coastweek* which is the local paper.

Gambling   *International Casino*, *Oceanic Hotel*, Lighthouse Rd, T312838.

Massage   *Lee Jim Hotel*, Durana Rd. *Splendid Hotel*, Msanifu Kombo St. *Kuona Hotel*, Tangana Rd. *Lee Jim Hotel*, Meru Rd. **Coast Massage**, 2nd Flr, Ambalal House, Nkrumah Rd. *Benita's Massage*, Room 107, *Manson Hotel*, Kisumu Rd.

Nightclubs   *Istanbul*, Moi Ave. Lively place. *New Florida Club and Casino*, Mama Ngina Drive. *Rainbows*, Mnazi Moja Rd. *Rainbow House Night Club*, corner of Moi Ave and Meru Rd. Popular disco and reggae club. *Sunshine*, Moi Ave. *Toyz* on Baluchi St. *Tiffany's* Ambalal House.

Sports (participant)   *Mombasa Sports Club* is located on Mnazi Mosi Rd. It offers a fairly wide range of activities. *Yacht and Rowing Club* in the southwest of the island close to the *Outrigger Hotel*. They have a busy programme – both races and social events. *Mvita Tennis Club*, near *Lotus Hotel*, off Nkrumah Rd.

Shopping   **Curios**   *Labeka*, Moi Ave, east of Tusks. Good selection of items.

Sea shells   Do not buy any shells at all. As a result of killing the animals that live inside the shells to sell them to tourists, populations have declined dramatically and many are seriously threatened. The vendor may tell you he has a licence – but if you want these species to survive into the next century you should not encourage this trade.

Souvenirs   That you will find in Mombasa are wooden carvings including Makonde carvings from Tanzania, soap stone carvings and chess sets, baskets, batiks and jewellery. There are lots of stalls in and around the market and around the junction of Digo Rd and Jomo Kenyatta Ave. There are also lots along Msanifu Kombo St; along Moi Ave from the *Castle Hotel* and down to the roundabout with Nyerere Ave; and around Fort Jesus. For kikois,

Deep-sea fishing

Most hotels up and down the coast do not own their own sports fishing boats, with the exception of Hemingways and the Pemba Channel Fishing Club. In order to maintain international standards of fishing such as governed by the IGFA (International Game Fish Association) and in keeping with the emphasis on conservation in sports fishing, KASA (Kenya Association of Sea Anglers) members support tag and release of billfish. It is a must for visitors to check out the company they are fishing with, and request information about the track record and safety equipment of the fishing boats advertising deep sea fishing. There are a number of companies that operate with less than satisfactory basic equipment, at cheap rates, with no safety back-up facilities. You are advised to check whether the company are KASA members before making your choice. Kenya has a nine month deep sea fishing season which runs from the beginning of August to around late April, although a few boats may sometimes fish through the rainy season as well. August through November is best for Tuna and Sailfish, and the main Billfish run is December to March. However, it is possible to catch big fish throughout the year. Before going out, it is advisable to find out who owns the fish caught, and how many people the boat can accommodate, since this varies from place to place. Boats vary from luxury 47 foot twin screw sport fishing cruisers down through a wide range of lesser craft both for inshore and offshore fishing. The bigger offshore craft boats will be equipped with all the tackle you need, most of it heavy gear in the 80 lb and 50 lb classes. These boats are fitted with VHF radio and are capable of going far out after the biggest fish. Some companies specialize in spin casting and bottom fishing.

Recommended Charter Boat operators: In Lamu: Peponi Hotel, PO Box 24, Lamu, T0121-33421/3, F0121-33029. Boat: Gem, 28 foot twin diesel. **In Malindi:** Kingfisher, PO Box 29, Malindi, T0123-21168/20123, F0123-30261. Boats: Snowgoose, 36 foot twin

diesel; Tina, 35 foot Striker; Nepture, 35 foot Bertram twin diesel; Snark, 31 foot twin diesel; Eclare, 33 foot Aquabell twin diesel. **Peter Ready**, PO Box 63, Malindi, T0123-21292, F0123-30032. Boat: Seahorse, 34 foot twin diesel. **In Watamu: Hemingways**, PO Box 267, Watamu, T0122-32624/32006, F0122-32256, Tx21373, Heways Ke. Boats: B's Nest, 35 foot Bertram twin diesel; Ol Jogi, 33 foot Bertram twin diesel; White Bear, 38 foot Sport fisherman twin diesel; Kaskazi, 24 foot twin outboards. **Tega Safaris Ltd**, PO Box 12, Watamu, T0122-32078. Boat: Tega, 33 foot Aquabell twin diesel. **In Mtwapa: James Adcock Fishing Ltd**, PO Box 95693, Mombasa, T011-485527. Boats: Vuma, 31 foot twin outboards; Oona, 25 foot twin outboards; Samvuke, 29 foot Sesse Canoe twin outboards for spin casting and bottom fishing. **In Mombasa:** Howard Lawrence-Brown, Hall Mark Charters, PO Box 10202, Mombasa, T011-485680/485808, mobile phone T254/0-071-400095, F011-485808/475217. Boats: Kipapa, 38 foot Commander Sportfisherman twin diesel; Bahari Kuu, 32 foot Catamaran Sportfisherman twin outboards. Hall Mark Charters' clients hold the IGFA All Africa record Wahoo 43.6 kilograms on 24 kilogram class line, and a Black Marlin 135.17 kilograms on 15 kilogram Class line. **Deep Water Sport Fishing**, Eligio Battaia, PO Box 82679, Mombasa, T491061/493756, F493756. Boat: Inca, 33 foot Rybovich Sportfisher twin diesel. **In Diani:** Nomad Boats, PO Box 1, Ukunda, via Mombasa, T/F0127-2156. Boats: Amani, 27 foot twin outboards; Mwinza, 27 foot twin outboards; Nomad II, 27 foot twin outboards. **In Shimoni: Pemba Channel Fishing Club**, PO Box 86952, Mombasa, T0-11313749, F0-316875. Boats: White Otter, 44 foot twin 120 Sabre diesels; Pingusi, 30 foot twin Perkins diesels; Countdown, 33½ foot twin Perkins diesels; Pandora, 27 foot twin outboards. **Sea Adventures Ltd** (Pat and Simon Hemphill), PO Box 56, Shimoni, T12/13 (Shimoni). Boats: Broadbill, 46 foot Sportfisherman twin diesels; Kamara, 32 foot Sportfisherman twin diesels.

kangas and other material or fabric go to Biashara St which runs off Digo St parallel to Jomo Kenyatta Ave. The bundles of sticks you see for sale on Kenyatta Ave are chewed and used to clean teeth. The darker sticks are chewed for stomach upsets.

👉 *Lunatic express*

Construction of the railway that was to be dubbed the "Lunatic Express" (see page 284) began in 1896. Until the railway was built the only means of getting inland was by foot and this was how the early explorers and missionaries travelled. It was soon realised that it was not economical for cash crops such as cotton to be grown in Uganda if they then had to face this protracted journey to the coast before they could be exported.

The railway was built using indentured labour from Punjab and Gujarat in India and many of these remained to form the Asian population that is found in East Africa today.

The railway was built through some extremely harsh environments and across some very difficult terrain. A further problem was the wildlife in the area and it was the "Man-Eating Lions of Tsavo" that really caught the public's imagination. During construction these lions attacked the camps, mauling and killing some of the workers.

Despite the problems - including the difficult engineering problems that were involved in climbing the Rift Valley escarpment - the railway reached Nairobi in 1899, Kisumu on Lake Victoria in 1901, but did not finally reach Kampala until 1928.

Transport   **Local   Car hire   Avenue Motors**, PO Box 83697, Moi Ave, T25162/315111; **Avis**, PO Box 84868, Moi Ave, T23048 and at the airport T43321; **Coast Car Hire**, PO Box 99143, Ambalal House, Nkrumah Rd, T311752; **Glory Car Hire**, PO Box 85527, Moi Ave, T313561; **Leisure Car Hire**, PO Box 84902, Moi Ave, T314935; **Ocean Car Hire**, PO Box 84798, Digo St, T313559/313083/23049. **Likoni ferry**: joins the mainland with the island. They go about every 20 minutes and are free for pedestrians and cyclists. Matatus to the ferry leave from outside the Post Office on Digo Rd – ask for Likoni.

Air   Mombasa is served by a number of different airlines, as well as by chartered planes for safaris etc. **Kenya Airlines** does the Nairobi-Mombasa-Malindi route once a day in both directions (except Saturday). It is a popular route so be sure to book well ahead and confirm your seat. The problem of double booking can be serious. Also serving this route are **Eagle Aviation**, T316054 (Mombasa); **Equator Airlines**, T2053 (Malindi); **Prestige Air Services**, T20860 (Malindi); **Skyways Airlines**, T432167 (Mombasa). All have 2 flights per day in both directions between Malindi and Mombasa. Baggage allowance is only 10 kilograms, and check in time is 30 minutes before take off. Airport tax is around US$1. **Tai Aviation**, cheapest to Lamu, US$140 return, PO Box 357, Malindi, T/F0123-31839. **Kenya Airways** flies 4 times a week to Zanzibar (US$60 plus US$20 departure tax). Moi International Airport is located on the mainland about 10 kilometres out of the centre of town. Kenya Airways operates a shuttle bus, about US$2. Taxi about US$9. Also public buses and matatus. Airport departure tax must be paid – currently US$1.50.

Train   Please see page 72 for details of train services, timetables and fares.

Road   Bus: there are lots of bus companies that go to **Nairobi** whose offices are to be found on Jomo Kenyatta Ave. They usually leave early morning and evening and take between 8 and 12 hours following the damage that El Niño inflicted on the roads. There are also 2 upmarket a/c shuttle services operating between Mombasa and Nairobi, called SavLine and The Connection – see page for booking details. Fares vary and are about US$9. Buses and matatus depart for **Malindi** frequently throughout the day and take about 3 hours. They leave Mombasa from Abdel Nasser Rd outside the *New People's Hotel*. Alternatively you can get together with a group and hire a Peugeot 504 station wagon as a share-taxi. They take 7 people and leave when full so get there early. They work out about the same price as the bus. For **Lamu** by bus (10 hours) Tawfiq US$8. Booking office on Jomo Kenyatta Ave. Early morning departure. However, *TSS Bus* on Digo St, PO Box 85059, T224541/222201/222916/222917, F223216. Well recommended. Seats bookable and no over-crowding with standing passengers. Heading south to Tanzania there are buses run by a company called *Cat Bus*, 3 times a week on Monday, Wednesday and Friday. They leave at 1600, and take about 8 hours to Tanga and 20 hours to Dar es Salaam. *Hood Buses*, US$3.50 to **Tanga**, US$8 to **Dar es Salaam**, US$9 to **Morogoro**, leave at 0900, driver and conductor listed on daily blackboard for the morrow's departures. The Mombasa/Lunga Lunga road is good although during the 97/98 El Niño rains several bridges and river crossings were washed away, many of which are still under repair.

Boat There have been boats (hydrofoils) from Mombasa to **Tanga**, **Zanzibar** and **Dar es Salaam** (see page 69). Although these have not been operating for a while partial resumption of the service has started. Mega Speed Liners now run a hydrofoil to Pemba US$30 and Zanzibar US$50 at 0900 Sunday. Book at *Kuldips Touring* on the south end of Mji Mpya Rd, or when boarding. Boat leaves from Kilindini Harbour. The cost to Dar es Salaam was about the same as the air fare (US$45). It is possible to take a dhow from Mombasa to **Tanga** and **Dar es Salaam** (see page 69). However, you must expect to wait around for a week or more for one to depart. It will take 1 or 2 days depending on the weather. Expect to pay about US$15 to Dar es Salaam, bring all your own food, and you will sit and sleep on the cargo. At one time it was also possible to get dhows to **Kismayo**, **Mogadishu**, **Berbera** and **Djibouti**. These are not currently an option with the civil war in Somalia.

Kenya

Directory

Banks There is a *Barclays Bank* on Moi Ave, PO Box 90183, T221952, where you can change TCs from 0900 to 1630 on weekdays and 0900 to 1400 on Sat. *Commercial Bank of Africa*, Moi Ave, PO Box 90681, Mombasa, T224711/224803, F315274; *Kenya Commercial Bank*, Moi Ave, PO Box 90254, T220978/223799. *National Bank of Kenya*, Nkrumah Rd, PO Box 90388, T311508/311733. *Standard Chartered Bank*, Moi Ave, PO Box 90670, T224351/2, F316750. **Bureau d'Exchange:** *Pwani Bureau d'Exchange*, opposite Mackinnon Market on Digo Rd, fast, efficient, good rates offered. Recommended; *Fort Jesus Forex*, near entrance to Fort Jesus on Nkrumah Rd.

Communications Post Office: Digo St, Mon-Fri 0800 to 1800, Sat from 0800 to 1200.

Consulates *Austria*, Mr T Gaal, PO Box 84045, Mombasa, Office T313386, Home T485550. *Belgium*, Mr F Van Burkom, PO Box 90141, Mombasa, Office T314531/220231, Home T471315. *Denmark* and Finland, Mr J Nielson, PO Box 99543, Mombasa, Office T316776, dir 316243, Home T471616, 471506. *France*, Mrs Z Blevins, PO Box 86103, Mombasa, Office T314935/315446, Home T485944/485253. *Germany*, Mr G Matthiessen, PO Box 86779, Mombasa, Office T314732/224938, Home T0127-20602114. *Greece*, Mr P Ch Lagoussis, PO Box 99211, Mombasa, Office T220898/224482, F222751, Home T485637. *India*, Asst Commissioner Mr JM Sharma, PO Box 90614, Mombasa, Office T224433/311051, Home T311819. *Italy*, Capt M Esposito, PO Box 80443, Office T314705/7, Home T472091. *Netherlands*, Mr LJM Van de Lande, PO Box 80301, Mombasa, Office T311043, Home T471250/472932, Tx21267, F315005. *Norway*, Mrs A Sondhi, PO Box 82234, Mombasa, Office T471771, Home T490415. *Sweden*, Mr I Hellman, PO Box 87336, Mombasa, Office T316172/3, Home T473468. *Switzerland*, E Habermachr, PO Box 85722, Mombasa, Office T316684/5, Home T485314. *United Kingdom*, Capt Richard GC Diamond, PO Box 80424, Mombasa, Office T312817/316331, Home T316502/316486. *United Republic of Tanzania*, Mr Juma A Ali, Deputy Consul-General, PO Box 1422, Mombasa, T228596, Tx21403 TZ CONS, Telegram: TANZAN CONS Palli House Nyerere Ave.

Cultural centres *Allianco Francaise*, Freed Building, Moi Ave. *German Institute*, Freed Building, Moi Ave. *British Council*, Sheetal Plaza, off Moi Ave just west of the tusks.

Hospitals & medical services Hospitals: *Aga Khan Hospital*, PO Box 83013, Vanga Rd, T321953. *Mombasa Hospital*, PO Box 90294, Mama Ngina Drive, T312190/312099. *Pandya Memorial Hospital*, PO Box 90434, Dedan Kimathi Ave, T314140. *Coast General Hospital*, PO Box 90231, T314201. **Pharmacies:** *Coast Medical Stores*, Digo Rd, T25600/26435, open from 0800 to 1230 and 1400 to 1600. *Digo Chemist*, Meru Rd, T316065, open 0800 to 1900 on weekdays, 0800 to 1500 on Sat and 0900 to 1300 on Sun.

Places of worship For Mosques see page 167 above. *Jain Temple*, on Langoni Rd, built in 1963 which is a splendid sight with a pair of lions flanking the entrance. The most important religious centre for Mombasa's Hindus is the *Lord Shiva Temple* which is located on the edge of the Old Town. The *Holy Ghost Cathedral* is located on the corner of Nkrumah Rd and Digo Rd and dates from 1918. There has been a church on this site since 1891.

Tour companies & travel agents *Across Africa Safaris*, PO Box 82139, Moi Ave, T315360/314394. *African Tours and Hotels*, PO Box 90604, Moi Ave, T23509/20627. *Airtour Suisse*, PO Box 84198, Moi Ave, T312565. *Archers*, PO Box 84618, Nkrumah Rd, T25362/311884. *Big Five Tours and Safaris*, PO Box 86922, Nkrumah Rd, T311462/311524. *Big Wave Holiday*, Grd Flr, Ambasal House, PO Box 90488, Mombasa, T2288039/222989. *Black Bird Tours & Travel Ltd*, Regal Chamber, Moi Ave, PO Box 40003, T225332. *Express Safaris*, PO Box 86031, Moi Ave, T25699. *Felix Safaris*, Electricity House, PO Box 40484, T227836. *Flamingo Tours*, PO Box 83321, Ambalal House, Nkrumah Rd, T315635. *Glory Tours and Safaris*, PO Box 85527, Moi Ave, T313561. *Highways*, PO Box 84787, T26886/20383. *Kenya Mystery Tours Ltd*, Canon Tower, Moi Ave, Grd Flr, PO Box 41800, T229247, F315927. *Kuldips Touring*, PO Box 82662, Moi Ave, T25928/24067. *Leisure Tours and Safaris*, PO Box 84902, Moi Ave, T24704/314846. *Lofty Safaris Ltd*, 1st Flr, Hassanali Bldg, Nkrumah Rd, PO Box 81933, T220241/315789, F314397. *Marajani Tours*, PO Box 86103, Moi Ave, T314935/315099. *Pollman Tours and Safaris*, PO Box 84198, Taveta Rd/Shimanzi, T316732/220926/229082/224732, F314502/312245, Tx21229. *Private Safaris*, PO Box 85722, Ambalal House, Nkrumah Rd, T316684/5. *Rhino Safaris*, PO Box 83050, Nkrumah Rd, T311755/311141/311536. *Rusco Tours and Safaris*, PO Box 99162, Maungano Rd, T313664/21137. *Savage Camping Tours*, PO Box 561, Diamond Trust House, near *Castle Hotel*, Moi Ave, T228236, F315545. *Sawa Sawa Tours*, PO Box 80766, Nkrumah Rd, T313187/3114790. *Southern Cross Safaris*, PO Box 90653, Nkrumah Rd, T471960, F471257. *Sunny Safaris*, PO Box 87049, Moi Ave, T23578/20162. *Thorn Trees Safaris*, PO Box 81953, Nkrumah Rd. *Transafric Tours and Travel Services*, PO Box 84198, Haile Selassie Rd, T26928. *Turkana Safari*, PO Box 99300, Moi Ave, T21065. *United Touring Company*, PO Box 84782, Moi Ave, T316333/4, F314549. It is possible to do a cruise of the Old Harbour and Kilindini Harbour. Ask at the *Castle Hotel* on Moi Ave, T315569, who arrange them. They take about 4 hrs and you can either do a lunchtime or evening cruise leaving at 1030 and 1800. They are not cheap, but the price includes food and live music. *Tamarind Restaurant*, T472263, also arranges lunch cruises which are excellent although, again, not cheap.

Tourist offices Moi Ave near the Tusks, T311231/225428. Open from 0800 to 1630 with 2 hrs off for lunch. It sells a map of Mombasa as well as guide books of Mombasa Old Town and Fort Jesus.

Useful addresses Police station: Makadara Rd, T311401.

South Coast

You are unlikely to visit Mombasa without going to the beach – this is the reason that most people come here as these beaches are some of the best in the world. The sand is white and very fine – it is actually coral that has been broken down by pounding waves over the centuries. There are a few well-developed areas, but you shouldn't have to go too far to find a quiet spot.

The coast is hot and humid all the year round although the rainfall varies. From April to June is the quietest season – this is when it is often overcast and muggy. However there is the definite advantage of cheaper accommodation and greater availability of places to stay.

*Running from Mombasa south, the main beaches are **Shelley**, **Tiwi** and **Diani**. The most popular beach on the south coast is Diani – it is also the most built up and not surprisingly is now the most expensive. However, most of the buildings have been designed well and local materials have been used so the hotels do not intrude too much. The hotels all have their own restaurants and bars and most of them arrange regular evening entertainment such as traditional African dancers and singers.*

Shelley Beach

This is the closest beach to Mombasa, ideal for a day trip if you are staying in the town. Swimming here can be problematic due to excessive seaweed. **Sleeping A** *Shelley Beach*, PO Box 96030, T451001/2/3/4, F315743. This is the only place to stay on this beach, it is located about 3 kilometres from the Likoni ferry and is well signposted, the hotel has over 100 rooms as well as some cottages that are ideal for families, there is a swimming pool very close to the sea, other facilities include tennis courts, watersports, glass bottom boat trips, restaurant, coffee shop and verandas, the hotel has wheelchair access. **B** *Savannah Cottages*, just south of Shelley Beach Hotel. Pleasant and relaxing atmosphere. **C** *CPK Guest House*, PO Box 96170, T451619. Not very near to the beach, but very good value, a church-run place.

Tiwi Beach

Going south from Likoni, Tiwi Beach is the next that you come to. It is about 20 kilometres from Likoni Ferry and is three kilometres off the main coastal road down a very bumpy track. It's the least developed of the beaches near Mombasa, so it's usually not swarming with package tourists. It is wise not to walk down this track – there have been muggings. This beach is wider than that at Shelley and it is particularly popular with families and with budget travellers as it has camping facilities and budget accommodation. It is ideal for children – the reef is quite close to the mainland which keeps the waves smaller than those at Diani. There is also lots for small children to do – hundreds of pools are exposed when the tide is out, all with plenty of marine life in them. There is also some quite good snorkelling here. It is possible to scuba dive too. *Tiwi Scuba Divers*, Tiwi Beach, PO Box 96242, Kwale Mombasa. Full beginners course and open water dive, four day course US$350, first discovery dive US$75. Refresher course and open water dives and equipment hire US$60, proof of qualifications required. British instructors – PADI/Bsac qualifications. If you walk up the beach in the direction of Shelly Beach for about one and a half kilometres you come to a rock pool in the shape of the African continent, this so called 'Pool of Africa' is quite spectacular. You can swim in the pool and even dive through a small tunnel to another pool aptly named Madagascar.

Before you go exploring on the reef check up on the tides (they are published in the local papers) and set out with plenty of time. It is very easy to get cut off when the tide comes in and it does turn quite rapidly. Also be sure you have a good pair of thick rubber soled shoes to protect your feet against the coral and sea urchins. Prone to large amounts of seaweed in April/May. Another advantage of Tiwi Beach is the absence of beach sellers. It is possible to walk south to Diani Beach at low tide, but again it is important to ensure you check the times of the tides to avoid getting stranded.

South coast

Port Reitz
Likoni
Ngombeni
Kwale
Waa
Shimba Hills National Reserve
Tiwi — Tiwi Beach
Ukunda — Diani Beach
Mwabungu — Galu Beach
Gazi — Gazi Beach
To Tanzania
Indian Ocean
Funzi — Funzi Island
Shimoni
Wasini Island

N

0 km   10

■ **Sleeping**
1 Beachcomber
2 Black Marlin
3 Caprichio
4 Coral Cove
5 Diani Reef & Dan Trench's
6 Funzi Beach Fishing Club
7 Jadini
8 Maweni Cottages
9 Pemba Channel
10 Robinson's Baobab

11 Savannah Cottages
12 Shelly Beach Fishing Club
13 Shimoni Reef
14 Seascapes Villas
15 Tiwi Villas
16 Warrandale
17 Tiwi Sea Castles
   Indian Ocean
   Beach Club
   Southern Palms
   Golden Beach
18 Trade Winds
   Two Fishes
   African Sea Lodge
19 Nomao Beach
   Safari Beach
   Paradise Union

Related map
The Coast, page 160

Kenya

Sleeping **A+** *The Indian Ocean Beach Club*, at the site of the 16th century Kongo mosque, overlooking the Tiwi River estuary, secluded 25 acres old coconut and baobab trees, moorish-style arched main building with smaller 'Makuta' thatched roof buildings, 100 rooms, en suite bathrooms, a/c, fans, phones, 2 restaurants, 3 bars, marine activities, courtesy bus shuttle to Diani shopping centre. Book through Block Hotels, PO Box 40075, Nairobi, T2-540780, F2-543810, or *Let's Go Travel*, Caxton House, Standard St, PO Box 60342, Nairobi, T2-340331/213033, F2-336890/214713. **A** *Golden Beach Hotel*, PO Box 31, Ukunda, T0127-2625, F0127-3188. Reservations through AT&H, Utaili House, Uhuru Highway, PO Box 30471, Nairobi, T2-336858, F2-218109. Rather ugly concrete hotel. **A** *Travellers Tiwi Beach Hotel*, PO Box 87649 Mombasa, T0127-51202/5, F51207. Opened in 1997, well designed and in keeping with the local environment, exceptional swimming pool, approximately 250 metres in length connected by channels and slides. **B-D** *Coral Cove Cottages*, PO Box 200, Ukunda, T0127-51295, F51062 or PO Box 23456, Nairobi, T/F02-582508. Has bandas (round thatched cottages) which vary in price – the six most expensive 2-bedroomed have bathrooms while the other four are cheaper and more basic, lovely location, a beautiful white sand beach, with swaying palm trees in a private cove, good value. The 2-bedroomed cottages are supplied with a personal cook/house-help/laundry-man at the inclusive rate of US$26 for 4 people per day. Cheaper cottages cost from US$3. **C** *Capricho Beach Cottages*, PO Box 96093, T0127-51231, F51010. Self-contained cottages, in a complex which has a swimming pool. **C** *Minilets*, PO Box 96242, T0127-51059/51054, next to *Twiga Lodge*. Has a lively bar, and is renowned for barbecues and curry dishes, chalets are set in sloping green garden. Not all the bandas are open. Simple but somewhat overpriced. **C** *Tiwi Sea Castles*, PO Box 96599 Likoni-Mombasa, T0127-51220/1/2, F51222. Very good rooms and facilities, bar, restaurant, swimming pool. Good service. **D** *Mawani Beach Cottages*, PO Box 96024, Mombasa, T0127-51008, F51225. Self-catering. **D** *Twiga Lodge*, PO Box 80820, Mombasa, T0127-51210/51267 or 225490. This is one of the oldest of the lodges on this beach. There are self contained or shared rooms and bandas or you can camp. The rooms are poor and overpriced. There is a good restaurant and shop. Nice beach at low tide. **E** *Camping*, facilities here are fairly basic but it is right on the beach and there is plenty of shade, there is a restaurant which does fairly good meals and snacks and a shop with most supplies that you will need. There were some security problems recently but Twiga Lodge camping appear to have tackled them. **E** *Sand Island Beach Self Catering Cottages*, PO Box 96006, Likani via Mombasa, T0127-51233, F0127-51201. Quiet and a little remote. **E** *Tiwi Villas*, 2-4 bedroomed villas, T0127-51265, F51265, PO Box 86775, Mombasa, next to campsite. Cheap food, suitable for divers.

Transport **Road Bus**: take a bus or matatu from Likoni and ask to be dropped off at Tiwi Beach. It is about 3 kilometres from the main road to the beach and unless there is a fairly big group of you then it is advisable to wait for a lift as there have been attacks on people walking down this road. You should not have to wait too long – and it is not worth the risk of going alone. There is also a newly established taxi service doing this route.

Diani Beach

Phone code: 0127 At about 20 kilometres this is the longest beach in Kenya and has a whole string of hotels. It is also the place to come if you want to do a bit of windsurfing or watersports including sailing, windsurfing, snorkelling and scuba diving. You can also go water-skiing or parascending, or can hire a bike or a motor bike. It is geared to the big spending package tourist which obviously has some disadvantages. However it is a classic paradise beach with endless dazzling white sand, coconut trees and clear sea.

The reef and tides At low tide you can go out to the reef which is worth doing at least once. At Diani you will need to take a boat if you want to go out to the main reef, although you should be able to wade out to the sand bank which is not too far. Of course this depends on the tides. The tides are controlled by the moon, in a monthly cycle. At full moon there are spring tides which means high High Tides and low Low Tides, while a fortnight later there will be neap tides with low Highs and high Lows. There are advantages to both – wind surfers may prefer neap tides as you will be able to go out for longer, while those who want huge waves at high tide, as well as going out to the reef during the low tide, the spring is probably better as it has the biggest contrasts. The timing of the tides changes and are published in local papers. Obviously if you are only at the coast for a few days there will not be much difference – but if you particularly want to do something (such as going out to the reef) it is worth looking up the tides and planning ahead so as to make the best of your time.

Vendors There are now hoards of hawkers who walk up and down the beach selling all sorts of things as well as offering themselves as models for photos. Most of the goods are hugely overpriced and are often of very poor quality. They may also try to sell you ivory and elephant hair bracelets. These are probably fake and anyway should not be bought if the elephant is not to go the way of the dodo. It may also surprise you to learn that some of the Masai who come round offering themselves for a photo (at a charge of course) are not Masai at all but are of other tribes.

At the far north of Diani beach just past *Indian Ocean Club*, is the **Kongo Mosque** (also known as the Diani Persian Mosque). It is rather a strange place – it is very run down but not really a ruin – and still has some ritual significance. The building is believed to date from the 15th century and is the only remaining building from a settlement of the Shirazi people (see page 356) who used to live here. There are a number of entrances and you should be able to push one of the doors open and have a look inside. **NB** Unofficial touts try to charge tourists US$20 each to have a look (they even have their own padlocks), refuse to pay.

Sights

Apart from the beach and the sea the other major attraction on this stretch of coast is the **Shimba Hills National Reserve** (see page 276). There are also the marine reserves, and you will see plenty of notices about trips in glass bottom boats. These can be excellent if you go to a good section of reef but on some of the trips you see little more than sand and seaweed (see Watamu Marine Park, page 196). Closer to the hotels is the **Jadini Forest** which is a small patch of forest that used to cover the whole of this coastal area. There are colobus monkeys and porcupine as well as other animals.

There is a really nice 'bushwalk' from Diani to Ukunda, starting opposite *Trade Winds* (about two kilometres) leading along the airport and Ukunda School. You will end up at a huge baobab tree, said by the locals to be the biggest in Africa, surrounded by several woodcarvers. The carvings are of good quality and are cheaper than at the beach. A colony of black and white vervet monkeys live in the tree. Crossing the village you will see some typical African huts. People are very friendly and don't mind you passing through the village.

The better hotels are all good value compared, say with similar standard hotels in the Seychelles or Mauritius. Prices vary with the season **Low** is April-June; **Mid** is July-October; **High** is December-March.

Sleeping

A+ *Diani House*, PO Box 19, Ukunda, T12612412. This is an extremely exclusive hotel that only takes 8 guests at any one time, it was a private house and is set in 12 acres of gardens and forest right on the beach, the price includes all meals and a trip to the Shimba Game Reserve. **A+** *Southern Palms*, PO Box 363, Ukunda, T0127-3721, 3360/4, F0127-3381. Facilities include boutique, hair and beauty salon, 2 swimming pools, 2 a/c squash courts, outside tennis courts, and gymnasium, water facilities including windsurfing, scuba diving (lessons available) and deep sea fishing.

A *Africana Sea Lodge*, PO Box 84616, T01261/2726, Tx22591. This is linked to the *Jardini Beach Hotel* and you can use the facilities of both – this is marginally cheaper than the *Jardini*, instead of standard rooms the *East Africana* has bandas, some of which are divided into 2, they are set in gardens, each have a little verandah and all are a/c with bathrooms, the facilities are the same as for the *Jardini* – some are shared although it has its own swimming pool. **A** *Diani Reef*, PO Box 35, Ukunda, T01261-2175/6/7. This is a comfortable hotel, all the rooms are a/c and the hotel has all the usual facilities including a craft shop, doctor, bar, restaurant and disco. **A** *Diani Sea Lodge*, PO Box 37, Ukunda, T01261-2114/5/2060. These are self catering cottages that are ideal for families and are popular with expatriates, they vary in size and price – but you hire the cottage and can get as many people in as you want, they all have a balcony and are simple but very pleasant and excellent value. **A** *Jadini Beach*, PO Box 84616, T0127-2021. This is linked to the *Africana Sea Lodge*, and you can use the facilities of both of the hotels, the *Jadini* has about 150 normal hotel rooms, while the *East Africana* has individual bandas, all rooms are a/c and have a balcony or terrace, facilities include swimming pool, squash courts, tennis courts, health club, watersports, bar, restaurant, meeting rooms, shops and evening entertainment including live dancing, films and disco. **A** *Robinsons Baobab*, PO Box 32, Ukunda, T0127-2623/2030, F2030, Tx21132. Set up on the cliff at the southern end of Diani this looks out across the sea, to get to the beach you have to climb down the steep steps, it used to be a very popular hotel with package tours who seemed to have their whole day planned out for them: 0800-0900 Early Morning Jog; 0900-1000 Breakfast; 1000-1030 Aerobics; 1030-1100 Coffee; 1100-1200 Postcard Writing and so on, it has about 150 a/c rooms as well as a number of bungalows suitable for families or groups, facilities include a library, restaurant, swimming pool, bar, watersports and diving facilities, shops, hairdresser and lots of organized activities, you can learn Swahili here. **A** *Safari Beach*, PO Box 90690, T0127-2726/3622, F2357. This is a large hotel with about 180 rooms, they are in round bandas which are grouped into villages set in wonderful gardens, all are a/c and very comfortable, facilities include meeting rooms, tennis courts, squash courts, swimming pool, bar, restaurant and watersports. **A** *Trade Winds*, PO Box 8, Ukunda, T0127-2016, F2010. One of the most northerly of the big hotels this is also one of the older ones on Diani, it has about 100 rooms all of which are a/c, it was well designed and is one of the most attractive of the hotels, facilities include swimming pool, watersports and very attractive gardens **A** *Two Fishes*, PO Box 23, Ukunda, T0127-2720, F2106. This is the hotel with the swimming pool that goes under part of the hotel and into the bar, it is one of the oldest hotels on Diani and for a long time had the most imaginative swimming pool – all the other hotels had straightforward rectangular pools, children love the idea of swimming under the hotel and there are a few water chutes and slides, non-residents can swim here but at a daily fee, it has been done up fairly recently.

B *Glory Palace Hotel* (**C** in low season), South Coast-Diani, PO Box 85527, T0-1272276, is located on the road between Ukunda and Diani. Offers a restaurant, swimming pool, and small simple rooms with s/c bathrooms, the rooms near the road are noisy, offers taxi service and car rental. **B** *Golden Beach*, PO Box 31, Ukunda, T0126-12625, F3188. This is one of the less attractive hotels and the architect would not get any prizes for blending into the surroundings, it is modern and very large with about 150 rooms all with bathrooms, facilities include meeting rooms, swimming pool, shops, restaurant, bar, tennis courts, gym, watersports facilities and wheelchair access. **B** *Leopard Beach*, PO Box 34, Ukunda, T01261-2110/1/2/3. This is one of the cheaper hotels on this stretch of beach and is not bad value, rooms are comfortable although perhaps a little shabby. **B** *Nomad Beach Bandas*, T01261-2155. Banda accommodation, good value and probably (with *Diani Sea Lodge*) the cheapest place to stay on Diani if you are not camping, there is a very good seafood restaurant here and watersports are available.

D *Diani Beachalets*, South Diani, PO Box 26, Ukunda, T01261-2180, also located at the southern end of the beach. Has a range of facilities including camping, some of the bandas have shared facilities while others have their own bathrooms and kitchens, there is a tennis court but no swimming pool or restaurant, there is also no shop so you will have to stock up before you get here. **D** *Four Twenty South Cottages*, South Diani, T01261-2034, located at the southern end. These cottages sleep 4 and have all facilities, you will need to bring bed linen, there is no shop on the site so you will have to buy food at Mombasa or else at the Diani shopping centre or Ukunda. **D** *Larry Peacock's*, close to Tradewinds is Larry Peacock's which has 3 rooms, the owner, a real eccentric, has been swanning around Diani for years and has always been known as 'The Peacock', the rooms are comfortable and the security is good, it is clean and friendly and you can use the facilities at *Trade Winds*.

E *Dan Trench's*, just behind the *Trade Winds Hotel*. Is famous amongst budget travellers, unfortunately it has seen better days but it remains popular being the only cheap place to stay on Diani, the facilities are basic and unfortunately it is not very safe so watch your belongings like a hawk, there is a small dorm and 1 banda, if you are staying here you can use most of the facilities at *Trade Winds*.

Camping E camping at *Dan Trench's* and *Diani Beachalets*, PO Box 26 Ukunda, T0127-2180. Good beach cottages sleeping up to 7 people US$5.50 per person, well appointed and managed.

Apart from the hotel restaurants there are a number of others. All do very good fish and sea- **Eating** food and you can rely on it being very fresh. Many of the hotels do special buffet lunches and dinners and these are usually very good value.

4 *Ali Barbours*, between *Diani Sea Lodge* and *Trade Winds*, T0127-2033/2163/3033, F2257. One of the most popular, you can either eat in the open air or else in a sort of underground cave, it does excellent seafood as well as French food.

3 *Bush Baby Restaurant*, opposite the *Two Fishes Hotel*. Open air restaurant, later on in the evening it develops into a disco and usually has quite a lively crowd. **3** *Nomads Seafood Restaurant*, PO Box 1, Ukunda, T0127-2155, F2391, at *Nomads Beach Bandas*, just south of Jadini. Probably one of the best restaurants on Diani, it does a very popular Sunday buffet lunch which is good value. **3** *Vulcano*, T1261/2004. Italian food and is not too expensive.

2 *Gallo's Restaurant*, PO Box 84616, T0127-3150, F2145, about 15 minutes' walk towards Mombasa from Dans Trench. Relatively expensive for the budget traveller but well worth a visit, next to Diani Shopping Centre, eclectic restaurant, run by a graduate of an American hotel school, fusion of local ingredients with international techniques. **2** *Hollywood*, located in the nearby village of Ukunda, opposite the Total Gas Station. Tasty Kenyan food at keen prices **2** *South Coast Fitness Centre*, has a restaurant which is fairly good value. **2** *Sundowner*, located on the southern part of the Diani Beach road, about 10 minutes' walk from the Diani Beach chalets. Serves excellent Kenyan food at low prices.

Most of the hotels arrange entertainment in the evenings. This includes traditional dancers **Entertainment** who are usually a group who do a range of dances from around Kenya. The hotels will often combine this with an evening barbecue. They also hold films shows.

Discos Almost all the hotels have discos which are of varying quality. Along the Diani Beach Rd there are also a number of discos not run by hotels. These include *Shakatak*, across the road from *Two Fishes Hotel*, German run with a restaurant and beer garden, entrance fee US$2. *Tropicana*, located at the AGIP Gas Station, open-air, plays only Reggae music, entrance fee US$1. *Casablanca*, located at the very southern end of Diani's Beach Rd, run by the *Neptune Paradise Hotel*, shuttle bus will pick up guests at certain times and bus stops, entrance fee US$1.

Sports (participant) Deep-sea fishing: *Nomad Boats*, PO Box 1, Ukunda via Mombasa, T/F0127 2156.

Air There is a small airfield at Ukunda which is used for small planes – usually charters for **Transport** safaris.

Kenya

Road From Likoni drive south on the A14, the main Kenya-Tanzania coastal road. All the turnings off are well signposted. For Diani, go as far as Ukunda village (about 22 kilometres) where there is the turning off to the smaller road that runs along Diani beach. At the T-junction, some hotels are to the left, while all the others are to the right.

Boat To get to the south coast, take the Likoni ferry from Mombasa Island. There are 2 ferries and they go about every 20 minutes throughout the day, although there are fewer late in the evening. You will be charged according to the length of your vehicle. Pedestrians go free.

Directory   **Banks** *Kenya Commercial Bank*, Ukunda Branch, PO Box 90254, T2197, Mombasa. *Barclays Bank of Kenya*, Diani Beach, PO Box 695, Ukunda-Kenya, T01261-2375/2448. **Useful services** If you are self-catering it is worth buying most of your supplies in Mombasa where it is cheaper. There are however a couple of places closer to the beach. Firstly there is the small village of **Ukunda** which is on the main road close to the Diani turn off. There is a post office here and a shop which before the *Diani Shopping Centre* was built was the best around. You can get most things here. Off the main road, on the road with all the hotels, is the much newer shopping area. This has sprung up in the last 10 years and has a couple of good supermarkets, banks (open 1000 to 1500), souvenir shops, petrol stations and you can hire a car here. There is also the *South Coast Fitness Centre* gym. You can hire go-karts here. For fresh fruit, vegetables and fish you will be able to buy off the vendors who come round all the self-catering places with their stock on their bicycles.

South of Diani

For many people Diani is the furthest south that they will go. In fact there are a few places to stay including the *Funzi Island Fishing Club* and the *Shimoni Reef Fishing Lodge* which are both located very close to the Tanzanian border. Both are very exclusive and in the **A+** price range although Shimoni is marginally the cheaper of the two. They both cater largely for keen fishermen. Before these two are reached, at the southern end of Diani is a small bay and Chale Island. This is a popular spot for day trips from Diani – boats take you out for swimming, snorkelling and beach barbecues on the island. Contact Nomad Safaris on Diani Beach for more details. Along this route you will not be able to miss the coconut plantations which cover a wide area.

Gazi
Colour map 3, grid B5

A village at the southern end of Diani, once significantly more important than it is now as it was the district's administrative centre. Here you will see the **House of Sheik Mbaruk bin Rashid**. There are said to be the bodies of eight men and eight women buried in the foundations of the house to give the building strength. He was also notorious for torturing people, and suffocating them on the fumes of burning chillies. In the Mazrui Rebellion of 1895 Mbaruk was seen arming his men with German rifles and flying the German flag. British troops did eventually defeat him and he ended his days in exile in German East Africa (mainland Tanzania). However, the house is now used as a school. It is looking rather run down. It once had a very finely carved door but this has been moved to the Fort Jesus Museum. You will have to ask directions for Gazi as it is not signposted on the main road.

Msambweni

About 50 kilometres south of Likoni is the village of Msambweni which is home to what is one of the best hospitals on the coast as well as a famous leprosarium. The beach here has recently been developed for tourists and there are some bungalows and a hotel. The beach is nice and there are some ruins in this area which are believed to have been a slave detention camp. **Sleeping A+** *Funzi Beach Fishing Club*, PO Box 90246, south of Msambweni, Mombasa, Tx21126. Only takes 12 people accommodated in tents on a beautifully secluded island to a very high standard, facilities for all watersports are available and are included in the price, as are all meals, drinks and transport. **B** *Beachcomber Club*, c/o *Let's Go Travel*, Caxton House, Standard St, Nairobi, PO Box 60342, T340331 F336890. **B** *Black Marlin*, PO Box 80, Msambweni, T90 (Msambweni). Being renovated, soon to reopen.

A small fishing village whose name means Place of the Hole. This is from the system of **Slave Caves** located to the west of the village. It is said that these caves were used by slave traders to hide the slaves before they were shipped out and sold to overseas markets. The other story associated with them is that they have been used as a refuge from various marauding tribes through the ages. To reach the caves take the path that begins opposite the jetty and walk up through the forest. When you get to the entrance you take a ladder down through a hole in the ground. The cave system is believed to extend about 20 kilometres underground.

Shimoni
Colour map 3, grid B5

In the far south is the **Kisite-Mpunguti Marine National Park** which has superb coral gardens and lots of sea life. You can take trips out to the Park – this is one of the glass bottom boat trips that are very good. For details contact *Kisite Dhow Tours*, T01261-2331 or T11-311752(Mombasa). At 0900 daily there is a snorkelling tour at Kisite National Park. Apart from the fish, coral and shells you may also see dolphins. This stretch of the coastline is also a bird watchers paradise. The small islands dotting the coastline have old established trees including baobabs with their thick gnarled trunks. Untroubled by elephants they dominate the island shelves in abundance. Coral seas of turquoise and dark green stretch away. Mountains rising straight up in the south over the ocean must mark the Tanzanian/Kenyan border.

Kisite is a flat little marine park, an atoll, with a dead coral shelf in the middle rising up off it like a table. The rest is worn to rough granular sand which is hot and uncomfortable to walk on. Unremarkable on the surface, what is truly amazing is what is in the waters around Kisite. The little convoy of dhows string out in a line, and drop anchor. The water is pure, warm and turquoise in colour, and is so salt saturated that it is difficult to swim in initially, as it seems to suspend you.

There are thousands of fish, in a dazzling array of sizes, shapes and colours just below the surface.

There is no shade or protection from the burning sun and wearing a shirt/long sleeved T-shirt whilst snorkelling is a wise precaution. Masks and snorkels are available but flippers are not always obtainable. **Sleeping A+** *Shimoni Reef Fishing Lodge*, south of Msambweni, beyond Funzi Beach, wonderful location, overlooking Wasini Island, c/o *Reef Hotel*, PO Box 82234, Mombasa, T471771. High standards. **A** *Pemba Channel Fishing Club*, PO Box 86952, Mombasa, T313749/225417, F316875, Mombasa, local: T2 (Shimoni). As the rates include full board this is very good value. It is older than the *Shimoni Reef Fishing Lodge* which caters almost exclusively for keen anglers, closed April-June (after fishing season). Deep-sea fishing also available from *Sea Adventures Ltd*, PO Box 56, Shimoni, T12/13 (Shimoni).

A wonderful place measuring one kilometre across and six kilometres along. It is totally undeveloped and there are no cars, no mains electricity, and no running water. There is no reliable fresh water supply on the island (it relies on the collection of rain water) which is the major factor that has limited the growth of the island's population and pace of development. They are building large culverts where they can store rainwater with some of the proceeds of the tourist trade. There is a small village on the island that includes the remains of an Arab settlement. There are the ruins of 18th and 19th century houses as well as a pillar tomb which has Chinese porcelain insets that have, so far, survived. The beach is worth exploring – you might well find bits of pottery and glass. Also interesting are the dead coral gardens which are found behind the village. They are above the sea although during the Spring tide they are covered as they are linked to the sea 100 feet below through a series of caverns. Some of the coral formations are said to resemble animal shapes (they call one the elephant).

Wasini Island

The local people run a restaurant, high on the hill in an open airy dining hall, with a thatch roof with bats sleeping high above you in the rafters. There are large rough hewn tables from which there are glimpses of the sea through the rhododendrons and palmetto. Lunch includes steamed sea crabs with claws the size of your fist, along with fresh lime and baked coconut rinds for dipping in salt. This goes down

Early coastal tourism

In the 1920s a return journey by ship from London to Mombasa through the Suez Canal took four weeks each way and cost £60. A hotel in Mombasa cost six shillings and eight pence.

The first beach hotel was established by a photographer from Goa, Hugo Coutinho, at Bamburi Beach, with thatched rondavels, palm frond beds, and they cost two shillings and ten pence a night. At Malindi, the first hotel was built by Pat Brady in 1932 and became known as Brady's Palm Beach and was on a site where the present Blue Marlin is located. Ernest Hemingway stayed there in 1934 (see Box, page 51). The next year a retired naval commander, Leo Lawford began a similar enterprise just to the south of Brady's and the hotel, subsequently much developed, still bears his name.

well with cold Kenya beer, but the wise drink water first. Bottled water is expensive here. There is not much of a beach on Wasini Island as it gets covered by the tide.

From Wasini Island you may want to organize a trip to the Marine Park (if you have not arranged this from Mombasa or Diani). Get a group together and ask at the *Mpunguti Restaurant*, who will be able to arrange a trip for you. This is said to be the best snorkelling in Kenya. It is not too expensive – especially as the price includes an excellent lunch. You can if you wish also hire a canoe and do it yourself but obviously will not know the best places to go.

On the east side of Wasini Island are the boat moorings of the wealthy, who tie up here between Hemingwayesque marlin and shark fishing adventures.

Sleeping **C** *Mpunguti Lodge*, this has a number of bandas and the food here is excellent – it is also very friendly, alternatively you can camp but if you want to be totally self-sufficient be sure to bring plenty of supplies from Mombasa as there is not much here, bring as much drinking water with you as you can carry. There are renovations in progress – a pavilion for meals, salt water toilets, overhead showers and a generator are planned. There's a restaurant, *Wesini Island Restaurant*, T0127-2331, but it's only open from July until April.

Transport To get to Wasini Island under your own steam either hire a taxi or take a KBS bus from Likoni to Shimoni (there are not very many). Alternatively take a matatu to Lunga Lunga and ask to be let off at the turning for Shimoni which is about 15 kilometres off the main road. From here you will have to hitch. From Shimoni, there is a dhow run by the Mpunguti Restaurant, otherwise a matatu boat. The last matatu back to Mombasa leaves between 1500 and 1600. Boats to Wasini Island cost around US$2 per person one way.

Lunga Lunga A village located about 95 kilometres south of Mombasa and is the nearest village to the border with Tanzania. It is about five kilometres from the actual border itself and can be reached by bus from Mombasa. Buses between Mombasa and Dar es Salaam or Tanga go about once a week in both directions taking about 20 hours to Dar and eight to Tanga. The border post is slow so you will have to be patient – it can take up to four hours. If you do not get a through bus you can take matatus but this involves a fair bit of walking. Coming from Kenya you cross through the Kenyan formalities and from here, unless you have your own transport, you will have to walk the six kilometres to the Tanzanian border at Horohoro. From here there are two buses a day to Tanga, but several *dala dala* (Tanzanian matatus).

North Coast

There is a whole string of beaches with lots of hotels on them to the north of Mombasa, including the major attractions of Malindi and Lamu. At these latter places there is much more choice for the budget traveller, and anyone who wants to avoid the package tours. There are major historical sites at Kilifi, Malindi and Lamu.

Mombasa to Kilifi

The strip of beach immediately to the north of Mombasa Island is well developed and there are lots of hotels. Most of them cater for package tours from Europe and usually each hotel caters for one nationality or another. None of them is cheap. All have facilities such as swimming pools, tennis courts, watersports etcetera and they all do their best to look after their guests very well, organizing all sorts of activities and trips.

Nyali Beach A+ *Mombasa Beach Hotel*, PO Box 90414, Mombasa, T471861/2/3/4/5, **Sleeping**
F472970. Run by Kenya Safari Lodges and Hotels, this hotel has about 150 rooms all of which are a/c with balconies, it is set up on a cliff looking over the beach and the sea, it is very well managed and facilities include conference rooms, tennis courts, golf, watersports, bar, restaurant and grill room. The newer section of the hotel is called the *Palm Beach Annex*, they are all a/c and most have balconies, there are also some cottages, facilities include meeting facilities, restaurant and grill room, tennis courts, 2 swimming pools, snack bar and nightclub. **A** *Nyali Reef*, PO Box 82234, Mombasa, T471771. This recently renovated hotel has about 160 rooms all of which are a/c and have balconies, facilities include meeting rooms, swimming pool, tennis court, sauna, restaurant and bar. **A** *Silver Beach*, PO Box 81443, Mombasa, T471771. This hotel is located fairly close to Mombasa and is popular with package tours, it has the usual range of facilities including swimming pool, restaurants and bar. **B** *Kidutu Hotel*, Links Rd, PO Box 86178, F472677. S/c, a/c, pool, games, not on beach.

Bamburi Beach A+ *Severin Sea Lodge*, PO Box 82169, Mombasa, T485001. This lodge consists of about 180 bungalows all of which are a/c and are very comfortable, facilities include 2 swimming pools, tennis courts, excellent watersports and sailing. **A** *Bamburi Beach*, PO Box 83966, Mombasa, T485611, Tx21181. Another of the older hotels this has recently been renovated, it has about 150 rooms all of which are a/c and have sea facing balconies, facilities include conference facilities and extensive sports provision including squash, gym and various watersports, there is a roof top bar and nightclub. **A** *Giriama Apartments*, PO Box 86693, T485726. Located on Bamburi Beach, these apartments are very comfortable and set in lovely gardens, swimming pool and restaurant. **A** *Travellers Beach Hotel*, PO Box 87649 Mombasa (North Coast), T011-485121/6, F485678. New development, spacious a/c rooms, swimming pool, restaurants. **A** *Whitesands*, PO Box 90173, Mombasa, T485926. One of the older and larger hotels, this has been refurbished recently, it is set in gardens and has meeting rooms, a swimming pool, and tennis courts.

   B *Kenya Beach*, PO Box 95748, Mombasa, T485821. A number of cottages, all a/c, set in gardens with a communal swimming pool, various watersports are available including deep sea diving. **B** *Ocean View Beach*, PO Box 81127, Mombasa. A rather old-style hotel, although most of the rooms are a/c they have no phone, however it does have a number of very modern facilities consisting of swimming pool, watersports including deep sea diving, bar, restaurant and disco. **B** *Plaza Beach*, PO Box 88299, Mombasa, T485321/485212. This hotel is reasonably good value, the rooms all have views of the sea and the restaurant, which specializes in Indian food, is especially good.

Shanzu Beach A+ *Dolphin*, PO Box 81443, Mombasa, T485801/ A very pleasant hotel, it has the full range of facilities. **A+** *Intercontinental*, PO Box 83492, Mombasa, T484811. A large hotel with nearly 200 rooms, all are a/c and have balconies, it has extensive meeting facilities, 2 swimming pools, 2 tennis courts, 2 squash courts and health club, bars, restaurants, nightclub and casino, it is set in large grounds and has a long beach front. **A+** *Serena Beach*, central booking PO Box 48690 Nairobi, T02-710511/2, F718100/2/3, serenamk@africaonline.co.ke, PO Box 90352, Mombasa, T485721. A very pleasant luxury hotel which has been designed to resemble Lamu architecture and it is clear that great care has been taken in its construction, it has about 120 rooms all of which are a/c, facilities include meeting rooms, tennis courts, swimming pool, watersports, bar, and restaurant.

Kenya

Mombasa North Coast

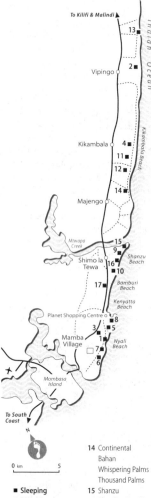

To Kilifi & Malindi

Indian Ocean

Vipingo

Kikambala

Kikambala Beach

Majengo

Mtwapa Creek

Shimo la Tewa

Shanzu Beach

Bamburi Beach

Kenyatta Beach

Planet Shopping Centre

Mamba Village

Nyali Beach

Mombasa Island

To South Coast

N

0 km   5

■ **Sleeping**
1 Bahari Beach
2 Jauss Farm
3 Kidutu
4 Le SOLEIL
5 Mombasa Beach
6 Nyali Beach
7 Nyali Golf & Country Club
8 Reef
9 Serena Beach
10 Severin Sea Lodge
11 Silver Star
12 Sun 'n' Sand
13 Tropicana Beach

14 Continental
   Bahan
   Whispering Palms
   Thousand Palms
15 Shanzu
   Flamingo Beach
   Dolphin
16 Rio
   Palm Beach
   Baherini Seahorse
17 Paradise
   Kenya
   Bamburi
   Travellers
   Whitesands
   Ocean View
   Piccolo
   Giriama
   Bora Bora Disco

Related map
The Coast, page 160

Kikambala Beach A+ *Sun 'n' Sand Beach*, PO Box 2, Kikambala, T0125-32008/055/123/124, F32133. A very pleasant hotel, good facilities, the beach here is particularly fine. **A** *Whispering Palms*, PO Box 5, Kikambala, T0125-32004/5/6, F32029. This is located on a quiet piece of beach and has been built with a high roof made of palm leaf thatch known as *makuti*, it has all the usual facilities including a swimming pool, watersports, restaurant, bar and entertainment.

B *Le Soleil Beach Club*, located 26 kilometres north of Mombasa and 3 kilometres from main Malindi-Mombasa Rd, 100 metres north of Continental Beach Cottages, PO Box 84737, T125-32195/6/32343, F32164, lesoleil@users.africaonline.co.ke. New development, very clean, TV and phones in rooms, a/c apartments, swimming pool, floating bar restaurant, snooker hall, range of water sports available, tennis courts, friendly staff. Recommended.

C *Continental Beach Cottages*, PO Box 124, Kikambala, T77(Kikambala). These are simple cottages that are rather out of the way set in peaceful gardens, some of them have a/c but they have seen better days and are rather grubby, you are charged for the cottage so can cram in as many people as you want, they are difficult to get to unless you have your own transport, however there is a swimming pool and a good beach, meals are available fairly cheap and basic. **C-E** *Jauss Farm*, PO Box 19, Vipingo, T0125-32218. This is located about 40 kilometres north of Mombasa and is a popular place for budget travellers, it offers a range of accommodation from camping to luxury cottages, the site is well-managed it has excellent facilities including a swimming pool, shop, video lounge and camping gear and diving gear is available to rent, it is secure, there are meals available and it is friendly, there are budget cottages which share the facilities with the campsite, or else luxury ones which are fully self contained, they also arrange budget camping safaris, the whole site is set in a fruit and dairy farm and has its own beach, to get there take a matatu to the sign post for Jauss Farm, about 2 kilometres north of Vipingo and from there it is a walk of about 1 kilometre, if you ring from the Post Office at Vipingo they will probably come and pick you up.

E *Kanamai Centre*, PO Box Kikambala 208, T46 (Kikambala). This centre used to be a youth hostel but you no longer need to be a member of the International Youth Hostel Association to stay here, it has a range of rooms including dormitories, doubles and singles, there are also a couple of self-catering cottages, they are basic but are good value and the beach is lovely, it is very clean and friendly and there is a dining room serving basic food, it is difficult to get to if you do not have your own transport you need to take a matatu as far as Majengo on the main road where you will see a sign saying Camping Kanamai, from here you will have to walk follow the road until you get to a fork take the left fork and then it is a little over 3 kilometres down a dusty track.

Camping **E** camping, at *Kanamai Centre* and *Jauss Farm*.

Eating If you are staying in one of the big hotels then the chances are that you will eat there most evenings. If you wish to try other places, you will usually need to have your own transport or else take a taxi.

4 *Harlequin Restaurant*, T472373. This is an excellent seafood restaurant, it has a wonderful position located overlooking Tudor Creek and the food is guaranteed to be very fresh. **4** *Le Pichet*, T585923. Another excellent seafood restaurant, this is located overlooking Mtwara Creek about 20 kilometres out of Mombasa in Kikambala, it is very popular so you are advised to reserve a table, there are lots of craft stalls surrounding the restaurant in response to the tourists who patronise it, they also organize an evening trip on a dhow – you go across the creek to a nearby beach and have your dinner under the stars, the trip includes the evenings entertainment of traditional African music and dancing, this trip is particularly popular so be sure to book ahead.

3 *Galana Steak House*, T485572. As the name suggests this restaurant is a carnivore's delight, it is located near Jomo Kenyatta Beach and is good value. **3** *Imani Dhow*, this is a superb grill restaurant located on Bamburi Beach. **3** *Libbas Restaurant*, T471138. Located in the Ratna Shopping Mall in Nyali this is a popular family restaurant, it specializes in Italian food – pizza and pasta. **3** *Rene's Restaurant*, T472986. Another Italian this is also good value, it is located in Nyali on Links Rd and in the evenings develops into a disco.

Entertainment **Sports** *Sun Line Tennis School and Club*, Jomo Kenyatta Beach. The courts are excellent quality and you will be able to arrange lessons if you wish.

As you head north the road crosses Tudor Creek, then reaches Mamba Village and Bamburi Nature Reserve. The road then runs parallel to Jomo Kenyatta Beach before crossing Mtwapa Creek. In this area is the Jumba la Mtwana site and Majengo village. A little further on is the Kurita Cottage Complex and the Vipingo Sisal estates. The next beaches are Bamburi Beach, and Kikambala Beach.

Mamba Village This is a crocodile farm located to the north of Mombasa close to the Nyali Golf Course on Links Road. Here you can see crocodiles of all ages and sizes from newborns to huge fully grown adults. There are film shows explaining some of the conservation efforts as well as the financial side of the venture. You can go for a camel ride here and it is a day trip in a pleasant setting which children in particular will enjoy. There is a very good restaurant. It is open all day during the week and on Saturday afternoons. For details contact PO Box 85723, Mombasa, T472709/472341/472361.

Further north along the main road is the **Bombolulu Craft Centre** which you might want to stop off at to do some of your souvenir shopping. PO Box 83988, Mombasa, T471704. The crafts are produced by the handicapped in the area and are generally of good quality and good value. A secondary school for the Physically Disabled is near here. You can also do a tour of the workshops.

Kenya

👉 *Sisal*

Sisal is used to make sacking and rope and before the invention of nylon was a particularly vital raw material. It requires a large amount of capital investment and for this reason is produced on large estates using wage labourers rather than on small-scale farms using family labour. It also has a very long maturation period requiring about six years from the time it is planted until it can be harvested. During the prosperous 1920s the demand for sisal was high, supply was inadequate and so prices were also high. As a result huge areas of sisal were planted but by the time they had matured the world economy was in slump and supply far outweighed demand. This lag in the supply of sisal makes it a difficult crop to manage. The harvesting of sisal is very demanding, and it requires a large labour force.

One of the biggest advantages of sisal is its ability to cope with a fluctuating and unreliable water supply and infertile soil. For this reason it has been grown in areas of the world where no other crops can survive.

During the Second World War the Americans were desperate to maintain their supply of sisal as sisal twine was vital for harvesting. As a result prices were controlled and the sisal farmer maintained a steady and healthy income during the war. However sisal is of less importance now compared to 50 years ago as the petroleum industry has produced substitutes such as nylon. This greatly reduced the world demand for sisal, although it recovered slightly when oil prices rose in the 1970s. It remains of local importance in Kenya, and many of the goods that you take home from Kenya have sisal in them – table mats, baskets, bags etc.

Bamburi Quarry Nature Reserve When you are at Likoni waiting for the ferry you will be able to see the Bamburi Cement factory. When quarrying of coral to make lime for the cement stopped in 1971 an effort was made to reclaim the land by reafforestation and a nature trail was then created. The reclamation scheme was ahead of its time and it attracted the attention of ecologists from all over the world. Part of the process included the introduction of hundreds of thousands of millipedes which helped convert the soil from infertile sand to soil able to support a forest in which the centre is now situated. Despite this, the whole area is still dominated by the Simbarite Ltd Quarry.

A fish farm produces tilapia; a reptile pit, a hippo called Sally which featured in one of the Root films, various antelope, monkeys, wart hog, buffalo and lots of different birds. Feeding time is at about 1600 and the trail is open from 1000 to 1800 during the week, 1000 to 1700 on Saturday and 1200 to 1700 on Sunday. Entrance US$3.50, children US$1. For further details contact Bamburi Farm, PO Box 90202, Mombasa, T48529. It is signposted on the main road towards Malindi and is 10 kilometres north of Mombasa, easily accessible by bus (bus stop outside).

Deep-sea fishing can be arranged by *Hall Mark Charters*, based 12 kilometres north of Mombasa on Mtwapa Creek, PO Box 10202, Bamburi, T011-485680/485808, Mobile phone T0-071-400095, F0-11-475217/485808, or by *James Adcock Fishing Ltd*, PO Box 95693, Mombasa T0-11-485527.

Kipepee Aquarium Located opposite the Bamburi Quarry Nature Reserve. There are about 15 large tanks filled with an estimated 150 different species of colourful fish, as well as the deadly stonefish. This is an extraordinarily well-camouflaged fish which lies in the sea completely still and is extremely painful if you tread on it. The collection has been put together by Jacques Allard who is often available to talk to visitors.

Kenya Marineland, PO Box 15050, Kikambala, T485248/485738/385866. Located in Mtwapa Creek this centre has underwater viewing rooms from where you can see turtles, barracudas, et cetera and watch sharks being fed. There are also boats for hire.

Baobab trees

These huge trees have enormous girths – which enable them to survive during very long dry patches. They live for up to 2,000 years. You will see some extremely large ones - there is one at Ukunda which has a girth of 22 metres and which has been given "presidential protection" to safeguard it.

The legend is that when God first planted them they kept walking around and would not stay still. So He decided to replant them up-side-down which is why they look as if they have the roots sticking up into the air. During droughts people open up the pods and grind the seeds to make what is known as "hunger flour".

About 13 kilometres from Mombasa is the Jumba la Mtwana site, a national monument located north of the Mtwapa Creek. The name means the house of the slave and this was once a slave-trading settlement believed to date from the 15th century. The site has only fairly recently been excavated and is now run by the National Museums of Kenya. At the entrance, fee (US$4), you can buy a short guidebook to the site, or else hire a guide. Within the site, which is spread over several acres there are three mosques, including the **Mosque by the Sea**, a number of tombs and eight houses. You will notice that architecturally they look little different from the houses of today in the area. This was a successful design that there was no need to change. The people of this town appear to have been very concerned with ablutions for there are many remains showing evidence of cisterns, water jars, latrines and other washing and toilet facilities.

*[margin: **Jumba la Mtwana**]*

Building with coral rag (broken pieces of coral) was something reserved for the more privileged members of the community, and it is their houses that have survived. Those that belonged to the poorer people would have been built of mud and thatch.

It is a lovely setting – close to the beach with shade provided by baobabs. To reach the site ask to be dropped off at the sign about a one kilometre beyond Mtwapa Bridge and from there it is a walk of about three kilometres. However you will probably be offered a lift as you walk down the track.

About a kilometre north of the Jumba site there is the Porini Village Restaurant which serves local dishes and puts on displays of traditional African dancing. The road continues north with the Kikambala beach running parallel to the right. You will then notice the very green, lush fields with hundreds of thousands of spiky plants growing in straight lines. This is sisal and much of this that you see is part of the **Vipingo Sisal Estates**. The estate covers an area of about 50,000 ha, and has not just fields, but factories, a railway and housing for the workers. You can do a tour of the estate and will see the spiky leaves being cut by hand and loaded onto a trolley and taken to the factory where the fibre is removed and dried.

There are also plantations of cashew nuts, mango trees and coconut trees. A few kilometres north of the sisal estate is the Kuritu Cottage Complex an example of a modern Swahili village. It is near to here that Denys Finch-Hatton had a beach cottage. He was hunter and pilot and lover of Karen Blixen, described in *Out of Africa*. As you get to the end of sisal estates you will reach the village of Takaunga located on the banks of a small creek.

This is a small village located 10 kilometres south of Kilifi and five kilometres off the main road. This is a sleepy kind of place located above Takaunga Creek. It has whitewashed houses, and a few shops. About a kilometre to the east there is a lovely beach which is only revealed at low tide. The swimming here is very good, and even when the beach is covered you can swim off the rocks – the water is beautifully clear. There are also some old ruins, and it is said to be the oldest slave port on the Kenyan coast.

*[margin: **Takaunga**]*

There are no hotels as such, but it is possible to obtain a room to rent. You should also if possible bring your own supplies and ask the family if they will cook them for you.

To get to Takaunga you can either take a matatu from Mombasa (there are two a day), or else take one to Kilifi and ask to be dropped off at the turning for Takaunga. From here it is a walk of about five kilometres – you are unlikely to get a lift as there is little traffic along this road.

Kilifi

3° 30' S, 39° 40' E
Colour map 4, grid C6

Kilifi Creek is located about 60 kilometres north of Mombasa. The town of Kilifi is situated to the north of the creek, while Mnarani village is to the south. In the time of the Portuguese, the main town was located to the south of the creek at Mnarani. Absolutely glorious location – the shore slopes steeply down to the water's edge, the view from the new bridge is spectacular.

Until very recently one had to cross the creek by ferry. A bridge, complete with street lights, has now been built with Japanese funding. There is a Ksh 10 toll – keep the receipt as you may be stopped by the police and asked for it.

The town has an interesting mix of people with quite a number of resident expatriates. The main industry in the town is the cashew nut factory which employs about 1,500 people. To the south there are the Mnarani Ruins. It is an easy going town with a nice beach.

Mnarani Ruins

The Mnarani Ruins was first excavated in the 1950s but renewed interest in the site has led the British Institute in Eastern Africa to work here again. The town was the place of one of the ancient Swahili city-states that are found along this coast. It is believed that the town was inhabited from the latter half of the 14th century until about the early 17th century, when it was ransacked and destroyed by a group of Galla tribesmen. It is thought that the inhabitants of the town locked themselves into the Great Mosque as they were attacked.

The ruins include one of the deepest wells (70 metres) along the coast, two mosques, part of the town wall and city gates and a group of tombs including a pillar tomb decorated with engravings of a wealthy sharif. Note particularly the tomb of the doctor which is easily the most ornate. At the ruins of the larger or **Great Mosque** can be seen the *mihrab* (which points towards Mecca) surrounded by carved inscriptions. There are many niches in the walls. To the left of the entrance, the smaller mosque is believed to date from the 16th century. There is a huge baobab tree nearby with a circumference of over 15 metres. The ruins are best known for the inscriptions carved into them – many of them remaining untranslated. However, in general they are much smaller and less impressive than the ones at Gedi.

To get to the ruins, turn off the main road to the south of the creek by the toll booth and go through Mnarani village. Turn left on to the old road and pass the now rusty ferry sign. There is a path signposted ("3 minutes and a short climb") and the ruins are a few 100 kilometres down this path and then a climb of about 100 steps. You also get a wonderful view of the creek from the ruins. Entrance US$1.75. Open 0700-1730.

There are also ruins nearby at **Kitoka** about 3 kilometres south of Kilifi. This is a smaller site – there is a small mosque and a few houses.

Sleeping

A *Mnarani Club*, PO Box 81443, Mombasa, T18/26 (Kilifi) or T125-22320. Located overlooking Kilifi Creek on Malindi Rd, this hotel is one of the oldest in the country. It has been beautifully rehabilitated, with 84 guest bedrooms, in natural wood finishes. There are smaller creek cottages designed for families. All rooms have a/c, mosquito nets and phones. It is set in marvellous gardens and has wonderful views, facilities include watersports (sailing, windsurfing and waterskiing), a bar, a good value restaurant overlooking the creek, and evening entertainment such as traditional dancing and music. Booking Agents: *Let's Go Travel*, Caxton House, Standard St, PO Box 60342, Nairobi, T340331/213033, F336890. **A** *Seahorse*, PO Box 70, Kilifi, T64/90 (Kilifi). Located looking out across Kilifi Creek on the northern side of the creek this also has good views and is a popular drinking spot for the resident expatriates and is considered to be Kenya's sailing centre, if you are hoping for some crewing this is the place to try your luck.

B *Baobab Lodge*, on cliffs to north, PO Box 40683, Nairobi, T222229, F332170. Attractive roundavels, pool, diving, path down to swimming cove. **B** *Kilifi Bay Resort*, PO Box 156, on Coast Rd about 5 kilometres out of Kilifi, T2511, F225. Well designed, with well-tended surroundings, located on cliffs with path down to beach, pool, diving.

D *Dhows Inn*, this small hotel is located on the south side of the creek on the new road leading to the bridge, rooms have bathrooms and mosquito nets, are clean and fairly basic but good value, the hotel has nice gardens and there is a popular bar and restaurant.

E *African Dream*, on road out of town to main road to Malindi, s/c rooms, oil lamps, a little overpriced. **E** *Bofa Beach Camp*, on coast road about 8 kilometres out of Kilifi, PO Box 660, T724483, Nairobi. Distance from town is a disadvantage, otherwise it is good value for a beach break, not terribly clean, water supplies erratic, soft drinks available. **E** *Gesarate*, PO Box 231, between centre and Masjid-ul-Noor Mosque on east side. Small courtyard, simple but comfortable. **E** *King 'enda*, close to bus station, PO Box 188. Fan, nets, good budget value. **E** *Tawfiq Hotel*, behind bus station. Nets, not s/c, basic but cheap. **E** *Tushaurane Boarding and Lodging*, this is a fairly new hotel located in the town centre, facilities are mostly shared, it is simple but it is clean and friendly and mosquito nets are provided.

Kenya

Kilifi

0 metres 250

Eating   **4** *Mnanari Club*, high standard, superb seafood, excellent atmosphere. **3** *Seahorse*, reliable international menu. **2** *Dhows Inn*, reasonable food. **2** *Topline Garden Bar and Restaurant*, PO Box 15, Kilifi, T0125-22234. **1** *Colombas Cold House*, on road into town, near bridge. Mostly juices, freshly squeezed. **1** *Gold Life*, at the bus station. Open air, neat and bright patio, excellent fruit juices. **1** *Kilifi Cafeteria*, near bus stand. Grills, snacks and juices, inexpensive.

Entertainment   *Top Life Gardens*, overlooking creek close to bridge, fine views, live band or disco on Friday, Saturday and Sunday. *Kaya Gardens*, north of KC Bank, disco Friday and Saturday.

Sports (participant)   *Microlitc Kenya*, PO Box 824, T/F22000.

Shopping   **Bookshops**   There is a small bookshop, just off the main street.

Transport   **Road   Bus**: Kilifi is about 50 kilometres from **Mombasa**, and 45 kilometres from **Malindi**. The buses which go between the two towns do pick people up here although they may be full. You may find it easier to get a matatu. Enquiries and bookings can be made at *Azzura Tours*, T2385, whose office is on the Kilifi's main road. *Tana Express* and *Tawfiq* have booking offices near Bus Station. To get to and from *Nairobi* from Kilifi the Tana Bus Company goes twice a day taking about 9 hours. The buses leave at 0730 and 1930. The Tana Express and Tawfiq have booking offices near the Bus Station.

Directory   **Banks**   There are 2 banks, in Kilifi which are open from 0830 to 1300 on weekdays and until 1130 on Sat. *Kenya Commercial Bank*, PO Box 528, T22034, Kilifi. **Communications**   There is a Post Office, next to the market. **Hospitals & medical services**   Dr Bomo has a *clinic* on the old Kilifi Rd in Mnarani. **Tour companies & travel agents**   You can hire cars at *Azzura Tours*, PO Box 2, Kilifi, T2385. You can also buy bus tickets and organize various trips. *Tuna Travel and Tours*, PO Box 592, Kilifi, T0127-3314, F3314.

North coast to Lamu

Parts of this area are rather more difficult to access than the southern section of the coast. However communications have improved in recent years and much of this part of the coast has been developed for tourists.

Kilifi to Malindi   The road from Kilifi continues north running parallel to the coast. As with much of the road from Mombasa it runs straight and true and is in quite good condition. Leaving Kilifi the road passes small villages dotted between lots of cashew nut trees which are surprisingly green-leafed at the end of the dry season. There are occasional stands of eucalyptus trees. Don't expect tropical rain forest as you approach the **Arabuko Sokoke Forest** – from the road the only discernible difference is that the scrub disappears and the trees are noticeably closer together. It is home to many species of birds – some of which are rare. Efforts to prevent the forest being cut down completely are being made but the constant needs for fuel and land in a country whose population is increasing so rapidly makes this difficult. The forest is home to a number of birds and the very small Zanzibar duiker which is only 35 centimetres high and is usually seen in pairs. Also found in this forest is the rare Golden-rumped elephant shrew. There are four endemic plants. The Forest Office is about one kilometre from the Watamu turning – obtain permission if you wish to explore the forest. They will also be able to advise whether the tracks which join the Tsavo National Park road to the north are passable. From Tsavo East to Malindi the distance is 100 kilometres but a four-wheel drive is necessary during the rainy season.

The road heads inland to skirt around the Mida Creek before coming to the village of Watamu. This is the location of **Watamu Marine Park**. A little further on and to the west of the road you will pass the Gedi National Park. This is located to the south of Malindi (see Game Parks Section). Close to the village of Watamu is the turnoff for the **Gedi ruins**. Beyond the Watamu turning, the road again passes through scrub with small villages interspersed. At the end of the dry season you will notice, both from the road and from the air, lots of bonfires. This is the villagers clearing their land ahead of the long rains when they will plant their crops. You will also notice termite mounds – some are well over two metres high and often fantastically shaped. Finally before reaching Malindi you will see signs to the **Malindi Marine Park** and the **Snake Park**.

Watamu

A small fishing village which in recent years has been seeing some fairly rapid tourist development. The atmosphere of the village itself is mixed – it is certainly feeling the impact of tourists. Watamu still maintains quite a lot of traditional village charm, despite the proximity of the tourist hotels. Watamu is known for its spectacular coral reef, and the coast splits into three bays: Watamu, Blue Lagoon, and Turtle Bay. Apart from the beach and the sea, the attractions of staying here are the nearby **Watamu Marine Park** and the **Gedi Ruins**. There are a number of resort hotels but not much in terms of budget accommodation. It is scenically quite attractive as there are a number of small islands just offshore – Turtle Bay is quite good for snorkelling as the small islands are only about 50 metres offshore at low tide. Watch out for speed boats ferrying fishermen to the large game boats. The water is much clearer here than at Malindi during the wet season. The most exciting way to the reef, two kilometres offshore, is to go in a glass-bottomed boat, which will cost between US$15-20 but is well worth it. The beach is relatively free of seaweed. Avoid the camel rides along the beach. If you can't afford deep-sea fishing, be at *Hemingways* at 1600-1700 when the days catch is recorded and the fishermen photographed. Tagged fish are apparently returned to the sea. Watamu is also a good place to hire bikes as an alternative way of exploring the surrounding area, including the Gedi ruins. There are a number of shops in the village, with reasonable rates. Look out for the new village school building which was completed by five unpaid British builders in a fortnight in early 1999. They were rewarded by being appointed as elders of the Giriama tribe and given Swahili names. Other places of interest are the **Snake Farm**, **Midi Creek Swamp**, the **Butterfly Farm** at Gedi Ruins, and **Dhow Building** on the beach.

Phone code: 0122
Colour map 4, grid C6

Kenya

Sleeping

A+ *Blue Bay Village*, PO Box 162, Watamu, T32626, F32422. Located a couple of kilometres to the south of the village in the most southerly of the 3 coves, this hotel is also popular with Italians, good facilities. **A+** *Hemingway's* (Formerly known as *Seafarers*), PO Box 267, Watamu, T32624/32624/320061/32052 (Watamu), 225255 (Nairobi), F32256 (Watamu). This has more of a mix of clientele although perhaps British, and expatriates living in Kenya dominate. The hotel has been renovated recently, it is to a high standard, but the rooms lack character, being a double storey concrete block with verandahs, facilities include 2 swimming pools, bar, an excellent restaurant, and watersports including deep-sea fishing fleet, own dhow. Trips to Tsavo National Park can also be arranged, good value out of season. **A** *Barracuda Inn*, PO Box 402, Watamu, T61/70/74. Located just to the south of the village this new hotel is Italian-owned and attracts a large proportion of Italians amongst their clientele, it is a wonderful building with fantastic thatched *makuti* roofs, the gardens are also very pretty and the staff friendly, closes in May.

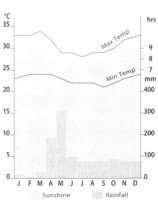

Climate: Watamu

B *Aquarius Watamu Hotel* (previously Watamu Cottages) PO Box 96, T32069, F32512, aquarius@users.africaonline.co.ke. Recently renovated, under Italian ownership. 40 a/c rooms, pool, gardens, Italian food, 100 metres from the beach facing Blue Bay Cove.

B *Ascot Residence Hotel*, PO Box 345. Not on beach, but good central location, bar, tennis, pizzeria, grill, boutique. Civilised Italian management, clientele include many retired Italians. Has spacious grounds and a pool. Friendly staff, large rooms, is splendid value. **B** *Ocean Sports*, PO Box 100, Malindi, T32008/32288 (Watamu), F32266. Located a little further south this has a series of cottages set in gardens, there is a large bar and restaurant and all the other usual facilities, the Sunday lunch is a huge buffet, popular with expatriates and particularly good value, will arrange big game fishing (US$140 per person a day), PADI and BASC, diving courses, goggling, tennis and squash, friendly atmosphere. Well recommended. Has a very well run dive shop/school, with British staff. **B** *Turtle Bay Beach Hotel*, PO Box 10, T32003/32080/32226, F32268, turtles@africaonline.co.ke . This hotel also has a mixed clientele, it is very relaxed and has all the facilities including watersports, it has a variety of rooms with or without a/c, will arrange a wide variety of tours in the area, organized as a club, encouraging residents to eat all their meals and take all their entertainment at the hotel, looks after guests very well and is excellently organized, a windsurfing course for beginners costs US$31, a 5-day PADI diving course costs US$250, exotic plants such as bouganvillea

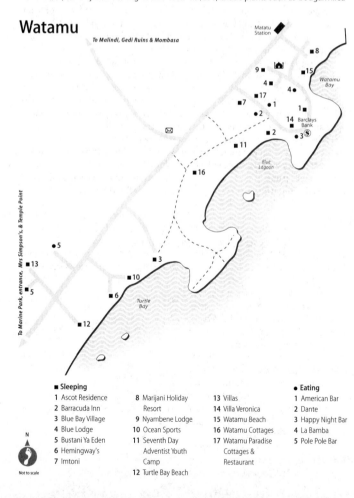

Watamu

To Malindi, Gedi Ruins & Mombasa

Matatu Station

Watamu Bay

Blue Lagoon

Turtle Bay

To Marine Park, entrance, Mrs Simpson's, & Temple Point

N

Not to scale

■ Sleeping		● Eating
1 Ascot Residence	8 Marijani Holiday Resort	13 Villas	1 American Bar
2 Barracuda Inn	9 Nyambene Lodge	14 Villa Veronica	2 Dante
3 Blue Bay Village	10 Ocean Sports	15 Watamu Beach	3 Happy Night Bar
4 Blue Lodge	11 Seventh Day Adventist Youth Camp	16 Watamu Cottages	4 La Bamba
5 Bustani Ya Eden	12 Turtle Bay Beach	17 Watamu Paradise Cottages & Restaurant	5 Pole Pole Bar
6 Hemingway's			
7 Imtoni			

and oleander are on sale at about US$1 each, tennis, basketball, programmes for children, cats restaurant, massage, excellent beach. **B** *Watamu Beach*, PO Box 81443, Mombasa T32001/32010. This hotel is the northernmost of all the Watamu hotels, it is located behind the village on the northern cove, it is a large hotel and is popular with German tourists, it is set in generous grounds, and facilities include swimming pool, bar, and restaurant, the beach here is lovely and there are lots of fishermen offering to take you out to the reef in their boats.

C *Hotel Golden Palm*, PO Box 14, T32444, Tx21459. **C** *Hotel Villas*, PO Box 150, T32298/32464, F32487. Not on the beach, but organizes transport to the shore, s/c villas with kitchens, a/c, pool, good value. **C** *Marijani Holiday Resort*, PO Box 282, T/F32448. Beautiful surroundings. Ocean front resort north of Watamu, near the African Safari Club, easily reached by Matatu as terminus 5 minutes walk away. A Kenyan/German enterprise offering a variety of accommodation from basic board to fully furnished s/c cottages available for short/long rental periods. Can arrange pick up from Mombasa Airport. Rooms have nets, fans, hot water, fridge, sunbeds and room-cleaning service. Phone/fax service available. Bicycle and surf board rental. **C** *Peponi Cottages*, PO Box 25, T32434 (Res), T32246. Recently built, small but reasonable rooms, with mosquito nets, small swimming pool, breakfast not included. **C** *Temple Point*, PO Box 296 T32057/8, Tx21051, F32289 at Watamu Marine Park.

D *Bustani Ya Eden*, PO Box 276, T32262. Small, 6 very pleasant rooms, rate very good for 2 sharing a room, s/c, fans, 300 metres to beach, speciality African and seafood restaurant, friendly Dutch/Kenyan couple run the place. **D** *Mrs Simpson Guest House*, PO Box 33, Watamu, T32032, Plot 28. Pleasant s/c double room, wonderful beach, friendly. **D** *Villa Veronica (Mwikali Lodge)*, PO Box 57, Watamu, T32083. This is one of the best of the budget hotels in Watamu, rooms have bathrooms attached, mosquito nets provided and are clean, it is a friendly family-run place, and the price includes breakfast. **D** *Watamu Paradise Cottages*, PO Box 249, Watamu, T32062, F32436. These cottages are situated close to the village near *Mustafa's Restaurant*, there is a swimming pool in the grounds and they are very pleasant.

E *Blue Lodge*, in village. Shared bathrooms, inexpensive and basic, has neither mosquito nets nor cool fans, so not comfortable. **E** *Iritoni Lodge*, only has 2 rooms but is clean and friendly. **E** *Nyambene Lodge*, in the village, basic rooms with shared facilities. **E** *Private Houses*, you can also usually rent a room very cheaply in a house in town if you ask around. **E** *Seventh Day Adventists Youth Hostel*, this is not a proper hostel and you can only stay here occasionally, facilities are basic. **E** *Watamu Cottages*, not to be confused with the *Watamu Paradise Cottages*, these are located about a kilometre out of town and are very popular, there is a swimming pool in the complex and they are used a lot by expatriate families, the price includes breakfast and they are really excellent value.

You can eat at all the big hotels which do various set menus and buffets – look around as there are sometimes real bargains. **Eating**

3 *Hotel Dante*, opposite *Mustafa's Restaurant*. Italian cuisine. **3** *La Bamba Country Lodge*, north of village. **3** *Watamu Paradise Restaurant*, part of the cottages of the same name, this serves good food including seafood and is good value. The nearby **3** *Mustafa's Restaurant*, particularly popular at night when it can get quite lively as the *Comeback Club*. **2** *American Bar*, north of village. Hamburgers and grills. **2** *Coco Grill Bar and Restaurant*, north of village. Grills and seafood. **1** *Happy Night Bar and Restaurant*, serves snacks and beers and is good value, occasional live music.

Sports (participant) Deep-sea fishing: *Hemingways*, PO Box 267, Watamu, T32624/32006, F32256. *Tega Safaris Ltd*, PO Box 12, Watamu, T32078. **Entertainment**

Local Bicycle hire: *Tuna Travel* near Mustapha's restaurant. **Transport**

Kenya

From Malindi to Watamu takes about half an hour, there are plenty of matatus and it will cost you about US$0.50. Hotel taxi from Malindi US$18; from Mombasa US$90. Note these taxis can seat 7, and on this basis cost is US$2.50 a head and US$13.

Directory

Banks There is a small branch of *Barclays*, in the village which is open in the mornings on Mon, Wed and Fri. The big hotels will change money out of these hours, although the rate will not be very good. **Tour companies & travel agents** *Tuna Travel and Tours*, PO Box 26, T322445. Located near Mustapha's restaurant. *Samurai Tours and Safaris*, PO Box 203, T32306 (office), T32252 (home). *Wildgame Tours and Safaris*, PO Box 131, T32311/32446, near Barclays Banks. *Blue Boy Safaris*, PO Box 162, T32626, F32422. *Sambu Tours and Travel*, T32482.

Watamu Marine Park

Along this coast close to Watamu village there is an excellent marine park which has been made a total exclusion zone. Obviously this was not all good news for some fishermen – but they seem to have adapted quite happily, and the influx of tourists has increased the incomes of the village. The park headquarters are someway south of Watamu at the end of the peninsula which guards the entrance to the creek. Unfortunately the road goes a little inland, hiding views of the sea. This is somewhat compensated by views of the creek – it is not that attractive though. You go out in a glass bottom boat to the protected area and some of the hundreds of fishes come to the boat to be fed. Glass bottom boats may seem rather expensive but are really well worth it and can be arranged at any of the hotels, or else at the entrance to the actual Park. You can also swim amongst the fish which is a wonderful sensation. There are lots of shells and live corals which are a splendid range of colours. If short of time, try the islands just offshore from *Hemingways*.

Gedi Ruins

Colour map 4, grid C6   This is one of Kenya's most important archaeological sites and is believed to contain the ruins of a city that once had a population of about 2,500. It was populated in the latter half of the 13th century, and the size of some of the buildings, in particular the mosque suggest that this was a fairly wealthy town for some time. However, it is not mentioned in any Arabic or Swahili writings and was apparently unknown to the Portuguese although they maintained a strong presence in Malindi just 15 kilometres away. It is believed that this was because it was set away from the sea, and deep in the forest. Possibly as a result of an attack from marauding tribesmen of the Oromo or Galla tribe, the city was abandoned at some time during the 16th century. Lack of water may have also been a contributing factor as wells of over 50 metres deep dried out. It was later reinhabited but never regained the economic position that it once had held. It was then finally abandoned in the early 17th century and the ruins discovered in 1884. The site was declared a national monument in 1948 and has been excavated since then. It has been well preserved. There is a small museum and visitors are welcome. You can buy a guide book and map of the site at the entrance gate. There are also informative guides – ask for Ali.

The site was originally surrounded by an inner and outer wall (surprisingly thin). The most interesting buildings and features are concentrated around the entrance gate, although there are others. Most that remain are within the inner wall although there are some between the two walls. All the buildings are built using coral rag and lime, and some had decorations carved into the wall plaster. You can still see the remains of the bathrooms – complete with deep bath, basin and squat toilet. There are a large number of wells in the site, some being exceptionally deep. The main buildings that remain are a sultan's palace, a mosque and a number of houses and tombs, a water system and a prison. Other finds include pieces of Chinese porcelain from the Ming Dynasty, beads from India and stoneware from Persia – some are displayed in the musuem, others in Fort Jesus, Mombasa.

The **Palace** can be entered through a rather grand arched doorway which brings you into the reception court and then a hall. This is the most impressive building on the site. Off this hall there are a number of smaller rooms – including the bathrooms. You can also see the remains of the kitchen area which contains a small well.

The **Great Mosque** probably dates from the mid 15th century, and is the largest of the seven on this site. It is believed to have been rebuilt fairly substantially more recently. Look out for the *mihrab* which indicates to the faithful the direction of Mecca, and being built of stone (rather than wood) has survived well. As you leave notice the carved spearhead which is located above the northeast doorway.

A great amount of trade seems to have been established here – silk and porcelain were exchanged for skins and most importantly ivory. China was keen to exploit this market and in 1414 a giraffe was given to the Chinese Emperor and shipped from Malindi. It apparently survived the trip. There was also trade with European countries – a glass bead has been found which originated in Venice.

There are in total 14 houses on the complex which have so far been excavated. Each one is named after something that has been found at its site – for example House of Scissors, House of Ivory Box. There is also one named after a picture of a dhow which is on the wall. In the houses you will again be able to see the old-style bathrooms. Deep pits were dug for sewage, capped when full and then used for fertilizer. Such techiques are still used in the Old Town district in Malindi.

The tombs are located to the right of the entrance gate and one of them is of particular interest to archaeologists as it actually has a date engraved on it – the Islamic year 802 which is equal to the year 1399 AD. This is known as the Date Tomb and has enabled other parts of the site to be dated with more accuracy. There is also a tomb with a design that is common along the Swahili coast – that of a fluted pillar. Pillar tombs are found all up the coast and were used for men with position and influence.

The site is in very pleasant surroundings – it is green and shady but can get very hot (cool drinks are available at the entrance). You may hear a buzzing noise. This is an insect that lives only for three or four days until it literally blows itself to pieces! There are usually monkeys in the trees above which are filled with the noise of many different types of birds. It is in fact also a wildlife sanctuary and is home to the

Gedi Ruins

magnificent, and now sadly rare, black and white colobus monkey. This monkey has suffered at the hands of poachers for their splendid coats but a few remain and you may see some here. Also in the sanctuary are the golden-rumped elephant shrew (only seen at dawn and dusk) and various birds such as the harrier hawk and palm tree vulture.

Kipepeo Project Just inside the entrance to Gede Ruins is a community-based butterfly farm which has trained local farmers living on the edge of the Arabuko-Sokoke Forest Reserve (see page 192) to rear butterfly pupae for export overseas. The project aims to link forest conservation with income generation for local communities and at present is the only butterfly farm in Africa of this kind.

At the central breeding unit at Gede Ruins it is possible to see all stages of butterfly development, learn about their natural history and see a selection of the species of butterflies present in the Arabuko-Sokoke Forest. Half an hour spent in this shady location offers an interesting contrast to the historic site of Gede Ruins as the emphasis is on providing a secure future for the Arabuko-Sokoke Forest and communities adjacent to it. Opening times 0800-1700, admission fees: non-residents, adults US$2, children US$1.

To get to the site, take the main Malindi-Mombasa road. The site is located about four kilometres to the north of Watamu. It is signposted from the village of Gedi and if you came by matatu you will have to walk the last one kilometre. You can hire a taxi from Malindi – it will cost about US$8. Entrance will cost around US$3.75, children US$1 and is open from 0700 to 1800 daily.

Malindi

3° 12′ S, 40° 5′ E
Phone code: 0123
Colour map 4, grid C6

Malindi is the second largest coastal town in Kenya after Mombasa. Although the history of the town dates back to the 12th century there are few remains of the ancient town.

A great attraction is the Malindi Marine Park with clear water and brilliant fish. It is also one of the few places on the East African coast where the rollers come crashing into the shore, there is a break in the reef, and it is possible to surf.

The beach is excellent and popular as it suffers less from the problem of seaweed compared to the beaches around Mombasa. Seaweed seems worse before the spring equinox and can make it impossible to swim. The more expensive hotels clear their section of the beach of seaweed. The surf is good during July-August and the only problem is that silt from the Galana River can make the water a rather red, muddy colour during the rainy season.

Safety The main parts of Malindi are safe, even at night. You should have no worries walking between *Lawfords Hotel* and the casino. Exercise caution elsewhere, however, and take a taxi if you need to go further afield.

History The earliest known reference to Malindi is found in Chinese geography in a piece published in 1060 written by a scholar who died in AD 863. This refers to Ma-lin, its people are said to be black and their nature fierce. However details in the piece are inaccurate and suggest that the writer was possibly referring to another town to the north of Malindi. The next reference, in 1150 is also thought to be inaccurate and actually to be Manda, a town to the south of Lamu. The first accurate description of the town is believed to be written by **Prince Abu al-Fida** who lived from 1273 to 1331. Archaeological evidence supports the theory that the town of Malindi was founded in the 13th century by Arabs. In any event, locals claim that there was a big Chinese trading influence. This is evidenced even today by the faces of the local people who still retain traces of Chinese features.

Fireworks at Malindi

In 1498 Vasco da Gama, sailing north up the East African coast had met with a hostile reception both in Sofala (now in Mozambique) and Mombasa. He needed to establish good relations with a town at the coast so that he could load fresh water and victuals and engage an experienced mariner to guide his fleet to the Indies. The bales of cotton cloth and strings of beads the fleet had brought with them to trade had proved useless – the coastal people had gold from Sofola, ivory from the interior, silk from the east.

Vasco da Gama decided to present some unusual items to the King of Malindi – a jar of marmalade, a set of decorated porcelain dishes and a candied peach in a silver bowl. He then invited the King and his people to witness a firework display on the shore. The King had a brass throne with a scarlet canopy brought down to the shore and with a court of horn players, flautists and drummers gazed out to the San Gabriel and da Gama's fleet. In quick succession the ship's canons fired shells into the air which burst over the King and his townsfolk on the shore. It was spectacular and exciting, and the King was impressed. At last the Portuguese had an ally for their conquest of the mainland.

Kenya

In 1498 **Vasco da Gama**, having rounded the Cape of Good Hope stopped off at various ports along the coast. At Mombasa he was not made welcome – indeed attempts were made to sink his ships. He quickly left and continued north stopping at Malindi where he found a much warmer reception. Why the response of the two towns should be so different is not clear – it may have been because of an on-going feud between the two local leaders as well as the gifts and pyrotechnic display (see Box). The good relations between Malindi and the Portuguese continued throughout the 16th century. In about 1500 the population of within the town walls was about 3,500, with another 2,000 Africans living in surrounding plantations. The town was governed by the Arabs who were the wealthiest group. The wealth came from the trade with India and the supply of agricultural produce, grown in the surrounding plantations largely by slaves, for passing ships. One of the visitors in this period was St Francis Xavier who passed by Malindi in 1542 on his way to India.

The town went into a period of decline in the 16th century and in 1593 the Portuguese administration was transferred from Malindi to Mombasa. Traders and labourers followed but the Arabs who remained behind had become too dependent on the Portuguese to manage without them. The decline was in part a consequence of the superiority of the harbour facilities at Mombasa. Neighbouring tribes, in particular the Galla, overran the town, and it is believed that Malindi was abandoned in the late 17th century. It lay in a ruined state for many years and it was not until 1861 that it was refounded by the Sultan of Zanzibar and again became prosperous.

In the period of the latter half of the 19th century Malindi was dominated by Zanzibar. Although Malindi continued to suffer as Mombasa expanded and took more trade, the town's prosperity did improve during this period and the use of slaves was undoubtedly an important factor. To get an idea of the scale, in the first year of resettlement in 1861 there were a 1,000 slaves working for just 50 Arabs. Malindi was not a major exporter of slaves as the demand within the town did not allow it. Malindi had a particularly bad reputation for its treatment of slaves.

The period under the **Imperial British East Africa Company** (IBEAC) began in 1887 when the Company acquired a 50-year lease from the Sultan of Zanzibar for territories in East Africa. The Company administered the area, collected taxes and had rights over minerals found. Bell Smith was sent to the town as officer for the Company and he began to lobby for the abolition of the slave trade. From around 1890 slaves who wished and were able to, could buy their freedom. For those who could not, the Company offered jobs, or found paid employment. Interestingly relatively few took up the opportunity and the process was a gradual one. It has been estimated that from 1888 to 1892 2,387 slaves were freed on the coast by the IBEAC and by 1897 there were still 5,442 slaves in the Malindi district.

In 1895 the British government purchased the assets of the IBEAC and established formally the East African Protectorate. The same year the Sultan of Zanzibar transferred the lease of the 10-mile coastal strip to the British Government for the sum of £11,000 per year. The Arabs, who had grown used to having slave labour, found it very difficult to adapt to actually paying workers, and the final blow was dealt in 1907 when the Protectorate government abolished the status of slavery. Merchandise trade developed, and in the early 20th century the most important exports were rubber, grain, ivory, hides and horns. Rubber was grown on European-owned plantations in response to a dramatic increase in the world price around the First World War. However, it was short lived as the world price subsequently fell and most of the plantations were abandoned.

During the second half of the British period the foundations were laid for what is now Malindi's most important industry – that of tourism. During the depression years Malindi's trade and agriculture had suffered not just from low world prices but also from drought. There continued to be a shortage of labour and the only crop that experienced an increase in production was cotton. The 1930s also saw the beginning of the tourist industry with the first hotel *Brady's Palm Beach Hotel* opening in 1932

Malindi North

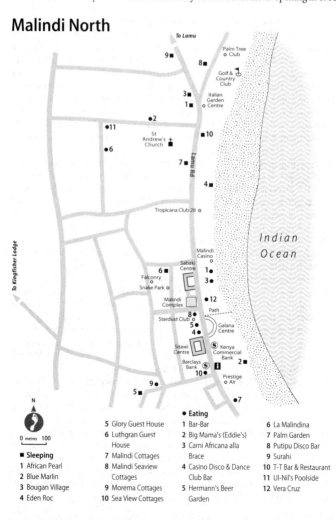

To Lamu

Palm Tree Club

Golf & Country Club

Italian Garden Centre

St Andrew's Church

Lamu Rd

Tropicana Club 28

Malindi Casino

Sabaki Centre

Falconry

Snake Park

Malindi Complex

Stardust Club

Galana Centre

Sitawi Centre

Kenya Commercial Bank

Barclays Bank

Prestige Air

Indian Ocean

Path

To Kingfisher Lodge

N

0 metres 100

■ **Sleeping**
1 African Pearl
2 Blue Marlin
3 Bougan Village
4 Eden Roc
5 Glory Guest House
6 Luthgran Guest House
7 Malindi Cottages
8 Malindi Seaview Cottages
9 Morema Cottages
10 Sea View Cottages

● **Eating**
1 Bar-Bar
2 Big Mama's (Eddie's)
3 Carni Africana alla Brace
4 Casino Disco & Dance Club Bar
5 Hermann's Beer Garden
6 La Malindina
7 Palm Garden
8 Putipu Disco Bar
9 Surahi
10 T-T Bar & Restaurant
11 Ul-Nil's Poolside
12 Vera Cruz

– famous visitors include Ernest Hemingway who visited in 1934. Most of the tourists at this time were settlers from the White Highlands. Expansion continued after the Second World War and Malindi became popular as a retirement town for European settlers. With the increase in air travel and affordability of holidays abroad the growth of Malindi as a tourist resort spiralled, spurred on by the popularity of package tours.

Today, Malindi is heavily influenced by the Italians who have been encouraged to invest by the Government. Many are attracted by the 'cheapness' of the area and many retirement villas have been built. This has not been altogether welcomed by the local people despite the obvious increase in jobs. A number of expensive shopping malls have sprung up recently which are full of expensive Italian goods and overpriced curios.

Although there is little left of the ancient walled town of Malindi, there are two remains in the town itself that are worth seeing. The oldest part of the town is clustered around the jetty – here is the **Jami Mosque** and two striking **Pillar Tombs**. These are thought to date from the 14th century. The Malindi Curios Dealers Associations have a huge market here. Behind the Jami Mosque lies a maze of small

Sights

Malindi South

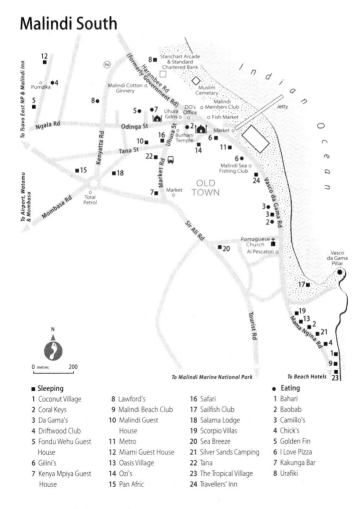

■ **Sleeping**

1 Coconut Village	8 Lawford's	16 Safari
2 Coral Keys	9 Malindi Beach Club	17 Sailfish Club
3 Da Gama's	10 Malindi Guest	18 Salama Lodge
4 Driftwood Club	House	19 Scorpio Villas
5 Fondu Wehu Guest	11 Metro	20 Sea Breeze
House	12 Miami Guest House	21 Silver Sands Camping
6 Gilini's	13 Oasis Village	22 Tana
7 Kenya Mpiya Guest	14 Ozi's	23 The Tropical Village
House	15 Pan Afric	24 Travellers' Inn

● **Eating**

1 Bahari
2 Baobab
3 Camillo's
4 Chick's
5 Golden Fin
6 I Love Pizza
7 Kakunga Bar
8 Urafiki

streets that form the Old Town district. The oldest surviving buildings are the mosques of which there are nine (including the Jami Mosque) which date from before 1500. Contempory account from the 14th century remark on two-stored houses with carved wooden balconies and flat roofs, the latter constructed from mangrove poles, coral and zinc mortar. None of these have survived. The smaller dwellings had timber and latticed walls covered with mud and mortar and woven palm frond roofs, called *makuti*. The density of the housing and the materials made old Malindi very vunerable to fire, and periodic conflagrations (the most recent in 1965) destroyed all the older dwellings. The mosques survived by virtue of having stone walls of coral blocks and mortar.

The two buildings of note from the British period are the **District Officers House** in front of Uhuru Gardens, and the **Customs House** behind the jetty. Both have verandahs, and are not in particularly good repair, but the District Officers House is a handsome and imposing structure.

In the centre of town, the **Uhuru Gardens** are being relaid. Close to the bus and matatu stand is the Malindi Wood Carvers located off Kenyatta Road, which is run as a co-operative. Ask to visit the workshops which are behind the shop. This is very interesting as many of the society's 350 members work in very poor conditions on a variety of wood. You will be able to see how some of the finely carved pieces are manufactured from the most unlikely looking material. Also in this area is the main market. Once again it is interesting to wander through as apart from clothing, vegetables and charcoal, you can see old cars being converted into pots and pans and other hardware.

On Government Road, between Uhuru Gardens and Kenyatta Road is the **Malindi Cotton Ginnery**. If you are in Malindi between September-January, the ginnery will be in operation. Much of the British-made machinery is over 70 years old, but still serviceable (see Box, page 421). There are some special machines for ginning kapok, used as an upholstery material. If you ask at the office, it is possible to look around.

If you walk inland from the jetty, past the Customs House, on the left you will see a **Maize Mill**. The owner will be happy to show you around. There is a British-made Yeoman mill dating from 1920, as well as some modern hammer-mills.

The area between here and Kenyatta Road to the northwest is the trading quarter – a hive of activity. Beyond it are the hotels and modern shopping malls. Note access to the beach can be gained by a footpath just beyond the Tourist Office and Galana shopping centre.

There are also a couple of monuments that date from the Portuguese period, in particular the **Vasco da Gama Cross**. This is situated on the promontory that is located at the southern end of the bay. It was erected to assist in navigation. The actual cross is the original and is made of stone from Lisbon, although the pillar on which it stands is constructed of local coral. You can reach it by turning down Mnarani Road.

The small **Catholic Church** close to the cross is also believed to date from the Portuguese period and is thought to be the same one that St Francis Xavier visited in 1542 when he stopped off at Malindi to bury two soldiers on his way to India. It is one of the oldest Catholic churches in Africa still in use today and the walls are original – the thatched roof has been replaced many times. Nearby are two graves, one of Sir Piers Edward Joseph Mostyn, the twelfth Baron Talacre, and the other of Geoffrey Herbert Locke of Tonbridge, Kent, England.

Both these monuments are about one kilometre south of the centre. However, it may be worth hiring a bicycle to visit them. You could then continue along the beach (follow the sign to Vasco da Gama Cross but carry on up the hill – there is a path descending to the beach) to the Marine Park. The sand is hard and flat – a much better alternative to cycling along the main road.

Outside Malindi there are Gedi Ruins, located 16 kilometres south Malindi, which are more extensive (see above, page 196).

Stamps, satchels and sardines

You may be approached in Malindi Old Town by a tall gentleman, with not many upper teeth. He asks if you might send some stamps to his daughter, who collects them. Come, my house is just round the corner, I can write out my address. He expands a little on himself – he is a fisherman, he has eight children, he caught a big tuna last night. Disappearing into a small Swahili house he emerges with his name and address, and a small basketware satchel. He says his wife makes them, and he would like you to have it as a gift. No, no, he cannot accept any payment. If you wish, you could buy him some sardines for bait for tonight's fishing. Off you trek to the fish market. A basket of small fish is selected and the visitor is requested to hand over US$5 to the fishmonger. Passing a stall later, you notice the little satchels on sale for about US$0.50.

Tana River You can take a cruise whilst in this part of Kenya. They are usually for two or three nights and are along the delta of the river Tana and tributaries situated to the north of Malindi. It is expensive – but you will be very well looked after and the food is excellent. The price includes all food, transport and day trips. You can be picked up from the airport or from Malindi, and will be taken by landrover to the camp on the river bank. While you are there you can swim, go on river trips, bird watching and animal tracking. For details and reservations: *Tana Delta*, PO Box 24988, Nairobi (T882826).

Malindi Marine Park This is popular and with good reason. The water is brilliantly clear, and the fish are a dazzling array of colours. There are two main reefs with a sandy section of sea bed dividing them. You can hire all the equipment that you will need and a boat here, but it is advisable to check your mask and snorkel before accepting. The fish are very tame as they have been fed on bread provided by the boatman. If you see any shells be sure to leave them there for the next visitor – the shell population has suffered very severely from the increase in tourism. The Park is located to the south of Malindi, and it is probably easiest to arrange a trip from Malindi. The price should include park entrance fees, transport to and from your hotel and the boat itself. Try and go at low tide as the calmer the sea, the better; also be sure to take some sort of footwear that you can wear in the water. You will also be taken to one of the sand bars just off the reef: take plenty of sun protection. You can organize the trip through your hotel, many of which seem to have arrangements with local boat owners. Be sure to enquire whether the rate includes the National Park entrance fee. Nearby is **Crocodile Paradise** with hundreds of crocs as well as snakes and other reptiles. ■ *0900-1750 daily.*

Lake Chem Chem Rhino Reserve This is about eight kilometres from town on the Tsavo Road. The road is quite bad but you can get a matutu to Ghardan. Get dropped off at the turning and then walk about 200 metres. There is only one rhino at the moment but you can go on a bird watching tour for about US$25, although it may be possible to negotiate a better rate with the park guards. The lake is dry for most of the year but the birds are supposed to be very good from May to August. Camel safaris are also organized for about US$60. Further information from Marcus Russell, Galdesa Office, T31084.

Arabuker-Sukoke Forest is about 20 kilometres south toward Mombasa, with the wildlife service post at the entrance just past Gedi and the road to Watamu. The forest runs for about 40 kilometres south to Kilifi and, at its widest, for 20 kilometres inland. The birds and butterflies are the main attraction as well as some small mammals.

Malindi Falconry This is located a little to the north of the town on the Lamu Road, and is said to be the only falconry in the country.

Snake Park. Situated close to the Falconry on Lamu Road. Avoid feeding time at 1600 Wednesday and Friday if you will be upset at the sight of live mice being fed to the snakes. ■ *PO Box 104, T21084, US$4 adults, US$2 children, open 0900-1800.*

Kenya

Akambo Village can be visited, T21245. It provides an example of the traditional life of the Kamba people (see page 288).

Gedi Ruins and National Park Located 16 kilometres south of Malindi, the National Park contains the ruins of this ancient village (see above, page 196). A visit can be combined with a trip to the Watamu Marine Park (see above, page 196).

Dhows Trips can be arranged through *Prince Safaris*, Silver Sand Road, PO Box 966, T20596, by the main jetty. There are several options: safaris, fishing or just sailing and involve a variety of activities including barbecues on the beach. Prices are around US$60 per person, minimum four to six people.

Deep-sea Fishing These can be arranged through your hotel or contact one of the following: *Malindi Sports Fishing Club*, PO Box 163, T20161; *Malindi Sea Fishing Club*, PO Box 364, T20410; *Kingfisher Safaris*, PO Box 29, T20123; *Slaters*, PO Box 147, Watamu, T12; *Peter Ready*, PO Box 63, T21292; *Von Menyhart*, PO Box 360, T20840; *Baharini Ventures*, PO Box 435, T20879.

Scuba Diving *Drift Wood Club*, PO Box 63, T20155/30569, at Silver Sands which charges about US$8 per dive, also a diving school; *Guarami Diving Centre*, Kirulini Village, T21267; *Venta Diving*, Club Jambo, at Casuarina Point by Marine Park, PO Box 444, T21245/20463; *Crab Diving*, at tropical village and *African Dream Hotels*, T20443/4, PADI course US$100 for five days.

Windsurfing Arrange through the centre next to the *White Elephant Hotel* at the south end of the beach.

Sleeping The great advantage that Malindi has over Mombasa is that there are inexpensive hotels located close to the beach. There are also plenty of luxurious hotels.

Tourism in Malindi is very seasonal, being packed into June-August. Outside these months you should bargain, and you can often, in the luxury hotels, obtain a very good special rate (perhaps a third of the asking rate).

Malindi has expanded enormously in the past decade, geared mostly to Italian and German tourists. Some superb restaurants and hotels have been constructed, but it is hard to avoid the view that there was a great deal of poor development. Off-season the large shopping complexes are empty, and about half of the large hotels are shut. In 1995 even the high-season was poor, and several hotels appear to have closed, and are doubtful about re-opening. Among these, to the north are *Vasco de Gama Villas*, *Bouganvillea*, and the old *Sinbad Hotel*. To the south, toward Casuarina Point are *African Dream Village*, *Kilili Baharini* and *White Elephant Sea Lodge*.

Town Centre The places in the town centre are mainly for the budget traveller. They often suffer from having more mosquitoes and being hotter as they do not get the sea breezes. They can also be noisy. **D** *Glory Guesthouse*, inland from Blue Marlin, past Swahili Restaurant, T30309. Some a/c, s/c, nets, restaurant, functional but well run and good value, part of Glory chain based in Mombasa.

E *Africa Lodge* (formerly *New Safari*), Tana Rd, close to bus station, entrance through restaurant, PO Box 589. A little rough and noisy, but cheap. **E** *Kenya Mpiya Guesthouse*, opposite market, PO Box 209, T31658. Some s/c, fans, no nets. **E** *New Lamu*, Tana Rd, about 50 metres from bus station, PO Box 333, T20864. Nets, not s/c, simple but good value. **E** *Pan Afric Guesthouse*, Tana Rd, close to junction with Tourist Rd, PO Box 589, T31148. Small, friendly, not s/c, nets, no fans, cheap. **E** *Salonna Lodge*, off Mombasa Rd, in town centre, PO Box 335. Small Swahili building, single storey, no fans, no nets, not s/c, cheap. **E** *Sea Breeze Hotel*, on Tourist Rd, on edge of Old Town, PO Box 533, T20718. Pleasant rooms, some s/c, balconies, restaurant, well-run establishment, thoroughly secure. Well recommended. **E** *Tana*, PO Box 766, T20234/20657. Well-run establishment, close to bus station, fans, net, restaurant, recently redecorated. **E** *Wanandil Lodgings*, on corner of intersection of Tana Rd and Mombasa Rd, PO Box 209, T2584. Above rather lively bar with some splendid murals, no fans, no nets, but cheap.

North of Malindi   These hotels are strung out on the Lamu Rd to the north of the town.
A+ *Club Che-Shale*, PO Box 492, T20063, F21257. Located about 8 kilometres north of
Malindi on a remote beach, this has 12 thatched bandas with bathrooms and verandas, they
vary – some are a bit run down, however it is a pleasant atmosphere and is located on a
lovely secluded beach, there is plenty to do here sailing, deep-sea fishing and snorkelling,
and there is a bar and restaurant which does top-class seafood dishes. **A+** *Eden Roc*, PO Box
350, T123/20480/1/2, Tx21225, F20265. This hotel is located on a cliff top overlooking the
bay in generous grounds, lily ponds, there are over 150 rooms, all a/c with bathrooms as well
as some cottages, tends to cater to European package tours, it has its own beach, though
water is 100 metres away, and facilities include swimming pool, tennis courts, watersports,
scuba diving, deep-sea fishing, golf, and disco, massage, hair plaiting (US$40 a full head).
A+ *Indian Ocean Lodge*, PO Box 171, T123/20394. This is a very exclusive hotel with just 5
rooms and a private beach, it has been built of local materials in the Lamu Arab style and tastefully decorated, and is set in marvellous colourful gardens, the price includes meals and there
are trips arranged, such as fishing, snorkelling and bird watching, you can also go on a trip to
the Gedi Ruins. **A+** *Kingfisher Lodge*, some 3 kilometres inland, PO Box 29, T21168. Thatched
cottages round a pool, a/c, fans, small and exclusive, transport to beach, tennis, squash, golf
and windsurfing available. **A** *Blue Marlin*, PO Box 54, T20440/1. This hotel was originally
named *Brady's Palm Beach Hotel* and was the first hotel to open in 1932, it is excellently run,
very friendly and has splendid facilities, Ernest Hemingway stayed here in 1934 (see page 51).
A *Lawford's*, PO Box 20, T20440. This was the second hotel to open in this part of the coast
being established in 1934, located very close to the town, under the same management as the
Blue Marlin, except *Lawford's* is slightly cheaper, a new wing was built in the late 1970s and the
hotel has singles, doubles and cottages, the rooms are nice although the restaurant only fair,
there are 2 swimming pools, meeting rooms and the hotel organizes trips out to the reef in
the glass bottom boat, water gymnastics, pool, volley ball, beach cricket.

   B *African Dream Cottages*, PO Box 939, T21296. These are self contained cottages which
each sleep 4, there is a swimming pool and a newly built restaurant and bar. **B** *Bougan Village*, north end of town on Lamu Rd, PO Box 721, T21205. Large complex, not on beach, but
shuttle to the shore where there is a bar and cafe, s/c, a/c, pleasant gardens, restaurant, bars,
pool, tennis courts. **B** *Palm Tree Club*, north end of town, just past Golf and Country Club, PO
Box 180, T20397, Tx21214. Not on beach, but shuttle to the shore, s/c, a/c, excellently furnished, restaurant, pool, horse riding, tennis, golf, bowling. **B** *Sea View Cottages*, these cottages are all self-contained with their own bathroom, the place has seen better days and this
really is not very good value, the swimming pool has had problems although these may have
been solved by now.

   C *Auberge du Chevalier Hotel and Restaurant Centre* (Kibokoni Riding Centre), PO Box
857, T21273, F21030. Cottage style accommodation, rather charmingly laid out, mostly for
riding enthusiasts. **C** *Lutheran Guest House*, T21098, located to the north of the town off the
Lamu Rd, PO Box 409, behind Sabaki Centre. This is good value and popular, there are a range
of rooms singles and doubles with or without own bathroom, there is also a self-contained
cottage, it is clean and the staff are very friendly. **C** *Malindi Cottages*, on Lamu Rd, opposite
Eden Roc Hotel, PO Box 992, T20304/91728, F21071. These cottages are self-contained and
fully furnished with excellent facilities, each sleep 5, and everything is provided, there is a
swimming pool in the complex.

   D *Big Mama's* (formerly Eddies), PO Box 385, T31324, north end of town. S/c, pool.
D *Fondo Wehu Guest House*, PO Box 5367, T0123-30017, about 10 minutes' walk from bus
station. Includes excellent breakfast and laundry. Well recommended.

   E *African Pearl*, PO Box 409, on road to Lamu, T21098. Courtyard, fans, quite small, not
s/c. **E** *Malindi Inn*, PO Box 17, T20564. S/c, fans, includes breakfast, bit away from centre, but
well run and good value. **E** *Morema Cottages*, on road to Lamu, T30822/16. Includes breakfast, good value. **E** *Pumzika*, small, new guesthouse, on road that runs from *Blue Marlin* past
Surahi Restaurant, s/c, hot water, good value.

South of Malindi   **A+** *African Dream Village*, PO Box 939, T20442/3/4, F20119. Run by the
same group that run the *East African Dream Cottages* further north, this caters for a slightly

Kenya

different type of holiday maker being a top quality beach resort with full facilities, these include swimming pool, gym, bars and restaurant, all rooms are a/c with bathroom and verandah. **A+ Sailfish Club**, PO Box 243, T20016. This is a very small and exclusive hotel with just 9 rooms, it is very much geared to big-game fishing. **A Coconut Village**, PO Box 868, T20928/30103, F30103. A popular family hotel with good facilities, the bar has been cleverly built into and around a growing tree, and the disco is under a thatched roof on the beach, but despite all this, it lacks some character. **A Coral Keys**, PO Box 556, Mama Ngina Rd, T30717/8, F30715, about 2 kilometres from town. Very attractive layout, 5 pools, tennis, beach bar, restaurant, videos, boutique. **A Kilili Baharini**, on Tourist Rd, about 4 kilometres from town centre toward Casuarina Point, PO Box 1068, T20169/20634, F21264. Pleasant hotel in thatched banda style, pool, restaurants, bars, a/c. **A Kivulini**, 7 kilometres beyond Casuarina Point, on main road south at Leopard's Point, PO Box 142, T20898. This is a relatively new hotel. Highly recommended. Again it has cottages set in wonderful gardens, and it has it's own private beach, the food is superb and the hotel is very well managed. **A Oasis Village**, Mama Ngina Rd, about 2 kilometres from centre, T30953. Well designed, pool, restaurant, bars. **A Scorpio Villas**, PO Box 368, T20194/20892, Tx21430, F21250, Mnarani Rd. This collection of about 17 villas is set in magnificent gardens, there are 3 swimming pools, a restaurant and bar and the beach is very close, the cottages are all fully furnished and self-sufficient and you even get your own cook, it is an excellently managed complex. **A Silversands Villas** (*Blue Club*), PO Box 91, T20842. This hotel has a range of rooms and villas, the cottages are thatched with *makuti* and are set in wonderful gardens, it is tastefully decorated with bits and pieces from across Africa, it is very friendly and well managed, and has a very good restaurant attached. **A Tropical Village**, PO Box 68, T20256/20711, Tx21089, F20788. High standard hotel this caters largely for package tours, with good facilities. **A White Elephant Sea Lodge**, PO Box 948, T20528/20223/30102, Tx21353, F30105. This is a lovely hotel and good value, the cottages are decorated tastefully and are set in magnificent gardens on a beautiful stretch of beach, there is a swimming pool and very good restaurant. **A Driftwood Club**, PO Box 63, T20155/30569, F30712. One of the older hotels in Malindi, this has managed to retain its unique character, it has a range of rooms including luxury cottages, doubles and singles (with own or shared bathroom), a/c, breakfast is included in the price and some of the rooms work out at very good value, facilities include snack bar, watersports including windsurfing and a squash court, temporary membership is very cheap, so a lot of people drop in to use the facilities, has a diving school facility on site. Reservations can be made directly through the Manager or through: The Bunson Group, PO Box 45456, Nairobi T221992/225465/337712, F214120, Tx22071.

B *Malindi Beach Club*, Mama Ngira Rd, about 3 kilometres from town. Well located.

C *Dorado Cottages*, Casuarina Point, close to Crocodile Paradise, about 5 kilometres from town centre, PO Box 868, T30104, Tx21459. Good value accommodation, fans, s/c, access by *matatus* running along Tourist Rd. **C** *Jambo Village*, Casuarina Point, close to Marine Park, about 6 kilometres from town, PO Box 444, T21245/20463. Villa rooms, fans, s/c, *Venta Diving* located here, access by *matatu* on Tourist Rd, then 1 kilometre walk to Marine Park. **C** *Mayungu*, some 15 kilometres south on main road beyond Casuarina Point at Leopard's Point, excellent beach, windsurfing. **C** *Stephanie Sea House*, Casuarina Point, close to Marine Park, 6 kilometres from Malindi Centre, PO Box 583, T20720/20430, F20613, Tx21333. Pool and restaurant.

D *Gossips*, previously called *Gilinis*, PO Box 380, on shore road near jetty, T20307. Italian owner, price does not include breakfast, fans, comfortable hotel with good restaurant. Well recommended. **D** *Ozi's*, T20218, F30421. Situated overlooking the beach very close to the jetty, this hotel has a range of rooms, it is simple, but clean and good value and is one of the most popular of the budget hotels, the price includes a very good breakfast. Tends to be noisy at night because of the proximity of the bus garage.

E *Da Gama's*, close to Portuguese Church on Vasco da Gama Rd, PO Box 5073, T30295. Above restaurant, fans, s/c, nets, pleasant atmosphere. **E** *Metro*, PO Box 361, T20400. This is popular and is located close to the *Gilini's*, fans, the rooms are, however, poky and stuffy and the water is unreliable, the people that run it are friendly, fans. **E** *Silver Sands Camp Site*, T20412. Located nearly 2 kilometres out of town this campsite is popular with overlanders and other campers, the facilities are fairly good although there are sea-water showers only and if you do not have a tent you can rent one, there is also a small tented camp (these are tents with a thatched roof over them to keep them cool) and a bathroom and electric lights, there are also bandas with beds and mosquito nets which have shared bathrooms, it is situated on a lovely stretch of beach, and has a friendly atmosphere, there is a snack bar and restaurant, and a well stocked shop, although it's very close to the *Driftwood Club* which does excellent food at a reasonable price, you can also hire bicycles here, for a proper shower and a swim you can join the *Driftwood Club* for the day. **E** *Travellers Inn*, PO Box 59, Vasco de Gama Rd, on Edge of Old Town. This is extremely popular amongst budget travellers and is good value, it is located just to the south of the fishing jetty and is clean and friendly, there are drinks and food available.

There is a range of restaurants and most of the restaurants in the hotels are open to non-residents – especially good value are their set menus and buffets. **Eating**

4 *Carni Africane alla Brace*, just south of casino. Pleasant lay out of tables under awnings in a courtyard, big open-air charcoal grill, game meats, gazelle, zebra, giraffe, crocodile.
4 *Fermento Bar*, Galana Centre, T31780. Only opens late, but serves Italian food and grills.
4 *La Malindina*, PO Box 5342, T20449/30197, this is located near the *Eden Roc Hotel*. Popular so book ahead in season, Italian food and Romanesque atmosphere by pool, rather special.

3 *Big Mama Hotel and Restaurant* (formerly *Eddies*), PO Box 485, T31324. This is a relatively new restaurant and is set in very pleasant surroundings with a swimming pool, it specializes in seafood which is delicious, and is open for lunch and dinner. **3** *Camillo's*, Vasco de Gama Rd, on edge of Old Town, T30251/2. Pleasant Italian restaurant. **3** *Da Gama's*, just north of Portuguese Church, PO Box 5073, T30295. Omlettes, grills, seafood, fixed price menu, pleasant decor with red table cloths and stone floor. **3** *Driftwood Club*, T30032. This is a nice way to spend a lazy day, you will need to join the Club as a temporary member – you will then be able to eat here as well as use their pool, the restaurant has a set menu, a huge Indian buffet, an à la carte menu as well as a snack menu. **3** *German Beer Garden*, T123/20533. This bistro, located to the north of the shopping centre, is good for snacks and a beer, it is particularly popular in the evenings. **3** *Gilini's*, PO Box 380, on shore near jetty, T20307. Pleasant location overlooking ocean, comfortable atmosphere, fine carved wooden chairs, Italian fish and meat dishes as well as some Indian food. **3** *I Love Pizza*, T123/20672, located on the Vasco da Gama Rd. This Italian restaurant is good value, it serves pizza, pasta, seafood dishes and other food. **3** *Lorenzo's Restaurant*, Italian Garden Centre, north end of town. Good standard Italian food, quiet out of season. **3** *Pescatori*, Vasco de Gama Rd, PO Box 102, T31198. **3** *Putipu Disco Bar*, opposite Galana Centre. Italian food, pastas, pizzas, grills. **3** *Rick's Café Americaine*, Italian Garden Centre, north end of town. Burgers and ribs, quiet out of season. **3** *Sportsmans*, at Falconry behind Malindi complex, T30456. Comfortable atmosphere, sound fare. **3** *T-T Bar and Restaurant*, opposite *Blue Marlin*. Grills, seafood, good coffee and ice cream. **3** *Vera Cruz*, opposite Malindi Complex. Grills, seafood.

2 *African Pearl*, north end of town. Moderately priced *al fresco* style restaurant. **2** *Chicks Restaurant*, near *Glory Guesthouse*. Mostly grills. **2** *Karen Blixen Café*, Galana Centre. Imaginatively designed, sandwiches, juices, coffee, parsols and outside tables, photos of Karen Blixen and Denys Finch-Hatton. **2** *La Galateria*, T123/20710, located on Lamu Rd. This is the best place in town for ice creams – they are excellent, good for a coffee and a snack. **2** *Malindi Sea Fishing Club*, PO Box 364, above *Kingfisher Safaris* office, just south of jetty, T30550. Temporary membership available for US$1, and well worth it as the food (grills, seafood) is modestly priced, comfortable club decor, bar, fishing photos, excellent views out over the ocean. **2** *Palm Garden Restaurant*, T123/20015, also located on Lamu Rd, opposite the Shell petrol station. You can sit in the shade of bandas, the food is fine – curries, chicken, seafood and so on – and it is very good value, there is also a bar and ice cream parlour which are rather run down.

Kenya

1 *Baobab Café*, PO Box 728, T31699/20489. This is located close to the Portuguese Church and has a wide ranging menu, you can have breakfast here, snacks and a beer or fruit juice, as well as full meals. **1** *Garden View Café*, by Uhuru Gardens. Pleasant location, simple fare. **1** *Golden Fin*, close to town centre. Clean and bright, grills and African dishes. **1** *Juice Bar*, in front of Malindi Complex. Excellent juices and local foods. **1** *Malindi Fruit Juice Garden*, is ideal for a break on a hot day, located close to the market, as the name suggests they do very good fruit juice as well as milk shakes. **1** *Travellers Café*, this is very popular with budget travellers and is close to the *Baobab Cafe*, it serves both Western and African food all of which are cheap, tasty and good value, and the beer is cold.

There are a couple of places in the town centre which are good for Indian and traditional African food – such as ugali and stew. These include the **1** *Bahari Restaurant*, close to the Juma Mosque. Excellent chapatis, beef stew, good value. Well recommended. **1** *Urafiki Bar and Restaurant*, located on Kenyatta Rd.

Bars *African Pearl*, north end of town. Pleasant gardens, live band on Sunday during high season (June-August). *Fermente Bar*, Galana Centre, T31750. Disco, karaoke and occasional live music, gets under way at about 2300. *Hermann's Beer Garden*, opposite Galana Centre. Open-air bar. *Iguana Bar*, Italian Garden Centre, north end of town. Quiet out of season, serves food, mostly grills. *Malindi Members Club*, large open air bar on beach side of Government Rd. It is not necessary to be a member. *Malindi Sea Fishing Club*, on shore road above *Kingfisher Safaris*, south of jetty. Temporary membership US$1, but well worth it as drinks are modestly priced, members congregate for lunch and sundowners, excellent vista over ocean. *Palm Garden*, at intersection of Kenyatta and Government Rd. Very pleasant atmosphere, with several bar areas. *Putipu Disco Bar*, opposite Galana Centre. Serves Italian food, pizzas, grills, wicker furniture, dance area. *T-T-Bar and Restaurant*, opposite *Blue Marlin*. Pleasant open air-style with thatched bandas, coffee, ice-cream and grills. *Vera Cruz*, opposite Malindi Complex. Huge concrete replica of the prow of Vasco de Gama's sailing ship, serving as a disco, bar and restaurant. *Wananchi Day and Nightclub*, Tana Rd, town centre. Lively local bar, with huge murals decorating the interior.

Entertainment There is plenty to do in the evenings in Malindi and there are a number of bars and discos. The bigger discos are found at the larger hotels. There is also occasionally live music – ask around at the different hotels. The *Malindi Casino* is open daily from midday, and entrance is free. Blackjack and roulette.

Cinema *Hero*, near market, mostly Indian films, pleasant building with a little courtyard.

Discos *Stardust Club*, starts fairly late in the evenings but is nevertheless very popular. *Casino Disco*, next to *Stardust Club*, attractive bars with thatched cover and dance area, no entry charge. *Ruputi Disco Bar*, opposite Galana Centre. *Fermento Bar*, Galana Centre. *Vera Cruz*, opposite Malindi Complex. The *Tropicana Club 28*, is situated up near *Eden Roc Hotel* and is small, friendly and popular. *Lawford's*, has a disco, as does *Coconut Village*, (open-air on the beach) and a number of the other large hotels. The bar at the *Coconut Village* is well worth seeing – it has been cleverly constructed into and around a tree. *Cacao Club*, at Scorpio Villas, south of centre, PO Box 102, T31198.

Live bands *Sea Breeze* play at the *Africa Pearl* at the north end of town on Sunday during the season (June-August).

Sports (participant) *Golf and Country Club*, north end of town, right fork off Lamu Rd. Tennis, golf and squash, daily membership available. *Malindi Sea Fishing Club*, PO Box 364, T30550, south of jetty. Has noticeboard for fishermen. **Deep-sea fishing**: *Kingfisher*, PO Box 29, Malindi, T21168/20123, F03261. UK agents: *Swahili Connections*, 8 Balls Lane, Thursford, Norfolk NR21 0BX, T01328-878173, F01328-878989. *Peter Ready*, PO Box 63, Malindi, T21292, F30032.

Videos If you want to see a film while you are here ask around at the hotels who often have video shows. Also the Malindi Fishing Club which has regular showings.

Bookshops There is a bookshop next to Barclays Bank at the *Sitawi Shopping Centre* – very limited choice.

Shopping

Handicrafts Craft shops have been forced to move due to works on the towns sewage system. They are mostly now located close to the beach and the jetty. In general the quality is reasonably good as are the prices – although you must expect to bargain. *Zai Noor Gift Shop*, near Uhuru Gardens, has wicker and basketry items as well as earthenware pieces. *Our Shop*, on the corner of Uhuru St and Government Rd has high quality handicraft items. *Nafisa Store*, on Government Rd, near Uhuru Gardens, also styled the 'Africa Curio Museum' is quite good, and the prices are reasonable. *Al Noor Gallery*, on Goram Mast Rd, near Uhuru Gardens is a high class establishment with antique items in wood and metal, including many pieces from Ethiopia. *Shezan*, just north of Galana Centre. Attractive antique items of Indian origin. *Kongonis*, just north of Portuguese Church, PO Box 605, expensive but high quality t-shirts, bead design sandals, sisal bags.

Local You will be able to walk around the town itself without any problems. If you want to go out at night then be prepared to take a taxi or ask your hotel to arrange transport. For day trips you can either organize them through the hotel, hire a car or else try the public transport. **Bicycle hire**: **Malindi Bike Rental**, near *Stardust Club*, PO Box 1177, T31741, about US$10 a day; **Sudi Sudi Safaris**, on shore road near jetty, PO Box 966, T20596, US$6 a day. **NB** If you are using a bike for more than a day, bargain for lower rate. It is possible to buy a new bike on Tana Rd, town centre US$100-120. *Silver Sands Camp Site*, *Ozi's Guest House* and a stall just outside the *Tropicana Club 28*. The quality of the bikes varies – so check thoroughly before you choose one.

Transport

Car hire: **Glory Car Hire**, centre of town, close to *Blue Marlin Hotel*, PO Box 994, T123-20065; **Kotsman Car Hire**, PO Box 262, Malindi, T20777/20988; **Avis Car Rental**, opposite *Blue Marlin hotel*. Some hotels also have motorbikes for hire (about US$35 per day). Arrange on a daily basis as there are not many places to visit.

Air The airport at Malindi is served by a number of different airlines, as well as by chartered planes for safaris et cetera. The airport is located about 3 kilometres south of the town – taxi to the centre costs about US$3; the hotels to the south will be about US$6. **Kenya Airlines**, does the Nairobi-Mombasa-Malindi route once a day in both directions (except Saturday). It is a popular route so be sure to book well ahead and confirm your seat. The Nairobi-Malindi fare is about US$100 one-way. Some travellers have reported problems with double booking. Also serving this route are **Eagle Aviation**, T21258 (Malindi)/316054 (Mombasa)/3119 (Lamu); **Equator Airlines**, T2053 (Malindi); **Prestige Air Services**, PO Box 146, T20861, Tx21065, SKYBIRD F20860; **Skyways Airlines**, T21260 (Malindi), 432167 (Mombasa), 3226 (Lamu); **TAI Aviation**, PO Box 357, T/F31839 office hours, T31837 after office hours. All their offices are situated on the Lamu road in Malindi. All have 2 flights per day in both directions between Malindi and Mombasa and Malindi and Lamu. Baggage allowance is only 10 kilograms, and check in time is 30 minutes before take off. Airport tax is around US$1.

Train There is no railway line to Malindi, but it is possible that you may want to reserve a sleeper on the Mombasa-Nairobi train. You can ask your hotel or a travel agent in Malindi to do this for you – but they will charge. Just as easy, and about a tenth of the price, is to ring and do it yourself, T011-312221.

Road Bus: there are plenty of buses between **Malindi** and **Mombasa** – there are 4 companies (Malindi Bus Service, Mombasa and Coast Express, Garissa Express and Tana River Bus Service) all of which have a number of departures each day. They all have offices in Malindi (around the Bus Station), Mombasa and Lamu but booking is not usually necessary. They mostly leave early in the morning and take about 2 hours, they cost about US$1. If you are in a real hurry you can take a matatu which go even faster and take under 2 hours. They leave when full throughout the day and cost about US$2. To **Lamu** there are also buses but the route is popular so you should book in advance. The trip takes about 5 hours and costs about US$4. They leave in the morning at between 0700 and 0800. If you miss these you might be able to get onto one of the Mombasa buses which get to Malindi about 0830 and go on at 0930 – but there is no guarantee that you will get a seat. The bus will take you to the jetty on the mainland from where you get a ferry across to Lamu (see page 226). **Taxis**: Peugeot 504 share-taxis do the Mombasa-Malindi route. These take 7 passengers and go in the mornings when full. They cost about the same as a matatu (US$2).

Directory **Banks** There are a number of banks in Malindi. *Barclays*, is located on the main coastal road (the Lamu road) opposite the *Blue Marlin Hotel* and is open on weekdays from 0830 to 1700 with a break for lunch from 1300 to 1430, and on Sat from 0830 to 1200. There is also a *Standard Chartered Bank*, close to the police station and post office. *Kenya Commercial Bank*, PO Box 9, T20148.

Hospitals & medical services *Malindi District Hospital*, PO Box 4, T20490. **Optician:** *Vijay Optico*, Lamu Rd, opposite Malindi Complex. **Pharmacy:** *Buhani Pharmacy*, Government Rd, near Uhuru Gardens.

Tour companies & travel agents In Malindi: *Duna Safaris*, PO Box 1001, T0123-21015/ 21121/31648, Mobile T071-414015, Tx21371, F0123-30258. *Falcony of Kenya Ltd*, Safari Section: PO Box 1003, T30455, F30455. *Galu Safari Ltd*, PO Box 650, Lamu Rd, T20493, F30032. *Haya Safari Africa Ltd*, PO Box 73, T220374, F20846. *Hewa Tours & Safaris*, PO Box 5322, T00254-123-21211/31730, F00254-123-30064. *Kingfisher Safaris*, south of jetty, PO Box 29, T20123. *North Coast Travel Services*, centre of town, near *Blue Marlin Hotel*, tours, safaris, car hire, railway and TNT services, PO Box 476, Office T0123-254-123/20531/30312, Home T0123-21294, Tx21450, North Coast, F30313. *Peacock Tours & Travel Ltd*, PO Box 689, T20097/31477, F20097, Uhuru St, opposite DO's office. Arranges adventure diving. *Pollman's Tours & Safaris*, PO Box 384, T0123-2028/30159, F0123-20820. *Scorpio Tours Ltd*, PO Box 368, T0123-21242/20194/20892, Tx21430, F0123-21250. *Sudi Sudi Safaris*, near jetty, PO Box 966, T20596. Deep-sea fishing, dhow trips, flights to game parks, bike hire. *Sunflower Safaris Ltd*, PO Box 1031, T20822. *Tusker Safaris Ltd*, PO Box 5348, T30525/30867, Galana Centre. *Zaitour Kenya Ltd*, PO Box 1059, T0123-30571/30116, F30571, Malindi Complex.

Tourist offices *The Tourist Office*, PO Box 421, T20747, and *Kenya Airways*' office are located on the same road opposite the shopping centre.

Useful information Tidal information: posted at Customs and Excise, just near jetty.

Malindi to Lamu

Soon after leaving Malindi you cross the Sabaki River, and then the turning for the village of **Mambrui**. This village is believed to be about 600 years old and all that remains of the ancient town is a mosque and a pillar tomb, which has insets of Ming porcelain. Further on you will eventually pass **Garsen**, a small town at the crossing of the Tana River where you can get petrol and drinks. It also has a Health Centre, PO Box 42, T35 (Garsen). From here the road turns back towards the coast and the town of **Witu**, another small old town. As you drive in this area you may see people of the Orma tribe as well as Somalis for this is getting close to the border. Both groups are pastoralists, and you will see their cattle which represent their wealth. Finally, about five hours after leaving Malindi, you will get to **Mokowe** and you will see the Makanda channel which separates Lamu from the mainland.

Lamu

A wonderful old stone town with its distinctive architecture, the carved doors, narrow streets, the absence of vehicles, its many mosques, the fishermen, the women dressed in black and wearing the *bui bui*. The town takes tourism seriously as this is the major source of income. In recent times Lamu has attracted free spirits from all over the world to this sleepy but fascinating place. Conservation and preservation all cost money and tourists are an excellent source of foreign exchange. Whatever the changes in the last few years, Lamu remains very popular with budget travellers and with good reason. *2° 16' S, 40° 55' E*
Phone code: 0121
Colour map 3, grid A6

The island has a population of about 12,000 people – almost half of whom are Bajun immigrants from the north. Expansion in tourism, but also the rapid growth of the population of the local peoples which has made population pressure a problem. The vast majority of the population are Muslim, and it is courteous for visitors to respect this during their stay. Aid from Saudi Arabia has been directed to the island in the form of a hospital, various schools and religious centres.

The island is about 9,000 acres in size. The coral rock is covered with sandy soil, and about a third of the island is covered with sand dunes. Although these render this part uncultivable the dunes serve an important purpose for they act as a filter for the water. Despite this, Lamu does often suffer from severe water shortages and supplies are often limited to certain times of the day. The island also has a fairly extensive area of mangrove swamps, and the only cultivable part of the island lies between the dunes and the marshy swamps. The conditions of Lamu are most suitable for coconut plantations and mango trees.

The Beach The southern shores of Lamu island have the best beach – 12 kilometres of almost deserted white sand which back onto the sand dunes. As there is no reef the waves get fairly big. To get there you have to walk through the southern part of the town towards Shela which will take you about 45 minutes and on to the beach. If you do not feel like walking you can take the dhow or motor boat which goes to Peponi's for US$0.30. It is possible to strike off directly southwest, but although it is shorter, the walk through the dunes can be hard work.

Safety Until very recently it would not have been considered necessary to include this section. As long as you are sensible there should not be a problem. However, a number of incidents over the last few years has meant that it is important to stress that there are certain dangers. Although the quayside (Harbour Road) and the main thoroughfare (Harambee Ave, previously *Usita wa Mui* or Town Street) are quite safe, do not walk around after dark in secluded parts of town without a companion. Do not go to remote parts of the island alone – always go with a group and ask your hotel whether there are any particular risks. On the beach if you are alone (especially women) you should not go out of shouting distance from other people. **Cautions**

Health Stomach upsets are fairly common, and it is wise to stick to bottled water or soft drinks. More serious is hepatitis – make sure you have a gamma globulin injection, or else the new treatment Havrix, which once completed, will last 10 years.

The town of Lamu was founded in the 14th century although there were people living on the island long before this. Throughout the years, and as recently as the 1960s, the island has been a popular hide-out for refugees fleeing from the mainland. **History**

The original settlement of Lamu was located to the south of the town, and is said to be marked by Hidabu hill. There was also another settlement between the 13th and 15th centuries to the north of the present town.

By the 15th century it was a thriving port, one of the many that dotted the coast of East Africa. However in 1505 it surrendered to the Portuguese, began paying tributes, and for the next 150 years was subservient to them, and to the sultanate of the town of Paté on the nearby island, part of the Omani Dynasty that ruled much of the East African coast.

Kenya

☞ *Shela Gold*

In 1915 a man called Albert Deeming was convicted of the murder of a woman and two children in Melbourne, Australia. He was sentenced to death but before his execution he prepared a document detailing the whereabouts of 50 kilos of gold bars, at current prices worth US$600,000, buried on Lamu Island.

In 1901, Deeming had boarded the bullion train from Pretoria to Laurenco-Marques (now Maputo in Mozambique), shot two guards and forced a third to open the bullion compartments. Grabbing as many bars as he could carry he jumped the train and made his way to the coast. At Delgoa Bay, he sailed by dhow to Lamu.

As a recent arrival on the island, locals were suspicious, and he resolved to hide the gold and return for it later. At a small European graveyard at Shela, in the lee of a sand-dune, enclosed by a coral stone wall, one of the graves was that of William Searle, a British sailor who died after falling from the rigging of his ship. Beneath Searle's gravestone, which he observed was cracked, Deeming buried the gold.

Deeming's belongings were eventually returned to his relatives in South Africa, and one of them made a visit to Lamu in 1919, but was unable to locate the grave.

In 1947 the documents passed to a Kenyan farmer, who with a couple of companions travelled to Lamu and found the Shela graveyard. Four graves were marked, but none of them had the name of William Searle. Convinced that this must be the graveyard described by Deeming they began probing the sands. They located a solid object and removed the covering of sand. It was a gravestone with a well-weathered crack. Deeming's instructions were that the gold was in a small wooden box at the head of the grave, at a depth of two feet. Despite extensive excavations they found nothing. They were curious over the fact that an area of sand appeared less compacted than that of its surroundings. Also, when they examined the gravestone it had some cracks that looked quite recent. They made discreet enquiries in Lamu Town. Four weeks earlier a party of three Australians from Melbourne had visited Lamu and had spent two days at the Shela sand-dunes.

By the end of the 17th century Lamu had become a republic ruled by a council of elders called the Yumbe, who were in principle responsible to Oman. In fact the Yumbe were largely able to determine their own affairs, and this period has been called Lamu's Golden Age. It was the period when many of the buildings were constructed and Lamu's celebrated architectural style evolved. The town became a thriving centre of literature and scholarly study and there were a number of poets who lived here. Arts and crafts flourished and trade expanded. The main products exported through Lamu were mangrove poles, ivory, rhino horn, hippo teeth, shark fins, cowrie shells, coconuts, cotton, mangoes, tamarind, sim sim (oil), charcoal and cashews.

Rivalries between the various trading settlements in the region came to a head when Lamu finally defeated Paté in the battle of Shela in 1813. However, after 1840 Lamu found itself dominated by Zanzibar which had been developed to become the dominant power along the East African coast. At a local level there were factions and splits within the town's population – in particular rivalries between different clans and other interest groups.

New products were developed for export including *beche de mère* (a seafood), mats, bags, turtle shell, leather, rubber and sorghum. Despite this, toward the end of the 19th century Lamu began a slow economic decline as Mombasa and Zanzibar took over in importance as trading centres. The end of the slave trade dealt a blow to Lamu as the production of mangrove poles and grains for export depended on slave labour. Additionally communications between the interior and Mombasa were infinitely better than those with Lamu – particularly after the building of the railway. Many of the traditional exports still pass through Lamu, particularly mangrove poles which contain an extract which resists termites and are used for traditional buildings as roof rafters along the Indian Ocean coast and in the Middle East. Poles can be seen stacked on the Promenade, just south of the main jetty, waiting to catch

Swahili culture

The coastal region is the centre of this distinct and ancient civilization. The Swahili are not a tribe as such – they are joined together by culture and language – Ki-Swahili – which is the most widely spoken language in East Africa. It is one of the Bantu languages and was originally most important as a trading language. It contains words derived from Arabic, Indian as well as English and Portuguese.

The Swahili civilization emerged from the meeting of East Africa, Islam, the classical world and eastern civilizations. Traders, as well as immigrants, from Asia and Arabia have had a gradual influence on the coast shaping society, religion, language as well as literature and architecture. These traders arrived at the ports of the east coast by the northeast monsoon winds which occur in March and April (the Kaskazi wind) and left around September on the southerly wind (the Kusi wind). Inevitably some stayed or were left behind and there was intermarriage between the immigrants and the indigenous people. Many families trace their roots back to traders from foreign shores and there is a complex social system.

Slavery was important to the coastal region and was not entirely an alien phenomenon. For long before slaves were being rounded up from the interior and shipped overseas, there was an important although rather different 'slave trade'. This involved a family 'lending' a member of the family (usually a child) to another richer family or trader in exchange for food and other goods. That child would then live with the family and work for them – essentially as a slave – until the debt had been paid off. However, in the same way as with bonded child labourers in India today, the rates of interest demanded often ensured that the debt could never be paid off and the person would remain effectively a slave. Later slavery became an important part of trade and commerce and the old system was replaced with something much more direct. Many slaves were rounded up from the interior (some of them 'sold' by tribal chiefs and village elders) and taken to the coast. Here they would either be sold overseas to Arabia via Zanzibar or put to work on the plantations that were found all along the coast. Successive measures by the British formally ended the slave trade by 1907 although it did continue underground for many years. When slaves were released they were gradually absorbed into the Swahili culture although their antecedents are known it means it is almost impossible to be rid of the stigma associated with being a slave.

Kenya

the dhows sailing north on the Trade Winds in September. In recent decades the tourist trade has helped improve Lamu's economic prospects.

The people of Lamu are a mixture of Swahili-speaking people of Arab and African **People of** ancestry – with much of the East African blood being brought in by the movement of **Lamu** slaves through this area. Some broad groupings can, however, be distinguished:

Swahili and Bajun Taking advantage of the monsoon winds, traders visited these shores annually in search of ivory, gold and slaves. Arabs, Indians, Persians and Chinese visited the coast and over the years some remained, intermarried with the local people and built up city states. The Afro-Arab peoples, who shared their Islamic faith and way of life became known as the Swahilis. Both the Swahili and the Bajun people claim Arab ancestry, although it is very much mixed with African blood. There is a rural-urban distinction between Bajun and Swahili with the Swahili mainly in the towns. The Bajun people also often claim Somali ancestry as well as Arabic origins.

Oromo or Galla The Oromo people (or Galla as they are also known), are nomadic pastoralists and mainland dwellers who for many years were a great influence on Lamu. While the Arabs and the Swahili speaking people of the islands and mainland were all Muslims, the Oromo retained their traditional beliefs. They were an aggressive people and a number of towns were abandoned as a result of their incessant pillaging. The ways of the Oromo have changed considerably since the

....

Swahili proverbs

A good house is not judged by its door.

What God has written cannot be erased.

The first wife is like a mother.
Used by polygamists to justify a second wife; also refers to the important part that the first wife plays in running the household.

A bird can be guarded, a wife cannot.

A woman you love for her being, not for her beauty.

A new mat is no pleasure to sleep on.

A young wife has a lot to learn.

Without children the house is sad and silent.

You cannot turn the wind, so turn the sail.

When the crocodile smiles, be extra careful.

A wise man talks about secrets only to his heart.

....

19th century and at the present they are suffering from pressure on their land.

Omani Arabs At the turn of the 19th century the Swahili and Bajun, including descendants of slaves, formed the majority of the population, with the *wangwana* (free or nobly born) ruling the communities. During the 19th century Omani Arabs started to arrive until eventually they became the most politically powerful group, despite being outnumbered a thousand to one by the Swahili and Bajun. A governor was appointed to the island who was usually closely related to the Sultan of Zanzibar, and he and other officials settled with their families.

Asians During the 19th century Asians, both Muslims and Hindus, came to Lamu to work as merchants and traders. While the Hindus often came on a more temporary basis and returned to India, many of the Muslim Asians came with their families and formed more permanent communities.

Sights **Old Town or Stone Town** Known to the local people as *Mkomani*. It is the largest stone-town on the East African coast, but easy to walk around. The town dates back to the 14th century although most of the buildings are actually from the 18th century and Lamu's Golden Age. The streets are very narrow, and the buildings on each side are two or three stories high. The streets are set in a rough grid pattern running off the main street which is called the *Usita wa Mui* (formerly Main Street) now known as Harambee Ave. *Usita wa Mui* runs parallel to the harbour and used to open out to the sea, although building from the mid 1800s onwards has cut it off from the quayside.

Mkomani is a very secluded place – the houses face inwards and privacy is carefully guarded. The families who live in these houses are mainly the patrician *wangwana* who keep themselves to themselves. The non-patricians who reside in *Mkomani* live there as clients of the patricians, employed or providing services and are often descendants of their patron's slaves. At the edges of the town live people of slave and immigrant ancestry.

Carved doors are one of the attractions for which Lamu has become known. The artesanal skill continues to be taught, and at the north end of the harbour you can see them being made in workshops by craftsmen and apprentices.

The maze of streets in the Old Town mean that it is easy to get lost – just bear in mind that Harambee Ave runs parallel to the waterfront and the all the streets leading into town from the shore slope uphill slightly.

Mosques There are a number of mosques on the island (over 20), but they are usually not very grand affairs and you may not even be able to tell what they are as some are little different from other buildings. You will need to seek permission before entering to look around.

The oldest mosque in Lamu is believed to be the **Pwani Mosque**, situated near the Fort which dates back to 1370. The **Jumaa** (or **Friday**) **Mosque** is at the north end of town and is the second oldest in Lamu, dating from 1511. Then comes the **M'na Lalo Mosque** (1753), more or less in the centre of town, just a little to the north of the Museum and set back from Harambee Ave. This mosque was built in Lamu's Golden Age, and it was followed by **Muru Mosque** (1821) on Harambee

Lamu weddings

In the traditional Lamu culture, children are often promised in marriage at an early age. A woman is not supposed to marry a man who is socially inferior, although a man can marry a woman who is socially inferior. Once the marriage has been agreed, the couple are not meant to meet. Bridewealth must be paid by the groom to the girl's parents. The bride spends the period in the run up to her wedding with the somo, *usually a close friend of her mother's, who advises the bride.*

Weddings themselves are held in the month preceding Ramadhan. In the days before the wedding the bride must go though a series of rituals which last about three days – including the washing of hair, the painting of the hands and feet with henna and the shaving of the skin. After this there are a series of ceremonies and celebrations which last about four days. The third day is perhaps the most important and has a number of ceremonies. The relatives of the groom go in a procession through the town until they reach the house of the bride. Here more singing and dancing occurs, gifts are exchanged and finally the `nikaha' takes place at which the marriage is formally contracted. More rituals take place before the groom may lift the curtain of the bride's sleeping alcove and then lift the veil that covers her face. In due course the somo *takes the bride for another ritual to remove the 'impurity' of intercourse and the*

sheet is shown to the woman of the family as evidence of the girl's virginity. After the bride has been presented publicly the couple return to the bride's sleeping alcove to remain in seclusion there for seven days.

One interesting feature that is fairly common in Lamu are ' secret marriages'. These are marriages that are kept from the parents or the first wife. They are often made between a young divorced woman who has some wealth of her own, or women of a lower rank who would not be approved by the husband's family. The ceremony is different and no property changes hands but such marriages gradually become general knowledge and become recognized, and children born to such alliances are legitimate.

Divorce is reasonably common. It is easier for a man to get a divorce – on grounds such as a woman's sterility, her adultery or persistent quarrelling. He simply needs to make it known to the Kadhi *(Islamic judge) or* Mwalimu *(teacher or Muslim healer) that he wants a divorce and on what grounds. If the marriage does not involve property, he may simply pronounce the triple repudiation or 'talaka'. It is much harder for a woman to get a divorce – she must give detailed reasons and provide substantial evidence. Otherwise she can try to provoke her husband so that he will initiate the divorce himself.*

Ave, **Utukuni Mosque** (1823) well into the interior part of the town, **Mpya Mosque** (1845) in the town centre; **Mwana Mshamu Mosque** (1855) in the northwest area of the town; **Sheikh Mohamed bin Ali Mosque** (1875), in the town centre; and the **N'nayaye Mosque** (1880) on the northwest fringe of town. Two mosques have been built in the 20th century, the **Riyadha Mosque** (1901) to the south of the town, and the **Bohora Mosque** (1920), fairly central, just inland of Harambee Ave.

The **Mwenye Alawi Mosque** (1850) at the north end of Main Street was originally for women, but it has since been taken over by the men. The small Ismaili community did have their own **Ismaili Mosque**, on the Kenyatta Road at the south end of town, but this is now in ruins.

Adjacent to the Riyadha Mosque is the **Muslim Academy**, funded by Saudi Arabia, and which attracts students from all over the world.

Lamu Museum, T1213073, incorporates a library and is located on Kenyatta Road. It is run by the National Museums of Kenya, and plays an important role in the conservation of old Lamu. The ground floor has a good bookshop with publication of the National Museum and the entrance has some photographs of Lamu taken by a French photographer, Guillain in the period 1846-9. In a lobby to the right is a Swahili kitchen with pestles and mortars, vermicelli presses. Also on the ground floor are examples of decorative 18th century *Kidaka* plasterwork, carved Lamu throne chairs with wicker seats, elaborately carved Lamu headboards.

To the rear are displays on the archaeological excavations of the Takwa Ruins (see page 226) on Manda Island, and at Siya and Shanga on Pate Island (see page 227)

On the first floor, the balcony has a display of large earthenware pottery. The balcony room has photographs and models of seagoing vessels, mostly dhows, and the various types and styles in use.

Just behind the balcony room is a display of musical instruments used in festivals and celebrations, including drums, cymbals, rattles, leg rattles.

The most celebrated exhibits are the two *Siwa horns*. These are in the shape of elephant tusks, with the mouthpiece on the side. The Lamu horn is made of brass, the horn from nearby Pate is of ivory. They date from the 17th century, are elaborately decorated, and are thought to be the oldest surviving musical instruments in black Africa.

Local tribes are featured in a side-room, and there are displays on the **Oroma** from around Witu, Garsen and southwest of Lamu; the **Pokot** from west of the Tana River and the **Boni** from the north of Lamu.

The jewelly includes nose rings, earrings, anklets and necklaces in bead designs and in silver. There are some illustrations of hand and feet painting, in henna, in black and red.

The two end rooms are examples of typical Swahili bridal rooms with furniture and dresses on display.

Inland from the Museum is the small **Swahili House Museum**. It is a traditional Swahili house, restored, with all the traditional furniture. There are three areas on the main floor. A centre aisle has beds off to the left and right. The beds are wooden with rope and raffia forming the base. The main room has a particularly fine **kikanda** plaster screen on the wall. Furnishings include a clock with an octagonal frame and a pointed pendulum case, a style found all along the East African coast. Outside is a well and a garden with frangipani. The museum is open daily, 0800-1800, with a small entrance fee.

Lamu Museum

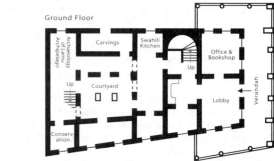

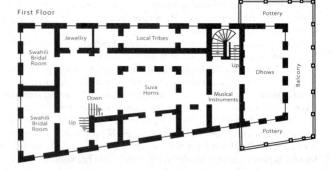

Lamu Fort The construction of the Fort was begun in 1809 and completed in 1821. The tile awning over the verandah at the front was originally of **makuti**, a thatch made from banana leaves. Inside is a central courtyard surrounded by internal walkways and awnings. The construction is of coral blocks, covered with mortar which has a yellowy-orange hue marked by black patches. It is possible to walk round the battlements, and they afford a good view of the nearby area. The Fort initially faced over the quayside, but there are now buildings between it and the sea. In the past it has served as both a fort and as a prison. Now it contains an exhibition on the environment, a shop and a library, plus a pleasant café overlooking the busy square at the entrance. Wedding parties take place inside the Fort – women only are allowed to attend the celebration. The invited guests sit downstairs and the town women stand up behind them. The bride sits on a bed, not participating in the dancing. There is a wedding banquet for the guests.

Tombs In the southwest part of town is a fluted **Pillar Tomb**, thought to date from the 14th century. It can be reached by going south and turning inland just after the Halwa Shop towards the Riyadha Mosque, and continuing beyond the mosque.

Another tomb is the **Mwana Hadie Famau Tomb**, a local woman believed to have lived here in the 15th or 16th century. This is situated a little inland from the museum.

The tomb had four pillars at the corners with inset porcelain bowls and probably a central pillar as well. A hermit took up residence in the hollow interior of the tomb, and became a nuisance by grabbing the ankles of passing women at night time. The solution was to wall up the tomb while the hermit was not at home.

The **Yumbe**, just inland and to the north of the museum was the location of the assembly of Lumu elders that ruled from 1650 to 1830. It is now ruined, but some fragments of the old building remain.

To the south end of the town, inland from Main Street, is the site of the old **Rope Walk**. Up to 1971, ropes were made here from coconut fibre, twisting the fibres between two wooden frames, for use on dhows. The ropes were thick, about 10 centimetres in diameter, and became very heavy when wet. Coconut fibre ropes have now been replaced by nylon ropes for use on seagoing vessels.

Behind the Fort is the **House of Liwali Sud bin Hamad**, a fine example of Swahili architecture. A Liwali was a governor appointed by the Sultan of Zanzibar. The house has now been subdivided, but it is still possible to appreciate how it looked when it was a single dwelling. On Main Street, just next to the *New Star* restaurant is the site of the offices of the **German East Africa Company**. Originally the Germans thought that Lamu would make a suitable secure base for their expansion into the interior (much in the same way as the British used Zanzibar). The agreement regarding British and German 'spheres of influence' in 1886 caused the Germans to turn their attention to Bagamoye, although they opened a post office in Lamu in 1888. Toward the rear of the town is the **whetstone** for sharpening knives, said to have been imported from Oman as local stone was not suitable.

At the northern end of the town, on the waterfront are Wood-carving Workshops, and the proprietors will happily show you around.

Further on, on the shore are boats being built and repaired at the **Dhow Boatyard**.

South of the jetty is the **Dhow Harbour**, and mangrove poles are stacked on the waterfront ready for loading on dhows catching the trade winds north to the Gulf.

St Mary's Church Next to the museum on the promenade. The only church on the island, walls of coral blocks, small tower, bell, roof of mangrove pole rafters, fine Swahili door.

Oil Mill on Main Street at south end, owner happy to show you around to observe the antique presses extracting coconut and sesame seed oil.

Generating Station Extreme south end of town, doors always open to let out the heat. Four huge diesel generators, three working and one stripped down for maintenance. Engineer happy to show you around.

Photography Bakar Studio, southern end of Main Street, photos of old Lamu, Lamu residents, visit of Sultan Khalifa from Zanzibar – the Sultan was too infirm to come ashore, and meetings took place aboard ship.

Donkey Sanctuary This is located in the northern part of the town close to the waterfront. It is run by the International Donkey Protection Trust, based in the UK. There is a small enclosure where sick donkeys are cared for. The remainder of the donkeys roam the town – there is fodder for them at the sanctuary – otherwise the other 50 or so spend much of their time on the rubbish tip at the north of the town, near the abbatoir (which they share with some Marabou storks) and on the tip in front of Salama Lodge.

Lamu Social Hall is a community meeting place at the north end of the prome- nade, Kenyatta Road. It is a fairly simple building, opened by Jomo Kenyatta in 1971. It has two small brass canons that were captured by the British at Witu, about 70 kilometres from Lamu, a small town on the route to Gersen.

Cat Clinic Established by Sir Cameron Razbi in 1993, provides free treatment.

Excursions One day dhow fishing excursions in the Manda Channel, followed by a barbecue on Manda Beach are excellent value at under US$10 per person. These are offered by many of the young men in the town. Snorkelling excursions can be at odd hours due to the times of the tide. They frequently take place very early in the morning. The best place is Manda Toto, which is a two to three hour dhow trip away. Unless you wish to stay overnight it may not be worthwhile. Avoid offers of snorkelling at Manda Island – it's an inferior experience.

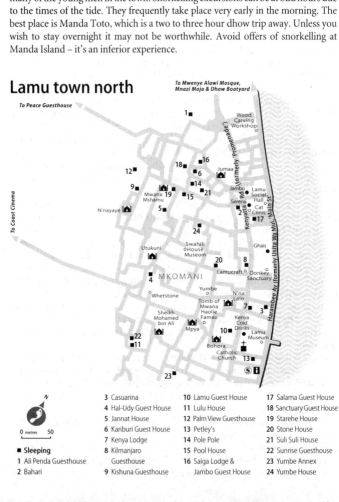

Lamu town north

Sleeping	6 Kariburi Guest House	16 Saiga Lodge &
1 Ali Penda Guesthouse	7 Kenya Lodge	Jambo Guest House
2 Bahari	8 Kilmanjaro	17 Salama Guest House
3 Casuarina	Guesthouse	18 Sanctuary Guest House
4 Hal-Udy Guest House	9 Kishuna Guesthouse	19 Starehe House
5 Jannat House	10 Lamu Guest House	20 Stone House
	11 Lulu House	21 Suli Suli House
	12 Palm View Guesthouse	22 Sunrise Guesthouse
	13 Petley's	23 Yumbe Annex
	14 Pole Pole	24 Yumbe House
	15 Pool House	

Kenya

Matondoni Village Here, on the western side of the island, about eight kilometres from town, you can see dhows being built and repaired. The easiest way is to hire a dhow between a group – you will have to negotiate the price and can expect to pay around US$10 for the boat. Alternatively you can hire a donkey – ask at the *Pole Pole Lodge* (situated up near the Jumaa Mosque – turn inland at the *Pole Pole Restaurant*). A third option is to walk – although leave early as it gets very hot. The walk will take a couple of hours and is quite complicated. You want to turn off the main street roughly opposite Petley's and keep walking west inland. Ask for directions from there – basically you want to keep going in the same direction of the telephone wires which go to Matondoni – if you follow these you should get there eventually.

Shela This village is another of the old stone-towns and is located to the south of Lamu town. It is a popular destination for beach lovers as it is just a 40 minute walk from Lamu. In the town are a number of old buildings including the **Mosque** which is situated behind Peponi's. The people of Shela were originally from the island of Manda and speak a dialect of Swahili that is quite different to that spoken in Lamu. The **Friday Mosque** was built in 1829 and is noted for its slender, conical minaret.

If the tide is low it is an easy walk, about 3 kilometres – down to the end of the harbour – and then along the beach. There is also a route inland, basically you need to head southwest and hug the shore. You can always hire a dhow which will take you for about US$0.50 a person, or get a group together and hire a motor boat run by Peponi's.

Dodori and Boni National Reserves In the far north of the Kenya coast close to the Somali border and are covered in the section on National Parks (see page 259). Because of the recent troubles in Somalia parts of this area have been out of bounds

Lamu town south

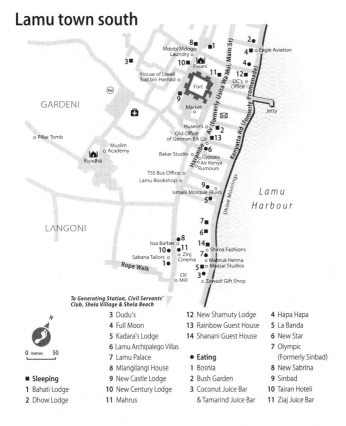

To Generating Station, Civil Servants' Club, Shela Village & Shela Beach

0 metres 50

■ **Sleeping**
1 Bahati Lodge
2 Dhow Lodge
3 Dudu's
4 Full Moon
5 Kadara's Lodge
6 Lamu Archipelago Villas
7 Lamu Palace
8 Mlangilangi House
9 New Castle Lodge
10 New Century Lodge
11 Mahrus
12 New Shamuty Lodge
13 Rainbow Guest House
14 Shanani Guest House

● **Eating**
1 Bosnia
2 Bush Garden
3 Coconut Juice Bar
  & Tamarind Juice Bar
4 Hapa Hapa
5 La Banda
6 New Star
7 Olympic
  (Formerly Sinbad)
8 New Sabrina
9 Sinbad
10 Tairan Hoteli
11 Ziaj Juice Bar

Percy Petley

The first lodgings in Lamu were established by the eccentric and somewhat belligerent Percy Petley. As he offered the only place where visitors could stay he amused himself by cursing his guests and informing them that the only food was stew and fish, and that the place was infested with rats. The rooms were divided by screens of coconut matting. The plumbing was simple. Outside was a long-drop lavatory. The bathroom was a bucket of water, discharged into a gully which ran across the floor, through another room, and out a hole through a hole to splatter down on to the street below. Any visitors meeting with the proprietor's displeasure were slung out to sleep on the beach. In the evening Petley would produce a box of local curios and abuse any guests who failed to make a purchase.

In the early days access was mostly by road, and Petley faced some competition in the 1930s when Jack MacDougall built a thatched rondavel Rest Camp, at Witu, a historic German settlement on the Lamu approach road half-way between Gasen and Lamu. As well as offering an edge in civility, MacDougall aimed to under-cut Petley with rooms at 50 cents. MacDougall's Rest Camp was burnt down a week after it opened.

to tourists for a while. If you want to go up here be sure to check with the local authorities and tour agencies.

Kiunga Marine National Reserve Located in the far northern part of the Kenyan coast, adjoining the Somali border, this Marine park suffers from being rather remote. It is possible to arrange a trip there through *Peponi's* at Shela, T3029.

Nearby islands **Manda Island** is quite close, **Pate Island** about 20 kilometres away, and **Kiwaiyu Island** 50 kilometres off. These islands are described in detail below, see page 226, page 227 and page 229. You will see notices advertising trips and will, undoubtedly, be offered trips from various people who usually act as a go-between for the dhow owners. Day trips are popular and because competition is tough the prices are almost standard. For longer trips you will need to be sure that everyone is clear who is arranging the food and drink (you or the dhow owner). Be sure to take lots to drink as it can get very hot. Another thing to remember is that the dhow is dependent on the tides and, if it has no outboard motor, on the winds. So bear in mind that a trip could easily turn into something longer through no fault of the dhow crew. It is unwise to set off with a very tight schedule. You would be advised to bring your own soft drinks or beer, buying the latter at the Kenya Breweries depot on the waterfront. The price will probably work out at about US$10 per person including food for a 3 day trip for a party of eight. You need to know that you will spend the odd night on the boat, so make sure you will be comfortable. Staying in any temporary lodging on one of the islands will be an extra (but nominal) expense.

Sleeping Price varies with the season. The peak periods are December and January for up-market travellers, and July, August and September for family visitors and budget travellers. Most of the more expensive hotels are not actually located in the Old Town, but are around the island or on nearby islands. At the lower end of the price range the main problems with the hotels in Lamu are twofold: firstly there are frequent problems with the water supply, you should expect to have cold bucket showers much of the time; secondly, many are very hot. The worst are those that do not catch the breeze, such as the ones on Harambee Ave. The only thing you can do is to try to get a room as high up as possible or on the waterfront. With many of these places you may be able to get a cheaper price if you agree to stay for a while. If you want, you can often sleep on the roof which is very cheap. Alternatively, for longer stays, it may be cheaper to rent a house – see page 222.

Lamu Town **B** *Amu House*, T3246, near the *Paradise Guest House*. This is very central, and a charming place, being a reworked 16th century Swahili house. **B** *Lamu Palace Hotel*, PO Box

83, T3272. New hotel on the harbour front at the south end of town, s/c, a/c, bar, pleasant patio restaurant, possible to negotiate a better rate off season, October-May, only other bar (apart from *Petley's*) in Lamu. **B** *Petley's Inn*, PO Box 4, Lamu, T3107. This is the only top range hotel in town, located on Kenyatta Rd next to the Lamu Museum on the harbour front, it was founded by an Englishman called Percy Petley in 1962 and only has 15 rooms, it is looking rather shabby these days but has a certain atmosphere, however it is really rather expensive for what you get, many of the rooms are very hot and stuffy, it has 2 restaurants and a rooftop bar with a good restaurant, the only hotel bar in the town, which of course makes it fairly popular, it has a swimming pool and sometimes holds a disco, one of the few places which serves chilled beers.

    C *Stone House Hotel*, inland from the Donkey Sanctuary, PO Box 192, T33544/33149 (Mombasa: PO Box 81866, T223295/227071, F221926). Well appointed and comfortable, Swahili canopy beds, excellent restaurant with imaginative menu. Well recommended. **C** *Yumbe House*, PO Box 81, Lamu, T/F33101, (Residence) 33280. This is a wonderful hotel full of atmosphere and excellent value, it is located in the heart of the old town next to the Swahili House Museum and is a traditional house of 4 storeys that has been skilfully converted into a hotel, it has a courtyard, and is airy and spacious, it is clean, friendly, has a good water supply and the price includes breakfast. Highly recommended. **C** *Yumbe Villa* (see *Yumbe House*), a traditional house with Zidaka niches in the ground floor room, located near the fort, clean, tidy, with traditional Lamu beds, mosquito nets, en-suite shower and toilet, a/c or fan, some have fridges, owned by the same family as *Yumbe House*.

    D *Kishuna*, northwest edge of town, PO Box 25, T3001. Quite a modern block, not well located or with a particularly attractive atmosphere, s/c, nets, fans, efficiently run. **D** *Lamu Archipelago Villas*, on waterfront at southern end, PO Box 339, T33368, T33111/33185 (home), F33368. Good location, s/c, includes breakfast, fans, nets, efficiently run, safe. Well recommended. **D** *Lulu House*, inland of town centre, close to Sheikh Mohamed bin Ali Mosque, PO Box 142, T33539. New establishment fashioned from a Swahili house around a charming centre courtyard with bougainvillea and a waterfall, roof restaurant with excellent views, table tennis. Well recommended. **D** *Mahrus*, PO Box 25, Lamu, T3001. This has a range of rooms with and without bathrooms, as well as 1 fully s/c Arab house for rent, it is modern and rather rundown and not very well run, the price includes breakfast.

    E *Alipenda*, just north of Lamu Town, PO Box 115 and 3119. Some s/c, fans, very comfortable. **E** *Bahari Hotel*, on Main St, to north end, PO Box 298, T3172. New establishment, pleasant internal courtyard, restaurant, s/c, fans, nets, popular, well run and nice atmosphere. **E** *Bahati Lodge*, situated to the north of the fort. Some of these rooms are better than others, the ones on the top floor are much cooler because they get the sea breezes and they also have good views, however it is fairly basic and perhaps not the cleanest. **E** *Casuarina Rest House*, PO Box 10, Lamu, T3123. Great location on the waterfront verandah overlooking harbour, on top of Kenya Commercial Bank (due to close), curious bell that sounds like a budgerigar, it is very clean, the rooms are spacious (it used to be the Police station) and it is well run and friendly, also has s/c apartments, there is a large rooftop area. **E** *Glory Guest House* (previously Dudu's Guest House), one of the nicest hotels in this range, it is located behind the Fort, and is a wonderful old house, the rooms are spacious and airy, and include bathrooms, there is a kitchen that you can use. **E** *Full Moon Guest House*, small hotel located right on the waterfront, above *Eagle Aviation* office. It only has 4 rooms with shared bathroom, but they are large, it is very friendly and is in an excellent position. **E** *Hal-Udy Guest House*, PO Box 25, T3001. Located in the heart of the old town, back from the harbour, this is a small hotel with 4 self contained suites, each has a bedroom, sitting room, with some lovely furniture, and cooking facilities, there is also a house boy, and this is particularly popular with expatriate families, it is especially good value if you are planning on staying for a few weeks. **E** *Lamu Sea Shore Lodging*, on waterfront, next to District Commissioner's office. Verandah, variety of rooms. **E** *Mtamwini Guest House*, located close to Fort. Old Swahili building, large cool rooms, all with bathrooms. **E** *New Century Lodge*, located behind Pwani Mosque, near Fort, PO Box 10. Very simple, not s/c, but comfortable atmosphere with rooms off central courtyard. **E** *New Kenya*, on Main St, close to Museum, PO Box 295. Good central location, simple, not s/c. **E** *New Sabrina*, Main St, south end, PO Box 294, T33552. Dormitory accommodation, but cheap. **E** *New Shamuty Lodge*, positioned close to the jetty on the waterfront this is a popular cheap hotel, bathroom facilities are shared and there is a rooftop. **E** *Pole Pole*, just inland, north end of town, PO Box 242, T33204. Highest building in Lamu, with good views from roof, s/c, nets, fans, can arrange donkey transport for excursions. **E** *Sanctuary Guest House*, situated in the northern part of town this has a range of self contained rooms and suites, it has good facilities, kitchen, garden and rooftop. **E** *Shanani Guest House*, on waterfront at southern end, PO Box 155, T3207. Good location, above a bakery overlooking harbour, secure.

Lamu Town Seasonal: **E** *Bush Guest House*, to rear of *Bush Gardens* restaurant, on Main St, PO Box 22. Small, efficiently run and well located, some rooms look out over harbour. **E** *Dhow Lodge*, on Main St to south of jetty. Closed in off-season, October-May. **E** *Hapa Hapa*, to rear of *Hapa Hapa* restaurant on Main St, PO Box 213, T3226. Fairly simple – some rooms look out over harbour. **E** *Jambo Guest House*, inland, north end of town, near Jumaa Mosque. Fans, nets. **E** *Kadara's Lodge*, on waterfront, in the far south of the town. Closed in off-season, October-April. **E** *Karibuni Guest House*, inland, north end of town, PO Box 209. Quite small. **E** *Kenya Lodge*, located a little inland from the waterfront this is one of the very basic hotels, it is reasonably clean but rather shabby and sometimes has problems with water supply although other times it can be 24 hours, some of the rooms are hot and stuffy so try and get one with a breeze. **E** *Kilimanjaro*, just inland from Donkey Sanctuary, PO Box 274. Pleasant, s/c, nets, fans, includes breakfast. **E** *Lamu Guest House*, PO Box 240, T3274. Situated at the back of the Lamu Museum and is good value, there are a range of rooms, the general rule is that top ones are usually the best because they catch the sea breezes, it is clean and friendly. **E** *New Castle Lodge*, PO Box 10, Lamu, T3123/3132. This is situated next to the Fort, it has a good position and is kept cool by the sea breezes, it has recently been done up so the prices may rise accordingly, it has both a dormitory on the roof and rooms with shared facilities, closed in off-season, October-May. **E** *Palm View*, northwest edge of town, PO Box 46, T3172. Quite small, some s/c, not particularly good location. **E** *Paradise*, inland from Main St, near Museum, PO Box 97, T3053. Swahili house, simple facilities. **E** *Rainbow*, on Main St, just south of Post Office, PO Box 10. A little basic. **E** *Saiga Lodge*, north end of town, near Jumaa Mosque. Fairly small and basic. **E** *Salama Guest House*, on Main St, northern end, PO Box 38, T3146. Simple accommodation, good location. **E** *Sunrise Guest House*, inland of town centre, near Sheikh Mohamed bin Ali Mosque, PO Box 20, T3175. Good value.

House rentals If you are planning to stay here for a while then it is probably worth getting together with a group to rent a house. Many of the houses are holiday homes of Kenya residents, they can be very good value if you are staying for a while and can fill the house, giving high quality accommodation at a very modest price. Even if you are not part of a group it is still often possible to rent a room. Other Kenya residents seeking to rent out houses post details on noticeboards at *Eagle Aviation*, the Museum and *Lamu Archipelago Tours*, all these located on the waterfront. **D** *Jannat House*, inland, north end of town, PO Box 195. **D** *Pool House*, inland, north end of town, PO Box 48. So-called because the house has a swimming pool. **D** *Starehe House*, inland, north end of town, near Mwana Mshamu Mosque, PO Box 10, T3123. Very charming old house. **D** *Suli Suli House*, inland, north end of town near Jumaa Mosque, PO Box 156, T3119. Handsome house with 8 rooms arranged round a courtyard. **E** *Mlangilangi House*, just by Pwani Mosque, PO Box 260. Comfortable, but a bit utilitarian.

Shela Village (about 3 kilometres south of Lamu Town) **A+** *Peponi's*, PO Box 24, Lamu, T3029. This is located on the beach next to the village of Shela. Highly recommended. It faces the channel that runs between Lamu and Manda and is a really wonderful setting with about 5 kilometres of private beach, the hotel is made up of a series of cottages each with a verandah and full facilities, there is an excellent restaurant which is for residents only, as well a bar and grill for non-residents, the hotel provides full watersports facilities, probably the best and most extensive on the island and organizes various excursions, it is very efficiently run by the Korschen's who are Danish, booking well ahead is definitely advised, it is closed from mid-April to end of June. **A** *Johori House*, house rental, PO Box 48, T33460, F33251. Well restored 18th century house, sleeps up to 6, excellent views. **A** *Kijani House*, on water's edge between *Peponi's* and Shela beach, PO Box 266, T3235/7, odd Swahili houses, fine gardens, traditional furniture, 2 small pools, excellent standards. Well recommended.

B *The Island Hotel Shela*, PO Box 179, Shella, Lamu, T0121-33290, F33568, situated approximately 200 metres from the beach, in the centre of Shela village, decorated in traditional Swahili style, 15 rooms with private bathroom, fans and mosquito nets. **B** *Shela Rest House*, PO Box 199, Malindi, or PO Box 255, Lamu, T20182, or 121/3251, this small hotel is located in the village of Shela close to *Peponi's*. It is a wonderful converted house and there are rooms as well as several self-contained suites – fine if you want to be self-catering.

C *Island Hotel*, town location, PO Box 179, T3290. Fans, s/c, rooftop restaurant. **C** *White Rock Pool*, between town and Shela beach, PO Box 296, T3234. Comfortable house with relaxed atmosphere, pool.

D *Shela Pwani Guest House*, PO Box 59, Lamu, Shela, T0121-33540. Very comfortable and friendly. **D** *White House*, on the waterfront, good value. Well recommended.

E *Samahani Guest House*, PO Box 59, Lamu, T3100. Located in the village of Shela this is particularly popular with budget travellers who want to be closer to the beach, it is basic but clean and friendly. **E** *Stop Over*, located right on the beach. Clean and simple but basic, has a good value restaurant.

Lamu Island **A+** *Kipungani Bay*, Lamu, c/o PO Box 74888, T/F33432, or T338084/335208, F217278 (Nairobi). This new lodge, with just 15 *makuti* thatched cottages which are made from local palm leaf mats with coconut thatched roof, is located at the southern tip of Lamu Island. They are all extremely spacious and comfortable and each has a verandah, they organize various excursions and snorkelling trips, there is a good restaurant and bar outside, and non-residents can visit for lunch, boats leaving from *Peponi's*. **E** *Peace Guest House*, a bit inland, set in gardens with camping facilities.

Manda Island **A+** *Blue Safari*, PO Box 41759, Nairobi, T338838. A small and exclusive Italian family-run hotel in an idyllic setting on Manda Island, thatched bungalows provide extremely comfortable accommodation and the hotel caters for those interested in watersports, scuba diving in particular, it is closed from May to September. **A** *Manda Island Village Resort*, PO Box 78, Lamu, T2751. As its name suggests this is located on Manda Island looking across to the village of Shela on Lamu, it has self sufficient cottages, a restaurant, bar and shop, excursions that the hotel organizes include trips to Lamu, deep-sea fishing and snorkelling trips.

Kiwayu Island **A+** *Kiwayu Safari Village*, PO Box 55343, Nairobi, T503030, F503144. Located to the north of Lamu on the Kiwaya Peninsula, this is managed by the same people as the *Kipungani Sea Breezes* and has been recently refurbished, it consists of luxurious thatched cottages, swimming pool, restaurant, bar and shops and has its own private airstrip, the hotel has a fleet of deep sea fishing vessels and is ideal for the enthusiast, the beach is also wonderful, and there is a full range of watersports on offer, and boat trips into the mangrove swamps, the food is excellent, closes for 2 months from mid-April, so check.

Eating There are lots of places to eat in Lamu which has responded magnificently to the demand for tourist menus. You will find lots of yoghurt, pancakes, fruit salads, and milk shakes as well as good value seafood. If you are looking for the traditional food that you find in up-country Kenya, such as ugali, beans, curries, chicken and chips, there are also a number of places that do these. They are mainly on Harambee Ave – particularly in the southern end of town.

Lamu Town **4** *Lamu Palace Hotel*, PO Box 83, T3272, southern end of waterfront. Pleasant restaurant looking out over the harbour, seafood, grills, Indian food, serves alcohol. **3** *Ali Hippy*, plump gentleman who approaches you in the street near Fort and offers traditional Swahili meal in his home with some musical entertainment. **3** *Bush Gardens*, on the waterfront with good view over harbour and is a very good seafood restaurant, it is friendly although can be extremely slow, especially when it gets full. **3** *Ghai's Restaurant* is named after the owner and cook, it is located up in the north of town close to the donkey sanctuary, its speciality is seafood although the quality can vary. **3** *Lamu Palace Restaurant*, south of the town on the waterfront. A very popular restaurant, it has a very nice atmosphere and a good range of food on the menu, make you sure you pop in and book before you go as it can get very full, the food is good – and there is also excellent ice cream. **3** *Petley's Inn*, restaurant and a grill house, the food at both of these is variable – snacks generally seem to be better than the full meals. **3** *Rumours*, Main St, toward southern end. High quality café with juices, cappuccino, ice-cream, sandwiches, pretty flower-filled courtyard to the rear. **3** *Stone Town Hotel*, inland from Donkey Sanctuary, PO Box 192, T33544/33194. Very good cuisine, crab and lobster, ginger tea, mango flambé, also a snack menu, juices, charming atmosphere with views out over Lamu.

2 *Hapa Hapa Restaurant*, on the harbour front. Barracuda is excellent, good fruit juices and snacks, lively place. **2** *La Banda*, on waterfront at south end of town. Good location, verandah overlooking harbour, comfortable atmosphere, mainly seafoods, grills, but also vegetarian dishes. **2** *Serena* (formerly *Yoghurt*, before that *Coral Inn*), charming garden atmosphere under *makuti* roof, wicker lamps, games (*bai* and dominoes), imaginative menu (pumpkin and ginger soup, seafoods, yoghurts and honey). Well recommended. **1** *Bosnia Café*, south end of Main St. Set up by soldier who served with the UN forces in Yugoslavia, first rate local food, pilau with chapati's, and cold juices. **1** *Coconut Juice Bar*, waterfront, southern end. Specialist juices, freshly made, with combinations of flavours comprising lime, peanut, chocolate, avocado, papaya, mango, coconut, banana. **1** *Jambo Café*, Harambee Ave, northern end. Popular with locals and is very cheap, it serves mainly traditional African food and also does good breakfasts. **1** *Kenya Cold Drinks*, located on Harambee Ave close to the museum. This is very good for a milkshake and a snack, serves really good spaghetti. **1** *New Star Restaurant*, in the southern end of town is reasonable and is very cheap, it has good breakfasts and opens very early – 0530 for the early birds. **1** *Olympic Restaurant*, (formerly *Sinbad*), south of the town also on the harbour front. Excellent pancakes and seafood, open, *Makuti* roofed eating area. **1** *Sabrina Restaurant*, southern end of town. Very cheap, has a reasonably wide range of food on the menu, and does breakfasts. **1** *Tairan Hoteli*, south end of Main St. Local café. **1** *Tamarind Juice Bar*, southern end of waterfront. Cold, straightforward juices and good milkshakes. **1** *Ziaj Juice Bar*, Main St. Handy for cinema next door.

Shela Village (about 3 kilometres south of Lamu Town) **3** *Barbecue Grill* at *Peponi's*. Excellent and open to non-residents, the food is very good value and is probably the best on the island. **2** *Stop Over Restaurant*, which serves simple, basic but good value food, it also has a great location right on the beach.

Bars Only 4 places serve alcohol. *Petley's*, on the waterfront north of the museum has a rather uninviting bar on the ground floor. There is a very much more attractive bar, at which you can sit, in the rooftop restaurant. *Lamu Palace Hotel*, located at the southern end of the waterfront, also has a bar. The *Police Post*, on the high ground inland from the Fort serves beer in the Mess – the guardians of the law are a friendly group, and you will get served if you buy the barman a drink. Has fine views out over the harbour, and there are 2 brass cannons in the front, commanding the bay. The *Civil Servants Club*, south along the waterfront, some distance past the generating station, and then up a steep path, is an unpretentious venue where you will be expected to buy a drink for the clientele, but the compensation, as with the *Police Mess*, is that the beer is cheaper than at either of the hotels with bars. Also there is *Peponi's* at Shela, which you can rely on for an ice-cold beer.

Bakery **1** *Bakery*, just to south of *New Star Restaurant* on Main St, pastries and fresh bread.

Entertainment **Cinemas** The open-air *Coast Cinema* inland from roughly behind the Museum, on the edge of town. There are films most nights in the peak period, and the programme is posted at the Museum. *Zinj Cinema*, excellent small cinema on Main St toward southern end, programme and times posted outside.

Discos The *Civil Servant's Club* (south end of town) has a disco most weekends.

Sports Watersports: organized from *Peponi's*, PO Box 24, Lamu, T0121-33421, F33029. Including windsurfing, surfing, snorkelling, deep sea fishing, sailing, and scuba diving.

Barber *Mohamed A Issa*, south end of Main St, PO Box 173. Haircut US$1, shave US$0.50. **Shopping**

Books The Museum has a very good collection of books on Lamu, its history and culture. There is also the *Lamu Book Centre* which has a reasonable selection as well as the local newspapers.

Henna Painting *Mabruk* on waterfront at southern end, traditional Swahili decoration for hands and feet, US$5-10.

Photography *Bakar Studio*, southern end of Main St. Has interesting collection of old photographs.

Souvenirs Hand-built model dhows. They are not too easy to carry around so try and get them at the end of the trip. Other woodcarvings are also good value here – chests, siwa horns, Lamu candlesticks, and furniture. Also in Lamu you will be able to get jewellery – silver in particular – as well as curios. You can get things made for you but be prepared to bargain. *Lamu Craft*, behind Donkey Sanctuary, PO Box 56, Lamu. Lamu carving, signs, candlesticks. *Casuarina Gift Shop*, behind *Casuarina Hotel*, on Main St, just north of Museum. Good selection of Lamu crafts and clothing. *Gypsies*, Main St, southern end. Expensive, high-quality carvings, Lamu chests, jewellery, clothing. *Shimi Fashions*, on waterfront at southern end, PO Box 18. Good selection of T-shirts and bags. *Maasai Studios*, waterfront, southern end, some very good, original design, clothing. *Zawadi* (Lamu Gift Shop), waterfront, southern end. Excellent, original design clothing and accessories, particularly skirts and patchwork waistcoats and bags. *Husein's*, Fakrudin Gulom Husein and brother, splendid carved door, copperware from Oman, jewellery.

Tailor *Sabana*, south end of Main St. Will undertake repairs very inexpensively.

Local Except for the District Commissioner's Land Rover, there are no vehicles on the island. **Transport** Even if they were allowed, the narrow streets would make driving impossible in town. Instead there are donkeys and bicycles.

Air There are flights to the airstrip on Manda Island and then get boat taxi or a dhow across. The companies serving this route are **Eagle Aviation**, T21258 (Malindi), 316054 (Mombasa), 3119 (Lamu); **Equator Airlines**, T2053 (Malindi); **Prestige Air Services**, T20860/1 (Malindi), 21443 (Mombasa); **Skyways Airlines**, T21260 (Malindi), 432167 (Mombasa), 3226 (Lamu). **Tai Aviation** offer cheap flights on 6 seater planes, 30 minute flight to Malindi US$30, book through *Lamu Archipelago Tours*. Prestige and Equator both have offices on Lamu close to the Standard Chartered Bank. All the companies have 2 flights per day in both directions between Malindi and Mombasa and Malindi and Lamu. Baggage allowance is only 10 kilograms, and check in time is 30 minutes before take off. There is no airport tax when you leave Lamu (although there is from Malindi). Fares are: Malindi US$35; Mombasa US$55; Nairobi US$100.

Road Bus: to Lamu go fairly regularly but the route is popular so you should book in advance. The trip takes about 5 to 6 hours from Malindi and costs US$4. They leave in the morning at between 0700 and 0800. You might also be able to take one of the buses from Mombasa that stop off at Malindi on the way, but these are often full so you will have to stand all the way which is not much fun. If possible sit on the left side of the bus (in the shade) and keep your eyes open for wildlife. If you are travelling from Mombasa, **TSS Bus** (in Mombasa on Digo Rd, PO Box 85039, 1224541/2222201; in Lamu on Main St, PO Box 3, T33059/33083) is recommended. The cost is about US$8, but seats are reserved and you will not be crushed by extra passengers crowding the gangway. The trip takes almost all day, arriving about 1700 at Lamu. There is tarmac to Malindi, a rough track to Garsen then a further 20 kilometres of tarmac after which there is a good graded coral and sand section to Makowe. With the current problems with bandits from Somalia, a convoy forms at Garsen and an armed escort joins the bus. The bus will take you as far as the jetty at Makowe on the mainland from where you get a ferry, about 7 kilometres, taking about 40 minutes, across to Lamu which costs about US$0.50.

Directory **Banks** Few on the island, *Standard Chartered*, located on the harbour front. It is only open in the mornings 0830 to 1300 on weekdays, and until 0830 to 1100 on Sat, and can get busy. It can also be painstakingly slow. The *Kenya Commercial Bank* (due to close soon), on the seafront, will change foreign currency and TCs, service slow. **Communications** Post Office: just to the south of the jetty Mon-Fri 0800-1230 and 1400-1700; Sat 0900-1200. There is a *poste restante* service. **Hospital & medical services** Hospitals: located in the southern end of the town to the south and inland from the Fort, PO Box 45, T3012. **Laundry** *Ndobi Mdogo*, behind Pwani Mosque, near Fort. **Tour companies & travel agents** *Lamu Archipelago Tours*, south end of waterfront, PO Box 339, T/F33368, T33111/33185 (residence). Efficient operation, will arrange reliable trips to nearby islands. *Tawasal Safaris and Tours*, PO Box 248, T33446/33533/33449, F33533/33513. **Tourist offices** Harbour front, next door to the bank. While the staff are friendly they have little information to give out.

Manda Island

Colour map 3, grid A6   This is the island which is located just to the north of Lamu and has the air strip on it. It is very easy to get to and is a popular day trip to see the ruins at Takwa.

The island is approximately the size of Lamu but has only a small permanent population – partly because of a shortage of fresh water and also because of the shortage of cultivable land. About a fifth of the island is made up of sand dunes and sandy flat land with just thorn bushes and palms. Another three fifths of the island is mangrove swamps and muddy creeks. Thus only about a fifth of the island's surface area is suitable for agriculture. The creek that Takwa is located on almost cuts the island in half during high tide. The main port is Ras Kilimdini which is located on the northern side of the island. In the 19th century this deep water harbour was considered to be superior to Lamu and was used by ocean-going vessels who would then take dhows across to Lamu.

The **Takwa Ruins** are those of an ancient Swahili town which is believed to have prospered from the 15th to the 17th centuries, with a population of between 2,000-3,000 people. For some reason it was abandoned in favour of the town of Shela on Lamu – it is not altogether clear why. The ruins consist of the remains of a wall which surrounded the town, about 100 houses, a mosque and a tomb dated from 1683. As with many of the other sites on the coast, the remains include ablution facilities. The houses face north toward Mecca as does the main street. There is a mosque at the end of the street which is thought to have been built on the site of an old tomb. The other feature of the ruins is the pillar tomb. It is situated just outside the town walls. The ruins have been cleared but little excavation has been done here. Only relatively little is known about the town – the biggest question that remains is if it was so well defended (as it clearly was with town walls, the sea and mangrove swamps as protection) why did the inhabitants leave so quickly? Entrance fee of US$2.

There are a number of good **snorkelling** sites off Manda Island. Perhaps the best is actually off the small island to the north of Manda, named Manda Toto. You will have to take a dhow to get here.

There are 2 hotels on Manda Island in the upper price brackets. **A+** *Blue Safari Hotel*,   **Sleeping**
T338838(Nairobi). Has 15 bandas, plus a bar and restaurant, at over US$400 a night it is
costly. **A** *Manda Island Village Resort* (see Lamu Sleeping, page 220), as well as **E** camping
close to the ruins.

You can get to Manda Island and the towns by way of motorized ferry as well as by dhow.   **Transport**
However dhow is the easiest as it will take you closest to the ruins, otherwise you will have to
walk across the island. The dhow will cost you about US$15 for a party of up to 8. Be sure you
know what is included in the price. It takes about an hour and a half and is dependent on the
tides. You may have to wade ashore through the mangrove swamp.

Paté Island

Kenya

About three times the size of Lamu and located about 20 kilometres to the northeast.   *Colour map 3, grid A6*
Unlike both Lamu and Manda, it does not have a large area taken up by dunes. The
island is divided into two parts – indeed it may have once been two islands but the
channel dividing them is so shallow that only the smallest boats can go down it. The
land is very low lying and the towns are situated on shallow inlets which can only be
reached at high tide. The only deep water landing point is at Ras Mtangawanda in the
west of the island, but as it is not a sheltered harbour it has never had a major settlement. Although it is fairly easily accessible it does not receive many visitors.

The town of Paté is only accessible from the sea at the right tide – otherwise you will   **Paté Town**
have to walk from the landing place. It is situated in the southwest corner of the
island and is one of the old Swahili towns that dot the coast. The town shows strong
Arabic and Indian influences, and was once most famous for the silk that was produced here. The old stone houses are crumbling and tobacco has been planted
amongst the ruins. The main ruins are those of **Nabahani** which are found just outside the town. Although they have not yet been excavated you should be able to
make out the town walls, houses, mosques and tombs.

   The age of the town is disputed – the earliest remains that have been found are
from the 13th century – although according to some accounts the town dates back to
the eighth century. The town was reasonably prosperous for up to 1600, although by
the time the Portuguese first arrived it had begun to decline. The Portuguese did not
have much success and by the 17th century had withdrawn to Mombasa. The final
decline of Paté was the war with Lamu. There had been an ongoing dispute between
the two islands. Over the years the port at Paté silted up, Lamu was used instead by
the bigger dhows, and the tensions increased. The situation reached a climax in 1813
when the army from Paté was defeated at Shela and the town went into a decline
from which it has never recovered.

Transport   To get to Paté from Lamu, you will have to take the motor launch to **Faza** or to
Mtangawanda and walk from there. To Faza the boat goes 3 times a week, Monday,
Wednesday, and Friday and takes about 4 hours. To Mtangawanda the trip takes about 3
hours. Once you get to Mtangawanda the walk will take you about an hour – the track is clear
and you will probably be accompanied by other people from the boat. To get back to Lamu
the boat leaves Faza on Tuesday, Thursday and Saturday. It does not always call at
Mtangawanda so you may have to walk to Faza via Siyu (quite a hike) and catch it from there.
You would be advised to take a guide (at least as far as Siyu).

A stone-built town dating from about the 15th century. It became most well-known   **Siyu**
as a centre for Islamic scholarship and is believed to have been an important cultural
centre during the 17th and 18th centuries. At one time is said to have had 30,000
inhabitants. Today there are probably fewer than 5,000 people living in the town and
the inhabited part of the town is slightly apart from the ancient ruined area. A creek

Kenya

separates the residential part of the town from the **Fort** which is believed to date from the mid-19th century when the town was occupied by forces of the Sultan of Zanzibar. The Fort has some impressive canons and has been partly renovated. The town itself is fairly dilapidated and outside the town are coconut plantations. It is a small fishing village which has a thriving crafts industry – you will be able to see leather goods being made as well as doors, furniture and jewellery.

About one hour's walk from Siyu there are the **Shanga Ruins**. There have been excavations in recent years and they show signs of unearthing impressive remains. There are buildings from the 13th and 14th century and many artifacts have been found dating back to the eighth and ninth centuries. There is a pillar tomb, a large mosque, a smaller second mosque, about 130 houses and a palace. The whole town was walled with five access gates and outside the wall is a cemetery containing well over 300 tombs. If you are visiting the islands by dhow and would rather not walk you can ask your boatman to take you to Shanga direct.

The channel which Siyu is sited on is so silted up that only the smallest boats can reach Siyu. It is therefore necessary to approach the town by foot – either from Shanga (about an hour), from Faza (about two hours), or from Paté (about eight kilometres). In the case of the latter two, unless you are happy to get lost and therefore walk for hours, you would be advised to take a guide, as the route (particularly from Paté) is complicated.

About a two-hour walk to the northeast of Siyu is the town of **Chundwa** which is situated in the most fertile part of the island. Being agriculturally productive the island is perhaps the most capable of self-sufficiency of all the islands in the archipelago, however, it does suffer from problems with the supply of fresh water.

Sleeping It is possible to rent rooms in local houses – there are no formal guest houses.

Transport The inlet is very shallow, and sea-going dhows and the motor launch from Lamu by-passes Siyu en route to Faza. It may be possible to persuade a small boat to sail or pole you round from Paté or Faza. Otherwise it is about a 10 kilometres hike to each of these places, and you probably need to hire a guide.

Faza About 20 kilometres from Paté Town, and 10 kilometres northeast of Siyu. Although the town of Faza is believed to date from the 13th century and possibly as early as the eighth century, there is little in the way of ruins left here. However the town is important in that it is the district headquarters of Paté Island and some of the mainland. It therefore has a number of modern facilities that are not found elsewhere on the island – such as post office, telephone exchange and some shops, restaurants and simple guest houses.

The town is believed to have been completely destroyed in the 13th century by the nearby town of Paté, rebuilt, and destroyed again in the late 16th century this time by the Portuguese. It was again rebuilt and joined forces with the Portuguese against Paté. However, its significance declined until recently when, being the district headquarters, it resumed its position of importance.

Close to where the ferries anchor are the ruins of the **Kunjanja Mosque**. You can see some the mihrab which points to Mecca and which is a beautiful example with fine carvings. There are some rather splendid Arabic inscriptions above the entrance. Outside the town there is the tomb of the commander of the Sultan of Zanzibar's army who was killed here, in action, in 1844.

Sleeping & eating There are 2 guesthouses in the town: **E** *Lamu House* and **E** *Shela House*, they are simple, basic and family run. Alternatively you can ask around to stay at a family house. You will probably be offered food at the place that you are staying – otherwise there is a simple restaurant in the village.

Transport   To get to Faza from **Lamu** take the motor launch which goes 3 times a week (on Monday, Wednesday and Friday) and takes about 4 hours. To get back to Lamu the boat leaves Faza at about 0600 on Tuesday, Thursday and Saturday. You have to take a small boat out to the launch so be sure to get there early. The journey to Lamu takes about 4 hours and will cost you about US$1.50. From Faza to any of the other towns you will probably have to walk – it is advisable to take a guide or ask around to see if anyone else is going who can show you the route. Generally when visiting Paté Island the best thing to do is to start at Paté Town, and walk through Siyu to Faza from where you will be able to get a boat back to Lamu.

Kiwaiyu Island

This island is located on the far northeast of the archipelago and is part of the **Kiunga Marine National Reserve**. Unfortunately this area has suffered from the problems to the north in Somalia, and so visitors are fewer than in previous years. The Marine Park has a reputation for being some of the best reef in Kenya.

Sleeping   There is an airstrip which serves the 2 luxury lodges below, as well as a launch which takes an hour to Lamu. **A+** *Kiwaiyu Mlango Wa Chanu Lodge*, on the Island, PO Box 48217, Nairobi, T331878, Tx22678. **A+** *Kiwaiyu Safari Village*, PO Box 55343, on the mainland, Nairobi, T503030. **D-E** *Kasim's*, has a number of bandas, located on the western shore of the island, the facilities are good and there is a dining and cooking area. **Camping** If you have a tent you can camp at **E** *Kasim's*.

Transport   To get there you can either take a regular boat or (and probably easier) you can get a group of 5 or 6 together and charter a dhow. This should include food and water as well as snorkelling gear and should work out at around US$15 per person. The journey is dependent on the winds and the tides and so be prepared for the journey in each direction to be anything between 8 and 36 hours.

Northern Kenya

This is a vast area of forested and barren mountains, deserts and scrubland occasionally broken by oases of vegetation and the huge Lake Turkana. Northern Kenya accounts for almost half of the country and yet only a fraction of the population live here. The people who do inhabit the area, the Samburu, Rendille, Boran, Gabbra, Turkana and Somali, are nomadic peoples crossing the region using ancient migration routes, existing as they have done for generations hardly affected by the modern world. The main reason tourists come up here is to see the wonders of Lake Turkana – the Jade Sea.

3° N, 36° E
Colour map 2, grid
A3/B3

Lake Turkana, the largest lake in the country, runs about 250 kilometres from the Ethiopian border in a long thin body of water which is never more than 50 kilometres wide. It stretches into the Ethiopian Highlands where several rivers, including the Omo River enter its waters.

Count Sammuel Teleki Von Szek is believed to have been the first white man to see the lake in 1888. In honour of his patron Von Szek named it Lake Rudolf, after the Austrian Archduke. President Jomo Kenyatta changed the name to Lake Turkana in 1975. This lake used to be far larger than it is today. Around 10,000 years ago it is believed the water level of the lake was about 150 metres higher and considered to be one of the sources of the Nile. At that time it supported a far greater number and diversity of plant and animal life. Now a combination of factors including evaporation and major irrigation projects in southern Ethiopia have brought the water level to its lowest in memory. As a result, the water is far more alkaline than in the past. The lake still supports a huge number of hippos and the largest population of Nile crocodiles in the world, about 20,000.

Giant Nile Perch are reported to grow from 200-400 lbs in the lake, but Nile Tilapia are a more commercial option as they are more palatable and are either dried or frozen before being marketed all over Kenya. There is also a profusion of birdlife including many European migratory species. Do not be fooled by its calm appearance, the lake's waters are highly unpredictable; storms build up out of nowhere and are not to be dismissed lightly as they are capable of sinking all but the most sturdy craft.

Northern region

Lake Turkana's **Central Island** is an active volcano which sometimes belches out smoke and sulphur laden steam. Central Island was established as a National Park in 1983, in order to protect the breeding grounds of the Nile Crocodile.

The climate up here is extraordinary. It can easily reach 50°C during the day with not a cloud in sight, then out of nowhere a storm will break whipping up a squall on Lake Turkana. For most of the year, the area is dry but when the rains do come, the rivers and ravines become torrential waterways sweeping over the parched plains. It is quite a sight, and it can leave you stranded until the water levels drop.

The environment in Northern Kenya supports many species not seen in other parts of the country such as the Grevy's zebra with saucerlike ears and narrower stripes. There are only about 10,000 left as they are hunted for their skins. The reticulated giraffe is only found here. Lake Turkana's **South Island**, 39 square kilometres, was established as a National Park in 1983 for the protection of the Nile Crocodile's breeding ground. South Island is also home to several species of venomous snakes, including vipers, puff adders and cobras. It is also an important breeding ground for hippos.

There are plenty of National Parks in Northern Kenya. On the eastern shores of Lake Turkana is the Sibilois National Park, just north of Isiolo you will find Samburu, Buffalo Spring and Shaba National Reserves, all three along the banks of the Ewaso Nyiro River covering an area of some 300 square kilometres. Further north still are the Parks at Maralal, Losai and Marsabit.

Travelling in Northern Kenya is a real adventure as there is almost no public transport in this desolate region. In fact, there is little traffic of any kind making hitching an unadvisable option. The western approach from Kitale is the simplest way for independent travellers without vehicles as there is transport to Kalokol on the lake on a fairly regular basis. Driving yourself is a possibility (a four-wheel drive is imperative), though this is not exactly trouble free. You will need to bring a number of tools in case of breakdown or getting stuck in the sand: a jack, sand ladders, a shovel and a rope. Also, you need to bring plenty of petrol, as it is in particularly short supply.

An alternative method of exploring Northern Kenya is to go on an organized tour. There are a number of organizations running tours, among them: *Best Camping*, PO Box 40223, Nairobi, T28091; *Birds Paradise Tours Ltd*, PO Box 22121, Nairobi, T25898. Offers both overland and flying safaris; *Safari Camp Services* PO Box 44801, Nairobi, T28936; *Special Camping Safaris*, PO Box 51512, Nairobi, T338325; *Zirkuli Expeditions*, PO Box 34548, Nairobi, T23949; *Turkana Air Safaris*, PO Box 41078, Nairobi, T26623. Air safaris only.

Most operators offer an eight to nine day tour heading up the Rift Valley to stop at Lake Baringo going on to Maralal and then to Lake Turkana via Baragoi and South Horr. The return journey goes via Samburu National Park and Buffalo Springs National Reserve. Some go via the Marsabit National Reserve crossing the Koroli Desert. Safaris cost between US$150 and US$180 which includes transport, food and camping. Most use open-sided four-wheel drive trucks, not built for comfort but sturdy and reliable. If you have a bit more money to spend, some companies arrange flying safaris. The flying safaris usually go to the western shores of the lake using the *Lake Turkana Lodge* on Ferguson's Gulf as a base. The cost is around US$320 for five days.

Seeing the western side of Lake Turkana by road involves a long rough trip. The desert and lake are beautiful. It is best to spend one or two nights at Marich Pass. Matatu touts try to overcharge travellers in Kitale. Expect to pay around US$3 for a matatu from Kitale to Marich Pass via Kapenguria. At Marich Pass transport on to Lodwar passes through around midday. In Lodwar the *New Salama Hotel* and *Restaurant* are cheap and good value. It is possible to get a matatu from Lodwar to Kalokol – there are about four matatus daily. Basic food and accommodation is available at *Tours Lodge*. The *Fisherman's Lodge* is scheduled to reopen this year. From Kalokol it is one hour's walk to the lake. You are advised to walk either in the early morning or evening as it gets extremely hot. A guide can be hired at *Tours Lodge*, US$2-US$4. It is essential to take adequate supplies of water as it is not possible to buy water at the lake.

Another consideration when exploring this region is the time of year. The majority of the inhabitants are Muslim and will adhere to Ramadan, a month of fasting. During Ramadan most stores and hotels are closed through daylight hours, though public transport and official business should continue as normal. The times of Ramadan vary each year. The British High Commission currently advises that tourists should not travel into the far northeast Kenya from Isiolo because of safety concerns.

The recent problems in Sudan and Somalia, and the influx of refugees into Kenya from these countries, means there is a high military presence in the north. Vehicles are escorted by armed guards, road blocks are common and vehicle searches are a part of everyday life. However, it is rare that this level of precaution is required. On the whole it is a safe area to travel, and you are assured a warm welcome wherever you go. The only area for which this may not be true is travelling north of Isiolo into the far northeast.

Marich Pass

1° 50′ N, 35° E
Colour map 2, grid B3

If you are coming up into Northern Kenya from Kitale, you travel a glorious route through the highlands, past the **Saiwa Swamp National Park** (see section on National Parks, page 251), through the northern gorges of the **Cherangani Hills**, coming into the desert plains through the **Marich Pass**. The views are incredible, looking down onto the plains from the lush highlands. There isn't much happening around here, the only town in these parts is **Ortum** where you should be able to find accommodation though it is pretty basic. If you do intend to stop and explore the area, the best place to stay is the **Marich Pass Field Studies Centre** (see below). This is an educational facility set up for groups to study various aspects of the environment in this area but it welcomes independent travellers. The centre has cordoned off about 12 hectares of wilderness and acts as a haven for species in the region including monkeys and baboons (who now live here) and has visits from wart hog, antelope, elephants and buffalo, as well as several species of birds. Marich Pass Field Studies Centre can arrange local guides for walks in the area and visits to the local Pokot villages.

Sights
Mount Sekerr is a few kilometres from the Study Centre and is a fairly easy climb over a couple of days. The views from the top (3,326 metres) are great looking onto forest glades and open moors.

Cherangani Hills is a good place to base yourself to explore (see Northern Rift Valley, page 139), offering some of the best walking in Kenya away from other tourists.

Elgeyo Escarpment About one and a half hours from the centre, with spectacular views out over the Kerio Valley.

South Turkana National Reserve is just northeast of the Marich Pass Field Studies Centre. Used by Turkana herdsmen as grazing land.

Sleeping
E *Marich Pass Field Studies Centre*, T0321-31541. Banda accommodation, there are toilets, showers, firewood and drinking water fresh from the well, a basic restaurant, and local shops for provisions, there is no petrol available.

Camping E Camping available at the *Marich Pass Field Studies Centre* (above).

Transport
Road The Pass is about 70 kilometres from **Kitale** going north. You can also reach it from **Eldoret** via Kabarnet and then on through the Kerio Valley joining the Kitale-Lodwar road

near Kapenguria. The other way is from **Lake Baringo** across the Kerio Valley though this way involves travelling a track through the northern face of the Cherangani Hills which becomes impassable after heavy rains when the streams which cross the track flood the road. The centre itself is off the main Kitale-Lodwar road to the north. It is clearly signposted north of the Sigor-Tot junction at Marich Pass. There is no public transport.

Lodwar

The only town of any size in the northwest of the region is Lodwar, the administrative centre. It is not nearly so isolated as in the past due to the opening of a surfaced road from the highlands and air connections to Nairobi, but it is still very much a backwater town with a pleasant enough atmosphere. It is currently the boom town in the region because of the possibility of oil discoveries, the development of the fishing industry at the lake, and the extension of a surfaced road from Kitale. This is a useful base if you intend to explore the lake from the western side. There is both a bank (though do not rely on it taking travellers' cheques), and a Post Office in town. The local people, predominately Turkana, are persistent in attempts to sell their crafts, but it is generally done in a friendly spirit.

3° 10' N, 35° 40' E
Phone code: 0393
Colour map 2, grid B3

Kenya

Sleeping At the moment most accommodation is at the bottom end of the market, though a luxury hotel is planned just outside the town by the Turkwel River. You will need a room with both a fan and mosquito protection if you intend to get any sleep.

D *Turkwel*, T0393-21201. Best accommodation in town, rooms come with a fan and bathroom, for slightly more you can hire a self-contained cottage with a full breakfast included in the price, bar is popular with Lingala music playing into the small hours.

E *Africana Silent Lodge*, basic, no nets, fan, communal showers clean, has a restaurant. **E** *Mombasa*, next to the JM Bus office. The best in this price range. **E** *Nawoitorong Guest House and Conference Centre*, just outside of town to the south. The centre was set up to support single mothers and drought victims but will take travellers, there are mosquito nets, and breakfast is provided. Recommended. Now also do dinners.

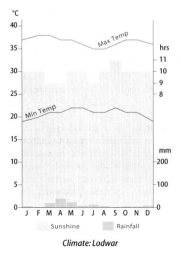

Climate: Lodwar

Shopping You can buy very large, beautiful baskets made by local women. Take care of your possessions as some of the children are accomplished thieves.

Transport **Road Bus**: buses go between here and Kitale daily, taking around 7 hours. There are also a few matatus which work the route though whether they reach their final destination depends on the number of passengers. The bus leaves from Kitale at 1500 and leaves Lodwar for Kitale at 0700. It is wise to take water and food for the trip as breakdowns and delays are common. Another point worth remembering is to book your seat on the return to Kitale the night before as the bus gets very full. The petrol station at Lodwar is the last place to buy fuel and food on the way to Eliye Springs.

Lake Turkana – West

From this side of the Lake it is possible to access Central Island National Park. The main virtue of this approach to the Lake is accessibility, as it is only 35 kilometres from Lodwar.

Kalokol

Colour map 2, grid B3   This is the nearest town to the lakeshore, a small and simple place, and the heat is quite oppressive. It is a few kilometres from here to the lakeshore itself. Getting water supplies in the dry season poses major problems. The women walk 3 kilometres to extract water from the river bed.

To get to the lake you will need to walk out to the Italian-sponsored fish processing plant (you can ask for a guide from *Oyavo's Hotel* if you want one). **Ferguson's Gulf** is the most accessible part of the lake, but not the most attractive. There are loads of birds here particularly flamingoes, and a number of hippos and crocodiles making swimming a fairly exciting activity. If you do intend to swim, ask the local people where to go.

To get onto the lake you can hire a boat from *Turkana Lodge* at Ferguson's Gulf to take you to the **Central Island National Park**. This is expensive: a cruiser costs around US$100 for eight or a long-boat for four costs US$45, but is well worth the trip. You will also be asked for a US$15 entrance fee by the park game wardens. The island is just five square kilometres with three small volcanoes on it. There are many reptiles on the island and if you arrive around April-May, you can witness crocodiles hatching and sprinting off down to one of the crater lakes. It is possible to negotiate with a local fisherman to take you out on his craft, though remember that the lake's squalls are a real danger, and there are crocodiles.

En route to Kalokol look out for the standing stones of **Namotunga** which have a spiritual meaning to the Turkana who gather here in December.

Sleeping &   **A** *Lake Turkana Fishing Lodge*, just across Ferguson's Gulf from Kalokol, PO Box 74609, Nai-
eating robi, T760226, F760546. Aimed at the top end of the market with self-contained bandas, this has a beautiful view across the lake and gets quite busy at weekends when parties from Nairobi are flown in, but is pretty deserted the rest of the time, set menu, which is changed regularly, good fish. Turkana Fishing Lodge does not appear to remain open all year round. **E** *Kalokol Tourist Lodge*, very simple, no tap water or mosquito nets, small restaurant. **E** *Oyavo's*, in Kalokol. The rooms are clean and cooler than you would expect, with palm leaf thatch roofs, food is basic, fish and rice, but sufficient, and there are warm beers and sodas.

Transport   **Road Bus**: buses go from **Lodwar** at 0500 (the driver honks his horn to announce his departure) arriving at Kalokol 1½ hours later.

Eliye Springs   A far more pleasant place to see the Lake from and the springs themselves under the palm trees bubble up warm water. However, you will need a vehicle to get here. There is a small village nearby where you can get some food and drink and no doubt some of the local people will want to sell you some of their handicrafts. The turn off for Eliye Springs is about half way along the Lodwar to Kalokol road. As it is 70 kilometres from Lodwar, your best bet would be to base yourself there, and travel up to the Springs. The last 10 kilometres is very sandy.

There is one basic place to stay, at the old Lodge but facilities are virtually non-existent. Follow the main sandy road straight to the lake, where the palm leaves are on the road. Basic rooms cost US$10, camping US$5, wonderful showers. Beer and soft drinks intermittently available after a truck delivery. No food.

Lake Turkana – East

Exploring the Lake from the east is far more exciting than the west, and you pass through a number of national reserves. Driving here takes skills and steel nerves and you will need a four-wheel drive vehicle. Few of the roads are surfaced, and the main A2 road is tricky to say the least. Avoid the rainy season as some routes become impassable. Public transport is available for most of the way, though not as easy as on the west.

Isiolo

Isiolo is an interesting little frontier town, not far but very different from the rest of the Central Province towns around Mt Kenya. Its at the end of the tarmac road heading north, which quickly becomes Samburu country. There's a busy goat, cattle and camel market here, in addition to the fruit and vegetable market. For travelling to Lake Turkana's eastern shores the best route is likely to be from Isiolo, 50 kilometres north of Meru, which is why it is included in this section though strictly it is in the Central Highlands. It is the last place with good facilities on your journey further north. The road to Isiolo is sealed and generally in good condition. There are a number of petrol stations, a bank and a post office (the last town to have these facilities until you reach either Maralal or Marsabit). It is also the last place to have a good supply of provisions, including an excellent fruit and vegetable market. Across the road from Barclays Bank is *Ali's Disco and Bar*, where you can drink and dance with the locals.

0° 24' N, 37° 33' E
Colour map 2, grid B4

Kenya

Isiolo is the nearest town to explore the **National Reserves** at **Samburu**, **Buffalo Springs** and **Shaba**, all grouped together 40 kilometres to the north (see National Park Sections, page 275).

Sleeping

C *Bomen*, PO Box 67, T0165-2225. Offers excellent value, relative luxury before roughing it trekking further north, all rooms have en suite bathrooms and they are well furnished, the hotel does excellent food and cold beers. **D** *Pasoda Lodge*, good double rooms with bath, restaurant. **E** *Jamhuri Guest House*, best of the cheap hotels and has been popular with travellers for years, the rooms are clean, have mosquito nets and the communal showers have hot water, you are ensured a warm welcome by the hosts here, has undergone recent renovation. **E** *Mashallah*, board and lodging, PO Box 378, T2142. The newest and tallest building in town, good value, very friendly and safe with a variety of rooms, great roof views – possible to see Mt Kenya summit on a cloudless day, very small parking area which would only accommodate a motorcycle. **E** *Mocharo Lodge Ltd*, nice clean rooms, with nets and desks in a small, new building. **E** *Silent Inn*, good value and it is quite quiet. **E** *Silver Bells*, very similar to its neighbour *Mocharo*, good value. Safe parking for cars and motorcycles.

Isiolo

To Samburu NP, Marsabit
NP & Lake Turkana

BP Petrol Station

Mashallah
D&L

Akamba
Bus Office

Silent Inn

Jamhuri

Bus for
Marahal

Bomen

Silver Bells

Mocharo

Market

Pasoda

N

To Nanyuki & Nairobi

0 metres 200

Eating

2 *The Bomens Restaurant*, has the widest choice and the tastiest food. Excellent place for a beer in the evening. **1** *The Interfast*, at Mashallah. Good basic food. **1** *The Silver Bells*, decent basic restaurant.

Kenya

Transport **Road** The Akamba office (next to Mashallah) runs a twice daily (0700 and 2000) 6 hours' ride to Nairobi, stopping at Nanyuki, Nyeri and other towns for US$6. The 'Babie Coach', a converted Isuzu truck, runs up and down between Maralal and Isiolo, leaving either place on alternate days. Departure time is 1100-1300 depending on the number of passengers. The trip takes about 5-8 hours depending on load and road conditions. Cost US$6. Buses run from Isiolo to Marsabit and Moyale on Tuesday, Thursday and Saturday, taking about 6 hours to Marsabit and a further 6 hours on to Moyale. On the way from Isiola to Marsabit you can stay at the campsite at the Catholic Mission at Laismais, which is approximately halfway to Marsabit. There are regular matatus to Meru and other near Central Province towns. Isiolo is also a good place to arrange a lift to Marsibat (14 hours) and Moyale (12 hours from Marsibat). Its a hot, dusty journey. The people in Mashallah are very helpful with this. There are no more buses north to Ethiopia. Sometimes you can hitch a lift on one of the trucks that travel in convoy to Moyale. They park near Barclays Bank.

Archers Post

Colour map 2, grid B4 About an hour north of Isiolo, this is a very small and hot outpost at the edge of Samburu and Buffalo Springs National Reserve. There are a couple of places where you can stay, as well as a few small shops and cafés. Curio sellers and tour guides for the parks are also around.

Sleeping **E** *Archers Safari Lodge*, small rooms, a bit rough and smelly. **E** *Kamanga Lodge*, slightly better of the 2, reasonably clean, mosquito nets and paraffin lamps, rooms are likely to heat up during the day as there is little shade around.

Wamba

0° 58' N, 37° 19' E A small town 90 kilometres northwest of Isiolo, and 55 kilometres from the
Colour map 2, grid B3 Samburu National Reserve. It is a useful place to stock up on fresh meat and other provisions. Also, there is **E** *Saudia Lodge* off the main street where you can get sound food and lodging in a family-run establishment.

Maralal

1° N, 36° 38' E High up in the hills looks down onto the Lerochi Plateau, about 240 kilometres from
Colour map 2, grid B3 Meru and 160 kilometres from Nyahururu. Long before the British administrators moved in, this was a spiritual site for the Samburu. The route from Isiolo passes though a wildlife haven and from the road you will be able to see zebra, impala, eland, buffalo, hyena and warthog, roaming a lovely area of gentle hills and forests. Maralal is home to Wilfred Thesiger, explorer and travel writer.

One of your first meetings with Maralal, if you alight here, will be with 'The Plastic Boys', an unendearing nickname for the local guides and curio sellers, who have been organized into a co-operative. It is not clear whether this has done them any good. They are persistent and can be rather irritating, but they are really harmless and friendly enough. If you are polite to them they will happily show you around Maralal. In return you are encouraged to visit their little shop on the town's outskirts and buy a little token. It is through them that trips in this area can be organized – by camel or donkey. You could even arrange a trek to Lake Turkana from here.

The town itself has all basic amenities including a number of good cheap hotels as this is the preferred route of safaris going up to Lake Turkana. There is a bank and post office and two petrol stations. Traditionally garbed Samburu are still very much in evidence here, brightening up the surroundings with their skins, blankets, beads and hair styles.

You can arrange to join a safari to Lake Turkana from here costing from US$300 upwards and taking eight days. Gametrackers charge US$500 for the Turkana tour.

B *Maralal Safari Lodge*, PO Box 45155, Nairobi, T211124, F214261, about 3 kilometres out of **Sleeping**
town towards Baragoi. A series of cottages with a main bar and restaurant, there is also a souvenir shop, the lodge is by a water hole which attracts a wide range of wildlife, and it is a nice place to go and have a beer (you don't need to be a resident to eat or drink here).

C-E *Maralal Hostel*, about 3 kilometres out of town. Excellent facilities (a library, self-service restaurant and bar, shop and a lounge), comfortable bandas or dormitory accommodation, bandas and restaurant are relatively expensive.

D *Buffalo Lodge*, good value, the bar here is lively, as it's a popular place. **D** *Yare Club and Camp*, PO Box 281, Maralal, T/F0368-2295, Nairobi contact: PO Box 63006, Nairobi, T/F213445. 3 kilometres out of town on the road to Isiolo. If requested the Isiolo-Maralal bus will drop you at their gate, this is a quiet place, although it can get pretty raucous in the evening once the bar gets going, the camping facilities are excellent, with lots of toilets and showers, all a stones throw away from the bar and restaurant, US$6 a night for the pitch, there are also a dozen charming bandas, all s/c (only cold water) and roomy. Adjacent to the bar is a games room with a couple of dart boards, a table tennis table and a pool table in the making. A token membership is required for their use. Malcolm, the English owner, is always around and is very helpful. His phone and fax can be used. Variety and taste from the kitchen leaves a little to be desired – Malcolm is rumoured to subsist solely on Yorkshire pudding, gravy and beer. With his resident camels, half-day, day and much longer treks are available.

E *Buffalo*, good basic hotel. **E** *Impala Lodge*, quiet and clean. Recommended. **E** *Jamaru Hotel*, the best place to stay and eat in town with a choice of rooms, walk through the restaurant to reach reception. **E** *Kariara*, cheap and basic for budget traveller. **E** *Kimanik*, good value.

Camping **E** Camping available at the *Maralal Hostel*, with good facilities.

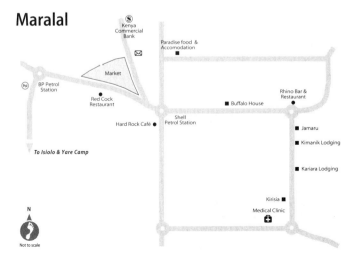

Maralal

Kenya Commercial Bank

Paradise food & Accomodation

Market

BP Petrol Station

Red Cock Restaurant

Rhino Bar & Restaurant

Buffalo House

Hard Rock Café

Shell Petrol Station

Jamaru

Kimanik Lodging

To Isiolo & Yare Camp

Kariara Lodging

Kirisia

Medical Clinic

N

Not to scale

Eating **2** *Hard Rock Café*, newly-opened, does excellent food, friendly staff. **2** *Yare Club and Camp*, T/F2295, 3 kilometres out of town on the road to Isiolo. Excellent variety of foods available.

Transport Daily bus to Isiolo US$7. **Warning** The area north of Maralal up to the Ethiopian border has had recent tribal clashes with many people killed. Tourists have been robbed. Check it is safe to travel locally.

Baragoi

1° 40′ N, 36° 50′ E
Colour map 2, grid B3

This next settlement on the route up to the lake marks the end of the Elbarta plains, climbing into the mountains. Baragoi is very easy to reach from Maralal, with many hitches and matatus available. It's an awful road in parts, particularly as there are a fair few steep climbs and descents. It takes from three to six hours depending on conditions. About 40 kilometres from Baragoi you will see what almost looks like a lunar landscape of semi-arid mountains and plains. Its a sight well worth a stop before the descent into the plain that takes you to Baragoi.

Baragoi is an important and expanding centre in this wilderness area. The locals jokingly say that the road is the 'International dividing line' between the Samburu and Turkana, and you will notice the design differences in their homesteads – the dome shaped of the Turkana and the flatter wider Samburu manyattas.

The nearby Baragoi secondary school produces an amiable bunch of English speakers, knowledgeable about the area. There are a few general stores here and you should be able to get petrol (sold out of barrels). However, at present there is no electricity or running water in Baragoi.

Sleeping **E** *Morning Star Hotel*, Paraffin lanterns and comfortable beds in clean rooms, shower and toilet separate – beware the latter because they use an ammonia based disinfectant which affects your breathing, this is by far the best place to stay, although a new hotel is planned soon. **Campsite** About 4 kilometres north of town, cross the River Baragoi and take first right, there is water, toilets and Samburu warriors will guard your possessions for US$3 a night.

Eating *Al-Mukaram*, good, cheap, breakfast of Mandaazi, eggs and tea, also good samosas. *Morning Star Hotel*, has an in-house butcher and nyama choma grill (barbecued meat including game). *Wid Wid Inn Hotel*, tasty meals prepared on demand, on main street. *Zaire Hotel*, new restaurant on the Nachola Rd. Recommended meals.

Baragoi

To Campsite & North

Bar Bosnia

Wid Wid Inn Hotel

Al-Mukaram

To Nachola & Zaire Hotel

N

Not to scale

Morning Star Hotel

Tours *Desert Rose Camels*, c/o Geo Safaris, PO Box 2406, Nairobi, T2-884258/59, F2-884445, operate walking and camel safaris through areas of inaccessible beauty.

Transport Regular matatus from Maralal cost about US$6. Irregular lifts to South Horr. Without your own transport, going north to the lake or Marsabit, requires putting the word out (and paying) and waiting, possibly for several days. To and from Isiolo – see Isiolo. To and from Nyahururu. To Nyahururu the first matatu usually leaves around 0300 (making it possible to get to Nairobi by 0900-1000), later matatus start at 0600 and then anytime onwards.

Between Baragoi and South Horr is an incredible lodge **A+** *Desert Rose Lodge* located in a beautiful setting. Excellent for hiking and relaxing in comfortable luxury. Book through Desert Rose Ltd., PO Box 4481, Nairobi, T228936/330130.

South Horr

The nearest village to the southern end of Lake Turkana. The village itself is set in a beautiful canyon and is an oasis of green between two extinct volcanoes (Mount Nyiro and Mount Porale). There is a Catholic Mission here with a nice site for **camping** nearby. There are a few **hotels** offering accommodation and food, though you will need to order your meal well in advance of actually eating it. There is also a **bar** with plenty of atmosphere, though there are only warm drinks. It would appear there is no petrol for sale here. There are some great walks in the mountain forests all around you and you could either hike through (it's a good idea to take a guide) or go on a camel trek (US$5-10 a day for a camel).

Colour map 2, grid B3

Loyangalani

One of the biggest villages on the lake shore, and is a collection of traditional huts, with thatched grass and galvanized iron roofs. The barren lava beds at the southern end of Lake Turkana peter out into the waters of the lake itself. The high salinity and soda mean nothing much grows around the shores.

Colour map 2, grid B3

A+ *Oasis Lodge*, PO Box 34464, Nairobi, T339025, F750035. Bungalows with electricity, it has a beautiful swimming pool and cold beers, non-residents are charged US$9 entrance. **A** *El-Molo Camp*, T02-724384, Nairobi. Well equipped with a swimming pool and a bar, there is also a restaurant which appears to open when you want, camping costs US$3 or there are bandas with full board available, you will need to bring your own fuelwood. **Camping E** Camping at *El-Molo Camp*, you need to supply your own cooking fuel. Bottled water, 1.5 litres, costs US$5. Take purification tablets or boil the water.

Sleeping

The village itself has a post office though no bank and no garage.

Useful services

Road The Loyangalini-North Horr-Marsabit road is virtually untravelled because the road is so terrible. Loyangalani to Baragoi by truck costs around US$8 per person. Trucks travel 1-2 weekly in both directions.

Transport

Marsabit to Moyale

Matthew's Range Off the Isiolo to Marsabit road, is just north of Wamba. This mountain range is thickly forested with its highest point reaching 2,375 metres. The area supports elephants, rhino, buffalo and other species and is in the process of being turned into a national reserve for rhino. There is also a spectacular array of butterflies and some unusual vegetation including cycad plants and giant cedars. There is **camping** nearby on the grounds of a derelict research centre, with no facilities, by a river, a beautiful spot. You are likely to be met by Samburu who will offer to guide you around the range for a small fee. The campsite is not easy to find, so ask for directions as there are tracks going all over the place. You will need to be self-sufficient here, so bring drinking water, food and fuelwood.

Marsabit

Rising to 1,000 metres above the surrounding plains, Marsabit is permanently green. The hills around the town are thickly forested making a nice change to the desert which surrounds the area. The main inhabitants of the town are the Rendille who dress in elaborate beaded necklaces and sport wonderful hair styles. They are nomadic people keeping to their traditional customs of only visiting the town to trade. **Marsabit National Park** is nearby and houses a wide variety of wildlife though it is difficult to see much through the thick forest (see National Parks section, page 264).

There is a bank and post office here, shops, bars, restaurants, hotels and three petrol stations. This is also a major trading centre in the area of livestock and the administrative capital in the district. For the past two years Marsabit has had no running water.

Sleeping
The cheapest place in town is **E** *Al-Jazeera*, communal showers, bar and restaurant. **E** *Bismillah*, not really recommended for its rooms, rather as a place for light snacks at good value. **E** *Kenya Lodge*, good value, there is a good restaurant attached serving Ethiopian style food including *ngera* (pancakes made from fermented batter) and stews. **E** *Marsabit Highway Hotel*, basic, simple hotel.

Camping Available at the Catholic Mission. It is also allowed at the gate of the National Park. However there are no facilities at the NP.

Entertainment
Disco At *Marsabit Highway Hotel* on Friday and Saturday nights. Bar stays open every night until 0200. Also has rooms.

Transport
Air It is possible to charter a plane from Wilson Airport, Nairobi or take one of the small private airlines directly to Marsabit (see Airlines Domestic and Charter, see page 71).

There are 2 petrol stations at Marsabit.

Road Bus: buses run from Isiolo to Marsabit on Tuesday, Thursday and Saturday taking around 6 hours. They return on Wednesday, Friday and Sunday though they may be delayed if there aren't enough passengers. The bus service was suspended temporarily, check locally. The revised service may be more limited. Pickup to see Marsabit National Park costs about US$45 for a half day. Alternatively try to hitch a ride with the water truck to the lodge in the park. All vehicles travelling around Marsabit, Isiolo and Moyale must travel in convoy to minimize the likelihood of being attacked. The journey to Moyale can take up to 9 hours passing through the Dida Galgalu Desert. The roads become virtually impassable when it rains.

Camel Safari In Marsabit it is possible to organize a Camel Safari to Lake Turkana (Loyangalani) costing US$150 per person including food and transport

Marsabit

To North Horr &
L Turkana

To Isiolo & Nairobi

Marsabit Highway
& Disco

Kenya Lodge

Al-Jazeera

Park Gate

To Park HQ

Campsite

Park Gates

N

Not to scale

To Marsabit NP

to North Horr. Trucks to North Horr run about twice weekly, costing around US$12. The safari takes 3 days from North Horr and is rather gruelling but very worthwhile. The landscape is magnificent and you camp under the stars of the desert sky. The tour is organized by 'Duba' who can be contacted at the Kenya Lodge in Marsabit. Duba has run this trip for the past 10 years and is described as very friendly and the best chapati cook in Kenya. Highly recommended by a recent traveller.

Marsabit to Lake Turkana

Maikona is a larger village with shops, but no lodges, though the Catholic Mission here is very friendly and is fairly sure to let you stay (donations gratefully received).

North of Loyangalani you come to **North Horr**. The Catholic Mission here may be able to supply you with petrol (at a price) or lodgings if necessary.

It is possible to strike southwest from North Horr to El Molo Bay on Lake Turkana (see above, page 230).

Moyale

Lies about 250 kilometres north of Marsabit and is on the Kenyan-Ethiopian border. The Kenyan side of the border closes at 1800 hours and the Ethiopian border is closed all day Sunday, as well as on Public and religious holidays. It is possible to cross into Ethiopian Moyale to do some shopping, or even stay overnight, leaving the car behind on the Kenyan side, prior to completing the border formalities. The bus going north to Addis Ababa leaves at around 0500, so it is not possible to leave Moyale by bus on the day of entry. The bus northwards leaves from *Brothers Hotel* courtyard on the Ethiopian side of this border town. This is a small town with a post office, basic shops and a police station which has only recently been supplied with electricity. It is developing slowly and there is now a bank here and two petrol stations. Petrol is much cheaper in Ethiopia than in Kenya.

3° 30′ N, 39° 0 E
Phone code: 0185
Colour map 2, grid B4

Sleeping
D *Medina Hotel*, central but a bit off the main road, clean and friendly hotel, nice balconies, communal showers, no restaurant. **E** *Barissah*, where you can rent a bed for the night in an unlockable room for less than US$2, there are no showers, but you can have a bucket wash. If this is not available, try the **E** *Bismillahi Boarding & Lodging*, which has the same basic level of facilities but is slightly more expensive at US$2.50 per night.

Eating & bars
1 *Barissah Hotel*, has the only bar in town and a simple restaurant. **1** *Somali Restaurant*, good basic food, around the corner from *Medina Hotel*. **Beer** is available at the Police barracks, where the officers are friendly towards visitors.

Transport
Road Bus: buses run from Isiolo to Marsabit and Moyale on Tuesday, Thursday and Saturday taking around 6 hours to Marsabit and a further 6 hours on to Moyale.

It is now possible to cross from here into Ethiopia, and it is reported that procedures are now much easier. In the past, officially only Kenyans and Ethiopians have been able to cross here. In practice a day crossing has been possible – the customs officials have been persuadable. On the Ethiopian side you used to have to go through the same rigmarole and were asked to leave your camera behind.

Northeast Kenya

The most remote part of the country is the northeast, a vast wilderness with almost no signs that humans have ever been here. The attraction is the scale of the place. Endless blue skies and flat landscapes hardly broken by anything, produce a sense of solitude that is hard to experience anywhere else. The landscape is made up of tracts of desert and semi-desert barely broken by settlements and with almost no public transport. Its inaccessibility combined with security problems around the Somali border make this area unappealing to even the most intrepid travellers – no tour companies operate in this region. Physically, the area is very flat with two important rivers flowing through, the Tana River and the Ewaso Nyiro. As you would expect, it is around these waterways that settlement is greatest and the national parks are based. The **Tana River Primate Reserve**, is based near Garsen though it is hard to get to. It was set up to protect the red colobus and crested mangabey monkeys (both endangered species). The other major national park in this region is **Meru National Park** based on the lowland plains east of the town of Meru (see National Parks section, page 268). It is advisable to check on the security situation before visiting the park as there have been some unpleasant incidents between tourists and poachers who have decimated the elephant and rhino population here.

This area has a long-standing bad reputation, though much of it would seem to have more to do with prejudice than justified danger. The majority of people living in this area are Somali and before the creation of country boundaries pastoralists roamed the area freely. In fact in colonial days, the area was known as Somali country. As countries in the region gained independence, Somalis unsuccessfully tried to claim this area as part of Somalia. Shortly after, the area was closed to visitors by the Kenyan authorities who wished to drill for oil. Years of neglect and almost no development leave it one of the poorest areas of the country. These problems have been exacerbated more recently by the civil war in Somalia resulting in a huge influx of refugees into northeast Kenya. There are a number of refugee camps now set up for them (and for Somali-Kenyans who can no longer support their way of life in this barren area). Somalis are blamed for most of the poaching in the region. Poachers pose a real threat to tourists being heavily armed and quite willing to attack if they feel it is justified.

Garissa
0° 25' S, 39° 40' E
Colour map 2, grid B5

This is the town in the northeast that is closest to Nairobi both geographically and culturally. It is on an alternative route back from Lamu to Nairobi. There are shops for provisions, and petrol and a bank. It is the administrative centre for the district. The heat is fierce and there is high humidity making it an unpleasant climate to stay in for long.

Sleeping **D** *Garissa Guest House*, just outside of town. Simple but adequate. **E** *Safari*, clean rooms and running water, there is a restaurant attached with reasonable food.

Transport **Air** There is a flight from Nairobi's Wilson Airport direct to Garissa if there is sufficient demand (see Airlines: Domestic and Charter, page 68). **Road** **Bus**: there are 3 bus routes travelling to and from Garissa. A bus goes from Eastleigh, **Nairobi** to Garissa direct on Monday, Wednesday, Friday and Sunday leaving at 0800. The journey takes about 8 hours. There is a bus from **Lamu** to Garissa leaving at 0700 and taking 8-10 hours. The other route is between Garissa and **Mandera** at the junction of the Kenya, Ethiopia, Somalia border, going on to **Wajir** on Tuesday, Thursday and Saturday and travelling on the next day to Mandera. Returns from Mandera Thursday, Saturday and Monday, to Wajir, and on to Garissa the next day.

Wajir
1° 42' N, 40° 5' E
Colour map 2, grid B5

This is 300 kilometres from Isiolo along the most remote route in the country. The area is a vast scrubland which seems to go on for ever. Due to security problems in this area following the Somali war, this unappealing journey becomes even more difficult. If you are going to try it, check the route has not been closed before setting out.

The town of Wajir itself is growing. The population and atmosphere of the place has more Arab than African influences and is far more interesting to visit than Garissa. The settlement developed around wells which have been fought over by rival clans for generations, water being such a valuable commodity in this area. In 1984, the rivalry between clans became more fierce than usual forcing the regional administration to act. It announced an amnesty for all those who surrendered their arms, but thousands of men and boys of one of the clans, the Degodia, did not avail themselves of this opportunity. They were rounded up to be interned by the government authorities in a military airstrip with no facilities where many died of exposure or dehydration. This tragedy has made the relationship between local people and the administration poor to say the least.

The **market** here is quite different from anything else you are likely to see in Kenya. It consists of a section of grass huts with a wide assortment of produce. Fruit and vegetables are not common, but you will find some beautiful pottery. A visit to the wells just outside of town to the north would also be quite interesting. A popular pastime among Somali men is to chew *miraa*, an appetite suppressant and mild stimulant.

Sleeping D *Nairobi Hotel*, showers, bar and a restaurant, good value. **E** *Malab*, by the bus station. Has a good reputation, provides fans and mosquito nets.

Transport Air There is an airstrip (see Airlines: Domestic and Charter, page 68). **Road Bus**: buses from **Garissa** to Wajir on Tuesday, Thursday and Saturday and travelling on the next day to **Mandera**. Returns from Mandera Thursday, Saturday and Monday, and on to Garissa the next day.

Mandera
3° 55′ N, 41° 53′ E
Colour map 2, grid A5

The furthest point in Kenya, 370 kilometres northeast further on from Wajir, on the Ethiopian, Somali and Kenyan border. The war has made this a particularly foolhardy expedition at the moment with marauding rival Somali clans. The main line of contact is on the private aircraft who fly in shipments of *miraa*. In the past, trade and communication with Somalia was more important than with Kenya as Mandera is far closer to Mogadishu, the capital of Somalia, than to Nairobi.

Until recently Mandera was a fairly small border town servicing the local community. Since the Somali civil war, it has become home to literally tens of thousands of Somalians putting an impossible strain on resources. The lack of water, always a problem, has become critical. Also, the stability of the place is severely tested by the prevailing conditions. *Miraa* is the big business in town.

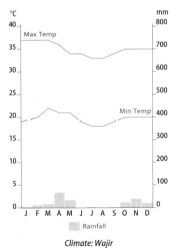

Climate: Wajir

Sleeping D *Mandera County Council Resthouse*, just to east of centre. Fans, showers, own bathrooms. **E** *Jabane*, town centre. Has showers and fans and reasonable restaurant. **E** *Mombasa Inn*, town centre. Simple, basic restaurant.

Transport Air There is an airstrip with several flights a day transporting *miraa* (see Airlines: Domestic and Charter, page 68). A flight costs US$50 to US$100 to Nairobi, depending on demand, and is negotiated with the *miraa* charterer. **Road Bus**: buses from **Wajir** on Wednesday, Friday and Sunday. Return to Wajir Thursday, Saturday and Monday, and on to *Garissa* the next day.

Useful services There is a post office, Police Station and bank.

Nairobi

South to Tanzania

This section looks at Southern Kenya from Nairobi down to the Tanzania border, and southeast to Kenya's coastline on the Indian Ocean. It is one of the most visited regions of the country with four of the country's major game parks. The Masai Mara towards the west of the region bordering onto the Serengeti in Tanzania, is one of the most exciting game parks in the world, teeming with wildlife and the site of the quite spectacular wildebeest migration. It is also the most likely place to see lions in Kenya. The scenery here is wonderful, with Mount Kilimanjaro in the background acting as the perfect backdrop to miles and miles of arid savannah plains covered with fragile grasslands and scrub bush. Tsavo West and Tsavo East on either side of the Mombasa-Nairobi road make up the largest park in the country, and Amboseli National Park is also very popular. All the parks are described in detail in the section on the National Parks, page 251.

There are many points of interest off the Mombasa road leading up from the coast. This road is one of the most important thoroughfares in the East Africa region as it runs the length of the country to Nairobi and then to Uganda, where it continues on to Kampala.

Mombasa Road

NB Ensure you have sufficient fuel for your journey – some petrol stations often run out.

The Mombasa road starts as a continuation of the Uhuru Highway in Nairobi, passing one of the city's drive-in cinemas and a number of housing estates. The first small town is **Athi River**, about 3 kilometres from Nairobi. **C** *Small World Country Club*, PO Box 78 (T239). Open 24 hours and is a lively spot. Also **D** *Congress Club*, with accommodation, a restaurant and discos at the weekends. The turning for **Machakos** is on the left just before the toll station across the Athi River.

Continuing along the road, the route passes through the **Kaputei Plains** with the Ngong Hills in the far distance. Most of this area is large scale cattle ranches with herds of gazelle and antelope. It is along here that you turn right for **Kajiado**. The next section of the route is through semi-arid country broken by the **Ukambani Hills**. The road up this long steep slope is poor, as years of heavy trucks making the laborious climb have dug deep ruts into the road. Just south of the road, by the rail line, is **Kima**, meaning mincemeat in Kiswahili. Kima was so named after a British Railway Police Assistant Superintendent who was eaten by a lion. Charles Ryall, using himself as bait, was trying to ambush a lion which had been attacking railway staff and passengers. Unfortunately the ambush went horribly wrong when he fell asleep on the job.

Further on is the town of **Sultan Hamud**. It sprung up during the making of the railway at Mile 250 where it was visited by the then ruler of Zanzibar and named after him. It has hardly changed since that time and is a pleasant enough place to stop off for a soda and snack.

Just to the southeast lie the alluvial **Masai Plains** and the road for **Amboseli National Park**. To get to Amboseli, you need to take the C102 road south at Emali towards Makutano where there is a cattle market on Friday visited by hundreds of Masai and Akamba herders. The route continues south to Kimana after which there is an access road to Amboseli National Park on the right. After Kimana the road continues south to Oloitokitok on the slopes of Kilimanjaro.

The first coffee growers

Coffee was first planted by John Patterson of the Church of Scotland Mission at Kibwezi, half-way between the coast and Nairobi, in 1891. The Arabica seeds had originally come from Aden and Arabica thrives best at high altitude. Kibwezi was too low for ideal growing conditions, but a crop did mature in 1896, some of which was sold in Europe, the rest used to provide other growers with seed. The French Catholic Street. Austin's Mission at Kitisutu, northeast of Nairobi, was one of the recipients, and set up a nursery to sell seedlings from 1900. Although it takes at least four years for a seedling to produce coffee, coffee growing really took off, so much so that by 1910 over 2,000 bags, each of 120 pounds in weight were harvested.

Back on the Mombasa road, you are now passing through Masai country, which is primarily featureless scrubland. There is a lodge at Kiboko which is about a third of the way through the journey (160 kilometres from Nairobi) and a good place to stop off for some refreshment. **C** *Hunter's Lodge*, PO Box 77, Makindu, T2021, is run by the wife of JA Hunter, a professional hunter with the Game Department. The gardens are quite pleasant with hundreds of species of birds, and there are wonderful views out over the Kiboko River. There is a swimming pool at the lodge though there is rarely any water to go in it.

If you fancy a break in your journey, an excellent place to stay is at **Makindu**, about 40 kilometres from Kiboko where a Sikh temple of the Guru Nanak faith offers free accommodation and food for travellers (offerings gratefully received). This is particularly handy on the return from Mombasa if you do not want to get back in to Nairobi late at night. Slightly further along the road (in the direction of Mombasa) is the *Makindu Handicrafts Co-operative* where around 50 people handcraft carvings for the tourist market, mostly of animals.

The road continues its route passing into more lush pastures with a proliferation of the wonderful and rather grotesque baobabs. The main trading centre at **Kibwezi** has some cheap places to stay including the **E** *Riverside Lodge*. There is no electricity in town as yet. This is the most important region in the country for sisal growing. Honey production is also much in evidence and you are likely to be offered some from sellers at the side of the road. Do try it before you buy to check its quality as sometimes it is adulterated with sugar. From Kibwezi the road passes through heavily cultivated land to the boundary of Akamba country at **Mtito Andei** – meaning vulture forest – about half way between Nairobi and Mombasa. There is a petrol station, a few places to eat and a curio shop. It is also the main gate to Tsavo West (see National Parks, page 279). Places to stay include the **A** *Tsavo Inn*, and the **D** *Okay Safari Lodge*.

From here the road runs through the centre of the parks Tsavo West and Tsavo East for around 80 kilometres. In the past, herds of elephants could be seen crossing the road in the grasslands making progress along this route slow. Now the grasslands are reverting back to thick bush and scrublands as there are so few elephants left (a combination of hunting and drought). On the right you will pass the Mbololo Hills Prison, formerly Manyani Detention Camp where the colonial forces incarcerated Mau-Mau freedom fighters. Today there is a prison industry showroom with hand-crafted furniture and a prison farm shop with a selection of produce.

Voi

The capital of this region, a rapidly developing industrial and commercial centre. This was the first upcountry railhead on the railway where passengers would make an overnight stop. There are a number of bungalows which were built in the early years of the century to accommodate passengers and provide dinner, bed and breakfast, but this is no longer offered as you can dine, sleep and breakfast on the

3° 25' S, 38° 32' E
Phone code: 0147
Colour map 4, grid C5

train. Voi is a good place to look for lodgings if you are visiting Tsavo East as it is not far from the gates and has many excellent cheap places.

Sleeping **C** *Tsavo Park Hotel*. New hotel near the bus station. Very good facilities, price includes breakfast. Recommended. **D** *Jumbo Guest House*, T0147-2059, near the bus station. Has cheap rooms with bath though it can be a bit noisy. **D** *Sagala View*, T0147-2267, 10 minutes from the bus station. Has good rooms. **D** *Voi Restpoint*, T0147-2079. Has 2 restaurants, and cooling fans in the rooms. **D** *Vuria Lodging*, T0147-2269. Fans and mosquito nets in all rooms, and flush toilets. **E** *Distarr Hotel*. Recommended. Very good restaurant, vegetable curry is excellent.

Transport **Train** This is a major stop on the railway, though the train pulls into Voi from Nairobi at around 0300 and from Mombasa at 1200. Please see page 72 for further details. **Road Bus**: there are also buses coming and going all day long between Mombasa and Nairobi. Buses leave to connect Voi with the border town of **Taveta** at 0930 and 1500.

Directory **Banks** *Kenya Commercial Bank*, PO Box 137, T2501/2622. **Hospitals & medical services** *Voi District Hospital*, PO Box 19, T2016 Voi.

Voi to Mombasa From Voi the road runs through the **Taru Desert** for another 150 kilometres down to Mombasa. This area is an arid, scorched wilderness and there is little sign of life. You will see several small quarries. These supply many of the hotels on the coast with natural stone tiles used in bathrooms and patios. The next small settlement is **Mackinnon Road** with the Sayyid Baghali Shah Mosque as its only landmark. 30 kilometres along the route you come to **Samburu** where to the left is a road to the **Shimba Hills**. If you are visiting the National Reserve here you can either camp on the edge of the range about 3 kilometres from the entrance, or stay at the **A+** *Shimba Hills Lodge* (see page 277).

Another 30 kilometres brings you to the busy market centre of **Mariakani**, a place of palm groves and an atmosphere quite different from upcountry Kenya. For the next 90 kilometres the scenery becomes progressively more tropical, the heat increases, as does the humidity and the landscape changes to coconut palms, papaya and other coastal vegetation. Eventually you enter the industrial suburbs of Mombasa.

Machakos

1° 30' S, 37° 15' E
Colour map 4, grid B4

Machakos has a long history as the capital of the Ukambani – the Akamba – who have lived in this part of Kenya for around 500 years. The town is named after Masaku, the Akamba chief who predicted the coming of the railway, the iron snake, and the plagues which followed (both smallpox and rinderpest decimated animal and human populations in the region). He died at the turn of the 20th century.

Machakos was also important in colonial times. John Ainsworth, Britain's first upcountry administrator made his headquarters here in 1889 and built a mudbrick fort, the site of which is on the right of the main road just north of town toward Nairobi. Reverend Stuart Watt and his wife arrived soon after and set up a mission which is now the Kenya Orchards Mua Hills Jam Factory. In 1895 the Church Missionary Society arrived and introduced wheat into the area. The importance of this area to the Imperial British East Africa Company made Machakos the ideal place to set up the first inland African Training Centre.

Little sign of its past remains to be seen except the clock tower which was erected in 1956 to mark a visit from Princess Margaret, sister of the British Queen. The clock no longer works. However, the tree-lined streets and attractive old buildings make it a pleasant town set in the Mua Hills, and the local people (who are predominantly Kamba) are very friendly. The colourful market selling locally grown produce as well as sisal baskets and other handicraft gives the town a bustling atmosphere.

Galla goats

The traditional Masai goat is comparatively small, males weighing up to 35 kilograms, females 30 kilograms. Growth is slow, a yearling seldom weighs more than 20 kilograms, females have a low rate of milk production, and they cease producing young at five or six years old.

Galla goats from northeast Kenya are bigger, produce more milk, grow more quickly, and the females can produce kids up to the age of 10. Most important is the Galla goat's superior ability to withstand drought, and its

rapid rate of recovery in putting on weight, restoring milk yield and starting reproduction when a drought ends. Being taller, they are able to feed on leaves of trees and shrubs that are out of reach of the smaller Masai goats. Galla goats from Isiolo, mostly males, are being introduced to develop both pure bred and cross-bred herds in the area around Kajiado. Some idea of the wealth of Masai goat herders can be gathered from the fact that a female sells at about US$50 and a male at US$75.

The weaving of sisal baskets (*vyondo*) is a major occupation of women in this area. A good place to get one is from the Machakos Handicrafts Centre, a self-help women's group. There is a small shop full of finished and half-finished baskets. The ones without leather straps are far cheaper, but all are considerably better value than in Nairobi and there is more choice.

About 75 kilometres out of Machakos along the road towards Kitui you come across the small village of **Wamanyu** which is the centre of wood carving activities in the country. A great grass rectangle in the centre of the village is surrounded by huts sitting in an ocean of wood shavings accumulated from years of work. Most of the wood carvings end up in Nairobi, but are considerably cheaper if bought here.

Sleeping

D *Kafoca Club*, T0145-21933, near the market. Pleasant, though quite basic, good restaurant. **D** *Machakos Inn*, just outside the town centre. You can also camp here. **D** *Masaku Motel*, T0145-21745, close to town centre. Inexpensive but adequate.

Eating

2 *Ivory Restaurant*, grills and some local dishes.

Transport

There is no shortage of transport between **Nairobi** and Machakos, you can take your pick from buses, matatus or the Peugeot taxis which run from Nairobi's country bus station on Pumwani Rd at the southeast end of River Rd. You should not have to wait more than half an hour for something. There is also transport from **Mombasa**, though not as frequent.

Kitui
1° 17' S, 38° 0' E
Colour map 4, grid B4

Kitui is in the middle of a semi-arid area which is frequently affected by drought causing malnutrition in this poor part of the country. Despite it being so close to Nairobi, it is quite undeveloped, and there is not much here of interest to travellers. Kitui used to be on the trade route of Swahili people in the 19th century, though there are few signs of this now apart from the mango trees planted in the town and the presence of the descendants of the Swahili traders.

Sleeping E *Gold Spot*, just to the east of the market. Own bathrooms. **E** *Kithomboani*, close to the market. Quite adequate.

Transport Road Bus: there are 3 buses a day to and from **Nairobi**, and 1 bus to **Mombasa** leaving at 1900.

Kajiado
1° 53' S, 36° 48' E
Colour map 4, grid B3

Directly south of Nairobi on the road to the Namanga border crossing to Tanzania. It is the administrative headquarters of southern Masai-land at the southern corner of the Kaputei Plains which run between Machakos and Kajiado. The town is in the middle of bleak grasslands which show little sign of the abundance of zebra, wildebeest and giraffe which used to roam here. The town is typically Masai and shows

Kenya

signs of their preoccupation with cattle. Simple accommodation and food and drink are available.

Transport The road to Kajiado forks right off the Mombasa highway just east of the Athi River crossing the Athi Plains. There are plenty of buses and matatus to Kajiado running between Nairobi and Namanga.

Namanga
2° 30' S, 36° 45' E
Colour map 3, grid A4

Namanga, the Kenya border town on the A104, you are advised to take great care when changing money, as there are many scams practiced both here and over the border in Arusha. It is important to have a rough idea of the current exchange rates for Ksh and Tsh. Do not allow yourselves to get separated if travelling by matatu or bus as coercive techniques are sometimes used to rip off the unsuspecting. Namanga is the nearest town to Amboseli National Park, and is a convenient stopover between Arusha and Nairobi.

Sleeping **D** *Namanga River Hotel*, set in beautiful gardens with good bars and restaurants, camping possible. **E** *Namanga Safari Lodge*, beautiful setting, wonderful gardens, excellent bars and restaurants, camping possible. Cheaper guesthouses also available.

Transport **Bus** Namanga-Nairobi takes 2½ hours and costs US$3. The Akamba Bus Company is recommended.

Directory **Tour companies & travel agents** *Kentan Travel Agency*, inquire at the *Namanga River Hotel*, can arrange day trips and longer trips to Amboseli at US$60 per person per day (4 people) and less for larger parties.

Oloitokitok
3° 37' S 30' E
Colour map 4, grid C4

This is a busy Masai town between the parks off the main road that runs from Amboseli in the southeast through to the Kimana Gate of Tsavo West. It is a useful place to stay between the parks, has a busy thriving atmosphere and the best views of any town in the area of Kilimanjaro. It is also a border crossing to the Tanzanian town of Moshi. The town has a bank and a post office, and there are market days on Tuesday and Saturday.

Sleeping As you would expect in a busy market town, there are plenty of cheap and clean lodgings and places to eat and drink. **E** *Mwalimu Lodge* is popular.

Transport **Bus**: there are buses and matatus along the road that links Oloitokitok with **Taveta**, running through Rombo (not marked on some maps), and thence to Voi. Transport is more available on Tuesday and Saturday, the market days. There are matatus and buses, but less frequent, west to **Tsavo** on the Mombasa Rd; east to **Namanga**; north to **Emali** on the Mombasa Rd. A route south runs into **Tanzania**, crossing the border at Kibouni, and on to Moshi. However, it is better to take the road through Kenya to Taveta and cross at Himo.

Taveta

3° 23' S, 37° 37' E
Colour map 4, grid C4

Taveta is a small town on the Tanzanian border next to Tsavo West National Park. It is fairly remote and inaccessible, but electricity was recently brought to the town and a bank has opened. It also has a District Hospital, PO Box 31, T06 Taveta.

Sights The town is near the privately run **Taita Hills Game Sanctuary**, which is actually south of the Taita Hills about 15 kilometres west of Mwatate. The Sanctuary is run by the *Hilton Hotel* chain who have two upmarket lodges here for guests on flying safari visits from the coastal resorts. They are **A+** *Salt Lick Lodge* and **A+** *Taiti Hills Lodge*. The *Salt Lick* costs around US$300 a night, and is noted for its strange design. It is basically a group of huts on stilts which are connected by open-air bridges over a

Grogan: Affairs, Torr's & Gertrude's garden

Shortly after Grogan was released from jail (see box, page 84) – or rather detention in a small bungalow on Ngong Hill with visitors and meals bought in – Grogan left for England with Gertrude, and a fourth daughter was born. He had stood for Parliament as a Conservative in Newcastle under Lyme in 1910, but lost to the Liberal candidate. He now busied himself writing two books on economic issues.

In the First World War Grogan worked in military intelligence. He had become somewhat distanced from Gertrude, and began an affair with a married European nurse of 26 (he was then 44). Her husband died, and she had Grogan's daughter, with Grogan continuing to support them both. He later had another affair with a young married woman who come from Britain to work in farming, and she subsequently bore him a daughter.

In 1928 Grogan financed the building of Torr's Hotel (named after the manager, Joe Torr) on the corner of what is now Kenyatta and Kimathi Avenue. The first floor lounge became the social centre of Nairobi.

Grogan was 65 at the outbreak of the Second World War, but he involved himself in administrative work. After the war Grogan developed his huge sisal estates at Taveta, and built a large house, now known as Grogan's Castle, on Girigan Hill.

Gertrude died in 1943 and Grogan built a children's hospital, Gertrude's Garden (still in use) on the grounds of their Muthaiga home.

In his later years he sold his saw mill, sisal estates and Torr's Hotel (it is now Grindley's Bank). In the last year of his life he left to live in Cape Town, where he died in 1967 at the age of 92. His daughter, Dorothy, was the only relative at his funeral.

number of water holes. The *Taiti Hills* is cheaper, and all rooms have a balcony. The lodge is resplendent with African wooden tables and batiks and rugs. Bookings for either should be made through the Hilton, Nairobi, PO Box 30624, T332564, F339462. The sanctuary is a pleasant place to visit with a good selection of wildlife for most of the year. Unfortunately it is extremely difficult to get to without your own transport as there is no public transport and it is rather off the regular tourist track and therefore not good hitching territory. There is also a tented camp owned by the Hilton chain, alongside the Bura River.

The **Taita Hills** are quite beautiful, densely cultivated and highly populated – in total contrast to the vast empty plains below. The fertile hills have made the Taita-speaking population relatively prosperous compared to other parts of the region. **Wundanyi** is the district capital here and the best accommodation is just outside town at the D *Mwasungia Scenery Guest House*. This is popular with people throughout the hills and consequently has a lively atmosphere and good food. On market days, Tuesday and Friday, it gets particularly busy.

Just outside Wundanyi is the **Cave of Skulls**, where the Taita would put the skulls of their ancestors. Traditionally, people would visit these caves if they needed to contemplate issues that were troubling them. The tradition is dying down as Christianity takes over from older beliefs, though the spot is left undisturbed. It's possible to ask someone from Wundanyi to guide you there.

Lake Chala is just north of Taveta, part of the lake being in Kenya and part being in Tanzania. This deepwater crater lake is about four square kilometres and is totally clear. It is a tranquil, beautiful place to explore by foot with **camping** possible, though you will need to bring all your own supplies. Getting there is not hard as there is a bus once a day from Oloitokitok, or Taveta. It's also safe to swim in.

Grogan's Castle is an extraordinary construction on an isolated hill quite near the main road. It was built by Ewart Grogan as a resort for the sisal estate managers in the area (see box, page 249). It has now fallen into disrepair, but retains spectacular views over Kilimanjaro and Lake Jipe.

Sleeping **B** *Chala*, T0149-2212. On the right hand side of the railway level crossing is the most comfortable hotel in town with a good restaurant and bar, staff will be able to help arrange excursions for you to points of interest in the area.

D *Kuwoka Lodging House*, T0149-228. Clean and pleasant and the best in this price bracket.

Eating The best places to eat in town are **2** *Taveta*, near the bus station, and the **2** *Taveta Border*, which has good fresh samosas, though food in Taveta is quite good on the whole, and relatively varied.

Transport **Train** The 1993 accord between the leaders of Kenya, Tanzania and Uganda includes a resolution to reopen the rail link between **Voi**, through Taveta, on to **Moshi** in Tanzania, and then to Tanga and Dar es Salaam. When the service does start, it will probably be weekly. Please see page 72 for details of train services, timetables and fares.

Road There are irregular matatus going to and from **Voi**, public transport being at its best on market days, Wednesday and Saturday. The road passes south of the Taita Hills past Wundanyi through Tsavo West.

Lake Jipe

Colour map 4, grid C4 Straddles Kenya and Tanzania, fed from streams on the Tanzanian side and from Mount Kilimanjaro. There are a number of small fishing villages around the Kenyan side, and its southeast shores lie inside Tsavo West National Park. Again, this is a peaceful place to stop off where you will be able to see hippos and crocodiles, and plenty of birdlife. You can hire a boat to take you round the lake, but there are some vicious mosquitos in this area, so be warned.

Sleeping **A** *Lake Jipe Safari Lodge*, PO Box 31097, Nairobi, T227623, Tx25508. Provides accommodation in bandas, and arranges trips on the lake. **E Bandas** and **E Camping** are available by the park entrance. The nearest settlement is **Mukwajoni**, a fishing village about 2 kilometres away from Tsavo West National Park. Supplies in the village are limited, except for fish, so bring everything you want from Taveta.

Transport Limited services, basically confined to a few matatus on Taveta's market days on Wednesday and Saturday. Depart Taveta 0600 and 1500 and leaves Jipe at 0730 and 1630.

National Parks and Reserves

Kenya has many national parks and game reserves which are home to a dazzling array of animals, birds, reptiles and plant species. They rate as amongst the best parks in the whole of Africa, and are certainly the most accessible in East Africa. Marine life is also excellent and is preserved in the marine national parks off Malindi and Watamu. Along with the wildlife, some of the parks have been gazetted to preserve the vegetation and unique locations such as Mount Kenya or the Kakamega Forest.

The Kenyan government has long been aware that the principal attraction of the country to tourists is its wildlife, and since 1989 have been keen to ensure it is available in abundance for tourists to see. Richard Leakey was appointed head of the Ministry of Wildlife in 1989 and put in force some drastic methods to reduce poaching. Poaching patrols are well trained and well equipped with Land Rovers and guns and there are extremely stiff penalties for anyone caught poaching. In 1990, 200 US-trained paramilitary personnel were deployed on shoot-to-kill patrols. The battle against poachers is a hard one. It is easy to see why people faced with poverty would resort to an occupation which appears to have such high risks, but also such high rewards (up to US$300 for a kilo of elephant tusk and US$2,000 for rhino horn).

The Kenyan government's policies have been controversial, and it has struggled to strike a balance between the demands of conservation and the needs of local people. Notwithstanding these problems Kenya's wildlife is one of its greatest assets and many of the parks and reserves offer a glimpse of a totally unspoilt, peaceful world.

Most of the game parks have to be explored from inside a vehicle, for safety reasons. The exceptions to this are Hell's Gate, parts of Nakuru and Saiwa Swamp National Park near Kitale.

The following is a guide to most of the parks and reserves, with just a paragraph on the smaller places saying where they are and what you are likely to see in them. For more details on nearby facilities such as transport, food and accommodation please look under the relevant regional section.

General information

A number of different terms are used to describe the parks and reserves of Kenya.

Park classifications

National Parks are wildlife and botanical sanctuaries and form the mainstay of Kenya's tourist industry. They are conservation points for educational and recreational enjoyment.

National Reserves are similar to parks but under certain conditions the land may be used for purposes other than nature conservation. Thus, some controlled agriculture may be allowed; in marine reserves there may be monitored fishing.

Biosphere Reserves were set up in 1989 and are protected environments which contain unique landforms, landscapes and systems of land use. There are four in Kenya, and only 271 in the rest of the world. Specific scientific research projects are attached to them, funded by UNESCO. They are protected under national and international law.

Kenya national parks

Kenya

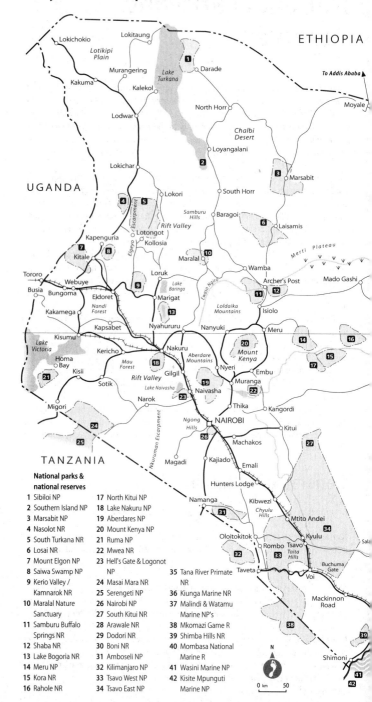

National parks & national reserves

1 Sibiloi NP
2 Southern Island NP
3 Marsabit NP
4 Nasolot NR
5 South Turkana NR
6 Losai NR
7 Mount Elgon NP
8 Saiwa Swamp NP
9 Kerio Valley / Kamnarok NR
10 Maralal Nature Sanctuary
11 Samburu Buffalo Springs NR
12 Shaba NR
13 Lake Bogoria NR
14 Meru NP
15 Kora NR
16 Rahole NR
17 North Kitui NP
18 Lake Nakuru NP
19 Aberdares NP
20 Mount Kenya NP
21 Ruma NP
22 Mwea NR
23 Hell's Gate & Logonot NP
24 Masai Mara NR
25 Serengeti NP
26 Nairobi NP
27 South Kitui NR
28 Arawale NR
29 Dodori NR
30 Boni NR
31 Amboseli NP
32 Kilimanjaro NP
33 Tsavo West NP
34 Tsavo East NP
35 Tana River Primate NR
36 Kiunga Marine NR
37 Malindi & Watamu Marine NP's
38 Mkomazi Game R
39 Shimba Hills NR
40 Mombasa National Marine R
41 Wasini Marine NP
42 Kisite Mpunguti Marine NP

World Heritage Sites are even more strictly protected under international law. Kenya signed the convention in 1989 but as yet no sites have been scheduled. Sites being considered are the Gede ruins, the Koobi Fora fossil beds, Mount Kenya, Hell's Gate and the Masai Mara.

Costs

The Kenyan Park entry fees have been revised from 1 March 1996, when a differential pricing structure was implemented. Environmentally fragile parks with an overload of visitors will now charge more, while those parks with low tourist volume and not threatened with environmental damage, will charge less, to encourage a wider spread of tourists within the National Parks.

Kenya Wildlife Services is also relaunching the annual park pass, allowing multiple entry into all the KWS Parks and Reserves, including any car driven by the pass holder. The only different ones are the Masai Mara and the Samburu-Buffalo Springs-Shaba complex which are administered locally as national reserves and set their own prices.

Remember to include the cost of tipping of the guides, cook and porters in your calculations. **Guidelines**: average tip is one day's salary irrespective of the duration of the trip.

When to visit

You are likely to see more animals during the dry season as they will congregate round water ways. Also, driving during the wet season becomes far harder in deep mud as none of the park roads are paved. However, prices can be up to a third lower in lodges during the rainy seasons.

Where to stay

Accommodation in the parks tends to be of two types, the ultra-expensive lodges or campsites. There is little or nothing in between. If you do not fancy camping and cannot afford the lodges, you may be able to stay in a nearby town and enter your chosen park daily though this is not an option for all parks such as the Masai Mara or Amboseli in the south. If you are on a luxury holiday, accommodation is excellent and there are a number of hotels in each of the major parks offering superb facilities. Camping is possible in designated sites

👉 **Park fees**

	Non-residents US$	Residents KShs
Category A		
Aberdares, Amboseli and Lake Nakuru		
Adults	27	250
Children	10	50
Student & organized groups	10	50
Category B		
Tsavo East and Tsavo West		
Adults	23	200
Children	8	50
Student & organized groups	8	50
Category C		
Nairobi, Shimba Hills and Meru		
Adults	20	150
Children	5	50
Student & organized groups	10	50
Category D		
All other parks		
Adults	15	100
Children	5	50
Student & organized groups	5	50
Mountaineering		
Adults	10	100
Children	5	50
Student & organized groups	5	100
Nairobi Animal Orphanage		
Adults	5	50
Children	2	10
Student & organized groups	2	10
Marine Parks		
Adults	5	100
Children	2	50
Student & organized groups	2	10
Vehicles, boats and aircraft fees		
Aircraft: single landing		
Less than 20 seats		1,000
20 seats or more		2,500
Vehicles: all parks and visitor groups		
Less than 6 seats		200
6-12 seats		500
13-24 seats		1,000
25-44 seats		2,000
45 seats or more		3,000

	Non-residents US$	Residents Kshs
Vehicles: stationed in park		
PSV's seats & commercial		
vehicles tonnes		20,000
PSV's 6-12 seats & commercial		
vehicles 2-5 tonnes		35,000
PSV's 13 seats or more &		
commercial vehicles 5 tonnes		70,000
Delivery vehicles		500
Boats: single entry		
All		200
Stationed in park		10,000
Annual pass for private boats		3,000
Accommodation and services		
Camping		
Adults: public campsites		
Category A, B, C	8	150
Category D	2	50
Adults: special campsites		
Category A	15	200
Category B	12	200
Category C	10	200
Category D	2	50
Children, organized groups		
& students	2	50
Public & special campsites		
(all other Parks)	2	50
Booking fee for special		
campsites per week		5,000
Bandas		
Adults	10	250
Children, organized groups		
& students	5	50
Field study centres		
Non-students	10	250
Students	10	50
Guide service		
Per person per guide per day		500
Per person per guide		
per half day (4 hours)		300
Annual passes (all parks)		
Individual		6,000
Couple		10,000
Children (each under 16)		1,000
Delivery vehicles		6,000

(for obvious reasons it is not wise camping outside these areas in a park full of wild animals). You will need to bring your own tent and other supplies as facilities tend to be extremely limited.

Self-drive This is the most convenient method of getting around the parks offering you greater freedom of movement, though it can be quite expensive. You will usually need to have a four-wheel drive vehicle, but it is not absolutely essential in many parks and outside the rainy season. If you are driving yourself, it is invariably an advantage to hire a local guide – the habits of the animals change, and the guide will know where to find them. Driving at night in the parks is prohibited.

Tours Arranged by many different companies and can be booked in Europe or in Kenya. There are a number of different types ranging from the luxurious to budget (see Tour Agents, page 79).

Kenya

Aberdares National Park

The Aberdares is a range of mountains to the west of Mount Kenya in the central highlands region, and the national park encloses around 715 square kilometres and is one of Kenya's only virgin forest reserves, situated 10 kilometres northwest of Nyeri town, and approximately 165 kilometres from Nairobi. The Aberdares come to a peak at about 4,000 metres and the middle and upper reaches are densely forested with bamboo thickets and tangled jungle. The Kikuyu call these mountains

0° 30' S, 36° 50' E

Aberdares national park

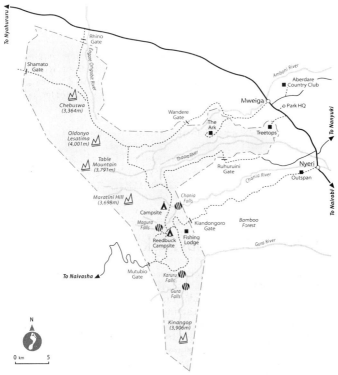

Nyandarua (drying hide) and they were the home to guerilla fighters during the struggle for independence. Nowadays the mountains house leopard, bongo, buffalo and elephant. At about 3,500 metres, where the landscape opens up, you may see lions, several cats and even bushbucks. Wildlife is comparatively scarce, but the views in the park are spectacular. Particularly good walks include hiking up the three peaks, Satima, Kinangop and Kipipiri. You can hire a guide to take you if you wish.

This park is not often visited either by individual travellers or tour companies primarily because of the weather. It rains often and heavily making driving difficult and seeing things impossible. The park is often closed during the wet season as roads turn into mud slides.

Sights The park is split into two sections, the high moorland and peaks and the lower salient which is dense rainforest and where much of the wildlife lives. The salient slopes are closed to casual visitors, you will need to apply for keys to enter this area from the warden. There are a number of spectacular waterfalls in the park including the **Chania Falls** and the **Karuru Giant Falls**.

Park information
See page 254 for costs

As accommodation is expensive and limited at the park, a sensible option is to stay at Nyeri (see page 113) and travel to the park from there by matatu.

A+ *The Ark*, centre of the park. The costs include full board, transfer to the hotel but exclude park entry fees, children under 7 are not allowed. You need to book in advance from *Lonrho Hotels*, Bruce House, Standard St, PO Box 58581, Nairobi, T723776. **A+** *Treetops*, just inside the park entrance. Recently restored, this is more basic than the *Ark*, and has small cabin-type rooms with shared bathroom facilities, there's a roof deck from where you can safely view the animals at night, the original tree-house was actually burnt down in 1955, but it was then very much for the elite, Princess Elizabeth was staying at *Treetops* when she became Queen Elizabeth II on the death of her father. You will need to book in advance from *Block Hotels*, PO Box 40075 Nairobi, T02-540780, F543810. Access to *Treetops* is from the *Outspan Hotel* in Nyeri, you need to arrive for lunch at 1130, the bus leaves for the Park at 1430.

D *Fishing Lodge*, T24 (Mweiga). Offers self-catering accommodation in the high park, there are 2 stone-built cottages each with 3 separate bedrooms of 2, 4 and 6 beds, you book your space with the warden at the front gate of the park, facilities are shared by everyone and include an open-fire for cooking and a communal eating area, you will need to take everything with you except water, including firewood.

Camping There is a site near the fishing lodge though it is extremely basic.

Transport The nearest bases are at Naivasha or Nyeri and it is easy enough to get a matatu to the gates of the park. From **Naivasha** follow the signs along the Upland road until you reach Ndunyu Njeru. From here the road only continues to the park, there are no services (food, petrol etc) from this point onwards. From **Nyeri** there are a number of matatus to the park, or you can rent a car and drive yourself. If you hire a vehicle, you will need a four-wheel drive.

Amboseli National Park

Background
2° 30' S, 37° 30' E

This park has long been one of the most visited in Kenya, and rightly so. It was first established as a natural reserve in 1948 and all 3,260 square kilometres of it was handed to the Masai elders of Kajiado District Council in 1961 to run with an annual grant of £8,500. After years of the destructive effects of cattle grazing and tourists on the area, 392 square kilometres of it were designated as a national park in 1973, after which the Masai were no longer allowed to use the land for grazing.

Decades of tourism have left well-worn trails, and much off-road driving has made the park look increasingly dusty and rather bleak. The late 1980s saw the start of an environmental conservation programme to halt erosion and Amboseli now has the toughest policy on off-road driving. Many new roads are being built which should improve access. The Kenya Wildlife Service has committed US$2mn to a rehabilitation programme, but this may not materialize.

Amboseli is in a semi-arid part of the country and is usually hot and dry. The vegetation is typical of savannah covered with the beautiful acacias which are so much a feature of East Africa. The main wildlife you are likely to see here are herbivores such as buffalo, gazelle, wildebeest, warthog, giraffe and zebra and there are lots of baboons. One of the most spectacular sites is the large herd of elephants here (some 700 live in the park) and you may be able to see the very rare black rhino which has nearly been poached out of existence. There are a few predators: lions, cheetahs, hyenas and jackals.

There have been environmental changes over recent years due to erratic rainfall. Lake Amboseli, which had almost totally dried up, reappeared during 1992/93. The return of water to the Lake flooded large parts of the park including the area around the lodges. Since then, flamingos have returned, and the whole park is far greener.

One of the main attractions of Amboseli is its location, with the stunning back-drop of Kilimanjaro. At dusk or dawn, the cloud cover breaks to reveal the dazzling spectacle of this snow-capped mountain, the highest in Africa.

A Masai community 25 kilometres east of Amboseli National Park has set up **Kimana Wildlife Sanctuary** – the first ever to be owned and run by the Masai. It contains elephants, lions, leopards and other game. Accommodation comprises three tented camps and one tourist lodge. The revenue generated goes to support local schools, dispensaries and reimburse the owners whose livestock has been killed by wild animals, or those who are particularly affected during times of drought.

Eselenkei Conservation Area, 17 kilometres north of Amboseli National Park, has also been established with local communities in mind. This 200 square kilometres area is being developed in a joint venture with a British tour operator *Tropical Places* and the Masai people. It will limit visitors to 60 at any one time. A lodge is being constructed using local labour. Again monies raised from the entrance fees and rent are paid to the Masai. Profits will be used for education and agricultural support.

Sights Near the park is the town of **Isinya** where you will find the *Masai Leatherworking and Handicrafts Centre*. Good buys are the handmade shoes and big leather bags. You will also be able to find some unusual Masai crafts such as marriage necklaces or beaded keyrings.

Amboseli National Park

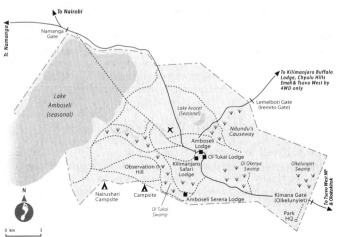

Best time to visit Best time to visit is just after the long rains in April-May as this is when the park is lush and green and you should be able to see more wildlife.

Park information
Please see page 254

Sleeping **A+** *Amboseli Lodge*, bookings through *Kilimanjaro Safari Club*, PO Box 30139, Nairobi, T227136, F219982. Good accommodation with pleasant gardens and a swimming pool, offers spectacular views out towards Kilimanjaro, but can get crowded. **A+** *Amboseli Serena Lodge*, bookings through *Serena Lodgings and Hotels*, PO Box 48690, Nairobi, T710511/2, F718100/2/3, E serenamk@africaonline.co.ke. A very attractive design, drawing on elements of Masai traditional dwellings, blending into the landscape, you can even get a lecture on Masai customs, or watch traditional dancers in the evening, quite the nicest place to stay but costly, it is near the Enkongo Narok Swamp which means there is always plenty of wildlife to see. **A+** *Kilimanjaro Safari Lodge*, bookings through *Kilimanjaro Safari Club*, PO Box 30139, Nairobi, T227136, F219982. Pleasant setting with white thatched cottages, good views of Mount Kilimanjaro. **B** *Ol Tukai Lodge*, located near the *Amboseli Serena Lodge*, these bandas were renovated in 1992 and are equipped with electricity, they occupy one of the finest viewing points in the park and are good value. Run by Block Hotels, PO Box 40075 Nairobi, T02-540780, F543810.

Camping There are 2 campsites in the Park with electric fences encircling them. Wonderful setting, be prepared to be visited by a selection of Masai from the local village trying to sell you artefacts. Facilities are basic, with a hole-in-the-ground toilet and a kiosk selling unrefrigerated drinks. The water supply is unreliable, so bring some with you. Alternatively, it is possible to stay in the border town of Namanga and visit Amboseli National Park as a day trip (see page 256, Namanga).

Eating If you intend to go camping or use the bandas, you will need to bring your own supplies of most things, though there is a kiosk at the campsite selling drinks. The lodges do allow non-residents to use their facilities and the *Amboseli Safari Lodge* is a nice place to stop off for a cold drink towards the end of the day.

Transport Air There is a daily flight from the private aerodrome at Wilson Airport to Amboseli on Air Kenya Aviation. It costs US$50 one way and leaves Nairobi at 0730 am and Amboseli at 0830. The journey takes 45 minutes.

Road The most common route is to drive from Nairobi along the A104 to Namanga (165 kilometres south), which is the border post between Kenya and Tanzania. The road is in good condition and there is a fuel stop here as well as a couple of shops selling Masai crafts. The prices are high but negotiable. From here to the park is 75 kilometres down an appalling road and there are no more petrol stations. The whole journey from Nairobi to Amboseli takes about 4 hours. If travelling by public transport, there is a bus from Nairobi bus station to Namanga. From there on in you will have to hitch. Alternatively, it is possible to get to the northern and eastern gates by driving down the A109 Nairobi/Mombasa road. Take the turning south at Emali to Makutamo. From there take the road southwest for the Lemeiboti/Iremito Gate. Alternatively, drive further south past the town of Kimana until you reach the C103 on the right. This is the road that traverses Amboseli National Park.

Arawale National Reserve

1° S, 40° E   North of Malindi, the Reserve is in Northeastern Province and is the only area in Kenya where Hunter's hartebeest can be found with their lyre-shaped horns. The thorny bushland also has zebra, elephant, lesser kudu, buffalo, hippo and crocodiles. There are no tourist facilities and as there is no gate into the reserve, there is no charge to visit.

Bisanadi National Reserve

This is adjacent to the northeast boundary of Meru National Park and is about 600 square kilometres. The area is mainly thorny bushland and thicket merging into wooded grasslands with dense riverine forests of raffia palm along the watercourses. You are likely to see the same sort of wildlife as in Meru National Park as it acts as a dispersal area during the rains. It is a particularly good place to find elephant and buffalo in the wet season.

0° 10' N, 38° 30' E

The reserve forms part of a chain of parks running from Meru northeast to Kora in the east. Kora is bounded by North Kitui National Reserve to the south and by Rahole National Reserve to the northeast. There are no facilities for visitors.

Boni National Reserve

This is one of the large, remote parks in the northeast of the country along the coast in Northeastern province. It is 1,340 square kilometres, the only coastal lowland groundwater forest in Kenya and has large concentrations of elephant and Harvey's and Ader's duiker in the dry season. It borders onto the better served Kiunga Marine National Reserve. No facilities for tourists.

1° S 41°, 30' E

Dodori National Reserve

The Dodori National Reserve is in Coastal Province and is 877 square kilometres extending from northeast Lamu District up to the Somali border. The vegetation consists of mangrove swamp, lowland dry forest, marshy glades and groundwater forest and is bisected by the Dodori River. It is a major breeding ground for topi and there are also elephant and lesser kudu. There are also substantial numbers of dugong and green turtle. Pelicans are particularly common birds here. There is **E** camping for visitors but it is essential to check with the police before choosing to stay as the park is often refuge to armed bandits or desperate Somali refugees.

1° 50' S, 41° E

Lake Naivasha & Hell's Gate

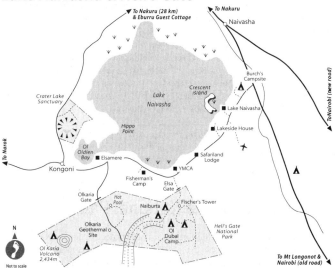

Hell's Gate National Park

0° 50' S, 36° 20' E This is to the south of Lake Naivasha in the Rift Valley and is one of the few parks you are allowed to explore on foot. Access is south of the YMCA at Lake Naivasha, through Elsa Gate and Olkaria Gate, south of Elsamere. The walk through the park is spectacular leading through a gorge lined with sheer red cliffs. There are many hot springs. The park is small, only 68 square kilometres and despite there being a wide variety of wildlife, including eland, giraffe, zebra, impala and gazelle, you may not see many of them as they are few in number. What you will see, though is the incredibly tame hyrax which looks like a type of guinea pig but is actually more closely related to the elephant, and a host of different birds of prey. Within the Park is a substantial geothermal project generating power from underground – lots of large pipes and impressive steam vents in the hills.

There are now several campsites within the National Park (see map) in addition to the campsite up the road by Lake Naivasha (see page 132) which also has bandas and is set in a beautiful shady garden.

Kakamega Forest National Reserve

0° 10' N, 35° 15' E This forest is only 45 square kilometres and is the eastern most corner of the Congo-West African equatorial rainforest. It lies about 17 kilometres north of Kakamega town on the Kisumu-Kitale road. It is extraordinarily beautiful with at least 125 species of trees. There are a number of animals which are found in no other part of the country, including the bush-tailed porcupine, giant water shrew, and hammer-headed fruit bat. There are also several primates including the colobus and blue monkey. For a small fee a guide will take you round the forest and this is well worth it as they are very knowledgeable about the forest flora and fauna. Look out for the Gabon viper, a particularly nasty snake which lives in the forest. The forest is also home to the hairy-tailed flying squirrel which can 'fly' as far as 90 metres. Camping and guides are both very cheap and the guides are very knowledgeable.

It is advisable to wear waterproofs if you plan to visit, as the rain is heavy and regular. But it is beautiful walking country.

Park information **Sleeping E** *Forest Rest House*, PO Box 88 Kakamega. Located within the forest reserve, it is small, having only 4 bedrooms, all with their own bathrooms, you will need to take your own food, but it is clean and friendly, advisable to book at weekends and during school holidays (Christmas, Easter and July-August) through: the Forester, PO Box 88. However you will need to bring your own food supplies from town although nearby there is a very small shop/restaurant where you can eat. In the National Reserve, there is a campsite and some furnished bandas, but with no food. The only other alternative to the *Rest House* is the **A** *Rondo Retreat Centre*, a religious centre only recently opened up to the public, a serene location. Book through Nairobi, PO Box 14369, or T0331-20145 on Thursday.

Transport Road Take the Kisumu road south of Kakamega for about 10 kilometres and turn left at Mukumu. Carry on down this road for about 7 kilometres when you will reach the village of Shinyalu where the forest is signposted. Take a right and after about another 5 kilometres you will reach the forest reserve.

Kiunga Biosphere National Park

1° 50' S, 41° 30' E Is 250 square kilometres from the northeast coastal border of mainland Kenya to the Paté Islands in the Indian Ocean in the district of Lamu. The coastal area is made up of scrublands and mangroves surrounded by microscopic marine plants and dugong grass. The vegetation is home to both the dugong and green turtle and a wide selection of reef fish. The coral here is extensive. As you would expect, there is a good variety of marine birds with colonies of various gulls and terns. The whole area contains more than 50 offshore islands, some of which house lesser kudu, bushbuck, monkeys, porcupines and wild pig. Poaching of the turtles and their eggs has been greatly reduced thanks to the efforts of the game wardens of Lamu.

There are a number of facilities for visitors despite the fact that this is one of the least developed of Kenya's marine reserves. There is swimming, sailing, water-skiing and diving here.

See under Lamu section, page 168. There are also some simple places to stay in **Park** Kiunga, the administrative centre of this area about 12 kilometres from the border **information** with Somalia, a village unspoilt by tourism.

Kenya

Kora National Reserve

On one of Kenya's most important waterways, the Tana River, the Reserve is 125 *0° 10′ S, 38° 45′ E* kilometres east of Mount Kenya in Coastal Province and covers 1,787 square kilometres. The land is mostly acacia bushland with riverine forests of doum palm and Tana River poplar. There is a wide variety of animal species here including elephant, black rhino, hippo, lion, leopard, cheetah, serval, caracal, wildcat, genet, spotted and striped hyena, and several types of antelope. The rivers hold lizards, snakes, tortoise and crocodiles. This area has had serious problems with poachers in recent years. George Adamson and two of his assistants were murdered here in 1989 by poachers. There are no tourist facilities.

Lake Bogoria National Reserve

This reserve is in the Rift Valley near Baringo, 80 kilometres north of Nakuru, size *0° 10′ N, 36° 10′ E* 107 square kilometres. This soda lake is shallow, up to two metres depth, and was formerly called Lake Hannington. It is mainly bushland with small patches of riverine forest. The shoreline of the lake is surrounded by grasslands where there are a number of greater kudu. The main reason people visit Lake Bogoria is to see the thermal areas with steam jets and geysers and the large number of flamingoes which live here.

This is the least-visited of all Kenya's Rift lakes, but it can conveniently be included in a visit to Lake Baringo and the Kerio Valley, all of which are in this extremely hot area of the Rift Valley. The Lake itself lies at the foot of the Laikipia Escarpment and its bottle-green waters reflect woodlands to the east.

Motorbikes are allowed into the park and the road is paved up to the hot springs, after which the road becomes very rough. It is not possible to drive all around the lake as the road is closed on the east side between just north of Fir Tree Camp to just east of Loboi Gate. Camping is allowed at the lakeshore but it is necessary to bring all food and drinking water with you. **Lake Baringo** is north of Lake Bogoria and houses schools of hippo and crocodile. However its greatest attraction are the numbers and varieties of birds. Over 400 species have been identified. On Gibraltar Island there is a very large colony of the Goliath heron.

Sleeping **A+** *Island Camp*, T2261, based on Ol Kokwe Island at the centre of Lake Baringo. **Park** This is some experience, even if only for a day-trip, there is a swimming pool at the highest **information** point of the camp, all tents have own bathroom with flush toilet and shower, as well as a shaded veranda, activities on offer include water-skiing and windsurfing (US$45 per hour). **A** *Lake Baringo Club*, T2259. Noted for its colourful gardens, it also has a swimming pool and serves good food, non-residents are welcome to use facilities on payment of a small fee, a resident ornithologist can accompany you on bird walks. **A** *Lake Bogoria Lodge*, recently been built inside the reserve near its northern entrance, which has a swimming pool, charge for use by non-residents. There is also accommodation at nearby Nakuru (see page 136).

Camping **E** *Fig Tree Campsite*, on the southern shore is pleasant and quite quiet, there is a freshwater stream running through the campsite which is just big enough to get into, baboons can be a problem. **E** *Acacia Tree* and **E** *Riverside* are both on the western shore, no facilities, so you need to bring all equipment, supplies and water.

Transport Road It is an easy drive from **Nakuru** taking less than an hour along the Baringo road. There are 2 entrances: at the southern end Mogotio Gate, which has some difficult roads; at the northern end there is better access via Loboi Gate. Motorcycles are allowed in this park.

Kenya

Lakes Baringo & Bogoria

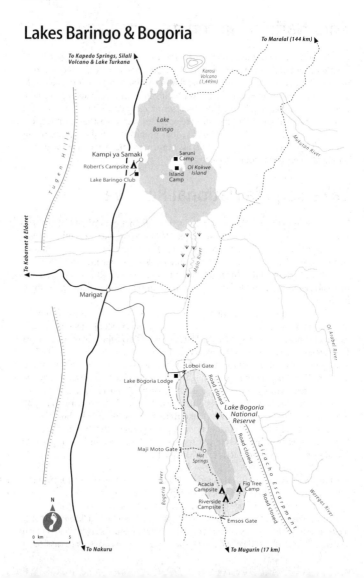

Lake Nakuru National Park

The park is just 3 kilometres south of Nakuru town in central Kenya, 140 kilometres northwest of Nairobi. It was established in 1960 as the first bird sanctuary in Africa. It is about 199 square kilometres and the lakes are fringed by swamps surrounded by dry savannah. The upper areas are forested. There is no entry by foot. There is a wide variety of wildlife: bats, colobus, spring hare, otter, rock hyrax, hippo, waterbuck, leopard, hyena, and giraffe but the most popular reason for visiting is the wonderful sight of hundreds of thousands of flamingoes. At one time there were thought to be around two million flamingoes here, about one third of the world's entire population, but the numbers have diminished in recent years. The best viewing point is from the Baboon Cliffs on the western shores of the lake. There are also more than 450 other species of birds here. The park has also established a special rhino sanctuary and contains 35 Black rhino and 10 White rhino in an enclosure, secured by electric fencing from poachers.

0° 30' S, 36° E

Kenya

Sleeping **A** *Lake Nakuru Lodge*, PO Box 70559, Nairobi, T224998, Tx22658, access from Ndarit Gate. Banda accommodation, swimming pool, good views of the lake. **A** *Sarova Lion Hill*, PO Box 30680, close to eastern shore of lake, T333248, F211472 (Nairobi), access from Lanet Gate. Each room has private bathroom and verandah, swimming pool, sauna and boutique, good views, popular with group tours. **E** *Florida Day and Night Club*, close to Main Gate, just beyond the outskirts of Nakuru. Basic but cheerful.

Park information
There is accommodation at nearby Nakuru (see page 136)

Lake Nakuru National Park

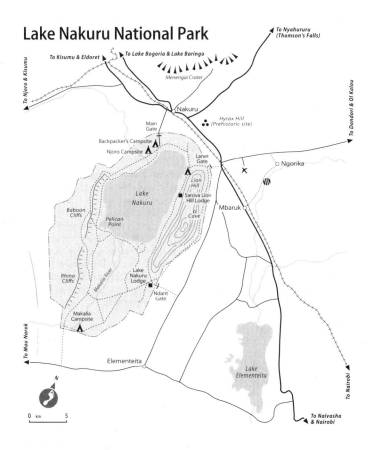

Camping This is available at **E** *Backpackers's Campsite*, just inside the Main Gate. **E** *Njoro Campsite*, about 1 kilometre into the park on the northwest side of the lake. **E** *Makalia Campsite*, by the southern boundary of the park and close to the waterfall. You will need a vehicle for these last 2 campsites. There are 2 other campsites by the northeast entrance, *Kampi ya Nyati* (Buffalo) and *Kampi ya Nyuki* (Bee). Both lead down to quiet viewpoints on the lakeshore.

Transport This is one of the easiest parks to visit being just outside Nakuru. You will need to be in a vehicle though you are allowed to get out at the lakeside.

Losai National Reserve

1° 30' N, 37° 30' E This is 1,800 square kilometres of thorny bushland situated in the Losai Mountains southwest of Marsabit National Reserve and about 175 kilometres north of Mount Kenya, in northern Kenya. The Reserve is a lava plateau with scattered volcanic plugs. No tourism is allowed at the moment as the area is trying to rehabilitate its elephant and black rhino populations which have been decimated by poachers. It is also unlikely tourism will develop for some time to come as it is virtually impenetrable even with four-wheel drive.

Malindi Biosphere Reserve

3° 12' N, 40° 15' E This strip along the coast is 30 kilometres long and five kilometres wide and includes Mida Creek. It lies about 80 kilometres north of Mombasa, around the Malindi and the Watamu Marine area, and includes the Watamu Marine National Reserve and National Park. The vegetation includes mangrove, palms, marine plants and various forms of algae which are home to various crabs, corals, molluscs, cowrie and marine worms. Coral viewing is popular here, as are boat trips and watersports. Whale Island is a nesting ground for roseate and bridled tern, and there are a number of other shore birds here.

Marsabit National Reserve

2° 45' N, 37° 45' Marsabit National Reserve is in Eastern Province 560 kilometres north of Nairobi in the district of Marsabit. The national reserve covers 2088 square kilometres and Mount Marsabit is undoubtedly the most attractive of North Kenya's extinct volcanic mountains. Its altitudes stretch from 420 metres where thorny bushland dominates the scenery to 1,700 metres above sea level. The upper reaches are covered in forest which merge into acacia grasslands. A number of birds and animals live here including 52 different types of birds of prey. You are likely to see elephants, greater kudu, various species of monkeys, baboons, hyena, aardwolf, caracal, cheetah, lion, gazelle, oryx and reticulated giraffe. A special feature of this area is the volcanic craters, several of which contain freshwater lakes. **Sokorte Guda Lake** is a wonderful spot to observe elephant and buffalo in the late afternoon, when they congregate for water.

Park information **Sleeping** There is alternative accommodation in nearby Marsabit (see page 240). **B** *Marsabit Lodge*, PO Box 45, Marsabit, T2044, bookings: Msafari Inns PO Box 42013, Nairobi, T330820, F227815. Excellent location overlooking a waterhole.

Camping Camping site (**E**) near the main gate.

Transport See under Marsabit, page 240.

Naipaul and Theroux I – Literary Lions

Paul Theroux was born in April 1941 in New England in the USA and attended university there before going to Malawi as a Peace Corp teacher. On finishing his assignment he travelled in west Africa and met a Nigerian girl, Yomo, who joined him when he got a job teaching English at Makerere University in Uganda.

VS Naipaul was born in 1933 in Trinidad. He won a scholarship to study English at Oxford. After graduating he settled down to the business of becoming a writer and making ends meet by doing bits of journalism and reviewing books. By 1965 he had published six novels, three of which had won prizes.

Theroux had never heard of Naipaul, but he lost no time in reading all his books when it was announced that the writer was to spend a year at Makerere with his English wife, Pat, funded by a US foundation. Naipaul was flattered by Theroux's knowledge of his writing – he would quote bits of A House for Mr Biswas. Until he could arrange to get a car, Naipaul asked Theroux to drive him around the main places of interest. They exercised together, Theroux running round the athletics track while Naipaul turned his arm over at the cricket nets, they took cucumber sandwiches and chocolate cake in a local teashop. From time to time he gave Theroux constructive criticism on his writing

Naipaul was an awkward cuss. It was clear he didn't much relish the idea of a year in Uganda – but he'd taken the award as his books hadn't realised much to live on, and he needed a spell away from hack work to finish the novel he had under way. He exercised his irritation at his situation by being withering about his colleagues at the University, referring to them as inferiors (or 'infies'). He didn't want to meet students, give lectures or contribute to seminars. Asked to judge a literary competition he insisted that the standard was so low that the best entry should only be given Third Prize. He was preoccupied with the idea that civilisation in Uganda was only a veneer and a collapse was inevitable. He never missed an opportunity to warn any fellow Asians he met of their impending plight. Yomo had gone back to Nigeria when it was apparent that she was already pregnant when she had joined Theroux in Kampala. They visited bars including the celebrated Gardenia in Bat Valley. Naipaul volunteered that at one stage he had been a great prostitute man – despite finding the episodes depressing and hating himself afterwards. Theroux argued that it was different in Africa – he has written engagingly about his casual liaisons with local girls – but Naipaul would have none of it. He announced he had given up sex.

The two spent some time together in Kenya (see box, page 158) and took a trip to Rwanda. After Naipaul left in 1966, Theroux visited him at Christmas in Stockwell, south of the river in London. He was introduced to Naipaul's literary friends, including his younger brother, Shiva, also a writer. Theroux returned to Uganda to finish his contract. They corresponded. Theroux married an English teacher he met in Kenya He took a job in Singapore for three years. In 1971 Theroux came to England and lived in a small house in Dorset. Although he'd had a novel published and another accepted, he struggled to make a living as a writer until he wrote a successful travel book, The Great Railway Bazaar.

Both authors travelled extensively, and the friendship continued. Naipaul was knighted in 1991. Pat Naipaul died in 1996 and he married Nadia Aliri, the little girl he'd first encountered in the Nairobi Street in 1966. Soon after, Naipaul stopped replying to Theroux's letters. They met by chance in a London street, and Naipaul indicated that the friendship was over. Theroux gives a highly readable account of his association with Naipaul in his 1988 book, Sir Vidia's Shadow.

Masai Mara Game Reserve

Background
0° 20' S, 35° E

The Masai Mara National Reserve covers some 1,672 square kilometres at between 1,500 and 2,100 metres above sea level. It is about 275 kilometres west of Nairobi. It is an extension of Tanzania's Serengeti National Park, a small part of the Serengeti ecosystem covering some 40,000 square kilometres between the Rift Valley and Lake Victoria. It is the most popular of Kenya's parks, with good reason. Almost every species of animal you can think of in relation to East Africa live on the well-watered plains in this remote part of the country. One of the most memorable and spectacular sites is the migration of hundreds of thousands of wildebeest, gazelle and zebra as they move from the Serengeti Plains in January on their way northwards arriving in the Masai Mara by about July-August as the dry weather sets in. They begin to return south in October. The main access to the Mara Reserve is through Narok town, the last stop for buying food, water and petrol.

The Masai Mara is not a national park but a game reserve, the difference being that people (the Masai) have the right to graze on the land and shoot animals if they are attacked.

The landscape is mainly gently rolling grassland with rainfall in the north being double that of the south. The Mara River runs from north to south through the park and then turns westwards to Lake Victoria. Most of the plains are covered in a type of red-oat grass with acacias and thorn trees.

The reserve is teeming with herbivores – numbering around two and a half million including: wildebeest, gazelle, zebra, buffalo, impala, topi, hartebeest, giraffe, eland, elephant, dik-dik, klipspringer, steinbok, hippo, rhino, warthog, bushpig. There is also a large number of lion, leopard, cheetah, hyena, wild dog, jackal as well as smaller mammals and reptiles. The number of animals suited to grasslands living in this area has increased enormously over the last 30 years due to woodland being cleared.

Masai Mara National Reserve

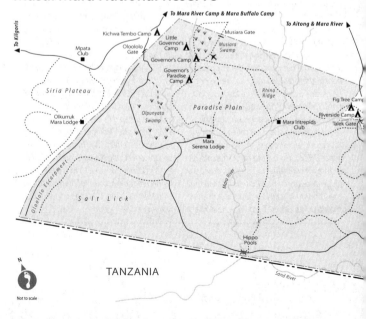

The Oloololo Escarpment on the western edge of the park is the best place to see the animals here, though it is also the hardest part to get around, particularly after heavy rain, when the swampy ground becomes impassable.

The accommodation in the Reserve is superb, and a stay in one of the high standard tented camps, with perhaps a dawn hot-air balloon safari (around US$300), is an unforgettable experience. It is advisable to book in advance if you don't want to be disappointed. Tented camps often include game drives in the price.

Sights

Just outside the Oloolaimutia Gate there is a Masai village, open to the public, which you can wander round taking as many photographs as you wish for US$7 per person.

Park information

Sleeping Lodges A+ *Mara Serena Lodge*, T710511/2, F718100/2/3 (Nairobi), E serenamk@africaonline.co.ke . Well designed, wildlife films, Masai dancing, balloon safaris, superb view over the Mara River. **A+** *Mara Sopa Lodge*, PO Box 72630, Nairobi, T336724/336088, F223843, mara@sopalodges.com. Strategically located near to Oloolaimutia Gate this 100 rooms lodge is one of the most popular lodges in this wildlife profuse area of the Masai Mara Reserve. Rondavel rooms with balconies and verandahs, grand African-style public areas, fine food and friendly staff, excellent swimming pool, conference rooms, balloon safaris and night game drives. **A+** *Rekero Farm*, outside Reserve to northwest, in Masai Mara Conservation Area, PO Box 56923, Nairobi, T506139, F502739. Expensive – only 4 guests in total, personally conducted safari walks available. **A** *Keekorok*, PO Box 40075, Nairobi, T02-540780, F02-543810. Oldest lodge, set in a grassy plain, swimming pool, wildlife and local culture lectures, shop, will arrange game drives, and dawn hot-air balloon trips. **A** *Olkurruk Mara Lodge*, outside Reserve, near Oloololo Gate, PO Box 30471, Nairobi, T336858, F218109. Good views from elevated site, small in comparison to other lodges, but friendly. **B** *Bush Tops*, outside reserve, nearest to Sekanini Gate, PO Box 44191, Nairobi, T882408. Fairly simple, but quite comfortable, can accommodate 20 guests, uses solar power.

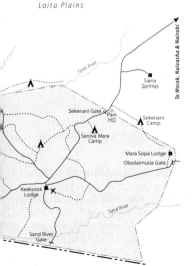

Loita Plains

To Narok, Naivasha & Nairobi

Talek River

Siana Springs

Sekenani Gate
Park HQ
Sekenani Camp

Serova Mara Camp

Mara Sopa Lodge
Oloolaimutia Gate

Keekorok Lodge

Sand River

Sand River Gate

Tented camps There are 4 'Governors' Camps', each with its own character. They are unfenced, but patrolled by Masai guards just in case the animals get too curious. All tents have private bathrooms with flush toilets and showers. You can even arrange a champagne breakfast! **A+** *Governors' Camp*, in area to north of park, accessed from Musiara Gate, PO Box 48217, Nairobi, T331871, F726427. Solid floors for tents, bar lounge, candlelit dinners, small museum, balloon safaris, no swimming pool, beautiful site by the Mara River. **A+** *Governors' Paradise Camp*, in area to north of park, accessed from Musiara Gate, PO Box 48217, Nairobi, T331871, F726427, located in bush along Mara River. Tents not on permanent floors, high standards. **A+** *Governors' Private Camp*, in area to north of park, accessed from Musiara Gate, PO Box 48217, Nairobi, T331871, F726427. Site can be booked for exclusive use, up to 16 people, minimum of 3 nights. **A+** *Little Governors' Camp*, in area to north of park, accessed from Musiara Gate, PO Box 48217, Nairobi, T331871, F726427. Solid floors for tents, access by boat ferry, pulled across the Mara River, really something special, on a splendid site, very high standards. **A+** *Mara Intrepids Club*, by the Talek River, PO Box 74888, Nairobi, T338084, F217278. Balloon safaris, swimming pool, shop, high standards. **A+** *Sekenani Camp*, close to Sekenani Gate, PO Box 61542, Nairobi, T333285, F228875. A place of much charm, with high standard tented accommodation with polished wooden floors, grand baths, hurricane lamps, quite excellent food, small camp, intimate and luxurious. **A** *Diners Tented Camp*, PO Box 46466, Nairobi, northeast corner, access from Olemutiak Gate, T333301, F224539. A touch more spartan than some of the other tented camps, excellent food. **A** *Fig Tree Camp*, PO Box 40683, Nairobi, T221439, F332170, just outside Reserve close to Talek Gate. Quite large, and also has some timber cabins with electricity, swimming pool, shop, balloon safaris. **A** *Kichwa Tembo Camp*, PO Box 74957, Nairobi, T219784, F217498, at the base of the Oloololo Escarpment by the Oloololo Gate. Does have some banda accommodation as well, balloon safaris, nature walks, visits to Masai village, swimming Pool. **A** *Mara River Camp*, PO Box 48019, Nairobi, outside the reserve, beside river, in pleasant site, T335935, F216528. Specialist ornithologist for tours, game drive, no swimming pool so cheaper than the others. **A** *Sarova Mara Camp*, PO Box 30680, Nairobi, near the Sekenani Gate, T333248, F211472. Good accommodation, beautiful views, swimming pool, large site, with 75 tents, so rather impersonal. **A** *Siana Springs* (formerly *Cottars' Camp*), PO Box 74957, Nairobi, just outside the Reserve, T219784, F217498. Unspoilt site, the tents are set out in 3 clusters: Acacia, Palm and Bamboo, but they are well spread out, specialist naturalist for walks and lectures, swimming pool. **A** *Talek River Camp*, inside the reserve, by the river, PO Box 74888, Nairobi, T338084, F217278. Sound facilities (but no pool), good value.

Camping The only option for budget travellers. You can camp outside any of the **E** *Park Gates*, (there are 5) for a small fee. The best of these locations are **E** *Sand River Gate*, with lavatories, water and a shop. Also **E** *Musiara Gate*, there are no facilities but you should be able to get water from the wardens. The most lively place to stay is the Masai-run **E** *Oloolaimutia Campsite* at the western side of the park where budget safari outfits usually stay. Water here is limited and you will have to buy it if you need it. The nearby *Mara Sopa Lodge* serves food and drink (warm beers) and has a lively atmosphere. There are camping facilities near **E** *Keekorok Lodge* and a place to buy food and drink. This is the only offical campsite in the reserve. **E** *National Park Campsites*, without any facilities are at 3 locations outside the Reserve beside the Mara River north of Mara River Camp. There are also **E** *Talek River Campsites*, close to the Talek Gate, at 12 locations.

Transport Air Flights leave twice-daily from Wilson Airport in Nairobi and take 45 minutes. They leave Nairobi at 1000 and 1500 and from the Masai Mara at 1100 and 1600. The fare is US$72 one-way.

Road The journey to the Masai Mara is fascinating in itself, crossing through the Rift Valley over dry range lands. The two major routes to the park are from Narok which is a small town to the west of Nairobi. From here to the park is 100 kilometres along unsurfaced roads. The other way is from Kisii, the road to the park being OK. Opportunities for hitching are very limited, you will really need transport to explore this park properly.

Meru National Park

0° 2' N, 38° 40' E Meru National Park is northeast of Mount Kenya and lies 85 kilometres east of Meru town on the north eastern lowlands below the Nyambene Hills. It is approximately 370 kilometres northeast of Nairobi. It straddles the Equator and has a road system of over 600 kilometres, which aids game viewing safaris. The late Joy Adamson hand reared the orphaned lioness Elsa here, later releasing her into the wild. It is mainly covered with thorny bushland and wooded grasslands to the west. Dense riverine forests grow along the watercourses surrounded by the prehistoric-looking doum palms. There are hundreds of species of birds including the Somali ostrich and animals include lion, leopard, cheetah, elephant, zebra, black rhino, giraffe, hippo, oryx, hartebeest and Grant's gazelle. There are few tourist package tours to this park making it one of the least trampled and unspoiled parks.

Sleeping **A** *Meru Mulika Lodge*, booking: Msafiri Inns, PO Box 42013, Nairobi, T330820, F1227815. Pool and a lovely terrace from which you can watch elephants, oryx and other animals at the Mulika Swamp, the Lodge has become somewhat rundown due to lack of custom, the food is not particularly good and the rooms are quite shabby, you may even be asked for petrol as there is no regular fuel supply. **D** *Leopard Rock Safari Lodge*, booking: PO Box 45456, Nairobi, T742926. Excellent value bandas with electricity, warm showers, fully equipped kitchens include a fridge and mosquito nets, it is best to bring your own food and drink, though there is a shop at the *Leopard Rock Safari Lodge* it is not very often open and when it is, has limited stocks.

Park information

Transport **Road** You will need your own vehicle. Head from Meru town to Maua which is the last place to stock up on petrol and supplies. Murera Gate is about 30 kilometres from Maua down an unpaved road, with magnificent views over shambas.

Mount Elgon National Park

In the Rift Valley on the western border of Uganda, covering 169 square kilometres. The peak of the extinct volcano Mount Elgon reaches 4,322 metres, the second highest mountain in Kenya, the topmost heights form the Kenya/Uganda border. The Kenya/Uganda border cuts through the caldera of this extinct volcano, giving half the mountain to Uganda, including the highest peak Wagagai (4320 metres), with Lower Elgon Peak (sometimes called Sudek Peak) (4307 metres) in Kenya. The park is approximately 30 kilometres northwest of Kitale. The park's boundaries go down to 2,336 metres. This area is known as Koitoboss meaning table rock by virtue of its

1° N, 34° 30' E

Meru National Park

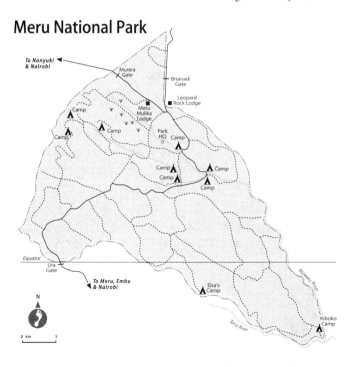

flat-topped basalt columns. There are a number of lava-tube caves, some over 60 metres wide which attract elephants in search of salt. Elgon is estimated to be more than 15 million years old.

The changes in altitude mean there are a number of ecological zones going from bamboo forest to afro-alpine moorlands. Animals likely to be seen here are: colobus monkey, elephant, leopard, giant forest hog, bushbuck, eland, buffalo, duiker and golden cat.

It is feasible to drive up to about 4000 metres and then hike over the moorlands to Koitoboss peak. From there it is possible to climb over the crater rim and descend to the floor of the caldera.

Climbing Mount Elgon Although it is possible to climb Mount Elgon at any time of year, the crater gets very cold and snow and hail are quite common so the best times are between December and March. It is possible to reach the summit and back in a day in dry weather when it is possible to drive to within a few hours hike of the highest point. There is not such a severe problem with altitude sickness as on Mount Kenya, but a night spent en route will lessen any problems that might arise. If you do not have a four-wheel drive vehicle, the ascent can be hiked in a fairly leisurely manner, spending three days on the way up and two down. You should be aware that it is illegal to enter the park zone without a vehicle. Mount Elgon was reclassified from a Forest Reserve to a National Park in 1993 – so standard fees are payable.

Equipment, porters, guides Camping gear and appropriate clothing can be hired in Nairobi at *Atul's*, Biashara Street, PO Box 43202, T25935. Cost about US$20 per day, with about US$200 in deposits. You should obtain one of the maps of the mountain showing the trails in some detail (see page 68). Porters for your gear, and guides, cost about US$3 a day, and are a sound investment, and can be recruited at any of the climb departure points. It is wise to ensure that the agreement with any guides or porters is clear. The guides are not obligatory, but if you don't have one, an armed Ranger must be hired for the day to take you to the Crater Rim. The Park Office in Budadiri will help to arrange everything. A recent traveller has highly recommended two guides, Lawrence Maina and James Wahoune, as being friendly, honest and competent. Contact them at PO Box 128, Naro-Moru, T0176-62265/62088.

Mount Elgon National Park

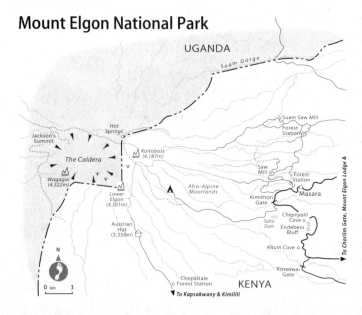

Park route, entry through the main Chorlim Gate to the park and then driving through the park to the end of the road track at Koroborte (3,580 metres). There is a campsite and water here. It is then about 3 hours to the Koitoboss summit.

Kimilili route This runs south of the route through the Park. Starting from the village of Kimilili, there is a track to Kapsakwany, eight kilometres away. Another two kilometres on is the turning to the forest Gate, which is a further two and a half kilometres. It is then 26 kilometres, which can be driven comfortably in dry weather, to the Austrian Hut (3,350 metres) where it is possible to stay or camp, with water nearby. There is a further three kilometres of driveable track. From here it is about a four-hour hike to Koitoboss summit. Currently closed for security reasons. The Sasa River route on the Ugandan side is a well-organized alternative (see page 638).

Kimithon route This runs north of the Park route. Starting from Enderbess, it is 16 kilometres to Masara village. About one kilometre further on take the right fork (not the left to the Kimithon Gate). The middle of three tracks leads to Kimithon Forest Station, where it is possible to camp. Koitoboss is then about six hours hike away. There may be problems with the Forest Station about using this route, but they can usually be negotiated.

Sleeping A *Mount Elgon Lodge*, just outside the main Chorlim Gate, bookings: Msafri Inns, Utali House, Uhuru Highway, Nairobi, PO Box 42013, T330820, Tx23009. It is not certain whether this lodge will remain open as it is run-down and consequently rather overpriced. **E** *Jasho Lodgings*, in Kimilili. Basic but sound. **E** *Lwala Paradise*, very basic, no water.

Park information

Transport **Road** The easiest way is from Kitale, the most popular being Chorlim Gate off the Enderbess road. The other gates can be reached from Kakamega (81 kilometres). You will be able to get a matatu from Kimilili.

Mount Kenya Biosphere Reserve

This reserve includes the Mount Kenya National Park, 715 square kilometres, which straddles the equator about 200 kilometres northeast of Nairobi in Central province. Mount Kenya, or Kirinyaga – the black and white striped mountain, is the sacred mountain of the Gikuya people, who believe that it is where their God 'Ngai' lived according to legend. The snow-capped peak is rarely visible during the day being surrounded by clouds, but it is usually clear at dawn and is quite an awesome sight. The upper base of the mountain is nearly 100 kilometres across and has two major peaks Nelion at 5,199 metres and Batian at 5,189 metres. Mount Kenya has a vital role in ecosystems in the area. It is Kenya's most important watershed and its largest forest reserve and the lower slopes make up the country's richest farmlands.

0° 5' S, 37° 20' E

The area has a variety of different vegetations over altitudes ranging from 1,600 to 5,199 metres. From bottom to top, it goes from rich alpine and sub-alpine flora to bamboo forests, moorlands and tundra. Over 4,000 metres there is some extraordinary vegetation including the giant rosette plants.

In the lower forest and bamboo zones, giant forest hog, tree hyrax, white-tailed mongoose, elephant, suni, duiker and leopard roam. Further up in the moorlands there are hyrax, duiker and Mount Kenya mouse shrews. In higher altitudes still there are the fairly common mole rat and the very rare golden cat.

Point Lenana at 4,986 metres is a strenuous hike, but quite manageable if you are an experienced climber. It is possible to reach **Mackinder's Camp**, about 4,175 metres, and back in a day – it requires going as far as the Meteorological Station (3,050 metres) on the Naro Moru route by four-wheel drive vehicle. This can be arranged through *Naro Moru River Lodge* (see below) for about US$20 plus park fees. The two peaks, **Nelion** and **Batian**, are only possible for very experienced climbers.

Climbing Mount Kenya

Take great care over equipment and altitude sickness precautions: otherwise the climb can be several days of sheer misery. It is essential to take effective rain gear as many of the huts have no drying facilities. The three most popular routes up the mountain are described here, and are best taken leisurely in six days, although they can be done in four. It is an interesting variation to ascend by one route and descend by another – it is important to keep the park fee receipts for the exit. An expedition to Point Lenana can be arranged for a group of four, including equipment, transport and food, for about US$120 per person through *Mount Rock Hotel* (see below).

Equipment, Porters, Guides Camping gear and appropriate warm and waterproof clothing can be hired in Nairobi at *Atul's*, PO Box 43202, Biashara Street, T25935. Cost about US$20 per day, with about US$200 in deposits. Alternatively hire at *Naro Moru River Lodge*, PO Box 18, Naro Moru, T0176-22018, at rates that are approximately 50 percent higher than in Nairobi. It is essential to bring effective rain gear as there are no drying facilities in some of the huts. You should obtain one of the maps of the mountain showing the trails in some detail (see page 68). Porters for your gear, and guides, cost about US$3 a day, and are a sound investment, and can be recruited at any of the climb departure points. It is wise to ensure that the agreement with any guides or porters is clear. A recent traveller has highly recommended two guides, Lawrence Maina and James Wahome as being friendly, honest and competent. Contact them at PO Box 128, Naro Moru T0176-62265/62088.

Health It is important to plan the climb to allow enough time for altitude acclimatisation. See Health section, page 40.

The climb **Naro Moru** approaches from the west and is the most direct and popular route. Naro Moru and Burguret are suitable starting bases. **Day 1**, from Naro Moru, is best spent travelling to the Meteorological Station at 3,050 metres. A ride can be hired from *Naro Moru River Lodge* part or all of the way. There are some bandas here or some permanent tents. **Day 2** is to Mackinder's Camp, through terrain that is often very wet underfoot. The camp has a bunkhouse and some tents. **Day 3** it is possible to make the final leg to Point Lenana, although it is more comfortable to spend Day 3 in and around Mackinder's Camp, getting acclimatized to the altitude, and **Day 4** climb to Point Lenana. **Day 5** it is possible to descend all the way down to Naro Moru (with a lift from the Meteorological Station), but it is more leisurely to return to Mackinder's Camp for a night, and then on to Naro Moru on **Day 6**.

Mount Kenya peaks

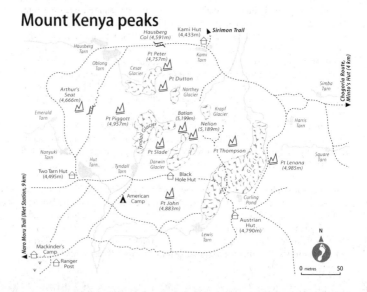

Chogoria approach is from the east, and is the most scenically attractive of the routes, although it can be wet. Chogoria village is the starting base. **Day 1**, from village to the Park gate by vehicle, and then it is about an hour of hiking to Urimandi Hut for the night. **Day 2** is a six-hour hike to Minto's Hut. **Day 3** it is possible to reach Point Lenana, but it is more comfortable to spend the day getting acclimatized in and around Minto's Hut, and **Day 4** climb to Point Lenana. **Day 5** it is possible to descend all the way down to Chogoria, (with a lift from the Park gate), but it is more leisurely to return to Minto's Hut for a night, and then on to Chogoria on **Day 6**.

Sirimon approaches from the north, and has a good repution for wildlife along the route. This route tends to be the driest, but can be a difficult climb. Naro Moru, Burguret or Nanyuki are possible starting bases. The trail starts 13 kilometres north of Nanyuki. **Day 1** from the trail start to the Park gates (about 10 kilometres) and then up to the end of the road track (a further nine kilometres) at 3,150 metres, where there is a bunkhouse and a campsite. **Day 2** is to Liki North Hut at 3,993 metres. **Day 3** it is possible to carry on past Kami Tarn, joining the Chogoria Trail about less than one kilometre from Point Lenana. However, if you are finding the climb and the altitude a strain, it is a good idea to spend a day acclimatising at Liki North Hut, or climb to Kami Hut, and on **Day 4** on to Point Lenana. **Day 5** it is possible to descend all the way with a lift from the end of the road track. However it is probably best to spend a night at Liki North Hut, and then to Nanyuki on **Day 6**.

Kenya

Sleeping Naro Moru A *Mount Kenya Mountain Lodge*, PO Box 123, Kiganjo, Nyeri, T0171-30785, F86011. Situated at 7,200 feet on Mount Kenya's slopes overlooking a water hole. A close up viewing bunker is connected to the hotel by a tunnel. **A** *Naro Moru River Lodge*, about 2 kilometres north of town centre, PO Box 18, Naro Moru, T22018 (Nanyuki). Some cheaper s/c cottages available. **E** *Naro Moru Hotel '86*, town centre, some self-contained rooms. **E** *Youth Hostel*, some dormitory accommodation. **E** camping possible at *Naro Moru Lodge*, and at the *Youth Hostel*.

Park information

Burguret B/C *Mountain Rock Hotel*, (formerly *Bantu Lodge*), 8 kilometres north of Naro Moru on the Nanyuki road, PO Box 33, Nanyuki, T62625/62098/62099. Log fires, good restaurant and bar, horse riding at about US$4 per hour, escorted forest walks.

Chogoria D *Meru Mount Kenya Lodge*, just inside park. Reasonable bandas with showers and log fires. **E** *Transit Motel*, in Chogoria village. Fairly basic.

Transport Road For **Naro Moru** and **Burguret**, Nyeri is the nearest major town, along the main Nairobi-Nanyuki road. For **Chogoria** the most direct route from Nairobi is through Embu. There are plenty of buses and matatus.

Mount Kulal Biosphere Reserve

This 7,000 square kilometres of land to the southeast of Lake Turkana in Eastern province has been made into one of Kenya's four biosphere reserves. The area includes many different types of environments ranging from mountain forest about 2,400 metres above sea level to desert with grasslands, dry evergreen forest, woodlands, bushlands and saltbush scrublands in between. It covers most of Lake Turkana, its volcanic southern shores, the Chalbi desert and the South Island National Park. There are two outstanding volcanoes in the reserve, **Teleki** and **Mount Kulal** which stands at 2,285 metres high. Both are a pretty straightforward climb if you are suitably equipped.

2° 30′ N, 36° E

Animals likely to be found here include giraffe, zebra, dik-dik, gazelle, elephant, cheetah, lion, black rhino, leopard, ostrich and crocodile as well as less common species such as gerenuk and greater kudu.

This area shows increasing evidence of human occupation from 10,000-12,000 years ago. Today the area is home to Samburu, Turkana and el-Molo around Lake Turkana, all of whom are pastoralists. There are no facilities for visitors to date.

Nairobi National Park

1° 18′ S, 37° E This park is just 10 kilometres southeast of Nairobi's city centre and despite its closeness to the city is home to over 100 recorded species of mammals. It is Kenya's oldest park having been set up in 1946. You are very likely to see zebra, giraffe, gazelle, baboons, buffalo, ostrich, vultures, hippos and various antelope. This is one of the best parks for spotting rhinos – the area is not remote enough for poachers. The concentration of wildlife is greatest in the dry season when areas outside the park have dried up. Water sources are greater in the park as a number of small dams have been built along the Mbagathi River. There are also many bird species, up to 500 different types. The park is small, only 117 square kilometres but is well worth visiting if you are staying in Nairobi. There are a number of minibus tours for either a morning or an afternoon.

Park information
See page 254 for costs

Sleeping *Nairobi Park Services Campsite*, PO Box 54867, Magadi Rd off Langata Rd, (past Brook House School) T/F2-890325, E shling@net2000ke.com or Allk@form-net.com . Opened in August 1997 this campsite offers budget facilities, bars and restaurant. Tented accommodation with 2 storey dormitory and bandas expected to be available soon. Hot showers, laundry facilities, western style toilets, secure fenced compound, vehicle parking, TV/Video US$3 per night. Can arrange game drives and camel safaris. Managed by Brendan Black and Dutch Pete.

North Kitui National Reserve

0° 15′ S, 38° 30′ E Adjacent to Meru National Park is North Kitui National Reserve in Eastern Province. It measures 745 square kilometres and is mainly bushland and riverine forest. The Tana River runs through where you are likely to see crocodiles and hippos. It forms part of a chain from Meru National Park to Bisanadi National Reserve east to Kora National Reserve then south to North Kitui National Reserve, which itself is bounded in the northeast by Rahole National Reserve. There are no tourist facilities.

Nairobi National Park

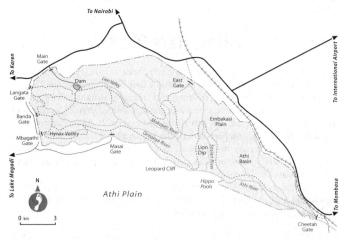

Rahole National Reserve

An enormous stretch of dry thorny bushland in Garissa district of North-Eastern Province about 150 kilometres ENE of Mount Kenya. It is home to elephant, Grevy's zebra and beisa oryx. There are no tourist facilities.

0° 5 N, 39° E

Ruma National Park

This park is 10 kilometres east of Lake Victoria in the South Nyanza district of western Kenya. The land is a mixture of tall grassland and woodlands of acacia, housing roan antelope, leopard, buffalo and topi. Giraffe, zebra and ostrich have recently been introduced. Camping is possible in the grounds. The Lambwe region is infested with tsetse fly which is fatal to man (sleeping sickness) and domesticated animals, but not to wild game. There are no camping facilities here and given the tsetse fly situation, you may want to give camping a miss. This area is fascinating with a mixture of small islands and peninsulas and is rarely visited by tourists.

0° 45′ S, 34° 10′ E

Kenya

Samburu/Buffalo Springs National Park

This was set up 20 years ago in this hot, arid lowland area just to the north of Mount Kenya, 325 kilometres from Nairobi and 50 kilometres from Isiolo town on the Isiolo-Marsabit road. The permanent water and forest shade on the banks of the Ewaso Nyiro River attract plentiful wildlife from the region including elephant, cheetah, giraffe, oryx, vervet monkeys, zebra and crocodiles. Leopards are regularly spotted. This is one of the pleasantest parks in Kenya and is not too crowded.

Samburu
0° 40′ N 37°, 30′ E

Elephant, zebra, giraffe, oryx, cheetah and crocodile can be found in the riverine forest of acacia and doum palm in this Reserve 85 kilometres north of Mount Kenya in Eastern Province, adjoining Samburu.

Buffalo Springs

Sleeping There are a surprising amount of facilities considering the two Reserves put together only cover some 400 square kilometres, catering for both luxury and budget tourists. Many of the more upmarket lodges offer discounts of up to 50 percent in the off-season

Park information
See page 254 for costs

Samburu & Buffalo Springs

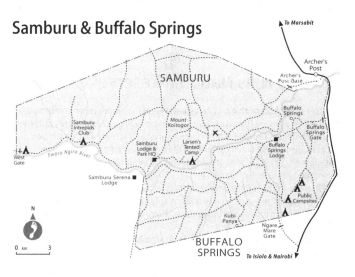

between April and July excluding Easter. **A+** *Larsens Tented Camp*, PO Box 40075, Nairobi, T540780, F543810, east of *Samburu Lodge*. Located by the river, small. Highly recommended. Offers game drives and excellent food, use of *Samburu Lodge* pool, they do not take children under 10. **A** *Buffalo Springs Lodge*, T0165/2259 (Isiolo), bookings: PO Box 30471, Nairobi, T336858, F218109. A pleasant relaxed lodge with good value bandas, swimming pool, excellent location. **A** *Samburu Lodge*, T2051 radiocall Nairobi, bookings: PO Box 40075, Nairobi, T540780, F543810. The oldest lodge in the reserve situated in the bend of the river, this is a wonderful place to stop off for a drink at the *Crocodile Bar* even if you do not stay, relaxed atmosphere in a beautiful setting, swimming pool, shop.

Camping E Camping is possible in *Buffalo Springs Reserve*, Ngere Mara, Ewaso Nyiro Bridge, and Maji ya Chumvi Stream near Buffalo Springs. The best is the one by Buffalo Springs Reserve which has showers and toilets. Baboons are a real nuisance here stealing anything not nailed to the ground. It is wise to have a guard provided by the Reserve, as there can be problems with theft and unwelcome visitors.

Transport Samburu is a couple of hours north of Nanyuki. Buses run here from Isiolo in the plains below on a regular basis.

Shaba National Reserve

0° 40′ N, 37° 50′ E 70 kilometres north of Mount Kenya the Shaba National Reserve in Isiolo District of Eastern Province is home to a number of gerenuk, gazelle, oryx, zebra, giraffe, cheetah, leopard and lion which roam around acacia woodlands, bushlands and grasslands. Shaba got its name from the volcanic rock cone in the reserve. The riverine areas are dominated by acacia and doum palms. There is one luxury lodge and three campsites. This is an extension of Buffalo Springs and Samburu National Reserve which lies to its west. The naturalists Joy and George Adamson who reared lions and returned them to the wild (the subject of *Born Free*, a book and film) had a campsite in Shaba Reserve.

Park information **Sleeping A+** *Sambura Serena*, Safari Lodge. Well designed overlooking the lazy Uaso Nyuro River which is abundant with birdlife and crocodiles. Central bookings Nairobi, PO Box 48690, T710511/2, F718100/2/3, E serenamk@africaonline.co.ke. **A** *Sarova Shaba Lodge*, PO Box 30680, Nairobi, T333248, F211472. A new luxury lodge, opened in 1989, offering excellent facilities, just to the east of Archer's post, overlooks river, well designed, swimming pool which curves around natural rock.

Transport Bus: buses to Archer's Post from Isiolo are fairly frequent.

Shimba Hills National Reserve

4° 15′ S, 39° 30′ E This is a small reserve 30 kilometres southwest of the Mombasa and quite possible to access on a day trip from the coast. The area is 192 square kilometres and is covered with forests and grasslands, riverine forest and scrubland. Due to strong sea breezes, the hills are much cooler than the rest of the coast making it a very pleasant climate. The rainforest itself is totally unspoilt and opens out into rolling downs and gentle hills.

There are a number of antelope, buffalo, waterbuck, reedbuck, hyena, warthog, giraffe, elephant, leopard, baboon and bush pig in the reserve. It is the only place in Kenya where you might see sable antelope. There is a nature trail which is pleasant to take and a picnic area.

It is possible to take a a half-day trip from Mombasa for US$25 (booking through travel agents, see page 79).

Adjacent is the **Mwalunganje Elephant Sanctuary** set up to provide access for the elephants between the Shimba Hills and the Mwaluganje Forest Reserve. There are approximately 150 elephants, mainly large bulls. Close range elephant viewing is virtually guaranteed.

Sleeping A+ *Shimba Hills*, PO Box 40075, Nairobi, T02-540780, F543810. Well designed round a water hole, which is illuminated at night for viewing, shop, children under the age of 7 are not allowed, but there is a bridal suite. E *Bandas*, located at a site about 3 kilometres from the main gate to the Reserve. Communal showers and lavatories. **Park information**

Camping E Camping at the Banda site.

Transport **Road** **Bus**: regular buses from Mombasa for Kwale, about 30 kilometres distant. From Kwale the Reserve is only 5 kilometres along a murram track.

Sibiloi National Park

Sibiloi National Park is one of the less known of Kenya's national parks despite its large size of 1,575 square kilometres. This is probably because of its isolated geographical location on the eastern shores of Lake Turkana – the Jade Sea – 960 kilometres by road from Nairobi via Marsabit, and about 320 kilometres from Marsabit town, in Eastern province. The landscape is grassy plains with yellow spear grass and doum palms. Within the park is Central Island holding the world's largest crocodile population of about 12,000. Other mammals include zebra, gazelle, oryx, hartebeest, topi, lion and cheetah. There are around 350 recorded species of birds. *4°N, 36°25'E*

In 1968 the Leakeys made many remarkable fossil finds of humans from 10,000-12,000 years ago. The Koobi Fora palaeontological site, 2,600 square kilometres, is here, as is a museum near the park's headquarters which houses the remains of prehistoric elephants among other things. This site has also yielded information about the environment one to three million years ago.

Lake Turkana

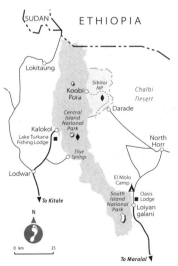

Camping E There are several campsites in the park but you will need to bring all your own supplies, including petrol. **Park information**

Transport It is about 120 kilometres from Lioyangalani along an unpaved trail through the desert to North Horr and then northwest to Alia Bay, the park headquarters. The most practical way of getting here is by air from Nairobi, or by boat from Ferguson's Gulf.

South Kitui National Reserve

This is the second national reserve in Kitui district. It is 1,800 square kilometres, adjacent to Tsavo East National Park but unfortunately no tourism is allowed at present. *1°50'S, 38°55'E*

South Turkana National Reserve

2°N, 35°45'E   Situated in the Rift Valley in Turkana District, this remote reserve is rarely visited and has no tourist facilities. It is 100 kilometres north of Kitale and if you do venture up here you are likely to see elephant or greater kudu in the dense thorn bush, riverine forest and scattered forest which make up its 1,000 square kilometres.

Tana River Primate National Reserve

2°30'N, 40°30'E   120 kilometres north of Malindi on the Tana River between Hola and Garsen. The highly diversified riverine forest has at least seven different types of primate including the red colobus and mangabey monkeys, and baboon. A number of other animals roam here including elephant, hippo, gazelle, duiker, river hog, giraffe, lion, waterbuck, bush squirrel and crocodiles. There is a research station for study of the primates.

Park information   **Camping**   E Camping available at *Mchelelo Camp* in an attractive site.

Transport There are buses running between Lamu and Garissa, and some of them detour to Mnazini village just to the south of the Reserve, from where it is possible to walk north along the river (there is a small boat ferry just before Baomo Village) to the campsite.

Tsavo National Parks East and West

3°N, 38°E   This is the largest national park in Kenya at around 21,000 square kilometres. It lies in the southern part of the country about 240 kilometres or halfway between Mombasa and Nairobi and is bisected by the Mombasa-Nairobi railway and road link. For administrative purposes it has been split into two sections, East (12,000 square kilometres) lying to the east of the Nairobi-Mombasa road/railway in the part of the park made famous by the 'Man Eaters of Tsavo' and west (9,000 square kilometres). The remoteness of much of the park makes it a haven for poachers but recent anti-poaching measures are having an effect. As a consequence, much of the northern area (about two thirds of East Tsavo) is off limits to the public in an attempt to halt poaching here which has decimated the rhino population from 8,000 in 1970 to around 100 today. Recent strict anti-poaching laws have been particularly successful in Tsavo and the number of elephants is increasing again. Both parts are fairly easily navigated with a good map as all tracks are clearly defined, and junctions are numbered.

   Tsavo East is the much less-visited side of the park where you will be able to see the wildlife without the usual hordes of other tourists. It mainly consists of vast plains of scrubland home to huge herds of elephants. The landscape is vast, and empty of any sign of humans, dotted with baobab trees. The Kanderi Swamp, not far from the main entrance at Voi Gate, has the most wildlife in the area. The main attraction of this part of the park is the Aruba dam built across the Voi River where many animals and bird congregate. **Mudanda Rock** towers above a natural dam and at certain times during the dry season draws hundreds of elephants. The **Yatta Plateau**, the world's largest lava flow, is found in Tsavo East.

   As time goes on, Tsavo East is opening itself up to package tourism, particularly the budget camping safaris. The wardens have even started to open up parts of the northern sector to upmarket low-profile camping and walking parties. This means the overwhelming feeling of solititude is slowly disappearing, though its vast size means you are likely to be alone for most of the time.

Tsavo West is the more developed part of the park combining good access, good facilities and stunning views over the tall grass and woodland scenery. The area is made up from recent volcano lava flows, which absorb rain water which reappears as the crystal clear Mzima Springs 40 kilometres away. The environment is well-watered and this combined with volcanic soils supports a vast quantity and diversity of plant and animal life. The main attractions are the watering holes by Kilaguni and Ngulia Lodges which entice a huge array of wildlife particularly in the dry season. During the autumn the areas around *Ngulia Lodge* are a stopover for hundreds of thousands of birds from Europe in their annual migration south.

Tsavo West National Park

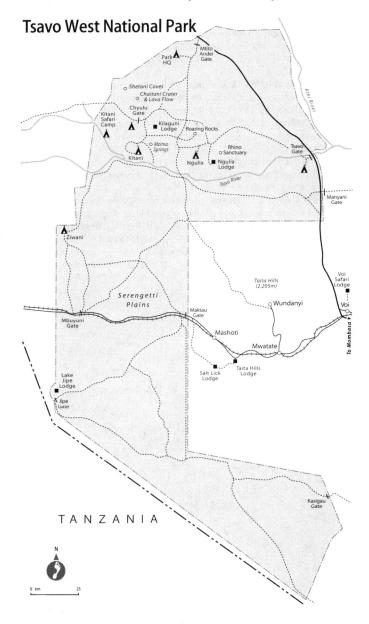

Kenya

Not far from the *Kilaguni Lodge* is the **Mzima Springs**, a favourite haunt of hippos and crocodiles. There is an underwater viewing chamber here, but the hippos have obviously decided against being studied so closely by moving to the other side of the pool. Also around the lodges are the spectacular Shaitani lava flow and caves which are well worth visiting. You will need to bring a good torch to explore them. Chaimu Crater to the south of *Kilaguni Lodge* can be climbed and though there is little danger of animals here, it is best to be careful.

At the extreme southwest of the park, bordering Tanzania, is the beautiful Lake Jipe, which is fed by underground aquatic flows from Mount Kilimanjaro. Here are found the Pygmy Geese and the Black Heron along with many other species of birds.

Wildlife you are likely to spot include: hyrax, agama lizards, dwarf mongooses, marabou storks, baboons, antelope, buffalo, zebra, giraffe, jackals and hyenas, crocodiles, hippos, leopards, lions, cheetahs. This part of Tsavo has some black rhino though most have been moved to the Rhino Sanctuary now.

Park information

See page 254 for costs

Sleeping Tsavo West A+ *Kilaguni Lodge*, PO Box 30471, Nairobi, T336858, F218109. Best lodge in the park and also the most expensive, every room faces the waterhole and has a verandah, swimming pool, Mt Kilimanjaro can be seen from the lodge. **A** *Lake Jipe Lodge*, PO Box 3107, Nairobi, T227623, Tx25508, near the Tanzanian border to the west. Swimming pool, isolated position, usually not crowded, views of the Lake and the Pare Mountains. **A** *Ngulia Safari Lodge*, PO Box 42, Mtito Andei, Kenya, T0147-30091, F30006. 52 roomed lodge, is slightly cheaper but still very good, the waterhole, again, is a big draw both for the animals and tourists, swimming pool, good location. Staff very knowledgeable on the wildlife and extremely helpful. The site of the lodge overlooks the Rhino Sanctuary and these can be viewed through the binoculars that are set up there. Visits to the sanctuary are restricted to between 4-6 each day. A leopard visits the lodges waterhole at dusk most nights to feed. **D** *Ngulia Safari Camp* and *Kitani Safari Camp*, T340331 (Nairobi). Offer self-service accommodation in the park in fully equipped bandas, including bathrooms with hot water, both places have a good friendly atmosphere and are popular with Kenyans and tourists alike, it's possible to arrange an early evening visit to one of the lodges from here for dinner and/or drinks. **Camping** Each of the gates at Tsavo, Mtito Andei and Chyulu have campsites (**E**).

Tsavo East

There is also a newer campsite at Ziwani on the western boundary of the park with full-size permanent tents and excellent food available.

Tsavo East A *Voi Safari Lodge*, PO Box 565, Voi, Kenya, T0147-30019, F30080. Slightly cheaper than the lodges of equivalent standard in West Tsavo and is much less crowded, it is 5 kilometres into the park from Voi Gate, swimming pool, good location. The animal hide by the waterhole, gives very good close up views at eye level. Baboons and rock hyrax wander freely through the hotel and gardens. Spectacular panoramic views. From here it is possible to arrange a drive to climb Mudando rock, where once the area is checked for lions, it is safe to climb. *Satao Camp*, this is a 'tented' permanent camp, the tents are pitched inside separate wooden roofs with a bathroom under the same roof but outside the tent, it overlooks a waterhole, where elephant, lions, zebra, etc come down in succession to drink at night, very well organized. **D** *Aruba Lodge*, PO Box 298, Voi, T2647, bookings: PO Box 14982, Nairobi, T720382. Close to the dam, banda accommodation, and very good value, there is a small shop nearby selling basic provisions, can be noisy at night. **Camping** There are sites (**E**) at Voi Gate, Kanderi Swamp, Aruba Lodge and at the Makwaju Campsite on the Voi River about 50 kilometres from Voi Gate. All have toilets, showers and running water.

Eating As usual, you should bring all your own provisions into the park including petrol and water. You should be able to eat or drink at any of the lodges if you so desire. There is a shop at Voi Gate in the east selling warm beers, sodas, bread and some vegetables and another shop in Tsavo West selling basic provisions.

Transport **Tsavo West** the park headquarters are off the Mombasa-Nairobi road at the northern end of the park through the Mtito Andei Gate. It is 30 kilometres from here to *Kilaguni Lodge* in the park. This is the busiest entrance to the park, and therefore the best one to aim for if you intend to hitch your way through the park. If you drive along the same Mombasa-Nairobi road for 48 kilometres you come to Tsavo Gate. Tsavo West is probably the easiest park to get around if you do not have your own car as there are plenty of buses from Nairobi to Mtito Andei, and your chances of getting a lift are fairly good. To get to the park from Voi, the easiest entrance is at Makatau near the Taita Hills and Salt Lick lodges. This road cuts across the park exiting at the Mbuyuni Gate in the west. It is easy to get to Tanzania from here via Taveta (see page 250).

Tsavo East you follow the same road as for Tsavo West (Nairobi-Mombasa road) and enter at the Park HQ at Voi Gate. There is a small educational centre at Voi Gate. If you are coming from Malindi, it is 110 kilometres up to Sala Gate on the eastern side of the park. There is a road cutting across to the Galana River and on up to Manyani Gate on the Mombasa-Nairobi road.

Kenya

Background

The land

Geography   Kenya is 580,367 square kilometres in area with the equator running right through the middle. Physically, the country is made up of a number of different zones. It lies between latitude 5° North and 4° 30′ South and longitude 34° and 41° East. The Great Rift Valley runs from the north to the south of the country and in places is 65 kilometres across, bounded by escarpments 600-900 metres high. This is probably the most spectacularly beautiful part of the country, dotted with soda lakes teeming with flamingoes. To the east of the Rift Valley lies the Kenya Highlands with Mount Kenya, an extinct volcano, which at 5,199 metres is Africa's second highest mountain. This is the most fertile part of the country, particularly the lower slopes of the mountain range. Nairobi sits at the southern end of the central highlands. The north of Kenya is arid, bounded by Sudan and Ethiopia. To the west lies Uganda and the fertile shores around Lake Victoria. Further south, the land turns into savannah which typifies Kenya and is mainly used for grazing.

The Indian Ocean coast to the east of the country runs for 480 kilometres and there is a narrow strip of fertile land all along it. Beyond this, the land becomes scrubland and semi-arid. Somalia borders Kenya in the northeast, and this is also a fairly arid area.

Climate   Kenya's different altitudes mean that the climate varies enormously around the country. Probably the most pleasant climate is in the central highlands and the Rift Valley, though the valley floor can become extremely hot and is relatively arid. Mount Kenya and Mount Elgon both become quite cool above 1,750 metres and the top of Mount Kenya is snow-covered. Mount Kenya and the Aberdares are the country's main water catchment areas.

Western Kenya and the area around Lake Victoria is generally hot around 30-34°C all year with high humidity and rainfall evenly spread throughout the year. Most rain here tends to fall in the early evening.

The country is covered in semi-arid bushland and deserts throughout the north and east of the country. Temperatures can go up to 40°C during the day and fall down to 20°C at night in the desert. Rainfall in this area is sparse, between 250 millimetres and 500 millimetres per annum.

The coastal belt is hot and humid all year round, though the heat is tempered by sea breezes. Rainfall varies from as little as 20 millimetres in February to 240 millimetres in May. The average temperature varies little throughout the year but is hottest in November and December at about 30°C.

Flora & fauna   Kenya is justifiably famous for its flora and fauna. In areas of abundant rainfall, the country is lush, supporting a huge range of plants, and the wide variety of geographical zones house a corresponding diversity of flora. The majority of the country is covered in savannah-type vegetation characterized by the acacia. The slopes of Mount Elgon and Mount Kenya are covered in thick evergreen temperate forest from about 1,000 metres to 2,000 metres; then to 3,000 metres the mountains are bamboo forest; above this level the mountains are covered with groundsel trees and giant lobelias. Mangroves are prolific in the coastal regions.

Kenya's wildlife is as diverse as its flora. On the savannahs you will be able to see the 'Big 5' of lion, leopard, buffalo, elephant and rhino as well as cheetah, gazelle, giraffes, zebra, wildebeest, warthog and a host of other species. Apart from these animals, there are flamingoes on the soda lakes and crocodiles in other waterways, many species of monkeys in the forests both by the coast or inland the amazingly tame rock hyraxes in Hell's Gate and many more. The birdlife is equally as varied including ostriches, vultures and many types of eagle, and even parrots up in Mount Kenya.

History

There is evidence that the forefathers of *Homo sapiens* lived in this part of East Africa 10-12,000 years ago. In the 1960s the Leakeys, Kenyan-born Europeans, began a series of archaeological expeditions in East Africa, particularly around Lake Turkana in the north. During these excavations they traced man's biological and cultural development back from about 50,000 years to 1,800,000 years ago. They discovered the skull and bones of a two to two and a half million year old fossil which they named *Homo habilis* who they argued was an ancestor to modern man. Since the 1970s, Richard Leakey, Louis and Mary Leakey's son, has uncovered many more clues as to the origins of mankind and how they lived, unearthing some early Stone Age tools. These findings have increased our knowledge of the beginnings of earth, and establish the Rift Valley as the Cradle of Mankind. Many of the fossils are now in the National Museum of Nairobi. Little evidence exists as to what happened between the periods 1,800,000 and 250,000 years ago except that *Homo erectus* stood upright and moved farther afield spreading out over much of Kenya and Tanzania. It is known that from 5,000-3,000 BC Kenya was inhabited by hunter-gatherer groups, the forefathers of the Boni, Wata and Wariangulu people.

Earliest times

Later still began an influx of peoples from all over Africa which lasted until about the 19th century. The first wave came from Ethiopia when the tall, lean Cushitic people gradually moved into Kenya over the second millennium BC settling around Lake Turkana in the north. These people practised mixed agriculture, keeping animals and planting crops. There is still evidence of irrigation systems and dams and wells built by them in the arid northern parts of Kenya. As the climate changed, getting hotter and drier, they were forced to move on to the hills above Lake Victoria.

Bantu expansion

The Eastern Cushitics, also pastoralists, moved into central Kenya around 3,000 years ago. This group assimilated with other agricultural communities and spread across the land. The rest of Kenya's ancestors are said to have arrived between 500 BC and 500 AD with Bantu-speaking people arriving from West Africa and Nilotic speakers from Southern Sudan attracted by the rich grazing and plentiful farmland.

The Kenyan coast attracted people from other parts of the world as well as Africa. The first definite evidence of this is a description of Mombasa by the Greek Diogenes in 110 AD on his return to Egypt. He describes trading in cloth, tools, glass, brass, copper, iron, olives, weapons, ivory and rhinoceros horn at Mombasa. In 150 AD Ptolemy included details of this part of the coast in his Map of the World. It was to be another few 100 years before the arrival of Islam on the coast and the beginning of its Golden Age.

Arab and Persian settlers developed trade routes extending across the Indian Ocean into China establishing commercial centres all along the East Africa coast. They greatly contributed to the arts and architecture of the region and built fine mosques, monuments and houses. Evidence of the prosperity of this period can be seen in the architecture in parts of Mombasa, Malindi and Lamu, and particularly in the intricate and elegant balconies outside some of the houses in the old part of Mombasa. All along this part of the coast, intermarriage between Arabs and Africans resulted in a harmonious partnership of African and Islamic influences personified in the Swahili people. This situation continued peacefully until the arrival of the Portuguese in the 16th century.

Mombasa was known to be rich in both gold and ivory making it a tempting target for the Portuguese. Vasco da Gama, in search of a sea route to India, arrived in Mombasa in 1498. He was unsuccessful at docking there at this time, but two years later ramsacked the town. For many years the Portuguese returned to plunder Mombasa until finally they occupied the city. There followed 100 years of harsh colonial rule from their principal outpost at Fort Jesus overlooking the entrance to the old harbour. Arab resistance to Portuguese control of the Kenyan coast was strong, but they were unable to defeat the Portuguese who managed to keep their foothold in East Africa.

Portuguese & Arab influence

☞ *The Uganda railway*

What it will cost no words can express;
What is its object no brain can suppose;
Where it will start from no one can guess;
Where it is going to nobody knows;
What is the use of it none can conjecture;
What it will carry there's none can define;
And in spite of George Curzon's superior lecture,
It clearly is naught but a lunatic line.

London Magazine Truth 1896

The end of Portuguese control began in 1696 with a siege of Fort Jesus. The struggle lasted for nearly two and a half years when the Arabs finally managed to scale the fortress walls. By 1720, the last Portuguese garrison had left the Kenyan coast. The Arabs remained in control of the East African coast until the arrival of the British and Germans in the late 19th century. In this period the coast did not prosper as there were destructive intrigues amongst rival Arab groups and this hampered commerce and development in their African territories.

The Colonial period The British influence in Kenya began quite casually following negotiations between Captain Owen, a British Officer, and the Mazruis who ruled the island of Mombasa. The Mazruis asked for British protection from attack by other Omani interests in the area. Owen granted British protection in return for the Mazruis abolishing slavery. He sent to London and India for ratification of the treaty, posted his first officer together with an interpreter, four sailors and four marines and thus began the British occupation of Kenya. At this time, interest in Kenya was limited to the coast and then only as part of an evangelical desire to eliminate slavery. However, 50 years later attitudes towards the country changed.

In 1887 the Imperial British East Africa Company (IBEAC) founded its headquarters in Mombasa with the purpose of developing trade. From here it sent small groups of officials into the interior to negotiate with tribesmen. One such officer Frederick Lugard made alliances with the Kikuyu en route to Uganda.

The final stage in British domination over Kenya was the development of the railway. The IBEAC and Lugard believed a railway was essential to keep its posts in the interior of Kenya supplied with essential goods, and also believed it was necessary in order to protect Britain's position in Uganda. Despite much opposition in London, the railway was built at a cost of £5mn.

Nairobi was created at the centre of operations as a convenient stopping point midway between Mombasa and Lake Victoria where a water supply was available. Despite many problems, the railway was completed in 1901 and was the catalyst for British settlers moving into Kenya as well as for African resistance to the loss of their lands.

From 1895 to 1910 the government encouraged white settlers to cultivate land in the central highlands of the country around the railway, particularly the fertile western highlands. It was regarded as imperative to attract white settlers to increase trade and thus increasing the usefulness of the railway. The Masai bitterly opposed being moved from their land but years of war combined with the effects of cholera, smallpox, rinderpest and famine had considerably weakened their resistance. The Masai were moved into two reserves on either side of the railway, but soon had to move out of the one to the north as the White settlers pressed for more land. Kikuyu land was also occupied by white settlers as they moved to occupy the highlands around the western side of Mount Kenya.

The number of Europeans in Kenya steadily increased from only about 3,000 at the beginning of the First World War to 80,000 by the early 1950s. The rise in numbers of people entering Kenya was helped by the British government's decision to offer war veterans land in the Kenya highlands. In order to increase the pool of African labour for white settler development (most Africans were unwilling to work for the Europeans voluntarily), but taxes and other levies were imposed. Furthermore, Africans were prevented from growing coffee, the most lucrative crop, on the grounds that there was a risk of coffee berry disease with lots of small producers. Thus many Africans were forced to become farm labourers or to migrate to the towns in search of work to pay the taxes. By the 1940s the European farmers had prospered in cash crop production.

Grogan: Cape to Cairo

Ewart Scott Grogan was born in 1874 in Eaton Square, Chelsea, London. He was to epitomize all that was good and bad in the early Kenyan pioneers.

His father was a wealthy estate agent who married twice, having 21 children, of which Ewart Grogan was the fourteenth. He went to school near Guildford, then to Winchester and finally to Jesus College, Cambridge to study law. In his third year, after a rugby game followed by some drinking, he locked a goat in the study of the Master of the college and was expelled without a degree.

For a while Grogan studied art at the Slade School in London before enlisting to fight against the Matabele, travelling up from Capetown to what is now Zimbabwe. When hostilities ended, Grogan took a hunting trip to nearby Beira where he contracted blackwater fever, coming close to death. When he recuperated he was involved in a brawl over a woman in a dancehall in which a Portuguese was killed.

A trip to New Zealand was suggested to consolidate his recuperation. There he fell for Gertrude Watt. Gertrude's stepfather was hostile to the notion of the couple marrying, and pointed out that Grogan had achieved very little in his 22 years. Stung, Grogan suggested a journey from the Cape to Cairo as a suitable test, and Gertrude's stepfather, virtually certain the expedition would fail, agreed.

Grogan planned to undertake a survey during his journey for the telegraph and railway planned by Cecil Rhodes. With a companion, Arthur Sharp, he assembled supplies and embarked for Beira – he reasoned the he had already covered the Cape to Beira leg prior to serving in Matabeleland. After a break for hunting, they set out.

Despite travelling by boat where ever possible, there was plenty of foot-slogging, deserting porters, stolen equipment, bouts of fever, and attacks by cannibals. He arrived in Cairo alone – Sharp had left at Toro in Uganda to head for Kenya and the coast.

Back in England, Grogan presented the Union Jack he had carried with him to Queen Victoria, lectured to the Royal Geographical Society, finished his book From Cape to Cairo, and married Gertrude on 11 October 1900. Continued in box, page 84.

As the number of Europeans moving into the country increased, so too did African resistance to the loss of their land and there was organized African political activity against the Europeans as early as 1922. The large number of tribesmen, particularly Kikuyu, moving into the growing capital Nairobi formed a political community supported by sections of the influential Asian community. This led to the formation of the East African Association, the first pan-Kenyan nationalist movement led by Harry Thuku. His arrest and the subsequent riots were the first challenge to the settlers and the colonial régime.

Jomo Kenyatta led a campaign to bring Kikuyu land grievances to British notice. In 1932 he gave evidence to the Carter Land Commission in London which had been set up to adjudicate on land interests in Kenya, but without success. During the war years, all African political associations were banned and there was no voice for the interests of black Kenyans. At the end of the war, thousands of returning soldiers began to demand certain rights, and discontent grew. Kenyatta had remained abroad travelling in Europe and the Soviet Union and returned in 1946 as a formidable statesman.

In 1944 an African nationalist organisation, the Kenya African Union (KAU) was formed to press for African access to settler occupied land. The KAU was primarily supported by the Kikuyu. In 1947 Kenyatta became president of KAU and was widely supported as the one man who could unite Kenya's various political and ethnic factions.

At the same time as the KAU were looking for political change, a Kikuyu group, Mau Mau, began a campaign of violence. In the early 1950s the Mau Mau began terrorist activities, and several white settlers were killed as well as thousands of Africans thought to have collaborated with the colonial government.

The Mau Mau era

The British authorities declared a state of emergency in 1952 in the face of the Mau Mau campaign and the Kikuyu were herded into 'protected villages' surrounded by barbed wire. People were forbidden to leave during the hours of darkness. From 1952 to 1956 the

Kenya

terrorist campaign waged against the colonial authority resulted in the deaths of 13,000 Africans and 32 European civilians. Over 20,000 Kikuyu were placed in detention camps before the Mau Mau finally were defeated. The British imprisoned Kenyatta in 1953 for seven years for alleged involvement in Mau Mau activities, and banned the KAU, though it is dubious whether Kenyatta had any influence over Mau Mau activities.

The cost of suppressing the Mau Mau, the force of the East African case, and world opinion, convinced the British government that preparation for independence was the wisest course. The settlers were effectively abandoned, and were left with the prospect of making their own way under a majority-rule government. A number did sell up and leave, but many, encouraged by Kenyatta, stayed on to become Kenyan citizens.

The state of emergency was lifted in January 1960 and a transitional constitution was drafted allowing for the existence of political parties and ensuring Africans were in the majority in the Legislative Council. African members of the council subsequently formed the Kenya African National Union (KANU) with James Gichuru, a former president of KAU, as its acting head and Mboya and Oginga Odinga, two prominent Luos, part of the leadership. KANU won the majority of seats in the Legislative Council but refused to form an administration until the release of Kenyatta.

In 1961 Kenyatta became the president of KANU. KANU won a decisive victory in the 1963 elections, and Kenyatta became prime minister as Kenya gained internal self-government. Kenya became fully independent later that year, the country was declared a republic, and Kenyatta became president. Kenya retained strong links with the UK, particularly in the form of military assistance and financial loans to compensate European settlers for their land, some of which was redistributed among the African landless.

Kenyatta The two parties that had contested the 1963 elections with KANU were persuaded to join KANU and Kenya became a single-party state. In 1966 Odinga left KANU and formed a new party, the Kenya People's Union, with strong Luo support. Tom Mboya, a Luo, was assassinated by a Kikuyu in 1969. There followed a series of riots in the west of the country by Luos, and Odinga was placed in detention where he remained for the next 15 months. At the next general election in 1969 only KANU members were allowed to contest seats, and two-thirds of the previous national assembly lost their seats.

The East African Community (EAC) comprising Kenya, Tanzania and Uganda, which ran many services in common such as the railways, the airline, post and telecommunications, began to come under strain. Kenya had pursued economic policies which relied on a strong private sector; Tanzania had adopted a socialist strategy after 1967; Uganda had collapsed into anarchy and turmoil under Amin. In 1977, Kenya unilaterally pulled out of the EAC, and in response Tanzania closed its borders with Kenya.

Kenyatta was able to increase Kenya's prosperity and stability through reassuring the settlers that they would have a future in the country and that they had an important role in its success at the same time as delivering his people limited land reform. Under Kenyatta's presidency, Kenya became one of the more successful newly independent countries. However, he became increasingly autocratic, and he was biased in favour of his own tribe over other interests.

Moi Kenyatta died in 1978 to be succeeded by Daniel arap Moi, his vice president. Moi began by relaxing some of the political repression of the latter years of Kenyatta's presidency. However, he was badly shaken by a coup attempt in 1982 that was only crushed after several days of mayhem, and a more repressive period was ushered in.

Relations between Kenya and its neighbours began to improve in the 1980s and the three countries reached agreement on the distribution of assets and liabilities of the EAC by 1983. At this time the border between Kenya and Tanzania was reopened.

In 1992 political parties (other than KANU) were allowed. Moi and KANU were returned (albeit without a majority of the popular vote) in the multiparty elections late in 1992.

In the 1997 Presidential elections Moi was again victorious, with an increased share of the vote. In the elections for the National Assembly KANU achieved a slender overall majority with 107 seats out of 210.

Culture

Tribal identity is still important in Kenyan life though this is changing as more people move into towns and tribal groups become scattered. Polygamy is still practised, though it is not officially condoned. The custom of a man taking more than one wife, is only recognized in the traditional systems, and not by official Kenyan family law. There is much resistance to western censure of polygamy. However, the practice is dying under the twin influences of economic realities and social pressure. Few men can now afford to take more than one wife. Among the better off, it is frowned upon for anybody in public life as it causes embarrassment when mixing with the international community. The Christian churches strongly disapprove.

People

Kenya has long been a meeting place of population movements from around the continent. This has resulted in there being as many as 70 different tribes living in Kenya with an estimated overall population of 29 million people. There are three main groupings based on the origins of these groups. The Bantu came from West Africa in a migration, the reasons for which are not clearly understood. The Nilotic peoples came from the northwest, mostly from the area that is now Sudan. They were mainly pastoralists, and moved south in search of better grazing on more fertile land. Finally there is the Hamitic group, made up of a series of relatively small communities such as the Somali, Rendille, Boran, Ogaden and others, all pastoralists, who have spread into Kenya in the north and northeast from Ethiopia and Somalia.

Kikuyu (Bantu)

Primarily based around Mount Kenya. This is the largest ethnic group with 21 percent. They are thought to have originated from the East and Northeast Africa around the 16th century. Land is the dominant social, political, religious and economic factor of life for Kikuyus and this attitude soon brought them into conflict with colonial interests when settlers occupied their traditional lands.

The administration of the Kikuyu was undertaken by a council of elders based on clans made up of family groups. Other important members of the community were witch doctors, medicine men and the blacksmiths. The Kikuyu God is believed to live on Mount Kenya and all Kikuyus build their homes with the door facing the mountain. In common with most tribes in Kenya, men and women go through a number of stages into adulthood including circumcision to mark the beginning of their adult life. It is not so common for women to be circumcised today.

It is said the Kikuyu have adapted more successfully than any other tribe to the modern world. Kikuyu are prominent in many of Kenya's business and commercial activities. Those still farming in their homelands have adapted modern methods to their needs and benefit from cash crop production for export, particularly coffee and tea. They have benefited by occupying a fertile area close to the capital, Nairobi.

Meru (Bantu)

Arrived to the northeast of Mount Kenya around the 14th century, following invasions by Somalis in the coast. This group is not homogenous being made up of eight different groups of people, accounting for five percent of Kenya's population. Some of the Meru were led by a chief known as the *mogwe* until 1974 when the chief converted to Christianity and ended the tradition. A group of tribal elders administer traditional justice along with the witch doctor.

The Meru occupy some of the country's richest farmland which is used to produce tea, coffee, pyrethrum, maize and potatoes. Another highly profitable crop grown by the Meru in this region is miraa, a mild stimulant particularly popular amongst Islamic communities and Somalis.

John Boyes

John Boyes was born in Hull, Yorkshire in 1845, and at the age of thirteen he walked to Liverpool and signed on as a cabin-boy. In 1898 his voyages saw him at Mombasa, where he took the offer and contracted to deliver a caravan of food supplies to the British troops engaged in suppressing the Ugandan mutiny. It was a tough trip for Boyes, he contracted malaria and was semi-conscious for three days, his donkeys fell prey to tsetse flies and his porters abandoned their load and deserted. Nothing daunted Boyes recruited porters who had deserted from other caravans and made the delivery, earning £100.

Boyes reasoned that it ought to be possible to buy supplies of food in Kikuyuland (north of Nairobi) and halve the travelling. Defying officials who tried to stop him, Boyes set off with porters and interpreter and was promptly captured by the Kikuyu warriors of Chief Kawics clan. While the Kiama of Kikuyu elders were deliberating his fate, there was a skirmish with another Kikuyu clan. Boyes dressed the wounds with an antiseptic powder, iodoform, and succeeded in establishing such good relations with the Kiama that he subsequently styled himself 'King of the Kikuyu'.

With his brusque Yorkshire manner, Boyes was never on cordial terms with the other European settlers and administrators, but when he died in 1912, the whole of Nairobi turned out to follow his funeral procession.

Kalenjin
(Nilotic)

It is a name used by the British to describe a cluster of tribes, the main being the Kipsigis (four percent of total population), Nandi (two percent), Tugen (one percent), Elgeyo (one percent), Keiyo, Pokot, Marakwet, Sabaot, Nyangori, Sebei and Okiek, who speak the same language but different dialects. They mainly live in the western edge of the central Rift Valley and are thought to have migrated from southern Sudan about 2,000 years ago. Most Kalenjin took up agriculture though they are traditionally pastoralists. Bee-keeping is common with the honey being used to brew beer. Administration of the law is carried out at an informal gathering of the clan's elders. Witch doctors are generally women, which is unusual in Africa.

Luyha (Bantu)

Based on Kakamega town in western Kenya, and making up 14 percent of the total. They are Kenya's third largest grouping after the Kikuyu and the Luo. They are cultivators, and small farmers are the mainstay of sugar-cane growing in the west. They occupy a relatively small area, and population densities are the highest anywhere in Kenya's countryside, with plot sizes becoming steadily smaller with the passing of each generation.

Luo (Nilotic)

Live in the west of the country on the shores of Lake Victoria. The second largest ethnic group with 14 percent of the total. They migrated from the Nile region of Sudan in around the 15th century. Originally the Luo were cattle herders but the devastating effects of rinderpest on their herds made it necessary to diversify into fishing and subsistence agriculture.

The Luo were also prominent in the struggle for independence and many of the country's leading politicians including Tom Mboya and Oginga Odinga were Luos.

The Luos have a different coming of age ritual to other tribes in the region which involved extracting the bottom four or six teeth, though this practice has fallen into disuse.

Kisii (Bantu)

Based on Kisii town in the west, south of Kisumu. Traditional practices have been continued, with sooth-sayers and medicine men retaining significant influence, despite the nominal allegiance of most Kisii to Christianity. Trepanning, the drilling of a hole in the skull, has been a time-honoured remedy for mental illness and headaches, and is still used occasionally today.

Kamba (Bantu)

Traditionally lived in the area now known as Tsavo National Park. They comprise 11 percent of the total population. Originally hunters, the Kamba soon adopted a more sedentary lifestyle and developed as traders because of the relatively poor quality of their land. Ivory was a major trade item as were beer, honey, ornaments and iron weapons which they traded with neighbouring Masai and Kikuyu for food.

The Akamba were well regarded by the British for their intelligence and fighting ability and they made up a large part of the East African contingent in the British Army during the First World War.

Akamba adolescents go through initiation rites at around 12 including male circumcision. In common with most Bantu tribespeople, political power lies with clan elders.

Swahili (Bantu)

Dwell along the coast, and make up less than one percent of the total population. Although they do not have a common heritage, they do share a common language, religion and culture. Ancestry is mainly a mixture of Arabic and African. Today the majority of coastal people are Muslims.

Masai (Nilotic)

Probably the best known tribe to people outside Kenya with their striking costume and reputation as fierce and proud warriors. They comprise two percent of Kenya's people. The Masai came to central Kenya from the Sudan around 1,000 years ago, where they were the largest and one of the most important tribes. Their customs and practices were developed to reflect their nomadic lifestyle and many are still practised today, though change is beginning to be accepted. The basic Masai diet, for instance, is fresh and curdled milk carried in gourds. Blood tapped from the jugular vein of cattle is mixed with cattle urine and this provides a powerful stimulant. Cattle are rarely killed for meat as they represent the owners' wealth.

Turkana (Nilotic)

Like the Masai, this group has retained its rich and colourful dress and have a reputation as warriors. They comprise two percent of the total population. They are mainly based in the northwest part of Kenya living in the desert near the Ugandan border. This is the most isolated part of the country and as a consequence the Turkana have probably been affected less by the 20th century than any other tribe in Kenya.

The Turkana are pastoralists whose main diet consists of milk and blood. Cattle are important in Turkana culture, being herded by men. Camels, goats and sheep are also important and are looked after by boys and small girls. Recently some Turkana have begun fishing in the dry season.

The traditional dress of the Turkana is very eye-catching and is still fairly commonly worn. Men cover part of their hair with mud which is then painted blue and decorated with ostrich feathers. The main garment is a woollen blanket worn over one shoulder. Women wear a variety of beaded and metal adornments many of which signify different events in a woman's life. Women wear a half skirt of animal skins and a piece of black cloth. Both men and women sometimes use the lip plug through the lower lip. Tattooing is still fairly common. Men are tattooed on the shoulders and upper arm each time they kill an enemy. Witch doctors and prophets are held in high regard.

Modern Kenya
Politics

Daniel arap Moi was elected to the Presidency in October 1978 following the death of Jomo Kenyatta, and began a programme to reduce Kenya's corruption and release all political detainees. Moi, a Kalenjin, emphasized the need for a new style of government with greater regional representation of tribal groups. However, he did not fully live up to his promises of political freedom and Oginga Odinga (the prominent Luo who had been a voice of discontent in KANU under Kenyatta) and four other former KANU members who were critical of Moi's régime were barred from participating in the 1979 election. This led to an increase in protests against the government, mainly from Luos. Moi began to arrest dissidents, disband tribal societies and close the universities whenever there were demonstrations. This period also saw the strengthening of Kenya's armed forces.

On 1 August 1982 there was a coup attempt supported by a Luo-based section of the Kenyan Air Force supported by university students. Although things initially appeared to be touch-and-go, the coup was eventually crushed, resulting in an official death toll of 159. As a result of the coup attempt, many thousands of people were detained and the universities again closed. The heavy Luo involvement led to Odinga being placed under house arrest and the information minister, also a Luo, being dismissed. Conciliatory moves from Moi followed these measures including an amnesty for political prisoners sentenced to death and an investigation of the civil service. The constitution was changed to make Kenya a *de jure* one-party state.

Moi decided to reassert his authority over KANU by calling an early election in which he stood unopposed. Inevitably he was re-elected but less than 50 percent of the electorate turned out to vote. Various measures were introduced to try to purge the political system of corruption and inefficiency though none resulted in any major changes. Students were seen as potential agitators and Nairobi University was regularly closed. By 1986 there were rumours of underground agitation from a group known as Mwakenya.

Mwakenya was a group formed of members from a wide spectrum of tribes and political interests, mostly well-educated, all brought together in opposition to the Moi presidency. The National Council of Churches became increasingly critical of political events as well, in particular voicing opposition to a new electoral system whereby voters were to queue publicly in line behind the candidate of their choice, replacing the secret ballot.

Moi's response to political criticism was to increase his power by transferring control of the civil service to the president's office and reduce the independence of the judiciary by giving the president the power to dismiss the attorney-general and the auditor-general without endorsement by a legal tribunal. He also expanded his cabinet to 33 ministers, many posts being filled on the basis of political patronage. With the fall of a couple of outspoken politicians, parliamentary opposition to Moi evaporated.

By 1987 international criticism of Moi's government was intensifying, particularly as allegations of human rights abuses increased. 1988 saw more student demonstrations, protesting against the arrest of seven student leaders. Nairobi university was closed and its student organisation banned. At the same time Moi made some minor concessions by releasing nine political detainees and dismissing some police officers. Later that year a general election, using the queue voting system, saw Moi re-elected for a third term of office. Of the successfully re-elected 123 (of 188), 65 were unopposed, and there were allegations that opponents had been intimidated or bribed into withdrawing. Following the election there was a government reshuffle. Mwai Kibaki, the vice-president, was replaced by Josephat Karanja, a relatively unknown politician.

In 1988 Moi again increased his control over the legal system by a new set of constitutional amendments. This time, the national assembly assented to allow the president to dismiss judges at will. Also, periods of detention were increased from 24 hours to 14 days. These latest changes were greeted with criticism by both foreign observers, the Church, and the judiciary in Kenya but went through parliament unopposed. Moi greeted these reproaches with proposals to arrest any 'roaming foreigners' and threatened to curtail freedom of worship.

In February 1990, the popular and internationally influential Luo minister of foreign affairs and international co-operation, Dr Robert Ouko was found murdered after his return from a visit to Washington DC, USA. There followed riots in Nairobi and Kisumu resulting in some 20 people being killed and thousands were arrested. Moi asked the British police to investigate Ouko's death, and the report named a minister, Nicholas Biwott, a Kalenjin kinsman of Moi, as one of the prime suspects. Pressure on the government to move to a multi-party sytem intensified, but Moi argued that this would play into the hands of tribalists in the pay of foreign masters seeking to undermine Kenyan unity.

A former cabinet minister Kenneth Matiba and Ogonga Odinga's son Raila Odinga were arrested for forming an alliance of people seeking to legalize political opposition. The US embassy intervened to grant refuge to one of the dissident leaders which caused a breakdown of accord between the Kenyan and US administrations. The US and British suspended aid disbursements, and within a matter of weeks, the Moi administration announced the introduction of a multi-party system. Several new political parties were registered in early 1992, the most important of which was the Forum for the Restoration of Democracy (FORD) in which Oginga Odinga was involved.

Tribal clashes abounded throughout Kenya in 1992, but were particularly violent in western Kenya resulting in as many as 2,000 people being killed and 20,000 being made homeless. In May the government banned all political rallies ostensibly to suppress the unrest, but they also placed restrictions on the press. The opposition parties accused the government of inciting the violence as a means of discrediting multi-party politics.

The opposition to KANU split, the main parties being FORD-Asili, led by Kenneth Matiba; FORD-Kenya, under Oginga Odinga; and the Democratic Party of Mwai Kibaki. The elections, at the very end of 1992, monitored by a commonwealth group, saw Moi re-elected but with only 36 percent of the popular vote. KANU won 100 of the 188 seats in the national assembly. The result saw a substantial opposition formed and the democratic process has improved as a result.

A new development has been the formation of a new party, Safina (meaning 'Noah's Ark' in Swahili) by Richard Leakey (a celebrated white Kenyan) and Paul Muite (a former FORD-Kenya MP). After a battle the party was finally registered a month before the polls in December 1997.

In the National Assembly KANU slipped a little with 107 seats out of 210 (in 1992 it was 100 out of 180). Kibaki's DP was the largest opposition party with 31 seats, and eight other parties won seats. Safina secured five seats, Richard Leakey was named as its nominated MP, and Safina is perhaps a force for the future.

Once again the opposition failed to unite effectively against Moi in the Presidential contest. Kenneth Matiba (the strongest contender in 1992) did not stand for President, and his party, FORD-Asili was reduced to one seat in the National Assembly.

Moi increased his share of the Presidential vote from 36 percent in 1992 to 40 percent. Kibaki made the best showing of the opposition with 31 percent.

It is reported that KANU is divided into two factions, each seeking to supply the eventual successor to Moi. One centres on Simeon Nyachae, a Kisii, and is known as 'KANU A'. The other, 'KANU B', is led by the Vice President George Saitoti, who styles himself as Masai, but is thought to be Kikuyu. Nicholas Biwott, the former minister named as a suspect in the Ouko murder rejoined the cabinet in January 1997 as Minister of State in the President's office, a move that will infuriate the international community. Biwott is aligned with Saitoti and 'KANU B'.

Early in 1999, Nyachae was removed from Finance and dropped from the cabinet. In April, Moi finally filled the post of Vice President (vacant since January 1988) by nominating Saitoti, the former incumbent. The identity of a favoured successor to Moi (who must leave office by the end of 2002) has been made no clearer by these manoeuvres.

In early 1997 there was a drought in the north, but journalists were banned from the area and the Public Security Act was invoked allowing detention without trial, the banning of demonstrations, prosecution for false reporting and the commandeering of private property. These developments did not create a favourable climate for free speech in the run-up to the election.

In July 1997 the IMF increased pressure on the Moi government by suspending a US$205mn loan pending commitment to fight corruption.

Moi's relationship with his neighbours has not been an easy one. Although Moi offered full co-operation with Museveni and the National Resistance Army (NRA) when they came to power in 1986, relations between Kenya and Uganda have often been strained. Moi was nervous that Uganda might supply arms to the Mwakenya movement. In 1987 the Kenya/Uganda border was temporarily closed as the two armies clashed, though the two countries later signed a treaty for co-operation. There have been problems with banditry and cattle raiding across the border with Ethiopia, and traffic has been moving in convoys with armed escorts north of Isiolo on the route to Moyale and Addis Ababa.

There were three incidents in early 1998 where tourists were killed during robberies. Although these fatal attacks on tourists are very alarming, Kenya overall continues to be a safe holiday destination provided precautions are taken to avoid unnecessary risks.

Economics

Kenya's economic strategy maintains reliance on a strong private sector in manufacturing and services as well as in the farming sector. Foreign investment is encouraged, although the regulations have recently been uncertain, and there are periodic efforts to increase local participation in foreign-owned enterprises. In the East African context, Kenyan economic management has been successful, and has achieved as much as can reasonably be expected of a country with no oil and without any major mineral deposits.

Economic structure

Population in 1998 is estimated at almost 30 million, and it is growing rapidly at 3.3 percent a year. This implies an increase in population of just under a million each year. Most people live in the rural areas, with only a quarter in the towns. Overall population density is high by African standards, over double the average. Given that a large proportion of the country is arid, the pressure on the land in the fertile areas, particularly in the central highlands and around Lake Victoria, is intense.

Income levels are modest. Converting the value of output to US$, using either the exchange rate or purchasing power method, indicates Kenya is a low-income economy, and among the 20 or so poorest in the world. Low levels of output per head, for quite a large population, mean that the total output is in the middle-ranking for Africa with regard to size.

Most families rely on agriculture for their livelihood, and 81 percent of the labour force is engaged in farming. However, incomes in agriculture are low, and the sector generates only 29 percent of GDP. Industry contributes 18 percent of output, but it must be remembered that there is little contribution from mining which boosts industrial output in many other African countries. Services is the largest sector at 54 percent, and it contains tourism, which is Kenya's largest source of foreign exchange.

Expenditure is reasonably well balanced, with 72 percent going on consumption, a respectable investment rate of 19 percent, and a modest level of government spending at 17 percent.

The economy is very dependent on foreign earnings, and 29 percent of output is exported. The main sources of export earnings are tourism which generate 27 percent of receipts, tea 16 percent, coffee eight percent and horticulture eight percent. Spending on imports is 37 percent of all expenditure. The main components of imports are machinery 24 percent, fuels 21 percent and vehicles nine percent.

Economic performance

Kenya has managed to expand output slightly faster than the rate of population increase in the 1980s. However, performance slipped in the 1990s and GDP grew at 2.2 percent 1991-95 while population has expanded at 3.3 percent. Good coffee prices in 1996 and 1997 boosted performance, but current growth rates have slipped to around two percent a year, which is less than the rate of population expansion.

The main impetus for growth has come from the services sector. Industry, too, has performed well. Agricultural growth has not kept pace with population expansion, and the main constraint is the limited amount of fertile land. Kenya is gradually changing to higher value, intensively cultivated, crops such as horticulture, but the process is slow and limited to areas in the central highlands.

Export volume performance has been good, with a 3.3 percent rate of annual expansion. However, import volumes have fallen, caused by deterioration in the terms of trade and the need for increasing payments to service external debts. Currently debt service takes up over a quarter of export earnings.

Aid receipts per head are about average for Africa – they would be higher if the international community were more confident about the government intention to tackle corruption.

Inflation averaged 10 percent a year in the period 1980-93. This fairly good performance faltered in 1991 and 1992, when prices increased by over 20 percent thought to be the result of irresponsible spending by the government in the run-up to the election. Subsequently there has been rather erratic inflation performance, but in 1995 prices seemed more under control with an increase of under five percent. Alas, with the election in 1997, inflation has increased to 12 percent, but has now been reined in to six to seven percent.

Kenya has been in receipt of structural adjustment loans from the World Bank. Policy changes involve gradual amendments to bring domestic prices in line with world prices. Moves to privatize parastatal enterprises have been resisted (although most agricultural marketing monopolies have now been ended), and the donor community is beginning to lose patience over this issue.

Recent economic developments

A series of financial scandals led to a suspension of IMF support in 1994, but a new agreement was signed in April 1996 for US$200mn. The programme anticipates continued liberalization, more privatization, civil service reform and a campaign against corruption. This subsequently ran into difficulties and payments were suspended pending better performance in controlling inflation and implementing the privatization programme. Negotiations for a new IMF deal were under way in early 1999.

The financial sector has been subject to a series of failures by privately-owned domestic institutions. There have been collapses of five financial groups, where three have shown evidence of irregularities, and two have suffered from the ensuing lack of confidence. Banking regulations have been tightened, and banks with foreign ownership and control, namely Barclays and Standard Chartered, have increased their share of banking business, realizing higher profits.

Efforts are being made to reform and improve the performance of the parastatal sector with changes in management personnel. The grain purchasing body, the National Cereals and Produce Board (NCPB), provides a continuing problem as maize is bought at well above the world price, and in recent years of good harvests, the Board is accumulating stocks and runs at a continual loss. Kenya seems inclined to solve problems in the parastatal sector by reforms rather than privatization, although the monopoly of the NCPB has been terminated by making it a purchaser of last resort.

The government claims that 105 enterprises have been sold under the privatization programme. Two big developments in this area is the reorganization of Kenya Posts and Telecommunications into three units (one to be a regulatory body) prior to privatization. Kenya Power and Lighting is to have the distribution network separated from generation.

Kenya's trade balance has been affected by the decline in world commodity prices since the mid-1980s, particularly the prices for coffee and tea, though coffee prices improved in 1996/97. Imports stand below the level achieved in 1980, when US$2.3bn of goods were imported. Some US$7bn of external debt is estimated outstanding. Debt service takes up just under a third of export earnings and at present this is within Kenya's ability to service, providing export revenues can be maintained.

Kenya's exchange rate policy involves periodic adjustments such that the official rate responds to the market rate. The black market in foreign exchange is not particularly vigorous, but there is evidence of some measure of currency overvaluation. The exchange rate has remained fairly stable depreciating slightly each year (by about five percent) against the dollar.

Foreign investment has been steady despite uncertainty regarding local ownership provisions, and the UK's Mirror Group is investing US$43mn in publishing, printing and newspapers. Phillips is expanding its involvement in assembly of electrical goods, and the World Bank's International Finance Corporation has lent up to US$29mn for private sector paper production.

The severe flooding resulting from the 'El Niño' rains in the past year has disrupted agriculture, transport and communications, and it will be a while before normal conditions are restored.

Despite the good economic performance since independence, and the avoidance of major stability problems, there are reasons to be cautious about Kenya's prospects. The tourism sector is now the main source of foreign exchange earnings, and this is very vulnerable to perceptions of deterioration of law and order in the country. The political situation has

Economic outlook

undoubtedly improved with the introduction of a multi-party system and a large contingent of opposition MPs in the national assembly. However, the outbreaks of violence before elections are worrying, and it remains to be seen if the present political system can deliver stability and security on a long-term basis.

Social conditions Literacy rates are good at 71 percent, and noticeably better than the African average. There is almost universal primary education with 95 percent enrollments. Secondary enrolments are also good, with almost 30 percent of children receiving education at this level. Tertiary education is limited, compared with the rest of Africa, but Kenya has expanded its university enrollments substantially since 1980.

Life expectancy at 58 years is better than the Africa average. Food availability with 86 percent of minimum requirements being met, give cause for concern. Population per doctor is high, but medical delivery is good, given the low income level, with the infant mortality rate significantly lower than the African average.

Females have good access to primary education, with the enrollment rate just a little below that of males. Female access is less good at the secondary level, with enrollments a quarter below those of males. Low income levels place heavy demands on women to contribute to family income by working outside the home, and female employment is almost 40 percent of the total. With such a high population growth rate, the fertility rate is lower than might be expected – it is below the Africa average. Contraception usage is high, with a third of women participating, and this should begin to reduce fertility rates and the population growth rate.

Environment Kenya has very little forest, only two percent of the total land area. High rates of population growth place demands on the forested area for cultivation and for fuelwood. Despite these pressures, Kenya has succeeded in preserving its forest area quite well, and over the past decade deforestation has only been at the rate of 0.1 percent a year.

Kenya has moderate domestic, agricultural and industrial water usage. Each year the usage of renewable fresh water resources is a manageable 7.4 percent.

Tanzania and Zanzibar

4

Tanzania and Zanzibar

Tanzania has unrivalled tourist attractions in its glorious game parks, the Indian Ocean coast, and a fascinating history embracing the earliest relics of man's evolution, the exotic influence of Zanzibar, early explorers, and the colonial presence of the Germans and British which began over a century ago. Tanzanians are friendly, warm-hearted and relaxed, the country is free from any serious tensions between ethnic groups and it has an enviable political stability.
Exchange rate September : Tsh 792.25 = US$1

Essentials

Before you travel

Getting in **Visas** Visas are required by all visitors except citizens of the Commonwealth (excluding UK citizens who **do** now need visas), Republic of Ireland, Sweden, Norway, Denmark, Finland, Romania. Citizens of neighbouring countries do not normally require visas. For other nationalities, visas can be obtained from Tanzanian Embassies, require two passport photographs, cost from between US$10 and US$50 (although this varies according to nationality) and are issued in 24 hours. An entry stamp is valid for non-visa visitors and is valid for 1-3 months. Your passport must be valid for a minimum of 6 months after your planned departure date from Tanzania.

It is straightforward to get a visa at the point of entry (ie border crossing or airport) and many visitors find this more convenient than going to an Embassy.

Travelling with your own car from Kenya requires leaving the vehicle log book with the Kenyan customs, and keeping a photostat copy for the Tanzanian side.

Tanzania charges US$65 for the car (multiple entry valid for 3 months) and car insurance US$34 per month.

Resident status for persons permanently employed in Tanzania can be arranged after arrival. Your employer will need to vouch for you, and the process can take several weeks. Resident status does, however, confer certain privileges (lower rates on air-flights, in hotels, game parks).

Vaccinations You will require a valid yellow fever vaccination certificate if you are arriving from a country where yellow fever occurs. Although visitors from Europe are not required to have one, it is strongly advised – you may find you are restricted in visiting neighbouring countries. However, recent travellers have been asked to produce a Yellow Fever Certificate on arrival directly from Europe, even though they have not passed through a high risk area.

Finding out In the UK: Tanzania Tourist Board, 80 Borough High St, London SE1, T0171-4070566. Tanzania
more Tourist Corporation also has offices in Dar es Salaam and Arusha: **Tanzania Tourist Board**, PO Box 2485 Dar es Salaam, T+51-111245/27673, F+51-113311, their internet site is http://www.tanzania-web.com; **Tanzania Tourist Board Information Centre**, PO Box 2348, Arusha, T+57-3842/3, F+57-8256, Tx42037. It has been an ineffective organization concerned only marketing its own state-run hotels, transport services, and the national parks. It is now being wound up and a new body is revamping information services but it remains to be seen how effective it will be.

The National Parks office in the Arusha International Conference Centre is a good source of information and has such booklets on the individual parks as are currently in print. **Tanzania National Parks**, PO Box 3134, Arusha, T+57-3471/3181, Tx42130 TANAPA TZ.

Travel and tour agents These are listed under the place of their location: Arusha, page 398; Dar es Salaam, page 344; Zanzibar, page 463. For the UK, page 520. Special interest safari operators, page 481. Specialist hunting tour operators, page 482.

Specialist tours Camel safaris *Adventure Centre*, PO Box 12095 Arusha, T057-7111, F057-8997. **Bike Tours** PO Box 75, Bath, Avon BA1 1BX, UK, T01225-480130, F01225-480132. Organizes cycling tours of northern Tanzania, Mt Kilimanjaro and the coast. Some camping, some lodge accommodation. Your luggage carried by vehicle. **Cycling Safaris** PO Box 10190, Mombasa, Kenya, T387326, F485454. Tours from Kenya to Tanzania with climb of Mt Kilimanjaro. **Walking** *Sherpa Expeditions*, 131a Heston Rd, Hounslow, Middlesex, TW5 0RD,

Tanzanian embassies and consulates

Angola, CP 1333 Luanda, T335205.
Belgium, 363 Ave Louise, 1050 Brussels, T26406500.
Burundi, Patrice Lumumba Av, BP 1653, Bujumbura, T24634.
Canada, 50 Range Rd, Ottawa, Ontario KIN 8J4, T613-2321500.
China, 53 San Li Tun Dongliujie, Beijing, T521408.
Egypt, 9 Abde Hamid Loufty St, Dokki, Cairo, T7041556.
France, 70 Boulevard Pereire Nord, 75017 Paris, T47762177.
Germany, Theatreplatz 26, 5300 Bonn 2, T0228-353477.
Guinea, BP 179 Donka, Conakry, T461332.
India, 27 Golf Links, New Delhi 110-003, T694351/2.
Italy, Via Giambattista Visco 9-00196, Rome, T06-3610898.
Japan, 21-9 Kamiyoga, 4 Chome Setagaya-ku, Tokyo 158, T03-4254531/3.
Kenya, PO Box 47790, Nairobi, T331056.
Mozambique, Ujamaa House, Avenida Marites Da Machava 852, PO Box 4515, Maputo, T744025.
Netherlands, a consulate is open Monday-Friday, 1000-1600, T0180-320939.

Nigeria, 8 Agor Odiyan St, Victoria Island, PO Box 6417, Lagos, T613594.
Russia, Pyatnitskaya, Ulitsa 33, Moscow, T2318146.
Rwanda, Ave Paul IV, BP 669, Kigali, T6074.
Saudi Arabia, PO Box 94320, Riyadh 11693, T45-42859.
Sudan, PO Box 6080, Khartoum, T78407/9.
Sweden, Oxtorgsgatan 2-4, PO Box 7255, 103-89 Stockholm, T08-244870.
Switzerland, 47 Ave Blanc, 1202 Geneva, T318929.
Uganda, 6 Kagera Rd, PO Box 5750, Kampala, T256272.
UK, 43 Hertford St, London W1Y 8DB, T0171-4998951.
USA, 2139 R St NW, Washington DC 20008, T202-9396128; and 205 East 42nd St, 13th floor, New York, NY 10017, T212-9729160.
RD Congo, 142 Boulevard du 30 Juin, BP 1612, Kinshasha, T32117.
Zambia, Ujamaa House, Plot No 5200, United Nations Av, PO Box 31219, Lusaka, T211422 211665.
Zimbabwe, Ujamaa House, 23 Baines Av, PO Box 4841, Harare, T721870.
See under Dar es Salaam (page 342) and Kigoma (page 426) for overseas country's embassies.

Tanzania & Zanzibar

UK, T0181-5772717, F0181-5729788. Organizes tours through Kenya to climb Kilimanjaro. Equipment can be hired if you don't have your own.

March, April and May can be months of heavy rain making travel on unsealed roads difficult. **Best time** Even in these months, however, there is an average of 4-6 hours of sunshine each day. **to visit**

See page 35 for detailed specialist advice. Malaria is the most serious risk. Take the tablets, use **Staying** vapour tablets on heated electrical pads, ask to have your hotel room sprayed each evening. **healthy** Cover your arms and legs at night and put repellent on your hands and face. If you observe mosquitoes in your hotel room, sleep under a net treated with insecticide.

It is not unusual to have a stomach upset on your first visit. Avoid drinking tap water and peel all fruit.

It is unwise to drink water, even when provided in a flask in a hotel. Stick to soft drinks, boil water in a travelling jug, or use water purifying tablets.

Currency Currently in circulation are TSh 200, 500, 1,000, 5,000 and 10,000 notes. Coins are **Money** TSh 50, 100: TSh 10 and 20 are little used.

The currency has suffered from extensive depreciation since 1983. Depreciation has been rapid since 1986, but has slowed down now that the main adjustments have been made. The rate is currently set by the market with only limited government intervention. In current conditions, the exchange rate will probably continue to depreciate at around 15 percent a year. In July 1998, it was around TSh655 = US$1 (it was TSh9 =$1 in 1983).

It is advisable to bring some foreign currency in small denomination notes and to keep at least one US$20 bill for when you leave. An endless source of annoyance is for a traveller to offer a US$20 TC to pay the airport departure tax, only to be told to go to the bureau and obtain dollars. Because of commisssion, the cheque will realize less than the US$20 required.

Visitors are advised to exercise caution at some of the border crossings. Conmen operate at Namanga, appearing to be 'official' but offering derisory exchange rates. It is important to have a rough guide to the exchange rate, US$1 = Tsh 755 July 1999.

Because of forgery, many banks now refuse to exchange TCs without showing them the purchase agreement – ie the slip issued at the point of sale.

Foreign exchange bureaux   The government has authorized Bureau de Change to set rates for buying foreign currency from the public. They will also sell foreign currency up to US$3,000 for *bona fide* travellers (you need to produce an international airline ticket).

Foreign exchange payments   In the state-owned and other large private hotels, rates are calculated directly in dollars, and must be paid in foreign currency. Airline fares, game park entrance fees and other odd payments to the government (such as the US$20 airport international departure tax) must be paid in foreign currency. There is pressure from the IMF and World Bank for Tanzania to end this requirement, so don't be surprised to find it is no longer the case at the time of your visit. At smaller hotels (B grade possibly, and certainly below) you can pay in local currency. You should pay all hotel bills other than the room rate (such as meals, drinks) in local currency – the rate used to convert the bill into dollars is usually markedly inferior to bureaus rates.

Black market   There is now no temptation to deal on the black market. The genuine street rate is no different from the bureau rate. You will be approached in the main towns, however, with offers of very high rates of exchange. The purpose is to trap you into circumstances where a swindle can be perpetrated. This will most likely take the form of an exchange in a back alley, hurriedly completed on the spurious grounds that the police are coming, only for you to find later that the Tanzanian currency is only a fraction of the sum agreed.

A more sophisticated ploy is to offer a generous rate for US$100, and to hand over the Tanzanian notes for you to count. When you produce the US$100 bill, the contact will express dismay. He says he has raised the Tanzanian shillings from several sources (the contact, in the old days of the thriving black market, always operated as a front for the real financier), and wants smaller denomination dollar notes to pay them off. He will suggest you hold on to the Tanzanian shillings while he goes off to try to break the US$100 bill. In a short while he returns. Alas he explains, he can't do it at the moment, but if you return later, he will have raised enough Tanzanian shillings from one source for the US$100. He hands you back the US$100, and you return the Tanzanian shillings. You are naturally a bit annoyed at the inconvenience. But not as annoyed as when you next try to change the US$100, only to find it is a high-class forgery (but clearly so from the quality of the printing and paper when you look at it closely), printed in Taiwan. Foreign exchange bureaux all have forgery detection machines.

Credit cards   These are now accepted by large hotels, airlines, major tour operators and travel agencies. Otherwise you need cash. Travellers cheques will not be taken by small hotels, restaurants and so on. It is wise to have a selection of small denomination dollar bills for any unforeseen needs.

It is not generally possible to get cash on a credit card such as Visa or Mastercard. It is possible to buy TCs from Rickshaw Travel, the American Express Agents, in Dar es Salaam (see page 345), on presentation of an American Express card, paying with a personal cheque.

Cost of living   In first rate hotels expect to spend US$150 a day. Careful tourists can live reasonably comfortably on US$60 a day and budget travellers can get by on US$20.

Getting there

The majority of travellers arrive in Tanzania through Dar es Salaam Airport. There are also **Air**
direct international flights to Arusha (Kilimanjaro Airport) and to Zanzibar. Carriers will usually
make the final leg of the journey from an airport in their own country, but will arrange
connecting flights from the other main European cities.

From **Europe** to **Dar es Salaam**, British Airways has 3 flights a week with a refuelling stop
in Nairobi. Passengers in transit are now allowed to disembark, making the total flight time
around 11 hours. Airlines with regular flights are Aeroflot, Air France, Egypt Air, Ethiopian
Airlines, Gulf Air, KLM, Swissair and Alliance (run by South African Airways). Air Tanzania has
suspended its service to London. To **Kilimanjaro** (Arusha/Moshi), flights by Egypt Air,
Ethiopian Airlines and KLM touch down on the way to Dar es Salaam. To **Zanzibar**, Gulf Air
has a direct flight.

From other part of **Africa**, there are regular flights by Air Botswana, Air Tanzania, Air
Zimbabwe, Kenya Airways, Royal Swazi, Zambia Airways, South African Airways. Air France
connects from **Comoros**.

Specialist agents will arrange economical fares from Europe, typically for fixed arrival and
departure dates, and for stays of a week or longer. Fares depend on the season. High season is
generally July-end March (expect to pay around US$900 return from Europe with a prestige
carrier, depending on country of departure), with the low season for April, May, June at around
US$750. You may do significantly better by shopping around. Gulf Air have occasionally offered
heavily discounted fares of around US$400 return. It is not generally cheaper to arrange a return
to Nairobi and a connecting return flight to Dar es Salaam. The connecting flights are not
reliable, and delay in Nairobi erode any cost advantage. For budget travellers, a return to Nairobi
and a road connection to Dar es Salaam can result in a savings of perhaps US$100.
    For specialist agencies offering discounted fares, see page 28.

Rail services link Dar es Salaam and Zambia, see page 306 for prices and timetable. Trains **Train**
used to run across the border to Kenya from Moshi. These were ended with the break-up of
the East Africa Community in 1977, but there are discussions on resuming the service.

The main road crossing is at Namanga, see page 407, on the road between Arusha and **Road**
Nairobi. This is reasonably quick and efficient and there are through buses and good roads all
the way. Other crossings are at Lunga Lunga, see page 360, between Mombassa and Dar es
Salaam. The road on the Tanzanian side is less good, but there are overnight through buses
between the two cities. There are also crossings at Taveta, between Moshi and Voi; at Isebania,
between Kisuma, and Musoma, see page 403; and across the border from Masai Mara Park
into the Serengetti. From Uganda there is crossing at Mutakulu, page 411, between Bukoba
and Masaka but there are no regular buses to the border on either side.
    From **Burundi** there is no feasible road access. From **Rwanda** there is a good bus link to
the border at Rusomo. There is a bus leaving very early each day from Ngara on the Tanzania
side and arriving at Mwanza in the evening.
    From **Mozambique** there appears to be no feasible road access.
    From **Zambia** there are buses to the border at Nakonde, see page 435. You have to walk
between the border posts (or use a bicycle-taxi) to Tunduma where there are buses to Mbeya.

From Kenya there have been boats from Mombasa to Tanga, Zanzibar and Dar es Salaam. The **Sea**
providers of this service change fairly frequently. The crafts in use are usually hydrofoils and
catamarans. The cost was about the same as the air fare from Mombasa (US$45).
    It is possible to take a dhow from Mombasa, see page 175. However you must expect to
wait around for a week or more for one to depart. It will take 1 or 2 days depending on the
weather. Expect to pay about US$15, bring all your own food, and you will sit and sleep on the
cargo.

Touching down

Tanzania & Zanzibar

Business hours *Most offices will start at 0800, lunch between 1200-1300, finish business at 1700, Monday to Friday; 0900-1200 on Saturday, although the introduction of competition from the private sector will probably lead to longer banking hours.*

Official time *3 hours ahead of GMT.*
IDD 255*. Double ring repeated regularly means it is ringing; short equal tones with short pauses means it is engaged.*
Weights and measures *Officially metric, but expect to pay for fruit and vegetables by the item.*

Shipping information Nedlloyd, PO Box 63361 Dar es Salaam, Mobitel 0811-325222, F46339, Tx41235/41145; **Nasaco Pangani dept**, PO Box 9082, Dar es Salaam, T112574, F44504, Tx41235/41145.

Ferry From Burundi there is a lake ferry to Kigoma from Bujumbura, every Monday. From Mpulungu (Zambia) there is a weekly ferry to Kigoma on Friday (see page 426 for further details). From Nkhata Bay (Malawi) there is a ferry to Mbamba Bay on Wednesdays. From Uganda there is a ferry from Port Bell, Kampala, see page 575, to Mwanza on Monday.

Customs There is now no requirement to change currency on entry. A litre of spirits or wine and 200 cigarettes are duty free. There will be no duty on any equipment for your own use (such as a laptop computer). Narcotics, pornography and firearms are prohibited. Duty is payable on fax machines, TVs, video recorders and other household electrical items.

Touching down

Airport information Dar es Salaam airport lies 15 kilometres west of the city, T+51-42111. There are foreign exchange bureaux, but limited hotel bookings or car hire facilities. Visitors are advised to proceed directly to a hotel where these things can be arranged. Flight information is virtually impossible to obtain by telephone at the airport. Contact airline direct.

There is still a problem with some of the Immigration officials at the airport, who mark your passport on entry with an incomprehensible squiggle. When you leave you are told you have overstayed and that you will have to pay a fine. Get a clearly marked period recorded in your passport on arrival.

Phone cards are available from shops just outside the airport and cost US$3. There are public telephones in the terminal buildings.

Airline offices Offices of these airlines in Tanzania are listed under Dar es Salaam, page 342, and Arusha, page 397.

Departure tax This is payable on leaving and is US$20 or £15, payable in foreign currency. A TC will need to be changed into dollars.

Transport **Local Bus**: there are official buses which cost around US$3 and go to the *New Africa Hotel* in the town centre. There are private buses (*dala dala*) which cost about US$1 but are very crowded, leaving when full. **Taxi**: a taxi to town will cost US$10-15 depending on your destination.

Rules, conduct & etiquette Travellers are encouraged to show respect by adhering to a modest dress code in public places, especially in the pre-dominantly Muslim areas like Zanzibar. Respect is accorded to elderly people, usually by the greeting *Shikamoo, mzee* to a man and *Shikamoo, mama* to a woman.

At work in offices men will wear slacks, shoes and open neck shirts. If you are visiting a senior official it is safest to wear a tie and a jacket and a suit is desirable. In the evening at social functions there is no particular dress code although hosts will feel insulted if you arrive

Geckos

You are bound to see these interesting little creatures on even a short visit. They are small lizards up to 180 millimetres long, that live in houses behind picture frames and curtains etc. They should not be killed. Not only are they totally harmless to humans but they are in fact very useful as they eat many of the other less pleasant insects. House geckos usually appear from their hiding places at nightfall and go off in search of food in the form of anything from flies, moths and cockroaches to spiders and centipedes. You will see them running across walls and ceilings with ease – they have suction cups on their feet which enable them to stick to almost any surface. On a white wall they appear pale and almost translucent for they are like chameleons in that they change colour to suit their background. They thrive in houses but in fact they live almost anywhere and are found all across Africa. There are actually a number of different species of gecko, some of which are very hard to tell apart, but the house gecko is the one that you are most likely to come across. The gecko's name in Swahili is mjusi kafiri.

They lay eggs, usually in pairs, which are soft and sticky and are spherical. They stick to a crevice of the wall, rock or tree on and the egg shell very quickly sets hard. The eggs are brittle but they are very firmly attached to the wall. In colour they are opaque or bluish white and are up to 10 millimetres in diameter. When the eggs hatch the young gecko emerges, measuring about 65 millimetres long, of which about half is the tail and the rest the head and body. As it grows the gecko's tail grows faster than the body, so for most of the animal's life the tail is longer than the rest. It is said that if the gecko is lined up in the right direction, with the light behind it, you can see through its ear openings all the way through its head. To see this you need a very still gecko.

The house gecko has a number of enemies including birds and snakes as well as small children who seem to get some kind of a pleasure from seeing the tails of these creatures wriggling around without a body. Tail dropping is the gecko's most important defense mechanism and is used whenever they feel under threat. The tail falls off (or is pulled off by the hunter) but continues to wriggle and so provide a distraction so that the gecko can run off and hide. It will quickly grow another – in fact you may well see a gecko with a half-grown tail. One interesting phenomena about tail regeneration is when the original tail only partly breaks off a new one starts to develop at the point of injury. This results in a fork-tailed gecko.

Tanzania & Zanzibar

for dinner in shorts, sandals or bare feet. Long hair on men makes local people uneasy. Visiting mosques requires removing shoes and modest dress.

Electricity 220 volts (50 cycles). However the system is notorious for power surges. Computers are particularly vulnerable and laptops which operate from a charged battery are wise for the traveller. Offices will invariably run desk-tops through a voltage regulator. New socket installations are square 3-pin. However, do not be surprised to encounter old round 3-pin (large), 3-pin round (small) and 2-pin (small) in old hotels. An adaptor is essential.

Safety Tanzania has become less safe for travellers in recent years. The overwhelming majority of people are trustworthy. The following are sensible precautions to observe.

It is unwise to venture into unpopulated areas after dark particularly alone – always take a taxi. There are notices displayed to the effect that muggers operate on the beaches between the hotels north of Dar es Salaam and this is certainly the case. Stay within the beach areas controlled by the security guards. There are warning signs in Bagamoyo, but you are quite safe if a local person, even a child, accompanies you (they would identify any assailant). Thieves on buses and trains may steal valuables from inattentive riders. Visitors driving in game parks without an experienced driver or game park official accompanying them may be at risk. Crime and hazardous road conditions make travel by night dangerous. Car-jacking has occurred in both rural and urban areas. The majority of these attacks have occurred on the main road from Dar es Salaam to Zambia, between Morogoro and Mikumi National Park.

Travellers are advised not to stop between populated areas, and to travel in convoys whenever possible. Banditry against boat travellers on Lake Tanganyika near the port of Kigoma is increasing.

Things left lying around may well get stolen. Always lock your hotel door (a noisy air-conditioner can made it easy for a sneak thief). Do not wear expensive jewellry, or watches and beware of having a camera or necklace snatched in a crowd. Leave your passport, spare cash, airline ticket and credit cards in the hotel safe unless you will be needing them. It is particularly risky to have all these items in a snatchable waistbelt traveller's bag. A better option is a slim money belt worn under clothing.

Recently thieves have begun to cut open bags and rucksacks of travellers on buses, trains or whilst camping and extracting valuables. It is difficult to guard against all eventualities but is probably prudent to keep documents and money on your person, divided into several sites eg in socks, under clothes, etc.

Areas of instability After hundreds of thousands of refugees from Rwanda and Burundi entered Tanzania in 1993-94, Tanzania closed its land borders with these countries. Military forces were deployed in the Kigoma and Kagera regions. Although most refugees have now returned home, the border areas which includes several minor game reserves and Gombe Stream National Park, remain tense.

Tricksters These are not common in Tanzania, but always be cautious when approached by a stranger with a sponsorship form.

Beggars It is difficult to have a rational policy towards beggars. It is best not to give to street children – they are often encouraged to skip school or forced to beg by their parents. It is quite unnecessary to pay to have your car 'watched'. See Advice and Hints, page 28.

Tipping Large hotels will add a service charge. In smaller places tipping is optional. In restaurants most vistors will tip about 10 percent of the bill.

Animal safety Finally when you visit game reserves, it is not advisable to leave your tent or bandas during
precautions the night. Wild animals wander around the camps freely in the hours of darkness. Exercise care during daylight hours too – remember wild animals are dangerous.

Where to stay

Hotels Places to stay have been polarized between those used by well-heeled tourists, and are expensive, at around US$200 a day, self contained with air-conditioning, hot water and swimming pools, and those used by local people (and budget travellers) at under US$10 a day, which may comprise a simple bed, shared toilet and washing facilities, irregular water supply. The expensive establishments used to be run by the monopoly Tanzania Tourist Corporation and the others by the private sector. However, this has now become more liberalized and more private hotels are opening and the competition is giving travellers better choice. There are now some acceptable places to stay (except, alas, in the parks) with fans or a/c, hot water and self contained at around US$20 a day. In many East African countries a system operates where tourists are charged approximately double the rate for locals for hotels – resident and non-resident rates. Frequently non-residents are unable to pay in Tanzanian shillings.

Some of the small beach hotels are in splendid locations and despite having only simple facilities are excellent value.

In the parks, camping in either a tented camp or a campsite is more atmospheric and certainly cheaper than staying in one of the lodges. Many of the camps advertise hot running water for showers. This is accurate when the sun is out, otherwise the water is cool or cold. *Tarangire Safari Lodge* is an exception, with hot water available day or night (see sleeping classification, page 31).

Daily selected country buses from Dar es Salaam to:

	Departure time			*Departure time*
Arusha			**Moshi**	
Air Msae Tourism Coach	0700		Air Msae Tourist Coach	0700
Bazzu	0900			
Fresh ya Shamba	0800		**Nairobi**	
Master City	0700		Bazzu	0900
Metro Coach	0830		Hood	0900
Royal Sumayi	0700		Tawfiq	1000
Royal Sumayi Luxury	0700			
Tawfiq	0900		**Njombe**	
			Lupelo	1000
Dodoma			Makete	0700
Super Champion	0800 and 1100			
			Singida	
Iringa			Azan Investment	1100
Scandinavia	1030			
			Tanga	
Masasi			AMTCO	0700
Tawaqal	1600		Zafanana	0630
			Atlantic	0600
Mbeya				
Kwacha	1200		**Kyela to Malawi**	
Safina	0900		Magoma Moto	0900
			Stage Coach	1330
Mombasa				
Hood	1100		*Please note that this timetable is subject to change. It is advisable to confirm departure times locally.*	

Getting around

Air Air Tanzania Corporation (ATC) has a schedule of domestic flights. However ATC has run into financial difficulties and some routes do not operate.

Dar es Salaam-Zanzibar is well served with daily flights scheduled from ATC (US$43) 2 flights a day from ZATA (US$35). **Zanzibar-Pemba** has a daily flight from ZATA and 2 flights on Wednesday and Friday (US$40). **Pemba-Tanga** has 2 flights a week by Jasfa (US$35). **Arusha-Dar es Salaam** has 3 flights a week by Aviators Services (US$120). **Dar es Salaam-Mafia**. 3 flights a week by Aviators Services (US$40).

Fares vary between US$50 per 100 kilometres on short-hauls to US$15 per 100 kilometres on the longer trips.

Train Train services are fairly reliable. There are two railway companies operating in Tanzania. Tazara is the name of the Tanzania-Zambia Railway Authority and the trains run from Dar es Salaam southwesterly to Zambia.

The Tanzania Railway Corporation operates services between Dar es Salaam and Kigoma with a branch line to Mwanza central line. The Northern line service to Tanga and Moshi has been discontinued.

Road There is now an efficient network of privately run buses across the country. On the main routes (Arusha, Morogaro) there is a choice of 'luxury', 'semi-luxury' and 'regular'. Fares are very reasonable – roughly US$2 per 100 kilometres. On good sealed roads they cover 50 kilometres per hour. On unsealed or poorly maintained roads they will average only 20 kilometres per hour.

Tanzania & Zanzibar

Tanzania Zambia Railway Authority (TAZARA) Trains Timetable

Ordinary train service:
Monday, Thursday and Saturday

Express train service:
Tuesday and Friday

Station	Arr	Dep	Station	Arr	Dep
Dar es Salaam		0900	Dar es Salaam		1734
Mzenga	1050	1056	Kisaki	2144	2154
Kisaki	1408	1423	Ifakara	0033	0043
Mang'ula	1648	1657	Mlimba	0257	0317
Ifakara	1745	1759	Makambako	0759	0811
Mlimba	2044	2117	Mbeya	1224	1244
Kiyowela	0051	0053	Tunduma	1529	1548
Makambako	0237	0247	Nakonde*	1454	1554
Chimala	0509	0511	Lugozi*	1724	1744
Igurusi	0536	0538	Kasama*	2056	2116
Mbeya	0750	0810	Mpika*	0023	0043
Idiga	0852	0854	Serenje*	0441	0501
Vwawa	1016	1018	Mkushi*	0651	0659
Tunduma	1120	1145	New Kapiri Mposhi*	0833	
New Kapiri Mposhi*	1500				

Station	Arr	Dep	Station	Arr	Dep
New Kapiri Mposhi*		0920	New Kapiri Mposhi*		1345
Tunduma	1305	1322	Mkushi*	1522	1530
Vwawa	1430	1438	Serenje*	1731	1751
Idiga	1608	1613	Mpika*	2152	2212
Mbeya	1655	1720	Kasama*	0122	0142
Igurusi	1954	1950	Lugozi*	0456	0516
Chimala	2024	2032	Nakonde*	0638	0658
Makambako	2300	2317	Tunduma	0804	0824
Kiyowela	0105	0108	Mbeya	1105	1125
Mlimba	0502	0527	Makambako	1611	1621
Ifakara	0803	0809	Mlimba	2113	2133
Mang'ula	0855	0900	Ifakara	2345	2350
Kisaki	1119	1131	Kisaki	0127	0137
Mzenga	1504	1510	Dar es Salaam	0648	
Dar es Salaam	1700				

*Denotes Central African Time (CAT), which operates in Zambia, is one hour earlier than Eastern African Time (EAT) which operates in Tanzania.

Ordinary fares to Mbeya
1st class   US$45
2nd class   US$30
3rd class   US$20

Express fares to Mbeye
1st class   US$50
2nd class   US$35
3rd class   US$25

For further information or clarification, please contact:
General Manager, Tanzania Zambia Railway Authority (Tazara), PO Box 2834,
Dar es Salaam, Tanzania
T865192/865187/864191-9/862480/862191/862479
F865192/865187/862474
Tx41097/41059

NB This timetable is subject to change. It is advisable to check details before travelling.

Tanzania Railway Corporation – trains and marine schedules

Passenger trains

Station	ETD	ETA	Station	ETD	ETA
Dar es Salaam-Morogoro[1]	1700	2030	Morogoro-Dar es Salaam[3]	0215	0850
Morogoro-Dodoma[1]	0015	0735	Dodoma-Morogoro[3]	1840	0135
Dodoma-Tabora[1]	0810	1825	Tabora-Dodoma[3]	0725	1810
Tabora-Mwanza[1]	1930	0535	Mwanza-Tabora[1]	2000	0600
Tabora-Kigoma[1]	1910	0630	Kigoma-Tabora[3]	1900	0630
Tabora-Mpanda[2]	2010	1030	Mpanda-Tabora[4]	1300	0245
			Moshi-Dar es Salaam[5]	1600	0700

[1] = Days of travel are Tuesday, Wednesday, Friday and Sunday
[2] = Days of travel are Monday, Wednesday and Friday
[3] = Days of travel are Tuesday, Thursday, Friday and Sunday
[4] = Days of travel are Tuesday, Thursday and Sunday
[5] = Days of travel are Saturday

Alternative services

There is not direct rail service betwen Mwanza and Kigoma. Change at Tabora.
An additional service on Monday alternates between Dar es Salaam-Mwanza and Dar es Salaam-Kigoma routes.

Marine services

Lake Victoria Services, see page 407. Lake Tanganyika Services, see page 426. Lake Nyasa Services (sometimes called Lake Malawi), see page 439. Zanzibar, see page 341

Passenger fares: selected stations/ports

Rail	First class	Second class (Sleeping)	Third class
Dar es Salaam-Kigoma	US$60	US$44	US$20.75
Dar es Salaam-Mwanza	US$59	US$43	US$20.50
Dar es Salaam-Tabora	US$43	US$32	US$15
Dar es Salaam-Morogoro	US$17	US$13	US$11

Reservations

These can be done for any class of travel from all over the world at the following telephone and fax numbers: 112529, 117833, 112565 (code: 00 25551).

For further information, please contact:
Director General or the Principal Commercial Manager (Promotion), Tanzania Railways Corporation, PO Box 468, Dar es Salaam.

NB Fares and schedules are subject to change without notice

Tanzania & Zanzibar

On the main routes it is possible to book ahead at a kiosk at the bus stand and this is wise rather than turning up at the departure time on the off-chance. It is sensible to avoid being placed on a make-shift gangway seat with only a small seat back, or sitting over the wheel arch where it's impossible to stretch your legs. The roads in Tanzania are of variable quality. The best roads are the tarmac roads from Dar es Salaam to Zambia and Dar es Salaam to Arusha. Most of the remaining roads are unmade sand and gravel with potholes: there are many rough stretches.

Swahili slang

It will not take you long to notice that many Swahili words sound remarkably similar to English words. Indeed Swahili, which is by origin a Bantu language, has been greatly influenced by Arabic and more recently the language has been further enriched by borrowings from other languages including English. There are also examples where two words are in common usage, each with the same meaning but with different origins. For example 'week' – juma or wiki – derived from Arabic and English respectively; 'handkerchief' – anakachifi or leso – derived from English and Portuguese; and 'report' – ripoti or taarifa – from English and Arabic.

Some words that have been adopted are very obvious and, for example, modern transport has produced a large number of words – for example basi (bus), treni (train), stesheni (station), teksi (taxi), petroli, tanki, breki. A rich man is mbenzi – he would be expected to drive a Mercedes. A traffic bollard is a kiplefti. Small sweet eating bananas were introduced from the West Indies, and are known as ndizi.

Other adoptions may not seem immediately obvious – for example 'electricity' is sometimes called elekrii but more commonly stimu is used. This is because when the word was originally coined nearly all the electricity generating stations were run by steam engines. In the same way the word for steamship, meli, derives from the fact that when the word was first used almost all the ships that were around would have carried mail. The dockyards are kuli which is from the dockyard workers who were known as coolies.

The Second World War also produced a number of words which were adopted into the Swahili language, many of them relating to animals. For example a submarine was papa which is the word for shark, a tank was faru which means rhino, an aeroplane is ndege ulaya which means white-man's bird.

Swahili, like all other languages, also has a large collection of slang words. For example the period shortly before pay day when all the previous month's money has been spent is known as mwambo which is derived from the word wamba, to stretch tight. This implies that the user is financially stretched.

Coins have also been given a variety of nicknames. Examples include ng'aru which

---

Sea & lake ferries   The ferries are reliable and pleasant. Between Dar es Salaam and Zanzibar there are several sailings each day, with a choice of hydrofoil or steam ship. On **Lake Victoria**, the main sailings are between Mwanza and Bukoba, though small islands and some other lakeside towns are served. On **Lake Tanganyika** boats go from Kigoma to various small ports south. Fares for non-residents greatly exceed those for residents. On **Lake Nyasa** (also known as Lake Malawi) there is a boat going from the northern port of Itungi to Mbamba Bay, the last Tanzanian port on the east shore.

The cost of travel varies between US$40 per 100 kilometres for 1st class hydrofoil travel to US$2 per 100 kilometres for 3rd class on a steamer.

Car hire   Car hire is expensive and is difficult to justify for in-town travel in view of the availability, cheapness and willingness-to-wait of local taxis. Drivers with a hired car are normally more trouble than they are worth in town.

Other local transport   **Dala dala**   Local private buses and passenger vehicles constructed from small trucks (called dala dala, it is said, because they charged a dollar, although this seems a high sum) are for the adventurous. Tanzania banned these vehicles until recently, and road transport was a state monopoly. However, inability to provide enough buses (Dar es Salaam required 250 minimum, and was down to 60 in 1989) led to unseemly fights to get on, huge queues, and many commuters were resigned to walking up to 20 kilometres a day. State corporations and private firms tended to provide their own buses for staff. Liberalization of transport is an enormous improvement but although the dala dala are steadily expanding, they get very crowded and there is usually a fight to get on. A modifed truck vehicle will carry 50, of which 30 will stand and you really need to hang on as it sways around. Dala dala are cheap, US$0.10 for any length of journey, and are frequent on main routes into and out of town. Fellow

Tanzania & Zanzibar

derives from the word to shine, ku-ngaa. During the colonial era the shilling, which had a picture of the king's head on it, was known as Usi wa Kinga meaning the king's face. Five and 10 cents pieces which used to have a hole in the centre were nicknamed sikio la Mkwavi meaning 'the ear of the Mkwavi'. The Kwavi people are a pastoral tribe who pierce their ear lobes and often used to hang coins from them as decoration.

A slang phrase for bribery that has come into common usage is kuzunguka mbuyu which literally translated means to go behind a baobab tree, the implication being that behind the baobab tree, which is an exceptionally wide tree, no-one will see the transaction that takes place. The slang term for liquor is mtindi which actually means skimmed milk – it was probably used to conceal what was really being drunk. The term for drunk that is frequently used is kupiga mtindi which translates to mean 'to beat up the liquor' and is used in the same way that we would use 'to go on a binge'. Someone who is drunk may be described as amevaa miwani which literally translated means 'he is wearing spectacles' but is used to suggest that he can't see well as a result of the alcohol – we might say he was seeing double. Another similar phrase is yuko topu which translates to 'he is full right up to the top'.

Clothes have also attracted various nicknames. For example americani, the name given to the cheap cloth that was imported from America during the colonial era and became very popular. Drainpipe trousers were known as suruwali ya uchinjo which means cut off trousers – because being so narrow they look as if part of them is missing. Many of the names given to items of clothing are derived from English words, such as tai (tie), kala (collar), and soksi (socks). The phrase used by off-duty policemen to describe their clothes also needs little explanation: kuvaa kisivilyan which means 'to wear civilian clothes', while a fashionable haircut is known as fashun.

Many of the examples here were collected by R H Gower, a colonial administrator, and father of David Gower, the former England cricket captain who was born in Tanganyika.

Tanzania & Zanzibar

travellers will be very helpful in directing you to the correct *dala dala* if you ask (most have a sign indicating their route and destination on the front), will advise on connections, fight on your behalf to try to get you a seat and get you off at your destination.

Taxis Hotels and town-centre locations are well served by taxis, very run-down but serviceable. It is wise to sit in the back if there are no front seat belts. Hotel staff, even at the smallest locations, will rustle-up a taxi even when there is not one waiting outside. If you visit an out-of-town centre location, it is wise to ask the taxi to wait – it will normally be happy to do so for benefit of the return fare. Up to 1 kilometre should cost US$1. A trip to the outskirts of Dar es Salaam such as the University (13 kilometres) would be US$7.50. There is a bargaining element: none of the cabs have meters, and you should establish the fare (*bei gani*? – how much?) before you set off.

Keeping in touch

Language

Facility in English is poor. Even well-educated, professional Tanzanians, although perfectly able to make themselves understood, write and express themselves awkwardly. A few words of Swahili are very helpful in dealing with local people. It can be confusing when place names are spelt in various ways in different reference sources. This is a reflection of the oral origin of languages which have been transliterated into English.

Postal services

Postal system is reliable. Airmail takes about 2 weeks to destinations in Europe and North America. Buy stamps at the hotel or at a postcard shop. The post offices are crowded and queueing is not observed.

Area codes

051 Dar es Salaam	**0575** Kilimanjaro	**056** Morogoro	**0635** Songea
057 Arusha	Airport	**055** Moshi	**0637** Sumbawanga
066 Bukoba	**0695** Kigoma	**059** Mtwara	**062** Tabora
054 Chake (Pemba)	**0525** Lindi	**068** Musoma	**053** Tanga
061 Dodoma	**059** Masasi	**068** Mwanza	**0658** Tukuyu
064 Iringa	**065** Mbeya	**0632** Njombe	**054** Zanzibar

DHL has offices in the major cities. Packages to Europe take 2 working days, to North America, 3 days.

Telephone Services Poor. However the system is being up-graded at present. Local calls often more difficult than international. If you have an important appointment to make or flight to confirm, send a driver or go in person.

In Dar es Salaam there is an efficient international service from Telecoms, off Samora Ave. Connections are quick and about a third the price of a call through hotels which are expensive for phone calls and faxes.

Tanzania **Country Code** 255

Food and drink

Food Cuisine in Tanzania is not one of the country's main attractions. There is a legacy of uninspired British catering (soups, steaks, grilled chicken, chips, boiled vegetables, puddings, instant coffee). Asian eating places can be better, but are seldom of a high standard. There are a few Chinese and Italian restaurants. Some of the best food is prepared on simple charcoal grills outside in beer gardens (see restaurant classification, page 31).

A variety of items can be purchased from **street venders** who prepare and cook over charcoal, which adds considerably to the flavour, at temporary roadside shelters (kiosks). Street cuisine is pretty safe despite hygiene methods being fairly basic. Most of the items are cooked or peeled which deals with the health hazard. Grapes require careful washing or peeling.

Savoury items include chips, omelettes, barbecued beef on skewers (*mishkaki*), roast maize (corn), samosas, kebabs, hard-boiled eggs and roast cassava (look like white, peeled turnips) with red chili-pepper garnish. Fruits variously in season include oranges (peeled and halved), grapes, pineapples, bananas, mangoes (slices scored and turned inside-out), paw-paw (*papaya*). In the evenings, particularly, but all day at markets, bus and railways stations there are traditional swahili coffee vendors with large portable conical brass coffee pots with charcoal braziers underneath. The coffee is ground (not instant), is sold black in small porcelain cups fished out of a portable wash-bowl, and is excellent. They also sell peanut crisp bars and sugary cakes made from molasses. These items are very cheap – a skewer of meat is US$0.25, an orange (US$0.05), a cup of coffee (US$0.05). They are all worth trying, and when travelling, are indispensable.

Drink **Local beers** (lager) are very sound and cheap (US$1 a litre). There is a wide variety of imported lagers from Kenya and South Africa particularly, but also from Europe at around 3 times the price of local lagers. Imported **wines** are good value at US$6 a bottle upwards for European and South African labels. Wines from Zimbabwe are quite pleasant. Tanzanian wines produced by the White Fathers at Dodoma, 'Bowani Wine', are reasonable. Wines made by the National Milling Corporation are undrinkable. **Soft drinks** are mainly limited to cokes, orange, lemon, pineapple, tonic and club soda. No diet sodas available. Fresh juices are very rare. Coffee is invariably instant. When fresh ground it is the local Arabica variety with a distinctive, acidic flavour.

Swahili

Swahili is not a difficult language. In Shadows on the Grass *(1960)* Karen Blixen called it *'a primitive ungrammatical* lingua franca', *an observation that will infuriate Swahili scholars, particularly in Zanzibar where they take pride in the beautiful and pure form of the language spoken there.*

Those new to Swahili often have difficulty with the use of pre-fixes for plurals. Thus mzungu *is a European,* wazungu *is Europeans.*

Swahili is the main language of instruction in primary schools, and everyone speaks it. As such it is continually absorbing new words and concepts (see box).

For those wanting to go further the Swahili Dictionary *compiled by DV Perrot (Teach Yourself Books) New York: Hodder and Stoughton, contains a concise grammar (despite Karen Blixen) and a guide to pronunciation.*

Goodbye	Kwa heri
Yes	Ndio
No	Hapana
Good	Mzuri
Bad	Mbaya
How much?	Bei gani
Where is?	Wapi
Why?	Kwa nini
Food	Chakula
Water	Maji
Room	Chumba
Bed	Kitanga
Toilet	Choo
One	Moja
Two	Mbili
Three	Tata
Four	Nne
Five	Tano
Ten	Kumi
Hundred	Mia
Thousand	Elfu

Swahili Basics

Please	Tafadhali
Thank you	Asante
Sorry	Pole
Hello	Jambo

Swahili Exotica

Parrot	Kasuka
Sick	Kutapika
As	Kama

Tanzania & Zanzibar

Entertainment

Cinemas Found in most large towns, they will show mostly Indian, King Fu and Western films of the action variety.

Music Most musical entertainment is in hotels where traditional dance programmes are staged for tourists, and there are live bands and discos. Hotels and social halls often stage fashion and musical shows where local entertainers impersonate Western pop stars. These events are all well-publicised in the local press.

Newspapers Tanzania has two English dailies, *Daily News* and the *Guardian*, as well as several Swahili dailies, but all are difficult to obtain outside Dar es Salaam. An excellent regional paper, *The East African*, published in Nairobi comes out weekly and has good Tanzanian coverage. The Kenyan daily, *The Nation*, is available in Arusha, Mwanza and Dar es Salaam from midday, and is a high quality source of regional and international news. There are a number of independent weeklies. The *Business Times* gives excellent coverage of commercial matters, *Family Circle* has served as a vehicle for criticism of the government, as does *The Express*. The Tanzanian press is worth sampling for the bizarre and curious local stories that appear (eg 'Vicar Kicks Worshippers Who Insist on Kneeling' – *Daily News* December 1992) as well as being the main vehicle for entertainment and sporting announcements.

Radio There are two government operated stations. Radio Tanzania on 1442 KHZ MW broadcasts in Swahili. The External Service at 1204 MW has programmes in English. News bulletins tend to contain a lot of local coverage. Programmes of African music are good, and the discussion programmes tend to be fairly serious, on health, development, education etc. In 1994 a new private station, Radio One, began broadcasting, mostly music and in Swahili. **BBC World**

Service is broadcast to Tanzania and can be received on radios with short waveband reception, see guide, page 33.

Sporting events   In large towns the main activities will be soccer matches. Fixtures tend to be arranged, or postponed, at short notice and details should be checked in the daily press. There are also cricket matches over weekends (predominantly a pursuit of the Asian community), golf, tennis and squash tournaments are held at clubs but open to the public. Occasional sailing regattas are held at the yacht clubs in Dar es Salaam and Tanga. Hash House Harriers (a paperchase running and social event) meet every Saturday afternoon in Dar es Salaam (details of the location of the meet can be obtained in the British Council offices on Samora Ave). Track and field meetings are staged, the Mt Meru marathon is an annual event in June, and there are boxing tournaments. For details see local press.

Television   In 1994 ITV began to transmit with a mixture of locally produced Swahili items and international programmes. Zanzibar has had television since the early 1970s, and the larger hotels will have a TV in one of the public rooms. It only operates in the evening, it is difficult to find a programme schedule, and a lot of videos are shown – it is said that if you hand a recent tape into the TV station they will put it out that evening. There is a flourishing video market with hire shops in all towns, though the quality is poor as most tapes are pirated.

Holidays and festivals

New Year's Day   1 January
Zanzibar Revolution Day (Zanzibar only)   12 January
CCM Foundation Day   5 February
Union Day   26 April
Mayday Workers Day   1 May
Farmer's Day   7 July
Peasant's Day   8 August
Prophet's birthday   10 September
Independence Day   9 December
Christmas Day   25 December
Boxing Day   26 December

Good Friday, Easter Monday, Id-ul-Fitr (end of Ramadan), Id-ul-Haji (Festival of Sacrifice), Islamic New Year, Prophet Mohammad's Birthday are other holidays which vary from year to year. Muslim festivals are timed according to local sightings of the various stages of the moon.

The Christian holidays will not be observed by all Muslims and vice-versa.

Further reading

History   Millar, C *Battle for the Bundu*. Superbly readable account of the First World War in German East Africa. Hibbert, C (1982) *Africa explored: Europeans in the Dark Continent,* London: Penguin. Fascinating detail on the early visitors and their motivations. Packenham, T(1991) *The Scramble for Africa,* London: Weidenfeld and Nicholson. The events that laid the foundations for the modern history of Tanzania.

Natural history   Grzimek, B (1959) *Serengeti Shall Not Die,* London: Collins. Classic account of the unique character of this world famous park. Douglas-Hamilton, I (1978) *Among the Elephants*, London: Collins. Interesting perspective on elephant conservation in Lake Manyara. Goodall, J (1971) *In the Shadow of Man,* London: Collins. Gives something of the flavour of what is involved in making a life's work of studying a particular species.

Dorst, J and Dandelot, PA (1970) *Field Guide to the Larger Mammals of Africa*, London: Collins. **Field guides**
Williams, J and Arlott, NA (1980) *Field guide to the Birds of East Africa*, London: Collins.
Larcassam, R (1971) *Hand guide to the Butterflies of East Africa*, London: Collins. Blundell, MA
(1987) *Field Guide to the Wild Flowers of East Africa*, London: Collins. Hedges, NR (1983) *Reptiles
and Amphibians of East Africa*, Narobi: Kenya Literature Bureau.

Waugh, E (1960) *A Tourist in Africa*, London: Chapman and Hall. A trip through Tanzania just **Travellers'**
prior to independence. Dahl, R (1986) *Going Solo*, London: Penguin. Impressions of a young **tales**
man sent out to work in the colonies.

Boyd, W *An Ice Cream War*. Neatly observed, humorous and sensitive tale set against First **Fiction**
World War campaign in East Africa. Boyd, W *Brazzaville Beach*. Although written as a West
African story, clearly based on Jane Goodall and the chimps of Gombe Stream.

Briggs, P (1993) *Guide to Tanzania*, Bradt: Chalfont St Peter. Very good for budget travellers and **Other Guides**
those planning hikes and treks. Else, D. *Guide to Zanzibar and Pemba*, Bradt: Chalfont St Peter.
Comprehensive, modern guide to the Islands. Good items of background information.
Spectrum (1992) *Guide to Tanzania and Pemba*. Nairobi: Camerapix. Quite glorious
photographs which serve to capture the special flavour of Tanzania and Zanzibar. Else, D.
Trekking in East Africa, Lonely Planet.

Tanzania & Zanzibar

Dar es Salaam

Dar es Salaam

6°50'S 39°12'E
Altitude: sea level
Phone code: 051
Colour map 3, grid B5

Dar es Salaam is the capital of Tanzania and the seat of government, although there are plans to move the capital to Dodoma. The city is located at sea level on the Indian Ocean coast and occupies an area of 90 square kilometres.

It is by some measure the largest city in Tanzania, and has grown rapidly since independence in 1961, roughly trebling in size. Almost all administrative, political and business activity is concentrated in the city although some government bodies and the main parliamentary sittings are in Dodoma, 480 kilometres to the west.

The city dates from 1857 and was successively under the control of Zanzibar, Germany and Britain before self-determination, and these influences have all left their mark. The first impression of the city on the journey in from the airport is of very shabby buildings and a dilapidated infrastructure. There is a marked contrast between the conditions of ordinary people (walking long distances, crowded on buses and makeshift transport, living in ramshackle dwellings, operating small businesses from temporary shelters) on the one hand, and the bureaucratic, business and international community which enjoys much higher standards. On closer acquaintance with Dar es Salaam the visitor is invariably surprised by the wealth of historical interest that has survived, appreciates the splendid coastal location, warms to the friendliness and relaxed manner of the inhabitants, and learns to seek out the special pleasures the city has to offer, which are not always apparent to the casual observer. There is a saying in Dar es Salaam that "the city has sun, climate, location – everything, in fact, except luck."

Ins and outs

Getting there **Air** As the main city, Dar es Salaam is the principal terminus for international travel and for the domestic transport network (see page 302). International and domestic flights depart from Dar es Salaam International Airport, along Pugu Rd, 13 kilometres from the city centre. *Dala dala* and minibuses run regularly, but are crowded and can be a problem with luggage. There is a shuttle bus service from *New Africa Hotel* on Maktaba St and the fare is about US$2. Taxis to the airport from the centre cost about US$15. The bus to the airport leaves from opposite the old GPO.

Train Central and northwestern areas run from the Central Railway station, Sokoine Drive, T110600. It is convenient for most hotels. Trains for the southwest leave from Tazara station some 5 kilometres from the centre. There are plenty of **dala dala** and a taxi costs about US$4.

Bus There are three main bus stations for up-country travel. **Iringa, Mbeya, Songea, Tanga, Mombasa**: bus station on UWT St at the intersection with Uhuru St on the City side of the Mnazi Moja open space. **Arusha, Moshi, Namanga, Nairobi**: bus station on Morogoro Rd at junction with Libya Road. **Bagamoyo, Morogoro, Dodoma, Mwanza, Kilwa**: bus station in Kariakooo on Msimbazi St (taxi from centre about US$3).

Boats Boats to Zanzibar, Tanga, Mafia Island, Lindi, Mtwara leave from the jetty on Sokoine Drive opposite St Joseph's Cathedral. Dhows sailing and motorized, leave

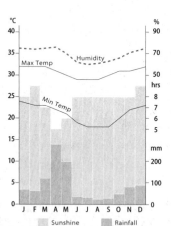

Climate:
Dar es Salaam

Sunshine   Rainfall

from the wharf just to the south of the boat jetty. The sea services to Mombasa have been suspended, but could resume at any time. Most of the companies request payment in US$.

Dala dala: (privately run buses, minibuses, pick-ups and lorries converted to carry passengers) are uncomfortable, hot and cheap at around US$0.20 for any length of journey. The front of the vehicle usually has a sign stating the destination. They leave the start of the route when full, and as that means packed, it is sometimes difficult to get on at intermediate stops, and virtually impossible to get a seat. It is, however, an extremely efficient system providing you can handle the congestion and having to stand. Fellow passengers are unfailingly helpful and will advise on connections. The main terminals in town are at the Railway Station (Stesheni) and the Post Office (Posta) on Maktaba St. **Taxis**: are readily available in the town centre, cost around US$1-2 per kilometre, and are battered but serviceable. **Always negotiate the fare before setting off**. If you are visiting a non-central location, eg Oyster Bay or Msasani Peninsula, and there is no taxi stand at the destination, always ask the driver to wait. — **Getting around**

The hottest months are December to the end of March with long rains March to May and short rains in November and December. The best season is June to October, although there is sun all the year round, even during the rains, which are short and heavy. — **Climate**

History

The name Dar es Salaam means 'Haven of Peace' and was chosen by the founder of the city, Seyyid Majid, Sultan of Zanzibar. The harbour is sheltered, with a narrow inlet channel protecting the water from the Indian Ocean. An early visitor, Frederic Elton in 1873 remarked that "its healthy, the air clear – the site a beautiful one and the surrounding country green and well-wooded." — **Zanzibar period 1862-86**

Despite the natural advantages it was not chosen as a harbour earlier due to the difficulties of approaching through the narrow inlet during the monsoon season and there were other sites, protected by the coral reef, along the Indian Ocean coast that were used instead.

Greater Dar es Salaam

Related maps
Dar es Salaam centre, page 320
Dar es Salaam Msasani Peninsula, page 326

Tanzania & Zanzibar

Majid decided to construct the city in 1862 as the result of a desire to have a port and settlement on the mainland which would act as a focus for trade and caravans operating to the south. Bagamoyo, (see page 346), was already well established, but local interests there were inclined to oppose direction from Zanzibar, and the new city was a way of ensuring control from the outset.

Construction began in 1865 and the name was chosen in 1866. Streets were laid out, based around what is now Sokoine Drive running along the shoreline to the north of the inner harbour. Water was secured by the sinking of stone wells, and the largest building was the Sultan's palace. An engraving of 1869 shows the palace to have been a substantial stone, two-storey building, with the upper-storey having sloping walls and a crenellated parapet, sited close to the shore on the present-day site of Malindi Wharf. In appearance it was similar in style to the fort which survives in Zanzibar, (see page 452). To the southwest, along the shore, was a mosque and to the northwest a group of buildings, some of two storeys with flat roofs and some with pitched thatched roofs. Most of these buildings were used in conjunction with trading activities and some of them would have been warehouses. One building which survives is the double-storeyed structure now known as the Old Boma, on the corner of Morogoro Rd and Sokoine Drive. The Sultan used it as an official residence for guests, and in 1867 a Western-style banquet was given for the British, French, German and American consuls to launch the new city. Craftsmen and slaves were brought from Zanzibar for construction work. Coral for the masonry was cut from the reef and nearby islands. A steam tug was ordered from Germany to assist with the tricky harbour entrance and to speed up movements in the wind-sheltered inner waters. Economic life centred on agricultural cultivation (particularly coconut plantations), traders who dealt with the local Zaramo people as well as with the long-distance caravan traffic.

Dar es Salaam suffered its first stroke of ill-luck when Majid died suddenly in 1870, after a fall in his new palace, and he was succeeded as Sultan by his

Dar es Salaam - 1891

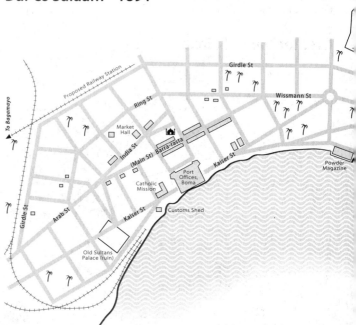

half-brother, Seyyid Barghash. Barghash did not share Majid's enthusiasm for the new settlement, and indeed Majid's death was taken to indicate that carrying on with the project would bring ill-fortune. The court remained in Zanzibar. Bagamoyo and Kilwa predominated as mainland trading centres. The Palace and other buildings were abandoned, and the fabric rapidly fell into decay. Nevertheless the foundation of a Zaramo settlement and Indian commercial involvement had been established.

Despite the neglect, Barghash maintained control over Dar es Salaam through an agent (*akida*) and later a governor (*wali*) and Arab and Baluchi troops (see page 347). An Indian customs officer collected duties for use of the harbour and the Sultan's coconut plantations were maintained. Some commercial momentum had been established, and the Zaramo traded gum-copal, rubber, coconuts, rice and fish for cloth, iron-ware and beads. The population expanded to around 5,000 by 1887, and comprised a cosmopolitan mixture of the Sultan's officials, soldiers, planters, traders, and ship-owners, as well as Arabs, Swahilis and Zaramos, Indian Muslims, Hindus and the odd European.

In 1887 the German East African Company under Hauptmann Leue took up residence in Dar es Salaam. They occupied the residence of the Sultan's governor whom they succeeded in getting recalled to Zanzibar, took over the collection of customs dues, and, in return for a payment to the Zaramo, obtained a concession on the land. The Zaramo, Swahili and Arabs opposed this European takeover, and this culminated in the Arab revolt of 1888-9 which involved most of the coastal region as well as Dar es Salaam. The city came under sporadic attack and the buildings of the Berlin Mission, a Lutheran denomination located on a site close to the present Kivokoni ferry, were destroyed. When the revolt was crushed, and the German government took over responsibility from the German East Africa Company in 1891, Dar es Salaam was selected as the main centre for administration and commercial activities.

German period 1887-1916

German development involved the construction of many substantial buildings,

and most of these survive today. In the quarter of a century to 1916, several fine buildings were laid out on Wilhelms Ufer (now Kivukoni Front), and these included administrative offices as well as a club and a casino. Landing steps to warehouses, and a hospital, were constructed on the site of the present Malindi Wharf and behind them the railway station. Just to the south of Kurasini Creek was the dockyard where the present deep-water docks are situated. A second hospital was built at the eastern end of Unter den Akazien and Becker Strasse, now Samora Ave. The post office is on what is now Sokoine Drive at the junction with Mkwepu St. A governor's residence provided the basis for the current State House. The principal hotels were the *Kaiserhof* which was demolished to build the *New Africa Hotel*, and the *Burger Hotel* razed to make way for the present Telecoms building. The Roman Catholic Cathedral is behind the customs jetty on Sokoine Drive and the Lutheran Cathedral is where Kivokoni Front forks away from Sokoine Drive.

(map labels) Ras Chokir (Arab Cemetery); Mjimwema; Graves; Government House; The Strand; Graves; Berlin Mission; N; 0 metres 150

(side tab) Tanzania & Zanzibar

The area behind the north harbour shore was laid out with fine acacia-lined streets and residential two-storey buildings with pitched corrugated iron roofs and first floor verandahs, and most of these survive. Behind the east waterfront were shop and office buildings, many of which are still standing, and can be recognized by their distinctive architectural style, (see page 539).

British period 1916-61

In the 45 years that the British administered Tanganyika, public construction was kept to a minimum on economy grounds, and business was carried on in the old German buildings. The governor's residence was damaged by naval gunfire in 1915, and was remodelled to form the present State House. In the 1920s, the Gymkhana Club was laid out on its present site behind Ocean Rd, and Mnazi Moja ('Coconut Grove') established as a park. The Selander Bridge causeway was constructed, and this opened up the Oyster Bay area to residential construction for the European community. The Yacht Club was built on the harbour shore (it is now the customs post) and behind it the Dar es Salaam Club (now the Hotel and Tourism Training Centre), both close to the present *Kilimanjaro Hotel*.

As was to be expected, road names were changed, as well as those of the most prominent buildings. Thus Wilhelms Ufer became Azania Front, Unter den Akazien became Acacia Ave, Kaiser Strasse became City Drive. Other streets were named after explorers Speke and Burton, and there was a Windsor St. One departure from the relentless Anglicization of the city was the change of Bismarck Strasse to Versailles St – perhaps surprising until it is recalled that it was the Treaty of Versailles in 1918 which allocated the former German East Africa to the British. The *Kaiserhof Hotel* became the *New Africa*, the *Burger Hotel* became the *Prince of Wales Hotel*.

The settling by the various groups living in the city into distinctive areas was consolidated during the British period. Europeans lived in Oyster Bay to the north of the city centre in large Mediterranean-style houses with arches, verandahs and gardens surrounded by solid security walls and fences. The Asians lived either in tenement-style blocks in the city centre or in the Upanga area in between the city and Oyster Bay where they constructed houses and bungalows with small gardens. African families built Swahili style houses, (see page 538), initially in the Kariakoo area to the west of the city. Others were accommodated in government bachelor quarters provided for railway, post office and other government employees. As population increased settlement spread out to Mikocheni and along Morogoro Rd, and Mteni to the south. An industrial area developed along the Pugu Rd, which was convenient for the port and was served by branch lines from the central and northern railway lines.

Independence 1961 to present

For the early years of independence Dar es Salaam managed to sustain its enviable reputation of being a gloriously located city with a fine harbour, generous parklands with tree-lined avenues (particularly in the botanical gardens and Gymkhana area), and a tidy central area of shops and services.

New developments saw the construction of high-rise government buildings, most notably the Telecoms building on the present Samora Ave, the *New Africa Hotel* for which the old Kaiserhof building was razed, the massive cream and brown Standard Bank Building (now National Bank of Commerce) on the corner of Sokoine Drive and Maktaba St, and the *Kilimanjaro Hotel* on a site next to the Dar es Salaam Club on Kivukoni Front.

With the Arusha Declaration of 1967, (see page 534), many buildings were nationalized and somewhat haphazardly occupied. The new tenants of the houses, shops and commercial buildings were thus inclined to undertake minimal repairs and maintenance. In many cases it was unclear who actually owned a building. The fabric of the city went into steady decline, and it is a testament to the sturdy construction of the buildings from the German period that so many of them survive. Roads fell into disrepair and the harbour became littered with rusting hulks.

The new government changed the names of streets and buildings, to reflect a change away from the colonial period. Thus Acacia became Independence Ave, the *Prince of Wales Hotel* became the *Splendid*. Later names were chosen to pay tribute to African leaders with Independence Ave changed to Samora, and Pugu Rd became Nkrumah St. President Nyerere decided that no streets or public buildings could be named after living Tanzanians, and so it was only after his death that City Drive was named after Prime Minister Edward Sokoine.

Old Dar es Salaam was saved by two factors. Firstly the economic decline which began in the 1970s, (see page 547), meant that there were limited resources for new modern blocks for which some of old colonial buildings would have had to make way. Secondly, the government in 1973 decided to move the capital to Dodoma. This didn't stop new government construction entirely, but it undoubtedly saved many historic buildings.

In the early 1980s, Dar es Salaam reached a low point, not dissimilar from the one reached almost exactly a century earlier with the death of Sultan Majid. In 1992 things began to improve. The colonial buildings have been classified as of historical interest and are to be preserved. Japanese aid has allowed a comprehensive restoration of the road system. Several historic buildings, most notably the Old Boma on Sokoine Drive, the Ministry of Health building on Luthuli Rd and the British Council headquarters on Samora Ave, have been restored or are undergoing restoration. Civic pride is returning. The Askari Monument has been cleaned up and the flower-beds replanted, the Cenotaph Plaza relaid, pavements and walkways repaired and the restoration of the Botanical Gardens has begun.

Walking tours

A walking tour (about half a day) of the historic parts of old Dar es Salaam might start at the **Askari Monument** at the junction of Samora Ave and Maktaba St. Originally on this site was a statue to Major Herman von Wissmann, the German explorer and soldier, who suppressed the coastal Arab Revolt of 1888-9 (see page 347) and went on to become governor of German East Africa in 1895-6. This first statue erected in 1911 depicted a pith-helmeted Wissmann, one hand on hip, the other on his sword, gazing out over the harbour with an African soldier at the base of the plinth draping a German flag over a reclining lion. It was demolished in 1916 when the British occupied Dar es Salaam, as were statues to Bismarck and Carl Peters. The present bronze statue, in memory of all those who died in the First World War, but principally dedicated to the Africa troops and porters, was unveiled in 1927. The statue was cast by Morris Bronze Founders of Westminster, London, and the sculptor was James Alexander Stevenson (1881-1937), who signed himself 'Myrander'. There are two bronze bas-reliefs on the sides of the plinth by the same sculptor, and the inscription, in English and Swahili, is from Rudyard Kipling.

Tour 1
See map page 320

Proceeding west towards the harbour, on the left is the *New Africa Hotel* on the site where the old *Kaiserhof Hotel* stood. The *New Africa Hotel* was once the finest building in Dar es Salaam and was the venue for the expats community to meet for sundowners. The terrace outside overlooked the Lutheran Church and the harbour, while a band played in the inner courtyard. Across Sokoine Drive, on the left is the **Lutheran Cathedral** with its distinctive red-tiled spire and tiled canopies over the windows to provide shade. Construction began in 1898. Opposite is the **Cenotaph**, again commemorating the 1914-18 war, which was unveiled in 1927, and restored in 1992.

Turning left along Kivokoni Front, there is a fine view through the palm trees across the harbour. Just past Ohio St, on the shore side, is the **Old Yacht Club**. Prior to the removal of the Club to its present site on the west side of Msasani Peninsular in 1967, small boats bobbing at anchor in the bay were a feature of the harbour. The Old Yacht Club buildings now house the harbour police headquarters. In the German period there were several warehouses along this part of the shore.

Tanzania & Zanzibar

Opposite the Old Yacht Club is the site of the German Club for civilians which was expanded to form the **Dar es Salaam Club** in the British period and is now the Hotel and Tourism Training Centre. It has a spacious terrace and a handsome bar. On the first floor are rooms that were used for accommodation, with verandahs facing inward and outside stone staircases. It is possible to use the bar, and to have a lunch prepared and served by the trainees. Evelyn Waugh once stayed at the DSM Club.

Passing the *Kilimanjaro Hotel*, on the corner of Mirambo St is the first of an impressive series of German government buildings. The first two, one now the High Court, and the other the present Magistrates Court on the corner of Luthuli Rd, were for senior officials. These had offices on the ground floor and spacious, high-ceilinged accommodation with verandahs, on the first floor (see architecture, page 539). In between is the old **Secretariat**, which housed the governor's offices. The first floor is supported by cast iron brackets which allow the verandah to over-hang. The verandah has been enclosed to provide more office space. On the other corner of Luthuli Rd is the German Officers' Mess, where some gambling evidently took place as it became known as the **Casino**. These buildings are exceptional, and it is a tribute to the high quality construction of the German period that they have

Dar es Salaam centre

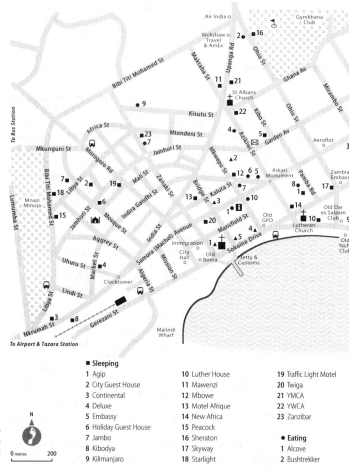

■ **Sleeping**
1 Agip
2 City Guest House
3 Continental
4 Deluxe
5 Embassy
6 Holiday Guest House
7 Jambo
8 Kibodya
9 Kilimanjaro

10 Luther House
11 Mawenzi
12 Mbowe
13 Motel Afrique
14 New Africa
15 Peacock
16 Sheraton
17 Skyway
18 Starlight

19 Traffic Light Motel
20 Twiga
21 YMCA
22 YWCA
23 Zanzibar

● **Eating**
1 Alcove
2 Bushtrekker

Related map
Greater Dar es
Salaam, page 315

N

0 metres   200

survived, with virtually no maintenance for the past 30 years. Construction was completed in 1893, and they have just passed their centenary.

On the shore side, just by the entrance to Luthuli Rd, was a landing pier in German times. Later, when a passenger pier was constructed opposite St Joseph's Cathedral, some landing steps replaced it, and these can still be seen. Further along Kivukoni Front, beyond the newer high-rise buildings is a group of single storey government offices constructed in the British period.

On the high ground past these offices is the site of the first European building in Dar es Salaam, the Berlin Mission. It was constructed in 1887, and was a fairly functional single storey rectangular building. Extensively damaged in the 1888-9 uprising it was rebuilt in two storeys with a corrugated-iron roof and an open gap between it and the walls which allowed ventilation. It was demolished in 1959 to make way for a hotel, which, in the event, was not constructed.

The eastern part of the city resembles an eagle's head (it is said the Masasani Peninsular is one of the eagle's wings). At the tip of the eagle's beak was a pier, just where the fishing village stands today, constructed in the British period for the use of the governor. This was just a little further round the promontory from the present ramp for the ferry which goes over to Kigamboni. Past Magogoni St is the Swimming Club, constructed in the British period and now mostly used by the Asian community.

Following Ocean Rd, on the left is the present **State House**, with a drive coming down to gates. This was the original German governor's residence. It had tall, Islamic-style arches on the ground floor rather similar to those in the building today, but the upper storey was a verandah with a parapet and the roof was supported on cast-iron columns. The building was bombarded by British warships in 1914 and extensively damaged. In 1922 it was rebuilt and the present scalloped upper storey arches added as well as the tower with the crenellated parapet.

The **German Hospital** is further along Ocean Rd with its distinctive domed towers topped by a clusters of iron spikes. It is an uneasy mixture of the grand (the towers) and the utilitarian (the corrugated-iron roofing). It was completed in 1897 and was added-to during the British period with single storey, bungalow-style wards to the rear.

Turning left past the baobab tree down Chimera Rd and taking the left fork, Luthuli Rd leads to the junction with Samora Ave. Here stood the statue of Bismarck, a replica of the celebrated Regas bust. The area either side of this boulevard, one of the glories of Dar es Salaam in the German era, was laid out as an extensive park. The flamboyant trees and *oreodoxa* (Royal Palms) still border the avenues.

Places to eat		Other	
3	Chinese	1	Catholic Cathedral
4	Garden Plaza	2	Club Billicanos
5	Happy Snack	3	Extelecoms House &
6	Hard Rock Café		Tanzania Coffee House
7	Internet Café (x 2)	4	Seyyid Bargash Building
8	Jungle Café	5	White Fathers' House -
9	RCL Internet Café		Atiman House
10	Salamandar		

Tanzania & Zanzibar (side margin)

Porters

From the days of the earliest explorers in the 19th century until railways and roads were built, the use of porters was vital to the opening up of East Africa. Anyone planning an expedition inland, whether an explorer, missionary, or trader, relied on porters (wapagazi) as the sole means of transport. Indeed the success of a trip into the interior depended largely on the health, strength and reliability of the porters. The use of draught animals was rendered impossible by the prevalence of the tsetse fly.

Porters came from many different tribes but broadly speaking there were two main groups. The first are the Nyamwezi/Sukuma who are usually bracketed together as their language and culture are very similar, and the second group was the Zanzibari/Swahili porters. `Zanzibari' porters were usually men who had travelled to the coast on an expedition and were then travelling back, while 'Swahili' porters were usually Muslim men of the coastal strip.

The Nyamwezi/Sukuma were generally considered to be the better porters and for many years were the mainstay of the caravan trade. They were an ingenious people and were very musical, singing songs as they walked. They carried their loads on one shoulder (unlike the Zanzibari/Swahili who carried them on their heads) and it is said that when they arrived at a place for the night they made great efforts to make themselves comfortable. The

Nyamwezi/Sukuma built themselves shelters and collected grass for matting, while the Zanzibari/Swahili porters were supposed to be much less bothered about their own comfort at the end of the day's walking, which some observers put down to laziness.

These were not the only groups who undertook porterage and others included men from around Rabai near Mombasa in Kenya. They were ex-slaves who found porterage a lucrative form of employment. However they were said to be the worst of all the porters – they had little sense of obligation to fulfil a contract, they would accept wages in advance, but they regularly absconded and were said to complain throughout the journey.

Porters from Uganda were supposed to be some of the best – they could carry heavier loads and endure longer marches more cheerfully than the other groups.

The loads that porters would carry varied a great deal. Around 1875 there were known examples of an single elephant's tusk weighing 55 kilograms being carried by one man – but this was very exceptional and usually it would be shared between two people. From the late 19th century until around the time of the First World War the loads weighed between 23 and 30 kilograms, although they would usually increase when a good food area was being passed through in order to be able to increase food rations.

In the First World War the load in the King's

The first Director of Agriculture, Professor Stuhlmann began laying out the **Botanic Gardens** in 1893. Initially there was also a vetinery station which was moved when the construction of the hospital began. The building to house the Agriculture Department as well as the Meteorological Station and the Government Geographer lies just to the southwest and was completed in 1903. It has recently been restored. By that time the gardens were well-established, Stuhlmann using his position as Chief Secretary from 1900-1903 to channel resources to their development. Stuhlmann went on to be Director of the Amani Agricultural Research Station (see page 381). The gardens became the home of the Dar es Salaam Horticultural Society which still has a building on the site. Recently the Gardens have undergone some rehabilitation with most of the exhibits now labelled. It is one of the few places to see the coco-de-mer palm tree apart from the Seychelles. Staff helpful but few of the plants are labelled.

To the left of the gardens is **Karimjee Hall**, built during the British era and which served as the home of the Legislative Council prior to independence. It then became the home of the National Assembly, the Bunge. In the same area is the original **National Museum** a single-storey stone building with a red-tiled roof and arched windows constructed as the King George V Memorial Museum in 1940, changing its

African Rifles was limited to 20 kilograms per man, while in the German forces loads were around 27 kilograms. On top of these weights the porter also had to carry all his own possessions and rations.

When the time came for choosing the porters it was probably the selection of the head porter that was most important to the success of the expedition. He had to oversee the porters and to be able to maintain the morale of the caravan at times of difficulty. If one of the porters was ill, it was up to the head porter to carry the extra load. He would often lead the singing and give a marching time to the porters. The other porters would be selected, followed by a negotiation of terms. A medical examination would take place so that only the most suitable men would be chosen. The men were usually given about two months wages in advance depending on the length of the trip.

The routine that most caravans seemed to follow was fairly similar. Before first light a bell would be rung or a bugle sound to wake up the camp. Sometimes a medical examination was carried out to deal with minor ailments and the porters would then collect up their loads – without having had anything to eat or drink. Their employer would usually have a cup of tea while his tent was packed away and then word went around to move on. As the men marched they would often sing, led by the head porter or else would chat among themselves. About two hours after dawn the leader of the expedition would have a light breakfast, but the porters themselves would continue on the journey. It seems incredible that they had the stamina to march for many hours without any sort of sustenance, while carrying a huge load – but that does seem to have been the general practice. The caravan would usually stop at around 10.00, as near to water as possible, having covered about 25 kilometres at a rate of about five kilometres an hour, before the main heat of the day. They would then set up camp for the night and the porters would at last get something to eat.

There is absolutely no doubt that the trade routes would not have been functionable without the porters and their importance cannot be overestimated. Employers of porters have almost invariably spoken in appreciative terms of them, and most were treated reasonably well. The impact of the porterage on the porters villages was also important – the absence of able-bodied men during the harvest would have been partially offset by their wages and goods that they would have bought. Also the passing of a large caravan through an area would have increased the demand for food supplies and thus stimulated domestic markets. The necessity for foot safaris did not vanish until the introduction of the railway and the motor vehicle.

name in 1963. A larger, modern building was constructed later to house exhibits, and the old building used as offices. ■ *Entry fee US$3. Student US$2.*

Turning left down Shaaban Robert St, on the other side of Sokoine Drive, in a crescent behind the Speaker's Office is the first school built in Dar es Salaam (1899) by the German government. It was predominantly for Africans, but also had a few Indian pupils, all children of state-employed officials (*akidas*). Walking west down Sokoine Drive we return to the *New Africa Hotel*.

A second half-day walking tour would begin at the *New Africa Hotel* and proceed west along Sokoine St past the National Bank of Commerce building on the right. On the corner with Mkwepa St is the German **Post Office** completed in 1893. Although the façade has been remodelled to give it a more modern appearance, the structure is basically unchanged. It was a pleasing two storey red-tiled building with a verandah on the first floor and a small tower with a pitched roof behind the main entrance which made for a more interesting roof-line. The windows were arched, and there was an impressive set of steps up to the main entrance. Just inside the entrance is a plaque to the memory of members of the Signals Corp who lost their lives in the First World War in East Africa. There are some 200 names listed with

Tour 2
See map page 320

particularly heavy representation from South Africa and India whose loyalty to the British Empire drew them into the conflict.

On the opposite corner to the Post Office is the site of the old customs headquarters, the **Seyyid Barghash** building constructed around 1869. The building on the corner with Bridge St is the modern multi-storey Wizaraya Maji, Nishati na Madim (Ministry of Water, Energy and Minerals) which is on the site of the old Custom House. Next door, sandwiched between the ministry building and Forodhani Secondary School is the **White Fathers House** – called **Atiman House**. It is named after a heroic and dedicated doctor Adrian Atiman, who was redeemed from slavery in Niger by White Father missionaries, educated in North Africa and Europe, and who worked for decades as a doctor in Tanzania until his death – circa 1924. Atiman House was constructed in the 1860s in the Zanzibar period. In fact the house, including a courtyard, is the oldest surviving house in the city, excluding administrative buildings. It was built as a residence for the Sultan of Zanzibar's Dar es Salaam wives, and sold by the Sultan to the White Fathers in 1922. In the visitors' parlour of the house are two extremely interesting old photographs of the waterfront at Dar es Salaam, as it was in German colonial times.

Continuing along Sokoine drive to the west, the next building is **St Joseph's Roman Catholic Cathedral**. Construction began in 1897, and took five years to complete. St Joseph's remains one of the most striking buildings in Dar es Salaam, dominating the harbour front. It has an impressive vaulted interior, shingle spire and a fine arrangement of arches and gables. Next to the Cathedral was Akida's Court.

On the corner of Morogoro Rd is the earliest surviving building, the **Old Boma** dating from 1867. On the opposite corner is the **City Hall**, a very handsome building with an impressive façade and elaborate decoration. Further along, on the corner of Algeria St is a three-storey commercial building with pillars and a verandah at first-floor level. The first two floors are from the Zanzibar period, with the third storey and the verandah being added later.

On the corner of Uhuru St is the **Railway Station**, a double-storey building with arches and a pitched-tile roof, the construction of which began in 1897. Between the station and the shore was the site of the palace of Sultan Majid and of the hospital for Africans constructed in 1895 by Sewa Haji (see box, page 354) but which was demolished in 1959.

Turning right in front of the railway station leads to the **Clock Tower**, a post-war concrete construction which was erected to celebrate the elevation of Dar es Salaam to city status in 1961. The Clock Tower is currently shrouded by scaffolding and boarding whilst being renovated. A right turn at the clock tower leads along Samora Ave and back to the Askari Monument. There are a number of buildings of stone construction that were erected by the local community, by Goan businessmen and by German commercial interests. The German buildings can be recognized by the two-storey style with a verandah at first-floor level, and by the use of pillars to support the first floor. Notable among these is the building that houses offices on the first floor, with the ground floor given over to shops and Salamandar Café, on the corner of Mkwepu St.

Other notable buildings in the City area include the present *Mbowe Hotel* on the corner of Mkwepu and Makunganya St, which was the *Palace Hotel*, and which dates from about 1920. On Mosque St is the **Darkhana Jama'at-Khana** of the Ismaili community, three-storeys high with a six-storey tower on the corner topped by a clock, a pitched roof and a weather-vane. It is in an ornate style with arches and decorated columns, and was constructed in 1930.

There are several other mosques, two (**Ibaddhi Mosque** and **Memon Mosque**) on Mosque St itself, one on Kitumbini St (the **Sunni mosque** with an impressive dome), and there are two mosques on UWT St, the **Ahmadiyya mosque** being near the junction with Pugo Rd and the other close by. On Kitsu St, there are two Hindu temples, and on Upanga Rd is a grand Ismaili building which is decorated with coloured lights during festival periods. This is the main Jama'at Khana.

St Albans Church on the corner of Upanga Rd and Maktaba St was constructed in the interwar period. St Albans is a grand building modelled on the Anglican Church in Zanzibar. This is the Anglican Church of the Province of Tanzania, and was the Governor's Church in colonial times. The **Greek Orthodox Church**, further along Upanga St, was constructed in the 1940s. **St Peter's Catholic Church**, off the Bagamoyo Rd, was constructed in 1962, and is in modern style with delicate concrete columns and arches.

The area to the northwest of India St, on either side of Morogoro Rd, was an Asian section of the city in the colonial period, and to a large extent remains so. The typical building would be several storeys high, the ground floor being given over to business premises with the upper storeys being used for residential accommodation. The façades of these buildings are typically ornate, often with the name of the proprietor and the date of construction prominently displayed. Two superb examples on Morogoro Rd, near Africa St, are the premises of M Jessa. One was a cigarette and tobacco factory and the other a rice mill.

Further to the west is the open Mnazi Mmoja (coconut grove) with the **Uhuru Monument** (dedicated to the freedom that came with independence). The original Uhuru monument is a white obelisk with a flame – the Freedom Torch. A second concrete monument designed by R Ashdown, was erected to commemorate 10 years of independence. This was enlivened with panels by a local artist. On the far side of the space is **Kariakoo**, laid out in a grid pattern and predominantly an African area. It become known as Kariakoo during the latter part of the First World War when African porters (the carrier corps, from which the current name is derived) were billeted there after the British took over the City in 1916. The houses are in Swahili Style (see page 538). The market in the centre and the shark market on the junction of Msimbazi and Tandamuti Sts are well worth a visit.

At the point of the eagle's beak, where the ferry leaves for Kivukoni, is the **Mzizima Fish Market**. Fresh fish can be purchased here. Mzizima is the name of the old fishing village that existed somewhere between State House and Ocean Road Hospital before Seyyid Majid founded Dar es Salaam in 1862. This stretch of sand was always known as **Banda Beach**, a well-known place for watching the ships coming in and out. Fishing boats, mostly lateen-sailed *ngalawas* are beached on the shore. There are some boat-builders on the site and it is interesting to observe the construction techniques which rely entirely on hand-tools.

Other sights

Further along Ocean Rd, past State House, are the grounds of the **Gymkhana Club**, which extend down to the shore. There were various cemeteries on the shore side of the golf course, European between the hospital and Ghana Ave, and a Hindu Crematorium beyond.

Gymkhana Club

At the intersection of Ocean Rd and Ufukoni Rd on the shore side is a rocky promontory which was the site of European residential dwellings constructed in the interwar period by the British. These are either side of Labon Drive (previously Seaview Rd). Continuing along Ocean Rd is Selander Bridge, a causeway over the Msimbazi Creek, a small river edged by marsh which circles back to the south behind the main part of the city. Beyond Selander Bridge, on the ocean side, is **Oyster Bay**, which became the main European residential area in the colonial era, and today is the location of many diplomatic missions. There are many spacious dwellings, particularly along Kenyatta Drive which looks across the bay. The area in front of the *Oyster Bay Hotel* is a favourite place for parking and socialising in the evenings and on weekends, particularly by the Asian community. Ice cream sellers and barbecue kiosks have sprung up in the last few years on the shore. In spite of the grand houses and embassies, unfortunately Oyster Bay has acquired a reputation for muggings and armed robberies, even in daylight hours, (see box on page 30).

Oyster Bay

Tanzania & Zanzibar

Kigamboni The ferry leaves from the harbour mouth, close to the fish market, where Kivukoni Front becomes Ocean Rd, at regular intervals during the day, crossing the mouth of the harbour to **Kigamboni**. The ferry takes vehicles, and this is the best way to reach this area as the approach from the land side circling the harbour inlet is a journey of about 40 kilometres over poor roads. Kigamboni is the site of Kivukoni College which provided training for CCM party members, but which is now being turned into a school and a social science academy. Just before the college, which

Dar es Salaam - Msasani Peninsula

Tanzania & Zanzibar

Related map
Greater Dar es
Salaam, page 315

faces across the harbour to Kivukoni Front is the Anglican Church and a free-standing bell. The Anglican Church was formerly a Lutheran Church. The Lutheran Church, a fine modern building, lies 500 metres into Kigamboni. On the Indian Ocean shore side, can be seen several small enterprises making lime by burning cairns of coral. The beaches on Kigamboni are the best close to the city, but they have not been developed as the ferry has been out of commission for lengthy periods in the past. A couple of unserviceable ferries can be seen beached on the main harbour shore.

Further along Ali Hassan Mwinyi Blvd, turning left at Mwenge, and then right at the petrol station leads to the **University of Dar es Salaam**. The university began life as a College in 1961 in a building still in existence in the area known as Mnazi Mmoja, on Lumumba St in the city, granting London University degrees. Initially it had only a law faculty as at the time law was not offered Makerere in Uganda or at Nairobi in Kenya. In 1964 the college moved to its present site on a hill some 10 kilometres west of the city. It become an independent university in 1970. The location is very attractive, and there are fine views across to Dar es Salaam from Observation Hill. Nkrumah Hall is a fine example of modern architecture and the ravine, crossed by a bridge, which runs from the faculty building to the post office and residential buildings, through trees, is particularly attractive. In the 1980s the fabric of the university buildings deteriorated considerably. In 1992, however, a rehabilitation programme started, and some of the former pride in the institution, buildings and site has begun to be restored. Transport to University of DSM: bus to Ubungo then bus to University (2 x US$0.20).

University

Museums

The museum gives a compact view of the main traditional dwelling styles of Tanzania, examples of artists and craftsmen at work, and, on Saturday and Sunday afternoons, there is a team of traditional dancers performing to drum music.

Makumbusho Village Museum

There are constructions from 13 groups with examples of dwelling huts, cattle pens, meeting huts and, in one case, an iron-smelting kiln. Among the artists and craftsmen resident is Issa Bahari, a Swahili from the coastal area who does ebony signs (US$7.50), and these are better value than in town. Issa will also carve a sign to your individual design. Allow three days for completion.

University of Dar es Salaam

Ardhi Institute
Gate House
Kileleni Housing
Mbugani Housing
University Rd
Kilimahewa Housing
UDASA Club
Darajani Housing
University Chapel
Simba Rd
Sinza Rd
Mosque
Nkrumah Hall
Weather Station
Uvumbuzi Rd
Sports Stadium
VC's House
To Mwenge & City Centre
Sam Njoma Rd
N
Not to scale
To Ubungo & City Centre

In one of the rooms of the Swahili banda is Helman Msole, a Fiba from southwest Tanzania with very striking paintings of village scenes and historical scenes on canvas (US$40 to US$80). Hand-painted postcards are US$2.50. Helman will paint a canvas from his collection (recorded on photos) in two days. Blassy Kisanga, a Chagga from Kilimangaro, depicts scenes with brown and black banana leaves on wooden panels (US$12.50 to US$40) and postcards (US$1.50). Petre Paulo Mayige, from Tabora makes clay figures of village scenes and *bao* games for US$7.50-40. Finally, Nyram Hsagula, a Swahili does the rather garish *tinga tinga* paintings on hardboard, as decorations on tins and bowls (US$2 to US$25). The art items are much a matter of taste –

Casuarina Cones

Casuarinas are also found in Australia. The theory is that they originated there – they are quite unlike most other trees in East Africa. It is thought that the seed-bearing cones were carried by the cold tidal currents from the west coast of Australia into the equatorial waters flowing west across the Indian Ocean to the shore of Tanzania and then north along the East African Coast in the Somalia current, eventually germinating after a journey of about 10,000 kilometres.

A particularly fine set of Casuarinas are to be seen along Ocean Road in Dar es Salaam.

the clay figures and the paintings of Helman Msole are not readily available elsewhere, and most visitors regard these as unusually good.

On Saturday and Sunday 1600-1800 a local dance troupe performs. It is a pity there is no guidance as to where the dances originate. The troupe is recruited from all over Tanzania and they end with a display of tumbling and acrobatics that is popular with children. There is a café, and an unusual compound, the Makumbusho Social Club, to which the public is welcome, with a number of small corrugated iron partly open-sided huts, each named after one of Tanzania's game parks. ■ *Open daily 0900-1900. This is situated along Bagamoyo Rd, about nine kilometres from the centre of Dar es Salaam, on the right-hand side of the road. There is a large sign indicating the entrance. It can be reached by taxi – about TSh 2,000 (US$4) – and it is advisable to ask the taxi to wait for you to return. A dala-dala, destination Mwenge, can be taken from Maktaba St, just opposite the post office for TSh 30 (US$0.10) and there are frequent returning dala-dala on this route. Entrance US$1, Tanzanians and all children free. Still photos US$2.50, video or cine US$10.*

National Museum The National Museum has collections of historical and archaeological items. The old photographs are particularly interesting. Traditional craft items are on display. Fossils from Olduvai Gorge are also kept there. ■ *Shabaan Robert St. Open 0930-1800. Entrance US$0.10 for residents; US$0.50 for non-residents; students free.*

Nyumba ya Sanaa This art gallery has displays of paintings in various styles as well as carvings and batiks. It is located by the roundabout on the intersection of Upanga and Ohio Sts.

Karibu Art Gallery On Bagamoyo Rd (beyond the Mwenge turn-off to the university) it has a good selection of carvings, paintings, pottery, jewelry and musical instruments. On Sunday there are traditional dance exhibitions.

Beaches

The shore close to Dar es Salaam is not particularly good for swimming. The best beaches are at Kunduchi, some 25 kilometres north of the city. A bus leaves from outside the *New Africa Hotel* in the City centre in the mornings and afternoons, and returns in the evening. *Silver Sands Hotel* and *Rungwe Oceanic Hotel* have fairly simple facilities. *Kunduchi Beach Hotel*, though a bit dilapidated, has an excellent beach, a swimming pool, and offers a variety of excursions to nearby islands and windsurfing. Snorkelling is variable as sometimes the water is not clear, especially during the rainy seasons. A band plays during the afternoons on Sunday. *Bahari Beach Hotel* is strikingly constructed from coral with thatched roofing for the main buildings and groups of rooms in similar style, and also has bands on Sunday and public holidays. These hotels make a charge for using their beaches for the day, around US$5-8.

To the south of Dar es Salaam and Kigamboni there are some very good beaches. To reach the nearest one, catch the ferry from the end of the Kivukoni Front. Once on the other side in Kigamboni, it is either a 30-minute walk along the coast (do not do this on your own as there are thieves here) or take a taxi. The second beach, which is the best one, is eight kilometres further and requires a car. Carry on directly south and branch off to the left. It is possible to get back to Dar via Mbagala and the Kilwa Road.

Excursions

In the peaceful rural hill town of Kisarawe it is hard to believe that you are just 32 kilometres southwest from the hustle and bustle of Dar es Salaam. During the colonial period Kisarawe was used by European residents of the capital as a kind of hill station to escape from the coastal heat. There is little to see in the town itself but the surrounding countryside is very attractive, in particular the nearby rain forest.

Kisarawe
Colour map 3, grid B5

Kisarawe can be visited on a day trip from Dar es Salaam. However, the best time for visiting the forest is early and late in the day and you may end up staying overnight. If so, *Zimbabwe Bar & Guest House* is cheap and basic, but it's reasonably clean and anyway you don't have much choice! The *Kigoma Restaurant* serves ugali and stew which is filling and couldn't really be bettered at US$0.75. *Getting there*: buses to Kisarawe leave from Narungumbe St (next to the Tanzania Postal Bank on Msimbazi St in Kariakoo) about once an hour. The trip takes one hour (plus a further 45 minutes or so waiting for the bus to fill up!) and costs US$0.75.

This reserve is situated about 3-4 kilometres from the centre of Kisarawe town. It constitutes one of the few remaining parts of a coastal forest which 10 million years ago extended from Mozambique to Northern Kenya. It was gazetted as a reserve in 1954, at which time it stretched all the way to the International airport in Dar es Salaam, and was home to many big game animals, including lions, hippos and elephants. Since then the natural growth of the metropolis, as well as the urban demand for charcoal (coupled with the lack of alternative sources of income), has seen a large reduction in the forested area. In the past few years a concerted effort has been made to counter this process and a nature trail has been established in order to encourage people to visit the area. You are unlikely to come across many animals in the forest but it is a very beautiful spot and the perfect tonic for those in need of a break from Dar es Salaam. Pugu Reserve contains flora and fauna which are unique to the forests of this district. Enquiries about the reserve can be made at the Forest Reserve Office in Kisarawe town. There is no charge at present, but this is likely to change in the near future.

Pugu Hills Forest Reserve

3-4 kilometres further on from the reserve is Pugu Kaolin mine, which was established by the Germans at the beginning of this century. Kaolin is a type of fine white clay that is used in the manufacture of porcelain, paper and textiles. The deposits here at Pugu are reputed to be the second largest in the world and should the market for it pick up, the mining of kaolin will clearly constitute a further threat to the survival of the remaining rain forest.

Pugu Kaolin Mine & the Bat Caves

If you continue through the mine compound you come to a 100 metre long, German built, disused railway tunnel (the railway was re-routed after the discovery of kaolin). On the other side of this are a series of man-made caves which house a huge colony of bats. At around 1800 or 1900 (depending on the time of year) the bats begin to fly out of the caves for feeding. It is a remarkable experience to stand in the mouth of the caves surrounded by the patter of wings as vast quantities of bats come streaming past you. To do this, however, you must be prepared to walk the 7-8 kilometres back to Kisarawe in the dark, so bring a torch.

Kisarawe

To Pugo Forest Reserve/ Nature Trail & Pugo Kaolin Mine

School

Zimbabwe Bar & Guest House

Bar

To Dar es Salaam

Kigoma

Forest Reserve Office

District Office

N

Not to scale

Tanzania & Zanzibar

Essentials

Sleeping
■ *on maps pages 320 and 326*
Price codes: see inside front cover

Hotels in Dar es Salaam are poor as far as luxury and middle grade accommodation is concerned and not particularly good value. Many deluxe travellers choose to stay at *Bahari Beach* some 25 kilometres north of Dar es Salaam. The luxury *Sheraton Hotel* opened in late 1995 while the *New Africa Hotel* is fully refurbished with a swimming pool, has recently opened and the competition should serve to up-grade the general standard. The lower end of the market, however, is good value, although it is always a sensible procedure to check the room and the bathroom facilities and inquire what is provided for breakfast. Ask about phone facilities as often the switchboard does not work. Check on the security of any parked vehicle. Recent travellers have reported that it is possible to negotiate lower rates, especially if you plan to stay a few days. In the upmarket hotels, at present, you are required to pay in foreign exchange. In the middle range it is usually possible to pay in Tsh, and this is an advantage if money is changed at the favourable bureau rate. Hotels will often change money at an unfavourable 'official' rate. Even if staying at an upmarket hotel it is advisable to pay for everything (except the room rate) with TSh exchanged at a bureau. It is not possible to get cash against a Visa card in Tanzania. A 20% VAT was officially introduced on 1 July 1998, and is added to all service charges.

At the top level *Kilimanjaro* is good value; in the middle range *Motel Afrique*, *Jambo Inn* and *Starlight*; at the cheap end, *Salvation Army* is quite excellent, while *Luther House*, and the two *YMCA* are also to be recommended.

A+ Sheraton Hotel, Ohio St, PO Box 791, T112416, T113525, F113981. Conference and banqueting facilities, shopping arcade and recreation centre with outdoor swimming pool. Rather gloomy, with a sombre brown and cream decor, good standards and service, a/c, has all mod-cons except tea/coffee-making facilities in the rooms, best rooms at the rear, smoking and non-smoking rooms available, British Airways office in hotel – useful for reconfirming your flight home, hotel will store luggage for you whilst on safari. **A Embassy**, PO Box 3152, 24 Garden Ave, T111181/117082-7, F112634, Tx41570/41666. Well run and comfortable, small pool on first floor with barbecue and bar, a/c, grill, restaurant, bar, hairdressers, chemist, travel agents. **A Karibu**, Haile Selassie Rd, T667761/668458, Oyster Bay area. Well run, good restaurant with Indian food a speciality, a/c swimming pool. **A Hotel Agip**, PO Box 529, Pamba Rd, T110819/20/21, Tx41276. Although recently refurbished in marble and mahogany style, the decor is looking careworn and the service is about adequate. No pool, a/c, good restaurant and snack bar, first floor bar, live music (duo) played on Saturday nights. A room at the front is recommended to avoid the noise of the a/c fans at the back, a recent traveller reported fraudulent use of his credit card billing him for additional nights – the signatures did not match. **A New Africa**, PO Box 9314, Maktaba St, T117139, T117050/1, Tx81049. A/c, 2 restaurants. The hotel does not provide twin beds. If you want separate beds you have to upgrade to 2 doubles and a sofa bed, called a Queen's Sofa, is put into the room. **A Oyster Bay**, PO Box 2261, Sekou Toure Drive, T668062/3/4, 5 kilometres from city centre. Beach location, although the beach is poor, a/c, good restaurant with excellent seafood, shopping mall, bamboo gardens, bar, pool. **A Oysterbay Executive Inn**, T668518/667963. **A Sea Cliffs**, PO Box 3030, northern end of Msasani Peninsula on Toure Drive, T600380/1/2/3/4/5/6/7, F600076. *Coral Cliff Bar*, pool and Ngalawa Bar, Dhow restaurant, Coffee Shop, gym, gift shop, pleasant style, white washed walls and thatched *makuti* roofing.

B Ambassador Plaza, PO Box 2114, Ali Hassan Mwinyi Blvd, T36006, Mx41801, about 4 kilometres from centre. A/c, well run, good restaurant, patio bar. **B Continental**, Mkrumah St. Some rooms a/c, patio bar, restaurant, shop. **B Etienne's**, PO Box 2981, Ocean Rd, T2093. Comfortable with relaxed atmosphere, some rooms a/c, restaurant, bar, garden bar with barbecue. **B Kilimanjaro**, PO Box 9574, Kivukoni Front, T113103/4, T332091, Tx41021, F39462. A little shabby but comfortable, the only pleasant pool in the city, a/c, 3 restaurants one of which, the Summit, affords a glorious view over the harbour, particularly charming at night,

24-hour Forex Bureau, bar and pool bar, hairdresser, bookshops, curios, chemist, travel agents, business services, creditcards accepted, professional ladies ply for trade at night in the Zebra Bar, plans are afoot to redevelop/privatize the operation. **B** *Mawenzi*, PO Box 332, Maktaba St, T29922/46561. Reasonably comfortable, some rooms a/c, pleasant patio bar, rather gloomy restaurant. **B** *Mbowe*, PO Box 15261, Indira Gandhi St, T20501/20188. Bar, run-down colonial establishment, central, some rooms out of service due to roof repairs. **B** *Motel Afrique*, PO Box 9482, Zanaki St. **B** *Palm Beach*, Upanga Rd, T28892. Very run-down, with creaky a/c, some rooms with own bathroom and hot water, between-the-wars style, a little away from the centre of town, airy and cool bar and restaurant, popular beer garden with barbecue. **B** *Peacock Hotel*, UWT, PO Box 70270, T114071/114126, F117962. Well run and centrally located, a/c, TV, restaurant, snackbar. **B** *Skyway*, PO Box 21248, Sokoine Drive, T27061. Some rooms a/c, basic restaurant and rather rough bar.

C *Jambo Inn*, PO Box 5588, Libya St, T35359/35531, some a/c, central. Hotel service has deteriorated, no hot water, nets, very noisy fan, no a/c, breakfast very unappetizing, some doors won't lock. However, restaurant serves Indian food and is one of the best in Dar es Salaam. **C** *Lutheran House Hotel*, PO Box 389, Sokoine Drive, T120734, behind the Lutheran Church on the waterfront. Excellent value, central and in considerable demand, is necessary to book as it is invariably full, recent renovations have been undertaken. **C** *Queen of Sheba Hotel*, PO Box 6308, T71780 off Shekilango/Mole Rds. S/c rooms, a/c available, safe parking, bar, restaurant, barbecue. **C** *Safari Inn*, PO Box 21113, Banda St, T21113, central. Fairly simple, but sound, similar price to *Jambo Inn* but is significantly better. Breakfast included, no restaurant. **C** *Starlight*, PO Box 3199, UWT St, T119391, 119387-9. Recently refurbished, well run and good value, a/c, near Mnazi Moja, no mosquito nets or screens on the windows. **C** *YMCA*, PO Box 767, Maktaba St, T110833. Central, no fans and can be hot, care required over belongings, basic facilities.

D *Deluxe Inn*, PO Box 2583, Uhwu St, T20873/25534. **D** *Keys*, PO Box 5330, Uhwu St, T20462, near Mnazi Moja. **D** *Kobodya*, PO Box 1019 Nkrumah St, T32937/31470. Central, straightforward. **D** *Mgulani Hostel*, run by the Salvation Army, a Christian Mission, PO Box 1273, Kilwa Rd, T51467, situated about 3 kilometres along Kilwa Rd to the south of the port area. Well run, outstanding value, easily accessible by *dala dala*, swimming pool. **D** *Marana Guest House*, PO Box 15062, Uhwu St, T21014, near Mnazi Moja. **D** *Mount Msambara*, PO Box 22770, Kango St, T37422/3, Kariakoo area. **D** *Traffic Light Motel*, PO Box 79, Maragwo Rd, T23438, central. Good value, well run, profits are used to fund a primary school for disabled children and a vocational training centre. **D/E** *YWCA*, PO Box 2086, Upanga Rd, T122439 and the *YMCA*, PO Box 767, T110833, are one block apart off Maktaba St. Women and couples accommodated, central, one traveller reported bed bug infestation. Good eating place.

E *Al Noor*, PO Box 3874, Uhuru St, T37082, Kariakoo area. **E** *Double Two*, PO Box 22102, Nyati St, T36027, central. **E** *Holiday Hotel*, PO Box 2975, Jamhuri St, T20675. Basic, clean, good terrace, excellent showers, advised by travellers that this hotel is the cheapest, has intermittent water supply problems, no parking facilities. **E** *Ismail*, Lumumba St, central. **E** *Mulapa Inn*, Wmumba St, central. **E** *New Happy*, PO Box 15042, Lumumba St, T34038, Kariakoo area. **E** *Zanzibar Guest House*, PO Box 20125, Zanaki St, T21197, central. Cheap, not very clean, communal showers, no hot water.

The beaches are poor near the city centre, with shallow water and rocky shorelines. Although **Beach hotels** they are an hour's journey (25 kilometres) from Dar es Salaam along poor roads many visitors choose to stay at one of the beach hotels to the north or south of the city. There is a regular bus shuttle service between the city and the beach hotels to the north leaving from the *New Africa Hotel* on Maktaba St. Please note that it is unsafe to walk along the beach between the northern hotels.

A+ *Ras Kutani Beach Resort*, bookings through Rickshaw Travel, PO Box 1889, T128485, 291125/35097, F29125/34556, Tx41162 or Selous Safari Co Ltd, PO Box 1192, T28985/35638,

F46980, Tx81016, across Kivukoni Ferry and 28 kilometres south of Dar es Salaam, 2-hour road journey or a 14-minute flight from Dar es Salaam costing US$50 return, the resort staff meet the flight. This is an excellent place to stay for a rest after a safari, some cottages are on a hill overlooking the ocean, charming thatched banda accommodation, good beach with lagoon, windsurfing, sailing, deep-sea fishing and diving can be arranged, some travellers have reported seeing hump-backed whales – visible about 3 times a year. **A** *Bahari Beach*, PO Box 9312, Kunduchi, T0811-327018/47101, 650475/6/7. Accommodation in thatched rondavels, a/c, large bar lounge, restaurant area under high thatched roofing, pool bar, swimming pool, band on Sunday and public holidays, sandy beach, garden surroundings, gift shop, tour agency, the most attractive and best run of the northern beach hotels. **A** *The Haven at Kunduchi*, PO Box 23272, Dar es Salaam, T0811-323443/325228, 650276, F0811-320525. Private beach, swimming pool, 6 acres of gardens, colonial atmosphere, 15 kilometres from Dar es Salaam. **A** *Jangwani Sea Breeze Lodge*, PO Box 934, Mbezi Beach off Bagamoyo Rd, 20 kilometres north of city, T647067, F811320714. **A** *White Sands*, PO Box 3030, Dar es Salaam, T35952/35524/35801/113678/116483, F39885/444/5, Tx41540, situated on Jangwani Beach, 20 kilometres north from Dar es Salaam. Reasonable beach, pool, restaurants, bars.

B *Kunduchi Beach*, PO Box 9313 Kunduchi, T47621/3. Somewhat run-down modern style accommodation, but good value, Islamic style architecture for main service areas, bar, pool bar, restaurant, swimming pool, charming beach palms and flowers, band on Sunday and public holidays, watersport facilities and trips to off-shore islands, close to fishing village (hotel restaurant will prepare fresh fish bought there for half menu price). **B** *Silver Sands*, PO Box 901 Kunduchi, T0812-781602/0811-320545, 650231. Now under new German management and pleasantly restored restaurant, bar.

C *Rungwe Oceanic*, PO Box 35639, Kunduchi, T47185. Good value, bar and restaurant, popular with budget travellers, has camping facilities.

E There are camping facilities at Kunduchi Beach, about 1.5 kilometres from where the ferry docks on the Kigamboni side of the harbour. There are also camping facilities at *New Silver Sands*, PO Box 60097, T0812-781602, F051-650428, 25 kilometres out of town. Since April 1998 managed by Michael, a very helpful South African who will organize tours to Zanzibar or the Marine Reserve. Car parking US$3 per night, you can leave the car/truck here while you make a trip to Zanzibar. Shuttle bus service can be arranged to Dar es Salaam airport. Has a good restaurant and 2 bars. Offers a phone/fax service. Also has good rooms, clean but crowded, theft of property can be a problem.

Eating
● *on maps*
Price codes:
see inside front cover

Variety is improving all the time in Dar es Salaam, with more tourists and new places opening. Particularly recommended are *Casanova's*, *Smokies*, *Summit* for atmosphere, *Simba Grill* for its buffet, dining and dancing, *Karibu* and *Jambo Inn* for Indian food, *Rickshaw* for Chinese, *Jungle Café* for pizzas, *Night of Istanbul* for Mediterranean, *Barbeque House* and *Happy Snacks* for inexpensive and delicious tandoori grills. If you go by taxi to venues in outer areas (*Casanova, Smokies, Rickshaw*) it is worthwhile asking the driver to wait.

4 *The Pearl*, run by *Bushtrekker*, corner of UWT and Upanga St, 1st floor, with views across Gymkhana Club grounds. International cuisine, pleasant atmosphere, good buffet at weekends. **4** *Casanova's*, Masaki St, T600268, F600269, Msasani Peninsular (30 minutes from centre in taxi). Delightful atmosphere often with live music, good Italian cuisine, currently one of the smartest Dar es Salaam restaurants. **4** *Karibu*, ground floor of *Karibu Hotel*, Haile Selassie, Oyster Bay (20 minutes from centre by taxi). Good quality Indian cuisine. **4** *Hotel Agip Restaurant*, first floor of *Hotel Agip*, Pamba St, T110819/12. Good standard Italian cuisine, decor rather gloomy. **4** *Oyster Bay*, *Oyster Bay Hotel*, Sekou Toure Drive (15 minutes from centre in taxi), T68631. First floor restaurant with views overlooking Oyster Bay, extensive menu and excellent quality, sea food platter is especially recommended and of daunting dimensions, excellent smoked sailfish. **4** *Rickshaw*, T601611/601919, off Chole Rd, Msasani Peninsular

(30 minutes from centre by taxi). Good quality Chinese cuisine in pleasant surroundings. **4** *Smokies*, off Chole Rd, Msasani Peninsular (30 minutes from centre in taxi), PO Box 23425, Dar es Salaam, T0812-780567. Rooftop, open air restaurant with views across Msasani Bay, buffet, dinner US$8, crowded at weekends, superior wine list.

3 *Alcove*, Samora Ave. Reasonable Indian food, also some Chinese, usually busy at weekends, one of the best restaurants in town. **3** *Bandari*, in *New Africa Hotel*, Azikwe St, T117050/117132. Uncomplicated international food. **3** *Cedars Restaurant*, on Bibi Titi Mohammed Rd, near the junction with Zanaki St. Offer good value Lebanese food, excellent local seafood. **3** *Chef's Pride Restaurant*, virtually opposite *Jambo Inn* Hotel, on road between Lubya St and Jamhuri St. Good food at excellent prices, fast service – Italian, Chinese, Indian and local dishes available. **3** *Chinese Restaurant*, basement of NIC Bldg, Samora Ave. Good standard of cuisine. **3** *Embassy Grill*, T30006, second floor of *Embassy Hotel* on Garden Ave, central. Steaks recommended. **3** *Empire*, in courtyard beside *Empire Cinema*, Maktaba St. Indian cuisine with live Indian music most nights. **3** *Garden Plaza*, T23520. International menu. **3** *Hard Rock Café*, PO Box 15261, T118249, F117869, Indira Gandhi St. Recently opened, pool table. **3** *Heri Restaurant*, Morocco Rd. Authentic Chinese food. Highly recommended. **3** *Jungle Café*, ground floor of *Agip Hotel*, Pamba St, central. Bright café atmosphere, good pizzas, espresso and capuccino coffee. **3** *Night of Istanbul*, UWT St and Zanaki St. Middle-Eastern cuisine of good standard plus international menu, it is possible to eat outside on the terrace, African wines from Zimbabwe, of drinkable quality available. **3** *Paradise*, off Old Bagamoya Rd, Mikocheni, T72730/0812-781743. Ethiopian Restaurant. **3** *The Rendez-Vous*, Samora Ave, near the junction at Morogoro Rd. Eat inside or out, a/c, good service. **3** *Sawasdee*, top floor of *New Africa Hotel*, Azikwe St, T117050/117132. Thai food, wonderful harbour views. **3** *Simba Grill*, T21281, first floor of *Kilmanjaro Hotel*, Kivukoni Front. Excellent buffet and dancing at weekends. **3** *Simonas*, Nmanga Rd. A new Croatian restaurant, very professional service and huge portions. **3** *Summit*, T21281, top floor of *Kilimanjaro Hotel*, Kivukoni Front. International menu, good value special menu, which runs out quickly, fine views across harbour especially at night.

2 *Barbeque House*, Vijimweni St, off Upanga Rd (outer central). Specializes in good quality tandoori grills. **2** *Best Bites*, American-style ice-cream parlour – excellent value at A H Mwinyi Blvd, Namanga along the Bagamoyo Rd, T0811-323164. **2** *Bruncherie*, ground floor of *Kilimajaro Hotel*, Kivukoni Front, T21281. Simple grills, steaks generally good value, open until midnight, rather shabby decor. **2** *Burger Bar*, opposite the *Salamanda* on Samora Ave. **2** *Central Fish*, Zaramo St, close to DTV roundabout. Roadside kiosk serving fish and chicken dishes. **2** *Chef's Pride*, just off Jamhuri St near Morogoro Rd, across the road from the Holiday Hotel. The food is good, serving local as well as Indian and Chinese dishes. **2** *Chicken King Restaurant*, Jamhuri St. Offers good local breakfasts. **2** *Etienne's*, *Etienne's Hotel*, Ocean Rd, T20293. Uncomplicated menu. **2** *Hajirah*, India St, next to Alliance Française. Good food but only open at lunchtimes. **2** *Jambo Inn*, Libya St, T35359/35531. Excellent Indian menu, huge inflated chapatis like air-cushions, outside and inside dining areas. **2** *Khalsa Sports Club*, Mtendeni/Mrima St, off Jamhuri St. Asia Club with nominal US$0.50 entrance fee, bar and restaurant, curried crab recommended, one of the few inexpensive restaurants where you can drink alcohol with meal. **2** *Madawa Restaurant*, opposite the Greek Orthodox Church on Ali Hassan Mwinyi Blvd. **2** *National Bank of Commerce Canteen*, Pamba Rd, off Samora Ave. Good charcoal barbecued meats, open lunchtimes only. **2** *New Zahir*, Mosque St, off Jamhuri St. Toothsome in expensive food, atmospheric, popular with locals, typical coastal dishes. **2** *Palm Beach*, *Palm Beach Hotel*, Upanga Rd, T28892. Rather uninspired menu of British food, set menu is good value, but runs out early, pleasant verandah atmosphere. **2** *The Retreat*, Mtendeni/Mrima St, off Jamhuri St. Favourite with the Hindu community, rather run down, but authentic South Indian cuisine, with the *masala dosa* specially recommended. **2** *Salamanda*, corner of Samara and Mkwepu (central). Once Dar es Salaam's smartest venue, closed in evening, pleasant ground floor area opening onto street, snacks and simple grills at lunchtime. **2** *Shalimar*, Mansfield St (central). Sound Indian cuisine, restaurant closes around 1830. **2** *Shari's Dar Bar*, UWT St. Simple charcoal grills, tandoori chicken, salad, fries, good value. **2** *Supreme*, Pugu Rd (outer central). Vegetarian, reasonable quality, but unbearably grim decor.

1 *Happy Snacks*, corner of Makinganya St and Simu St (central). Street café, exceptional tandoori charcoal grilled chicken, fries and chapatis. **1** *Husseini's Ice Cream Parlour*, corner of India St and Zanaki St. A Dar institution run by an old coastal family, serving juices, shakes and snacks. **1** *Sno-cream*, near *Shalimar*, Mansfield St. Serves excellent ice cream, this is an old-fashioned ice cream parlour, done out in Disney style, it is almost opposite the Cathedral Bookshop, next door to *Shalimar Restaurant*. **1** *Tanzania Coffee Board*, coffee shop on ground floor of Telecoms building on Samora Ave (central). Lunchtimes and early evening only, outside patio, rather drab, snacks, disappointingly only serves instant coffee. On corner KLM office, *Eesiq* takeaway is very famous, good food.

Bars All the bars in Dar es Salaam are associated with hotels. Range of local beers is limited to two local lagers, Safari and Pilsner, until a reported six new small breweries come on stream. Variety of beers available has expanded in recent years as import restrictions have relaxed and a variety of Kenyan, South African and European beers are available. Specially recommended are the beer gardens at *Palm Beach*, *Etiennes* and *Oyster Bay* for tropical atmosphere, *Kimicho* for the prettiest local girls, *Agip* and the *Zebra* for a quiet central meeting place.

Agip, Pamba St. First floor bar, secluded pleasant atmosphere. Sedate patio bar at the *Continental Hotel*, Nkrumah St. *Embassy*, Garden Ave. First floor bar, rather dull. *Etiennes*, Ocean Rd. Pleasant beer garden, rather drab bar inside hotel. *Kimicho* at Mamanga Shopping Centre, just off Ali Hassan Mwinyi Blvd. Secluded bar with thatched roofing to open-air area, popular with the smartest local girls. *Ambassador Plaza Inn*, Ali Hassan Mwinyi Blvd. Outside patio bar has moved upstairs. *The New Happy Hotel*, rooftop bar, Lumumba/Ungoni sts, with views over Mnazi Mmoji. *The Empire Cinema Bar*, Maktaba St. Nice bar, also does excellent food if you can ask for it. *New Africa*, Azikiwe St. Secluded bar has moved upstairs. *The Khalsa Sports Club*, Mtendeni/Mrima St. Good place for a beer or two, jolly club just outside the centre. On Ali Hassan Mwinyi Rd, next to the *California Dreamer* disco, is a classic Tanzanian outdoor bar/nyama choma spot. For those staying at the Salvation Army there are some good bars nearby in the grounds of the Saba Saba exhibition centre. *Oyster Bay*, Sekou Toure Drive, pleasant well appointed bar to rear of hotel overlooking Bamboo Gardens. *Palm Beach*, Upanga Rd. Very popular beer gardens, coloured fairy lights. *Zebra Bar*, Kilimanjaro Hotel, Kirukoni Front, central. Large lounge, quiet.

Entertainment **Cinema** Europeans and visitors seldom visit the cinema, which is a pity as the general audience reaction makes for an exciting experience. Programmes are not announced in the *Daily News*, but the *Express*, *Family Mirror* and the Swahili *Uhuru* all carry details.

There are six cinemas, showing mostly Indian, martial arts or adventure films. Entrance about US$1. The most popular are the *Empire*, Maktaba St opposite the Post Office; *Empress* on Samora Ave; *New Chox* on Nkrumah St; *Odeon* on Zaramo St; *Starlight* on Kisutu St; *Drive-Inn-Cinema* is on Old Bagamoyo Rd, just before Morocco Rd.

The *British Council* on Ohio St has fairly regular film shows on Wednesday. The *Alliance Française* on Maktaba St opposite the *New Africa Hotel* shows films from time to time. Announcements in *Daily News*.

Classical music Concerts by touring artists, are presented by the British Council, the Alliance Française and occasionally other embassies. Announcements in *Daily News*.

Fashion shows Popular occasions, often for charity, held at *Diamond Jubilee Hall* and *Embassy Hotel* Pool. Often accompanied by pop music impersonaters. Announcements in *Daily News*.

Gambling *Las Vegas Casino*, corner of Upanga Rd and Ufukoni Rd. Roulette and Vingt et Un. *Classique Casino*, on Bagamoyo Rd. *Club Billicanos*, Simu St, is applying for a gambling licence, as is a hotel under construction on Msasani Peninsula.

Music special visits by popular African bands and artists and Indian groups occur regularly and are presented at *Diamond Jubilee Hall, Bahama Mama's, Club Billicanos, Pearl Restaurant* at *Bushtrekkers*, Cnr Upanga Rd & Ohio St has resident band Tuesday-Saturday. Announcements in *Daily News*.

Zaita is mainly Congolese, the *Tanzanites* are from the Arusha area, **BICO Stars** are from Dar es Salaam. **Shikamoo** is a famous band of the 1960s with an exceptional saxophonist and lead guitarist. They play regularly at *Bahama Mama's* and at various social clubs such as Langata in Kinondoni, Kawe along the Old Bagamoyo Rd and Mwenge off the Bagamoyo Rd just before Sam Njoma Rd. There are some music announcements in the *Daily News*, but a more comprehensive listing is in the Swahili *Uhuru* – get a local informant to translate.

Theatre *Little Theatre*, Haile Selassie Rd, off Ali Hassan Mwinyi Blvd, presents productions on an occasional basis, perhaps 2-3 times a year, usually musicals, very popular, particularly the Christmas Pantomime, announcements in the *Daily News*. **The British Council**, Ohio St, occasionally presents productions, announcements in the *Daily News*. **Diamond Jubilee Hall**, Maliki Rd, Upanga. Occasional visits by companies from India performing a bill of variety acts, announcements in *Daily News*.

Most nightlife gets under way late – things tend not to warm up until the bars close at around 2300. Many venues open (and close) at short notice. Check the local *Daily News*. **Nightlife**

California Dreamer disco next to Las Vegas Casino on corner of Upanga Rd and Ufokoni Rd. Bright and busy during the week and packed at weekends, girls free before 2300 during the week, rather a lot of street lighting, US$4-US$6. **Kilimanjaro Pool**, Kivukoni Front, US$2-4. Live bands on Sunday by the pool, attracts the older set, becomes crowded during Christmas, Easter and Summer vacations. **Classique Casino**. **Coco Beach**. **La Dolce Vita**, Sekou Toure Drive, US$2-4, Friday, Saturday. Open-air, pleasant atmosphere with thatched roofing, the smart place with *Bamboo Gardens* closed. **Club Billicanos**, Simu St, US$5-10. Discos most nights, ocasional live band or cabaret entertainment, strobe lighting, smoke machines, revolving glitter balls, expensive, but popular at weekends, though often quiet during the week. **Continental**, Nkrumah Rd, US$2-$4. Discos Friday and Saturday, popular with locals. **Tazara Hostel**, Kilimani Rd, off Bagamoyo Rd, US$4. Bands at weekends. **Msasani Bay Villa**, off Kimnei Ave in Msasani Village. Discos at weekends. **Simba Grill**, *Kilmanjaro Hotel*, Kirukoni Front, US$4. You need not dine, but is essentially a dining and dancing venue with a live band and usually some cabaret, through to 0100. **Bahama Mama's**, Morogaro Rd, US$2-3, 15 kilometres from town centre. Large open air venue, Shikamoo, a legendary jazz and rumba band from the 1960s play there regularly.

There are no department stores in Dar es Salaam. The Shopping Malls at *Oyster Bay Hotel* and **Shopping**
Casanova's have high quality goods that are imported and expensive, both on Msasani Peninsular. Otherwise shops are located along Samora Ave (electrical goods, local clothing, footware) and on Libya St (clothing and footwear). Supermarkets with a wide variety of imported foods and wines are on Samora Ave between Pamba Ave and Azikawe St, on the corner of Kaluta St and Bridge St and in the *Oyster Bay Hotel* Shopping Mall. A popular loca tion for purchase of fruit and vegetables is the market on Kinondoni Rd. Fresh fish and seafood can be bought at the market on Ocean Rd just past the ferry to Kivukoni. The shop in the foyer of the *Kilimanjaro Hotel* has a good selection of postcards, and will also sell stamps.

Locally produced tie-dye material can be obtained cheaply about US$2 a metre from the women who congregate at the corner of Aggrey St and Indira Ghandi St. Tie dye also available at one of the craft shops in the complex at Mwenga.

The Supermarket next to the *Hotel Afrique* is currently the most central available. The selection of goods is a bit limited.

Books can be bought secondhand at the stalls on Samora Ave and on Pamba St (off Samora). The best bookshop is in the *Casanova* shopping mall on Msasani Peninsular. Another excellent bookshop is the **Cathedral Bookshop** on Mansfield St (behind St Joseph's Cathedral). There is a small bookshop in the foyer of the *New Africa Hotel*; the **Tanzanian**

Tanzania & Zanzibar

Bookshop, Indira Gandhi St, leading from the Askari Monument; *Tanzania Publishing House*, Samora Ave, but all 3 have only limited selections.

Curios and crafts *Lalji Ramji* has a counter in the *Kilimanjaro Hotel* foyer and he is there 1100-1600 daily to sell old stamps and coins. These are coins from the German period. A one Heller copper coin can be purchased for US$2. Copper coins from the British period can be obtained in a 1 cent, 5 cents and 10 cents set of 3 for US$1.50. They have holes in the centre so they could be carried on a loop of string. There are also silver (US$4) and nickel (US$1.25) 1 shilling coins. They have a lion on one side in front of an unrecognisable East African mountain. The silver coins can be made into earrings. There are some reproduction postcards from the German period showing the Governer's residence and the post-office, and Mr Ramji has a collection of antique postcards for sale, a sample of which he will bring in on request. Mr Ramji's grandfather came from India in 1880, and it looks unlikely that the business or the supply of antique items survive him.

There is also a good curio shop on Mkwepu St between Samora Ave and City Drive. This shop is particularly good for antique brass and copper items. Excellent quality modern wood products can be obtained from *Domus*, PO Box 6724, T42418/42244/42248, F25551, Tx41741 SYSCON TZ, on India St. Other curio shops are *Silver Curios* on Asikiwe St opposite the *New Africa Hotel*. There are 2 curio shops in the *Kilimanjaro Hotel*.

Traditional crafts particularly wooden carvings are sold along Samora Ave to the south of the Askari Monument. Good value crafts can be purchased from stalls along Ali Hassan Mwinyi Blvd near the intersection with Haile Selassie, and at Mwege, along Sam Njoma Rd close to the intersection with Ali Hassan Mwinyi Blvd. Easily the best place for handicrafts in Dar es Salaam, and for ethnografia from all over Tanzania and further afield (notably the Congo). There is a large number of shops and stalls offering goods at very reasonable prices. The market is about half an hours journey from the town centre, easily reached by dala-dala (destination: Mwenge).

Flowers can be bought along Samora Ave and in the *Kilimanjaro Hotel* foyer. Plants, containers and makrame holders are available along Ali Hassan Mwinyi Blvd near the Haile Selassie intersection.

Hairdressers European Unisex hairdressing at *Kilimanjaro Hotel* and at *Embassy Hotel*. Also at Namanga Shopping Centre. Small African style hairdressers are to be found in all non-European residential areas.

Sports (participant) **Fishing** Marine fishing can be arranged through *Kunduchi Beach Hotel*, PO Box 9313, T47621/3, 25 kilometres north of Dar es Salaam.

Golf, tennis, squash At *Gymkhana Club* on Ghana Ave, visitors can obtain temporary membership. The *Gymkhana Club* is however very expensive, even by first world prices. *Upanga Sports Club* on Upanga Rd just past the Greek Church also has squash facilities. An informal group meets for tennis at the University of Dar es Salaam courts on the campus 15 kilometres to the north of the city at 1700 every day.

Gym *The Fitness Centre*, off Chole Rd on Msasani Peninsula has a gym with weights and also runs aerobics and yoga classes.

Hash House Harriers Meet regularly in Dar es Salaam on late Monday afternoons. Details from British Council, Ohio St or British High Commission, corner of Samora Ave and Azikiwe Street.

Sailing The *Yacht Club* is located on Chole Rd on Msasani Peninsula. Visitors can obtain temporary membership.

It was magic, Brian

In 1993, Simba, Tanzania's most prominent football club, qualified for the African Club Championships. They had a marvellous run, putting out teams from Burundi, Angola and Algeria to meet Stella Artois of Côte d'Ivoire in the final. The first leg was away in Abidjan, and Simba held Stella to a goalless draw. Hopes were high. Surely Simba would now win the second leg at home in Dar es Salaam and lift the cup – a first triumph for Tanzania in any international competition.

The press warned that Simba's only problem would be over-confidence. It's the usual practice for each team to have a resident witch-doctor to put bad magic on the opposition players (not that much different, really, from European football where players observe absurd superstitious rituals and managers wear lucky suits). Both Simba and Stella would expect to have spells put on them, but all-in-all, things would cancel out, and the teams would be able to get on with the football.

Stella, however, pulled a master-stroke. Amid much publicity their players and officials arrived a week before the game and booked into a beach hotel north of Dar es Salaam for acclimatization and final preparations. Simba's

medicine man began a suitable course of treatment. Alas, this was a decoy team. The real players were bussed in secretly from Nairobi the night before the game.

The National Stadium was packed. The President and most of the Ministers were there, having left early from a graduation ceremony at the University of Dar es Salaam. Simba began brightly. Early in the first half, a cross from the left was met by an unmarked Simba striker at the far post. All of the National Stadium was on its feet (well, most were of necessity already on them – they were joined by the VIPs in the stand) as the ball was headed toward the top corner. The Stella goalkeeper appeared from nowhere, got the mearest finger-tip to the ball, deflected it onto a post, and it stayed out. The stadium went very quiet (except, that is, for a handful of fans from Simba's great rivals, Yanga, who suddenly sensed the game might turn out better than they ever dared hope). A few minutes later Stella scored against a listless Simba, and added another in the second half. Simba were kutapika kama kasuka and Stella sur la lune. The press blamed over-confidence. But all of Tanzania knew better.

Swimming   Can be had at the **Kilimanjaro Hotel** (entrance US$4 adults, US$2 children), the **Karibu Hotel** (US$4), the **Embassy Hotel**, **University of Dar es Salaam**, and **Salvation Army Hostel** on Kilwa Rd. New pools will be opening at *Sheraton* and *New Africa* hotels. In the sea, the best location is at the **Swimming Club** on Ocean Rd near Magogoni St. Otherwise the best sea beaches are some distance to the north and south of the city.

Athletics   Meetings at National Stadium. Details in *Daily News*.

Sports
(spectator)

Cricket   Almost entirely a pursuit of the Asian community. There are regular games at the Gymkhana Club, off Ghana Ave and at Janqwani Playing Fields off Morogoro Rd at weekends. Announcements in *Daily News*.

Golf, tennis, squash   Tournaments each year at the Gymkhana Club, off Ghana Ave, announcements in *Daily News*. Also further information about squash from Col SMA Kashmiri Chairman Tanzania SRA, c/o Africonsult Ltd, PO Box 21242, Dar es Salaam, T32299/44811/34097, F31842.

Soccer   The main African pursuit, and is followed by everyone from the President and the Cabinet down. Matches are exciting occasions with radios throughout the city tuned to the commentary. Terrace entrance is around US$1 (more for important matches). It is worth paying extra to sit in the stand. Details of games announced in *Daily News*. There are two main venues, the **National Stadium** on Mandela Rd to the south of the city and **Karume Stadium** just beyond the Kariakoo area, off Uhuru St. There are two divisions of the National league, and Dar es Salaam has two representatives, **Simba** and **Young Africans** (often called *Yanga*),

The Dala-dalas of Dar es Salaam

It may seem hard to believe considering the routine overloading of passengers, their substantial contribution to the levels of atmospheric and noise pollution in the town, and the life threatening driving techniques of their drivers, but the dala-dalas of Dar es Salaam represent a welcome development to the average 'Mbongo' (resident of Dar, meaning literally 'person with brains'). In the bad old days of the 1980s the public transport sector suffered the same shortages as most of the country's other sectors. Buses, both local as well as inter-city, were unreliable, infrequent and even more crowded than they are today. However, with the deregulation of the Tanzanian economy under former President Mwinyi, and the increasing tolerance of all kinds of private initiative (Mwinyi is known as 'Ruksa' in Tanzania – Swahili for 'permission') wealthier Tanzanians recognized a profitable area for investment in Dar es Salaam's inadequate transport network. Although the rate of return has no doubt declined with the spectacular rise in the number of dala-dalas, ownership of one or more mini-buses remains, along with the

construction and rental of property, a favourite 'mradi' (income generating project) for Dar es Salaam's middle class. Judging by the numbers squeezed into their interiors and the speed they travel between destinations those returns are still handsome.

Realizing that they can in no way monitor the amount of passengers using their buses, the dala-dala owners stipulate a specified amount of money to the 'crew' who they hire to operate the vehicle which they expect to receive at the end of each day; the remainder constitutes the crew's wages. It is a system which appears to work to everyones' advantage other than that of the passenger, who suffers the consequent overcrowding and the suicidal driving as dala-dala competes with dala-dala to arrive first and leave fullest. In a forlorn attempt to reduce the number of accidents involving buses, the Tanzanian government in early 1997 passed a law requiring all public service vehicles to install speed governors, designed to restrict speeds to under 80 kilometres per hour. However, dala-dala and coach operators soon worked out ways to override them, or simply disconnected them completely, and within

and there is intense rivalry between them (see box, page 337). Simba, the best known Tanzanian club, have their origins in Kariakoo and are sometimes referred to as the 'Msimbazi Street Boys' – they have a club bar in Msimbazi St. Initially formed in the 1920s as 'Eagles of the Night', they changed their name to 'Sunderland FC' in the 1950s. After independence all teams had to choose African names and they became Simba. The national team *Taifa Stars* play regularly at the National Stadium, mostly against other African teams.

Transport **Local Car hire**: can be arranged through most travel agents (see below) Specialist companies are **Avis**, T30505/34562/34598, F37426/37442, Tx41361. **Bugoni Super Auto Garage**, PO Box 25087, T63708. **Evergreen Cabs**, corner of Zanaki and Indira Ghandi St, PO Box 1476, T183345/7, T/F183348, F113841/112914, Tx41180. **Europcar**, 2 Nelson Mandela Express Way, PO Box 208, Dar es Salaam, T0811-786000/325990, F0811-326770, europcar@raha.com. **Hertz** (*Savannah Tours*, PO Box 20517, T115624/114339/138088, F113748, savtour@twiga.com), rates US$40 daily plus US$0.38 per kilometres for a medium saloon. **Kara Motors**, PO Box 64, T33549. **White Cabs**, PO Box 2107, Zanaki St, T23078/30454/33450, Tx41181. **Yellow Cabs**, Upanga Rd, PO Box 6100, T35981.

Air Tanzania Corporation (ATC), T110245/8. This is the state-owned carrier. Often there are delays of several hours for a flight and a whole day needs to be allocated to a leg of air travel. ATC generally has daily flights scheduled to Zanzibar and Arusha and once or twice a week to Bukoba, Kigoma, Mwanza, Tabora, Dodoma, Mtwara, Mafia, Kilwa and Pemba. ATC has suffered from severe operating difficulties, and flights are cancelled and the schedules changed all the time. The line is rather unkindly dubbed 'Air Total Chaos' by local folk. The only sensible procedure is to call in at the ATC office on Ohio St and Garden Ave and check what is currently available. Flights are cheaper for residents, and not particularly expensive weeks the drivers were proceeding with their old reckless abandon.

The basic crew of each dala-dala is made up of three people: the driver (clearly picked for the ability to drive fast rather than well), the ticket collector, and the turnboy (in Dar slang 'Mgiga debe' – literally 'he who forces things into a tin can'), whose job it is to harangue passengers who fail to make room for one more, as well as to entertain the remainder of the bus with hair raising acrobatic stunts hanging from the door of the bus (there is at least one Mpiga debe currently working in Dar who has just one leg – it's not hard to imagine how he lost the other one). Supplementing this basic crew at either end of the journey is a tout, who bawls out the intended destination and route, attempting to attract, or, if necessary, to intimidate (at times this stretches to actual manhandling of passengers) people into entering his dala-dala. He is paid a fixed amount for each bus which he touts for. In addition, when business is slow, there are people who are paid a small amount to sit on the bus pretending to be passengers in order to give the impression that it is fuller than it actually

is to the potential passenger, who will then enter the dala-dala assuming it will be leaving sooner than the next one along.

The dala-dala network radiates from three main termini in the town centre.

Posta at 'Minazi Mirefu' ('Tall palm trees') on the Kivukoni Front opposite the old Post Office; Stesheni close to the central railway station; and Kariakoo (around the Uhuru/Msimbazi Street roundabout for destinations south and at the central market for those in the north). From each of these you can catch dala-dalas to destinations throughout Dar es Salaam, although the four main routes are along Ali Hassan Mwinyi to Mwenge (for the Makumbusho Village Museum, Mwenge handicrafts market and the University); along the Kilwa Road to Temeke, Mtoni and Mbagala (these take you to the Salvation Army); to Vingunguti via Kariakoo and Ilala (for the Tazara railway station); and along the Morogoro Road to Magomeni, Manzese and Ubongo. For a dala-dala going to the airport ask for Uwanja wa Ndege at Minazi Miretu. Satari njema (happy travels!).

for tourists. A single flight to Zanzibar is about US$25, about US$100 to Arusha and US$200 to Mwanza, but bear in mind that fares are subject to frequent alteration. There are plans for ATC to be sold to South African Airways, who are reportedly eager to take over ATC's international routes, but are less keen on running the domestic network.

Other domestic air services are fairly unstable. Air transport has recently been opened up to private operators, several of whom have started services only to close them when it was apparent that the immediate market was unviable. The best advice is to explore the private carriers through one of the Dar es Salaam travel agents (see above). **ZATA** generally has 2 daily flights each way to Zanzibar and cost of a single is US$38. **Aviators Services**, T6386 (Arusha) has 3 flights a week to Arusha, 1100 Monday, Wednesday, Saturday and the cost of a single is US$126. Three or four flights a week to Mafia, 1100 Tuesday, Wednesday, Friday, Sunday, single US$42. **Dar Aviation, Coastal Air** and **Sky Tours** all offer flights from Dar es Salaam to Mafia Island. They all cost about US$85 per person one way. It is possible to charter planes through Air Tanzania but that is very expensive. **Coastal Travels Ltd**, Dar es Salaam, T51-37479/80/30934/31216, F46045/843033. Can arrange flights to Mafia, Zanzibar, Selous, Ruaha and Ras Kutani. It can arrange flights to link with Selous airstrips including Mtememe (Rufiji River Camp), Siwandu (Mbuyuni Luxury Tented Camp), Beho Beho and Kiba (Sand Rivers). Some travellers have reported that the service can be chaotic, running hours late. **Zanair** links with Zanzibar, T843297. **Precisionair** serves Mwanza, Zanzibar, Arusha, Kilimanjaro and Bukoba, PO Box 70770, T30800, Tx41928. **Nahab Air Safaris** arrange charter flights, T843201/2. **Tanzanian Air Services Ltd** (Tanzanair). Charter air service, PO Box 364, Dar es Salaam. Airport T844101/843131/2/3. Sheraton Hotel office T113151/2/112416 ext 7884, F112946, Mobile 0811-406408, simon.tanzanair@raha.com. **Tanzanair** flies to Arusha, Dodoma, Kilimanjaro, Morogora, Moshi and Mwanza.

Train The **Central Railway Station** is located off Sokoine Drive at the wharf end of the city at the corner of Railway St/Gerezani St, T110600. This station serves the line that runs through the central zone to Kigoma on Lake Tanganyika and Mwanza on Lake Victoria and the line that goes north to Tanga and Moshi. The continuation of the line from Moshi to Taveta, Voi, and the Kenyan rail network has been closed since the break up of the East African Community in 1977. However, there are new initiatives to revive co-operation between Kenya, Tanzania and Uganda. The rail link from Kenya to Uganda has been restored, and the possibility of reopening the Moshi-Voi link is being explored.

The **Tazara Railway Station** is located at the junction of Mandela Rd and Pugu Rd, and is about 5 kilometres from the city centre, T860344-7. It is well served by *dala dala* and a taxi from the centre costs about US$4. This line runs southwest to Iringa and Mbeya and on to Tunduma at the Zambia border. It is a broader gauge than the Central and Northern Line.

Please see pages 306/307 for details of train timetables and fares.

On the **Tazara** line, Express trains go all the way to Kapiri Mposhi in Zambia. It takes about 40-50 hours to get to Kapiri Mposhi and for those who are so minded it is possible, with a little luck, to link up with transport which will get you all the way to Harare on the same day. The local trains, which stop at the Zambian border, are a little slower, and take approximately 23 hours to get to Mbeya. First class cabins on both trains contain four berths and Second Class six.

There is a 50 percent discount on Tazara trains for students with ID, although you need to first collect a chit which you have to take to the Ministry of Education (at Luthuli St/Magogoni St in Kivukoni) to get stamped. In Mbeya they make you go to a school which is located a mile or so from the station in order to get a letter confirming you are a student.

All cabins on Tanzanian trains are sexually segregated unless you book the whole cabin.

Road The road is sealed all the way to Malawi, but there are bad stretches especially from Morogoro into the mountains.

If you are making a long journey you can book a seat at kiosks run by the bus companies at the bus stations. Larger buses give a considerably more comfortable ride and are to be recommended on safety grounds as well. If you are taking a shorter journey (Morogoro or Bagamoyo, say), the bus will leave when full. You can join an almost full bus, and leave promptly for an uncomfortable journey, either standing or on a makeshift gangway seat. Or you can secure a comfortable seat and wait till the bus fills, which can take 1-2 hours for a less busy route such as that to Bagamoyo. On the larger and more travelled routes (Arusha, Mbeya) there is now a choice of 'luxury': 'semi-luxury' and 'ordinary'. **Arusha**: fare is around US$20 luxury, US$16 semi luxury and US$12 ordinary and takes about 9 hours. The road has improved considerably and journey times are getting shorter. **Bagamoyo**: fare is US$1 and takes up to 3 hours. The road is very poor. **Dodoma**: fare is about US$6 and takes about 6 hours. Train is really the only feasible option on the Dodoma to Tabora and Kigoma route. **Mbeya**: fare is around US$15 luxury, US$10 semi-luxury and US$7 ordinary and journey takes about 12 hours. **Tanga**: fare is roughly US$6 and takes about 5 hours. **Mtwara**: fare is about US$10 and takes up to 24 hours.

Sea Boat: **Canadian Spirit** runs once a week to Mafia and Mtwara (1st class to Mtwara US$15, 2nd US$10, takes 24 hours), avoid using it during the rainy season as it gets massively overcrowded, and overloaded with cargo because the roads down south are often impassable at that time of year. Outside the rainy season it offers a good service. **M/S Sepideh** boat to Zanzibar, Pemba and Mombasa, PO Box 1428 DSM, economy class Zanzibar US$30, Pemba US$30, Mombasa US$65. The cost of transporting a motorcycle to Zanzibar is US$20 plus US$5 charge for the porters to bring it on board. You will need to pay porters to take the bike off the boat in Zanzibar – negotiate a rate beforehand. The ferry **Azam Marine**, T33013/0811-334347, takes 4 hours, cost US$10 – excellent during the day, on the return journey to Dar es Salaam travellers have reported having to remain on the boat until the Customs open at 0600. *Azam Marine* now operate 2 Australian-built catamarans 3 times daily, giving a comfortable and fast service to Zanzibar. **The Muungano** is the slowest ferry at 4

Sea Ferries to Zanzibar			
Name of ferry boat	**Schedule**	**Fare** **Tsh**	**Duration**
Sea Express T255-51-137049 F255-51-116723	DSM Depart: 1000 1515 ZNZ Depart: 0700 1200	**Residents** 1st class 11,500 2nd class:10,500 **Non resident** 1st class U$40 2nd class U$35	70 minutes
New Sea US Fast Ferries T811-334347 or 134013	DSM Depart: 1115 1600 ZNZ Depart: 0700 1330 1600	**Residents** 1st class 12,500 2nd class 10,500 **Non resident** 1st class U$40 2nd class U$35	90 minutes
MS Sepideh N T0811-326414 Note: DSM-Pemba: daily DSM-Tanga: Saturday	DSM Depart: Daily except Sunday 0730 ZNZ Depart: Daily except Saturday 1600	**Resident** 12,500 **Non resident** Salon U$35 VIP U$40	90 minutes
Sea Star Service T0812-789393 or 781500	DSM Depart: 0730, 1145 1400, 1615 ZNZ Depart: 0815, 1015 1415, 1615	**Resident** Economy 8,000 1st class 9,000 **Non resident** Economy US$25 1st class U$30	**90 minutes**
Flying Horse T255-51-124504	DSM Depart: 1230 ZNZ Depart: 2000 arrive DSM 0600	**Resident** 1st class 8,500 2nd class 8,000 3rd class 7,500 VIP class 9,500 **Non resident** US$25	2 hours
Port tax US$5			

hours US$10. **Zanzibar Sea Ferries**, runs a daily ferry to Zanzibar, overnight, 3rd class only, as it is a cargo ship, takes 6 hours, fare approximately US$6 plus US$5 port tax (which can be negotiated or avoided). **Tanzania Coastal Shipping Company**, PO Box 9461, T110102 is a cargo service that takes some passengers and serves Tanga, Mombasa, Mafia, Kilwa, Lindi and Mtwara, sailings are irregular, slow and cheap. Mtwara costs US$5 and takes 36 hours. **Dhows** are irregular, slow and cheap, a motorized dhow will take 12 hours to Mafia, and sail-powered up to 24 hours, cost US$3 to US$6, you sit or sleep on the cargo and need to take your own food. **Mega Speed Liners** travel to Zanzibar, Pemba and Mombasa, T38025. **Adecon Marine**, located at Sokoine Drive, go to Mafia and Mtwara. **Zanzibar Shipping Corp** travel to Mtwara, Zanzibar and Pemba, T152870.

Tanzania & Zanzibar

Directory   **Airline offices** International: *Aeroflot*, PO Box 2758, Eminaz Mansions, Samora Ave, T113332. *Air France*, PO Box 2661, Upanga Rd, T36653/4/37378/9. *Air India*, PO Box 1709, UWT St, opposite Peugeot House, T117036/117041. *Air Tanzania*, PO Box 543, ATC Bldg, Ohio St, T110245/6/7/8. *Air Zaire*, PO Box 2564, IPS Bldg, Samora Ave, T20836/25988. *Alitalia*, PO Box 9281, AMI Bldg, Samora Ave, T23621/24318. *Alliance Air*, corner Bibi Titi, Mohamed St and Maktaba St, PO Box 5182, T117044/5/8. *British Airways*, PO Box 2439, based at the Sheraton Hotel, Ohio St, T113820/1/2. *Egypt Air*, PO Box 1350, Matsalmat Bldg, Samora Ave, T113333. *Ethiopian Airlines*, PO Box 3187, TDFL Bldg, Ohio St, T20863/20933. *Gulf Air*, PO Box 9794, Raha Towers, Bibi Titi St/Maktaba St, T22112/22814. *Kenya Airways*, PO Box 8342, Peugeot House, Upanga Rd, T119376/7. *KLM*, PO Box 3804, T113336/7. *Lufthansa*, PO Box 1993, Upanga Rd, T22270/110672/113339. *PIA*, PO Box 928, IPS Bldg, Samora Ave, T26944. *SAS*, Upanga Rd, PO Box 1114, T22015/22013. *Swiss Air*, PO Box 2109, Luther House, Sokoine Dr, T118870/1/2. *Zambia Airways*, PO Box 21276, IPS Bldg, Samora Ave, T46662. *Air Zimbabwe*, c/o *Easy Travel*, T123526/121747. Domestic and charter: *Dar Air Charters*, PO Box 18104, Old Terminal 1, Pugu Rd, T42332. *Dar Aviation*, c/o Coastal Travel, PO Box 3052, Upanga Rd, T37479/37480. *Tanzanian Air Services*, PO Box 364, Azikiwe St, T30232.

Banks A private sector bank has opened for business, *Standard Chartered*, located in the Plaza on Sokoine Drive close to the Askari Monument. The state-owned banks are improving, but are still notoriously slow and inefficient – it can take 2 hrs to cash a TC. There are branches of the *National Bank of Commerce* on Samora Ave next to the *Twiga Hotel*; and on the corner of Sokoine Drive and Azikiwe St. Hours are 0830-1230 on weekdays and 0830-1200 on Sat.

   Foreign Exchange Bureaux: are to be found in almost every street in the city. Hours are usually 0900-1700 Mon-Fri and 0900-1300 on Sat. *National Bureau de Change*, opposite the Extelecom Bldg on Samara Ave, offer very favourable rates. 24 hr bureaux are at the airport terminal along Pugu Rd and in the foyer of the *Kilimanjaro Hotel*. Although these bureaux offer convenience, they offer an unfavourable rate. Rates vary between bureaux and it is worth shopping around. Some hotels, *Starlight* is an example, offer extremely unfavourable rates. *Coastal Travel*, India St/Ali Hassan Mwiniyi St, offer cash in advance on credit cards at reasonable rates. American Express: *Rickshaw Travel*, PO Box 1889, on Upanga Rd, opposite the *Sheraton Hotel*, T29125/35097, F29125/35456, Tx41162, will issue TCs to card-holders.

Communications Service on local calls can be variable. The Dar es Salaam exchange is being up-graded, and whole areas of town can be impossible to reach. There are now many private telephone/fax offices all over town where you can make and receive phone calls and faxes. International outgoing calls can be much easier. Hotels will usually charge up to three times the actual cost.

   Internet Access: next door to the Zanzibar GH in Zanaki St. Cheap rates with efficient, quiet, friendly staff. Open Mon to Sat 0830-2200. The office has 3 modern machines, charges US$3 per hour. *The Internet Café*, near the *Hard Rock Café*, charges US$4.50 per hour for the use of the computer. *RCL Internet Café*, PO Box 14324, T139818, Mobile 0811-608937, F113862/139817, rcl@rcl.co.tz, corner of Zanaki St and Kisutu St, opposite *Buy Best Cash & Carry* Supermarket. Open Mon-Sat 0830-2200, Sun 1000-1400, and 1700-2200. Total internet access. Send and receive emails/faxes. Charges US$3 per hour. There are lots of cyber cafes springing up in Jamhuri St offering fast and cheap communication home. *Cyberspot* recommended. Post Office: main post office on Maktaba St. Other offices on Sokoine Drive, near Cenotaph; behind the bus stand on Morogoro Rd and Libya St. Post offices are generally crowded. Sharooq's shop in the *Kilimanjaro Hotel* foyer will sell stamps. DHL: office is on Upanga Rd near Selander Bridge.

Embassies (E), High Commissions (HC) and Consulates (C) You can usually be sure that diplomatic missions will be open in the mornings between 0900 and 1200. Some have afternoon opening, and some do not open every day. Even when a mission is officially closed, the staff will usually be helpful if something has to be done in an emergency. *Albania (E)*, PO Box 1034, Msese Rd, T34945. *Algeria (E)*, PO Box 2963, 34 A.H Mwinyi Rd, T117619, F117620, algemb@entafrica.com. *Angola (E)*, PO Box 20793, 78 Lugalo Rd, T117673, F32349. *Argentina (E)*, Msasani Peninsula, T41628/4313. *Australia (HC)*, PO Box 2996, NIC Investment House, Samora Ave, T20244/6. *Austria (C)*, PO Box 312, Samora Ave, T112900. *Belgium (E)*, NIC Investment House, 7th Floor, Samora Ave, T112688/113466, F117621. *Brazil (E)*, PO Box 9654, IPS Bldg Samora Ave, T668170. *Bulgaria (E)*, Mikocheni, A H Mwinyi Rd, T72140/116274. *Burundi (E)*, PO Box 2752, Lugalo Rd, T113710, F115923/117615. *Canada*, PO Box 1022, Canadian High Commission, 38 Mirambo St, Garden Ave, T112831/2/3/4/5, F116896. *China (E)*, PO Box 1649, 2 Kajificheni Cl, T667212/667586/667694, F666353. *Cuba (E)*, PO Box 9282, Lugalo Rd, T115928, F115927. *CIS (former USSR) (E)*, PO Box 1905, Kenyatta Dr, T666005, F666818. *Cyprus (C)*, PO

Box 529, *Motel Agip*, Sokoine Dr, T113450/21975. *Czechoslovakia (E)*, PO Box 3054, Jubilee Mansion, Upanga Rd, T46971/23360. *Denmark (E)*, PO Box 9171, Ghana Ave, T113887/8/118844, F116433. *Egypt (E)*, PO Box 1668, 24 Garden Ave, T113591/117622, F112543. *Finland (E)*, PO Box 2466, Mirambo St/Garden Ave, T119170, F119173, finemb@twiga.co. *France (E)*, PO Box 2349, Ali Hassan Mwinyi Blvd, T666021, F667702. *Germany (E)*, PO Box 2083, NIC Investment House, Samora Ave, T117409/15, F112944. *Greece (C)*, PO Box 766, Upanga Rd, T110329/22931. *Hungary*, PO Box 4153, 194 Chaka Rd, Oyster Bay, T668573, F667214. *India (HC)*, PO Box 2684, NIC Investment House, Samora Ave, T117175, F118761. *Indonesia (E)*, PO Box 522, 229 Upanga Rd, T119119/118133, F115849. *Iran (E)*, PO Box 5802, Upanga Rd, T34622/3. *Ireland (E)*, PO Box 9612, Msasani Rd, T666211/666348, F667214. *Italy (E)*, PO Box 2106, Lugalo Rd, T115935/7, F115938. *Japan*, PO Box 2577, 1081 A H Mwinyi Rd, T115827, F115830. *Kenya (HC)*, PO Box 5231, NIC Investment House, 14th Flr, Samora Ave, T112955/8, F113098. *Korea (E)*, PO Box 2690, United Nations Rd, T117628. *Libya (E)*, PO Box 9413, Mtitu St, T31666/35063. *Madagascar (E)*, PO Box 5254, Malik Rd, T29442. *Malawi (HC)*, PO Box 23168, IPS Bldg, Samora Ave, T113238. *Mozambique (E)*, PO Box 1007, 25 Garden Ave, T116502. *Netherlands (E)*, PO Box 9534, ATC Bldg Ohio St, 2nd Floor, T118566/7/8/118593/4/5/6/7, F112828. *Nigeria (HC)*, PO Box 2925, Ali Hassan Mwinyi Blvd, T666000, F666834. *Norway (E)*, PO Box 2646, Mirambo St, T113366/113610, F116564, norw/embassy@twiga.com. *Pakistan (HC)*, PO Box 2925, 149 Malik Rd, Upanga, T117630, F113205. *Poland (E)*, PO Box 2188, 63 Ali Khan Rd, Upanga, T115271, F115812. *Romania (E)*, PO Box 590, 11 Ocean Rd, T115899. *Rwanda (E)*, PO Box 2981, Upanga Rd, T117631. *South Africa (HC)*, PO Box 10723, Mwaya Rd, Oyster Bay, T600484/5, F600618/600683/4. *Spain (E)*, PO Box 842, Kinondoni Rd, T666936/666018, F666938. *Embassy of Sudan*, PO Box 2266, Upanga Rd, T/F117641/115811. *Sweden (E)*, PO Box 9274, Mirambo St/Garden Ave, T111239/111240/111265, F111340, sweden@ www.interafrica.com. *Switzerland (E)*, PO Box 2454, Kinondoni Rd, T666008/9, F666376. *Syria (E)*, PO Box 2442, Ali Khan Rd, T117656/118782. *Uganda (HC)*, PO Box 6237, Extelcom Bldg, Samora Ave, T117646/7, F112913. *UK (HC)*, PO Box 9200, Bank House, Samora Ave, T112953/117659/64, F112951, BHC.Dar@raha.com. *USA (E)*, PO Box 9123, located at 36 Laibon Rd (off Ali Hassan Mwinyi Rd), Dar es Salaam, T666010/5, F666701, office hours, 0730-1600. *Yemen (E)*, PO Box 4646, United Nations Rd, T117650. *Yugoslavia (E)*, PO Box 2838, Upanga Rd, T46378. *RD Congo (E)*, PO Box 975, 438 Malik Rd, Upanga, T31672. *Zambia (HC)*, PO Box 2525, Ohio St, T116811/118481, F112974. *Zimbabwe*, PO Box 20762, Longido St, T116789/112912.

Hospitals & medical services Hospitals: the main hospital is *Mihumbili Hospital* located off United National Rd, T151351. *Oyster Bay Hospital* is an efficient and accessible small private medical centre (follow the signs along Haile Selassie Rd). *Kilimanjaro Hotel* will recommend a physician in an emergency. The *Aga Khan Hospital* is located on Ocean Rd at the junction with Ufukoni Rd, T114096/37917/30081/2/3. *Ocean Road Hospital* is on Ocean Rd at junction with Chimara Rd. All these hospitals are well equipped and staffed. The *Zenco Clinic*, Samora Ave, close to the Salamander Restaurant is very good and central, fees US$1 for a consultation, US$1 for a malaria test which takes about 20 mins. **The Flying Doctors:** Nairobi (emergency), T02-501280, Tanzania office for information on membership, T116610. **Pharmacies:** are located in all shopping centres. There is a good chemist in the *Kilimanjaro Hotel* foyer and one in the Namanga Shopping Centre along Bagamoyo Rd. Small **dispensaries** are located in the main residential areas.

International Institutions *European Union*, 38 Mirambo St, PO Box 9514, Dar es Salaam, T117473/4/5/6/118965/66/67/68/69/70//1, F113277, EC-TAN-@Twiga.com. *Food and Agriculture Organisation*, Tetex building, Pamba Rd, Dar es Salaam, T113070/1/3/4, F11250, Tx41320, FAOTZA@FIELD.fao.org. *ILO*, 40 A H Mwinyi Rd, Dar es Salaam, T666029/4/6/7, Tx41126 ILO DAR TZ. *UNDP*, PO Box 9182, Dar es Salaam, T112799/11280/1/5, F113272, Tx41284 ABD UNDEVPRO. *UNESCO*, Comtech Bldg, Old Bagamoyo Rd, Dar es Salaam, T75706, F75705 or UNDP 113272, TxUNDP 41284 UNDEV PRO, *UNHCR*, 18 Kalenga Rd, near MMC, Dar es Salaam, T150075, F152817, Tx41406 HCR TAN TZ. *UNICEF*, Bibi Titi Rd, PO Box 4076, Dar es Salaam, T152164, F151603, Tx41103 UNICEF TZ. *World Bank*, PO Box 2054, Dar es Salaam, T114575/7/116197, F113039, Tx41273 INTBAFRAND DSM. *World Health Organisation*, next to Government Chief Chemist, Sokoine Rd, PO Box 9292, Dar es Salaam, T113005/22225, F113180, Tx41110.

Libraries *Alliance Française*, Library facilities, French TV news. *Cultural Centre*, Mavuno House, Azikiwe St, T119415. The *British Council*, PO Box 9100, on the corner of Ohia St and Samora, T116574/5/6, F112669. Has an excellent library, with reference, lending, newspapers and magazines. It is well worth joining the lending section if you are in Dar es Salaam for any length of time. *US Information Service*, 3rd Floor of the Tanganyika Motors Bldg, PO Box 9170, T117174/37101/37111, has good reference facilities and has recently moved to new premises at the Lufthansa Bldg, at the junction of Bibi Titi Mohammed Rd and Upanga Rd. *National Central Library* is on Bibi Titi Mohammed Rd near the Maktaba St intersection, T150048/9. The library at the University of Dar es Salaam currently charges US$50 to use it, even for reference purposes.

Places of worship Churches: *Roman Catholic Cathedral* is on Sokoine Drive opposite the Customs jetty. *Lutheran Church* is at the junction of Kivukoni Front and Sokoine Drive. *St Alban's Church*, the Anglican Church, is situated at junction of Maktaba St and Upanga Rd. *Greek Church* is on Upanga Rd. **Mosques:** are located on Zanaki St; there are three on Mosque St (one is Ismaili); 2 on UWT St at the Pugu Rd end; on UWT St near Morogoro Rd; on Kitumbini St; on Ghandi St; on Upanga Rd (Ismaili); off Chole Rd on Msasani Peninsular. **Temples:** there are two on Kisuki St which runs off India St near the Mawenzi roundabout on Maktaba St.

Tour companies & travel agents A variety of companies offer tours to the game parks, the islands (Zanzibar, Pemba, Mafia) and to locations of historical interest (Kilwa, Bagamoyo). It is well worth shopping around as prices (and degrees of luxury) vary. Among the most experienced companies are: *AMI Travel Bureau, Coastal Travel, Hippo Tours & Safaris, Kearsley Travel and Tours, Rickshaw Travel, Savannah Tours, Sykes, Takims Safaris, Valji & Alibhai.* **Across Tanzania Safaris**, PO Box 21996, Makunganya St, T219961/23121. *Adventure Centre*, Goliondoi Rd, PO Box 12799, Arusha, T057-7111, F8997. *Africa Expeditions*, PO Box 1857, Mindu St, T34574/38985. *All African Travel Agents*, PO Box 1947, T20886. *AMI Travel Bureau*, PO Box 9041, AMI Bldg, Samora Ave, T115777/8/9. *Azania Tours and Travel*, PO Box 3707, UWT St, T36959. *Bahari Enterprises & Safaris*, PO Box 15384, T63422/9. *Bon Voyage Travel*, Osman Towers, Zanaki St, T33080/25951. *Bushtrekker Safaris*, PO Box 5350, *Bahari Beach Hotel*, T31957/32671, Tx41178. *Coastal Travel*, PO Box 3052, Upanga Rd, T37479/80. *East African Holidays*, PO Box 2895, Samora Ave, T25989. *Easy Travel & Tours Ltd*, Avalon House, 1st Flr, Sokoine Drive/Zanaki St, PO Box 1428, T123526/121747, F113842/114479, easytravel@raha.com. *Emslies Travel Ltd*, TDFL Bldg, Upanga Rd, T114065/115553. *Flag Tours and Safaris*, PO Box 16046, T37075. *Four Ways Travel Service*, PO Box 2926, Samora Ave, T22378. *Glide Safaris*, PO Box 4427. *Gogo Safaris*, PO Box 21114, Bagamoyo Rd, T0811-321552. *Hakuna Matata*, The Arcade, Old Bagamoya Rd, T700230/1. *Hoopoe Adventure Tours*, India St, PO Box 2047, Arusha (UK: T0181-4288221, F0181-4211396, hoopoeUK@aol.com). Highly recommended. *Hippo Tours & Safaris*, PO Box 1658, Mkwepu St, T36860/71610. *Hit Holidays*, PO Box 1287. An excellent travel agency, UWT St (near *Rickshaw Travels*), T0811-324552. *Holiday Africa Tours & Safaris*, PO Box 2132, Africa St, T111357/8. *Hotel Tours & Management*, PO Box 5350, T31957/32671. *Iramba Tours*, PO Box 21856, T44482. *J M Tourist*, PO Box 21703, T22433, Tx41207. *Kearsley Travel and Tours*, PO Box 801, Kearsley House, Indira Gandhi St, T115183/4, F35012/29085, Tx41014/41615. *Leisure Tours & Safaris*, PO Box 6100, T32251. *Mashado Tanzania*, Central Reservations: PO Box 14823, Arusha, T57-6585, F8020, Mashado@ habari.co.tz, Mobitel T+255-811-510107/1/2, F+255-811-510104/3. *Mill Tours & Safaris*, PO Box 19604, T22114. *Molenveld Travel Bureau*, PO Box 456, Samora Ave, T0811-324609. *Multi Tours and Travel*, PO Box 6940, Zanaki St, Osman Towers, T30501/22147, F32138. *Panorama Tours*, PO Box 7534, Bakwat Bldg, corner of Morogoro Rd and UWT St, T115508. *Parklands Tours*, PO Box 19630, T68586. *Parkway Tours and Safaris*, PO Box 6945, Tanzania Publishing House, Samora Ave, T36731. *Pwani Tours & Safaris*, PO Box 50007, Cnr Kaluta St and Morogoro Rd, T22433/32261. *Reza Travel & Tours*, Jamhuri St, opposite Caltex Station,

T334458/34814. *Rickshaw Travel* (American Express Agents), PO Box 1889, Sheraton Hotel, Ohio St, T115620, F29125/35456, Tx41162. *Safari Tours*, PO Box 9442, THB Bldg Samora Ave, T28422/28737/28765. *Savannah Tours*, PO Box 20517, T115624/114339/138088, F113748, savtour@twiga.com. *Searock International*, PO Box 3030, T32703/33589. *Selous Safaris*, PO Box 1192, T34535, F28486, Tx81016. *Skylink Travel & Tours*, TDFL Bldg, Ohio St, T115381/30110. *Southern Tanganyika Safaris and Tours*, TDFL Bldg, Ohio St, T0812-781971. *State Travel Service*, PO Box 5023, Bank House, Samora Ave, T112747/110038, F29295, Tx41508. *Sunshine Safari Tours*, PO Box 5575, T22700. *Sykes*, PO Box 1947, Indira Ghandi St, T110552/115542, F29330, Tx41046. *Takims Holidays Tours and Safaris Ltd*, Sales Office: DTV Bldg, Jamhuri St, Dar es Salaam, T110346/7/8/30037/23394, Cable AIRFLY Head Office: Mtendeni St, PO Box 20350, Dar es Salaam, T31260/37384, F116659/60, takims@twiga.com, offer an IATA accredited travel agency as well as a bureau de change in Dar es Salaam, long established company with an office in Arusha (see page 399), London contact: "Tanzania Experience", T0171-6245128/0171-3289521, F0171-6258333 and 0171-6244100. *Tankar*, PO Box 5286, T3109. *Tent with a View Safaris*, Muleweld Tours, PO Box 40525, Samora Ave Dar, T38120/23205. *Tourcare Tanzania*, PO Box 22878, T42496. *Trans Africa Guides*, PO Box 853, T30192. *Vacational*, PO Box 6649, T34350/21015, F34160, Tx81012. *Valji & Alibhai*, PO Box 786, Bridge St, T20522/26537, F112988, Tx81052. *Walji's Travel Bureau*, PO Box 434, cnr Zanaki St and Indira Ghandi St, T111157. **Hunting Safari agents:** *Cordial Tours*, PO Box 1679, Jamhuri St, T35264. *Gerald Posanisi Safaris*, PO Box 45640, T47435.

Tourist offices Tourism has recently come under new management and this is expected to improve services. The Tourist Information Centre is located at the UN Bldg, Samora Ave, T31555/20373/23491.

Useful addresses Police: main police station is on Gerazani St near the railway station, T115507. Also stations on Upanga Rd on the City side of Selander Bridge; on Ali Hassan Mwinyi Blvd at the junction with Old Bagamoyo Rd.

Tanzania & Zanzibar

Dar es Salam

North Coast: Bagamoyo and Tanga

Bagamoyo is one of the most fascinating towns in East Africa, with a host of historical associations. Access is only really feasible by road, and although the surface has been repaired for the part of the distance, the major part is very rough. It is quite possible to make a day trip from Dar es Salaam, although an overnight stay is perhaps best. Tanga was an important port in the period up to independence when sisal was Tanzania's main crop, and the main growing area was between Kilimanjaro and the coast. The Usambara Hills are a very attractive, and Lushoto and Amani can be visited either on the way to Tanga, or when travelling to Kilimanjaro and Arusha.

Bagamoyo

History
6°20'S 38°30'E
Colour map 3, grid B5

The coastal area opposite Zanzibar was first settled by fishermen and cultivators. Towards the end of the 18th century, 12 or so Muslim diwans arrived to settle, build dwellings and establish their families and retinues of slaves. These diwans were all related to Shomvi la Magimba from Oman. They prospered through levying taxes whenever a cow was slaughtered, or a shark or other large fish caught, as well as on all salt produced at Nunge, about three kilometres north of Bagamoyo.

The town was threatened by the Kamba around 1800, and an uneasy alliance of the Shomvi, the Zaramo and the Doe, was formed to hold them off. In return for their support against the Kamba, the Shomvi agreed to pay a tribute to the Zaramo of a third of the revenues from their commercial activities, mostly the sale of slaves and ivory.

In 1868, the diwans granted land to the Holy Ghost Fathers to establish a mission. The Zaramo challenged the right of the diwans to make this concession but, following intervention by the French Consul, Zanzibar (firstly under Sultan Majid, and, after 1870, under Sultan Barghash), put pressure on the Zaramo to accept the settlement.

Bagamoyo's location as a mainland port close to Zanzibar led to its development as a centre for caravans and an expansion of commerce in slaves and ivory soon followed. There was also growing trade in sun-dried fish, gum copal (a residue used in making varnishes that accumulates from the *msandarusi* tree in the soil near its roots), and the salt from Nunge. Copra (from coconuts) was also important, and was used to make

North coast

KENYA

Shengena (2,462m)
Mlalo
Magambo (2,230m)
Lushoto
Soni
Usambara Mountains
Amani
Korogwe
Segera
Muheza
Tongoni
Tanga
Pemba Channel
Pangani River
Pangani
Mkata
Zanzibar Channel
Mligasi River
Sadani
Miono
ZANZIBAR
Wami River
Msata
Bagamoyo
To Morogoro
Chalinze
Mlandizi
Ruvu River
DAR ES SALAAM
Lunga Lunga

0 km 25

Mangroves

Up and down the coast of East Africa you will come across stretches of mangrove forests. Ecologically these can be described as evergreen saline swamp forests and their main constituents are the mangroves Rhizophora, Ceriops and Bruguiera. These are all described as viviparous, that is the seeds germinate or sprout when the fruits are still attached to the parent plant. Mangrove forests support a wide range of other plants and animals including a huge range of birds, insects and fish.

Economically mangrove forests are an important source of building poles, known on the coast as boriti, which were once exported in large quantities to the Arabian Gulf. Their main property is that they are resistant to termite attack (see box, page 542). Mangrove bark is also used as a tanning material and charcoal can be obtained from mangrove wood. As with so many natural resources in East Africa care needs to be taken in the use of mangrove forests. Their over-exploitation could lead to the delicate balance that is found in the forests being upset, with serious consequences for these coastal regions.

soap. A boat-building centre was established which supplied craft to other coastal settlements.

In 1880 the population of the town was around 5,000 but this was augmented by a substantial transient population in residence after completing a caravan or undertaking preparations prior to departure. The numbers of those temporarily in town could be considerable. In 1889, after the slave trade had been suppressed reducing the numbers passing through significantly, it was still recorded that 1,305 caravans left for the interior, involving 41,144 people.

The social composition of the town was varied. There were the initial Muslim Shomvi and the local Zaramo and Doe. Among the earliest arrivals were Hindus from India, involving themselves in administration, coconut plantations and boat-building. Muslim Baluchis, a people based in Mombasa and Zanzibar, and following for the most part the profession of mercenary soldiers, also settled and were involved in trade, financing caravans and land-owning. Other Muslim sects were represented, among them the Ismailis who settled in 1840 and by 1870 numbered 137. A handful of Sunni Muslims from Zanzibar established shops in Bagamoyo, some Parsees set up as merchants, and a small group of Catholic Goans was engaged in tailoring and retailing.

Caravans from the interior brought with them Nyamwezi, Sukuma and Manyema porters. They might remain in town for six months or so before joining an outgoing caravan, and they resided for the most part in an insalubrious shanty settlement known as *Kampi Mbaya* ('bad camp') which was just off the main caravan route out of town close to the caravanserai. Some remained to take up life as fishermen or working the Nunge salt deposits.

In 1888 the German East Africa Company signed a treaty with the Sultan of Zanzibar, Seyyid Khalifa, which allowed the company to collect customs duties along the coast. The Germans rapidly made their presence felt by ordering the Sultan's representative (the Liwali) to lower the Sultan's flag, and on being refused, axed down the flag-pole.

Later in the year a dispute between a member of the company and a townsman culminated in the latter being shot. The Usagara trading house of the company was beseiged by irate townspeople, 200 troops landed from the *SS Moewe*, and over 100 local people were killed.

Further resentment was incurred when the Germans set about registering land and property, demanding proof of ownership. As this was impossible for most residents there was widespread fear that property would be confiscated.

One of the diwans, Bomboma, organized local support. They enlisted the help of Bushiri bin Salim al-Harthi who had earlier led Arabs against the Germans in Tabora. Bushiri had initial success. Sections of Bagamoyo were burned and Bushiri

Lay down my heart

I'm weary for travelling has taken its toll
Lay down my heart and calm my soul
Happy haven, Bagamoyo

While far away, in my heart I saw
A shimmering pearl on a jade-green shore
Coast of palms, Bagamoyo

Laden with spices and ivory
Dhows sail in on the sparkling sea
Bustling harbour, Bagamoyo

There the women are pretty and fine
All year round they drink palm wine
Garden of love, Bagamoyo

Under the stars hear the laughter ring
From lovely girls as they dance and sing
Velvet nights, Bagamoyo

My spirits lift as the drum beats roll
Lay down my heart and calm my soul
At last I'm home, Bagamoyo

On the long journey from the interior, travelling east to the Indian Ocean, caravan porters looked forward to their arrival at Bagamoyo, a place of cool sea breezes, greenery and high-living. As they marched, the porters sang to keep up their spirits. The verses above, originally in Swahili, were recorded in 1890, by Hauptmann Leue a German colonial administrator.

The name of the town is said to be derived from Bwaga-moyo which would be translated as `lay down my heart'. A two-edged interpretation has arisen. The first is that like the caravan porters the weary traveller from the interier could `lay down his heart' at Bagamoyo, resting and recuperating. More poignantly, the second interpretation is that as they were to be transported overseas, the last part of Africa the slaves would ever see was Bagamoyo. It was there they should `lay down their hearts'.

formed up in Nzole about 6.5 kilometres southwest of the town ready for an assault. The German government now felt compelled to help the company and Herman von Wissmann was appointed to lead an infantry force comprising Sundanese and Zulu troops. Admiral Denhardt, commanding the German naval forces played for time by initiating negotiations with Bushiri whose demands included being made Governor of the region from Dar es Salaam up to Pangani, payment of 4,000 rupees (about US$10,000 in present-day values) a month, and the right to keep troops.

By May 1889 Wissmann had consolidated his forces and built a series of fortified block houses. He attacked Nzole and Bushiri fled. The alliance of the diwans and Bushiri weakened, and in June the Germans retook Saadani and in July, Pangani. Bushiri was captured and executed at Pangani in December. Bomboma, and another of the diwans leading the resistance, Marera, were both executed, and other diwans were deposed and replaced by collaborators who had assisted the Germans.

It was now clear that the German government intended to extend their presence and in October 1890, rights to the coast were formally purchased from the Sultan of Zanzibar for four million marks.

In early 1891 German East Africa become a formal colony, but in April it was decided to establish Dar es Salaam as the capital. Commercial activity in Bagamoyo revived, and in the last decade of the century rebuilding began with the construction of new stone buildings including a customs house and the Boma which served as an administrative centre.

The caravan trade resumed and there was a further influx of Indians together with the arrival of Greeks who established a European hotel. Wm O'Swald the Hamburg trading company arrived and Hansing established vanilla plantations at Kitopeni and Hurgira. An important Koran school was established in the town.

Despite these developments Bagamoyo was destined for steady decline as its harbour was unsuitable for deep draught steamships and no branch of the railway was built to serve the port. The ending of the German rule further reduced commercial presence in the town, and the present century has seen Bagamoyo decline steadily, lacking even a sealed road to link it to Dar es Salaam.

At the south approach to the town, on the road from Koale is the **Old Fort** (some- **Sights in Old**
times referred to as the Old Prison). It is the oldest surviving building in Bagamoyo **Bagamoyo**
having been started by Abdallah Marhabi around 1860 and extended and strength-
ened by Sultan Baghash after 1870 and then by the German colonialists. It was used
as a police post until 1992. Initially one of its functions was to hold slaves until they
could be shipped to Zanzibar. It is said there is an underground passage through
which the slaves were herded to dhows on the shore, although this passage is not
apparent today. It is currently being restored and the plan is that it will provide
teaching rooms for the nearby **Chuo cha Sanaa** (Art College). The caretaker will
allow you to look round, and it is clear that the work will result in a particularly hand-
some building. The construction is whitewashed, three storeys high, with buttresses
and battlements and an enclosed courtyard.

On the path to *Badeco Beach Hotel*, off to the right is the **German cemetery** with
some 20 graves dating from 1889/90, and most are of Germans killed during the
uprising led by Bushiri in those years (see page 347). A German deed of freedom for
a slave is reproduced on a tree. The cemetery is well tended, surrounded by a coral
wall. In the ground of the *Badeco Beach Hotel* is the site of the tree reputedly used by
the German administration for executions. The site is marked by a plaque.

Continuing along India St on the left is an old two storey building **Liku House**
with an awning supported by slender iron columns and a central double door. This
served as the first administrative headquarters for the German from 1888 until the
Boma was completed in 1897. Emin Pasha stayed there in 1889 (see box, page 351).

The **Boma** is an impressive two storey building topped by crenellations, con-
structed in a U-Shape. There are pointed arches on the first floor and rounded
arches on the ground floor. This was the German administrative centre from 1897,

Tanzania & Zanzibar

Bagamoyo

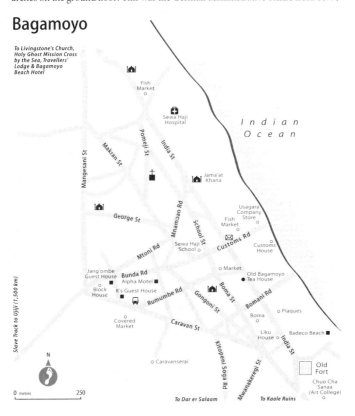

Krakatoa

In August 1883, a volcano erupted on the island of Krakatoa in the strait of Sundra, just east of Java, in present-day Indonesia. The explosion was enormous, and it is said that it was heard in Rodrigues, 3,000 miles away in the Mascarene Islands of the Indian Ocean. 100 kilometres-an-hour gales were registered for six weeks in the Indian Ocean islands. A huge wave, 20 metres high, hit the islands and the East African coast. At Bagamoyo, although the impact was lessened by the fact that it was partly shielded from the direct path of the wave by Zanzibar, local people still reported a sudden five metre tidal surge that was repeated with gradually diminishing force, six times, during the next 24 hours as the wave was reflected to-and-fro between the west coast of Zanzibar and the mainland. Huge quantities of ash from the eruption floated up into the atmosphere, catching the light to cause the most glorious sunrises and sunsets for several years.

If you are walking on the shore you may find a piece of pumice stone – grey honey-combed rock, often used for removing stains on skin – it originates from the foaming volcanic lava after the Krakatoa eruption over 100 years ago and has been brought by the current that sweeps from the South China Seas to Africa.

and it currently serves as the headquarters for the District Commissioner. The building is undergoing some restoration, and it is possible to look round. On the inland side of the building is a well constructed by Sewa Haji, (see box, page 354).

On the shore side is a semi-circular levelled area on which was a monument erected by the Germans with brass commemorative plaques. With the fall of Bagamoyo to the British, the monument was razed and replaced with the present construction which commemorates the departure of Burton and Speke to Lake Tanganyika from nearby Kaole in 1857. The old German plaques have been reset in the walls which support the levelled area, on the shore-side. To the left is an Arabic two storey building fronted by six columns, a fretted verandah and curved arch windows, said to be the **Old Bagamoyo Tea House**, and is thought to be one of the oldest buildings in the town, constructed by Abdallah Marhabi in 1860. In front of the Boma is the **Uhuru Monument**, celebrating Tanzania's independence in 1961, and a bandstand.

Continuing north along India St there is a particularly fine residential house on the right with columns and arched windows, just before Customs Rd. This leads down to the **Customs House**, built in 1895 by Sewa Haji and rented to the Germans. It is a double storey building with an open verandah on the first floor, buttresses, arched windows, and lime-washed. It looks onto a walled courtyard and is currently undergoing restoration. Opposite the Customs House are the ruins of the **Usagara Company Store** built in 1888 with the arrival of the German commercial presence. The unusual construction had stone plinths on which were mounted cast-iron supports for the timber floor, raised to keep the stores dry. The cast-iron supports have cups surrounding them in which kerosene was poured to prevent rats climbing up to eat the stored grain. At one end of the building is a tower, held up by a tree growing through it.

Halfway down Customs Rd is the covered **Fish Market** with stone tables for gutting fish. When not used for this purpose they are marked out with chalk draughts boards for informal games with bottle-tops. At the top of Customs Rd, just before the intersection with India St is the **Post Office**, with a fine carved door and a blue-painted upstairs verandah. Further north along India St are a series of Arabic buildings, one of which, the first on the right after the square to the left, is being restored as a hotel.

Continuing north, on the right, is the **Jama'at Khana**, the Ismaili mosque, which dates from 1880, double-storeyed with a verandah and carved doors. On the right beyond the mosque is the hospital, now part of Muhimbili Teaching Hospital in Dar es Salaam, which is based on the original Sewa Haji Hospital, constructed in 1895. On the death of Sewa Haji in 1896, the hospital was run by the Holy Ghost Mission,

The Bagamoyo banquet of Emin Pasha

Emin Pasha was born to a Jewish family in Germany and his original name was Schnitzer. At various times he presented himself as Turkish and Egyptian, and considered becoming either Belgian or British. `Pasha' is a Turkish title given to the governor of a province. He had a Turkish wife, left behind in Prussia and he took an Ethiopian mistress with whom he had a daughter. All who met him were impressed with his charm, generosity, his scholarly interest in natural history and his devotion to his daughter. General Gordon recruited him in Egypt and appointed him Governor of Equatoria in Southern Sudan. When Gordon was killed in the fall of Khartoum in 1885, Emin Pasha was stranded. The plight of the gallant defender of the Empire captured the imagination of the British public and a public subscription was got up to finance a rescue expedition led by HM Stanley. Far from being beleaguered and starving, an exhausted Stanley found Emin Pasha and his Egyptian forces living comfortably with harems and slaves. An attack by the Sudanese however caused them to flee. The Pasha's troops had melted away by the time Stanley, together with a decimated force and the Pasha in tow, reached the coast at Bagamoyo in December 1889.

The Germans laid on a great reception and there were 34 at the banquet on the first floor of Liku House. Roasts, fresh seafood and champagne were served. A naval band played below the balcony. In the street the returning porters celebrated their return with an orgy. Emin Pasha circulated, captivating the guests with his charm. Suddenly there was an uproar from outside. The guests rushed to the balcony to see revellers surrounding the figure of Emin Pasha, covered in blood, who had tumbled from the balcony.

It took six weeks in the Sewa Haji Hospital for the Pasha to pull through. When he had recovered, a telegram from the Kaiser persuaded him to set off into the interior again to negotiate treaties with native leaders to extend Germany's power.

Three years later, in 1892, at his camp in present-day Zaire not far from Kisingani, struggling with failing eyesight to catalogue his collection of insects, plants and flowers, he was surrounded by Arab slavers who slit his throat.

and then from 1912 by the Germans. The present hospital has some handsome old buildings and some more modern blocks. It has a rather charming air, with goats lolling on the covered walkways between the wards.

At the northern end of the town on the right is substantial **Mosque** and Muslim school with curved steps up to the carved door over which is a delicate fretted grill. The building is fronted by six columns and there is a verandah to the rear.

Other buildings of interest in Bagamoyo Town include the **Sewa Haji School** (see box, page 354), a three storey construction with filigree iron-work and constructed in 1896.

Close to the intersection of Sunda Rd and Mongesani St at the Western approach to the town is the white **Block House**, constructed in 1889 by Herman Wissman during the Bushiri uprising (see page 347). There is a mangrove pole and coral stone roof and an outside ladder which enabled troops to man the roof behind the battlements. The walls have loopholes through which troops could fire, standing on low internal walls, which doubled as seating, to give them the height to fire down on their adversaries. Behind the block house is a disused well.

The **slave track** to the interior departed from this point – a 1,500 kilometre trail which terminated at Ujiji on Lake Tanganyika. Off Caravan St is the **Caravanserai**, a courtyard with single-storey buildings at the front and a square, two storey building with a verandah at the centre (the corner of which is collapsing). It was here that preparations were made for the fitting out of caravans to the interior.

Chuo cha Sanaa This is a school for the arts where music, drama, dance and painting are taught. Most students are Tanzanian, but there are several from Europe, America and the Far East. The main buildings are located along the road to Koale to the south of

Tanzania & Zanzibar

Bagamoyo. They are a mixture of a Viking house and a traditional African home, recently constructed, with help from a Swedish Aid Project, and are very impressive. The main building has a Greek-style open amphitheatre, with proscenium stage covered by a 15 metre high thatched canopy. The amphitheatre stage backs onto a second theatre area, which is roofed and enclosed. Attached to the stage are workshops and offices. Students can be observed in the area round the dormitories practising their skills. Visitors are welcome to observe the training.

Livingstone's Church This is a simple construction with a tin roof, curved arch windows and wooden benches. Its formal name is the Anglican Church of the Holy Cross. Above the entrance is the sign 'Through this door Dr David Livingstone passed' referring to the fact that his body was kept in the church prior to it being returned to England.

Cross by the Sea A monument in green marble surmounted by a cross is located on the path leading to the sea from Livingstone's Church. It marks the spot where, in 1868, Father Antoine Horner of the French Holy Ghost Fathers crossed from Zanzibar (where they had operated a Mission since 1860) and stepped ashore to establish the first Christian Church on the mainland.

Holy Ghost Mission Opposite the path to the Cross by the Sea is **Mango Tree Drive** which was established in 1871 as the approach to the Mission. There is a statue of the Sacred Heart, erected in 1887 in front of the **Fathers' House**. The Fathers' House is a three storey stucture with an awning over a verandah on the top floor and arches on the other two floors. It was begun in 1873 and the third storey finally added in 1903. In 1969 the building was taken over by MANTEP as a training centre for educational management.

Behind the Fathers' House is the **First Church**, construction of which started in 1872. It comprises a stone tower topped with arches with a cross at the centre and crosses on the pediments at each corner. The main building is a simple rectangular structure with a tin roof, unusually situated behind and to the side of the tower so that the tower sits at one corner.

It was to here on 24 February 1874, that the body of David Livingstone was brought by the missionary's African followers, Sisi and Chuma, who had carried their master 1,500 kilometres from Ujiji. Speke, Burton, Grant, Stanley, Peters, Emin Pasha and Wissmann all visited the church at one time or another.

Following the path to the right of the First Church is a cemetery where the early missionaries are buried. Further down this path is a small shrine built by freed slaves in 1876 with the sign 'Salamnus Maria', picked out in flowers.

A great baobab tree, planted in 1868, stands to the side of the the first church. At the base can be seen the links of the chain where Mme de Chevalier, a mission nurse, tethered her donkey.

The **New Church**, constructed of coral blocks, started in 1910 and completed in 1914, stands in front of the First Church. A small iron cross commemorates the centenary, in 1968, of the Holy Ghost Mission in Bagamoyo.

The **Mission Museum** is housed in the **Sisters' Building**. The displays present a history of Bagamoyo and there are relics and photographs from the slave period. One intriguing exhibit is the uniform presented by HA Schmit in 1965, that he wore during the East African Campaign under von Lettow (see page 530). Adjacent to the Mission Museum is a craft workshop with *Ufundi* ('craftsmen') picked out in flowers.

One of the main activities of the Holy Ghost Mission was to purchase slaves and present them with their freedom. A certificate of freedom was provided by the German authorities. These freed slaves had originally been captured hundreds of kilometres away in the hinterland, and the Mission undertook to rehabilitate them in **Freedom Village** located just to the north of the main Mission buildings.

These are located five kilometres south of Bagamoyo. The route is the road past **Kaole Ruins** Chuo Cha Sanaa (Bagamoyo Art College). It is quite possible to walk, but it is advis- *Colour map 3, grid B5* able to take a guide for security. At present there are no taxis in Bagamoyo.

The ruins are on the coastal side of the present day village of Koale. The site consists of the ruins of two mosques and a series of about 30 tombs, set among palm trees. Some of the tombs have stones pillars up to five metres in height.

The older of the two mosques ('A' on the site plan) dates from some time between the third and fourth centuries and is thought to mark one of the earliest contacts of Islam with Africa, before the main settlement took place. The remains of a vaulted roof constructed from coral with lime mortar can be seen which formed the *mbirika* at the entrance. Here ceremonial ablutions took place, taking water from the nearby well. There is some buttressing with steps which allowed the muezzin access to the roof to call the faithful to prayer. The recess (*kibula*) on the east side, nearest to Mecca has faint traces of an inscription on the vaulting.

The stone pillars that mark some of the tombs were each surmounted by a stone 'turban' and the remains of some of these can be seen on the ground. Delicate porcelain bowls with light green glaze were set in the side of the pillars and the indentations can be seen. The bowls have been removed for safe-keeping and are in the National Museum in Dar es Salaam. These bowls have been identified as celadon made in China in the 14th century and are the main indication of the likely age of the structure. Some of the tombs have frames of dressed coral and weathered obituary inscriptions. Bodies would have been laid on the right side, with the face toward Mecca.

Tanzania & Zanzibar

Kaole Ruins

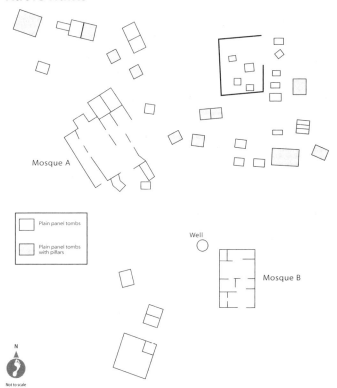

☞ *Sewa Haji – Bagamoyo Philanthropist*

Sewa Haji's father came from the Hindu Kush, in what is now Pakistan, to Zanzibar, setting up general stores in Zanzibar and Bagamoyo in the 1860'. Sewa Haji was born in 1851, one of four children, and when two of his brothers died in 1869, he found himself, at the age of 18, in charge of the two family firms, Haji Karji and Ratansi Mayi and Co.

The firms supplied caravans operating out of Bagamoyo with cloth, beads, copper wire, brass vessels, gun-powder and shot, and purchased ivory, rhino horns and hippo teeth from them on their return. Equipment and supplies would be provided on credit, financing part of the caravan. The firm also acted as an agent in recruiting porters. Sewa Haji accumulated substantial land holdings around Bagamoyo, including the Old Fort which he sold to the Germans in 1894, while renting them the Post Office and the Customs House. In 1892 Sewa Haji donated 20,000 hectares to the Holy Ghost Mission in Bagamoyo. The same year he donated the three-storey building in the centre of town for a multiracial (African and Asian) school, an exceptionally enlightened move at the time. He established hospitals in Zanzibar, at Bagamoyo (the original building forms part of the present hospital) and in Dar es Salaam (near the present Malindi Wharf, it was demolished in 1951).

Sewa Haji died and was buried in Zanzibar, in 1894, at the age of 46. He had accumulated very consideraable wealth through his shrewd business dealings. Most of his land and houses in Bagamoyo were bequeathed to the German government on the understanding that the income be used to support lepers and the hospitals.

Mosque 'B' is of later construction and has been partially restored. It is similar to the triple-domed mosque at Kilwa Kisiwani, see page 370, in style, and it is thought that the builder may well have been the same.

The community that gave rise to these ruins would have been founded during the Muslim period AD 622-1400. The first Muslim colonies were established from AD 740 by sea-borne migrations from the Persian Gulf down the East African coast as far as Sofala, the area round the Zambezi River. The settlement at Koale would have traded mangrove poles, see page 347, sandalwood, ebony and ivory. It is suggested that Koale might have had several hundred inhabitants. The dwellings would have used timber in their construction and thus would have been less durable than the all-stone mosques and tombs. Being on more fertile soil inland, as the dwellings collapsed they rapidly became overgrown. The settlement went into gradual decline as the shore became more densely packed with mangroves, making its use by dhows difficult, and commercial activity shifted to Bagamoyo.

Sadani Game Reserve This is located on the coast about 50 kilometres north of Bagamoyo. However it is really inaccessible without hired transport. The best route is to turn off the Chalinze to Tanga Rd for Miono. The track can be impassable in the rainy seasons. There is a very rundown rest house in Sadani Village. The main track in the reserve runs south from Sadani Village to where there is a ferry across the Wami River. This ferry cannot take vehicles. The track continues to Ngiapanda which is about 10 kilometres west of Bagamoyo. This latter may be a possible route for trekkers. The reserve has elephant, leopard, lion, giraffe, buffalo and zebra.

Essentials Local guide Mr Esa has been fulsomely praised by visitors. He is a young student, very knowledgeable, keen and attentive. Some travellers have reported that they found the local people unwelcoming, and were advised by their guide to keep within close reach of their vehicle. They were also advised locally not to take any photographs.

Several new developments are in the process of construction. Bagamoyo is in a glorious location, with a splendid, curved, palm-fringed beach. There are only a few beach hotel rooms in town, and it is advisable to book. The currently available hotels are all good value. Inquire through *Coastal Travel*, PO Box 3052, Upanga Rd, T37479/37480. *B Livingstone Village*, mobile T0811-324645, recently opened complex.

Sleeping
■ *on map, page 349*
Price codes:
See inside front cover

C *Bagamoyo Beach Resort*, PO Box 250, Bagamoyo (sometimes referred to as the 'Gogo'), T83 (Bagamoyo) or T31235 (Dar es Salaam), at the north end of town – continue along India St. French management, a/c, hot water showers, most of the 22 rooms are comfortable but the style is a little uninspired with tin roofs and concrete walls, there are a few traditional-style rooms with thatched roofs, but they do not face over the ocean, simple restaurant, pleasant open-air bar overlooking beach with thatched roof, has a beach kindergarten, offers conference facilities up to 45 people for seminars and workshops, new sports facilities – windsurfing, snorkelling and diving, excursions can be arranged to Zanzibar, the mangrove swamps of the Ruvu River offer a wide variety of birdlife, including kingfishers, herons, ibis, bee eaters and the migratory flamingoes, the road to Bagamoyo is currently being upgraded.

D *Badeco Beach Hotel*, PO Box 261, T18 (Bagamoyo). Glorious location right on the beach at south end of town, small, with 15 rooms, 9 self-contained, some currently under construction, thatched bandas along shore, garden planted with bouganvillea, small restaurant, but with excellent and imaginative seafood menu. Camping available. **D** *Travellers' Lodge*, PO Box 275, T051-116222, Ext 77, F116236, at north end of town on India St. 4 small bungalows and 4 rooms, pleasant traditional thatched style, excellent bar. Camping in the grounds.

E *Alpha Motel*, PO Box 85, T56 (Bagamoyo), in town, on Rumumba Rd, near covered market. Pleasant shaded outside bar. **E** *Jang'ombe Guest House*, PO Box 268, Mangesani Rd, near intersection with Mtoni Rd. **E** *K's Guest House*, PO Box 15, T15 (Bagamoyo), in town centre opposite covered market on Caravan St. Camping also available at *Gogo Beach Resort*.

Eating Hotels are the main places. There are some snack bars near the covered market on Caravan St. **2** *Badeco*, excellent seafood, charming small restaurant. **2** *Bagamoyo Beach*, simple food.

Bars Only in hotels and the best are *Travellers Lodge*, *Badeco Beach* and *Bagamoyo Beach*, all of which overlook the sea.

Entertainment At weekends there are entertainments provided by the *Nyumba ya Sanaa* (Bagamoyo Art College) and they including music, dance and drama. They are well attended and the atmosphere excellent. You need to ask at the college for times and programmes.

Shopping There are some small general and pharmacy stores on School St. The covered market on Caravan St is excellent for fruit, vegetables, meat and dried fish. Fresh fish at fish market on Customs Rd. There is a curio stall with crafts on sale at the *Badeco Beach Hotel*. Sea shells can be bought by the Customs House.

Sports Marine fishing can be arranged through *Badeco Beach Hotel* and they have plans to introduce a range of watersports. **Football matches** at ground on road to Kaole, south of town.

Transport **Local** Not a single taxi at present. All destinations in Bagamoyo are walkable. It is a good idea to hire someone (US$0.50) to carry any bags and being with a local person provides security. There are signs warning of muggers, but local residents suggest this is to boost the guide business. It is as well to be careful, however.

Road The only feasible mode at present. There are plans for a boat from Dar es Salaam which will avoid use of the poor road. There is sometimes a weekend shuttle from Dar es Salaam on the *Twiga* – check at the Msasani slipway. Buses leave from the bus stand opposite the covered market on Caravan St. To Dar es Salaam costs US$1 and takes 2 to 3 hours.

Tanzania & Zanzibar

The legend of the Shirazi migration

Ali ben Sultan Hasan of Shiraz in Persia (now Iran) had a dream in AD 975 in which a rat with jaws of iron devoured the foundations of his house. He took this as a sign that his community was to be destroyed. The court in Shiraz ridiculed the notion but his immediate family and some other followers resolved to migrate. They set out in seven dhows from the nearby port of Bushehr and sailed through the mouth of the Persian Gulf, into the Indian Ocean. There they were caught in a great storm and separated, making landfalls at seven different points on the East African coast where they established settlements. Among these were Tongoni and Kilwa.

Directory **Banks** Foreign exchange bureaux: there are none at present in Bagamoyo. *Badeco Beach Hotel* will change money in emergency. National Bank of Commerce is located off road to Dar es Salaam to south of town (follow the sign). **Communications** Post Office: Customs Rd. **Hospitals & medical services** Hospital: *Bagamoyo District*, T8 (Bagamoyo), located on India St. **Places of worship** Churches: Holy Ghost Roman Catholic Mission north of town. Small church on Pomji St in town. **Mosques:** India St north end of town. Small mosque on George St, off Mangesani St. **Useful addresses** Police: at intersection of Caravan St and Boma St at south end of town.

Tanga

History
5°5'S 39°2'E
Phone code: 053
Colour map 3, grid B5

The African groups in the Tanga area, excluding those in the coastal belt, number six. The Pare who now inhabit the Pare Hills came originally from the Taveta area of Kenya in the 18th century. The Zigua inhabited the area to the south of Tanga and have a reputation for aggression and Bwana Heri attacked and defeated the force of the sultan of Zanzibar in 1882. The Nguu clan to the west occupy the Nguu hills and the Ruvu clan inhabit the Pangani islands. The Shambaa are around the Lushoto area and are closely allied with the Bondei who occupy the area between Tanga and Pangani. Both these groups have tended to be pushed inland by Swahili and Digo settlement at the coast. The Digo originated in Kenya but were forced south by expansion of their neighbours to inhabit the coastal strip between Tanga and the Kenyan border, forcing out the Bondei in their turn. The Segeju inhabit part of the coast between Tanga and Kenya. They originated in Kenya from a war party that was cut off by flooding of the Umba River which meets the sea at the border. They thus decided to settle in Digo country. In a rather touching display of male solidarity they decided to avoid any falling out over who should possess the only female in the party by killing her. As a result they have been forced to intermarry with the Digo and the Shirazi.

The coastal people are termed Swahili and are descendants of Africans and Arabs following Islam. Among the Arab immigrants are the Shirazi who are said to be originally from around Shirazi in Persia (now Iran) who came to the East African coast via Muscat in the 10th century. The Shirazis had a hierarchy of rule from the Diwan, centred on Pangani, through Jumbes to Akidas. Tributes were extracted from most domestic events such as marriages and deaths. The role of the Akida was to organize the young men and they acted as headmen for caravans to the interior. With the gradual decline of the caravan trade, being an Akida in the area became little more than a sinecure entered into by paying fees to a Jumbe and extracting taxes from the populace.

European period Carl Peters and the German East Africa Company arrived in 1885 and in 1888 leased a 16 kilometres wide strip from the sultan of Zanzibar along the entire coast of what is now Tanzania, between the Ruvuma and the Umba Rivers. The Germans appointed agents (calling them Akidas), though they were often not of the same tribe as the people they administered, to collect taxes and enforce law and order.

With the advent of European settlement and trade, Somalis arrived, trading in cattle but seldom intermarrying. Islanders from the Comoros also settled, but were generally difficult to distinguish in both appearance and speech from the Swahili.

Agriculture in the Usambara area expanded (see page 381), and with the construction of the railway to Moshi Tanga became a flourishing port. Tanga was the site of a substantial reversal for the British during the First World War. Allied troops, including 8,000 Indian soldiers found it difficult to disembark through the mangrove swamps and were repulsed by the well-organized German defence and some hostile swarms of bees that spread panic among the attackers. Over 800 were killed and 500 wounded, and the British abandoned substantial quantities of arms and supplies on their withdrawal.

German settlers dwindled after this and were steadily replaced by Greek plantation owners. Tanga's prosperity declined with the collapse in sisal prices in the late 1950s and the large estates were nationalized in 1967. Some have now been privatized, and sisal has made a modest recovery.

Sights in Old Tanga

The open space in the centre of town is Uhuru Park. It was originally Selous Square, named after the celebrated naturalist and hunter (see box, page 517). At the junction of the square with Eukenforde St are the German buildings of **Tanga School**, (see box, page 360), the first educational establishment for Africans.

On Market St to the east of Uhuru Park is **Planters Hotel**. This once grand wooden building is now rather run-down, but is reputed to have seen wild times as Greek sisal plantation owners came into town for marathon gambling sessions at which whole estates sometimes changed hands. Arches with columns and plinths. First floor wooden verandah. Ground floor bar with huge antique corner cabinet of miniatures.

Proceeding north across Independence Ave leads to the **Tanga Library**. The West Wing was opened in 1956 and the East Wing in 1958 by the then Governor Sir Edward Twining. There is a courtyard behind with Moorish style arches. To the west is the **Old Boma,** a substantial structure in typical style. Further to the west, in a location leading down to the shore is **St Anthony's Cathedral**, a school and various mission buildings.

Following Independence Ave back towards the east is the **Clock Tower** and the **Post Office**. On the corner of Independence Ave and Usambara St is the **Court House**. This is a very fine building with an interesting tiled roof, offices on the mezzanine level, a fluted façade and fretwork over the windows. It is in use today, and dates from the German period. Just opposite is **Tanga ropeworks** where you can see examples of the ropes and twine made from sisal, known as 'white gold' in the 1950s. Crossing over the railway line along Hospital Rd to Ocean Drive to the south is Karimjee School and off to the left is the old Tanga Club of the British period.

Further east is the **Old Hospital,** another handsome German building, with newer hospital buildings beside.

The **Railway Station** is on Ring St. There are two railway offices nearby, and this group dates from the German era.

Amboni Caves
Colour map 3, grid B5

These are natural limestone caves formed during the Jurassic Age some 150 million years ago, when reptiles were dominant on land. There are 10 caves, extending over a wide area, lying mostly underground, accessed through openings in the gorges of the Mkilumizi River and the Sisi River. They form the most extensive cave system in East Africa, and there are chambers up to 13 metres high with stalactites and stalagmites. They are also very dark, and potentially lethal. The location is of religious significance to local people, and offerings are made to ensure fertility in one of the shrines. A guide wil escort you round the caves, illuminating the chamber with a burning torch. The caves were used by the Mau Mau during the troubles. It is essential to take your own powerful torch and go in pairs using a guide. There have been fatalities when people have explored the caves on their own. The caves are home to many bats.

Tanzania & Zanzibar

The caves are 8 kilometres to the north of Tanga on the road to Lunga Lunga at the Kenyan border. They are badly signposted. A taxi to the caves from town will cost about US$5 (ask the driver to wait). Alternatively you can take a bus or a dala dala for US$0.50. These are not frequent however. Alternatively a visit to the caves is within easy reach by bicycle if you have the time. It is a very nice way of meeting local people and exploring the area, the birds are numerous and occasionally you may spot wildlife like the dikdik.

Galamos Sulphur Springs
Colour map 3, grid B5

These were discovered by a local Greek sisal planter, Christos Galamos. They are hot and sulphurous, and are said to relieve arthritis and cure skin ailments. A small spa was erected, but it has now fallen into disrepair. It is still possible to bathe in the springs, however. The springs are located close to Amboni Caves, see above, off the Tanga to Mombasa Rd.

Tongoni Ruins
Colour map 3, grid B5

These ruins date from the Shirazi period and the Tongoni settlement was started at the end of the 10th century. The community would have been similar to that at Koale (see page 353), but almost certainly larger and predating it. It was to the west of the site of the ruins and only the traces of two wells remain. There are 40 tombs, some with pillars, and the remains of a substantial mosque. The mosque is of the type found along the north part of the East African coast. There is a central *musalla* (prayer room) with arches leading to aisles (*ribati*) at each side. The mosque is constructed of particularly finely dressed, close-grained coral, especially on the lintel of the *kiblah*, the side of the building which faces toward Mecca. The roofs were coral on mangrove rafters, and the deterioration of the rafters is responsible for their collapse.

There are depressions in the pillars where there were porcelain bowls, all apparently removed during the German period. It is said that Tongoni was founded by Ali ben Sultan Hasan at much about the same time as he established the settlement at Kilwa (see page 368). There are Persian inscriptions at Tongoni which would seem to establish a link with Shiraz.

The Tongoni ruins are 20 kilometres south of Tanga on the road to Pangani about 1 kilometre away. Buses or *dala dala* from Tanga cost about US$0.50 and will take up to 1 hour. A taxi will cost about US$12.

Excursions By boat to nearby islands and Pangani can be arranged locally.

Sleeping In town the *New Era* is recommended for value and efficient operation; *Inn by the Sea* for its location; the *Planters Hotel* and *Tanga Hotel* for their colonial atmosphere.

B *Inn by the Sea*, PO Box 2188, T44614, located close to Mkonge on Ocean Drive. A/c, good location. **B** *Mkonge*, PO Box 11544, T44542/6, F43637, located about 1 kilometre from the centre to the east along Hospital Rd which leads into Ocean Drive. It is set in what was designed as Amboni Park on grounds by the sea, it is based on the Sir William Lead Memorial Hall which became the club for the sisal growers, it is sometimes known as the *Sisal (Mkonge) Hotel*, and there is a mosaic of a sisal plant on the floor of the foyer, a/c, bar, restaurant, disco at weekends, swimming pool, one of the *Bushtrekker* hotels. **B** *Raskzone Hotel*, east of centre off Hospital Rd, PO Box 5101, T43897, F43897. A/c, restaurant, garden bar.

C *ASA Hotel*, clean, safe, close to the bus stand. **C** *Marina*, PO Box 835, T44362, on junction of Boma Rd and Eukenforde St. Fairly new, bar, restaurant, a/c. **C** *Panori Motel*, east of the centre, south of Hospital Rd, PO Box 672, T46044, F43295. A/c, restaurant with Indian and International food, well run and comfortable.

D *Centaur* on Railway Rd south of Uhuru Park. Recently constructed, bar, restaurant. **D** *Coastal Pride* on corner of Independence Ave and Boma Rd. Fairly simple, fans. **D** *Fourways*, located at intersection of Market St and Guinea St. Recently constructed bar, restaurant. **D** *MK Inn*, extremely good value, very clean, safe, breakfast included, best place in town for the budget traveller. Situated close to the bus stand. **D** *New Era*, east of town centre to the south of Hospital Rd, PO Box 1430, T43466, F47523. Really excellent value, good food, safe car parking, 1 a/c room. **D** *Planters*, T2041, on Market St just east of Uhuru Park. Historic hotel from colonial era, dilapidated, extensive verandah overlooking street, bar, cold water only. **D** *Tanga*, PO Box 602, T45857, on Eukenforde Rd at west end. Colonial-style, rather dilapidated, bar, reasonable restaurant, fans.

Camping   Available (US$2) at *New Era* (see above).

2 *Annabelle*, south of Usambara St. Excellent grills, fresh juices. Highly recommended. **Eating**
2 *Avenue*, bar, restaurant, serves good food (close to dhow harbour). **2** *Chinese Restaurant* on corner of Customs Rd and Independence Ave. As well as Chinese it serves International food, it is possible to eat outside in the garden. **2** *Patwas Restaurant* off Market St just south of market. Well-run, with a good Asian menu. **1** local restaurant located in front of the *Planters Hotel* is recommended, as very popular and cheap. **1** *Coffee Marketing Board* on corner of Usambara Rd and Eukeberg Rd. Snacks and coffee (alas, instant). **1** *Food Palace* (Solisme Av). Clean, good snacks but closes at 1500. **1** *Market Restaurant*, Market St, behind market. Simple and cheap.

The verandah at the *Planters Hotel* is recommended for atmosphere. The *Yacht Club* along   **Bars**
Ocean Drive is a focus for the expatriate population.

Cinema   Tanga has four cinemas, one in Ngamiani, the Swahili district about 1 kilometre on   **Entertainment**
the left along the Pangani Rd; one off Pangani Rd behind the station; one off Market St, near Swahili St; and one off Usambara St and Market St. Do not have high expectations that they will be operating. **Disco**   There are discos at the weekend at the *Mkonge Hotel*.
Video   *Marina Hotel* on Boma Rd shows videos in the bar.

Tanga

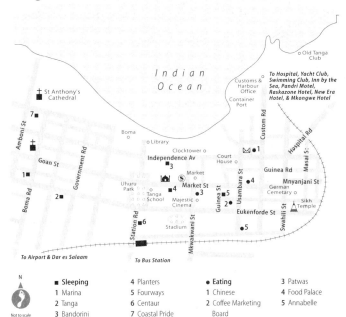

■ **Sleeping**	4 Planters	● **Eating**	3 Patwas
1 Marina	5 Fourways	1 Chinese	4 Food Palace
2 Tanga	6 Centaur	2 Coffee Marketing	5 Annabelle
3 Bandorini	7 Coastal Pride	Board	

Tanzania & Zanzibar

Tanzania's first school

Tanga school was established in 1892. It was initially run by the German Colonial Society, and the government took over responsibility in 1895. Paul Blank was the first headmaster, retiring in 1910. The German language, reading, and writing were taught in one large room and three different groups were taught, 0700-0800 adult 'coloured', 0800-1000 children, 1600-1730 houseboys.

In 1897 there were 86 enrolments, and the pupils began boarding, sleeping in bunk beds and cooking their own food. In 1899 the present buildings were started, with the pupils doing most of the construction, bringing coral from the beach for the walls. The school was now reorganized into a primary section with four years of schooling, a section training teachers, and a craft section. The best pupils were selected to go on to teacher training, and on graduating an assistant teacher started at one rupee a month (about US$3 in present-day values), rising yearly by a rupee to five rupees. On promotion to senior teacher the salary was 12 rupees with an extra five rupees if the teacher was in the band.

The craft element of the school expanded, covering carpentry, printing, book-binding, tailoring, blacksmithing, bricklaying, and masonry. In 1905 a secondary school was built, and the trade school became separate in 1907. By 1911, the staff comprised four Europeans, three craft instructors and 41 African teachers, and had begun to admit Indians.

Discipline, as typical of the period, was strict. Corporal punishment was common. On one occasion, when pupils complained of being forced to attend school against their will, they were punished for their insolence with a week in chains.

The school closed with the outbreak of war in 1914. The British, with a fine sense of priorities, took over the band when they captured Tanga in 1915, but did not reopen the school until 1920.

Shopping *Tanga Ivory Carvers*, near Post Office on Independence Ave, PO Box 1135, T43278. Good quality craft work, no ivory on sale these days.

Sports (participant) **Golf** The *Golf Club* is along the main road running beside the railway as it heads west. **Sailing** At the *Yacht Club* on Ocean Drive. **Swimming** At *Bathing Club* on Ocean Drive before the *Yacht Club*, and at *Mkonge Hotel* for US$2. **Tennis and Squash** At the *Aga Khan Club* which is behind the *Aga Khan School* off Swahili St, south of the railway line. Also at the *Tanga Club* off Ocean Drive. **Windsurfing** At *Baobab Beach Hotel*, 8 kilometres south of Tanga.

Sports (spectator) **Cricket** At the *Aga Khan Club* which is behind the *Aga Khan School* off Swahili St, south of the railway line. **Soccer** The soccer stadium is on the intersection of Eukenforde St and Mkwakwani St. You will need to consult the *Daily News*, or a local enthusiast, for fixtures.

Transport **Local** **Taxis**, **buses** and **dala dala**: can be obtained in Uhuru Park. However, all of Tanga is walkable, although taxis are advisable after dark. **Bicycles**: can be hired at several places in town – **Ali Musso**, PO Box 2344, can be found between 7th and 8th St.

Train All train services from Dar es Salaam to Tanga have unfortunately been terminated.

Road Bus and *dala dala* leave from the bus stand for **Dar es Salaam** from 0800, the trip takes 4 to 6 hours and a regular bus costs US$3 and a luxury one US$4. For **Moshi** the bus takes 4 to 6 hours and costs US$4. To **Lunga Lunga** at the border with Kenya costs US$1, is slow as the road is poor and can take between 1 and 3 hours. The roads are unmade dirt roads until the Amboni Sisal Estates, where tarmac begins, although there are some pot-holes developing. To **Pangani** buses take 3 hours and cost US$1.

Sea **Boat**: Tanzanian Coastal Shipping Line, a cargo service, runs boats up and down the coast which take passengers. However, they are irregular, slow, and you need to ask at the port. The **Zanzibar Sea Ferry Ltd**, which operates the *Sepidah Boat* from Dar/Zanzibar/Pemba, goes to Mombasa via Tanga on Saturday, returning the following day. Other shipping companies (*Virgin Butterfly; Canadian Spirit; Sea Horse*) have operated services calling at Tanga at various times. Again, you will need to ask at the port. **Dhows** operate from Tanga. You will need to ask if any are sailing at the port. Routes to and from Tanga are not sailed that frequently.

Banks *National Bank of Commerce* is on Market St near *Planters Hotel*, does not change American Express TCs without showing them the purchase agreement. **Communications** Post Office: on Independence Ave near Msambara St. **Hospitals & medical services** Hospital: on Ocean Drive to east of town centre. **Libraries** Tanga library off Independence Ave near the Old Boma. **Places of worship** Churches: *St Anthony's Cathedral*, west of the Old Boma. There is a Roman Catholic Church in Ngamiani. **Mosques:** the main mosque is off Independence Ave near Uhuru Park, and there are three other mosques in Ngamiani. **Temple:** to be found off Ring St, near Guinea St. **Tour companies & travel agents** *Karimjee Travel Services*, near Post Office on Independence Ave, PO Box 1563, T41099/46195/46534, Tx45132. **Useful addresses** Police: off Independence Ave near Tanga library.

Directory

Pangani

The town, on the north side of the river of the same name, has good beaches and is a fine location for a quiet beach vacation. There are some handsome old Arab houses, but these are in poor repair.

During the 19th century Pangani, situated at the mouth of the river, was a prosporous port. The community was ruled by an Arab Liwali, five Shirazi Jumbes and a network of Akidas. Indian traders financed parties under Akidas to collect ivory and rhinoceros horn in the interior, and there was some trading in slaves. The town prospered as the ivory and trade in slaves flourished. It was at Pangani that Bushiri, leader of the Arab revolt of 1888/89, was finally captured and executed (see page 347).

The mouth of the Pangani River is crossed by a sand bar. This provided shelter for dhows, and prevented them being pursued by steam vessels when the slave trade was being suppressed after 1873. However it also meant that deeper draft vessels could not use the port, and traffic drifted steadily to the newer facilities at Tanga, subsequently accelerated by the rail line linking Tanga to Dar es Salaam and Moshi.

History

5° 25' S, 38° 58' E

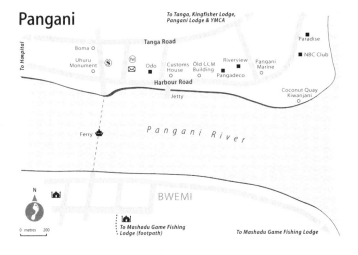

Pangani

In 1930 the population was around 1,500, but the substantial houses on the north side of the river built, largely by slave labour, have fallen into disrepair. The economy of the town shifted to reliance on the sisal plantations, the Pangani being served by shallow draft steamers, but sisal declined drastically in price with the advent of synthetic fibres from the mid 1950s on. There are still many coco-palms and some fishing.

Sights The old **Customs House** and the old **CCM Building** are both fine structures, unfortunately in poor repair. The **Boma** is a handsome building. Just by the ferry is a plaque recording the capture of Pangani by the British on 23 July 1916, and the **Uhuru Monument**, celebrating Independence. It is possible to hire a boat, through *Pangadeco Hotel*, to travel up the river, costing around US$4 per hour, and it will take up to 10 people. There are crocodiles on the river and many birds.

Three marine islands can be visited and there is fishing and snorkelling, although the quality of the latter can be disappointing in the rainy seasons when the water is not clear. The islands are Marve Mdogo, Mwamba Marve and Mazivi. Again, boats can be arranged through *Pangadeco Hotel.*

Sleeping **A+** *Mashado Pangani River Lodge*, Central Reservations c/o PO Box 14823, Arusha, Tanzania, T+255-576585, F8020, Mashado@habari.co.tz, Mobitel T811-510107/1/2, F811-510104/3 or see page 50 for UK agent. The lodge has 40 rooms and suites, described as the best that is available in Tanzania, a/c pool activities include offshore deep water game fishing and inshore fishing, horse riding, guided walking safaris, game viewing, river trips, tennis, swimming, snorkelling and diving, located high on the bluff on the south side of the river, pitched at big-game fishing in the Pemba Channel (one of the world's great game-fishing waters). **A** *Tinga Tinga* is a newly opened resort, operated by an Australian man and his Kenyan-born wife, beautiful rooms including a spacious, well appointed bath, good if relatively expensive food in restaurant, lovely location right on the beach, offers horseback riding as well as watersports.

B *Pangani Lodge*, PO Box 118, T0811-440044, F440045, on the cliff 5 kilometres north of Pangani. Good value, excellent site, steps down to cove, offers diving, restaurant, bar.

E *NBC Club*, PO Box 90, T55, near east end of Harbour Rd. Only 5 rooms and often full. **E** *Pangadeco Beach*, PO Box 76, T72, located at the east end of Harbour Rd. Very simple, you need to give notice of meals required well in advance, bar. **E** *Paradise Guest House*, Harbour Rd. **E** *Riverside Inn*, PO Box 4, on the river between the bus stand and the ferry. Simple and cheap. **E** *Udo Guest House*, close to ferry. **E** *YMCA*, PO Box 84, on Tanga Rd, about 8 kilometres from Pangani. Spartan but good value.

Transport **Road** Is the only feasible transport, and then the only regular bus services are from Tanga. However there are several buses each day. They take around 3 hours, depending on the season and cost US$1. There is a ferry to the south bank of the river, but no buses from the other side.

South Coast to Mtwara and West to Songea

The south coast receives few visitors due to its inaccessibility. However if you have the patience, or can go by plane, you will be well rewarded. Off the coast is the island of Mafia, which is a proposed marine park. It is an idyllic setting and a paradise for scuba divers and snorkellers.

A thoroughly recommended excursion is to hire a sailing dhow at Kisiju (see below) for about US$15 a day and sail to Mafia, stopping off at little islands en route. Further south is the town of Kilwa, with the small island of Kilwa Kisiwani just off the mainland. This is the location of the Kilwa ruins and although very remote the ruins make the trip worth the trouble. Further south still are the towns of Lindi and Mtwara. These are best known for being in the area where Makonde carvings are made. However they receive very few visitors due to their isolation.

Kisiju

This is a coastal village, rather spread out, on a small river, about 80 kilometres south of Dar es Salaam. Its main interest is that dhows leave here on a regular basis for Mafia Island and for small islands on the way. The dhows take household goods and manufactures to the islands, and they return with cargoes of fish, cashews, rice, coconuts, charcoal and cassava. There are several small eating places in the village. If you need to stay the night, ask for Mr Shanzi, and he will arrange for you to stay in a local house for about US$1.

Colour map 5, grid B5

South coast

If you wish to sail around the very pretty islands close to Kisiju, as well as Mafia and the small islands nearby, it is possible to hire a sailing dhow at Kisiju for around US$15 a day and make an excursion. You need to take your own food, water, charcoal, sleeping bags, tent and sea-sickness pills. Plenty of fish can be bought cheaply on the islands, and on the smaller ones, there will be no other tourists.

Sleeping A+ *Amani Beach Club*, 10 a/c beach facing rooms, tradition-styled buildings, beach bar restaurant, marine sports, 1½ hour drive from Dar es Salaam or light aircraft, swimming pool, tennis court, opportunity to spot rare birds in the 40 acres of woodland. Agents *Val Investments Ltd*, PO Box 1547, Dar es Salaam, T600020/601721, F602131.

Transport **Road** Mini-buses and pick-ups with cargo for the dhows leave from the Esso petrol station on the Kilwa Rd in Mtoni (see map of Greater Dar es Salaam, p 259). The journey to

Tanzania & Zanzibar

Kisiju takes 4 hours and costs US$ 2. **Sea**   About 10-15 dhows sail each day for **Kwali**, **Koma** and **Mafia**. There is a sand-bar at the mouth of the river and dhows can only leave at high tide. You need to take your own food and drink, and be prepared to sleep on the cargo. Sea-sickness pills are recommended for inexperienced sailors. **Kwali** is only about 1 kilometre from Kisiju, and, depending on the tides and the winds, will be reached in under an hour of sailing for about US$1 **Koma** is about 10 kilometres from Kisiju, will take about 2 hours of sailing and cost about US$2. A motorized dhow will reach **Mafia** in 12 hours, a sailing dhow in 24 hours, and will cost US$3 to US$6.

Kwali Island   Very close to Kisiju (about 1 kilometre). Small fishing village of about 300 families. Perhaps three dhows a day go there from Kisiju. It is possible to walk round the island in about an hour. There are one or two small eating kiosks, proving simple fare. It is possible to stay in a local house for about US$1. There are onward dhows to **Koma** and **Mafia**.

Koma Island   About 10 kilometres from Kisiju and Kwali, and a very pretty island. Not many inhabitants, and it is mainly used by dhows as a base on their way south to fish. You will need to be self sufficient if you decide to stay. Onward dhows to **Mafia**.

Mafia Island

7°45'S 39°50'E
Colour map 3, grid B5

There are a number of attractions to Mafia Island which include historical remains, deep sea fishing, and diving. The population of Mafia are mainly fishermen; the other industries are coconut palms and cashewnut trees. The plantations are left over from those established by the Omanis. The coconut industry is particularly important and the largest coconut factory in East Africa is found on Mafia at Ngombeni Plantation. It produces copra (dried kernels), oil, coir yarn and cattle cake. However the poor soil has meant that the island has never been able to support a very large population.

History   The name Mafia is derived from an Arab word *morfieyeh* which means a group, and refers to the archipelago. There is evidence of foreign settlers on Mafia from as early as the 9th century. From the 12th to the 14th century it was an important settlement and the remains of a 13th century mosque have been found at Ras Kismani. By the 16th century when the Portuguese arrived it had lost much of its importance and was part of the territory ruled by the king of Kilwa. There is little left of the site of the settlement of the 12th to 14th century although old coins and pieces of pottery are still found occasionally, particularly to the south of Kilindoni where the sea is eating away at the ruins. On the nearby island of Juani can be found extensive ruins of the town of Kua. The town dates back to the 18th century and the five mosques go back even further to the 14th century. In 1829 the town was sacked by Sakalava cannibals from Madagascar who invaded, destroyed the town and dined on the inhabitants.

Evidence of Chinese visitors to the Mafia Island group comes in the form of Chinese coins dating back to the 8th and 9th centuries which suggest that the Far East was then trading with these islands.

It is thought that the Shirazi people from Persia may have settled on the islands of Juani and Jibondo for strategic reasons. In AD 975 Ali ben Sultan Hasan (see box, page 356), founded the sultanate of Kilwa and it is said that one of his sons, Bashat, settled in Mafia. The Shirazi, under Bashat, found the native Mwera people were settled on the islands – they also inhabited a large stretch of mainland and other islands of the coast. It is thought that the Mwera intermarried with the Shirazi. It was around this time that Islam reached Kilwa and no doubt then spread to these islands. There are believed to be some remains dating from the Shirazi period, including that of a mosque, on Jibondo Island. The Shirazi's influence was at its greatest from the 11th to the 13th centuries and from their headquarters at Kilwa they dominated the coast.

The Legend of Ras Kismani

The town of Ras Kismani was originally settled by the Sakalava from Madagascar. The townspeople built a large ship, and when it was completed they invited the local people of Kua to a feast. During the celebrations, the Sakalava seized several children and laid them on the sand in the path of the ship as it was launched.

The Kua people planned revenge at their leisure. Seven or eight years later they invited the Sakalava of Ras Kismani to attend a wedding at Kua. The celebrations were in a special room beneath a house. Gradually the hosts left, one by one, until only an old man was left to entertain the guests. As he did so, the door was quietly bricked up, and the bodies remain to this day. A message was sent to the head man at Ras Kismani that the account was now squared. Within a month, Ras Kismani was engulfed by the sea.

Their main income was from gold from inland, and they also commanded huge customs duties on all goods that passed through Kilwa.

The town of Kisimani Mafia is thought to have been founded during the period of Shirazi and Arab domination. There were some suggestions that Kua also dated from this period but it is now believed that most of these remains are more recent, with just a few dating back further. Kisimani Mafia lies on the west tip of Mafia overlooking the delta. Kua is located on Juani, a much smaller and less hospitable island – very hot with a poor water supply. It is thought possible that some Shirazis from Kisimani Mafia were driven out of the town by Arabs and founded Kua where they would be left alone. The ruins of Kisimani are being eaten away by the sea; the larger part of the town has already been engulfed. However one observer has suggested that the size of the town has been exaggerated and the story that much of the town lies under the sea derives from the rather curious coral reef and ridge in this sea which could have been mistaken for the remains of a town.

this time the island was under the control of Kilwa. In April 1498 Vasco da Gama sighted the island of Mafia as he sailed on his first journey towards Mombasa. Portugal's influence spread quickly and during the 16th century a number of visits were made to Mafia and revenues were collected. However it was a period when expeditions were fitful – they would be launched to collect revenue and were then followed by years of neglect. In 1635 a Portuguese commandant, subordinate to the Governor of Mozambique, was stationed here and a small fort was erected on the east side of the island with a garrison of about 10 to 15 men. This fort is thought to have been at Kirongwe although no trace of it has been found.

The islands of Chole and Juani had to make payments to passing Portuguese ships in the form of coconut fibre and gum copal. The population of the islands was believed to have been concentrated on the island of Jibono and at Kua on Juani as at some stage (the date is not known) the town of Kisimani had been destroyed. The islands seem to have been used as a port of call for repairs to ships as well as a kind of safe haven when there were troubles on the mainland as, eg in 1570 when Kilwa was invaded by the Zimba people and about 1,000 Arabs are thought to have been killed and eaten.

Portuguese was loosening and by 1697 Portugal had lost control of her East African posts, except for Mozambique. This was followed by a difficult period for the inhabitants of the islands with pirates active in the seas around Mafia. The next major event in Mafia's history was an invasion from Madagascar by war canoes. The exact date that this occurred is not known although it is thought to have been during the time of Sultan Said, between 1810 and 1835. According to tradition, the Sakalava came from Madagascar in 80 canoes each with four men. They sacked Kua and all those who did not escape were killed or carried off as slaves. At this time Kua was the chief town on Mafia and the population was believed to have been large. The news of the raid was sent to Zanzibar and an expedition was sent by the sultan to chase the invaders. The sultan's troops found the raiders on a small island nearby and they were taken as prisoners back to Mafia. Kua however was never rebuilt and instead Chole Island, which had until then been home only to a slave population, became the seat of the sultan's government.

The influence of the Omani Arabs grew although it is not known exactly when the Arabs settled on the Mafia islands. It was not until 1840 after the sultan moved their headquarters from Muscat to Zanzibar that his control over the coast reached its zenith. By 1846 he had established garrisons up and down the coast and there is little doubt that his influence on the Mafia group was considerable. Trade grew enormously and Mafia took part in this with gum copal trees being planted in large numbers. The islands were ruled by a series of governors called Liwalis appointed by the sultan of Zanzibar and after the sacking of Kua the government was moved to Chole. Chole Island is less than 1 square kilometre and many of the influential Arabs built houses on the island so that about half the island was covered. It has been noticed that at least one of these Liwalis had a eye for orderly town planning for many of the streets ran parallel to one another. This was unusual for Arab towns on the East African coast and comparisons with the narrow and windy streets of other towns show that this was clearly an exception.

From the beginning of the 19th century traders from all over the world had been plying these coastal waters. 'Americani' cloth proved itself to be perhaps the most popular of all the traded goods amongst the resident population. The trading of goods and of slaves was soon to be followed by the interest of European politics. However it was not until the end of the century that this affected territorial rights. Under the Treaty of 1890, Mafia, Zanzibar and Pemba were initially allotted to the British sphere. However it was later agreed that Mafia should go to Germany in exchange for Germany renouncing her claims on Stephenson Rd which was between Lake Nyasa and Tanganyika. The island was therefore included in the purchase of the coastal strip from Sultan Seyyid Ali and the German flag was raised in 1890.

The Germans established a headquarters at Chole and in 1892 a resident officer was posted here together with a detachment of Sudanese troops. A large two storey boma was constructed with various other buildings such as a gaol. The site seemed ideal with good anchorage for dhows, but with the opening of a regular coastal steamship service a deeper harbour was needed and the headquarters were moved to Kilindoni in 1913.

During the First World War it became clear that Mafia represented an extremely useful base from which attacks could be launched. In particular the British needed a base from which to attack the *SS Königsberg* which was wrecking havoc on her fleet up and down the East African coast. In January 1915 a British expeditionary force under Colonel Ward landed on the island at Kisimani and the islands were captured with little resistance. A garrison of about 200 troops remained on the island.

The *Königsberg* had been damaged and gone into the mouth of the river Rufiji for repairs. This delta, with its many creeks and maze of streams proved the perfect hiding place. It was important to the British to find and destroy it before any further damage could be done. In 1915 a British war plane was assembled on Mafia and took off from there. It spotted the ship, and boats went into the delta to destroy it. It was the first example of aerial reconnaissance being used in warfare. A description by a local man of the intense activity of the British fleet at the time was that the search lights 'turned night into day'. The wrecked remains of the hulk of the crippled boat could be seen until 1979 when it finally sank into the mud out of sight.

For a short period the islands were under military rule, and were later administered under Zanzibar. In 1922 the islands were handed over by the government of Zanzibar to become part of the Tanganyika Territory under the United Nations Mandate.

Sights **Boat-building** 20-25 metre 100 tonne boats under construction on the shore. Timbers prepared by hand, and the frame of the boat made from naturally V-shaped forked branches of trees.

Ruins at Kua Kua is on Juani Island to the south of Mafia Island. The remains are located on the west side of the island of Juani. The ruins cover a large area of about 14 hectares. In 1955, when the site was cleared of bush, one observer stated that he believed that these ruins were 'potentially the Pompeii of East Africa'. The remains however need much work on them for them to be brought up to anything like this standard. There are several houses, one of which was clearly double-storeyed. Beneath the stairs leading to the upper level is a small room in which slaves could be confined for punishment. Under the building is the *haman* (bathroom), with a vaulted ceiling of curved coral blocks. A soil pipe runs from the remains of an upper room to a pit below. Two mosques and a series of tombs, some with pillars are nearby. The evidence suggests that the town did not have a protecting wall and that the inhabitants were mainly involved in agricultural pursuits on the island rather than in sea-trading.

Kua was famous for the supposed curative properties of milk obtained there. There is a cave on the island formed by the action of the sea. The water streaming out of the cave as the tide turns is reputed to cure *baridi yabis* ('cold stiffness' – rheumatism) and other ailments. The cure is not effective, however, unless the hereditary custodian of the cave is paid a fee and the spirits of the cave appeased by an offering of honey, dates or sugar. Local fishermen will take you to Kua for US$1.

Nororo Island Small island with fishing community of about 50 local boats 12 kilometres off north coast of Mafia. Two small *hotelis* selling rice, ugali and fish. Possible to camp on beach in a thatched shelter.

Baracuni Island Very beautiful small island with fine beaches. Used as a base for fishing dhows. About 12 kilometres off northwest coast of Mafia and an hour's sailing from Nororo. You need to have your own food, water and tent if you want to stay.

Deep sea diving Many people will come here to experience some of the best deep **Activities** sea diving in Tanzania. There is something here for everyone from the most experienced diver to those who want to snorkel in the shallower pools. The coral gardens off Mafia are marvellous – wonderfully vivid fish, shells, sponges, sea cucumber and spectacular coral reefs. Two of the most beautiful reefs are the Okuto and Tutia reefs around Juani and Jibondo Islands a short distance from Chole Bay. About one kilometre off Mafia's coastline there is a 200 metre deep contour along the seabed of the Indian Ocean. The depth contributes to the wide variety of sea life. Mafia Lodge will provide equipment, but the quality is variable and you may prefer to bring your own. The best time for diving is between November and March. During April to September the monsoon winds blow so hard, making it impossible to dive outside the lagoon. Visibility also deteriorates a little.

There is a proposal that Mafia should become a marine park. This has been under discussion for some time now and implementation is imminent. The aim would be to create a series of zones around the island providing areas with differing levels of protection, while not ruining local fishermen's livelihoods. The preliminary scientific study for this is currently being carried out by Frontier Tanzania manned almost entirely by volunteers in collaboration with the University of Dar es Salaam. The Worldwide Fund for Nature has also become involved and if the model is successful it will be used in other marine parks around the country.

Fishing This is at its best from September-March when the currents and the northeast monsoon (*kaskazi*) mean that there is an enormous variety of fish. When the south monsoon (*kusi*) blows during the rest of the year fishing can be rather sparse. Some of the 'big game' fish that can be caught in the area include marlin, shark, kingfish, barracuda and red snapper. There is a fishing club where there are records kept of some of the record catches. Mafia Island, and some of the uninhabited islands around, are also a breeding site of the green turtle. Sadly you would be very lucky to see these as they are now close to extinction as a result of man's activities – being killed both as adults for their meat and as eggs. Another threatened species is the dugong which lives in sea grass such as that found between Mafia and the Rufiji delta, giving rise to the legend of the mermaid (see box, page 369). This strange beast is protected by law, but hunting continues.

Sleeping   **A** *Kinasi Lodge* is a new complex 100 metres up the beach from *Mafia Lodge*, its beach is not quite as nice as its rivals but Kinasi Lodge has a beautiful main complex in old coastal traditional style with a bar, patio and dining room, its furnished tastefully, with attractive pottery, accommodates 20 people, no a/c or phone, Kinasi Lodge also arranges diving and has sailboats. **A** *Mafia Island Lodge*, PO Box 2, Mafia, or PO Box 2485, Dar es Salaam, T23491, Tx41061. 40 rooms, a/c, bar, restaurant, watersports, lovely setting overlooking Chole Bay, recently refurbished, food is good but a bit unvaried – mostly seafood, nice bar, the lodge has its own beach, there are windsurfing boards and Hobicats for rent, there is also a small diving centre at Mafia Lodge run by a divemaster, dives are US$40 per person with all equipment, there are oxygen facilities with a DAN oxygen provider for safety. **D** *Lizu*, restaurant, bar, simple and tidy, fans, disco at weekends, can be rather noisy when the disco operates.

Transport   **Air**   **Air Tanzania**, PO Box 543, ATC Bldg Ohio St, Dar es Salaam, T46643/4/5, Tx42137, is scheduled to fly into Mafia once a week taking 45 minutes. However, the flight is often cancelled – check at the Ohio St office. **Aviators Services**, T6386 Arusha or c/o Scantan Tours, PO Box 1054, T8170, fly from Dar es Salaam to Mafia at 1100 on Tuesday, Wednesday, Friday, Sunday, and return the same day at 1200. The fare is US$85 one way. **Dar Aviation**, **Coastal Air** and **Sky Tours** are new operators who offer flights from Dar es Salaam to Mafia. They all cost about US$85 per person one way.

The airport is about 20 kilometres from *Mafia Lodge* and a Lodge vehicle will collect you – they charge US$10 if you are not staying at the Lodge. There are no taxis on the island – indeed there are few vehicles of any sort.

Sea   The crossing from Dar es Salaam to Mafia can be rough, and sea-sickness pills are strongly recommended. **Tanzania Coastal Shipping Line**, PO Box 9461, Dar es Salaam, T26192, Tx41532, operate a service of sorts, but is infrequent and unreliable. **Canadian Spirit** stops at Mafia Island once a week on its way to Mtwara from Dar es Salaam. Scheduled to leave Mafia on Thursday for Mtwara, and on Friday for Dar es Salaam, although these schedules change. Fare to Mafia is about US$10 1st class and US$7 2nd, and takes about 6 hours. **Dhows** can be taken from the dhow harbour in Dar es Salaam. They depart irregularly but there are usually 2-3 a week. From Kisiju (page 363) there are dhows leaving every day. A motorized dhow takes 12 hours, and a sailing dhow up to 24 hours. Passengers sit and sleep on the cargo. You need to take your own food and drink. Costs US$3 to US$6.

Kilwa

9°0'S 39°0'E
Colour map 3, grid C5   *Kilwa is a group of three settlements, and it is of exceptional historical interest, magnificently situated on a mangrove fringed bay which is dotted with numerous small islands.*

If Kilwa was in Kenya the place would be full of tourists; it is an extraordinarily rewarding place to visit. As it is, it gets just a handful of visitors each week. Kilwa grew up as a gold trade terminus and when its fortunes faded some magnificent ruins were left behind. These are said to be some of the most spectacular on the East African coast. The town is divided between Kilwa Kisiwani (Kilwa on the Island), two kilometres offshore; Kilwa Kivinje (Kilwa of the Casuarina Trees) on the mainland; and Kilwa Masoko (Kilwa of the Market) which was built as an administrative centre on a peninsula, and which is the site of the main present-day town.

There is a superb beach within a stone's throw from Kilwa Masako centre, and another even better one a few miles north of the town (ask for Masako pwani).

The Mermaids of the Rufiji Delta

Around the island of Mafia and the Rufiji Delta lives an animal called the dugong (known in Swahili as the nguva) and it is this sea living creature that is believed to have given rise to the story of mermaids. The animal is now threatened with extinction but not many years ago they were reasonably common in these waters. One observer reported seeing seven being landed in the time that he was stationed at Mafia – a period of under two years.

Looking at a specimen of these animals it may be wondered how the story of a beautiful half-woman, half-fish came into being. The animals have a large tail measuring up to one metre across and in total they measure up to three metres long. They are rather walrus or seal-like although their heads are larger – not at all like that of a

beautiful woman. However these animals do display a certain human posture when feeding their young. The female supports the young with her flippers, and treading water she raises her head and teats above the water. Also the tail is very mermaid-like particularly when they dive down into the water and it can be seen most clearly.

The dugongs live in the sea grass that is found in deltas such as the Rufiji and its habitat is restricted to places where it can browse without fear from sharks and other predators. It is entirely herbivorous and defenceless, and not being an agile swimmer, is extremely vulnerable. Sadly this vulnerability has been the dugong's downfall for its population has suffered at the hands of hunters and its survival is now threatened. The nearest relative to the dugong is the freshwater

Tanzania & Zanzibar

Kilwa Kisiwani contains the ruins of a 13th century city of the Shirazi civilization which are well preserved and documented. The town was founded at the end of the 10th century by Shirazis (see box, page 356), and flourished with the core of commercial activity based on the trade of gold from Sofala (in present-day Mozambique). It grew to be the largest town on the south coast and prospered to the extent that Kilwa could maintain an independent status with its own sultan and coinage.   **History**

The large stone town that grew up thrived and the architecture was striking. The largest pre-European building in Equatorial Africa was located here – the Husuni Kubwa. However Kilwa's fortunes were reversed in the 14th century. Vasco da Gama was said to have been impressed by the buildings of Kilwa and in 1505 a large Portuguese fleet arrived and took the town by force. Their aim was to take control of the Sofala gold trade and they did this by erecting a garrison and establishing a trading post in the town from where they set up a gold trade link with the interior. Without the gold trade the Shirazi merchants were left with little to keep the wealth growing and the town quickly went into decline. Having taken over the gold trade, and thus triggered off the decline of the town, the Portuguese decided there was little point in staying in Kilwa, an outpost which was expensive to maintain. They therefore withdrew from Kilwa and continued the gold trade from further afield.

Deprived of the main source of income, the town continued to decline. In 1589 disaster struck when a tribe from nearby called the Zimba attacked the

Kilwa area

town, killing and eating many of the inhabitants. In the 17th century, with the arrival of the Oman Arabs, Kilwa began to revive and many of the buildings were taken over by the sultans as palaces. The slave trade (see page 529), made a significant impact on this area and Kilwa Kivinje on the mainland flourished from the caravan route from the interior which terminated at the port.

Sights **Kilwa Kisiwani** This demands at least half a day. Small dhows in the harbour at Kilwa Masoko will take you across the two kilometres channel for US$5. The Cultural Centre will organize a half day boat trip for US$10, and the boat will take up to 6 people. It is necessary to get a permit to visit the site from the Cultural Officer at the District Headquarters, which is on the road leading to the harbour. There is a guide on the island who will take you through the ruins giving some background information on the buildings. For those interested in finding out more about the ruins *One thousand years of East Africa* by John Sutton is highly recommended (and is available in Dar es Salaam from the museum bookshop).

Gereza Fort The original Gereza was built in the 14th century but the one that is standing there today was built by the Omani Arabs in the 19th century on the site of the original on the orders of the Imam of Muscat. It is a large square building built of coral set in lime. The walls are very thick with circular towers at the northeast and southwest corners. It has an impressive entrance of fine wood carving and some, although not all, of the inscription is legible.

Great Mosque (Friday Mosque) This mosque is said to have been built in the 12th century and is probably the largest of this period on the east coast. It was excavated between 1958 and 1960 and parts of it have been reconstructed. The oldest parts that remain are outer sections of the side walls and the north wall. The façade of the *mihrab* (the aspect that points towards Mecca) is dated from around 1300. The domed chamber was supposed to have been the sultan's prayer room. The water tanks and the slabs of stone were for rubbing clean the soles of the feet before entering the mosque.

Great House A large one-storey building is said to have been the residence of the Sultan and the remains of one of the sultans are said to reside in one of the four graves found within its walls. The building is an illustration of the highly developed state of building and architectural skills in this period with examples of courtyards,

Kilwa Kisiwani

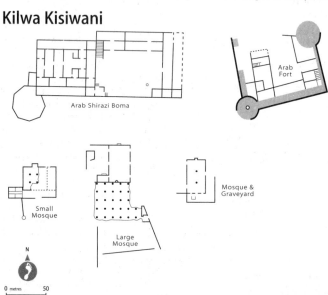

Arab Shirazi Boma

Arab Fort

Small Mosque

Large Mosque

Mosque & Graveyard

N

0 metres 50

reception rooms, an amphitheatre which is unique to this part of the world, latrines, kitchens and cylindrical clay ovens.

Small Domed Mosque This is without a doubt the best preserved of all the buildings in Kilwa. It is an ornamental building with beautiful domes located about 150 metres southwest of the Great House. The long narrow room on its east side is thought to once have been a Koran school.

House of Portico Little remains of this once large building. There are portico steps on three of its sides from where it gets its name and its doorway has a decorated stone frame.

Makutini Palace (Palace of Great Walls) This large fortified building is believed to date from the 15th century. It is to the west of the Small Domed Mosque and is shaped in roughly a triangle. Its longest wall that ran along the coast is in ruins. Within the complex is the grave of one of the sultans.

Jangwani Mosque The ruins of this stone building are concealed under a series of mounds to the southeast of the Makutini Palace. This mosque was unique for having ablution water jars set into the walls just inside the main entrance.

Malindi Mosque This Mosque to the east of the Gereza Fort was said to have been built and used by migrants from Malindi on the Kenya coast.

Husuni Kubwa This building is thought to be the largest pre-European building in Equatorial Africa. It is located between 1-2 kilometres to the east of the main collection of ruins on top of a steep cliff. It is certainly an exceptional construction with over 100 rooms and a large conical dome that reaches about 30 metres above the ground. The mosque has 18 domes on octagonal piers, separated by high barrel vaults. The piers are decorated with bowls of white porcelain set in the plaster.

Husuni Ndogo This is a smaller version of Husuni Kubwa and they are separated by a small gully. It is said to have been built in the 15th century with walls one metre thick and towers in the corners.

Excursion to Kilwa Kivinje

This is 29 kilometres north of Kilwa Masoko and can be reached by *dala dala,* heading for Manguruturu, costing about US$1. There are half-a-dozen or so each day.

Kilwa Kivinje is an attractive historical trading centre whose heyday was in the days of the slave trade in the 18th and 19th centuries, but which remained the district headquarters up till 1949. It retains many interesting old buildings dating back to the 19th century as well as the colonial period and is somewhat reminiscent of Bagamoyo.

Kilwa Kivinje

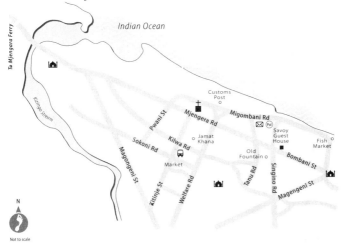

Tanzania & Zanzibar

There is a handsome old boma on the shore which dates from the German period as does the covered market. Several fine houses stand along the main street, but are rather dilapidated. There is an old mosque in the centre, and to the east of the town is a cemetery with tombs and pillars.

Sleeping **E** *Savoy Guest House*, located near the Old Boma in Kilwa Kivinje, fans, simple and adequate.

Songomonanara and islands

There is a group of islands to the south of Kilwa Kiswani. It is necessary to hire a motorized dhow in Kilwa Masoko to get there, and it will cost US$20 for up to six people. If you have the time it is very worthwhile to spend a few days visiting some of the more distant islands, camping out on isolated beaches. This is the ideal way to take in all that the islands offer.

The ruined buildings at Songomonanara are exceptional. The settlement is surrounded by the remains of a wall. The main mosque is distinguished by stonework in a herringbone pattern and there is a double row of unusually high arches at one end.

The Sultan's Palace is extensive, with high walls, and it was evidently at least two storeys high. The doorways, faced with slender stonework, are particularly fine.

The building to the east of the palace has a room with a vaulted roof and porcelain bowls are set in the stonework. There are three other smaller mosques, two of which abut the surrounding wall. Some of the other ruins leave little to be distinguished, although rectangular windows and door frames are a feature of the group. Fragments of porcelain and earthenware abound, and some relics have been identified as Egyptian dating from the 14th and 15th centuries.

About three kilometres south of Songo Mnara is **Sanje Majoma Island** also containing the ruins of a number of once beautiful houses, complete with courtyards

Songomanara

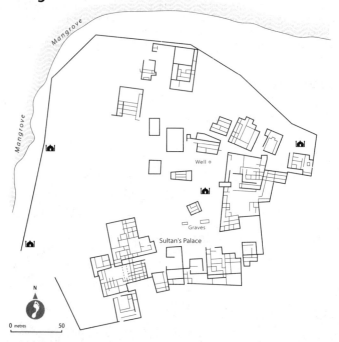

and stone arches. **Sanje ya Kati** is another nearby island which was once settled by the Shanga people who are now extinct. In the 13th century they were considered a force to be reckoned with and they resisted foreign control.

E *Hilton Guest House*, self-contained rooms, basic but tends to be noisy. **E** *Kilwa Guest House*, simple but basic. **E** *New Majaka Guest House*, located on right of road which leads from main Mangurukivu Rd to the market. Fans, only single rooms, clean and tidy. **E** *Pande Guest House*, similar to the others. **E** *Salama Guest House*, on road from Milwa Kirinje and Mangurukuru. Fans, double rooms available, restaurant, bar. **Sleeping**

1 *Masoko by Night*. Charcoal grilled chicken (*kuku*) and beef (*mishkaki*), breakfast options are especially poor. The restaurant next door to the *Hilton* serves excellent fish sambusas. For lunch or dinner the best bet is the small hotel opposite the bus stand. It is a modest place but the food is better there than at the other restaurants. **Eating**

Air Air Tanzania, PO Box 543, Ohio St, Dar es Salaam, T46643/44111, Tx42137, has had a flight once a week to Kilwa Masoko, but it appears to have been discontinued. The fare is around US$100 one-way, US$40 for residents. A charter is a possibility, particularly if you are a party see Air Charter operators in Dar es Salaam section, page 342. **Transport**

Road Bus: direct to Kilwa from **Dar es Salaam** leave from Kariakoo, Msimbazi St at 0500, take 13 hours and cost US$6 Confirm exact departure time and book a ticket the day before you travel. Return from Kilwa at 0500 daily. Alternatively take one of the numerous buses heading for destinations south of Kilwa, such as Mtwara, Lindi or Nachingwea. These leave Dar between 0700 and 0900 from the Kisutu bus stand on Morogo Rd in Dar. It is advisable to book at least a day in advance. Seats closer to the front are recommended as the going is rough. This bus will drop you off at Nangurukuru, a village 35-45 kilometres from Kilwa Masoko, from where you have to transfer to a minibus or pickup to complete the journey US$1. The cost from Dar to Nangurukura is around US$10. The journey takes between 7 to 9 hours. There is a simple guesthouse in Nangurukuru if you arrive late. In order to travel south to Lindi, Mtwara or Masasi you have to catch buses coming from Dar es Salaam at Nangurukuru. They start arriving from about 1400 onwards. The journey takes 5 hours minimum as the road is poor. You'll be lucky to get a seat. There are numerous minibuses/pickups between Kilwa Kivinje and Kilwa Masoko daily.

Kilwa Masoko

Sea This stretch of ocean can be rough – travel sickness tablets are recommended. **Tanzania Coastal Shipping Line**, PO Box 9461, T25192, Tx41532, and **Shipping Corporation of Zanzibar**, PO Box 80, Zanzibar, T30300/30749, Tx57215, run irregular freighters taking passengers. Enquire at port in Dar es Salaam or Zanzibar. **Canadian Spirit** from Dar es Salaam has sailings, at one time regularly once a week to Mtwara (connect to Kilwa by bus), and costs US$15 1st class and US$10 2nd class. Trip takes 24 hours. Confirm departure times and days at port in Dar es Salaam.

It is possible to get a **dhow** from Dar es Salaam, but it is a matter of going to the dhow anchorage every day and asking about departure. You may need to go via

To Fire Station, Aerodrome & Masoko Pwani

Market

Masoko By Night

Bar

Mnyalukolo Bar o School

Jimbiza Beach

Silent Inn Bar

Mokorongoni Beach Bar

District Office

N

Harbour

0 metres 200

■ **Sleeping**
1 Hilton Guest House & Restaurant
2 Hotel
3 Kilwa Guest House
4 Mjaka Guest House
5 Pande Guest House

Mafia. A motorized dhow will take 24 hours and a sailing dhow 48 hours. Costs US$6 to US$12. Sleep on the cargo and take your own food and drink.

Lindi

9°58'S 39°38'E
Phone code: 0525
Colour map 3, grid C5

Lindi translates from Ki Mwera (a local language) as 'a pit latrine'. The town is another little visited place which has a great deal of charm, albeit faded. The centre has many attractive colonial buildings. It is a town of around 40,000 inhabitants. Poor communications, and the collapse of the Ground Nut Scheme (see page 534), one site for which was at nearby Nachingwea have hampered development. Initial settlement was by Shirazi migrants, (see page 356). It was a destination for slave caravans from the interior in the 19th century, being the main seaport for Lake Nyasa (now Lake Malawi). The Germans chose Lindi as the administrative headquarters of the Southern Province, a huge administrative area which encompassed the whole of the south of Tanganyika right across to Lake Nyasa (renamed Lake Malawi). A custom house and store for the German East African Company were constructed close to the fort which dates from the Arab period. These, and other buildings of the colonial period, are now very dilapidated.

The beach is excellent and it is possible to take a ferry across the bay to the village on the far side. You can stay here very cheaply.

The modest mosque next to the bus station possesses a wonderful elaborately carved and colourful door.

Litipo Forest Reserve There are numerous little known forest reserves dotted throughout Tanzania, including many that exist to help preserve some of the remaining patches of the coastal rainforest which millions of years ago covered the whole coastal area. Several of these reserves are in Lindi district, the most accessible of which is west of Litipo. The reserve here consists of a patch of rainforest lying between two small lakes. It is a beautiful spot and although you are unlikely to see many animals there the area is rich in birdlife. In order to see the reserve you will need to spend at least one night at the village of Rutamba. There is a basic rest house in Rutamba called the *Ali Baba* where a room costs US$1.50.

To get into the reserve go along the road leading to Tandangogoro village and take one of the patches leading north which go into the reserve. To get more information about Litipo it may be advisable to ask for the forest reserve officer who is usually stationed at Rutamba.

Getting there: if you are going to Litipo you need to catch one of the buses to Rutamba which leave daily from opposite the Caltex station on Ghana St in Lindi. These go at either 1000 or 1200 and the journey, although only 30 kilometres or so, takes at least three hours. There are daily buses back to Lindi each morning.

Rutamba area

Sleeping

E *City Guest House*, corner of Msonobar St and Amani St, 3 blocks in from the ferry. Fans, has a superb location by the beach but a rather tatty interior, rather basic. **E** *Coast Guest House*, about 500 metres north of ferry on beach. Fans. **E** *Lindi Beach Hotel*, just south of ferry on beach. Fans, has a superb location by the beach but a rather tatty interior, rather run down. **E** *The Shiriton Guest House*, located close to the bus station. Probably the best of the local accommodation, rooms are large, clean and comfortable enough. **E** *South Honour Guest House*, Amani St, 3 blocks back from the ferry. Fans, nets, simple, with agreeable staff. **E** *Town Guest House*, junction of Eilat St and Makonde St, 5 blocks in from the shore. Fans, nets, clean and simple.

Eating & bars

All of the hotels have restaurants, and there are snack bars round the bus station. Fresh fruit can be purchased at the market on Jamhuri St. **2** *The DDC Club* offers excellent nyama choma and chips mayai. **2** *The Maji Maji Restaurant* does good fish and rice. **2** *National Bank of Commerce (NBC) Club*, pleasant location on beach. Charges entrance fee for non-members (US$0.50), fairly simple meals. **2** *The Old NBC Club* located behind the beach, is the best place in town for a drink. **2** *The Sayari Hotel* has very good breakfasts. **1** *K's Cold Drinks*, Eilat Rd, 3 blocks in from the beach. Cheap meals.

Transport

Air Air Tanzania, PO Box 543, Ohio St, Dar es Salaam, T46643/44111, Tx42137, has had a flight once a week which has touched down at Lindi, but it appears to have been discontinued. The fare is around US$100 one-way, US$40 for residents. A charter is a possibility, particularly if you are a party – see Air Charter operators in Dar es Salaam section, page 342. Alternatively fly to Mtwara and connect by road.

Lindi

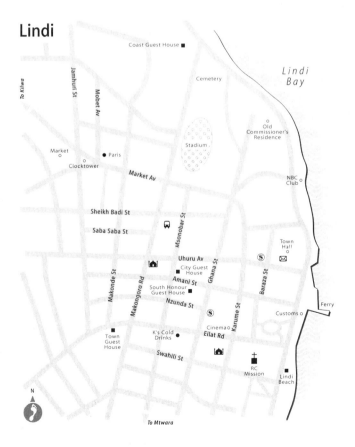

Tanzania & Zanzibar

Road Really the only feasible way unless you have time to wait for boats, or wish to charter a plane. Buses leaves from Kisutu bus stand on Jamhuri St/Morongoro Rd in **Dar es Salaam** at 0600-0900, take 14-20 hours and cost US$13. Bus to Dar es Salaam leaves at 0500 from bus stand on Makongaro Rd. To **Mtwara** buses run fairly frequently and cost US$1.70 and take about 2 hours. There are several daily direct buses. The journey takes about 4 hours and the fare is US$3. To Nachingwea and Newela there are daily buses. The fare to Nachingwea costs US$5, the journey time is 5-6 hours, and to Newala it costs US$4 and the journey time is 6 hours. The road rising up to the Makonde plateau is pretty grim.

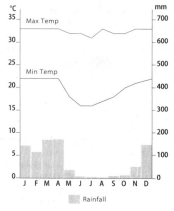

Climate: Lindi

Sea Tanzania Coastal Shipping Line, PO Box 9461, T25192, Tx41532, and **Shipping Corporation of Zanzibar**, PO Box 80, Zanzibar, T30300/30749, Tx57215 run irregular freighters taking passengers. Enquire at port in Dar es Salaam or Zanzibar. **Canadian Spirit** from Dar es Salaam has sailings, at one time regularly once a week to Mtwara (connect to Lindi by bus), and costs US$15 1st class and US$10 2nd class. Trip takes 24 hours. Confirm departure times and days at port in Dar es Salaam. It is possible to get a **dhow** from Dar es Salaam, but it is a matter of going to the dhow anchorage every day and asking about departure. You may need to go via Mafia. A motorized dhow will take 24 hours and a sailing dhow 48 hours. Costs US$6 to US$12. Sleep on the cargo and take your own food and drink.

Mtwara

10°20'S 40°20'E
Phone code: 059
Colour map 3, grid C5

Mtwara is a sizeable town of around 80,000. It was largely by-passed by the Shirazi settlers. German administration was centred on Lindi, and Mtwara came to prominence during the British period. Mtwara has been a centre for agricultural processing, and there is a factory for shelling and canning the cashew nuts that are grown extensively in the southeast. The town itself is set a little way from the shore. Mtwara boasts a magnificent sheltered harbour. There are some good beaches, but they are about two kilometres from the town centre. Even the better priced hotels are good value for a beach vacation.

Sleeping **B** *Mtwara Beach*, located on beach 2 kilometres out of town to the north. Restaurant, bar, recently renovated. **D** *Shangari Club Beach*, location 2 kilometres north of town. Good restaurant, bar. **E** *Kisutu Guest House*, located 1 kilometre south of town centre, near market and bus station. Fans, nets, simple. **E** *Kusunva Guest House*, town centre just off Aga Khan Park. Simple fare. **E** *Maibras Guest House*, about 500 metres north of town on the way to the beach. Rather basic. **E** *National Bank of Commerce (NCB) Club*, on corner of Tanu Rd and Uhuru Rd in town centre. Restaurant, bar, fans, nets, good value, used by travelling government officials and often full, pleasant beer garden. **E** *Ngomeke Guest House*, in centre of town on Bazaa St. Fairly simple. **E** *Super Guest House*, town centre opposite post office. Rather basic. **E** *Tanzania Cashew Marketing Board (TCMB) Club*, close to beach, 2 kilometres north of town. Originally the Cashew Association of Tanganyika (CATA) Club for the growers in the colonial period and still known as the CATA Club, restaurant, bar, fans, nets, good value and a comfortable atmosphere.

Eating & bars **2** *Shangani Club* on the the beach. Recommended. **2** *Mtwara Beach Hotel*, on beach, is reasonable. **1** *Paradise*, in town centre just off Aga Khan Park is cheap and good value.

Air Air Tanzania, PO Box 543, Ohio St, Dar es Salaam, T46643/44111, Tx42137, has had a
flight once a week. The fare is around US$100 one-way, US$40 for residents. A charter is a
possibility, particularly if you are a party – see Air Charter operators in Dar es Salaam section,
page 342.

Transport

Road Bus: from **Dar es Salaam** buses leave from Kisutu bus stand on Morogoro Rd at 0500,
take pretty much 24 hours and cost US$8. Buses leave for Dar es Salaam at 0500 from the bus
stand on Market St. Book ticket day before and confirm departure time. Buses to **Masasi**
leave fairly frequently, cost US$4. Regular buses to **Lindi** which cost US$1.

Sea This stretch of ocean can be rough – travel sickness tablets are recommended. **Tanzania Coastal Shipping Line**, PO Box 9461, T25192, Tx41532, and **Shipping Corporation of
Zanzibar**, PO Box 80, Zanzibar, T30300/30749, Tx57215 run irregular freighters taking passengers. Enquire at port in Dar es Salaam or Zanzibar. **Canadian Spirit** from Dar es Salaam
has sailings, at one time regularly once a week, and costs US$15 1st class and US$10 2nd
class. Trip takes 24 hours. Confirm departure times and days at port in Dar es Salaam. It is possible to get a **dhow** from Dar es Salaam, but it is a matter of going to the dhow anchorage
every day and asking about departure. You may need to go via Mafia. A motorized dhow will
take 24 hours and a sailing dhow 48 hours. Costs US$6 to US$12. Sleep on the cargo and take
your own food and drink.

This is a small village 11 kilometres to the west of Mtwara on the Mtwara to Lindi
road. The beaches are excellent. There are several fine two storey town houses in
Arab style with elaborate fretwork balconies. There is an old slave market and a fort
dating from the German period. Mikindani was the port from which Livingstone
departed on his final journey to the interior in 1867 (see page 425). *Dala dala* from
Mtwara to Lindi will take you for US$0.50. A taxi will cost US$15 for the return trip.

Mikindani
Colour map 3, grid C5

Tanzania & Zanzibar

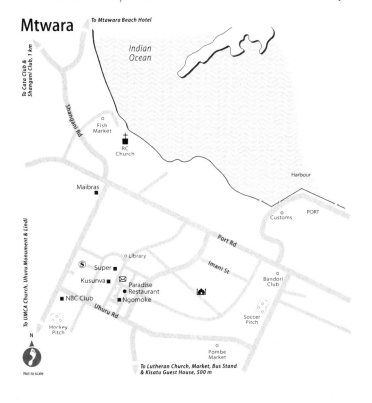

Mtwara

To Mtwara Beach Hotel

Indian
Ocean

To Cata Club &
Shangani Club, 1 km

Shangani Rd

Fish
Market

RC
Church

Harbour

Maibras

Customs

PORT

Port Rd

To UMCA Church, Uhuru Monument & Lindi

Library

Imani St

Super

Kusunva

Paradise
Restaurant

Bandori
Club

NBC Club

Ngomoke

Uhuru Rd

Soccer
Pitch

N

Hockey
Pitch

Not to scale

Pombe
Market

To Lutheran Church, Market, Bus Stand
& Kisatu Guest House, 500 m

Lip plugs

About 40 years ago it was fairly common to see elderly women wearing lip plugs amongst the people of south Tanzania. Lip plugs were worn by a variety of ethnic groups and principally amongst tribes that had originated from what is now Mozambique. The tribes that wore the lip plug most commonly included the Makonde, Mwera, Mukua, Mawiha and Metu.

The procedure that was necessary for the wearing of a lip plug began when a girl was just five or six. One of the older women in the tribe would pierce the girl's upper lip using a thorn and would then thread a blade of grass into it. Three days later another blade of grass would be inserted this time a little larger. This would be repeated about three times until a millet stalk about the thickness of the little finger would be inserted. A week later a second thicker stalk would be inserted and would be left in place for about a month. By this time the lip would have healed and from then on a series of lip plugs would be inserted each just a little wider in diameter than the last so that the upper lip would gradually be stretched. The first three plugs usually have a circumference of about 50 millimetres. The first plug was worn for about two months and the second for about four months. When the third plug was inserted a number of

markings would be cut into the girl's face – usually about three vertical lines each side of the eyes. When the girl reached puberty a plug of about 125 millimetres in circumference would be used and kept in place until the birth of her second child when it would be replaced by a larger one. In Makonde plugs of about 100 millimetres in diameter were fairly common.

The plugs were mostly made of ebony. They would be hollowed out and often were highly polished. The plugs would be prepared by the older men of the tribe. The wearer of the plug could not remove it at any time in public – in fact it would only have been taken out to be washed. There was also the much rarer practice of having a lip plug in the lower lip. The practice of wearing a lip plug caused problems as the pressure of the plug displaced and distorted the teeth.

The origin of the lip plug is not clear and there are a number of different suggestions. One is that they were introduced to stop the women being taken away as slaves in the slave-raiding days. However others suggest that lip plugs were in use long before the slave trade and they were originally used as an ornament. No special rights were associated with the wearing of a plug and there was no religious significance attached to them.

A new hotel is due to have started operation at Mitengo Beach, and is expected to be in the B price range.

Makonde plateau This area is occupied by the Makonde people. They have three claims to distinction. The first is the exceptional ebony carvings with groups of exaggerated figures, the traditional work related to fertility, and good fortune. The second is their spectacular *sindimba* dancing with the participants on stilts and wearing masks. The third is that Makonde women are celebrated throughout Tanzania for their sexual expertise. The best place to experience the atmosphere of the Makonde is to visit **Newala**. The road passes through dense woodland as it climbs up to the plateau from the coast.

Transport Bus: you need to stay at least one night in Newala as there is only one bus a day to and from **Mtwara**. It leaves Newala at 0500 and Mtwara at noon. It costs US$6 one way. There are several small lodging houses in Newala. There is a daily bus from Masasi at 1200, leaving from Newala at 0500.

Masasi The other main Makonde town is **Masasi**, surrounded by granite hills some 140 kilometres southeast of Lindi and 190 kilometres from Mtwara. In 1875 Masasi *Phone code: 059* (*Altitude:* 1,440 feet) was selected by Bishop Steere of the Universities Mission to *Colour map 3, grid C5* Central Africa as a place to settle freed slaves and it has been an important mission centre since then. Nowadays it is a pretty undistinguished town, although it is strikingly located in between a series of large gneiss kopjes. It is an important junction for

Nachingwea, Tunduru/Songea, Lindi, Mtwara and Newala and the Makonde plateau. There are some pleasant walks around town head towards the kopjes and there is a cave which contains rock paintings nearby. It is possible to take a trip to Nachingwea, where remnants of the Ground Nut scheme are apparently still in evidence. These reputedly include rusting ex-Sherman tanks which were bought from the American army in the Far East after the Second World War and coverted into tractors for the scheme.

E *Chilumba Guest House*, slightly better than the other accommodation in Masasi. **E** *Katami Guest House*, simple but clean. **E** *Mahenge Guest House*, basic accommodation. **E** *Masasi Hotel*, on the road to Lindi from the town centre. Has nets and fans, bar and restaurant. **E** *Muruwa Guest House*, basic clean rooms. **E** *The New 4 Ways Guest House*, closest to the bus stop but slightly more expensive than the others. There are several basic hotels which serve food, none of which are oustanding.

Sleeping

Road Bus: There are several buses to Lindi and to Mtwara daily; to Lindi it costs US$3 and takes about 4 hours, to Mtwara US$3.50 and 5-6 hours. Buses to Newala (US$1.50 and 2-3 hours) and to Nachingwea (US$1.50 and an hour or so) are twice daily. Several buses go to Dar es Salaam each day, these cost US$13 and the journey takes 18-22 hours. There is usually one bus per day going to Tunduru which costs US$6 and takes 7-8 hours. There are no direct buses to Songea, you have to go to Tunduru and overnight there. Be prepared for breakdowns or punctures on journeys between Masasi-Tunduru and Tunduru-Songea. The buses are in a sorry state and the roads are atrocious (impassable without a four-wheel drive during the rainy season). For those travelling across the south it is worth knowing that the average speeds of the buses plying the awful roads between Masasi and Mbamba Bay are around 25 kilometres an hour or less!

Transport

Tanzania & Zanzibar

Masasi

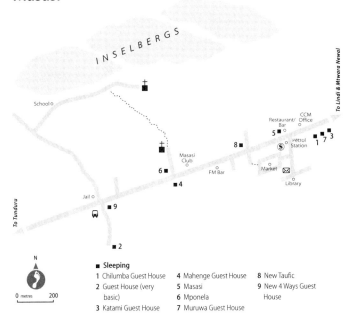

■ Sleeping
1 Chilumba Guest House
2 Guest House (very basic)
3 Katami Guest House
4 Mahenge Guest House
5 Masasi
6 Mponela
7 Muruwa Guest House
8 New Taufic
9 New 4 Ways Guest House

Tunduru

11°5'S 37°22'E
Colour map 3, grid C4

From Masasi to Tunduru you pass through mile after mile of miombo scrub whose monotony is only spared by some impressive gneiss kopjes which are scattered about the countryside for the first few hours after leaving Masasi.

After the journey from Masasi or Songea you'll be pleased to reach Tunduru (*Altitude*: 2,300 feet). It's a pleasant enough town in its own modest way, attractively situated with fine views over the surrounding undulating countryside, but there's little to keep you here for more than one night. Unless you are a gem dealer, that is; the surrounding area is rich in gemstones, including amethyst, diamonds and sapphires.

Sleeping **D** *Hunter II Guest House* is reasonable with toilet, shower but is very overpriced. **E** *Ngaunje Guest House*, clean, simple accommodation. **E** *Yakiti Guest House*, **E** *Mnazi Mmoja Guest House* and **E** *The Hunter Guest House*, are all simple, clean, basic accommodation.

Eating The best place to eat is the **Al** *Jazira* restaurant which is owned and run by a friendly Zanzibari man living in Tunduru. Be prepared to pay more for your drinks in Tunduru. The state of the road you came in on today (along with the state of the one you'll [probably] be leaving on tomorrow) leads to sodas being around twice the normal price.

Transport There are daily buses from Masasi to Tunduru leaving in the morning which cost US$6 and take 7-8 hours. There is at least one bus leaving for Songea early every other morning; these cost US$10 and the journey lasts about 10-12 hours. Try to book a seat in front of the back axle, this can make a big difference considering the state of the road. There are also Land Rovers (ask for ëgari ndogo) which do this trip carrying passengers. You will pay more for these – up to US$16.50. They are quicker although more uncomfortable than a bus – unless you happen to get a front seat – but they may be the only thing going on a particular day. There are also lorries taking passengers in the back.

Tunduru

■ Sleeping
1 Hunter Guest House
2 Hunter II Guest House
3 Mnazi Mmosa Guest House
4 Ngaunje Guest House
5 Yakiti Guest House

● Eating
1 Al Jazira
2 Restaurant/Bar
3 Restaurant/Bar

North to Kilimanjaro, Moshi and Arusha

Most Tourists that come to Tanzania are likely to see at least part of the northern circuit. There is so much packed into what is, by African standards, a small area. Here you will find the Serengeti National Park, Mount Kilimanjaro National Park, the Ngorongoro Crater Conservation Area and Olduvai Gorge. Each of the national parks is dealt with separately in the National Park section. The major towns in this area are Arusha and Moshi, but the small towns of Lushoto and Amani are very attractive and well recommended. The road through the well-cultivated Usambara and Pare Mountains is spectacular, and there is good hiking in the hills.

Although listed in this section because of their proximity to the main Dar/Arusha road, the towns of Amani, Korogwe, Mombo and Lushoto are administered from the Tanga Region.

Amani

Delightful small town based on the Agricultural Institute and Botanical Garden established by the Germans in the heart of mountain vegetation.

Colour map 3, grid B5

In 1898, at Amani in the cool Usambara hills, the Germans established an agricultural research institute that was the envy of Africa. With the twin benefits of the north railway from Tanga to Moshi and the Amani Institute, the Usambara area flourished under settler farming. By 1914, 40,000 hectares were under sisal, 80,000 hectares under rubber, 14,000 hectares under cotton as well as extensive areas of tobacco, sugar, wheat and maize.

Northern region

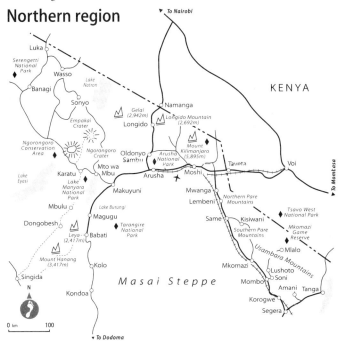

Tanzania & Zanzibar

One of the great lessons of farming in Africa is that crops have to be carefully adapted to local conditions. Amani tested soils, experimented with insecticides and developed new varieties. After 1914, Amani turned its hand to the war effort, developing a local quinine for use against malaria from cinchona bark and manufacturing chocolate, tooth-powder, soap and castor oil.

In May 1997 the **Amani Nature Reserve** was established to protect the biodiversity of the flora and fauna of the sub-montane rain forests of the East Usambara Mountains. This joint venture of the Tanzanian and Finnish Governments seeks to protect an area with one of the greatest numbers of plant and animal diversity in the world. Their biological significance has been compared to the Galapagos Islands. The rain forests also provide the water supply for 200,000 people in Tanga.

The total area of the Amani Nature Reserve is 8,380 hectares, which includes 1,065 hectares of forests owned by private tea companies under the management of the East Usambara Tea Company. It also includes the Amani Botanical Garden, established in 1902, one of the largest botanical gardens in Africa.

The Amani Nature Reserve Information Centre is housed in the recently rehabilitated old German Station Master's house in Sigi, built in 1905. A small resthouse has also been constructed nearby. The East Usambara Catchment Forest Project has made efforts to strengthen the villagers' rights to manage their own forests, and pilot farm forestry activities have been started in a number of villages in an effort to improve local land husbandry.

There have been a dozen forest trails established, including three drive routes. A guidebook for the East Usambaras has been written by Graham Mercer. The development of the tourist services is being co-ordinated at the Old German Resthouse in Amani.

For further information contact M Katigula, Project Manager or Stig Johansson, Chief Technical Advisor, East Usambara Catchment Forest Project, PO Box 5869, Tanga, Tanzania, T/F53-43820, usambara@twiga.com.

Today Amani is a medical research centre run by the Tanzanian government. Bird life and small animals such as monkeys abound. It is excellent hiking country.

Sleeping **D** *IUCN* (International Union for Conservation of Nature) is recommended. Good food, clean room in a Scandinavian wooden hut, IUCN belongs to a research project of the rainforest. **E** *Rest House*, run by the medical centre, charming colonial atmosphere and really excellent value.

Transport **Road Bus**: you will need to make a connection at Muheza on the road linking Tanga to the Dar es Salaam to Moshi highway. There is a bus which leaves Muheza at around 1400 each day for the 25 kilometre trip to Amani which takes about an hour and costs US$0.50. In the mornings the bus leaves Amani when full, usually around 0800. The bus may not go up to the top and you may have to walk or hitchhike the last 2-3 kilometres.

Korogwe

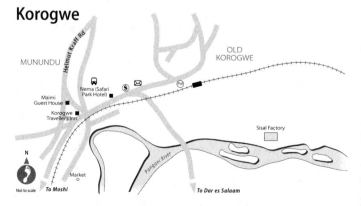

Korogwe

Korogwe is a small town that you pass through on the way from Tanga or Dar es Salaam north to Moshi. It lies at 52 metres, on the north bank of Pangani/Ruvu Rivers, of which the fertile valley with many settlements stretches away west. The local people are of the Zigua and Wasambaa but call themselves Waluvu. It is a local administrative centre due to its position near the local sisal estates, the Dar es Salaam-Nairobi road and railway and its proximity to the Usambara and Pare Mountains. There are a few shops, a market, a hospital and a Christian Mission.

5°0'S 38°20'E
Colour map 3, grid B5

Sleeping

D *Korogwe Transit Hotel*, on the main road between Arusha and Dar es Salaam. Probably the best hotel in town, mosquito nets, private bath but cold water most of the time, front rooms have a balcony but are very noisy due to the proximity of the main road, ear plugs recommended for front rooms, camping possible. **D** *Korogwe Travellers Inn*, on the main road. Bar, restaurant, fans, quite reasonable. **E** *Miami Guest House*, central, fans, nets, basic. **E** *Mountain View Resort*, PO Box 444, Korogwe, Tanga, T235. Owned and operated by an elderly man and his family who are outstanding hosts, as it is off the main road it is much quieter than other local accommodation, clean, mosquito nets, private bathrooms, running water, wonderful setting about 1 kilometre from bus stop, local food outstanding at the attached restaurant/bar, also has a campsite. **E** *Nema* (previously *Safari Park Hotel*), near bus stand. Fans, nets, simple fare.

Transport

Road Frequent buses pass through from Dar es Salaam, Tanga and Moshi (see these towns for details).

Mombo

Small town on the Dar es Salaam to Moshi highway. Little of interest – its main activity is the provision services for travellers. The BP service station offered fabulous service to a recent visitor – four people cleaned the car and three filled it up! **E** *Usambara Inn*, restaurant and beer garden, fans.

Colour map 3, grid B5

Soni

This is on the road from Mombo to Lushoto, and is close to the capital of the Shambaa people at Vugu. The Shambaa were well organized militarily, and supported Bushiri in the 1888/9 Arab revolt (see page 347). There is a pretty waterfall, and Soni is a good staging-post for hiking in the Usambaras.

Colour map 3, grid B5

Sleeping **E** *Msufino Lodgings*, located in village. Resaurant, bar, simple but adequate. **E** *Soni Falls*, about 1 kilometre from village. Restaurant, bar, comfortable and good value.

Eating **2** *Riverside Café*, good basic food served. Has the advantage that you can see the buses arriving whilst eating.

Transport **Local** **Bus**; regular buses run from Mombo to Lushoto.

Lushoto

Lushoto is located about 1½ hours off the main Korogwe-Moshi road. The road up to Lushoto via the small town of Soni is spectacular as it twists and turns through the mountains.

4°4'S 38°20'E
Colour map 3, grid B5

   Lushoto was the town chosen by early German settlers for vacation residences, when it was called Wilhemstal. It is reminiscent of Indian hill stations. The cool fresh air (it is 1,500 metres above sea level) and lush, green surroundings were greatly appealing and it was once thought that it might develop into the capital of the colonial administration. The Germans planned the site as their version of the ideal colonial town. Many of the surrounding farms and government buildings are originally German. There is a very fine Dutch-style Governor's House. Other reminders of the

Tanzania & Zanzibar

German connection are the horse-riding arenas, a golf course and the red tiles on the roofs of the buildings. Set in a valley in the Usambara (sometimes known as Asamabara) Mountains it can get quite cold from June to September so come prepared with warm clothes. The viewpoints on the southern and western side of the Usambaras are noted for the spectacular views of the plains of Mkomazi and Handeni. Kilimanjaro can be seen on the horizon and at the end of the day the sunset turns the area into unforgettable colours.

Sights This area is very much a place to enjoy the views and countryside. It is fertile and verdant, cultivated with maize, bananas etc, and there are plenty of tracks to walk along. One such walk takes about 45 minutes from Lushoto and ending at the 'Viewpoint' where the view of the hills and the Maasai Plain below really is breathtaking. Take the road out of town towards Irante and head for the Children's Home. Ask around and you'll be shown the track.

The **Usambara Mountains Tourism Programme** is a local tourism initiative advised and supported by SNV, the Netherlands Development Organisation, and GTZ, the German Development Organisation. It aims to involve and ultimately profit the small local communities who organize tourist projects off the usual circuits. These include one day walking modules from Lushoto to the Irente viewpoint overlooking Mazinde village 1,000 metres below, a walking tour of Usambara farms and flora, the growing rock tour from Soni and the Bangala river tour, which includes wading through the water. There are also longer modules walking into the Western Usambara Mountains via the villages of Lukozi, Manolo and Simga to reach the former German settlement of Mtae, or the tour to the Masumbae Forest Reserve.

The guides are all former students of the Shambalai secondary school in Lushoto, speaking fair to good English, and can tell you many interesting facts and stories about the history and daily life in the Usambara Mountains. They also hope to earn some income through their work as guides. The profits from the tourism ventures help fund local irrigation systems, afforestation and soil erosion control measures.

Lushoto is one of only two places in the world where you will find the Usambara Violet (its other habitat is in Mexico). There are lots of different churches and missions in Lushoto which are worth visiting. Missions were established by the Protestant Mission Society; Holy Ghost; Liepzig Mission; Seventh Day Adventists; African Protestant Union. The town holds a fine market (close to the bus station) which is very colourful and lively. There is good fishing in the mountain streams, one of which runs through the centre of the town.

Sleeping **B** *Grants Lodge*, Mizambo, Lushoto, PO Box 859, Tanga, T/F053-42491, at Tanga ask for Sarah or David, tanga4@twiga.com or grants@lt.sasa.unep.no, www.grantslodge.com. Lovely brick built house, open fire place. Tasty home-cooked food – soups are excellent as is the hot chocolate, 5 rooms, welcoming atmosphere, newly decorated. Can organize walking safaris with photocopied instructions. Car safaris. Range of reference bird books in the library. Highly

Lushoto

District Offices

Forestry Office

Cricket Ground

RC Church

Cemetery

Mission Hospital

Lutheran Church

Market

Milimani Guest House

To Mombo & Lawns Hotel

Kilimani Guest House

N

Not to scale

To Lawns Hotel (1 km)

Tanzania & Zanzibar

recommended. Payment US$ or Tanzanian shillings. Travellers' cheques accepted. To get to Grants Lodge if driving towards Moshi/Arusha, drive through Lushoto until you see a large sign on the right saying SECAP (Soil Erosion Control and Agro Forestry Project), which is just after a large church and the jail (Gereza) on the left. Begin counting kilometres at SECAP and drive uphill as it winds to the right. The old governor's office, now the District Commissioner's office is visible straight ahead. Continue to the silvaculture traffic circle approximately 1 kilometre where there is a sign for Grants Lodge. From there take a hard left and proceed uphill to a T-junction at Magamba – a distance of approximately 5.4 kilometres, where there is another signpost for Grants. At Magamba turn right and drive approximately 7.5 kilometres which brings you to the entrance of Grants Lodge. There is a blind curve to the left shortly after you enter the driveway, so be alert for oncoming traffic. Drive past the school and you have arrived.

C *The Lawns Hotel*, old colonial-type hotel, wonderful views, verandah, restaurant and bar, very good breakfast, but is a bit run down, running water, staff very accommodating. It is situated about 1 kilometre south of the town. Run by a Cypriot. Good source of information about Tanzania. From here you can organize hikes to 'Viewpoint'.

E *Kilimani Guest House*, basic but friendly, bar and restaurant. **E** *Lushoto Sun Hotel*, popular with tourists, has a restaurant. **E** *Milimani Guest House*, near bus station. Restaurant, bar, simple but adequate, safe parking for cars and motorcycles, there is a charge for a guard. **E** *New Friends Corner Hotel*, clean rooms, warm water but cold showers. **E** *Rombo Hotel* on the same side of the road as the *Milimani*. Very cheap, no single rooms. Small bar serves sodas and beer and they also serve food – chips, omelette and meat. At night Zairean music is played loudly until 2300. **E** *Teachers Club Guest House*, friendly, new, opposite *Milimani*, no parking facilities.

1 *Green Valley Restaurant* is very close to the market and bus station and serves reasonable, cheap food. **1** *Msumbiji Restaurant* at the far right hand corner of the bus stand. Serve fresh bread rolls every day. Food very reasonably priced. **Eating**

Road Bus: Lushoto is located off the main Korogwe-Moshi road. Bus from **Mombo** which takes about 1½ hours and costs US$1. You can also get a direct bus from **Tanga**, but it is slow, taking up to 6 hours, and costs US$2. The roads are excellent, all sealed. Hitching may be preferable to using the very overcrowded matatus as there are plenty of westerners in four-wheel drives who will give lifts in this area. **Transport**

Useful addresses The *bank*, which offers poor exchange rates, and *post office* are both on the main street. There is a *municipal office* beyond the Post Office on the left where it is possible to get a visa extended. **Directory**

Located about 25 kilometres north of Lushoto. Unusual village of two storey dwellings with fretted balconies. The Usambaras provide a spectacular backdrop. **F** *Afilex Hotel*, central. Simple but adequate. **E** *Lonido Guest House*, central, near bus stand. Rather basic, oil lamplights. *Getting there:* 1 bus a day to and from Lushoto. Leaves Mlalo around 0700 when full, and returns at midday, takes 2 hours and costs US$.50. **Mlalo**

A small town on the Moshi-Tanga road, it is a base for a visit to Mkomazi Game Reserve, which is the Tanzanian extension of the Tsavo National Park. **D** *Elephant Motel*, simple but adequate, staff helpful if arranging to hire a vehicle to get to Mkomazi. **Same**
Colour map 3, grid B4

Close by, off the beaten track to the south of Lembeni, is **Nglulu**, a rural village in a beautiful valley between the North and South Pare Mountains. There is not much in the way of tourist facilities but the **E** *Ngulu Guest House*, PO Box 85, Mwanga Moshi, T81 (Mwanga) is in a spectacular location. Clean, basic rooms with separate toilet **Lembeni**
Colour map 3, grid A4

block (cho) and washing facilities (bafu). The village is approximately 10 kilometres off the main road, well worth a visit if you are looking for cheap accommodation in a wonderful setting.

Kisangara   Off the main Moshi-Dar road, almost halfway between Mwanga and Lembeni, is a small town at the foot of the North Pare Mountains. Nearby there is a high school and vocational school located in the village of Chanjale. Here Grace Mngara and her husband Msafiri Banduka run one of the best kept secrets of rural Tanzania. The couple have both travelled to Europe and the States and have used their experience to create a farm with an education-environmental focus, with tree plantings, water retention schemes and sustainable food crops. They will help organize local tours, hikes into the mountains or will help you design a unique safari.

They have rooms available in their home (**C**) to rent, or (**E**) camping or (**D**) bandas to let. The Tanzanian food is superb. Contact Grace or Msafiri Hasna - Habari Za Shamba, PO Box 205, Mwanga-Moshi, F055-51113.

Mwanga   Mwanga is the district capital and is situated approximately halfway between Same
Colour map 3, grid A4   and Moshi, 50 kilometres southeast of Moshi. Huge palm trees grow abundantly in the water that streams downhill from the Northern Pare Mountains. From Mwanga there is a good sand road, which winds upwards to **Usangi,** the centre of the Northern Pare Mountains. This little town is surrounded by 11 peaks, and is an important economic centre producing beer, bricks, stoves, pottery and clothing. There is a colourful market held on Mondays and Thursdays, where local farmers come to sell their produce. This is one of the most fertile regions in East Africa.

The **Northern Pare Mountains Tourism Programme** is a cultural tourist programme supported by the Tanzanian Tourist Board and the Dutch (SNV) and German (GNV) Development Organisations. Local people take you on a walking tour of the area, staying in local homes with outstandingly good food. The guides speak reasonable English, most of them are farmers or local craftsmen. The scheme is co-ordinated at Lomwe Secondary School, in the centre of Usangi, T7, where a teacher is available to make further arrangements for your stay. In the mountains there are areas suitable for camping. Profits from these tourist projects are used to buy energy saving stores to reduce deforestation as they use only one third of the firewood, and help to reduce the workload of women. The walking tours from Usangi include the Mangata view tour, from where you have excellent views of Lake Jipe and Mount Kilimanjaro. The Goma Caves can be visited, where a century ago the Pare Chiefs dug deep caves to hide from rival tribes, and later the Colonial rulers. The table mountain Kindoroko and its forest reserve can be reached from the Goma Caves. On the other side of the forest stone terraces and irrigation systems in the village of Kisangara Juu can be seen before returning to Usangi via a route through the moorland.

Old churches and graves of the first missionaries are a reminder of the early German influence at the village of Shigatini which is accessed through a forest. Farmers have established irrigation systems, soil conservation measures, tree nurseries and are happy to show you around. A recent traveller reported that the tour guides were extremely well informed, proud of their culture and knew a lot about the pre-colonial era. Their vivid stories and knowledge of the local flora and the medicinal uses of the plants greatly enhanced the experience. The facilities were superb and food was delicious.

Moshi

3°22'S 37°18'E   Moshi, at 890 metres above sea level, is set at the base of Mount Kilimanjaro. The
Phone code: 055   town is located about 580 kilometres from Dar es Salaam, 76 kilometres from
Colour map 3, grid A4   Arusha and 280 kilometres from Nairobi. This is the end of the railway line and rail is the most popular approach after air. The population is about 180,000.

A Chagga story about Mount Kilimanjaro

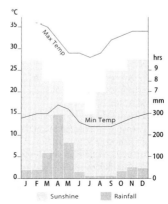

The Chagga people who live on the lower slopes of Mount Kilimanjaro have a large number of stories about the mountain. This one is commonly told and relates a quarrel between two sisters, Kibo and Mawenzi which are the names of the two peaks of the mountain.

The sisters who lived in different huts and each cooked and ate her own meals in her own hut. Kibo was the more careful and always had a store of food in case of a rainy day. Mawenzi however was much more extravagant and often finished her food before the next harvest. To fill the gap she decided that at meal times she would put out her fire deliberately and go to Kibo to ask for fresh fire embers to restart her fire. She

knew that when she went to Kibo her sister would always ask her to share her meals. Sure enough, whenever Mawenzi went over to Kibo to ask for embers, Kibo offered her food. However one day she went too far and three times in a row she asked for fire embers saying that her fire had gone out again. Each time she was offered food until finally on the third visit Kibo grew angry and hit Mawenzi across her back with a big ladle. It is this that explains the rugged appearance of the Mawenzi peak. There is also a moral – that too much spoon-feeding is a bad thing. After this incident Mawenzi decided that she had better look after herself better and she never allowed her fire to go out again.

Moshi is the first staging post on the way to climb Mount Kilimanjaro (see section on National Parks, page 498), and it is a pleasant place to spend a few days organizing your trip. The two peaks of this shimmering snow-capped mountain can be seen from all over the town and it dominates the skyline except when the cloud descends and hides it from view. It is a fertile area (the soil is volcanic) and there are lots of melt-water streams fed by the snow. This is where Arabica coffee, the higher quality of the two coffee types, is grown by the Chagga. This has helped the Chagga to become one of the wealthiest of the Tanzanian groups. However, not all of the wealth generated by the sale of coffee makes its way back to the growing community. Local small farmers have been known to receive only half the Moshi export price. By the time the coffee is sold in London their purchase price amounts to only one tenth of the London price. Moshi was the site of the signing of the Moshi Declaration after the war with Uganda in February 1979.

West Kilimanjaro The road running in a northerly direction from Boma ya Ngombe on the Moshi-Arusha road, passes through Sanya Juu and Engare Nairobi to reach Olmolog. This was the main area for European farming in Northern Tanzania prior to Independence. The boundaries of the old estates are marked on the existing Kilimanjaro Ordnance Survey map. After Independence most estates were nationalized. However, lack of capital and management skills has now forced the Tanzanian government to invite foreign commercial interests back, in the hope of increasing production of cereals, seed beans, beef and dairy products.

A drive in this area can include estate visits and a trip through the **Londorossi forest** glades. Most estate managers are happy to receive visitors. Of particular interest is the parastatal owned Rongai ranch, where African 'cowboys', mounted on horseback, herd Boran cattle and Persian black-headed sheep in Texas style.

Climate: Moshi

....

Cultivation on the slopes of Mount Kilimanjaro

Mount Kilimanjaro rises high above the East African plateau and for this reason is considerably better watered than the land surrounding it. In particular the lower southeast slopes of the mountain on the Tanzania side are very fertile with two rainy seasons in March-May and November-December. The southeast slopes receive the most rain while the northwest slopes also have two rainy seasons but at different times from the southeast. The southwest and northeast sides are drier.

Rain is brought in on the rain-bearing winds that come from over the Indian Ocean, and the higher the land, the more rain that falls. On the tropical grassland savannah at the base of the mountain the rainfall is approx 380-510 millimetres, while half way up the mountain at the forest zone the rainfall is about 1,500 millimetres. Above about 3,000 metres the temperatures fall to below zero and vegetation ceases.

The Chagga people who live on the slopes of Kilimanjaro take advantage of these differences in rainfall. They cultivate between about 900 and 1,400 metres and in some places up to 2,440 metres. On the lower slopes just above the tropical grassland savannah they cultivate annual crops such as millet, maize and beans, while higher up, on what is called the kihamba land they plant coffee and bananas and keep livestock. This obviously means a lot of work, especially as inheritance can lead to a farmer owning several scattered plots.

A variety of bananas are grown. There are some that are savoury, are known as matoke and are cooked by steaming for a few hours. Others are used for making traditional beer. A banana garden takes three years to establish, but once it has been established it needs relatively little time spent on it. The stems and leaves of a banana tree are also used as fodder for cattle, and for mulch for coffee trees.

Coffee is the main cash crop in the area. The volcanic soils of Mount Kilimanjaro are ideally suited to coffee cultivation. There are two types of coffee grown in East Africa – Robusta and Arabica – each having different climatic requirements. Arabica is the type that is grown on the slopes of Mount Kilimanjaro as it requires high altitude. It is the superior of the two coffees and attracts better prices. Coffee cultivation demands considerable attention; the plants spend their first year in a shaded nursery before they are transplanted into the fields. They need careful pruning to ensure good yields – this is particularly important for Arabica. Care must also be taken to keep the coffee well weeded.

On a man's death his land is traditionally divided up between his sons. As in many other parts of East Africa, this tradition, combined with the high birth rate, has meant that the average size of holding is divided into three or four plots when it is inherited. Many farms are now under one hectare and often smaller.

....

A valuable source of information in this area is retired forestry officer Mr Stanislavs Malya, PO Box 76, Sanya Juu, who now owns a small bar on the roadside at Sanya Juu.

Sights Many visitors do not stay long in Moshi, but go on to Marangu, the village at the entrance to Kilimanjaro National Park and arrange the trip up the mountain from there. There are however some things that are worth visiting in Moshi itself. These include the **Mwariko Art Gallery** on Mufutu St which exhibits local arts and crafts and the **Mweka Wildlife Museum**. This is a part of the College of Wildlife Management which is the major centre for training in conservation and wildlife management in Africa.

A leathercraft workshop which also makes pressed flower cards and jewellery, batik, carvings, is situated in southeast Moshi. *Shah Industries Ltd,* PO Box 86, Moshi, T52414, F51010, employ many disabled workers producing high quality goods. Goods available at Our Heritage, Hill St, PO Box 86, Moshi.

About 100 kilometres out of Moshi on the road towards Dar es Salaam is the **Nyumba ya Mungu** (House of God) dam on the Pangani River. This is a pleasant place to stop for a picnic.

Moshi is an unusual African town, insofar that it no longer has many European or Asian residents, unlike nearby Arusha. There are a number of African-owned hotels catering for visiting African traders and administrators. This offers travellers an opportunity to converse with English-speaking Africans in the bar and sample African food. It also offers travellers a chance to break away from the segregated tourist ghettos of the foreign owned hotels. Moshi has a vibrant shanty town, with markets, dukas and bars, with distinctive noises and smells. Moshi is safe by day, but don't go out after dark without a local escort.

Sleeping

B *Keys*, PO Box 933, T2250, Tx43159, just to the north of the town centre. Restaurant and bar, special rate for residents. **B** *Moshi*, PO Box 1819, Moshi, T3701, Tx42318, town centre. Restaurant and bar, rather run-down, government owned.

Moshi

L *Moshi View Hotel*, Kiusa St, PO Box 13, Moshi, T55-50993/4, F50994, has 16 self-contained rooms, en suite bath/toilet, hot water, ceiling fans, a/c available, *Cave Bar and Restaurant* offers Tanzanian and international food, rooftop bar with panoramic views including Mt Kilimanjaro, weather permitting, offers a genuine African experience. **C** *Motel Silva*, on Kiadha St, south of market. No hot water, rooms with balconies, good restaurant. **C** *New Kindoroka*, central, close to market. Restaurant, bar, well run. **C** *YMCA*, PO Box 85, T52362. Clean, no hot water, shared bathroom facilities, gymnasium, shop, travel office.

D *Coffee Tree Hostel*, PO Box 184, Moshi, T2787, town centre (2 floors of a large office block). Good views of Kilimanjaro, ideal for the bus station, communal bucket showers, wonderful views, will store rucksacks and baggage, local food available. **D** *Newcastle*, PO Box 2000, T3203/4382, close to the market, on Mawenzi St. New, hot water.

E *Hotel Buffalo*, superb value, budget hotel, sited 2 blocks south and west of the bus station, new clean, hot water with/without bathroom. Highly recommended. Good restaurant and bar. Will store luggage for you if you want to go on safari. **E** *Mlay's Residential Hotel*, Market St, opposite the market, good basic accommodation, restaurant downstairs. **E** *Rombo Cottage*, T2112, off road to Marangu. Hot water, own bathroom, bar and restaurant, good value and atmosphere, safe parking for cars and motorcycles. Charges higher for foreign travellers than local residents. **E** *Suncourt Inn*, off the road to Marangu, restaurant, bar, reasonable.

Camping There is camping near the *Golden Shower Restaurant*, which is 2 kilometres from Moshi on the road to Marangu. It is also possible to camp at the *Keys Hotel*.

Eating

All of the hotel restaurants will serve non-residents.

2 *Chinese Restaurant*, near CCM HQ. Well recommended. **2** *El Ghaneens's*, between the bus station and the mosque. Indian food. **2** *Golden Shower*, 2 kilometres from Moshi on the road to Marangu, has a good atmosphere. The owner, John Bennet, is the son of the legendary character 'Chagga' Bennet ex-First World War Royal Flying Corps ace, and economic adviser to the former Kilimanjaro Native Co-operative Union. He is a wonderful source of local information. There is an excellent cheap restaurant opposite Tambo Cottages. **1** *Chrisburger*, close to the clock tower, has a lovely garden out the back.

Transport

Air There is an airport halfway between Moshi and Arusha. This is Kilimanjaro International Airport, Moshi, T2223. It is served by both international flights as well as by Air Tanzania. Air Tanzania flies to Dar es Salaam and back twice a day but booking in advance is essential. Some people say its worth avoiding the hassle of Air Tanzania altogether and getting one of the international flights (such as Air France, and Ethiopian Airlines) which stop off at Kilimanjaro. The Air Tanzania office is next to the *Moshi Hotel* by the clock tower and from here a shuttle bus leaves 2 hours before the scheduled flight departure and costs US$3.

Road There are daily buses to and from **Dar es Salaam**. They leave Dar es Salaam from the Morogoro Rd bus station. Fare is around US$20 luxury, US$16 semi-luxury and US$12

ordinary and takes about 9 hours. The road has improved considerably. For **Tanga** the bus takes 4-6 hours and costs US$4. To **Marangu** there are lots of *dala dala* (US$1) or you can share a taxi (US$15). It is possible to get a direct bus to Mombasa, cost approximately US$13, 12 hours.

Communications Telephone: International calls can be made from the post office.
  Hospitals & medical services Hospitals: Moshi is home to what is said to be the best hospital in Tanzania – the *Kilimanjaro Christian Medical Centre (KCMC)* which is located a few km out of town; *Maweizi Moshi District Hospital*, located in town.
  Places of worship Church of England: *St Margaret's Church*, English language service at 1030 on most Sun (1 km from town centre).
  Tour companies & travel agents It is cheaper to book tours for Mt Kilimanjaro from Moshi than from either Arusha or Marangu. *Afri Galaxy Tours & Travel Ltd*, CCM Building, Taifa Rd near YMCA, PO Box 8340, T50268/53666/55873, F53666/51113, Kit@form-net.com. *Come and Go Safari Tours Ltd*, c/o Moshi View Hotel, PO Box 13, Moshi, T50993. Can arrange climbs of Kilimanjaro and tours of all National Parks, the manager Mr OL Nassari is very helpful. *Elmslies Tours*, PO Box 29, Old Moshi Rd, T2701/4742. *Fortes Safaris*, PO Box 422, Lumumba St, T41764. *Fourways Travel*, PO Box 990, Station Rd, T2620. *Kibo Safari Adventure*, T50367/51878, F50609. Led by Mr Athanas Minja. *Kilimanjaro Crown Birds Agency*. Based in the *New Kindoroka Hotel*, offers a good, friendly service. Can arrange a 5 day Kilimanjaro climb by the Marangu route for US$450 and a 6 day climb for US$540 all inclusive of guides, fees, transport, food etc. Their guide Mohammed is recommended. Kilimanjaro NP entry fee is US$20 per day and the hut fees are US$40 per day. *Mauly Tours & Safaris*, PO Box 1315, Rombo Av, T2787; *Trans-Kibo Travels Ltd*, PO Box 558, T4734, 2923 which is located in the YMCA. Organizes climbs of Kilimanjaro, see also National Park Section, page 498. *Zara Travel Agency*, PO Box 1990, T54240/50808, F53105/50233, zara@form-net.com, *Kilimanjaro Climb & Safari*, climb US$550 for 5-day 'Coca Cola route' – sleep in huts, US$720 for 6-day 'whiskey route' – sleep in tents, the safari charges are US$90 per person per day for a tour of Serengeti/Ngorongoro. Recommended.
  Useful addresses Bank and the **post office** can be found in the centre of town near the clock tower. **Immigration office:** where you can renew your visa, is also near the clock tower in Kibo House.

Marangu

This is the closest village to Kilimanjaro National Park, the entrance to which is five kilometres away. It is more expensive than Moshi, and budget travellers are advised to plan an assault on the mountain from the latter. Most people visit Marangu only to attempt the climb to the summit of Mount Kilimanjaro. However, Marangu and nearby **Machame** are excellent centres for hiking, bird watching and observing rural Africa.

The Ordnance Survey map of Kilimanjaro (1:100,000) is an essential guide for walks. The main tracks in the region radiate from the forest boundary, through the cultivated belt of coffee and bananas, to the road which rings the mountain.

There are many possible choices. One recommended hike is to take the murram road running westwards past the *Kibo* hotel. After about five kilometres take the track running northwest up the Mai River valley, past Maua Seminary. From Maua a track winds in a southwest direction to connect with the Kirua road above the Mworoworo Dam. Walkers can either go south to Kirua or proceed via Kidia to Old Moshi, where local transport will be available to take you back to Moshi town.

A *Kibo*, PO Box 137, Moshi, T52503 or PO Box 102, Marangu, T4, about 1 kilometre from Marangu village, old German building. Restaurant, bar, gardens, well organized, but up-market, Evelyn Waugh stayed here in 1959, finding it 'so comfortable' with a 'cool verandah', Kilimanjaro climbs can be organized from here. **A** *Marangu*, PO Box 40, Moshi, T51307, F50639, marangu@africaonline.co.ke, 40 kilometres from Moshi, 7 kilometres from Park gate. Long-established family owned and run country style hotel, warm and friendly atmosphere, self contained cottages with private baths and showers, hot water, set in 12 acres of gardens offering stunning views of Kilimanjaro, swimming pool, croquet lawn, one of the original operators of Kilimanjaro climbs with over 40 years' experience. **B** *Babylon Lodge*, PO Box

227, Marangu, T5 Marangu, 500 metres from the Post Office on the Jarakea Rd. Clean and comfortable, sited in well kept gardens, built into the hillside, all 18 rooms have private facilities, owner Mr Lgimo is very helpful. **Camping**: *Babylon Lodge*, rather less good value at US$10; *Kibo Lodge* charges US$6, and with use of hotel facilities is good value.

Transport   **Local   Dala dala**: regular *dala dala* to and from Moshi (US$1). **Taxi**: US$15.

Arusha

3°20'S 36°40'E
Phone code: 057
Colour map 3, grid A4

Arusha is a pleasant town set at an altitude of 1,380 metres above sea level. The road between Dar es Salaam and Arusha is now sealed. The journey by bus takes about eight hours. The drive up to Arusha passes through the semi-arid grass plains gradually becoming greener, more cultivated and more heavily populated. Mt Meru appears on the right with its fertile cultivated slopes. Arusha is 50 kilometres from the Kilimanjaro International Airport, 95 kilometres from Moshi, 680 kilometres from Dar es Salaam and 272 kilometres from Nairobi. It is probably the busiest Tanzanian town after Dar es Salaam and has a population of around 350,000.

The town is at the base of Mt Meru and is a wonderfully fertile area producing coffee, wheat, sisal and maize. In 1900 the town was just a small German military garrison but it has expanded and flourished. It was once the headquarters of the now defunct East African Community. Many of the wide roads are lined with flame trees, jacaranda and bougainvillaea and if you are lucky enough to be here when they are in bloom it is a fantastic sight.

It was here that the Arusha Declaration was signed in 1967 which marked the beginning of Tanzania's commitment to socialism. Arusha is the starting place for safaris in the north part of Tanzania – the Serengeti, Ngorongoro, Manyara, Olduvai Gorge, and Arusha National Parks. The huge **Arusha International Conference**

Arusha

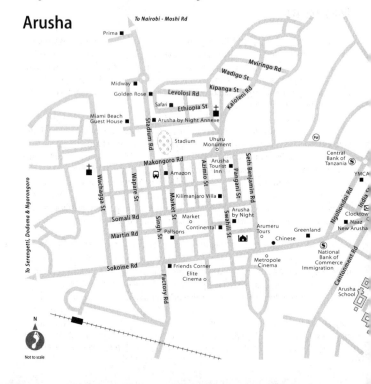

Centre (AICC), PO Box 3081, Arusha, T8008/ 2595/ 2953/ 3161/ 3181, F6630, Tx42032 AICC TZ, here is a legacy of the role that Arusha played as capital of the East African Community. It is made up of three main blocks – the Kilimanjaro, Ngorongoro and Serengeti wings. It has all the facilities that would be expected of an international conference centre including a hall with a seating capacity of 800, an interpretation system, meeting rooms for groups of varying sizes. The centre also has within it a bank, post office, foreign exchange bureau and cafeteria as well as various tour operators and travel agents.

The **National Museum** is at the top end of Boma Rd in the old German administrative **Sights** building. One display of interest is the tracing of the evolution of man based on the findings at Olduvai Gorge (see page 490). The **Arusha Declaration Monument** is set on a roundabout past the police station on the Makongoro Rd. The Declaration of 1967 outlined Tanzania's economic and political policies. There is a small museum here dedicated to the Declaration outlining the history of Tanzania's political and economic development. **Arusha School** dominates the area on the left bank of the Temi River. It is sited on sloping ground, dominated by huge eucalyptus trees and surrounded by a large swathe of playing fields. A typical low-slung, grey granite colonial-style main building with standard pink *bati* roof and large casement windows, arranged around courtyards with colonnaded loggias. Remaining buildings are run-of-the-mill whitewash and tile-classrooms, dormitories and sanatorium. Exception being the Silver Jubilee Library donated by the Round Table, who met in an old wooden lodge in the grounds. There was always a strong Church of England connection. Nyerere's two sons were taught there. It also hosted the meeting of the OAU Heads of State in 1966, which included Nyerere, Obote, Kaunda, Moi (as Vice President) Haile Selassie and Nasser. Sadly the school and grounds are now very neglected.

About 25 kilometres from Arusha, west and off to the right on the road to Makuyuni (see map, page 381) is the **Meserani Snake Park**, with crocodiles and lizards as well, with gardens and a restaurant. Alas safety is becoming an increasing concern in Arusha. Muggings have become more common. Sokoine Rd is unsafe at night, unless you are in a big group. Taxis are advised at night.

The best hotels in the Arusha area are out of **Sleeping** town. They have fine gardens, good standards and charming atmosphere in the foothills of Mt Meru. They are recommended above similar priced hotels in Arusha or its outskirts. They really require that you have your own transport. Recent reports stress security concerns especially after dark. If using the 'hotel safe', people are advised to check their money when deposited and on collection. There are reports of false receipts being issued, and less money returned on collection. At the other end of the market there are a number of cheap hostels around Levolosi Rd. They cost around US$8 and are good value. Recent travellers have advised that it is possible to negotiate lower room rates if you plan to stay a few days.

Mountain Hotels (see map, page 381) **A** *Mountain Village Lodge*, PO Box

376, T2699/2799/8967, F8749, Tx42107, out of town, 15 kilometres along Moshi Rd. Thatched bomas, excellent gardens, splendid location, overlooking Lake Duluti, very good restaurant. **A** *Mount Meru Game Lodge*, PO Box 659, T7179, about 20 kilometres off Moshi Rd near Usa River. High standard establishment in splendid garden setting, very good restaurant. **A** *Ilboru Safari Lodge*, T057-7834, PO Box 8012, Arusha, 2 kilometres from centre on Mt Meru itself, a taxi ride from town. Beautiful gardens, very friendly. Highly recommended. **B** *Dik Dik*, PO Box 1499, T8110, about 20 kilometres off Moshi Rd near Usa River. Swimming pool, good restaurant, pleasant grounds, well run establishment and good value, very proficiently run by Swiss owners, no reduction for residents. **B** *Lake Duluti Mountain Lodge*, PO Box 602, Arusha, located 11 kilometres from Arusha about 1,500 metres off the Moshi Rd. **B** *Tanzanite*, PO Box 3063, T32 (Usa River), about 11 kilometres along road to Moshi, near Usa River. Swimming pool, tennis, restaurant, good value.

Town hotels   A+ *Novotel Mount Meru*, Moshi Rd, PO Box 877, T2711/2712/8804/8737, F8503/8925. Full facilities including swimming pool, set in pleasant gardens, recently renovated. **A** *Equator*, PO Box 3002, T3127, Tx4215, town centre, Boma Rd. Restaurant, bar and beer garden, disco at weekends. **A** *Impala*, PO Box 7302, T8448/51, F8220/8680, Tx42132. Close to conference centre, pleasant garden and patio, good restaurant, gift shop, Bureau de Change, arranges tours and safaris through Classic Tours. **A** *New Arusha*, PO Box 88, T4241, Tx42125, town centre, near clock tower. 2 bars and beer garden, restaurant and fast food restaurant, bookshop and craft shop, swimming pool, rather run-down. **A** *New Safari*, PO Box 303, T8545/7, Tx42055, central, on Boma Rd. Restaurant and outdoor bar, weekend disco. **B** *Arusha*, PO Box 1530, Pangani St, T8863. Fans, hot water, reasonable value. **B** *L'Oasis Lodge*, PO Box 14280 Arusha, T57-7089, 2 kilometres out of town, 800 metres down the road opposite the *Mt Meru Hotel*, in the quiet residential area of Sekei with wonderful views of Mt Meru. Small, quiet family-run hotel. Good food, Masai 'roundhouse' style, safe car parking, all 11 rooms have en suite facilities. **B** *Pallson's*, PO Box 773, T2485, F7263, off Sokoine Rd, near market. Restaurant overpriced, service terribly slow, has seen better times, East Indian/Chinese food. **B** *Seventy Seven*, PO Box 187, T3800, Tx42055, off Moshi Rd, about 2 kilometres from centre. Pleasant bar and restaurant, prefabricated rooms, efficient but a bit utilitarian, substantial discount for residents. **B** *Tanzanite Hotel*, 16 kilometres from Arusha towards the airport. Bookings via *Savannah Tours*. Currently being revamped, swimming, popular with locals at the weekend, chalets set in verdant gardens, small animal sanctuary, child friendly, nature trail, bike safaris planned, lovely surroundings. **C** *Equator Hotel*, very central, good rooms, lovely garden, quiet area away from the noise, appears a bit run down, very popular with Canadians, it is possible to get a cheaper rate than advertised if booked through an agent or by negotiation. **C** *Golden Rose*, PO Box 361 Arusha, T8860 Stadium Rd, self contained, hot water, telephones, balconies, bar and restaurant, reported to have a rather noisy generator at the back. **C** *Mezza Luna Hotel*, PO Box 14365, Arusha, T4381. Recommended Italian family-run hotel with an outdoors restaurant under thatched roofs, excellent furnishings and high quality service and food, local African band play most evenings. **C** *Naaz*, PO Box 1060, T2087, central, near clock tower on Sokoine Rd. Restaurant, hot water, good value. **C** *Outpost*, PO Box 11520, T/F051-8405, Serengeti Rd, off the Old Moshi Rd, near the *Impala*

Hotel. Run by a Zimbabwe couple, Kathy and Steve Atwell, who are wonderful hosts, staff superb, very welcoming. Popular with ex-pats. Accommodation either in the main house, spacious rooms, or in bandas. Within walking distance of the *Mezza Luna* and the *Mambo Jazz Café*. **C** *Williams Inn*, just around the block from *Sunny Safaris*. Recommended. **D** *Amazon Tourist*, Market St, rather basic. **D** *Arusha by Night Annexe*, PO Box 360, on corner of Stadium Rd and Makongaro Rd, T6894. Basic, good value, difficult to get a booking, will not accept local currency. **D** *Jambo*, PO Box 1101 Town Centre. **D** *Meru House Inn*, Sokoine Rd, PO Box 10558, T057-7803, F8220/8929, near the main Meru Post Office. With attached restaurant, clean, friendly staff, hot water, own generator, can help arrange safaris including walking safaris into local farmland areas, safe and relatively quiet, it is possible to negotiate rates – lower for lengthier stays. *Roots Café* is now open at the Meru. Free transport is offered from the main bus station or take a taxi and *Meru House* will pay for you. **D** *Miami Beach Guest House*, off Stadium Rd. Reasonable, clean and basic but noisy, no hot water, has a small, good value restaurant. **D** *Midway*, near Stadium on Stadium Rd. Restaurant, good value. **D** *YMCA*, PO Box 118, India St, centre. No hot water, shared bathrooms. **E** *Arusha by Night*, PO Box 360, Swahili St, T2836. Basic, but good value, discos every night and can be noisy. **E** *Continental*, Swahili St. Very basic, but cheap. **E** *Friends Corner*, corner of Sokoine Rd and Factory Rd. Simple but reasonably good value. **E** *Greenlands*, Sokoine St, east end. Rather basic. **E** *Kilimanjaro Villa* Swahili St, very simple. **E** *Kitundo Guest House*, behind the *Golden Rose Hotel*. Reports of theft from locked rooms, so leave no valuables in your room, good and cheap local bars and restaurants in the vicinity. **E** *Mashele Guest House*, good breakfast, nets and fans available, close to the football stadium, has a small restaurant, good food. **E** *Meru Guest House*, Sokoine Rd, opposite the Regional Airways office, at the end of town towards Serengeti, and the snake park. Offers excellent value, safe parking for cars and motorcycles, friendly, safe, clean, hot showers. **E** *Prima Guest House*, Stadium Rd toward Moshi and Nairobi Rd, rather basic. *Rahaleo Guest House*, north of the stadium. Basic, clean and cheap. Recommended. **E** *Safari Guest House*, Ethiopia St, north of Stadium, simple fare. **E** *Shimbwe Guest House*, Ethiopia St. Clean, hot water in the mornings, communal showers, nets, bar but relatively quiet GH.

Camping *Kinyoro Campsite*, 1 kilometre along Old Moshi Rd. *Maasai Camp*, 3 kilometres along road to Moshi, hot water, restaurant, US$3. *Lake Duluti camping ground*, about 11 kilometres from town toward Moshi, restaurant, US$3. *Arusha Vision Campground*, T057-3461, centre of town next to the *Hotel Equator*. Quiet and peaceful, safe, guarded all night, can provide tents, the owner 'J4' and his American wife also run a small travel agency and are very helpful, this is the cheapest camp ground but also the most basic and central. Recently there have been security problems. J4 is very helpful. Camping is available at the *Meserani Snake Park*, PO Box 13669, T/F00873-682087337 (cellular), 25 kilometres out of town. Very popular site for tourists looking for something different, basic toilets and showers, interesting snake park. Barry Bale from South Africa offers a fun atmosphere, and trekkers are welcome. The bar serves very cold beers and sodas. Has hot showers. If camping you get free entry to the Snake Park. Local crafts people sell their goods. There is a small zoo in addition to the snake park. Camel rides and treks can be arranged and ox treks into the bush are planned. *Club Africa*, 1 kilometre beyond *Novatel Mt Meru*. Excellent security, camping US$3 per person per night. Camping also possible at the *Tanzanite Hotel*.

4 *Hotel Seventy Seven*, comfortable atmosphere, live band plays for diners most nights. **Eating**
4 *Mount Meru Hotel*, International menu, very pleasant coffee shop.

3 *Shanghai Chinese Restaurant*, on the Sokoine Rd near the bridge, beside the new post office. Extensive menu, recent reports indicate that standards have deteriorated, however the hot and sour soup is highly recommended. **3** *Hotel Equator*. Good restaurant with a varied menu. **3** *Mandarin*, near the *Impala Hotel* on Serengeti Rd, south of the old Moshi Rd. Seating inside and outside at the back. **3** *Mezza Luna*, T4381, on the old Moshi Rd near the *Impala Hotel*. Generous glasses of South African wine, good cappucino, terrific Italian food, live African band. **3** *Pallsons*, Market St. Good quality Indian food, very slow service. **3** *Pita*

Pizzeria, Maasai St, down from the centre of the market. Serves pizza, pasta, steaks, hamburgers and salads, clean and cool inside. **3** *Safari Grill*, next to the *New Safari Hotel*. Good standard. **3** *Shanghai*, Uhuru Rd, next to the new Post Office. Excellent food but rather pricey.

2 *Big Bites*, on Swahili St. Serves good tandoori's and curries**. 2** *Golden Rose Hotel*, good standard and sound value. **2** *Kuleana*, next to the *New Mwanza Hotel* is a pizza parlour, open 1100-2000. Excellent pizzas, bread and expresso, this is a project run by the Centre for Children's Rights, and employ street children as waiters, a visit is strongly recommended. **2** *Mambo Café*, on the old Moshi Rd, 5 minutes walk from the Clock Tower. Serves 'comfort food', hamburgers, fries/catsup, submarine sandwiches and milkshakes. **2** *McMoody's*, on the corner of Sekoine and Market St. Serve McDonald's-inspired fastfood, not quite as good as the original but offers a change to most food available, also serve fries and shakes. **2** *Mike's Maasai Camp*, 3 kilometres west on the old Moshi Rd. Good food and bar, excellent place to meet people, serves hamburgers, chips, pizzas and Mexican food. **2** *New Safari Hotel Garden Bar*. Recommended for traditional meat barbecues. **2** *Picknick Restaurant* behind the *Golden Rose Hotel*. Serves good and cheap meals, local food and fish/chicken/egg with chips, friendly and has a bar which sells beer. **2** *Roots Café*, at Meru House Inn, Sokome Road. Serves good cheap meals. **2** *Sher-E-Punjab Bar and Restaurant* (previously *Meenar Restaurant*) on Ngoliondoi Rd. Serves excellent Tandoori food, T3688. **2** *Sherry Bar*, pleasant African outdoor bar on Arusha/Nairobi Rd – 1 kilometre west of Simeon Rd. Clean and comfortable. **2** *Spices & Herbs Ethiopian Restaurant* (formerly *Axum*), approximately 1 kilometre from Clock Tower next to *Impala Hotel* on Old Moshi Rd, Kijenge district, T2279. Simple Ethiopian dishes, full bar and jazz club.

1 *Ark Grill*, on Swahili St. Friendly place serving European food. **1** *Naura Yard Bar* which is on Sokoine Rd near the bridge. Simple but sound. **1** *Silver City Bar*, attached to the YMCA. Good value.

Market very good for fruit, locally made basketware, wooden kitchenware and spices, colourful, good bakery and coffee on Sokoine Rd not far from the clocktower.

Entertainment **Bars and discos**: there are a number of popular bars including the *Naura Yard Bar* next to the Chinese Restaurant on Sokoine Rd near the bridge. On Sunday this holds a free, very loud, disco. Another popular spot is the *Silver City Bar* attached to the YMCA. The bar at the *Hotel Equator* has live bands at the weekend which are very popular. *Mambo Jazz Café* near the *Mezza Luna*, great atmosphere. There is another very good and popular disco held at the *New Safari Hotel* each weekend called the *Cave Disco*. If you want to dance during the week there are nightly discos at the *Hotel Arusha by Night*. *Club 21*, over the *Ethiopian Restaurant* off Ngiro Rd, gets very lively at times. *Seventy Seven* has discos on Friday which attracts mostly locals, good music including Congolese soca.

Cinemas: *Metropole Cinema* is on Sokoine Rd (formerly Uhuru Rd); *Elite Cinema*, off Sokoine Rd, south of the market. Both these cinemas show mostly Asian films, martial arts and adventure movies.

Shopping **Bookshops**: there is a bookshop at the New Arusha Hotel which sells international newspapers and magazines as well as books. There is a new bookshop on Stadium Rd, just before the roundabout, when leaving town. However, the best bookshop by far is situated in the *Mambo Café*, a five minute walk down Moshi St. The *Mambo Café* is set in a lovely old colonial villa and incorporates a café, bookshop and craft shop.

Craft shops: there are some good craft shops on Ngoliondoi Rd and near the clock tower with some very good examples of carvings. They are probably cheaper here than elsewhere.

Markets: the market is behind the bus station along Market St and Somali Rd and there are lots of shops along Sokoine Rd.

Mount Meru Marathon is held yearly in Arusha and attracts competitors from all around **Sports** the world. **Golf**: 9 hole golf course is available at the *Gymkhana Club* which is out towards the High Court, temporary membership is available. **Horseback riding**: at Usa River about 15 kilometres out of Arusha as well as at Lake Duluti which is 11 kilometres out of Arusha on the Moshi road. **Swimming**: is available at the pool at the *Novotel Mount Meru*, this is open to non-residents for a temporary membership fee.

Air Kilimanjaro International Airport, Moshi T+55-2223, is halfway between Arusha and **Transport** Moshi. It is served by international flights as well as by Air Tanzania. Air Tanzania flies to Dar es Salaam and back twice a day but booking in advance is essential. It is also possible to catch one of the international flights (such as Ethiopian Airlines and KLM) which stop off at Kilimanjaro. *Aviators Services*, T6386. Has 3 flights a week to Dar es Salaam, 1400 Monday, Wednesday, and Saturday, and the cost one-way is US$126. *Eagle Aviation Ltd* at the Adventure Centre, T057-7111, F057-8997. Offers a coach service to Kilimanjaro Airport, flights to Mombasa 3 times weekly, Monday, Wednesday and Sunday. The **Air Tanzania Office** is on the Boma Rd. **Ethiopian Airlines** also have offices on Boma Rd. To get to the airport you can get the STS shuttle bus which costs US$3 and leaves about 2 hours before flight departure. It stops at the Air Tanzania office, *Mount Meru Hotel* and *Hotel Seventy Seven*. Taxi to the airport is about US$20. **Precision Air**, PO Box 1636, T6903/2818/7319/F8204, Tx42148/50008. Have flights to Bukoba, Dar es Salaam and Zanzibar, occasionally over booked, but very good reputation to date.

Road The bus station is located in Zaramo St just to the north of the market. There are reported to be thieves operating around the Arusha bus station. There are regular buses and *dala dala* to and from **Moshi**. Trip costs US$1 and takes 1½ hours. You can also get a shared taxi for which you can expect to pay at least US$35. **Dar es Salaam**: fare is around US$20 luxury, US$16 semi luxury and US$12 ordinary and takes about 9 hours. The road has improved considerably and journey times are shortening. Large buses are safer than mini-buses. Taqwa offer a fast reliable service. **Tanga**: daily buses (Tanga African Motor Transport), US$7 (luxury) and US$4 (ordinary). You can also get buses from here up to **Mwanza**. Public transport from Musoma to Arusha now goes via Nairobi. It is possible to get to Mwanza via Singida and Shinyanga, although you may need to change buses, and the trip will take the best part of 2 days. **Nairobi**: *Dala dala* only take 4 or 5 hours from here, depart, regularly through the day, and the border crossing is efficient. A regular bus leaves every morning to go through to Nairobi, it calls at *Mount Meru Hotel* and *Hotel Seventy Seven* and costs around US$8.

There are two shuttle services to Nairobi US$15-US$20. Departures at 0800 and 1400 daily. *Riverside Shuttle*, c/o Riverside Car Hire, Sokoine Rd, near Chinese Restaurant, PO Box 1734, Arusha, T057-2639, F057-3916. *AA Tours and Safaris Ltd*, Sokoine Rd, near Piita Pizzeria, PO Box 281, Arusha, T057-3665.

Banks The *Central Bank of Tanzania* has a branch on Makongoro Rd near the roundabout with **Directory** Ngoliondoi Rd. There is an AmEx office on Sokoine Rd near Friends Corner, and there are now many Forex offices in town. The *National Bank of Commerce* is on Sokoine Rd down towards the bridge. *Stanbic Bank*, near Uhuru Monument. The *Impala Hotel* will give cash advances but there is a large fee – approximately 25%. Good exchange rates are given at the bank opposite the Post Office at clocktower called National Bureau de Change.

Communications **Post Office**: the main Post Office is by the clock tower opposite the *New Arusha Hotel*. **Telephone**: Recent travellers have reported that the cheapest place to make calls or send faxes is the TTCA on Boma Rd, opposite the tourist office. Very efficient service. International telephone calls can be made from the *New Safari Hotel*. Phone calls to Australia US$6 per minute and US$6 per fax page. **Internet Access**: Available close to the Post Office and also in the AICC building.

Hospitals The *Mount Meru Hospital* is opposite the AICC on Ngoliondi Rd.

Tour companies & travel agents There are a number of tour operators based in Arusha who organize safaris to the different National Parks in the north. There are some in the International Conference Centre as well as others along India St, Sokoine Rd and Boma Rd. When choosing a safari company and before handing over any money on a 'share Land Rover/Land Cruiser or minibus' basis, it is advisable to try to meet your driver/guide and to examine the vehicle, in order to check out the former's command of English and the roadworthiness of the vehicle. Travellers have reported that rival tour companies sometimes double up, with 2 or 3 groups sharing the same cars and other facilities – all paying different amounts. As a result itineraries are changed without agreement. It is advisable to draw up a comprehensive written contract of exactly what is included in the price agreed, before handing over any money. Sometimes agents for rival tour companies are very persistent and may follow travellers to promote their company. It is also prudent to explicitly mention that unused park fees will be refunded as the park fees are for 24-hr periods. At the tourist office there is a '**black list**' of rogue travel agencies, unlicensed agents and the names of people who have convictions for cheating tourists. It is recommended that you cross check before paying for a safari. In addition, when going on safari you are advised to check at the Park gate if all the fees have been paid, especially if you plan to stay for more than 1 day in the park. Also check that the name of the tour company is written on the permit. Sadly there is a lot of cheating going on at present, and many tourists have fallen victim to well organized scams. The tourist office also has a list of accredited tour companies in Arusha. The *National Parks of Tanzania Headquarters* is on the 6th flr of the Kilimanjaro wing of the Arusha International Conference Centre, PO Box 3134, Arusha, T3471/2, Tx42130. It has a park guides as well as the National

---

Tours to all National Parks in Tanzania

* Luxury Lodge Safaris
* Luxury & Budget Camping Safaris
* Photographic Safaris
* Mount Kilimanjaro & Mount Meru Climbing
* Walking, Camel Riding and Serengeti   Baloon
  Safaris
* Beach Holidays

P.O. Box 7267
Tel:255-57-7145/8184 Fax: 225-57-8094
ARUSHA – TANZANIA

We accept all major credit cards.

HOOPOE ADVENTURE TOURS TANZANIA LTD

Hoopoe Adventure Tours will take you anywhere you want to go in Tanzania, Kenya and Ethiopia at a price you can afford. Travel with us and our experienced Driver Guides by 4WD Landrover on an unforgettable safari in the wilds of East Africa. Enjoy the panoramic views, comfort and excellent food at our luxurious Kirurumu Tented Lodge, overlooking the spectacular Rift Valley scenery of Lake Manyara National Park. We arrange Mountain climbs, Walking safaris, Fly-ins and Zanzibar trips, and cater for special interests with tailor-made, professionally led safaris both lodging and camping. Safari camps are mobile and either simple but comfortable, or more traditional and deluxe.

Enjoy East Africa to the full with **HOOPOE ADVENTURE TOURS**. For further information contact the London office for ease of communications.

"A traveller without knowledge is like a bird without wings"
(Mushariff-Ud-Din 1184-1291)

TANZANIA	U.K. Suite F1	KENYA
India Street	Kebbell House	Off Enterprise Rd
P.O. Box 2047	Carpenders Park	P.O. Box 14662
Arusha	Watford WD1 5BE	Nairobi
	Tel: (44 181) 428 8221	
	Fax: (44 181) 4211396	
	Email: HoopoeUK@aol.com	

Parks Quarterly Reports. **Horse riding safaris** are becoming increasingly popular and can be arranged from Arusha. Most of these begin from Usa River which is 22 km from Arusha on the Moshi road. These are discussed in more detail in the National Parks Section. *Tanzania Game Trails* arranges such safaris. Among the most experienced tour organizers are *Abercrombie and Kent, Adventure Centre, Classic Tours and Safaris, Hoopoe Adventure Tours, Ker and Downey Safaris, Savannah Tours* and *Takims*.

Abercrombie and Kent, PO Box 427, T8347, F8273, Tx42005. **Adventure Centre**, Goliondoi St, PO Box 12799, T057-7111, F057-8997. **Adventure Tours and Safaris**, PO Box 1014, T6015. **African Gametrackers**, PO Box 535, T2913/7791. **AICC Tours**, PO Box 3801, T3181 (ext 23). **Angoni Safaris** (located in the AICC Bldg). Recommended. **Arumeru Tours and Safaris**, PO Box 730, T7637/2780. **Blue Bird Tours**, PO Box 1054, T3934. **Bobby Tours**, PO Box 716, T3490. **Classic Tours and Safaris**, PO Box 7302, T7197, F8220. **Come to Africa Safaris**, AICC Complex, Serengeti Wing, 5th Floor, Room 511, PO Box 2562, T4530, F4601, Mobile 0811 650420. **Dorobo Tours and Safaris**, PO Box 2534, T3699. **Eagle Tours and Safaris**, PO Box 343, T2909. **Easy Travel & Tours Ltd**, Clock Tower Centre, Joel Maeda Rd, 2nd Flr, PO Box 1912, T3929, F7322/4110, easytravel@habari.co.tz. **Executive Travel Services**, PO Box 7462, T2472/3181, Tx42136. **Flamingo Tours**, PO Box 2660, T6976/6152, Tx42003. **Fly-Catcher Safaris**, PO Box 591, T3622. **George Dove Safaris**, PO Box 284, T3090, 3625. **Hoopoe Adventure Tours**, India St, PO Box 2047. UK address: Suite F1, Kebbell House, Watford, WD1 5BE, T0181-4288221, F0181-4211396, HoopoeUK@aol.com). This company has been consistently well recommended by a number of travellers. **K and S Enterprises**, PO Box 1318, T6465. **Ker and Downey Safaris**, PO Box 2782, T7755/7700, Tx42013. **King Safari Club**, PO Box 7201, T3958. **Laitolya Tours and Safaris**, PO Box 7319, T2422/2984. **Let's Go Marve Holidays**, PO Box 2660, T3613. **Let's Go Travel**, The Adventure Centre, PO Box 12799, T2814/7111, F8997/4199. **Lions Safaris International**, PO Box 999, T6422. **Lost Horizons**, PO Box 425, Tx42047, F057-2123. **Mashado, Tanzania**, PO Box 14823, T57-6585, F8020, Mashado@ habari.co.tz, mobitel: T+255 811 510107 or 01/02, F+255-811-510104 or 03. **Nature Discovery**, T057-8406, F4063, for alternative routes and trekking safaris. **Ostrich Tours & Safaris Ltd**, PO Box 12752, T/F4140. **Peacock Tours and Safaris**, Regional CCM Bldg, Makongoro Rd, PO Box 10123, Arusha, T57-7884, F8256, peacock@yako.habari.co.tz. Company and driver "Linus" highly recommended by recent travellers (98). **Ranger Safaris**, PO Box 9, T3074/3023, Tx42063. **Roy Safaris Ltd**, PO Box 50, T2800 and 2115, F8892, Tx42021 ATL TZ. Recommended as offering an excellent service. **The Safari Company**, T057-7932, F6620, paulmatthysen@ yako.habari.co.tz. Do the Kili climb as well as Lake Tanganyika trips. **Sandgrouse Adventure Tours & Safaris Ltd**, PO Box 11661, T3485/ 4065, F4095. **Savannah Tours**, PO Box 3038, T331662/332550, savtour@twiga.com. **Serengetti Select Safaris**, PO Box 1177, T6186. **Shallom Tours and Safaris**, PO Box 217, T3181. **Simba Safaris**, PO Box 1207, T3509 3600, Tx42095. **SNV**. The Dutch development aid organisation, based in the AICC building, organizes some tourist projects which involve and profit the local communities. They tend to be run by local entrepreneurs and are off the beaten track, giving a very different tourist experience. An example is the Usambara Mountains Tourism programme (see page 384) or the Northern Parc mountains walking tours (see page 386) and the Mto Wa Mbu cultural programme (see page 485). **State Travel Service**, PO Box 1369, T3300/3113/3152, Tx42138. **Star Tours**, PO Box 1099, T2553. Recent travellers have advised against this tour company, as the new owner Clemence Muta has been unreliable, check with the tourist office 'black list' for an update of the situation. **Sunny Safaris Ltd**, PO Box 7267, T7145/8184, F8094, sunny@arusha.com. Recent travellers report excellent service. **Takims Holidays Tours and Safaris**, Rm 421, Ngorongoro Wing, AICC, PO Box 6023, T3174/7500. **Tanzania Game Trails**, PO Box 535, Tx42075. **Tanzania**

Tanzania & Zanzibar

Guides, PO Box 2031, T3625. *Tanzania Wildlife Corporation*, PO Box 1144, T3501. *Tanzanite Wildlife Tours*, PO Box 1277, T2239. *Tarangire*, PO Box 1182, T3090/3625. *The Safari Co*, PO Box 207, T8424, F8272, mia@marie.gn.apc.org. Can organize private safaris. Highly recommended. *Shidolya Safaris*, AICC Conference Centre, PO Box 1436, T8506/2813, F4160/8242. Drivers/cooks/guides are excellent, recommended for lodge/camping safaris but not the Kilimanjaro climb. *United Touring Company*, PO Box 2221, T8844/5, F8222. *Tracks Travel*, PO Box 142, T3145. *Tropical Tours Tanzania* at Moshi Rd, near the clocktower. German Swiss managed, offer excellent tours but are not one of the cheapest. *Wapa Tours and Safaris*, PO Box 6165, T3181. *Wildebeest Migration Safaris*, AICC Building, 6th floor room 650/651/652, PO Box 13964, T3364, 3962, F8497, mobile 0811 510349, wildebeest@form-net.com. Feedback about this company has been mixed. *Wildersun Safaris and Tours*, PO Box 930, T6471/3880. *Wild Spirit Safari Ltd*, PO Box 2288, T/F574215. French/Tanzanian team offering a range of safaris, offer good tours for a fair price US$80 a day camping safari to Serengeti and Ngorongora Crater. *Wildtrack Safaris*, PO Box 1059, T3547. *W J Travel* Service, PO Box 88, T6444.

For details of other safari companies both within Tanzania and overseas, see page 47. We have been asked to mention that *Paradise Safaris*, also known as *Paradies Safaris Ltd*, located at the Elity Cinema Building, 2nd Flr, Jacaranda St, managed by Ms H Kiel has offered poor quality service to some of our contributors. Paradise Safaris is on the 'black list' - see beginning of section. The cost of taking foreign registered cars into the National Parks in Tanzania means that it is usually cheaper to hire a driver/guide and cook with their own vehicle to go on safari. J4 at Arusha Vision Campground is very helpful. **Hunting Safaris:** *Bushmen Company*, PO Box 235, T6210. *King Tours and Hunting Safaris*, PO Box 7000, T3688.

Tourist offices The Tourist Office is on Boma Rd (T3842) but it is not overly helpful unless you are making a booking for a TTC hotel or lodge.

Useful addresses **Immigration Office** is on Sinoni Rd.

Monduli Monduli is a small town off the main road from Arusha to the Northern Circuit. It is not commonly used by tourists, so it remains very cheap. **E** *The Blue Annex* in the centre of town offers a simple room, opening out on to a courtyard, separate toilet and bucket shower block. Space to park a vehicle, local meals available next door.

Mount Hanang This is the ninth highest peak in East Africa, with an altitude of 3,417 metres. It lies to
Colour map 3, grid B3 the southwest of Babati, and is a challenge for more adventurous trekkers. There is accommodation at the old *Fig Tree Hotel* which has a bar, dining-room and three detached rondovels for guests. It was run by Baron von Blixen and his second wife, Cockie, between 1928-32. The Prince of Wales was entertained to lunch there by the von Blixens during his safari in 1928.

Mount Mount Longido, altitude 2,629 metres, is situated 100 kilometres north of Arusha on
Longido the road to Namanga. The town of Longido lies on the main road, at the foot of the
Colour map 3, grid A4 mountain. The mountain rises up steeply from the plains and forms an important point of orientation over a wide area. To climb Mount Longido is an excellent preparation for Mount Meru or Mount Kilimanjaro. The Masai guides will point out lots of wildlife and this area is rich in birdlife.

The **Longido Cultural Tourism programme**, supported by the Tanzanian Tourist Board and SNV, the Netherlands Development Organisation, is an excellent way of supporting the local Masai people and learning about their lifestyle and culture. There are several walking tours of the environs, from half day 'bird walk' from the town of Longido across the Masai plains to the bomas of Ol Tepesi, the Masai word for Acacia tree. On your return to Longido you can enjoy a meal cooked by the BAWATA women's group. The one day walking tour extends from Ol Tepesi to Kimokonwa along a narrow Masai cattle trail that winds over the slopes of Mount Longido. On clear days there are views of Kilimanjaro and Mount Meru and from the north side there are extensive views of the plains into Kenya. The tour includes a visit to a historic German grave. There is also a more strenuous two day tour climbing to the top of the steep Longido peak, following buffalo trails guarded by Masai warriors armed with knives and spears to protect you. Accommodation is in local guest houses or camping. Part of the money generated by this cultural tourism project goes to rehabilitate the cattle dip in Longido. The Masai lose about 1,500 head of cattle per annum, mainly because of tick-borne disease. Since Masai life is centred around their livestock this creates serious problems as reduced herd size means less work, income and food. Regular cattle dipping eradicates tick-borne diseases and the renovated cattle dip will be available to all local Masai families at low cost. Further details of these tours can be obtained from the Tanzanian Tourist Information centre in Arusha, T057-3302. The tours are co-ordinated locally by Mzee Mollel, a local Masai who studied in Zambia and Australia, who is partially paralyzed following an accident. Mzee is happy to answer any enquiries about the Masai way of life.

Lake Natron

Soda lake on the border with Kenya, about 200 kilometres to the northwest of Arusha. There are many thousands of flamingoes, and it has many more of these birds than either Lake Magadi in the Ngorongoro Crater or Lake Manyara. The lake is seldom visited, and you are unlikely to see any other tourists. The route from Arusha is through an area rich with wildlife, depending on the season, particularly ostriches, zebra and giraffe. Numerous Masai herd cattle. **Engaruka** is 63 kilometres north of Mto wa Mbu on the road to Oldoinyo Lengai and Lake Natron. The village of Engaruka lies at the foot of the rift valley escarpment. The Masai cattle graze on the surrounding plains. Dust cyclones often arise at the horizon. They are feared as the 'devil fingers' that can bring bad luck when they touch people.

Colour map 3, grid A4

Engaruka is one of Tanzania's most important historical sites. 500 years ago the farming community developed an ingenious irrigation and cultivation system. Water from the rift escarpment was channelled into stone canals which led to terraces. For some unknown reason the farmers left Engaruka around 1700. Several prominent archaeologists, including Louis Leakey, have investigated these ruins but to date there are many questions left unanswered about the people who built these irrigation channels, and why they abandoned the area.

The ruins are deteriorating because with the eradication of the tsetse fly, Masai cattle now come to graze in this area during the dry season, causing extensive damage.

There are plans to develop a cultural tourism programme here with the local people and the Tanzanian Tourist Board and SNV, the Dutch Development Organisation, and to use the monies generated to exclude cattle from the ruins and start conservation work.

If you follow the river upstream from the campsite, with a bit of wading from time-to-time, there is a fine waterfall after a hike of about an hour.

Road Access is really only feasible by four-wheel drive vehicle. The turn-off from the Arusha Ngorongoro road is just before Mto wa Mbu. The drive from Arusha to the lake takes about 6 hours, and is fairly straightforward. From the lake it is possible to drive northwest to Lobo Lodge in the Serengeti through Sonjo and Wasso, or southwest to Ndutu Safari Lodge in the Ngorongoro Crater but you will need a guide, as the tracks are not clear in parts.

Transport

There is a campsite near the southwest corner of the lake, just off the track, beside a river. You will need to take your own tent, food, water and cooking facilities.

Sleeping

This lake is situated on the remote southern border of the Ngorongoro Conservation Area, on the western wall of the Rift Valley.

Lake Eyasi
Colour map 3, grid A3

It has no tourist facilities and is rarely visited. Two ancient tribes inhabit this area. The Hadza people who live near the shore are hunter-gatherers. Nearby there is a village of Datoga pastoral herdsmen. Access to Lake Eyasi is from the Kidatu-Ngorongoro road.

Lake Victoria and Environs

This area is fairly cut off and transport links are poor. The road to Mwanza is in a poor state and the towns along the lake are most easily reached by the ferry. The problems of accessibility were made worse by the closure of the border with Kenya from 1977 to 1983. However now that this has reopened there is more through traffic. Mwanza is a busy town, and there is much activity in exporting fish from Lake Victoria. Bukoba, on the west side of the lake is in a very attractive setting. Haya men from this region are tall, and Haya women have a reputation for great beauty.

Lake Victoria, bordered by Kenya, Tanzania and Uganda, is the largest freshwater lake in Africa and the second largest in the world. Occupying a shallow depression at an altitude of 1,135 metres, it covers 69,490 square kilometres and is one of the chief sources of the Nile.

Musoma

1°50'S 34°30'E
Phone code: 068
Colour map 3, grid A3

This small port with a population of about 65,000 is set on the east shores of Lake Victoria close to the border with Kenya. It is a bustling and friendly town with many visitors who are on their way to or from Kenya. It is also close to the Serengeti National Park and so should be one of the centres for safaris to the park. However because of the border closure and its inaccessibility it has not developed as such (see section on National Parks, page 494). It has a climate of hot days and cool nights.

Sleeping **D** *Musoma*, PO Box 282, T176. Restaurant, 30 minutes walk out of town, on the lake shore. **D** *Stigma Hotel*, Mukendo Rd. Some rooms have ensuite bathroom (shower), prices can be negotiated. **D** *Tembo Beach Hotel*, PO Box 736, T/F622887, hotel town office T622386/622085. Situated at Old Musoma Pier, 1.5 kilometres south of Musoma town, private beach on a peninsular. Variety of accommodation from self contained units to camping, bar and restaurant facilities newly opened with wonderful views of the lake. **E** *Banana Bar Lodge*, central, on Mukendo St, opposite National Commercial Bank. **E** *Bubata Lodge*, on Mukendo St in town centre. Fair. **E** *Embassy Lodge*, town centre. **E** *Mennonite Centre*, some way from the ferry terminal, clean. **E** *Musabura Guest House*, town centre. **E** *Orange Tree*, central. **E** *Sengerema Guest House*, town centre. **E** *Silver Sands Inn*, on Lake shore. Comfortable and good value. **E** *Tema Guest House*, town centre.

Musoma

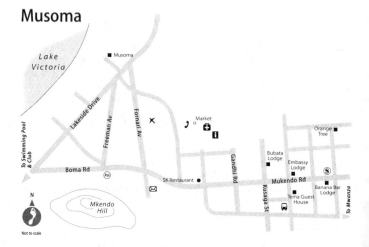

2 *Freepark*. Open air, good atmosphere and excellent value food. 2 *Orange Tree Hotel*. Reasonable. 2 *SK Restaurant*. Indian cuisine, good value.

Air Air Tanzania flights go to Mwanza, see page 407, twice a week, although schedules are subject to cancellations and alterations. Link to Musoma by road. **Train** To Mwanza by road and then please see pages 306/307 for details of train services, timetables and fares. **Road Bus**: Mwanza: the road is reasonable in the dry season, and there are regular buses leaving from the bus station, which is behind Kusaga St in the centre. The trip takes up to 6 hours, and costs US$4. Ask to be dropped off at the Ndabaka Gate, which is 10-15 kilometres south of Bunda on the main road. The gate itself is about 5 minutes walk from the main road. The guards are not very helpful at the gate, and normally will not allow you to wait for a lift there, telling you to go back and get your own transport. It is possible to wait for lifts at the turn off from the main road. Then you have to pay the Park entry fee. The tracks in the park are bad, taking 5 hours to reach the Senonara Wildlife Lodge. Negotiate a price for the lift – around US$8-10. **Arusha**: buses no longer go through the Serengeti and across the top of Lake Manyara Park. Public transport from Musoma to Arusha now goes via Nairobi, Kenya. From Mwanza there is a bus that travels painfully slowly over very difficult roads south of the Serengeti, taking an age to reach Arusha. Road travellers from **Dar es Salaam** say that the quickest road route is to Arusha, then across the border at Namanga to Nairobi, then Nakuru, Kericho, Kisii or Nakuru to Kisumu and back across the border. The roads are good all the way except for the stretch from the border to Musoma. Check if you need a visa to enter Kenya. **Sea Ferry**: the ferry for Kisumu to Mwanza used to stop at Musoma, but this is not now the case.

Mwanza

This is the largest Tanzanian port on Lake Victoria and with a population of 400,000 it is Tanzania's second largest town. It lies on a peninsula that juts into the lake. It is surrounded by rocky hills and the land is dominated by granite outcrops some of which are very impressive and look as if they are about to topple. The road approach is spectacular, tunnelling through some of the great boulders on the route. As the railway terminus and major lake port, Mwanza is a bustling and lively town. The produce from the lake region is gathered here and is then transported to the coast by

2°30'S 32°58'E
Phone code: 068
Colour map 3, grid A2

Lake Victoria region

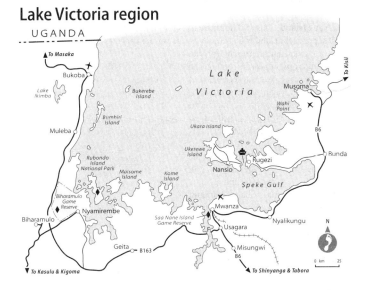

👉 *Early cotton*

Cotton textiles were a key item in European industrialization. By the end of the 19th century USA was the largest producer with 60 percent of world production, followed by India 10 percent and Egypt nine percent.

European manufacturers had to import all their raw cotton, and Germany was aware that it had no colonies or protectorates which could supply the raw material (unlike England, with India and Egypt), and its textile manufacturers were heavily dependent on the USA. The American Civil War and the blockade of Southern ports in 1860-62 reduced cotton exports to Europe by 80 percent, and the price of raw cotton increased tenfold.

Determined to have its own source of supply, the German Colonial Office thought East Africa was the most promising of its territories. A Cotton Commission was set up, a levy was raised from cotton manufacturers in Germany and made available to small African farmers, plantations and settler farmers for developing cotton. Areas chosen bordered the Northern Railway from Tanga, inland from Dar es Salaam to Morogoro, along the Rufiji River, and down the coast to Kilwa. In 1906 an experimental station was opened at Mpanganja on the Rufiji. Free seed was given to African farmers. Ginneries were set up. Mr JHG Becker, a German-American cotton expert from Texas was recruited as Cotton Inspector. First trials began in Zaramo areas near Bagamoyo in 1886 under DOAG, the German East Africa Company (Deutsche Ostafrikanisole Gesellschaft). These suffered set-backs in the Maji-Maji uprising of 1888-90 (see page 530).

Further research stations were set up at Myombo, Kibong`oto, Mabama, Mahiwa and Mwansa, and Agricultural Officers planted one hectare demonstration plots. Trials showed the Abassi variety from Egypt with long, silky pure white fibres did best in local conditions. Problems arose from locust attacks, leaf-curl and ball-worm.

Most success was in Mwanza region where Julius Weigand, a German entrepreneur, distributed seeds free to Africans and bought the crop and nearby Ukerewe Island where the White Fathers did the same. In the period 1890-96 when under Governor Gotzen, compulsory labour (24 days a year) was introduced on communal cotton farms. These areas contribute 80 percent of Tanzania's cotton output today.

the railway. The lake is dotted with islands of varying sizes from the smallest specks, unmarked on maps, to Ukerewe which is heavily populated. Fishing is a major commercial activity is this area, although coffee, tea and cotton are also important.

Sights **Saa Nane Island** This wildlife sanctuary is not far from Mwanza in the lake and has on it hippo, zebra, and wildebeest as well as various caged animals. It is a pleasant place to spend an afternoon with the rocky outcrops appearing out of the grassy landscape. You can get a boat out from Mwanza, leaving the jetty one kilometre south of the centre off Station Rd about five times a day. There is an admission charge of US$0.50. The combined boat and entry fee is about US$1.50. This place gets very busy at the weekends. The boats depart at 1100, 1300, 1400, 1500 and 1600 hours.

Bujora Sukuma Village Museum This is located 15-20 kilometres from Mwanza on the Musoma road. It can be reached by taking a local bus from the bus station near the market in Mwanza to Kisessa and from there walking the remaining one kilometre. The exhibits

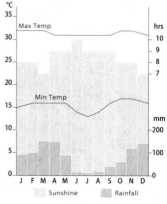

Climate: Mwanza

Bark cloth

Bark cloth is a product of the Lake Victoria region. It has been used in the past as a material for making ceremonial clothes and more recently you see it for sale to tourists as table mats etcetera.

The preparation of the cloth is a long and complex process and making good quality bark cloth is a very real skill. The process begins with the scraping down of the outer bark. It is then slit from top to bottom and a cut made around the top and bottom of the tree trunk. Using a ladder the bark is gradually removed beginning at the bottom and working upwards. It is removed from the entire circumference of the tree trunk so that the piece of bark should be fairly large. It is then rolled up and taken back to the house of the cutter. The next step in the process is to scorch the side of the bark that was closest to the tree. This 'melts' the sap and helps in the softening and stretching processes. The bark is scorched

by laying the bark on the ground and placing dry banana leaves on it. These are set on fire and are very quickly taken off the bark so that it is not burnt too much. The bark is then rolled up in fresh banana leaves to prevent it from drying out and is left overnight.

The next day the process of pounding the bark begins. This is done in two stages using a special beater with ridges on it. As the bark is beaten it gradually gets thinner and wider. The process of stretching the bark is next and is usually undertaken by two or three people. The bark is alternatively beaten and stretched until it is stretched out and fixed with stones and left in the sun to dry. By this stage it is a thin and totally malleable piece of cloth. If it is good quality the bark cloth will be large and of a uniform thickness, however it is common for several pieces to be sewn together and for there to be the odd thin patch.

are of the traditions and culture of the Sukuma who make up the largest tribe in Tanzania. They include a traditional house, shrines, and traditional instruments including a drum collection. It was originally set up by missionaries from Quebec. There are regular traditional dances held there which include the impressive Sukuma snake dance or *Bugobogobo*, usually on a Saturday.

Another place to visit whilst in Mwanza is the **Rubondo National Park** (see section on National Parks, page 523).

Ukerewe, Kome and Maisome Islands These three islands are scenically very pretty, but there is little to attract the tourists. Ukerewe Island to the north of Mwanza can be reached by ferry, taking about three hours, leaving Mwanza at 0900 and Nansio, the main town on Ukerewe at 1330. It is also possible to go by road, east round the lake to Bunda and then west along the north shore of Speke Gulf, crossing by ferry to Ukerewe Island. There are no regular buses on the last leg of this route and it is necessary to hitch. There are some small hotels and a series of cheap restaurants.

Kome and Maisome Islands are served by the ferries to Myamirembe which leave Mwanza on Monday (0800) and Thursday (2100). Kome takes about three hours to reach and Maisome about seven hours. Ferries return from Nyamirembe on Tuesday (0800) and Friday (1900).

Botanical Gardens These were located on the road to Mwanza Airport to the north of the city centre by the lake shore. They have fallen into total disrepair now. However the location is attractive.

Sleeping **B** *New Mwanza*, PO Box 25, T40620, Tx46284, central, on Post St. Restaurant, bar, a/c, pleasant and convenient. **B** *Tilapia*, on lake 1 kilometre to south of town centre. On Station Rd near ferry to Saa Nane Island. Chalet style accommodation, swimming pool, restaurant, pleasant and comfortable.

C *Iko Hotel*. New hotel. **D** *Delux*, PO Box 1471, T2411. Town centre, on corner of Uhuru St and Nkrumah St. Restaurant and lively bars, popular. **D** *Lake*, PO Box 910, T2062. Off Station Rd close to stadium. Restaurant, outdoor bar, noisy and busy, fans, nets, good value.

Tanzania & Zanzibar

E *Geita Guest House*, central position. Basic, communal showers, mosquito nets. **E** *Mlangowa Guest House*. Central, good value. **E** *Pamba Hostel*, on Station Rd near roundabout. Shared facilities, noisy, especially at the weekends, serves a continental breakfast, restaurant, bar. **E** *Sayi Mlekwa Guest House*, PO Box 639, Karuta St. Fan and mosquito nets, friendly, cheap and clean, good local restaurants nearby, close to train station. **E** *Shinyanga*, Lumumba St. Just off centre, rather run down. **east** *Victoria*, on Mitimirefu Rd. Shabby but cheap.

Camping: Available at the **Sukuma Museum**. The **New Blue Campsite**, Capri Point Road, US$1.75 per night.

Eating **2** *Delux Hotel*. Indian food, good value. **2** *Kidepo Grill*, in *New Mwanza Hotel*. Live music at weekends and occasionally other nights. **2** *Lake Hotel*. Varied menu, reasonable value, owner will prepare a special meal if ordered in advance for a group, lacks a bit of atmosphere. **2** *Sitar*, corner of Liberty St and Lumumba St. Indian food, slow service but food excellent, also has Chinese food. **2** *Tilapia*, Station Rd. Near ferry to Saa Mane, nice location overlooking part of lake. Good standard and popular, restaurants inside in the basement and outside on roof, Chinese and Indian food. **1** *Blue Café*, on corner of Post St and Nyerere Rd. Simple but good value. **1** *Nile Café*, off Post St near Nyerere Rd. Straightforward food. **1** *Pizzeria Kuleana*, Post St, near the *New Mwanza Takeaway Service*. Cappuccino US$1, pizza US$2-US$5, ice-cream US$1, excellent value, they support street kids. **1** *Salma Cone*, corner of Barti St and Nkrumah St. Serves coffee, snacks and ice cream.

Shopping There is an excellent supermarket on the site of the previous *U Turn Restaurant*, corner of Nkrumah and Hospital St. This sells frozen meat, toiletries, canned drinks including Diet Coke, English biscuits and chocolate bars, English choc ices, fairly expensive but has an excellent range of products.

Mwanza

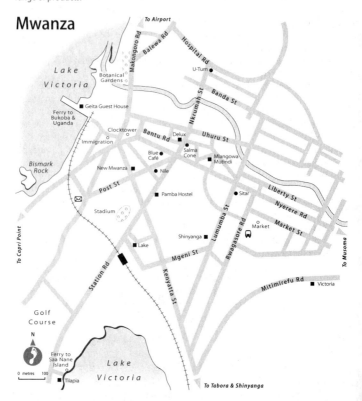

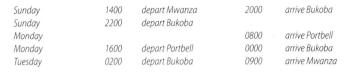

Ferry timetable

Sunday	1400	depart Mwanza	2000	arrive Bukoba
Sunday	2200	depart Bukoba		
Monday			0800	arrive Portbell
Monday	1600	depart Portbell	0000	arrive Bukoba
Tuesday	0200	depart Bukoba	0900	arrive Mwanza

Passenger fares (US$)

Station	First class (shared cabin - 2 people)	Second class (shared cabin - 4 people)	Second sitting	Third class
MZP/PBL	35	30	25	20
BKB/PBL	30	25	20	15

Captain's (owner's) cabin fare (US$)

MZP/PBL	55
BKB/PBL	40

Car: US$80 plus port tax US$5

Air There is an airport at Mwanza served by **Air Tanzania** (Dar es Salaam: PO Box 543, **Transport**
T46643/4/5. ATC Building, Ohio St). There should be at least one flight every week. However it is not uncommon to turn up at the airport with a valid and confirmed ticket and be turned away due to overbooking. Fare is around US$100, but half that for residents.

Train The railway line, built in the 1920s during the British administration was completed in 1928. It forms the extension of the Central Line and was considered vital for the development of the northwest area. Please see pages 306/307 for details of the train services, timetables and fares. The train from Dodoma/Mwanza takes approximately 26 hours and costs US$35 1st class, US$23.50 2nd class sleeping and US$18.50 2nd class sitting.

Road To **Arusha** buses no longer go through the Serengeti and across the top of Lake Manyara Park. However, by taking this Mwanza/Arusha bus (via Shinyanga, Singidi) it saves paying the National Park fees twice. The buses do not run every day. Road travellers from **Dar es Salaam** say that the quickest road route is to Arusha, then across the border at Namanga to Nairobi, then Nakuru, Kericho, Kisii (or Nakuru to Kisumu) and back across the border and south through Musoma. The roads are good all the way and the stretch from the border to Musoma has a brand new highway. Check if you need a visa to enter Kenya. There is at least one bus a day to Kisumu in Kenya, leaving at around 0700. The bus journey from Mwanza to Musoma takes about 4 hours.

Lake Ferry: this is easily the most reliable and comfortable way to travel on to the town of **Bukoba**. Tanzanian Railways have responded constructively to the sinking of the MV Bukoba ferry – their boats are better maintained and no longer overloaded. They have domestic ferries serving destinations within Tanzania. The boats, though old, have recently been refitted. There is a ferry each day (but not Wednesday from Mwanza, not Thursday from Bukoba), leaving at 2100 taking between 8 and 11 hours depending on the ports of call. Fares are US$16, US$13 and US$9. First class provides a berth in a 4 person cabin, second in a 6 person cabin. Earplugs can be a bonus. **Nyamirembe** is served by 2 ferries a week, from Mwanza at 0800 on Monday and 2100 on Thursday and from Nyamirembe at 0800 on Tuesday and 1900 on Friday. The journey takes 10 hours. Its ferries call at **Kome** and **Miasome Islands** and cost US$5 (2nd class) and US$3 (3rd). **Ukerewe Island** has a daily ferry, leaving Mwanza at 0900 and returning around 1300. The trip is 3 hours, and costs US$1.50. There were ferries to and from **Kisumu** in Kenya until the border closed in 1977. Although it reopened in 1983, the ferries have not returned. However there have recently been co-operation initiatives between Kenya and Tanzania, and hopes are high that the ferry will resume.

Services to Port Bell (Kampala) for Uganda have restarted in February 1999 on the MV Victoria. There is a weekly service. In addition, according to the Tourist Information centre near the Parliament building, there are still cargo ships that take passengers, although it is an uncomfortable journey.

Directory **Communications** Post Office: is on Post St. The quickest and cheapest place to send a fax is from the Fax Centre – across the road but close to the post office on Post St. **Hospitals & medical services** *The Bugando hospital* is located on a hill about 1 km out of town and was built in the 1970s with Israeli support. **Tour companies & travel agents** *Fourways Travel Service*, PO Box 990, Mwanza, T2273/2620. Very helpful travel agency, managed by Sharad J Shah. **Useful addresses** Immigration office: is on the road leading off from the clock tower towards the lake.

Bukoba

1°20'S 31°59'E
Phone code: 066
Colour map 3, grid A2

Bukoba is now the main urban area west of the lake, but for several centuries, until Bukoba was established at the end of the 19th century, **Karagwe**, some 100 kilometres inland, was the principal centre. The Bahinda of the interior operated feudal systems where chiefs took tributes from their subjects. The wealth of the area was based on cattle which were raised successfully despite problems with tsetse flies (see box, page 507). Bukoba, set in a bay between lush hills is Tanzania's second largest lake port, with a population of 47,000. However it receives few visitors. It was founded in 1890 by Emin Pasha. It is a lovely part of Tanzania – green and fertile and with a very relaxed way of life. The major food crop here (as in much of the area around the lake) is matoke. This is the green banana which you will see grown everywhere. It is peeled, wrapped in banana leaves and cooked very slowly by steaming. The major commercial crop is coffee which has contributed significantly to the wealth of the area. There is a coffee factory near the jetty. Unfortunately the world price has fallen in recent years with notable effects on the people of this district.

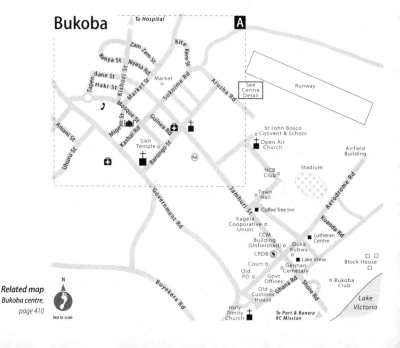

Related map
Bukoba centre,
page 410

The Hen and the Hawk: a Bukoba Fable

Once upon a time a hen and a hawk who were friends lived together in the same hut. One day, during a great famine the hen went off in search of food. She was successful for she met a man who had some bananas. As she was carrying her load home she met the hawk who asked her how she had got the bananas. The hen, standing on one leg and hiding the other in her feathers, replied that she had paid for them with her foot. The hen told the hawk that he must also buy some food with his foot.

The hawk agreed that this was indeed fair and went off in search of some food. He met a man and offered his leg in return for some food. The man agreed, cut off the hawk's leg and then gave him a some food. The hawk had great difficulty walking home with only one leg, trying to balance the load.

When the hawk eventually reached home he saw the hen standing on two legs. He was extremely angry with the hen, saying that although the hen was supposed to be his friend she had cheated him. The hawk told the hen that he could not forgive her and would kill her. The hen replied that he would never succeed in killing her for she would run away. Sure enough the hen ran away and lived with man, while the hawk and all his descendants remain determined to kill the hen and its offspring. This is why the hawk will always try to kill any hen that it sees.

There are quite a few aid projects in this area so a number of expatriate aid workers live here. Huge deposits of nickel and cobalt have been discovered in the area, and there are plans to exploit these.

The Haya people have high educational standards, and, together with the Chagga from around Kilimanjaro, are strongly represented in academic life, government service and business. This feature of Tanzania has been attributed to climate. Both Kilimanjaro and Kagera (West Lake) are at high altitude and are cool, thus proving to be attractive locations for early missionaries from Europe. Both Catholic and Protestant mission activities were particularly strong, and competition between the two groups led to superior educational facilities being offered to attract converts.

Sights Near the lake shore is a group of buildings from the German period – the regional administrative offices, magistrates courts, old post office and *Duka Kubwa*, the first general store in the town. Across the road from the *Lake View Hotel* is a German cemetery. Further west is the area with European housing up in the hills. Beyond the aerodrome runway to the east is Nyamukazi Fishing village. Between **Lake View Hotel** and the lake shore is the former British Club where there was a cricket pitch, a golf course and tennis courts, now called the *Bukoba Club*.

The centre of town has many Asian style buildings, now very shabby.

The **Matos Mesericordia Cathedral** (Roman Catholic) is an extraordinary building, huge scale, spectacular style, now being refurbished.

The **Lutheran Cathedral** is an altogether more modest and practical construction in modern style.

Coffee has long been the economic mainstay of the region and there is a coffee factory at the eastern end of the Kashaj Rd, past the school. There is a second factory on the lake shore by the wharf, south of the administrative centre, and it is usually possible to be shown

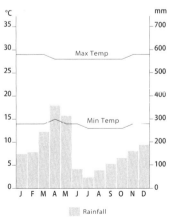

Climate: Bukoba

round. Continuing south in from the wharf is the **Bunena Roman Catholic Mission** buildings with a spire, gardens and a cemetery. The walk from the wharf to Bunena is through some pretty fishing settlements.

Sleeping **D** *Lutheran Centre*, PO Box 98, T20027, F20954. Very comfortable accommodation, simple but excellent food, hot water, a/c. **D** *Coffee Tree Inn*, PO Box 412, town centre. **D** *Lake*, PO Box 66, T176. Beautiful building, rather dilapidated, on the lake shore; **D** *New Banana*, PO Box 311, T20861/92, Zam Zam St, east of the Market. Restaurant, central and well run, outside area with tables, quite popular. **E** *Bunena Mission*, about 5 kilometres from town centre along Shore Rd. Dormitory accommodation. **E** *International Mtiga Guest House*, PO Box 92, Hamugembe area, on Uganda Rd. Has a bar, no frills. **E** *Kahawa Guest House*, PO Box 1263, T578, Arusha Rd. Cheap and reasonable. **E** *Kolping House*, Private Bag, Bunena, T21289, Arusha Rd. Small, very clean, well run, good value. **E** *Kwa Bizi*, on the corner of Nyara Rd and Kashaza. Rather simple. **E** *Lily Villa Guest House*, next door to the Kahawa Guest House, very clean, owner speaks good English. Recommended. **E** *May Day Hotel*, Sokoine Rd. Quite a lively bar, accommodation somewhat rudimentary. **E** *New Highway*, PO Box 1319, T23014, Hamugembe, on Uganda Rd. Basic, but very cheap. **E** *New World*, PO Box 954, T303. Very simple, central location. **E** *Rukindo Guest House*, T21140, Hamugembe, on Uganda Rd. Simple accommodation. **E** *Sukira Guest House*, PO Box 1756, Hamugembe area, on Uganda Rd. Simple and inexpensive **E** *Super Star Guest House*, PO Box 870, Hamugembe, on Uganda Rd. Shared bathrooms. **Camping** possible at the **Lake Hotel**, US$3.50 per person per night.

Eating Reasonable if a bit uninspired. **2** *Coffee Tree Hotel*, adequate. **2** *Lake Hotel*. **2** *New Banana*, food a bit above average. **2** *Rose's Café*, Kashai Rd. Good cheap local food, friendly owner.

Entertainment *Garden Tree Hotel*, disco on Saturday. *Grande View Bar*, disco on Friday and Saturday, US$1, located in Hamugembe, on road to Uganda, about 1 kilometre. *NBC Club*, just to west of Jamhuri St. Disco Friday and Saturday.

Transport **Air** Bukoba is served by **Air Tanzania** (Dar es Salaam: PO Box 543, T46643/4/5. ATC Building, Ohio St) but the usual problems apply of unreliability and overbooking. The fare is

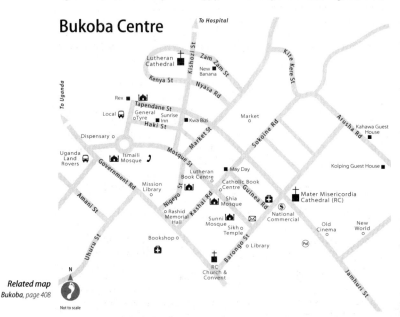

Bukoba Centre

Related map
Bukoba, page 408

Not to scale

roughly US$250 one-way to Dar es Salaam. Most travellers fly to Mwanza (which has more frequent flights) and then take the ferry. **Precision Air**, a relatively new company, fly here twice a week, flights tend to be overbooked but travellers report good service.

Road Land Rovers leave at 0700 for Kampala from near Telecomms at start of Uganda Rd, cost about US$14 and takes 7 hours, booking through Bukoba Machinery and General Supplies, Haki St near bus station, PO Box 82, T20545. There are also Land Rovers waiting at the ferry arrival area, they will take you to the Ugandan border – cost approximately US$2.50. Local buses west to Bugene and Kaisho US$4 and south to Biharamulo US$9.

Lake Ferry: this is easily the most reliable and comfortable way to travel to **Mwanza**. The boats, though old, have recently been refitted. There is a ferry most days (not Wednesday from Mwanza, not Thursday from Bukoba) leaving at between 2000 and 2100 and arriving next morning at around 0800. Fares are US$9, US$6 and US$3. A US$5 port tax may be levied, but it is occasionally possible to negotiate a lower fee. 1st class provides a berth in a 4 person cabin, 2nd in a 6 person cabin. Earplugs can be a boon.

The lake ferry service to Port Bell, Uganda restarted in February 1999. See page 407 for details of timetable and fares.

Karagwe
2° 0s, 31° 0' E

Located inland, this was an important centre until Bukoba came to prominence with the introduction of access by steamer across Lake Victoria to Mwanza and the rail link to the coast. The surrounding area is rich and fertile and cattle thrive particularly well.

In the past two years Karagwe has served as a base for the non-government organizations coping with the exodus of refugees from Rwanda. The refugee camps are to the west of the border, but supplies come through Bukoba and then Karagwe. There are several small hotels charging around US$15 per night. They are very basic, with shared bathrooms and no running water.

Transport Buses from Bukoba take about 4 hours to cover the distance of about 100 kilometres, and cost around US$2.50.

Muleba
2° 0' S, 31° 30' E
Colour map 3, grid A2

Small port about 70 kilometres south of Bukoba, occasionally called Mulemba on older maps. Centre of the collection and dispatch of coffee grown in the surrounding area. The quayside is a grand sight when the lake steamers, en route from Bukoba and Mwanza, are in – bags of charcoal and coffee being loaded, great bunches of bananas piled on deck, joyful reunions at homecomings, tearful partings as scores of relatives and workmates come to bid travellers farewell.

Transport Road Buses from Bukoba take about 2 hours to cover the distance of about 100 kilometres, and cost around US$1.50. **Boat** Lake steamer from Bukoba and Mwanza.

Biharamulo
2° 25' S, 31° 25' E
Colour map 3, grid A2

Continuing south from Mulemba skirting the edge of the Game Reserve (not much wildlife visible from the road) is Biharamulo, a well laid out town which served as an administrative centre during the German period. There are some fine buildings from the German period, and the entrance to the town is through a tree-lined avenue. The **Old Boma** has been restored. At present the town houses government offices, is a market for the surrounding area, and is the nearest town to the Biharamulo Game Reserve (see page 524). Large market, bank, and post office with telephones and fax.

Sleeping E *Sunset Inn*, opposite the bus stand. Spartan rooms with communal bathrooms, serves food all day.

Transport Buses from **Bukoba**, leave when full, usually around 1100, takes about 6 hours to cover about 200 kilometres, and costs around US$5. The road is unsealed and in poor shape. Also buses to **Mwanza**, about 3 hours and US$3.

Tanzania & Zanzibar

Dar es Salaam

Central: Morogoro, Dodoma, Tabora, Kigoma

The central route to Kigoma in the far west passes through a number of different landscapes and vegetational zones. The distance between the towns is large and much of this route is sparsely populated. The major towns which you pass through are Morogoro, Dodoma, and finally Tabora before reaching Kigoma. The central railway line is the focus of this route, and it follows the old slave and caravan trail from the coast to Lake Tanganyika. The road is good only as far as Dodoma, just over a third of the distance to Kigoma.

Chalinze
Colour map 3, grid B5

Chalinze lies 100 kilometres to the west of Dar es Salaam. A small town, essentially a truckstop, the main fuelling centre for travellers to North and South Tanzania out of Dar es Salaam. There are six fuel stations, hundreds of little bars, everyone accommodated for. It is also a big HIV centre. Chalinze is a buzzing place in the evenings, and a good place to break a journey for 30 minutes.

Morogoro

6°50'S 37°40'E
Phone code: 056
Colour map 3, grid B4

Morogoro lies at an altitude 500 metres above sea level and is based at the foot of the Uluguru Mountains which reach a height of 2,138 metres. The mountains provide a spectacular backdrop to the town, and the peaks are often obscured by dramatic, swirling mists. It was here that Smuts was confident he would confront and destroy the forces of von Lettow in the First World War – only to be bitterly disappointed (see page 530).

Morogoro has been particularly unlucky in that the two main enterprises which were expected to provide substantial employment in the area, the Groundnut Plantation at Kongwa on the route to Dodoma (see page 416) and the Morogoro Shoe Factory (state-owned), have been failures.

Central region

The countryside is green and fertile, and large sisal plantations predominate. The town is an important agricultural marketing centre with a population of 120,000, and fruit and vegetables from here are transported the 195 kilometres to Dar es Salaam. The market is probably the largest in the country; it is busy, bustling and worth visiting to soak up the atmosphere. You may well stop here en route to Mikumi National Park which is 100 kilometres further down the road – few visitors seem to stay. It was en route to Morogoro that Edward Sokoine, the Prime Minister, widely expected to be Nyerere's successor, was killed in a road accident in October 1984. The Agricultural University in Morogoro has been named after him.

Sights

The old German **Boma** is situated to the south of the town in the foothills of the Uluguru Mountains, along Boma Rd. The Ulugurus dominate Morogoro, with a range of impressive summits rising over 7,000 feet. The lower slopes are densely cultivated, and the terracing is quite a feature. Higher up it is forested and there are some splintered rock bastions. Further back they rise to over 8,000 feet. The Railway Station is a German building, as are the main buildings of the *Savoy Hotel,* though they are not particularly distinguished.

At the top of Kingalu Rd there is a rock garden, laid out around a mountain stream. It is very pretty, and there is a café.

Further along Boma Rd, well into the Ulugurus is **Morningside**. It is one of the summits above Morogoro and a relatively popular climb. The area is reminiscent of Switzerland with pretty valleys and good fishing in the mountain streams. The villa, with an ornate façade and a verandah, formerly a hotel, is situated just below the forest line. There is a road up and a communications mast at the top. Morningside is almost 10 kilometres from the centre of Morogoro, and it is necessary for Europeans to obtain permission to visit from the District Commissioner's Office on Dar es Salaam Rd just opposite the *Acropole Hotel.*

Excursions

By dala dala one can do a nice three-hour trip to **Mgeta**, located in the Uluguru Mountains. The road leading there is very rough, and you have to walk from time to time, but it offers excellent countryside views. However, it is advisable not to take this trip during the long rains season, as the buses are prone to get stuck.

Mgeta is a small town, people are friendly. There is a pleasant 10 kilometre hike to the village of **Bunduki** through farming area. Bunduki is a hill station, surrounded by eucalyptus trees and has trout fishing. Alternative access is via Mikumi. **Sleeping** *Mgeita Guest House,* centre of Mgeta, 200 metres from the Matutu stop, US$2, rarely has water, mosquito nets, clean, one of two buildings in town with electricity, regular video shows on offer. **Eating** No restaurants, foodstalls offer chips and meat, daily market has fruit, some shops offer soft drinks and tinned food. For longer stays bring your own food from Morogoro.

Sleeping

B *Morogoro* (Bushtrekker Hotels), PO Box 1144, T3270, Tx55100, 1 kilometre from town. Comfortable accommodataion in chalet-style rooms, main buildings were previously thatched, but now the roofing has been replaced with corrugated iron sheeting, restaurant, bar, swimming pool (currently not in service), conference centre.

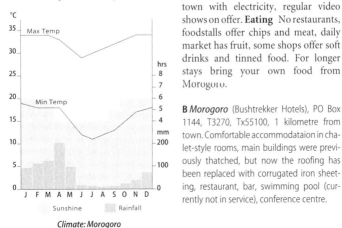

Climate: Morogoro

C *Hilux*, along Dar es Salaam Rd going out of town on the left. Comfortable, pleasant outside beer garden at the back, restaurant, bar. **C** *Savoy*, PO Box 35, T3245, just opposite the Railway Station. This was the former *Banhof Hotel* constructed in the German Period and the scene of an elaborate prank by von Lettow in the First World War (see page 530), it is now rather shabby and run by the government.

D *Acropole*, PO Box 78, Dar es Salaam Rd. Bar, restaurant, family-run. **D** *Kola Hill Hotel*, PO Box 1755, Morogoro, T2872. One of the nicest hotels in rural Tanzania, set on a hill overlooking the city, breathtaking views, well maintained, mosquito nets, hot and cold water, private bathrooms, nice restaurant serving local and international food, exceptional value. Highly recommended. **D** *Masuka Village*, PO Box 1144, T3270, along Boma Rd. New hotel with accommodation in bandas. **D** *Sofia*, just off Madataka St. Good value, comfortable, small pleasant restaurant and bar. **D** *Uluguru Hotel*, PO Box 1557, Morogoro, T4093/3489. A new establishment downtown that is clean, has a nice restaurant and bar, comfortable rooms, mosquito nets, running hot and cold water, TV in the bar.

E *Luna*, corner of Madaraka and Uhuru, reasonable value. **E** *Longido Guest House*, clean quiet guesthouse, communal showers, no hot water, mosquito nets, fans, laundry facilities, none of the staff speak English. **E** *Masinga Hotel*, very clean, communal showers, fan, mosquito nets, friendly staff. **E** Guesthouse opposite the market behind the petrol station, safe parking for cars and motorcycles, clean rooms.

Eating **2** *Mama Pierina*, on Station Rd. Comfortable establishment, menu. **2** *Morogoro Hotel*, has reasonable restaurant if perhaps a bit uninspired. **2** *New Green*, on Uhuru north of Mandaraka. Indian food, good standard. **1** *Asif Restaurant*, on Uhuru north of Mandaraka. Indian food. **1** *Sofia Hotel*, uncomplicated but sound, cosy atmosphere.

Entertainment There are two **cinemas** – Shan and Sapna. A film here is an experience. There is also a **disco** or live band each Saturday at the *Morogoro Hotel*, and a disco at the *Luna Hotel*. The *Hilux Hotel* shows **videos** in the garden bar.

Morogoro

Harvest Dance of the Turu

The Turu are found in central Tanzania and each year put on a dance which is one of the most colourful and elaborate of all dances in East Africa. The dance is held to celebrate the gathering of the harvest and usually lasts about three weeks. The men and youths paint their faces and bodies and wear elaborate head-dresses. The women play only a minor role in the dance and they do not dress themselves especially for it, wearing only their normal clothes.

It is only the men and youths who actually partake in the dancing. They gather into small groups and there is competition between the groups for the best performance. A group of about a dozen individuals stand shoulder-to-shoulder facing in the same direction. To begin with there is comparatively little movement – just a slow and rhythmic rising on their toes and contortions of the body. They all hold bows or staves which they strike together in unison. The dance gradually builds up in intensity. At various stages of the dance groups of women and girls (about the same number as the corresponding group of men and youths) line up opposite the men and youths for a few minutes. However they do not stay long before they retire to the sidelines to be spectators throughout the rest of the dance. At intervals leaders of the groups separate themselves from the group and dance alone nearby. These leaders are usually more elaborately dressed and decorated and their dances will usually be of greater intensity that those of the groups.

Shopping There is an excellent German shop in Morogoro, selling pastries, cheese cake and ice cream of international standard. Next door there is a magnificent meat shop, stocking smoked hams and cheeses. These shops are located close to the Cathedral on the Dar es Salaam Rd on either Boma Rd or Mahein St. The building is easily identified as it is an all white multi-storied building. There is an unmade road alongside the Cathedral and both shops are about 50 metres down there on the left. There may be a business connection with the church. They are open from 0930-1200 and 1400-1700 Tuesday to Friday, 0930-1230 Saturday. There is strict adherence to these times and the shops are closed on Sunday and Monday.

Transport **Air** Morogoro has an airstrip, but there are no regular flights.

Train Please see pages 306 and 307 for details of train services, timetables and fares.

Road The 196 kilometre road to Morogoro from Dar es Salaam is tarmac. There are numerous buses making the trip, and the fare is around US$3. Buses leave from several locations – by the *Sofia Hotel* just of Madaraka St, from the bus stand on the corner of Boma and Madaraka, and on the road out of town toward Dar es Salaam. There is a good choice of buses, and it is safest (the road is busy and notorious for accidents) and most comfortable to opt for a large coach rather than a minibus.

At Morogora the road divides north west to Dodoma and south west to Mikumi NP and then on to Iringa.

Mikumi village is about 10 kilometres south of the National Park. There is a lot of transit traffic. It has a number of small cheap hotels. The entrance fee to the National Park is US$10 per 24 hours. It is possible to visit the National Park in the afternoon, sleep overnight in the village and return to the National Park the following morning.

Dodoma

Dodoma, the new capital of Tanzania, has a population of about 100,000. It is a dry, windy, and some say desolate place to choose for a capital, lying at an altitude 1,133 metres above sea level which gives it warm days and cool nights. It is located 512 kilometres west of Dar es Salaam.

Dodoma itself was formerly a small settlement of the semi-pastoral Gogo people. Caravan traders passed through the plateau and it developed into a small trading centre. It owes its growth to the Central Railway as the Germans hoped to take advantage of Dodoma as a trading and commercial centre. During the First World War Dodoma was important as a supply base and transit point. In the years after the war, two famines struck the area and an outbreak of rinderpest followed. The British administration were less keen than the Germans to develop Dodoma as the administrative centre, for its only real advantages were its central position and location on the railway line. From 1932 Cape to London flights touched down here and Dodoma received all Dar es Salaam's mail which was then transferred by rail.

As it is located in the very centre of the country, Dodoma has been designated the new capital and some of the Tanzanian government ministries are in the process of moving. As this process continues parts of Dodoma look rather like a giant building site. Besides this, and being the CCM party political headquarters, the most notable things about Dodoma are probably that it is the only wine-producing area in the country. Few tourists stay long here, although as the designated administrative centre the city is becoming fairly important for foreign businesses.

There is a ranch of 33,500 hectares at nearby Kongwa which produces beef and high quality breeding cattle. It was originally a site for the ill-fated Groundnut Scheme (see page 534). A cattle crossbreed was developed here, known as Mpwapwa Sahiwal. However it has not been an enormous success and has been registered as an endangered species.

Dodoma

Wildlife of East and
Southern Africa

"Well, make up your mind", said the Ethiopian, "because I'd hate to go hunting without you, but I must if you insist on looking like a sunflower against a tarred fence."

"I'll take spots, then," said the Leopard; "but don't make 'em too vulgar-big. I wouldn't look like Giraffe – not for ever so."

"I'll make 'em with the tips of my fingers," said the Ethiopian. "There's plenty of black left on my skin still. Stand over!"

Then the Ethiopian put his five fingers close together (there was plenty of black left on his new skin still) and pressed them all over the Leopard, and wherever the five fingers touched they left five little black marks, all close together. You can see them on any leopard's skin you like, Best Beloved. Sometimes the fingers slipped and the marks got a little blurred; but if you look closely at any Leopard now you will see that there are always five spots—off five fat black finger-tips.

"Now you are a beauty!" said the Ethiopian. "You can lie out on the bare ground and look like a heap of pebbles. You can lie on the naked rocks and look like a piece of pudding-stone. You can lie out on a leafy branch and look like sunshine sifting through the leaves; and you can lie right across the centre of a path and look like nothing in particular. Think of that and purr!"

How the Leopard got his spots
Just So Stories, Rudyard Kipling

Wildlife of East and Southern Africa

Text: adapted from original version by Margaret Carswell with additional material from Sebastian Ballard. Photographs: BBC Natural History Unit Picture Library, Bruce Coleman Collection, Tony Stone Images, Gus Malcolm.

Contents

The big nine

It is fortunate that many of the large and spectacular animals of Africa are also, on the whole, fairly common. They are often known as the "Big Five". This term was originally coined by hunters who wanted to take home trophies of their safari. Thus it was, that, in hunting parlance, the Big Five were Elephant, Black Rhino, Buffalo, Lion and Leopard. Nowadays the Hippopotamus is usually considered one of the Big Five for those who shoot with their cameras, whereas the Buffalo is far less of a 'trophy'. Also equally photogenic and worthy of being included are the Zebra, Giraffe and Cheetah. But whether they are the Big Five or the Big Nine, these are the animals that most people come to Africa to see and with the possible exception of the Leopard and the Black Rhino, you have an excellent chance of seeing them all.

■ **Common/Masai Giraffe** *Giraffa camelopardis* (top). Yellowish-buff with patchwork of brownish marks and jagged edges, usually two horns, sometimes three. Found throughout Africa in several differing subspecies. ■ **Reticulated Giraffe** *Giraffa reticulata* (right). Reddish brown coat and a network of distinct, pale, narrow lines. Found from the Tana River, Kenya, north and east into Somalia and Ethiopia. Giraffes found in East Africa have darker coloured legs and their spots are dark and of an irregular shape with a jagged outline. In southern Africa the patches tend to be much larger and have well defined outlines, although giraffes found in the desert margins of Namibia are very pale in colour and less tall – probably due to a poor diet lacking in minerals.
■ **Buffalo** *Syncerus caffer* (above). Were considered by hunters to be the most dangerous of the big game and the most difficult to track and, therefore, the biggest 'trophy'. Generally found on open plains but also at home in dense forest, they occur in most African national parks, but like the elephant, they need a large area to roam in, so they are not usually found in the smaller parks.

■ **Cheetah** *Acinonyx jubatus* (left). Often seen in family groups walking across plains or resting in the shade. The black 'tear' mark is usually obvious through binoculars. Can reach speeds of 90km per hour over short distances. Found in open, semi-arid savannah, never in forested country. Endangered in some parts of Africa but in Namibia there is believed to be the largest free-roaming population left in Africa. More commonly seen than the leopard, they are not as widespread as the lion. ■ **Lion** *Panthera leo* (below). Nearly always seen in a group and found in parks all over East and Southern Africa. ■ **Leopard** *Panthera pardus* (bottom). Found in varied habitats ranging from forest to open savannah. They are generally nocturnal, hunting at night or before the sun comes up to avoid the heat. You may see them resting during the day in the lower branches of trees.

Wildlife of East and Southern Africa

■ **Black Rhinoceros** *Syncerus caffer* (right). Long, hooked upper lip distinguishes it from White Rhino. Prefers dry bush and thorn scrub habitat and in the past they were found in mountain uplands such as the slopes of Mount Kenya. Males usually solitary. Females seen in small groups with their calves (very rarely more than four), sometimes with two generations. Mother always walks in front of offspring, unlike the White Rhino, where the mother walks behind, guiding calf with her horn. The distribution of this animal has been massively reduced by poaching and work continues to save both the Black and the White Rhino from extinction. You might be lucky and see the Black Rhino in: Etosha NP, Namibia; Ngorongoro crater, Tanzania; Masai Mara, Kenya; Kruger, Shamwari and Pilansberg NPs and private reserves like Mala Mala and Londolozi, South Africa.

■ **White Rhinoceros** *Diceros simus* (right). Square muzzle and bulkier than the Black Rhino, they are grazers rather than browsers, hence the different lip. Found in open grassland, they are more sociable and can be seen in groups of five or more. More common in Southern Africa due to a successful breeding programme in Hluhluwe/Umfolozi NP, South Africa. The park now stocks other parks in the region. ■ **Elephant** *Loxodonta africana* (above). Commonly seen, even on short safaris, throughout East and Southern Africa, though they have suffered from the activities of war and from ivory poachers. It is no longer possible to see herds of 500 or more animals but in Southern Africa there are problems of over population and culling programmes have been introduced.

Wildlife of East and Southern Africa

■ **Hippopotamus** *Hippopotamus amphibius* (top). Prefer shallow water, graze at night and have a strong sense of territory, which they protect aggressively. Live in large family groups known as "schools". ■ **Mountain zebra** *Equus zebra zebra* (above). Smallest of the three zebras shown here, with a short mane and broad stripes, it is only found in the western cape region of South Africa on hills and stony mountains. ■ **Common Zebra (Burchell's)** *Equus burchelli* (left). Generally, broad stripes (some with lighter shadow stripes next to the dark ones), which cross the top of the hind leg in unbroken lines. The true species is probably extinct but there are many varying subspecies found in different locations across Africa, including: **Grants** (found in East Africa) **Selous** (Malawi, Zimbabwe and Mozambique) and **Chapman's** (Etosha NP, Namibia, east across Southern Africa to Kruger NP). ■ **Grevy's Zebra** *Equus grevyi*, (bottom left) larger than the Burchell's Zebra, with narrower stripes that meet in star above hind leg, generally found north of the equator. Lives in small herds.

Larger antelopes

On safari the first animals that will be seen are almost certainly antelope, on the plains. Although there are many different species, it is not difficult to distinguish between them. For identification purposes they can be divided into the larger ones which stand about 120 cm or more at the shoulder, and the smaller ones about 90 cm or less.

■ **Common** *Kobus ellipsiprymnus* and **Defassa** *Kobus defassa* **Waterbuck** 122-137cm (right). Very similar with shaggy coats and white marking on buttocks. On the Common variety, this is a clear half ring on rump and round tails; on Defassa, the ring is a filled in solid white area. Both species occur in small herds in grassy areas, often near water. Common found in East and Southern Africa, Defassa only in East.

■ **Nyala** *Tragelaphus angasi* 110cm (above). Slender frame, shaggy, dark brown coat with mauve tinge (males). Horns (male only) single open curve. As the picture shows, the female is a very different chestnut colour. Like dense bush and found close to water. Gather in herds of up to 30 but smaller groups more likely. Found across Zimbabwe and Malawi.
■ **Eland** *Taurotragus oryx* 175-183cm (right). Noticeable dewlap and shortish spiral horns (both sexes). Greyish to fawn, sometimes with rufous tinge and narrow white stripes down side of body. Occurs in groups of up to 30 in both East and Southern Africa in grassy habitats.

■ **Sable antelope** *Hippotragus niger* 140-145cm (left) and **Roan antelope** *Hippotragus equinus* 127-137cm (bottom left). Both similar shape, with ringed horns curving backwards (both sexes), longer in the Sable. Female Sables are reddish brown and can be mistaken for the Roan. Males are very dark with a white underbelly. The Roan has distinct tufts of hair at the tips of its long ears. Found in East and southern Africa (although the Sable is not found naturally in East Africa, there is a small herd in the Shimba Hills game reserve). Sable prefers wooded areas and the Roan is generally only seen near water. Both species live in herds. ■ **Gemsbok** *Oryx gazella* 122cm (below). Unmistakable, with black line down spine and black stripe between coloured body and white underparts. Horns (both sexes) straight, long and look v-shaped (seen face-on). Only found in Southern Africa, in arid, semi-desert country. Beisa Oryx occurs in East Africa.

Wildlife of East and Southern Africa

■ **Greater Kudu** *Tragelaphus strepsiceros* 140-153cm (above). Colour varies from greyish to fawn with several white stripes on sides of the body. Horns long and spreading, with two or three twists (male only). Distinctive thick fringe of hair running from the chin down the neck. Found in fairly thick bush, sometimes in quite dry areas. Usually live in family groups of up to six, but occasionally larger herds of up to about 30. ■ **The Lesser Kudu** *Tragelaphus imberis* 99-102cm is considerably smaller, looks similar but lacks the throat fringe of the bigger animal. Has two conspicuous white patches on underside of neck. Not seen south of Tanzania.

■ **Brindled or Blue Wildebeest** or **Gnu** *Connochaetes tauri- nus* (right)132cm. Often seen grazing with Zebra. Found only in Southern Africa. ■ **The White bearded Wildebeest** *Connochaetes taurinus albojubatus* is generally found between central Tanzania and central Kenya and is distinguished by its white 'beard'.

■ **Hartebeest**, 3 sub-species, (right) and **Topi** (above). In the Hartebeest the horns arise from boney protuberance on the top of head and curve outwards and backwards. **Coke's Hartebeest** *Alcephalus buselaphus* 122cm, also called the **Kongoni** in Kenya, is a drab pale brown with a paler rump. **Lichtenstein's Hartebeest** *Alcephalus lichtensteinii* 127-132cm, is also fawn in general colouration, with a rufous wash over the back, dark marks on the front of the legs and often a dark patch near shoulder. The **Red Hartebeest** *Alcephalus caama* is another subspecies that occurs throughout Southern Africa, although not in Kruger NP. **Topi** *Damaliscus korrigum* 122-127cm. Very rich dark rufous, with dark patches on the tops of the legs and more ordinary looking, lyre-shaped horns.

Smaller antelopes

■ **Impala** *Aepyceros melampus* 92-107cm (left). Bright rufous in colour with a white abdomen. From behind, white rump with black lines on each side is characteristic. Long lyre-shaped horns (male only). Above the heels of the hind legs is a tuft of thick black bristles (unique to Impala), easy to see as the animal runs. Black mark on the side of abdomen, just in front of the back leg. Found in herds of 15 to 20 in both East and Southern Africa.

Wildlife of East and Southern Africa

■ **Thomson's Gazelle** *Gazella thomsonii*, 64-69cm (left) and **Grant's Gazelle** *Gazella granti* 81-99cm (above). Superficially similar Grant's, the larger of the two, has slightly longer horns (carried by both sexes in both species). Colour of both varies from bright to sandy rufous. Thomson's Gazelle can usually be distinguished by the broad black band along the side between the upperparts and abdomen, but some forms of Grant's also have this dark lateral stripe. Look for the white area on the buttocks which extends above the tail on to the rump in Grant's, but does not extend above the tail in Thomson's. Thomson's occur commonly on plains of Kenya and Tanzania in large herds. Grant's Gazelle occur on rather dry grass plains, in various forms, from Ethiopia and Somalia to Tanzania.

Wildlife of East and Southern Africa

■ **Vaal Rhebuck** *Pelea capreolus* 75cm (right). Sometimes confused with the Mountain Reedbuck where the two species coexist. The Rhebuck has a long, slender neck and a woolly coat and narrow, pointed ears. Brownish grey in colour, its underparts and the tip of its short bushy tail are slightly paler. The horns (male only) are quite distinctive: they are vertical, straight and almost parallel to each other. It lives in family groups of up to 30. They are usually found in mountainous or hilly regions where there are patches of open grasslands. ■ **Springbuck** *Antidorcas marsupialis* or Springbok, 76-84cm (below). The upper part of the body is fawn, and is separated from the white underparts by a dark brown lateral stripe. A distinguishing feature is a reddish brown stripe which runs between the base of the horns and the mouth, passing through the eye. The only gazelle found south of the Zambezi River. You no longer see giant herds, but you will see Springbuck along the roadside as you drive between Cape Town and Bloemfontein in South Africa.

■ **Steenbok** *Raphicerus campestris* 58cm (right). An even, rufous brown colour with clean white underside and white ring around eye. Small dark patch at the tip of the nose and long broad ears. The horns (male only) are slightly longer than the ears: they are sharp, have a smooth surface and curve slightly forward. Generally seen alone, prefers open plains, often found in more arid regions. A slight creature which usually runs off very quickly on being spotted. Common resident throughout Southern Africa, Tanzania and parts of Southern Kenya. ■ **Sharpe's Grysbok** *Raphicerus sharpei* 52cm (bottom). Similar in appearance to the Steenbok, but with a white speckled rufous coat. Nose dark brown, white belly. Horns (male only) are very short and sharp, rising vertically from the forehead. Prefers stony and hilly country, often seen amongst kopjies, could be confused with the klipspringer. Lives alone except during the breeding season. Often seen under low bushes, which they browse upon, looking for new shoots and any small fruits. Limited distribution in East Africa, but common along the mountainous areas of the rift valley. In South Africa you are likely to see the **Cape Grysbok**.

■ **Oribi** *Ourebia ourebi* 61cm (left). Slender and delicate looking with a longish neck, sandy to brownish fawn coat. Oval-shaped ears, short, straight horns with a few rings at their base (male only). Like the Reedbuck it has a patch of bare skin just below each ear. Live in small groups or as a pair. Never far from water. Found in East and Southern Africa. ■ **Kirk's Dikdik**, *Rhynchotragus kirkii* 36-41cm (below). So small it cannot be mistaken, it is greyish brown, often washed with rufous. Legs are thin and stick-like. Slightly elongated snout and a conspicuous tuft of hair on the top of the head. Straight, small horns (male only). Found in bush country, singly or in pairs, East Africa only.

Wildlife of East and Southern Africa

■ **Bohor Reedbuck** *Redunca redunca* 71-76cm (above). Horns (males only) sharply hooked forwards at the tip, distinguishing them from the Oribi (top). Reddish fawn with white underparts and short bushy tail. Live in pairs or small family groups, in East and Southern Africa. Often seen with Oribi, in bushed grassland and always near water. ■ **Suni** *Nesotragus moschatus* 37cm (left). Dark chestnut to grey fawn in colour with slight speckles along the back. Head and neck slightly paler with a white throat. Distinct bushy tail with a white tip. Longish horns (male only), thick, ribbed and sloping back. One of the smallest antelope, they live alone and prefer dense bush cover and reed beds in East and Southern Africa.

Wildlife of East and Southern Africa

■ **Gerenuk** *Litocranius walleri* 90-105cm (right). Disinct long neck, often stands on hind legs to browse from thorn bushes. Likes arid, semi-desert conditions. Only found in Kenya and possibly Uganda.
■ **Bushbuck** *Tragelaphus scriptus* 76-92cm (below). Shaggy coat with variable pattern of white spots and stripes on the side and back and 2 white, crescent-shaped marks on front of neck. Short horns (male only) slightly spiral. High rump gives characteristic crouch. White underside of tail is noticeable when running. Occurs in thick bush, especially near water. Either seen in pairs or singly in East and Southern Africa.
■ **Klipspringer** *Oreotragus oreotragus* 56cm (bottom right). Brownish-yellow with grey speckles. White chin and underparts, short tail. Distinctive, blunt hoof tips. Short horns (male only). Likes dry, stony hills and mountains. Found only in Southern Africa.

■ **Common (Grimm's) Duiker** *Sylvicapra grimmia* 58cm (above). Grey fawn colour with darker rump and pale colour on the underside. Dark muzzle. Prominent ears divided by straight, upright, narrow pointed horns. This particular species is the only duiker found in open grasslands. The duiker is more commonly associated with a forested environment. Common throughout Southern and East Africa, but difficult to see – it is shy and will quickly disappear into the bush.

Other mammals

Although the antelopes are undoubtedly the most numerous animals to be seen on the plains, there are many other fascinating mammals worth keeing an eye out for. The following are some of the more common mammals that you may see in East and Southern Africa.

■ **Warthog** *Phacochoerus aethiopicus* (left). Almost hairless and grey with a very large head, tusks and wart-like growths on face. Frequently occurs in family parties and when startled will run at speed with their tails held straight up in the air. Often seen near water caking themselves in the thick mud which helps to keep them both cool and free of ticks and flies. Found in both East and southern Africa.

Wildlife of East and Southern Africa

■ **African Wild Dog** or **Hunting Dog** *Lycaon pictus* (above). Easy to identify since they have all the features of a large mongrel dog: a large head and slender body. Their coat is a mixed pattern of dark shapes and white and yellow patches, no two dogs are quite alike. Very rarely seen, they are seriously threatened with extinction. Found on the open plains around dead animals, but not a scavenger. They are in fact very effective hunters, frequently working in packs. ■ **Dassie** (left, above Rock hyrax, left below Tree hyrax) *Dendrohyrax arboreus*. There are three main groups of this small, guinea-pig-like rodent: the rock hyrax, the yellow spotted hyrax and the tree hyrax. Tree hyraxes are nocturnal and feed in trees at night. They have longer fur than the rock hyrax. The rock hyrax, also nocturnal, lives in colonies amongst boulders and on rocky hillsides, protecting themselves from predators like eagle, caracal and leopard by darting into the rock crevices if alarmed. Found only in Southern Africa.

■ **Bat-eared fox** *Otocyon megalotis* (right). Distinctive large ears (used for listening for prey underneath the surface of the ground) and very short snout are unmistakeable. Greyish-brown coat with black markings on legs, ears and face. They are mainly nocturnal, but can be seen lying in the sun near their burrows during the day. Found in East and southern Africa.

■ **Civet** *Viverra civetta* (right). Yellowish-grey coarse coat with black and white markings and black rings around eyes. Nocturnal animal rarely seen and quite shy. Found in woody areas or thick bush. ■ **Black-backed Jackal** *Canis mesomelas* 45cm (bottom). Foxy reddish fawn in colour with a noticeable black area on its back. This black part is sprinkled with a silvery white which can make the back look silver in some lights. Often seen near a lion kill, they are timid creatures which can be seen by day or night.

■ **Serval** *Felis serval* 50cm (left). Narrow frame and long legs, with a small head and disproportionately large ears. Similar colouring to a cheetah, but the spots are more spread out. Generally nocturnal, they are sometimes seen in bushy areas, near rivers or marshes. Found in both East and Southern Africa. ■ **Spotted Hyena** *Crocuta crocuta* 69-91cm (below). ■ **Brown Hyena** *Hyaena brunnea* (opposite page, centre). High shoulders and low back give characteristic appearance. Spotted variety is larger, brownish with dark spots, a large head and rounded ears. The brown hyena, slightly smaller, has pointed ears and a shaggy coat, more noctural. Found in both East and Southern Africa.

Wildlife of East and Southern Africa

■ **Caracal** *Felis caracal* (left). Also known as the African lynx, it is twice the weight of a domestic cat, with reddish sandy colour fur and paler underparts. Distinctive black stripe from eye to nose and tufts on ears. Generally nocturnal and with similar habits to the leopard. They are not commonly seen, but are found in hilly country, sometimes in trees, in both East and Southern Africa.

Apes

Baboons

◼ **Chacma** *Papio ursinus* (top). Adult male slender and can weigh 40kg. General colour is a brownish grey, with lighter undersides. Usually seen in trees, but rocks can provide sufficient protection from predators. Occur in large family troops, have a reputation for being aggressive where they have become used to man's presence. Found in East and Southern Africa. ◼ **Hamadryas** *Papio hamadryas* (right). Very different from the other two species, the male being mainly ashy grey with a massive cape-like mane. The face and buttocks are bright pink, and the tail does not appear broken. Females lack the mane and are brownish in colour. ◼ **Olive Baboon** *Papio anubis* (top, opposite page). A large, heavily built animal, olive brown or greyish in colour. Adult males have a well-developed mane. In the eastern part of Kenya and Tanzania, including the coast, the Olive Baboon is replaced by the Yellow Baboon *Papio cynocephalus*, smaller and lighter, with longer legs and almost no mane in adult males. The tail in both species looks as if it is broken and hangs down in a loop.

■ **Vervet** or **Green Monkey** *Cercopithicus mitis* (above). Appearance varies, most commonly has a black face framed with white across the forehead and cheeks. General colour is greyish tinged with a varying amount of yellow. Feet, hands and tip of tail are black. They live in savannah and woodlands but have proved to be highly adaptable. You might think the Vervet Monkey cute: it is not, it is vermin and in many places treated as such. They can do widespread damage to orchards and other crops. On no account encourage these creatures, they can make off with your whole picnic, including the beers, in a matter of seconds. Found in East and Southern Africa. ■ **Chimpanzee** *Pan troglodytes* (left) and the **Gorilla** *Gorilla gorilla* (centre, page 16) are not animals you will see casually in passing, you have to go and look for them. They occur only in the forests in the west of the region in Uganda, Rwanda and Zaire. In addition there are some Chimpanzee in western Tanzania.

Wildlife of East and Southern Africa

Reptiles

◼ **Blue-headed Agama** *Agama atricollis* (opposite page, top) and **Orange-headed Agama** *Agama agama* (right) up to 20cms long. Only the males have the brightly coloured head and tail. They run along walls and rocks and are frequently seen doing 'press-ups'. You will notice them around your lodge or camp site. They make lovely photos, but are not easy to approach. The Blue-headed is the most common and more widespread of the two.

◼ **Monitor lizard** *Varanus niloticus* (centre and right) up to 200cm long, about half this being tail. Greyish brown in colour, with lighter markings. It stands fairly high on its legs and constantly flickers its tongue. It is fairly common and you have a good chance of seeing one, especially near water. Found in both East and Southern Africa.
◼ **Crocodile** *Crocodilus niloticus* (above, hatchling). Particularly common on the Nile in Uganda, but also occurs elsewhere in East and Southern Africa. Though you might expect to find it in Lakes Edward and George, it does not occur here, but is plentiful in the other large nearby lake – Lake Albert.

■ **Green Chameleon** *Chamaeleo gracilis* (below). Well-known and colourful reptiles, there are several species of Chameleon, but this is the most common and is fairly widespread. ■ **Tree Frogs** *Hylidae*, (bottom). There are many different sorts of tree frog. They are all small amphibians which are not often seen, but occasionally one can be found half way up a door post or window frame which it has mistaken for a tree. They are usually bright green or yellow, often with pretty markings.

Wildlife of East and Southern Africa

Water and waterside birds

Wildlife of East and Southern Africa

Africa is one of the richest bird areas in the world and you could spot over 100 species in a single day. The birds shown here are the common ones and with a little careful observation can all be identified, even though they may appear totally strange and exotic. To make identification easier, they have been grouped by habitat. Unless otherwise stated, they occur both in East and Southern Africa.

■ **Greater Flamingo** (96) *Phoenicopterus ruber* 142cms (right). The larger and paler bird of the two species found in Africa has a pink bill with a black tip. ■ **Lesser Flamingo** (97) *Phoenicopterus minor* 101cms, deeper pink all over and has a deep carmine bill with a black tip. Both occur in large numbers in the soda lakes of western Kenya.

■ **Hammerkop** (81) *Scopus umbretta* 58cms (top left). Dull brown in colour with a stout, moderately long bill. Distinctive large crest which projects straight backwards and is said to look like a hammer. A solitary bird usually seen on the ground near water – even roadside puddles. Builds an enormous nest in trees, large and strong enough to support the weight of a man. ■ **Pied Kingkisher** (428) *Ceryle rudis* 25cms (above). The only black and white kingfisher. Common all round the large lakes and also turns up at quite small bodies of water. Hovers over the water before plunging in to capture its prey. ■ **Blacksmith Plover** (258) *Vanellus armatus* 30 cms (right). Strongly contrasting black, white and grey plumage. White crown, red eye, black legs. Common resident found around the margins of lakes, both freshwater and alkaline, also close to rivers and cultivated lands. Distinct, high-pitched call which it utters when it that feels its nest or young are threatened.

■ **NB** The number in brackets after the birds' names refers to the species' 'Roberts' number, which is used for identification purposes in Southern Africa. This code is not used in East Africa, but it can still help in cases where the same species has a different local name.

■ **Fish Eagle** (148) *Haliaeetus vocifer* 76cms (left). This magnificent bird has a very distinctive colour pattern. It often perches on the tops of trees, where its dazzling white head and chest are easily seen. In flight this white and the white tail contrast with the black wings. It has a wild yelping call which is usually uttered in flight. Watch the bird throwing back its head as it calls. ■ **Goliath Heron** (64) *Ardea goliath* 144cms (below). Usually seen singly on mud banks and shores, both inland and on the coast. Its very large size is enough to distinguish it, but the smaller **Purple Heron** (65) *Ardea purpurea* 80cms, which frequents similar habitat and is also widespread, may be mistaken for it at a distance. If in doubt, the colour on the top of the head (rufous in the Goliath and black in the Purple) will clinch it.

■ **African Jacana** (240) *Actophilornis africana* 25cms (left). This is a mainly chestnut bird, almost invariably seen walking on floating leaves. Its toes are greatly elongated to allow it to do this. Its legs dangle down distinctively when in flight. Found in quiet backwaters with lily pads and other floating vegetation.

Wildlife of East and Southern Africa

■ **Paradise Flycatcher** *Terpsiphone viridis* male 33cm, female 20cm (right). Easily identified by its very long tail and bright chestnut plumage. The head is black and bears a crest. The tail of the female is much shorter, but otherwise the sexes are similar. It is seen in wooded areas, including gardens and is usually in pairs. In certain parts, notably eastern Kenya, its plumage is often white, but it still has the black head. Sometimes birds are seen with partly white and partly chestnut plumage. ■ **Egyptian goose** (102) *Alopochen aegyptiaca* (below) 65cm. Brown to grey-brown plumage. Distinct chestnut patch around the eye and on the centre of the breast; wings appear white in flight. Red/pink legs and feet. This is a common resident found throughout the region except in arid areas. Occurs in small flocks and pairs. Most likely to be seen around the margins of inland waters, lakes, rivers, marshes, pans and cultivated fields.

■ **Crowned Crane** (209) *Balearica pavonina* 100cms (right). It cannot really be mistaken for anything else when seen on the ground. In flight the legs trail behind and the neck is extended, but the head droops down from the vertical. Overhead flocks fly in loose V-shaped formation. Not a water bird, but quite common near Lake Victoria, it also occurs in much of the rest of East Africa as well.

Birds of the open plains

■ **Ground Hornbill** (463) *Bucorvus cafer* 107cm (left). Looks very like a turkey from a distance, but close up it is very distinctive and cannot really be mistaken for anything else. They are very often seen in pairs and the male has bare red skin around the eye and on the throat. In the female this skin is red and blue. Found in open grassland.

Wildlife of East and Southern Africa

■ **Bateleur** (146) *Terathopius ecaudatus* 61cm (above). A magnificent and strange looking eagle. It is rarely seen perched, but is quite commonly seen soaring very high overhead. Its tail is so short that it sometimes appears tailless. This, its buoyant flight and the black and white pattern of its underparts make it easy to identify. ■ **Secretary Bird** (118) *Sagittarius serpentarius* 101cm (left). So called because the long plumes of its crest are supposed to resemble the old time secretaries who carried their quill pens tucked behind their ears. Often seen in pairs hunting for snakes, its main source of food.

■ **Ostrich** (1) *Struthio camelus* 2m (right). Male birds are predominantly black, while the females are usually a dusty dark brown. Found both in national parks and on open farm land. The original wild variety has been interbred with subspecies in order to improve feather quality. In South Africa the region known as the Little Karoo was once the centre of a boom during which millions of birds were kept in captivity. The Ostrich is sometimes seen singly, but also in family groups.

■ **Kori Bustard** (230) *Otis kori* 80cm (top left). Like the Secretary Bird, it quarters the plains looking for snakes. Quite a different shape, however, and can be distinguished by the thick looking grey neck, caused by the loose feathers on its neck. Particularly common in Serengeti National Park and in the Mara. ■ **Red-billed Oxpecker** (772) *Buphagus erythrorhynchus* 18cm (above). Members of the starling family, they associate with game animals and cattle, spending their time clinging to the animals while they hunt for ticks. ■ **Cattle Egret, Forktailed** (71) *Bubulcus ibis* 51cm (right). Follows herds and feeds on the grasshoppers and other insects disturbed by the passing of the animals. Occasionally too, the Cattle Egret will perch on the back of a large animal, but this is quite different from the behaviour of Oxpeckers. Cattle Egrets are long legged and long billed white birds which are most often seen in small flocks. In the breeding season they develop long buff feathers on the head, chest and back.

Woodland birds

■ **Superb Starling** *Spreo superbus* 18cm (left) and **Golden-breasted Starling** *Cosmopsarus regius* 32cms (below). Both are common, but the Superb Starling is the more widespread and is seen near habitation as well as in thorn bush country. Tsavo East is probably the best place to see the Golden-breasted Starling. Look out for the long tail of the Golden-breasted Starling, and the white under tail and white breast band of the Superb Starling. Both are usually seen hopping about on the ground.

Wildlife of East and Southern Africa

■ **Little bee-eater** (444) *Merops pusillus* 16cm (above). Bright green with a yellow throat, conspicuous black eye stripe and black tip to a square tail, lacks the elongated tail feathers found in many other species of bee-eater. Solitary by day, but at night often seen bunched in a row. Favours open woodlands, streams and areas where there are scattered bushes which can act as perches. Look out for Carmine bee-eater colonies in sandbanks along rivers. This beautiful bird is an intra-African migrant. ■ **Drongo** (541) *Dicrurus adsimilis* 24cm (left). An all black bird. It is easily identified by its forked tail, which is 'fish-tailed' at the end. Often seen sitting on bare branches, it is usually solitary.

■ **Red Bishop** (824) *Euplectes orix* 13cm (right). Brown wings and tail and noticeable scarlet feathers on its rump. Seen in long grass and cultivated areas, and often, but not invariably, near water. Almost equally brilliant is the **Blackwinged Bishop** *Euplectes hordeaceus* 14cm. Distinguished by black wings and tail and obvious red rump.

■ **Red-cheeked Cordon-bleu** *Uraeginthus benegalus* 13cm (below). Brown back and bright red cheek patches. They are seen in pairs or family parties and the females and young are somewhat duller in colour than the males. They are quite tame and you often see them round the game lodges, particularly in Kenya and parts of Uganda and Tanzania but not in Southern Africa.

■ **Red-billed Hornbill** (458) *Tockus erythrorhynchus* 45cm (above). Blackish-brown back, with a white stripe down between the wings. The wings themselves are spotted with white. The underparts are white and the bill is long, curved and mainly red. Use the tops of thorn trees as observation perches. ■ **White-crowned Shrike** (756) *Eurocephalus rueppelli* 23cm (right). Black wings, tail and eye stripe, brown back. Throat and breast white, with a distinct white crown. Always seen in small parties, making short direct flights from one vantage point to the next. Walks confidently on the ground amongst debris in the dry bush country they tend to favour. Look out for them in 'feeding parties' in acacia woodlands. Similar in appearance to the White-headed Buffalo Weaver *Dinemellia dinemelli* 23cm, though not related.

■ **Helmeted Guinea Fowl** (203) *Numida meleagris* 55cm (left). Slaty grey with white speckles throughout, bare around the head which is blue and red with a distinct horny 'casque' – the helmet. A common resident in most countries, found close to cultivated lands and open grasslands. Highly gregarious, during the day the flocks tend to forage on the ground for food; rarely do they take to flying and even then it is usually only for a short distance. At night the birds roost communally, making a tremendous din when they come together at dusk. Look out for them near water, they tend to approach the source in single file.

■ **Red-billed Francolin** (194) *Francolinus adspersu* 35cm (below). Medium sized brown bird, finely barred all over. Legs and feet red to orange, yellow eye with bare skin around it. This particular species is found throughout central and northern Namibia, Botswana and western Zimbabwe. Other similar species with only minor variations are found throughout East and Southern Africa. An annoying bird which makes itself known at dawn around campsites with a harsh cry that speeds up and then suddenly stops.

■ **D'Arnaud's Barbet** *Trachyphonus darnaudii* 15cm (above). Quite common in the dry bush country. A very spotted bird, dark with pale spots above, and pale with dark spots below. It has rather a long dark tail which is also heavily spotted. Its call and behaviour is very distinctive. A pair will sit facing each other with their tails raised over their backs and wagging from side to side and bob at each other in a duet. All the while they utter a four note call over and over again. "Do-do dee-dok". They look just like a pair of clockwork toys.

■ **Lilac-breasted Roller** (447) *Coracias caudata* 41cm (left). The brilliant blue on its wings, head and underparts is very eye-catching. Its throat and breast are a deep lilac and its tail has two elongated streamers. It is quite common in open bush country and easy to see as it perches on telegraph poles or wires, or on bare branches.

Wildlife of East and Southern Africa

Urban birds

The first birds you will see on arrival in any big city will almost certainly be the large numbers soaring overhead. Early in the morning there are few, but as the temperature rises, more and more can be seen circling high above the buildings. The following (with the possible exception of the Quelea) are often seen in either in towns or near human habitation, although you may see them elsewhere, such as arable farmland, as well.

■ **Black-headed Weaver** *Ploceus cucullatus* 18cm (right). Male has a mainly black head and throat, but the back of the head is chestnut. The underparts are bright yellow and the back and wings mottled black and greenish yellow. When the bird is perched, and seen from behind, the markings on the back form a V-shape. Often builds its colonies in bamboo clumps.

■ **Marabou Stork** (89) *Leptoptilos crumeniferus* 152cm (above, with fish eagle devouring a flamingo). Overhead, its large size, long and noticeable bill and trailing legs make it easy to identify. Although this bird is a stork it behaves like a vulture, in that it lives by scavenging.
■ **Hooded Vulture** (212) *Neophron monachus* 66cm (right). Medium size vulture, dark brown, pink head. This is one of the smallest of the vultures and is unable to compete with other vultures at a carcass. Often solitary, feeding on small scraps of carrion as well as insects and offal.

■ **Red-billed quelea** (821) *Quelea quelea* 13cm (left and below). Similar colour and markings to a common sparrow, black face and a distinct thick red bill. Widespread throughout tropical Africa, a quiet bird when alone or in pairs. Best known for their destructive abilities around harvest time. They gather into flocks of several hundreds of thousands and can wipe out a seed crop in a single day. When they reach plague proportions they are treated as such and destroyed.

Wildlife of East and Southern Africa

■ **Scarlet-chested Sunbird** *Nectarinia senegalensis* 15cm (above). Male is a dark velvety brown colour with scarlet chest. Top of the head and the throat are iridescent green. The tail is short. One member of a large family of birds which are confusingly similar (particularly the females), rather like the weavers. Often perches on overhead wires and in parks and gardens, especially among flowers, allowing you to get a good look at it.
■ **African Pied Wagtail** (711) *Motacilla aguimp* 20cm (left). Black and white with a white band over the eye, black legs. Common where resident throughout the region. Associated with human habitation, sports fields, city parks and drains, also seen on sand bars along river beds. A very tame bird which you may be able to approach in some hotel gardens.

Animal location charts

Wildlife of East and Southern Africa

	Kenya											Tanzania									Uganda			
	Aberdare	Amboseli	Marsabit	Masai Mara	Meru	Mt Kenya	Nairobi	Lake Nakuru	Samburu/Shaba	Shimba	Tsavo	Arusha	Katavi	Kilimanjaro	Lake Manyara	Mikumi/Selous	Ngorongoro Crater	Ruaha/Rungwa	Serengeti	Tarangire	Kidepo Valley	Lake Mburo	Murchison Falls	Queen Elizabeth
Big Nine																								
Lion		•		•	•		•	•	•		•		•		•	•	•	•	•	•	•	•	•	•
Leopard	•	•	•	•	•	•	•		•		•	•	•	•	•	•	•	•	•	•	•	•	•	•
Cheetah		•		•	•	•	•		•		•						•		•	•	•			
Elephant	•	•	•	•	•				•	•	•	•	•	•	•	•	•	•	•	•	•		•	•
Buffalo	•	•	•	•	•	•	•	•	•	•	•	•	•	•	•	•	•	•	•	•	•	•	•	•
Black rhino				•													•							
Zebra		B	G	B	BG	B	B	B	BG		BG	B	B		B	B	B	B	B	B	B	B		
Giraffe		M	R	M	R		M	Ro	R		M	M			M	M	M	M	M	M	Ro		Ro	
Hippo		•		•	•		•	•	•		•	•	•		•	•			•	•			•	•
Larger Antelopes																								
Hartebeest		K		K	K	K					K				K	L	K	L	K	K	J		J	
Gnu		•		•			•								•	•	•		•	•				
Topi				•									•						•				•	•
Waterbuck	C	C		D	C		CD	D	C		C		D		C	C	C	C	CD	C	D	D	D	D
Roan				•									•						•					
Sable																•		•						
Oryx			Bo		Bo						Bo	Fo							Fo	Fo				
Kudu		Gkl	I		I						I	I			Gk		Gkl							
Eland	•	•		•	•		•	•	•		•				•	•	•	•	•	•	•			
Smaller Antelopes																								
Oribi				•	•																	•	•	•
Reedbuck	•	•		•	•		•	•			•				•	•	•	•	•				•	•
Impala	•	•		•	•		•	•	•		•				•	•	•	•	•	•			•	•
Thomson's Gazelle		•		•	•		•	•											•		•			
Grant's Gazelle		•		•	•		•	•	•		•				•	•	•	•	•	•				
Bushbuck	•	•		•	•		•	•	•		•				•	•	•	•	•		•	•	•	•
Dikdik		•		•	•		•	•	•		•				•		•	•	•	•				

B = Burchell's Zebra   G = Grevy's Zebra
M = Masai Giraffe   R = Reticulated Giraffe
Ro = Rothchild's Giraffe   K = Kongoni (Coke's Hartebeest)
J = Jackson's Hartebeest   L = Lichtenstein's Hartebeest
C = Common Waterbuck   D = Defassa Waterbuck
Bo = Beisa Oryx   Fo = Fringe-eared Oryx
Gk = Greater Kudu   I = lesser Kudu

The **Kondoa Irangi Rock Paintings** These are the nearest attraction to Dodoma and are among the finest rock paintings in the world. They can be reached about 180 kilometres down the Great North Rd to Arusha in the Great Rift Valley. The rock paintings are a fine example of ancient art and a further reminder of the existence of ancient man in this part of Africa. The rock shelters were used in the later Stone Age by the Bushmanoid tribes who were mainly hunters. Many of the shelters have fantastic views over the plains for miles around. The paintings vary in quality, size, style and colour. At Kolo where interesting paintings are most accessible, guides may be hired. Other sites worth a visit are Kinyasi, Pahl, Swera and Tumbelo.

Sights

Mount Hanang, sometimes called the forgotten mountain, East Africa's ninth highest, rising some 6,000 feet above the Mangati Plain is accessed off the road from Dodoma to Arusha, southwest of the town of *Babati*, northwest of Singida.

B *Dodoma*, PO Box 239, T20451. Double self-contained rooms, old German Hotel, now extended, close to the Railway Station, bar, a little run down, no hot water, convenient location, very loud disco at the weekends, however the hotel has recently changed management to a private hotel company from Mwanza. **C** *Dodoma Inn*, PO Box 411, Dodoma, T23204/21012.

Sleeping
The town can be very busy when parliament is in session or there is a CCM meeting, and it is wise to book ahead.

D *Nam Hotel*, second best hotel in Dodoma, PO Box 1868, Dodoma, T22255/22263. Comfortable 3-storey hotel, cold running water, private bathroom, mosquito nets and optional TV, clean restaurant serving predominantly European food, bar and restaurant are noisy at weekends, appears safe, good value. **D** *National Vocational Training Centre*, T061-22181, F061-24343. Single and double rooms with bathrooms, recently built Scandinavian style, training centre for chefs and waiters, best place to eat, has a good bar, excellent meeting rooms, fax, phones and photocopiers, own water well and hot water, 15-minute walk from station, next to new Parliament building.

E *Christian Council of Tanzania Guest House*, T21258, past railway station going out of town. Canteen, cold showers, water supply are petrol barrels, refilled every 3-4 days, toilets very off-putting, mosquito nets, extremely basic, food not recommended. **E** *Horombo Malazi Guest House*, central and simple. **E** *Ujiji Guest House*, near the bus station.

All hotels serve meals to non-residents. It might have been expected that the transfer of the seat of government would have seen the emergence of some reasonable restaurants. This doesn't appear to have been the case. Tanzanian's do not eat out extensively, and the diplomatic community has remained in Dar es Salaam. **1** *Ali Baba's Cave* near the Zuzu roundabout at the junction of Fifth St and Tembo Ave. Serves delicious ice cream. Only opens in the late afternoon till evening.

Eating

Climate: Dodoma

NK Disco, Tembo Ave. Good music and there is a room upstairs where you can watch kung-fu movies all night.

Entertainment

Air There is an airport at Dodoma and theoretically there are regular flights by **Air Tanzania** (Dar es Salaam: PO Box 543, T46643/4/5. ATC Building, Ohio St). However cancellations, delays and rescheduling are a real problem. Fare is about US$80 one-way. Now that the National Assembly meets at Dodoma, the flights are often full with VIPs.

Transport

Train Please see pages 306/307 for details of train services, timetables and fares.

Road Bus: buses go to **Arusha** daily theoretically taking 13 hours. However it can take half as much again as the road is poor. They can fill up so it's advisable to book a seat a day in advance. Costs US$8. The road to **Dar es Salaam** is surfaced all the way, however there is a 30-40 kilometre stretch which is badly potholed. Buses go daily, and cost about US$5. The road to Dar es Salaam is good and car journey time is about 6 hours.

Tabora

5°25'S 32°50'E
Phone code: 062
Colour map 3, grid B2

The railway continues along the old caravan trading route reaching Tabora. This town was founded in 1820 by Arab slave traders and is of enormous historical interest. From 1852 Tabora was the Arab's slaving capital ('Kazeh') in Unyanyembe, the Nyamwezi Kingdom (Tanzania's second-largest tribe) with famous chieftains Mirambo and Isike. Ivory and humans were bartered in exchange for guns, beads and cloth. Its heyday was in the 1860s when half a million caravan porters annually passed through the town. Many trade routes converged at Tabora. The Germans realized this and constructed a fort. Isike later fought the Germans here in 1892, and the Germans captured the town in 1893.

The building of Mittelland Bahn (the Central Railway) in 1912 increased the town's importance. It fell to Belgian forces from the Congo after 10 days fighting on 11 September 1916. Tabora was a 'railway town' by the time the British took over. Tabora school 1925 was important for nurturing future leaders including Nyerere. The explorers Burton, Speke, Livingstone and Stanley all used the town as an important base for their journeys into more remote areas. The town has a population of 100,000. It is here that the railway divides, one line going on to Kigoma, the other north to Mwanza. For this reason people often stay a night in order to change trains.

Sights Tabora is dominated by the **Fort** (or Boma) on a hill overlooking the town built by the Germans at the turn of the century. This is southeast of the town centre along Boma Rd at the junction of Boma Rd and School St. Do not take pictures as it is a Military Building.

Tabora

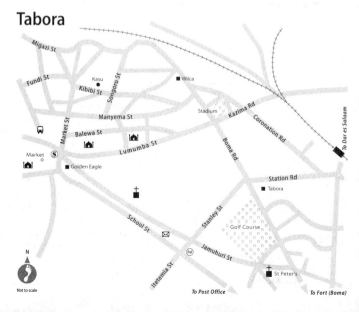

Not to scale

The Miombo woodland of Tanzania

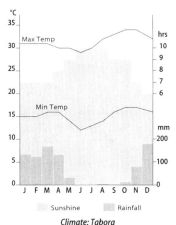

A type of woodland called miombo is found in large parts of the south, central and western part of Tanzania. One of the major towns in the heart of miombo country is Tabora. At a glance these areas appear to be ideally suited for agricultural and other development. However this area is infected with the tsetse fly (see page 507) which is a serious hinderance to settlement and so parts of it are very thinly populated.

If you are visiting miombo country around the rains it is a very colourful sight – all hues of reds, pinks and browns – and plenty of shade. However in the dry season all the leaves fall and bush fires are common. There is little shade and the slate grey bark of the trees seems to shimmer in the heat. One of the most successful economic activities in areas of miombo is the cultivation of tobacco. This has been introduced in the Urambo area and is ideal as tsetse fly make it unsuitable for livestock.

Kwihara Museum   This is probably one of the major attractions of Tabora. It is located about 10 kilometres outside the town and is dedicated to Dr Livingstone. The museum is in the house that Livingstone occupied for about 10 months before setting off on the final leg of the journey in 1872 that was to be his last. He died less than a year later at Chitambo, Zambia. The museum, although run down, is interesting and contains various letters, maps, pictures etc associated with Livingstone as well as other early missionaries and explorers.

Sleeping **B** *Rafiki*, PO Box 310, T2482, town centre. **C** *Tabora* (*Railway Hotel*), PO Box 147, T2172, town centre. Hot water, bar, restaurant. **D** *Golden Eagle*, Songeya Rd, central. Reasonable value. **D** *Wilca*, Boma Rd. Comfortable and well-run. **E** *The Moravian Guest House*, friendly and pleasant. **E** *YMCA*, hostel accommodation, spartan.

Eating **2** *Wilca*, simple menu but food is well prepared. **1** *The Mayor Hotel*, PO Box 1191, Tabora, T3411, behind Market St, behind the National Bank of Commerce. Excellent breakfasts available.

Transport **Air**   There is an airport at Tabora and theoretically there are regular flights by **Air Tanzania** (Dar es Salaam: PO Box 543, T466434/5. ATC Building, Ohio St). Monday and Friday DSM to Tabora, Kigoma and back. Wednesday DSM to Tabora and back. However cancellations, delays and rescheduling are a real problem. Fare is about US$150 one-way.

Train   The Kigoma and Mwanza trains stop at Tabora. Please see pages 306/307 for details of train services, timetables and fares. The railway station is 3 kilometres outside the town. A taxi there costs US$1-2.

Road   There are no direct buses to Mwanza. Take the daily bus to Shinyanga and change buses there for the onward journey, but the roads are poor. Buses to Dodoma are scheduled daily, but a more reliable route is via Ngeza and Singida. There is a twice-weekly bus to Mbeya, taking roughly 24 hours over very poor roads. The road from Tabora west to Kigoma is not feasible in the wet months.

°C / hrs / mm

Max Temp

Min Temp

Sunshine   Rainfall

Climate: Tabora

Tanzania & Zanzibar

Shinyanga

3°45'S 33°27'E
Colour map 3, grid B3

Shinyanga is a large, sprawling town with buildings and roads in poor condition, mostly built in the 1940s and 1950s when the area was thriving on gold, diamonds and cotton. During that time a large number of Europeans lived here and many vets from the UK were employed at a research station involved in eradicating rinderpest.

The region is known for its cattle production and African dew-lapped cows can be seen everywhere. Some gold is found in the area and mined in open-cast pits with the ore broken in large mortar and pestles.

Much cotton grows in the region and is brought to the area's ginneries for processing. Rice is also grown and just outside town are several large circular covered stores where the surplus is kept to be distributed in the event of crop failure. The area has been deforested, the timber being used for firewood and now the region is hot, dry and dusty.

The inhabitants are very friendly and there is no problem walking around, especially in the day time. Education has always been very important in Shinyanga and now there is a large college on the road to Kamborage Stadium. There is a sizeable Indian community and also many Africans of Arab descent, hence the large number of Muslims.

There are no large shops, but a great number of stores selling only a few items, many with a dressmaker and sewing machine outside. Everyday there is a busy market selling just about everything.

Electricity and water supply is unreliable and when there is water (not every day) it is so muddy it has to be filtered as well as boiled. The water treatment works built by the Germans in the mid-1980s is no longer in use.

Shinyanga has a large number of Marabou Storks and during the breeding season these huge birds have nests on most of the Acacia trees in town. During the heat of the day the adult birds shade the young with their vast wings. Kites frequently swoop down to pick something off the road, and Shinyanga has many birds of all types and sizes.

Mosquitoes are a big problem as they breed in the swampy areas where rice is grown. It is essential to take prophylactics and to report to a doctor any unusual symptoms as malaria now seems to take many forms and if untreated can be fatal. This region is known for having drug resistant malaria strains. The poor water leads to a discolouration and pitting of the teeth among local people – use boiled water for teeth cleaning.

Sights **Kamborage Stadium** is where soccer matches are played – football is a very popular pastime in Shinyanga with more pitches in the town.

Further along the road to Mwanza can be seen a large white meat processing factory which has never been used and cattle are still transported live by rail to Dar es Salaam. There is a left turning which takes you through a sisal lined village of thatched mud huts towards a large kopje (a hill) and the remains of a **zoo,** the only inhabitant left is a huge crocodile. The café and bar are now no longer used, but this area makes a most attractive place to walk particularly when the many flamboyant trees are in

Shinyanga

To Mwanza

To Old Shinyanga

Kamborage
Stadium

RC
Church

o Cinema

Market

Butiama

Shinyanga

African Inland
Church

N

0 metres 50

To Nzega

Cotton

Cotton grows well in East Africa and, unlike cereal crops, can survive low rainfall. Planting time varies between countries according to the rains. It is a low shrubby plant with pinky white flowers similar to a dog rose. A few months after planting the buds form – lower buds first. Cotton is often grown by a village co-operative, planting and harvesting is by hand and women, men and children all participate. Buds are harvested and taken to the local village go-downs (warehouses) until enough has been collected for transportation to the ginneries. Lorries can be seen making their way to ginneries, cotton piled high, travel made more hazardous with the rains and many vehicles become stuck in the mud.

The gins remove the seed and waste material to produce lint. The soft lint is then compressed into bales weighing about 180 kilograms. Lint is exported all over the world to make cotton products. There is an incredible amount of seed in proportion to lint. Some seed is saved for planting but most is crushed to produce a crude cooking oil, and the residue, called cake, is used for cattle food.

Ginneries in East Africa have from 12 to 50 'roller' gins. A small but increasing proportion have `saw' gins and these are approximately ten times more efficient, although it is felt the lint can be superior from a roller gin. It is rare for all gins to be working, spares being a problem. The engineering fitters do their best to improvise, with patches on pipes and buckets catching water leaking from the hydraulic press.

flower – here also can be seen small ebony trees, the wood used for cooking before they get much chance to grow.

Beside the zoo is the reservoir serving the region, **Lake Ningwa**, and local lads can often be seen catching small fish. It is also a popular place for migrating waterfowl.

Another 15-20 minutes along the road on the right you come to a turning for **Mwadui Mine**, there is a tree lined road leading up to the compound. In the 1960s it was a flourishing diamond mine with its own hospital, churches, supermarket, and schools, and a considerable number of Europeans were employed. A Dakota flew weekly to Nairobi from the on-site airstrip for shopping trips. The same Dakota still flies to Dar es Salaam and onward to South Africa, with diamonds.

De Beers are refurbishing the mine, but only industrial diamonds are now found. The mine covers a huge area and sometimes it is possible to get a permit to look around. During the mine's heyday there was a **Yacht Club** a few miles away on the other side of the main road, it is still a most attractive red-tiled clubhouse set in lovely shrubbed gardens, but all is now neglected. The small area of water on which the club is located, **Lake Songwa**, no longer has sailing boats.

eaving Shinyanga going south to Nzega, across the railway lines, you shortly come to a brightly painted **Catholic Church** and small hospital on the right. This road has a lot of use with lorries bringing cattle and cotton to Shinyanga station and many heavy vehicles and car transporters travelling onward to Dar es Salaam via Nzega. It is deep sand during the dry season and very sticky with the rains.

Within a few kilometres houses give way to plains and baobab trees, to the left is a vast open area and the smoke of the engine at **Manonga Ginnery** in Chomachankula village can be seen way off in the distance with large blue hazy hills behind. Large eagles can be seen on the plains around here, they feed on some of the many snakes. Further along the main road is a strange sight – an **oasis** with a group of palms which provide Shinyanga with a good supply of dates. The baobabs have a crop of heavy seed pods which the children harvest to sell in the market as they are popular with a taste similar to sherbet.

Further on is a large area used as paddy fields during the rains and often oxen can be seen here working. Away to the left on the plains is the main **gold region** where settlements have sprung up having the atmosphere of gold rush towns.

Tanzania & Zanzibar

Sleeping **B** *Mwoleka*, en suite facilities, it is clean, has quite good food and a locked compound for vehicles. **C** *Shinyanga* is being refurbished and may now be serving food, bedrooms are en suite, noisy as close to railway. **C** *Three Stars*, rooms en suite and passable food, vehicle parking is in the street but beside the railway and so quite noisy. **D** *Butiama*, north of the Post Office. Bar, serves food. **D** *Safari*, fairly central, modest standard.

Eating **2** *Green View Bar*, on road to Mwanza. Serves charcoaled chicken in the evening and is a most attractive place with lots of shrubs, seating is in thatched rondavels, Masoi, the owner, makes patrons welcome, to one side of the road leading to the bar there is a football pitch used by the locals and most evenings the teams of shirts verses no-shirts can be seen playing. **2** *Mama Shitta's Café*, in the centre of town. Serves the best African food to be found anywhere, especially if a booking is made in advance, local dishes cooked over charcoal – beef, roast potatoes with crispy onions, rice, many vegetables, wonderful value, cold sodas are available and the staff will bring back cold beer from the nearby bar.

Transport **Air** A grass airstrip is a few kilometres out of town toward Mwanza. When the cows are shooed off, **Air Tanzania Corporation** makes an occasional landing. More commonly a plane lands to bring missionaries to or from nearby *Kolondoto Hospital* and sometimes it is possible to get a seat to Mwanza or Nairobi. It is also occasionally possible to get a seat on the Mwadui Mine plane to Dar es Salaam.

Train Please see pages 306/307 for details of train services, timetables and fares. The rolling stock is in poor condition, the concertina between carriages long gone and the external doors swing open and shut disconcertingly during journeys. The staff are polite and helpful. Much freight, cotton bales and cows are loaded at Shinyanga Station.

Road Shinyanga is 162 kilometres from Mwanza, but as the roads are so bad in this region most people speak of time taken for a journey and not distance. When the road has been graded Shinyanga/Mwanza can be driven by car in just over 2½ hours but 4 more hours can be added to this time during the rains. There are a great number of buses in every direction daily.

Directory **Hospitals & medical services** On the main Shinyanga/Mwanza road about 20 mins out of town is *Kolondoto Hospital*, run by the African Inland Church. Several American doctors and nurses working here, some for over 30 years. It is the best place to go if taken ill in the region.

Kigoma

4°55'S 29°36'E
Population: 80,000
Altitude: 800m
Phone code: 0695
Colour map 3, grid B1

Kigoma is a small sleepy town on the edge of Lake Tanganyika 1,254 kilometres west of Dar es Salaam. It has one main road that is tree-lined. Most people come here on their way to Burundi or Zambia across the lake on the steamer *MV Liemba* or else on their way to **Gombe Stream National Park** (see Section on National Parks, page 520). The **Railway Station**, the terminal point of the line from Dar es Salaam, has been marked by the German colonialists by a very imposing building. Whilst here, it is well worth making a trip to Ujiji which is 10 kilometres south of Kigoma (see page 426). The major industry is fishing. This is mostly done by night with pressurized paraffin lamps mounted on the rear of

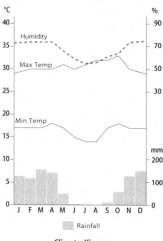

Climate: Kigoma

The graveyard at Kigoma

At the graveyard at the top of the hill at Kigoma there are three gravestones dating back to the late 19th century. The oldest is that of Rev J B Thompson who died at Ujiji on 22 September 1878; the second is that of Rev A W Dodgshun who also died at Ujiji on 3 April 1879; and the third is that of Michel Alexandre de Baize who died on the 12 December of the same year, also in Ujiji. The first two graves are those of two members of the London Missionary Society (LMS) while the third, not actually a missionary, was sent on behalf of the French Government. The LMS, following a donation of £5,000 from a Robert Arthington of Leeds, sent an expedition of four ministers and two laymen to establish a mission on the shores of Lake Tanganyika. The leader of the party was a Rev Roger Price. Dodgshun and Thompson were two of the other ministers.

Thompson had had seven years experience as a missionary in Matabaleland, while Dodgshun was a young man who had only recently left training. Based on his experiences in South Africa, Price decided to try to use bullocks to carry some of the equipment on their journey inland. However this was impossible as none of the animals survived due to the tsetse fly which was rampant in the area. Price then decided to return to the coast to try and persuade the missionary authorities to establish a whole string of mission stations along the road that headed into the interior, instead of heading straight for the lake.

The expedition that continued onto the Lake divided into two with Thompson taking the forward party, and Dodgshun following on behind. The advance party reached Ujiji on 23 August 1878, and Thompson who had been seriously ill during the early part of the journey, again fell ill. He had never really recovered and on 22 September 1878 he died. Meanwhile Dodgshun was having many problems and did not reach Ujiji until 27 March 1879, by which time he was very unwell. He died just one week later.

Michel Alexandre de Baize (known as Abbe De Baize) had gone out to Africa under the auspices of the French government. He was a young man, with no experience of Africa or of exploration. He had been generously equipped with a large sum of money by the French government and had a huge array of supplies and equipment. His provisions included such weird and wonderful things as rockets, fireworks, coats of armour and a barrel organ. He planned to travel across Africa from east to west and set off from Bagamoyo with a small army of about 800 men. However, all sorts of troubles beset him. He was attacked at night, many of his porters deserted which meant that much of his equipment had to be abandoned and many of his supplies were stolen (often by the deserting porters). When he reached Ujiji he apparently became upset that the White Fathers failed to come out to greet him. He is said to have paraded Ujiji firing his revolver. He received assistance from the LMS before setting off for the north shores of Lake Tanganyika. During that stretch of the journey he offended a local chief and set fire to a number of huts and had to be rescued by the LMS at Ugaha. He then fell ill and the LMS again came to his aid. When he was well enough he returned to Ujiji where he again fell ill. He died on 12 December 1879.

The LMS finally abandoned their station at Ujiji in 1884. The graveyard has fallen into disrepair. It is difficult to find. Walk in the direction of Ujiji, after the CCM building turn to the right.

---

the boat over the water to attract the fish. The sight of hundreds of flickering lamps bobbing up and down and reflected in the lake waters is really quite a spectacle. There are a large number of refugee camps close to Kigoma following the unrest in RD Congo and Rwanda. The fishing villages south of the town are very charming and merit a visit (half day walk).

Sleeping **C** *Aqua*, on lake shore. Comfortable and new. **D** *Lake Tanganyika View Hotel* (previously called the *Railway Hotel*), accepts payment in Tsh, T64, overlooking the lake, beautiful views, very clean, 24-hour water, toilet and shower in room, price includes breakfast, has a bar and restaurant, will arrange private boat trips to Gombe Stream or Mahale Mountains National

Tanzania & Zanzibar

Mv Liemba

In 1910, having made rapid progress with the Central Railway line, the Germans began to consider further consolidation of their presence in Central Africa. A ship was ordered in 1913 from the shipbuilders Jos L Meyer at Papenburg on Ems at a cost of 406,000 marks (which was equal to £20,000 at the then current rate of exchange). The cost of transporting the ship and reconstructing it in Tanganyika was a further £16,000.

The first steamer was the Gotzen and in 1913 a second ship was ordered from the same company, called the Rechenberg. In November 1913 the first ship was completed and it then had to be taken apart, packed up and sent in three consignments to Dar es Salaam. From here it was taken by railway to Kigoma where it was put back together again. It was held up in Dar es Salaam for some months while the railway to Kigoma was completed. However in 1914 all the pieces of the Gotzen arrived in Kigoma and it was fitted back together. The first trial runs took place in June 1915 and average speeds of around eight knots were reached.

The steamer was the flagship of the German flotilla on Lake Tanganyika and was used during the First World War as armed transport, particularly to carry troops down the lake from Kigoma to Kasanga (which was then known as Bismarkburg). The Gotzen was the largest ship on the lake at this time and could carry about 900 men in a quarter of the time that it took the dhows to do the same journey. In June 1916 the Gotzen was attacked by Belgian aeroplanes but was not too seriously damaged. In Jul of the same year, when the railway to Kigoma was captured, the Germans decided to scuttle the Gotzen. She was filled with cement and sunk off the mouth of the Malagarasi River.

After the war, when the Belgians were in charge of the lake province, they raised the Gotzen and towed her to moorings at Kigoma harbour. It was not successful and she sank again in deep water. In March 1921 the British took over at Kigoma from the Belgians and the decision was made to attempt once more to raise the vessel. Initially the cost of salvage was estimated at £7,500 but in fact the operation took much longer, and cost much more than had been thought. The final bill for raising, refitting and reconditioning the steamer came to about £50,000. This included the money that the Belgians had spent in their attempt and compared with the German cost of building, transporting and reconstructing the steamer in the first place which came to £36,000.

The ship was to be renamed and various suggestions were put forward. Some examples of suggestions included Livingstone because of his connections with Kigoma, or Kagura which is the name by which Livingstone was known across much of South Africa and which means 'man with a little dog'. The decision that was finally made was to name the steamer Liemba as this was the name by which Lake Tanganyika had originally been known by the people living around it. The vessel was rechristened on 16 May 1927 and in trials held in May the average speed that was maintained was 8.5 knots – not too bad for a ship that had spent from 26 July 1916 to 16 March 1924 at the bottom of the lake and which is still in operation.

Park, nice lakeshore walk road south, past the power station and local prison which resembles a medieval fort, holds a disco on Saturday. **E** *Mwanga Guest House*, PO Box 57, T88, town centre. **F** *Kigoma*, town centre. Spacious rooms, good value, bucket shower, laundry facilities, no mosquito nets, serves reasonable food and has a noisy bar, very basic, suspect mattresses. **F** *Lake View*, town centre. Boasts a working shower and toilet system. **F** *Mapinduzi*, very basic, doubles only.

Eating **3** *Lake Tanganyika View Hotel*, previously called the Railway Hotel, good. **2** *Kigoma Hotel*, adequate, if a little uninspired. **2** *Lake View*, simple but good value meals. **1** *Ally's*, along Ujiji Rd going east. Quite reasonable.

There are a lot of little restaurants opposite the railway station serving cheap local food.

Dr Livingstone

David Livingstone was born on 19 March 1813 in Blantyre in Scotland. He had a strict Scottish upbringing, and his first job was in a factory. He studied during the evenings and at the age of 27 finally qualified as a doctor. In 1840 he joined the London Missionary Society, was ordained in the same year and set off for Africa. On the voyage out he learnt to use quadrants and other navigational and mapping instruments which were to prove vital skills during his exploring of uncharted parts of Africa. In 1841 he arrived in South Africa and journeyed north from the mission in the search for converts. In the first few years as a missionary he gained a reputation as a surveyor and scientist. His first major expedition into the African interior came in 1853 and lasted three years. It was in 1855 that he discovered Victoria Falls. When Livingstone returned to England in 1856 he was greeted as a national hero, was awarded a gold medal from the Royal Geographical Society, and honoured by the City of London, making him a Freeman of the City.

He returned to Africa two years later in 1858 and began his quest for the source of the Nile in 1866. This trip was funded by a grant from the British Government which enabled Livingstone to be better equipped than during his previous expedition. During this journey little was heard of from Livingstone and rumours reached Britain of his apparent death. Henry Morton Morton Stanley, a newspaper reporter for the New York Herald was sent by James Gordon Bennett, his publisher, to find Livingstone. On 1871 Stanley found Livingstone's camp at Ujiji, a small town on the shores of Lake Tanganyika and the famous phrase 'Dr Livingstone, I presume?' was Stanley's greeting. At the time of the meeting Livingstone had run short of supplies, in particular quinine, which was vital in protecting him and his companions from malaria.

Livingstone set out on his last trip from near Tabora in Tanzania and continued his explorations until his death at Chitambo in what is now Zambia. His heart was buried at the spot where he died, his body embalmed and taken by Susi and Chumah, his two servants, to Bagamoyo (see page 352) from where it was shipped back to England. He was buried at Westminster Abbey and a memorial was erected at Chitambo. After Livingstone's death Stanley returned to Africa to complete Livingstone's expeditionary work. He began in Bagamoyo in 1874 and travelled inland reaching Lake Victoria and Lake Tanganyika as well as Uganda and the Congo.

Transport

Air Flights to Kigoma from Dar es Salaam are costly at over US$200 one-way. Theoretically there are regular weekly flights by **Air Tanzania** (Dar es Salaam: PO Box 543, T46643/4/5. ATC Building, Ohio St). However cancellations, delays and rescheduling are common. Air Tanzania run a minibus from their office by the roundabout to the airport.

Train Please see pages 306/307 for details of train services, timetables and fares. The journey from Kigoma to Dar es Salaam is a total of 1,254 kilometres and it takes about 36 hours although it may be worth getting off at Morogoro and doing the last stretch by road, saving a few hours. The difference between 1st and 2nd class is that in 1st class there are only 2 beds in the compartment. In 2nd class there are 6 beds, and men and women are separated unless you book the whole carriage.

It is easy to buy fruit and small meals in the stations along the way. There is also a reasonable restaurant car which offers beef or chicken with rice or chips for US$3, and warm drinks including beer, book ahead if at all possible.

Kigoma

To Gombe Stream National Park

To Mahale Mountains National Park Office

Lake Tanganyika

Not to scale

Local people fear theft on the train, especially at stations. The women frequently lock themselves inside their compartment and don't go out at night. Police ride on the train.

Road There are local buses to Kasulu and Ujiji, but no long distance services. Buses leave from outside the railway station.

Lake Ferry: the ferry on Lake Tanganyika is the *MV Liemba*. The *MV Liemba* leaves at 1600 on Wednesday for Mpulungu (Zambia), arriving there on Friday morning. It stops at lots of small ports on the way. If travelling to Mbeya, and wanting to remain in Tanzania, it may be worth disembarking at Kasanga or at Kipili (journey time 24 hours). The latter may be preferable because you arrrive in daylight. Kigoma-Kipili 1st class US$35, 2nd class US$30, 3rd class US$23; Kigoma-Kasanga 1st class US$47, 2nd class US$40, 3rd class US$31; Kigoma-Mpulunga (Zambia) 1st class US$50, 2nd class US$40, 3rd class US$35; Kigoma-Bujumbura (Burundi) 1st class US$25, 2nd class US$20, 3rd class US$15. Plus US$5 port tax. Journey described by travellers as "quite a hairy affair". The return to Kigoma is at 1600 on Friday, arriving Sunday morning in Kigoma, a 40 hour journey. 3rd class are benches or deck space, 2nd class cabins are small, hot and stuffy with 4 or 6 bunks. 1st class cabins have 2 bunks, a window, fan. Meals and drinks are available on the ferry and are paid for in Tanzanian shillings.

Gombe Stream National Park (see page 520) can only be reached by lake taxis (small boats with an outboard motor) which are hired at Kigoma (ask around for the best price). The journey takes about 3 hours.

Directory **Banks** *National Commercial Bank* is next to the market. **Communications** Post Office: is about 500m to the north of the main roundabout past the Caltex station. **Embassies & consulates** The *Burundi Consulate* is just off the main street and the *RD Congo Consulate* is next door to the police station. **Hospitals & medical services** Hospital: there is a hospital a kilometre or so down the road towards Ujiji. **Useful addresses** Research centre: the Mahale Mountains Wildlife Research Centre has an office in Kigoma where you can ask about transport to the park and accommodation availability there.

Ujiji

This village 10 kilometres south of Kigoma is a small market village with a thriving boat building industry. It used to be the terminus for the old caravan route from the coast. The Arab influence brought inland by the caravans is clear to see. The houses are typical of the coastal Swahili architecture and the population is mainly Muslim. It is however most famous for being the location where the words 'Dr Livingstone, I presume' were spoken by Henry Morton Stanley. The site where this is thought to have occurred is marked by a plaque, between the town and the shore, on Livingstone St. There are also two mango trees that are supposed to have been grafted from the one under which they met.

The post office on Kigoma Rd is a substantial structure dating from the German period. Further south on Kigoma Rd, past the hospital, is the **White Fathers' Mission**.

Sleeping & **E** *Matanda Guest House* is plain and cheap. There are several other small guest houses and
eating eating places on Kigoma Rd between Livingstone St and the Post Office.

Transport **Local Bus**: regular buses to and from Kigoma. The bus station is next to the market on Mnazi Moja St.

South along Lake Tanganyika is a small port named **Kipili**. Just a few kilometres north is a very pretty town called **Kirando**. **E** *Bahama Guest House* on the main road, near the bus stop. Very basic but cheap, no mosquito nets, cheap and tasty food available next door.

To link to the road to Mbeya take a bus to **Sumbawanga**. The buses leave at 0700 and cost around US$8. The roads are poor and it is a very slow journey taking about 24 hours. Plan to stay overnight in Sumbawanga before continuing your journey.

This is a lovely large town with some impressive buildings, in particular, the Roman Catholic church. There is a large market selling second-hand clothes, and a separate market selling a wide range of fruit, vegetables and fish. The town is very clean, with a newly laid tarmac road.

Sumbawanga
Phone code: 0637
Colour map 3, grid C2

Sleeping & eating E *Zanzibar Guest House*, behind the bus station. Clean, communal bath facilities, mosquito nets. *Upendo Inn*. Recommended.

Transport Regular bus service to Mbeya. Be warned of serious competition from ticket sellers – there is room to bargain. Expect to pay around US$5. Buses leave at 0600 and arrive in Mbeya at 1300. In the morning several four-wheel drives leave from the petrol stations for the Zambian border or to Kasanga. The journey takes the best part of the day.

Tanzania & Zanzibar

Ujiji

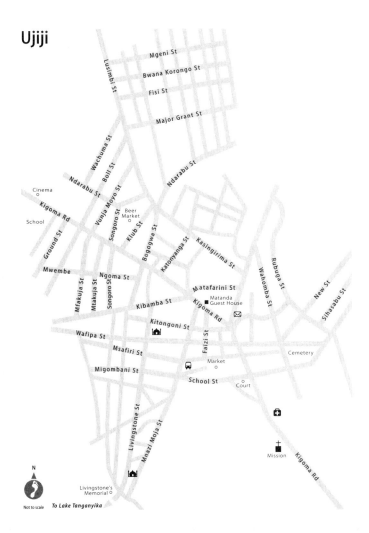

Ujiji to Mbeya

Nuzi & Southwest of Sumbawanga on Lake Tanganyika is a lovely unspoilt village called
Kasanga **Nuzi**, which is surrounded by palm trees. Nuzi has no electricity or piped water but
is very charming. There is only one very basic hotel, bucket shower, no mosquito
nets. However, there are lots of mosquitoes in this area.

Nuzi is a short walk away from the next, larger village of **Kasanga Bismarck** (5
kilometres, sometimes called Kasanga). It is possible to arrange for a local fisherman
to take you by boat from Nuzi to Kasanga. The trip takes about half an hour and costs
about US$1 per person.

Shopping is very expensive in Kasanga. It is difficult to buy mineral water, toilet
paper, fresh fruit and snacks. There are 2-3 local restaurants serving local food – the
fish is cheap and very good. Kasanga has one guest house. If waiting to board the lake
ferry one can visit the nearby ruins of the German Fort Bismarckburg.

Close by, near the border with Zambia, are the **Kalamba** waterfalls which merit a
visit. These falls are said to be the second highest in Africa and there are many crocodiles there.

Tanzania & Zanzibar

Dar es Salam

Southwest: Iringa and Mbeya

The southwest has much to offer in the form of huge untouched areas of great beauty and wildlife and has only recently been 'discovered' by many tourists. The parks in the southwest are increasingly popular particularly with those who want to avoid the tourist trails. The area's isolation is as much a part of its attraction as a problem. The major towns in the southwest are Iringa and Mbeya. Road communications are good, and Mbeya is on the TAZARA railway.

Beyond the Mikumi National Park the road climbs into the Kitonga Hills which are part of the Udzungwa Mountains. It is quite a journey, with sharp bends, and dense forest all around. Part of the road runs alongside the Ruaha River gorge. Eventually the road levels out to the plateau on which Iringa is sited.

The southern highlands of Tanzania form one of the largest blocks of highland within East Africa. They mostly have a high rainfall and because of their altitude are cool. Like the rest of south Tanzania (and unlike the highlands to the north) they have one long wet season and one long dry season. As with most highlands areas in East Africa they are associated with the Rift Valley System and there has been much volcanic activity in the area over the years. It is probably their inaccessibility that is the most notable feature about the southern highlands. Until the construction of the TAZARA railway Mbeya was 650 kilometres from the nearest railway and this meant that development of the area was slow. However the high rainfall and rich soil have meant that this area is agriculturally productive in both food crops and some coffee and tea which are the major cash crops in the area.

Ifakara

Southeast of Iringa. For those with a penchant for getting off the beaten track a visit to this isolated central Tanzanian town is recommended. Ifakara is a verdant, tree dotted old trading station situated close to the Kilombero River in a highly fertile agricultural area. The most important crop of the local Pogoro people is rice and there is thriving trade in this commodity between Ifakara and Dar es Salaam. Tropical hardwoods (from the rainforests north of Ifakara) are also being sent from here to the coast for export. In the town itself there are no obvious sights as such although the Secondary School (built in the 1930s) and Church are quite interesting, as are some of the Indian traders shops along the main street which are mostly constructed after the Second World War.

Colour map 3, grid C4

The countryside surrounding Ifakara is very attractive and being flat is ideal for cycling around (bikes can be hired from the town centre); it is also rich in birdlife. The Kilombero River flows past about six miles to the south of the town. At Kivukoni there is a ferry crossing for the road to Mahenge. There are hippos in the river here and it is possible to arrange a trip in a dug out canoe to see them. North of Ifakara the Udzungwa mountains rise scenically from the Kilombero plain.

Ifakara

To Railway Station (7 km) & Morogoro

Petrol Station

Diamond Guest House
Agip Petrol Station
Market
Bike Hire
Zanzibar
Hood Buses
Furahia
Goa Guest House
Kayuga Guest House
School
Zanil Buses
Bar

To Kivukoni (7 km) & Mahenge

N

0 metres 200

To Malinyi

Tanzania & Zanzibar

Sleeping **E** *Goa Guest House* is the best of the local lodges; a clean, simple double (self-contained). If it is full both the **E** *Diamond Guest House* or the **E** *Kayuga Guest House* are also currently located and similarly priced. Confusingly, there are two Diamond Guest Houses in Ifakara.

Eating The *Furahia Restaurant*, near the market, is the best of a bad bunch – try their baggia and egg chop for breakfast, you'll probably have difficulty finding anything else you'd want to eat at that time of day in Ifakara! It is perhaps advisable to have meals at the Mission (next to the Church) which you can arrange in advance.

Transport The best way to travel to Ifakara from Dar es Salaam is on the ordinary Tazara train, not the international train which arrives at 0100. The station is situated 7 miles north of the town centre. Please see pages 306 and 307 for details of train services, timetables and fares. Buses also go from Kariakoo to Ifakara daily. Leaving Ifakara the trains depart at rather inconvenient times, however, there are several companies running buses. By far the best of these is Zanil's which has daily buses leaving at 1000 for Morogoro and Dar es Salaam. Book a seat on the left hand side for good views of the Udzungwa mountains. For the more adventurous there are also daily bus services to Mahenge and Malinyi (towns to the north and west of Ifakara).

Iringa

7°48'S 35°43'E
Phone code: 064
Colour map 3, grid B4

With a population of 90,000 Iringa is a fair-sized town. At an altitude of 1,635 metres Iringa is 502 kilometres from Dar es Salaam on the main Tanzania-Zambia road beyond the Mukumi National Park. A fertile area, it is an important farming centre and maize, vegetables, fruits and tobacco are grown here. The town itself, set on a plateau, commands a panoramic view over the surrounding countryside. The pleasant climate attracted settlers to the area and German architecture can still be seen in the town. The streets are lined with trees, all planted when Tanzania was German East Africa. The area is of some historical interest for near Iringa, at Kalenga is where

Southwest region

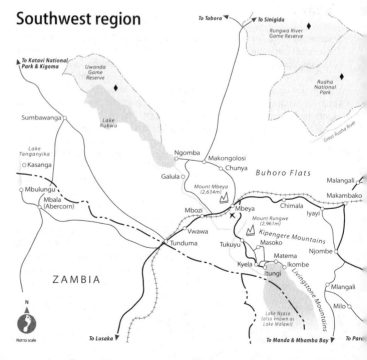

Chief Mkwawa fought off the Germans in an uprising of 1894. He was finally defeated in 1898, but refusing to be captured by the Germans he committed suicide. His head was severed from his body and sent back to Germany. It was finally returned to Tanzania in 1954 and is on display at the small museum at **Kalenga**. This town is within easy reach of Ruaha National Park (see section on National Parks, page 513).

The road from Iringa to Mbeya goes through mixed woodland and savannah as well as cultivated land. Gradually it opens up to more open savannah. There are various roads that you can take off the main road that will lead you into the Usangu Plains. About 25 kilometres from Mbeya on the right hand side of the road is the Mwambalisi River which is fairly spectacular during the rainy season. At about 37 kilometres from Mbeya is the Mlowo River and one of its waterfalls can be seen.

The old **Boma**, the **Town Hall**, the **Hospital** and **Post Office** in the centre of town are an impressive legacy of German colonial architecture.

Isimila Stone Age Site This is considered to be one of the finest stone age sites in **Sights** East Africa. The site was once a shallow lake, now dried up. The tools found there are believed to date from 60,000 years ago. Also amongst the finds were animal bones, including those of two now extinct forms of hippopotami (*H Gorgops*) and giraffe (*Sivatherium*). A small museum was built on the site in 1969 and displays some of the tools, fossils and bones found during excavations. Cost US$2.

Isimila Gully This is upstream from the stone age site and is a spectacular natural phenomenon. Erosion over the millennia has left standing several pillars which tower above you.

Isimila can be reached by buses going to Mbeya, and is about 20 kilometres from town. There is then a walk to the site of about two kilometres. A taxi from Iringa will cost US$20.

To Dodoma

Mikumi National Park

Mikumi

Ruaha

Mazombe

Iringa

Udzungwa Mountains National Park

Kidatu

Idodi

Isimila

Rumili

Ulete

Little Ruaha River

Ifakara

Kibau

TANZAM Railway

Mahenge

Ilonga

Selous Game Reserve

Lukumburu

B4

To Songea, Mbamba Bay & Mtwara

B *The Old Farm House*, Kisolanza Farm, Box **Sleeping** 113, Iringa, F064-2505. Charming old farmhouse with new thatched roofed guest cottages, situated 50 kilometres southwest of Iringa adjacent to the Dar es Salaam-Mbeya Rd, has been the home of the Ghaui family for over 60 years, pleasant climate at an altitude over 1,600 metres, large freshwater dam offers excellent swimming and fishing, nearby golf at Mufindi. A separate site for **campers** and overlanders is available in a secluded area away from the main house. The site has showers, wc, stone built barbecue and plenty of shade. Fresh food, including bread, meat and eggs available from the farm. Very friendly management, beautiful site. Telephone messages can be left via the phone at Iringa Stores, T255-642073. Personal callers can go to the farm. From Iringa (travelling towards Mbeya) pass by Ifunda (on your right), and when you reach Ulete Mission (again on your right) Kisolanza Farm will be found shortly afterwards on the left hand side of the road. **C** *Iringa* (*Railway Hotel*), Box 48, T2039, town centre, comfortable colonial hotel, built by the Germans in anticipation of the arrival of a railway line

Iringa

To Dodoma

Not to scale

which never materialized. **C** *NR Hotel*, off Uhuru Ave, near bus station. Popular with ex-pats and Japanese, excellent restaurant, slow service, chefs cooking recommended. **D** *Isimila*, Box 216, T2605, Uhuru Ave, secure parking. **E** *Akbar*, Store St. Simple, basic. **E** *Cat Hotel*, previously *Hoteli ya Kati*, under new management. Friendly, very basic, on Uhuru Ave, past library, run down, but nice garden. **E** *Iringa Venus*, central. Simple but reasonable value, plumbing unpredictable. **E** *Jawal*, Store St, central, basic. **E** *Lubombwe*, just off Pangani St. Fairly simple. **E** *Taj*, Uhuru St close to Uheme St. Modest but comfortable. **E** *Tembo*, Pangani St. Simple but reasonable.

Eating **2** *Iringa Hotel*, solid fare and reasonable value. **2** *Lantern Restaurant*, pleasant location, sound cuisine. **2** *Taj Hotel*. Recommended. International and Indian food, safe parking for motorcycles. **2** *NR Hotel*, off Uhuru Ave, near bus station. Excellent food when the chef is on duty. **1** *Hasty Tasty*, on Majumbu St. Simple but reasonable. **1** *Hoteli Ya Kati*, good value.

Transport **Road** This really the only feasible mode. Buses from Dar es Salaam leave from the Mnazi Moja bus stand. They take about 8 hours and cost US$9. To Mbeya costs US$3 and takes 3 hours.

Mbeya

8°54'S 33°29'E
Phone code: 065
Colour map 3, grid C3

Population 160,00, altitude 1,737 metres. Set in the lush and fertile part of Tanzania, against the Mbeya Range, this town has a most scenic setting. The town was founded in the late 1920s when the gold mines at Lupa became active, and continued to grow after they shut down in 1956. It has developed into a bustling town and is an ideal base from which to explore the Southern Highlands. It is only 114 kilometres from the Zambian border being the last main station on the Tazara railway before the border and is a popular overnight stop. Because of this location it is an important trading centre. However being 875 kilometres from Dar es Salaam it has been rather isolated until the construction of the railway and the sealed road. The Mbozi area to the south of Mbeya is an important arabic coffee and maize growing area.

Sights **Chunya** is an old gold-mining and tobacco market town 65 kilometres to the north. It is rather inaccessible without your own transport. There are some small guest houses and some faded buildings from its more prosperous era in the interwar period.

The DC's Hat

During the colonial period, a District Commissioner in Mbeya region established the custom of going for a walk at 1700 each evening. As he reached the furthest point from home, he would hang his hat on a tree. The first African to see the hat was obliged to take it immediately to the District Commissioner's residence. This custom was vigorously observed by the locals who feared the District Commissioner would find out that they had ignored the hat and that they were in trouble.

Mbozi Meteorite is a 15 tonne mass, one of the world's largest, southwest of Mbeya, along the road to Zambia, with the turn-off just after Mbowa. It is a good 10 kilometres from the highway.

The **Ngozi Crater Lake**, south of Mbeya, is worth a visit but you will need a guide to get there – see entry on page 436.

Walking This is walking country and you will be able to get some really tremendous views of the surrounding countryside. The mountain to the north of the town is **Kaluwe** (otherwise known as Loleza Peak) and rises to 2,656 metres. It can be reached in about two hours and is well worth it if you have a spare afternoon. Go about 150 metres from the roundabout towards the water works, turning left down a gravel track before you reach them. You will pass a quarry and a few houses before getting to the path that climbs up the mountain where you will find the views merit the fairly steep climb. In the wet season the highland flowers are also impressive. Recent travellers report that there are security concerns for walkers, and that the environs of Mbeya are no longer considered to be safe for tourists unless accompanied by a guide.

Mbeya Peak, rising to 2,809 metres, is the highest peak in the range and looms to the north above the town. There are two possible routes – one a harder climb than the other. The first is down a track about 13 kilometres down the Chunya Rd. From the end of this track the climb will take about one hour, including a walk through eucalyptus forest and high grass. The second, and more difficult climb, is only recommended for those prepared for a steep climb and, in parts, a real scramble. This begins from the coffee farm at Luiji. There is very charming accommodation here at **C** *Utengele Country Resort*. At the top you can catch your breath and admire the view for miles around.

Another worthwhile, but energetic trek is to **Pungulume** (2,230 metres) at the west end of the range. It is approached from the road at its base near Njerenji. Alternatively follow the ridge from Mbeya Peak. This particular trek should be avoided in the wet season.

Probably one of the best viewpoints in the area is known as **World's End**. From here you will see the Usangu Flats and the Rift Valley Escarpment; the view is really quite breathtaking. To get to it go about 20 kilometres down the Chunya Rd to a forest camp and take the track off to the right.

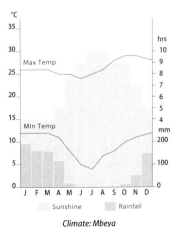

Climate: Mbeya

Sleeping

B *Utengube Country Hotel*, PO Box 139, F065-4007, 90 kilometres from the Zambian border. Restaurant, bar, comfortable rooms.

Tanzania & Zanzibar

Has a swimming pool and tennis court. Under new management since 1997. **C** *Mbeya Peak*, PO Box 822, town centre. **C** *Mkwezulu*, PO Box 995, southwest of centre, on road to Tazara railway. **C** *Mount Livingstone*, PO Box 1401, opposite mosque on Lumumba St, T3331, Tx51175. Noise from disco can be irritating, ask for a room away from it, beautiful gardens and good food. **C** *Rift Valley*, PO Box 1631, T3756, Tx51256, town centre. **C** *Tembo Tourist Resort*, 25 kilometres on the road to Tunduma. **D/E** *The Central Tourist Lodge*, a reddish building on a hill behind the bus stop has excellent (**D**) single rooms and good value (**E**) doubles without toilet, it is extremely convenient for catching the early buses to Dar es Salaam. **E** *Moravian Youth Hostel*, clean and friendly, no food available, intermittent water supply, safe parking for cars and motorcycles, the road leading to the Moravian YH is the haunt of muggers who wait for tourists late at night and early in the morning, you are advised to get a taxi back late at night, and if you are catching an early bus see if you can pay one of the askaris to accompany you to the bus stand. **E** *Warsame Guest House*, central position. Communal showers, no hot water, clean and quiet.

Camping: **E** *Karibuni Centre*, 500 metres off the Tanzam Highway at the Mbalizi Evangelical Church, PO Box 144, T065-3035, F4178. Run by a Swiss Missionary in a forest area, good food, safe car parking, has a small guest house or camping facilities.

Another campground between Mbeya and Iringa is on the main road to Dar approximately 50 kilometres before Iringa. Look for the sign, in an old farmhouse - see entry on page 431.

Eating **2** *PMS Corner Restaurant*, friendly staff, good cheap local food. **2** *Rift Valley Hotel*, lengthy menu, food unmemorable, overpriced. **2** *Scotch Box*, despite its name an Indian Restaurant and bar in the centre of town does reasonable food. **1** *Eddy Coffee Bar*, previously *Tanzania Coffee Shop*, near the market in Sisimba St has very good food, especially the fish. Recommended. Excellent vegetarian fare.

Transport **Air** There are once-weekly flights scheduled into Mbeya, by **Air Tanzania** (Dar es Salaam), PO Box 543, T46643/4/5, ATC Building, Ohio St). However, flights are currently erratic. Fare is about US$150 one-way. Being so close to the Mbeya Range makes for a fairly spectacular, if dramatic, landing.

Mbeya

Not to scale

Train Please see pages 306 and 307 for details of train services, timetables and fares. Trains are often full and booking in advance is essential through the Tanzanian-Zambia Railway Authority (Dar es Salaam: PO Box 2434, T64191, Tx41466). The journey takes about 2 days. The TAZARA rail station is outside the town on the Tanzam highway – the main road linking Dar es Salaam to Zambia. **Warning**: Take great care of your possessions at the railway and bus stations as local thieves target travellers, especially backpackers. Thieves and pickpockets also operate on the minibuses linking the stations.

Road Buses are very regular to **Dar es Salaam**. Fare is around US$15 luxury, US$13 semi-luxury and US$9 ordinary and journey takes about 10-12 hours. The best companies are Fresh ya Shamba (every other day) and Safina. The road goes through the Mikumi National Park (see section on National Parks, page 511). There are two buses a week to Tabora: the road is poor, they take about 24 hours and cost around US$10. There are frequent small buses to the Zambian border at **Tunduma** (US$1.70), or to Kyela close to Lake Nyasa (Lake Malawi) for the Malawi border, both taking about 3-4 hours and costing US$2.50. Few buses or minibuses from Mbeya travel all the way to the Malawi border, but transport is fairly easy to Kyela. Ask to be dropped off at the turn-off to the border before you reach the town of Kyela. From there it is approximately 5 kilometres to the border and you should be able to get a lift. After Tanzanian immigration formalities you cross the bridge over the Songwe river to the Malawi immigration on the other side. It's a friendly border. Your yellow fever card may be checked.

Buses for Morogoro – take the Dar es Salaam bus and get off at the junction outside Morogoro. Takes 8-9 hours and costs US$10. Buses to Songea: there are 3 buses daily costing US$6.50 and taking 6-7 hours. Buses to Njombe leave several times a day, costing US$5 and taking 3-4 hours. Buses to Iringa cost US$5, take 4-5 hours and leave several times a day. Buses to Tundema are frequent, cost US$1.70 and take 1-2 hours.

Banks *National Bank of Commerce*, close to Market Square. **Communications** Post Office: near the Library. **Directory**

Tukuyu

This is a small town about 40 kilometres south of Mbeya, on the road to Lake Nyasa (Lake Malawi). It was an administrative centre for the Germans and there is a group of colonial buildings to the southeast of the town. Tukuyu is a pretty dreary town, on the other hand it has a glorious location in the scenic Poroto mountains. There's nothing to keep you in the town itself but a great deal to see in the surrounding countryside. Tukuyu is an important tea growing area and the

9°17'S 33°35'E
Altitude: 5,300 feet
Phone code: 0658
Colour map 3, gridC3

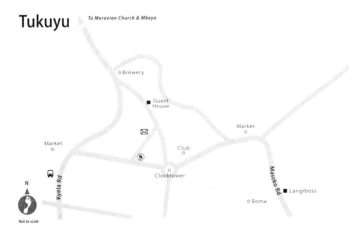

Tukuyu

To Moravian Church & Mbeya

Brewery

Guest House

Market

Market

Club

Kyela Rd

Clocktower

Masoko Rd

Langiboss

Boma

N

Not to scale

(side margin, vertical text) Tanzania & Zanzibar

road to Kyela is lined with the picturesque fields of the mostly foreign owned plantations.

It is a good centre for trekking. It is necessary to engage a guide, and the *Langiboss Hotel* can arrange one. Among the local attractions are **Mount Rungwe**, the most important mountain in this area, which is accessed from Isangole 10 kilometres north of Tukuyu, and it will take at least a full day to climb; **Masoko Crater Lake** 15 kilometres to the southwest; Kapalogwe Falls, south of Tukuyu, the falls are spectacular, around 40 metres high in an attractive lush setting. Half way down there is a cave behind the falls which it is possible to enter. There's good swimming at the bottom in the pool the falls cascade into. To reach them go about six kilometres down the main road towards Kyela to the Ushirika village bus stop. From there it's about two and a half hours to walk or it's possible to hire a bicycle at the main road (with or without rider!). **Ngozi Crater Lake** about 20 kilometres north of Tukuyu in the Poroto Mountains, is a beautiful lake lying in the collapsed crater of an extinct volcano the sides of which plunge down steeply from a rainforest covered rim. To get there catch a dala-dala going to Mbeya up to Mchangani village (this takes 1-1½ hours). It's probably advisable to arrange for a guide at Mchangani to take you up to the lake as the route is by no means obvious. It's a two-hour walk from the main road to Ngozi. The second half of the walk entails a steep climb through rainforest before you emerge at the crater rim. From here the views across the lake are spectacular. You could camp at the top, in which case you would be there for sunset and dawn which would be rather special. **Daraja la Mungu** (Bridge of God), also known as Kiwira Natural Bridge, this is an unusual rock formation spanning a small river close to Tukuyu. To get there take a dala-dala going to Mbeya and get off a Kibwe (12 kilometres north of Tukuyu). Here change to one of the Land Rovers waiting at the beginning of the road branching off to the left (ask for Daraja la Mungu). It's a further 12 kilometres down this rough road. There are apparently also hot springs (maji ya moto) a little further on.

Sleeping　**D** *Langiboss*, about 1 kilometre from the town centre on the road to Masoko. Modest but well run, food available if you order in advance. The *Bombay Restaurant* offers cheaper fare of similar quality.

Transport　**Road Bus**: there are regular buses running from Mbeya to Kyela. To Dar es Salaam the buses come early (around 0500-0600) and cost US$16.50. Journey time around 11 hours.

Kyela

Colour map 3, grid C3　Kyela is a small commercial centre loated in a rich agricultural area to the northwest of Lake Nyasa. The countryside surrounding the town is verdant and fertile, abounding in banana plants, mango trees, maize, bamboo and also rice, which is particularly prized throughout Tanzania, much of it being transported to Dar es Salaam after harvest. Unfortunately the town itself doesn't match its attractive surroundings; it is dusty and characterless and on arrival you'll probably be keen to get out as soon as possible! However, if you're hoping to catch the ferry to Mbamba Bay or Nkhata Bay (in Malawi) at least one night in Kyela is necessary, as this is the access town for the ferries that leave from Itungi. This corner of southwestern Tanzania, south of Mbeya, is home to Nyakyusa, who, along with the Chagga of Kilimanjaro and the Haya of Bukoba region, are one of the country's most prosperous and successful ethnic groups.

Kyela

Biritura Guest House
Kilimanjaro Guest House
Bar
Jafina Bus
Pattaya Central Guest House
Matema Beach Bus
Upete Bus
Market
New Steak Inn
Livingstone Cottage Guest House
Hassan
Buses to Matema, Ipinda
Buses to Tukuyu, Mbeya & border

0 metres 200

To TRC Office & Itungi Port

Fortunately several good guesthouses have recently been built in Kyela, an indication of the **Sleeping**
increased trade and rising prosperity in the area. Best of all is the **D** *Pattaya Central* which
has spotless rooms that, according to the owner, will all have their own television by the time
you read this! The only drawback, TV or not, may be the noise resulting from its central location. **E** *The Bikutuka Guest House* is another good place; cheaper, shared bathroom, quieter
due to its residential location. **E** *The Kilimanjaro Guest House*, close to the market, has clean
rooms and is cheaper still. **E** *Livingstone Cottage* on the road to Mbeya is similar to the
Kilimanjaro Guest House.

The New Steak Inn is a new and surprisingly plush restaurant for a Tanzanian town of this **Eating**
size and does good basic dishes. There is another Arab-run restaurant just down the road
which serves all the Tanzanian regulars and is fine.

Road Bus: to Dar es Salaam, you have to be an early riser to catch a bus going to Dar es **Transport**
Salaam. They leave between 0440-0500 and pick up passengers at Tukuyu and sometimes
Mbeya also. The most reliable (and safe) company is Safina whose fare is US$16.50. **Warn-
ing**: Matema Beach coaches have rather a bad reputation. To **Mbeya**: there are numerous
minibuses going to Mbeya which if you're very lucky will take 3 hours, normally will take 4
hours, and can take up to 6 hours or more. Be prepared! It costs US$2.50. To **Tukuyu**: catch a
bus going to Mbeya. It takes 2-3 hours and costs US$1.20. To **Itungi (for the Nyasa ferry)**:
takes 30 minutes and costs US$0.60. If you're catching the Thursday ferry then you'll need to
get up very early. To **Matema**: very difficult to reach on public transport. See under Matema.
To the border with Malawi: some of the minibuses to Mbeya go via the border. There are
also occasional Land Rovers. It costs US$0.60 and is about 30 minutes away. **Ferry** To Lake
Nyasa, the boats are run by Tanzanian Railways Corporation (TRC). Tickets are best bought on
the afternoon before departure from the TRC building which is located 1 kilometre down the
road to Itungi on the right. A bus leaves the TRC office for Itungi at around 0500. See the timetable under Mbamba Bay.

Matema

The Lutheran Mission guesthouse at this beautifully located lakeside village is justi- *Colour map 3, grid C3*
fiably a favourite amongst expatriate workers in Tanzania. It is situated at the foot of
the Livingstone mountains on a magnificent beach which sweeps around the northern tip of Lake Nyasa.

The Kisi, one of the peoples who make up the population of the surrounding area,
are well known throughout Tanzania for their pottery skills. There is a market to the
south of Matema which can be reached by dug-out and in the centre of Matema village itself large piles of Kisi pots can be seen bound up awaiting transportation to
Mbeya, Iringa and even as far away as Dar es Salaam.

There are supposed to be hippos and crocodiles in the river which flows into the
lake about two miles or so west of the guesthouse. It is a pleasant walk anyway, along
the beach and then returning on a path slightly inland.

Matema

Dug-outs can be hired which take you
across to the far shore where there is
good snorkelling (you need to have your
own equipment). It's not as good as
some spots further south in Malawi
though. Dug-outs can also take you to
the Kisi pottery market. Beach safe for
swimming, reportedly clear of bilharzia.

On the northeastern side of Lake
Nyasa are found the **Livingstone
Mountains**, which are among the most
spectacular in all Tanzania – 5,000 feet
of vertiginous rock, meadows and

waterfalls plunging into the calm waters of Lake Nyasa. The old German mission stations of Milo and Perimiho are a major feature of this area. They were later converted to UMCA stations.

Sleeping There is only the **E** *Lutheran Guest House* which with its superb location and good rooms is all you could ask for, some rooms have up to 5 beds in them and are ideal for families, has good value accommodation in bandas and is well recommended, simple and spotlessly clean. It is possible to camp.

Eating The guesthouse does good breakfasts (which are included in the price of the room) and very reasonable school dinner-type lunches and dinners for US$2.50.

Transport The only way I can account for Matema being so little visited is the difficulty in getting there by public transport. Buses to Matema are painfully slow, uncomfortable and extraordinarily overcrowded. If you are lucky you'll catch a direct bus from Kyela to Matema. The distance is 35 kilometres and it costs US$0.65. If you're not lucky then you'll get a bus to Ipinda and change there (after a considerable wait); if you're unlucky then you might have to spend the night at Ipinda (there's a basic but reasonable guesthouse there) and hope to get a bus on to Matema the following morning. Leaving Matema: however you get to Matema you're going to want to spend a few days there if only to put off the return journey! There are buses leaving daily early in the morning to Kyela, and occasionally to Mbeya via Tukuyu. Alternatively, a fellow guest with their own transport may assist you. Unfortunately the Lake Nyasa Ferry no longer stops at Matema.

Mbamba Bay

11°13'S 34°49'E
Colour map 3, grid C3

This is mainly a transit point for travellers en route for Songea. The route from Songea to Mbamba Bay is very scenic, passing up, down and around the green hills and mountains surrounding Mbinga before descending to Lake Nyasa. The road is bad, however, and the journey is pretty awful in the rainy season. Mbinga has become an important centre for the growing of Arabica coffee.

Mbamba Bay (known in the German colonial period as Sphinxhaven) is a modest village located on a glorious bay surrounded by hills on the eastern shore of Lake Nyasa (to Malawians, Lake Malawi). Most people coming to Mbamba Bay will be here to connect with (or arriving on) the ferries (Swahili = 'ëmeli') going north to Itungi or across the lake to Nkhata Bay and will probably only stay overnight. The scenic surroundings of Mbamba Bay, however, may well entice you into waiting for a later ferry. There's nothing much to do here, but what a setting for doing nothing! If Mbamba Bay was in Malawi the place would be heaving with tourists, as it is you're likely to have the place to yourself.

The magnificent Mohalo Beach, reportedly over 20 kilometres in length, lies 4-5 kilometres south of Mbamba Bay. It can be reached by walking along the road to Mbinga and taking a right at the junction after 1.5 kilometres or so or alternatively by hiring a dug out canoe to take you around the headland (this takes about 45 minutes). It is an ideal place for camping. There is another long beach to the north of the village.

Sleeping **E** *Nema Beach Guest House* is the best place for longer stays but inconvenient for overnights, it is located on its own beach about a mile from the centre of the village.

Mbamba Bay

Maruyu Guest House

Satellite Guest House

Hotel

Government Rest House
TRC Office
Bar

Pier

Nema Guest House

Good snorkelling

Good snorkelling

Lake Nyasa

To Mbinga, Songea
(& Mohalo Beach 3-4 km)

0 metres 100

Sailing schedule for MV Songea

	Arrive		Leave	
Mbamba Bay	Tuesday	0500	Tuesday	1400
Itungi	Wednesday	0900	Thursday	0800
Mbamba Bay	Friday	0500	Friday	1100
Nkhata Bay (Malawi)	Friday	1300	Friday	1800
Mbamba Bay	Friday	2100	Friday	2400
Itungi	Saturday	1700	Monday	0800

Sailing schedule for MV Ilala

	Arrive		Leave	
Mbamba Bay	Tuesday	0430	Tuesday	0730
Nkhata Bay (Malawi)	Tuesday	1100	Tuesday	1300
Monkty Bay (Malawi)	Thursday	0600	Sunday	1130

NB The boats are subject to delays from time to time

E *The Government Rest House*, a signless pink building next to the ferry, has basic self-contained rooms, it has an excellent location on the beach. If you want to stay in the village there are the **E** *Satellite* and the **E** *Mabuyu Guest Houses* which both have clean doubles without toilet/shower.

Eating Limited. There is a simple hotel on the roundabout. The restaurant at the *Nema* isn't bad, but it's inconvenient if you're not staying there.

Transport **Road Bus**: for buses to Songea, see Songea. **Boat** The ferry journey up the lake to Itungi, cruising along the eastern shore of Lake Nyasa with the impressive Livingstone mountains looming at the background. Highly recommended. 1st class cabins are for 2 people and small but comfortable. Try to get a cabin facing the lakeshore for the view. The ship's clerk on board the boat allocates the cabins. In third class you get a wooden bench and plenty of company. Second class seems to have disappeared! Fares for non-residents are US$16 plus US$5 port tax for 1st class and US$6 plus US$5 port tax for 3rd.

Njombe

Njombe

To Songea

Sangamela Annex
Guest House

o Market

Africa Guest
House

Market
o

New Tazama Lwira
o   ■ Ufunguo Guest
Total Petrol   House
Station

New Mpori
Guest House

Mbalache   ■   New Magazeti
Guest House   ■   Highland Green Inn

District
Library
o

N

Ⓢ

0 metres   100

To Chani Hotel

To Mabandaro
& Tranzam

Set amongst attractive green rolling highlands Njombe is another undistinguished Tanzanian town which has a wonderful location. The surrounding hills are excellent walking country and are easily accessible from the town. Being 6,100 feet above sea level the climate here is cool all year round. There are several wattle and tea plantations in Njombe district some of which can be seen on the road to Iringa and Mbeya.

9°20'S 34°50'E
Colour map 3, grid C3

The town was set up in rich farming country of the Southern Highlands, possibly because of the aerodrome, an early refuelling point en route to South Africa. Nearby is a spectacular waterfall, and wattle estates and tanning factory on the hill opposite (Kibena). The UMCA Diocesan HQ, Bishops House and Cathedral are worth a visit. Very much the centre of missionary activity. Old hotel bought by the mission. Single high street, usual stores included at one time Sachadena's Fancy Stores. This is on the route from Songea to the Mbeya-Iringa highway. There are frequent buses between Mbeya and Songea which pass through Njombe.

Sleeping **D** *Miliwana Hotel*, central, very comfortable. **E** *Africa Guest House* is of a similar standard. **E** *Mbalache Guest House* is the best value in town, good rooms available with or without showers and toilets. If you have transport, the **C** *Chani*, a few kilometres out of town is highly recommended.

Eating For a town of its size Njombe is particularly poorly served for restaurants – but then you won't have come here for the cuisine! Despite its unappealing façade and interior the *New Tazama Lwira Hotel*, located to the south of the market, does good basic meals. *The New Magazeti Highland Green Inn* is the best place for a drink; the bar there is very cosy.

Transport **Road Bus**: to **Dar es Salaam**, two direct buses daily leaving 0500-0600, journey time 9-10 hours. Fare US$15. To **Arusha**: Hood Transport runs buses twice weekly on Monday and Friday, leaving at 0800 and arriving 2200. Fare US$21.50. To **Songea, Iringa and Mbeya**: there are numerous buses daily, they all take around 3-4 hours and costs around US$4.50. There are also four-wheel drive (gari ndogo) going to Ludewa on Lake Nyasa (where you could link up with the ferry) for US$7.50. It will probably be fairly tough going though.

Songea

10°40'S 35°40'E
Altitude: 4,000 feet
Phone code: 0635
Colour map 3, grid C4

This town was comparatively isolated until the construction of the sealed road from the Iringa-Mbeya highway.

The journey from Tunduru to Songea is tough going and not particularly scenic, undulating miombo scrub mostly, until you begin to ascend the hills approaching

Songea

To Njombe · To Tunduru

Esso Petrol Station

Njombe Rd

Tunduru Rd

Angoni Arms (Closed)

District Office

Saba Saba

Matomondo St

Jamhuri Rd

Sokoine Rd

Jail

Market

Caltex Petrol Station

Day & Night Pharmacy

BP Petrol Station

Mission St

Makita Rd

Total Petrol Station

To Mbamba Bay

N

0 metres 50

■ **Sleeping**
1 Deluxe
2 Jordan River Guest House & Bar
3 Madamba Family Guest House
4 New Jamaica Guest House
5 New Mbalache Guest House
6 Okay Lodge
7 Yapender Annex Lodge
8 Yapender Lodge

Tanzania & Zanzibar

Songea, by which time you'll probably be too knackered to appreciate the scenery anyway!

Songea is the provincial headquarters of Southern Province. It's a pleasant enough place, although there is little to keep you in the town itself. On the other hand, it is surrounded by attractive rolling countryside and hills which are good for walking. Matogoro peak is within easy reach to the southeast of the town – take one of the tracks leading off the road to Tunduru. It is situated in part of the Matogoro forest reserve most of which stretches to the east of the peak itself. There are fine views from the top.

Songea and the surrounding area is home to the Ngoni, a group descended from an offshoot of the Zulus who came from South Africa in the mid-19th century. Tobacco is the main cash crop in the area, although Mbinga, to the south, is an important centre for coffee growing.

Sleeping

If you've just arrived from Tunduru you'll be pleased to hear that Songea has some excellent guesthouses. The **D** *Yapender Annex Lodge* has spotless, spacious self-contained double rooms. Just down the road the **D** *Okay Lodge* also has good self-contained doubles. The rooms at the **D** *Yapender Lodge* are the same price as those at the Annex but not as good value. Best budget hotel is the **D** *New Mbalachi Guest House*, which has the added advantage of being very close to the bus stand. To reach it go to the back of the station and walk down the passageway between the Caltex pumps and the Day & Night dispensary. Actually located at the bus stand is the **E** *Madamba Family Guest House* where rooms are very cheap but noisy. **E** *The New Jamaica Guest House* on Matomondo St, has cheap, basic rooms. **E** *The Deluxe Hotel* on Sokoine Rd, has cheap and not so cheerful rooms. The Angoni Arms looks very pleasant but has been closed for the past few years.

Eating

There are few culinary highlights in Songea. Best bet is probably the restaurant at the *Okay Lodge* which does descent simple meals such as fish and chips or ugali and stew.

Transport

Road Bus: there are several buses leaving daily to Dar es Salaam all leaving early. Best company is Kiswele Bus. The journey takes around 12 hours and costs US$12.50. Three buses a day go to Mbeya costing around US$6.50 and taking 6-7 hours. Buses to Njombe are numerous, costing US$4.50 for the 3-4 hour ride. To Mbamba Bay (outside the rainy season) there are two daily buses leaving between 0600-0700. The journey takes 8-10 hours, US$10. Book a seat the day before. There is at least one bus leaving Songea for Tunduru leaving early every other morning. Costs US$10. Try to book a seat in front of the back axle in view of the appalling state of the roads.

Tanzania & Zanzibar

Zanzibar and Pemba

6°12′S 39°12′E
Phone code: 054
Colour map 5

The very name Zanzibar conjures up exotic and romantic images. There are two main islands making up Zanzibar, Unguja and Pemba. Zanzibar Town is on Unguja Island, but Unguja Island is popularly refered to as Zanzibar. The town is steeped in history, is full of atmosphere and immensely attractive. There are excellent beaches on the east coast. The island is about 96 kilometres long and is separated from the mainland by a channel 35 kilometres wide. The main rains are from March to May, and the best time to visit is from June to October.

Zanzibar is perhaps most famous for once being the home of the slave trade, and an important trading post for spices and cloves. Once Zanzibar was the world's most important supplier of cloves but it has now been overtaken by producers in the Far East. Cloves do remain the most important export of the island, while tourism is now the largest source of foreign currency. On the western part of the island there are clove plantations with trees 10-20 metres tall.

The island has been a stopping-off point for traders going up and down the coast for many years and as a result has seen many different travellers including Greeks, Egyptians, Persians and Chinese. European explorers and missionaries also visited the island and it was used as a starting point for their travels inland. The legacy of these early visitors is shown in the people, architecture and culture.

Since 1964, when the rule of the Sultans ended, Zanzibar has neglected its heritage. In a union with the mainland, Zanzibar sought to progress by socialist policies and a modernising philosophy. The relics of this period are to be seen in the brutal concrete blocks constructed to the east of Creek Rd in Zanzibar Town. Fortunately the glorious old Stone Town escaped unscathed, and with a change of heart toward the past, is now being restored.

Tourist facilities and prices of accommodation, tours and excursions have all increased rapidly over the past couple of years. Prices quoted may therefore be inaccurate at times.

History The origin of the name Zanzibar is disputed. The Omani Arabs believe it came from Zayn Zal Barr which means 'Fair is the Island'. The alternative origin is in two parts – the early inhabitants of the island were from the mainland and were given the name *Zenj*, a Persian word which is a corruption of *Zangh* meaning negro. The word *bar* which means coast was added to this to give negro coast.

The earliest visitors were Arab traders who brought with them Islam which has remained the dominant religion on the island. They are believed to have arrived in the 8th century. The earliest building that remains is the mosque at Kazimkazi which dates from about 1100.

For centuries the Arabs had sailed with the monsoons down from Muscat and Oman in the Gulf to trade in ivory, slaves, spices, hides and wrought-iron. The two main islands, both of roughly similar size, Unguja (usually known as Zanzibar Island) and Pemba, provided an ideal base, being relatively small islands and thus easy to defend. From here it was possible to control 1,500 kilometres of the mainland coast from present day Mozambique up to Somalia. A consequence of their being the first arrivals was that the Arabs became the main landowners.

In 1832 Sultan Seyyid Said, of the Al Busaid Dynasty that had emerged in Oman in 1744, moved his palace from Muscat to Zanzibar. Said and his descendants were to rule there for 134 years. In 1822, the Omanis signed the Moresby Treaty which made it illegal for them to sell slaves to Christian powers in their dominions. To monitor this agreement, the United States in 1836 and the British in 1840, established diplomatic relations with Zanzibar, and sent resident Consuls to the islands.

The slaving restrictions were not effective and the trade continued to flourish. Caravans set out from Bagamoyo on the mainland coast, travelling up to 1,500 kilometres on foot as far as Lake Tanganyika, purchasing slaves from local rulers on the way, or, more cheaply, simply capturing them. The slaves, chained together, carried ivory back to Bagamoyo. The name Bagamoyo means 'lay down your heart' for it was here that the slaves would abandon hope of ever seeing their homeland again. They were shipped to the slave market in Zanzibar Town, bought by intermediary traders, who in turn sold them on without any restrictions.

All the main racial groups were involved in the slave trade. Europeans used slaves in the plantations in the Indian Ocean islands, Arabs were the main capturers and traders, and African rulers sold the prisoners taken in battle to the traders. Alas, being sold into slavery was not the worst fate that could befall a captive. If a prolonged conflict led to a glut, the Doe tribe from just north of Bagamoyo would run down excess stocks of prisoners by the simple expedient of eating them. Nevertheless, it is the perception of the African population that the Arabs were mainly responsible.

Cloves had been introduced from Southeast Asia, probably Indonesia, prior to the advent of Sultan Seyyid Said. They flourished in the tropical climate on the fertile and well-watered soils on the western areas of both Zanzibar and Pemba islands. Slaves did the cultivation and harvesting and the Sultan occupied plots such that by his death in 1856 he had 45 plantations. Other plantations were acquired by his many children, as well as by numerous concubines and eunuchs from the royal harem. In due course cinnamon, nutmeg, black pepper, cumin, ginger and cardamom were all established, their fragrances were everywhere and Zanzibar became known as the 'Spice Islands'. Slaves, spices and ivory provided the basis of considerable prosperity, mostly in the hands of the Arab community, who were the main landowners, and who kept themselves to themselves and did not intermarry with the Africans.

This was not true of a second group that came from the Middle East to settle on the East African coast. In AD 975 Abi Ben Sultan Hasan of Shiraz in Persia (now Iran) is said to have had a dream in which a rat with iron jaws devoured the foundations of his house. He took this as a sign that his community was to be destroyed. Other members of the Court in Shiraz poured scorn on the notion, but Sultan Hasan, his family and some followers decided to migrate. They set out in seven dhows from the nearby port of Bushehr and sailed through the mouth of the Persian Gulf into the Indian Ocean. Here they were caught in a great storm, separated, and made landfalls at seven separate places along the East African coast, one of which was Zanzibar, and established settlements. Intermarriage between Shirazis and Africans gave rise to a coastal community with distinctive features, and a language derived in part from Arabic which became known as Swahili. In Zanzibar the descendants of this group were known as the Afro-Shirazis. They were not greatly involved in the lucrative slave, spice and ivory trades. They cultivated coconuts, fished and became agricultural labourers. Those Shirazis that did not intermarry retained their identity as a separate group.

Two smaller communities were also established. Indian traders arrived in connection with the spice and ivory trade, and, as elsewhere in East Africa, settled as shopkeepers, traders, skilled artisans, money-lenders, lawyers, doctors and accountants. The British became involved in missionary and trading activities in East Africa, and had exercised themselves in attempting to suppress the slave trade. Germans had begun trading on the mainland opposite

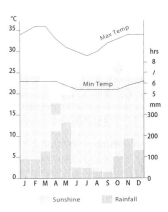

Climate: Zanzibar

Tanzania & Zanzibar

☞ *A Zanzibar excursion from Kenya*

Zanzibar is easily accessible from Kenya and is highly recommended as an extension to your Kenyan holiday. It is a very exotic place and quite different from the Kenyan mainland. 90 percent of the population are Muslim. Allow perhaps five nights: it is worth staying in Stone Town for perhaps two of these and the remainder of your time on the East coast. Spice Tours are excellent especially if the spices are in season.

Arrival

For many travellers who arrive from Mombasa, Zanzibar can seem a little daunting which can quickly tarnish the island's romantic image. For a start, there is a degree of bureaucracy at both Mombasa and Zanzibar airports which involves queuing apparently pointlessly in several lengthy lines – this can be hot and irritating. Having the correct documentation and particularly a current Yellow Fever certificate will help. If you don't have one, you will not be allowed on the plane until it has been obtained (this will certainly cost money one way or another).

Money

Make sure that you take a lot of hard currency in small denomination notes. It is easy to

forget that Zanzibar is an international destination and you will have to pay the full departure tax of US$20 on leaving both Mombasa and Zanzibar. In 1994, there was a small bank in the airport immediately before you exit the baggage retrieval area. It does NOT accept travellers cheques or Kenyan shillings but will change US dollars, Pounds sterling, Deutsche Marks and some other hard currencies. Rates are not very good so change a small amount in order to have sufficient funds to get a taxi or bus into town. US$20 or equivalent should suffice.

Despite official denials, many hotels still insist on being paid in US dollars. Very few will accept travellers cheques and even fewer credit cards. Some hotels and restaurants will accept Visa credit cards, but charges are steep at 15-20 percent commission in the £ or US$, plus a 20 percent worse exchange rate. Often they will want paying in advance. If you run short of hard currency, go to the Bank of Tanzania behind the fort. This is the only bank where you can change travellers cheques for hard currency. Again it will not change Kenyan shillings. Officially you will only be able to change 50 percent into dollars, the remainder will be given to you in Tanzanian shillings.

Zanzibar. Things needed to be sorted out with the Sultan of Zanzibar, who controlled the 10 mile coastal strip that ran for 1,500 kilometres from Mozambique to Somalia. Germany bought their strip of the coast from the Sultan for £200,000. The British East African Company had been paying the Sultan £11,000 a year for operating in the Kenyan portion. In 1890, Germany allowed Britain to establish a protectorate over Zanzibar in return for Heligoland, a tiny barren island occupied by the British, but strategically placed opposite the mouth of the river Elbe, 50 kilometres from the German coast. In 1895 Britain took over responsibility for its section of the mainland from the British East African Company and agreed to continue to pay the £11,000 a year to the Sultan. The British mainland territory (later to become Kenya) was administered by a Governor, to whom the British representative in Zanzibar, the Resident, was accountable.

The distinctive feature of Zanzibar as a protectorate (Kenya had become a colony in 1920) was recognized in 1926 when the British Resident was made directly responsible to the Colonial Secretary in London. Germany had by this stage lost control of its section of the mainland when, as a result of its defeat in the First World War, the territory was transferred to British control to become Tanganyika.

The colonial period Further legislation in 1873 had made the slave trade illegal, the slave market in Zanzibar was closed and the Protestant Cathedral erected on the site. But slavery lingered on. The trade was illegal, but the institution of slavery existed openly until Britain took over the mainland from the Germans in 1918, and covertly, it is argued, for many years thereafter. Many former slaves found that their conditions had

There is no problem in paying for restaurants or tours in local currency. There are many Foreign Exchange Bureaux which open long hours and give good rates – the one at the Hotel International near the market is recommended.

Hotels

If your hotel is in Stone Town (and this is highly recommended), don't be surprised when the vehicle stops amidst run down buildings. This will be the closest the vehicle is able to go before the narrow alleys begin. A walk of 5-10 minutes with your luggage is common especially if you are staying near the centre (eg Spice Inn). Make sure that the taxi driver actually takes you to the hotel but don't assume that he will carry your luggage. With this in mind, take as little luggage as possible. Telecommunications from Kenya are not always reliable, so don't be surprised if the hotel has not heard of you – keep insisting that they find a room. Finally, don't expect to be able to sleep in, there are many mosques in Stone Town: the morning call to pray invariably starts well before dawn.

Orientation

The bewildering maze of streets can be disorientating and has a very Arab feel. Only bicycles, scooters and hand carts are able to use the narrow alleys. You must constantly make way for those with wheels – listen out for the tinkling of bells and the 'quack-quack' of horns. You should within reason follow Muslim dress code to avoid offence, although in Zanzibar this is fairly relaxed.

Stone Town covers quite a small area and once accustomed to it, you will be able to walk around confidently and enjoy the atmosphere as well as the architecture and lovely doors. The door to a house was built to reflect the wealth and social status of its owner. They were often elaborately carved or decorated with brass studs.

Remember it is quite safe to walk around, even at night. The streets are poorly lit in places so you may find a torch useful. You will fairly quickly find a guide to help you back to your hotel if you do become lost (a small tip will be expected). Do not be afraid to ask at your hotel reception for help either – they usually have someone on hand to guide you.

Further information can be found in the Tanzania Essentials section on page 298.

changed but little. They were now employed as labourers at low wage rates in the clove plantations. Zanzibar continued to prosper with the expansion of trade in cloves and other spices. The fine buildings that make Zanzibar Stone Town such a glorious place were constructed to a high standard by wealthy Arab slavers and clove traders, British administrators and prosperous Indian businessmen and professionals. These structures were so soundly built they have survived for the most part without repairs, maintenance and redecoration from 1964 to the present.

The wealth of the successive Sultans was considerable. They built palaces in the Stone Town and around Zanzibar Island. Islamic law allowed them to have up to four wives, and their wealth enabled them to exercise this privilege and raise numerous children. Until 1911 it was the practice of the Sultan to maintain a harem of around 100 concubines, with attendant eunuchs. The routine was established whereby the Sultan slept with five concubines a night, in strict rotation. The concubines had children, and these were supported by the Sultan.

Social practices changed with the succession of Khalifa bin Harab, at the age of 32, as Sultan in 1911. He was to reign until his death, in 1960 at the age of 81. The harem and concubines were discontinued – apart from anything else, this proved a major economy measure. Gradual political reforms were introduced, with successively more democratic representation until the Sultan was a constitutional monarch with no significant legislative or executive powers. With the influences from Oman and Shiraz, Zanzibar is overwhelmingly Islamic (97 percent) – the remaining three percent are Hindus, Christians and Sikhs. Moreover, the practice of Islam was tolerant and relaxed. Social pressures on non-Muslims are minimal. A member of the British

High Commission tells of being on the verandah of the palace at sundown with Sultan Khalifa bin Harab. They scanned the skies, as Ramadan would begin officially when the Sultan glimpsed the moon. They drew blank, and the visitor was offered a whisky and soda. The next night there was a sliver of silver low down on the horizon, and the Sultan apologized for the fact that he felt he was not able to be so hospitable.

The office of the Sultan was held in considerable awe. As the Sultan drove each day to spend the afternoon a few kilometres away at his palace on the shore, his subjects would prostate themselves as he passed. In 1959, when it was suggested that there should be elected members of the Legislative Councils, and Ministers appointed to deal with day-to-day matters of state, the Sultan received numerous delegations saying change was unnecessary and the Sultan should retain absolute power. The present Sultan is still addressed as 'Your Highness' when Zanzibaris visit him. British protocol decreed that the Sultan should qualify for a 19-gun salute on ceremonial occasions. This placed Zanzibar on an equal footing with Tonga. At the coronation of Queen Elizabeth in 1953, the diminutive and reserved Sultan was consigned to share a carriage with the formidable physical presence of Queen Salote of Tonga, who insisted on driving through the pouring rain with the hood down so she could wave to the crowds. As they passed, a bystander asked Noel Coward if he knew who was sharing the carriage with Queen Salote. "Her lunch", was the reply. It says much for the Sultan's sense of humour that this was the first item of news about the coronation that he recounted to the British Consulate staff on his arrival back in Zanzibar.

British American Tobacco had several plantations on the mainland. One of the tasks assigned to new trainees from Britain was to sail to Zanzibar with a consignment of cigarettes, each stamped in gold with the Sultan's monograph. The trainee then had to go through the Palace, taking the stale contents out of the cigarette boxes in each room and replenishing them with new cigarettes. It was not possible to give the old cigarettes away as local people refused them when they saw the monogram. They were taken down to the beach and burnt.

David Reed, writing for Readers Digest in 1962, described Zanzibar as the "laziest place on earth – once a Zanzibari has caught a couple of fish, he quits for the day, to retire to his bed, or the heavenly chatter of the coffee house". He developed his theme – "Once a clove has been planted, its lethargic owner has only to sit in the shade and watch as its tiny green buds grow into handsome pounds sterling. Even when the market is in the doldrums, a good tree may produce as much as £6 worth of cloves a year for its owner. In better times, it simply rains money on those who sleep below."

Despite these impressions of tropical torpor under a benevolent ruler, there were significant tensions. Several small Arab Associations combined to form the Zanzibar National Party (ZNP) in 1955. The leader was Sheikh Ali Muhsin, educated at Makerere University in Uganda with a degree in Agriculture. The leadership of the party was Arab, and their main objective was to press for independence from the British without delay. Two African associations, active with small landless farmers and agricultural labourers, formed the Afro-Shirazi Party (ASP) in 1957. The leader was Sheikh Abeid Karume, at one-time a school-teacher, a popular and charismatic personality, with great humorous skills which he exercised to the full at public meetings.

Although the ZNP tried to embrace all races, the fact was that they were seen as an Arab party, while ASP represented African interests. Arabs comprised 20 percent of the population, with Africans over 75 percent. Election to the Legislative Council in 1955 were organized on the basis of communal rolls – that is, so many seats were allocated to Arabs, so many to Africans, and so on. This infuriated the ZNP who wanted a common electoral roll so that they could contest all seats. They boycotted the Legislative Council. When a ZNP member broke ranks, he was assassinated, and an Arab was executed for his murder. The next elections, in 1957, were held on the basis of a common roll, and the ZNP did not win a single one of the six seats that were contested. ASP took five and the Muslim League one. More damaging, Ali Muhsin insisted on a head-to-head with Karume in the Ngambo constituency, and was soundly beaten, polling less than 25 percent of the votes cast. ZNP's confidence that they could draw broad-based support was very badly dented. In the next four years, the ZNP greatly increased its efforts with youth and women's organizations and published five daily papers. It was also felt that wealthy Arab land-owners and employers flexed their economic muscles to encourage support for ZNP among Africans. ZNP was greatly assisted in 1959 by a split in the ASP. Sheikh Muhammed Shamte, a Shirazi veterinary surgeon with a large clove plantation in Pemba, formed the Zanzibar and Pemba People's Party (ZPPP). Two other ASP members of the Legislative Council joined Shamte, and ASP was left in a minority with just two seats.

The dispute was a clash of personalities as much as anything, the more urbane Shamte finding it difficult to rub along with the rough and ready manner of Karume. A contributing factor was that ASP contested the 1957 elections on a pro-African platform, particularly playing to fears that ZNP would only allow Arabs to vote in future elections and would reintroduce slavery.

In the run-up to Independence, there were three more elections. In the first, in January 1961, ASP won 10 seats, ZNP took nine and ZPPP was successful in three. A farce ensued in which both ASP and ZNP wooed the three ZPPP members. One supported ASP and the remaining two supported ZNP, creating a deadlock with 11 apiece. In the event, ZNP and ASP formed a coalition caretaker government on the understanding that new elections be held as soon as possible.

For the June 1961 elections a new constituency was created, to make a total of 23 seats. ASP and ZNP won 10 each, and ZPPP three. However, ZPPP had committed itself to support ZNP, and this coalition duly formed a government. However, ASP had gained a majority of the popular vote (albeit narrowly at 50.6 percent) and this caused resentment. The improved performance of ZNP in the two elections after the debacle of 1957 was bewildering to ASP. There were serious outbreaks of violence, and these were clearly along racial lines and directed against Arabs. There were 68 deaths of which 64 were Arabs.

In 1962 a Constitutional Conference was held at Lancaster House in London, attended by the main figures of the three political parties. A framework was duly thrashed out and agreed, with the Sultan as the constitutional Head of State. The number of seats was increased to 31 and women were given the vote. Elections in 1963 saw ASP gain 13 seats, ZNP 12 and ZPPP six. A ZNP/ZPPP coalition government was formed under the leadership of Muhammed Shamte of ZPPP. Once again ASP had the majority of the popular vote with 54 percent. Independence was set for later that year, on 10 December.

The old Sultan had died in 1960 and was succeeded by his son Abdullah bin Khalifa, who was to reign for less than three years, dying of cancer in July 1963. His son, Jamshid Bin Abdullah (see box, page 450), became Sultan at the age of 34.

It has been described as 'the most unnecessary revolution in history'. At 0300 on the night of 12 January 1964, a motley group of Africans, armed with clubs, pangas (long implements with bent, curved blades, swished from side to side to cut grass), car springs, bows and arrows, converged on the Police Headquarters at Ziwani on the edge of Zanzibar Stone Town. There were two sentries on duty. **The revolution**

As the mob came into view one sentry managed to fire a couple of shots and kill two of the attackers. For a moment the assault was in the balance. John Okello (see box, page 448) was the leader of the attacking force. As his supporters faltered, Okello rushed forward, grappled with the sentry, seized his rifle and bayonetted him. The other sentry was hit by an iron-tipped arrow. The door was beaten in and Okello shot a policeman at the top of the stairs. Encouraged, the attackers stormed the building. In a matter of moments the police had fled, and the mob broke into the armoury. Armed, they moved on to support other attacks that had been planned to take place simultaneously at other key installations – the radio station, the army barracks, and the gaol. There was some brisk fighting, but the inexperienced defenders had little stomach for the fight against rebels intoxicated by their early success. By midday, most of the town was in the hands of Okello's forces.

John Okello – drifter who destroyed a Dynasty

John Okello was born in Uganda in 1937. There is no record of him having had any early schooling. He left home at the age of 15 and did a variety of jobs whilst travelling, including work as a domestic servant, a tailor and as a building labourer. Eventually he worked as a mason in Nairobi and went to evening classes where he learnt to read and write. In 1957 he was given a two-year prison sentence for a sexual offence. On his release he travelled to Mombasa, and did some casual building jobs. In 1959 he crossed illegally, at night, in a dhow, to Pemba. While doing odd jobs he attended some ZNP political meetings. Later he began a stone-quarrying business, and joined ASP, campaigning for them in the three elections in the run-up to Independence.

After the third election, Okello moved to Zanzibar Island. The Shamte administration was anxious that the police force contained many African recruits from the mainland, and began to replace them with inexperienced Zanzibaris. It was in this context that John Okello began to form plans to overthrow the government, recruiting mainly from Africans who were not Zanzibaris (including some disaffected former policemen) who feared that they may be expelled by a pro-Arab government. Okello warned his followers that after Independence all male African babies would be killed, Africans would be ruled as slaves, and 3,000 Africans would be slaughtered in reprisal for the 64 Arabs killed in the 1961 disturbances. By November Okello was having visionary dreams and commanding his men to abstain from sex until after the revolution and not to wear other people's clothes, in order to keep strong. He designed a Field Marshal's uniform and pennant for himself. Final battle instructions indicated who should be killed (males aged between 18 and 55), who could be raped (no wives of men killed or detained, and no virgins). The Sultan and three specified politicians were to be killed and the remainder captured. Some of his followers thought that Independence Day, 10 December 1963, would be an appropriate day for the revolution, but Okello thought it would be a pity to spoil the celebrations for the many overseas visitors.

Okello led the crucial attack on Ziwani Police Station on 12 January 1964, which overthrew the government and resulted in the flight of the Sultan into exile. Following this coup Okello pronounced himself Field-Marshal, and for a while assumed the title of Leader of the Revolutionary Government. As a semblance of order was restored, it was clear that Okello was an embarrassment to the ASP Government, and by 11 March he was expelled, resuming his former career of wandering the mainland, taking casual employment, and languishing for spells in prison.

As the skirmishes raged through the narrow cobbled streets of the historic Stone Town, the Sultan, his family and entourage (about 50 in all) were advised to flee by the Prime Minister and his Cabinet. Two government boats were at anchor off-shore. The Sultan's party was ferried to one of these, and it set off to the north-west to Mombasa, in nearby Kenya. The government there, having gained Independence itself only a month earlier, had no desire to get involved by acting in a way that might be interpreted as hostile by whatever body eventually took control on the island. The Sultan was refused permission to land, and the boat returned southwards down the coast to Dar es Salaam in Tanganyika. From there the party was flown to Manchester and exile in Britain.

Following the assault on the Ziwani Police Headquarters at 0300 on the 12 January, all other strategic targets were swiftly captured and Okello began the business of government by proclaiming himself Field Marshal, Leader of the Revolutionary Government, and Minister of Defence and Broadcasting. Members of the ASP were allocated other ministries, with Abeid Karume as Prime Minister. Meanwhile there was considerable mayhem throughout the islands, as old scores were settled and the African and Arab communities took revenge upon one another. Initial figures suggest that 12,000 Arabs and 1,000 Africans were killed before the violence ran its course.

The British kept themselves aloof, refusing military assistance to the Sultan and Shamte. A cruiser with troops was moored in the Pemba Channel, and the High Commission sent Morse signals to it and was allowed to receive an envoy and some supplies each day. After a particularly hot day, a request was signalled for two bottles of calamine lotion. On arrival with the envoy, the consignment was seized and a member of staff of the High Commission was hauled out to explain to the Field Marshal why bottles of high explosive had been requested. Okello waved one of the bottles, and pointed out that if he took the top off they would all be blown sky-high. The officer unscrewed the other bottle and dabbed a little lotion on his sun-burnt forehead.

A trickle of countries, mostly newly independent African states and Soviet regimes recognized the Karume regime fairly promptly. In February 1964 Karume expelled the British High Commissioner and the Acting US Charge d'Affaires as their countries had not recognized his government.

Army mutinies in Kenya, Tanganyika and Uganda earlier in the year, the presence of British troops in the region and some ominous remarks by the US Ambassador in Nairobi about communist threats to the mainland from Zanzibar, all served to make Karume anxious. He felt very vulnerable with no army he could count on, and what he saw as hostile developments all around. He needed some support to secure his position.

On 23 April, Karume and Julius Nyerere signed an Act of Union between Zanzibar and Tanganyika to form Tanzania. Later the mainland political party merged with ASP to form Chama Cha Mapinduzi (CCM), the only legal political party in Tanzania.

The union

The relationship between Zanzibar and the mainland is a mess. It is neither a proper federation nor a unitary state. Zanzibar retains its own President (up to 1995, *ex officio* one of the Vice-Presidents of the Union). It has a full set of ministries, its own Assembly, and keeps its own foreign exchange earnings. Mainlanders need a passport to go to Zanzibar, and cannot own property there. No such restrictions apply to Zanzibaris on the mainland. Despite comprising less than five percent of Tanzania's total population, Zanzibar has 30 percent of the seats in the Union Assembly. The practice of rotating the Union Presidency between Zanzibar and the mainland meant that from 1985-95 two of the occupants of the top three posts (the President and one of the two Vice-Presidents) come from Zanzibar. Zanzibar has not paid for electricity supplied by the mainland's hydro-electric power stations for over 15 years.

Despite all these privileges (which annoy the daylights out of many mainlanders) the Zanzibaris feel they have had a rough time since 1964. The socialist development strategy pursued by Tanzania after 1967 has seen living standards fall in Zanzibar. Where once the inhabitants of Zanzibar Town were noticeably better off than the urban dwellers in mainland Dar es Salaam, they now feel themselves decidedly poorer. They consider that if they had been able to utilize their historical and cultural links with oil-rich Oman they would have benefitted from substantial investment and development assistance.

The legitimacy of the Act of Union has been called into question – it was a deal between two leaders (one of whom had come to power unconstitutionally) without any of the democratic consultation such a radical step might reasonably require.

Separatist movements have emerged, pamphletting sporadically from exile in Oman and Scandinavia, and suppressed by the Tanzanian government. A Chief Minister in Zanzibar, Seif Sharrif Hamad, was dismissed when it was thought he harboured separatist sympathies. Later he was detained for over two years on a charge of retaining confidential government documents at his home.

Multiparty elections were set for the end of October 1995. No-one appears to have thought through what this would mean for Zanzibar.

When political parties were sanctioned again, a cluster of organizations applied to get themselves registered, including a group based on the old ASP in Zanzibar. One of the successes of Tanzania, on the mainland at any rate, has been the absence of any serious tribalism. The government was determined to ensure the new parties

☞ **Jamshid Bin Abdullah – Eleventh Sultan of Zanzibar**

Jamshid Bin Abdullah, the 11th Sultan of Zanzibar in the Al Busaid Dynasty, was born in 1929. He was educated by private tutors in Zanzibar, and at the suggestion of the British Resident he then attended the Royal Naval College at Dartmouth in the UK, where he is reported to have been very unhappy. He served as an officer for a period in the British Navy. A handsome man, of modest stature, he established a reputation as something of a playboy with a string of girlfriends including the European wife of a Zanzibari Indian. A favourite pastime was hunting wild pigs on the islands, on foot, with rifles and spears.

After the revolution in 1964 the Sultan was granted exile in the United Kingdom, and went to live in Portsmouth where there has long been a Zanzibari community. He has not been allowed to return to Zanzibar, and indeed, in all these years he has not wanted to. He divorced his first wife (a Zanzibari) who retains a house of her own in Portsmouth and shuttles between Hampshire and Oman where most of her children, and the children of the Sultan's second wife (also a Zanzibari), reside. The Sultan has never visited Oman – he has maintained a very private existence – reading, following world events, concerning himself with his family, a few close confidants, and the remaining members of his retinue.

When he arrived in the United Kingdom in 1964, the British authorities recalled that the agreement for the annual payment for the surrender of the rights to the Kenyan coastal strip was made with the Sultan personally, rather than with the Government of Zanzibar. It was arranged that the Sultan should be paid the annual sum of £11,000 as long as he remained resident in the UK. Should he move overseas, there would be a single lump sum payment of £250,000 which would discharge the obligation. The Sultan has lived modestly in Portsmouth. Although in 1964 the annual payment was worth around £100,000 in today's values, it must be remembered that there was a retinue of perhaps 50 that followed him into exile. Journalists who called on him in the early years made much of the contrast between life in a humdrum Portsmouth suburb and the opulence of his former existence in his various palaces in exotic Zanzibar. The Sultan tired of these visits, and for almost 30 years he has declined to be interviewed or have his photograph taken. He has aged very little, and he is easily recognizable as the figure that fled in 1964. He is not anxious to go back to Zanzibar, but he will return if there is a desire by his community for him to do so.

were broadly based and not merely representatives of a particular race, region or religion. This was to be achieved by requiring each party to obtain 200 members in each of at least 13 of Tanzania's 25 regions. The Registrar of Political Parties has had 2,600 names and addresses checked for each of Tanzania's thirteen registered parties. This, it was felt, would scupper a group like the re-formed ASP, based on a region, and which might campaign in Zanzibar on a pro-separation ticket. In the event, the Zanzibaris appear to have bought an already registered party, the Civic United Front (CUF), off the shelf.

The former Chief Minister and detainee, Sharrif Hamad, was the CUF candidate for the Zanzibar Presidency. Support for CUF in the islands prior to the election was very strong. It was hard to find anyone in Zanzibar or Pemba, who wasn't actually a member of CCM, who said they weren't going to vote for CUF. In the event, it is thought that Hamad and CUF were victorious by a narrow margin in both the Presidential and Assembly elections. A recount was called, and independent observers claim that forged voting papers supporting CCM were introduced. In the event, the incumbent Salim Amour was declared President with 50.2 percent of the vote (Hamad had 49.8 percent) and with two constituencies changing hands at the recount, CCM formed the islands' administration with 26 seats (to CUF's 24). CUF and Hamad were incensed at the outcome, and CUF have boycotted the Zanzibar Assembly. The international community pressed for a re-run of the election under international monitoring and control – the 1995 election only had international observers, who were powerless to prevent the alleged fraud at the recount.

Zanzibar town

Even with a map it is suprisingly easy to get lost as the narrow winding alleys and overhanging balconies mean it is difficult to mantain a sense of direction. Alternatively hire a guide who will show you all the sights. A local artist John da Silva (T32123) gives walking tours that are particularly attractive if you are interested in the architecture of the island, cost US$25. Emersons has a security man who will provide an all day tour for US$10, although some of his information on buildings is suspect. As you wander around the streets you will notice that the ground floor of many of the buildings is taken up by shops and businesses, whilst above are the homes of the Zanzibaris. Exploring on foot during the day or night will give you a real feel of this wonderful town and its people. Walking around Zanzibar has previously been very safe, recent incidents, however, would advocate more caution.

The area to the west of Creek Rd is known as the old **Stone Town**, recently declared a World Heritage Site, and a tour will take at least a day. It is such a fascinating place that it is easy to spend a week wandering the narrow streets and still find new places of charm and interest. A good place to start the trip is from the **Central Market** located on Creek Rd. This was opened in 1904 and remains a bustling, colourful and aromatic place. Here you will see Zanzibarian life carrying on as it has done for so many years – lively, busy and noisy. Outside are long, neat rows of bicycles carefully locked and guarded by their minder while people are buying and selling inside the market. Fruit, vegetable, meat and fish are all for sale here as well as household implements, many of them locally made, clothing and footwear. **NB** The chicken, fish and meat areas are not for the squeamish.

Nearby, also on Creek Rd, is the **Anglican Church of Christ** which was built in 1887 to commemorate the end of the slave trade. The altar is on the actual site of the slave market's whipping post. The columns at the west end were put in upside down, while the bishop was on leave in the UK. Inside are impressive marble pillars and stained glass windows. Other points of interest are the small wooden crucifix said to have been made from the wood of the tree under which Livingstone died in Chitambo in Zambia. If you can, try to go up the staircase of the church to the top of the tower from where you will get an excellent view of the town. It is sadly run down and needs all the funds it can get. Next door, under the St Monica restaurant, you can visit the underground slave pens.

Also on Creek Rd is the **City Hall** which is a wonderfully ornate building currently undergoing renovation.

Mathews House is located close to *Africa House Hotel*, just to the south of Ras Shangani at the western tip of the town, and before the First World War was the residence, with characteristic overhanging balconies, of Lloyd Mathews (1850-1901). Mathews was a naval officer who was put in charge of the Sultan's army in 1877 (he was a mere Lieutenant of 27 at the time). Later he became Chief Minister, and was known as the 'Strong Man of Zanzibar'. The **Africa House Hotel** was once the British Club. Also in this area is **Tippu Tip's House**, named after the wealthy 19th century slave-trader, which has a splendid carved wooden door and black and white marble steps. Tippu Tip was the most notorious of all slavers and

Colour map 5, grid B1

Tanzania & Zanzibar

Greater Zanzibar

To Kibweni Palace
To Welezo & Dunga
Maruhubi Palace
Funguni Creek - Bwawani Plaza
Dhow Harbour
STONE TOWN
Creek Rd
Malawi Rd
Fruit Market
Uhuru Park
To Tunguu
Nyerere Rd
Zanzibar Channel
Mazizini-The Fishermans Resort
To Fumba
N
Not to scale
Mbweni Ruins
To Airport

Related map:
Zanzibar - Stone Town, page 454

Freddie Mercury

In 1946 Farokh Bulsara was born in Zanzibar to parents who were Parsees – followers of the Zoroastrian faith. The Zoroastrian Fire Temple in Zanzibar is located on Vuga Road to the east of Zanzibar Stone Town. His father worked as a civil servant for the British colonial government on the islands. The Parsees had a great affinity with the British, and Mr Bulsara senior was a cricket enthusiast, spending much of his leisure time at the ground at Mnazi Moja. The family lived in a house in the square behind the present Post Office. When he was nine, Farokh was sent to boarding school in India, and he never subsequently returned to the place of his birth.

In 1970, while studying graphics at Ealing College, he joined up with some students at London University's Imperial College of Science and Technology. He changed his name to Freddie Mercury and they formed the group Queen.

The influence of his Zanzibar background is expressed in the lyric of Queen's best-known song Bohemian Rhapsody *with 'Bismillah will you let him go'. Bismillah means 'the word of God' in the Islamic faith, and it has become a rallying cry for Muslim groups pressing for Zanzibar to break away from Tanzania.*

Freddie Mercury died in 1992, his body being cremated at a Zoroastrian funeral ceremony in London.

Livingstone's arch-enemy – the latter's report of the massacre at Nyangwe, in the Congo, where Tippu Tip had commercial hegemony, led ultimately to the abolition of the slave trade.

At the western tip of the town is the building known now as **Mambo Msiige** which was once owned by a slave trader. It is said that he used to bury slaves alive within the walls of the building in accordance with an ancient custom. Since then the building has been used as the headquarters of the Universities Mission to Central Africa and later as the British Consulate.

The **Old Fort** (also known as the Arab Fort or Ngome Kongwe) is located in the west of the town next to the House of Wonders. This huge structure was built in 1700 on the site of a Portuguese church, the remains of which can be seen incorporated into the fabric of the internal walls. The tall walls are topped by castellated battlements. The Fort was built by Omani Arabs to defend attacks from the Portuguese, who had occupied Zanzibar for almost two centuries. During the 19th century the Fort was used as a prison and in the early 20th century it was used as a depot of the railway which ran from Stone Town to Bububu. It is possible to reach the top of the battlements on the west side and look at the towers. The central area is now used as an open air theatre, and renamed the Zanzibar Cultural Centre. On Friday at 1930 film nights are held, and on Tuesday, Thursday and Saturday there is a Zanzibar buffet barbecue with African dance and drums.

The Fort also houses an Art Gallery, several small shops selling crafts and spices, plus a tourist information desk. There is also a charming café, with tables in the shade of a couple of large trees.

On the south side of the Fort you can take a walk down Gizenga St (used to be Portuguese St) with its busy bazaars. This will lead you to **St Joseph's Catholic Cathedral**, and on the opposite side of the road the **Bohora Mosque**.

Beit-el-Ajaib (House of Wonders) is Zanzibar's tallest building and is located close to the fort opposite the Jamituri Gardens. It was built in 1883 by Sultan Barghash and served as his palace. It has fine examples of door carving. At the entrance are two Portuguese canons which date from about the 16th century. It is a four-storey building and is surrounded by verandahs. In 1896 in an attempt to persuade the Sultan to abdicate, the palace was subjected to bombardment by the British navy. Inside the floors are of marble and there are various decorations which were imported from Europe, there are also exhibits from the struggle for independence. The building served as the local headquarters of Tanzania's political party CCM, but there are now plans to open it to the public.

On Mizingani Rd there is the **Beit al-Sahel (People's Palace)** which is located to the north of the House of Wonders. It was here that the sultans and their families lived from the 1880s until their rule was finally overturned by the revolution of 1964. This has now been opened as a museum. There are three floors of exhibits and it is well worth a visit. There is a wide variety of furniture including the Sultan's huge bed. Lookout for the formica wardrobe with handles missing – obviously very fashionable at the time. Good views from the top floor. Open Tuesday-Saturday 1000-1800, entrance US$3. The palace has grounds which can sometimes be viewed, containing the tombs of Sultan Seyyid Said and his two sons Khaled and Barghash. Also along this road is the **Na Sur Nurmohamed Dispensary**, situated between the House of Wonders and the Arab Fort, a very ornate building which was donated to the community by a prominent Ismailian Indian Sir Tharia Topan. It has recently undergone renovations funded by the Agha Khan Cultural trust. The Dispensary now houses the Zanzibar Cultural Centre. Inside is a small tourist development with fixed priced shops, including a jeweller, curio and clothes boutique and a small very pleasant 2 restaurant with a shady courtyard. There are cultural events with taarab, Zanzibari traditional drummers in an open air stadium. Prices: US$12 including barbecue, US$5 for show only.

Further up Mizingani Rd is the **Dhow Harbour** which is a lively and bustling part of the Malindi quarter. It is at its busiest in the morning when the dhows arrive and unload their catches, and buyers bargain and haggle over the prices.

Livingstone House is located on Malawi Rd. It used to be the offices of the Zanzibar Tourist Corporation. Currently it appears to be closed, but it is possible to look around inside if you speak to the caretaker. In 1866 it was used by Livingstone as a base whilst he was staying on the island before what was to be his last journey into the interior. It was from Zanzibar that he arranged his trip inland, organizing porters, supplies and guide.

The **Hamamni Persian Baths**, in the centre of Stone Town, were built by Sultan Barghash for use as public baths and have been declared a protected monument. If you want to have a look inside them ask for the caretaker, Hakim Wambi, who keeps the key and he will let you in and show you around. As there is no water there any more you have to use your imagination as to what it was like in the old days. Hakim also runs the Zanzibar Orphans Trust from the building opposite the baths. He will show you around – donations are gratefully received.

The **Museum** is located in two buildings and although fairly run down and shabby has some interesting exhibits relating to Zanzibar's history. It was built in 1925 and has relics and exhibits from the Sultans, the slave traders and European explorers and missionaries. Livingstone's medicine chest is here and the story of the German battleship the *Königsberg*, sunk during the First World War in the Rufiji Delta, is documented. There are also displays of local arts and crafts. It is located near the junction of Creek Rd with Nyerere and Kuanda Roads at the south end of the town. If you are 'out of season', it has a most interesting exhibit on clove production. There are giant tortoises in the grounds of the Natural History museum next door. The entrance fee is US$1 for both buildings.

Tours

In order to maximize your time in Zanzibar it is worth considering going on a tour. This applies especially if you do not have the time to stay on the east coast and transport can be a problem. Most companies offer a range of tours:

City Tour Half day: includes all the major sites of the Stone Town – market, national museum, cathedral, Beit al-Sahel and Hamamni baths. Cost US$15.

Spice Tour About 4 hours: includes pleasant stops at various villages to taste the freshly picked local fruits and herbs (see spice and copra production). The highly decorated

Zanzibar - Stone Town

Tanzania & Zanzibar

Map labels:

Dhow Harbour

To Bwawani Hotel

Clove Distillary

MALINDI

Fish Market ○

■ Malindi Guest House

Warsame Guest House ■

Ciné Afrique Café ○ ○ Mitu Spice Tour

Fungi Rd

Malindi Rd 🏠 ● Sinbad Sailors

Minara Mosque

To Tourist Office

Creek Rd

■ Narrow Street

Al Jabr ●

KOKONI

Pyramid Guest House ■

🅸 Tourist Information Centre

🏠 Shia-Ithna-Asheri Mosque

HURUMZI

Markets

🚌

OldSlave Market

To New Post Office

■ St Monica's Guest House

Karume Monument ○

Jamhuri Gardens

House of Representatives

MNAZI MMOJA

---

persian baths at the Kidichi are often included. You may be offered a swim on the west coast – however, the water is usually cloudy and useless for snorkelling. **NB** This tour is highly recommended, but only during the harvest – out of season you may get weary of looking at leaves that look very similar. Cost: US$20. An option besides going on an agency organized Spice tour is to get a taxi driver to show you around. US$30 should be the maximum price for 4 people in the car, which competes favourably with some of the organized agency tours.

East Coast Full day: the tour may include a visit to the Jozani Forest where the rare red colobus monkey is found (recommended). Cost: US$35 (US$15 if you only go to Jozani).

North Coast Full day: this can be combined with the spice tour and usually ends at the beach at Nungwi. The Mangapwani slave caves are sometimes also included. Cost: US$35.

Dolphin Tour Dolphin Tours are increasingly promoted part of the tourist industry in Zanzibar. Wander along Forodhani Gardens or up Kenyatta Rd and you will be approached by men offering Spice/Dolphin tours. Prices vary a lot from US$10-75. The quality of the boats are also variable, from leaky wooden to fibreglass. Many of the small boats do not run to a timetable but wait to fill up, usually accommodating 6-8 tourists.

The dolphins swim in pods off Kizimkazi Beach, on the southwest of the island, and are not always readily spotted. It takes about an hour for the boats to reach Kizimkazi Beach, and you are advised to leave early. Loud noises or splashy water entries will scare off the dolphins. If you see a school, do not chase them in the boat. Get reasonably close and the helmsman will turn off the engine. Slide gently into the water, swim with your arms along your body and duck dive/spiral – do interesting things to attract their attention. Dolphins are curious mammals but they are wild. If you are lucky they will surround you and nudge you. Try not to touch them and do not feed them.

Tanzania & Zanzibar

Swimming with the dolphins is not recommended if you are a nervous swimmer. The dolphins are found in the open sea, which frequently has a marked swell. Dolphin's idling speed equates with a reasonable swimmers top speed aided by fins.

There is research being conducted into cetacean behaviour in relation to tourists, to ascertain whether this incredible experience from our point of view may pose long term problems for the dolphins.

Whilst at Kizimkazi Beach it would greatly benefit the local people if a donation was made for their library. There is a book which you can sign and a locked donation box in the rondavel of the guesthouse in Kizimkazi, which has basic food and cold beer available.

Tour operators   Your hotel will be able to arrange the above for you but it may be better to contact one of the specialist companies (see page 463). See below for further details of excursions outside of Zanzibar Town (page 464).

Safety   Safety is becoming an increasing concern in Zanzibar. There have recently been several violent robberies, at knifepoint, of tourists even during daylight hours in Stone Town and its environs. There is speculation that the perpetrators are mainland Tanzanians, as Zanzibaris are noted for their honesty. Travellers have reported that the police do not appear to be actively seeking out these gangs of robbers. Be careful walking after dark, especially in poorly lit areas. Avoid alleyways at night, particularly by the Big Tree. Valuables can usually be left at your hotel safe as an extra precaution. A drawback of wandering around Stone Town, especially near the *Africa House Hotel*, is the number of young men who tout for business to travellers, offering taxis, spice tours, or trips to Prison Island. Some can be very persistent. It is better to deal directly with one of the many tour companies for excursions. Use taxis to get back to the hotel. Exert caution on quiet beaches.

It is not uncommon for travellers to be stopped by the police while driving to one of the beaches. The police may say that they are thirsty or try to claim that your papers are not in order – basically they are looking for a small bribe to supplement their meagre incomes. If you ask for a receipt they will frequently wave you through.

A couple of recently published colour maps of Zanzibar Island, town and the sea (US$5 each) are highly recommended to help plan your stay (see Maps, page 463).

Sleeping   Zanzibar has a relaxed and sympathetic attitude to visitors. However, the islands are
■ *on map, page 454*   predominently Muslim and although Zanzibaris are too polite to raise the issue, they feel
Price codes: uncomfortable with some Western dress styles. In the towns and villages (that is, outside the
see inside front cover   beach hotels and resorts) it is courteous for women to dress modestly, covering the upper arms and body, with dresses to below the knee. Wearing bikinis, cropped tops or shorts cause offence. For men there is no restriction beyond what is considered decent in the west.

All non-residents are expected to pay for hotel accommodation in US dollars even for somewhere very cheap. However the relaxation of currency controls and the introduction of foreign exchange bureaux has meant that local currency is becoming more generally accepted and paying the bill in Tsh is invariably cheaper (but see box, page 444). A few hotels and restaurants now accept Visa credit cards, charges are very steep, at 15-20 percent commission in the £ or US$, plus a 20 percent worse exchange rate. The main exception is *Bwawani Hotel*, which is government-owned. Recent travellers have told us that it is possible to negotiate hotel rates, even in high season, by speaking to the Manager and booking for several days stay. The explosion of interest in Zanzibar has resulted in many houses being turned into hotels and guest houses. Nevertheless it has been the case that the town has been full in June, July and August, and the overspill has been accommodated in tents on the beach. It is advisable to book. If you don't want to stay in the heart of Stone Town, there are places to the north (Mtoni and Bububu) and the south (Mbweni) via the coast roads.

Some hotels in Zanzibar are charging up to 8 percent 'commission' if you use TCs to pay your bill, far more than the forex bureau charges.

Recent visitors to Zanzibar (May 1999) have reported that the authorities will no longer allow camping on beaches. It has not been possible to verify this ruling, as to whether it was just a local decision or whether the whole island is affected. We would be pleased to hear about this from travellers.

A+ *The Fisherman's Resort*, PO Box 2586 Mazizini, T30208/33957, F30556, 10 minutes south of Stone Town, situated in a secluded cove overlooking the nearby islands. Village layout with restaurants, bars, health club, conference rooms, diving and watersports centre, a/c, fridge, private safe, s/c bathrooms, private terraces. **A+** *Zanzibar Reef Hotel*, just outside Zanzibar City, 10 minutes south from Stone Town. Magnificent rooms with good bathrooms, fine swimming pool, lovely clean beach, bit shallow for swimming. **A+** *Zanzibar Serena Inn*, Shangani St at Shangani Square, PO Box 4151, T33587, 33051, F0811-333170, 33019, zserena@cctz.com. One of the nicest hotels in East Africa, stunning restoration of two historic buildings in Stone Town funded by the Aga Khan Fund for Culture to provide a sea front hotel, with 52 luxury rooms and swimming pool. Restaurant has an excellent but pricey menu. Wonderful location with first class service. Pool-side snack menu also recommended – delicious smoked sailfish. Central reservations: Kenya: Williamson House, 4th Ngong Ave, PO Box 48690, Nairobi, T254-2-711077, F718103; Tanzania: 6th floor, AICC Ngorongoro Wing, PO Box 2551, Arusha, T255-57-8175/6304, F4058/4155, Serena@marie.gn.apc.org. **A** *Bwawani Plaza International Hotel*, PO Box 670, T30200, F31840, 101525,1213@ Compuserve.com, located overlooking the Funguni Creek. It's a dull and characterless modern concrete building, now under recent new private ownership, improved facilities and offers a variety of different cuisines, a/c, swimming pool (currently out of service), tennis courts, restaurant, bar and disco on Saturday. **A** *Emersons*, PO Box 4044, T32153, F33135, located fairly centrally at 1563 Mkunazini Rd (but quite hard to find: look for a small brass plaque). This old house has recently been restored by an American hotelier after whom it is named, there are 8 rooms which vary in size and price and whether they have a bathroom attached, they are beautifully decorated and are named by colour, no air conditioning, only provides breakfast as the ground-floor café is closed. **A** *Emersons and Green*, Hurumzi St, is a second *Emersons* hotel, also in Stone Town, no air conditioning, with a spectacular rooftop restaurant – open-sided, no shoes, sit on cushions, not cheap but worthwhile – a really magical experience, beautiful rooms with old Zanzibari furniture and fittings.

B *Chavda*, PO Box 540, T32115, F31931, newly renovated building in heart of Stone Town, off the Shangani Rd. Nice large rooms, rooftop bar, restaurant. **B** *Dhow Palace Hotel*, Stone Town, T33012, F33008. Private bathroom, a/c variable effect, fans, fridge, phone, antique furniture and courtyard, minimal breakfast, Muslim hotel so no bacon or booze on premises. **B** *Inn by the Sea Hotel*, T31755, on the way to Mbweni, good location. As its name suggests, near to the ruins of Kirk House (see page 464). **B** *International*, PO Box 3784, T33182, F30052. Part of the *Narrow Street Hotel* Group, comfortable, a/c, fridge, TV, phone, restaurant, bureau de change, approached through the market which adds to the atmosphere. **B** *Mazsons Hotel*, Kenyatta Rd, PO Box 3367, Stone Town, T33694, 33002, Mobile 0811-320655, F33695. A/c, fridge, TV, only charge US$1 commission on TCs used to pay the bill. **B** *Spice Inn*, PO Box 1029, T30728/30729/28826. Used to be very popular, exudes atmosphere, the rooms vary so ask to take a look before you decide, price including breakfast, some rooms with a/c available, shared or private bathroom. **B** *Shangani Hotel*, PO Box 4222, T/F33688, on Kenyatta Rd in Stone Town near the Old Post Office. Services include a/c, fridge, TV, some rooms s/c bathroom, gift shop, roof top restaurant, laundry service. **B** *Tembo Hotel*, opposite the *Fisherman's Restaurant*, Forodhani St, T33005, F33777. Recommended, pool, has a terrace for sundowners, great location right on beach, food is good – no alcohol. The shop has a reasonable, if limited, range of books, films, and the usual tourist souvenirs. Staff very friendly. One of the nicest hotels in Stone Town.

Tanzania & Zanzibar

C *Baghani House*, PO Box 609, Stone Town, T811-321058, F33030, next to *Zanzibar Hotel*. Private house with 6 rooms, a/c, fans, TV; *Livingstone's Bar*. **C** *Clove*, PO Box 1117, T31017, F32560, located on Hurumzi St, T31785. Self contained with fridge and fan, hot water, good bar at rooftop level, cheap, basic food available. **C** *High Hill*, PO Box 907, T30000/32550, located on Nyerere Rd and is rather out of the way and difficult to get to. Modern, a/c rooms available, price including breakfast, hot water. **C** *Hotel Kiponda*, PO Box 3446, T33052, on Nyumba ya Moto St, central location with good restaurant. **C** *St Monica's Guest House*, PO Box 5, T32484, New Mkunazini St. Very clean and comfortable, own restaurant, price including breakfast. **C** *Tufaah Inn*, Stone Town, T30326, F30225. Some a/c, fans.

D *Africa House*, PO Box 317, T30708, located on Kaunda Rd. This used to be the British Club in the pre-independence days, very run down, rambling traditional building, it has had problems with its water supply, it has a good bar overlooking the sea and the staff are fairly indifferent to guests, warm beer, worth having a 'sundowner' simply to see the tourists, private or shared bathrooms, a/c also available, Annexe I in Narrow St, T32620, Annexe II, T33006. **D** *Blue Ocean Hotel*, good rooms, management fairly orthodox Muslims male/female couples are expected to be married. **D** *Coco de Mer Hotel*, PO Box 2363, Stone Town, T30852, F33008. Including 10 rooms, restaurant, bar, fans, near Old Fort. **D** *Flamingo Guest House*, PO Box 4279, Mkunazini St, T32850, F33144, good value. **D** *Golf Hotel*, T33963. Includes a/c, fans, TV, fridge. **D** *Karibu Inn*, Stone Town, T/F33058. 15 rooms, fans, double rooms have fridges. **D** *Kids Play Guest House*, PO Box 2632, Mwembetanga, T/F30475. S/c rooms, a/c, fridge and satellite TV, free pick-up service – at the edge of Mapem beani ground, excellent breakfasts. **D** *Kiponda Hotel*, Stone Town, T33052, F33020. Rooftop restaurant, sea views, fans. **D** *Kokoin Hotel*, PO Box 1256, T/F31584, Mobile 0812 750232, located in the heart of Stonetown behind the BP Shell garage in Dakajani. Offer a free pick-up service from the airport and the port, hotel very clean with en suite bathroom, hot water, fans and nets and TV, some rooms have a/c. **D** *Lail-Noor Guest House*, PO Box 132, T31086, Maisara, 5-minute walk from Stone Town, close to the beach. S/c bungalows, transport to town. **D** *Malindi Guest House*, PO Box 609, T054-30165, located on Malindi St at Funguni Bazaar – excellent value and a wonderful atmosphere, central courtyard with plants, plenty of space to relax, clean and prices including breakfast. **D** *Mtoni Marine Centre*, T30285. 4 kilometres north of Stone Town near the Maruhubi Palace ruins offers excellent facilities at a reasonable cost – see entry under North, page 465. **D** *Narrow Street Annexe II*, PO Box 3784, T32620, F30052, located on Kokoni St, off Creek Rd. Despite the rather unprepossessing exterior the rooms themselves are quite pleasant and all have baths attached, restaurant, friendly staff. **D** *Pearl Guest House*, T32907, sited in the Stone Town, close to the Shia-Ithna Asheri Mosque. Rooftop views, 100-year-old building, if prearranged by phone, will arrange collection from port or airport at no extra cost, very helpful. **D** *Pyramid Guesthouse*, Kokoni St, PO Box 254, T33000, 30045, Mobile 0811-328460/1. Charming staff, modest, but well recommended. **E** *Riverman Hotel*, Mkunazini St. Spacious restaurant, near Ciné Afrique, PO Box 1805, T/F333188, cheap and clean with good facilities. **D** *Stone Town Inn Hotel*, T/F33658. A/c, fan. **D** *Victoria Guest House*, T32861. Located on Victoria Rd – good value, friendly staff. **D** *Wazazi Guest House*, rather basic. **D** *Zanzibar*, PO Box 392, T30708, F31827. This is located close to the *Africa House Hotel* and is good value, it is a fine example of Zanzibari architecture and has a wonderful atmosphere.

E *Bottomsup*, in the very centre of Stone Town. Run down, very small breakfast, attracts international backpackers, fans and nets available, friendly, good terrace. Recommended. **E** *Garden Lodge Resthouse*, Kaunda Rd, PO Box 3413, T33298, located at Vuga opposite the National Library/High Court. It has lovely gardens, peaceful and quiet with friendly staff. **E** *Manch Lodge Vuga*, Old Town off Vuga Rd. Friendly, clean, best rooms on top floor, huge breakfast. **E** *The Haven Annexe* at Mtoni, T32511 (previously the *Mtoni Sunset Beach Hotel*), about 4 kilometres north of the town off the road to Bububu. Modest but extremely good value. **E** *The Haven Guest House*, PO Box 3746, T33454, Mobile 0811-320204, 0811-327406, located behind the Cultural Musical Club off Vuga Rd. Owned by Mr Hamed, who is also the proprietor of the Annexe, safe, secure place to stay, plenty of hot water, nets and fans, breakfast included in the price, spotlessly clean and very friendly. **E** *Manch Lodge*, Vugu Bed & Breakfast, PO Box 3060, T31918. **E** *Warere Guest House*, including a large breakfast, clean, nets and fan, located close to *Malindi Guest House*, livelier than the *Malindi*, can arrange cheap transport to east coast beaches.

There are a number of moderate standard eating places in Zanzibar and you will not usually need to reserve tables. Many of them have good fresh seafood.

Eating
● on maps
Price codes:
see inside front cover

The only first rate restaurant is **4** *Emerson's*, T32153/30609, and *Emersons and Green*, where you can eat in wonderful surroundings in two different rooftop restaurants, if you are not staying there you need to book a day ahead as space on the roof is limited. **4** *Hotel Kiponda*, T33052. Another relaxing rooftop restaurant serving speciality seafood dishes. **3** *Pagoda*, T31758, Mobile 0812 750168. Has really excellent spicy Chinese cuisine, generous portions, slightly out of Stone Town, located at Funguni close to *Bwawani Hotel*, free transport provided to and from your hotel.

3 *Blues* (formerly the *Floating Restaurant*), T320413, F33098, res@halcyontz.com. Recently extensively upgraded by a South African company which is also renovating the old seafront hotel d'Afrique Central, lovely position, very professional staff. Recommended. On the dock in front of the old Fort which is a good place to watch the children somersaulting from the seawall into the water. **3** *Fisherman Restaurant*, PO Box 3530, T33658, Mobile 0811- 334872, 0812-750071, F33480. Located on Shangani St has good food but is very overpriced. **3** *La Lampara*, good Italian. **3** *Maharaja*, Kenyatta St, opposite High St Vugu, PO Box 1436, T/F30359, Mobile 0811-328243. Excellent food. Recommended. Try the delicious prawn curry. **3** *Sea View Indian Restaurant (Tomane Palace)*, PO Box 666, T32132, has a splendid location which overlooks the harbour. You can eat inside or out and there is a wide range of food on the menu, however service is slow, and if you want to sit on the balcony you would be advised to book ahead.

Among the others, the **2** *Africa House Club* has a mediocre restaurant and cold beer. Slightly cheaper is the **2** *Dolphin Restaurant*, Shangani St, PO Box 138, T31987, which is popular and sells mainly seafood plus some other dishes (nothing special). **2** *The Bistrot*, Stone Town, off Shangani St. Simply decorated inexpensive restaurant with a small but groovy bar. Lots of reggae, delicious fresh fish, generous portions. Popular with backpackers/locals, cold beer. Very noisy. Sited close to the Old Orphanage, **2** *Cultural Centre Restaurant*, at the Na Sur Nurmohamed Dispensary, Mizingani Rd, between the House of Wonders and the Arab Fort, hosts cultural events like taarab, Zanzibari traditional drummers in an open-air stadium, barbecued food. **2** *Cumlurs*, Shangani St, PO Box 546, T31919, 1 minute walk from Africa House. Specializes in Goan cuisine; other places including the **2** *Divers Restaurant*, in Old Town (opposite Eagle Bureau de Change). Serves good cheap, local food. **2** *House of Spices*, Khood St, T33520. Pizza place close to *International Hotel*. **2** *Luis Yoghurt Parlour*, Gizenga

Tanzania & Zanzibar

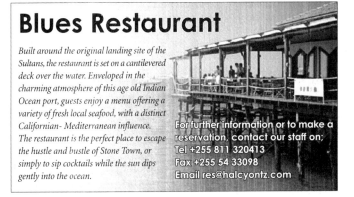

Id-Ul-Fitr Festival

At the end of Ramadan there is a festival called Id-ul-Fitr. It lasts about four days and is a time of general celebration. If you are in Zanzibar at this time go down to Makunduchi which is in the southeast part of the island where there is a carnival atmosphere.

St, is very small and serves excellent local dishes including Lassi yoghurt drinks, milk shakes, fresh fruit juices, spice tea, opens 1000-1400 and 1800-2200 Monday to Saturday. Closes for long periods in off season while the owner goes on holiday. **2** *Luna Mare*, Gizenga St, PO Box 3424, T31922. Reasonably priced Indian food. The **2** *Narrow Street Hotel* on Kokoni St has good food (but not to everyone's taste). If you want a seafood meal it's best to order in advance.

2 *Pichy's Bar*, situated on the seafront. Speciality is pizza. *Two Tables Restaurant* is very charming, on the veranda of a private house, local food and drink (non-alcoholic), situated very close to Victoria House – look out for the signs as no entrance from the street. The **2** *Zee bar and Zee pizza*, oven spice shop, very good.

Other good value places include the café at the **1** *Ciné Afrique* and *Chit Chat*, Cathedral St, PO Box 4099, T32548. Moderate prices, seats 36, serves snacks, refreshments and quick meals. Finally there are a large number of vendors with charcoal grills selling a variety of foods in the **1** *Jamituri Gardens* (also known as *Forodhani*), between the fort and the sea. Here you can get excellent meat or prawn kebabs, corn on the cob, cassava and curries all very cheaply. Fun to wander around even if you don't feel hungry. If you're thirsty, try some fresh coconut milk from one of the local stalls. Try 'African Pizza' (*mantabali*) well worth a try. Excellent foodstall next to the *Fisherman Restaurant*, very popular. **2** *Fuji Snackbar & Restaurant*, Bububu, 6 kilometres, north of Stone Town. Serves snacks and quick meals. Ideal for travellers on the Spice Tours or for those going to Nungwi.

It is not possible to purchase bottles of spirits in shops anymore, only available in bars. Bring your own supply from the mainland if required.

Entertainment The most popular bar in the town is that at the *Africa House Hotel* which looks out across the ocean. The beers are sometimes cold and plentiful although rather expensive, and it is a good place to meet people. Get there early if you want to watch the sun set: seats are quickly taken. Other bars include the *Wazazi Bar* next door to the *Africa House Hotel*. It is cheap, popular, and there is music (sometimes live) and it stays open fairly late. *Livingstone* and *Stanley* Bars in Baghani are open until 0200 where this is good music. Finally the *Starehe Bar*, located on Shangani St, overlooks the harbour and tends to be less crowded than the *Africa House Hotel*. It sometimes holds discos. There is a disco next to the *Fisherman's Restaurant* on Shangani St. The *Bwawani Hotel* has popular disco's on Saturday.

Scuba diving Zanzibar is a great place to go diving. There are two scuba diving schools in town which both offer good value. *Zanzibar Dive Centre-One Ocean*, PO Box 608, T33686, F31242, located behind/under *Africa House Hotel*. Italian owned, very friendly, 2 dhows used to go to several coral reefs, PADI certificate course US$300 for open-water diving. If you have a scuba certificate, 1 dive including boat trip to the reef costs US$35 and 3 dives US$90, including equipment hire costs. The inexperienced are offered 'fun dives' for US$30, which includes 30 minutes instruction in the basics of scuba diving from an experienced instructor, plus a 6 metre deep dive in the coral reef, snorkelling is US$15 a trip, safety highest priority, with fully-trained dive masters/instructors. Recommended. *Dive Africa Watersports* (previously known as Indian Ocean Divers), mobile 0811-323096 Stone Town and T0811-326574, Paradise Beach, PO Box 2370, T/F33860, located beside the *Sea View Indian Restaurant*. They offer a similar package as *Zanzibar Dive Centre One Ocean* and have the same quality and experience. The PADI Open Water Diver course costs US$300, but you can keep the theory book. The coral reef near Zanzibar Town is well preserved. Depending on the season one can see a lot of coral fish, stingrays, scorpion fish, doctor fish and large shoals of sardines. The deepest possible dive is only 26 metres. *The Zanzibar Dive Adventures*, PO Box 2282, Zanzibar,

Tanzania & Zanzibar

T/F32503. For diving in the north and northeast. *Dive Africa Watersports*, Mizingani Rd, between the 'Big Tree' and the Harbour Customs office. Use RIBs not dhows, are part of a larger chain teaching PADI in East Africa.

Shopping

The Market Place off Creek road sells mainly fresh fruit and vegetables. However the shops nearby sell kikois and kangas, wooden chests and other souvenirs. If you want batiks or paintings, a visit to the small art gallery above *St Monica's Guest House* is worthwhile. The *Rashid A Nograni Curio Shop* and the *Chanda Curio Shop* sell carvings, wooden boxes, brass and copper coffeepots and jewellery. You can pick up good reading material at *Musoma Bookshop* just behind the Central Market. *Stone Town Memories*, T33300, Gizenga St, deal in old artefacts and handicrafts. *The Gallery*, Gizenga Rd, has an excellent range of new and secondhand books, and a huge range of curios. It also sells excellent post cards taken by the owners son. Accepts credit cards. *Abeid Curio Shop*, T33832, Cathedral St, sells old Zanzibari furniture, clocks, copper and brass ware. In the area near Mlandegi Bazaar there is a wide choice of Kangas and Kofias – the traditional Muslim head covering. Also available are bread baskets, woven flat trays from Pemba and Mafia, plus wooden artefacts. Zanzibar is a good place to buy film (mostly Konica) and tends to be cheaper than Kenya. Outside the *Hammamni Public Baths* there are ceramic bowls for sale, which the Zanzibarians use to decorate their homes. Originally Dutch in design. Visitors are advised not to buy products of rare and endangered species such as green turtle.

Transport

Air Air Tanzania (PO Box 773, T30297/32441/30213) is scheduled to have 2 flights daily in each direction between **Dar es Salaam** and Zanzibar which costs US$43 and takes about 20 minutes. The Air Tanzania office is on Vuga St and closes for lunch (1230-1400). You can also fly to Zanzibar from **Mombasa** on **Kenya Airways** for US$35 (plus US$20 airport tax). The Kenya Airways office is close to the Oman Air office, behind the Ijuna Mosque, PO Box 3840, Zanzibar, T32041-2-3. **Gulf Air** also have direct flights from Europe, PO Box 3179, Zanzibar, T33379/33221. As always book in advance as this is a popular route. **ZATA**, Zanzibar Airport, T33569 32001; or c/o Jasfa, PO Box 4203, T/F30468; or Pemba 2016, has 2 flights most days between Zanizibar and **Dar es Salaam**. Depart Zanzibar 0930 and 1600 (1700 on Wednesday and Saturday) Depart Dar es Salaam 1300 (not Monday, Thursday, Saturday) and 1730 (1815 Wednesday and Saturday). The fair is US$41 one-way. ZATA also has 2 flights most days to **Pemba**. Depart Zanzibar 0730 (not Sunday) and 1400 (Wednesday, Friday, Sunday only). Depart Pemba 0830 (not Sunday), 1615 (Wednesday and Sunday only), 1500 Friday. Fare US$46 one-way. There is a relatively new private airline called **Precisionair** which has regular flights between Zanzibar, Dar es Salaam and Arusha. Reputed to offer an excellent service so far. However, it is essential to follow the instructions to reconfirm – flight times are frequently at variance with that printe`d on the tickets.

If you are returning from Zanzibar to Dar es Salaam, you could try and get a seat on the plane which brings the daily newspapers over. Tickets are sold from the Musoma Bookshop (T32652) and cost $40.

There are buses between the airport and the town for a US$0.50. Alternatively you can get a taxi for about US$6-US10. Zanzibar Airport, T I-54-32001/32872.

Dhows: a cheaper alternative from **Dar es Salaam** is by motorized dhow (nicknamed *yongo* which is Swahili for milipede). These go each way most days leaving early in the morning (about 0600) costing about US$3 and taking up to 8 hours. It is hot and there is no food or water on board so take your own. To get back to Dar es Salaam book from the Malindi Sports Club opposite Sinbad Sailors Restaurant 1 day in advance. This is strictly speaking illegal as there have been some restrictions on non-Tanzanians travelling by dhow. You can also get a dhow to **Pemba** and **Mombasa**. For Pemba book at the Malindi Sports Club. For Mombasa they go once or twice a week. Ask for details at the Institute of Marine Science on Mizingani Rd. It costs about US$3 and takes about 6 hours to Pemba, to Mombasa US$10 and takes about 24 hours.

The *Zanzibar Shipping Corporation* runs a weekly service between Dar es Salaam, Pemba and Zanzibar. The Zanzibar booking office is at the wharf, and the fare is about US$2-3. It's an unreliable service and not recommended unless you're on a very tight budget with time to spare.

Tanzania & Zanzibar

👉 **Sea Ferries to Zanzibar**

Name of ferry boat	Schedule	Fare Tsh	Duration
Sea Express T255-51-137049 F255-51-116723	*DSM Depart:* *1000* *1515* *ZNZ Depart:* *0700* *1200*	**Residents** *1st class 11,500* *2nd class:10,500* **Non resident** *1st class U$40* *2nd class U$35*	*70 minutes*
New Sea US Fast Ferries T811-334347 or 134013	*DSM Depart:* *1115* *1600* *ZNZ Depart:* *0700* *1330* *1600*	**Residents** *1st class 12,500* *2nd class 10,500* **Non resident** *1st class U$40* *2nd class U$35*	*90 minutes*
MS Sepideh N T0811-326414 **Note:** DSM-Pemba: daily DSM-Tanga: Saturday	*DSM Depart:* *Daily except Sunday* *0730* *ZNZ Depart:* *Daily except Saturday* *1600*	**Resident** *12,500* **Non resident** *Salon U$35* *VIP U$40*	*90 minutes*
Sea Star Service T0812-789393 or 781500	*DSM Depart:* *0730, 1145* *1400, 1615* *ZNZ Depart:* *0815, 1015* *1415, 1615*	**Resident** *Economy 8,000* *1st class 9,000* **Non resident** *Economy US$25* *1st class U$30*	*90 minutes*
Flying Horse T255-51-124504	*DSM Depart:* *1230* *ZNZ Depart:* *2000* *arrive DSM 0600*	**Resident** *1st class 8,500* *2nd class 8,000* *3rd class 7,500* *VIP class 9,500* **Non resident** *US$25*	*2 hours*

Port tax US$5

Getting around the island You can hire **minivans** which seat 8 passengers through one of the tour agencies. It will cost about US$40 for the van. At the southern end of Jamituri Gardens it is possible to hire **four-wheel drives** that are parked there for US$30 a day. Hiring a taxi to take you across the island is cheaper if negotiated directly, rather than through a tour agent. Pickup vans (known as *dala dalas*) with wooden benches in the back are the cheapest way of getting around the island. It will cost about US$2 per person to the east coast and is a hot, dusty and not very comfortable journey. You can hire **bicycles** (there is a shop close to the Tourist Bureau on Creek Rd) for US$5 a day and there is a US$50 deposit. **Motorbikes** can be hired for US$20 per day from behind the tax office close to Jamituri Gardens. Vespas can be hired for US$25 and Honda 125ccs for US$30 per day (rates negotiable). Left side of Post Office (recommended) and opposite Post Office. **Buses** to the east coast go from the bus station on Creek

Rd opposite the Market. To Chwaka takes 1½ hours, to Jambiani takes 3 hours, and to Bwejuu takes 4½ hours, costing US$2.50-3. There is a bus which returns from the East Coast to Stone Town leaving at 0630. However, this means that you need to get your baggage to the bus stop under your own steam. Travellers have reported that trips may be offered to remote parts of the island at an agreed price, eg to Jambiani by minibus/landrover. However, on arrival, they were forced to pay 3 times the agreed original price. The return trip cost 4 times the original one-way quote.

Banks The chaotic *People's Bank of Zanzibar*,T054-11138/9, F054-31121, is located close to the fort. There is also a branch at the Airport Terminal, T054-1118/9 and 11138/9, F054-31121. Close by is the *Tanzania Commercial Bank*. However banks often give an inferior rate compared with the foreign exchange bureaux. There is a foreign exchange bureau opposite the Tourist Bureau at north end of Creek road. *Malindi Exchange* opposite Ciné Afrique, next to Zanair offer good rates reputed to be the best in town T30903, F30052, and *Darajani Bureau de Change* on the Darajani Rd, T33820, F30052. Near the Post Office is the efficient and friendly *Shangani Bureau de Change*, T31660, F33688. *The Forex Bureau* around the corner from *Mazsons Hotel* is reported to offer excellent exchange rates.

Communications Post Office: the post office is located out of Stone Town past the Karume Monument. Bus A or M from the market will take you there. Poste Restante and faxes are held there. The Poste Restante charge is US$0.15 per letter held for collection. Ask to see all letters if you are expecting mail as the local sorting and filing can be erratic. There is another Post Office in the Shangani area.

Hospitals & medical services There is a state hospital (V I Lenin) on Kaunda Rd. Also private Clinic – *Mkunazini Hospital*, near to the market. British trained doctor. Pay fee to register, wait to see doctor then pay for any prescription necessary. Pay again when go to collect medicine: this may be at the clinic or in a nearby drug-store. An interesting way to pass a few hours if not too ill. A good clinic is *Zamedic*, PO Box 1043, Bububu, near the cinema, T/F33113. Ask for Dr Mario Mariani.

Tour companies & travel agencies *Mitu*. Contactable at the café next door to the Ciné Afrique early in the mornings or in the evenings. Get a group of 4 together, and Mitu an elderly Indian (or one of the people he has trained) will take you on one of his own guided tours visiting the Marahubi Palace, 2 spice plantations, the Kidichi Baths and a 1 hour trip to relax on the beach. They are good value. However they have become very popular and you may find yourself in a large group. Cost US$10 per person including vegetarian lunch. Get there by 0900, departure 0930, returns 1600. Advance bookings in Dar es Salaam: Coastal Travels Ltd, PO Box 3052 Upanga Rd, Dar es Salaam, T1 37279/37480, F36585. Bookings are also taken at the office next to the Ciné Afrique from about 0800 on the day. *Adventure Afloat* organize *African Boat Safaris*, PO Box 4056, Zanzibar, T/F30536, T31832, Mobile 0811 320166, c/o Mbweni Ruins Hotel, Marine Channel 72 (156.625 MHz). Excursions to see the dolphins, game fishing and dhow trips available. UK office, 21 Linton St, London N1 7DU, T0171-3540771. *Chema Bros Tours*, PO Box 1865, Shangani Rd, T33385. *Classic Tours*, c/o Emerson's House, T83629. *Dolphin Tours*, PO Box 138, New Mukanazini Rd, T33386. *Eco Tours*. Recommended for the Dolphin Tour US$15 per person including transport, guide, lunch, boat and snorkelling gear. *Equator Tours and Safaris*, PO Box 2096, T33799, F33882, Tx57070 RDZ TZ. *Faizin Tours & Travel Agency*, PO Box 702, T32501. Also have a branch at Pemba. *Jasfa Tours & Safaris*, PO Box 4203, Shangani Rd, T/F30468, Res 31457. Good reputation and will confirm flights, organize hotel bookings, etc. *Mreh Tours & Safaris*, PO Box 3769, T33476, F30344. *Orient Expeditions*, T30813. *Rainbow Tours & Travel*, T33469, F33701. Car and bike hire, tours, hotel bookings, flight confirmations. Recommended. *Ras Tours & Safaris*, T31078. *Sama Tours*, PO Box 2276, Changa Bazaar St, T33543. *Sun and Fun Safari Tours*, PO Box 666, Shangani Rd, T32132. *Triple M Tours Africa House Club*, T30708/30709. *Tropical Tours & Travel*, Kenyatta Rd, Shangani, T/F30868. Good reliable agency. *Zanea Tours*, PO Box 620, Shangani Rd, T30413. *Zanzibar Safari Tours*, PO Box 4052, Kenyatta Rd, T31463. *Zanzibar Tourist Corporation*, Creek Rd, PO Box 216, T32344. Incompetent. *Zenj Tours*, PO Box 3355, T31894/30384.

Tourist offices *Commission for Tourism*, PO Box 1410, Zanzibar, T33485/6/7, F33448. There is a *Tanzania Friendship Tourist Bureau* located on Creek Rd, at the north end. Sells map of island but otherwise not terribly helpful. Maps: excellent colour *Map of Zanzibar* available with town map on one side and the Island map on the other. Includes hotels, beach resorts, flora and fish. *Zanzibar at Sea* illustrates the diving, snorkelling and game fishing facilities and Mnemba Atoll, by Giovanni Tombazzi 1996, distributed by MACO Ltd, PO Box 322, Zanzibar, T/F54-33778, US$5 each.

Directory

Tanzania & Zanzibar

Changuu Island (Prison Island)

Colour map 5, grid B1   Also known as Prison Island (just off Stone Town), this island was once owned by an Arab who used it for 'rebellious' slaves. Some years later in 1893 it was sold to General Mathews, a Briton who converted it into a prison. However it has never actually been used as such and was later converted to serve as a quarantine station for East Africa in colonial times. The prison is still relatively intact and a few remains of the hospital can be seen including the rusting boilers of the laundry. There is good snorkelling, wind surfing and sailing from the beautiful little beach. Jelly fish can sometimes spoil bathing and snorkelling however. The island is also home to giant tortoises which are supposed to have been brought over from Aldabra (an atoll off the Seychelles) around the turn of the century. The tortoises are no longer roaming freely over the island because many were stolen. Now they are kept in a large fenced area. Recent visitors report that a US$4 landing fee has been imposed.

Grave Island which is nearby, has no facilities, but there is an interesting cemetery with headstones of British sailors and marines who lost their lives in the fight against slavery and in the First World War.

Sleeping   **B** *Reef Hotel*, south of Zanzibar Town, T30208, F30556. Includes a/c, TV, phone, pool, traditional dance shows and buffet. **C** *Changuu Island Resort*, PO Box 216, T32344, F33430, Tx57144. Simple and reasonable with cold beers, also has facilities for snorkelling, wind surfing and sailing, plans are afoot for a huge holiday complex to be built by Lonrho.

Transport   **Local**   You can get there through one of the tour agencies. Or a boat will take you across to the island for about US$5. There is a US$1 landing fee. Day trips can be arranged from *Africa House Hotel*. Alternatively ask around on the beach in front of the *Sea View Indian Restaurant*.

South of Zanzibar town

Kiungani,
Mbweni &
Chukwani
Colour map 5, grid
B1/C1

This route will take you past Kiungani where there was once a hostel built in 1864 by Bishop Tozer for released slave boys. A little further on are the ruins of **Mbweni Settlement** which was also established for rescued slaves. This was built in 1871 by the Universities Mission to Central Africa. In 1882 St John's Church was built in the same place for the use of the released slaves. There is a fine carved door and a tower.

Also at Mbweni is **Kirk House** which was built by Seyyid Barghash in 1872. Kirk came to Zanzibar as part of Livingstone's expedition to the Zambezi as the Medical Officer. He played an important role in the fight to end the slave trade and in 1873 was appointed His Majesty's Agent and Consul General in Zanzibar. He was also a botanist, introducing a number of plants to the island said to have originated from Kew Gardens, including cinnamon, vanilla, mahogany and eucalyptus.

Further south at Chukwani are the **Mbweni Palace Ruins**. This was once a holiday resort of Sultan Seyyid Barghash and it had a wonderful position overlooking the sea. However it has been totally neglected and as a result is slowly crumbling away. The main palace has completely disappeared, although some of the other buildings do remain and may be toured. The ruins are located to the south of the town off the airport road. **A** *Mbweni Ruins Hotel*, PO Box 2542, T31832, F30536, Mobile 811 320855, mbweni-ruins@twiga.com. Built in the spacious grounds of the ruins of the first Anglican Christian missionary settlement in East Africa in 1871, seafront, pool, garden setting, art gallery, a/c, fans.

Chumbe Island
Colour map 5, grid C1

Approximately four kilometres off-shore southwest from Chukwani Palace ruins lies the **Chumbe Island Marine Sanctuary**. This is a wonderful reef with coral gardens which can be viewed from glass-bottomed boats. Snorkelling is available. Tours are organized from the *Mbweni Ruins Hotel*, US$68 per trip.

Changuu Tortoises

The earliest trade routes from Europe to India and the Far East, before the building of the Suez Canal in 1856, went down the west coast of Africa, round the Cape, and northeast through the Indian Ocean Islands. On such a long journey, ships put in to ports along the route to replenish water and victuals. On the Indian Ocean leg giant tortoises, turtles and dodos proved easy to catch for meat that was salted and stored. Reunion, Rodrigues and Mauritius were the principle sources.

By 1750, the tortoises on Mauritius were facing extinction, and 30,000 tortoises were brought in from Diego-Garcia 5,000 kilometres to the west in the Indian Ocean.

The new supply could not meet with demand, however, and by 1850 tortoises were extinct in Mauritius, Reunion and Rodrigues, as well as in the Farquar Islands in the Seychelles. In 1884, in an effort to make sure that some tortoises survived, tortoises were shipped from the Aldabra Islands in the Seychelles, and were used to establish protected colonies in Mauritius, the Chagos Islands near Diego Garcia, and on Changuu Island off Zanzibar. As tortoises can live for 150 years, some of the tortoises you can see on Changuu began their lives on Aldabra, 1,000 kilometres to the southeast, more than 120 years ago.

North to Ras Nungwe

These are located about three kilometres to the north of the town. They were built in 1882 by Sultan Barghash for his harem of many (said to be 99) women. The palace was almost completely destroyed by a fire in 1899. All that remains are the pillars and aqueducts which brought water to the palace from the nearby springs. The site is very overgrown, and marble from the baths has long since been stolen.

Maruhubi Palace ruins
Colour map 5, grid B1

Between the ruined palace of Maruhubi and Mtoni to the north is **Mtoni Marine Centre,** PO Box 992, Zanzibar. There are two kinds of accommodation on offer, **B** *Mtoni Club*, T32540, F865692, Mobile 811 323226/321381, a/c, self-contained rooms with verandas, beachfront restaurant, thatched roofs. **C** *Mtoni Village*, T30285, simple, comfortable, self-contained rooms by the beach, private jetty, safe moorings, all marine activities, closest beach to Stone Town, dhows trips can be arranged and excursions to Jozani Forest etc. Safe parking for motorcycles.

Beit-ell-Ras Palace Ruins Building began on this palace for Seyyid Said in 1847, but was left unfinished when he died. Some of the impressive stone arches can still be seen. The rest was used in the construction of the Bububu Railway at the start of this century, which linked the centre of the town with the village. The line wasn't viable, and closed in the 1920s.

Fuji beach This can be easily reached from Bububu village, and is a great place to take a relaxing swim if you've been exploring the area. A good place to stay is the **D** *Bububu Beach Guest House*. Access to the Stone Town is easy, as there is a shuttle at 0900 and 1800. In the evening they pick up their guests in Stone Town at around 2100 and drive them back to the guest house. Alternatively any Matatu with the letter B from the main road will get you to Fuji beach. Five kilometres north of Fuji Beach, past Chuini Palace is **Mawimbini Village Club,** Chuwini Village, PO Box 4281, T31163, offering water sports – diving, snorkelling, sailing, windsurfing and boat excursions.

Built on the highest point of Zanzibar Island by Sultan Seyyid Said in 1850, they were for his wife who was Persian, and are decorated in an ornamental stucco work that is in the Persian style. The remarkably preserved Baths have a series of domed bath-houses with deep stone baths and massive seats.

Persian Baths at Kidichi
Colour map 5, grid B1

Tanzania & Zanzibar

This is quite a contrast to the plain baths nearby at **Kizimbani**, which were built within Said's clove tree and coconut plantation.

Mangapwani slave caves
Colour map 5, grid B1

Located about 20 kilometres north of the town, these were used to hide slaves in the times when the slave trade was illegal but in fact continued unofficially. One particular trader, Mohammed bin Nasser, built an underground chamber at Alwi which was used as well as the naturally formed cave. The cave itself is said to have been discovered when a young slave boy lost a goat that he was looking after. He followed its bleats which led it to the cave containing a freshwater stream. The discovery of the cave (although it was used to hide slaves and thus helped the slave trade continue illegally), was actually a blessing in disguise, as the freshwater stream was a boon to the confined slaves. You may well see women carrying water from this very same stream today. If you want to get there independently the caves can be reached by taking the bus from Creek Rd opposite the market.

Tumbatu Island, located northwest of Zanzibar, contains Shirazi ruins of a large ancient town dating from the 12th century. There are about 40 stone houses remaining.

Mvuleni ruins
Colour map 5, grid A2

These are in the north of the island and are the remains of the Portuguese attempt to colonize Zanzibar.

Nungwi
Colour map 5, grid A2

At the north tip of the island is **Nungwi**, located about 56 kilometres from Zanzibar town. Down on the beach, local men are often working in groups to build dhows. Boat enthusiasts can observe how dhows are constructed. Lorries will take approximately one hour from town – order from the hotel, US$4 per person one way.

Nungwi is a pleasant fishing village, and has a number of good, white, beach-side bungalows. There are several good beaches and it is a good place for snorkelling and diving. Snorkelling equipment can be hired from local shops. A number of places organize 'sunset cruises' on traditional dhows US$15 per person. The name of this resort is derived from the Swahili word *mnara* meaning lighthouse. Built in 1886 by Chance and Brothers, this 70 foot lighthouse was operated by a kerosene burner for its first 40 years, when it was converted to an automatic system. It flashes for half a second every five seconds. Currently the lighthouse is in a restricted area, with access permitted only by special request. Photographing the lighthouse is prohibited. Nungwi has arguably the best beaches, with little seaweed and the water is a little cooler than the east side. The tide does not go out for miles either. However, it is developing fast. Remember to respect local custom if you go in to the village. Women should cover their arms, shoulders and thighs. Men are expected to cover up too.

Maviko ya Makumbi: As you walk along the beach there are mounds of what look like stones, known locally as 'Heaps of Stones', which are in fact deposits of coconut husks, which is made into coir and may be used to make ropes, matting and decorations. Each Heap of Stones belongs to a family or sometimes an individual, and some are 60 years old, passed down from one generation to the next. The coconuts are buried in the mud for 3-6 months, which accelerates the decay of unwanted parts of the coconut, leaving the coir. The sea water helps to prevent insect infestation. The coir is hammered which helps to separate it from other vegetable matter. Again, it is recommended that if you see a group of women working on the Maviko ya Makumbi, that you request permission before taking a photograph.

Boat building has been a traditional skill for generations using historic tools and a 12 metre boat takes approximately six months to build. Goats are slaughtered when certain milestones are reached, eg raising the mast, and verses and prayers are read from the Koran. Upon completion a big ceremony is organized, with all villagers invited. Before the launch the boat builder hammers the boat three times in a naming ceremony.

You can buy basics at the small shops along the beach front but it is much cheaper to go into the village where water, bread and other basics are available. There are two natural aquariums near the lighthouse at the northern tip of the island. **Mnarani Aquarium** was established in 1993 by a local resident in an attempt to help restore the local turtle population which had been rapidly declining in recent years. Turtles in optimum conditions have a life expectancy of over 150 years. Four varieties of turtle are endemic to Zanzibar; the hawksbill (Ng'amba); the green turtle (Kasakasa); the leather back turtle (Msumeno) and the longer head turtle (Mtumbi). In the aquarium are five green turtles which have a light grey/yellowish shell and two hawksbill turtles, which have a yellowish/red shell. Their diet is seaweed and the hawksbill also eats fish. Any turtles hatched at the aquarium are released into the sea. It is possible to hand feed these protected turtles with seaweed. Entry cost is US$1.60. Visitors are advised not to buy any turtle products on offer, to discourage this illicit trade. As in other parts of the island beach robberies have been reported.

Sleeping A *Ras Nungwi Beach Hotel*, Zanzibar, T07714-088822, res@halcyontz.com or juliet.halcyon@virgin.net. 68 kilometres from Stone Town near Nungwi (north). All major credit cards accepted, excellent dive centre with good diving on the reef, deep sea fishing. The hotel is closed for a few weeks in low season April and June. Mastercard and Visa accepted but attract a 10 percent surcharge.

B *Mnarani Beach Cottages*, PO Box 3361, Zanzibar, T/F33440, Mobile 0811-334062, Mnarani@cctz.com, www.raha.com/mnarani.htm. 12 cottages, located right by the sea, next to the beach, friendly management, clean, comfortable and well maintained, great service and a good atmosphere, reductions can be negotiated in low season, caters for middle budget tourist/traveller, sited up near the lighthouse, 20 minute walk from the main strip, service includes bar, seafront restaurant, international cuisine, laundry facilities, hot water, snorkelling, fishing and diving trips. **B** *Saleh's Beach Bungalows*, close to Ras Nungwi.

C *Amaans*, PO Box 2750, Mobile 0811 327747, F0811-30556. Clean, basic, share showers and toilets, has a restaurant too, transport by minibus can be arranged from hotels in Zanzibar Stone Town, situated right on the beach, breakfast included, 3 bars and restaurant on site serve good quality food. Scuba diving centre. **C** *Imani Lodge*, Bububu Beach. Recommended. **C** *Paradise Beach Club*, run by Indian Ocean Divers, has pleasant bar/restaurant, if you wish to sleep out under the stars try out one of the two bandas next to the Baraka Bungalows on the beach at US$5 per person, breakfast not included in the price. **D** *Baraka Guesthouse*, simple bungalows close to Nungwi Village, including breakfast, communal showers, cheap restaurant with generous portions, close to the beach, mosquito nets, clean. **E** *Kigoma Guest House*, PO Box 1496. No phone, slightly more basic than Baraka and Amaan but quieter, popular with budget travellers, very friendly staff, nets, fans and en suite. **E** *Morning Star Guesthouse*, PO Box 7092, in the village. New, very clean, friendly staff,

Tanzania & Zanzibar

Diving and fishing in Zanzibar

There are many new developments catering for diving and deep sea fishing on the north and northeast coast. These include:
A+ Mnemba Fishing Club, **Mnemba Island**, lies 15 minutes by boat from northeast Zanzibar. Private island resort, offers watersports, big game fishing, 'Barefoot luxury', bookings via Archers Tours, Nairobi, PO Box 40097, T254-2331825, F254-2212656, Tx22082, very expensive, costs US$300 per person per night. **A** Mapenzi Beach Resort, located at **Pw Mchang**, T0811-325985, F0811-325986. Marine sports centre.
B Matemwe Bungalows, in **Matemwe**, T/F31342. Marine Sports centre, snorkelling, fishing and sailing, good food, friendly staff, hotel has an excellent relationship with the local village residents. **C** Mtoni Marine Centre (north of Zanzibar Town), T/F32540. Water sports, adjacent to ruins, seafront, restaurant and bar. **B** Mawimbini Hotel Village, T/F31163. Italian hospitality in a club setting. **E** Makunduchi Beach Bungalows, T32344, F33430. Government-run beach house.

including breakfast, own bathroom and shower, 6 rooms. **E** *Safina Guest House*, PO Box 2050. No phone, self-contained, fan, breakfast, has 11 rooms, soon to have 14.

Eating The cheapest and tastiest place to eat is the *Gossip Restaurant* between Paradise and Amaan guesthouses. Set menu, usually coconut rice with coconut sauce, tuna steak or king fish, calamares or octupus, sweet potatoes and chapattis. There are several other restaurants and two bars at prices that range from US$3 to US$7.

Diving: diving is good, 2 dive shops, both with representatives in Stone Town, *Dive Africa Watersports* (previously known as *Indian Ocean Divers*) and *Zanzibar Dive Centre-One Ocean Divers* – see information on page 460.

South of Nungwi, about 20 minutes along the beach, is a small resort called **Kendwa Rocks**. It is reached by a boat which is free for residents at the two hotels at Kendwa Rocks which leaves at 0930 daily. **E** *Kendwa Rocks Hotel* and the nearby similar **E** *White Sands Hotel*, PO Box 1933, T32854, Mobitel: 0811 337462. There are bandas and a campsite, basic food available. It is reported that next door there is also a fancy resort costing US$30 a night. Boat rides to Tumbatu Island can be organized. Snorkel and kayaks can be hired. *Getting there:* Their Land Rover meets the minibuses which bring tourists from Stone Town to Nungwi daily.

There are many new developments catering for diving and deep sea fishing on the north and northeast coast. These include: **A** *Mnemba Fishing Club*. **Mnemba Island** lies 15 minutes by boat from northeast Zanzibar, private island resort, offers watersports, big game fishing, 'Barefoot luxury', bookings via Archers Tours, Nairobi, PO Box 40097, T254-2-331825, F254-2-212656, Tx22082. Very expensive, costs $300 per person per night. **A** *Mapenzi Beach Resort*, located at Pw Mchang, T0811-325985, F0811-325986. Marine sports centre, good food, friendly staff, hotel has an excellent relationship with the local village residents. **C** *Mtoni Marine Centre*, (north of Zanzibar Town), T/F32540. Watersports, adjacent to ruins, seafront, restaurant and bar. **B** *Mawimbini Hotel Village*, T/F31163, Italian hospitality in a club setting. **E** *Makunduchi Beach Bungalows*, T32344, F33430. Government-run beach house.

East coast

The east part of the island is not too difficult to get to but has a remote, 'get away from it all' feel, which is part of its attraction. Recently the road to Paje has been sealed – the trip there by minibus takes just over an hour. Cost there US$2 per person, back US$3. Here you will see the fishermen go out in their dhows, while the women sit in the shade and plait coconut fibre which they then make into every-thing from fishing nets to beds. In principle you still have to pay for accommodation in foreign currency and book at the tourist office in Zanzibar but these regulations are being relaxed.

Communications with the east coast are poor. For the most part it is necessary to book through an agent in Zanzibar or in Dar es Salaam – or take a chance on getting a room when you arrive. This is particularly risky from June to September. However, the number of places offering accommodation are increasing significantly. It is reported that licence applications had been made for a further 200 hotels in Zanzibar.

Central and northeast

This route takes you across the centre of the island. Just over 20 kilometres down the road are the Dunga Palace ruins which were built by Chief Mwinyi Mkuu Ahmed bin Mohamed Hassan. Unfortunately there is little left of the palace today beside a few arches and bits of wall, and the area has been taken over by a plantation. At the end of this route you will reach Chwaka Bay – see section on the East Coast, page 471. Also on the east coast to the north of Chwaka is Uroa, another beach resort.

Dunga & Chwaka to Matemwe

This is located 32 kilometres from Zanzibar town and is a popular beach. Has one of the islands main fish markets. It was also popular as a holiday resort with slave trad-ers and their families in the 19th century. The beach is lovely and the fishing is said to be good. Swimming is impractical at low tide – long walk out.

Chwaka
Colour map 5, grid B2

Sleeping B *Chwaka Beach Hotel*, T33943, F30406. Accepts credit cards, curio shop and bar. **D** *Bungalows* (two), run by the Tourist Office at Chakwa. **D** *East Coast Guest House* and restaurant, cheap with basic facilities, friendly, good food. **D** *Kichipwi Guest House*, book through Ali Khamis, PO Box 25, Zanzibar.

Lovely unspoilt fishing village located 10 kilometres to the north of Chwaka, Uroa is close to the Dongwe Channel. It offers suitable diving for novices.

Uroa
Colour map 5, grid B2

Sleeping A+ *Uroa Bay Village Resort*, PO Box 3389, T32552, F33504 or c/o *Coastal Travels*, PO Box 3052, Upanga Rd, Dar es Salaam, T37279/37480, F36585. Italian-run establishment, high standard, swimming pool, tennis courts, watersports, selective game fishing, water ski-ing and diving school – SSI & PADI. **A** *Tamarind Beach Hotel*, T33041, 33060, F33041/2. Dive centre offering fishing, snorkelling, game fishing, sailing, surfing and parasailing, *Buddies Divebase*, located between Uroa and Chwaka, European-run, no pool, pleasant restaurant and open-air bar. **B-C** *Kiwenga*, 10 kilometres north of Uroa, has a Club Village, T0811-325304, watersports and tennis. **C** *Sun and Sand Beach Bungalows*, Stone Town office, T32449. Comfortable accommodation. **C** *Uroa Bay Hotel*, T32552, F33584. **D** *Blue Sea Guest House*, near *Uroa Bay Hotel*, cheap, basic accommodation.

Five kilometres north of Uroa, **D** *Pongwe Beach Hotel*, new nice bungalows, small, good beach. Book through *Fisherman's Tours* in Stone Town.

Pongwe
Colour map 5, grid B2

10 kilometres north of Uroa, unsealed road from Pongwe.

Kiwengwa

Sleeping A+ *Kiwengwa Club Village (Francorossa)*. New luxury development, beautiful, good diving, *Orca Diving Centre*, c/o Kiwengwa Club Village, PO Box 4095, T0811-326205, professional diving centre offers PADI courses. **B** *Pongwe Beach Hotel*, beach bungalows, comfortable. South of the village is a new development **C** *Reef View*, bandas and bunga-lows, bar and restaurant.

45 kilometres from Stone Town and 15 kilometres north of Kiwenga is the small vil-lage of Matemwe.

Matemwe
Colour map 5, grid A2

Tanzania & Zanzibar

Clove production

It has been estimated that there are about six million clove trees on the islands of Zanzibar and Pemba and they cover about one 10th of the land area. The plantations are found mainly in the west and northwest of the islands where the soil is deeper and the landscape hillier. To the east the soil is less deep and fertile and is known as 'Coral landscape'.

Cloves were at one time only grown in the Far East and they were greatly prized. On his first trip back from the East, Vasco da Gama took a cargo back to Portugal and they were later introduced by the French to Mauritius and then to Zanzibar by Sayyid Said who was the first Arab sultan. At this time all the work was done by slaves who enabled the plantations to be established and clove production to become so important to the economy of the islands. When the slaves were released and labour was no longer free, some of the plantations found it impossible to survive although production did continue

and Zanzibar remained at the head of the world production of cloves.

Cloves are actually the unopened buds of the clove tree. They grow in clusters and must be picked when the buds are full but before they actually open. They are collected in the sprays and the buds are then picked off before being spread on the ground to dry out. They are spread out on mats made from woven coconut palm fronds for about five days, turned over regularly so that they dry evenly – the quicker they dry the better quality the product.

There may be many clove trees on Zanzibar now – but there were even more in the past. In 1872 a great hurricane passed over the island destroying many of the trees and it was after this that Pemba took over from Zanzibar as the largest producer. Zanzibar however has retained the role of chief seller and exporter of cloves so the Pemba cloves first go to Zanzibar before being sold on.

Sleeping B *Matemwe Bungalows*, PO Box 3275, T33789, F31342. To the north of the village offers simple accommodation. Recommended. The bandas are built from local materials, coral stone walls and dried palm leaf roofs and all the bandas are surrounded by colourful flowers and have an ocean view. The food is the fresh fish catch of the day and meat dishes are also available. The area is unspoilt with white sandy beaches and excellent snorkelling is possible at the nearby coral reef. A professional diving centre is planned to open soon.

South east

Bwejuu,
Makunduchi,
Kizimkazi
Colour map 5, grid C3

There is a small nature reserve, **Jozani Forest**, located about 40 kilometres to the southeast of Zanzibar town which is home to the last few remaining protected red colobus monkeys, one of Africa's rarest primates. Only 1,500 are believed to have survived. In Zanzibar Kiswahili, the name for the red colobus monkey is *Kima Punju* – 'Poison Monkey'. It has associations with the kind of poisons used by evil doers. Local people believe that when the monkeys have fed in an area, the trees and crops die, and dogs will lose their hair if they eat the colobus. Although legally protected the colobus remain highly endangered. Their choice of food brings them into conflict with the farmers, and their habitat is being destroyed due to demands for farmland, fuel, wood and charcoal. The monkeys appear oblivious to tourists, swinging above the trees in troups of about 40, babies to adults. They are endearing, naughty and totally absorbing. There is a visitors centre where you pay US$3 per person for a guide, US$1 of which goes to the people of Pete and Jozani villages. There are a series of nature trail walks in Jozani Forest. Stout shoes are recommended as there are some venomous snakes. The rare Zanzibar leopard can occasionally be sighted. Lizards, civets, mongooses and Ader's duiker are more plentiful and easier to see.

Jozani-Chwaka Bay is also an excellent place to spot birds, including spotted flycatchers, greenbuls, kingfishers and cattle egrets.

About 1 kilometres south of the Jozani Forest Visitor Centre there is the **Pete-Jozani Mangrove Boardwalk**. From the visitor centre the walk takes you through coral forest to an old tamarind tree which marks the beginning of the board-walk. The transition from coral forest to mangroves is abrupt. The boardwalk, which is horseshoe shaped, takes you through the mangrove swamp – the forest in the sea. Mangroves anchor the shifting mud and sands of the shore and help prevent coastal erosion. There are 18,000 hectares of mangrove forests along the muddy costs and inlets of Zanzibar. When the tide is out the stilt-like roots of the trees are visible. Crabs and fish are plentiful and easily seen from the boardwalk.

The Jozani-Chwaka Bay Conservation Project is a partnership between the Commission for Natural Resources, Zanzibar, and CARE Tanzania, and is funded by the government of Austria. The construction costs of the boardwalk were paid for by the government of the Netherlands, with local communities providing labour. Part of the profits made from tourists are returned directly to the local villagers. Going there by taxi will cost around US$25 (for four people inside one car), which is competitive to agency offered tours.

The road continues south to the village of Kitogani. From here you can take a road across to the coastal village of Paje on the east coast about 50 kilometres from Zanzibar town. Also on this coast is the resort of **Bwejuu** (see Coastal section, page 471). There are a series of other villages on the coast as you head south before you reach **Kizimkazi**, the southernmost village. There is little of significance in this small fishing village beside the ancient mosque. However this was once the site of a town built by King Kizi and his mason Kazi from whom the name Kizimkazi originates. There is a Dolphin tour from Kizimkari for US$13.

Found near Kizimkazi in the south of the island this mosque contains the oldest inscription found in East Africa – from AD 1107. The mosque has been given a tin roof and is still used. However its significance should not be underestimated for it may well mark the beginnings of the Muslim religion in East Africa. It was built by Sheikh Abu bin Mussa Lon Mohammed and archaeologists believe that it exists on the site of an even older mosque.

Shirazi Dimbani Mosque ruins
Colour map 5, grid C3

Small village on the east coast mainly relying on fishing. There is a low rectangular mausoleum in the village, inset with old plates and dishes. This design is believed to be Persian in origin.

Paje
Colour map 5, grid C3

Sleeping D *Ndame Guest House*, PO Box 229, T31065, reasonable. **D** *Padje Ndame Village*, PO Box 3781, T/F31065. Very quiet and relaxing, food OK, rather unspoilt. **D** *Paje by Night*, T30840. Very rustic verging on ethnic. **D** *Paradise Bungalows*, run by a Japanese woman, attached restaurant food is excellent but fairly expensive, has to be ordered in advance.

This is considered to be the best of the eastern beaches. White sandy beaches for kilometres with lovely palm trees and good swimming areas. 65 kilometres from Stone Town. Excellent snorkelling at low water in the lagoon at the end of the jetty, 15 minutes along the beach by bike. Hire bicycles to get there from *Dere Guest House*, see below. It is possible to book a tour to see and swim with the dolphins from Jambiani. Cost US$13 per person including mask and snorkel. Important to bring flippers in order to follow the dolphins. Nice experience. Recommended.

Bwejuu
Colour map 5, grid C3

Sleeping A-B (depending on the season) *Breezes Beach Club*, PO Box 1361, T0811-326595, F0811-333151. Opened 1998, 1.5 kilometres north of Sunrise Hotel, well appointed club. **B** *Sunrise Hotel-Restaurant*, PO Box 3967, T/F0811-320206, 2 kilometres north of the village. All rooms s/c with fans, bungalow rooms all face towards the sea, French seafood cuisine in garden, Belgian chef/owner. Recommended. Best quality place to stay in this part of the island, try the chocolate mousse while supplies of Belgian chocolate hold out, also famed for its spiced pudding. **C** *Palm Beach Inn*, T33597, F32387. This is simple and basic, some bungalows have been added, there is now running water or electricity just buckets and paraffin lamps, for many adding to the charm, the food is fresh and good and the staff friendly, if you want to drink while you are there, take your own alcohol. **C** *Bwejuu Beach Hotel*, another simple place and popular with budget travellers, all rooms and bathrooms are shared, there is a bar here and beers are usually cold, good swimming when the tide is high in the afternoon. **D** *Bwejuu Beach Bungalows*, T33430. Government-run beach hotel. **D** *Bwejuu Dere Beach Resort*, PO Box 278, T31047. Offer s/c or shared bathroom, excellent value, safe parking for motorcycle, restaurant food unremarkable. **D** *Dere Guest House*. Simple facilities, and good straightforward food, hires out bikes and snorkelling equipment. **D** *Twisted Palm*. Simple accommodation on the beach, 5 rooms, very relaxing. You can get a simple but excellent meal at *Jamal's Restaurant*.

Jambiani
Colour map 5, grid C3

Situated on the southeast coast of the island. Great white sharks are found off shore beyond the coral reef.

Sleeping **C** *Jambiani Beach Hotel*, run by the very friendly and helpful Mr Abu, bookings through, PO Box 229, Zanzibar. **C** *Oyster Hotel*, PO Box 4199, Mobile/F0811-333125, town office 31560. Brand new hotel, very congenial, Tanzanian owned, good food, closer to the beach than Sau Inn. Staff mostly locals, rooms clean, light, good mosquito screens, bike rental, sea sports. Recommended. **C** *Sau Inn*, PO Box 1656, T322215, Mobile 0811 320623/337440. Best guest house on the beach. Recommended. Bar & restaurant, sports facilities, volley ball, tennis, snorkelling and diving. **D** *Gomani Guest House*, most beautiful in Jambiani, uncomplicated but comfortable. **D** *Horizontal Inn*, owned by local Zanzibaris, simple and good value. **D** *Imani Beach Lodge Annex*, T33476, F31329. Small lodge caters for up to 14 people, bar and restaurant, bike hire available. **D** *Jambiani Beach Bungalows*, T32344. Government-run beach house. **D** *Manufaa Guest House*, small rooms but clean, price drops by US$1 the second night, friendly, breakfast included. **D** *Shehe Guest House*, bungalows good value. **D** *Visitors Inn*, good value bungalows.

Pemba Island

5°0'S 39°45'E
Colour map 3, grid B5

The island of Pemba is located 40 kilometres to the north of Zanzibar and is about 70 kilometres long and 23 kilometres wide. It has not, so far, been developed as a holiday spot and so is much less touristy. There is however an airport on the island and there are plenty of attractions.

Zanzibar is connected to the African continent by a shallow submerged shelf. Pemba, however, is separated from the mainland by depths of over 3,000 feet. During September and March the visibility around Pemba has been known to extend to a depth of 150 feet. Underwater photographers will enjoy the sharks, tuna and barracuda around Pemba.

Numerous fine, deserted beaches are dotted round the coast and there are 27 islands, most with good sandy beaches. The shores are fringed by mangrove forests. The coral reefs are excellent for snorkelling and diving. In deeper waters there are great game fish such as marlin and barracuda, and the Pemba Channel, between Pemba and the mainland, is one of the world's great game fishing waters. There are some important ruins with historical sites, towns with handsome Arab architecture and charming Swahili villages.

The island is perhaps most famous for its clove production. In addition there are coconut palms, mango trees and bananas. Much of the island was covered in vegetation until clove cultivation began at the beginning of the 19th century, and great swathes were cleared for clove trees and other cultivation. Three small areas of forest remain: Ras Kiuyu Forest is at the north tip of the Ngezi peninsular in the northeast; Msitu Kuu Forest is just south of Wingwi in the northeast; and Ngezi Forest is west of Konde in the north. Msitu Kuu has antelope and monkeys, while the Pemba flying fox inhabits the Ngezi Forest. **Ngezi Forest Reserve** covers 1440 hectares. Despite its coastal location it contains tree species which occur on the East African mainland from lowland mountain forests, eg Quassia undulata. Other trees with Madagascan links are also present, eg musa acuminata, Typhanodorun lindleyanum. Ngezi has its own plant species and subspecies which are unique to it. Half the Reserve is covered by lush moist forest containing thick undergrowth. Several bird species, some unique to Pemba, live in the Reserve, including Hadada, the African Goshawk, the Palm-nut vulture, Scops Owl, the Malachite Kingfisher and the Pemba White eye.

The narrow coastal belt of the Forest Reserve is covered with thick bush. The ground is ancient coral rag, often sharp edged containing pockets of soil. Mangrove forests grow on the tidal coastal creeks and the incoming tide sees seawater running deep up streams forming brackish swampy areas.

The central Reserve area contains heather dominated heathland where the soil is leached sand. The heather, Philippia mafiensis, is only found on Pemba and Mafia Islands.

Pemba's Flying Fox is found in Ngezi, a large fruit eating bat. Tree mammals include the Pemba Vervet Monkey and the Zanzibar Red Colobus monkey. An indolent-looking Hyrax can also be seen climbing in the trees eating leaves. The Pemba Blue Duiker, an antelope about the size of a hare, is also found in Ngezi Forest Reserve. However, it is very shy and is rarely spotted. Feral pigs, introduced long ago by the Portuguese, can be found along with the Javan Civet Cat, which was probably brought to the island by south-east Asian traders for the production of musk for perfume. The only indigenous carnivore in Ngezi is the Marsh Mongoose, which normally lives by ponds and streams.

Pemba Island

The island is much hillier than Zanzibar and the higher rainfall ensures that the vegetation flourishes.

The major income for islanders is from cloves – the clove production of this island is actually about three times that of Zanzibar – and it is the mainstay of the island's economy. Also, unlike Zanzibar production is largely by individual small scale farmers who own anything from 10 to 50 trees each. Most of the trees have been in the family for generations. They were first introduced to the island at the beginning of the 19th century from Indonesia. The production is very much a family affair especially during the harvest when everyone joins in the picking. Harvest occurs about every five months and everything is geared towards it and even the schools close. The cloves are then laid out in the sun to dry and the distinctive fragrance fills the air.

Climate There are long rains from March to mid-June and short rains in November and December. The timing of the rains is thought to be more erratic than in the past, and they can often vary by a month or so, and sometimes the short rains hardly seem to occur at all.

The hottest period is after the short rains, running from December through to February, with temperatures up to 34°C at midday. The period just before the long rains, in February, can be particularly oppressive, with high humidity.

The most comfortable time of year is June to October, with lower temperatures, little rain and plenty of sun, made bearable by the cooling Trade Winds from the southeast, known as the *Kusi* or the South East Monsoons. From October to March the winds change, blowing from the northeast, and they are known as the *Kaskazi* or the North East Monsoons.

Culture The island is overwhelmingly Muslim, with more than 95 percent of the population following Islam. It is tolerant of other cultures, and alcohol is available at hotels, some guest houses and in the police messes (where visitors are welcome). Local inhabitants do, however, like to observe modest dress and behaviour and it is a courtesy not to appear in swimwear or shorts in the streets, and for women to wear long skirts or trousers.

An unusual feature is the bull-fighting that takes place in October and November at the end of the cool season. It is thought that bull-fighting was introduced by the Portuguese during the 16th and 17th centuries when they established forts and settlements in the Indian Ocean, most notably at Mombasa, Lamu and Zanzibar. Why the practice endured in Pemba and not elsewhere remains a mystery. It is a genuinely sporting event in that there is sparring between the bull and the fighter, but the bull is not weakened with lances or killed at the end – the pragmatic Pembans consider the animal too valuable to sacrifice in this way. Two villages where fights are staged are Wingwi in the northeast and Kengeja in the south.

At Tumbe in the north, at the end of the cool season in October, there is a boat race. Teams of men compete, paddling dug-out canoes and the day is completed with a feast provided for contestants and onlookers.

Chake Chake

5°15'S 39°45'E
Phone code: 054
Colour map 3, grid B5

This is Pemba's main town located on the west coast of the island. The town sits on a hill overlooking a creek and is fairly small. A new sports stadium has also recently been built. The market and bus stand are both located in the centre of town close to the mosque. There have been some strikes and riots since the multi-party elections at the end of 1995. Pemba is the stronghold of the CUF opposition party, who dispute the outcome of the elections.

Sleeping & eating
There is currently very little hotel choice in town. One (*Chake Chake*) is fairly central – the others are a 15-minute walk on the road to Wete. **B** *Hoteli ya Chake Chake*, PO Box 18, T52069,

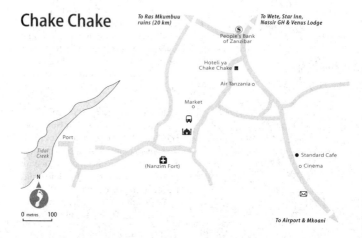

Chake Chake

To Ras Mkumbuu
ruins (20 km)

To Wete, Star Inn,
Nassir GH & Venus Lodge

People's Bank
of Zanzibar

Hoteli ya
Chake Chake

Air Tanzania

Market

Port

Tidal
Creek

(Nanzim Fort)

Standard Cafe

Cinema

N

0 metres 100

To Airport & Mkoani

F33430. It is government owned, all rooms have bathrooms and a fan – it is a clean and friendly place, the hotel has a restaurant with a fairly limited menu, and a bar. **C** *Nassir Guest House*, PO Box 385, T2028. No restaurant or bar. **C** *The Star Inn*, PO Box 109, T52190. Has 7 rooms, restaurant and a bar. **C** *Venus Lodge*, PO Box 183, T52294. Restaurant but no bar. Alternative places to eat are **2** *Balloon Bros*, just south of mosque on main street, charcoal grill, cold drinks, pleasant patio with thatched bandas. **2** *Best Colours*, PO Box 62, T52383, opposite *Hoteli ya Chake Chake*. Small but smart, friendly and good value; and the *Standard Café* by the cinema.

Air   The airport, T2357, serving the island is located about 5 kilometres out of town. The daily   **Transport**
Gulf Air flight from Dubai brings in tourists to Pemba direct. **Road**   There are buses or *dala dalas* between Chake Chake, Wete and Mkoani, but these tend to operate in the mornings only. Also from Wete to Tumbe and Michiweni in the north of the Island. It is possible to hire vehicles at around US$35 a day by asking at the hotels. Similarly with bicycles at US$10 a day. **Sea**   The 'Sepideh' boat operates a normal scheduled service between Dar es Salaam, Zanzibar, Pemba and Mombasa. There is also a Dhow service to Tanga.

Airline offices   *Air Tanzania*, PO Box 92, T2162 (town), T2357 (airport). Situated on the road to   **Directory**
Mkoani, opposite the National Bank of Commerce.

Banks   *People's Bank of Zanzibar*, PO Box 135, T2351/2367, F2139, Tx5740. Open 0830-1530 Mon-Fri and 0830-1200 Sat, it is the only bank on the island to change TCs. *Pemba Bureau de Change*, PO Box 283, T528058, opposite *Hoteli ya Chake Chake* accept TCs.

Tourist offices and information   There is a tourist information office next to the *Hoteli ya Chake Chake*, T2121, but it has no maps and little information. An excellent map can be obtained from the Ministry of Lands and Environment situated behind the Esso station near *Hoteli ya Chake Chake*.

Tour companies & travel agents   *Partnership Travel*, PO Box 192, T2278. Located opposite *Hoteli ya Chake Chake*. *Hamisa Touristers*, PO Box 389, T52343. Near People's Bank of Zanzibar, ferry bookings.

Around the island

Nanzim Fort, located in Chake Chake, is now housing the Ministry of Women and Children. There are some handsome administrative buildings nearby in Moorish style with verandahs, and a **clocktower**.

About 20 kilometres west of Chake Chake, these are probably Pemba's most impor-   **Ruins at Ras**
tant ruins and are believed to date back about 1,200 years, the site of a settlement   **Mkumbuu**
originating in the Shairazi period (see page 356). The ruins include stone houses and pillar tombs and the remains of a 14th century mosque. Access is best by boat, which can be hired informally at the shore. Zanzibar Tourist Corporation Office at the *Hoteli ya Chake Chake* has a boat for hire at about US$70 for the day for a party of six, and from Ras Mkumbuu it is possible to go on to **Mesali Island** where the marine life on the reef is excellent for snorkelling and there is a fine beach.

About 10 kilometres southeast of Chake Chake, this settlement is thought to date   **Ruins at Pujini**
back to the 15th century. It is believed to have been built by a particularly unpleasant character, nicknamed Mkame Ndume which means 'a milker of men' because he worked his subjects so hard. The memory remains and local people believe that the ruins are haunted. The settlement and the palace of Mkame Ndume were destroyed by the Portuguese when they arrived on the island in about 1520. It is best to visit by hiring a bicycle (ask at the hotel).

Tumbe is at the north end of Pemba and is a busy fishing village. Local fishermen contract to provide catches for firms which chill the fish and export it from the mainland. Tumbe can be reached by bus from Chake Chake.

Wete This town is located on the northwest coast of Pemba and serves as a port for the clove trade. It is a pleasant town on a hill overlooking the port. Clustered close to the dock area is a pleasant group of Colonial era buildings. On the north side of the market is a craftsman making very fine carved doors.

From Wete travel to the north of the island to **Vumawimbi beach** or to **Panga ya Watoro beach** on the other side of the north-west headland. North of the latter beach is a big hotel, near a manta reef, which specializes in scuba diving, where you can buy a wholesome if expensive lunch. The best way to get to the beaches from Wete is to hire a motorcycle – enquire at the Sharooq Guesthouse. It is possible to cycle there but the terrain is hilly. The last dala dala leaves from Wete at around 1300.

Sleeping **B** *Hoteli ya Wete*, PO Box 66, T4301, F33430. Government-owned, it has a restaurant and bar. **D** *Sharooq Guest House*, PO Box 117, T4386. Located just near the market and bus stand, it is good value and has a restaurant with the best food in town. If you are just visiting Wete you can leave luggage here for the day while you explore for about US$0.25. Food can be provided if pre-ordered. Own generator. Can arrange trips to local islands, or bicycle hire.

Eating Other places to eat besides the hotel including **1** *Garden Café*, next to the hospital. Pleasant outdoor eating area. **1** *Laki Supisa*, near *Sharooq Guest House*. **1** *New 4-Ways Restaurant*, and **1** *Pop-In Restaurant*, which are both located opposite *Hoteli ya Wete*. **1** *Salim Café*, on the main road near the post office. Sells coffee, milk, ice-cream, etc.

Bars Located at *Hoteli ya Wete* and at the *Police Mess*, down toward the docks, where guests are welcome.

Directory **Banks** *People's Bank of Zanzibar* on the main road and *Wete Bureau de Change*, PO Box 258, T54072, close to the Post Office. **Useful addresses** Also on the main road is the **post office** and the **police station**. The market and matatu stand are located in the centre of town.

Mkoani This town is located to the southwest of the island and is the principal port. If you come to Pemba from Zanzibar by boat this is where you will arrive. It is a little town of some charm on a verdant hill rising up from the shore. Just back from the dock are the offices of **Azam Marine** and **Zanzibar Ferries** and a small café. Nearby is a traditional **bakery** with a large earthenware vessel, surrounded by a wattle and mud cylinder, with a charcoal fire underneath. Pieces of dough are slapped on the inside of the vessel and levered off with a wooden spatula when they are cooked, and sold for US$0.10.

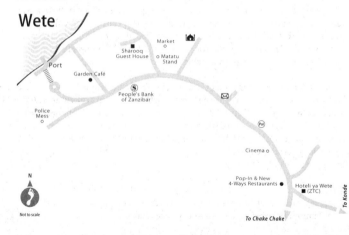

South of the dock there are steep steps down to the **market** by the shore, where small boats leave for Makoongwe Island.

Following the winding road to Chake Chake which runs up the hill inland from the port, the old colonial **District Commissioners Office** is on the right. There is a bandstand in front of the compound. On the left is Ibazi **Mosque**, with a fine carved door.

Sleeping A *Kiweni Marine Resort*, Kiweni Island, T0811-325367, F0811-325368. Also tent accommodation. **B** *Hoteli ya Mkoani*, T56271, F33430. Restaurant and bar. **B** *Pemba Reef Diving Lodge* at Kigomasha, radio contact. **C** *Star Inn* (Jodeni Annex), PO Box 109, T52190, Tx30954. A short walk (10 minutes) north along the shore, nicely located on a bluff overlooking the sea, simple restaurant. Recommended.

Eating Apart from the hotels, **1** *Koani*, PO Box 64, T60304/6002, further along the main road, before the hospital, simple fare. **1** *Nguru*, close to hospital, opposite CCM office.

Other services *Ali Atem Photocare*, PO Box 31, T56248. Sells film and will develop photos.

Transport Local There is one main road in Pemba running from Msuka in the north to Mkoani on the south which is served by public transport. Although the vehicles themselves are not the most comfortable they do provide a fairly good service. From Chake Chake the No 6 goes to Wete and the No 3 to Mkoani. From Chake Chake to Wete takes about 45 minutes and costs US$0.30. Besides this, it is very difficult to get around. **Rental** Motorcycles and bicycles can be rented at the hotels – negotiation is necessary as ever. The motorcycle is the most comfortable form of transport on the island, more so than cars, as pot holes are more readily avoided. Car rental can be arranged with the government hotels costing US$35 a day with a driver. **Air** There are **Air Tanzania** flights to Pemba from Zanzibar and Tanga about 3 times a week. The flights are usually fairly empty – bookings can be made at the Air Tanzania office in Chake Chake. The airport departure tax is about US$1 but you do not have to change money on arrival. Public transport to and from the airport only operates when there is a flight due. **ZATA**, Zanzibar Airport, T33569/32001; or c/o Jasfa, PO Box 4203, T/F30468; or Pemba 2016. This also has 2 flights most days to between **Zanzibar** and Pemba. Depart Zanzibar 0730 (not Sunday) and 1400 (Wednesday, Friday, Sunday only). Depart Pemba 0830 (not Sunday), 1615 (Wednesday and Sunday only) 1500 Friday. Fare US$46 one-way. ZATA also flies to **Tanga** twice a week on Wednesday and Sunday, leaving Pemba at 1445 and Tanga at 1530. The fare is US$42 one-way. **Sea** Check Sea Express and Flying Horse (see page 462) who have recently started services connecting Pemba with Zanzibar and Dar es Salaam. Otherwise, from Zanzibar, **dhows** arrive at Mkoani and from Tanga they arrive at Wete. Bookings from Zanzibar (which is easier and more reliable) can be made at the Malindi Sports Club in Zanzibar and the trip takes 6-8 hours, and costs around US$3. You can also get a dhow to **Mombasa**. Departures are from Wete, cost about US$7 and take about 12 hours for a motorized dhow, and 24 hours for a sailing vessel.

Tanzania & Zanzibar

National Parks and Game Reserves

The parks and game reserves of Tanzania are without rival anywhere in the world. Some are world famous, such as Serengeti, Ngorongoro, Kilimanjaro and Gombe Stream, and have excellent facilities and receive many visitors. Many rarely see tourists and make little or no provision in the way of amenities for them. The differences between national parks and game reserves depends on the access by local people. In national parks the animals have the parks to themselves. In game reserves however the local people, in particular pastoralists such as the Masai, are allowed rights of grazing. Game reserves are often found adjoining national parks and have usually been created as a result of local pressure to return some of the seasonal grazing lands to pastoralists.

It is essential to tour the parks by vehicle. In fact, walking is prohibited in all parks except Selous, Gombe Stream and Mahale Mountain National Parks, and Gombe Stream and Mahale Mountains are the only parks that can really be enjoyed without a vehicle. You will either have to arrange a drive in a park vehicle with a guide (the least expensive option), join an organized tour by a safari company, hire or have your own vehicle. It is a waste not to take a guide – the cost is modest, and without one, you will miss a lot of game, and not go to the promising locations for viewing.

Arrangements are most conveniently made through tour operators who will generally offer a variety of tours of differing durations, luxury and expense. Lists of major operators are given below (see page 481). If you are making your plans from either Dar es Salaam or Arusha, there are lists of operators with offices in these locations (see page 344 for Dar es Salaam, and page 398 for Arusha). For many people a camping safari is the most attractive option, the conditions are very comfortable while being less expensive than staying in lodges. A list of camping safari specialists is on page 481, but most tour operators will offer camping as well as lodge and hotel based touring.

Balloon safaris, US$375 per person, can be arranged from the Serena Serengeti. They are an absolutely amazing experience with a champagne breakfast afterwards.

Hunting safaris are very specialized and expensive operations, and hunting is strictly controlled to ensure conservation. It is possible to hunt all the big game with the exception of rhinoceros, as well as most of the minor species and birds. A hunting safari is usually for a minimum of seven days. A list of specialist hunting operators is given below (see page 482).

Rules of the National Parks The rules of the national parks are really just commonsense and are aimed at visitor safety and conservation. The Parks are open from 0600-1900 and at other times driving in the parks is not permitted. Walking is prohibited in all parks except Selous, Gombe Stream and Mahale Mountain National Parks, so you must stay in your vehicle at all times. Do not drive off the main track. This causes damage to the vegetation and is strictly banned. Do not ask your driver to do this in order to get closer to game. Blowing your horn is prohibited, as is playing radios or tape recorders. The speed limit is 50 kph but you will probably want to go much slower most of the time as at 50 kph you will miss a lot of game. Chasing the animals is strictly prohibited, as is feeding the animals – this includes animals that gather around the lodges. Take all litter home with you, and be careful when discarding cigarette butts as the fire risk is high particularly during the dry season.

Tour operators Until 1989 only Tanzanian registered tour operators were allowed to operate in Tanzania. That has now changed and overseas-based companies have established themselves in Tanzania. There are a large number of safari companies and organized safaris are the most common way of seeing the parks. Safaris to Serengeti National Park, Ngorongoro Conservation

Fees

The fees for the parks have to be paid in hard currency unless you are a resident of Tanzania in which case you pay in local currency. The fees for each 24-hour period are as follows:

Park permit entry fees (non nationals)

Kilimanjaro, Arusha, Tarangire, Lake Manyara and Serengeti National Parks

Adult	US$25
Child 5-16 years	US$5
Child under 5	Free
Vehicle entry:	
Up to 2,000 kilogrammes	US$30
Over 2,000 kilogrammes	US$150

Katavi, Mikumi, Ruaha, Rubondo and Udzungwa National Parks

Adult	US$15
Child 5-16 years	US$5
Child under 5	Free

Gombe Stream National Park

Adult	US$100
Child 5-16 years	US$20
Child under 5	Free

Mahale National Park

Adult	US$50
Child 5-16	US$20
Child under 5	Free

Permit for camping in any period of 24 hours, or part thereof (non nationals)

Established campsites

Adult	US$20
Child 5-16	US$5
Child under 5	Free

Special campsites

Adult	US$40
Child 5-16	US$10
Child under 5	Free

Guide fees (non nationals)

Fees for the service of official guide	US$10
Fees for the service of official guide who accompanies the Tourist outside his normal working hours	US$15
Walking safaris guides	US$20

Special sport fishing fees

Applicable only to Gombe, Mahale and Rubondo Island National Parks (sport fishing allowed between 0700 and 1700 only)

Adult	US$50
Child 5-16	US$25
Child under 5 years	Free

Huts, hostels, rest houses fees

(rates are payable per head per night)

Kilimanjaro National Park:	
Mandara, Horombo and Kibo	US$40
Meru - Miriakamba and Saddle	US$20
Other huts - Manyara, Ruaha, Mikumi etc	US$20
Hostels - Marangu, Manyara, Serengeti, Mikumi, Ruaha and Gombe (strictly for organized groups with permission of park wardens in charge)	US$10
Rest houses - Serengeti, Ruaha, Mikumi, Arusha, Katavi	US$30
Rest house - Gombe	US$20

Rescue fees

Mounts Kilimanjaro and Meru
The park shall be responsible to rescue between the point of incident to the gate in any route. The climber will take care of other expenses from gate to KCMC or other destination as he/she chooses.
The rates are payable per person for trip (non-Tanzanian):   US$20

Tanzania & Zanzibar

Area, Lake Manyara National Park, Tarangire National Park and Arusha National Park are best arranged from Arusha if you have not arranged it before you arrive in Tanzania. For trips to Mikumi National Park, Ruaha National Park and Selous arrangements are best made in Dar es Salaam, while trips to Gombe Stream National Park and Mahale Mountain National Park can be arranged from Kigoma.

More extensive lists of tour and travel companies are given in the sections for Dar es Salaam (see page 344) and Arusha (see page 398). The lists here are of experienced operators.

Tanzanian national parks & game reserves

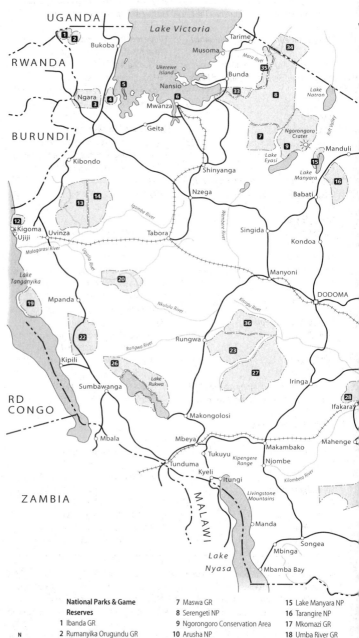

National Parks & Game Reserves

1 Ibanda GR
2 Rumanyika Orugundu GR
3 Burigi GR
4 Biharamulo GR
5 Rubondo Island NP
6 Saa Nane Island GR

7 Maswa GR
8 Serengeti NP
9 Ngorongoro Conservation Area
10 Arusha NP
11 Mt Kilimanjaro NP
12 Gombe Stream NP
13 Moyowosi GR
14 Kigosi GR

15 Lake Manyara NP
16 Tarangire NP
17 Mkomazi GR
18 Umba River GR
19 Mahale Mts NP
20 Ugalla River GR
21 Sadani GR
22 Katavi NP

Tanzania & Zanzibar

Hotel & Lodge Safaris

Abercrombie & Kent, PO Box 427, Arusha, T7803, F7003, Tx42005. *Bushtrekker Safaris*, PO Box 3173, Arusha, T3727 or PO Box 5350, Dar es Salaam, T31957/32671. *Classic Tours & Safaris*, PO Box 7302, Arusha, T7197, F8220. *Easy Travel and Tours Ltd*, Clock Tower Centre, Joel Maeda Rd, 2nd Flr, PO Box 1912, Arusha, T3929, F7322/4110, easytravel@habari.co.tz. *Equatorial Safaris*, PO Box 2156, Arusha, T2617, F2617, Tx42103. Located in Serengeti Block, AICC (Conference Centre). *Hoopoe Adventure Tours*, India St, PO Box 2047, Arusha (UK: T0181-4288221, F0181-4211396, hoopoeUK@aol.com). *Ker and Downey Safaris*, PO Box 2782, Arusha, T77557700, Tx42013. *Let's Go Travel*, The Adventure Centre, PO Box 12799, Arusha, T2814/7111, F8997/4199, located in Goliondoi Rd. *Mashado, Tanzania*, PO Box 14823, Arusha, T255-576585, F8020, Mashado@habari.co.tz, Mobitel T255-811510107 or 01/02, F255-811-510104 or 03. *Sandgrouse Adventure Tours & Safaris Ltd*, PO Box 11661, Arusha, T3485/4065/4244, F3485/4095. *Savannah Tours*, PO Box 3038, Arusha, T331662/332550, savtour@twiga.com. *Selous Safaris*, PO Box 1192, Dar es Salaaam, T34535, F28486, Tx81016. *Simba Safaris*, PO Box 1207, Arusha, T3509 3600, located between Ngoliondoi Rd and India St, Arusha. *Sunny Safaris Ltd*, PO Box 7267, Arusha, T7145/8184, F8094, sunny@arusha.com. *Takims Holidays Tours and Safaris*, PO Box 6023, Arusha, T3174/7500, located Room 421, Ngorongoro Wing, AICC, Arusha, or PO Box 20350, Dar es Salaam, T2569130037, located Jamhuri St. *Tanzania Safari Tours/Rufiji River Camp*, PO Box 20058, Dar es Salaam, T64177/63546, located on Pugu Rd, Dar es Salaam. *The Safari Co*, PO Box 207, Arusha, T8424, F8272. *United Touring Company*, PO Box 2211, Arusha, T8844/5, F8222 (UK: T0181-9056525). Located on corner of Sokoine St and Ngoliondoi Rd, Arusha. *Valji & Alibhai*, PO Box 786, Dar es Salaam, T20522/26537, F46401, Tx81052, located on Bridge St. *Wildersun Safaris and Tours*, PO Box 930, Arusha, T38806471, Tx42021, located on Sokoine Rd, Arusha. *World Archipelago*, PO Box 2174, Arusha, T6079/7931/7880, F6475.

Camping safaris

Sengo Safaris, PO Box 207, Arusha, T3181 ext 1518/1519/1520, located Room 153-3, Ngorongoro Wing, AICC, Arusha. *Dove*

Poaching

This is a serious problem in Tanzania. An example of the devastation that the poacher has wrought on Tanzania's wildlife can be seen by examining the estimated national elephant population which fell from around 200,000 in 1977 to 89,000 in 1987 – a fall of some 55 percent in just 10 years. These figures give rise to the fully justified concern for the future survival of some of these species. It is important that the ivory trade is discouraged and every tourist can help in this by not buying any ivory of any description. This rule should extend beyond ivory to other living creatures. For example there was a time when on a trip to the coast you would be sure to see a great many extremely beautiful shells along the reef. As a result of the tourist trade you are now less likely to see them in the sea and more likely to see them being sold to tourists on the road side. Many people collect the brightly coloured star fish found on the reefs. However these quickly die and fade once they are out of the water. Their population has undoubtedly been affected as a result of tourists collecting them. If you want these species to survive do not buy or collect any such souvenirs.

If you want to become involved in any conservation activities in Tanzania there are a number of societies and organizations you can contact. These include the Tanzania Wildlife Protection Fund, PO Box 1994, Dar es Salaam; The Wildlife Conservation Society of Tanzania, PO Box 70919, Dar es Salaam; African Wildlife Foundation, PO Box 48177, Nairobi, Kenya or 1717 Massachusetts Avenue NW, Washington DC, 20036, USA; Frontier Tanzania, PO Box 9473, Dar es Salaam or Studio 210, Thames House, 566 Cable Street, London, E1 9HB, England.

Safaris, PO Box 284, Arusha, T3090/3625, located Sokoine Rd, near clock tower, Arusha. *Arumeru Tours and Safaris*, PO Box 730, Arusha, T2780, located Seth Benjamin Rd, Arusha. *Wildlife Safari*, PO Box 1207, Arusha.

Hunting Safaris *Bushmen Company*, PO Box 235, Arusha, T6210. *Cordial Tours* PO Box 1679, Jamhuri St, Dar es Salaam, T35264. *Gerald Posanisi Safaris*, PO Box 45640, Dar es Salaam, T47435. *King Tours and Hunting Safaris*, PO Box 7000, Arusha, T3688. *Tanzania Wildlife Corporation*, PO Box 1144, Arusha, T3501/2, Tx42080.

Costs Safaris vary in cost and length. On the whole you get what you pay for. Obviously the longer you spend actually in the Parks, rather than just driving to and from them, the better. To see Ngorongoro Crater and Lake Manyara you will need, absolute minimum, three days and two nights. To see these two plus Serengeti you will need four days and three nights, and if you add Tarangire to these three you will need six days and five nights.

The costs will also vary enormously depending on where you stay and how many of you there are in a group. For a **tented camp or lodge safari** the cost will average out at about US$100-140 per person per day. This assumes that there is a group of at least six of you. If you want to go in a smaller group you can expect to pay substantially more, and if you are alone and not prepared to share a room/tent then you will have to pay a 'single supplement'. You will have to pay in hard currency and the price will include accommodation, park fees, food and transport.

For a **camping safari** you can expect to pay about US$60-80 per person per day including park entrance fees, cost of vehicle and driver, camping fees and costs of food. This assumes you get a group of at least five together.

In addition 'tipping' is an additional expense. A guide may expect US$5 a day, and half of this for the porters. Toursist may be coerced into tipping between US$50 and $100 for the guide, but you are advised not to tip before completion of the trip.

Hunting safaris are extremely expensive and require considerable preparation.

Car rental Car rental is not as well organized in Tanzania as it is in Kenya. There are fewer companies from which to hire vehicles (although this is changing) and it is expensive. Also many of the vehicles are poorly maintained and you may find it difficult to hire a car without a driver. The

Tanzania & Zanzibar

National Parks & Game Reserves

The following is a list of the 12 national parks and one conservation area which together hold a population of over four million wild animals.

List of National Parks in Tanzania

Name of Park	Area (sq km)	PO Box	Telephone
Arusha	137	3134 Arusha	3471
Gombe	52	185 Kigoma	-
Katavi	2,253	89 Mpanda	-
Kilimanjaro	756	96 Marangu	50 Marangu
Lake Manyara	320	3134 Arusha	3471
Mahale Mountains	1,613	1053 Kigoma	-
Mikumi	3,230	62 Mikumi	Radio 6037
Ruaha	12,950	369 Iringa	Radio 6037
Rubondo	457	111 Geita	Telex 42130
Serengeti	14,763	3134 Arusha	3471
Tarangire	2,600	3134 Arusha	3471
Udzungwa Mountains	1,000	-	-
Ngorongoro Crater	2,288	776 Arusha	3339

In addition, there are 17 Game Reserves in Tanzania among which the World's largest is the Selous Game Reserve.

List of Game Reserves in Tanzania

Reserve's Name	Area (sq km)	Region
Selous	55,000	Coast, Morogoro, Lindi, Mtwara and Ruvuma
Saadani	300	Coast
Rungwa	9,000	Singida
Kizigo	4,000	Singida
Moyowosi	6,000	Kigoma
Ugalla	5,000	Tabora/Rukwa
Uwanda	5,000	Rukwa
Maswa	2,200	Shinyanga
Burigi	2,200	Kagera
Biharamulo	1,300	Kagera
Rumanyika-Orugundu	800	Kagera
Ibanda	200	Kagera
Umba River	1,500	Tanga
Mkomazi	1,000	Kilimanjaro
Kilimanjaro	900	Kilimanjaro
Mount Meru	300	Arusha
Saa Nane Island	0.5	Mwanza

hire charge for this will depend on where you get the vehicle from. Dar es Salaam is usually cheaper with a Land Rover or VW kombie costing US$20 plus US$1 per kilometre plus US$5 for the driver. A Nissan minibus will cost about US$25 plus US$1 per kilometre. (Both have a minimum mileage of 100 kilometres per day.) In Arusha a Land Rover will cost about US$40 plus US$1 per kilometre. You will have to pay the entrance fees for the car and the driver and although it will work out expensive this method does allow for greater flexibility than an organized safari. Most of the Tour and Travel agents listed will be able to arrange vehicle hire (see page 344 for Dar es Salaam; page 398 for Arusha; specialist car hire for Dar es Salaam, page 338).

Tanzania & Zanzibar

Facilities **Hotels and lodges** These vary and may be either typical hotels with rooms and facilities in one building or individual bandas or rondavels (small huts) with a central dining area. Most have been built with great care and blend very well into the environment.

Tented camps A luxury tented camp is really the best of both worlds. They are usually built with a central dining area. Each tent will have a grass roof to keep it cool inside, proper beds, and verandah and they will often have a small bathroom at the back with solar heated water. But at the same time you will have the feeling of being in the heart of Africa and at night you will hear animals surprisingly close by.

Campsites There are camp sites in most national parks. These are both normal which cost US$10 (TSh 100 for residents) per person per night and 'special' camp sites which cost US$40 (TSh 200) per person per night. Both cost US$5 (TSh 40) for children per night. You will almost always need to be totally self sufficient with all your own equipment. The campsites usually provide running water and firewood. Some campsites have attached to them a few bandas or huts run by the park.

The northern circuit

The Northern Circuit is an extremely popular route as it includes the best known of the national parks in Tanzania. It is an incredible resource and the country is obviously very keen that full advantage of it should be taken. It is therefore seeing rapid and increasing tourist development and while it is not yet as developed as some of the Kenyan parks, nor are there as many visitors, this can be expected to change in the future.

Popular routes take in Lake Manyara National Park, Ngorongoro Crater Conservation Area (with the Olduvai Gorge) and the Serengeti National Park. However there are a number of other major attractions. In particular, keen climbers and walkers visit the area to climb Mount Kilimanjaro and Mount Meru in Arusha National Park. The Tarangire National Park, as a dry season retreat for many animals, is a superb game viewing opportunity and is also located in the north of the country.

Lake Manyara National Park

Approach
3° 40' S, 35° 50' E
Colour map 3, grid A4

Many visitors go to Lake Manyara National Park on a safari circuit which will include Ngorongoro and Serengeti. The park is located 130 kilometres west of Arusha and is reached via the Arusha-Serengeti road (see maps, pages 381 and 488). The drive from Arusha takes about two and a half hours, the road is good tarmac for the first 80 kilometres, then the road is rough: it is an enjoyable journey. The entrance to the Lake Manyara National Park is off the left of the Great North Rd at Makuyuni. From here there is a track that goes past the lake and through the village of Mto wa Mbu to the park entrance at the foot of the Great Rift Escarpment. Lake Manyara National Park is small enough to be ideal for a day visit. The main road is good enough for most vehicles; although some of the tracks may be closed during the wet season. Taking a guide with you is recommended as they will be much better at spotting the game – in particular the lions – than you.

The village of **Mto wa Mbu** (meaning Mosquito Creek) is a small busy market town selling fruit and vegetable produced by the fertile surrounding farms. You will also be surrounded by people trying to sell you arts and crafts. Many of the children tend to be aggressive. However they seem to be more expensive here than in Arusha. At the gate of the national park is a small museum displaying some of the bird and rodent life found in the park.

The **Mto wa Mbu Cultural Tourism programme**, supported by the Tanzanian Tourist Board and SNV, the Dutch Development Organisation, offers an opportunity to support the local inhabitants and learn about their lifestyle. Walking safaris with Masai guides through the farms in the verdant oasis at the foot of the Rift Valley can be arranged. There are walks to Miwaleni Lake and waterfall where papyrus plants grow in abundance, or an opportunity to climb Balaa hill which overlooks the whole town. The Belgian Development Organisation ACT have enabled locals to grow flowers commercially for export and there are colourful flower fields, with the wonderful backdrop of the Rift Valley.

The area around Mto wa Mbu was dry and sparsely populated prior to the irrigation programmes which began in the 1950s, which transformed the area into an important location where fruits and vegetables are grown on a large scale. The accompanying population growth turned Mto wa Mbu into a melting pot of cultures. There is greater cultural diversity in this area than elsewhere in Tanzania, where you can sample Chagga banana beer, or see a farmer from the Kigoma region make palm oil. The Rangi use papyrus from the lakes to make beautiful baskets and mats and the Sandawe continue to make bows and arrows which are used to hunt small game. On the surrounding plains the Masai tend their cattle.

The cultural tours are organized at the Red Banana Restaurant in Mto wa Mbu on the main road, or at the TTB Information Centre in Arusha, Boma Rd, T057-3302. Alternatively you can rent a bicycle and cycle through the banana plantations to see the papyrus lake. The landscape is awe inspiring with the escarpment rising vertically up into the sky on the one side and the semi-desert stretching away to the horizon on the other.

Background

The word 'Manyara' is derived from *emanyara* the name of a plant used by the Maasai used in the building of their kraals. The plant's Latin name is *Euphorbia tirucalli*. Lake Manyara National Park was established in 1960. It is set in the Great Rift Valley and covers an area of 325 square kilometres, of which 229 square kilometres are the lake. However within this small area there is a diversity of habitats including open grasslands with rocky outcrops, forests and swamps as well as the lake itself. The best times to visit are December to February and May to July.

Ian Douglas-Hamilton has given an account of the conservation of the elephant population in *Among the Elephants* 1978, London: Collins.

Lake Manyara NP

Formation

The lake is believed to have been formed about two or three million years ago when, after the formation of the Rift Valley, streams poured over the valley wall. In the depression below, the water accumulated and so the lake was formed. It has shrunk significantly and was probably at its largest about 250,000 years ago.

Wildlife

The major attraction to the Lake Manyara National Park are the tree-climbing lions. Unfortunately there is no guarantee that you will see them. However there are other things to see – elephants, hippo, plain animals as well as a huge variety of bird life, both resident and migratory. At certain times of the year Lake Manayara is home to thousands of flamingoes which form a shimmering pink around the lake shore. As with all the other parks poaching is a problem and it affects elephants in particular. It was a shock when the census of 1987 found that their population had halved to under 200 in the last decade.

Routes   The road from the park gate goes through the ground water forest before crossing the Marere River Bridge. This forest, as its name suggests, is fed not by rainfall, but by ground water from the high water table fed by seepage from the volcanic rock of the rift wall. The first animals you will see on entering the Park will undoubtedly be baboons. About 500 metres after this bridge the road forks. To the left the track leads to a plain known as **Mahali pa Nyati** (Place of the Buffalo) which has a herd of mainly old bulls cast out from their former herds. There are also zebra and impala in this area. This is also the track to take to the Hippo Pool. The pool is formed by the Simba River on its way to the lake and is home to hippos, flamingoes and many other water birds. Some of these tracks may be impassable in the wet season and you may have to turn round and go back the way you came.

Back on the main track the forest thins out to bush and the road crosses the Mchanga River (Sand River) and Msasa River. Shortly after this latter bridge there is a turning off to the left which leads down to the lake shore where there is a peaceful picnic spot. Soon after this bridge the surroundings changes to one of Acacia woodland. This is where the famous tree climbing lions are found, so drive through very slowly and look out for a tail dangling down through the branches.

Continue down the main road crossing the river Chemchem and on to the Ndala River. Here you will probably see elephants although their numbers have been reduced severely in recent years as a result of poaching. As the park is small they tend to stray across into the surrounding farmland where great damage is done to crops. Outside the park boundaries there is little to stop them being killed. During the dry season the elephants may be seen digging in the dry river bed for water. At the peak of the wet season the river may flood and the road is sometimes impassable as a result. Beyond the Ndala River the track runs closer to the Rift Valley Escarpment wall which rises steeply to the right of the road. On this slope are many different trees from those on the plain and as a result they provide a different habitat for various animals. The most noticeable are the very impressive baobabs with their huge trunks.

The first of the two sets of hot springs in the park are located where the track runs along the wall of the escarpment. These are the smaller of the two and so are called simply *Maji Moto Ndogo* (small hot water). The temperature is about 40°C, heated to this temperature as it circulates to great depths in fractures that run through the rock that were formed during the formation of the Rift Valley. The second set of hot springs is located further down the track over the Endabash River. These, known as *Maji Moto*, are both larger and hotter, reaching a temperature of 60°C. You are supposed to be able to cook an egg here in about 30 minutes. The main track ends at *Maji Moto* and you have to turn round and go back the same way. In total the track is between 35 and 40 kilometres long.

Sleeping   **A+** *Maji Moto Camp*, is the only tourist resort inside Lake Manyara NP sited among acacia trees on the southern shore of the lake. Accommodation is a luxury permanent camp, affording a panoramic view of millions of flamingos, pelicans and waders. Nearby are the hot sulphuric springs (Swahili: Maji Moto). UK Agents: World Archipelago, 6 Redgrave Rd, London SW15 1PX, T+44-181-7805838, F+44-181-7809482, 100711.3161@compuserve.com. Arusha Agent: PO Box 2174, Arusha T57-6079/7931/7880, F57-6475. Nairobi Agent: PO Box 40097, Nairobi T2-331825/223131-2, F2-212656, or Conservation Corporation Africa – a South African company – Nairobi Office: PO Box 74957, T2-750928/750780/750813, F2-746826. **A+** *Lake Manyara Serena Lodge*, PO Box 2551, Arusha, T6304/4159, F4155/8185. Set on the edge of the eastern Rift Valley's Mto Wa Mbu escarpment overlooking the lake, offers Camel Safaris, nature walks included in *The Times*' 1999 list of the World's top 100 hotels. **A** *Lake Manyara Hotel (TAHI)*, PO Box 3100, Arusha, T8802/3113, 100 rooms, swimming pool and shop, located 10 kilometres from the park gate, 300 metres above the park on the escarpment overlooking the lake and park – wonderful views. **E** *Kudu Guest House*. Basic but friendly, including breakfast and dinner, located in Mto wa Mbu. **E** *Starehe Bar and Hotel*, located about 100 metres down a left turning off the road from Mto wa Mbu to Ngorongoro. Clean and friendly, cold water only, good food.

Tented Camp *A Kirurumu Tented Lodge* (contact through Hoopoe, page 481), built on the Gregorian Escarpment of the Great Rift Valley, stunning location overlooking Lake Manyara and over towards Mount Losimongori, well appointed (tents on solid platforms under thatched roofs), with splendid views, located close to park. Recommended. Excellent service. Accommodation and meals free for children aged up to six years. From 7-12 years the cost is 50 percent of full board shared rates.

Bandas 10 bandas located just before park entrance. Booking through Tanzania National Parks Headquarters, PO Box 3134, Arusha or Chief Park Warden, Lake Manyara National Park, PO Box 12, Mto wa Mbu.

Youth Hostel Located at the park headquarters. Booking through Tanzania National Parks Headquarters, PO Box 3134, Arusha or Chief Park Warden, Lake Manyara National Park, PO Box 12, Mto wa Mbu. Sleeps 48 people. Facilities are basic.

Camping Two camp sites located at the entrance to the park. Both have water, toilets and showers. Mosquito nets are essential. Bring sufficient food and drinking water. The camp site in the park is expensive and facilities are minimal. *Twiga Campsite and Lodge* is situated about 2 kilometres before the park entrance, restaurant, beautiful rooms, safe parking, curio shop.

Ngorongoro

The Ngorongoro Conservation Area is 190 kilometres west of Arusha, 60 kilometres from Lake Manyara and 145 kilometres from Serengeti and is reached via the Arusha-Serengeti road (see map, page 381). The drive from Arusha takes about four hours and is a splendid journey with a view of Mount Kilimanjaro all the way arching over the right shoulder of Mount Meru. You will go across the bottom of the Rift Valley and pass the entrance to the Lake Manyara National Park on the left of the Great North Road at the foot of the Great Rift Escarpment. Just beyond the entrance to the park the road climbs very steeply up the escarpment and at the top the turning to the Lake Manyara Hotel is off to the left. From here the country is hilly and fertile and you will climb up to the Mbulu Plateau which is farmed with wheat, maize and coffee. 25 kilometres from Manyara at Karatu (known as Safari Junction), is the turning off to Gibbs Farm, which is five kilometres off the main road. You turn right towards the Park entrance and on the approach to Lodware Gate as the altitude increases the temperature starts to fall. Your first view of the crater comes at Heroes Point (2,286 metres). The road continues to climb through the forest to the crater rim.

Approach
3°11'S 35°32'E
Colour map 3, grid A3

Embagai Crater can be visited in a day from any lodge at the Ngorongoro rim. It has a more interesting landscape than wildlife. You can walk down to the lake at the bottom of the crater. Buffalo, hyenas and leopards may be seen. This is an isolated beautiful place, four-wheel drive access only. Need to be accompanied by a ranger, because of the buffalos.

The Ngorongoro Conservation Area was established in 1959 and covers an area of 8,288 square kilometres. In 1951 it was included as part of the Serengeti National Park and contained the headquarters of the park. However in order to accommodate the grazing needs of the Masai people it was decided to reclassify it as a conservation area. In 1978 it was declared a World Heritage Site in recognition of its beauty and importance. The crater has an area of 265 square kilometres and measures

Background

Tanzania & Zanzibar

between 16 and 19 kilometres across. The rim reaches 2,286 metres above sea level and the crater floor is 610 metres below it. The best times to visit it are December to February and June to July. During the long rains season (April to May) the roads can be almost impassable and so access to the crater floor may be restricted.

The name 'Ngorongoro' comes from a Masai word *Ilkorongoro* which was the name given to the age group of Masai warriors who defeated the previous occupants of the area, the Datong, around 1800. The sounds of the bells that the Masai wore during the battle, that were said to have terrified their enemies into submission, was 'koh-rohng-roh' and it is from this that Ngorongoro comes. The Masai refer to the Ngorongoro Southern Highlands as 'O'lhoirobi' which means the cold highlands; while the Germans also referred to the climate calling these the 'winter highlands'.

Ngorongoro has been called the 'Garden of Eden' and 'Paradise on Earth'. Obviously for this reason it has attracted a large number of tourists which has affected it a great deal. When you come here be prepared for the fact that many other people have the same idea. If you are expecting to have a pride of lions to yourself think again – it is more likely that there will be a mob of minibuses surrounding it. Some people find this a huge disappointment and feel there is an almost zoo-like atmosphere to the crater. However, you can expect to see almost all of the big game including a pool full of hippo. There are an estimated 30,000 animals living in the crater. As this is a conservation area rather than a national park you will also see some of the local Masai people grazing their cattle here. Poaching has affected the animal population and in particular the rhino population is believed to be under 15. Recent reports indicate that there are few giraffes left in Ngorongoro.

Formation Ngorongoro is believed to date from about 2.5 million years ago – relatively modern for this area. It was once a huge active volcano and was probably as large as Kilimanjaro. After its large major eruption, as the lava subsided its cone collapsed

Ngorongoro Conservation Area

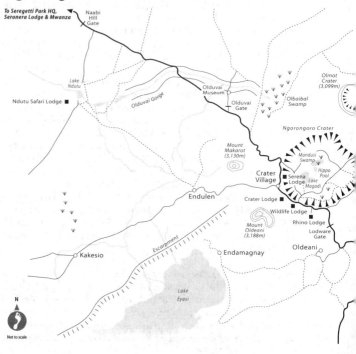

inwards leaving the caldera. Minor volcanic activity continued and the small cones that resulted can be seen in the crater floor. To the northeast of Ngorongoro crater are two smaller craters Olmot and Embagai. From the crater on a clear day you should be able to see six mountains of over 3,000 metres.

Route

In the crater itself, for most of the year, only four-wheel drive vehicles are allowed. Sometimes in the dry season other vehicles will be allowed but do not rely on this. Whether you have your own vehicle or hire one there you will have to take a park ranger with you which costs US$15 per day. Four-wheel drive Land Rovers can be hired in Crater Village where you pick up the ranger, which is cheaper than hiring through the lodges. There is a US$10 charge to go down into the crater.

Where the road gets to the rim of the crater you will see memorials to Professor Bernhard Grzimek and his son Michael. They were the makers of the film 'Serengeti Shall Not Die' and published a book of the same name (1959 London: Collins). They conducted surveys and censuses of the animals in the Serengeti and Ngorongoro Parks and were heavily involved in the fight against poachers. Tragically Michael was killed in an aeroplane accident over the Ngorongoro Crater in 1959 and his father returned to Germany where he set up the Frankfurt Zoological Society. He died in 1987 requesting in his will that he should be buried beside his son in Tanzania. Their memorials remain as a reminder of all the work they did to protect this part of Africa.

Access to the crater is by way of two steep roads which are both one way. You enter by the Windy Gap road and leave by the Lerai road. The Windy Gap branches off the Serengeti road to the right and descends the northeast wall of the crater to the floor of the crater 610 metres below. The road is narrow, steep and twists and turns as it enters the crater which is rather like a huge amphitheatre.

Encounters with animals are frequent and there is a wide variety of game in the crater. These include lion, elephant and rhino as well as buffalo, Thompson's gazelle, wildebeest and zebra. You are also likely to see ostrich and Lake Magadi, the soda lake at the floor of the crater, is home to thousands of flamingoes.

Lerai Forest is a good place for a picnic lunch. Beware of dive-bombing kites snatching your lunch.

Lake Eyasi, the 'forgotten lake', larger than Manyara or Natron is nearby at the foot of Mount Oldeani, a slope of some 3,000 feet – see page 401. Abercrombie and Kent organize mobile camping trips to Lake Eyasi. See Arusha tour companies for details.

Sleeping & eating

A+ *Ngorongoro Serena Lodge*, PO Box 2551, Arusha, Tanzania, T4159/6304, F8185/4155, Serena@marie.gn.apc.org. Luxury development to the highest international standards, built out of wood and pebbles, stunning hotel perched on the rim of the crater. Telescope provided on main balcony to view the crater. Friendly staff, good food, environmentally aware – has its own nursery in the gardens to plant indigenous plant species. 25 percent of staff are

Embagai Crater
Embagai
Nainokanoka
Mount Lolmalasin (3,648m)
Sopa Lodge
Lemala
Lositete
Mbulumbulu
Kitete
Gibbs Farm Lodge
Rotia
Karatu
Mto wa Mbu
Lake Manyara Lodge
Lake Manyara National Park
Lake Manyara
To Arusha

(side margin) Tanzania & Zanzibar

local Masai. **A+** *Ngorongoro Sopa Lodge*, PO Box 1823, Arusha, T6886/6896/6703, F8245, info@sopalodges.com. Luxury all-suite lodge with 100 suites on the exclusive eastern rim of the crater, all suites enjoy uninterrupted views into the crater, spectacular African rondavel design with magnificent lounges, restaurant and conference and entertainment areas, swimming pool and satellite TV, fabulous place but it is way off the beaten track, involving an extra 45-50 kilometres journey (one way) over poor quality roads. **A** *Gibb's Farm* (Ngorongoro Safari Lodge), PO Box 1501, Karuta, TKaruta 25, F57-8310, Tx42041. Discount between Easter and end of June, on the outer slopes of the crater located at the edge of a forest facing the Mbulu Hills to the southeast, original farm built by German settler in 1930s to cultivate coffee, sold to James Gibb in 1948 after the Second World War, and is currently run by his widow, Margaret Gibb, fine atmosphere, open log fires, excellent gardens. **A** *Ngorongoro Crater Lodge*, PO Box 751, Arusha, T7803, Tx42065 (bookings can be made through Abercrombie and Kent, Sokoine Rd, PO Box 427, Arusha, T7803 3181). Discount between Easter and end of June. Old lodge built on rim of the crater in 1937, individual cottages, good views, lovely old bar with roaring log fire. **A** *Ngorongoro Forest Resort* was formerly Dhillons Lodge, owned by a local Sikh family, is located on the left side of the approach road from Manyara, well before you get to the other lodges. **A** *Ngorongoro Wildlife Lodge*, PO Box 887, Arusha, T057-8150/2404, F8150. Modern building on the rim of the crater with wonderful views, 75 rooms, heated, geared to fast throughput of tours, bar with log fire. **C** *Ngorongoro Rhino Lodge*, PO Box 776, Arusha, T3466, on the rim of the crater. Lovely site but does not have the views of some of the other lodges, can sometimes camp here if you have your own tent. **D** *Simba Camp Site*, located about 2 kilometres from Crater Village. Facilities include showers, toilets and firewood, facilities have deteriorated overall and water supplies are irregular, it is important to make sure that you have sufficient water to keep you going for the night and the game drive the next day. **E** *Usiwara Guest House* (Drivers Lodge), located in Crater Village near the post office. Basic, will need sleeping bag, can get food here.

Ushirika Co-op Restaurant also does cheap simple food. You can usually buy food in the village but the stock is limited so you would be advised to bring supplies with you.

Road   If you have your own transport, you will have to hire an official guide in Karatu. Camping available in Karatu at the *Safari Junction Camp*, clean, secure, hot water, US$3 per person – 25 kilometres from Ngorongoro Crater.

If you are without transport, you will have to go with an organized safari from Arusha.

Olduvai Gorge

Approach   This lies within the Ngorongoro Conservation Area to the northwest of the crater (see map, page 488). The site is located about 10 to 15 minutes off the main road between Serengeti and Ngorongoro.

Background   Olduvai Gorge has become famous for being the site of a number of archaeological finds and has been called the 'cradle of mankind'. The name Olduvai comes from the Masai word *oldupai* which is the name for the type of wild sisal that grows in the gorge.

Archaeological finds   Olduvai Gorge aroused interest in the archaeologcal world as early as 1911. This was when a German, Professor Katurinkle, whilst looking for butterflies in the gorge, found some fossil bones. These caused great interest in Europe and in 1913 an expedition led by Prof Hans Reck was arranged. They stayed at Olduvai for three months and made a number of fossil finds. At a later expedition in 1933 Professor Reck was accompanied by two archaeologists, Dr Louis Leakey and his future wife Mary.

The Leakeys continued their work and in July 1959, 26 years later, discovered 400 fragments of the skull *Australopithecus-Zinjanthropus Boise*i – the 'nutcracker man' who lived in the lower Pleistocene Age around 1,750,000 BC. A year later the skull and bones of a young *Homo Habilis* were found. The Leakeys assert that around 1.8

to 2 million years ago there existed in Tanzania two types of man, *Australopithecus-Zinjanthropus Boisei* and *Homo Habilis'*. The other two, *Australopithecus Africanus* and *Arobustus*, had died out. *Homo Habilis* with the larger brain, gave rise to modern man. *Habilis* was a small ape-like creature and, although thought to be the first of modern man's ancestors, is quite distinct from modern man. Tools, such as those used by *Homo Erectus* (dating from 1-1½ million years ago), have also been found at Olduvai as well as at Isimila near Iringa. Other exciting finds in the area are the footprints found in 1979 of man, woman and child at Laetoli (this is a site near Oldovai) made by 'creatures' that walked upright. Dating back 3.5 million years they pushed back the beginnings of the human race even further. In 1986 a discovery at Olduvai by a team of American and Tanzanian archaeologists unearthed the remains of an adult female dating back 1.8 million years. In total the fossil remains of about 35 humans have been found in the area at different levels.

Prehistoric animal remains were also found in the area and about 150 species of mammals have been identified. These include the enormous Polorovis with a horn span of two metres, the Deinotheruium which was a huge elephant-like creature with tusks that curved downwards and the Hipparion, a three-toed horse-like creature.

At the site there is a small museum which is open until 1500. It may, however, be closed during the wet season, April to end June. It holds displays of copies of some of the finds as well as pictures of what life was like for Olduvai's earliest inhabitants. You can go down into the gorge to see the sites and there will usually be an archaeologist to show you around.

Sleeping There is nowhere to stay on the actual site so you will have to make this a day trip. The nearest place to stay, apart from the Ngorongoro lodges and campsites, is **A** *Ndutu Safari Lodge*, PO Box 1182, Arusha, T3625, sleeps 70, bar and restaurant, beautiful setting overlooking Lake Ndutu, located about 90 kilometres from the Ngorongoro Crater near southern boundary of Serengeti National Park.

Serengeti National Park

Approach
2°40'S 35°0'E
Colour map 3, grid A3

The Serengeti is usually approached from Arusha along a fairly good road (see map below). From Arusha you will pass the entrance to Lake Manyara National Park and through the Ngorongoro Conservation Area. Shortly before the park boundary there is the turning off to Olduvai Gorge. Seronera, the village in the heart of the Serengeti is 335 kilometres from Arusha. Approaching from Mwanza or Musoma on the lake shore take the road east and you will enter the Serengeti through the Ndaraka Gate in the west.

Background Serengeti is the most famous of Tanzania's national parks. The name is derived from the Masai word 'siringet' meaning 'extended area'. It was established in 1951 and at 14,763 square kilometres is Tanzania's second largest national park (after Selous). It rises from 920-1,850 metres above sea level and its landscape varies from the long and short grass plains in the south, the central Savannah, the more hilly wooded areas in the north and the extensive woodland in the Western corridor. The Maswa Game Reserve adjoins the western border of the Serengeti National Park. The main rainy season is from November to May.

Serengeti is perhaps most well known for the annual migration which takes place across the great savannah plains (see map below). This is a phenomenal sight: thousands and thousands of animals, particularly wildebeest, as far as the eye can see.

Wildlife During the rainy season the wildebeest, whose population has been estimated at around 1.5 million, are found in the eastern section of the Serengeti and also the Masai Mara in Kenya to the north. When the dry season begins at the end of June so the annual migration commences as the animals move in search of pasture. They concentrate on the remaining green patches, forming huge herds. It is also around this time that the rutting season starts and territories are established by the males who then attempt to attract females into their areas. Once mating has occurred, the herds merge together again and the migration to the northwest begins. The migrating animals do not all follow the same route. About half go west, often going outside the park boundaries and then swing northeast. The other half go directly north. The two groups meet up in the Masai Mara in Kenya. To get to the west section of the Serengeti and the Masai Mara, where they will find pasture in the dry season, the wildebeest must cross a number of large rivers and this proves too much for many of them. Many of the weaker and older animals will die during the migration. Needless to say predators follow the wildebeest on their great trek and easy pickings are to be found. They return to the east at the end of the dry season (November) and calving begins at the start of the wet season.

Other animals for which Serengeti is famous include lions some of which migrate with the wildebeest while others remain in the central plains (the population was estimated at 3,000 in 1978) and cheetah (500). However, because this park is so vast, they are in fact spread fairly thinly on the ground. The elephant population in Serengeti has been decimated by poaching and is estimated to have fallen from around 2,500 in 1976 to under 500 in 1986.

Serengeti National Park

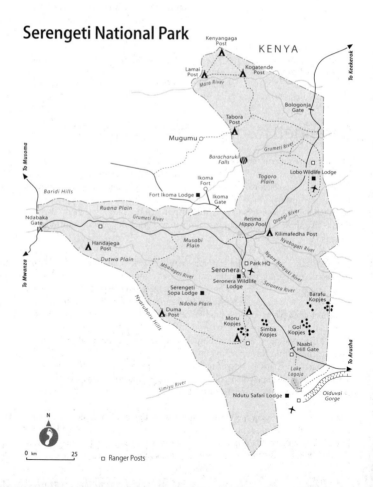

□ Ranger Posts

If you are approaching the Serengeti from the southeast you will first reach the Short Grass Plains. The flat landscape is broken by the Gol Mountains which are seen to the right and by kopjes. The grass here remains short during both the wet and dry seasons. There is no permanent water supply in this region as a result of the nature of the soil. However during the rains water collects in hollows and depressions until it dries up at the end of the wet season. It is then that the animals begin to move on.

Naabi Hill Gate marks the end of the Short Grass and beginning of the Long Grass Plains. Dotted across the plains are kopjes. These interesting geological formations are made up of ancient granite which has been left behind as the surrounding soil structures have been broken down by centuries of erosion and weathering. They play an important role in the ecology of the plains providing habitats for many different animals from rock hyraxes (a small rabbit-like creature whose closest relation is actually the elephant) to cheetahs.

A number of kopjes that you might visit include the Moru kopjes in the south of the park to the left of the main road heading north. You may be lucky enough to see the Verreaux Eagle which sometimes nests here. These have a cave with Masai paintings on the wall and a rock called Gong Rock after the sound it makes when struck with a stone. There are also the Simba Kopjes located on the left of the road before reaching Seronera, which, as their name suggests are often a hide out of lions.

Passing through the Long Grass Plains in the wet season from around December to May is an incredible experience. All around, stretching into the distance, are huge numbers of wildebeest, Thompson's gazelle, zebra etc.

The village of **Seronera** is in the middle of the park set in the Seronera Valley. It is reached by a gravel road which is in fairly good condition. It contains a small museum noted for its giant stick insects – located near the lodge. In the approach to Seronera the number of trees increases – particularly the thorny Acacia trees. The valley itself is home to a large number of animals and is a popular viewing area. You can expect to see buffalo, impala, lion, hippo and elephant. If you are really lucky you might see leopard; however they are few and far between, are nocturnal and spend most of the day in trees, so the chances of seeing them are fairly remote.

Tanzania & Zanzibar

Serengeti migrations

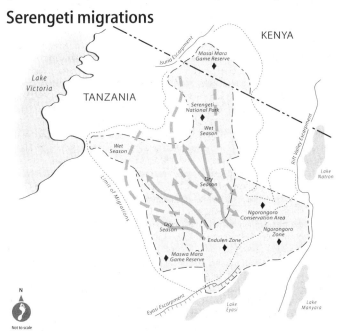

About five kilometres north of Seronera the track splits. To the right it goes up to Banagi and Lobo beyond, and to the left to the so-called Western Corridor, about 20 kilometres north of Banagi Hill which is home to both browsers and grazers. At its base is the Retina Hippo Pool which is located about six kilometres off the main track at Banagi. Banagi was the site of the original Game Department Headquarters before it became a national park. North of here the land is mainly rolling plains of both grassland and woodland with a few hilly areas and rocky outcrops.

In the northeast section of the park is Lobo. Wildlife remain in this area throughout the year including during the dry season. Lobo is the site of the Lobo Lodge, 75 kilometres from Seronera. Further north is the Mara River with forest on both sides of its banks. This is one of the rivers that claims many wildebeest lives every year during the migration. You will see both hippo and crocodile along the river banks.

If you take the left hand track where the road splits north of Seronera you will follow the Western Corridor. (This is also the route to take if you are heading for Mwanza.) The best time to follow this track is in the dry season (June to October) when the road is at its best and the migrating animals have reached this area. Part of the road follows the Grumeti River on your right. On the banks of this river you will also see huge crocodiles basking in the sun. The Musabi and Ndoha Plains to the northwest and west of Seronera respectively can be viewed if you have a four-wheel drive. The latter plain is the breeding area of topi and large herds of up to 2,000 will often be found here.

Sleeping

The Park Headquarters are at Seronera and there are airstrips at Seronera and Lobo.

In the Western corridor of the Serengeti, 93 kilometres west of *Seronera Lodge* and 50 kilometres east of Lake Victoria, there is a luxurious permanent tented camp called the **A+** *Grumeti River Camp* which overlooks a tributary of the Grumeti River, which is teeming with hippo and crocodiles, the wildebeest migration also passes through this area, this is real African bush country and boasts an abundance of birdlife including Fisher's Lovebird, central bar/dining area, has 10 self-contained custom made tents with private shower and wc, solar power electricity minimizes noise and pollution. Agents: *World Archipelago Ltd*, 6 Redgrave Rd, London SW15 1PX, UK, T44-181-780 5838, F44-181-780 9482, 100711.3161@compuserve. com. Arusha: PO Box 2174, T57-6079/7931/7880, F6475, Conservation Corporation Africa, Nairobi, PO Box 74947, T2-750928/750780/750813, F2-746821. **A+** *Klein's Camp*, is a sanctuary located on a private ranch, on the northern-eastern boundary of the Serengeti National Park just south of the Kenyan border, it is named after the American Big Game Hunter, Al Klein, who in 1926 built his base camp in this valley, the ranch is located between the Serengeti Park and farmland and makes it a natural buffer zone, there are 8 stone cottages with thatched roofs, each with en suite facilities, dining and bar facilities are in separate rondavels with commanding views of the Grumeti River Valley, solar power electricity reduces pollution and noise. Agents: *Archers Tours & Travel Ltd*, PO Box 40097, Nairobi, T254-2-331825/224069/223131, F254-2-212656, Tx22082, or *Conservation Corporation Africa*, PO Box 74957, Nairobi, T2-750928/750780/750813, F2-746826. **A+** *Mashado Serengeti Kusini*, PO Box 14823, Arusha, T57-6585/4398, 0811 510101, F8020/4409, Mashado@ habari.co.tz. Located at the Hambi ya Mwaki-Nyeb Kopjes in the Southwest Serengeti, near the border with the Maswa game reserve, well off the usual tourist track, the camp is situated in a conchoidal outcrop of large boulders or kopjes, offering superb views, the camp is accessed by car from Arusha, and closes during the rainy season April/May, for UK agent see page 50. **A+** *Migration Camp*, T07714-088822, res@halcyontz.com or juilet.halcyon@virgin.net. The camp is built within the rocks of a kopje in the Ndassiata Hills near Lobo, overlooking the Grumeti River giving excellent views of the migration masses to and from the Southern Plains, facilities include jacuzzi, swimming pool, restaurant, the camp has many secluded vantage points linked by timber walkways, bridges and viewing platforms, resident game includes lion, leopard, elephant and buffalo. **A+** *Serena Kirawira Camp*, Western Serengeti, central reservations: Serena Hotels, PO Box 2551, Arusha, T255-57-8175/6304, F4058/4155, Serena@marie.gn.apc.org. A luxuriously appointed tented camp in the secluded Western corridor of the National Park, area famous for giant crocodiles, tree climbing lions and the annual wildebeest migration. **A+** *Serengeti Serena Lodge*. Idyllic central location with superb views towards the Western corridor, set high overlooking the plains, this lodge is constructed to reflect the design of an African village.

Central booking – see entry above for *Serena Kiriwira Camp*. **A+ *Serengeti Sopa Lodge***, PO Box 1823, Arusha, T6886/6896/6703, F8245, info@sopalodges.com. Luxury all-suite lodge with 75 suites in the previously protected area of Nyarboro Hills near to Moru Kopjes. Excellent views of the Serengeti plains through double storey window walls in all public areas, multi-level restaurant and lounges and conference facilities, double swimming pool and satellite TV, way off the beaten track involving an extra 45-50 kilometre drive over poor roads (one-way). **A *Lobo Wildlife Lodge***, PO Box 3100, Arusha, T3842, Tx42037. Book through the Tanzanian Tourist Corporation in Dar es Salaam (see page 345) or Arusha (see page 400), 50 percent discount from Easter to 30 June, 75 rooms, located northeast of the Seronera village, swimming pool, shop, also built overlooking the plains, good restaurant and bar. **A *Ndutu Safari Lodge***, PO Box 6084 Arusha, T57-6702, 8930, F57-8310, Tx42041. Accommodates about 25 in rooms and about 40 in tented camp, located about 90 kilometres from the Ngorongoro Crater near southern boundary of Serengeti National Park, wonderful view of Lake Ndutu and the plain beyond, excellent for service, food and welcome. **A *Seronera Wildlife Lodge (TAHI)***, PO Box 3100, Arusha, T3842, Tx42037. Book through Tanzanian Tourist Corporation in Dar es Salaam (see page 345) or Arusha (see page 400), 50 percent discount from Easter to 30 June, 75 rooms. Fantastic building constructed on and around a kopje with wonderful views of the plains around, restaurant, shop, electricity mornings and evenings, bar and viewing platform at the top of the kopje – beware the monkeys, calm, efficient and friendly. Recommended.

Kijirishi Tented Camp, PO Box 190, Mwanza, T40139/41068, Tx46213. *Balloon Safaris*, US$375 per person available at *Seronera Lodge*, 1 hour balloon flights, champagne breakfast and transport to and from your lodge (see page 50 for details).

Camping: be prepared to be totally self-sufficient and bring food with you as there is little available in Seronera Village. **C *Special camp sites*** at Seronera, Lobo, Ndutu, Nabi Hill, Hembe Hill. **D *Public camp sites*** at Lobo, Nabi Hill and Kirawira. **D *Camp sites*** at Seronera

Migration Camp - Serengeti

Our luxury tented-camp is situated in the Northern Central Serengeti, overlooking the Grumeti River. As well as enjoying the resident game, the camp is nestled along the ancient migratory route of the wildebeest and zebra, which congregate around the site for several months of the year.

The spacious tents are comfortably furnished with en-suite bathrooms and balconies. They are orientated westwards with spectacular views of the river and the breathtaking Serengeti sunsets.

Our luxurious honeymoon suite is currently unique to the park with its own private, outdoor bath. Bush meals by the river, early evening game drives in open Landcruisers, a freshwater swimming pool and a well-stocked library are some of the facilities that our guests enjoy.

For information or booking enquiries, please don't hesitate to contact our staff:
E mail res@halcyontz.com or juliet.halcyon@virgin.net or tel: 07714 088822

Tanzania & Zanzibar

Tanzania & Zanzibar

The Snow Sepulchre of King Solomon

Legend has it that the last military adventure of King Solomon was an expedition down the eastern side of Africa. Exhausted by his battles the aged King was trekking home with his army when they passed the snow-covered Mount Kilimanjaro. Solomon decided this was to be his resting place. The next day he was carried by bearers until they reached the snows. As they steadily trudged up to the summit they saw a cave glittering in the sunlight, frost sparkling in the interior, icicles hanging down to close off the entrance. As they watched, two icicles, warmed by the sun, crashed to the ground. They carried the old king inside and placed him on his throne, wrapped in his robes, facing out down the mountain. Solomon raised a frail hand to bid farewell. The bearers left with heavy hearts. The weather began to change and there was a gentle fall of snow. As they looked back they saw that icicles had reformed over the entrance.

close to the Seronera Wildlife Lodge. **B** *Kijereshi Lodge* at the end of the Western corridor, partly luxury tents and bungalows, convenient if you want to pass through the corridor and visit the Grumeti River with hippos and crocodiles.

Kilimanjaro National Park

Approach
3°7'S 37°20'E
Colour map 3, grid A4

There are a number of approaches to Mount Kilimanjaro (see map, page 381). The easiest is to fly to Kilimanjaro International Airport and on the approach you will get a magnificent view of the mountain (provided it is not covered by cloud). The park entrance is about 90 kilometres from the airport which takes about one and a half hours. Alternative routes are to go to Moshi by train or road and from there to Marangu (see map, page 498). Marangu is the village at the park entrance at the base of the mountain. It is located 11 kilometres north of Himo which is a village 27 kilometres east of Moshi on the road to the Kenya border. It is also cheap and easy to get to Kilimanjaro from Kenya by taking a matatu from Nairobi to the border (about four hours) and from there another matatu to Marangu Gate.

Formation

Kilimanjaro was formed about a million years ago by a series of volcanic movements along the Great Rift Valley. Until these movements the area was a flat plain lying at about 600-900 metres above sea level. About 750,000 years ago volcanic activity forced three points above about 4,800 metres – Shira, Kibo and Mawenzi. Some 250,000 years later Shira became inactive and it collapsed into itself forming the crater. Kibo and Mawenzi continued their volcanic activity and it was their lava flow that forms the 11 kilometre saddle between the two peaks. When Mawenzi died out its northeast wall collapsed in a huge explosion creating a massive gorge. The last major eruptions occurred about 200 years ago and Kibo now lies dormant but not extinct. Although Kibo appears to be a snow clad dome it does in fact contain a caldera of 2.5 kilometres across and 180 metres deep at the deepest point in the south. Within the depression is an inner ash cone which rises to within 60 metres of the summit height and is evidence of former volcanic activity. On the southern slopes the glaciers reach down to about 4,200 metres whilst on the north slopes they only descend a little below the summit. Kilimanjaro has well defined altitudinal vegetation zones. From the base to the summit these go: plateau, semi-arid scrub; cultivated, well-watered southern slopes; dense cloud forest; open moorland; alpine desert; moss and lichen.

Background

Some people will come to Tanzania just to climb Kilimanjaro, the highest mountain in Africa. The national park was established in 1973 and covers an area of 756 square kilometres. The altitude rises from 1,829 metres at the Marangu Gate to 5,895 metres at Kibo Peak. Although it can be climbed throughout the year it is worth

The Meaning of Kilimanjaro

Since the earliest explorers to East Africa, people have been intrigued by the name Kilimanjaro and its meaning. There is in fact no simple explanation. The Chagga people do not actually have a name for the whole mountain – they have names for the two peaks – Kibo and Mawenzi. Kibo (or kipoo which is the correct term in Kichagga) means 'spotted' and refers to the rock which can be seen standing out against the snow on this peak, and Mawenzi (or Kimawenze) means 'having a broken top' and again describes its appearance.

The question of the origin of the name Kilimanjaro for the mountain as a whole has been much discussed and a number of theories put forward. Most of these break the word down into two elements: kilima and njaro. In Swahili the word for mountain is actually mlima while kilima means hill – so it is possible that an early European visitor incorrectly used kilima because of the analogy to the two Chagga words Kibo and Kimawenzi.

The explorer Krapf said that the Swahili of the coast knew it as Kilimanjaro 'mountain of greatness' but he does not explain how he came to this conclusion. He also suggests it could also mean 'mountain of caravans' (kilima = mountain, jaro = caravans) but while kilima is a Swahili word, jaro is a Chagga word. Other observers have suggested that njaro has at some time meant 'whiteness' and therefore this was the 'mountain of whiteness'. Alternatively njaro could be the name of an evil spirit, or a demon which causes colds. The first known European to climb Mount Kilimanjaro does make reference to the spirit, mentioning 'Njaro, the guardian spirit of the mountain' and this seems quite a plausible explanation. There are many stories in Chagga folklore about spirits who live on the mountain. Most spirits tend to be kind and have good intentions although there is one who is supposed to destroy anyone who climbs up beyond a certain point. However there is apparently no evidence of a spirit called Njaro, either by the Chagga or by the coastal peoples.

Another explanation involves the Masai word njore for springs or water. The suggestion is that the mountain was known as Mountain of Water because it was from there that all the rivers in the area rose. The problems with this theory are that it does not explain the use of the Swahili word for 'hill' rather than 'mountain', and also it assumes that a Swahili word has been put together with a Masai word.

The final explanation is from a Kichagga term kilelema which means 'which has become difficult or impossible' or 'which has defeated'. Njaro can be derived from the Kichagga words njaare a bird, or else jyaro a caravan. The suggestion is that attempts to climb the mountain were a failure and thus the mountain became known as kilemanjaare, kilemajyaro or kilelemanjaare meaning that which defeats or is impossible for the bird or the caravan. The theory has the advantage of being made up of all Chagga parts. It seems possible either that this was the name given to the mountain by the Chagga themselves, or else people passing through the area, who heard the Chagga say kilemanjaare or kilemajyaro meaning that the mountain was impossible to climb associated with their own kilima and so the name caught on and was standardized to Kilimanjaro.

avoiding the two rainy seasons (late March to mid-June and October to beginning of December) when the routes become slippery. Probably the best time to visit is January to February and September to October when there is usually no cloud.

When, in 1848, the first reports by the German missionary Johannes Rebmann of a snow-capped mountain on the equator arrived in Europe, the idea was ridiculed by the Royal Geographical Society of Britain. In 1889 the report was confirmed by the German geographer Hans Meyer and the Austrian Alpine mountaineer Ludwig Purtscheller who climbed Kibo and managed to reach the snows on Kilimanjaro's summit. At the centenary of this climb in 1989, the Tanzania guide was still alive and 118 years old. Mawenzi was first climbed by the German Fritz Klute in 1912.

The mountain was originally located in a part of British East Africa (now Kenya). However the mountain was given by Queen Victoria of England as a gift to her cousin, and so the border was moved and the mountain included within German Tanganyika.

Climbing Mount Kilimanjaro

Officially anyone aged over 12 may attempt the climb. The youngest person to climb the mountain was an 11 year old, while the oldest was 74. However it is not that easy and estimates of the number of people that attempt the climb and do not make it to the top vary from 50-80 percent. The important things to remember are to come prepared and take it slowly – if you have the chance, spend an extra day half way up which will give you the chance to acclimatize.

Being well equipped will also increase your chances of succeeding in reaching the summit. In particular be sure you have a warm sleeping bag, insulating mat, thermal underwear, gloves, wool hat, sun glasses or snow goggles, sun cream, large water bottle and first aid kit. If you are going on any route apart from Marangu you are advised to take a tent and stove. Although organized climbs will provide food, some people recommend that you should take your own freeze-dried food and cook it yourself. This will decrease the likelihood of getting diarrhoea and thus having to turn back.

Altitude sickness is often a problem while climbing Kilimanjaro. If you know you are susceptible to this you are advised not to attempt the climb. Symptoms include bad headache, nausea, vomiting and severe fatigue. It can be avoided by ascending slowly and if at all possible spending an extra day half way up to acclimatize. It can be cured by descending to a lower altitude. There is a drug called Diamox which helps if taken before the ascent. Other more serious conditions include acute pulmonary oedema and cerebral oedema. In the former, the sufferer becomes breathless, turns blue in the face and coughs up froth. The latter is even more serious – symptoms are intense headache, hallucinations, confusion and disorientation and staggering gait. It is caused by the accumulation of fluid on the brain and can cause death or serious brain damage. If either of these conditions are suspected the sufferer should immediately be taken down to a lower altitude to receive medical care. It is however normal to feel breathless and fatigued at high altitudes and these are not precursors to the more serious conditions.

Marangu is the usual route for tourists and only experienced climbers should use

Kilimanjaro National Park

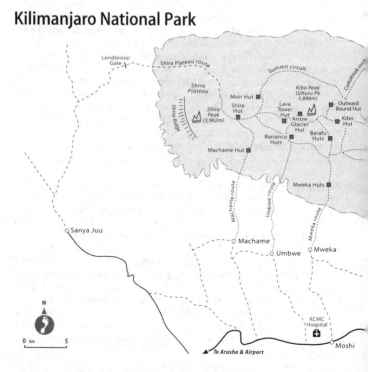

the other routes. A guide is compulsory on all the routes. However if you are going on one of the other routes although you must take a guide with you, be sure to have a good map and compass as he may not know the route. Do not be tempted to go it alone to avoid paying the park and guide fees – above the tree line the path is not always clear and you will be in big trouble if you are caught. It is also well worth hiring porters – they are not too expensive and will increase your enjoyment enormously.

Costs Climbing Mount Kilimanjaro is a fairly costly experience. The costs are much higher than those imposed in the Alps or the Andes. But everyone who does it agrees that it is well worth it. Park fees US$25 per 24 hours, camping or hut fees US$40 per person per day (whether you use the huts or not). Rescue fee (insurance) US$20 per person, guide US$8-10 per guide per day, depending on the trail you choose. Porter US$5-6 per porter per day, depending on the trail chosen. All the big tour operators have to charge an additional 20 percent VAT on the total invoice. In addition an arrangement fee may be charged by the tour operator – around 10 percent. On to this you must add getting to the start of the trail, food, hiring equipment and tips for the guide and porters. The cheapest you will probably manage to do it will be around US$450, but it will more likely be closer to US$600 or more. Organized climbs do not usually work out much more expensive than doing it yourself and are considerably less hassle. **Tipping** Be aware that on the last day of the tour your guide will request a tip for himself and his porters. The guide may try to negotiate a daily rate of US$15 for the guide, US$10 daily for the assistant guide, US$8 daily for the cook and US$5 for each porter. A reasonable tip for the whole trip is in the region of US$30 for a single guide, and US$10 for each porter. Even this amount is very high in comparison to the local income.

Anyone planning to climb the mountain is advised to buy the *Map and Guide* by Mark Savage. This is difficult to obtain in Tanzania but you can get it in Kenya or before you leave from England (32 Seamill Park Crescent, Worthing, BN11 2PN, UK). Another guide particularly useful if you want to climb the mountain (rather than walk up like the rest of us) is the *Guide to Mount Kenya and Kilimanjaro* edited by Iain Allan and published by the Mountain Club of Kenya.

Tour operators There is one tour operator at Moshi (*Trans-Kibo Travel* PO Box 558, Moshi, T47342923, located inside the YMCA) and two at Marangu, the village at the gates of the National Park, contactable through *Kibo Hotel* or *Marangu Hotel* (see page 391). *Shah Tours* – Mr Shah specializes in Kili tours, helping to join up groups, T055- 52370/52998, F51449, kilimanjaro@eoltz.com. Recent travellers have reported that some of the tour operator's personnel have not given them the best advice about routes up the mountain. The Machame route, although the most attractive, is not suitable for all visitors, in particular older persons or people of any age who are not very fit.

Websites Kilimanjaro Adventure Travel; www.kilimanjaro.com, Africa Park East; www. africaparkeast.com, Terra Ferma; www.terraferma.com.

Tanzania & Zanzibar

R   *An unusual way up Mount Kilimanjaro*

> *On the 11 March 1962, three French parachutists, Jean-Claude Dubois, Bernard Couture and Jean-Claude Camus, landed on the crater of Mount Kilimanjaro and broke the world record for the highest parachute landing drop. They had had some problems finding a plane that would fly high enough, and organising a ground rescue team, but the jump itself went off without incident and they landed less than 50 metres from the targetted landing zone. Two of the three were doctors, and they studied the repercussions on the human body of an abrupt change in altitude. Having landed in the crater at around midday, they descended immediately and reached the* Marangu Hotel *at one o'clock in the morning.*

There are a number of different trails. The most popular is the Marangu trail, which is the recommended route for older persons or younger people who are not in peak physical condition. The climbing tends to be much more strenuous than anticipated, which when combined with lower oxygen levels accounts for a failure rate to reach the summit of between 20-50 percent.

Marangu trail This is probably the least scenic of the routes but being the gentlest climb and having a village at the start and accommodation on the way means that it is the most popular.

The national park gate (1,830 metres) is about eight kilometres from the *Kibo Hotel*. This is as far as vehicles are allowed. From here to the first nights stop at Mandara Hut (2,700 metres) is a walk of about four hours. It is through shambas growing coffee as well as some lush rainforest and is an enjoyable walk although it can be quite muddy. On the walk you can admire the moss and lichens, the vines and flowers including orchids. The Mandara Hut, near the Maundi Crater, is actually a group of huts which can sleep about 200 people. Mattresses, lamps and stoves are provided but nothing else. This complex was built by the Norwegians as part of an aid programme. There is piped water, flushing toilets and firewood available. There is a dining area in the main cabin.

The second day will start off as a steep walk through the last of the rainforest and out into tussock grassland, giant heather and then on to the moorlands. There are occasional clearings through which you will get wonderful views of Mawenzi and Moshi far below. You will also probably see some of the exceptional vegetation that is found on Kilimanjaro including the giant lobelia, Kilimanjaro 'everlasting flowers' and other uncommon alpine plants. The walk to Horombo Hut (3,720 metres) is about 14 kilometres with an altitude gain of about 1,000 metres and will take you anything between five and seven hours. This hut is again actually a collection of huts that can accommodate up to 200 people. There is plenty of water but firewood is scarce. Some people spend an extra day here to help get acclimatized and if you are doing this there are a number of short walks in the area. It is a very good idea to spend this extra day – but there is the extra cost to be considered.

On the next day of walking you will climb to the Kibo Hut which is 13 kilometres from Horombo and is at 4,703 metres. As you climb, the vegetation thins to grass and heather and eventually to bare scree. You will feel the air thinning and will probably start to suffer from some altitude sickness. The route takes about 6-7 hours up the valley behind the huts, past 'Last Water' and onto 'The Saddle.' This is the wide fairly flat U-shaped desert between the two peaks of Mawenzi and Kibo and from here you will get some awe-inspiring views of the mountain. After Zebra Rocks and at the beginning of the saddle the track forks. To the right, about three hours from Horombo Hut, is Mawenzi Hut and to the left across the saddle is Kibo Hut. Kibo Hut is where the porters stay and from here on you should just take with you the absolute bare essentials. It is a good idea to bring some biscuits or chocolate with you for the final ascent to the peak, as a lunch pack is not always provided. Kibo Huts sleep about 120 people. There is no vegetation in the area and no water unless there has been snow recently so it has to be carried up from Last Water. Some people

Tanzania & Zanzibar

decide to try and get as much sleep as possible before the early start, while others decide not to sleep at all. You are unlikely to sleep very well because of the altitude and the temperatures anyway.

On the final day of the climb, in order to be at the summit at sunrise, and before the cloud comes down, you will have to get up at about 0200. One advantage of beginning at this time is that if you saw what you were about to attempt you would probably give up before you had even begun. You can expect to feel pretty awful during this final five hour ascent and many climbers are physically sick. You may find that this climb is extremely slippery and hard going. As the sun rises you will reach Gillman's Point (5,680 metres) – it is a wonderful sight. From here you have to decide whether you want to keep going another couple of hours to get to Kibo Peak (5,896 metres). The walk around the crater rim to Kibo Peak is only an extra 200 metres but at this altitude it is a strenuous 200 metres. At the peak there is a fair amount of litter left by previous climbers. You will return to Horombo Hut the same day and the next day return to Marangu where you will be presented with a certificate.

This climb is short and steep but is a wonderfully scenic route to take and as a result **Umbwe trail** is becoming increasingly popular. However it is not recommended for inexperienced climbers. To get to the start of the trail take the turning off the Arusha road about two kilometres down on the right. From there it's 14 kilometres down the Lyamungu road, turn right towards Mango and soon after crossing the Sere River you will get to Umbwe village. Ask at the mission school to leave your vehicle here.

From the mission the track continues for about three kilometres up towards the forest to Kifuni village. From there it's another six kilometres before you get to the start of the trail proper. There is a sign here and the trail branches to the left and climbs quite steeply through the forest along the ridge that is between the Lonzo River to the west and Umbwe River to the east. You will reach the first shelter which is a cave (2,940 metres) about 6-8 hours from Umbwe. This is Bivouac I which is an all weather rock shelter formed from the rock overhangs. It will shelter about six or seven people. There is firewood nearby and a spring about 15 metres below under a rock face.

If you made an early start and are fit you can continue on to Bivouac II. From the cave, continue up, past the moorland and along the ridge. It is a steep walk with deep valleys on each side of the ridge and this walk is magnificent with the strange 'Old Man's Beard' – a type of moss – covering most of the vegetation. The second set of caves is Bivouac II (3,800 metres) about 3-4 hours from Bivouac I. There are two caves – one about five minutes further down the track which will both sleep three or four people. There is a spring down the ravine about 15 minutes to the west.

From the second set of caves the path continues less steeply up the ridge beyond the tree line before reaching Barranco Hut (3,900 metres). Barranco Hut is about five hours away from the first caves. The path is well marked. The hut is a metal cabin which sleeps 6-8 people. About 200 metres beyond the hut is a rock overhang which can be used if the hut is full. There is water available about 250 metres to the east and firewood available in the area.

Just before reaching the hut the path splits in two. To the left, climb the west lateral ridge to the Arrow Glacier Hut (now defunct) towards the new Lava Tower Hut (4,600 metres) about four hours away. Up this path the vegetation thins before disappearing completely on reaching the scree slopes. Having spent the night here you will want to leave very early for the final ascent. Head torches are imperative and if there is no moon the walk can be quite difficult. Climb up between Arrow Glacier (which may have disappeared completely if you are there towards the end of the dry season) and Little Breach Glacier until you get to a few small cliffs. At this stage turn to the right heading for the lowest part of the crater rim that you can see. This part of the walk is on scree and snow and parts of it are quite a scramble. Having reached the crater floor cross the Furtwangler Glacier snout to a steep gully that reaches the summit plateau about another 500 metres west of Kibo Peak.

If you take the path to the right from Barranco Hut (east) you will cross one small stream and then another larger one as you contour the mountain to join the Mweka Trail. The path then climbs steeply through a gap in the west Breach. From here you can turn left to join the routes over the south glaciers. Alternatively continue along the marked path across screes, ridges and a valley until you reach the Karangu Campsite which is about a further 2-3 hours on from the top of the breach. A further couple of hours up the Karangu valley will come out at the Mweka-Barafu Hut path (part of the Mweka Trail). If you go left down along this you will get to the Barafu Hut after about 1-1½ hours. If you go straight on for about three hours you will join the Marangu Trail just above the Horombo Hut.

Machame trail   This trail is considered by some to be the most attractive of the routes up Kilimanjaro. It is located between Umbwe Trail and Shira Trail and joins the latter route at Shira Hut. The turn-off to the trail is to the west of Umbwe off the main Arusha-Moshi road. Take this road north towards Machame village, and leave your vehicle at the school or hotel there. From the village to the first huts takes about nine hours so be sure to start early.

Take the track through the shambas – small farms – and the forest to the park entrance (about four kilometres) from where you will see a clear track that climbs gently through the forest and along a ridge that is between the Weru Weru and Makoa streams. It is about seven kilometres to the edge of the forest, and then 4-5 hours up to the Machame Huts (3,000 metres). The two Machame Huts, on the edge of the forest, will sleep about seven people each. There is plenty of water down in the valley below the huts and firewood available close by.

From the Machame Huts go across the valley, over a stream, then up a steep ridge for about three or four hours. The path then goes west and drops into the river gorge before climbing more gradually up the other side and onto the moorland of the Shira Plateau to join the Shira Plateau Trail near the Shira Hut (3,800 metres). This takes about five hours in total. From the Shira Plateau you will get some magnificent views of Kibo Peak and the Western Breach. The Shira Hut (3,800 metres) sleeps about six people and is used by people on the Shira Plateau Trail as well as those on the Machame Trail. There is plenty of water available to the north and firewood nearby. From here there are a number of choices. You can go on to the Barranco Hut (5-6 hours, 3,900 metres) or the Lava Tower Hut (four hours, 4,600 metres). The path to Arrow Glacier Hut is well marked. The ascent includes scrambling over screes, rocks and snow fields – tough at times. Probably only suited to experienced hikers. It goes east from Shira Hut until it reaches a junction where the North Circuit Route leads off to the left. The path continues east crossing a wide valley before turning southeast towards the Lava Tower. Shortly before the tower a route goes off to the right to Barranco Hut and the South Circuit Route. To the left the path goes to Arrow Glacier Hut and the Western Breach.

Shira Plateau   This route needs a four-wheel drive vehicle and so for this reason is little used. How-
trail   ever if you do have access to such a vehicle and are acclimatized you can get to the Arrow Glacier Hut in 1 day.

The drive is a complex one and you may need to stop and ask the way frequently. Pass through West Kilimanjaro, drive for five kilometres and turn right. At 13 kilometres you will pass a small trading centre on the left. At 16 kilometres you will cross a stream followed by a hard left. At 21 kilometres you will enter a coniferous forest which will soon become a natural forest. The plateau rim is reached at 39 kilometres. Here the track continues upwards gently and crosses the plateau to the roadhead at 55 kilometres. From here you will have to walk. It is about one and a half hours to Shira Hut (3,800 metres). From here you continue east to join the Umbwe Trail to the Lava Tower Hut. The walk is fairly gentle and has magnificent views.

Mweka trail   This trail is the most direct route up the mountain. It is the steepest and the fastest. It begins at Mweka village, 13 kilometres north of Moshi, where you can leave your vehicle at the College of Wildlife Management with permission.

The trail follows an old logging road which you can drive up in good weather, through the shambas and the forest, for about five kilometres. It is a slippery track which deteriorates into a rough path after about two hours. From here it is approximately a further six kilometres up a ridge to the Mweka Huts (3,100 metres) which are about 500 metres beyond the tree line in the giant heather zone. In total the first day's walk takes about 6-8 hours. There are two huts here which each sleep about eight people. Water is available nearby from a stream in a small valley below the huts five minutes to the southeast and there is plenty of firewood.

From the Mweka Huts follow the ridge east of the Msoo River through heathlands, tussock open grassland and then onto the alpine desert to the Barafu Hut (4,400 metres) about 6-8 hours. These metal shelters sleep about 12 people. There is no water or firewood available so you will need to bring it up from Mweka Hut.

From the Barafu Huts the final ascent on a ridge between Rebmann and Ratzel glaciers takes about six hours up to the rim of the crater between Stella and Hans Meyer Points. From here it is a further hour to Uhuru Peak. At the lower levels the path is clearly marked, but becomes obscured further up. It is steep being the most direct non-technical route. Although specialized climbing equipment is not needed, be prepared for a scramble.

Loitkitok trail

This approach from Kenya is closed to the public and is not recommended. However you may be able to obtain special permission from the park's department to climb it. See the warden who is based in Marangu. You may have problems getting porters to go up this route.

This, and the Shira Plateau Trail, both come in from the north unlike the other trails. From the Outward Bound School take the path towards the border road and on reaching it turn left down it. Cross over the bridge over the Kikelewa River and go a further 150 metres. Here you will see a rough track leading through the plantations. Take this track, you will recross the Kikelewa and continue up through the forest, and on to the heather and moorlands until you reach the caves. It is a total of approximately 5-6 hours to the caves.

From these caves follow the path which heads towards a point just to the right of the lowest point on the Saddle. You will pass 'Bread Rock' after about one and a half hours. The track then divides, to the right is the Outward Bound Hut which you will almost certainly find locked. The path continues upwards to the Saddle towards the Kibo Huts – a climb of about 3-4 hours. To the left the another path crosses towards the Mawenzi Hut.

Sleeping

A *Ashanti Lodge*, PO Box 339, Marangu, T206. **A** *Kibo*, PO Box 102, Marangu, T4. Old German hotel, cool and comfortable, fine gardens, Evelyn Waugh stayed here in 1959 and was delighted with the place. **A** *Marangu*, PO Box 40, Marangu, T51307, F50639, B-Bennett@ tt.gn.apc.org, 40 kilometres from Moshi, 7 kilometres from Park gate. Long established family owned and run country style hotel, warm and friendly atmosphere, self contained cottages with private baths and showers, hot water, set in 12 acres of gardens offering stunning views of Kilimanjaro, swimming pool, croquet lawn, one of the original operators of Kilimanjaro climbs with over 40 years' experience. **B** *Aishi Hotel*, PO Box 534, Moshi T/F54104, situated south of Machame National Park gate near Machame village. 14 rooms with private facilities, set in well kept gardens, spotlessly clean and very well furnished. **C** *Kilimanjaro National Park Hostel*, PO Box 96, Marangu, T 50, located at entrance to park. Bunk beds and bedding supplied, you will need to bring your own food.

Tanzania & Zanzibar

Arusha National Park

Approach
4°0'S 36°30'E
Colour map 3, grid A4

Arusha National Park is situated about 25 kilometres east of Arusha and 58 kilometres from Moshi (see map, page 381). The road is a good one and the turning off the main road, about 35 kilometres from Kilimanjaro International Airport, is at Usa River and is clearly signposted. There are two lodges at Usa River. From the airport the landscape changes from the flat dry and dusty Sanya Plain which gradually becomes greener, more fertile and more cultivated. Take the turning (on the right if you are heading towards Arusha) and follow the gravel road for about 10 kilometres until you reach the Ngurdoto Gate. This is coffee country and you will see the farms on each side of the road. On reaching the Park entrance this changes to dense forest. At the entrance a small museum provides information for the visitor on the bird, animal and plant life of the park. The vehicle used by John Wayne in the film *Hatari* was at one time on view in Arusha National Park. It had a metal seat over the inside front mudguard from which the 'Duke' lassoed rhino in Ngorongoro.

Background

The Arusha National Park, which contains within its boundaries Mount Meru, was established in 1960. The film *Hatari* was made here in 1962 by Howard Hawks, starring John Wayne, Elsa Martinelli, Red Buttons and Hardy Kruger. The park has actually changed its name a number of times from Ngurdoto Crater National Park to Mount Meru National Park and finally to Arusha National Park. It covers an area of 137 square kilometres and rises from 1,524 metres at the Momella Lakes (also spelt Momela) to 4,572 metres at the peak of Mount Meru. Although it is only small because of this gradation there is a variety of landscapes, a variety of ecosystems and therefore a wide variety of flora and fauna. Within the park are the Ngurdoto Crater and the Momella Lakes. The best time to visit is from October to February.

Formation

Mount Meru is believed to have been formed at around the time of the great earth movements that created the Rift Valley, about 20 million years ago. The crater was formed about 250,000 years ago when a massive explosion blew away the eastern side of the volcano. A subsidiary vent produced the volcano of Ngurdoto which built

Ngurdoto Crater Arusha national park

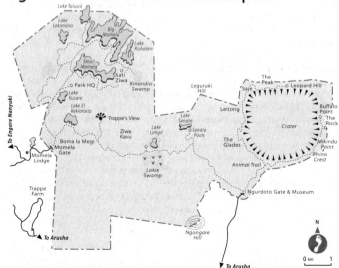

up over thousands of years. In a way similar to Ngorongoro, when the cone collapsed the caldera was left as it is today. Ngurdoto is now extinct, while Meru is only dormant, having last erupted about 100 years ago. The lava flow from this eruption can be seen on the northwest side of the mountain. It was at around this time in 1872 that the first European, Count Teleki, a Hungarian, saw the mountain.

Wildlife

Arusha National Park contains many animals including giraffe, elephant, hippo, buffalo, rhino (if you're lucky), colobus monkey, bush buck, red forest duiker, reed buck, waterbuck and wart hog. In fact Arusha is supposed to contain the highest density of giraffes in the world. There are no lions in the park although you may see leopard.

Routes

Within the park there are over 50 kilometres of tracks. However no road has been built into the Ngurdoto Crater in order to protect and preserve it. From the Ngurdoto Gate a road leads off towards the Ngurdoto Crater. This area is known as the 'connoisseur's park' – rightly so. The road climbs up through the forest until it reaches the rim. At the top you can go left or right, either going around the crater clockwise or anti-clockwise. The track does not go all the way round the rim of the crater so you will have to turn round and retrace your tracks back to the main road. You will be able to look down into the animals in the crater below but will not be able to drive down. The crater is about three kilometres in diameter and there are a number of viewing points around the rim from which you can view the crater floor, which is known as the 'park within the park'. These include Leitong Point (the highest at 1,850 metres), Glades Point, Rock Point, Leopard Hill, Rhino Crest and Mikindani Point. From this latter point you will be able to view Mount Kilimanjaro in the distance.

From the gate if you take the left track you will reach the Momella Lakes. This track goes past the Ngongongare Springs, Lokie Swamp, the Senato Pools and the

Meru Crater - Arusha National Park

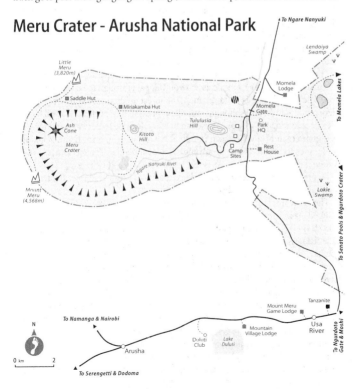

Tanzania & Zanzibar

two lakes Jembamba and Longil. At the peak of the dry season they may dry up but otherwise they are a good place to watch the animals and in particular the bird life. At various spots there are observation hides. At Lake Longil there is a camping and picnic site in a lovely setting.

From here the track continues through the forest which gradually thins out and through the more open vegetation you will be able to see Mount Meru. The Hyena Camp (Kambi ya Fisi) is reached where you will probably see a pack of spotted hyenas. Beyond this there is a small track leading off the main track to Bomo la Mengi which is a lovely place from which to view the lakes. Unless the cloud is down you will also be able to see Kilimanjaro from here. The main track continues past two more lakes – Lake El Kekhotoito and Lake Kusare before reaching the Momella Lakes.

The Momella Lakes are shallow alkaline lakes fed by underground streams. Because they have different mineral contents and different algae their colours are also different. They contain few fish but the algae attracts lots of bird life. What you see will vary with the time of year. Flamingoes tend to move in huge flocks around the lakes of East Africa and are a fairly common sight at Momella Lakes. Between October and April the lakes are also home to the migrating waterfowl which are spending the European winter in these warmer climes.

The track goes around the lakes reaching the Small Momella Lake first. This lake often has a group of hippos wallowing in it. Follow the road anti-clockwise and you will pass Lake Rishetani which is a fantastic emerald green colour. Along this route you will be able to stop off at the various observation sites. The next lake that you will get to is the Great Momella Lake which has a huge variety of bird life and is a lovely spot. The last two lakes are Tulusia and Lekandiro where you may see animals grazing.

Mount Meru The other major attraction of Arusha National Park is Mount Meru (4,565 metres) the second highest mountain in Tanzania and also the fifth highest in all Africa. The mountain lies to the west of the Ngare Nanyuki road in the western half of the Park. There is a road that leads up the mountain from Momella, passing through an open space called Kitoto from where there are good views of the mountain, to about 2,439 metres and from there you must walk. The road up Mount Meru requires a four-wheel drive vehicle and even this may have problems in the wet season.

The climb takes 2-3 days depending on whether you have a vehicle or not (and also on how fit you are). On the ascent you will pass through the changing vegetation. The first change is to lower montane forest at about 2,000 metres, then to higher montane forest. Although you will not need to hire porters, you will have to take a guide/ranger with you. These can be hired for US$10 per day from the Park headquarters in Momella as can porters if you decide you want them. Booking a guide and accommodation in advance is recommended: The *Warden, Arusha National Park*, PO Box 3134, Arusha.

Be prepared for a steep climb, and take plenty of warm clothes as the temperatures fall dramatically at night.

The walk up Mount Meru involves a 3,500 metres altitude hike, frequently climbed up and down within three days. The last section of the walk to the summit is very steep. It is easy to underestimate the problems associated with this walk – altitude sickness and frostbite. Snow is not unknown at the summit. Nobody checks if you have appropriate equipment for your climb. Recommended reading *before* the climb: page 40, **Health Information**, re: Altitude. During the wet season be sure to have a good pair of walking boots. You will also need to provide all your own food. The road climbs up the mountain up to the heath zone at about 2,439 metres from where you can climb to the peak. Follow the track from the roadhead until you reach the first hut. Alternatively if you do not have transport you can walk from the park headquarters to Miriakamba Hut which takes about three hours. The first mountain huts sleeps about 48 people, while the second, Saddle Hut, sleeps about 24 people. Both huts provide firewood. It is a three hour walk between the two huts and having reached Saddle Hut you can spend the afternoon climbing Little Meru (3,820

Tsetse Fly

The tsetse fly is a little larger than the house fly and is found over much of East Africa including Tanzania. Its presence is a serious threat to human habitation because it is a carrier of two diseases. The first is a human disease known as 'sleeping sickness' and the second is a disease which affects cattle that is called trypanosomiasis known as nagana amongst the people of Tanzania. This disease can be deadly to cattle while leaving man uninfected or can affect both man and cattle. In the former areas people can live and can cultivate the land but cannot keep cattle, whilst in the latter areas the presence of the tsetse fly has meant that large areas of Tanzania are uninhabitable by human beings and are left to the wild animals. Interestingly the tsetse fly does not affect wild animals. When it was realised that humans would never be able to live in these areas, but that wild animals could, large areas were designated to be game reserves in the early colonial era.

There are eight different species of tsetse fly found in Tanzania of which four are most important. The different species are each suited to a different type of environment and vegetation. Unfortunately there is a species of fly for almost all conditions in East Africa. Areas where there are no tsetse include land over about 1,830 metres, and areas with under 400 millimetres of rainfall. Tanzania is probably the worst affected of all the countries of East Africa.

Since the colonial period great efforts have been made to control the movement of tsetse fly. This was done by moving people out of certain areas and clearing the bush. A belt of five kilometres wide is cleared of bush and people moved into this belt in a dense settlement. This belt provides a barrier which the tsetse cannot move across. Spraying has also been used. However a lapse in the efforts is all that is needed for the fly to return to areas that have been cleared.

metres) which takes about one and a half hours. From Saddle Hut climb up to the rim of the mountain and around to the summit (4,572 metres) before returning to the Momella park headquarters.

A+ *Mashado Arusha Mountain Lodge*. In September 1997 a start is being made on the construction of a low-impact 40 bedroom lodge within the park boundaries, due to be completed in 1998. **A** *Momella Game Lodge*, PO Box 418, Arusha, T3798/3038. Accommodates 40 people, located just outside the park near the Momella Gate, wonderful views. **A** *Mount Meru Game Lodge*, PO Box 427, Arusha, T7803, Tx42005, located along turn-off from Usa River, 22 kilometres from Arusha. Small, well-run, excellent cuisine, fine gardens and charming atmosphere. **B** *Ngaresero Mountain Lodge*, PO Box 425, Arusha, T Usa 38. Located 16 kilometres from Arusha at Tengeru in the Mt Meru foothills. **B** *Tanzanite*, PO Box 3068, Arusha, T Usa 32, Tx42038. Located along turn-off from Usa River 22 kilometres from Arusha. Swimming pool, tennis, good value. **C** *Rest House*, sleeps 5, located near the Momella Gate, bookings through the Warden, Arusha National Park, PO Box 3134, Arusha. **D** *Camp sites*, there are 3 sites in the park, all have water and toilets and provide firewood, book through the *Park Warden, Arusha National Park*, PO Box 3134, Arusha.

Sleeping

Tarangire National Park

Tarangire National Park is reached on the main Arusha-Dodoma road (see map of National Parks). From Arusha the road leaves the bustling town and enters the heavily cultivated countryside. You will pass maize, coffee and banana plantations. A few acacia trees start to appear and you will probably see groups of Masai grazing their herds along the road. About 85 kilometres from Arusha at Makuyuni the main road up to the Serengeti and Ngorongoro branches off to the right. Continue along the Great North Rd towards Tarangire which is signposted – it is about 120 kilometres from Arusha.

Approach
3° 50'S, 35° 55' E
Colour map 3, grid B4

Background The Tarangire National Park, established in 1970, covers an area of 2,600 square kilometres and lies at 1,110 metres above sea level. Its name is from the Tarangire River which flows through the park throughout the year. The best time to visit is from July to September when, being the dry season, the animals gather in large numbers along the river. Although you may not see as many animals here as in other places, Tarangire is a wonderful park. There were fewer people here than in Ngorongoro and that is very much part of the attraction.

One of the most noticeable things on entering the park are the baobab trees which rise up from the grass. With their massive trunks they are instantly recognisable. As the park includes within its boundaries a number of hills, as well as rivers and swamps, there is a variety of vegetation zones and habitats. The river rises in the Kondoa Highlands which are located to the south and flows north throughout the length of the park. It continues to flow during the dry season and so is a vital watering point for the animals of the park as well as those from surrounding areas.

Wildlife The Tarangire National Park forms a 'dry season retreat' for much of the wildlife of the southern Masailand. The ecosystem in this area involves more than just Tarangire

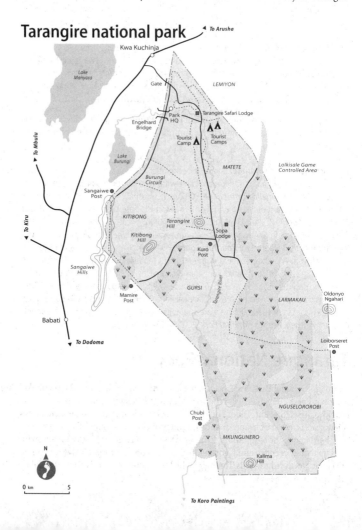

Tarangire national park

National Park. Also included in the ecosystem are the Lake Manyara National Park to the north and a number of 'Game Controlled Areas'. The largest of these are the Lake Natron Game Controlled Area further north and the Simanjiro Plains Game Controlled Area towards Arusha. The Mto wa Mbu Game Controlled Area, the Lolkisale Game Controlled Area, and Mkungunero Game Controlled Area are also included in the ecosystem. The key to the ecosystem is the river and the main animal movements begin from the river at the beginning of the short rains around October and November. The animals that move north during the wet season include wildebeest, zebra, Thompson's gazelles, buffalo, eland and hartebeest. The elephant population in this park was estimated at around 6,000 in 1987. At the height of the rainy season the animals are spread out over an area of over 20,000 square kilometres. When the wet season ends the animals begin their migration back south and spend the dry season (July-October) concentrated around the river Tarangire until the rains begin again.

The number of species of birds recorded in Tarangire National Park has been estimated at approximately 300. These include migrants which fly south to spend October to April away from the winter of the northern hemisphere.

Part of the reason that this area was put over to national park status is that being a tsetse fly infested area it is not suitable for stock rearing (see box, page 507).

Routes

The park is large enough for it not to feel crowded even when there are quite a few visitors. There are a number of routes or circuits that you can follow that take you to the major attractions.

Lake Burungi Circuit

This track covers about 80 kilometres. It begins at the Engelhard Bridge and following the circuit clockwise, goes along the river bank. Continue along through the Acacia trees until about three kilometres before the Kuro Range Post where you will see a turning off to the right. Down this track you will pass through a section of Combretum-Dalergia woodland as you head towards the western boundary of the park. The route continues around and the vegetation turns back to parkland with acacia trees and then back to Combretum as the road turns right and reaches a full circle at the Englehard Bridge. If you are very lucky you may see leopard and rhino in this area although the numbers of rhino have reportedly decreased.

Lemiyon area

This circuit covers the northern area of the park bound on each side by the eastern and western boundaries of the park and to the south by the river. This is where you will see the fascinating baobab trees with the large silvery trunks and gourd like fruits. These huge trunks enable the trees to survive throughout a number of rain failures and they are characteristic of this type of landscape. Also here are the acacia trees which are the food of giraffe. Other animals that you expect to see are wildebeest, zebra, gazelles and elephant.

Tarangire migrations

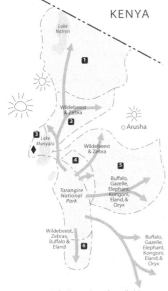

KENYA

Lake Natron

Wildebeest & Zebra

○ Arusha

Lake Manyara

Wildebeest & Zebra

Buffalo, Gazelle, Elephant, Kongoni, Eland, & Oryx

Tarangire National Park

Wildebeest, Zebras, Buffalo & Eland

Buffalo, Gazelle, Elephant, Kongoni, Eland, & Oryx

1 Lake Natron Game Controlled Area
2 Mto wa Mbu Game Controlled Area
3 Lake Manyara National Park
4 Lolkisale Game Controlled Area
5 Simanjiro Game Controlled Area & Plains
6 Mkungunero Game Controlled Area

N

Not to scale

Kitibong Hill circuit This track covers the west section of the park and is centred on Kitibong Hill. It includes acacia parkland in the east and Combretum-Dalbergia woodland in the west, the Gursi floodplains to the south and the foothills of Sangaiwe Hill which are along the western boundary of the Park. This area is home to a variety of plains animals including buffalo and elephant.

The Gursi & Lamarkau circuit The area is in the south of the park. The grasslands found here are home to many plain grazing species. You are also likely to see ostrich here. During the wet season a large swamp forms in what is known as Larmakau – a corruption of the Masai word *'o'llakau'* which means hippo, which can be seen here.

Without a four-wheel drive vehicle you will not be able to see much of the southernmost section of the park and during the wet season it is often impassable to all vehicles. There are two areas in the south – Nguselororobi to the east and Mkungunero in the southwest corner. The former of these is mainly swamp, with some plains and woodland, and if you are lucky you might see cheetah here. Mkungunero has a number of freshwater pools which serve to attract many different species.

Sleeping **A+** *Oliver's Camp* in the eastern part of Tarangire National Park offers a small luxury twin bedding camp, which accommodates 12 guests, carefully designed to blend into the Kikoti landscape, bookings c/o Abercrombie and Kent, PO Box 427 Arusha, T7803, F7003. **A+** *Tarangire Sopa Lodge*, PO Box 1823, Arusha, T6886/6896/6703, F8245, info@sopalodges.com. Luxury all-suite lodge with 75 suites, opened in 1995, opulent lounges, bars and restaurant, excellent food and barbecues, large landscaped swimming pool and conference facilities, probably Tanzania's most luxurious safari lodge. **A+** *Tarangire Swala Camp*, Mashado Central Reservations, PO Box 14823, Arusha, T57-6585, F57-8020, Mashado@habari.co.tz, camp accessed by air from Arusha. Located on the edge of the Gursi swamp which makes the camp a first class site for ornithologists, comprises 8 extremely comfortable guest tents, en suite facilities, special activities at the camp include informal talks by a scientist involved in conservation – related research camp closed during the rainy season April-June, for UK agent see page 50. **B** *Tarangire Safari Lodge*, PO Box 2703, Arusha, T7182, Tx42126, sleeps 70. Luxury tented camp with hot water, showers, toilets etc, good restaurant and bar, swimming pool, overlooking the river – wonderful setting, this area is relatively free of tsetse flies, best tented location for game viewing. **C** *Six special camp sites*, enquire at Park HQ, water and firewood are provided. **D** *Two public camp sites*.

Mkomazi Game Reserve

4°S, 38°E This national park of 3,600 square kilometres lies about 100 kilometres north of Tanga and is adjoined to Kenya's Tsavo National Park (see map, page 381). **The Mkomazi Rhinos project**, coordinated by the Tanzania Wildlife Protection fund, has taken a lead role in relocating four black rhino from South Africa to Mkomazi Reserve and Ngorongoro. The released rhino are kept in intensive protection zones and it is hoped that they will breed, after which they will be relocated within Tanzania to other traditional natural habitats. It is an expensive programme. The cost of transferring 10 rhinos is put at US$1.1 million. There are no hotel facilities in this Park, although there are some in the form of the **E** *Elephant Motel* located in the nearest town Same.**Same** is a small town on the Moshi road at the foot of the Usambara Mountains. This is the road that leads to **Lushoto** (see page 383) a lovely town in the hills. There is a campsite located at Ibeye which is within the Reserve, if you are prepared to be self sufficient.

Central and southern parks

Mikumi National Park

This park is located in central Tanzania about 300 kilometres west of Dar es Salaam (see main map, page 480 and southwest region map, page 430). Mikumi National Park has an important role as an educational centre for students of ecology and conservation. From Morogoro the main Tanzania-Zambia road continues west. The road travels through well populated cultivated land for about 100 kilometres before reaching the boundary of Mikumi National Park. It only takes about four hours from Dar es Salaam on a good road and so is popular with weekend visitors. The national park is on both sides of the road so drive with care. The southern boundary is close to Selous Game Reserve.

Approach
7°26'S 37°0'E
Colour map 3, grid B4

Bunduki is a hill station, amid stands of eucalyptus, with trout fishing, can be accessed via Mikumi.

Mikumi National Park, established in 1964, covers an area of 3,230 square kilometres and is set at 549 metres above sea level. The park lies in a horseshoe of towering mountains – the Uluguru range which rises to 2,750 metres. The park lies between the villages of Doma and Mikumi from which it takes its name. 'Mikumi' is the Kiswahili name for the Borassus palm, a type of palm tree that is found in the area. The best time to visit is from September-December.

Background

There is a lot of wildlife to be seen in this park including elephant, buffalo, giraffe, the famous tree-climbing lions, leopard, zebra and many sorts of antelope.

Wildlife

At Mikumi it is well worth taking a guide for a short time when you first arrive – this isn't expensive compared to the other costs involved (about US$10) and can greatly improve chances of seeing the rarer types of game.

Tanzania & Zanzibar

Mikumi national park

To Morogoro

Mwanambogo Dam

Chamgore

Mkata Flood Plain

Mgeta River

Visada Circuit

Kisingura Circuit

Kikoboga

HQ

Gate

Gate 2

Ikoya Loop

To Iringa

Mikumi

Mkata River

N

0 km   5

■ **Sleeping**
1 Mikumi Wildlife Camp
2 Mikumi Wildlife Lodge

Other
▲ Camp Sites
∘ Waterholes

Routes From the park gate the road leads to the floodplain of the Mkata River which is particularly important for the wildlife. To the north the floodplain remains swampy throughout the year, whilst in the south water channels drain to the Mkata River. Here you will see amongst other animals elephant, buffalo and hippo.

About 15 kilometres northwest of the park gate there are some hippo pools where there are almost always a number of hippos wallowing in the mud.

Other areas worth visiting are the Choga Wale area and Mwanambogo area. The latter of these can only be reached in the dry season. The track is to the east of the flood plain and heads north towards the Mwanambogo Dam. The Kisingura Circuit is another popular drive as is the Kikoboga area where you are likely to see elephant particularly during December and January.

The road that goes along the river is a good one to take for viewing. It passes through a patch of woodland and some swampy areas before coming onto the grasslands of the Chamgore. Chamgore means 'place of the python' and here there are two waterholes which are always ideal for spotting game. Hill Drive leads up the foothills of the Uluguru Mountains and from here you will get wonderful views all around. The vegetation is miombo woodland and the ebony tree grows here.

To get to the south part of the park take the track which branches off opposite the Park entrance which heads towards an area called Ikoya. Here you will see sausage trees (*Kigelia africana*) with their distinctive pods hanging down. This is also where you may see leopard.

Ruaha east & south-east

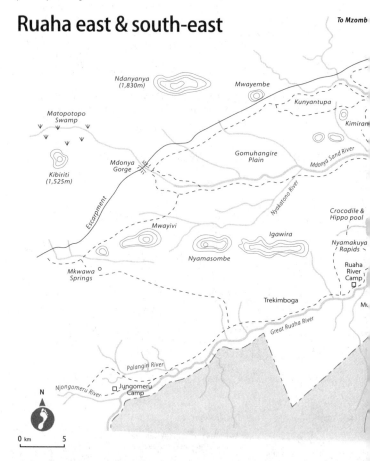

B *Mikumi Wildlife Lodge*, PO Box 2485, Dar es Salaam, T23491, located down a left turning off the main road about half way across the park, discount of 50 percent between Easter and end of June. Built of local materials on a hill 500-600 metres from a waterhole, restaurant, bar, swimming pool (but currently out of service), shop and petrol station, bathrooms need renovation. **C** *Mikumi Wildlife Tented Camp*, T Dar es Salaam 68631, located about 300 metres off the main road to the right, near the park headquarters. Very comfortable, accommodates about 10 people, bar and restaurant, booking through *Oyster Bay Hotel*, PO Box 1907, Dar es Salaam, T68631. **D** *Youth Hostel*, located at park headquarters. Bookings through Chief Park Warden, Mikumi National Park, PO Box 62, Morogoro, sleeps 48 people, basic. **D** *Camp site*. Located about 4 kilometres from park entrance gate. Water and firewood usually available, otherwise very basic. **E** *Mikumi Medical Centre Guest Cottages*, excellent place to stay, run by a Dutch organization who have funded the building of the guest cottages so that they might provide a continuing source of income for the medical centre, the facilities include a fully equipped kitchen, shower room with hot water, lounge/dining room and a number of bedrooms with fans and nets, the medical centre can be found by driving from the park entrance to Mikumi – keep going until you cross the railway and it is on the left a few hundred metres on, there are Hospital (road signs by the entrance).

The National Park is about 10 kilometres north of the small village of Mikumi, which has a number of cheap hotels and guest houses. It is possible to visit the park one afternoon, stay overnight in Mikumi village and return to the National Park the following morning, paying the National Park entry fee of US$25 per 24 hours once. **Accommodation: E** *Genesis Hotel*, rooms, camping, restaurant, secure**. Camping** also available at the *Southern Highland Estate*, 28 kilometres from Mikumi.

Sleeping
There is an airstrip near the park headquarters for light aircraft

Ruaha National Park and Rungwa Game Reserve

Ruaha National Park is located 130 kilometres west of Iringa and from Iringa it is a drive of about four hours (see map, page 430). It is the most remote park in Tanzania, and visitor numbers reflect that: 2,500 pa in Ruaha, 45,000 for Tarangire and 150,000 for the Serengeti. Initially the road passes through densely populated countryside until the population gradually thins out. The vegetation becomes miombo woodland and about 60 kilometres from Iringa the turning off to the right to the park is indicated. It is another 50 kilometres down this road to the park boundary and from there about 10 kilometres to Ibuguziwa where you cross the Ruaha River and pay the Park entrance fees. About one kilometre beyond the river there is a junction. To

Approach
6°55'S 33°32'E
Colour map 3, grid B3

Tanzania & Zanzibar

the right the track goes to Msembe and the park headquarters and to the left to Ruaha River camp. A new scheduled air service runs twice weekly by Coastal Travel in Dar es Salaam, cost US$140 each way.

Background Ruaha National Park was classified a national park in 1964 having been a part of Rungwa Game Reserve until then. It covers an area of 12,950 square kilometres and ranges from 750 metres to 1,900 metres above sea level. The Park gets its name from the river which forms part of its boundary. The name *Ruaha* is from the word *Luvaha* which means great in the Hehe language and the river certainly is this. It is vital to the economy of the country for it supplies much of Tanzania with electricity through hydro-electric power from the dam at Kidatu. Further downstream the Ruaha joins with the Ulanga to make the Rufiji River. Visiting is only possible during the dry season. In the wet the tracks are mostly impassable and when the grass is long, game viewing is almost impossible so the best time to visit is from July-December. The park's inaccessibility means that not many people visit it although the Ruaha River camp is very popular.

Wildlife There is a wide variety of wildlife in this park including elephant, ostrich, greater and lesser kudu, gazelle, and other antelope and, in the river, hippo, packs of cape hunting dogs and crocodile. There are over 400 recorded species of bird in the park. It is a huge park and is largely underdeveloped and inaccessible. Unfortunately poaching in this park is a serious problem and the animal population has suffered enormously from this. In particular rhinos which were once found here are probably now extinct. Also the elephant population has fallen tremendously from over 22,000 in 1977 to under 4,000 in 1987. The 4,000 elephant still represents the largest number in any National Park in Africa. Ruaha is unrivalled for buffalo and hippo too and the bird count is unsurpassed in Tanzania, possibly all East Africa. The fall in the number of elephant population is probably the most dramatic decline in all the national parks of Tanzania. However efforts are being made to improve the situation and the Friends of Ruaha Society (PO Box 60 Mufindi, or, PO Box 786 Dar es Salaam) is the motivating force behind this. They, together with the park's wardens have improved the roads and signposting and thus the game drives have improved. They have also increased the anti-poaching patrolling.

Routes There are four major vegetation zones within this park. The river valleys; the open grassland; the miombo woodland (see box, page 419); and undulating countryside where baobabs dominate.

Around Msembe is bush country with acacia and baobab trees, and elephants are often found here. Along the river, particularly during the dry season, many animals congregate. You can expect to see elephants, giraffe, baboons, wart hogs, buffalo, zebra, all sorts of antelope and if you are lucky leopard and cheetah. In the river itself are both hippo and crocodile.

The Mwagusi Sand River joins the Ruaha about 10 kilometres from Msembe. If you cross this river and follow the track you will get to Mwayembe Hill and the escarpment where there is a salt lick often frequented by elephant and buffalo.

The Mdonya Sand River joins the Ruaha between the ferry and the park headquarters. From the ferry a drive southwest will take you past the Nyamakuyu Rapids and Trekimboga to where the Jongomero joins the Ruaha about 40 kilometres upriver. This is a good place to see hippo and crocodile. Roan and Sable antelopes can be seen, which are difficult to see elsewhere. There are supposed to be rhino in the western part of the park, but the location is kept secret.

Sleeping The park headquarters are located at Msembe which is 112 kilometres from Iringa and 615 kilometres from Dar es Salaam. It is halfway from Dar es Salaam to the Zambia border town of Tunduma. There is an airstrip at the Park headquarters for light aircraft, and 3 flights a week from Dar es Salaam (contact Foxtreks, see below).

A *Mwagusi Camp*, owned and run by Chris Fox (Foxtreks Ltd), PO Box 84, Mufindi, Tanzania and Foxtreks, PO Box 10270, Dar es Salaam, T37479, F46045, Tx41150. The site overlooks the Mwagusi Sands River, which does not dry up and so attracts all kinds of wildlife to drink there, it's a tented camp with en suite showers, hot water is limited, the site accommodates 16 people and is 30 minutes away from the airstrip. As soon as you disembark from the plane you are amongst the wildlife, highly recommended if you want to see the wildlife and not many other human beings, the owner will take you on Game Drives and is very experienced, alternatively short guided walking tours are available, giving you an opportunity to 'touch the wild', animals wander freely through the camps. **A+** *Ruaha River Lodge* (Foxtreks, PO Box 10270, Dar es Salaam, T37479, F46045, Tx41150), the direct telephone and fax booking number for Ruaha River Lodge is 255 811 327706, Fox@tt.sasa.unep.no. Price includes full board, bandas accommodation, located 18 kilometres south of Msembe on and around a kopje overlooking the Ruaha River, restaurant (a recent traveller reported that the food was mediocre) and bar, vehicle hire available, wonderful setting, excellent value, you will undoubtedly enjoy your stay here. Some bandas are on a hill, others overlook the river, the bandas have WC and shower, essential because many animals roam the campsite during the night, nearby there is a hippo pool – worth a visit. During the dry season – October – the animals remain in this vicinity. **D** *Rondavels and campsite*, located at the park headquarters, bookings through Chief Warden, Ruaha National Park, PO Box 369, Iringa. Other campsites around the park.

Udzungwa Mountains National Park

This has recently been been classified as a national park, previously it was a national forest reserve. The conservation team effort programme is designed to benefit the local people and improve their social amenities of health and education, water supplies and transport to encourage them to fully co-operate in the conservation programme with the National Park Management. Funds raised by tourism will directly benefit the local people.

This is a forest area and covers an area of approximately 1,000 square kilometres lying between 300 and 2,800 metres. Since the mountains are so steep there has been little development apart from at the foothills, where sugar is cultivated. There are no roads or tracks through the park but guided walks are available. The shortest walk takes you to the Prince Bernhard' waterfalls. The Mwanihani trail can be walked in two days, climbing to a height of over 2,000 metres. A tent, all food and water must accompany you as there are no fixed facilities. This great altitudinal range makes for a great diversity of vegetation and thus habitats for many different species. These

7° 50' S, 37° E

Udzungwa Mountains National Park

include the Iringa-Uhehe Red Colobus monkey and the Sanje mangabey, as well as elephant, buffalo, lion and leopard. To the south lies the green Kilombero valley, with the jagged slopes of the Mbarika Mountains 100 kilometres away, clearly visible rising out of the lowlands.

As yet there are no facilities here but it is close enough to Mikumi National Park for those facilities to be used (see map, page 430). The best time to visit is from September-December.

Selous Game Reserve

Background
9° S, 38° E
Colour map 3, grid C5

This enormous reserve in south Tanzania, first established in 1922, is the largest park in Africa and the second largest in the world, covering an area of 55,000 square kilometres. This makes it about twice the size of Denmark. However, the size of the Park is misleading insofar that visitors are restricted to the area north of the river Rufiji. South of the Rufiji is completely undeveloped and forbidden to visitors. The density of animals in this park is lower than that of other parks.

Travellers have reported that Selous Game Reserve is now overrun with tourists from July to September. The cheapest camp is US$110 per night, without park fees. It is relatively untouched by man and being here gives you a feeling of being somewhere where little has changed for hundreds of years. The park is named after a Captain Frederick Selous who was killed in action in January 1917 whilst scouting in the area (see box, page 517). The best time to visit is from July-October. The camps and lodges are closed at the peak of the wet season from April-June when the rains render many of the roads impassable.

Selous game reserve

Related map
A Selous Game Reserve - Beho Beho, page 518

Frederick C Selous: Greatest of the White Hunters

Born in 1852 in London, the young Selous went to Rugby school. An early expedition saw Selous trek to a lake 25 kilometres from Rugby, strip-off, swim through the icy water to a small island and shin up a tree to collect eight blue heron's eggs. On returning to school he was rewarded by being made to copy out 63 lines of Virgil for each egg. Inspired by the writings of Livingstone, Selous determined to visit Africa. After toying with the idea of becoming a doctor, he travelled to South Africa in 1871, and rapidly established himself as a supreme tracker and hunter.

Hunting was tough. The rifles were heavy muzzle-loaders, and powder was carried loose in one pocket, ignition caps in another and a supply of four ounces of lead bullets in a pouch. It was not uncommon for a hunter to be knocked out of the saddle by the gun's recoil and accidents were common.

Selous killed numerous game in his early years, partly for trophies in the case of lion and rhinoceros, for ivory in the case of elephants, and anything else as meat for his party. Later he was to become more restrained, virtually giving up trophy hunting. His skills were based on absorbing the skills of African hunters and trackers, and in 1881 he published the first of a series of highly successful books on his methods and exploits, A Hunter's Wanderings in Africa. In 1887 he began a career of paid work leading safaris for wealthy clients, which culminated in a huge expedition organised for President Roosevelt in 1909. A young British diplomat in South Africa, H. Rider Haggard, based his character Allan Quatermain on Selous and his adventures in his novel King Solomon's Mines, published in 1895.

During one visit to England, Selous took delivery of a new .450 rifle at his hotel an hour before he was due to catch the boat train from Waterloo to return to Africa. There was no time to test the sights and alignment on a rifle range, so Selous ordered a cab to stand-by, flung open his bedroom window, squeezed off five shots at a chimney stack, checked that the grouping was satisfactory with his binoculars, swiftly packed the rifle and skipped down to the cab, forcing his way through a throng in the lobby, pausing only to remark that he had heard some shots on his floor, and the manager had better look into it.

By 1914, Selous, now married, had retired to Surrey and busied himself with running his own natural history museum. At the outbreak of war, despite being 63, he was determined to serve in East Africa, where he felt his skills would be useful. He joined the Legion of Frontiersmen, a colourful outfit which included French Legionnaires, a Honduran general, a handful of Texan cowboys, Russian émigrés, some music hall acrobats and a light-house keeper.

In January 1917, scouting in the campaign against General von Lettow Vorbeck, see page 530, he was killed by a German sniper at Behobeho on the Rufiji River. Behobeho Camp is now part of the Selous Game Reserve. In 1985, the Rugby School Natural History Society was renamed the Selous Society.

History This Game Reserve has an interesting history. In the days of the slave trade the caravan routes passed through the park. It is said that the occasional mango groves that can be seen grew from the mango stones discarded by the caravans on their way to the coast. In the early 20th century during German colonial rule some of this area was designated into game reserves but in those days big game hunting was the most significant activity. In 1910 Kaiser Wilhelm gave part of the reserve to his Kaiserin as an anniversary gift. This is how the nickname 'Shamba la Bibi' meaning 'The Woman's Field' came to be. During the First World War the area was the location of confrontation as described in William Boyd's novel *An Ice Cream War*.

Wildlife There are supposed to be over a million animals in this park and it is probably best known for its large numbers of elephant. However poaching has been an enormous problem in the past and the numbers have been reduced substantially in recent years. A very disturbing report that came out in 1988 estimated that the elephant population had fallen by 80 percent in Selous in just 10 years from 1977 (census estimated population at 22,852) to 1987 (population estimated at 3,673). However, more recent estimates of the numbers of elephant show an increase. Rhino have also been seriously affected and their population in Selous is estimated to have fallen from 2,500 in 1976 to less than 50 in 1986. Other animals you may see include lions, buffalo, hippo, crocodile. The proximity of areas for trophy hunters exacerbates the difficulty of viewing the animals. Part of the reason for the lack of human habitation in this area is that it is infested with the tsetse (see box, page 507). For this reason using insect repellent on any exposed areas of your body is a good idea. Although sleeping sickness is rare, the flies do have a nasty bite.

Routes Much of this enormous park is without tracks and in the wet season is completely inaccessible. The best explored area is to the north where the lodges and camps are located. Central to the park is the Great Rufiji River. This river and its associated water system has the largest catchment area of any river in East Africa, and is probably the most significant feature of the park. It rises from the south and becomes the Rufiji where the Luwegu and Mbarangandu join together. Other rivers join it and further north it swings east before it is forced through Stiegler's Gorge. At its delta, opposite Mafia Island, millions of tonnes of silt are deposited every year during the wet season. During this season it swells to such an extent that is renders much of the park inaccessible. During the dry season it subsides and the sand banks are revealed.

Stiegler's Gorge is found in the north of the reserve at the junction of the Rufiji and Ruaha rivers (see Beho Beho map, page 518). It is a bottleneck as the water from this huge catchment area is forced through the narrow gorge. The gorge is named after a German explorer who was killed here by an elephant in 1907. The gorge is about 100 metres wide and the same depth and if you have a head for heights there is a cable car which spans it. There was a plan to build a hydro-electric dam here. This project was to be undertaken by the Rufiji Basin Development Authority (RUBADA) with Norwegian funds. However it has been put on hold and the Stiegler Gorge Safari Camp is made up

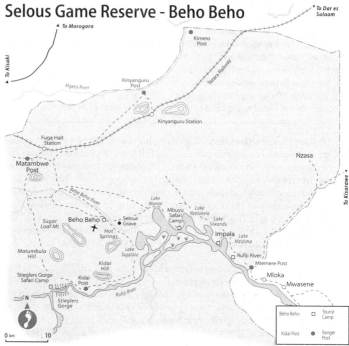

Selous Game Reserve - Beho Beho

To Dar es Salaam

To Morogoro

To Kisaki

To Kisarawe

Kirnero Post

Mgeta River

Kinyanguru Post

Tazara Railway

Kinyanguru Station

Fuga Halt Station

Nzasa

Matambwe Post

Beho Beho River

Lake Manze

Lake Nzelakela

Sugar Loaf Mt

Beho Beho

Selous Grave

Mbuyu Safari Camp

Lake Siwandu

Hot Springs

Impala

Lake Mzizima

Matumbula Hill

Lake Tagalala

Kidai Hill

Rufiji River

Mtemere Post

Stieglers Gorge Safari Camp

Kidai Post

Mloka

Mwasene

Stieglers Gorge

Rufiji River

Related map
Selous Game Reserve,
page 516

N

0 km   10

| Beho Beho | □ | Tourist Camp |
| Kidai Post | ● | Ranger Post |

of what were to be the housing facilities of the expatriate workers on the project.

Beyond the gorge the river widens out again and splits to form a number of lakes – Tagalala, Manze, Nzerakera, Siwando, and Mzizima. This swampy area is home to many animals who congregate there especially when water is scarce during the dry season. In particular elephant, buffalo and of course hippo gather here, sometimes in large numbers.

Other attractions in the park include the hot springs known simply as Maji Moto (hot water in Kiswahili). These are located on the eastern slopes of Kipalala Hill and the water flows down into Lake Tagalala. You get to them by walking (with a ranger at all times) up the ravine. The water is heated deep in the earth by thermal activity and emits the strong smell of sulphur. The highest springs are the hottest whilst further down they cool down enough for you to be able to swim in them.

Tours

Apart from seeing Selous by road, the other popular ways are by foot and by boat. This is one of only two national parks where you are allowed to walk. All four camps can arrange a walking safari. You will normally set off early in order to avoid the worst of the midday sun when most of the animals retire for a siesta. You must be accompanied by a ranger. Animal sightings tend to be rarer on walking safaris; as the animals frequently shy away from humans. However, it is very pleasant to be able to stretch your legs and get a different perspective of the country.

Rufiji and Mbuyu Safari Camps can both arrange boat trips up the river Rufiji. Boat trips are a wonderful way of seeing this park.

The south part of the park is characterized by a feeling of great emptiness. The Lewegu, Mbarangandu and Njenji Rivers flow through the area, much of which is heavily forested. There are a series of steep cliffs in the south formed by geological faults.

Sleeping

The Park Headquarters are located at Matambwe. Please note that two separate companies have similarly named camps in this Park.

A+ *Mbuyuni Tented Camp* is a new luxury development, WCs, showers, solar electricity and swimming pool, bookings through Selous Safari Co, PO Box 1192, Dar es Salaam, T34535, F28486. Animals wander freely in the camp during the night. Boats and fishing equipment are available in both camps. The wildlife is excellent and camp visitors include elephant and hippo. **A+** *Sand Rivers*, just eight cottages offering comfortable accommodation, overlooking the Sand Rivers which is teeming with hippo and crocodiles, contact Abercrombie and Kent, PO Box 427, Arusha, T7803, F7003. **A+** *Selous Safari Camp*, on the Behobeho River. Individual huts with hot water and shower, view overlooking the lakes, restaurant and bar, **A** *Mbuyu Safari Camp*, T051-124897/111139, F116413/647583, stgs@Kuiga.com, http://www.mbuyu.eastafrica.net. Bookings through Southern Tanganyika Game Safaris and Tours Ltd, PaO Box 2341, Dar es Salaam, T812-781971 or 812-782421 (ask for Mbuyu), F116413 or 811-324662, aircon@twiga.com. Named after the large baobab tree that the camp is sited around, accommodates about 30 people, located on a high bank overlooking the river Rufiji, luxury tented camp, all tents with hot water and shower, lovely setting, restaurant and bar, fishing equipment, boats and Land Rovers for hire, boat safaris, fishing excursions, walking safaris, all provided with an armed ranger and experienced guide can be arranged from here, specialize in overnight camps off road in the bush. If you wish to visit the grave of Captain F.C. Selous near Beho Beho, which is an all day drive, book the trip shortly after arrival at the camp. Access to the Mbuyu Safari camp is cheaper by train vs small aircraft. The camps close from Easter until the beginning of June because of the rains. Mbuyuni may remain closed for longer because of its location on the floodplain. **A** *Rufiji River Camp*, bookings through Hippotours & Safaris Ltd, PO Box 13824, Dar es Salaam, Kilimanjaro Office T36860, Tx41685 TAIRTZ, Mikocheni Office T75164/75610, F75165, Radio Call HF 5189.00 LSB, located overlooking the Rufiji River, accommodates about 20, tented camp with hot water, WCs and showers integrated in the tents, recently electricity has become available, restaurant and bar, fishing equipment, boats and Lnd Rovers for hire. **A+** *Sand Rivers* Just 8 cottages offering comfortable accommodation, overlooking the Sand Rivers which is teeming with hippo and crocodiles. Contact Abercrombie & Kent, PO Box 427, Arusha, T7803, F7003.

Safari companies Because of the problem of accessibility (remember that in the wet seasons it can be difficult to go by road) most people go to Selous on organized safaris. Companies to contact include: **Abercrombie and Kent**, Sloane Square House, Holbein Place, London SW1W 8NS, UK, T071-7309600 or the local contact number PO Box 427, Arusha, T7803, F7003. **Coastal Travel** (see page 344) have a 2-day, 1-night fly-in package for US$230 (extra day US$110) in Mbuyu Safari Camp, boat trips and game drives US$25, walking guides US$10. **Easy Travel & Tours Ltd**, Avalon House, 1st Flr, Sokoine Drive/Zanaki St, PO Box 1428, Dar es Salaam, T123526/121747, F113842/114479, easytravel@raha.com. **Ecosafaris**, 146 Gloucester St, London SW7, UK, T071-3705032. **Hoopoe Adventure Tours**, UK Suite F1, Kebbell House, Carpenders Park, Watford WD1 5BE, UK, T0181-4288221, F0181-4211396, HoopoeUK@aol.com. **Karibu Safari**, Imaginative Traveller, 14 Barley Mow Passage, Chiswick, London W4 4PH, UK, T0181-7828612, 0181-7423049, F0181-7423045. **Selous Safaris**, PO Box 1192, Dar es Salaam, T34535, F28486, 788 Bath St, Cranford, Middlesex, TW5 9UL, UK, T081-8979991. **Southern Tanganyika Game Safaris & Tours Ltd**, PO Box 2341, Dar es Salaam, T24897, F38758. **Wildlife Safari**, Old Bakery, South Rd, Reigate, Surrey RH2 7LB, UK, T01737-223903, F01737-241102, Tx94081633. **World Archipelago Ltd**, 6 Redgrave Rd, London SW15 1PX, UK, T0181-7805838, F0181-7809482, 100711.3161@compuserve.com.

Transport **Air** There are a number of approaches to the park. The most convenient is certainly by air and there are airstrips at all the camps. The flight takes about 45 minutes from Dar es Salaam.

Train Take the TAZARA railway as far as Fuga. From here, with prior arrangement, the lodges will collect you. This will be expensive unless you get a group together to share the costs.

Road If you have your own vehicle take the Dar es Salaam-Kibiti-Mkongo road. The road is tarmac to Kibiti (250 kilometres from Dar es Salaam) which is also the last place you will be able to get petrol. It will take about 7-8 hours by road from Dar es Salaam. The other road you can take is the Dar es Salaam-Morogoro-Matombo-Kisaki road which will take you into the north section of the park to Stiegler's Gorge Camp. This road should only be attempted in the dry season and will require a four-wheel drive vehicle.

Western Game Parks

Gombe Stream National Park

Approach
4°38'S 31°40'E
Colour map 3, grid B1

Gombe Stream National Park is about 16 kilometres from Kigoma and can only be reached by boat from there (see map, page 412). You can get a boat fairly easily, they normally leave around 0800 and the trip takes about three hours and costs about US$3. They return to Kigoma at around 1700. They do not run on Sunday. The boats continue to Banda, on the border of Burundi, so you can approach the Park from both ways. The main purpose of the Park is research

Gombe stream national park

rather than tourism and the facilities there are minimal. Entrance fee: US$100 per person per 24-hour period, one has to take a guide who costs US$10 per trip. *Getting there*: a hired taxi boat from Kigoma will cost at least US$60 for the trip – be prepared to barter. However, the local taxis are reluctant or refuse to return to Kigoma from Gombe in the afternoon.

Background The major attraction of the park are the chimpanzees that were made famous by Jane Goodall. In 1960 she set up the area as a chimpanzee research station. She wrote a book on the findings of her research called *In the Shadow of Man*. Her work was later filmed by Hugo van Lawick the wildlife photographer. This attracted much publicity to the Reserve and in 1968 the Gombe Stream National Park was established. It covers an area of 52 square kilometres making it the smallest park in Tanzania. It is made up of a narrow, mountainous strip of land about 16 kilometres long and five kilometres wide that borders Lake Tanganyika. The mountains, which rise steeply from the lake at a height of about 681 metres to over 1,500 metres, are intersected by steep valleys which have streams running in them and are covered in thick gallery forest (that is, the river banks are wooded, but beyond is open country). The park headquarters is located at Kasekela. The park can be visited all the year around. One point worth noting is that, being so closely related to humans, chimpanzees get many of the same diseases. You will not be allowed to visit Gombe if you have a cold or any other infectious illnesses.

Wildlife There are approximately 200 chimpanzees in the park divided into three family troupes. They each mark their territory fiercely. One of the groups often goes down to the research station so you can observe them from there. Alternatively there are a number of observation points around the park and the wardens usually know where to go to see them. However there is no guarantee that you will see the chimpanzees during your visit. They are less visible here than at Kibale Forest in western Uganda.

Routes It is compulsory to take a guide with you into the forest. From the guest house there is a trail leading up to the research station about two kilometres away and a lovely waterfall a bit further on. If there are no chimps at the station itself you will have to ask one of the guides to take you into the forest to try and track them down. Another route you can take (which does not require a guide) is along the lake shore.

Mahale mountains national park

Sleeping There is a *hostel* that sleeps about 15 people. It is advisable to book ahead in Kigoma. Beds and mattresses are provided but all cooking equipment and food should be brought with you from Kigoma. Camping is allowed with permission, in fact the park is becoming so popular that it is a good idea to have your own tent and stove.

Mahale Mountains National Park

Approach There is no main road to the park although there is a track of sorts. The easiest way to get to the park is by boat from Kigoma (see map, page 412). There are no roads in the park so you

Colour map 3, grid B1

Tanzania & Zanzibar

will have to walk. It is very remote and difficult to get to and for this reason is visited by few tourists. Entrance fee: US$100 per person per 24-hour period. Obligatory guide US$10 per trip.

Background This is another chimpanzee sanctuary established in 1985 as a national park covering an area of 1,577 square kilometres, and lying at an altitude of over 1,800 metres. Mahale has five times the number of chimps as Gombe Stream. The highest peak reaches 2,460 metres and the prevailing winds from over the lake, when forced up to this level, condense and ensure a high rainfall. The best time to visit is from May-September during the drier months.

Vegetation & The park is largely made up of montane forests and grasslands and some alpine bam-
wildlife boo. The eastern side of the mountains is drier, being in the rain shadow, and the vegetation there is the drier miombo woodland (see box, page 419) which is found over much of West Tanzania and East RD Congo. The wildlife found in this park is more similar to that found in Western Africa than Eastern. It includes chimpanzee, porcupine, colobus monkeys (both red and the Angolan black and white). The range and numbers of animals found here has increased since the ujaama villagization programme of the 1970s. Indeed animals such as the leopard and lion have reappeared in the area. The park is probably best known for its chimpanzee population and they have been the focus of much research by scientists from around the world. There are an estimated 1,000 in the Park divided into 20 family troupes of about 50 each.

Sleeping **E** *Guest House* at Kasiha village. Facilities are minimal, bring all food requirements from Kigoma.

Camping Allowed in designated areas. If possible take your own equipment although you may be able to hire it. Check at the MMWRC (Mahale Mountains Wildlife Research Centre) in Kigoma for current availability of accommodation and transport.

Transport **Sea Boat**: to get to the Park, take the lake steamer (*MV Liemba* or *MV Mwongozo*) from Kigoma, see page 426. You get to Lagosa (also known as Mugambo) after about 6 hours at about 0300 and will have to get a small boat to take you to the shore. From Lagosa you will have to hire another boat to take you the 3-hour journey to Kasoge. As you are relying on the lake steamer you will have to stay until the next ferry comes, which is usually about a week although it is not very reliable.

Katavi National Park

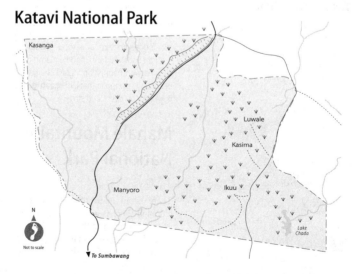

Ugalla River Game Reserve

The Ugalla River Game Reserve, located to the west of Tabora, is approximately *6° 30' S, 32° E* 5,000 square kilometres (see map, page 412). Its inaccessibility and lack of facilities mean that it receives few visitors. If you do manage to get there, and are prepared to be totally self sufficient, there is a wide variety of game.

Katavi National Park

Katavi National Park is located in the west of Tanzania, close to Lake Tanganyika *7° S, 31° E* (see map, page 412). It is 40 kilometres southeast of Mpanda town astride the main Mpanda-Sumbawanga road. It was upgraded to a national park in 1974 and covers an area of 2,253 square kilometres. Travelling from Tunduma (the border town of Tanzania and Zambia) to Kigoma the road passes through the Park. The best time to visit is July-October. However, like the Ugalla River Game Reserve its isolation and lack of facilities has meant that it receives few visitors.

The Park is made of miombo woodland (see box, page 419), acacia parkland as well as some grassland plains. There is also a large swampy area around the Katuma River which joins the two lakes in the park – Lake Katavi and Lake Chada. Wildlife that you may see in the park includes hippo, crocodile, zebra, elephant, buffalo, all sorts of antelope as well as lion and, if you are lucky, leopard.

The nearest hotels and other facilities are at Mpanda which is 40 kilometres away. If you have your own camping equipment you can use the sites in the Park.

Lake Victoria

Rubondo Island National Park

Rubondo National Park is an island located northwest of Mwanza. It has an area of *2° 30' S, 31° 45' E* about 240 square kilometres which includes the main island and a number of *See page 524 for* smaller ones. The best time to visit is November-February. *map*

There are a number of different vegetation types on the island which provide differing habitats for a variety of animals. With a high water table the island is able to support dense forest. Other vegetation includes more open woodland, savannah grassland, and swamps. There is little 'big game' on the island although some has been introduced including giraffe, elephant and rhino. Other animals include crocodile, hippo, bushbuck, sitatunga (a swamp-dwelling antelope only found here and in Selous) vervet monkeys and mongeese. The park has wonderful bird life. You are likely to spot fish eagle, martial eagle, sacred ibis, saddle billed stork, kingfishers, water fowl, cuckoos, bee eaters and sunbirds. There are animal hides from where you can view the wildlife.

There are camping facilities on the island but they are very basic so you are advised to take all your own equipment. All food supplies must be taken with you.

The park headquarters are located at Kageye. There is an airstrip here suitable for light aircraft. No vehicles are allowed on the island although there is a lorry that can be hired to drive visitors around. Boats and camping should to booked in advance: The Park Warden, Rubondo Island National Park, PO Box 11, Geita, or send a message through the National Parks radios, or through the Schumann's Garage (T40037) in Mwanza.

Tanzania & Zanzibar

Approach The quickest and easiest access is by air. Other cheaper ways are by hiring a boat directly from Mwanza. Alternatively you can drive the six or seven hours to Nungwe (300 kilometres via Gieta) from where it is a two-hour boat journey or you can drive the 10 hours to Nyamirembe (via Gieta) from where the boat journey is about 30 minutes. It is wise to check on availability of boats at Schumann's Garage (T40037) in Mwanza before departing.

Biharamulo Game Reserve

2° 30', 31° 30° E Adjacent to Rubondo Island National Park on the mainland (see map, page 403) is the Biharamulo Game Reserve which covers an area of 1,300 square kilometres. This is located to the south of Bukoba on the main Mwanza to Bukoba road but has no facilities and receives very few visitors. It is possible to hunt in Biharamulo – see page 400 for Hunting Safari Agents.

Rubondo Island national park

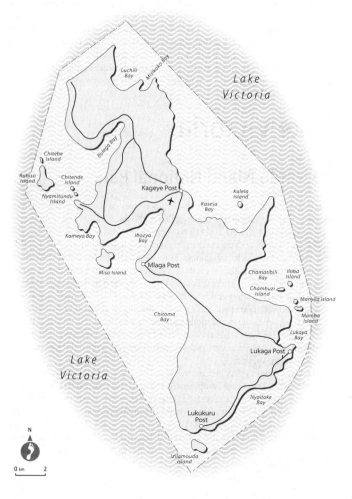

*For text,
see page 523*

0 km   2

N

Saa Nane Island

This wildlife sanctuary is situated in Lake Victoria just off Mwanza (see map, page *2° 30' E, 33° E* 403). It can be visited as a day trip from Mwanza. It is mainly savannah grassland broken by rocky outcrops. The animals here include zebra, wildebeest, hippo as well as some caged chimpanzees, lions and leopards.

Marine protected areas

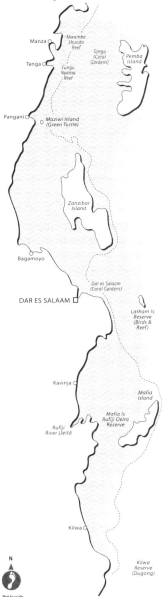

Manza

Mwamba
Shundo
Reef

Tanga
(Coral
Gardens)

Pemba
Island

Tanga

Fungu
Nyama
; Reef

Pangani

Maziwi Island
(Green Turtle)

Zanzibar
Island

Bagamoyo

Dar es Salaam
(Coral Gardens)

DAR ES SALAAM

Latham Is
Reserve
(Birds &
Reef)

Kavinja

Mafia
Island

Mafia Is
Rufiji Delta
Reserve

Rufiji
River Delta

Kilwa

Kilwa
Reserve
(Dugong)

N

Not to scale

Marine parks of Tanzania

The National Parks Department of Tanzania has been planning to set up some marine parks since the 1960s. The first to go ahead will probably be Mafia Island. This has been the site of detailed scientific study on the part of Frontier Tanzania, a non-profit making organization based in London, manned almost entirely by volunteers. It is proposed that a series of zones should be established to enable multi-use of this area by local fishermen as well as tourists in a manner to ensure the conservation of the coral gardens and many sea-living species found around the island. In a joint venture with Frontier Tanzania (also known as the Society of Environmental Exploration – see box, page 482) and the University of Dar es Salaam, the scientific research for the proposal is being undertaken and these zones are being created. The World Wildlife Fund is also involved. It is hoped that careful planning will ensure that the local people will support the park. If this method is successful it will be used as a model for other marine parks in the country. Currently the major threat to the area is dynamite fishing and mining for coral which is used as a building material, and as a source of lime.

Other possible sites of marine parks include Tanga Coral Gardens which are made up of three reefs – Mwamba Wamba, Mwamba Shundo and Fungu Nyama. They are located between 10 and 15 kilometres out to sea. Around Dar es Salaam there are coral gardens near the islands of Mbudya and Sinda which may be developed into a marine park. At Latham Island a reserve has been established, being a site of nesting sea birds and the rare green turtle. Around Kilwa,

Tanzania & Zanzibar

in the south is another likely site for a marine park, being one of the few places where the dugong is found.

Other game reserves

There are a number of other game reserves in Tanzania each thousands of square kilometres in area (see main map, page 480). These include **Saadani** (300 square kilometres) and is located on the coast. Saadani has a beach camp. The animals come down to the beach especially at night. There is now a permanent safari camp in **Saadani Game Reserve**, with seven en suite tented bandas, US$65 per person full board, and three tented bandas with shared facilities at US$55 per person.

Saadani has plentiful game including giraffe, hartebeest, waterbuck, wildebeest, eland, buffalo, hippo, crocodile, reedbuck, Colombus monkey and warthog. Also present but harder to see is lion, leopard, elephant, sable antelope, greater kudu and beisa oryx. A highlight is the thousands of flamingoes found in the salt marshes in the Vami river estuary. There is also an extensive range of bush, river and sea birds.

Access by road from Dar es Salaam (DSM) takes four and a half hours – 109 kilometres west to Chalinze, 52 kilometres north to Mandera, then 60 kilometres along dirt track to Saadani via the towns of Miono and Mkange. The Reserve entrance is just after the railway line, and the Reserve is signposted from the Mandera junction. A new road from DSM to Bagamoya is currently under construction. On completion it will halve the journey time.

Cheapest access is by train from DSM on Friday and Sunday at 1600 arriving at Mvave station at 2030 (the next station after Wami town). A Land Rover from the camp will pick up arriving guests from the station. The return train to DSM comes from Moshi, arriving at Mvave at 1430 on Sunday and Tuesday and reaches DSM at 0700.

Charter flights from Zanzibar US$200 fro a five-seater provided you can fill the plane, or US$320 from DSM.

From late 1997 a regular dhow service is planned to run between Zanzibar and Saadani.

In Saadani Game drives cost US$25 per person. Boat safaris US$25 per person and Foot safaris US$12 per person.

Bookings can be made through *Tent with a View*, PO Box 40525, Dar es Salaam, T0811-323318, F051-113688. The main booking agent is *Rickshaw Travel* based on the ground floor of the Sheraton Hotel, who charge a small commission.

Kigosi, 4,000 square kilometres, is found in Singida Province. **Moyowosi**, 6,000 square kilometres, in Kigoma Province; and **Uwanda**, 5,000 square kilometres, located in Rukwa Region. **Burigi**, 2,200 square kilometres, and **Ibanda**, 200 square kilometres, are located in Kagera Province. **Rumanyika Orugundu Game Reserve** covers an area of 800 square kilometres and lies in the Kishanda Valley also in Kagera Province, accommodates buffalo, elephant, eland as well as other antelope. Rumanyika Urugundu is near Biharamulo, in the Kagera Salient, mostly in the Kishanda valley of north Karagwe district. It is basically a rainforest reserve among high mountains, but with one of the largest concentrations of rhino in Tanzania. No lodge or hotel. **Umba Game Reserve**, 1,500 square kilometres, is found in Tanga Province. However none of these reserves have been developed and they do not contain any facilities.

Background

Present-day Tanzania comprises a union between the former mainland Tanganyika and the islands of Zanzibar. Its modern history has involved three profound changes of direction from colonialism to socialism to capitalism. Like a traveller uncertain of the way, these diversions have slowed progress. As a result Tanzania has not developed as rapidly as its northern neighbour, Kenya. Its cities have few modern buildings, living standards have remained more-or-less unchanged since independence in 1961, and the considerable mineral, agricultural and tourist resources of the country have been only partially exploited.

In the past few years, however, there have been significant improvements. Roads have been repaired, foreign investment has increased rapidly, new businesses are springing up everywhere. For the visitor, there are many new hotels, lodges, restaurants and tourist facilities.

NB The installation of new telephone exchanges in Tanzania has led to a radical overhaul of telephone numbers. In case of difficulty, call T116803/4 in Dar es Salaam, which is a Tanzania Telecommunications Company enquiry number.

The land

Tanzania, in the East Africa region is a large coastal country which lies just below the Equator and includes the islands of Pemba and Zanzibar between 1° S and 11° S latitude and 30° to 40° E longitude. It is bounded by Kenya and Uganda to the north, Rwanda, Burundi and RD Congo to the west, Zambia, Malawi and Mozambique to the south. Temperatures range from tropical to temperate moderated by altitude. Most of the country consists of high plateaux but there is a wide variety of terrain including mangrove swamps, coral reefs, plains, low hill ranges, uplands, volcanic peaks and high mountains, as well as depressions such as the Rift Valley and lakes. Dar es Salaam is the main port and there are hydro-electric schemes on the river Rufiji. Mineral deposits include diamonds, gold, gemstones (tanzanite, ruby, emerald, green garnet, sapphire), graphite, gypsum, kaolin and tin.

Geography

There is a long dry season, June to October, followed by short rains in November and December. January to March can be very hot, and are followed by heavy rains in April and May. The timing of the rains has been less regular in recent years and the volume also varies from year to year, and from region to region. Short rains have tended to spread from November to May with a drier spell in January and February. In northeast Tanzania, the long rains are in March to June. A quarter of the country receives an annual average of 750 millimetres of rain, but in some areas it can be as high as 1,250 millimetres. The central area of the country is dry with less than 500 millimetres per annum. In many areas two harvests can be grown each year.

Climate

History

Without any written records, relatively little is known about the early history of Tanzania. However, with the use of oral history, archaeology, linguistic analysis and anthropology, a certain amount can be deduced. Archaeological finds at Olduvai Gorge have provided evidence of human evolution. At this site bones from the Australopithecine stage of human development have been found of two types. These are *Zinjanthropus* known as Nutcracker Man and *Homo Habilis* known as Handy Man. They lived together about two million years ago and it is thought that Homo Habilis, capable of using tools, is the ancestor of modern man – Homo Sapiens. Olduvai Gorge has become known as the cradle of mankind. The era of Australopithecine man probably lasted several million years.

Tanzania & Zanzibar

By about 500,000 years ago the *Homo Erectus* stage came into being which was somewhere between Australopithecine and *Homo Sapiens*. The brain was larger and the hands more nimble and therefore better capable at making tools. The development of tool-making is clearly seen at Olduvai Gorge. The different layers of rock contain tools of different ages which show the development from crude tools to more efficient and sharper implements. Another collection of such tools can be found at Isimila near Iringa (see page 431).

The middle stone age saw the further development of tools, advances in human ingenuity and craftsmanship and the use of fire. Progress accelerated into the late stone age which began about 100,000 years ago. There are a number of sites from the late stone age in Tanzania which are particularly well known as they are sites of rock painting. The hunter-gatherers were probably related linguistically and racially to the Bushmen and Hottentots of South Africa. Interestingly the Sandawe that now live in the area of the rock paintings speak a form of the Khoisan or 'click' language which otherwise is not spoken in East Africa and which is characteristic of the Bushmen.

The virtual disappearance of these people was a result of the migration and expansion of other people who were more numerous and more advanced. The most significant factor about these migrating people was that instead of being hunter-gatherers they were food producers – either by agriculture or by keeping livestock. They spoke the language of the Cushitic group (legendary biblical descendants of the Cush in Ethiopia, Somalia and north Sudan) and came from the north from around 1,000 BC onwards. They did not have iron-working skills and this meant that the efficiency of their agriculture was limited.

Later still, during the past 1,000-2,000 years, two other groups migrated into the area. These were both Negroid but were of different linguistic groups – the Bantu from the west and the Nilo-Hamite pastoralists from the north. A process of ethnic assimilation followed and the Cushitic intermarried with the newcomers and adopted their languages. The Bantu possessed important iron-processing skills which greatly improved agricultural efficiency and this enabled population growth. There was not one single migration but a series of waves of various groups, expanding and contracting, assimilating and adapting. The present ethnic mix is as a result of this process over many centuries.

The most recent of the Nilotic migrations was by the Masai. By about 1800 AD they had reached the area around Dodoma where their advance was stopped by the Gogo and the Hehe, (see page 543). Their reputation as a warrior tribe meant that the north part of Tanzania was largely avoided by slave traders and caravan routes.

As a result of these migrations north and central Tanzania has great ethnic diversity. In this part of the country there are Khoisan, Cushitic, Nilotic and Bantu speaking peoples. The rest of the country is entirely Bantu speaking; indeed about 95 percent of Tanzanians born today are born into a family speaking one of the Bantu dialects. Swahili itself is a Bantu tongue and this has developed into the national language and as such is a significant unifying force.

Initially Swahili was a coastal language and developed as the language of trade. The earliest visitors to Tanzania were Arab traders who arrived on the coast, and the influence of these traders can be seen by the coastal settlements such as Kilwa. These coastal towns were very much orientated to sea-going trade and away from the interior and until the beginning of the 16th century the coast and the interior had very little contact with each other. However the development of long-distance trade led to the integration of the two. Caravan routes went from the coast to the Congo and Buganda. By the 13th century there was a bustling trade on the coast with the gold and ivory trades becoming particularly important. Initially the trade was dominated by the Persians, Arabs, Egyptians, Indians and Chinese. The Arab influence increased and with it the spread of Islam. The major trading objects were gold, ivory and rhino horns in exchange for guns, textiles and beads.

By the mid 15th century the Portuguese had arrived on the scene. Vasco da Gama noted the beauty of the town of Kilwa, and attempted to take control of the gold trade from the interior. The Portuguese were later expelled by the Arabs and the influence of the Arabs increased again. A period of reduced trading activity followed until the latter half of the 18th century when trade flourished again and the commodity traded was slaves.

Around 1776 the only trading route inland went southwest from Kilwa to the area around Lake Nyasa and this became increasingly important through the slave trade. During the 18th century Kilwa became East Africa's major slave-trading port, drawing first on the peoples of southeast Tanganyika and then on the Lake Nyasa area.

During the 19th century the trade pattern shifted. This was as a result of the changes in the supply of ivory. During the first half of the 19th century, most of the ivory came from within what was to become Tanganyika. However as Tanganyika's elephants were destroyed, so the price of ivory rose rapidly. Prices at Tabora are reported to have increased tenfold between 1846 and 1858. Thus the hunters looked further afield and eventually left Tanganyika altogether. As the hunters moved away the chiefs in these areas lost their major source of revenue. It was this that led some of them to look to the new trade in slaves.

Caravan routes into the interior developed by the 19th century and trade centres developed at places such as Ujiji and Tabora. Humans and ivory were exchanged for guns, beads and cloth. The slaves were largely obtained by bartering with the local chiefs rather than by force. Some of the more militarized tribes raided their neighbours and 'prisoners of war' were then sold on to the Arabs as slaves. Convicted criminals were often sold as slaves and this penalty was sometimes extended to include their families.

The slave trade

The size of the slave trade remains speculative. However it has been estimated that approximately 1.5 million slaves from the interior reached the coast and 10 times that number died en route. Bagamoyo was a terminus of the trade and from there they were taken to Zanzibar which developed into a important trading centre. The slaves were either put to work in the plantations of Pemba and Zanzibar or were shipped to the Middle East.

By the 1830s Zanzibar had become sufficiently prosperous from slaves and spices for the Omani Sultan Seyyid Said to move his capital from Muscat to Zanzibar itself. For some time Britain tried to suppress the slave trade by signing various agreements with the Omani Sultans. However it was not until 1873 that the slave trade was officially abolished when an agreement was signed between Sultan Barghash (Seyyid Said's successor) which forbad the seaborne trade. However this prohibition was implemented only slowly and the practice continued in the mainland for some years. By the 1880s the internal market for slaves had become more important than the external.

The first Europeans in this part of Africa were missionaries and explorers. In 1844 John Krapf, a German missionary working for the Church Missionary Society of London arrived in Zanzibar. He was joined by John Rebmann who was to become the first European to set eyes on Mt Kilimanjaro in 1848. The two British explorers Burton and Speke, sent by the Royal Geographical Society, arrived in Zanzibar in 1856 and journeyed along the caravan routes into the interior. In 1858 Speke came across the huge expanse of water which he named Lake Victoria. Dr Livingstone (see box, page 425) was perhaps the most celebrated of all the missionaries, being found, after no news of him for several years, by HM Stanley, a newspaper reporter.

The first Europeans

By the 1880s numbers of Europeans were arriving in East Africa as missionaries, big game hunters, traders and adventurers. There were some with political ambitions including two Germans Carl Peters and HH Johnson, who wanted to see this part of Africa under the control of Germany. They formed the Society for German Colonization from which emerged the German East Africa Society. Emissaries of the Society signed 'protective treaties' with unsuspecting and often illiterate chiefs from the interior. These so-called treaties of friendship were then used by the German East Africa Company to exploit the areas that they covered with the apparent agreement of local authorities.

Both Germany and Britain made claims over East Africa which were resolved by a series of agreements between the two countries. The Berlin Conference of November 1884 to February 1885 was convened by Bismarck and was important in demarcating European spheres of influence in Africa. This saw the recognition of the German 'protective treaties' and by early 1885 several chiefdoms were formally placed under the control of the German East Africa Company. Three years later the Germans were shaken by an uprising of both Arabs and Africans and the German government took control in 1891. The Anglo-German

Tanzania & Zanzibar

Agreement of November 1886 defined the north boundary from the coast inland to Lake Victoria. A month later another agreement saw the defining of the boundary with Mozambique. These and various other treaties saw Zanzibar, Pemba and a 16 kilometre coastal strip go to the Sultan under British Protectorate rule in 1890, while what is now mainland Tanzania, Rwanda and Burundi became German East Africa. It was not until 1898 that German rule was secured and consolidated with the death of Mkwawa, chief of the Hehe who had resisted German domination.

Mount Kilimanjaro Whilst Germany and Britain were deciding the north boundary, Kaiser William I insisted that Mt Kilimanjaro should be German because it had been discovered by a German, John Rebmann. Queen Victoria generously 'gave' the mountain to her grandson, the future Kaiser William II on his birthday in 1886. Although no official record exists the Queen is supposed to have explained, by way of justification for her royal 'gift', that 'William likes everything that is high and big'. The boundary was thus moved so that Kilimanjaro is now found within Tanzania. As can be seen on the present map, instead of marking the boundary by pencilling it in with a ruler from the coast to Lake Victoria in one go, a freehand detour was made when the ruler hit the mountain, before carrying on again with the ruler and pencil on the far side.

The German colonial period There were a number of phases of German colonial rule. The first around the turn of the century saw attempts at establishing a settler economy. This was to be based in the north highlands and agriculture was to be the basis of the economy. However this was initially not a great success. Revolts occurred in Bagamoyo, Pangani and Tanga which were all crushed. The best-known uprising was the Maji Maji rebellion (*maji* means water in Swahili) which occurred in the south of the country from 1905 to 1906. Discontent was initially aroused over a cotton scheme which benefited the Africans little although they were obliged to provide all the manual labour. The uprising was unique in Eastern Africa for it was cross-tribal and included a large area – almost the whole of the country south of Dar es Salaam. With only spears and arrows, but believing themselves to be protected by sacred water (hence Maji Maji), the rebels were pitted against German troops equipped with rifles.

The uprising led to a major reappraisal of German colonial policy. The administrators realized that development would be almost impossible without a contented local population. This period saw the building of the railway to Tabora to open up the area to commerce, and crops such as coffee and groundnuts were encouraged. Economic activity increased and a world boom led to the reemergence of a settler cash crop economy as the most significant part of colonial policy. In particular the boom saw prices of sisal and rubber soar. Most farming took place along the coast and on the slopes of Mount Kilimanjaro and Mount Meru. Inland the threat of the tsetse fly hindered development as domestic animals could not be raised in affected areas. Missionary activity led to the growth of clinics and schools.

The First World War With the outbreak of hostilities in Europe, the German commander General Paul von Lettow Vorbeck realized that his meagre forces could not defeat the British. He resolved to aid Germany's efforts in the European theatre of war by tying up as many British military resources as possible. Von Lettow, his German officers and African troops conducted an astonishing rearguard campaign, retreating from Kenya through what is now Tanzania and Mozambique, being undefeated when Germany surrendered in Europe.

Paul von Lettow had arrived in Dar es Salaam at the start of 1914 to take command of the German forces. He was 44 years old, son of a general, a professional soldier and experienced in bush warfare from service in German South West Africa (now Namibia).

His forces consisted of around 2,500 Schutztruppe *askaris* in 14 field companies, and he promptly signalled his intentions by capturing Taveta across the border in Kenya. The British assembled a force of 5,000 mainly British, South African, and Indian troops and von Lettow withdrew to begin his epic, 4,000 kilometres, four-year campaign. When faced by overwhelming odds von Lettow fell back, but at defendable positions, although always

Central and northern railways

The first railway to be constructed in Tanganyika was the Tanga (Northern) line which began when the German authorities decided in 1891 that a metre-gauge line should be built from Tanga to Muheza, and then on to Korogwe. Eventually this line would be continued on to Moshi and Arusha. A small port was built at Tanga to land equipment and material and the construction of the line began in 1893. Labour was scarce and at times had to be imported from Mozambique making progress slow. It took two years for the laying of just 40 kilometres as far as Muheza. Financial difficulties caused the construction to be halted periodically and the line finally reached Korogwe in 1902 and Moshi in 1911. Unfortunately much of this line, built at great expense over a long period of time, was destroyed by the Germans as they retreated in 1914.

Meanwhile the central route of the old slave trail to Lake Tanganyika was receiving attention. Dar es Salaam had been made the capital of the German protectorate in 1891 and talk of the construction of a railway began soon after. However, delays again ensued and it was not until 1905 that construction began on a line from Dar es Salaam to Morogoro. This was to be built by a private company with a grant from the Imperial German Government. The Maji Maji rebellion created problems with the supply of labour, but the line reached Morogoro in December 1907. By 1914 the line had been extended as far as Kigoma although it was clear that this line had little commercial value and traffic was extremely light.

Planning continued for other lines but the First World War intervened and much of the work already carried out was destroyed. Most of the bridges between Dar es Salaam and Kigoma were blown up, and the rolling stock destroyed. A line was built during the war, linking the Tanga line to the Kenya railway system which facilitated the advance and occupation of Tanga by the British.

Following the war many repairs were carried out so that the goods traffic on the railways increased. However the problems returned with the depression of the 1930s which severely affected revenues. The non-metre gauge lines were closed and about 40 percent of the staff were laid off. The Second World War saw an increase in the activities of the Railways, and following the war the 'Groundnut Scheme' (see box, page 534), involved the hasty construction of a branch line from Lindi on the coast to Nachingwea, one of the areas where groundnuts were to be grown. However the scheme was a monumental failure, the expected traffic never materialized, and the line was abandoned.

In 1948 the railway and port services in Tanganyika were amalgamated with the Kenya and Uganda railways under the East Africa High Commission. A regional authority, East African Railways & Harbours (EAR&H), ran the railways until 1977 when the East African Community collapsed, severing the rail link through Taveta to Kenya, with Tanzania assuming responsibility for its own network.

Friends of Railway Heritage are currently restoring steam locomotives. Contact Andreas Huber at Tanzania Railway Corporation, PO Box 468, Dar es Salaam.

hopelessly out-numbered, he inflicted fearful losses on his adversaries, most notably at Tanga and Kibata (see page 356). The British fared better when commanded by the South African, Jan Christian Smuts, for 11 months in 1916. A rare combination of intellectual, politician and soldier, Smuts was later to be Prime Minister of South Africa. Smuts found himself pursuing an infuriatingly elusive foe. He was convinced that he would trap and destroy von Lettow's troops in Morogoro, where retreat to the south was blocked by the Ulunguru Mountains. But as his forces marched into the town they heard a mechanical piano playing *Deutschland Uber Alles* in the *Bahnhof Hotel*, and in the empty Schutztruppe barracks, on every item of furniture, was a piece of human excrement.

Never defeated, at the end of the campaign von Lettow and his force numbered 155 Germans 1,156 Schutztruppe *askaris* and about 3,000 camp-followers made up of porters and *askari* wives and children, many of the latter born during the campaign. Over 250,000 Allied troops had been thrown against them at one time or another during the four years.

Tanzania & Zanzibar

The Schutztruppe – an African fighting elite

It was recognized by the Germans from the start that white troops in East Africa would be nothing more than a 'walking hospital'.

Under German officers, an African fighting force of askaris was recruited, thoroughly drilled, trained, disciplined, and well paid – 30 rupees a month for privates (about US$80 in present-day values) and 150 rupees for non-commissioned officers.

The Shutztruppe became an elite. The uniform was a khaki jacket, trousers and puttees and a black leather belt with ammunition pouches. Head gear was a kepi – rather like a khaki fez with a chin-strap and a gold Imperial eagle on the front. The non-commissioned officers decorated their kepis with feathers. Each soldier had his own servant (an askari-boy). When travelling, a

Schutztruppe private would send his askari boy ahead to a village with a cartridge. This was an order to the local headman to have ready four beds (one for the askari, one for his rifle, one for his ammunition pouch and one for his uniform) – and some 'blankets' – a selection of the village girls.

Tough, resilient, and brave, around 150 askaris made up a field company that included two machine-gun teams. With several hundred porters carrying food and ammunition, it was highly mobile. During the First World War, the British were contemptuous of these African troops, considering they would collapse when faced with European and Indian forces. In the event, the Schutztruppe was never defeated, and inflicted fearful losses on the British and their allies.

Von Lettow returned to Germany, in 1920 entered politics and for 10 years was a Deputy in the Reichstag. In 1929 he was guest of honour in London, with Smuts, at the anniversary dinner of the British East African Expeditionary Force. In 1930 he resigned from the Reichstag and in 1935 Hitler suggested he become Ambassador to Britain. Von Lettow declined. It is said he told Hitler to 'go fuck himself', but von Lettow subsequently denied he had ever been that polite.

In 1958, at the age of 88, von Lettow returned to Dar es Salaam. He was met at the dockside by a crowd of elderly Schutztruppe askaris who carried him shoulder-high to an official reception at Government House.

In 1964 the German Bundestag finally voted the funds to settle the back-pay owing to the Schutztruppe at the surrender in 1918. Over 300 veterans, some in faded and patched uniforms presented themselves at Mwanza. Only a handful had their discharge papers. Those that didn't were handed a broom and taken through arms drill, with the orders given in German. Not one man failed the test. The same year, at the age of 94, von Lettow died.

With defeat in the First World War the Germans lost control of German East Africa. The northwest, now Rwanda and Burundi, went to the Belgians. The rest was renamed Tanganyika, and the British were allocated a League of Nations mandate.

The British period From 1921 Britain introduced the policy of Indirect Rule which had proved effective in other parts of colonial Africa. This involved giving a degree of political responsibility to local chiefs and ruling through them. Economic development between the wars was negligible. Tanganyika had few exportable products. Unlike Uganda, there was no major cash crop such as cotton suited to production by small African farmers. The most significant export was sisal, a spiky plant which yields fibres that can be made into ropes and twine, but this required long-term large-scale capital-intensive investment and was not suitable for small-scale African production. It was produced almost entirely by British and Asian companies with a local workforce. The most successful African cash crop was coffee grown by the Chagga on the slopes of Mt Kilimanjaro. Coffee growing was extended to Africans by the British in 1922. Previously only settlers were allowed to grow coffee on estates established by the Germans from 1910.

Most British settlers went to Kenya where there was already a sizeable settler community and the highlands provided an attractive climate. Moreover the British presence seemed more secure in Kenya, which was a colony. The League of Nations mandate required Britain to prepare Tanganyika for eventual self-government, and the British kept expenditure on administration, infrastructure and education to a minimum.

The 1920s saw the emergence of the first African political groups. In 1922 the African Civil Servants Association of Tanganyika Territory was formed in Tanga, and in 1929 the Tanganyika African Association (TAA). Throughout the 1930s and 1940s, unions and agricultural cooperatives developed. These were not primarily political associations although their formation obviously led to an increased political awareness.

The major issues upon which attention was focused were land-use policies, aimed in particular at soil conservation, and the eviction of Africans to make way for white settlers. The African population in 1950 was about eight million, compared to an Asian population of 55,000 and European population of 17,000. However Europeans and Asians dominated in local government councils even in areas that were almost exclusively African. These were issues upon which the TAA focused. In 1953 Julius Nyerere became the leader of the TAA and the movement towards independence developed momentum. In July 1954, at a meeting of all political elements, the Tanganyika African National Union (TANU) was created with the slogan *Uhuru na Umoja* (Freedom and Unity).

There were two major strengths of this movement as against similar movements in other parts of Africa. Firstly there was no dominating tribal group, and secondly Swahili had

Tanzania & Zanzibar

Von Lettow's campaign

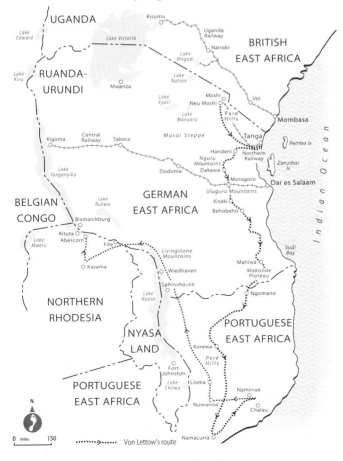

The ground nut scheme

Immediately after the Second World War there was an attempt by the British Labour government to grow ground nuts on an enormous scale. Three sites were chosen in the south, near Lindi at Nachingwea; just north of Morogoro at Kongwa; and at Urambo west of Tabora on the central railway line. The scheme aimed to alleviate the world-wide shortage of edible oils following the war. The operation was to be capital-intensive, with a military style approach to planning, and there was immense enthusiasm among the British who went out to run the programme and became known as 'ground-nutters'. It was thought that with modern methods and enough machinery it would be impossible for the scheme to fail. However, it was a complete disaster. When finally abandoned a total of £36.5mn was written off. This huge sum was equal to a little less than the entire Tanganyikan government expenditure from 1946-50.

The reasons for failure were numerous and included inadequate planning which meant the environmental and climatic problems were not properly considered; unsuitable machinery; and failure to test the scheme by way of a pilot project. Other difficulties included insufficient rain in the areas to support the ground nuts and inadequate capacity in the transport system to keep the tractors supplied with fuel. Although it was supposed to be a capital-intensive project the inappropriateness of the machinery meant that it actually was more efficient to clear the land by hand. The project is held up as an example of everything that was wrong with attempting to impose European agricultural techniques without adequate consideration of local African conditions.

Kongwa is now a ranch, Urambo has been given over to tobacco, and at Nachingwea, oilseeds and cereals are grown.

developed into the major language encouraged by German colonial policy and this served as an important unifying force. A further point of relevance in the run up to independence was that after the Second World War Tanganyika was given UN Trustee status in place of the mandate. Both the mandatory system and the trusteeship system were very important as they meant that controversial issues could be referred to the UN Council unlike in other colonial territories. In December 1956 Nyerere addressed the UN General Assembly's Fourth (Trusteeship) Committee. This gave Nyerere a platform to present the views of Tanganyikans to the outside world.

The first elections were held in two phases, in September 1958 and February 1959, and TANU won a sweeping majority. These were multiracial elections but even the European and Asian candidates owed their success to TANU. Tanganyika attained Independence on 9 December 1961 with Nyerere as the first Prime Minister. The constitution was subsequently changed, Tanzania becoming a republic with Nyerere as President.

Post-independ -ence Tanzania In 1964 Zanzibar and Tanganyika merged to form Tanzania (see page 449). An awkward union has resulted in which Zanzibar has retained its own President, Parliament, a full range of Ministries and handles most of its own finances. The President of Zanzibar is, *ex officio*, one of the Vice-Presidents of Tanzania. Despite having a population that is less than five percent of the total, it has almost a third of the seats in the Tanzanian Assembly.

After independence there was pressure to replace Europeans with Africans in administration and the business sector. There was also considerable demand for basic education and health services. Although economic progress was significant in these early years, there was an impatience at the slow pace of development, and Nyerere made plans for a bold, radical change.

This culminated in the 1967 Arusha Declaration. It was a programme of socialist development accepted by TANU and which was then amplified in a number of pamphlets by Nyerere. The two main themes of this programme were egalitarianism and self-reliance and it was broadly based on the Chinese communist model. It has been said that Tanzania took the Chinese model, mistakes and all and then added a few mistakes of its own. Politicians were subject to a leadership code which required that they had no private

Julius Nyerere

Julius Kambarage Nyerere was born in 1922 in Butiama, east of Lake Victoria. He was the Roman Catholic son of a Zanaki chief. His father died having reportedly had 26 children by 18 wives. The name Nyerere means 'caterpillar' in the Zanaki language and was supposed to have been given to Nyerere's father because at the time of his birth (around 1860) the countryside was infested with these creatures. Nyerere attended a boarding school in Musoma and, from 1937, the Tabora Government Secondary School. He was baptized in 1943 into the Catholic Church and the same year he entered Makerere College, Uganda. After Makerere he returned to Tabora where he taught history and biology at St Mary's Catholic Boys School operated by the White Fathers. In 1949 he went to Edinburgh University and in 1952 obtained his Master of Arts. In 1953 he married Maria Gabriel Magigo who was also a Catholic of the Msinditi tribe and was to become its first woman teacher. He paid the traditional bride price of six head of cattle for her and they have seven children.

Nyerere subsequently took a teaching post at the Catholic Secondary school of St Francis at Pugu a few kilometres west of Dar es Salaam and it was from here that he became involved in politics. In 1954 he became president of the Tanzania African Association and was instrumental in converting this into the political organization TANU. He was appointed a temporary member of the Tanganyika Legislative Council in 1954, and a full member of the Legislative Assembly in 1958 where he remained until his assumption of the Presidency in 1962. He resigned as President in 1985. Nyerere has become known as Mwalimu which means teacher and he is undoubtedly one of Africa's greatest statesmen, admired for his integrity, modest lifestyle and devotion to equality and human rights.

Tanzania & Zanzibar

sources of income, and no more than one house or car. Banks, plantations and all major industries were nationalized. The cornerstone of the programme was the villagization and agricultural collectivization programme known as *Ujamaa*, see below. This, and efforts in the rest of the economy, would, it was hoped, lead to the development of a just and prosperous society. Education was considered to be one of the most important aims of the programme and as a result Tanzania achieved some of the highest literacy rates in Africa. In the initial years there was success, too, in extending basic health care in the rural areas.

Ujamaa

An important element in post-independence Tanzanian philosophy was *Ujamaa*, a programme for advancement in the rural areas. This was supposed to be the voluntary movement of people into villages with a major objective being to raise output through collectivization and large-scale agricultural production. Emphasis was also on the social benefits – the provision of services such as piped water, electricity, schools and clinics. Self-reliance was the key and the villages were meant to be set up and run by the villagers themselves.

There were three phases of villagization in the decade from 1967. The first was voluntary movement on a locally selective basis combined with compulsory movement in Rufiji and Ilandeni which were areas worst affected by drought and flood. From 1970 to 1973 this was replaced by a 'frontal approach' whereby incentives were given for people to move to villages, which included financial and technical assistance. The reluctance of people to move on their own accord meant the targets were not reached and so after 1973 these methods were replaced by a willingness to use force in support of rapid villagization. The results were dramatic. In 1970 the villagized population stood at about 500,000, or less than five percent of the population. After the first year of compulsory movement Nyerere claimed that there were over nine million people – or about 60 percent of the mainland population, living in villages. Force was justified on the grounds that people could not always see what was best for them and had to be shown the way. Viewed in the light of easier provision of social benefits the *Ujamaa* programme was partially successful.

The Uhuru railway

The enthusiasm for building this line dates back to Cecil Rhodes who envisaged a Cape-to-Cairo railway linking all the territories then under British control. However it was not until the 1970s that the link between Zambia and Tanzania was finally completed, and there is still a gap from Gulu in Uganda to Kartoum in Sudan.

The line is important for two reasons, one political and the other economic. The line was to link landlocked Zambia with the coast of Tanzania and in so doing to free Zambia from her economic dependence on what was then white-ruled Rhodesia (now Zimbabwe). Until the line was built all Zambia's exports and imports had to be carried by rail through Rhodesia to reach the ports of Mozambique. Just a year after Zambia's independence, Rhodesia's Unilateral Declaration of Independence (UDI) increased tension, and the country felt that this dependence on the hostile regimes of Southern Africa had to end. The objective of building a railway line that would enable Zambia's trade to avoid going through white-ruled Africa thus became paramount.

There was also economic reasoning behind the arguments for a rail link between the Zambian copperbelt and Tanzania. The extensive mineral deposits as well as the rich agricultural land in southwest Tanzania added to the economic viability. Until the line was built there was actually little contact between the two countries. The so-called 'Great North Road' that joined the two was actually over 1600 kilometres of dirt track which was frequently rendered impassable during the rainy season. There was thus little trade between the two countries. In the immediate post-independence era the establishment of links between African countries, and the commitment to African unity that this implied were also considered important political objectives.

Various requests for assistance – both financial and technical – in the building of the line were made to Britain, the US, Germany, the Soviet Union and the World Bank as well as others. However they were all reluctant to commit such a large sum of money for a single development project, and in 1965 China offered to finance and build the line. This was seen as China's most ambitious move into Africa and in 1967 the agreement between China and the governments of Zambia and Tanzania was signed. A survey was made of the route and construction of the line began two and a half years later. The West put much emphasis at the time on the ulterior motives of China in becoming involved in development of East

---

However attempts to farm collectively were disastrous and agricultural output fell. The programme was vigorously resisted in the major coffee-growing areas of Kagera (west of Lake Victoria) and in Kilimanjaro region. By 1977 the Ujamaa programme was effectively abandoned although considerable villagization remains.

In 1973 it was decided to move the capital city from Dar es Salaam on the coast to Dodoma in the centre. The position of this city is suitable in so far as it is on communication networks and is located in the centre of the country about 320 kilometres inland. However it is also a dry and desolate area. The major problem with the plan has been the cost of moving. A Presidential official residence, the Prime Minister's office, and a National Assembly building have all been established there. The cost has forced the rest of central government to remain in Dar es Salaam for the time being.

In 1975 a law was passed which gave legal supremacy to TANU as the national political party, and in 1977 TANU and the Afro-Shirazi party (which had taken control in Zanzibar after the revolution) merged to form Chama Cha Mapinduzi (CCM) the 'party of the Nation'.

The 1970s saw the gradual disintegration of the East Africa Community (EAC) which involved Kenya, Tanzania and Uganda in a customs union and provision of common services. Tanzania and Kenya had different ideological perspectives, and the three countries could not agree on the distribution of the costs and services of the EAC. Things came to a head over East African Airways. The failure of Tanzania and Uganda to remit funds to Kenya caused Kenya to 'ground' the airline (conveniently when all the planes were sitting on the tarmac in

Africa and some saw it was an attempt to thrust communism into the heart of Africa – calling it the 'Red Railway'. The white rulers in southern Africa also felt threatened and saw it as an attempt to undermine their political and economic domination as well as providing logistical support to guerilla fighters in Rhodesia and South Africa. The Chinese themselves, however, called it the 'Friendship Route', aimed at strengthening the newly independent African states against the forces of Imperialism. Rumours of CIA involvement in attempts to discredit the Chinese and their motives abounded: for example there was a picture published (said to be a forgery by the CIA) showing a poster requesting Chinese volunteers for the railway. The text of the poster said that those who helped in the construction of the line would be offered 'good land' when the line was completed. This was said to be an attempt by the CIA to stir up anti-Chinese sentiments in Zambia and Tanzania.

China committed a loan of some US$166mn for the railway, and construction began in April 1970. One of the first buildings to be completed was the reception centre for the Chinese workers when they first arrived. Also built were a hospital, staffed by Chinese doctors, an equipment depot, repair workshops and a huge passenger station. The whole project employed about 25,000 Chinese, 50,000 Tanzanians and 15,000 Zambians and was extremely labour intensive.

The line was a great engineering feat completed in just five years. 300 bridges were built and 23 tunnels totalling eight kilometres were cut into rock. The line was 963 kilometres in Tanzania and 885 in Zambia making a total of 1848 kilometres plus a further 185 kilometres of sidings. Because of the problems of access to land-locked Zambia, and as all the equipment and rails were imported from China, construction took place from the Tanzania end and progressed south. An immediate problem was that the port at Dar es Salaam became seriously congested and found it difficult to cope with the enormous increase in traffic.

Despite the successful completion of the project, it led to little genuine warmth and understanding between the two African countries and China. African students have been the object of hostility in China in recent years. Apart from official duties and functions the Chinese kept themselves very much to themselves during the construction period. A reflection of this is the Chinese boast that there was 'not one baby'.

Tanzania & Zanzibar

Kenya) and Tanzania reacted by closing the border with Kenya in February 1977. The border was only reopened in 1983 after the ownership of the assets the EAC was finally agreed.

In 1978 Tanzania's relations with neighbouring Uganda worsened and skirmishes on the border were followed by an announcement by Amin that Uganda had annexed the Kagera salient. This is an area of about 1,800 square kilometres of Tanzanian territory west of Lake Victoria. The OAU applied pressure which caused Uganda to withdraw but fighting continued. In January 1979 a Tanzanian force of over 20,000 invaded Uganda, Amin's army capitulated and the Tanzanians rapidly took control of the southern part of the country. The invading force had withdrawn by 1981 having spent the interim period in Uganda overseeing the election of Milton Obote for the second time. A remarkable feature of this episode is that, despite being the only African country ever to win a war this century, this event is not celebrated in Tanzania. The only monument is a small pyramid on columns, located on the road from Bukoba to Masaka, just south of the border. It is dedicated to the 16 Tanzanian soldiers who died in the war.

In 1985 Nyerere decided to step down as President of Tanzania (the first President in post-independence Africa to retire voluntarily). He remained as Chairman of the party (CCM) before retiring from politics completely in 1990. Vice-President Sokoine, who had been widely thought of as Nyerere's successor, was killed in a car crash in October 1984. Ali Hassan Mwinyi, who was then President of Zanzibar, was nominated to be the sole candidate for President and was elected in October 1985.

Throughout the early 1980s Tanzania was put under pressure to accept economic reforms suggested by the World Bank and IMF. These financial institutions, as well as Western governments, aid donors and foreign investors argued that the socialist development strategy had led to a crisis involving falling incomes, decaying infrastructure, deteriorating health and educational provision, and a climate of petty corruption. For many years Tanzania resisted changes, but eventually the climate of opinion changed and in 1986, under Mwinyi, a market economy strategy was adopted, and Tanzania began an economic recovery.

In 1993, Tanzania allowed political parties other than CCM to form. In October 1995 there were elections in which CCM won a substantial majority of seats in the Union Assembly. The Presidency was won by the CCM candidate, Benjamin Mkapa, Mwinyi having retired after two terms in office.

The main opposition in Zanzibar, the Civic United Front (CUF) ran CCM very close in both the Zanzibar Assembly and in the race for the Zanzibar Presidency. There were allegations of election fraud, supported by evidence from international observers. CCM has formed the administration in Zanzibar, and Salim Amour was returned as Zanzibar's President.

Art and architecture

There are five main styles of buildings in Tanzania. The most common are traditional African dwellings constructed variously of poles, mud, straw, cattle-dung and thatch. The styles of these traditional dwellings vary from one region to another. The second style, found on the coast and in Zanzibar shows strong Arabic and Islamic influence and these buildings date from the earliest arrivals of these peoples. During the German colonial period, a substantial number of impressive public buildings were constructed with a distinctive design adapted to the tropical conditions. The British introduced mainly bungalow-style dwellings along lines developed in India. The Indian community constructed commercial and residential buildings in tenement style, but often with elaborate Eastern decorations. Finally there are the concrete office-blocks of the modern era.

Traditional African dwellings Among the main ethnic groups with distinctive building styles are: the **Nyaleylusa**, from the south between Mbeya and Lake Malawi with isyenge dwellings of bamboo walls and thatched roofs; the **Nyamwesi** from between Mwanza and Tawith msonge dwellings of thatch roofs and timber and mud walls; the **Masai** from the north border with Kenya, west of Arusha, with manyatta half-sphere dwellings of a timber frame entirely covered with mud reinforced with cow-dung; the **Makua** from the coast to the south near Mtwara with dwellings of mud-covered timber walls and thatch; the **Zaramo** from around Dar es Salaam with msonge dwellings all of thatch; the **Ha/Rundi** of west Tanzania region inhabiting grass-thatch msonge dwellings; the **Haya** from west of Lake Victoria with msonge elephant grass huts; the **Ngashi** from around Songea in the south with fairly extensive dwellings in msonge style; the **Fiba** from west of Lake Rukwa in the south with conical msonge dwellings; the **Gogo** from Tabora in central Tanzania with tembe dwellings which feature a dried mud-covered roof; and the **Hele** from Winga to the south with tembe dwellings.

The **Swahili**, the Arabic/Bantu group from along the coastal strip have banda with coral walls and lime mortar made from burnt coral with mangrove pole and clay tile roofs, ornately carved doors and usually a verandah. Later dwellings have corrugated iron roofs. Typically there is a central corridor with rooms off each side on solid coral and mortar floors. A stone slab in the front, shaped like a couch, is for sitting outside in the evenings.

Construction was typically of coral, bound together with lime mortar. The ground floor would be solid coral and mortar, while upper floors were coral and mortar on mangrove rafters (mangrove contains a chemical which discourages termites). The building have thick walls and are cool. Decorations often involved crenellations on towers, and carved doors. Examples would be the Fort in Zanzibar, and the Old Boma in Dar es Salaam.

Arabic period

The German colonists constructed durable buildings, with high ceilings to keep rooms as cool as possible, invariably of two stories with the upper floor designed to catch any breezes through open arches. Construction was in stone often on a steel frame. Steel girders were used to support floors and verandahs. Roofs were tile or corrugated iron coated with red-oxide paint. The use of steel allowed the construction to be strong, yet not as heavy in appearence as the Arabic buildings. Crenellations, fort-like towers and Islamic arches were incorporated, giving the buildings a distinctive style. In almost all Tanzanian towns, the German built railway station, main hotel, hospital and administration building (Boma) will still exist.

German period

The British were not inclined to embark on an ambitious programme of public buildings as Tanzania was a protectorate (not a colony) destined for eventual self-determination. Government buildings were single-storey bungalows with over-hanging galvanized-iron roofs to provide an awning giving shade, supported by slender iron poles. Residential dwellings had clay-tiled roofs, again mostly single-storey. Some two-storey dwellings would have tile awnings over the lower windows to give shade, and to throw rainwater away from the house preventing it spattering in through the window. Examples of government buildings are the newer wards to the rear of the old German hospital in Dar es Salaam. Also in Dar es Salaam, British colonial bungalows are dotted throughout the Oyster Bay area and two-storey dwellings are grouped along Ali Hassan Mwinyi Rd, previously Bagamoyo Rd.

British period

The temples and mosques of the Indian community are constructed in traditional style. The Hindu and Ismaili buildings are often several storeys high with elaborate arches and columns. The commercial and residential buildings also tend to be several storey's high, decorated with inscriptions marking the owners and the date of construction, and with the upper storeys embellished with elaborate, arches, columns and façades. The centres of all main towns contain examples.

Indian architecture

Some bold attempts to introduce interwar suburban architecture took place, most notably the Selander Bridge Police Post in Dar es Salaam, with curved windows at the corners. Nearby *Palm Beach Hotel* is another example. There was wide experimentation with forms and materials. Reinforced concrete and the use of plank shuttering allowed the construction of external features such as cantilevered fire-escapes, prominent lift shafts, projecting stair wells etc while the use of coral, terrazzo, mosaic and terrilium added to the richness and variety of texture. Style and creativity were exhibited by the use of glass-paned louvres, flat roofs and anodized aluminium fittings. Unfortunately, a lack of maintenance has had a deleterious effect on many of these modern buildings. Otherwise concrete construction for office buildings and large Mediterranean style residential houses with arches and tiled-roofs have been the order of the day. There are numerous examples of the latter on Msasani Peninsular, and along the road to Bagamoyo between Mwenge and Kunduchi Beach.

Modern era

Tanzania & Zanzibar

People

The population is made up of largely mixed Bantu groups, the largest being the Sukuma and the Nyamwezi, but there are 129 recognized tribes. Swahili is the official language, but English is widely spoken. The country is sparsely populated. The majority of the population is concentrated in the north. The fertile lower slopes of Mt Kilimanjaro have population densities as high as 250 persons per square kilometres, causing severe land shortage, whereas the average density is 31 persons per square kilometre.

East Africans are frequently divided into 'tribes'; but exactly what makes a tribe is often difficult to define. A tribe usually refers to a group of people with a common language and culture. They possess a common name and recognize themselves to be distinct from their neighbours. Sometimes the group may be fairly distinctive and easy to define – but other times the divisions are much less clear. There are some observers who believe that the concept of 'tribe' is largely an artificial one imposed from outside since the colonial period. Certainly there are some 'groups' who only attained full identity and unity after the arrival of Europeans. Putting this debate to one side, the term 'tribe' is used frequently and the people of Tanzania have been classified into such groups.

129 different tribal groups have been distinguished in Tanzania. They vary from groups of over a million people to tribes of just a few hundred. It is obviously impractical to look at all these groups here so only the most important are examined. The largest ethnic groups are the Sukuma and the Nyamwezi although no group makes up more than 15 percent of the population. About a dozen of the largest groups make up about 50 percent of the population. Most of these groups are of Bantu origin (although there are some Nilotic groups as well) and about 95 percent of the population is Bantu-speaking – the most important Bantu language is Swahili, a language which is the mother tongue of the people of Zanzibar and Pemba as well as some coastal people. Swahili became a *lingua franca* before the colonial period in some areas and this was encouraged by both the Germans and the British. It is very widely spoken and in 1963 it became Tanzania's national language.

Sukuma This is Tanzania's largest ethnic group and makes up between 10 and 13 percent of the population. The name means 'people of the north' and the group lives just to the south of Lake Victoria. The ethnic consciousness of this group is fairly recent and is not entirely pervasive. In the pre-colonial period they were organized into a large number of small chiefdoms. They practise mixed agriculture, with both cattle-herding and cultivation. This is also an important cotton growing area.

Nyamwezi The Nyamwezi people are found to the south of the Sukuma people in north Tanzania and in many ways are similar to the Sukuma. Like the Sukuma they were formerly made up of a large number of very small chiefdoms. Some of these chiefs tried later to dominate wider areas. Their identity is fairly recent and rather fragile. They are primarily a cultivating people and have established a reputation as traders.

Makonde These people are located in the southeast part of the country and are fairly isolated, being on the Makonde Plateau. Although they are one of the five largest groups the Makonde have been little affected by colonial and post-colonial developments. They are renowned for being a conservative people who are determined to defend their way of life. This is facilitated by the difficulty in reaching this part of Tanzania. Even today communications with the southeast are poor, particularly during the wet season. The Makonde are perhaps most famous for their beautifully-crafted woodcarvings which are sold all over Tanzania. Makonde people are also found in Mozambique.

Chagga The Chagga (or Chaga) people are found around the south slopes of Mount Kilimanjaro and constitute the third largest group in Tanzania. They are greatly advantaged by living in a fertile and well-watered region which is ideally suited to the production of coffee. They were also one of the first groups to be affected by the Christian missionaries, in particular the Roman Catholics and Lutherans, and this meant that the initial provision of education in the area was ahead of many other areas. The high level of education and opportunity of cash-cropping have resulted in a comparatively high level of income, and also a relatively high level of involvement in community activity. One example of the form that this has taken is through cooperative action in the production and marketing of coffee.

Chagga customs and beliefs The Chagga believe that the god that they called Ruwa was greater than all the other gods that they worshiped. They believed all men had their origin in him and that as he did not trouble them with petty demands unlike some other gods he must love men. He is believed to live in a place in the skies which they called *nginenyi* which means blue skies. Sacrifices would be made to Ruwa when someone was ill or when there was a famine or epidemic. Usually prayers would be said and then a goat would be slaughtered. The goat should be a male of uniform colour without any spots, and it should not have had its tail docked. Sacrifices would also be offered to the spirits of the dead. When a person dies it is believed that they would live in the new world but in a different form. The spirits of the dead would be able to return to the world to demand what is due to them from their relatives. Their physical presence would not be noticed but they would be seen in dreams or through the noises made by animals.

Haya The Haya people are different from most other ethnic groups in Tanzania. They are located in the far northwest of Tanzania, to the west of the shores of Lake Victoria. Culturally and linguistically they are more closely related to the interlacustrine Bantu who are found to the north and west of the Haya. Like the interlacustrine Bantu they are organized into a few centralized states. Although the Haya have common traditions, social system, culture, and language as well as territorial identity, they are divided into several chiefdoms which suggests that in this case political unity is not an essential part of tribal identity. The Haya are cultivators growing coffee and plantains and live in densely populated villages. In a similar way to the Chagga the Haya have had high levels of education and this, combined with the production of coffee, has had a clearly beneficial effect on the economy of the area.

Haya pregnancy and childbirth What follows is a description of some of the traditions which were originally recorded in the late 1950s by a Dr Moller who was the District Medical Officer in the area at the time. There is little doubt that some aspects will have changed since then, particularly with the increase of births in clinics and hospitals.

A Haya woman is usually married at about 17 or 18 years old and once married would be kept in seclusion until the birth of her first child. She is known during this period as *omu-gule*, and is not allowed to leave the house during the day. She is kept in a special part of the house and is under the watchful eye of her mother-in-law.

Once a woman discovers that she is pregnant the first person that she must tell is her mother-in-law or, if she is not available, another senior member of her husband's family. Only then can she inform her mother and her husband. There are a number of taboos imposed during pregnancy including that the mother must not walk through any entrance backwards or the labour will be difficult, and she must chew all her food very carefully and eat very slowly. This is because it is thought that the child may be hurt by the food falling on it, and if the mother eats too quickly the child, who is also eating, may choke. There are various food taboos that apply and the mother is also given a variety of herbal medicines throughout her pregnancy.

When labour begins a midwife is sent for. These are usually elderly women who have learnt their trade from their mothers and will in turn pass it on to their daughters. As labour progresses the midwife will check that no clothing on or belonging to the mother has a knot in it as it is thought that this will adversely affect the labour. The woman is allowed to drink during labour, but not to eat. When the waters break the woman is made to lie down. Herbal drugs are sometimes given to try to speed up the labour. It was believed by a doctor who observed numerous labours that many of these drugs were actually harmful and did little good to the mother or child.

Edible insects

There are a number of different insects which are eaten in East Africa. The most common are locusts, grasshoppers and flying ants. Locusts are collected when they arrive in swarms (which happens much less frequently now that their populations are more under control) while grasshoppers are collected particularly by children while they look after cattle. They have their wings and spiny legs removed and are either fried in butter, roasted, or are sun-dried.

Termites (or white ants) are the other most commonly eaten insect. Some people say that it serves them right, as anyone living in Africa will quickly come to regard termites as a real nuisance. Any piece of wood that has not been treated is very quickly devoured by these insects. Support poles in a vegetable garden disappear almost overnight. They will also, given the chance, eat away an entire house – all that the termites will leave of ceilings is a thin layer of paint. At certain times of the year, in particular after a prolonged period of heavy rain, the adult form of this insect (which is the flying phase) will appear in huge numbers. They emerge from the mounds or, where there is no mound, from holes in the ground, and fly off to begin new colonies. If you are around when they fly out (they somehow synchronize their exit from the mounds so that thousands leave at the same time) you may wake up to find the ground covered in these insects and their discarded wings. You will also see everybody collecting the insects – sometimes eating them immediately or else taking them home to be lightly fried in butter. They have a rather nutty flavour. You are likely also to see birds, cats and dogs gorging themselves on this 'manna from heaven'. You may also see people setting 'traps' to collect the flying ants. These involve constructing a sort of `tent' over the hole from which the ants would appear. A small opening is left at one end and as the termites struggle to get through this opening many of them fall into a bowl that has been sunk into the ground at the threshold of the opening. Many will lose their wings in the struggle and can then easily be collected.

The queen termite is a sought-after delicacy. There is just one in each mound or colony and they are usually about 125-150 millimetres long. The huge sausage-like body is far too big for the head and thorax and it is incapable of moving anywhere. It is little more than a highly specialized egg-producing factory (producing one a minute every hour of its reproductive life). To reach a queen involves a lot of digging into the termite mound – the colony is usually at least as much below the ground as it is above – so it is unusual for someone to dig up a mound just to get a queen. If however a mound is being dug away anyway then the digger will certainly try to reach the queen.

Caterpillars are also eaten in parts of East Africa. Particularly popular are the caterpillars of the silk Anaphe infracta which are found in nests on the branches of the trees on which they feed. These communal nests contain large numbers of caterpillars and they can be cooked and eaten fresh or else dried and stored.

Finally, another insect which is eaten occasionally in some parts of East Africa is the 'lake fly' which is found in swampy areas around lakes. These flies are known as Kungu on Lake Nyasa. You may see huge swarms of this tiny fly as they fly around the lake shores in a cloud-like formation. Traditionally they were captured by swinging a large basket, which is on long handles, around the head. As they gather in the bottom of the basket the minuscule flies are squashed together into a solid mass. These are then moulded into cakes and dried in the sun. This practice seems to be much less common nowadays than 50 years ago.

The placenta is sometimes called the 'brother' or 'dead brother' of the child born. This may lead to women saying that they had two children, when in fact only one was born and the other was the placenta. The placenta is treated like a corpse and is disposed of in the same way. It is wrapped in bark cloth and is buried inside or near a hut. There are a number of taboos relating to the placenta and its disposal and the violation of these taboos was thought to be punished by various skin diseases.

Blessing the year

This ceremony has been observed amongst the Rangi and Wasi peoples living in the Mbulu District near Lake Manyara in the north. Three groups of men take part in the ceremony: they are the elders and grandfathers, the adult men (from initiation upwards) and the boys (the uninitiated). No women or people from other tribes are allowed to take part. Special dress is not worn at the ceremony. The participants gather around a sacrificial tree and the ceremony involves the chanting and singing of various songs followed by the sacrificing of a lamb. One of the men then whisks or agitates a liquid in a gourd which quickly generates a large quantity of foam. When the foam overflows onto the ground it is scattered around while the man calls out "Howa! Howa!". A number of the other men repeat the process of whisking the liquid and scattering the foam. Meanwhile the lamb is skinned and the juices of the stomach contents squeezed into a half gourd which is then hung from a branch of the tree using strips of the sheep's skin. Beer is then distributed amongst the men. A young girl is brought to sit at the base of the tree with a gourd containing seeds from all the plants grown in the area and some beer. his will later be carried around the boundaries before being returned to the tree. The seeds will then be divided up between all the participants who will mix them with seeds when planting the next ear's crops.

The 'bound-beating' party then sets off with the half gourd containing the liquid which is scattered using twigs from the tree. The party contains two leaders, hornblowers and all the other participants except the elders. As the party goes around the area to be blessed they are given local beer at the houses that they pass. Large quantities of beer are consumed and the ceremony continues late into the day. The elders meanwhile roast the remains of the sheep using firewood from the sacrificial tree. They then eat the meat and drink the beer.

The cord is tied with a piece of string made from a kind of tough grass, and traditionally it was cut using a sharpened slice of reed. There is a belief that any blood that is lost during delivery can be used for witchcraft and this will cause barrenness of the woman from whom the blood originated.

Finally it is believed that the man who first has intercourse with a woman is the father of her first child. The traditional belief is that the first intercourse did cause pregnancy but it 'broke off' and the child was 'hiding in the back' to be born later. This is called a long pregnancy or *bisisi* and the child is known as a 'bisisi-child'. Thus if a couple marry but fail to produce children and later separate, the first child born to the woman belongs to the first husband – even if the child is born many years later. This means that any man who can prove that he has had the first intercourse with a woman can justly claim the first child of that woman as his. This is of considerable legal, social and economic importance to this district. Also from the period of the first birth, until the cord has dropped, the woman returns to her 'virginal status' – thus any man who has intercourse with her during this period can claim the next child of the woman as his. For this reason a newly-delivered woman is guarded very carefully during this period by her husband's family. To make things even more complicated, it seems that 'real' intercourse is not necessarily essential – sometimes 'symbolic' intercourse is all that is needed.

Hehe

The Hehe people live in the central south region of Tanzania around Iringa. They have a strong sense of being Hehe, and have their own more or less distinctive social system and culture with a unifying political system. However within this group there are differences in the way of life and social systems between those who live in the drier eastern parts of the region and those who live in the wetter uplands to the west. These are caused by environmental factors as well as the effects of distance. Despite this, one observer has suggested that there is a greater unity and identity amongst the Hehe than there is with any other group of people.

Tanzania & Zanzibar

Last of the cannibals

In 1891, the Polish writer Henryte Sienkiewicz (later to win a Nobel Prize for Literature in 1905) as part of a safari through Africa went on a hunting expedition from Bagamoyo to the Mission at Mandara in Kilimanjaro region. En route they passed though the territory of the Doe on the south bank of the Pangani River.

Sienkiewicz had been advised by the Holy Ghost Fathers Mission in Bagamoyo before departure that the King, Muremi-Pira, then about 70, from time to time, and in conditions of the utmost secrecy would purchase a prisoner from whom he would take a *filet au sauce naturelle.* This practice was frowned-upon by the German community, and the chief was continually apprehensive that he would be called to account by the Bagamoyo authorities. Since he preferred cutlet *homo sapiens* to beef, the restrictions, apart from the occasional treat, had reduced him to a vegetarian diet.

The Holy Ghost Fathers always had a fairly good indication as to when a lapse occurred as a cow, by way of a guilt offering, would arrive at the Mission.

The Doe had been a pastoral community in regular conflict with their neighbours which had not been unpleasing to the previous Arab administration since the enhanced availability of captives from both sides served to increase the supply of slaves in Zanzibar and lower their price. The problem of casualties, and captives surplus to the slavers' requirements was solved in a fairly simple manner by eating them.

Sienkiewicz and his companions felt reasonably secure during their visit as the Doe believed that if they ate a white their country would disappear. One disconcerting custom, however, was the king's practice of serving guests with a mead made from local honey, garnished with dead caterpillars, in a human skull.

Masai The Masai inhabit the north border area with Kenya, but are found as far south as Morogoro and Tabora. They are a spectacular group of tall, slender cattle-herders, living off milk, blood and meat. Young men leave to become *moran* before returning to begin family life. As *moran* they carry spears, wear distinctive red garments and have elaborately decorated faces, bodies and hair. The women have shaven heads and often wear many coils of beads on their necks and shoulders.

Shirazi The Shirazi is the name given to people who are a mixture of Africans and people who are said to have come at a very early time from the Shiraz area of Iran. They are divided into three 'tribes' called the Hadimu, Tumbatu and Pemba. The Africans are descendants of mainlanders who came to the islands of Zanzibar and Pemba often as slaves although later on of their own accord. Descendants of the Shirazis have intermixed with other Swahili people and have become more African in race, speech and culture.

Swahili This is the general term given to the coastal people who have a Muslim-orientated culture. They are the descendants of generations of mixing of slaves, migrant labourers and Afro-Arabs.

Other African groups The **Hi** people are a very small group of click-speakers. They are hunter-gatherers and live on the southwest shores of Lake Eyasi which is found in the central north part of Tanzania. Other click speakers that are found in Tanzania include the **Hadzapi** and the **Sandawe**. The Hadzapi live in the same area as the Hi and the groups are believed to be closely related. The Sandawe live in the interior central region of Tanzania to the north of Dodoma. The **Dorobo** are a small group of hunter-gatherers who are found throughout Masailand and are also found in Kenya.

Non-Africans This group makes up under one percent of the population of Tanzania and comprises Europeans, Asians and Arabs. In the mid 1970s it was estimated that there were 1,500 European citizens (compared to 23,000 in 1961 at the time of independence, and 17,000 in

Traditional alcoholic beverages

A variety of grains is used in the making of the traditional beer in Tanzania known in Swahili as pombe. The procedure followed varies in different parts of the country.

In many parts, including Dar es Salaam, millet is used. It is allowed to germinate for three days before being sun dried – it is then called kimea. The kimea is ground and mixed together with ungerminated flour before being added to hot water and left to stand for a while before being boiled. The liquid is then left to cool and mixed with a suspension of kimea and cold water. Fermentation begins and more flour may be added. The whole mixture is then shaken up and roughly filtered. The pombe is left overnight and the next day is ready to drink. The whole process takes several days and is a skilled job often undertaken by women. The stage at which yeast is added varies – indeed in some cases no yeast is added at all and instead the sprouted millet provides wild yeasts. The alcoholic strength of pombe is 9-11 percent proof – double the strength of European beers.

Another local brew is tembo which is made from part of the coconut palm. However its preparation and consumption has dropped over the years. At the turn of the century everywhere that could grow the palms did and very large quantities of tembo were drunk. The flower head of the palm is used. The top is cut off and the juice within it allowed to collect in a gourd overnight. The next morning a further section of the flower head is sliced off and the juice again allowed to collect. Collections are made about three times during the day until the whole of the flower head has been used. This liquid which has been collected ferments quickly and spontaneously. The alcoholic content of tembo is higher than that of pombe and increases with time before it goes sour. The strength is 14-16 percent proof. Once it has gone sour the liquid can be used as a sort of vinegar.

Tembo is not the strongest of the locally made 'traditional' drinks in Tanzania – a spirit called moshi which is also known as brandi can be up to 90 percent proof. It is made using a still which traditionally would have been constructed of gourds. Nowadays however it is more likely that an old petrol tin (debe) will be used. The exact method varies, but it is based on a brew of pombe or tembo which is successively distilled.

Tanzania & Zanzibar

1967), and about 40,000 Asians (compared to 75,000 in 1967). A recent figure for the number of Arabs is not known although there were about 30,000 in 1967 living on the mainland. Until the 1964 revolution Arabs were the dominant group in Zanzibar although they constituted only about 20 percent of the population.

Modern Tanzania

Politics

Since independence in 1961 to 1995, Tanzania had single party rule. Julius Nyerere was President until 1985, followed by Ali Hassan Mwinyi until 1995 when Benjamin Mkapa won the multiparty elections. There has been negligible internal unrest since the revolution in Zanzibar in 1964 (see box, page 448), closely followed by a suppressed army mutiny on the mainland. The invasion of Uganda in 1979, and a subsequent period of peace-keeping occupation, although costly, had minimal disrupting effect on the economy.

The current situation in Zanzibar is a cause for concern. It is argued that the Union, created in 1964, although following constitutional procedures, has no political legitimacy as the Zanzibar party to the agreement seized power undemocratically after the 1964 revolution (see page 447). In addition, there are the cultural and religious differences with the mainland stemming from the population of Zanzibar being overwhelmingly Islamic. Zanzibaris feel the Union with the mainland has held back their development, and that they would have benefited in terms of aid and foreign investment if they had been able to forge stronger ties with Islamic states, particularly in the Gulf, where they have strong historical links (see page 442).

The structure of the Union is awkward. It is not a proper federation as Zanzibar has its own President, Assembly and Ministries, while the mainland does not. Until the 1995 elections, the Zanzibar President was *ex officio* one of the Vice Presidents of the Union. Despite having a population that is under five percent of the Union, Zanzibar has 30 percent of the seats in the *Bunge*, the Tanzanian National Assembly.

In 1994, a group of mainland MPs pressed for the creation of a Tanganyika Assembly, and the reorganization of the Union into a proper federation. Though there was logic behind this move, the extra cost of another bureaucratic layer was a considerable drawback, and the proposal was dropped when the former President, Julius Nyerere, expressed his disapproval.

Various Zanzibari separatist groups have formed in exile, some wishing merely for independence, others pressing for an independent Islamic state. The splits within the separatist movement have enabled the government to contain the problem to date. A former Chief Minister of Zanzibar, Shariff Hamad, who was suspected of sympathy to the separatist cause, was removed from office and detained.

In 1994 Zanzibar joined the Organization of Islamic States (OIS), which, although unconstitutional as Zanzibar is not an independent state, appeared to be tolerated by the government. However, Nyerere, whose liberal and egalitarian philosophy is uncompromisingly secular, denounced the move, and Zanzibar was forced to withdraw.

For the multiparty elections in October 1995 thirteen opposition parties were formed. The strongest was NCCR-Maguezi led by a former Interior Minister from CCM, Augustine Mrema, who has considerable popular appeal. CUF, in which Shariff Hamad, the dismissed former CCM Chief Minister on the Isles, is the driving force, had nominal support on the mainland, but was very strong in Zanzibar.

Prior to the election there was a good prospect that Zanzibar would elect a CUF president, and have a majority of seats in the Zanzibar Assembly. The Assembly could then instigate a referendum on the separation issue, and most observers judged that this would be carried. Given the commitment of Tanzania to democratic self-determination in the past, it would be difficult to resist the break-up of the union. Indeed Tanzanians seemed to be preparing themselves to face up to such an eventuality – "let us end the Union, if that is what the Zanzibaris want, while we are all still smiling" – was a sentiment frequently heard on the mainland. Former President Nyerere, architect of the original Act of Union, has observed that he feels Zanzibar will always be a headache, and that if he could tow it away from the Tanzanian coast to the centre of the Indian Ocean, he would.

The CCM Presidential candidate was Benjamin Mkapa, from the south, a former journalist, diplomat, Foreign Minister, and latterly Minister for Science, Technology and Higher Education. The opposition parties failed to unite behind a single candidate, and NCCR-Maguezi fielded Augustine Mrema (also supported by CHADEMA, a party strong in the north); CUF put up Professor Ibrahim Lipumba, a pro-market economist; and the United Democratic Party (UDP) were represented by John Cheyo, a businessman. Mkapa won comfortably with 62 percent of the vote, over Mrema with 28 percent.

In the Union Assembly elections, run on a first-past-the-post-basis, CCM got 219 seats, NCCR-Maguezi 19, CUF 28 (mostly from Zanzibar), CHADEMA four, and UDP four. Some irregularities were reported, but the general impression of observers was that the election was a reasonable reflection of the nation's political preferences.

By contrast, the elections for the Zanzibar Assembly and President were a disaster as far as both credibility and the medium-term future of the Islands are concerned. The initial outcomes of both sets of elections indicated narrow victories for Shariff Hamad and CUF over the incumbents, Salim Amour and CCM. Recounts were demanded, and pro-CCM ballot papers appear to have been smuggled into the count. Finally Salim Amour was declared President with 50.2 percent of the vote (to Hamad's 49.8 percent), and with two constituencies changing hands at the recount, CCM took 26 seats and CUF 24 (which included all the seats in Pemba).

CUF boycotted the Zanzibar Assembly, and the donor community exerted pressure for a rerun of the election under International control. Norway and Sweden and the EU suspended aid to Zanzibar. CCM held firm however, and CUF's attention will be centred on ensuring a good showing in what they hope will be free and fair elections in 2000.

The Mkapa presidency has begun well with a determined stance over corruption. Three ministers (the Finance Minister, the Deputy Finance Minister and the Minister for Wildlife and Tourism), have all been forced to resign because of corruption allegations.

The opposition has fared less well. The major success has been that the NCCR-Maguezi presidential candidate, Augustine Mrema, won a by-election in a Dar es Salaam constituency. However, this was followed by an apparent split between the party General Secretary, Mabere Marondo and Mrema. Constitutional reform has emerged as a key issue, with the opposition unhappy with the power of the central executive to appoint Regional Commissioners and members of the Electoral Commission.

In August 1998 there was a bomb blast at the American Embassy on the main road through an ocean-side residential suburb. The outrage, which killed 10 people and coincided with a similar bomb blast in Kenya, was attributed to an Islamic extremist group in Afghanistan led by a Saudi, Omar bin Ladin. This incident is seen as a one-off – there is no terrorist group active and resident in Tanzania.

Overall, however, Tanzania's stability has remained excellent. The government has remained secure, despite the advent of multiparty democracy and an economic policy that has changed from socialism to capitalism.

Economics

Economic strategy underwent a profound change in 1967 when financial and business enterprises were taken into public ownership and a major reorganization of the agricultural sector was introduced involving collective production and relocating the population into villages. By 1977, the collectivization of agriculture had virtually been abandoned. In 1986 Tanzania signed an agreement with the IMF which heralded the beginnings of a reversal of economic strategy to more encouragement for the private sector and reliance on market forces, rather than on planning and central control.

Economic structure

In terms of both population and geographical area, Tanzania is a large country in the African context. The population has been growing rapidly at 2.8 percent a year, and in 1999 there were an estimated 32.8 million people. This gave a population density of 3.3 persons per square kilometre, rather higher than the African average. However, the distribution of the population is very uneven, with the areas around Mount Kilimanjaro and west of Lake Victoria heavily populated, while in the south and southwest there is much uncultivated fertile land. Urbanization is not as advanced as elsewhere in the continent, and only 23 percent live in the towns.

Despite its large area and population, Tanzania produces only a modest output of just over US$2bn of GDP, converted to US$ using the exchange rate. Using purchasing power parity conversion, GNP per head is US$580 a year. Both these measures put Tanzania in the poorest two or three countries in the world.

Agriculture is the most important sector, producing 56 percent of GDP, and, more importantly, providing the livelihood of 85 percent of the population. Maize is the staple food with cassava and rice also grown. Wheat and barley (the latter for brewing) are grown in the highlands of Kilimanjaro, Arusha and Mbeya regions. The industry sector is small at 14 percent of GDP, employing only five percent of the work force. The services sector is relatively small too, at 30 percent of GDP, generating 10 percent of employment. Both industry and services are relatively high-income sectors, with incomes three times the average.

A large proportion of income goes on consumption (82 percent), as is to be expected in a low-income economy where the main activity is subsistence agriculture. Investment is 26 percent of GDP. Government expenditure is low at nine percent of GDP, and this reflects inability to raise revenue through taxation, combined with spending limits to curtail inflation.

Tanzania & Zanzibar

Export dependence is high at 31 percent of GDP. The main sources of export income are coffee (31 percent) and cotton (13 percent) with tea and tourism other important earners. New export crops include beans, green beans and cut flowers grown around Mount Kilimanjaro and shipped by air to Europe. Imports are the equivalent of 54 percent of GDP, and this high level is only possible as a result of the high level of donor assistance. The main imports are manufactures and metals (20 percent), machinery and transport equipment (19 percent), fuel (14 percent), foodstuffs (nine percent).

Economic performance

GDP growth is averaging five percent a year, and this is faster than the rate of population expansion, allowing living standards to show an improvement.

Agriculture has slowed as the main growth sector, with output expanding at 2.5 percent a year but is being aided by reforms in marketing arrangements and improvements in transport. Industry has grown slowly at 2.5 percent a year and has been hampered by the slow pace of reform of the state-owned sector. Services have picked up to grow at 5.5 percent a year and are driven by strong expansion in tourism.

Export volumes have recovered to compensate for output falls in the early 1980s. Input volumes have fallen also. Firstly they have been reduced by lowered export receipts due to poor export performance, and this has been compounded by a deterioration in the terms of trade, caused by a fall in export price relative to the price of imports.

Inflation was high at 24 percent a year 1980-93. There has been slow but steady improvement in recent years, and in the first part of 1999, the rate was running at 12% a year. The government has found it difficult to raise revenue and has run budget deficits to finance its expenditure.

Aid receipts at $US34 per head are a little below the African average. However, debt service is quite high at 21 percent of export receipts.

Recent economic developments

In June of 1986, the Tanzanian government reached agreement with the IMF, after resisting IMF terms since 1979. The main measures involved a substantial devaluation of the currency, rises in producer prices for key export crops, and a budget which aimed to keep government spending constant in real terms. These changes, together with the revelation that the government was to register individual land-holdings, marked a decisive movement away from planning and government intervention in the economy, which had been the main feature of Tanzania's economic strategy since 1967. However relations with the IMF deteriorated as a result of slow sell-off of the state-owned sector and evidence of corruption in revenue collection. IMF lending was suspended in 1992, and in 1995 some major donors suspended support. It was hoped that the new Mkapa administration would herald a new agreement with the donors, but the unsatisfactory political outcome in Zanzibar has precluded this.

As part of the reform programme, the government has ended the monopoly of the National Milling Corporation (NMC) in the purchase of domestic foodstuffs. There is now private trading in all the major crops including coffee, cotton, tea and sugar. Several key hotels are run by international corporations, and other hotels and tourist facilities have been made into private companies. Lonrho has indicated its willingness to invest in Tanzania, and is reported to be extending its tea holdings, and to be involved in brewing and tractor production.

Air Tanzania has been taken over by Alliance Airlines from South Africa, and the new group also includes Uganda Airways. The group runs two flights a week to London. A South African company is to run trains on the rail network, and the central line from Dar Es Salaam to Dodoma has re-opened following the disruptions caused by the El Nino rains.

Export volumes have shown some improvement, and the response to the increased producer prices for coffee and tea will become apparent over the next five years, as there is a lag between new plantings and the first crops.

The banking sector is in poor shape with Meridien collapsing and the National Commercial Bank (state-owned but scheduled for privatization) posting losses of US$186mn in 1994. As a result government has insisted that commercial banks keep high levels of reserves at 12 percent of their deposits.

Zanzibar is proposing to allow 'off-shore' banks (deposits will be held in foreign currencies and they will not be subject to Central Bank regulations). A German investment bank is launching the initiative for the Zanzibar Investment Corporation (ZICO).

The exchange rate has continued to depreciate. It stood at TSh 17.50=US$1 in mid 1985 and by 1995 had fallen to TSh 578=US$1. The exchange rate is now reasonably stable. Some depreciation is to be expected given that Tanzania's inflation rate is quite high. In the first part of 1998, the value of the shilling had fallen to TSh 668 = US$1.

Tax collection is reported to have improved, and a VAT system has been introduced on the mainland.

The current aid programme concentrates heavily on rehabilitation of infrastructure. There is a massive US$700mn scheme to improve roads coordinated by the World Bank. Other projects include an US$8mn programme to upgrade electricity supplies also funded by the World Bank, and schemes to upgrade port facilities in Dar es Salaam financed by Sweden and Norway. Railway rehabilitation is being undertaken by various donors. The Petro-Canada International Assistance Corporation is engaged in a US$27mn oil exploration programme funded by the World Bank. A new mine 'Golden Pride' has been opened in the central area and expects to export US$50mn of gold a year. Sutton Resources of Canada is engaged in a US$20mn development at Bulyanhulu where a gold deposit estimated at 3.5 million ounces has been discovered (worth US$1.5bn).

The tourism sector is booming, with arrivals doubling since 1990 and receipts tripling.

Economic outlook

Assuming that Tanzania maintains its record of political stability, and perseveres with a steady programme of liberalizing economic reforms, general prospects are good.

Social conditions

Adult literacy figures are not available for recent years, but in 1980 it was estimated at around 80 percent. Although this followed a widespread literacy campaign, it is widely thought to have been an over-estimate. Certainly literacy rates have slipped in recent years, and a more realistic estimate is thought to be around 60 percent.

It will prove difficult to maintain even this literacy level with primary enrolment at 68 percent. Secondary education has received very low priority and at five percent is well below the African average of 14 percent. Tertiary education enrolment rates are under one-half of one percent.

Life expectancy is about the African average, and provision of medical care, indicated by numbers of doctors per head, is slightly better than the average elsewhere on the continent. However, infant mortality rates are high, and are a reflection of the concentration of medical services in the urban areas and comparative neglect of the majority of the population in the countryside.

Despite being a fertile country with unused agricultural land, nutrition levels leave something to be desired with average daily calorie supply about 10 percent below the recommended daily minimum.

A big effort has been made to improve the status of women in recent years, and enrolment levels for females are only slightly below the rate for males at the primary level. However, at the secondary level, a quarter less women are enrolled. Low income levels lead to many women needing to work outside the home, and 87 percent are so engaged, compared to 60 percent in the rest of Africa. The burden of home-care and work are compounded by high fertility rates of close to six children per female. Only 10 percent of women are using contraceptives, and this rate of uptake is about half the African average.

In the latter part of the Colonial era (1960/61) a waiter or barman in a good hotel would earn TSh 150 (US$10 per month) at a time when a bottle of beer cost TSh 2.50 (US$0.20). In other words one day's pay was the equivalent of the price of two bottles of beer. In 1997 the same waiter would expect to earn TSh 25,000 (US$40 per month) whilst a bottle of beer now costs TSh 450 (US$0.75). A day's pay continues to equate to the price of two bottles of beer.

Environment Tanzania has a large area of forest, about 36 percent of its total land area. However, a fast expanding population has led to demands for agricultural land. Poor provision of electricity, and inadequate income levels to allow purchase of bottled gas have led to a high demand for fuelwood. As a result the forest area has been declining at 1.2 percent a year, much higher than the African average.

In general there is adequate rainfall in Tanzania, although uneven distribution can lead to pockets of drought. Domestic usage per head is very low, and commercial usages are modest, and there is little strain on overall water availability, with only 0.6 percent of annual renewable freshwater supplies being utilized.

Uganda

Uganda

Uganda is a land-locked country on the northern shore of Lake Victoria in the centre of Africa. The Equator runs through the country. The north is arid except where the Albert Nile runs through it. The rest of the country is extremely fertile. There are some fine parks and wildlife; attractive countryside with tremendous mountain ranges, lakes, rivers and waterfalls; and a rich cultural background among the people.

Uganda's recent history, however, was scarred by a descent into chaos and anarchy from the early 1970s until 1986. Untold numbers died; skilled people of both African and Asian origin fled overseas; residents of towns sought refuge in the countryside eking out a bare survival existence. Institutions of excellence, such as the famous Makerere University, collapsed. Buildings, roads, factories and farms were destroyed, or fell into disrepair.

Happily Uganda has made a tremendous recovery under President Museveni. Law and order has been restored, it is a secure country for travellers once again (except for some parts of the north and south west), the economy is booming, facilities for tourists are mostly restored and it is once again a fine place to visit.

The north is off-limits as a result of rebel activity. Extreme caution is required in visiting the gorilla areas in the southwest in the wake of the killing of tourists and rangers at Bwindi in March 1999.

The Ugandan Government has now put in place a series of measures to better protect travellers. The area around the Biwindi Impenetrable Forest is now among the most heavily regulated in the world. A few soldiers accompany the tourists on the walks and all campsites have 24 hour armed guards.

Exchange rate (September 1999) USh1,470 = US$1

Uganda

Essentials

Before you travel

When to go **Best time to visit** The heavy rainy season is March to May, and there are lighter rains in November and December. It is probably best to try to avoid March to May. Generally there is some sunshine each day even in the rainy seasons.

Getting in **Visas** List of countries whose nationals do **not** require a visa to enter Uganda: Angola, Antigua, Bahamas, Barbados, Belize, Burundi, Comoros, Cyprus, Eritrea, Fiji, Gambia, Grenada, Italy (Diplomatic Passport holders only), Jamaica, Kenya, Lesotho, Malawi, Malta, Mauritius, Madagascar, Rwanda, Seychelles, Sierra Leone, Singapore, Solomon Islands, St Vincent and Grenadine, Swaziland, Tanzania, Tonga, Vanuatu, Zambia and Zimbabwe.

   Please note that nationals of countries not listed above have to obtain a visa prior to their travel to Uganda. Should you be in doubt as to whether you require a visa, consult your nearest Uganda Diplomatic or Consular Mission.

   Citizens of all other countries require visas, except if in transit and remaining in the airport.

A visa application must include a valid passport for at least six months; a completed application form; 2 passport-size photographs; the appropriate fee; letter of invitation or introduction if travelling on business; a registered, stamped, self-addressed envelope if applying by post. Visa applications are processed in one to two working days. Visas are issued by the Ugandan representatives (listed below).

Visa Fees US$24 Transit visa (valid for 24 hours); US$32 Student visa (valid for three months from date of issue); US$40 Single entry visa (valid for three months from date of issue); US$88 Multiple entry (valid for six months from date of issue); US$168 Multiple entry (valid for one year from date of issue).

Transit Visa Applicants are required to have obtained entry visa for the country of destination. A valid airline air-ticket to country of destination has to be produced on application.

   Journalists are required to notify, in advance, and obtain accreditation and clearance from the Director of Information, Ministry of Information and Broadcasting, PO Box 7142, Kampala, T254410/232734/235764, F256888 Tx61188.

Customs **Duty-free** Cigarettes and tobacco 250gms; wines and spirits 1 lire; toilet water and perfume 0.5 litre (perfume 0.25 litre max). Equipment for personal use. **Pets** require permit in advance from Ministry of Agriculture, Animal Industry and Fisheries, PO Box 102, Entebbe, T20981/9. **Game Trophies** Permit required from Chief Game Warden, The Ministry of Tourism, Wildlife and Antiquities, PO Box 4241, 1 Parliament Ave, T232971/2, F242247.

Vaccinations A certificate indicating vaccination against Yellow Fever is required.

Money The Ugandan shilling floats against other currencies, and the exchange rate can be expected to depreciate steadily as prices have been rising faster in Uganda than in the rest of the world. In September 1999, the exchange rate was USh 1,470 = US$1. Best rates are offered on US$50 or US$100 notes. The rates are 5-10% better in Kampala.

Banks Money can be exchanged in banks or in the foreign exchange bureaux that have recently been established. The bureaux tend to offer better rates than the banks and to stay open longer hours. However some of the comission rates charged are steep. Money can be changed in the large hotels 24 hours a day. There is now no effective black market, and

Ugandan embassies and consulates

Australia*, Canberra.
Belgium, Ave de Tervuren 317, 1150 Bruxelles, T7625825, F7630438.
Canada, 231 Coburg St, Ottawa, T7897797, F2326689.
China, Beijing.
Cuba, Havana.
Denmark, Copenhagen.
Egypt, Cairo.
Ethiopia*, PO Box 5644. Addis Ababa, T513088, F514355, Tx21143.
France, 13 Ave Raymond Poincaré, 7116 Paris, T47274680, F47559394.
Germany, Düerenstr. 44, 5300 Bonn 2, T228-355027, F228-351692.
India, New Delhi.
Italy, Via 9 Pisanelli 1, Rome 00196, T63605211, F63225220, F330970.
Japan, 2-2 Shoto 2 Chome, Shibuya – KU Tokyo, T4693641/2/3, Tx23937.
Kenya, PO Box 60853, Phoenix House, Kenyatta Ave, Nairobi, T2-330801.

Libya, Tripoli.
Nigeria, Abuja.
Rwanda, Ave de la Paix, Kigali. BP 656, T76495.
Saudi Arabia, Riyadh.
South Africa, Pretoria.
Sudan*, Khartoum.
Tanzania, Dar es Salaam.
United Kingdom, Uganda House, Trafalgar Square, London WC2 5DX, T0171-8395783, F0171-8398925.
USA, 5909 16th St NW, Washington DC20011, T7260416, F7261727, also New York.
Russia, Moscow.
RD Congo, Kinshasha.
Zambia*, Lusaka.

* denotes office does not issue visas.

Overseas representation in Uganda
See Kampala page 576.

Uganda

persons approaching visitors in the street and offering implausibly favourable rates of exchange are invariably engaged in some exercise designed to cheat the traveller.

US dollars are the best form of cash to carry. It is helpful to have some US currency in small denomination notes to avoid changing too much at an unfavourable rate when that is the only option, and for last minute transactions when leaving. However it is difficult to exchange or spend bills of denominations of less than $20.

It is possible to get money out on most credit cards at Barclays on Kampala Rd. This costs an additional US$3 for checking your card with Nairobi! Asian hoteliers and traders will occasionally exchange US$ for cash at reasonable rates – however, such transactions may be illegal.

Warning Dollar bills with the *slightest* mark or tear will be rejected – even if they pass the 'electronic counterfeit detectors' which are in use everywhere. Take notes issued after 1990 with the security strip.

Cost of living It is possible to stay in the better hotels, eat well and travel in reasonable comfort for US$30 a day. On a strict budget, it is possible to stay, travel and eat for US$10 a day.

Credit cards Credit cards are accepted by the large hotels, airlines, main car hire firms, tour and travel agents. American Express is the most widely accepted card, with Visa, Diners and Mastercard also taken by some establishments.

Tourist information See Kampala page 577 for the main tourist office. Ugandan Embassies and High Commissions around the world have a tourism attaché who will advise (see above).
Mountain Clubs of Uganda, PO Box 4692, Kampala. *Safari Uganda Association*, PO Box 3530, Kampala, T233566, F235770. *Uganda Tourist Association*, PO Box 5011, T245092, F41245092. *Uganda Tourist Board*, PO Box 7211, Kampala, IPS Building, Parliament Ave 14, T041-242196/7, F2421888. *Widlife Clubs of Uganda*, PO Box 4596, T256354.

Tour & tour operators For those based in Uganda, see Kampala page 576; Kasese page 597; Fort Portal page 602.

United Kingdom *One World Tours*, 80 Stuart Rd, London SW19 8DH, T0181-9466295, F0181-9461985. Specialize in tourism that supports conservation and traditional life. *African Adventures*, 55 Huddlestone Rd, London NW2, T0181-4512446. *Nile Safaris*, Meadow Cottage, Watlington, Oxford OX9 5HR, T01491-612033, F01491-613356. Organize a variety of tours covering the main attractions from 1 day to 19 days.

Getting there

Air Direct flights are only available from five cities in Europe and five in Africa. There are no direct flights from America. For all other points of departure, connecting flights are necessary. An economical way to access Uganda is to obtain a cheap excursion flight to Nairobi and then to travel overland or take a local connecting flight from Kenya Airways. Otherwise Aeroflot tend to be able to offer the most competitive fare, but it will mean flying through Moscow.

Europe Sabena Brussels, Belgium. **British Airways** London, United Kingdom. **Aeroflot** Moscow, Russia. **Air France** Paris, France. **Lufthansa** Frankfurt, Germany.

Africa Ethiopian Airlines Addis Ababa, Ethiopia. **EgyptAir** Cairo, Egypt. **Air Zambia** Lusaka, Zambia. **Sudan Airways** Khartoum, Sudan. **Kenya Airways** Nairobi, Kenya.

The national carrier is **Uganda Airlines**. They are anticipating starting scheduled services to other African counties, covering: Nairobi and Mombasa, **Kenya**; Dar es Salaam, **Tanzania**; Harare, **Zimbabwe**; Kigali, **Rwanda**; Johannesburg, **South Africa**.

Specialist Agencies for discounted fares, see page 28.

Train In 1997 the passenger rail service in Uganda was discontinued. There is only a freight service since then.

Road **Kenya** There are buses that run from Nairobi to Kampala, crossing at **Malaba** and **Tororo**, taking about 15 hours and costing around US$15. There is a variety of standards of service. It is possible to do the journey in stages in minibuses or Peugeot taxis, but buses are more comfortable and safer.

There are also a border crossings at **Busia**, but no through buses, but convenient for Kisumu; and at **Suam** to the north of Mt Elgon.

Tanzania The route is south from Masaka to Bukoba. The road is not very good and this crossing is not used very much, although traffic is increasing. There are matatus from Masaka which go as far as Kyotera and from there you will have to get a lift to the border, crossing at **Mutukula**, with one of the trucks going across – this is not usually a problem. If you get to the border shortly before dark you may want to stay at the small guesthouse which is on the Uganda side of the border – there is nothing on the Tanzania side until you get to Bukoba. For crossing the border you will need to have patience as you go through the rather long drawn out process. The road on the Tanzania side is worse than the Uganda road but there are four-wheel drive vehicles operating on the route. They go when full.

Rwanda In normal times, there are frequent daily minibuses between Kabale in Uganda and the **Katuna** border post, the trip taking an hour. There are frequent minibuses to Kigali from Katuna until mid afternoon and they take about 2 hours. Check locally.

The other crossing is from Kisoro in Uganda to Ruhengeri in Rwanda via **Cyanika**. This route is not as busy and it may be harder to get a ride from here. There is an hour time difference between Uganda and Rwanda, Uganda being an hour ahead.

Touching down

Electricity *220 volts. You will encounter a variety of sockets, particularly in the older hotels, and an adaptor is advisable.*
IDD *256. Ringing tones are either a double ring repeated regularly or long equal tones separated with long pauses. Equal tones with equal pauses indicate engaged.*

Hours of business *Business and offices Monday to Friday 0800-1245 and 1400-1700.* *Banks* *Monday to Friday 0830 to 1400.* *Post Offices* *Monday to Friday 0830 to 1700.* *Shops* *Generally from 0800 to 1700 or 1800 Monday to Saturday.*
Offical time *Three hours ahead of GMT.*

RD Congo The most reliable crossing is **Kisoro** to Rutshuru. Minibuses from Kisoro to the border, about 10 kilometres and costing US$0.50, and on the RD Congo side a motor-taxi (motorbike) to Rutshuru.

Alternatively Kasese to Beni via **Kasindi** There is infrequent public transport along this route. Some minibuses from Kasese to the border at Kasindi. The leg from Kasindi to Beni can be awkward, some minibuses, but a motor-taxi (motorbike) is probably the best possibility. There are small hotels on both the Uganda and RD Congo side of the border in case you are stuck there late at night.

Finally, it is possible to cross the border from Kasese to Rutshuru, the border post being at **Ishasha**. There are infrequent minibuses on this route and hitching is possible.

The crossing to the north of Lake Albert, at **Arua**, although possible, is extremely difficult to access and security is less certain.

Sudan The current impossible political situation in Southern Sudan rules out the routes from Juba to Gulu, which in normal times allow crossings at **Moyo** and **Nimule** to the west and east of the Nile respectively.

Vehicle entry If you are driving into Uganda, you must be registered in your home country, with registration plates, log book, and insurance against third party risks. A thirty day licence will cost between US$20 (2,000 kilogram vehicle) and US$100 (10,000 kilogram).

Lake ferry **Tanzania** Weekly ferry service from **Mwanza** to Kampala (Port Bell) has recently recommenced following the ferry disaster in 1996. A new ferry has been donated by Finnish Aid. The water hyacinth problem (see box page 612) has created great difficulties for large vessels on Lake Victoria. The Port Bell Ferry Office telephone number is 221336. As an alternative to the ferry the locals report that it is possible to get the cargo ferry to Mwanza, expect to pay a landing fee of US$6.

Timetable Sunday: 1400 departs Mwanza, 2000 arrives Bukoba, 2200 departs Bukoba; Monday: 0700 arrives Port Bell, 1600 departs Port Bell, 2300 arrives Bukoba; Tuesday: 0100 departs Bukoba, 1000 arrives Mwanza.

Fares Mwanza to Port Bell (via Bukoba): cabin US$55; 1st US$35 (shared cabin); 2nd US$30 (shared cabin); 2nd US$25 (sitting); 3rd US$20. Bukoba to Port Bell: cabin US$40; 1st US$30; 2nd US$25 (sleeping); 2nd US$20 (sitting); 3rd US$15.

Touching down

Airport information Uganda's international airport is at Entebbe, 30 kilometres from the capital, Kampala. There is a **departure tax** of US$20 on leaving Uganda by air. **Transport to town** A taxi to Entebbe costing US$3 and then a matatu (minibus) to Kampala US$1. Taxi from airport to Kampala US$20. Thomas Cook International Timetable – Table 3295 lists limited Public Bus Service, and some hotels in Entebbe (*Sophies Motel*) and the *Sheratour Hotel* run a courtesy bus to and from the airport (see page 580).

Rules, customs & etiquette As in much of Africa, it is considered a courtesy and a mark of respect to dress neatly and smartly. If you have an appointment with a senior government official or member of the business community men should wear a collar and tie or safari suit; women should be conservatively dressed with a medium length skirt.

Safety Rebel activities in the north of the country mean that Gula is the northernmost point that seems advisable to visit. Rebels supported by Sudan have carried out terrorist attacks in Arua and Kitgum. Before travelling upcountry, consult the Consular section of the British High Commission in Kampala, T257054. Prior to the tragic events of March 1999 the situation in Rwanda and Burundi had not affected Uganda although many aid agencies are based here. Sometimes Congolese rebels have come over the border into Uganda as happened in the Ruwenzori region in December 1996. In March 1999 four park rangers and eight tourists were killed at Bwindi by members of Rwanda's International guerillas. Since then the Ugandan authorities have greatly increased security meaures to protect travellers. Gorilla tracking at Bwindi and Mgahinga National Parks resumed in April 99.

You are advised to check with your External Affairs Ministry before visiting these potential hotspots. Overall, Uganda is very safe, with far less petty crime than is found in Kenya. Bag snatching remains uncommon. It is sensible to take taxis at night outside the centre of towns; not to walk about in dark or deserted areas; and to be careful about belongings in crowded areas.

Where to stay

Hotels The most luxurious hotels used by business travellers and up-market tourists have prices set in dollar terms, and are similar in cost and value to those in Kenya. On the other hand, devaluation of the Ugandan currency has made most other accommodation, particularly that used by ordinary Ugandans, good value. There is plenty of budget accommodation at less than US$5 a night, and reasonably comfortable lodgings can be had for between US$10 and US$20. Accommodation in the parks is good value and generally the best lodges are not above US$20-US$30 a night, see Sleeping classification, page 31.

Getting around

Air Several companies now offer flights internally, including Eagle Airlines, United and CEI Aviation (see page 575). It is also possible to charter light aircraft to fly to airstrips around the country (see Kampala page 575). These are located in **East** Tororo and Moroto; **North** Soroti, Lira, Gulu, Chobe, Paraa (for Murchison Falls National Park), Pakuba, Katarum (for Kidepo National Park); **West** Masindi (for Queen Elizabeth National Park), Kasese; **South West** Mbarara.

Train Since 1997 the Uganda Rail Network only operates a freight service.

Road There are good roads on the main routes, and travel is comfortable and swift.

Buses are safer, slower and cheaper than other modes. Bus travel is roughly US$0.02 per kilometre. Most buses and matatus wait until they are full before departure. That can take a long time on Sunday and holidays. However a few bus companies adhere strictly to listed departure times, so avoid being late. Post Office buses are generally safely driven and well maintained (see page 574).

Matatus are minibuses; or pick-up trucks converted to carry passengers; or cars or station wagons carrying passengers. They are privately owned, and operate on the basis of departing from the terminus when full. Minibuses are fine for short journeys, a Peugeot station wagon is more comfortable and safer for a longer journey. Costs are roughly US$0.04 per kilometre.

Taxis Generally available in large towns. Always advisable to agree the fare before departure. In small towns 'taxi' mopeds and bicycles are common. These can be useful for travel where public transport is scarce, for example Entebbe/Kasenyi (for Sese Islands) or Sanga/Lake Mburu National Park.

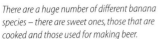

Bananas

There are a huge number of different banana species – there are sweet ones, those that are cooked and those used for making beer.

Matoke *(green banana) is the main item of the Baganda diet. There are actually 14 varieties of matoke alone. These include* Muvubo, Musakala, Nakitembe, Kisubi, Ssiira, Nnambi *and* Manwoge.

The sweet bananas eaten as fruit are known as Ndizi *(the small ones) and* Bbogoya *(larger). Other varieties include* Gonja *which is eaten cooked – either baked, roasted or fried and which can be dried and stored. The main types used for making beer are* Kisubi, Mbidde *and* Kabula.

Car hire There is a wide choice of tariffs and some extra charges you might not expect (for example 'up country driving'). Prices are often quoted in US$, but have to be paid in local currency, converted at a rate determined by the local operative. Drivers are an asset in case of a breakdown, but some can be obstructive and morose. Self drive saloon US$50-60 per day, plus US$0.40-50 per kilometre per day over 100 kilometres, plus tax (15%). Toyota landcruiser including driver, US$130 per day, plus US$0.60 per kilometre after 100 kilometres per day, including fuel.

Lake ferries There are steamers and ferries and small cargo boats that sail between ports on the shore of Lake Victoria and the Sese Islands.

Food and drink

Food Simple meals are good value, but the range and variety of food is limited. Local food includes *ugali*, which is maize ground and boiled to form a stiff dough: and *matoke*, which is boiled plantains (cooking bananas). Indian additions to the menu include *chapatati*, a flat bread, and *pilau* which is a rice and meat together with a vegetable curry, see restaurant classification page 31.

Drink Imported wines, spirits and beers are widely available. Uganda produces a range of soft drinks and beers that are are quite acceptable and good value compared with the imported alternatives.

Keeping in touch

Language Official language is English, and it is widely spoken, although for most Ugandans it is their second language. Swahili is also spoken (see box, page 308), but not as widely as in Kenya and Tanzania.

Postal services Services are reliable and letters take about 10 days airmail from Europe. There is a Post Restante service in Kampala (Post Restante, GPO, Kampala Rd, Kampala). Most post offices offer a fax service – cost US$2 per page outgoing overseas, US$0.50 for an incoming fax. Postcards and letters cost US$0.50.

Telephone services International calls can be made from the GPO office on Kampala Rd in Kampala. Phonecards are required – offered by Uganda Telecom and private companies. Uganda **Country Code** 256. **Area Codes** Kampala 041. Entebbe 042. Jinja 043. Busai 044. Fort Portal 0483. Kabale/Kisora 0486. Kasese 0483. Mbale 045. Masaka 0481.

Media **Newspapers** The main newspaper is *New Vision*, published in English. Although it is government-owned it has considerable editorial freedom. It contains good listings of up-coming events in Uganda. The Kampala newspapers are surprisingly independent and informative.

Uganda

Radio Radio broadcasts mainly in English, but some in Swahili and Luganda. **BBC World Service** is broadcast to Uganda, and can be received on a short wave band radio, see guide, page 33.

Television There is a colour television service run by the government and broadcasting for about 6 hours every evening, mostly in English.

Sporting events There are regular football matches in the main towns, hockey and cricket in Kampala.

Holidays and festivals

New Year's Day 1 January
NRM Day 26 January
Good Friday April
Easter Monday April
International Labour Day 1 May
Independence Day 9 October
Christmas Day 25 December
Boxing Day 26 December

Health

Health/ disease risks It is not uncommon for travellers, particularly those visiting the country for the first time, to have some form of stomach upset. Plenty of fluids are advised, and a rehydration preparation such as *Dioralyte* can be invaluable.

Still pools and lakes present a risk of bilharzia, and it is wise to ask local advice before taking a swim. Swimming in chlorinated pools is the safest option.

Uganda has a high prevalence of AIDS.

Malaria Malaria is a serious risk, and the appropriate prevention tablets, sleeping under a treated net and the use of insect repellents after dark are essential.

Water It is not safe to drink local water. It should be boiled or treated with sterilization tablets. The local soft drinks and, provided the seals are intact, bottled water are quite safe.

For more details see the Health Section page 35.

Further reading

General Hansen B and Twaddle M (eds), 1988, *Uganda Now*, London: James Currey, an excellent series of essays on the political, economic and social problems that have plagued Uganda since independence.

History Miller C, *Lunatic Express*, weaves the history of East Africa round the story of the building of the Uganda Railway, from Mombasa to Kampala, well researched, engagingly written, and with a fine eye for the bizarre and amusing. Moorehead A, 1960, *The White Nile*, London: Hamish Hamilton. Highly readable account of exploration to find the source of the Nile.

Natural History Blundell MA, 1987, *Field Guide to the Wild Flowers of East Africa*, London: Collins. Dorst J and Dandelot PA, 1970, *Field Guide to the Larger Mammals of Africa*, London: Collins. Hedges NR, 1983, *Reptiles and Amphibians of East Africa*, Narobi: Kenya Literature Bureau. Larcassam R, 1971, *Handguide to the Butterflies of East Africa*, London: Collins. Williams J and Arlott NA, 1980, *Field Guide to the Birds of East Africa*, London: Collins.

Kampala

Kampala

The population of Kampala, the capital of Uganda, has increased in recent years to about 800,000. It is a compact city and the spread of suburbs is really a fairly recent phenomenon. The city centre is located about seven kilometres to the north of Port Bell on the shore of Lake Victoria and the average height above sea level is 1,230 metres. It is a friendly city and in the last few years security has improved dramatically so that nightlife is beginning again. Accommodation in the city is rather limited, and relatively expensive. The city was always known for its greenery, but in recent times much of this has been lost. Makerere University, at one time the intellectual centre of East Africa but now sadly faded, is located in the city outskirts.

0°20 32°30′E
Population: 800,000
Altitude: 1,230m
Phone code: 041
Colour map 2, grid B2

History

Early Days

The name Kampala came from a Bantu word Mpala meaning a type of antelope which, it is said, the Buganda chiefs used to keep on the slope of a hill near Mengo Palace. The name Hill of the Mpala was given specifically to the hill on which Captain Fredrick Lord Lugard, a British Administrator, established his fort in December 1890. At the Fort, which was also an administrative post, Lugard hoisted the Imperial British East African Company flag in 1890, which in 1893 was replaced by the Union Jack. The Fort at Kampala Hill as it became known (now known as Old Kampala Hill) attracted several hundred people and a small township developed.

As time went on traders erected shops at the base of the hill, and by 1900, the confines of the Fort had become too small for administrative purposes and it was decided that the Colonial Offices and government residences that were in Kampala (at this time most offices were at Entebbe) should be moved to Nakesero Hill. The shops and other commercial premises followed.

Kampala grew and the town spread over the surrounding hills – until it became known, like Rome, to be built on seven hills. These historical hills are Rubaga, Namirembe (Mengo), Makerere, Kololo, Kibuli, Kampala (Old Kampala) and Mulago. On top of three of these hills, Rubaga, Namirembe and Kibuli, places of worship were built – Catholic, Protestant and Muslim respectively.

In 1906 Kampala was declared a township, and the railway joining Kampala with the coast reached Kampala in 1915. In 1949 it was raised to municipality status, in 1962 it became a city and in October of the same year, it was declared the capital. The city has continued to grow and now covers 23 hills over an area of nearly 200 square kilometres.

Independence & after

Like the rest of Uganda Kampala has suffered enormously in recent years. Prior to these years Kampala had developed into a green city – it was spacious and well laid out and had developed into the cultural and educational centre of Eastern Africa. During the Amin period the most dramatic changes to Kampala came with the expulsion of the Asian community. Until then trade was almost

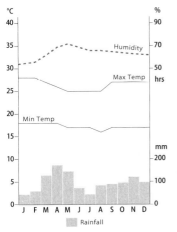

°C / % / hrs / mm

Humidity

Max Temp

Min Temp

J F M A M J J A S O N D

Rainfall

Climate: Entebbe

Uganda

entirely in the hands of Asians and because of this large areas of the town itself were Asian-owned. Apart from their residences – which were concentrated around Old Kampala – their businesses were also handed over to officials in the Amin administration and these premises were allowed to gradually fall apart. By the early to mid-1980s there were many business premises and blocks of flats that had not been touched for over a decade and were very dilapidated.

With the return of stability to the country Kampala has also gradually been recovering. One of the most obvious of these changes is the sight of premises that have been refurbished from top to bottom. Many of these are in fact Asian properties which have been returned to their original owners as part of Museveni's attempts to attract investment to the country. Other buildings have also been renovated and the roads repaired, and Kampala is gradually smartening itself up. Having said that, there are still parts of the city that remain in a very poor state of repair.

Visitors to Kampala often comment on the greenness of the city and the number of trees. Much of this has been lost in the last five to 10 years. This is due to two factors. Firstly there has been a massive building boom since 1986 in Kampala, and this has led to previously empty areas being divided up and built on. One example of this is Kitante Valley (which runs from the golf course to the museum) which a few years ago was public land, on which pupils at Kitante School used to go cross country running. It has now been built up almost entirely. Secondly the bricks used for building are made locally and they are made by being baked in furnaces which are fuelled by

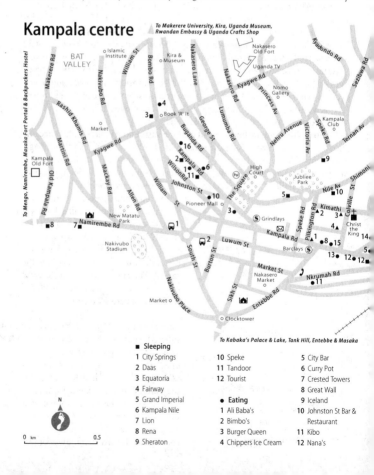

Kampala centre

To Makerere University, Kira, Uganda Museum,
Rwandan Embassy & Uganda Crafts Shop

■ Sleeping		
1 City Springs	10 Speke	5 City Bar
2 Daas	11 Tandoor	6 Curry Pot
3 Equatoria	12 Tourist	7 Crested Towers
4 Fairway		8 Great Wall
5 Grand Imperial	● Eating	9 Iceland
6 Kampala Nile	1 Ali Baba's	10 Johnston St Bar &
7 Lion	2 Bimbo's	Restaurant
8 Rena	3 Burger Queen	11 Kibo
9 Sheraton	4 Chippers Ice Cream	12 Nana's

woodfuel. As you drive into Kampala you may notice these furnaces dotted all over the countryside – trying to keep up with the tremendous demand for bricks – and in the process decimating Kampala's trees.

Sights

Note that a convenient and cheap way of travelling about town is to use a 'motor-taxi' – a motor-bike. They are available on Kampala Road and any cruising bike can usually be hailed and hired.

Kampala Club PO Box 9048, Tiernan Avenue, T230577. Elegant, red-roofed, colonial-style. Essentially for members, but it is possible to look in to savour the atmosphere. Busiest early evening. Tennis, squash and swimming pool nearby.
Railway Station South of centre. Solid colonial style completed in 1928 (see boxes pages 285 and 174). The final stretch of line, west to Kasese, was opened in 1956, and the ceremonial copper fish-plates and bolts are on display.

Kisubi Tombs

These are situated a few kilometre out of town on Nabulagala Hill off the Kampala-Hoima Road. They are the site of the tombs of the Kings known as the Kabakas of Buganda. The site contains the tombs of Muteesa I (1856-1884), Mwanga II (1884-1897), Sir Daudi Chwa (1897-1939), and Edward Muteesa II (1939-1966). Mwanga II was exiled to the Seychelles in 1899, died there in 1903 and his body was returned to Uganda and buried at Kisubi in 1910. Muteesa II was removed from his position soon after independence during the Obote I régime and died three years later in 1969 in London. His body was returned to Uganda in 1971 and buried at Kisubi in an attempt by Amin to appease the Baganda. During Museveni's rule Muteesa II's son has been allowed to return to Uganda and in July 1993 he was crowned as the Kabaka at Budo.

■ *The tombs are open from 0900 to 1800 throughout the week and there is a small charge, and for this you will get a very knowledgeable guide.*

The largest building, which is the tomb house, is called *Muzibu-Azaala-Mpanga*. It is a large thatched round house which although it can be said to reflect traditional Ganda architecture is actually a modern structure built during the colonial period by a British company of architects. You can have a look at the plans for the building in the small shop. There is a guidebook for sale, as well as a variety of souvenirs.

There is a two-doored house, *Bujjabukula* which you pass through as you enter the main enclosure, as well as the drum house *Ndoga-Obukaba*. There are also a number of smaller buildings of similar design around the outside,

(Map of central Kampala showing streets including Siad Barre, Clement Hill Rd, Hannington Rd, Siad Barre Av, Kitante Rd, Nile Av, Yusuf Lule Rd, De Winton Rd, Jinja Rd, Parliament Av, Kampala Road, with locations: Tanzanian High Commission, City Hall, National Theatre, Parliament, Immigration. To Kololo, To Lugogo, Port Bell & Jinja.)

13 Nile Grill
14 Sgt Peppers
15 Slow Boat
16 Tandoor

▲ **Others**
1 Air France & British Airways

2 Ethiopan Airlines, Air Tanzania & Aeroflot
3 Uganda Airlines
4 Uganda Bookshop

🚌 **Buses**
1 Main Bus Station
2 Matatu Park

Uganda

within the inner enclosure. Originally there was an outer fence that enclosed the whole of the area – over six kilometres in length as well as the inner wall – but only the inner wall remains.

Just outside the main tomb to the right is a small cannon which was presented to the Kabaka Muteesa I as a gift by Speke and Grant in 1862. Visitors remove their shoes and enter to sit in the cool, dark interior on mats. There are pictures of the different Kabakas and some of their belongings – including a large number of spears and a stuffed leopard. The main hut is divided into two by a barkcloth curtain behind which are the tombs, in an area closed to visitors, called the *Kibira*. Each of the graves has a corresponding platform just outside the *Kibira*.

The descendants of the wives of the Kabaka's live in huts around the main tomb and look after it – they are usually sitting inside making mats – and you are expected to leave a tip for them (around US$3) in the bowls provided. The duty that they perform is called *Ejisanja* – looking after the house and making mats.

The Kabaka's lake & palace Located close to the Kabaka's capital this lake was constructed from about 1885 to 1888 by Kabaka Mwanga. The original plan was to link it up with Lake Victoria but this was not to be as Mwanga was deposed. The lake got into a fairly terrible state and became very stagnant. The Kabaka-to-be reopened the lake in 1993 (see box page 565) and unveiled a statue to Mwanga. The lake is a pleasant secnic stretch formed by damming two small streams from the north, with two small islands in the centre. It is possible to walk round most of the lake shore.

The hilltop palace at Mengo, just west of Kampala, has been returned to the Kabaka. The Palace was once the pride of Buganda, with its high walls, beautiful gardens and lake. It is a handsome building with a cupola in classical style, and it faces across the valley north toward the *Bulange* building, off the Natete Road, which serves as an assembly and administrative centre for the Buganda.

A group of Ugandan royalists is working to prepare the Palace for the return of the Kabaka. By tradition the King is forbidden to enter the palace until he has been anointed by witch doctors, soothsayers and healers.

Namugongo Shrine The Namugongo Martyrs Shrine is located about 12 kilometres out of Kampala off the Jinja Road. This is the site were 22 Ugandan Christian converts were burnt to death on the orders of Kabaka Mwanga in 1886. On the visit of Pope Paul VI to Uganda in 1969 the victims were canonized and since then the shrine has been an important site for Ugandan Christians. On the site there are two churches – one built by the Roman Catholic Church, and the other by the Church of Uganda. The steel structure, built in traditional style, has artistic work on its interiors depicting scenes from this episode and, in the centre, preserved in glass, are some of the remains of one of the martyrs, Kaloli-Lwanga. Nearby is an artificial lake that is believed to have been formed from a well that belonged to one of the Kabaka's soldiers who was staying in the area. There is a public holiday every year on 3 June in remembrance of the martyrs.

Kampala Museum Most of the displays have been renovated and the rest are in the process of being restored. Many of the items were looted during 1970-86 and a big effort is being made to return the museum to its former standard. Displays include a number of items from archaeological sites from around the country; models of dwellings, settlements and hunting scenes; wood-carvings, metal-work and leather-craft, pottery, weapons; a collection of musical instruments including many drums and a large and impressive canoe. The first printing press used in Uganda is on view. It was used to print the Bible in Uganda. Every so often the museum holds live traditional music afternoons. The Museum is home to the Uganda Society, the Historic Building Society, and the Uganda Food and Drink Society. ■ *Located out of the town centre on the Kira Road, open 0900 to 1700. US$1.50.*

The Coronation of the Kabaka

This event eventually took place at the end of July 1993. There had been a number of delays from when it was first announced that the son of Edward Muteesa II could return to Uganda and be crowned. An amendment had to be made to the constitution and it was made clear that the new Kabaka would not have any political powers but would be a cultural leader. The occasion also gave rise to much discussion as to the future of the other four kingdoms in Uganda – the people of at least one of these kingdoms (the Ankole) did not want their king to return.

Finally it was declared that the coronation could go ahead and suddenly the Baganda found they had a huge amount to organize before the great day. There were invitations to be sent out, a hill-top to clear, large grass thatched constructions to be built, a road to be surfaced, not to mention all the traditional rituals that the Sabataka (the one who was to be King) had to perform before he could be pronounced the Kabaka. These included the tuning of the drums and a series of visits to culturally important sites around Buganda.

In the weeks before the coronation day hoards of volunteers gathered at the site at Namugongo near the famous Kings College, Budo, and set about clearing the hill-top. Groups of women sat around cleaning and preparing the reeds used for the construction of walls of the buildings. They were dressed in the Ugandan busuti, many made from bark cloth. The atmosphere was one of great anticipation, and they frequently broke into song.

Eventually the great day arrived. Events began at day break with a mock cane fight in which the Sabataka had to prove his worthiness to become the Kabaka. Thousands of people began to arrive in traditional dress and gathered on the hill top. It was a wonderful site, with fine views of Buganda all around, and as the sun rose, the mist gradually cleared.

Foreign dignitaries took their places in the shade of a pavilion. President Museveni and his wife were the last of the guests to arrive and the president was greeted extremely warmly as the Baganda thanked him for returning their King to them. The ceremony was split into two parts – the first being the traditional one under a tree, and the second, in view of many more people, was the religious ceremony when prayers were said. The Sabataka was carried into the enclosure where the coronation was to take place and took his seat on a barkcloth-covered throne underneath the traditional tree. As part of the ritual he prodded a cow (in the past he would have killed it) and as the ceremony progressed he was dressed in layers of barkcloth covered by animal skins.

Just after the actual crowning dark clouds started to gather and the wind suddenly rose. There had been no rain in the area for a few weeks and now it looked as if there was to be a thunderstorm, which would forebode ill. But after just a few spots of rain the clouds cleared and the sun came out – as the Bagandans said: God is being kind to us.

Uganda

Block house on a small hill to the southwest of the centre of Kampala. There is a half-finished mosque with a huge, slender, concrete minaret. It is difficult to know if the Old Fort still exists, or whether it was demolished to make way for the mosque. Entry, in principle, through a gate on the west side of the hill, just next to the abandoned Aga Khan Sports Club, but access is restricted. **Kampala Old Fort**

Brick construction, concrete rendered perimeter walls, with rifle slits. Now houses the Police Quartermaster's Depot, and access is restricted. **Nakasero Old Fort**

This small building is Uganda's National Art Gallery where art work by local artists as well from other parts of East Africa are displayed. Exhibitions are advertised in the local press, but there is invariably something on display. There is also a shop attached with both artworks and crafts available. It was once a private house and is set in spacious grounds. **Pearl Gardens** restaurant is an excellent outside café. It is located in Kololo on Victoria Avenue – there is a signpost opposite the main *Sheraton* entrance gate. ■ *0900 to 1700 on weekdays, and from 0900 to 1500 on weekends.* **Nommo Gallery**

The Uganda Museum

The possibility of establishing a museum in Kampala was first put forward in 1907 when the grand sum of £200 was allocated for the purpose. The Officer in Charge of the Botanical, Forestry and Scientific Department, Mr Dawe, was informed that the collection of items for display should begin immediately or the money would lapse. Circulars were sent out to a number of private individuals as well as to Colonial Officials asking for exhibits.

Within a matter of months a considerable number of items had been collected and until a permanent building was built they were housed at Coronation House in Kampala. The original museum was built on the site of the Old Fort in Kampala and when the contents outgrew their home it was moved to the larger site currently in use. Sadly many of the specimens collected in the earlier period of the museum's history no longer survive.

Tulifanya Gallery, PO Box 926, T254183. Small, but charming art gallery in Hannington Road, run by Maria Fischer. African artists. Pleasant café in gardens.

National Theatre The National Theatre is located on Dewinton Street at the end of Parliament Avenue. It was built in the 1950s and first opened in 1959. There is something presented most weekends – dances, drama and music. There is a notice board outside that announces the events planned. The British Council shows films once a month, and the Alliance Française holds French classes. Occasionally there are visiting musicians from around the world – they are usually advertised in the main daily paper *New Vision* and on posters around town.

Parliament Buildings The Parliament Buildings complex is located on Parliament Avenue (the road that has undergone the most name changes in Kampala – it has been Obote Avenue twice and this is the third time it has been Parliament Avenue) and is the seat of the Uganda Government. The archway at the entrance is the symbol of Uganda's independence and on it there are often perched what must be one of the world's most sinister birds – the marabou stork. If you look at the pillars from behind you will notice that there are quite a few gun shot holes – only the ones at the front have been filled in. On the metal gates at the entrance there are the emblems of the original districts of Uganda. Inside, at the entrance to the main Chambers (which is far as visitors can go) there are engravings representing the different modes of life in all the districts.

Makerere University This is the oldest University in East Africa and for many years had a fine international reputation. However, it has suffered greatly in the past two decades and is now struggling to return to its former high standards. Despite the rather shabby look at present, the original impressive appearance is unmistakable. The main campus contains the administrative buildings, the academic faculties, the library, seven halls of residence, the Guesthouse, staff residences as well as recreational facilities include the Student Guild and a swimming pool.

Within the Faculty of Fine Art there is a gallery which holds exhibitions of students works and is open from 1000 to 1800 Monday to Saturday. The building dates from 1923, and there is a permanent display of sculptures. In the basement is a Victorian art printing press bearing the Royal Arms, with handsome cast-iron feet and the maker's name Payne & Sons, Otley, Yorkshire, England.

Sikh & Hindu Temples In the town centre close to the matatu park are two temples – one Hindu and the other Sikh. One of these was used as a school for some years but has now returned to its original use.

Kibuli Mosque On Kibuli Hill is the mosque, which as a result of recent cutting down of trees is now visible from Kampala town centre. Prayers are held here five times a day.

Uganda

This brick red Anglican Cathedral, with its impressive dome is visible from much of **Namirembe** Kampala and is located at the top of Mengo. Particularly interesting is the graveyard **Cathedral** which includes the graves of both the Cooks (who established Mengo Hospital) and the remains of Bishop Hannington – who was murdered in 1885 (see box, page 584). The congregation is called to the service by the beating of drums instead of by bells and if you are staying at *Namirembe Guesthouse* you will certainly hear them.

This is the Catholic Cathedral and was restored in preparation for the visit of the **Rubaga** Pope to Uganda. It is a huge building and has an illuminated cross outside. Inside **Cathedral** the Cathedral are the remains of the first African Catholic Bishop and the first African Archbishop of Kampala Diocese, Joseph Kiwanuka.

The Bahai Temple is situated about four kilometres out of Kampala on Kikaya hill **Bahai Temple** off the Gayaza Road. It is the only Temple of the Bahai religion that is found in Africa. This religion believes that each religious manifestation forms a successive chapter in one great and continuous revelation of God. People of all faiths are therefore welcome to visit this temple for prayer and meditation at any time. There are services held here on Sundays at 1030. A wonderful view of the Temple can be seen from the end of Kira Road in Kampala, just beyond the Museum to the left. From the temple itself there are excellent views of Kampala and the surrounding countryside.

Excursions from Kampala

Pleasant day-trips, either in your own vehicle or by public transport, can be made to **Entebbe** (see page 578), **Jinja** (see page 582) and the **Mpanga Forest Reserve** (see page 607).

Essentials

A+ *Sheraton*, PO Box 7041, Ternan Ave, T344590/6, F256696/234252, Tx61517. Located in **Sleeping** the centre of Kampala, this 245-room hotel is ideally set within the 9 acres of the Jubilee gardens (which are beautifully maintained by the hotel and open to the public), it has meeting *Price codes:* rooms to cater for conferences from 4 to 500 people, a complete recreation centre with a *see inside front cover* swimming pool, squash courts, tennis court and health club open to hotel guests and members only, in the foyer there is a good coffee bar which is a perfect meeting place, e-mail services and internet access is offered in the business centre. All rooms have balconies. The *Hippo Barbeque* restaurant offers good value for money buffets for lunch and dinner daily, the *Rhino* pub with large TV screens showing satellite sports and music channels, has draught beer, pool tables, darts, serves Sunday brunches and a snack menu is available, the *Sheraton Kampala* hotel offers airport transfers for hotel guests and is a 45-minute drive from Entebbe Airport.

A *Equatoria*, Junction of Bombo Rd and Kyagwe Rd This is a newly refurbished, Indian-owned hotel, it has 2 restaurants including the excellent *Chop Sticks* with Chinese cuisine. **A** *Grand Imperial Hotel*, Nile Ave, PO Box 7195, T250681/8, F250605/6, Tx61580. Pleasant conversion of a colonial building, very central, a/c, 3 restaurants, 4 bars, ballroom, pool, saunas, jacuzzis, steam and spa baths, massage, shopping mall, satellite TV. Outgoing international telephone charges are exorbitant. **A** *Nile Hotel International*, Kampala, PO Box 7057, 32 Nile Ave, T258080 and 235900/9, F259130. Luxury 4-star fully a/c hotel, aimed at business traveller. Has an International Conference Centre connected to the hotel: capacity 1,550, shopping centre, duty free shop, Art Gallery, Bank Forex Bureau and postal services, airport shuttle service, several bars, cafeteria and restaurants, set in 7 hectares of grounds, with a swimming pool.

B *Diplomate*, T/F267690/625, Tank Hill. Out of the hustle and noise of the city centre, offers an excellent barbecue on the terrace – all you can eat for US$10 per person, the *Diplomate* is

■ *on map page 562*

Uganda

awkwardly placed if you are without transport, relatively expensive. **B** *Fairway*, PO Box 4595, 1/2 Kafu Rd, T259571/4, F234160, fairway@starcom.co.ug. Located opposite the Golf Course close to the Kampala Club this is a pleasant hotel with nice grounds, it is also one of the more friendly hotels in Kampala. **B** *Havana Hotel*, 28 Mackay Rd, PO Box 2251, T250762/343532, F343533, havana@starcom.co.ug located close to the new taxi park. Good Indian restaurant, adequate facilities, safe parking, some rooms have a/c. **B** *Hotel Africana* , Plot 2-4 Wampewo Avenue, PO Box 10218 Kampala, T348080/6, F348090, africana@starcom located in the pleasant lower Kololo area. Modern hotel, 75 rooms with a/c, Satellite TV, Health club, sauna, gym, free temporary membership to Golf course next door, business centre, shops, restaurant. Free airport and City shuttle service. **B/C** *Palais Dacha Guest House*, Muntungo Hill, Kampala, PO Box 24520, T/F223827. Located 3 km southeast of the city centre, 1km from Port Bell harbour. Spacious gardens, airport transport by prior arrangement, own generator. satellite TV. Offer long term and whole villa rental tates for up to 10 people. Self-catering available by negotiation otherwise traditional cuisine/bar **B** *Speke*, PO Box 7036, Speke Ave, T243244. One of the oldest hotels in town and has recently been renovated, it is very attractive with striking murals and portraits of John Harnnington Spere. Although there are three restaurants and a bar, they are all franchise operations owned by different operators so nothing can be charged to your room – cash payments only taken. **B** *Shanghai Hotel*, behind the *Sheraton Hotel*. Very clean. Free laundry service, breakfast in room, other meals in restaurant, no bar. Recommended.

C *Antler's Inn*, Bat Valley, opposite *Uganda Crafts*. Nicer than it looks from the outside, it caters mainly for businessmen, and if you are planning to be in town for a fairly long time you can usually negotiate for a reduction in the price, the staff are very helpful and friendly and it is good value, restaurant does breakfast only. **C** *Athina Club House*, Windsor Crescent, T341428. Located by north end of the golf course in Kololo. Very comfortable, Mediterranean atmosphere, pleasant restaurant under awning, with lunchtime buffet. **C** *Colline*, PO Box 7, T290212, located in Mukono about 20 kilometres to the east of Kampala, signposted on the left of the road. There is traditional music and drumming most Sunday afternoons. **C** *Lion*, PO Box 6751, Namirembe Rd, T243490. Clean and comfortable, hot water, good value. **C** *Reste Corner*, PO Box 9153, 31 Tank Hill, outside the city centre, T267910, F267938. Hotel rooms or cottages available, conference facilities, fairly modern. **C** *Silver Spring*, on the Port Bell Road. There are either small cottages, or cheaper bandas which are particularly popular. Reported to have become rather shabby with slow service. There is a swimming pool which is free to guests, a gym, sauna, restaurant and bar, poor value. **C** *Tandoor*, Kampala Rd, PO Box 12034. Small, rather cramped, but well-run and good value. Renovation work may still be in progress.

D *College Inn*, Wandegaya, close to the university campus. It is a friendly place and is clean although rather basic. **D** *Hill Crest*, PO Box 4037, Nakasero Rd, T343624, F234265. Good area, gardens, bar (jazz on Friday), restaurant, camping in grounds. **D** *Kidikuru Economic Hotel*, Portal Ave, T257192. Sound value. **D** *Lusam Inn Guest House*, Plot No 197, Namirembe Rd, PO Box 11434, T250920/250808/250892/250891, F245769. **D** *Luwero Guesthouse and Restaurant* on Nakivubo Place, near bus station, next to stadium. Basic and clean. **D** *Makerere University Guest House*, University campus. Biggest problem with it is the noise from the Student Guild which has loud music until late at night, rooms facing away from the Guild are quieter, food is available (both European and African), breakfast is included. **D** *Namirembe Guest House*, Mengo, close to Mengo hospital, and just below the Cathedral. There is a range of rooms – singles, triples and dormitories – in the original building and in the new extension, the extension has hot water showers and is generally nicer, but more expensive, some dormitory accommodation. **D** *Noble*, has moved from Nakivubo Rd to William St on the block east of Bombo Rd. Renovations underway to include a restuarant. Basic single room, friendly helpful service including breakfast delivered to the room, noisy on Saturday nights. **D** *Rena*, Namirembe Rd, on the way up to the Cathedral. Shared bathrooms, bar and restaurant, very good value. **D** *Samalien Inn Guest House*, Plot No 25, Nakivubo Place, PO Box 11434, T250920/245737, F245769.

E *Backpackers Hostel and Camp Site* (previously Natate Backpackers Hostel), Kalema Rd, Luguffa, PO Box 8643, Kampala, T41-272012/258469, F272012, backpackers@infocom .co.ug, www.traveluganda.com. Probably the best of all the budget accommodation in Kampala, it is run by an Australian (John) who is working on a sustainable agriculture project. There is the choice of double rooms, dormitory, floor space or camping space, you can cook your own food. There is a good notice board, the only slight disadvantage being its location which is a little way out of Kampala. Can get noisy and crowded with overlanders trucks. Restaurant and hot showers. The campsite has recently been resited 2 kilometres closer to town on the Kalema Rd in Lungujja, approximately 100 metres from the Masaka Rd. Tent US$3.50 each, dormitory US$8, double US$12-US$14, food US$2-5, breakfast from US$1, Nile Rafting can be arranged from here with a New Zealand company called *Adrift*. A one day trip costs US$95 including lunch. They will arrange a pick up in Kampala or Jinga. To get to Natate take a matatu from the centre of town from the Matatu station opposite Nakivubo Stadium, US$0.40 out, US$0.20 back. There is a pole with an attached sign 'Backpackers' at the new taxi-park in Kampala. **E** *St John Bugolobi Guest House*, on the Port Bell Road. Popular with travellers, clean and friendly, good value. **E** *YMCA*, Bat Valley. Popular with campers and backpackers and is probably the cheapest place in town, it is however very basic – you have the choice of the floor (with a mattress if they haven't run out) or camping outside, the main problem is that during the day it acts as a school – so you have to pack up and move out by 0700, if you have a tent you can camp in the grounds, although being on the main road you have little privacy and security is poor, having said all this the staff are friendly and for years it has been the best place to meet other travellers.

Camping See *YMCA* and *Backpackers Hostel* above. Also *Hill Crest* on Makasero Rd, quite central (US$5).

4 *Andy the Greeks*, Windsor Crescent in Kololol, near *Athina* Club House. Popular, with a lively Hellenic atmosphere. **4** *China Great Wall*, Kampala Rd near the Diamond Trust building. Chinese cuisine. Generous portions and reasonable standard. **4** *The Lion Restaurant*, at the *Sheraton* does a buffet lunch which is popular. Also at the *Sheraton* there are other restaurants and snack bars – they are rather expensive but the quality of the food is excellent. **4** *Maharajah*, Speke Hotel, Nile Ave. Good quality Indian cuisine, pleasant setting with a rock garden, cream table-cloths, large parchment parasols and, in their flowering season, a carpet of blue Jacaranda petals. **4** *Shangai* behind the *Sheraton Hotel*. Has excellent Chinese food. **4** *Sheraton's Garden Restaurant*, good buffet. **4** *Sitar's*, Bat Valley. Indian restaurant, is generally considered to be the best in town, the menu is extensive, the food is excellent and there is a nice atmosphere.

Eating
● *on maps*
Price codes:
see inside front cover

3 *Ali Baba's*, Kampala Rd, T244149/163. Sound Indian cuisine. **3** *Burger Queen*, Kampala Rd opposite City Square, upstairs. There are seats inside as well as outside on the cool balcony, international and African food with a good selection of hamburgers, steaks and fish, try fish fingers – rather different to the Birds Eye variety, good standard and value. **3** *Café Roma*, in Tank Hill Shopping Mall. Serve good quality pizzas. **3** *Chadenel Restaurant*, near the *Grand Imperial Hotel*. Serves a good variety of grilled fish and meat dishes. **3** *DAAS Ethiopian Restaurant*, Kampala Rd. Interesting food. **3** *Fasika*, located in the village at the bottom of Tank Hill, just off the Gaba Rd in Kabalagala. Serves traditional Ethiopian food and on Wednesday and Saturday there is a buffet, it is a good way of sampling Ethiopian food as you get a chance to try a bit of everything. **3** *Golden China Restaurant*, Jinja Rd. Good Chinese food. **3** *Le Chateau*, Gaba Rd opposite *Pulsations*. French cuisine and great steaks. **3** *Nile Grill*, Uganda House, Kampala Rd. This popular drinking spot also does some food, relatively expensive for the size of the portions, useful meeting place, there are regularly live bands in the evenings when it is packed to overflowing. **3** *Parrots Café*, an open-air restaurant opposite British High Commission on Parliament Rd. Serves good burgers and meat and fish dishes. Very attractive courtyard café. **3** *Sergeant Peppers*, off Parliament Ave, close to British High Commission. Pizzas. **3** *Sikoni Restaurant*, Pioneer Mall, Kampala Rd. Lively patio café, omelettes, spaghetti, curries, club sandwiches, ice-cream. **3** *Swagat Restaurant*,

Uganda

junction of Kampala Rd/Kyagwe Rd. Indian Food which caters for European tastes. **3** *Tandoor Restaurant*, Kampala Rd (the Bombo Rd end), formerly the Odeon Cinema. Downstairs is *Fido Dido*, which serves ice-cream and snacks, very clean and modern, excellent ice-cream.

2 *Africa Guest House*, opposite the bus terminal on 4th floor. Good views of the city, very popular place among locals for a beer.

2 *Bimbo Ice Cream Parlour*, Siad Barre Ave, has been taken over – no place to take distinguished guests. The ice cream is of poor quality and full of ice crystals. **2** *Chippers Ice Cream*, T254512, across from Hotel Equatoria, Bombo Rd, just past Book 'R'. Currently the best ice cream parlour in Kampala. **2** *Curry Pot*, Kampala Rd, Bat Valley end. It has a rather limited menu but the food is alright. **2** *Hot Loaf Bakery*, next to UCB. Has very good cakes. **2** *House of Foods*, Plot 26 Luwum St, next to Barclays. Local dishes, snacks, pizzas, friendly service. **2** *Johnston St Bar & Restaurant*, Johnston St. Indian food, kebabs, grills, snacks. **2** *Kibo Restaurant*, Nkrumah Rd, opposite UCB Building. Fish and chips and other basics. **2** *Munchies*, American style fast food: burgers and pizza, good quality and cheap, relaxed atmosphere. Located at Kampala Rd/Kyagwe intersection. **2** *Nana's*, Kampala Rd, close to the *Nile Grill* in the Uganda House complex. Although not as popular as the Nile it is just as pleasant with seats outside, the service is good and it serves good fruit juices and snacks. **2** *Nectarine Bar and Restaurant Crested Towers*, Siad Barre Ave. This has become a fashionable hang out in recent years, it has rather an odd atmosphere however, and is more of a bar than restaurant. **2** *Slow Boat*, Kampala Rd, next to *China Great Wall*. Grills, spaghetti, snacks, sandwiches and good curries, service tends to be very slow.

1 Good local food at the night market in Natate, US$0.50 per head.

Entertainment **Bars** *Grand Imperial Hotel*, Nile Ave. Upper Deck Bar, jazz band by the pool, piano in coffee lounge. Well recommended. *Al's Bar*, lively disco with lots of local girls. Open until 6am. *Slow Boat*, next to the *China Great Wall*. Comfortable bar. *Kabalagala*. This is one of the areas on the outskirts of Kampala that established themselves as night spots when it was not safe to drive across town. Originally there were mainly shops with just a couple of bars which served warm beers – now it is lively with bars, restaurants, and well-stocked shops. The bars have chairs outside on the pavement and include the *Tex Bar* (one of the oldest) and the *Afrianex*. *Half London*, Gaba Rd beyond the turning for Tank Hill. Thriving and popular place for eating and drinking. There is often a live band here and it can be too noisy to talk. However there is a good atmosphere and the service is fairly good. There is food available – steak, fish, chips and excellent pizzas.

Gambling *Kampala Casino*, 1st floor, Pan Africa House, Kimathi Ave, T243630/243628. Black Jack, Pontoon, Roulette, Punto Banco, Stud Poker, slot machines. Bar and restaurant open from 1200, casino from 1400. *Equatoria Hotel*, corner Bombo Rd and Kyagure Rd. Newly established casino.

Music see the *New Vision* for announcements of where the local bands are playing. Particularly popular are *Big Five Band*, *Afrigo*, *De Joe's Band*, *Super Rocket Band*, *New Generation Band*. *Nile Grill*, Kampala Rd. One of the most popular places in town, particularly for the wealthier section of the Kampala community. *Simba Sounds*, Friday, Saturday. Members of the audience will often get up on the stage and join the musicians. *Nile Hotel*, Nile Ave, *Nile Quintet Band*, Wednesday. *Little Flowers*, Bombo Rd, *Big Five Band*, Saturday. *Hotel Equatoria*, Bombo Rd, *De Joe's Band*, Sunday. *Slow Boat*, Kampala Rd, *Super Rocket Band*, Wednesday, Thursday, Friday. *Fairway Hotel*, Kitante Rd, *Afrigo Band* with *Moses Matoru*, Friday. *Roof View Bar*, has live Congolese music 7 nights a week, sited between Nakirubo Stadium and BZ Matata Park, open 9-12 midnight, beer US$1.50. *Hill Crest Hotel*, Makasero Rd. Live jazz and blues on Fridays at 2200.

Nakivubo Stadium

At the end of the First World War a certain amount of money remained in what was known as the Gifts and Comforts Fund. This had been raised by public subscription for the purpose of sending comforts to African soldiers serving in the war zone. The Government of Uganda, who administered the fund, decided that the money should be used for a memorial to those who had died during the war. Many schemes were considered by the Committee and finally it was decided that a sports ground should be built and dedicated to the war dead.

The Government allocated a piece of land between Makerere and Mulago and a football ground was quickly and inexpensively constructed, with the help of prison labour. However, it did not take long for the Government to realize that this piece of land was totally inadequate for the intended purposes and future development on this piece of land would be difficult. It was decided to sell the land to Makerere College and the memorial authorities were given nearly 12 acres of land in the Nakivubo Channel.

The work began again. The land was ideal in that it was central and flat, but it was little more than a marsh. Much of it was under papyrus and very rough. The prison authorities were unable to provide labour this time and workers proved difficult to procure. It was decided therefore to send recruiters to West Nile district and they brought back nearly 200 labourers. Deep drains were cut and levelling was completed. The old Nakasero-Mengo road had to be moved and a new one on the east side constructed. Finally the ground was ready for football and on the 10 April 1926 the ground was officially opened by the Governor of the Protectorate, with a match between the Uganda Kobs and a team selected by the Uganda Football Association.

Nightspots *Al's Bar*, on the Gaba Rd, southwest of centre (take a taxi). Great atmosphere, very popular, disco (no entrance charge), celebrated for its glamorous local girls. *Ange Noir*, Plot 77A Jinja Rd and 1st St, T230190, Industrial Area. Currently the hottest nightspot in town. They have recently introduced a dress code – dress smartly and no flip flops. They also have a large notice at the entrance saying "No Firearms Allowed". At time of writing they have different music on each night of the week – for example Saturday is disco, Sunday is African – but in practice by the end of the evening there is little difference. This is the only club in Kampala that has fluorescent lights, nets on the ceiling, even a smoke machine. Mostly the young smart set. *Blue Note*, on Gaba Rd, close to *Al's Bar*. Quieter than its neighbours. *Capital*, Tank Hill Rd, southwest of centre (take taxi). Disco, bar, food. *Half London*, on Gaba Rd (next to *Al's Bar*). Excellent live music on Wednesday and Saturday, bar and restaurant. *Little Flowers*, Bombo Rd, Bat Valley Part of the Uganda Crafts/UNICEF/and Sitar restaurant complex. Not as popular as it used to be, but still blasts its music across Bat Valley. *Starlight*, close to Nakasero Market on the Kampala Rd side. From the outside it looks very unimpressive and a bit of a dive. Inside the bar and dance floor are actually outdoors, in a sort of courtyard – it is very popular with local people. Foreigners and travellers here are relatively rare, although it is very friendly. *Silks*, off Jinja Rd, near industrial area. Unexceptional disco. *Viper Room*, Hotel *Equatoria*. Rather gloomy atmosphere.

Sport (participant) Climbing and trekking: *Mountain Club of Uganda*. John Woodall (Chairman), Room 5.21, Ministry of Finance, T241772 or Deo Lubega (Secretary), Room 1A8, Blacklines House, T254240. **Golf**: Located on Kitante Rd opposite the *Fairway Hotel*, *Uganda Golf Course* has 18 holes. Opened in 1909, and the club trophy, the Wilson Cup, has been competed for every year since 1926 (except 1979-81). Pleasant bar and patio café. Visitors can play for US$30 a round. Club Secretary, PO Box 624, Kampala, T257345. **Rafting**: On the River Nile, US$95 per person for 1 day's rafting with a New Zealand company *Adrift*, T041-268670, Mobile 075-707668, F041-341245. UK: Adrift UK Ltd, Wessex House, 127 High St, Hungerford, Berkshire, RG17 ODL, T01488-684509, F01488-685055, Safari_Drive@compuserve.com/raft@adrift.co.uk, www.adrift.co.uk. USA representative: c/o Bio Expeditions Worldwide, PO Box 2028, Truckee, California 96160, T1-800-2467238,

The Canoe Regatta at Munyonyo

The landing site at Munyonyo has a history dating from the late 19th century and from the time of Kabaka Muteesa I. It was used by Kabakas from Muteesa onwards and canoe races were first introduced during the reign of Daudi Chwa – however, it was not until 1986 that the modern races were reinstated.

In 1871 Kabaka Muteesa I fell in love with the place and a hunting lodge was built for him there. Here he could indulge in some of his favourite pastimes – canoeing on the lake and hunting for hippos. After embracing the Moslem faith, Muteesa I used his lodge at Munyonyo during the month of Ramadan as a retreat. He ordered the construction of two canoes which he named Waswa and Mbaliga. These were used by later Kabakas after Muteesa's death in 1884.

Following Muteesa's death his 17 year-old son, Mwanga Basammula, became Kabaka. He also used the lodge at Munyonyo – especially when his palace at Mengo was undergoing repairs following a fire.

Kabaka Daudi Chwa also used Munyonyo for a place for relaxation, and he was the first of the Kabakas to hold an organized canoe race. In turn his son, Muteesa II, also spent time at the lakeside, buying a yacht which he named Nguwu. This was kept at Munyonyo until the political unrest of the mid-1960s between the Baganda and the Obote Government which resulted in the Kabaka's exile. The yacht was taken by government troops to Luzira where it remains.

In 1986, when peace began to return to Uganda, a group of Baganda royalists got together and organized a canoe race to mark the centenary of the Uganda Martyrs. One year later it was repeated in the presence of Prince Ronnie Mutebi. Since then it has become an annual event and in 1993 it was brought forward to July so that it could be part of the coronation celebrations.

Munyonyo is a small landing site on Lake Victoria which is located down the Gaba Road. Normally a matatu goes as far as the turning off the main road and then there is a walk to the shore, but on the day of the regatta you will have no problems getting public transport all the way. Food and drink are available – mainly roasted meat and grilled maize. On the day of the races a festive mood descends on the area and thousands of Baganda arrive for a day out. The men are dressed up in the traditional white kanzus, the women in brightly coloured busutis, many wearing hats to show which clan they support. In past years the teams all represented clans of the Baganda. However, at the 1993 race there was a change to the rules and the teams represented clubs rather than clans. This meant that a European team was able to enter, proving extremely popular with the crowd as they were thoroughly beaten in every race.

Once the guests of honour have arrived and taken their places the teams set off. There are a number of races. In the first the teams race to the nearby island and back. The major race of the day is also the longest and that is all the way around the nearby island. During much of the race the teams are out of sight and dancers and musicians entertain the crowds. It is also possible, on payment of a small fee, to go for a trip in one of the motor canoes that follow the racing canoes during the contest. As the boats turn the corner of the island the attention of the crowd returns to the race as the onlookers strain their eyes to see who is leading. As they come closer the cheering begins, and if the race looks likely to be close the crowds go wild. Part of the tactics involves trying ram other competitors. It is altogether an exciting and entertaining day.

F1-916-5826865, H2Omarc@aol.com. Transport from the *Sheraton Hotel* and (Natate) *Backpackers Hostel*. However, for experienced rafters, there is an exciting trip from Masindi to Murchison Falls, International River Grade 5. See entry on page 637. **Tennis**: *Lugogo* on Jinja Rd. *Sheraton Hotel* in City Centre.

Sport (spectator) Kololo Indoor Stadium, near Lugogo on Jinja Rd. Tennis, cricket and hockey. **Canoe Racing**: Annual event, the date of which has varied (most recently in July). At Munyonyo on Lake Victoria (see box, page 572). **Cricket**: *Lugogo*, on the Jinja Rd. Exceptional location in a natural amphitheatre was originally a quarry set in the side of a hill. Regular games between local clubs. Europeans, Indians and Africans all participate. **Football**: The most popular sport in Uganda. Matches at the Nakivubo War Memorial Stadium near the taxi park. As well as international matches for the Africa Cup, there are also league matches. Supporters are extremely loyal. Even if you are not a great football fan you will find the occasion fun. **Tennis**: *Lugogo* on the Jinja Rd. Clay courts and occasional tournaments. The Centre Court is well appointed with stands and banked seating.

Bookshops *Books 'R' It*, 87 Kampala Rd. Large selection of imported books, pop, fiction, adventure, romance etc, takes shillings and hard currency, western orientated shop, reasonable collection of history books on Uganda. *Pauline Book Shop* Kampala Rd near *Curry Pot* restaurant. Has an outstanding selection of worldwide religious books. *Aristoc Booklex* on corner of Kampala Rd and Colville St. Highly recommended, excellent selection of African literature, Ugandan history, politics and economics, physics, geography, also stocks text books and stationary. *Uganda Bookshop* Colville St just past the Blacklines building, off Kampala Rd. It is one of the best bookshops in town but even here the stock is fairly limited. Other bookshops around Kampala tend to mainly sell stationery and text books.

Shopping

Antiques A very interesting selection of old photographs, postcards, engravings, books, stamps, coins and paper money can be purchased at *Roberto Andreetta's Antiques*, Main Courtyard, Hotel Equatoria, Kampala (junction of Bambo Rd and Kyagwe Rd), T041-254759, F041-250128. *Antiques and Knicknacks*, *Sheraton Hotel*. Antique brass and copper measures, cut-glass lamps, polished oil-lamps, padlocks, saxaphones, trumpets.

General *Pioneer Mall*, on Kampala Rd/City Sq intersection. Modern mall indoor/outdoor with food, ice cream, clothing shops, video rental, gift shops, travel bureau etc, relaxed atmosphere. *Minimarket*, Kampala Rd, located in the new shopping centre opposite City Square. This supermarket is run by a European and caters largely for the expatriate community. Prices are high and most of the goods are imported. *Tank Hill Shopping Mall Family Shop*, run by an Austrian, has a good selection of sausages, cheeses and home-made bread. *Quality Cut*, a Belgian-owned butchers with recommended meat and sausages. *Hot Loaf Bakery*, Kampala Rd, next door to the *Nile Grill*. Actual bakery is out on the Jinja Rd. Apart from many different breads it sells lovely pastries, pizzas and croissants. *Beaton's Cookies*, Kampala Rd, just round the corner from *Hot Loaf*, in the same shopping complex. Small shop which specializes in cookies. Expensive by Ugandan standards – but very good. *The Crafts Village*, near the National Theatre, Derwinton Rd. Has a wide selection of local goods. Goods have marked prices but can be negotiated. *Nakasero Market*, town centre. The largest and best fruit and vegetable market in the town centre. The prices are slightly high because it caters mainly for expatriates. It is divided into two, and all around the edge are small shops. In the lower market (built in 1929) there are stalls with a wonderful range of unusual spices. As you approach the market you will be inundated with offers from boys to carry your bag. *Owino*

Market, a huge and bustling market by the Nakivubo Stadium, sells everything from pots, pans, sheets, bags, clothes. As with all similar markets you should be prepared to bargain. There is also a large second-hand clothes section and if you pick carefully you will be able to find very good quality. Do not be surprised if you find designer labels from the west going very cheap here. Any repairs or alterations can be done for you while you wait. This area is due to be redeveloped soon. *Shauri Yako Market*, by the Nakivubo Stadium is particularly good for second-hand clothes from Europe. Don't be put off by the idea of buying second-hand – the quality is usually very good and you will invariably pick up a bargain.

Handicrafts   *Uganda Crafts*, this is the largest craft shop in Uganda and has a wide range of products from all over East Africa. The goods are made by the disabled. There is a Uganda Crafts Village on the Entebbe Rd. Prices are fixed and the quality generally good. It's located on the Bombo Rd, just north of the junction with William St. *African Village* is a compound of over 30 small shops and kiosks next to the National Theatre. Batiks, prints, carved folding chairs, wooden sculptures, bark-cloth, jewellery, antique masks, all reasonably priced.

Transport   **Local**   Unless you are staying outside the centre of town you probably will not need to use public transport much as most places are within easy walking distance. **Motor taxis** are motor-bikes which will ferry you around cheaply and quickly – most trips can be negotiated for US$0.50 to US$1. They can be seen plying around the centre, particularly on Kampala Rd. The **Post Bus** is well driven with some luggage space and they run to a fixed timetable. They depart from the front yard of the main Post Office on Kampala Rd. Runs include Kampala/Lira via Jinja/Tororo/Mbale. There are other routes, one of them to Mbarara which leaves at 0800. The fares are similar to other buses (Kampala/Mbale US$6). The stops to load and unload mail don't appreciably add to the journey time. May only run on PO working days. **Bus**: cheaper than matatus but are less regular, have fewer routes and are extremely crowded. They have the advantage of going across town so on some routes you do not have to change buses. They stop around City Square and are usually marked by destination. Kampala to Kabale costs US$10 and takes about 6 hours. The bus to Mbarara costs US$5 and takes 3 hours. The bus to Masindi takes 3 hours and costs US$5; Kampala to Fort Portal, 7 hours, US$7; Kampala to Masaka, 2 hours, US$2, leaves Kampala at around 1400 for the bordertown to Tanzania, Mutuleula. There are 2 bus services to Kigali, Rwanda from Kampala: Komesa and Kibungo, cost US$15, leaves at 0800 from big bus area in Namirembe Rd. There is also a special terminal for buses to Kenya in Burton St. **Car hire**: City Cars, T232335, F232338. **Matatu**: matatus are minibuses running along the main routes and leaving the terminus when full. They are the cheapest way of travelling between the centre and the suburbs. At the matatu park very few of the vehicles are marked, and there is no system of route numbering, but the matatus all have regular stations in the park. Keep an eye on your belongings and put any jewellery or smart watches out of sight – particularly in the evenings. Most matatus stop running at about 10 in the evening; some run later, although they usually charge more. The fare to most places in town is US$0.30; to Entebbe it is US$1. There are two matatu parks, one opposite the Stadium in Namiremba Rd, the second in Kiwanuka St some 400 metres away. **Taxis**: if you have a lot of luggage or miss the last matatu you can get a private hire – this may be a matatu or a taxi. You will have to bargain the fare – from Kampala city centre to one of the suburbs will cost around US$3.

Air   The main international airport is at Entebbe 37 kilometres from Kampala. Many of the larger airlines are starting to use Entebbe after many years of absence – including British Airways which flies in twice a week. A service flies from Entebbe to Kisoro since 1998. The return flight costs about US$100. There are plenty of matatus shuttling up and down to Entebbe town – getting to and from the airport itself is not so easy. Having arrived at the airport you can of course take a taxi (US$30) all the way to Kampala although there is a tendency to overcharge new arrivals. If you are trying to save your money the best thing to do is try to persuade the taxi to take you to Entebbe town and from there take a matatu which will only cost you US$1. However, not surprisingly the taxi drivers may refuse to do this in the hope you will go with them all the way to Kampala. Thomas Cook International

Mugala's chair

The word entebbe *means chair and there is a legend attached to this name. Mugala was the head of the Mamba (or lungfish) Clan. Apparently Mugala used to command his domain from a royal enclosure not far*

from the present Entebbe Airport, seated in a chair carved out of the rock. Eventually he seat was submerged by the Lake but he area continued to be known as ntebbe.

timetables – Table 3295 lists a limited public bus service. There is a free bus shuttle to the *Sheraton* Hotel which connects with most of the international flights incoming and outbound. You do not have to stay at the *Sheraton* to use it.

Train There are no passenger rail services in Uganda since 1997. The network is only used for freight transportation.

Road The most common approach to Kampala from Kenya is by road. If you have your own transport then you can choose whether to cross the border at **Busia** or **Malaba**. If you are planning on using public transport you can go all the way from **Nairobi** on an overnight bus. There is now more than one company that go direct – meaning it is no longer necessary to change buses at the border. Akamba was the first company to offer this service but there is now competition. All the buses leave Kampala at 1500. The Akamba office is on Lagos street in Nairobi and they have a number of buses that go each day at 0700 getting in at about 1000 the next morning. The Kampala Office is on Dewinton St near the National Theatre. They return to Nairobi at 1500 – book a day ahead to be sure to get a seat. The bus stops at about 0200 in the morning at Kericho – but there is little to eat there – and gets in to Nairobi at about 0530 the next morning.

Boat The ferry service to Tanzania restarted. See page 557 for details. There is a twice weekly steamer service to the **Sese** Islands. Recent information indicates that the ferry has sometimes been suspended for security reasons.

Airline offices *International Air Tanzania*, Airline House, United Assurance Bldg, 1 Kimathi Ave, T234631/134673. *British Airways*, Kampala Rd, behind the Kampala Club, T256695/257414. *CEI Aviation* Metropole House, 8-10, Entebbe Rd, Kampala, T255825, F236097. *Eagle Airlines*, Box 312, Kampala, T042-20513 ext 3020. *Egypt Air*, Metropole, 8/10 Entebbe Rd, T241276/233960. *Ethiopian Airlines*, Airline House, 1 Kimathi Ave, T254796/7. *Kenya Airways*, Airline House, 1 Kimathi Ave, T233068/344304/256506. *Sabena*, Sheraton Hotel Arcade, T259880/234200. *Uganda Airlines*, Airline House, 1 Kimathi Ave, T232990. *Zambia Airlines*, 1 Kimathi Ave, T244082/244067. **Domestic and charter:** Anyone hoping to see Uganda, particularly the north, who is short of time and wants some comfort is likely to use one of the charter airlines. *Bel Air Ltd*, Spear House, T242733/243800. *Speedbird Aviation Services*, PO Box 10101, Kampala, T231290/231729, 1st Floor, *Sheraton Hotel* Arcade or *National Insurance Building*. Airport Office, T042-20689 (Entebbe). **Directory**

Banks The relaxation of the foreign exchange regulations has meant that there are a large number of foreign exchange bureau all over town. These offer a quick and efficient service 5 days a week, and on Sat mornings. The rates around town may vary by a few shillings but not by an enormous amount. Banks also change money – but it takes longer, and they are only open in the mornings. Changing TCs can present a problem at some of the banks, as there have been a number of forged TCs in circulation. You may be asked to produce the original sale receipt for the TCs. The Barclays Bank in Luwum St won't cash TCs – you have to go to the Head Office. *Barclays*, PO Box 2971, Kampala Rd, T232597. *Crane Bank*, Kampala Rd, near the Speke, are reported to offer excellent rates without surcharges. Open all day Mon- Fri and Sat mornings. *Grindlays*, PO Box 485, Kampala Rd, T230074/231151. *Standard Chartered Bank*, PO Box 7111, Speke Rd, T258211.

Communications Post Office: the main Post Office is situated in the centre of town on Kampala Rd and is open from 0830 to 1700. The post is expensive – to Australia a 3 kg parcel cost US$80 airmail or US$25 by sea – takes 6-7 months to arrive. Most post offices offer a fax service, US$2

Uganda

overseas, US$0.50 for an incoming fax. **Telephone:** international telephone calls can be made from the card phones outside the post office. There is a Starcom telephone booth at the Backpackers Hostel where you can ask your caller to return your call. YMCA also offer cheap phone calls. Most international calls made from the hotels are at exorbitant rates – often not realized until you check out. There are several email and internet facilities in Kampala. The Sheraton Hotel bureau T344590 charges US$10 an hr online.

Cultural centres *British Council*, Parliament Ave, IPS Bldg, PO Box 7070, Kampala, T257054. Has films, concerts and talks, library and all UK newspapers, excellent facilities. All British Councils offer e-mail facilities and for a small fee they will send and receive messages. *Ugandan-German Cultural Society*, PO Box 11778, T259617, F251648, Nakasero Rd, 1000-1900 Mon-Fri, 1400-1900 Sat.

Embassies (E), High Commissions (HC) and Consulates (C) *Algeria*, 6 Kololo, Acacia Ave, T232689. *Austria*, 6 Entebbe Rd, behind the UCB building, T235796. *Belgium* (E), Parliament Ave, T230659/250304. *Burundi* (E), Plot 7, Bandeli Rise, in Bugolobui area, T221697, has moved from Nakasero area, serves non-Ugandans. Visa for Burundi US$20, 2 photos issued in 24 hrs. *Canada*, T258141. *China*, 112 Luthull Ave, T220379/220263/220691. *RD Congo*, 22 Kololo, T346605. *Denmark* (E), 17/19 Hannington Rd or 3 Lumumba Ave, T256783/256687/250928/235659/250926. *Ethiopia* (E), 7 Hse 7A Okurut Cls, near Uganda Museum on Kira Rd, T241325/241149. Visas for Ethiopia cost US$63 and are issued in 24 hrs. *France* (E), PO Box 7218, Embassy House, 9/11 Parliament Ave, T24210/242176. *Sheraton* Hotel Bldg, T347223. *Germany* (E), PO Box 7294, 15 Philip Rd, T343136/256768. *Greece*, 17 Kampala Rd, T230056/230952. *Ireland*, 12 Acacia Ave, T344344/344348. *Italy* (E), PO Box 4646, 10 Hill Lane, Kololo, T256879/241566/250448. *Japan*, 15 Rm 8 Kawalya Kagwa Cls, T347983. *Kenya* (HC), PO Box 5220, Gaba Rd, T267694/268536/267042. *Libya*, 26 Kololo Hill Drive, T258674. *Netherlands*, 8 Nakasero Ln, T234527/234708/234802/231861. *Nigerian*, 28 Elizabeth Ave, T343465/235401. *Norway* (E), 20 Upper Kololo Terrace, T341789/243621. *Russia*, 24 Bazarabusa Drive, T221393/221396/343808. *Rwanda* (E), PO Box 2468, Plot 2, Nakaima Rd, T224045, opposite Uganda Museum, Kira Rd. Visas for Rwanda, single entry US$20, multiple entries US$30, 2 passport photos, valid 3 months, immediate issue. 3 Bandali Rise, T221816/341338. *South Africa*, 8 Kisozi Complex, Kyagwe Rd, T231007/231011/231013. *Sweden*, Impala House, Kimathi Ave, T236031/236636. *Switzerland* (C), PO Box 4187, T67305/41574. *Tanzania* (HC), PO Box 5750, 6 Kagera Rd, T236245/342890. *UK* (HC), PO Box 7070, 10/12 Parliament Ave, T257054/5/257303. *USA* (E), PO Box 7007, British High Commission Building, 10/12 Parliament Ave, T259791/2/3, T269467/233902/220058. The following countries handle diplomatic affairs for Uganda from their Nairobi Embassies or High Commissions (see page 104): *Australia*, *Austria*, *Canada*, *Japan*, *Greece*, *Zimbabwe*, *Zambia*.

Hospitals & medical services There are several hospitals but the quality of care varies. *Nsambya*, PO Box 7161, T268016. A private Catholic Mission hospital was undoubtedly the best through the difficult years although the difference is now reduced. *Mulago*, adjoining Makerere University, PO Box 7161, T268016. Has had an enormous amount of foreign aid invested in it. The infrastructure is recently much improved (there is running water etc), and there are doctors available. Many of the staff suffer from apathy (not really surprising considering the wages that they get paid) and it is often necessary to pay to get attention. You will also have to buy drugs at local pharmacies. At the *International Health Centre* in the Pentecostal Church building, an excellent medical service is available. A malarial blood testing service takes 20 mins and malaria treatments are in stock. Health Centre T341291.

Tour companies & travel agents *Abercrombie & Kent*, PO Box 7799, T242495/9, F242490. *Afrique Voyages*, PO Box 10895, T251366, F242437. *Air Masters*, PO Box 5649, T250267, F255288. *African Pearl Safaris*, PO Box 4562, Embassy House, Parliament Ave, T233566/235700, F235770. An Australian/Ugandan partnership, does trips to the gorillas as well as to most other parts of Uganda. *Afri Tours and Travel Ltd*, 18 Shimoni Rd, Flat A2 (opposite *Nile International Hotel*), PO Box 5187, T233596, F232307. Specialize safari planning, domestic air charters, hotel and lodge bookings and conference planning, are the concessionaire for *Sambiya River Lodge & Tented Camp*. *Belex Tours*, PO Box 10542, T231387/244590, F234252. *Blackline Tours*, PO Box 6968, Blacklines House, Dewinton Rd, T255520, F254240. *Crimux Tours*, PO Box 4458, T258266, F250324. *Delmira*, PO Box 9098, T235499, F231927, delmira@imul.com. *Express Transport*, PO Box 353, T259029. *Hippo Tours*, PO Box 16183, T230727. *Flyway*, PO Box 6263, T233207. *Hot Ice*, PO Box 151, Kampala, T242733, F244779. Run by a British family who have lived in East Africa for many years, very experienced and versatile. *Jet Tours*, PO Box 5710, T245158, F235292. *Jumbo Tours*, PO Box 11420, T255317. *KEB Creative Tours*, PO Box 87663,

T250839. *Luxury Tours*, PO Box 10842, T256815. *Nile Safaris*, PO Box 12135, Farmers House, Parliament Ave, T245092, F245093, Tx61283. Tours ranging from 1 day to 19 days. *Pearl Africa Travel*, PO Box 1102, T232730. *Rwenzori Mountain Tours and Travel*, PO Box 10549, Impala House, T321290, F241754. *Safari Seekers*, PO Box 7493, T235165, F245597. *SM Tours and Travel Ltd*, PO Box 5184, 54 Kampala Rd, T254738, F258785. *Spear Touring Safaris*, PO Box 5914, T232395, F257239. *Speedbird*, PO Box 10101, Kampala, 1st Floor. *Sheraton Hotel* Arcade or National Insurance Building, T234669, F234252. *Sunshine Tours*, PO Box 5011, Kampala Rd, Georgiadis Chambers, T243255, F231927. *Uganda Incoming Tours*, PO Box 2633, T230910. *Uganda Voyages Ltd*, PO Box 10805 3, Parliament Ave, T242437/251366/251367, F242437. *Vacational Tours*, PO Box 10460, T236211, F236211. *Value Tours*, PO Box 8316, T250072. *Volcanoes Tours*, PO Box 22818, T346464/5, F341718, volcanoes@infocom.co.ug, www.VolcanoesSafaris.com (also in the UK: PO Box 16345, London, SW1X 0ZD, T0171-2357897, F0171-2351780, volcanoes@mailbox.co.uk), offers tailor-made safaris, also runs 3 properties. *VIP Tours*, PO Box 4443, T234658.

Tourist offices *The Uganda Tourist Board*, staff are very helpful, but may 'forget' to tell you about local disturbances. It is advised to cross check with the embassies for this advice. The office is situated on the 1st floor of the little shopping centre above a small courtyard on Kimathi Ave near the junction with Parliament Ave, T342197, F342188, utb@starcom.co.ug. *The Uganda Wildlife Authority*, PO Box 3530, Headquarters, Plot 3, Kintu Rd, Nakasero, T346287/8/9/90, F346291, director@uwahq. uu.imul.com, www.visituganda.com is the authority in charge of all Uganda's National Parks and game reserves. The main office is close to the *Sheraton* Hotel on the Kintu Rd (300 metres). Arrange to pay for and collect permits to see the gorillas from here. Take matuta for museum but stay on for another kilometre, friendly, take bookings for Mgahinga NP made over the radio, and you don't have to pay in advance. Bwindi bookings must be paid for. Gorilla tours are frequently reported to be fully booked when enquiries are made here. However, on arrival at the National Parks there are often vacancies. Alternatively, the Backpackers Hostel and Campsite is an excellent source of up to date information about Uganda. The visitors book is a compilation of many travellers experiences.

Uganda

Entebbe

0°4'N 32°28'E
Phone code: 042
Colour map 2, grid B2

Entebbe is the home of Uganda's international airport. Entebbe became famous in 1976 when an Air France plane from Israel was hijacked and was forced to land there. The Jewish passengers were held hostage as demands were made for the release of prisoners in Israeli jails. All but one of the prisoners were rescued when Israeli paratroopers stormed the airport building. The raid actually took place in an old part of the airport which is no longer used. You can see the control tower of this building on the drive to the new terminal. The airplane from the hijack is being converted into a beach bar near the airport.

Entebbe is situated on the shores of Lake Victoria, about 30 kilometres from Kampala, and until 1962 was the administrative capital of the country. On the drive down to Entebbe you will pass a signpost of the **Kajansi Fish Farm** which used to be home to a number of huge crocodiles. It is a very good birdwatching spot.

At the turn of the 19th century the colonialists built their administrative centre at Entebbe and some government offices are still located here, including the Ministry of Works, Ministry of Agriculture and Ministry of Health. State House, the official residence of the Head of State is also located in Entebbe.

One relic from former times is the **Cannon** in the square in front of the Entebbe Club, captured from the Germans during the First World War (see page 530). It bears the maker's name and date, Krupp of Essen, 1917.

Colonial Entebbe Walking along the criss-cross of lanes between the main road and the lake shore there are a number of beautiful old buildings. Most of these were built when Entebbe was the capital of the Uganda Protectorate – they have painted red roofs and wide verandahs and are used mainly as Government departments and ministries. Particularly attractive, and recently repainted is the Ministry of Agriculture building which dates from the 1920s.

Botanical Gardens The Botanical Gardens were established around the turn of the century by the Protectorate Government and the first curator was a Mr Whyte. There was originally a natural forest and the gardens were used as a research ground for the introduction of various exotic fruits and ornamental plants to Uganda. There are species in the gardens from all over the world and they include plants like cocoa trees, and rubber plants that were introduced to see how well they would thrive in Uganda's climate and soils.

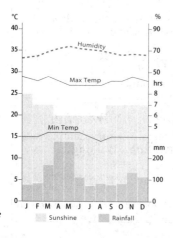

Climate: Entebbe

Throughout all the troubles the Gardens were relatively well maintained and have survived quite well. However, some of the trees have died natural deaths and have not been replaced. Many of the trees still have their metal labels on them, and there is a small patch of virgin forest down close to the lake shore. Walking through this (there are well maintained paths) you will experience lots of different noises and smells, and it is worth remembering that large areas of Uganda were once forested like this patch. For people spending longer in Uganda, there is also a very good plant nursery. The Johnny Weismuller 'Tarzan' films were shot in the Botanical Gardens.

■ *To get there from Kampala, take a matatu – they go every few minutes and take about 45 minutes, costing US$1. Stay on until the turning off to the right to Entebbe town which is just after a Shell petrol station. Walk down Portal Road (which heads towards the Lake Victoria Hotel and the airport) for about a 100 yards when you will see Lugard Avenue forking off to your left. Follow this until you see the sign for the Botanical Gardens on your left. There is a small charge for using camera or video recorder. No café or snack bar so take a drink on a hot day.*

Entebbe Wildlife Education Centre

At Entebbe is the zoo which was originally established as an animal orphanage and gradually developed into zoo with a wide range of species. Up until fairly recently it was a fairly miserable sight, and a place to avoid. However it has just been renamed the Entebbe Wildlife Education Centre and attempts are being made to improve the conditions. Large amounts of aid money are being spent on the rehabilitation. The master plan has been designed by experts from the New York Zoological Society and it will incorporate an educational centre as well as dormitories for school children and other visitors. The proposals for the Centre itself include replicating some of the country's ecological zones, such as savannah, wetlands and tropical forest. The main features will be a forested reserve for primates and an island surrounded by moats for chimpanzees.

The **Geological Museum** past the Wildlife Education Centre is unfortunately now derelict.

Kigungu Landing

Located about five kilometres off the Airport Road is the place where the first Catholic Missionaries to Uganda, Rev Fr Simon Lourdel and Brother Amans of the Society of White Fathers, landed on 17 February 1879. There is a small brick church marking the spot and a memorial plaque. There is a small fishing village here nearby.

Kasenyi Fishing Village

This fishing village is located six kilometres off the Entebbe-Kampala road. Both traditional and more modern techniques are used today – often a canoe with an outboard motor attached. Nile perch and tilapia are amongst a number of species caught. You will be able to see fishermen mending their nets and boats and it is possible to arrange a trip to some of the nearby islands.

Uganda

Entebbe

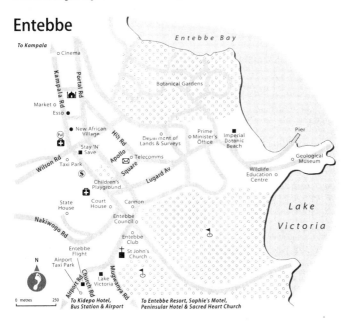

It is possible to get local boats to the Sese Islands. Boats leave for all the islands at about 1500 US$7.50. However, getting out to the boats is quite an experience. The shoreline has 20 metres of mud and weeds. Local men on the shore will carry people on their shoulders to and from the boats. Competition among the men can be fierce and the experience intimidating on the return journey, when the boat is suddenly surrounded by men all shouting and trying to pull you and your bags out of the boat. The best advice is to sit on your bags and clearly indicate your choice of porter.

Sleeping   **A+** *Lake Victoria*, PO Box 15, Circular Rd, T20644/20645/21078, F20404. Newly refurbished hotel, is often described as the best in Uganda, the facilities are excellent and include a swimming pool and the nearby golf course, swimming for non-residents at US$7, snacks and drinks available and hot showers. The wine list is reported to be rather expensive and somewhat limited. If you are flying out of Entebbe on the early morning British Airways flight you can get a discount to stay here and you will be provided with transport to the airport the next morning, ask for details at the British Airways office in Kampala.

A *Botanic Beach Hotel*, off Lugard Ave on route to Botanical Gardens, PO Box 90, T20800/23/32/66. Fairly modern, bars, restaurant, comfortable and quiet, free transfer to airport, has been undergoing very extensive renovations recently, very loud disco on Saturday.

B *Entebbe Resort Beach*, PO Box 380, T20934/20941/21012, F21028, left after the *Entebbe Club* and go through the golf course towards the lake. Banda accommodation, there is a beach although as with all of Lake Victoria remember that swimming here you risk contracting bilharzia. **B** *Peninsular Hotel*, south of centre, PO Box 390, T042-20391. Restaurant and bar, good standard, small (8 rooms).

C *Sophie's Motel*, Plot 3, Alice Reef Rd, south of centre, PO Box 6186, Kampala, T041-321370/320885, mobile 75-645471/2, F041-321384. Range of rooms, pleasant location, quite small, 6 rooms, 3 in the main building and 3 chalets, more rooms are being added, has a courtesy bus to and from the airport. Recommended. **C** *Stay 'n' Save*, corner of Kampala Rd and Wilson Rd, PO Box 7666, Kampala, T21044. Quite central, but not particularly good value. **D** *The Entebbe Flight Motel*, new mid-range accommodation, conveniently sited for the airport. **E** *Kidepo*, beyond the *Lake Victoria Hotel* on the airport road. It is rather basic and not particularly good value, but is convenient if you cannot get to Kampala, or have an early flight.

Camping   at Entebbe Resort, beach, excellent facilities. Highly recommended. US$10 per person.

Eating & bars   Apart from the hotels themselves the best place to eat is the **2** *Entebbe Club*, it is very pleasant with tables outside and serves up a fairly limited menu – include steak, fish and chips and such like, this was the club for colonial officials. Doesn't do food in the evenings.

1 *China Garden*, Kampala Rd, near *Stay 'n' Save*. Newly opened, good service. **1** *Esso Restaurant*, Kampala Rd. Simple fare. **1** *New Africa Village*, Kampala Rd. Pleasant garden bar.

Entertainment   **Sport (participant) Golf**: At *Entebbe Club*, US$10 for 18 holes. **Sport (spectator) Cricket**: Played in the middle of the Golf course, very pleasant, spectators can watch from the Entebbe Club.

Shopping   **Crafts** on the road down to Entebbe there are a number of stalls selling everything from pottery, mats, baskets and a huge range of fruit and vegetables. Prices are not as cheap as you would expect – the sellers obviously are used to people buying on their way to and from the airport. They include brightly coloured woven baskets which are made by Nubian women. Generations of Nubians have lived close to Entebbe – but they have maintained their cultural identity.

Maps the Department of Surveys and Mapping has its office in Entebbe – turn left opposite the playground, walk down the road and it is on the left. The staff are very helpful and will do their best to dig out the maps that you want. This is also a good source of Kenyan maps, which are not available in Nairobi for security reasons. Get a receipt if you do buy anything, as there are reports of the money disappearing into the wrong hands. Many however are out of stock although the department is in the process of re-printing many of the old series.

Air Airport tax (departure) for international flights is US$20 per person.   **Transport**

Road Minibus from the matatu park in **Kampala**. They go every few minutes and take about 1 hour, costing US$1. From the airport to Entebbe town a taxi should cost about US$3. **Bus**: Kampala to Jinja: 1½ hours, US$1.

Kampala

East from Jinja to Tororo and Mount Elgon

Compared to the west of Uganda the east part receives relatively few visitors apart from those passing through on the way to and from Kenya. Some travellers however do stop off at Jinja and interest in climbing Mount Elgon from the Uganda side is once again increasing.

Jinja

0°25'N 33°12'E
Phone code: 043
Colour map 2, grid C2

The town of Jinja is located on the road to Kenya 80 kilometres from Kampala and 143 kilometres to the Kenyan border. It is perhaps best known for being the source of the Nile and is located at the head of Napoleon Gulf, on the northern end of Lake Victoria, the second largest freshwater lake in the world (after Lake Superior). During the bad times in Uganda, Jinja, like most other towns in the country, fell into disrepair. However there was one important exception to this – through the enthusiasm of one individual in the Jinja Parks Department the gardens, roundabouts and verges were kept immaculately – the flower beds were always planted and weeded and the lawns mowed. In recent years Jinja, has recovered impressively, the roads are being repaired and the town centre rehabilitated. As you walk through the town you will see the old colonial and Asian bungalows in their spacious gardens. Many of these are now overcrowded and dilapidated, although some have been renovated.

Sights　**Source of the Nile**　The source of the Nile was actually at the site of the Rippon Falls. These were submerged during the construction of the Owen Falls Dam, however ripples can still be seen from the picnic area. It is lovely to sit on the lawn in the shade listening to the birds and watching the swirling river below. The islets and rocks recorded by Speke (see box, page 582) have disappeared with the building of the Owen Falls Dam. There is a plaque marking the spot from which the Nile begins its journey through Uganda, Sudan and Egypt.

To get to the Source of the Nile you can either walk or take a bicycle taxi from the town centre – you will have no problems finding someone to take you. If you are walking, go along Bell Avenue out beyond the Sports Club and then turn left along Cliff Road. Entrance fee US$1.00. On the other side of the river is a monument indicating the spot where Speke stood, when he first sighted the source of the Nile. There is no public access but the site can be reached on foot, via a circuitous route with the assistance of the local populace.

....

Speke and the source of the Nile

During his 1860-63 journey with Grant from Zanzibar to Khartoum via the west shore of Lake Victoria (see box page 285) Speke was the first European to see the source of the Nile in 1862, from the other side of the inlet to the present picnic area. He recorded the moment thus:

　"Most beautiful was the scene, nothing could surpass it! It was the very perfection of the kind of effect aimed at in a highly-kept

park; with a magnificent stream from 600 to 700 yards wide, dotted with islets and rocks, the former occupied by fishermens' huts, the latter by terns and crocodiles basking in the sun, flowing between fine high grassy banks, with rich trees and plantains in the background. The expedition had now performed its functions; old Father Nile without any doubt rises in the Victoria Nyanza."

....

Uganda

Owen Falls Dam The Owen Falls Dam was built in 1954 and it supplies most of Uganda, and a good part of Kenya, with electricity. During the turmoil of the Amin period a group of dedicated engineers managed to keep the generators going almost without interruption. The falls themselves were hidden during the construction of the dam, but the dam and the new falls that it creates are impressive in themselves. The main road from Kampala to the east crosses the dam, so if you are travelling by bus or in a matatu try and get a seat on the appropriate side (left if you are heading east) in order to get a good view. Because of the dam's strategic and economic importance and its perceived vulnerability you are not allowed to take photographs.

Bujagali Falls Downstream from the Owen Falls Dam are the Bujagali Falls. These can be reached by crossing the Owen Falls Dam (if you are coming from Kampala) and turning northwards at the Kyabazinga roundabout. The Bujagali Falls are approximately nine kilometres from Jinja (two-hour walk), go straight on from Clive Road, past the roundabout, continue for a further seven kilometres, entrance fee US$2. It is a spectacular area with about one kilometre of raging water. There is a legend that says that a man called Mr Bujagali sometimes sits on the river on a bark cloth mat.

There's a bar, campsite and restaurant called the **Bujagali Falls Campsite**. Good security. Opened in 1997 and recently taken over by *Adrift* - for details see page 571. Beautifully situated. From here the White Water Rafting on the White Nile is

Uganda

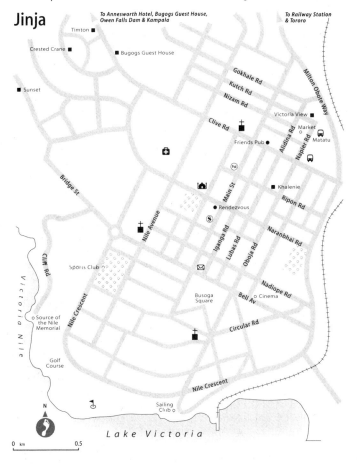

Bishop Hannington

Coming from Kampala, a little beyond Jinja on the right, is a place called Buluba (meaning the place of Luba, once chief of the area) which is the site of some historical interest. For it was here that Bishop Hannington, who in 1884 was consecrated as the first Bishop of the Diocese of Eastern Equatorial Africa, met his death. Hannington kept a detailed diary during his journeys and it is through these, and the stories from the survivors, that we know what happened.

James Hannington had first visited East Africa in 1882 as the leader of a party of reinforcements for the Victoria Nyanza Mission in Uganda. However, he had suffered severely from dysentery and had been forced to return to Britain. However, after being made bishop he began to plan his return to Africa. At this time the route into Uganda was from Zanzibar, through what is now Tanzania, to the south of Lake Victoria. However, in 1883 a new route was used, through Kenya, via Busoga, to the north of the Lake. This route through Masai country was more direct and had less harsh climatic conditions.

However, in October 1884 the Kabaka of Buganda, King Mutesa I, died and was succeeded by his son Mwanga. The missionaries in Uganda now found themselves in a position that had changed from one of tolerance to one of suspicion. Hannington arrived on the East African coast in January 1885 and made plans to use the Masai route. The missionaries in Buganda, on hearing of this, wrote that the current political situation in Buganda was such that entering by what was considered to be the back door, through Busoga, was extremely dangerous. However, the warning arrived about two weeks after Hannington set off.

Hannington's only real mistake was that he did not stick to his plans as set out in a letter to the missionaries in Buganda. He told them that he would go overland as far as Kavirondo on Lake Victoria where the mission boat should meet him and he would enter Buganda by boat. This would mean he would avoid entering Uganda through Busoga, which was so sensitive. Mwanga had been told that those entering Buganda from the East (that is, Busoga) would destroy the Kingdom of Buganda. Indeed the mission boat did go to the northeast of the Lake in early October, but hearing nothing of the Bishop it left after two days. The missionaries based in Buganda assured Mwanga that the Bishop would not enter through Busoga, so when he did, it appeared as a calculated deceit.

On the 21 October Hannington reached the headquarters of Luba, the chief of the area of Busoga. He was imprisoned, and on the orders of messengers from Buganda, speared to death and his porters massacred.

In March 1890 a small boy who had been with Hannington but who had survived, arrived in the camp of Jackson, another missionary, who was on his way to Uganda. He had with him Hannington's skull (although the lower jaw bone was missing) which was identified by his gold teeth, the soles of his boots, a rubber hot water bottle and the lid of an Army and Navy canteen. There was also another smaller skull, which was believed to be that of Pinto who was the Goan cook who had accompanied Hannington. The remains eventually found their way to Kampala and on 31st December 1892 they were buried on Namirembe Hill.

---

organized in conjunction with *Adrift*. Sited eight kilometres out of town on the Kampala Road, well signposted.

Sleeping **C** *Bugogo Guesthouse* (near *Annesworth*). Comfortable. Recommended. **C** *CC Hotel and Tourism Training Institute*, previously called the *Crested Crane*, PO Box 444, 4-4 Hannington Square, T21513/4/5. This sprawling building has clearly seen better days, it is rather lacking in character and distinctly shabby. However, as it is a training establishment for hotel staff, they are very helpful and look smart. Food available on the first floor. **C** *Hotel Daniel*, 300 metres south of *Sunset*. Comfortable, same price bracket. **C** *Sunset*, this hotel has a fine location overlooking the Owen Falls Dam and is set in lovely gardens, it is rarely full and it is possible to negotiate the price down, does not take plastic.

Uganda

D *Annesworth*, PO Box 1253, 3 Nalufenya Crescent, T20086. Located not far from the *Crested Crane Hotel* and is one of the old Asian buildings. **D** *Timton*, Clive Rd roughly opposite the *YMCA*. Also converted from an old Asian built building, not bad value, camping possible. **D** *Triangle*, same area as the *Annesworth* and *Tim Tom*. Reasonably comfortable, excellent food, varied menu.

E *Kahlenje*, Ripon Rd, centre of town. Clean and friendly, good value. **E** *Khalinie*, Lubas Rd. Friendly and fairly clean, with own shower. **E** *Penguin Guesthouse*, very basic, cheap, security a bit lax, sited near the *Hotel Triangle*, just out of town. **E** *Victoria View Inn*, close to the market in the town centre and is good value, it is clean and friendly, sited on Kutch St, down by the lake.

Camping *Paddlers Inn, Backpackers Lodge and Campsite*, Lubogo Rd, Jinja, next to the old Triangle Hotel, T30079/22381, F22050. Camping, double rooms, dormitories, restaurant, bar, gym, volley ball, videos, hot showers.

Eating There are a few in town worth trying besides those attached to hotels. **2** *Friend's Pub*, Clive Rd near the market. Fairly straightforward grills. **2** *Munch's Corner*, Main St/Clive Rd next to Caltex. Good cheap Indian food, friendly and clean. **2** *Rendezvous*, Main St. Simple menu, but reasonable value.

Entertainment **Sport (participant)** There is a **Golf Club** on the shore of Lake Victoria and the Victoria Nile off Nile Crescent. The **Sailing Club** is off Nile Crescent. There is **tennis** and **squash** at the **Sports Club** where Nile Crescent swings north. **White water rafting**: Rafting starts 10 kilometres south of Bujagali Falls, see page 636 for details under entry for Bujagadi Falls Campsite.

Money No credit cards accepted. *Forex bureaux* give better rates and quicker service than banks.

Transport **Bus** Jinja to Kampala, 1½ hours, US$1.50. **Matatu** Jinja to Busia, US$3. From Kampala to Jinja by matatu takes 1-2 hours and costs US$2.50. Bicycle taxis are called *Boda-Bodas*. Matatus in Uganda tend to be better than in Kenya. Nissans with individual (rather than bench) seats frequently used.

Tororo

Situated in the far east of Uganda this is close to the border with Kenya and many people pass through on the way to and from the border crossing at Malaba. Its major claim to fame is the rock named after it, which can be seen from miles around. Built during the colonial period in the late 1940s the Tororo Cement Works made an important contribution to the development of Uganda as it took away the necessity of importing cement from Kenya. It functioned well until Amin's time. As everything in Uganda began to fall apart so did the roof of the cement works – it collapsed under the weight of cement dust as no-one bothered to sweep it.

0°45'N 34°12'E Colour map 2, grid C2

From Jinja the road to Kenya continues first northeast and then swings east. You will pass through the town of Iganga. This has wide streets bordered by shops and houses with broad verandas. The road to the border is good and you will pass through fairly typical Ugandan scenery – clusters of small huts surrounded by farmland, as well as areas of verdant bush and elephant grass with the occasional anthill sticking up. There are stretches of hills, between which are marshy swamps. There are also many mango trees in this part of Uganda and during the mango season they can be bought on the roadside. As you approach the border you can either continue straight on to Tororo for the Malaba crossing or take a right turning to Busia. There is a road block at this turning which is there to stop smugglers – it seems to do little more than collect bribes. From about this point you should be able to see the Tororo rock sticking up in the distance.

Tororo Rock The Tororo rock is a volcanic plug which rises to about 1,800 metres above sea level. It is possible to climb and the views from the top are fantastic. There are steps and ladders to help you get to the summit, and the climb takes about an hour.

Sleeping **C** *Rock*, PO Box 42, T4458/4426. Located a few kilometres out of town beyond the golf course, run by *Uganda Hotels* this is a pleasant enough establishment, set in gardens. **D** *Crystal*, medium-sized hotel with views of Tororo Rock, rooms are self-contained and have balconies, simple and clean, restaurant and bar, good value. **E** *Co-op*, one of the cheaper hotels in Tororo, not particularly good value and has water supply problems. **E** *Tororo Christian Guest House*, rather run down with irregular water supply.

Transport **Road** Tororo is 217 kilometres to Kampala, about 3½ hours by matatu or bus. They go frequently – however if you are heading for Kenya there is little reason to stop over at Tororo now that Akamba Bus do a direct service from Kampala to Nairobi.

Mbale

1°8'N 34°12'E
Phone code: 045
Colour map2, grid C2

This town in the eastern part of Uganda in the foothills of Mount Elgon, giving it a pleasant climate. Mbale shows clearly the Asian influence on towns in Uganda – in particular many of the buildings have the distinctive verandah that is seen all over East Africa. It is a bustling market town and for many years you could buy all sorts of things in Mbale smuggled from Kenya that were unobtainable in Kampala. During the colonial years eucalyptus plantations were planted all around Mbale as an anti-mosquito measure. During the past 25 years the trees have gradually been cut down and malaria, which was once eradicated from the area, has returned. There is a large **Commonwealth War Graves Cemetery**. Mbale is also home of the **Islamic University**, one of only two such institutions in Africa, founded in 1988.

Nkokenjeru Not far from Mbale is a large rock called Nkokenjeru which means the White Rock. On this, Idi Amin planned to build to huge international hotel and conference centre. The building began with the construction of the road – almost a motorway – up to the top of the rock. That was as far as it got and the complex itself was never begun. There are wonderful views and it is sometimes possible to see peregrine falcons which live on the rock.

Imbalu dances If you happen to be in this area during even years you may manage to see some of the local festivities of the Imbalu people, as well as the mass circumcision ceremonies of the Bugisu and Sebei people. The festivities reach a climax during December and involve singing, dancing, drumming and general merrymaking (see box, page 587).

Rock art paintings About 25 kilometres northwest of Mbale are the **Kakoro Rock Paintings** which are on a koppie near the village of Kabwangasi. To get there take a matatu going north on the road to Kumi to Nakaloke. From there take a bicycle taxi as there is little alternative traffic on this road. Kakora is approximately 12 kilometres from Nakaloke.

Bugisu circumcision

The Bugisu have a strong belief in their rites – and the ceremony of circumcision is very much an important part of the life cycle. All men must undergo circumcision and males who die before they have been circumcised will be circumcised before they are buried in order to complete their life on earth.

Circumcision takes place every other year and is performed on young men aged between 14 and 25. The circumcision season is said to be marked by the appearance of a strange bird whose singing marks the beginning of the preparations. The elders gather under the clan tree – which is said to be older than the memory of man itself. They then begin training the candidates for the rituals, which last three days.

On the first day the young man is smeared with sorghum paste all over the body. He wears the traditional dress of animal skins and a head dress, puts three heavy bangles on each leg and then visits his relatives, singing and dancing. The songs he sings are mainly praising his forefathers and the gods. Every so often he stops and leaps high in the air.

On the second day his hair is cut and he is allowed to bathe – the last opportunity before the ceremony proper begins. This symbolizes the death of the past and of what he has been, and a new beginning. The white sorghum paste is again smeared on his body. The singing and dancing continues and this evening is one of great celebration amongst the people of the village.

On the morning of the circumcision the young man wakes at first light and is again smeared with sorghum paste. He then sets off to visit his maternal uncles who give him gifts of cows or goats which are part of the bride price paid by his father. As the day progresses and the sun gets overhead the man returns home where he is taken down to the river by the men who wash him thoroughly from the waist to the knees. He is then brought at a slow pace to the ground which is traditionally used for these ceremonies. On the ground is a Y-shaped stick which he picks up and holds behind his head. The circumcision itself is fairly quickly over and a whistle is blown to announce that the candidate has been successful. Occasionally it happens that a man will try to run away – but this is looked upon with great shame as the epitome of disgrace and cowardice.

Traditionally once a man has been circumcised he can sit in on tribal meetings and participate in decision-making, and is allowed to marry. Only once you have been through what is known as the pain of the knife can you be called a man, and it is said that, just like birth and death, it can only be done once in one's lifetime. Recent travellers have indicated that they have been allowed to witness part of the circumcision ceremony in and around Budadiri.

Uganda

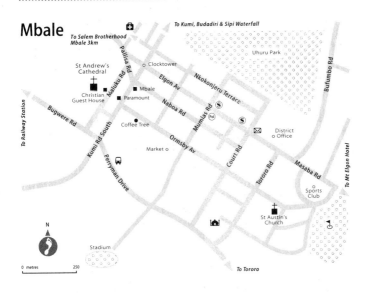

Mbale

To Salem Brotherhood
Mbale 3km

To Kumi, Budadiri & Sipi Waterfall

Uhuru Park

Pallisa Rd

Clocktower

St Andrew's
Cathedral

Elgon Av

Nkokonjeru Terrace

Bufumbo Rd

Maluku Rd

Mbale

Christian
Guest House

Paramount

Naboa Rd

Mumias Rd

To Railway Station

Bugwere Rd

Coffee Tree

Kumi Rd South

Ormsby Av

District
Office

Market

Court Rd

Masaba Rd

To Mt Elgon Hotel

Perryman Drive

Tororo Rd

Sports
Club

St Austin's
Church

N

Stadium

0 metres 250

To Tororo

Ask permission from the local farmer before climbing the koppie. Further north are the **Nyero Rock Paintings** near the town of Kumi (see page 590).

Sleeping **C** *Mount Elgon*, PO Box 670, T3612. Located a little way out of town, run by *Uganda Hotels* it has recently been done up and is a comfortable place to stay, set in peaceful gardens, chalet accommodation, nice afternoon snacks. **C** *West End Guest House*, off the main road from Kampala opposite the Lions Playground (signposted). Clean and well run. Evening meals rather limited.

D *Mukwano Hotel* (previously New Michaelsworth). All rooms s/c with balcony. Bucket showers. **D-E** *Salem Brotherhood Mbale*, PO Box 1558, T/F045-33368. Salem Brotherhood is a Christian NGO providing medical care and community support. It is partly funded by the SB in Germany but also raises funds through income generating projects like a conference centre, the guest houses and sale of handicrafts. All profits made go towards the running of the Health Centre and Children's Home. There is a variety of accommodation from self-contained to camping facilities. Fresh home-grown food is available. Highly recommended. Located northwest of the town on the road to Kolonyi.

E *Christian Guest House*, this has a range of rooms and is good value. Recent travellers report it has become very run down and dirty, and has a restaurant attached. **E** *Mbale*, rather run down, basic but cheap. **E** *Mount Elgon View*, clean and friendly, in the building of the *Forex and Nile Beer Rooftop* restaurant. Irregular water and power supply. **E** *Paramount*, a pleasant clean hotel with a bar and restaurant, this is not bad value, however, this hotel is currently closed – possibly long-term, no current sign of renovation work. **E** *Sunrise Inn*, PO Box 2607, T3090. Newly opened, about 500 metres further out on the road past *Mount Elgon Hotel*. Sunrise Inn is very popular and needs to be booked well in advance. Very good meals – probably the best in Mbale.

Camping Available at *Sipi Falls Rest House*, US$3.

Eating **3** *Mount Elgon*, the best place to eat in Mbale, if you don't mind a 30-minute walk, the food is very good and the setting makes the walk and cost worth while. **2** *Coffee Tree Bar and Restaurant*, town centre, good value. **1** *Wimpys*, Cathedral Rd. Does good steak rolls at US$2 each.

Transport **Road** Mbale is 272 kilometres from Kampala, about 3 hours or less via the new tarmac road from Iganga on the Jinja-Tororo road. It is 1½ hours from Busia on the Kenyan border.

Directory **Tourist Offices** There is a tourist office in Mbale, located not far from the *Mount Elgon Hotel*, which provides information about climbing Mt Elgon. The tourist office also stocks the informative leaflet and map of the Mount Elgon Forest Exploration Centre, and can confirm accommodation availability there. There are maps as well as up to date advice, and anyone planning to climb the mountain is advised to visit the office.

Budadiri, is a small village about 20 kilometres from Mbale near the entrance to the National Park. It is a more convenient base to stay prior to climbing Mount Elgon. Matatus run frquently between Mbale and Budadiri from the taxi park at the outskirts of Mbale. The route for drivers is to take the Kumi road from Mbale for six kilometres before turning right onto the Moroto road. The turn off for Budadiri is three kilometres along the Moroto road on the right. Only basic food supplies are available in Budadiri. Buy tinned foods or luxuries in Mbale. **Sleeping** **E** *Wagagai Hotel*, next to the NP office offers basic accommodation or camping. **E** *Lwala Paradise Hotel*, simple and basic rooms. On Mount Elgon the only option is camping, although a recent traveller reported that there are huts at each camp where you can sleep.

North to Soroti and Gulu

The north of Uganda can be divided into the northwest, north and northeast. The northwest covers what is known as West Nile – that is, anything beyond Murchison Falls and includes Pakwach, Nebbi, Arua and Moyo. The north includes Lira, Gulu and Kitgum. The main towns in the northeast are Soroti, Karamoja, Moroto and Kotido. There are conflicting reports as to how safe it is to travel. In late 1995 the precaution of only travelling in convoy was relaxed. However, in early 1996 attacks on travellers and on Gulu and surrounding areas appear to have increased.

*The northeast of Uganda, bordering on Sudan to the north and Kenya to the east is one of beautiful scenery ranging from mountains to vast, flat, empty plains. It is a magnificent part of Uganda and so totally different to the southern part of the country. For information about **Kidepo National Park**, see section on National Parks, page 639.*

The inaccessibility of the north of Uganda, as well as the relative insecurity of the area compared to the rest of Uganda discourages visitors. However, some European residents have indicated that the security concerns have been overstated. Although security in the north has improved dramatically in the last five years, this part of Uganda does still suffer from being one of the most heavily armed. There is a high proportion of male adults carrying guns and raids by bandits are not uncommon. Its remoteness and under development made it ideal terrain for the retreating soldiers of Obote after Museveni came to power and some bands of dissidents still remain, particularly between Gulu and Arua.

The most noticeable threat to date is the Lord's Resistance Army who do not appear to be affiliated with any particular religious or political group. Though they are small, in 1994 they kidnapped an expatriate working for the World Food Programme, taking his vehicle. He was released a few days later unharmed but the Ugandans he had been travelling with remained as captives. More recently, hundreds of children, mostly from the Acholi tribe, have been kidnapped by the Lord's Resistance Army who are believed to be backed by the Sudanese government. The children have been used as fighters and sex slaves. President Museveni has recently pledged to protect the Acholi people from further raids.

In an effort to increase the safety of people travelling to the north, the government have set up army posts in isolated areas, particularly the national parks, and operate travel curfews.

A main feature of travel into the north is not so much the beauty of its scenery which is quite breathtaking at times, but more the fact that it gives the visitor a glimpse of the history of the country over time from the Arab slave traders of centuries ago through the colonial era to the turmoil in Uganda from the 1970s to 1986. The current presence of tens of thousands of refugees from southern Sudan, together with the activities of the international aid agencies, has made the area around Arua an important trading zone.

All the main churches have missions in the north and their representatives in Kampala are a reliable source of information on the current situation. For example at certain times it is considered prudent to only drive in convoy. Don't let this put you off completely – but be aware of the situation.

Soroti

Although not that far north, there is something about Soroti which gives it a northerly feeling. It is a hot and airless town with a frontier atmosphere. It is the site of the **Soroti Flying School**, set up to train pilots for the whole East African region.

The drive from Soroti to Moroto is mainly through acacia thorn bush. Every so often you will see a herd of scrawny goats being looked after by a couple of young

1°43'N 33°35'E
Colour map 2, grid C2

Uganda

The Karimojong

The Karimojong are one of the tribes inhabiting the more southerly part of the district of Karamoja, which is situated in the northeast corner of Uganda. Their language is Nga Karimojong.

The marriage system is polygamous, the number of wives being limited solely by financial circumstances. No boy is allowed to marry until he has been admitted by the elders to the status of manhood. Up to this time a boy must pluck out all his pubic hair. When the time comes (there are usually a group presented at the same time) his father gives him a bull which the boy kills and shares with his male relatives. He smears himself with the dung from the entrails and gives his mother the head, neck, hump, stomach and ribs. His hair is cut by an adult male friend leaving a tuft at the back to which a short string is attached. Traditionally when the hair grows back he moulds it into two buns, one on top of the head and one at the back, with coloured clay.

When a youth has obtained manhood he may seek a wife. It is usual that he will already have at least one lover (although a girl is only supposed to have one) and if his father approves, a lover may be taken as his wife.

When a woman is about to give birth she is assisted by her female relatives. The umbilical cord is tied with fibre and cut near to the body. If the baby is a boy the cord is cut with the arrow used for bleeding cattle but if it is a girl a knife is used. The cord is buried in the cattle enclosure.

When someone dies the body is wrapped up in a hide and buried in a goat enclosure. If the person is a pauper without friends the body would simply be thrown outside the kraal and left to the wild animals.

When a husband dies the widow passes into the possession of his principal brother. He will bring a sheep to her door which he will then kill and they will smear themselves with dung from its entrails. From this time onwards she belongs to him. If there is no brother then she will pass to the son of a co-wife.

boys, or perhaps some cattle with some Karamajong guarding them. Most of the time it is very hot and dusty but at certain times of the year there are the most fantastic thunderstorms. On this road as you pass from Teso into Karamoja you go between two hills called **Akisim** and **Napak**. They are quite impressive as they can be seen for some miles around as they stand up above the plains. They mark the boundary into Karamoja.

Nyero Rock Paintings These are located in Kumi district and consist of three painted shelters close to each other. Paintings are in red and white pigment and are mainly of geometric shapes. They are believed to be between 300 and 500 years old and are regarded as being amongst the best rock paintings in Eastern Africa.

Other attractions in the area include **Moru Apeso Rock** viewing and climbing and the **River Awoja** where there is a campsite.

Sleeping C *Soroti*, PO Box 397, Serere Rd, T269. Run by *Uganda Hotels*.

Transport **Air** *CEI Aviation*, Metropole House, 8-10 Entebbe Rd, Kampala, T255825, F236097. Offer return flights to Soroti for US$380. *Eagle Airlines* and *United* offer flights at similar prices and fly daily. **Road** Soroti is a drive of about 5 hours from Kampala – a distance of about 385 kilometres. It is 128 kilometres from Lira, 113 kilometres from Mbale and about 200 kilometres from Moroto. Kampala-Moroto is less than 600 kilometres, via Soroti, and the road journey can be done in one day. There are now several buses between Kampala and Moroto.

Moroto
2°28'N 34°42'E
Colour map 2, grid B2

In the northeast of the country lie the vast open spaces of Karamoja. Here rocky mountains interrupt the plains making it an arid land of great scenic beauty. Mount Moroto, which reaches a height of about 3,400 metres above sea level offers challenging climbing to the enthusiast. It is the traditional area of the pastoralist Karamojong people (see box above).

Labwor and **Nangeya** hills to the northwest of Moroto are noted for their giant inselbergs, volcanic plugs that remain after the erosion of the cones. **Matheniko**, **Pian**, **Upe** and **Bokora** are all designated game reserves in the area around Moroto, stretching from north of Mount Elgon up to Kotido. However the title 'game reserve' is somewhat inappropriate, as there appears to be little or no game left – the result of the local firearm availability.

Sleeping **C** *Mount Moroto*, PO Box 54, T97, run by *Uganda Hotels*.

Transport **Air** The easiest way to reach Moroto. Charter flights go fairly regularly from Entebbe. **Road** Kampala to Moroto is a distance of some 840 kilometres so is not for the feeble-hearted.

Situated 352 kilometres from Kampala in the north. Lira Spinning Mill is the main economic activity in town and has recently been renovated. Town Park has fine trees and a bandstand.

Lira
2°17′N 32°57′E
Colour map 2, grid B2

Sleeping **D** *Lira*, PO Box 350, T24. Scandinavian construction, water in bowls, candles and oil lamps, laundered clothes pressed with a charcoal iron.

Transport Matatus from **Gulu** – not particularly frequent.

Gulu

Gulu is the largest town in northern Uganda and is located on the northern edge of the Murchinson Falls National Park and many people pass through it on the way to either the Murchinson Falls or to Kidepo National Park.

2°48′N 32°17′E
Colour map 2, grid B1

Bakers Fort If you have the time while you are passing through Gulu you might want to go to see Bakers Fort which is located at Patiko, about 30 kilometres north of Gulu. This was founded by Sir Samuel Baker in 1872 when he was Governor of Equatoria Province. It was built as a base from which to crush the slave trade and was later occupied by Gordon and Emin Pasha (see box, page 351). There are said to be rock paintings at Samuel Baker's camp.

The handicrafts made in the area around Gulu range from baskets to earthenware, as well as ironwork.

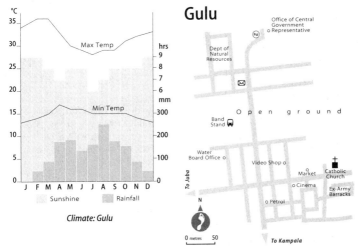

Climate: Gulu

Gulu

Uganda (side tab)

Sleeping   **C** *Acholi Inn*, PO Box 239, Gulu (Gulu) T108. Run by *Uganda Hotels* and offering fairly good services.

E *Church of Uganda Guesthouse*, simple but sound. **E** *Hotel Roma*, central, 250 metres from the bus park. Very friendly, basic but clean. Breakfast available. Recommended. **E** *Luxor Lodge*, opposite the lorry park. Fairly basic.

Transport   **Air**   There is an airstrip at Gulu which is used by small aircraft. There are no scheduled flights to Gulu but there are charter flights from Entebbe.

Road   Gulu is a distance of 328 kilometres from Kampala and is accessible via **Lira** from the east and **Masindi** from the west. The roads are not very good, worse than many areas of the country. The bitumen road stops at Karoma where you can go straight for Gulu or left for Pakwach and Arua. From here onwards you are travelling on roads which do not appear to have been touched for decades and the going is extremely slow, particularly after the rains. If you drive you must remember to buy enough petrol where you can as there are only service stations in the more developed towns, that is Gulu, Pakwach and Arua. Also, it is not wise to drive after dark because of the possibility of being stopped by guerrilla fighters or bandits. Indeed you are not able to drive through the National Park after dark and before entering you have to register your vehicle with soldiers at the check-point on the edge of the park before entering or leaving as a safety measure. **Bus**: there are daily buses to Gulu. All traffic north passes through Masindi.

Pakwach
2°28'N 31°27'E
Colour map 2, grid B1

Pakwach is a tiny town on the western edge of the park. It is little more than one street but has everything a traveller is likely to need. Despite its primitive conditions (there appears to be no sanitation in town, though there is electricity) it is a very pleasant place to stay. Being on the edge of the river, its environment is green and fertile and it is a restful place where people are very friendly.

The main reasons for being here are either to visit the park or stop by the Nile, or to cross into RD Congo. Pakwach is only a few kilometres from the border and it is easy to cross at the northern tip of Lake George. However, the notorious corruption of Congolese officials, including customs officers, means an expensive crossing particularly if you want to take your vehicle with you.

Sleeping and eating   There are a number of small hotels. A popular venue is the **E** *Training Centre* at the end of the town. Turn left down a murram road towards the lake. An NGO has developed facilities for training purposes, but which can be used by the general public. The rooms are clean and equipped with mosquito nets. There are toilets and sinks in each room but the sanitation system does not operate yet. Water is brought to you daily. The rooms cost less

Pakwach

than US$5 per night. You can also order food here which is substantial local cooking and costs around US$3-5 per meal. There are several other small restaurants. The only place in town which seems to sell cold drinks is on the right hand side at the western end of the town. It has no name but is easily identified by its garish electric lights and loud music. Beers and sodas are the same price as in all rural areas of Uganda.

Arua

3°1'N 30°58'E
Colour map 2, grid B1

Small town in northwest, located close to border with RD Congo about 500 kilometres from Kampala. Sudanese backed rebel terrorist activities occur from time to time, area probably best avoided.

Sleeping and eating C *White Rhino*, PO Box 359, T157. Water from well in garden, oil lamps and candles. *The Grid*, good value restaurant and bar frequented by aid workers, so called because it is exactly on 3 ° latitude north and 31 ° longitude east.

Transport Air Irregular flights, charter (see page 575) or with an aid agency, US$50-100 one way. **Road Matatus** and **buses** from Bomba Rd in Kampala. Take about 6 hours and cost US$12. Leave at 0300 to avoid travel in the heat. Are popular, so it is necessary to book in advance. Travellers carry lots of luggage and merchandise, so it is wise to arrive well before departure (1 hour) to ensure there is room for you and your luggage.

Moyo/Adjumani

This is one of the northernmost administrative centres in Uganda, on the border with Sudan. It is the headquarters of West Moyo, East Moyo and Obongi. It is actually on the border and is one of the major crossing points between the two countries. *3°20'N 31°50'E Colour map 2, grid B1*

It is a beautiful part of Uganda and the mountains of southern Sudan can be seen in the distance standing out against the rather flat landscape all around you. Deforestation was rife in these parts as it has been host to waves of refugees from Uganda and southern Sudan since the 1960s. In some ways this adds to the beauty of the place as you can see for miles and at night the deep inky blackness of the landscape with bright stars above is lovely, though it has obviously had a rather negative impact on the environment and on people's livelihoods.

Moyo town itself looks much like all the other towns in the north. Before independence much of this area was under cotton cultivation and therefore there were good roads, a reasonable telephone and electricity system and thriving trade centres. However, the area has suffered terribly from Uganda's troubled history. Amin came from the neighbouring district to the west and following his fall and the retreat of many of his soldiers through this area the bulk of the population were forced to flee into the Sudan. Subsequent waves of people fled to and from the area until 1986 when the NRM come to power and the majority of the Ugandans returned.

The history of Sudan has also played its part on this area and the 27-year-long civil war in that country has caused tens of thousands of refugees to seek safety in northern Uganda.

The insecurity and isolation of the area is apparent in the appalling roads, a non-existent telephone system (except for the poles which are still along the roadside) and an electricity system which relies on generators and is unreliable. The cotton industry has collapsed and with it went the wealth, commerce and trade of the area. There have been some recent improvements. Electricity came to nearby Adjumani in late 1994 and is expected to make its way to other areas over the next few years.

Adjumani

To Pakele
To UNHCR Airfield
Shops
Catholic Mission
ACORD
Dept of Entomology
Shops
MSF
Library
Office of the Assistant Central Government Representative
N
Old Cotton Ginnery
To River & Oliji
0 metres 100

An irony in this bleak picture is that you can buy coffee, whisky, international brands of cigarettes and other luxury items, or shop in the market near Adjumani, which is now a substantial trading area. This is because of the presence of the Sudanese refugees who now outnumber the local population and who are supported by a number of NGOs and UN agencies.

Uganda

Sleeping As there are so few visitors to Moyo, there are no hotels or guest houses. However, is is possible to stay with some of the NGO workers. They can provide you with a bed for the night and food. Costs should be negotiated at the time. If intending to stay in Moyo, take plenty of mosquito repellent, as mosquitoes are prevalent in the area.

Transport **Air** There are daily flights from Entebbe to UNHCR-maintained airfields at Adjumani, Arua and Moyo. Flights are organized by the Ministry of Agriculture and Fisheries in Kampala.

Road The best route is to Gulu continuing north to Adjumani, the administrative centre of the Moyo district and on to Moyo. This route takes you through Pakele and Dzaipi, both small towns with nothing of interest to look at, but useful places to stop for a soda or roasted meat. There is petrol in Pakele. An alternative is via Pakwach if visiting the Murchison Park then to Arua. There is public transport to Arua and Adjumani. Parts of the route between Gulu and Adjumani have been very unsafe of late. In the early part of this year (January-April) over 100 villagers have been killed and their homes destroyed by the Lord's Resistance Army. UNHCR in Kampala can provide security assessments of the route by road.

West to Fort Portal and Kasese

Kampala

Uganda

The west of Uganda can be reached directly from Kampala by taking the Mubende-Fort Portal road, and this route is covered here. However many travellers opt to take the southwest road to Mbarara (covered in the southwest section, page 607), and then north either via the Queen Elizabeth National Park or direct to Fort Portal.

Mubende town is a small pleasant town which few tourists visit. It is about halfway between Kampala and Fort Portal and if you are particularly interested in archaeology you may want to stay here on the way to the Bigo site.

Mubende
0°33'N 31°22'E
Colour map 2, grid C1

Bigo Earthworks consist of a series of trenches and mounds, not far from Mubende, on the Mubende-Masaka road. It is something of a mystery as to who constructed them and why. The main outer trench forms an oval enclosure measuring some five kilometres around the perimeter, its flanks resting on the Katonga and Kachinga rivers. Within the massive enclosure is a subsidiary complex of earthworks with an entrenched inner stronghold in which there are two artificial mounds about three metres high which were probably look-out posts. From the top of these mounds – they are likely to have been taller at the time of construction – a clear view would have been had of the surrounding countryside.

South region

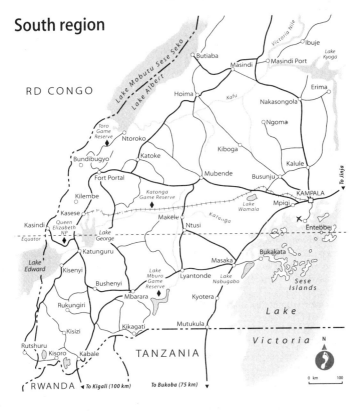

The remains of two forts of considerably smaller dimensions can be found at **Kasonko**, five kilometres northeast of Bigo and at **Kagago**, three kilometres north-west. They consist of a rampart and a ditch sunk into the slopes of small hills and do not have inner fortifications. It is believed that the constructors of Bigo also built these low flanking strong points as part of an all-round defensive system.

To get to Bigo turn off the Masaka-Mubende road at Makole. Follow this rather poor road for about 10 miles which is as far as you can go by vehicle. From here it is a walk for about five kilometres through the bush.

Sleeping E *Nakaima*, pleasant and good value, there is a restaurant here, which does the usual range of food.

Bushenyi
0°35'S 30°10'E
Colour map 2, grid C1

Bushenyi is the district centre and there is a hospital, a few shops, a couple of cheap guest houses and two petrol stations.

The road from Bushenyi to Kasese is excellent, courtesy of one of the western governments. At first the road goes up and down through forested hills, before it reaches the escarpment down to the Rift Valley. As you descend you will be able to see ahead of you Lakes George and Edward. From the cooler heights you descend into the hotter, dustier floor of the Rift Valley which the road crosses, passing through the Queen Elizabeth National Park (see National Parks, page 626). The vegetation around is mainly acacia bush and the grass is sprinkled with the occasional ant hill. A causeway crosses the Kazinga Channel – a natural channel that joins the two lakes. A bit further on you cross from the southern to the northern hemisphere – on each side of the road there is a large round wheel marking the Equator. The countryside around is mixed bush and some cultivation, including what was, for many years, Uganda's most important cash crop, cotton.

The Crater Lake Pavilion is sited on a hill top approximately 250 metres from the Bushenyi – Kasese Road, north of the Kazinga Channel, 25 kilometres south of Kasese. This overlooks a large shallow circular crater lake. The pavilion was opened in 1956 by Taro Rukidi III.

Kasese

0°13'N 30°3'E
Phone code: 0483
Colour map 2, grid B1

This is the terminal of the western railway in Uganda and you might visit it on the way to a trip up the Rwenzoris, to Kibale Forest or to the Queen Elizabeth National Park (64 kilometres away). For information about climbing the Rwenzori Mountains, see page 646; for Queen Elizabeth National Park, see page 626. Kasese is extremely hot, and the mosquitoes are most troublesome at night. A very dusty town, which gives you the feeling of the Wild West.

Kilembe Copper Mines Located 13 kilometres to the west of Kasese are the mines which were once an important source of foreign exchange for Uganda. They later closed down although there were rumours of them being reopened by the Japanese. It is possible to hire a bicycle and cycle to the mines. It is a long hard slog up (especially as the bikes are nothing special) but wonderful on the way down. Contact the manager of the *Saad Hotel* (see below) for bicycle rent.

Rwenzori Mountains, sometimes known as the Mountains of the Moon are best accessed from Kasese. The snow-peaked mountains were recently turned into a National Park. Mount Stanley in the Rwenzori range is the third highest mountain in Africa. The upper peaks are too difficult for ordinary hikers. The Rwenzeri Mountains are frequently closed to public access because of clashes between rebel ADF and government forces.

C *Margherita*, PO Box 90, T4015. Best hotel in Kasese and is set in beautiful surroundings, it is located with the Rwenzori Mountains on one side and a golf course on the other, there is something magnificent about the vegetation in this area – especially when the trees are in flower, it is situated about 3 kilometres down the road to Kilembe to the west of town and so unless you have your own transport is not very accessible, it is one of the *Uganda Hotels* Corporation chain and although it has seen better days the setting makes it worthwhile, there is a good restaurant.

Sleeping

D *Saad*, clean and fairly friendly, the rooms are doubles with their own facilities, and there are also beds in a dormitory, the restaurant is good (although there is no alcohol served on the premises because the owner is Muslim), the tilapia (fish) is recommended, bicycles for hire, videos screened, there are ongoing problems with the plumbing and the hotel is frequently without running water.

E *Ataco Holiday Inn*, all rooms have shared bathrooms, restaurant and bar, straightforward and basic. **E** *Highway Bar and Lodge*, shared bathrooms, not especially friendly. **E** *Kaghasera*, double rooms with own bathrooms, fairly basic and simple, not bad value. **E** *Moonlight Lodge*, on the Margherita Rd next to the Shell station, showers, friendly staff and mosquito nets (essential), very good local restaurant inside. **E** *Paradise Bar and Lodgings*, rather basic with shared bathrooms.

Camping In the grounds of the *Margherita Hotel* at US$5 a person, they expect you to eat and drink at the hotel. The site is behind the building, and not very attractive. Camping is also available at *Virina Gardens*, which also offers accommodation in rondavels.

The most popular places in town are the **2** *Margherita* (if you have a car or don't mind the walk) or else **2** *Saad Hotel*; **2** *Al-Hajji Yassin*, close to bus park. Local food: matoke and beans; rice and beans.

Eating

There are quite a few shops situated close to the market where you can buy food suitable for hiking – such as dried soups imported from Kenya.

Shopping

Kasese

To Margherita Hotel (3km),
Golf Club & Kilembe (10 km)

Rukidi III Rd

Kilembe Rd

Portal Rd

Emin

Ruwenzori Rd

Ruwenzori
Mountain
Services

Alexandria St

Speke St

To Fort Portal & Airport

Market

Market

Paradise Lodging

Kaghasera

Margherita Rd

Al-Hajji Yassin

N

Ataco Holiday
Inn

Highway
Lodge

Stanley St

Saad

0 metres   100

To Railway Station (750m)

Air Charter flights go to Kasese airport, although as they are more often than not taking tourists they are more likely to go direct to the Mweya Lodge landing site in Queen Elizabeth National Park (see page 631).

Transport

Road Kasese is 418 kilometres from **Kampala** via Mubende and Fort Portal. The more common route used, because the road is better, is via Mbarara. Buses leave from the Shell station on the main road. The matatus leave from the matatu park south of the centre. Buses to Kabale US$6, take 6 hours. Buses to Kampala US$8, take 7 hours. Matatus to Fort Portal US$4 takes 2 hours. Daily bus service from Fort Portal, Kasese, Mbarara to Kabale depart at 0600 from Fort Portal. Matatu to Ibanda/Rwenzoris US$1.50, tend to be infrequent.

Tour companies & travel agents *Rwenzori Mountain Services*, PO Box 33, Alexandra Rd, Kasese, T493-259175. Organize 2/4 day short tours and 6-7 day circuit tours of the Rwenzori

Directory

Uganda

Mountains. If you want to climb the peaks the tour will take 8-12 days. Equipment can be rented in Kasese but it is unlikely to be modern. Take good rain equipment because there is no real dry season. Take a stove – cooking over charcoal can be slow. Walking sticks are the most important equipment for the trip, along with waterproof boots. *Lake Kitandara Tours* is a new company offering a variety of tours to the Queen Elizabeth NP, hikes around the base of the Rwenzori Mts and walking tours around Kasese.

Nyakalengija Nyakalengija is a small village on the fringe of the Rwenzoris. Agricultural area, also depends on the income from guides and porters.

Matatu from Kasese to Ibanda US$1.50. Walking to Nyakalengija from Kasese takes about one hour. There is a mountaineering club hotel which is clean and friendly, costing US$9. There is one restaurant serving mostly African food, run by a local woman, service tends to be slow.

Bigodi The nearest village to the forest, six kilometres from Kanyanchu River campsite. To get from Bigodi to Kanyanchu you can hire bicycles from the lodges below. They will also organize tours of the Bigodi swamp, where there is a variety of birdlife and monkeys. **C** *Omucuso Lodge*, just outside Bigodi. Has about 10 bedrooms and serves excellent food – rather better than the usual menu. **C** *Safari Lodge*, new and fairly popular. **E** *CVK* is on the Fort Portal-Bigodi road 10 kilometres before Kibale Forest, located on one of the lakes. Tents and bandas available, the owner is a lecturer at Kabale University, very kind and interesting host, food and soft drinks available. **E** *Safari Hotel*, Nkingo Village, near the National Park, follow the sign post on the yellow gate to Nkimbo village. Friendly, economic accommodation.

Fort Portal

0°40'N 30°20'E
Phone code: 0483
Colour map 2, grid B1

Heading to Fort Portal, from Kasese, a distance of about 75 kilometres, is another beautiful drive. The road climbs out of the dry plain in which Kasese sits and gradually enters the hilly greenness that surrounds Fort Portal.

Located a little over 300 kilometres to the west of Kampala and 70 kilometres north of Kasese at 5,000 ft above sea level, Fort Portal is situated at the foothills of the Rwenzori Mountains known as the Mountains of the Moon. Small, quiet and refreshing it is one of Uganda's most pleasant towns.

Fort Portal is now the regional headquarters for Kabarole, Kasese and Bundibugyo districts. The town currently has a population of about 32,000 people. The town enjoys an excellent climate, almost temperate in nature with moderate sunshine and heavy downpours during the rainy season. The main rains are from March to May and from September to November – although there are no real dry seasons. The annual temperatures are about 25-28° C. The climate is mainly influenced by the surrounding environment – particularly the hills and mountains. The River Mpanga meanders through the municipality, its source being the tributaries from the Rwenzoris. It is this river that is the main source of water for the town.

From the town there is a beautiful view of the **Rwenzori Mountains**. They are snowpeaked – although cloud often covers the peaks themselves. The Rwenzori Mountains were recently turned into a fully fledged national park and the animals found in the park include elephants, leopards, many sorts of monkeys and a huge range of birdlife (see National Parks, page 626).

The countryside surrounding Fort Portal is tea country and in the old days this was an important export for Uganda. During the colonial period many of the plantations were run by Europeans on land leased (rarely owned) from the Government. Labour migrated from other parts of Uganda, particularly the southwest to work on the estates usually for six months after which they would return home. Many migrants made this same journey year after year. In recent decades, however, many of the plantations have fallen into disrepair – if a tea tree is not picked over a long period of time it is difficult to revive it into a useable state. However efforts have been made on some of the plantations – but the years of neglect are obvious if you compare them to plantations around, for example, Kericho in Kenya.

Some people base themselves at Fort Portal while organizing a trek up the Rwenzoris but, in fact, although not so pleasant, Kasese is more convenient for this as it is closer to the starting point at Ibanda. You might also pass through on the way to the **Murchison Falls National Park** or to **Bundibugyo** in Semliki Forest to see the hot springs and the pygmies. Another place of interest is the **Bunyuruguru Crater** lake which is situated between Kibale Forest and the main Kasese-Fort Portal road.

History of Fort Portal

Fort Portal was founded in 1893 under the name of Fort Gerry, and was later renamed Fort Portal after Sir Gerald Portal a British explorer who mounted an expedition to the area in 1900. Gerald Portal was the British Consul General of Zanzibar who arrived in Uganda in late 1892 and died of malaria there. He was instrumental in the signing of agreements with the leaders of the Kingdoms of Uganda that led to the formalizing of Protectorate status for the country. Fort Portal is in the centre of the Toro Kingdom and the town started as a base from where the British colonial power protected the then Omukama (or King) of Toro. In 1876 Toro was captured by the Banyoro king, Kabalega, but the British expelled him in 1891 and replaced him with a new Toro king, Kasagama. In later years Catholic and Protestant missionaries followed the colonial administration in order to establish churches, schools and hospitals. By 1900 the town was expanding rapidly. The development of the town was helped by the booming trade in food and cash produce. In the 1930s Europeans and Indians came and started large tea estates, and shops and residential premises were built. The growth of the town was also helped by the establishment in 1952 of the railway line from Mombasa as far as Kasese for the transportation of copper from the mines at Kilembe. A cement factory was set up at Hima along the Fort Portal-Kasese road. As with the other Kingdoms in Uganda, Toro was abolished in 1966 during Obote's first term of office. However, it was restored by Museveni in 1993.

Fort Portal

Sights

Toro Palace Ruins Close to Fort Portal, on one of the highest hills around the town, is the site of the former palace of the King of Toro (Omukama). It was built in the 1960s for the then Omukama, Rukidi III (son of Kasagama, the British installed King) but was destroyed when the Kingdoms were abolished and is now only a ruin. It is not a particularly attractive site but there are good views of the Rwenzoris from the hill on which it stands.

Fort Ruins The Fort after which the town is named, is now the site of the town's golf course, where it is now little more than a collection of rocks. It is said that one of these rocks contains the footmarks of General Gerald Portal's men.

Karimbi Tombs These are the burial ground for the former Toro royal family, where both Kasagama and Rukidi III are buried. Located about five kilometres along the Fort Portal-Kasese Road.

Uganda

Nearby attractions There are a number of tourist attractions accessible from Fort Portal and if you are a group then you might be able to organize a day trip. *Kabarole Tours*, and *Semliki Safaris* both based in Fort Portal are very friendly and helpful and will be able to arrange trips.

Bundibugyo is located the other side of the Rwenzori Mountains from Fort Portal and the two main attractions there are the **hot springs** and the **pygmy tribes** who live in the forests nearby. The journey to Bundibugyo through the mountains is spectacular.

Lake Saka This small crater lake is located about eight kilometres out of Fort Portal and can be visited quite easily. Take the road that goes towards the *Mountains of the Moon Hotel* and go beyond the market and post office, until you reach a turning to the left down Saka road roughly opposite the golf course. Follow this road which leads to the lake.

Bunyuruguru Crater Lake Field This is a collection of crater lakes located about 30 kilometres to the south of Fort Portal between the main Fort Portal-Kasese road and Kibale Forest. It is an attractive place with good views from the crater rim and abundant birdlife. However without your own transport this is not all that easy as there is not very much traffic going along the road to the lakes. The lakes are situated between Kasenda and Rwaihamba villages which are 10 kilometres apart. On Monday and Thursday, when there is a market at the latter village there are a few vehicles to Rwaihamba from where you will have to walk. *Kabarole Tours* can arrange transport. **C** *Crater Valley Beach Resort*, campsite offers bandas with continental breakfast or camping at US$7.50 per person. Food is available and it is sound and cheap. Water supply comes in buckets. The lakes are reportedly bilharzia free, but there are leeches. There is a nice walk to the 'Top of the World' taking in four of the five craters. Another pleasant walk is to walk all the way around the Lake, journey time 1½ – 2½ hours depending on how many locals you meet.

The road through Kibale Forest is gravel, but in good condition. The road to Mubende is gravel, and sections are poor in wet weather, but it is undergoing improvement. From Mubende to Kampala the road is sealed.

Lake Nkuruba, a beautiful, small crater lake within the Bunyuruguru region, 20 kilometres south of Fort Portal, not far from Kibale Forest. Conservation area. It offers reportedly safe swimming and good views. **Transport** from Fort Portal by matatu or pickup a few times daily. 17 kilometres from Fort Portal on the Kibale road the road forks, left to Kibale Fores (25 kilometres) and right for Nkuruba (eight kilometres). Getting there can be difficult. It is easiest to get there on Monday and Thursday when there is a market in Rwaihamba, a village two kilometres from the lake. **Lake Nkuruba Nature Reserve** Nkuruba is the only crater lake remaining unspoiled by deforestation. The Nature Reserve is a community project funding education and health for the community. There are three camping areas in tranquil surroundings. Hokwegondeza campsite is situated on the lakeside in the forest. Entangantangano campsite is up on the crater rim overlooking the lake. Rwenzori campsite is sited higher still, with breathtaking views of the mountain range. Home grown vegetables and freshly baked salt bread available. On Mondays and Thursdays there is a busy market, plus a nearby trading centre for essentials. You may also wish to walk to other nearby lakes (one to three hours) like Lake Lyantonde Conservation and Tourism project. Guided walks available.

Pygmies In the Semliki River Valley is Ntandi village and near to this is the Semliki Forest which is home to the pygmies. There is one matatu a day that leaves Fort Portal early in the morning for Ntandi. The pygmies themselves can be visited. However many visitors are disappointed. Not surprisingly the pygmies have been quick to learn their novelty value and demand considerable sums of money from tourists. Recent reports indicate that the pygmies have started building roadblocks and demanding money. Failure to comply with these demands has resulted in people having their vehicles smashed up. Disconcertingly, they appear to spend the largest proportion of this money on drink and drugs, often staggering around unaware of what is going on. It is difficult to find anyone who has visited the pygmies and considers it a worthwhile part of their trip to Uganda.

Itwara Forest Located to the northeast of Fort Portal this is another forest with a large number of small mammals as well as a great range of birdlife. Primates that are found include chimpanzees, black and white colobus, blue monkey, red-tailed monkey, and red colobus. Also found are the African palm civet, the giant forest squirrel and the scaly-tailed flying squirrel.

Kibale Forest To the north of Kasese and south of Fort Portal is Kibale Forest which forms a unique habitat for animals, birds and plants. Kibale lies at an altitude of about 1,230 metres above sea level. The forest provides a rich habitat for more than 250 species of animals and over 300 of birds. The animal species include 11 primate species including black and white colobus monkeys and chimpanzees.

Guided forest walks are available from knowledgeable staff, and the centre has become a major focus of research for scientists from around the world. The forest has a campsite at Kamyanchu which is about 35 kilometres south of Fort Portal. It is on an elevated grassland located within the forest itself and has a beautiful view of the Rwenzori Mountains. Interesting features outside the forest include a number of crater lakes, one of which has a fascinating natural lava formation making a bridge under which water flows. Kibale forest is divided into seven zones for management purposes: research, natural reserve, civic-cultural, recreation, harvest, community and protection (see page 642).

Sleeping

C *Mountains of the Moon*, about 2½ kilometres from the town centre. This is a lovely, but run-down old colonial hotel, it is set in beautiful grounds, there is a restaurant which does good steak and chips, service variable. The water supply, both hot and cold is reported to be unreliable recently. Ideal for a drink in the garden in the afternoon or in the bar during the evening. Recent travellers report that this hotel will not accept travellers' cheques in settlement of the bill. **C** *The Ruwen Zori View Guest House*, PO Box 709, Fort Portal, Lower Kakiiza Rd, Plot 15 Boma, T/F0256-48322102, sited about 200 metres beyond the *Mountain of the Moon Hotel*. Excellent hotel, way above usual standards. Outstanding food served for dinner. Hosted by Ineke Jongerius and Maurice Barnes, a Dutch/English couple. Recommended by several travellers.

E *CVK*, excellent value, friendly and pleasant host who teaches at Kabale University, also has accommodation by the lakeside 10 kilometres before Kibale Forest. **E** *Christian*, one of the best of the cheap hotels, this is clean and simple, it is popular with Peace Corps and is a friendly place, food is available. **E** *Exotic Lodge*, next to the tourist information office. Basic. **E** *Hotel Nkingo Village Safari Camp and Guest House*, PO Box 733, Fort Portal, located in Kibale forest south of Fort Portal, on the Fort Portal-Kamwenge road, four-wheel drive or matatu at 0900 from Port Portal. Very basic, guest rooms or choice of private campsites, camping US$3, cooking grills, firewood and water, basic latrines, bush showers with hot water, restaurant, chicken in red wine and baked pineapple pie worth trying, and bar, laundry services available, run by the engaging Charles Lubega. **E** *Hot Springs*, this is a simple good value budget hotel, there is good food available and it is popular. **E** *New Linda Guest House*, on the road to Kasese, close to the centre. Quieter rooms at the back, friendly staff. **E** *Wooden*, situated in the middle of town. Popular with travellers, bar and restaurant, no water, only in buckets, power cuts at night, probably the best place to stay overnight, although slightly more expensive than other places in the same price bracket, not too

Uganda

friendly but is close to the matatu station. Has a very noisy night club. Sleep impossible before 2am except if there is a power cut. Expect to be woken again at 6am by the shouting of touts at the matatu station.

Camping *Crater Valley Kibale Lodge*, PO Box 769, Fort Portal, T483-22035, F22636, Kabopoza@starcom.co.ug.

Eating **2** *Don's Plaza*, on the main street in the centre. Currently the 'in-place' where locals and ex-pats meet for an evening beer, open at weekends until the last guest leaves. **2** *Linda's Place*, located on the road to Kasese between the gas station and the *Church of Uganda Guest House*. High quality food. Recommended. **2** *Mountains of the Moon*, a bit out of town, but nice setting and varied international menu. **1** *Western Tourist*, good value. *Selget Restaurant* at the Matatu Station. Serves good breakfasts, US$0.50. *SM Takeaway*, Bwamba Rd. Friendly, cheap, restaurant.

Entertainment **Sport** **Golf**: the town has a 36-hole course which is open to members and those from affiliated clubs. Temporary membership is also available. Other facilities that are available include **table tennis**, **tennis** and **squash**. The course is a 20-minute walk toward the *Mountains of the Moon Hotel*. **White Water Rafting**: At nearby Murchison Falls available c/o *Adrift* – see entry on page 636.

Shopping A visit to the Cloth Market close to the Post Office is worthwhile.

Transport **Air** The nearest airport is Kasese – this is for small airplanes only and there are no longer any scheduled flights, only charters. **Eagle Aviation**, Box 312, Kampala, T042-20513 (Entebbe), ext 3020. Fly on Friday and Sunday from Entebbe to Fort Portal, US$75 one way, US$150 return, they use the unreliable airstrip at Lake Sakam. When muddy or misty one has to go to Kasese to fly to Entebbe.

Road Fort Portal is accessible by road, by two alternative routes from **Kampala**. The first is through Mubende district and is 320 kilometres long but is only partly paved; the other is through Masaka, Mbarara, Bushenyi and Kasese and is 430 kilometres. By bus the journey takes about 8 hours, goes through exceptionally beautiful countryside. There are frequent matatus to and from **Kasese** taking about 2 hours, cost US$4. Fort Portal to Kampala: bus leaves at 0700 but you must be there at 0530, takes 7 hours, US$7 per person. Matatus to Masindi/Hoima (changing in Kagadi) cost US$10. It takes 7 hours to reach Masindi. Bus to Kabale takes 8 hours and costs US$9.

Public transport to Kabale Forest from Fort Portal. Take the bus at 0500 from the stage for Buhinga Hospital on the bridge on the Kamwenge road, journey time is 2 hours.

Directory **Banks** There are two banks in Fort Portal – the *Co-operative Bank* and the *Uganda Commercial Bank*. It is very difficult to cash TCs as there have been a lot of forged TCs in circulation recently. You may be asked to produce the original sale receipt for the Tcs. **Libraries** Public library at Fort Portal has an excellent selection of books. **Places of worship** Every religion is represented at Fort Portal – there are several mosques and churches of Anglican, Roman Catholic, Pentecostal, Seventh Day Adventist, and Church of Uganda denominations. **Tour companies & travel agents** *Kabarole Tours* and *Semliki Safaris* specialize in arranging excursions to places of interest around Fort Portal.

Fort Portal to Hoima

Heading for Hoima and Masindi from Fort Portal be prepared for a bad road – this road is not used much and in parts is both very steep and almost impassable. However, if you have the time and a good four-wheel drive you will be rewarded with going though one of the most lovely parts of Uganda. The first part of the journey is through low cultivated hills. But as you proceed north it changes to a mountainous,

The Spirit of Ndahura

Situated not far from Kibale and Kisomroro is a hot spring call Rwagimba, which, literally translated, means that which pushes or jets out. The hot waters from the spring run into two rock pools which lie, one below the other, within a few yards of the ice-cold waters of the Ruimi river.

The spring is widely known for the healing powers of its hot sulphurous waters, which are used both for washing and drinking, particularly by those suffering from skin diseases. The healing powers of the spring are supposed to be under the spiritual sway of Ndahura, who was a Muchwezi warrior whose career ended disastrously in defeat and small pox. His name became so closely connected with small pox that it was actually known as Ndahura's disease.

The spring is jointly owned by two clans – the Bachwamba and the Basambu, and its keeper is always a Muchwamba man married to a Musambu woman. Although the man is the keeper he cannot exercise full powers, for it is the woman who is the actual priestess of the spring. It is in her that, from time to time, when she becomes possessed, the spirit of Ndahura becomes immanent. The spirit of Ndahura is not normally regarded as being immanent in the spring itself but in the shrine which is maintained near to the keeper's house, where small offerings of food and beer are made. The spirit of Ndahura only becomes immanent in the spring when the waters are troubled. This seems to occur fairly rarely and in the rest of the time people seem happy to use the spring to bathe in and to help reduce aches and pains.

partly-forested area and every so often the road reaches a spot where you can look around for miles. It really is fantastically beautiful. The forest is interspersed with patches of cultivation, but this is one of the poorer parts of Uganda being so cut-off.

Hoima

The most direct route to Hoima from Kampala is on a poor road via **Kiboga** but the journey is an interesting one and runs through the bush. After about 30 miles the tar road becomes murrum and gradually deteriorates. The landscape is hilly with a scattering of huge boulders amongst the farmland. The town of Kiboga is about 120 kilometres from Kampala and is strung out along the road, it is rather shabby and run down.

1°40'N 31°30'E
Colour map 2, grid B1

Soon after leaving Kiboga the road begins a gradual descent into the plain beyond which Hoima, the capital of Bunyoro, is located. The plain is punctuated by the occasional bare hill, and Hoima itself is spread across two such hills. Hoima can be seen from quite a distance, the town is surrounded by eucalyptus trees planted as an anti-malarial measure during the colonial era. On entering the town you pass through the instantly recognizable old colonial part of town – the bungalows surrounded by wide verandahs, set in large gardens, and the fading government offices. The town centre sits overlooking a deep valley with a number of buildings, including one of the town's churches on the opposite side.

Katasiha Fort This is located about three kilometres along the Butiaba road which leads north out of town towards Lake Albert. The Fort was established in 1894 by Col. Colville when he was trying to subdue Kabalega, the King (Omukama) of Bunyoro. All that survives of the Fort are a rampart and a ditch.

Nearby attractions

Mparo Tombs These are situated four kilometres along the Masindi road which is to the northeast of Hoima. They are the tombs of the former Omukamas of Bunyoro – Kabalega and his son Tito Wimyi who died in 1923 and 1971 respectively. The building is similar to the Kasubi tombs in Kampala although not as grand. As with those tombs it is guarded by an old woman who will allow you to go in and take a

Bunyoro Coronation

As part of the programme to restore traditional structures as with the Buganda (see box, page 565), the monarchy was restored with the coronation of the 42-year-old, British-educated, Solomon Iguru in 1994.

The previous King, Sir Tito Winyi IV, had been crowned in 1924, but deposed in 1967 when Obote abolished the monarchies (see page 659). It is the tradition that the King nominates his successor from among his heirs. There was a wide choice as King Winyi had several wives and 104 children. His choice of Solomon was disputed by another son, John who claimed that, as the eldest son of the only wife to have been married in a Christian ceremony, he was the legitimate heir. The High Court of Uganda, however, decided in favour of Solomon.

The coronation took place on 11 June at Hoima where the King has a palace, a large, strong construction with two wings and a blue tiled roof, where the Rukerato, the Bunyoro parliament is located. The ceremony was attended by President Museveni, the King and Queen of Toro and a representative of the Kabaka of Uganda. As the previous coronation had been 70 years ago, the procedures were uncertain. In the event it began with representatives of various religious denominations giving their blessing. Various ceremonial objects were presented to the King: slippers to help him travel; a spear to kill anyone despising his people; a dagger for protection; a kaliruga, a club to beat anyone vexing him; a kujunju, a staff to punish offenders; an empese, a hoe symbolizing fathership of the people; a bow and quiver for fighting enemies; a leopardskin bag to assist in trading; a bamboo whistle to sound the war alarm; a kasisi, a vessel to ensure peace; and a second hoe to ensure good harvests.

The ceremony also included the presentation of 20th century 'slippers' in the form of a Land Cruiser from President Museveni; some centenary pottery from Leeds, where the new King had studied; followed by traditional music, drumming and dancing.

JJ Pearlman

look around. Be sure to remove your shoes before entering and leave a small donation. Inside there are some of Kabalega's belongings. He was the Omukama who fought against the British at the end of the last century, until he was captured in 1894.

Sleeping **D** *Kopling House*, a new, clean, pleasant hotel, set in a well kept garden with smallish rooms, private facilities and good mosquito nets, good restaurant, medium range, serves local and international dishes, friendly staff. Recommended. **E** *Hoima Inn*, basic accommodation. **E** *Kwebiiha Hostel*, fairly simple. **E** *Nsamo Inn*, new, clean and comfortable, good value. **E** *Red Cross Hostel*, clean, though a touch spartan.

Eating **2** *Nsamo Inn*, reasonable restaurant, with fairly simple food. **1** *Ebony Bar and Restaurant*, straightforward local food, mostly grills.

Transport **Road** The town of Hoima is located about 200 kilometres from **Kampala** via Kiboga, a drive of about 3 hours. Unfortunately because the road is not good there is little traffic on this road. There are alternatives – it can be reached via **Masindi** – it is about 70 kilometres from Masindi – making a total of about 270 kilometres from Kampala, or from **Fort Portal**. If you are doing the latter on public transport you will probably have to change vehicles at least once, usually at Kagadi.

Masindi

1°43'N 32°2'E
Colour map 2, grid B1 Many people pass through Masindi on the way to the Murchison Falls National Park. Apart from the Park there are a few things near to Masindi which you may also want to do. Masindi has a market and is livelier than Fort Portal but has few tourist facilities. For information about Murchison Falls National Park (also known as Kabalega NP) see section on National Parks, page 634.

Masindi can either be reached via Hoima (see above), or else by taking the more direct road. The latter leaves Kampala heading north (starting at the Wandegeya roundabout near Makerere University) and passes through Bombo and Luwero, before swinging westwards, taking about five hours from Kampala. About 30 kilometres out of Kampala you will go through the town of **Bombo** – very much an army town. You pass row upon row of barracks. It began as an army town at the beginning of this century with the Sudanese Volunteers in the King's African Rifles – they were always known as the Nubians. The area became known as the Luwero Triangle and was very severely affected during the Obote II régime when army atrocities resulted in the killing of many thousands of people. Houses were looted and then burnt to the ground, along with the surrounding shambas. It did not take long for the vegetation to grow up again and the sight of the remains of a house with bush growing through it is not unusual. As a result of the events in the area Luwero has received considerable attention from aid workers and foreign governments.

Kihande Palace A couple of kilometres out of town is the palace of the Omukama, the former king of Bunyoro. This is situated on Kihande Hill but is no longer in use as a palace. The Bunyoro kingdom and its kingship was one of those abolished in 1967 during the Obote I régime.

Bundongo Forest This wildlife area, about 30 kilometres west of Masindi on the Butiaba road, lies between Masindi and Lake Albert, and is renowned for the presence of chimpanzees and therefore receives a fair number of visitors. Before the opening up of Kibale Forest for viewing chimpanzees, Budongo was considered to be the most accessible of Uganda's forests where chimpanzees could be viewed. More recently however most visitors go to Kibale and the researchers are less willing to take people to see the chimps here. There are however plans to set up a tourism project that will enable tourists to visit the chimps here. Other animals found in the forest include the scaly-tailed flying squirrel, the giant forest squirrel, the tree pangolin and the black and white colobus monkey. Budongo Forest also has an extremely rich birdlife with an estimated 90 bird species. These include the cuckoo falcon, crowned hawk eagle, great blue turaco, the great honey guide and the dwarf kingfisher.

There is a daily bus which will drop you off at the turning for Nyabyeya Forestry College from where it is a short walk. On the way back you should be waiting at the turn off early in the morning as there are few matatus after about 0900.

There is a *guesthouse* at the Forestry College which has rooms and camping available. It is cheap but you will need to bring your own food.

Masindi Port This is different from Masindi itself, and is about 40 kilometres to the east. It is located on Victoria Nile at the western end of Lake Kyoga which extends across much of central Uganda. In the days when steamers on the Nile were an important form of transport the two sets of falls in the Murchison Falls National Park were major obstacles to travelling up the Nile. Coming from Lake Victoria, the steamers went up Victoria Nile and into Lake Kyoga. Passengers and goods then disembarked at Masindi Port and travelled overland to Butiaba on Lake Albert. From here they continued their journey north. Masindi Port has now declined in importance, and is mainly a market town.

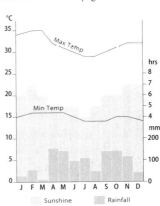

Climate: Masindi

The Prince of Wales hunting lodge

Between the road and the escarpment on the way down to Lake Albert there was once a hunting lodge which was built for Edward, Duke of Windsor, when he was the Prince of Wales in the 1930s. Gradually, during the 1960s and 1970s, it fell into disrepair and brick by brick was removed by the local people so that little of it now remains.

Lake Albert Excursions to Lake Albert can be made from Masindi. Head for the town of **Butiaba Port** on Lake Albert – a distance of about 70 kilometres. The drive on the escarpment to the Rift Valley is an experience in itself. Once you get to Butiaba ask the local fishermen and you should be able to hire a boat for the day.

Sleeping **C** *Masindi*, PO Box 11, Butiaba Rd, T23, about a kilometre out of town. Because it is never anywhere near full you can usually negotiate the price, run by the *Uganda Hotels*. **E** *Codia Lodge*, fairly simple, restaurant. **E** *Emmest Guest House*, basic and unpretentious. **E** *Kyaterekeva Guest House*, sited between the market and matatu park. Mosquito nets, friendly service. **E** *Soft Lodge*, there are 2 *Soft Lodges* in Masindi which offer moderate accommodation and are clean and friendly.

Eating *The Traveller's Corner*, next to the Post Office. Serves good food.

Entertainment **Sports (participant)** **Tennis**: courts available for temporary membership. **Sports (spectator)** **Football**: there is a sports stadium in Masindi and matches are held there on a regular basis.

Transport **Road** Masindi is a drive of about 3½ hours from **Kampala**, a distance of about 200 kilometres. There are regular buses and matatus.

Bulisa
Colour map 2, grid B1

Bulisa is a small village 30 kilometres from Paraa, the headquarters of the Murchison Falls NP. There is only one hotel, **E** *Bulisa Corner Hotel*, friendly staff, food served mostly Matooke and Ugali, very basic facilities. *One African Place*, restaurant opposite the hotel. Also serves mostly local food. *Getting there:* No public transport. It's possible to rent a bike for US$8, check the condition of the brakes before setting off as there's a steep descent shortly after the park entrance gate. The bike ride takes around 2-2½ hours. Start early if visiting the park (0600) in order to catch the boat on the Nile which leaves at 0900. **NB** There are many tsetse flies in the area. You have to pay the park entrance fee at the gate US$23.

Wanseko
Colour map 2, grid C1

Wanseko lies on the shore of Lake Albert close to the Nile estuary about six kilometres northwest of Bulisa. The views across the lake of the Blue Mountains in RD Congo are magnificent. Wanseko is a small town with few facilities, but there is a wide variety of birdlife living in the reed beds near the estuary. **E** *The Wanseko Lodge*, a friendly basic hotel, food available. *Getting there:* The bus to Masindi stops overnight at Wanseko, and leaves very early in the morning.

Southwest to Kabale and Kisoro

The southwest runs from Kampala to Kabale and Kisoro, and includes as well the Sese Islands. The main tourist attractions in this area are the Impenetrable Forest with the mountain gorillas, the Sese Islands, Lake Mburo National Park and the less frequently visited Lake Nabugabo and Mpanga Forest Reserve.

*The road leading out of Kampala through Masaka and on the southwest of the country is one of the best in Uganda. You will pass through some swamps and small patches of forest and the surrounding countryside seems fertile and well watered. About 40 kilometres out of Kampala you will reach the village of **Mpigi** and if you are hoping to buy any traditional music instruments (particularly drums) this is the place to do so. You will see drum makers and their stalls on the side of the road. Near to here is the Mpanga Forest Reserve which you might want to visit either on the way south or else it makes an easy day trip from Kampala.*

Mpanga Forest Reserve

This is not a well known tourist location, it is a small (450 hectares) patch of the type of forest that once was found almost all over the northern section of the lake fringe, but which has now been mostly destroyed. This has been partly as a result of extending cultivation into forested areas; but is also the result of the policies (see box, page 507) of the colonial period that were aimed at reducing the incidence of sleeping sickness (*trypanosomiasis*), spread by the tsetse fly. The area was preserved during the colonial period partly for research purposes and so remains as a small reminder of what was once all around.

The forest has a number of clearly marked footpaths and you are unlikely to get lost. However, a guide will help you get more out of your visit. There are a variety of monkeys living in the forest and there is a wide range of birdlife.

There are no facilities for overnight stays at Mpanga Forest, although if you have your own tent you could probably camp. There is certainly a lovely site in a clearing in the forest but apparently you are supposed to get written permission from the Forestry Department in Kampala in order to camp actually in the forest although this may not be strictly necessary any longer. If you are stuck there are a few basic hotels in Mpigi village.

To get to the forest on public transport take a matatu that goes through Mpigi (any of the Masaka matatus will do) and once you have passed the turning for Mpigi village itself continue for about three kilometres. Here the road dips and goes through the southern part of the forest, where you should ask to be let off. To the right, just beyond the dip, is a turnoff down an unmarked track which goes to the forest station. Follow this for about 500 metres keeping to the right when the path forks and you will reach the forest station. Here you must meet the ranger to let him know that you are planning to visit the forest – entrance however is free. He should be able to give you some information sheets about the forest and arrange for a guide if you want one.

Masaka

About 75 kilometres from Kampala you will cross the Equator which is marked. Further along the road, about 150 kilometres from Kampala, is **Kinoni** which is one of the best places to buy papyrus mats. Another 20 kilometres further on is

0°21'S 31°45'E
Phone code: 0481
Colour map 2, grid C1

Kyazanga where you can buy snacks of roasted meat, sodas and roasted bananas (*gonja*). Masaka is about two hours from Kampala.

Masaka was intensively damaged during the Tanzanian invasion of 1979, and much of the destruction has not been repaired. Leaving the town to the west is the road to Tanzania which was the route along which the Tanzanian troops advanced.

Sleeping **D** *Laston*, this is about 500 metres from the bus station. Recent reports of this hotel have been less favourable. **D** *La Nova*, not particularly good value, it is a fair step from the bus station and is often full, few creature comforts, frequent disruptions to the electrical power supply. **D** *Victoria End Rest House*, town centre. A very basic hotel, there is a range of rooms, central, probably one of the best places to stay. *The lodge* situated on the corner near *La Nova* has been recommend. It's in the **D** price range, clean facilities with hot water.

E *Executive Lodge*, Plot 51 Hobert St. Basic accommodation, somewhat shabby. **E** *Exotic Guesthouse*, not recommended. Standards have declined. **E** *Masaka Backpackers' Cottage and Campsite*, PO Box 834, T0481-21288, F0481-20514, 4 kilometres Masaka, Bukoba-Kyotera Rd. Actually situated in the village of Nyendu, semi-rural hilly site. Cooking

Masaka

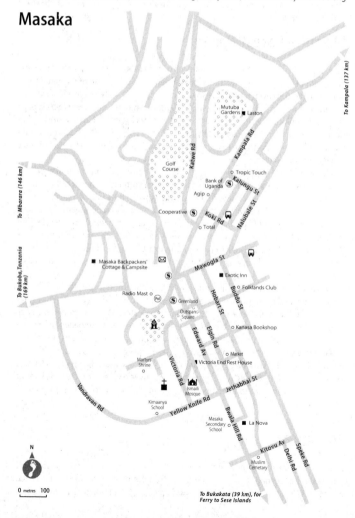

facilities, single rooms and dormitory. Taxi/minicab shuttle to Kirimya disembark Kasanvu and follow the signs.

2 *Laston*, good value and reasonable standard. **1** *Elgin Inn and Restaurant*, fairly cheap and **Eating** basic, downstairs from *Victoria End Resthouse*. Good local food, friendly, US$1.50. **1** *Exotic Inn*, simple fare.

Road There are frequent matatus and buses to Masaka from **Kampala**. Get to either one of **Transport** the 2 bus stations in Kampala early in the morning as most leave soon after daybreak, bus takes 2 hours, cost US$2. Alternatively go to the matatu station as they continue later in the day. Masaka is a distance of 128 kilometres from Kampala. Masaka is also where you change to pick up matatus to Bukakata for the Ssese Islands and for the overland journey to Mutukula on the Tanzanian border. Shared taxi: Masaka: Nyendo US$0.30. Pickup Nyendo-Bukakata US$2.

Boat Bukakata-Luku/Buggala Island, US$1, first boat leaves around 1300. Sometimes the ferry will not run if there are too few passengers and cars. Pickup: Luku-Kalangala, US$1 around 1700, from Kalangala back to Luku at 0630.

How to get from the Ssese Islands to Mutukula (Tanzanian border) Kalangala to Luku: pickup US$1.50; Lulu to Bukakata: boat US$1; Bukakata to Nyendo: pickup US$1; Nyendo to Masaka: shared taxi US$0.30; Masaka to Mutukula: matato US$2.50. The journey is possible to complete in one day, but it takes a lot of waiting around. Check the exchange rate before leaving Uganda and change left over shillings at the border, as Uganda currency is not exchangeable elsewhere. Get your exit stamp before the immigration Office closes at 0500 because the only bus for Bukoba leaves Mutukulu at 1700. The Immigration Office reopens at 0800. Hitching a lift to Bukoba could involve a very lengthy wait, as traffic is sparse.

West from Masaka

After leaving Masaka and heading west the countryside gradually gets drier and more hilly and the density of population falls as you move into Ankole which is populated by pastoralists.

About half way between Masaka and Mbarara is the trading centre of Lyantonde. There is a turning to the right and 100 kilometres to the north is **Ntusi** where there is an archaeological site.

Masaka to Tanzania (Bukoba)

From Masaka you can head for Tanzania – this is not nearly as pleasant as the alternative route using the Port Bell-Mwanza ferry (see page 557) – but as that only goes once a week many travellers prefer to go by road. The road is not very good and this route is not used very much, although traffic is increasing. There are matatus from Masaka which go as far as Kyotera and from there you will have to get a lift to the border, crossing at Mutukula, with one of the trucks going across – this is not usually a problem as pickups are often waiting for you in Kyotera. Journey time about six to eight hours. The road takes you through the district of Rakai which has become infamous as a result of being devastated by the AIDS epidemic. Evidence of it can be seen in the number of abandoned homesteads and shambas.

Very little traffic comes this way, possibly only 10-20 vehicles a day. Theoretically this should mean crossing the border is quick but it does not. It takes between 30 minutes and two hours to get through the Ugandan-Tanzanian bureaucracy here and you require a letter from the government in Kampala confirming that the vehicle you were using is yours and not for sale. You need to pay US$100 for driving a vehicle into Tanzania. The reason for all this bureaucracy is said to be that many traders used to buy vehicles (new or secondhand) in Uganda and sell them in Tanzania which affected the local market and reduced government revenue from sales tax

Crocodiles in Lake Nabugabo

During the colonial period Lake Nabugabo was a popular holiday resort in Uganda for expatriates. One of the reasons why swimming here was preferred over swimming in Lake Victoria was that there was supposed to be an absence of crocodiles. One report of a crocodile seen in 1932 was dismissed, but when a dog was snatched while swimming in the lake in 1946, a meticulous search was made. So much for no crocodiles – in a period of about three months a total of 10 crocodiles were seen and shot in the lake. These included a particularly huge male which was 4.5 metres long, with an enormous girth, 167 centimetres round the body, 140 centimetres round the neck and 125 centimetres round the base of the tail. This was estimated to be at least 30 years old.

The lake was cleared of crocodiles with the aim of making it safe for swimmers. However, exceptionally heavy rains later that year flooded the land between the two lakes and crocodiles reappeared. It is doubtful whether there are currently crocodiles in Lake Nabugabo – but you might want to check with local residents before you dive in.

on luxury items. If you can cope with the bureaucracy, this trip is well worth making as the scenery is lovely and there are many nice shady places to stop and have a soda en route.

If you get to the border shortly before dark you may want to stay at the small guesthouse which is on the Uganda side of the border – there is nothing on the Tanzania side until you get to Bukoba. For crossing the border you will need to have patience as you go through the rather long drawn out process. The road on the Tanzania side is worse than the Uganda road but there are four-wheel drive vehicles operating on the route. They go when full.

In the far south of Uganda, on the Tanzania border there was once a hotel. It was on an island in the Kagera river at a place called **Kitagatoa** and was reached by a pulley system across the river. The place was run by a very eccentric English woman called Toni. *Mutukula Safari Lodge*, highly recommended, clean, excellent value, meals available US$2 per person.

Lake Nabugabo

This is a small oval lake, slightly less than five miles in length and about three miles wide. It is located about two miles from the western shore of Lake Victoria, from which it is separated by rough undulating country. Because of the mineral content of the lake it is said that bilharzia does not occur here and this has made it popular for swimming. It is a very peaceful place to relax for a couple of days in the friendly Church of Uganda resort.

Sleeping There is a guesthouse at Lake Nabugabo which is run by the Church of Uganda (which also runs the *Namirembe Guesthouse* in Kampala). There are a range of bandas to rent which are clean and comfortable. There are two family bandas and two doubles (both have a sitting room and their own shower) – as well as a dormitory. Food is available at the restaurant if you order it in advance – but no alcohol is served on the premises. It is occasionally full at weekends. Check with the *Namirembe Guesthouse*, Mengo close to Mengo hospital, just below the Cathedral, in Kampala. **Camping** is permitted but bring equipment.

Transport **Road** Lake Nabugabo is located about 16 kilometres from Masaka, a few kilometres off the Masaka-Bukukata road. Getting to get to it by public transport from Masaka is easiest if you happen to be in Masaka on a Monday, Wednesday or Friday. This is because this is the day when a bus goes to Butukula for the Sese Islands. It leaves at about 1400 from the main Masaka bus station, and goes past the turning to Lake Nabugabo which is clearly signposted. Alternatively take a matatu from Masaka to Nyondo (two kilometres from Masaka) and change there to get onto the Bukutula road – you will probably end up getting a shared taxi. From the main road the lake is about 4 kilometres but traffic along here is scarce and it is probably quicker to walk than wait for a lift. The easiest alternative of all is, of course, to arrange a special hire from Masaka all the way – it will only cost you US$10-15 depending on your bargaining powers, and good value if you are in a group. The resort can be reached by road from Kampala in a few hours which makes it a popular weekend destination for Kampala residents.

Sese Islands

This collection of islands (sometimes spelt Ssese) is situated in the northwestern part of Lake Victoria and are an increasingly popular tourist destination. There are 84 islands in the group, and they are very attractive. Apart from being a birdwatcher's and botanist's paradise, the islands are particularly suited to those keen on walking. Being cut off, the islands have retained an easy-going atmosphere – a wonderful place, with friendly people.

0°21'S 32°20'E
Phone code: 0481
Colour map 2, grid C2

There are forests to walk around and plenty of paths to follow – you will see monkeys, hippos, crocodiles as well as many species of birds. The hippos tend to avoid the habitated islands, having been frightened away to the more isolated areas of the lake. It is now very rare to see both crocodiles and hippos, unfortunately. The islands are hilly and in the uncultivated parts, are still forested. The most important crops on the island are cassava, bananas, sweet potatoes and coffee.

The main island is **Buggala Island** (sometimes spelt Bugala) which is about 34 kilometres long and whose main towns are Kalangala (sometimes spelt Kalengala) and Luku. It has a bus and matatus which link the main towns. The second largest island is **Bukasa Island** and other islands which are easy to visit are **Bubeke** and **Bufumira**.

The island has about 50 kilometres of road on it and really the best thing to do is simply to set off and explore – either by foot or by bicycle (which can be hired from *Andronica's* at Kalangala). All around are wonderful views of the lake and all the other islands – some forested, others cultivated and others a mixture of both. The forests do contain a certain amount of wildlife – although nothing spectacular. There are various species of monkey and a profusion of birdlife. A popular trip is to Mutambala Beach which is off the Kalangala-Luku road – some people do swim despite the risk of bilharzia. There are beautiful walks around the island.

Buggala Island

Sese Islands

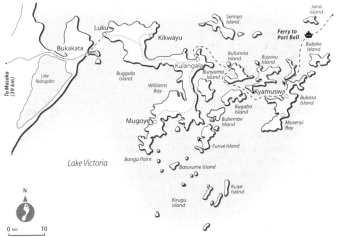

Water hyacinth

The attractive water hyacinth plant is posing a serious threat to the ecology of Lake Victoria. This fast-growing plant is rapidly choking the shores of the Lake and in the past five years the spread of the plant has been phenomenal. Murchison Bay, which is the part of the Lake that can be seen from some of the hills surrounding Kampala, has been severely affected and huge islands of the weed can be seen floating in the Lake.

The plant, which reproduces very fast, covers the water surface completely, starves the water of oxygen with a serious impact on all other species, both plant and animal. It also makes navigation through the water very difficult.

People who rely on fish as the major component of their diet, such as those living on the Seses, are reported to have had to invest in stronger and more expensive fishing nets as a result of the hyacinth.

Efforts are being made to find a solution to the problem. Pulling up the weed appears to be ineffective as the smallest piece of root left behind will regrow rapidly. Other suggestions that have been made include the introduction of a beetle from West Africa that will eat the water hyacinth. Extensive tests are being undertaken to ensure that the beetles will not then eat everything else in sight.

Other islands Although most people stick to Buggala Island there is no reason why you should not venture further afield. Provided you are flexible and not in any hurry you can explore the other islands at your leisure. **Bukasa** is a particularly attractive island – it has a smaller population, is more forested and has a wider range of wildlife. There are two beautiful beaches on the island as well as a waterfall. For further information on how to reach these ask at the *Agnes' Guest House*. **Bufumira Island** can be visited from Kalangal for the day, as can many of the uninhabited islands. Either talk to one of the fishermen or arrange it through *Andronica's Lodge*.

Sleeping There are no hotels in the upper price brackets and if you come to the Seses you should expect to stay in fairly basic accommodation. There are only a few lodges on the islands – all other accommodation is with families. If you ask around someone will be able to put you up, and you will undoubtedly be made to feel most welcome.

Buggala Island Kalangala D *Malaanga Safari Lodge*, (also known as *PTA Andronica Lodge*) PO Box 1165, Kalangala, Masaka, T26. Run by the very friendly Mr Andronico Semakula, (known to everyone as Mzee Andronico) and his daughter, this lodge provides food and lodging, it is the sort of place that some people love and others hate, you will certainly meet other travellers here, but this is a place that has not had to face much competition and so standards have been allowed to slip, recent reports of poor hygiene and cockroaches, not always enough food for all guests. Reports of wildlife in the mattresses may prompt you to ask around elsewhere for other accommodation, there is also a small library and bicycles are available for hire, there is food available at the lodge – but there are much cheaper, and equally good, places nearby, Mzee Andronico is a bit of a character – he is a retired teacher and likes to exercise his business skills so you may have to negotiate over the price of the room, he is full of stories and will be able to tell you all about the island. **E** *Panorama Cottages*, US$15 for 2 persons, but you can share the cottage with more, good food, friendly service, near fishers' village, easy to find from the main road, close to the jetty, generator not on when there are few guests. **E** *Church of Uganda Hostel and Campsite*, this has opened recently and is close to *Andronica's*, it is clean, friendly and cheaper than *Andronica's*, recent travellers report that it looks somewhat desolate and in need of maintenance. **Camping** The 1998 El Niño rainfall has had a great local impact. Lake Victoria's water level rose about 2 metres. The Hornbill campsite lost its beach and the Nsera campsite was flooded. The lake level is likely to go down again but some of the camping facilities may take time to be re-established. **E** *Church of Uganda Hostel*. **E** *Hornbill* campsite, friendly but located 500 metres down a steep track, near the lake with a private 'beach', also has a couple of basic huts. *Nsera Beach Resort*, 2.5 kilometres from Kalangala (downhill) then turn right. Bandas, camping or tree house. Large undercover communal area, pier for swimming and western style ablutions. Excellent for bird-watching. Very friendly, peaceful and relatively undiscovered. Water has been tested as bilharzia free – due to continuously moving water. Managed by the eccentric 'Friday'. Possible to get a boat directly there from Kesenyi fishing village from just outside of Kampala. Memorably sited but exposed to winds from the south, pleasant individual huts US$10, treehouse US$7.50, camping US$1, single bandas US$5, doubles US$7.50.

Luku E *Luku Guest House*, Bugala Island. Run by Mr Kalwangi this is another small and simple lodge, it is useful for people who arrive from Bukakata and is located about a kilometre from the pier, food is available and it is possible to camp. **E** *Sikopian Lodge* (*Scorpion Lodge*), this is a new hotel with 3 doubles and 5 singles, as well as camping space available, serves food and has bicycles available for rent, cold water only and no electricity. **Camping**: at both *Luku Guest House* and *Sikopian Lodge*.

Bukasa Island E *Agnes' Guest House*, located on the second largest island this has a beautiful location overlooking the lake, it is a friendly place – there are both rooms and space for camping, a limited range of food is available.

Camping Apart from the places mentioned you can theoretically camp anywhere on the islands – although obviously you should ask if you are going to be anywhere near people's houses. It is meant to be very safe here – but it goes without saying that you should keep your valuables with you at all times and don't flaunt your wealth.

Transport

Local To get between the islands ask one of the **fishermen** and agree a price. There are **matatus** on the island of Buggala. Other than that the best way to see the islands is to walk around them.

There are several ways of reaching the Seses. You can either go on the steamer *MV Barbus* from Port Bell; the ferry via Masaka; or finally via the village of Kisenyi by ferry or small boat. Which ever way you get to the Sese Islands you may well find yourself arriving as it is getting dark. The first thing to do is a formality – you are required to inform the Police Post of your arrival on the island. Recent travellers indicate that this formality to register with the Police is not always adhered to – but it is probably best to check locally.

Ferry The alternative is to go from Masaka by the Bubakata Ferry, which goes to **Luka** and has the advantage that the journey is shorter. Again the timetable has changed recently – the ferry used to go daily – but now goes 3 times a week on Monday, Wednesday and Friday. Uganda Transport Company runs a bus from Kampala, leaving early in the morning, which goes via Masaka and on to the ferry terminal at Bukakata. Here it takes the ferry to Buggala Island and then drives the last 20 miles to **Kalangala**. Here is the very popular *Hornbill Campsite*, which has good facilities, excellent cheap food, boats and a bar. Own tents are required. Beautifully sited on the beach. Plans are in hand to build bandas on the site. The return journey is run on Tuesday, Thursday and Saturday, leaving at 0600 in the morning. **Small boat**: from Masaka take a matatu to Nyondo from where you should get a share taxi to Butukula to catch the ferry to the town of Luku in the northwest of **Buggala**. Besides the ferry are smaller boats that shuttle between the two on which you should be able to negotiate a ride with. Once in Luku, if you are heading for Kalangala, you may have to wait a while as there is not much traffic along here. There are a couple of places to stay in Luku so it is not really a problem if you arrive late.

The *Port Bell* steamer sank in 1996 when around 100 people drowned in a storm. The captain was reportedly drunk and is being held on manslaughter charges. A new ferry, paid for by Finnish aid, came into service in early 1999. See page 557.

Uganda

☞ *Ankole cattle*

These are the very large horned cattle that are famous throughout the country. Large horns are considered to be very beautiful and they are highly prized possessions. You will even see some cattle whose horns are so large that they are unable to raise their heads, or their heads are constantly leaning to one side.

Alternative routes are tough, even by African standards. Residents of Bukasa tend to sail directly to Kisenyi, rather than travel to the mainland via the other islands. The Kisenyi-Sese Islands route is usually done in open boats. 5 hours is a typical journey time, and it can be especially miserable in heavy rain and after dark. Travellers may find it cheaper to travel from Kalangala to Bukasa Island via Kisenyi (US$5 x 2).

Mbarara

0°35'S 30°40'E
Colour map 2, grid C1

Mbarara is an important trading centre and is a crossroads for travellers heading towards the Rwenzori Mountains and Kabale in the southwest. The town of Mbarara also suffered over the past 20 years but not to the same extent as Masaka. Just before you enter the town centre you will see in the middle of a roundabout a statue of an Ankole steer with its impressive horns. The town is home to one of Uganda's new universities.

Mbarara is the centre of the Kingdom of Ankole. The Kingdom was, like the other kingdoms of Uganda, broken up soon after independence but as part of Museveni's policies all the kingdoms were offered the chance to have their kings back – on the understanding that they were to be cultural figures only without any political role. The palace of the Omugabe (King) of Ankole is located in Mbarara on a hill on the outskirts of town. The buildings have been taken over by the army and huts have sprung up all around the main buildings, as accommodation for the wives and families of the soldiers. Although you will probably not be able to walk around the building (which is in poor repair) you can drive past it. There is the one main building and a few secondary ones. To the right of the main structure is the building which used to house the royal drums. A few miles to the west of Mbarara is the Nkokonjeru which is the burial place of the last two Omugabe of Ankole, Kahaya II and Gasyonga II.

Library on Main Street. Attractive old colonial single-storey building, well-sheltered courtyard with foliage in front, currently being repaired.

The **Aga Khan School** Just on the eastern edge of town is an impressive building combining neo-classical and Indian architectural styles. There are three arches at the front with double mock columns. Portico windows face the building and above the main entrance are crossed flags and the date of construction (1948).

Safari land, just outside town on the road to Kabale, is built in a rocky location and has little walkways and hidden nooks and crannies which contain, among other things, a London Bus, a Wild West Garden and a Jungle Fever enclosure.

About 45 kilometres from Mbarara is **Lake Mburo National Park**, and about 70 kilometres away is the **Kitagata Hot Springs**.

Sleeping

B *Lake View*, PO Box 165, T21394/8, F21399, located on the western outskirts of town and as its name suggests it overlooks a lake, the lake is said to be the King of Ankole's lake and nearby on top of a hill you will be able to see his palace. In front of the hotel is an interesting collection of concrete sculptures of traditional figures by S Rwemizhumbi. Modern, four storey building. Restaurant, bar, business centre, gym, sauna, pool, beauty salon, gift shop.
B *Safariland Park*, PO Box 1512, T21692, south of the road to Kabale, about 3 kilometres from town, self-contained accommodation, hot water, European toilets, restaurant, bar, theme-park decor on a craggy site.

C *University Inn*, PO Box 1410, T20334/5/7, double rooms with bathrooms, set in very pleasant gardens, the water supply is not terribly reliable but the surroundings make it worth staying here, restaurant, bar.

D *Agip Motel*, on the main road from Kampala on the lefthand side as you approach from Kampala. It is modern and comfortable and has a bar which is popular with local business men. **D** *Buhimuriro GH*, PO Box 1255, T12894, south end of town. Shared ablutions, hot water. **D** *Mayoba Inn*, PO Box 326, T21910/21161, north end of town. S/c rooms, hot water, European toilets. Reception upstairs, through bar. Restaurant, mainly grills.

E *Africa GH*, PO Box 1378, T21712, F21304, main street. Shared ablutions, squat toilets, hot water. No bar or food, gate closes at midnight. **E** *Andrews Inn*, PO Box 1310, T20244, situated about 1 kilometre off to the right just before you reach Mbarara. Unless you have your own vehicle it is rather out of the way, there is a range of rooms, hot water, self-contained, restaurant and bar. **E** *Bunhorro*, located up to the right of the main road near the church, cheap and simple food available. **E** *Church Of Uganda Hostel*, next to the bus station. Dormitory accommodation. **E** *Entry View GH*, PO Box 1252, north end of town. Shared ablutions, European toilets, hot water, local food, bar. **E** *Kikome Rest House*, PO Box 527, on the northern edge of town. Shared bathrooms, squat toilets, cold water, comfortable enough, but fairly simple. **E** *Mbiringi Hotel*, PO Box 843, T21162, north end of town. Shared squat toilets, hot water, bar, (no food), good value. **E** *Memory Lodge*, PO Box 357, T20934. Central, hot water, shared ablutions, no food or bar. **E** *New Safari*, central. Very simple, shared squat toilets, no food or bar. **E** *Pelican*, centre of town. Good value, rooms clean and comfortable. **E** *Sabena Club*, located about 3 kilometres out of town, down a turn-off roughly opposite the *Lake View Hotel*. There is food available. **E** *Silver Inn*, PO Box 357, located off the main road to the right just after the *Motel Agip*. The rooms are basic but clean, hot water, shared European toilets, bar, good value.

Camping At *Safariland*, the *Sabena Club* and *Katatumba Hotel*, below.

Outside Mbarara A-E *Katatumba Hotel*, PO Box 1177, Mbarara, T20152/20090, F21300. Luxurious resort-style hotel and has a fine variety of facilities – sauna, tennis courts, horse-riding, satellite television and camel-riding, there is a range of accommodation available – there are self contained rooms in bands **A** to **C**, then there are economy rooms (**D-E**), if you have equipment you can camp for US$5, there is an excellent restaurant and bar, run by the same people as the *Hotel Diplomate* on Tank Hill in Kampala.

B *Pan Africa*, PO Box 1169, Mbarara Resort-style hotel, located 40 kilometres from Mbarara on the road to Kabale. The staff are friendly and they will try very hard to persuade to do one of their many activities, these include guided tours around coffee farms, banana plantations, a trip to the Hot Springs at Kitagata.

Mbarara

To Masaka & Kampala

To Andrews Inn

To Masaka & Kampala

Shell

Total

Mackansyh St

Nile

Lucky Supermarket

Library

Gold Trust

Bulemba Rd

Cinemao

Mbarara United Club

Community Rural Development Bank

Uganda Commercial

All in One Bar

Market

Aga Khan Mosque

Aga Khan School

Vision Empire Disco

Muscleflex Gym

N

0 metres 50

To University & Lake View Hotels, Kabale & Kasese

■ Sleeping
1 Africa Guest House
2 Church Hostel
3 Buhimariro Guest House
4 Entry View
5 Kikomgs Rent House
6 Kings Lodge
7 Mayoba Inn
8 Mbiringi
9 Memory Lodge
10 Motel Agip
11 New Safari Guest House
12 Pelican
13 Ruhinda Bar & Lodge
14 Safariland
15 Silver Inn

● Eating
1 Akaanye Pub
2 Comar Café
3 Island Grill
4 Mbarara Coffee House
5 Pram Take-Away
6 Pub Mercury
7 Sek Eats
8 Tree Shade Café

Uganda

Eating **2** *Mbarara Coffee Shop*, Main St. Fish, local stews, grills, curries, spaghetti. **2** *Pram Take-Away*, Main St. Grills, chapatis and samosas. Pleasant forecourt.

1 *Island Grill*, just west of Main St. Variety of grills, good value. **1** *Seko Eats*, next to Island Grill. Grills and local dishes.

Bars *Pub Mercury*, on main through road, has a pleasant verandah.

Entertainment **Sport** *Mbarara Sports Club*, southwest of town centre. Squash, tennis, golf. *Muscleflex Gym*, at the southern end of town, US$3 a day.

Transport **Air** There is a small airport at Mbarara but there are no scheduled flights any longer – only charter.

Road Mbarara is located nearly 300 kilometres from **Kampala** and about 150 kilometres from Kabale. The road is excellent – one of the best in the country. There are buses to and from Kampala every day. They leave from both the UTC bus station and the private bus station from 0600. Returning to Kampala there are also early morning buses or else you might also be able to get onto the bus that has come from Kabale, although this is sometimes full by the time it reaches Mbarara. There are of course also matatus although many people choose to avoid them as they drive particularly fast on this road. There are also buses from Mbarara to **Kasese** and **Fort Portal**, a distance of about 180 kilometres on a newly improved road.

Directory **Banks** *Uganda Commercial Bank*, 0830-1600 Mon-Fri, 0930-1300 Sat. *Nile Bank*, Main St, 0830-1600 Mon-Fri, 0930-1300 Sat. *Gold Trust Bank*, Main St, 0830-1600 Mon-Fri, 0900-1200 Sat.

Kabale

1°15'S 30°0'E
Phone code: 0486
Colour map 2, grid C1

The road from Mbarara to Kabale is good – you pass through the pastoral areas – a mix of dry plains and some more undulating countryside. Shortly before you reach Kabale the terrain changes and becomes more hilly and greener. Before long the scenery becomes increasingly dramatic with very steep slopes. If you are driving through this area very early in the morning the valleys are filled with mist.

Kabale is located in the southwestern corner of Uganda, an area which is characterized by great diversity of topography, landscape and vegetation. Parts of this area are densely forested while the rest is extremely heavily populated and intensively cultivated. You will see some hillsides that have been terraced to increase the cultivable area. This was undertaken during the colonial era.

The old part of the town is located up the hill – here you will find the government offices – many dating back to the early colonial period, the hospital, the church and the White Horse Inn. The other essential part of colonial life – the golf course – is also on the hill. It is all very spaciously laid out with well kept flower beds and mowed lawns in between. The newer part of the town is spread out along the main road, down in what used to be a swampy valley – it is wide with the buildings set back from the road.

The area around Kabale is ideal for hikers – it is often described as the Little Switzerland of Africa. There are tracks and paths through the hills and local guides.

Sights **Lake Bunyonyi** A popular day trip which you can either walk to or else hire a bike. Walking from Kabale takes about 1½ hours (13 kilometres). Take the road towards Kisoro and Kisizi, there is a turn-off after one kilometre, there is a signpost to Lake Bunyonyi on the left hand side. The more direct route shown on the map of Kabale has the disadvantage of very poor roads. It takes about an hour from here. Getting pickups can be difficult, US$0.50 as traffic is infrequent. If you are cycling then be prepared for a long hard slog up and a wonderful run down. Once you get to Lake Bunyonyi you will almost certainly be offered a canoe trip across to **Bwama island**

in the lake. You can expect to pay US$1-2 per person to be rowed across. Nice place for bird watching. On the island there is a school with pupils aged 5-17. (Originally it was a leper settlement.) The school is run by a social worker and a hard working headmaster, Mgababa Jasper, PO Box 1114, Kabale, Uganda. Jasper has done an excellent job with the school and children, and welcomes visitors. Jasper has built a small campsite and a nice little hut with a double bed and a bucket shower on an adjacent island. It is very quiet, lots of birdlife and costs US$4 – proceeds go towards the running of the school. The school has a 'sponsor a child' programme costing US$11 for an entire year. A campsite has recently opened for travellers and volunteers. Again all proceeds go to help the school, costs US$2 per person per night. More information available at the *Visitors Hotel* in Kabale. The school-children make craft items for sale to tourists and there is a shop on the island. There is a new campsite at Karibuni Beach. Enquire at the *Visitors Hotel* for the local entrepreneur who rents dug out canoes. Prices by negotiation – appear to vary considerably. There is also camping at the *Old Lodge* at the first hill on the lake shore. Cold beers and sodas available, but no food. A little further on is another campsite used a lot by overlander's trucks. **Bunyonyi Overland Camp** and Parking. New development, several travellers have recommended this campsite. Ecologically built with local materials. Offers secure car parking US$1 per car per night. Campsite well equipped with a variety of accommodation, hot showers, swimming and canoeing, bird watching, volley ball, tortoise pond, biking and fishing. Restaurant serves locally caught crayfish. Fully stocked bar. Charges from US$2-8 depending on type of accommodation. Emergency VHF radio contact with *Highland Business Centre*. Car hire and transport can be arranged. Laundry facilities. Contact: Highland Business Centre, 1 Kazooba Rd, PO Box 710, Kabale, T0486-23743/1, F23742. In Lake Bunyani there is a campsite on **Bushara Island**, with fully furnished tents. Bushara Island Camps are part of a project to minimize soil erosion and increase the agricultural yield of local farmers. The tourist revenues pay the salaries of agroforestry workers who support the local farmers. Excellent for bird watching. Landing fee for day visitors US$1. Contact Highland Business Centre (as above) or Bushara Island Camps, Box 794, Kabale, T/F486-22447. From Bunyonyi Overland Camp follow the lake shore around to the southeast and you will find the old Resort Hotel. The owners of the Backpackers Campsite in Kampala have bought Idi Amin's villa on the lake. It's in a beautiful location, very quiet. Renovation is planned to start soon and various grades of accommodation will be on offer, including camping. The only restaurant on the lakeshore is the *Bamboo Tours Hotel*, very good crayfish with chips, try the Congolese beer. Locals claim that Lake Bunyonyi is the only lake in Uganda that is bilharzia free.

Hot Springs These are some 10 kilometres to the south of Kabale. You can either hire a bike or walk, although you may need a guide to find it. Many of the local people have traditionally used the Hot Springs for their ablutions and find the presence of tourists embarrassing. Before you set off check that there are no problems – being so close to the Rwanda border this is a sensitive area.

Kisizi Waterfalls This 90 foot waterfall near to the village of Kisizi about 30 kilometres from Kabale can be visited by matatu from Kabale. They leave about once an hour and take two hours. *Kisizi Hospital* has a small guest house which

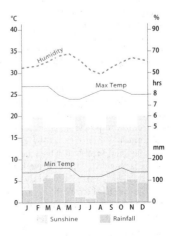

Climate: Kabale

☞ *Naipaul and Theroux IIi – Lions on Tour*

Around the middle of 1966 Naipaul and Theroux (see box, page 265) planned a trip to Rwanda. Naipaul got himself comprehensively kitted out in safari clothing, waterproof walking boots and a stout walking stick. Equipped to ascend Kilimanjaro, Naipaul got into Theroux's car. Leaving Kampala before dawn, they motored down to Masaka, and through Mbarara. At Kabale, Theroux suggested a bite to eat at the White Horse Inn. Naipal revealed that he'd had words with the manager on a previous visit, but sportingly agreed to wait in the car while his companion lunched Unfortunately Theroux was turned out of the restaurant as he hadn't brought a tie, and he had to make do with a sandwich in the bar.

Pressing on to Kisoro, Theroux took a wrong turn and ended up at the border crossing to what is now R D Congo. Turning back, they crossed into Rwanda, passed through Ruhengeri in the late afternoon, and decided to push on to Kigali, arriving after dark. After looking at various hotels that

didn't meet with Naipaul's approval – presumably because the proprietors were not nutty enough – they fronted up at the American Embassy and were lodged in the official guest house for the night.

Next day, unimpressed by the small-town atmosphere of the capital they left for Gisenyi on Lake Kivu. They were put up in the Miramar, where Naipal was irritated by the only other guests, a large family of boisterous Belgians. Taking a walk along the Lake Shore, and viewing the deterioration and neglect that had set in during the few years since the end of Belgian rule, Naipal was, as ever, deeply pessimistic about Africa's prospects.

Next day they motored to nearby Goma, where Naipal took the opportunity to lecture a local Asian businessman on the impending doom. They stayed another night in Gisenyi before driving back to Kampala. This was their last adventure together in Africa. Shortly afterwards Naipal departed leaving Theroux with the gift of an orange tie and the assurance that he would do well as a writer.

has accommodation available for rent when not required by official hospital visitors. Unfortunately it is not possible to pre-book the rooms as the hospital has not got a phone/fax. Visitors are encouraged to check out this option as any money generated goes towards the cost of running the hospital.

Gorillas Kabale is the town that you will pass through, and probably stay a night or two, if you are planning a visit to the gorillas – which can be done in Uganda or RD Congo. (For Uganda see National Parks Section, page 650). Be warned if you want to see them in Uganda you must book your day and buy your tracking permit in Kampala – there are no facilities to make the booking in Kabale and many people who turn up there are disappointed (you can, however, take up a cancellation). If you have been told in Kampala that there are no spaces but have decided to risk it and see if anyone has cancelled it is worth hanging around Kabale for a couple of days and talking to people on the way back. They will be able to tell you if there is a huge backlog of people on the waiting list at Buhoma and whether it is worth you going straight there or waiting in Kabale for a few days (a National Park permit is valid for three days only).

Recent travellers report that the gorilla tracking permit system is so unreliable that they advise going straight to Kisoro, arranging a lift from there to Mgahinga Park (costs US$20, regardless of the number of people) and getting on the stand-by list. From the six people that go to see the gorillas every day, four have booked and two will normally go from the stand-by list. However, information on obtaining a standby has varied, and it may be that the situation varies. If you fail to see the gorillas, the permit fee is refunded. If there are too many people on the stand-by list Mgahinga are prone to radio down to Kabale to say the gorillas have crossed into the Congo and the excursion is off. Alternatively they contrive that the booked visitors only arrive after the guides have departed. With no-one turning up from the booked list, all six people can be selected from the stand-by list. Petty bribery by the stand-by visitors has resulted in this situation. It is possible to camp in the park for US$3, or there are some beds in a hut. The road to the park is not sealed but it is in good condition.

Bwindi **Impenetrable/Mgahinga Gorilla National Parks Information Office**, PO Box 723, Kabale, Uganda, has recently opened in Kabale near the Co-operative Bank next to the Hot Loaf bakery. Helps tourists to get to the National Parks, possible places to stay, campsites, info about places to visit in Kigezi Mountains. Has tourist maps, postcards and handicrafts.

Sleeping

The accommodation at Kabale can be overcrowded due to foreign aid traffic for Rwanda and Burundi passing through. There are also a lot of NGO officials staying in Uganda before venturing into less safe areas.

B *White Horse Inn*, PO Box 11, Lwamafa Rd, Kabale, T23336/37/99, F23717. This is the best hotel in Kabale and is one of the *Uganda Hotels* Corporation chain, it has recently been done up. Brick verandah off dining room. High standards – in the past V S Naipaul has been

Uganda

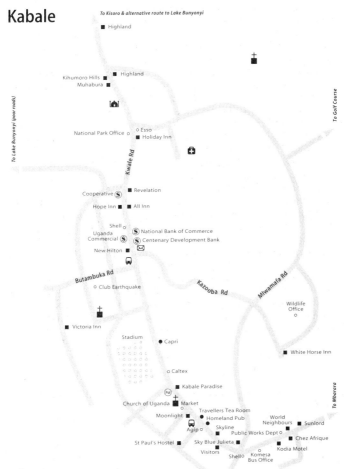

Kabale

To Kisoro & alternative route to Lake Bunyonyi

Highland

Highland

Kihumoro Hills
Muhabura

National Park Office ○
○ Esso
Holiday Inn

Kwale Rd

To Lake Bunyonyi (poor roads)

To Golf Course

Cooperative ⑤
Revelation

Hope Inn ■ ■ All Inn

Shell ○
Uganda
Commercial ⑤
⑤ National Bank of Commerce
⑤ Centenary Development Bank

New Hilton ■

Butambuka Rd

○ Club Earthquake

Kazooba Rd

Mlwamafa Rd

Wildlife
Office
○

Victoria Inn

Stadium

Capri

○ Caltex

White Horse Inn

Kabale Paradise
Church of Uganda
Market

Travellers Tea Room

Moonlight
Homeland Pub
World
Neighbours
Sunlord

Agip ○
Skyline
Public Works Dept ○
Chez Afrique

St Paul's Hostel
Sky Blue Julieta
Visitors
Shello
Komesa
Bus Office
Kodia Motel

To Mbarara

N

0 metres 100

To Rwanda

banned and Paul Theroux thrown out of the restaurant (see box page 618). Cottages with steep shingle roofs connected by walkways. Tennis court, pool table. Pleasant lounge, bar and restaurant. Set in wonderful gardens, service is slow, the access road is only negotiable with a four-wheel drive in the rain.

C *Victoria Inn*, PO Box 741, Kabale, T0486-22154/22134. Located in the southwestern part of town the Victoria Inn has about 20 very clean rooms all with their own bathrooms with running water, there is hot water available in buckets, and an electricity generator, wood fireplace, brick pathways, restaurant and bar.

D *Highland*, PO Box 95, T22175, F23742. North end of town on road to Kisoro. Guarded internal parking lot, running water, although there is only bucket hot water, also Business centre Forex office, good value.

E *All Inn*, PO Box 727, T24307. Shared facilities, hot water, European toilets. Restaurant and bar. **E** *Capri*, PO Box 641, T24124, F23200. Only 4 rooms, hot water, European toilets, shared facilities. Recommended for value. **E** *Chez Afrique*, PO Box 668, T23508. European shared toilets, bar, no food. **E** *Holiday Inn*, PO Box 866, T23550. Hot water, shared ablutions, squat toilets. Restaurant with grills and local food. Bar with billiards, darts, draughts, chess. **E** *Hope Inn*, PO Box 2234. Shared ablutions, hot water, squat toilets. Restaurant and bar. **E** *Hotel Revelation*, PO Box 752, T23292, F23290. Shared ablutions, European toilets, hot water, phones, TV. Restaurant with grills and local food, bar, good value. **E** *Kabale Paradise Hotel*, PO Box 285, T22083. Rather basic, shared bathrooms, squat toilets, no hot water. **E** *Kasiizi Hospital Guest Accommodation*, PO Box 109, T271776, F34143. Due north of Kabale, about 30 kilometres by road, turning off the road to Mbarara, just before Rwahi. Two cottages available. Kasiizi falls nearby. Daily bus to Kabale, leaves Kabale at noon, Kasiizi at 0700. **E** *Kuhimoro Hills Hotel*, PO Box 475, T22131. Simple style, shared squat toilets, hot water. **E** *Moonlight*, PO Box 822, T23317, near market. Shared bathrooms, squat toilets, simple meals, bar. **E** *Muhabura Inn*, very basic, shared ablutions. Bar but no restaurant. **E** *New Hilton*, Main St. Rather basic. Restaurant and bar. **E** *St Paul's Training Centre and Hostel*, take the left turning off the main road beyond the market and it is located a little way down on the right, it is signposted. Cheapest of all the places in Kabale, there are basic meals available. **E** *Skyblue Julieta*, (PO Box and Tel same as *Victoria Inn* above) opposite the matatu stop. All rooms have common facilities, running water is intermittent but plenty of buckets of hot and cold water are provided, well organized, safe parking for motor-cycles, the *Skyblues* are run by a very helpful manager called Elisa who will give you all sorts of useful advice. **E** *Skyline Hotel*, PO Box 78, T24071. Fairly basic. Shared bathrooms, European toilets, hot water. Restaurant with grills and local dishes. Bar. **E** *Sunland Hotel*, PO Box 617, south end of town on Mbarara Rd. Some self-contained rooms. Hot water, food and bar. **E** *Visitors*, PO Box 128, T22239. Next door to the matatu stop and they usually send someone to meet all the buses. It is very friendly and is slightly cheaper than the *Skyblue*, the rooms are a bit shabbier but there is a lovely verandah, meals good, water at times, ask for one of the back rooms as very noisy at the front, restaurant downstairs with grills, local food, curries, spaghetti. **E** *World Neighbours Inn*, PO Box 664, south end of town on Mbarara Rd. Clean and simple. European toilets (shared). Bar. No restaurant.

Eating There are no separate restaurants, but all the hotels provide meals. The **3** *White Horse* is the most expensive, and quite reasonable quality. Popular are **2** *Highlands* does very acceptable food. **2** *Visitors* and the central **2** *Skyblue Julieta* and the food is good value. **2** *Capri Restaurant*, PO Box 641, T24124, F23200. Bright, neat and clean, wide variety – Chinese, Indian, Russian, Italian, Greek, Hungarian, French dishes. Set menu of curry, rice and fruit salad recommended. Good fruit juices. **2** *Homeland Pub*, popular restaurant and bar just opposite bus station. Grills and local dishes. Pleasant courtyard. **1** *Hot loaf bakery* opposite Uganda Commercial Bank sells excellent pizzas and pastry, best cakes in Uganda. **1** *Travellers' Tea Room*, near market and bus park. Mostly snacks – eggs, chapattis, samosas, sambunas, donuts.

Sport Visitors can have a round of golf at the course to the northwest of town, for around US$15.

Local One of the features of Kabale is the bicycle taxi with a padded seat for the passenger behind the saddle. As Kabale is flat, it is cheap and quick for travel about town.

Road Kabale is a distance of about 400 kilometres from **Kampala**. There are daily buses direct in both directions. They leave Kampala (from both the UTC bus station and the private bus station) around 0600 and arrive in Kabale sometime early in the afternoon. The bus costs US$10 for UTC and US$12 for the private buses. If you miss the bus you may want to get a matatu. There is actually little to be gained by doing this – the time of departure is not fixed and you wait until it is full. They usually leave about mid-morning and take about an hour less than the buses. Return departs at 0600. You can either go down to the bus station itself or else wait outside the central Skyblue Julieta, ready (preferably with a torch) to wave and whistle to be picked up. It is a lovely journey as the sun rises as you leave Kabale. Alternatively, the Daily Post bus runs between Kampala and Kabale (except Sundays). Departs at 0645 from Kabale.

If you are heading for **Kasese** or **Fort Portal** take the bus as far as Mbarara and change there, possible in one day, but takes a lot of patience.

For transport to Bwindi National Park ask at the National Parks Information Office. It's best on Friday because there is a market in Buhoma on Saturday.

There are 2 possible routes to **Rwanda**. The first is the border post of **Gatuna** (also known as Katuna) which is the more direct route. Alternatively you can go via Kisoro to **Ruhengeri** which is the longer, about 3 hours, but a more scenic route. Buses (AMK Express, Horizon Express) for Rwanda via Katuna stop at the Kiomesa office, south of town on the Mbarara Rd at around 1000-1100. Visas are available at the border US$20. Matatus to **Kisoro** go occasionally throughout the day. This is a wonderful journey and some say that this is the most beautiful part of Uganda. Kabale to Bwindi pickup, takes 4 hours, US$10 per person.

Banks and Forex Bureau *National Bank of Commerce*, Main St. 0830-1500 Mon-Fri, 0900-1300 Sat. *Highlands Forex Bureau*, Highland Hotel.

Kisoro

Kisoro is in the extreme southwestern corner of Uganda about 510 kilometres from Kampala, and just over 80 kilometres from Kabale. At the moment the town is suffering rather from the lack of traffic through to Rwanda. The **Mufumbiro Mountains** are located in this corner of the country – made up of three extinct volcanoes: Muhabura (4,125 metres), Mgahinga (3,474 metres) and Sabyinyo (3,674 metres). These are located on the border of Uganda, RD Congo and Rwanda and are known as the Virunga Range. Anyone planning to visit the Congolese gorillas will come to Kisoro, and once the Mgahinga National Park is fully developed this will also be an added attraction (see National Parks, page 653). Near to Kisoro to the north is **Lake Mutanda**. Ask around for a guide to take you there or else head back up the Kabale road for about two kilometres and the turnoff is on your left. This lovely walk offers superb views over Lake Mutanda. By using the 50,000:1 map available from the tourist office it is easy to find your way should you not wish to use a guide.

1°17'S 29°48'E
Colour map 2, grid C1

Visiting the gorillas in RD Congo is possible although some of the tour operators are anxious about the political situation. This changes almost from week to week and obviously you will have to talk to local people to establish the current situation.

The basic difference with Uganda is that the Congolese gorillas are much more used to humans – many people would say that they are over-habituated. It is one thing to get close to these animals so that you get a good view, but it is another to feel that you are really in little more than a zoo. In Uganda you truly feel that these are wild animals – and you are entering their world, leaving a genuine feeling of awe for the gorillas. Rules and regulations, which are largely ignored in RD Congo, are made solely to increase the chance of the long term survival of the gorillas. Those involved in gorilla-tourism in Uganda are trying to learn from the mistakes made in RD Congo, and to a lesser extent in Rwanda, and not repeat them.

To get to RD Congo you will need to get a lift in a truck to the border via Kisoro – ask around at the matatu station and someone should be able to put you in touch with someone heading in that direction. Alternatively take a matatu to Kisoro (there should be a few each day, as well as a bus once a day) and ask around for a lift for the remaining nine kilometres to the border. At the border you will be met by a guide who will offer to take you to the huts and from there to see the gorillas. If you refuse him you will probably end up walking about eight hours as you will not know the short cuts – with a guide it should take you about two hours. This is where the tipping begins and it is from here that the costs of seeing the gorillas are so difficult to estimate. Basically, although the permit to see the gorillas is cheaper in RD Congo than in Uganda and transport to them is cheaper, there are many more hidden costs involved in a trip to RD Congo. You will need to take into account the extra cost of visas for entering RD Congo and then re-entering Uganda, tips to the border officials, tips to the guides, and so on. It is also more costly in that once you reach the huts that you stay in for the night, everything, including accommodation, food and drinks are all expensive.

Kisora has a superb market which is held on Monday and Thursday. This market used to take place on the Congolese-Ugandan border until the tense political situation prompted its move. It is very colourful and attracts traders from Uganda, RD Congo and Rwanda. Highly recommended.

Sleeping **A** *Mount Gahinga Rest Camp*, on the edge of Mgahinga NP. Luxury thatched cottages or tents (also see entry, page 654). Run by *Volcanoes Tours* (see entry for *Travellers Rest* below for booking details). **A** *Travellers Rest*. This is a well known hotel amongst gorilla experts for it was once known as the unofficial gorilla headquarters. This was because in the mid-1950s the game warden, Walter Baumgartel, self styled 'King of the Gorillas', was also the owner of the Travellers Rest. He was one of the first people to take an interest in gorillas and their protection. Amongst the scientists who stayed here were Diane Fossey and George Schaller and it became a centre for primate experts from around the world. Baumgartel left Uganda in the late 1960s and the hotel was later taken over by the *Uganda Hotels* Corporation. Recently renovated by *Volcanoes Tours*. Booking details: *Volcanoes Tours*, PO Box 22818, Kampala, T041-346464/5, F041-341718, Mobile 075-741718, volcanoes@infocom.co.ug.

Kisoro

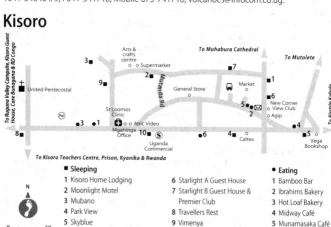

■ **Sleeping**
1 Kisoro Home Lodging
2 Moonlight Motel
3 Mubano
4 Park View
5 Skyblue

6 Starlight A Guest House
7 Starlight B Guest House & Premier Club
8 Travellers Rest
9 Vimenya
10 Western

● **Eating**
1 Bamboo Bar
2 Ibrahims Bakery
3 Hot Loaf Bakery
4 Midway Café
5 Munamasaka Café
6 St Johns Pub

B *Kisoro Guesthouse*, 1 kilometre from town towards RD Congo border. Well appointed, also run by *Volcanoes Tours* – see above.

D *Sky Blue*, PO Box 225, T76. Shared bathrooms, hot water, simple but comfortable.

E *Kisoro Home Lodging*, very basic, but cheap. **E** *Moonlight Hotel*, PO Box 282. Rather basic, shared bathrooms. **E** *Mubano*, PO Box 198. All rooms have bathrooms, there are doubles and triples only, there is an excellent restaurant attached. **E** *Park View*, PO Box 92. Shared bathrooms, hot water, restaurant with good simple fare. **E** *Starlight 'A' and 'B'*, PO Box 89, T3001. Simple, shared bathrooms, hot water. *Starlight 'B'* has *Premier Club* bar attached. **E** *Starlight Hotel*, PO Box 89. Some self-contained rooms, hot water, no food. **E** *Virunga Hotel*, situated behind the Park headquarters. Recently opened, clean, friendly, good food, located on just the other side of the fence of the *Mubano Hotel*. **E** *Western Hotel*, currently closed, but is expected to re-open. Fairly simple, shared bathrooms. **E** Village cooperative bandas just outside the Mgahinga park entrance recommended. New and clean. Good food.

Camping Available at *Virunga Hotel*, US$6 per tent, and *Mubano*, at US$4 per tent. *Rugana Valley Campsite*, PO Box 4, 1.5 kilometres west out of Kisoro. Tents US$4, also lodge accommodation (**E**). Organizes hikes and hill-climbing.

1 *Hot Loaf Bakery*, just past the Mgahinga NP booking office on the main road. **1** *Ibrahim's Bakery*, close to market. Fresh bread, donuts, samosas. **1** *Midway Café*, west end of town. Simple fare, grills and snacks. **1** *Munamasaka Café*, near market. Basic snacks. **Eating**

St John's Pub. Busiest place in town. Disco on Fridays and Saturdays. *Bamboo Bar*, *Premier Club*, *New Corner View Club*, all fairly simple bars. **Bars**

There is a basic *Supermarket* just after the *Virunga* Hotel. Markets held Monday and Thursday – fresh fruit and vegetables available. *Art and Craft Centre* next door to supermarket. **Shopping**

Road The Mgahinga NP is about 13 kilometres from Kisoro. A boda-boda motorbike taxi ride there is a cheap option although you may have to walk over some of the roughest parts of the route. **Transport**
    There are matatus to **Kabele** occasionally throughout the day. There are matatus to the Rwanda border to cross to **Ruhengeri**, taking about 3 hours, a more scenic route and it is said that this is the most beautiful part of Uganda.

Air Kisoro now has an airstrip which opened in August 1998. Close to the town. You can fly from Entebbe to Kisoro. Return flight costs around US$100.

Uganda

National Parks

The National Parks covered in this section are the Queen Elizabeth National Park, Murchison Falls, Kidepo, Lake Mburo, Kibale Forest, Rwenzori Mountains, Bwindi Impenetrable Forest and Mgahinga Gorilla National Park. Apart from the ten parks covered in this section, there are another five designated (their locations are marked on the National Parks and Game Reserves map). However, they do not have any facilities and are, at present, unpromising to visit.

For up-to-date information on the parks, and to buy a gorilla tracking permit you should visit the Uganda Wildlife Authority, PO Box 3530, T041-346290, F236291, in Kampala. This has recently changed location and can now be found a little way out of town on the Kintu Road 300 metres past the Sheraton Hotel. Take a matatu from the matatu park toward Makerere University and Kira road, past the museum.

Uganda national parks & game reserves

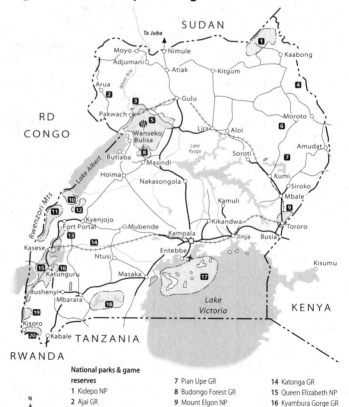

National parks & game reserves

1 Kidepo NP	7 Pian Upe GR	14 Katonga GR
2 Ajai GR	8 Budongo Forest GR	15 Queen Elizabeth NP
3 Achwa Lolim GR	9 Mount Elgon NP	16 Kyambura Gorge GR
4 Matheniko GR	10 Toro GR	17 Sese Islands GR
5 Murchison Falls NP	11 Rwenzori Mountains NP	18 Lake Mburo NP
6 Bokora Corridor GR	12 Semliki Valley Wildlife Reserve	19 Bwindi NP
	13 Kibale Forest GR	20 Mgahinga Gorilla NP

0 km   55

Uganda

Ugandan Park Fees

Prices are per person and subject to change

Category A *(entrance per day)*
Murchison Falls, Queen Elizabeth, Bwindi Impenetrable and Mgahinga Gorilla National Parks

Adult	US$15
Youth 5-18 years	US$8
Children under 5 years	Free

Category B
All other protected areas in the UWA system

Adult	US$7
Youth 5-18 years	US$3
Children under 5 years	Free

Ranger guide fees

Per half day	US$10

Accommodation
(prices in Ush)

	Single	Double	Triple	Extra person
Category A: ensuite	20,000	30,000	40,000	5,000
Category B: basic/traditional	10,000	15,000	20,000	3,000

NB Advanced booking requires a 50% non-refundable advance payment.
prices are per person unless otherwise stated

Do-it-yourself camping

per person per night	US$10

Vehicle entry fees
Only for Murchison, Queen Elizabeth, Kidepo, Lake Mburo National Parks and all Wildlife Reserves

Motor-cycles	US$20
Minibuses, cars and pick-ups	US$30
Rescue fees	US$10

NB Foreign registered vehicles carrying tourists are allowed in the country as long as the driver has an international driving licence and pays at the point of entry temporary vehicle licence which is determined by Uganda Revenue Authority basing on the capacity, purpose of use and duration of stay. The minimal sum is US$50.

Gorilla tracking
Bwindi Impenetrable National Park*
 US$250 plus park entry fee advance booking
 US$150 stand-by
*U$30 non refundable booking fee for advance booking 6 months to one year.
Mgahinga Gorilla National Park* US$175
*US$50 deposit fee for 2 months advance booking.

Chimpanzee tracking

Kyambura George	US$30

Primate walk

Kibale National Park	US$10

Launch cruise/boat trip	US$20
Queen Elizabeth National Park *(2 hours)*	
Minimum charge per cruise US$120	
Murchison Falls National Park *(3 hours)*	
Minimum charge per cruise US$150	
Lake Mburo National Park *(2 hours)*	
	US$40 per trip

Guided nature walk
All protected areas

	Half day (upto 5 hours)	Full day (over 5 hours)
Adult	US$5	US$7.50
Youth	US$2.50	US$3

Mountaineering*

	Up to 5 days	Up to 10 days
Rwenzori Mountains National Park		
	US$250	US$350
Mount Elgon National Park		
	US$90	US$10
		per every extra day

*Includes park visitation fee
Rwenzori mountaineering is suspended until further notice.

Virunga Volcano climb
Magahinga Gorilla National Park US$30
Includes park visitation fees

Uganda

National Park bylaws

Camping and camp fires permitted at official sites only.

Off-road driving prohibited.

Driving between 1915 and 0630 is forbidden.

Blowing of motor horns is prohibited.

A speed limit of 40 kilometres per hour should be observed.

Carrying of arms or ammunition is forbidden.

Dogs are not allowed in the Park.

Littering in the Parks is an offence.

Queen Elizabeth (Rwenzori) National Park

The Queen Elizabeth National Park lies across the Equator in the southwest of Uganda. It is bordered to the southwest by Lake Edward and to the northeast by Lake George. The two lakes are joined together by the 33-kilometre long Kazinga Channel. The park covers an area of 1,978 square kilometres, mainly flat and gently undulating terrain which rises from the lakes 910 metres to 1,390 metres above sea level at the crater area to the north of the Kazinga Channel. To the northeast are the Rwenzori Mountains, often known as the Mountains of the Moon, which rise to over 5,000 metres. On a clear day it is possible to see the Rwenzoris.

There are two centres for touring the Park, from Mweya Lodge in the north, and *Ishasha River Camp* in the south. After covering the general history and ecology of the park, accommodation, travel details and viewing routes are first presented for the northern (*Mweya Lodge*) sector, and then for the southern (*Ishasha River Camp*) sector.

Prehistory In the early 1930s Sir Vivian Fuchs discovered fossils from the Early Pleistocene period along the Kazinga Channel, but it was not until some years later that prehistoric material was found. From the finds and work in Queen Elizabeth National Park it is possible to indicate a little of the prehistory of this area. The fossils that have been found are water snails and other molluscs, crocodiles (which do not occur in Lakes George or Edward), hippos (including the pygmy variety), members of the pig family and various fish including Nile Perch.

No tools belonging to the Early Pleistocene have been found in the fossiliferous ironstone bands, which are readily seen outcropping along the Kazinga Channel. Elsewhere in Africa this was an important period in human evolution and in East Africa ape-men of the Australopithecine family were beginning to make recognizable stone tools and became effective hunters rather than scavengers. Over a large area of the Queen Elizabeth National Park, and possibly as far north as Murchison Falls, transient lakes existed in the comparatively shallow trough of the Rift Valley. It seems that these early palaeolithic hunters would have lived around these lakes hunting their prey whose bones are often found in the ironstone bands.

Following the faulting in the middle Pleistocene, the Rift Valley became more pronounced and the lakes more permanent. Stone tools found in the deposits from the period have been hand-axes of quartz and quartzite and pebble tools, which are water worn pebbles flaked to give a sharp cutting edge.

At Mweya on the peninsula of land leading to the present lodge, stone tools have been found in gravels which date from a slightly later period. The material found in a 1958 excavation consisted of all the types of tools of a fully developed Acheulean hand-axe culture – hand-axes, cleavers, round stone balls and waste flakes. Similar tools have been found on the south bank of the Kazinga Channel.

The stone balls were thought to be wrapped in skin and attached to thongs and used to throw at animals. Hunting was probably conducted by making drives using wooden spears. The hand-axe, stone-bladed, was a standard tool, an all-purpose cutting implement. The cleaver (or straight-edged hand-axe) was used for skinning or chopping whilst the waste flakes, resulting from the making of the tools would have been used to scrape skin, and sharpen spears. The tools were made quickly and had a short life. The constant search for food would account for the widespread nature of the stone tools as well as their profusion – it is likely that many temporary camps around the lakes and water holes were established.

Judging from the profusion of waste flakes of quartz dating from the Late Stone Age, right along the Kazinga Channel, the Queen Elizabeth National Park continued to be an area eminently suitable for hunting, fishing and fowling until recent times. It is not known when agriculture was introduced although this was probably some time before the end of the first millennium AD, from which time the area became progressively pastoral. It is unlikely that a large population was ever supported. Surface collections of pottery indicate that the Kazinga Channel and lake shore regions, where fishing supplemented agriculture, were always more populous than the drier plains. The present depopulation of the Park is largely a result of the ravages of

Queen Elizabeth National Park

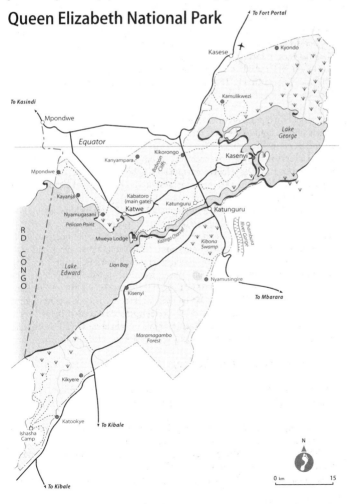

Uganda

Elephants in the Queen Elizabeth National Park

A recent report suggested that the herd of about 200 elephants that shuttles between the Queen Elizabeth National Park and neighbouring Parc Virunga in Zaire now stay longer in Uganda. The habits of this herd are said to have become an index of the level of security in the two neighbouring countries. The study also suggested that the age composition of the herd reflected the years of poaching and other forms of disturbance, with a third of the population under five years of age and an unusually large proportion of orphans. It was also found that there were hardly any bull elephants over 45 years old, and tuskless elephants dominated, due to selective killing by poachers.

rinderpest (see box, page 642) and smallpox in the 1890s and then the arrival of tsetse (see box, p age 507) at the beginning of this century. In 1910 the seriousness of the animal trypanosomiasis and human sleeping-sickness led the officials to move the inhabitants to areas free of the tsetse fly.

Modern History In 1925 the Lake George Game Reserve was declared and was followed in 1930 by the Lake Edward Game Reserve. These were later enlarged to include the crater areas and the area south of the Kazinga Channel. The Kibale Forest Corridor Game Reserve, to the north of Lake George, was also established to provide a corridor for elephants to pass to and from Kibale Forest. The park was renamed the Kazinga National Park and was gazetted in 1952. In 1954 it was renamed again following the visit by Queen Elizabeth II. The park headquarters were established in Mweya and in 1960 the Nuffield Unit of Tropical Animal Ecology, later renamed the Institute of Ecology, was also developed there.

Ecology The Park lies in the area of Africa where two types of vegetation meet – the rainforest which stretches out to the west for thousands of kilometres to the shores of the Atlantic, and the Eastern and Southern Africa grassland. The Park, like much of Uganda, gets two rainy seasons each year – from March-May and from September to November. However there is often rain during the rest of the year and prolonged droughts are unusual. The temperature varies from a minimum of 18° C to a maximum of 28° C.

Animals that occur in the Queen Elizabeth National Park include hippos, lions (well-known for being tree-climbers), elephants, buffalo, Uganda kob, waterbuck, bushbuck and topi. Smaller animals that occur (although are not necessarily seen easily) include warthog, hyenas, mongoose, red-tailed monkey, black and white colobus monkey, baboon, vervet monkey, and chimpanzees. Giant forest hogs occur in the Park – you are particularly likely to see them on the escarpment on the way up to Mweya, just outside the Maramagambo Forest. They look rather like large shaggy warthogs for which they can be easily mistaken. The Park is famous for its wide range of birdlife – an estimated 540 species have been recorded. In marshy and waterside areas larger species such as cormorants, goliath herons, egrets, spoonbills, and sacred ibis can be seen. Others include fisheagles and pied kingfishers.

Northern Sector (Mweya Lodge)

This is the most visited part of the park, partly because access from Kampala is better, and because there is a wider choice of accommodation.

Routes **Launch Trip on the Kazinga Channel** The journey takes about two hours and you can expect to see plenty of hippos and a wide range of birdlife. For information ask at the information desk at Mweya Lodge. The launch goes twice a day and costs US$60 for up to 10 people – and for parties of more than that US$6 each. You should not have too much difficulty in getting a group together. You can also organize game

Uganda kob

This is probably the most numerous mammal in the Queen Elizabeth National Park with an estimated population of about 17,000. They prefer low-lying, open country without too much bush. Female kob and their young form loose herds of about 50, and during the dry season they join up with males and with other groups to form herds of up to 1,000 in areas where green grass is still available. Uganda kob once found in southern Sudan, throughout Uganda, into western Kenya and down into northern Tanzania. They are now limited to western Uganda and eastern Zaire.

Male Uganda kobs mate with females in what is known as a breeding territory. Other antelopes breed in a similar way, but kobs have a more refined system that involves them using permanent grounds known as leks. Within a lek, there are a cluster of small, usually roughly circular, breeding territories. The males will defend their territory by ritualized displays and by fighting when necessary. They defend their territory for a fairly short time, usually a few days, before they have to wander off to find food and water, or if they are chased away by another male. The females range freely within the lek and appear to favour males that hold territories in the centre of the lek. For this reason there is most activity within the central area of the lek, with these males constantly being challenged by other males. When a male loses his territory he will go off to join other males in a bachelor group and will later try to regain his territory.

The leks can be recognized by the flattened grass that is the result of being trampled on over many years. They are usually located in open grassland near to water. During a prolonged dry season leks are usually abandoned and the herds join together in search of food and water.

Uganda

drives through Mweya Lodge if you do not have your own transport. Shorter boat trips to see a small island with nine orphaned chimpanzees US$15 per person can be booked at Mweya Lodge. It is not possible to walk around the island but visitors are taken in small groups to an observation platform where the chimps can clearly be seen. The guardians of this new facility are well informed to answer visitors' questions about the project.

Channel Track and North of the Kazinga Channel This area is perhaps the most popular for game drives and there is a network of roads that enable you to choose a length of drive that suits you. If you plan your route there is no need to double back on yourself. Generally the roads are passable although after heavy rain patches of thick sticky mud may make some routes difficult. Hippo trails cross the road every so often – it has been observed that individual hippos tend to use the same route every night when they go inland to feed. If you do come across any hippos on land be sure to give them a wide berth and do not come between them and the water. There are hyenas, buffaloes, Uganda kob, and down by the Kazinga Channel and Nile monitor lizards. The most elusive of animals, the leopard, lives in this area – but they are extremely difficult to spot.

Crater Area There are seven Crater Lakes in this area, although only four of these are accessible on the existing roads. These are Katwe, Kikorongo, Munyanyange and Nyamanuka. They are all alkaline although to differing degrees. The name Nyamanuka literally translated means animal smell and is so-named because there is a strong smell of sulphur which is emitted from the water. Lake Katwe is known throughout Uganda for being an area of salt production (see box, page 630) and has been producing high quality salt for many years.

Take the track opposite the Main Gate at Kabatoro to the Baboon Cliffs and follow it through the rolling grasslands. The road is generally good although after rain there may be some muddy patches suitable only for four-wheel drive vehicles. The grasslands are torched regularly as the dominant plants are all species whose growth is encouraged with regular burnings. There is no permanent fresh water in this area

Salt

The salt industry at Katwe is hundreds of years old and over many years has provided the local inhabitants with an important source of income. About 25 kilometres from Butiaba on the eastern shores of Lake Albert is the village of Kibiro where salt is produced in a process that appears to have changed little in over seven centuries. The only change is that the containers used, formerly pottery, are now metal.

There is archaeological evidence of production going back 700-800 years. The first written reports of production came from Speke in 1863 and Grant in 1864 who described it as perfectly pure in colour and taste. Emin Pasha (see page 351) was the first to give a first-hand description of the production methods used.

The basis of the salt production are the hot springs which are found here at the base of the Western Escarpment. One unusual aspect is that both the production and marketing of salt is solely by women. The salt gardens are owned by women and ownership is by female inheritance. It is not possible to buy a salt garden, although recently it has become possible to hire one.

The main method of salt collection is by evaporation and the rate of production depends on the weather. First, what is called a salt garden is prepared. This can be of any size and shape, and the area is cleared of grass. In the second stage dry soil is scattered over the wet exposed surface.

The loose soil is left to dry and as it does so it draws salty moisture from below and the moisture evaporates by the heat of the sun.

This process increases, the salt content of the scattered soil at the end of the day is scraped together and heaped up so that if it rains all the salt will not be lost. The spreading and drying process continues for a few days depending on the weather, and as the salt content of the scattered soil increases, the colour changes to a greyish brown.

Once a sufficiently high concentration is reached the third stage begins. This is a process whereby the soil impregnated with salt is leached with water so that all the salt dissolves into the water. To do this the loose soil is put in a container with holes in the bottom and water is poured through it and collected in a second container held underneath the first. The liquid collected is dark brown and has a very high salt content.

This liquid is then taken indoors to special salt-boiling buildings for the final stage of boiling the solution to evaporate the water. Firewood is used and its supply is one of the major restrictions on the amount of salt that can be produced. As the brine boils the water evaporates and after an hour or two the salt starts to form. By the final stages the salt is white and porridge-like and is poured onto a mud platform where it immediately solidifies. As more salt is ladled on, a salt cone grows until it is about three to four kilograms. The number of cones that a saltworker will be able to take to market will depend on how much firewood she can gather and how much brine she can prepare. These in turn depend on the size of the female labour force working on her gardens.

---

so, apart from the rainy season (March-June), you are unlikely to see many animals. During the rains, however, there are often herds of both buffalo and elephant. There are always plenty of birds (particularly grassland birds) and the area is particularly popular with ornithologists.

The track to Baboon Cliffs is worth taking for the views alone. The road continues upwards, and thorn trees (*Acacia gerrardii*) become more common. About 12 kilometres from Kabatoro the track ends at Baboon cliffs and here you get a splendid view of the park and surrounding countryside. The crater of Kyemango is below and in the distance Lake George can be seen. To the north are the Rwenzoris and on a clear day you will be able to see the snow caps.

Lake George and Lake Kikorongo To follow this route travelling west, take the right turning just after the main gate at Kabatoro and drive towards and then across the main Kasese road. The track continues towards Lake George and the fishing village of Kasenyi through open grassland. About 10 kilometres from the main road look to your left and you should be able to see a Uganda Kob lek (see Box, below).

Just before you reach Kasenyi you will see the small crater lake of Bunyampaka which is also used for salt panning on a small scale. You can take the track around the rim of the crater lake from Kasenyi that will also lead you to the Channel. Alternatively you can return along the main track and after six kilometres turn right. This leads you to the village of Hamukungu, turn left and you will pass through a large swamp and then pass the crater lake of Kikorong before reaching the main Kasese road. On this latter route you may see elephant and in the swamp there is the possibility of seeing the shoebill, while there are sometimes flamingoes in the Kikorongo Crater Lake.

Lake Katwe and Pelican Point To get to Lake Katwe take the left turning just after the Main Gate and head for the now abandoned village of Kabatoro. About five kilometres from this is Katwe town and on your right are the crater lakes of Katwe and Munyanyange. These provide Katwe inhabitants with their main sources of income, by salt panning and fishing. They are outside the Park boundaries so it is possible to leave your car. You should be able to visit the salt works at Lake Katwe on payment of a small fee. You may be able to get a guide to show you around and explain the methods by which salt is evaporated and purified. As Lake Munyanyange is an alkaline lake it is sometimes the home of lesser flamingoes in varying numbers. It is possible to walk around the rim of the lake.

The road continues beyond Katwe. It is not in very good condition and if there has been recent rain then you would be advised to avoid this route unless you have a four-wheel drive. From the track you will be able to see the Nyamagasani Delta and the Kihabule Forest before you reach Pelican Point. **NB** Pelican Point is difficult to access by car due to road conditions. There is however, a nice picnic spot on the side of a former ranger's station, overlooking the Nyamagasani delta.

South of Kazinga Channel Take the main road and cross the Kazinga Channel. About five kilometres south of the crossing turn right along the Ishasha road and follow it south. This route is mainly through grasslands, and about eight kilometres after the turning there is a kob lek on your left (see box, page 629).

Lake Nyamusingiri and Maramagambo Forest This is one of the longer trips taking a full day and requires a four-wheel drive. Go back to the main Kasese road and turn east towards the Kichwamba escarpment. Cross the Katunguru bridge and continue along the road for about 12 kilometres before turning right and starting to climb up the escarpment. The road takes you through both grasslands and acacia woodland, to your right you should be able to see the Kibona swamp, while ahead of you is the Maramagambo forest.

Lake Kasanduka and the start of the Maramagambo forest is reached about nine kilometres along this track, and a further three kilometres is Lake Nyamusingiri. There are trails into the forest although you are advised to take a rancher who knows the forest. Chimpanzees live in the forest but are not habituated so you are unlikely to see them. Other primates that you may see are black and white colobus and red-tailed monkeys.

Chambura River Gorge The Chambura Gorge marks the boundary between the Queen Elizabeth National Park and the Chambura Game Reserve. The Gorge was formed by a river which flows off the Kichwamba escarpment and into the Kazinga Channel at Katunguru. The Gorge is 10 kilometres long and supports thick forest which is home to many different forest-living species. These include chimpanzees, but so far visits to these chimpanzees by tourists are not organized at present, although one tour operator *Hot Ice* (see page 576) has plans to begin chimpanzee viewing trips. On each side of the Gorge is savannah, and the view from the edge is spectacular. You can walk along the top of the Gorge and look down onto the forest. This gives a wonderful view of the tops of the trees and any birds or animals that may be feeding off them.

The easiest way to get to the Gorge is to take a park ranger with you who will be able to advise you on up-to-date conditions locally. One possible route is to take the road from Katunguru for about eight kilometres towards the escarpment. There is a turning off to the left shortly before the road begins to climb the escarpment and from here it is about two kilometres to the edge of the Gorge. Once you get to the Gorge it is possible to climb down the 200 metres into it. This is a bit of a scramble as it is fairly steep. You pass from dry grasslands at the top, to thick forest and the river at the bottom. Mweya Lodge should be able to organize a trip to Chambura River Gorge between a group.

Sleeping **B** *Mweya Lodge*, PO Box 22, Kasese T0493-4266, managed by *Uganda Hotels*, PO Box 7173, Kampala, T234296. Located on the Mweya Peninsula on a bluff overlooking Katwe Bay, the original lodge was built in the mid-1950s but in 1967 was replaced with the present building. It has 75 beds, some nicer than others. The singles have a prison cell-like atmosphere, but all very clean. There's a good restaurant with lavish food, with a strong Indian input. In the lobby there's a huge TV set, plus piped music, which is predominantly Indian, or Hammond-organ, excellent value, competent manager. The terrace has wonderful views overlooking the water, there is a small shop here and you can change money. The lodge is rarely full although as it is a popular destination for Kampala residents at weekends, non-residents can eat at Mweya Lodge, breakfast good value, US$6.50, dinner US$9-10, major renovations are planned shortly. Very friendly staff. Will change travellers' cheques. **C** *Chambura River Gorge Camp* run by *Hot Ice* (see page 576). **E** *Institute of Ecology*, next to *Mweya Lodge*. There are singles and doubles available, all with shared facilities, there is no bed linen provided so it is pretty basic but is clean and comfortable, meals available. **E** *Student Hostel*, 1 kilometre from the Ecology Institute. The cheapest place to stay, however it is very basic and not especially good value. **E** *Christian Guesthouse*, US$7. Highly recommended.

Camping There are also a number of campsites near Mweya Lodge. **A** *Jacana Camp*, upmarket luxury camp run in conjunction with *Abercrombie and Kent Tours*, Tank Hill, PO Box 7799, Kampala, T/F259181. There is also one on the south side of the peninsula overlooking the Kazinga Channel. This is the most convenient if you want to use some of the Lodge's facilities. Another two are located off the Channel Track – the first is 4 kilometres from the Lodge and the second is 6 kilometres. Each of the campsites has a pit latrine, water and firewood provided. It is also possible to camp at a Student Hostel, but you need to bring all equipment and food.

Transport **Air** Services can be chartered from Kampala to the Airstrip at Mweya Lodge or alternatively to Kasese, which is 64 kilometres from the Park.

Road From **Kasese** take matatu going in the direction of Katwe on the north shore of Lake Edward – they go every day in the morning. Ask to be dropped off on the main road at the turning for the Park entrance which is a hundred yards down a track. From the gate it is about 6 kilometres to Mweya – you can either try to hitch and this is not as difficult as it sounds or you can ask the people at the gate to radio for a vehicle to be sent to pick you up. This latter option will cost you about US$10-15 split between however many there are in your group. However, this collection service from the main gate to the Lodge appears to have been suspended according to travellers who have visited recently.

It is 435 kilometres from **Kampala**, via Mbarara, a journey which takes about 6 hours. The Kazinga channel is crossed on an iron bridge and then onto the small village of Katunguru. From Katunguru there are two different routes. You can either continue on the main road towards Kasese turning left after 5 kilometres and then a further 15 kilometres to the Main Gate at Kabatoro passing Lake Nyamanuka. From the Main Gate it is 8 kilometres to the Lodge. Alternatively you can turn left immediately after Katunguru and follow the road to the Katunguru Gate from where it is 20 kilometres to the Lodge along the Channel Track. The road from **Fort Portal** and **Kasese** in the north is sealed. The western route north from **Mahinga** and **Bwindi** parks is gravel and some sandy sections can be difficult when wet.

Southern Sector (Ishasha River Camp)

Mainly open partly-wooded grasslands and more heavily populated with animals, the southern part of the Park is quite beautiful. It is less accessible, than the northern part (and offers some new accommodation of two bandas and three excellent campsites) and so receives substantially fewer visitors. **Ishasha River Camp** is located in the far southwestern corner of the Park, close to the RD Congo border. The Park Sub-headquarters are at Ishasha which is over 120 kilometres south of Mweya. The 'tree climbing lions' of Ishasha are not easily seen, and some travellers have declared them mythical! However, the birdlife is excellent.

Routes

South Kigezi Route The route covers a distance of about 14 kilometres and begins at the bandas. Close to the bandas is a large hippo wallow which apart from being home to hippos is also a watering point for various antelope and buffalo. The birdlife here is also fairly extensive – there are herons, storks and ibises.

In the woodland in this southern area there are the famous tree-climbing lions. They are rarer now and it has been suggested that their habit of climbing trees is less common. In this area you may also see topi. These are splendid animals with beautiful coats. They are also found in Lake Mburu National Park in Uganda, and only a few other National Parks in Kenya and Tanzania.

North Kigezi Route A rarely visited part of the park. There are plans to rehabilitate the roads. It is an area of grassland with patches of woodland. There are elephants in this area – these are the ones that move between Uganda and RD Congo (see box, page 628), although they are very shy. The northern route is reputed to be the best section of the national park for viewing the lions.

Sleeping at Ishasha River Camp

At *Ishasha* the only accommodation available are simple **bandas** with beds for up to 6 people and campsites. These were built during the colonial period and seem to have had little done to them since. For **camping** there are three sites which are very pleasant – both are located on the banks of the river, which is teeming with hippos, in the riverine forest and have firewood and pit latrines provided but little else. There is no food available so you must come fully self-sufficient. Each site is very private and has a gazebo with a cement floor to shelter from the sun or rain. The charge is US$15 per person. You are not allowed to camp outside the park, even with a bribe.

Transport to & from Ishasha Camp

From **Mweya Lodge** take the main Kasese-Mbarara road south and turn off (right) at Katunguru. Although this is a route used by commercial traffic it has not had any maintenance for many years and its condition deteriorates sharply during the rains and may become impassable. The heavy trucks bound for RD Congo, Rwanda and Burundi frequently get stuck on this road, blocking all lighter traffic for hours and sometimes days on end. About 100 kilometres after joining the road at Katunguru you will see a turning to the right with a sign to the Katookye gate. From the entrance gate to the camp is a further 7 kilometres.

An alternative route from **Mweya Lodge** is much longer in terms of distance via Ishaka to Rukungiri. It is not a very well signposted route – Ishaka is on the main Kasese-Bushenyi-Mbarara road about 6 kilometres before Bushenyi. This is the route if you are coming from **Kampala** via Mbarara. From Ishaka take the road south to Rwashamaire and then west to Rukungiri. If you are travelling independently there are matatus from Ishaka to Rukungiri. From Rukungiri head for Ishasha village and a few kilometres before you reach it the road joins the main road from Katunguru. Turn up this road and follow it for 7 kilometres to the entrance gate. If you do not have your own vehicle you will have to get off at this junction and walk it or try to hitch a lift to the entrance gate. Once at the gate it is another 7 kilometres to the camp. It is usually possible at a cost of about US$12 to get a Park vehicle to come and collect you. Boat trip on Kazinga channel US$8 per person or US$88 per boat if fewer than 11 persons.

Murchison Falls (Kabalega Falls) National Park

2°15′N 31°30′E The Murchison Falls National Park is the largest National Park in Uganda and covers an area of nearly 4,000 square kilometres and offers some of the most spectacular scenery in Uganda. Until about 20 years ago the waters of the Nile were forced through a narrow gap in the rocks to fall through a series of foaming, roaring cascades down a drop of about 50 metres, creating one of the world's most spectacular waterfalls. However, in 1961, a year of particularly heavy rains and floods in Uganda, the waterfall broke through another gap in the rocks so that there are now two breaches.

The park is not in the risky area of the north, and is worth visiting for the variation in its scenery more than its wildlife. It covers about 3,900 square kilometres and the further north you travel, the more savannah-like terrain becomes. The south of the park is green and lush with many small settlements and banana or matoke (like plantain) everywhere. The further north you travel the more dry and hot it becomes and the sparse are human settlements. Parts are quite extraordinary with long alleys of palm trees and other exotic plants stretching from left to right into the horizon in a wide avenue. The date palms apparently were planted by Arab slave traders centuries ago marking their route into and out of inland black Africa.

Many animals and birds still live in the park including Ugandan kobs, buffaloes, hippos, baboons and crocodiles. Lions, elephants and antelope are rarer.

A chilling sight travelling along the main road north is the visible impact of the civil war and retreating armies on this part of the country. The roads are appalling, there are few vehicles and all around you are signs of poverty and decline. Throughout the park there are concrete or brick buildings that have either been blown up or are falling down through neglect. Soldiers are stationed at various points to ensure the safety of those travelling, but the low pay they receive means most have to farm to survive. Their uniforms are ragged and their weapons old.

Prehistory The area around Chobe in the eastern part of the Murchison Falls National Park has been a popular habitat for man from early times for a number of reasons. Firstly it has good animal and vegetable resources; it also had a good agricultural potential; and later iron-ore suitable for primitive smelting technology was present in the area.

Murchison Falls National Park

The earliest artefacts found in the area of Chobe date from the Middle Stone Age, when the banks of the Nile were peopled with small groups of hunters and gatherers, who may also have done some fishing. Some rough pebble tools, large flakes, some picks and a hand-axe have been found dating from this period, when it is believed that the Nile was flowing at a higher level than at present.

Throughout the Middle and Late Stone Age agriculture and the domestication of animals were not known to the river bank dwellers – they continued to eke out an existence based on hunting and gathering. However over the years the manufacture of stone tools became more sophisticated and some new types of tool appeared for the first time. The abundance of flakes and chippings in places along the eroded banks of the river suggests that these may have been places where tools were made rather than actual settlements.

Along the banks pottery fragments, iron-ware and iron slag has been collected dating back as far as 2,000 years. The bulk of the finds, however, are much more recent, and dating from the last 200 years. The settlers who are thought to have first introduced iron technology to this part of Africa left behind a very distinctive type of pottery known as dimple-based ware. This is characterized by bevelled rims and incised cross-hatched or grooved decoration, and is to be found over much of the Lake Victoria basin. Related pottery types occur over most of the sub-continent; but the most northerly occurrence of this archaeological complex yet discovered is at Chobe.

Most of the pottery fragments found in recent years carry decorative motifs identical to those used by the people surrounding the National Park today. They consist of concentric circles, raised bosses and zigzag chevrons applied to the wet clay with a carved wooden roulette or a knotted cord.

Launch Trip

Everyone who visits Murchison Falls National Park is recommended to go on this trip. It is operated by Uganda National Parks from Paraa to the Falls themselves. The cost is US$120 for up to six people – so if you can gather a group together it is not too expensive but there is a minimum charge of US$20 per additional person. There is also the US$23 National Park entrance fee on top of this. During the ride you can expect to see crocodiles and hippos. Other game that are found at Murchison Falls include elephants, buffalos, giraffes and a range of antelopes. You can arrange for the boat to stop at the base of the Falls while you walk up the footpath to the top, which gives an excellent the views of the Falls. The launch trip usually runs twice daily from Paraa at 0800 and 1500. The round trip takes about three hours.

Sleeping

There will shortly be accommodation of approximately 300 beds available in this National Park. The tourist population may not support this rapid expansion, leading to a deterioration of some of the facilities. There used to be two high standard lodges in Murchison Falls

Murchison Falls (Kabalega Falls)

National Park – *Chobe Safari Lodge* and *Paraa Safari Lodge*. They were both virtually destroyed during the troubles and have been closed for some years. There is talk of reopening **Chobi Safari Lodge**, which is situated on the northern bank of the Nile. Recently the **Paraa Safari Lodge** has been renovated, with large rooms with balconies. **A+ Sarova**, PO Box 22636, Kampala, T041-251211/5, F251209. **Paraa Lodge**, which is located in the western part of the National Park was looted, bombed and burnt down, it was then rebuilt in 1987, only to be looted again a few months later. Beautiful pool/bar area. Nicely built hotel, 100 beds, lies on the north bank of the Nile. Swimming pool.

A *Nile Safari Camp*, 6 double tents with wooden bathrooms, two 4-person similar wooden bandas, situated 5 kilometres downstream from the ferry, wonderful views of the Nile. Presidential Suite consists of 3 intelligently connected double rondavel-like rooms, dining in lovely open dining room or on deck, bar, fine swimming pool, safaris available, has enthusiastic South African management, the most upmarket camp in Uganda, very polished operation (book through **Inns of Uganda**, PO Box 2288, Kampala, T258273, F233992, iou@swiftuganda.com). **A** *Sambiya River Lodge*, Masindi Rd. Opened in December 1995, within Murchison Falls National Park on the banks of the Nile tributary, open fronted lodge with a swimming pool, has 20 thatched cottages with private bathroom, soon to be expanded to 100 beds, good value for money. Local four-wheel drive tours, cruises, fishing, walking tours available, contact *Afri Tours and Travel*, PO Box 5187, Kampala, T233596, F232307 or Let's Go Travel, Caxton Hse, Standard St, PO Box 60342, Nairobi, Kenya, T254-2-340331/213033, F254-2-336890/214713. **A** *Sambiya River Tented Camp* is in the centre of Murchison Falls National Park, 10 kilometres north of Waringo gate. Executive double tents, solar powered hot showers/fans, bar, full kitchen service, concession: *Afri Tours and Travel*, PO Box 5187, Kampala, T233596, F232307, or *Let's Go Travel*, Caxton Hse, Standard St, PO Box 60342, Nairobi, Kenya, T254-2-340331/213033, F254-2-336890/214713.

C *Rabongo Cottages*, the only high standard accommodation currently available at Murchison Falls, run by *Hot Ice* (see page 576).

D *Bandas*, more basic accommodation is available south of the river, built in about 1988, there are simple bandas which are kept fairly clean and have mosquito nets and bedding provided, the bandas can be booked through the Uganda National Parks (PO Box 3530, Kampala, T256534), if you ask in advance meals can be made for you, or else if you bring your own food you can borrow a charcoal stove, cost US$24 per person per night.

Camping Possible here at the site of the bandas (see above), cost US$10 per person per night. Camping is available at the top of Murchison Falls, 1 hour from Paraa by four-wheel drive.

Entertainment **Sports** **White water rafting**: One of the country's most popular tourist attractions, all in holidays or river-only prices, from Masindi to Murchison Falls (International River Grade 5) along the White Nile are organized by *Adrift*, in Kampala, T041-268670, Mobile 075-707668, F041-341245 or see page 571 for UK and USA representative details. There is no human habitation on the river. Many of the rapids are larger and more powerful than most better known rapids, with the river splitting into 5/6 channels at places. In some sections the rapids are too large to raft and there is a 5-kilometre stretch which is unrunnable. This involves some heavy carrying of equipment/supplies for the whole crew. Trip suitable only for experienced rafters. *Adrift* run a one day white water rafting trip starting at Jinja, and a 5-day package from Jinja to Murchison Falls. New for 1999 is a holiday which combines rafting on the White Nile and exploring the islands of Lake Victoria by sea kayaks – contact *Adrift* for details. Package tours can be arranged from UK and elsewhere or local white water rafting river trips are available.

Transport **Air** There is an airstrip at Paraa and charter flights do fly here from Entebbe. Alternatively you could fly to Masindi and continue by road from there.

Road (own vehicle) Murchison Falls can be reached by road from Kampala via Masindi. From Masindi there are two routes to Paraa but one is in much better condition than the other. From Masindi take the road to Butiaba on the shores of Lake Albert and from there head north, through the village of Bulisa to the park entrance (see map, page 624). It is a very attractive drive looking across the Rift Valley towards the Lake and across to RD Congo on the other side. The alternative route is more direct and goes through the park and forest – but it is only suitable for reliable four-wheel drive vehicles. Alternatively if you are heading for Chobe (not very likely until the lodge re-opens) take the road from Kampala towards Gulu. At Kigumba turn right to Karuma and from here it is a further 15 kilometres to Chobe.

Road (Public Transport) Getting to Murchison Falls National Park by public transport involves a number of changes. From Hoima or Masindi you want to head for Bulisa which is north of Butiaba and about 30 kilometres from the Park entrance gate. It is a small town where you will probably have to stay the night. There is a simple lodge **E** *Bulisa Corner Guest House*. From Bulisa you can either try and hitch or failing that can hire a bicycle from the Bulisa Corner Guest House. It is 27 kilometres to Paraa and is mostly flat. Motorbike hire with driver is another possibility to get to the park from Bulisa, cost US$20 one way.

Mount Elgon National Park

Uganda

Near Mbale is an extinct volcano believed to have had its last major eruption about 10 million years ago, located on the border of Uganda and Kenya. It has gradual slopes up to the peaks on the crater rim which means that non-mountaineers can climb it (see below). Wagagai at 4,320 metres is the highest peak, and the fourth highest East African mountain. The foothills around the base of Mount Elgon, known to the locals as 'Masaba', are also a good hiking area, and here are caves to visit as well as Sipi Falls (see below). Endemic flora includes the giant lobelia, giant heather and giant groundsel. Wild flowers abound. Mammals include tree hyrax, bushpig and buffalo, blue monkey, baboon and black and white colobus monkeys. There are frequent sightings of casqued hornbill, the crowned eagle, Ross' touraco and the lammergeier. This area is well known for its high quality Arabica coffee and you are likely to see coffee plantations in this area. They are mostly small-scale farms using family labour.

The **Mount Elgon Forest Exploration Centre**, which lies within the National Park boundaries, was set up as an educational facility for local schools. However, travellers to the area can also utilize their expertise to explore Mount Elgon's foothills. There are three interconnected walking trails, of three kilometres, five kilometres and seven kilometres length. The seven kilometres Mountain Bamboo Loop leads to an outlook area where Mount Elgon can be seen on a clear day. The five kilometre walk takes you to the Chebonet Falls and to a climb up a rock chimney. The three kilometre Ridge View Loop route is an easier ascent to the ridge and connects to pathways to the main viewpoint. There is accommodation (dormitory) at US$12 per person. Camping costs US$7.50 plus an entry fee of US$7 per person. Basic meals are available or self-catering.

The centre is 11 kilometres from Sipi by road (four-wheel drive required) towards Kapchorwa for six kilometres before taking the right turn which is signposted. Matatus will take you as far as this turning, then it is five kilometres to the centre.

Climbing Mount Elgon

Until very recently anyone wishing to climb Mount Elgon approached it from the Kenya side and most of the recently published mountaineering and hiking guides reflect this. However, recently efforts have been made to improve facilities on the Uganda side to enable climbers to approach it from here. Take care, however, as recent travellers have been ambushed by machine gun carrying poachers.

Encompassing the largest surface area of any extinct volcano in the world, Mount Elgon rises through a series of gradual slopes punctuated by steep cliffs to a height of

4,321 metres above sea level. Volcanic foothills, cliffs, caves, gorges and waterfalls combine with panoramic views across wide plains to create some of the most spectacular scenery in Uganda. Elgon's upper slopes are cloaked in tropical montane forest while above this lies a vast tract of Afro-Alpine moorland. This unique vegetation extends over the caldera – a collapsed crater covering over 40 square kilometres at the top of the mountain.

The time to avoid is the long rains which are April and May. Climbers should first head for the village of Budadiri where the climb begins. **E** *The Wagagai*, offering basic accommodation, houses the Mount Elgon Club and they can arrange the climb for you – guides, porters, food etcetera. Follow the sign 'Family Maternity Home' at the gate. The facilities on the mountain itself are currently minimal. A tourist office is now open in Budadiri, helpful for hiring guides, porters etcetera for Mount Elgon. Only 700 visitors have signed in over the past year and the Park Rangers haven't been paid for months, which indicates how relatively unused and quiet this access to Mount Elgon is at present. If you plan to get to the top expect the climb to last four days. However, if you are less ambitious there are many different walks that you can take, that range from easy hikes to hard climbs. The Tourist office in Budadiri or in Mbale can give you maps and make suggestions to suit your requirements.

The climb itself is straight forward and can be accomplished easily by non-mountaineers. The trail is steep in places but it is possible to reach the caldera and return to the roadhead within three days of setting off walking at a comfortable pace. With an extra two days you could also reach Jackson's Summit on the highest point, Wagagai, or visit the hot springs at the head of the Suam gorge.

The Caves of Mount Elgon There are numerous caves on Elgon and one of the most interesting and most readily accessible is that situated within the spur on which Bulago Camp stands. Its entrance is impressive, being some 30 feet wide and 10 feet tall, and (during wet weather) is partially hidden in spray from a small waterfall which drops down of banks of ferns which almost block the mouth. Just inside the main chamber are flat ledges cut into the rock, which are believed, at one time, to have been used as sleeping berths by the Bugisu when hiding from their enemies. The size of the main chamber is approximately 60 feet by 150 feet in depth, with a height over 15 feet.

According to native legend the tunnel at the far end of the cave to the left leads to another much larger cavern. This is supposed to be full of water to a considerable depth. Whether this is true or not is not known – but certainly water can be seen trickling from the tunnel.

The main cavern has no stalactites or stalagmites, nor any rock paintings. There are instead a number of garnet-like stones, embedded in a nest of a fine scintillating material resembling spiders' webs. The floor of the cave is flat and soft and is littered with the droppings of bats. Looking out towards the entrance of the cave, especially when the sun is shining through the waterfall, giving off rainbows, is a lovely sight.

Other well known caves on Mount Elgon include one opposite Sipi Camp. However this bears no comparison either in size or interest to the one described above.

Sipi Falls These are situated in the lower slopes of Mount Elgon at an altitude of 1,750 metres, close to the village of Sipi and are 40 kilometres and a drive of about 1½ hours from Mbale. The waterfall and the surrounding area are very pretty and a pleasant place to spend a few days unwinding. The Sipi Falls Rest Camp is built around a small cottage with just two rooms – originally built as a holiday house for the Governor and officials during the colonial period. This tourist resort has greatly expanded and is wonderfully situated overlooking the main falls.

Non-resident users of the facilities are charged an entrance fee of US$3 per person to visit the site or use the restaurant facilities. Accommodation is either bandas with adjoining bush showers and toilets or camping (relatively expensive charges). There is a restaurant which caters for local and western preferences.

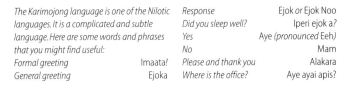

Karimojong phrases

The Karimojong language is one of the Nilotic languages. It is a complicated and subtle language. Here are some words and phrases that you might find useful:		*Response*	Ejok *or* Ejok Noo
		Did you sleep well?	Iperi ejok a?
		Yes	Aye *(pronounced* Eeh*)*
		No	Mam
Formal greeting	Imaata!	*Please and thank you*	Alakara
General greeting	Ejoka	*Where is the office?*	Aye ayai apis?

There is a steep trail that takes 20-30 minutes to walk from near the post office in Sipi village to the base of the main falls. A small entry charge is levied. This pathway continues past the falls, crossing the river to caves. In addition, there are three smaller waterfalls above the main falls, and it is possible to swim in the pool below one of these falls. Guides are available but it is possible to visit the second waterfalls without a guide by taking the road out of Sipi towards Suam for approximately one kilometre.

Sleeping **A-B** *Sipi Falls Rest Camp* (see entry above) run by *Volcanoes Tours*, PO Box 22818, Kampala, T041-346464/5, F041-341718, Mobile 075-741718, volcanoes@infocom.co.ug. Climbing expeditions to Mount Elgon can be organized from here. **E** *Elgon Masai Lodge*, popular with budget travellers, clean rooms, bucket showers.

Camping *Elgon Sipi Falls View Campsite and Backpackers*. New campsite just next to the Sipi Falls Rest Camp. The location is excellent but the facilities are rather basic. *The Crow's Nest* is a new backpacker campsite recently opened. Owned by local people and set up with the help of two former Peace Corps volunteers, the Crow's Nest offers panoramic views of Mount Elgon and the four waterfalls. There is a small nature trail encircling the campsite. There are showers, western toilets, a bar and small restaurant on site. Tents and sleeping bags can be hired. Banda accommodation is available US$10. The Crow's Nest is 500 metres distance from Sipi Village on the Mbale road and is sign-posted, on your right if coming from Sipi Village.

Eating **2** *Sipi Falls Hotel* across the road from the *Elgon Masai Hotel*, serves good local food and cold beers.

Kidepo National Park

Kidepo is one of the most spectacular National Parks in Uganda but being the most isolated it is also one of the hardest to visit. However while it may not have the animals of many of the National parks, it is one of the few remaining places in the world where you get a real feeling of wilderness.

3°N 32°E

Kidepo National Park is located in the far northeast of Uganda on the border of Sudan and close to the border with Kenya (see map, page 624). The area adjacent to the National Park is inhabited by the Ik people, hunters and farmers, who are described unflatteringly in Colin Turnbull's 1972 book "The Mountain People". It is about 840 kilometres from Kampala, and is an area of about 1,334 square kilometres with an altitude that ranges between 1,350 metres and 2,750 metres. The Napore Nyangea Mountain Range is located to the west of the camp and the Natera hills to the east. In the distance to the north you will be able to see the peak of Mount Lotukei. The vegetation is typical savannah with some acacia woodland.

One problem which Kidepo National Park suffers from more than the other National Parks in Uganda is that of water supply. This is a problem that the plants and animals of the area have adapted themselves to well. Low rainfall in the form of a long and severe dry season of almost six months is characteristic of Karamoja as a whole. The effect of this régime is best appreciated between October and March

Uganda

when the National Park is progressively baked, bleached and burnt by sun and often fire. Every scrap of moisture, except that which manages to survive in a few water-holes and dams, turns to dust under the scorching breath of the tireless northeast wind. Unattractive that this might sound it is in fact perhaps the best time to visit for these conditions are good for game-viewing. Animals are more tied to the available water sources, and there tends to be a concentration of animals around Apoka, the Park headquarters at the height of the dry season. This is the time when animals tend to leave Kidepo Valley, which dries out very rapidly once the rains have ceased, and head for the comparatively lush savannas and woodlands of Narus valley where there is enough water to see them through until the rain breaks again in March or April. Once the rains begin the animals drift back to the Kidepo Valley, and from April-October, when the grass is shorter this is probably the best viewing area. The **Kanangarok hotsprings** which cross the Kidepo River are worth a visit.

The Kidepo River is a sand river, which only flows visibly for a few days of the year. However, below the sand, at depths that vary from a few centimetres to a few metres, there is water. How deep it is depends on how far into the dry season it is. The animals of the Park dig holes to reach the water. This also explains why on the banks of an apparently dry river the vegetation is often more green and lush than elsewhere in the Park. Kidepo is an ornithologist's delight, with over 460 bird species, including the ostrich and kori bustard.

Game in Kidepo suffered badly during the recent turmoil and lawlessness. The animals include lion, buffalo, elephant, zebra and a wide range of antelope. Land Rovers US$2 per kilometre can be hired at Apoka Park Headquarters.

Museum The National Park has a museum which is open to visitors. There are some pieces of skeletons as well as some insect specimens. There are also some photographs of some of the rangers involved in earlier efforts at conservation.

Security Northern Uganda has been subject to intermittent unrest and bandits are by no means uncommon. The Lords Resistance Army (LRA) or Kony rebels have been active in this area, with reports that children and teenagers have been abducted from the area around Gula.

Kidepo Valley

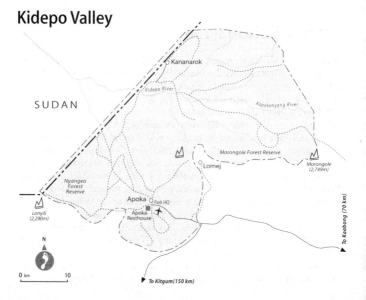

A *Apoka Resthouse* (recently renovated), 32 beds, nets, generally very comfortable. Nearby the *Apoka Rest Camp* has several double bandas, US$22 daily, campsites US$10 per day. **Sleeping**
E *Student Hostel*, 15 renovated bandas managed by the Park Administration, with support from some Germans working for the Game Department. The standard is good, with warm showers, helpful staff, comfortable beds and mosquito nets. Bring your own food, including fresh fruit and vegetables, basic foodstuffs can be bought on the way in Kaabong or Kotido.

Camping there are four sites close to *Apoka Lodge*.

Air You can charter a light aircraft from Kampala which will take about 2-3 hours, and will **Transport** cost somewhere in the region of US$1,000 per person for a 2-day and 1 night all inclusive stay. Contact *Bel Air* (see page 575).

Road The drive up to Kidepo should not be undertaken lightly and before you contemplate a trip you should speak to people who can give you up to date information, such as *Bel Air* (see page 575). This part of the world is heavily armed and when you arrive there you will notice the high percentage of Karimojong men who carry guns. There have been periods when, because of the bandits, it has not been safe to travel in this area and it may therefore be advisable to drive up in a convoy. The drive to Kidepo is a 2-day journey by four-wheel drive from Kampala via Moroto, but road conditions need to be checked before departure.

Travel agents Delmira: T256-41-235499, F231927, delmira@imul.com, operate tours into the park. **Directory**

Lake Mburo National Park

Lake Mburo National Park is one of the newest of Uganda's National Parks. For many years there has been a great deal of dispute between the use of this area by man as against game. This began during the colonial period when the area was declared to be a hunting ground for the Ankole royalty. After independence it became a game reserve and in the early 1980s was finally gazetted as a National Park. However, to establish the Park it was necessary to resettle large numbers of people and their herds of cattle, and this is still a fairly controversial issue.

It is probably the Park most easily accessible from Kampala and is a landscape of open plains, acacia grasslands and marshes. Around the lake itself is thicker riverine woodland while much of the rest of the park is acacia woodland.

Animals that are found in Lake Mburo National Park include impalas, zebras, topi, oribi, land, klispringer, buffalos, waterbucks, reedbucks and warthogs. Baboons and vervets are commonly seen and the Lake contains hippos and crocodiles, while buffaloes can often be found in the marshes. Leopards are present but they are rare. Interesting birds include crested crane (Uganda's national emblem), saddlebill storks and Abyssinian ground hornbills. There is also a wide range of water birds.

One of the great advantages of Lake Mburo National Park is that you can walk around the park (rather than having to drive in a vehicle) as long as you are accompanied by a ranger. In addition to this you can also walk between the camp and the lake without a ranger – a distance of about a kilometre. A game drive in the Park vehicle can be arranged, however, they can often be restricted at short notice when the Rangers' vehicles are out of action. It is possible to hire a motor launch to go onto the lake, but this service is intermittently suspended if the outboard motor is out of action.

D *Rwonyo Rest Camp*, there are double and single bandas as well as one 4 bed family **Sleeping** banda, which are simple but comfortable, bedding and mosquito nets are provided, and showers are shared, meals are available and are cheap and simple. Bandas cost US$20 per person per night. *Kachira Bush Camp*, run by *Hot Ice*, tented camp, thatched roof, wooden floor, with toilets and showers. Reportedly more upmarket than Rwonyo Camp.

Rinderpest

The first recorded outbreak of Rinderpest in East Africa occurred in 1889 in what was then Somaliland. It is generally believed that the disease followed the introduction of cattle from India and Aden for use by the Italian army during the first expedition to Abyssinia. Once established, Rinderpest spread like wildfire over the whole of East Africa reaching Lake Tanzania by 1890.

The devastation resulting from the disease was terrible. Lugard was in Africa at this time and tells of the misery and suffering that the pastoral tribes, such as the Masai and the Bahima, endured as a result of this disease. Many were made destitute with cattle mortality rates generally over 90 percent. In some areas, not a single animal survived. It is believed that many people also perished along with their animals – often of malnutrition. Many species of game were almost exterminated – buffalo, eland, warthog and wild pig were particularly badly affected.

Camping there are 4 sites in the Park where the facilities are basic – the one on the lakeshore is the most popular, cost US$10 per person per night.

Transport   **Road (own vehicle)** The Park is located 230 kilometres (about 4 hours) from Kampala along the Mbarara Rd. Take the main road through Masaka and the turning is marked 13 kilometres past the Lyantonde trading centre. If you are coming in the other direction, from Mbarara, a turning to the park at Sanga, about 25 kilometres from Mbarara, is probably better. 'Taxi' mopeds and bicycles can be useful for travel in areas with poor public transport, for example from Sanga to Lake Mburo National Park. The moped drivers are allowed to drive you through the park to the camp. Specify "no short cuts" while bargaining the fare! From Mbarara the Park headquarters are about 47 kilometres, a journey which will take about 1½ hours. Unless there has been recent rain the road is not too bad although at certain times of the year four-wheel drive is recommended.

Road (public transport) There are a number of possibilities. You can arrange a special hire from Mbarara for about US$35. There is a National Parks vehicle which goes between Mbarara and the Park on most weekdays – obviously this not very reliable. If you know what day you will be going you can arrange it through the Uganda National Parks Office in Kampala – they have a radio contact with the Park. If there is not a vehicle going they can arrange to meet you at Sanga, on the Masaka to Mbarara road for about US$20. If you get to Sanga early you can walk – it is about 13 kilometres and is fairly flat but be sure to take plenty of water. From the Park entrance to Rwonyo camp is a further 8 kilometres and you may have to wait until someone is ready to escort you. Coming from Kampala is easiest as at the weekends as the park is fairly popular with Kampala residents and lifts are possible.

Kibale Forest National Park

Kibale Forest, which covers an area of about 560 square kilometres, was, until recently a Forest Reserve but has now been taken over by the Uganda National Parks (see main map, page 624). There is now an emphasis on conservation, sustainable utilization and non-consumptive uses of the forest. The viewing of chimpanzees in their natural environment is the main tourist attraction.

Nature trails into the forest have been created and quite apart from the chimps the walks in the forest are wonderful. Tracking to the habituated chimp troops is conducted by trained guides who will also be able to tell you about the forest. The group of chimps in the Kanyanchu community is believed to be the largest group in Kibale Forest, numbering about 45. Individuals are named and include Miika, a strong and authoritative male; Mutaganya a female; Nkojo a male identified by a scar; Nkazi a female with a swelling on her chin; Kaara with a stiff digit on its right hand. The forest is believed to contain the highest concentration of primate species in East Africa –

these include chimpanzees, black and white colobus monkeys, red colobus monkeys, blue monkeys and baboons. Other animals that are found in the forest include elephants, buffaloes, bush pigs, and duickers. However many of these are very shy and you will be lucky to see them. There is also a huge range of birdlife and an estimated 140 species of butterfly.

More trails are being constructed and efforts are being made to restrict the number of people that go along these in any one day. Plans are also underfoot to have a number of new campsites in the park – all will be within the grassland part of the park. An information centre and exhibition hall will also be established.

The emblem of Kibale Forest is a black and white colobus monkey designed by Lysa Leland, a researcher and photographer who with her husband Tom Struhsaker, worked in Kibale for many years, long before its popularity took off.

Forest walks

There are organized excursions to the chimps twice a day leaving from Kanyunchi at 0700 and 1500. The morning walk is reported to offer a better opportunity to see the primates. The revenue from the Swamp Walk goes to the local community who are building a school nearby. A three-day hike is planned – starting on the Kampala-Fort Portal Road which borders the forest, with two night forest camp, estimated to cost around US$100 all in, including food, porters and accommodation. The earlier walk is meant to be better as you have a better chance of seeing the chimps. Tourists are not allowed to walk in the forest unaccompanied and you must take a guide – but you will find their knowledge will greatly increase your enjoyment of the walk.

Sleeping

A+ *Mantana Kibale Camp*, luxury well-appointed campsite run by Abercrombie and Kent, PO Box 7799, Tank Hill, T/F259181. **E** *Hotel Nkingo Village Safari Camp and Guest House*, PO Box 733, Fort Portal, located in Kibale Forest south of Fort Portal on the Fort Portal-Kamwenge road. Matatu from Fort Portal at 0900 from Matatu Park. Guest rooms or choice of private campsites, cooking grills, firewood and water, basic latrines, bush showers, restaurant and bar, bring warm clothing for nights and rain wear, laundry services available. Excellent food, well spiced and delicious baked pineapple pie. **E** *Kanyanchu River Campsite*, situated about 35 kilometres from Fort Portal. It is simple and is not geared for the tourist looking for luxury. There are five covered camping sites – which are invaluable during very wet weather as well as an open camping site. It is a wonderful setting, surrounded by thick forest and the design of the site has been well thought out. There are long drops, washing facilities, drinking water and firewood available but there is no food so bring anything you need. Tents and paraffin lamps are available for rent.

Transport

Road **Own vehicle**: the Kanyanchu River Camp is located 35 kilometres east of Fort Portal. If you are coming direct from Kampala on the Kampala-Mubende-Fort Portal Rd and have a four-wheel drive you can take the right turning through the Katonga Game Reserve. Coming from Fort Portal, Bigodi and the Kanyanchu River Camp are located off the Fort Portal-Kamwenge-Mbarara road. **Public transport**: travellers without their own vehicles can get one of the matatus from Fort Portal that leave about 3 times a day in the morning and take about 2 hours. In the other direction they leave Kamwenge very early, before sunrise at 5 am from the stage for Buhinga Hospital on the bridge, on the Kamwenge Rd, and take about 2 hours. Returning to Fort Portal you have to catch the pickup at about 0700 – after this time you will have to try to hitch, which is difficult along this road. If you are using the road on a Tuesday there is a market at Rukunyu (a village between Bigodi and Kamwenge) so there is more traffic. Alternatively hire a *boda-boda* (motor cycle taxi) from Fort Portal.

Uganda

Rwenzori Mountains National Park

".. you may be familiar with the Alps and the Caucasus, the Himalayas, and the Rockies, but if you have not explored Rwenzori, you still have something wonderful to see." *DW Freshfield (Explorer, 1906)*

The Rwenzoris (Ruwenzoris) lie along the border of Uganda and RD Congo, rising to a height of about 5,600 metres above sea level (see main map, page 624). The range is about 100 kilometres in length and is about 50 kilometres wide. It was formed from a block which was tilted and thrust up during the development of the Rift Valley. These beautiful, often mist-shrouded, mountains are non-volcanic and offer mountaineers and walkers superb country and wonderful views.

The Rwenzoris are also known as the Mountains of the Moon – they were first described as such by Ptolomy because they were believed to be the *Lunae Montes* predicted by the ancient Greeks to be the source of the Nile.

A number of the mountain peaks are named after early explorers to Uganda and some of those in the centre of the range have permanent snow cover – these include Mount Stanley (5,109 metres), Speke (4,889 metres), Baker (4,843 metres), Gessi (4,797 metres), Emin (4,791 metres) and Luigi di Savoia (4,626 metres). On Mount Stanley are the twin summits of Alexandra (5,044 metres) and Margherita (5,109 metres). There is some divergence on the actual heights of these peaks, and other sources mark them as being significantly higher.

Geology Rwenzoris are young mountains at less than 10 million years old. Until that time, the area was part of a huge plain that extended to the Atlantic coast to the west and rivers flowed to the west. A series of movements of the earth's crust resulted in major rifting and in the Rwenzori area an uplifting of the underlying rock. The Rwenzoris are made up of quartzite and gneiss.

Although not the highest, the Rwenzori range is certainly the largest and most important group of snow mountains in Africa. Mount Kilimanjaro (5,968 metres) and Mount Kenya (5,225 metres) are both higher, but are single volcanic peaks. Rwenzori, whose highest point is the Margherita peak of Mount Stanley (5,109 metres) is a massif composed of six separated mountains all of which carry

Rwenzori Mountains

To Roccati Pass & Mt Emin

Peaks:
Albert (5,101m)
Margherita (5,109m)
Alexandra (5,092m)
Moebius (4,925m)

Mt Gessi

UGANDA

Lake Bukurungu West

Skull Cave (3,810m)

Kihuma (4,321m)

Portal Peaks

Mt Speke (4,889m)

Mt Portal (4,370m)

Lake Rutara

Irene Lakes (4,900m)

Bigo Hut (3,444m)

Mt Stanley (5,109m)

Bujuku Hut (3,900m)

John Mate Hut (3,505m)

Nyamiliju Hut (3,322m)

Kibatsi Bog

Bigo Bog

Bujuku River

Elena Hut (4,541m)

Lake Bujuku (3,962m)

Scott Elliot Pass (4,372m)

Kinyangoma (4,361m)

Mt Baker (4,843m)

Kurt Schafer Bridge

To Nyakalengija (10 km)

Kitandara Lakes

Kitandara Hut (4,032m)

Kabamba (3,779m)

Guy Yeoman Hut (3,505 m)

Kichuchu

Nyabitaba Hut (2,651m)

Freshfield Pass (4,282m)

Maburka River

Mahoma River

N

Mt Luigi di Savoia (Selta 4,627m)

Karaguta (2,940m)

0 km   2

Weissman (4,547m)

RD CONGO

■ Hut
□ Rock Shelter

Exploration of the Rwenzori Mountains

It is now generally accepted that Ptolemy (c AD 150), when writing of the Mountains of the Moon, the legendary source of the Nile, was referring to the Rwenzori massif. Interestingly Speke, on his discovery of the Virunga volcanoes in 1861, did at the time associate them with Ptolemy's Moon Mountains.

It was in 1864 that the first European saw the Rwenzoris – this was when Baker observed, to the south of Lake Albert, a huge mountain mass which he named The Blue Mountains.

In 1876 Stanley looked across at the Rwenzoris from the escarpment above Lake George but, like other explorers before him, had failed to appreciate the importance of this natural feature. It was another 12 years before the ice caps were first seen and it was Sir Henry Stanley who was the first to proclaim the existence of the Rwenzoris as snow mountains. In his book Darkest Africa he claims to have made the discovery himself, but in fact two members of his expedition had seen the snows a month before him. They were Surgeon Parke and Mountenoy-Jephson who saw the snows on 20 April 1888. The following year, another member of the expedition, Lieutenant Stairs, ascended the mountains up to a height of over 3,050 metres.

It is to Stanley that we owe the name Rwenzori (often spelt Ruwenzori). The word means the place from where the rain comes.

The word was transcribed by Stanley as Runzori; hence Rwenzori. No name appears to have been given to the mountains by the local residents and their custom was to name the rivers running off the mountains rather than the actual peaks.

In the summer of 1891 Emin Pasha's companion Dr F Stuhlmann climbed up the Butagu valley to a height of 4,062 metres and had the first close glimpse of the snow. A few years later in 1894-95 G F Scott Elliott, a naturalist, also made a number of expeditions which were of significant botanical importance. In 1900 an expedition by C S Moore proved the presence of glaciers; and shortly afterwards Sir Harry Johnston reached the Mobuku glacier at a height of 4,520 metres. The first purely non-scientific climb, and the first by a woman, was in 1903 by the Reverend A B and Mrs Fisher. The twin peaks of Mount Stanley, Alexandra (5,044 metres) and Margherita (5,105 metres), were climbed for the first time in June 1906 by an expedition led by the Duke of Abruzzi. This expedition produced important scientific results and an excellent topographical survey of the range was completed with information on the areas of the glaciers. It was this expedition that named most of the main peaks, the Duke naming first (the smallest), Luigi de Savioa, after himself.

permanent snow and glaciers. The general axis of the range is north-south and the snow peaks, divided by lower snow-free passes, lie roughly along this axis along the middle of the range. The mountain range is about 120 kilometres long and 50 kilometres wide. Unlike all the other great mountains of central Africa, Rwenzori is not of volcanic origin but is the result of an upthrust associated with the formation of the western Rift Valley, in which it stands.

There are six separated glaciated groups and the glaciers are the equatorial type. That is they are more truly ice-caps than ice-rivers; movement is very slight as can be seen from the clearness of the streams and the absence of large moraines (accumulations of debris carried down by the glaciers). There have been times of much greater glaciation in earlier eras on the Rwenzoris, reaching thousands of feet below the current levels, and many of the valleys are characteristically shaped by ice erosion. The existing glaciers are in retreat.

One of the most delightful aspects of the Rwenzoris is the diversity of plants and trees. Cultivation rarely extends above about 2,000 metres around the base of the mountain, and in many places it is considerably lower. Ascending, the climber passes from the foothills where most of the vegetation is elephant grass up to about 1,800 metres. From there is the montane or true forest which is a mixture of trees, bracken and tree ferns. In this zone, which extends to about 2,500 metres, it is possible to see orchids. Higher still is the bamboo zone which continues up to about 3,000

Vegetation & wildlife

metres. The vegetation here also includes tree heather and, in moister patches, giant lobelias. The next, fairly extensive, zone is the heather forest, which extends from about 3,000 metres up to about 3,800 metres. The humid climate at this altitude causes vigorous development of mosses and lichens which cover the ground and the trunks of living and fallen trees. At this level, on the better drained slopes are tree groundsels and shrubby trees while the wetter parts are distinctly boggy. This zone also has brambles, orchids and ferns – all of which form a tangle which make passage through them difficult. The highest vegetative zone, extending from about 3,800 metres to the snowline, is alpine. From here most of the common herbaceous plants disappear leaving tree heaths, giant lobelias and senecios. Reeds grow in the marshes and shrubby bushes with everlasting flowers (*Belichrysums*) are abundant. The rocks are covered with a loosely adhering carpet of moss. Above about 3,000 metres there is little sign of life except hyrax and other small rodents. Birds are also fairly sparse.

People The Bakonjo live on the Rwenzoris, a Bantu tribe who speak Lukonjo which is believed to be one of the earliest forms of Bantu speech. They are a short and sturdy people and frequently find work as guides and porters as many are excellent climbers. Apart from when they are acting as guides and porters, they rarely actually go high up into the mountain range believing that a god called Kitasamba lives in the upper reaches of the mountains. You may see small grass huts with offerings to Kitasamba in them on your ascent.

Climbing the Rwenzoris For the past couple of years it has not been possible to safely climb these mountains because of political unrest and trans-border fighting and rebel attacks. The situation in this southwestern region is changeable so check before finalizing your travel plans.

The Rwenzoris are suitable for almost all climbers and walkers who are reasonably fit. There are hiking routes in the foothills for those with no climbing experience – all that is needed is a little stamina and waterproof clothing. More demanding is the ascent of Mount Speke which is a simple glacier requiring limited mountain experience. Most difficult are some of the routes on Mounts Stanley and Baker, and only those with experience in rock, snow and ice climbing should attempt these.

The Rwenzoris have a reputation for being wet – and with good reason. The best time of the year to visit them are from the end of December to February and from mid-June to mid-August. The rest of the year there is often a lot of rain and apart from making the walk or climb slippery, the views are not so good with mist sometimes shrouding the mountain, in particular the peaks, and blocking off the views.

The situation as regards climbing the Rwenzoris is changing almost constantly. There has been a lot of political unrest in the area and the mountains are frequently closed to public access due to clashes with rebels. Up to date information is best gathered from other travellers who have recently completed the climb. In the middle of 1993 the *Rwenzori Mountains Services (RMS)*, PO Box 33, Kasese, who maintain the huts and trails, sharply raised their prices. Safari companies such as *Semliki Safaris* (Fort Portal), who have a site at Ntandi, have responded by setting up their own campsites along the route, competing directly with the RMS. The total price that you can expect to pay, very roughly, for an eight-day trek will be in the region of US$278 but these prices have risen steeply in the past few years. This includes all fees, porters, guides, equipment hire and food. Most equipment that you may need can be hired from the RMS and food bought in Kasese. It is wet for much of the year and cold at night – so come well prepared with waterproofs and plenty of warm clothing. Pack everything inside your rucksack in plastic bags.

It is obligatory to take porters and a guide. Porters carry loads of 22 kilograms excluding their own blankets and supplies. The headman does not carry a load although is expected to relieve a tired member of the party. Guides are also necessary. It is important to get absolutely clear what the charges are going to be – they depend on the number of days taken up on the trip and the stages covered.

You should take all the food that you will need. A stove is certainly worth taking – apart from the environmental impact of cutting wood for cooking, the wood is almost without fail wet and difficult to light.

For more serious climbers who intend to climb the peaks be sure that your guide is experienced. The best written work is Osmaston and Pasteur's *Guide to the Rwenzoris* although it is rather out of date as far as the huts go, the actual description of climbs and so on, has not changed. This is not available in Uganda but can be obtained from *Stanfords Map and Travel Bookshop* (Longacre, Covent Garden, London WC2E 9LP, England). The other good guide with a detailed map is Wielochowski's *Rwenzori Map and Guide* which is available from the author (32 Seamill Park Crescent, Worthing BN11 2NP, England), and also in some bookshops in Nairobi.

You should allow about 10 days for the trip and the most popular route (the Circuit) should take you six to seven days. This is described below. This is obviously just one suggestion – you can break the route up with more frequent stops – for example Day 1 to Nyabitaba; Day 2 to Nyamileju; Day 3 to Bigo Hut; Day 4 to Lake Bajuku; Day 5 to Kitandara; Day 6 to Buy Yeoman and Day 7 back to Nyakalengija.

Day 1 Begin by heading for Nyakalengija (1,600 metres) three miles from Ibanda **The Circuit** and 22 kilometres from Kasese, where the trail begins and from there take the path to the Nyabitaba Hut (2,651 metres) about 10 kilometres. If you have made arrangements through the RMS they should be able to arrange transport to their office at Nyakalengija where you will pay your fees et cetera. You can also park vehicles here fairly safely, and camp if you want to start the walk early the next day. From Nyakalengija head through a coffee plantation and a field and on into some elephant grass. The path gradually deteriorates as you enter the bush and the cultivation disappears and is replaced by elephant grass and nettles. There is the Mubuku River on your right (which has trout – introduced by the British). You descend to the edge of the river and then climb up and into the forest. Cross two streams and continue for several kilometres before crossing the Mahoma River. The final ascent is up a moraine ridge to Nyabitaba – before you get to the hut itself there is a small rock shelter. There is a large rock shelter a little beyond the hut – which many people use in preference to the hut, alternatively, you can camp in the clearing by the hut. The Nyabitaba Hut is a two-roomed hut built in 1987 which sleeps up to 12 people. There is a water supply at the hut.

Day 2 Nyabitaba (2,651 metres) to John Mate Camp (3,500 metres). This is the most difficult day of the circuit, and will take you at least seven hours. You follow the ridge through the forest and then fork down steeply to the left to the Mabuka River. This you cross using the Kurt Schafer Bridge which was built in 1989 after the old one collapsed. From here you climb up again on the other side – the path gradually gets harder becoming a slippery scramble – and continue on to the bamboo forest. The walk through the bamboo forest is relatively easy but before reaching Nyamiliju there is a long hard climb upwards. It is here that you will start to go through the heather and groundsel towards Nyamiliju – in fact Nyamiliju actually means place of beards – a name that refers to the moss and lichen that hangs from the trees. There is an old hut at Nyamiliju (3,322 metres) which is a round uniport with a wooden floor. It is not much used any longer as most people prefer to push on to John Mate Hut. But if you wish to go slower, it is there, and has a good water supply. There is also a nearby rock shelter which some people prefer to use but there is no room for tents here. If you are lucky, and it is clear, you should be able to see Mount Stanley and Mount Speke as well as the glaciers, and Nyamiliju can make a good lunchtime stop. From Nyaniliju it is a further two hours to John Mate Hut (3,505 metres) climbing up through the giant heather and groundsel forest. The trail is much less clear – start by crossing the stream just below the rock shelter and carry on towards the river, although don't actually cross it. Continue from the heather forest until it opens out a bit, and up two fairly steep moraines before you reach the camp. The hut is modern and in good condition. It is close to the Bajuku River from where you can collect water.

Day 3 John Mate (3,505 metres) to Lake Bujuku (3,962 metres). On the third day you go through the muddy bog of Bigo, past the Bigo Hut and on to the Bujuku Hut. Begin by crossing the river and then head for the left-hand edge of the valley skirting around the bog. You will find it almost impossible to avoid getting muddy. Bigo Hut (3,444 metres) sleeps 12 and is in fairly good condition and there is flowing water nearby. There is also a rock shelter here, which the porters tend to use.

From Bigo Hut you can choose a number of different routes. You can go north to Roccati pass which runs between Mounts Gessi and Emin; or northeast to Bukurungu pass between Gessi and the Portal Peaks; or southwest to Lake Bujuku. The latter route is the most popular for Circuit users and is the one described below.

From Bigo (3,444 metres) to Lake Bujuku (3,962 metres) you cross the Kibatsi Bog to what is known as the Cooking Pot Cave (marked as a Rock Shelter on the map, page 644) and from there to the Lake Bujuku hut with its beautiful setting. Begin by following the route which swings southwestwards with Mount Stanley on your right (west) and Baker on your left (east). The path starts off rather steep but levels off as you round the southern spur. You will shortly reach the Kibatsi bog which will take you two to three hours to cross and from the bog there is another steep climb. Here you reach Cooking Pot Cave, where the track splits into two. Take the right (northwest) route to the huts. The left fork leads to the Scott Elliot pass and you will return here tomorrow to continue the Circuit. The Lake Bujuku Hut is actually two huts which sleep up to 14 people and are in fair condition. There is water available close by. It is one of the loveliest settings of all the huts on the routes, with Mount Stanley and an incredible ice cave in the Peke glacier on Mount Speke clearly visible.

Lake Bujuku Hut is the base for those planning to climb Mount Speke (4,889 metres). Serious climbers hoping to reach the highest point on the range, Margherita Peak on Mount Stanley (5,109 metres) should base themselves at Elena Hut (4,541 metres). This is located about two kilometres off the circuit and is about three or four hours from Bujuku or Kitandara huts.

Day 4 Lake Bujuku (3,962 metres) to Kitandara (4,032 metres). This walk is a fairly light one, taking about half a day, and you climb to the highest point on the circuit at the Scott Elliot Pass. Begin by returning to the Cooking Pot Cave and from there take the southerly path that leads to the Scott Elliot Pass (4,372 metres). The track takes you through groundsel to a scree slope. At the head of this is a rock buttress – the pass is to the right. There is a cleft in the rocks to the left and from here the descent continues with the vertical cliffs of Mount Baker on your side. Before reaching Lake Kitandara the path rises then descends again. The two huts at Lake Kitandara are also in a wonderful setting – next to one of the two lakes and close to the foot of Elena glacier.

Day 5 Lake Kitandara Hut (4,032 metres) to the Kamamba Rock Shelter (3,779 metres) or to Guy Yeoman's Hut. If you go on to Guy Yeoman's Hut this is a walk of about five hours. The day begins with a steep climb to the Freshfield Pass (4,282 metres), followed by a descent down to a rock overhang called Bujongolo. This is where the first expedition to explore the mountains in 1906 based themselves. A little further on is a second, and larger rock shelter called Kabamba located close to a waterfall, where you can spend the night. Alternatively you can continue onto the Guy Yeoman Hut (3,505 metres) which is one of the newer sites.

Day 6 Guy Yeoman (3,505 metres) to Nyabitaba Hut (2,651 metres), or on to Nyakalengija (1,600 metres). Continue your descent via Kichuchu where there is another rock shelter. From Kichuchu the descent continues through bog and bamboo forest and then across the Mubuku River. Having forded the river, follow the path along a ridge and down to the Nyabitaba Hut (2,651 metres). Alternatively you can go via Lake Mahoma where there is a hut, if you want to spend an extra night. From Nyabitaba Hut you then have to retrace your steps back to Nyakalengija, about another three-hour hike.

Air Chartered flights go to **Kasese** from where you can complete the journey by road.   **Transport**

Road The Rwenzoris are approached from **Ibanda** in Mubuku Valley. Ibanda can be reached from Kampala via Mbarara and Kasese from where it is a further 18 kilometres.

Alternatively from Kampala to Fort Portal and then 75 kilometres on the Fort Portal-Kasese road before turning off for Ibanda. Coming from Kasese, about 10 kilometres along the main Kasese-Fort Portal road, there is a turning off to Ibanda. Take this for about 12 kilometres – it is a fairly good gravel road. On reaching Ibanda you will see a sign-post for the Rwenzori Mountaineering Service on the right hand side of the road and this is where you will need to go to organize guides, porters et cetera.

Semliki National Park

The Semliki (or Bundibugyo) National Park, 70 kilometres northwest of Fort Portal, located in the Bundibigyo District north of the Rwenzori Mountains, was gazetted in 1993. The Semliki River forms its northern and western boundary, and the eastern boundary is the Fort Portal to Bundibugyo Road. The unspoilt Semliki Forest extends over the border to RD Congo where it is known as the Ituri Forest, which continues down to the Congo River. The Semliki River separates Uganda from RD Congo. The National Park covers 222 square kilometres. It contains many species of animals and birds that are not found elsewhere in East Africa. Larger mammals such as elephant, leopard and buffalo, exist in the forest but although evidence of their presence can be observed, the animals themselves are rarely seen. A large number of smaller mammals are found in the forest including a black and white colobus, chimpanzees, brazza monkey, African palm civet, giant forest squirrel, black mangabey and many others. The birdlife at Semliki is phenomenal with about 400 species recorded, including the Gabon Woodpecker, Hartlaub's duck, five varieties of greenbill and four of hornbill.

Within the park the most popular attractions are the **hot springs** at **Sempaya**. Heated underground, the springs come to the surface at temperatures close to boiling. The largest spring has a geyser shooting up through clouds of steam.

There is a campsite next to the NP headquarters on the side of the Bundibugyo Rd, costing   **Sleeping**
US$10 per person per night plus park fee.

Ntandi Village, home to the Pygmies, is just across the Bundibugyo Road – see entry on page 600. Confusingly, **The Semliki Valley Wildlife Reserve**, previously called the Semliki Game Reserve or, before that, the Toro Game Reserve, is a separate reserve from the National Park. The road from the Ntoroko fishing village on the southern shore of Lake Albert to the main Semliki Road at Isojo, runs through the valley Wildlife Reserve. The Reserve is mostly open savannah with swampy areas in the north of this 510 square kilometre reserve. The tourist facilities here are under-developed but plans are in hand to organize trips to see the chimpanzees and boat trips for bird-watching.

Sleeping A *Semliki Safari Lodge*, T/F041-25-9700, gwg@swiftuganda.com, built by the *Green Wilderness Group*, is establishing trails through the swamps and forest enabling visitors to see the primates and elephants.

Uganda

Security is a major concern in this area. The guerrilla activities of the Allied Democratic Front (ADF) have caused problems since 1997. Thought to be Congolese refugees, the brutal attacks on local people has had the effect of driving these villagers into the towns of Nyakuka and Bundibugyo. In June 1998 the ADF attacked a technical college in Kichwamba, killing about 60 people. Check at Fort Portal for a current update before visiting this area.

Transport Four-wheel drive preferable as the road is poor 20 kilometres after leaving Fort Portal. There are no buses but lifts from trucks which usually leave Bundibugyo before 0800. Ask to be dropped at Isojo close to the Park entrance.

Bwindi National Park (Impenetrable forest)

Bwindi Impenetrable National Park covers an area of 321 square kilometres and is located in Southwestern Uganda on the edge of the Western Rift Valley. It lies along the Uganda-RD Congo border in Kabale and Rukungiri districts. Bwindi Forest was first gazetted to the status of a forest reserve in 1932 and in 1961 as an animal sanctuary. From 1961 it was under the joint management of the Forest and the Game Departments, until 1991 when it became a National Park and was taken over by Uganda National Parks.

The forest has had a number of names in the past including Bwindi, and Kayonza. In the local language Bwindi means a Place of Darkness, a result of the thick vegetation. The other popular name is the Impenetrable Forest – a perfect description.

Mountain gorillas There are only three countries in which it is possible to visit mountain gorillas (*Gorilla beringei*) namely Uganda, Rwanda and RD Congo. With the problems in Rwanda continuing, visiting the gorillas there has been rendered impossible. Currently RD Congo is the main competitor to Uganda and has been running gorilla tours for a number of years. Since April 1993 it has been possible to visit the gorillas in Bwindi National Park. Booking through the Uganda National Parks headquarters, see page 619, or the office in Kabale, see page 619 for recent information on the booking procedures and its short-comings. The maximum numbers are rigidly applied, demand is high, and can be booked up a year ahead (there are cancellations). Overseas travel firms for example Abercrombie & Kent, and the Kampala-based Safari Companies take the majority of places, so go through them if tours appear full. Try to see the Mubara group which is bigger (13).

However, since the tragic events of march 1999 when tourists and park rangers were murdered by guerillas there has been a huge decline in the number of gorilla tourists. Currently it is easy to get a permit.

It has been estimated that there are only about 630 remaining specimens of the Mountain Gorilla in the world – and about half of these are thought to be in Uganda. The vast majority of these are in Bwindi although there are a few at Mgahinga National Park, which is part of the Virunga volcano range which extends across Rwanda, Uganda and RD Congo. The development of gorilla tourism and habituation of the gorillas is proceeding with great care in order to avoid dangers such as the gorillas catching human diseases.

There are two ways of seeing the gorillas. The first is to go it alone organizing transport, permits and camping equipment et cetera yourself. The alternative is much easier but for many is prohibitively expensive: that is to pay a tour operator to organize the whole trip including transport, accommodation and permits. These can be arranged in the USA, in Europe, in Kenya or else in Kampala (see Tour Operators listed in Kampala section page 576).

Bwindi gorilla visit

Early in the morning, the day we were to go gorilla-tracking, I awoke to a dawn chorus of birds and monkeys echoing across the forest valley to our camp. Opening my tent I watched as the mist lifted from the trees and the forest came to life. After struggling to get our fire going we had a quick breakfast and then set off. We were introduced to our Ugandan guide for the day who explained some of the rules of the park such as no smoking, eating or drinking once we reached the gorillas. More disconcertingly, he then went on to explain what to do in the event of a silver-back charging us. Above all, we were told, we must stay still, crouch down and keep our heads down. We should at all times follow his instructions while he and the two trackers would speak in gorilla language to reassure the boss of the group that we were friends not foes.

The 1st part of the walk was the easiest, being along a sunlit path decorated by scores of dancing butterflies. About 45 minutes into the forest we turned off this and the hard walking began. From here it was about two and a half hours up and down the steep valley sides – ascending, we pulled ourselves up with the help of nearby trees and on the way down slid most of the way on our backsides. We traversed three valleys before we reached the place where the gorillas had spent the previous night. This spot is marked by the nests of branches and leaves that the gorillas make for themselves and huge piles of dung. From here the trackers hacked through the thick bush following the trail of the gorillas. Occasionally the pungent sweetness of jasmine descended. Everywhere cicadas hummed, punctuated occasionally by the haunting shrieks of chimps. We tried to spot them in the trees around – but in vain. Suddenly the trackers stopped – we are very close, they told us, so this was the last chance for a drink and a snack.

After this rest we walked on – the atmosphere changed as we realized we were so close. About 15 minutes later we suddenly heard a loud grunt – it sounded very close and my heart missed a beat but, peering through the bush, I could see nothing. The grunting continued – I would have sworn it was less than a metre away but the bush was so thick that still I could see nothing. Our guide started to reply to the gorilla making a deep coughing noise and we slowly crept around keeping a fair distance away from the source of the grunting. Peering into deep green vegetation, I could see nothing. Suddenly I caught sight of an enormous hand reaching up from ground level to pluck a green shoot. At the end of the arm was the face of a female sitting with her young close by. She was staring at us but was remarkably unconcerned at our presence as she continued to eat her meal. As we watched our eyes were drawn upwards to the sounds of two infants playing in the trees – they were absolutely delightful as they clambered up the branches and pushed each other down again. We still hadn't seen the silverback, but knew where he was, as he was the source of the deep grunts. Slowly he emerged from the bushes, familiar from films and photographs, but in the flesh he was quite awe-inspiring. Everything about him was bigger than I'd imagined and as he moved through the undergrowth it collapsed around him.

We stayed with the family group for about an hour before returning to our camp, thoroughly delighted with the experience. The route back was more direct but a downpour slowed our progress. I had always been led to believe that in a rainforest the tree canopy overhead prevents most of the rain reaching the forest floor – but it soon became clear this was not so. I put on a raincoat but within minutes the warm and heavy rain had soaked through it. As we left the forest the rain stopped almost immediately, and we returned dripping to the camp for a cup of hot coffee.

Uganda

Independent gorilla excursions If you are planning to go it alone the first thing to do is to obtain tracking permit as the permits sell out weeks in advance. See page 625 for information about fees. If you have not booked, or find there are no spaces you can go to Bwindi and hope that someone fails to turn up. At the moment it seems that most people who turn up and wait at the campsite do eventually get on a tour. (See page 619 for information on recent booking experiences.) You are strongly advised to check your permit before leaving Kampala as some unscrupulous tour operators have been selling permits to visit gorilla groups which have disbanded. Some companies have also been selling the US$250 permits for US$350, which is illegal. Some reports have been received that "extra" visits have been laid on by park staff. This is illegal and increases the risk that the gorillas will become stressed or aquire human viral/bacterial diseases. If you fail to see the gorillas, the charge is refunded.

The gorilla viewing is excellent. At present M group of 13 animals is the recommended option. K group is comprised of five gorillas as the troop broke up in May 1996 due to internal strife. Another group of gorillas has now been habituated and viewing of this troop started in 1997.

It has been reported that no standby permits are being issued at Bwindi since the breakup of K group. However there has been conflicting information on this. The main hope for those without a booking is to wait for a permit holder to get a cold (which disqualifies the permit) or try a reputable tour operator like Delmira for a cancellation. Delmira appears to have overtaken Hot Ice and others as the major tour operator. It is run by a Dutch lady, Mirjam Blaak, who appears to be well known locally. Good shoes and dirt-resistant clothes are essential as it is very muddy. It is also appreciated if tourists share their lavish lunches as some porters and guides have just a banana.

You can go on half-day guided tours of the forest for US$10 – there is a waterfall nearby which you can visit which makes a nice walk. The forest has been estimated to have at least 120 species of mammals of which 10 are primates. There are chimpanzees, black and white colobus, red-tailed monkeys and vervets. Other species include giant forest hog, and bushbucks although these are both rare and shy animals. There are an estimated 20 elephants which have survived in the forest – their population has been brought near to extinction over the past 20 years. The forest maintains a huge range of birdlife – over 330 species. The plant and insect life is also phenomenal – there are about 150 tree species as well as a wide range of ferns, orchids, mosses and lichens.

Sleeping At Bwindi (Buhoma) there is now a wide range of accommodation. **A+** *Abercrombie and Kent "Five Star Luxury" Tented Camp*, not luxury but comfortable with lots of atmosphere, 7 tents plus bar and dining room, staff are willing and helpful, but the camp is a little disorganized, well sited. **A** *Mantana Tented Camp*, simpler tented camp than A and K situated in a rather damp forest patch, very helpful staff. **B** *African Pearl Lodge*, nice little houses, some self-contained, opposite the National Parks Office, communal showers may be used by those staying at the campsite, recent feedback indicates that this company has become overpriced and less reliable, with 'extra' costs being incurred after bookings have been paid for in full. **D** Bandas, **E** Campsite, *Buhoma Community Campground*, a co-operative camp group owned by locals is sited next to the Park HQ. The Coop has a gazebo dining area, attractive campsites, running water, bucket showers and a pit toilet, there are 2 x 4 bedroomed bandas, very clean. Highly recommended. Good campsite worth supporting, food and basics available at the H and P canteen, cheap, tasty and wholesome. US$3.

Transport **Road (public transport)** Buses leave between 0600 and 0700 every morning from **Kampala** take 6 hours and cost US$6, Matatus leave when full – usually mid-morning – from Kampala, take about 5 hours and cost US$11. From **Kabale** it is a journey of 3 hours to the campsite at Buhoma – but transport links are difficult. Because you have to start tracking at 0830 in the morning it is strongly advised that you get to Buhoma the night before. If you are late you lose your booking and do not get any money back.

To get to the campsite you have a number of choices. You can either hire a pickup, or go as far as possible on public transport and walk part of the journey. *M/S Tour Operators*, PO Box 640, 147/149 Kabale Rd, Kabale, T22700, can arrange transport.

The cheapest alternative is to take a public pickup as far as possible and then walk the rest of the way. The campsite is at Buhoma, and the pickups go part of the way, leaving from the Kabale matatu stand at about 0800. The nearest village is Butagota from where it is a 14 kilometres hike. Using public transport you shouldn't pay more than US$4 one way.

If you are relying on public transport and want to be sure not to miss your allocated day, you should allow at least one spare day. There is plenty to do around the forest itself, and your park entrance fee lasts 4 days.

Mgahinga Gorilla National Park

This, the smallest National Park in Uganda at just 36 square kilometres, was established in 1991. It is found in the far southwest of the country in Kisoro District. It makes up the northeastern part of the Virunga Volcano range which extends into RD Congo and Rwanda.

The protection of gorillas on the Ugandan side of the Virunga volcanoes began in the mid-1950s when a game warden, Walter Baumgartel, took an interest in them. Baumgartel left Uganda in the late 1960s and in the years that followed there was much encroachment into the forest particularly along the lower slopes of Mount Muhavura, Gahinga and Sabinyo. Poaching was also a threat and many of the gorillas retreated into better protected areas in the neighbouring countries. It has been estimated that the gorilla population of the Mgahinga National Park declined by about 50 percent between 1960 and the early 1980s and is currently believed to be 45.

It was not until 1989 that gorillas began to receive some protection under the Gorilla Game Reserve Conservation Project which began to operate along the Virunga Volcanoes on the Uganda side. This became the Mgahinga Gorilla National Park Project in 1991. Gorilla tracking tours have recently started. They take four people who book from Uganda National Park Headquarters in Kampala, and two people who book from the National Park Tourist Information Office in Kabale, see page 618. It is not always possible to see gorillas in Mgahinga as they move over to RD Congo but recent travellers report that gorillas have been easier to see. Tourists should check from Kampala or the information office Kabale to confirm whereabouts of the gorillas first.

In Mgahinga National Park there is at least one group of 10 habituated gorillas. Recent travellers have indicated that there are now more than one group of habituated gorillas in this park, and that as a result it has become easier to get permits to see them. Gorilla tracking begins at 0830 sharp daily, late arrivals may lose their place.

Other animals that are found in Mgahinga include a small number of elephants, buffaloes, giant forest hogs, the rare golden monkey, and the rare blue monkey. The golden monkey is only found in the Virunga Volcano range and two other forests in central Africa. The monkey gets its name from the colour of its fur, which unfortunately puts it under threat from poachers. The project leader has adopted and tamed a young elephant which you will see around the camp.

The summit of Mount Muhavura forms the highest point of the park at 4,127 metres and has a small crater lake which tourists may want to visit. The vegetation in the Park includes montane, alpine and subalpine flora at each of the different levels up the volcano as vegetation varies with altitude. The lowest vegetation zone of the mountain is mainly bamboo and this is the area where the gorillas are likely to be found. The alpine zone is dominated by the impressive giant senecios and giant lobelias which are found at an altitude of between 3,600 and 4,200 metres. It is possible to climb to the peaks of Gahinga and Muhavura if you are reasonably fit. This can be organized at the Mgahinga National Park office in Kisoro, where they collect entrance fees, et cetera. If you do not feel fit enough for this there are other shorter walks that can be arranged, including a visit to a the Garama Cave. Cost US$13 per person including the Ranger fee but not the park entrance fee. In addition to the Park entrance fee (US$15 per person) you will be charged for a trip to the peaks (US$30 per person in a group, US$40 if you are on your own. This includes the Rangers fee). Climbing to the peak of Mount Muhavura involves paying a rescue fee of US$10. Camping in the base camp of Muhavura costs US$10 per person in a tent. The climb takes approximately seven hours. If climbing other lower peaks you are not obliged to pay the rescue fee. Shorter walks within the park cost US$5 per person. All such walks must be accompanied by a ranger which costs US$10 (or US$5 for half a day) for the group. The Rangers expect to be tipped after the climbs – the amount is at your discretion.

Camping   **A** *Mount Gahinga Rest Camp* set in dramatic scenery in the shadow of the Virunga volcanoes is a good base from which to see the gorillas, or climb Mounts Muhavura and Gahinga. Run by *Volcanoes Tours*, PO Box 22818, Kampala, T041-346464/5, F041-341718, Mobile 075-741718, volcanoes@infocom.co.ug. UK representative, PO Box 16345, London, SW1X 0ZD, T0171 -2357897, F0171-2351780, volcanoes@mailbox.co.uk, www.VolcanoesSafaris.com. **E** Lovely campsite at the park entrance with water and firewood, tents and banda, meals available.

Transport   See travel to Kisoro, page 623.

Background

In the last eight years, Uganda has made a remarkable recovery. Peace has returned to the main parts of the country, although there are still some armed bands marauding in the north. Many Asians and skilled Africans have returned, and the economy has begun to allow improved living standards. Many of the features that were so attractive to visitors before 1970 are there to be enjoyed again and Uganda offers excellent value in wildlife viewing.

The land

Uganda, in the East African region, is a medium-sized landlocked state bordered by Sudan, Kenya, Tanzania, Rwanda and Zaïre. Uganda lies between latitude 4° North to 1° South and longitude 30° West to 33° East. It forms part of the central African plateau, dropping to the White Nile Basin in the north. Lake Kionga and Lake Albert lie in the Rift Valley and much of the territory to the south is swampy marsh. To the east is savannah and the western part of the country forms the margins of the Congo forests. Generally the south is agricultural and the north is pastoral.

Geography

There are hydro-electric schemes on the Owen Falls Dam. Mineral resources include copper, tin, bismuth, wolfram, colombo-tanalite, phosphates, limestone, gold and beryl (a gemstone).

Temperature varies little; there is an equatorial climate modified by altitude. Rainfall, greatest in the mountains and the Lake Victoria region, reaches an annual average of up to 200 centimetres. Elsewhere it averages 125 centimetres but the dry northeast and parts of the south receive up to 75 centimetres. The dry season varies between one month in the centre and west, to the months of June, July and August in the south. There are two dry seasons in the north and northeast in October and December to March, making two harvests possible.

Climate

Uganda

History

Before the arrival of the British there were as many as 30 different ethnic groups in the area that now forms modern Uganda, each with its own language, culture and social organization.

The political organization of these different states ranged from those with a highly developed centralized system of government, through small chiefdoms, to areas with no obvious system of government. Buganda, Toro, Bunyoro and Nkore, were of the first type, and all had a highly developed centralized system of government with a monarch in place. Around 1830 Toro broke away from Bunyoro when Prince Kaboyo rebelled against his father. For some time Bunyoro was the strongest and most powerful of the four, but from the second half of the 18th century they were overtaken by Buganda. In Nkore the system was rather different as the minority pastoral Bahima ruled over the majority agriculturalist Bairu.

Other areas had no obvious system of government and interpersonal relations were controlled by fear of spirits and the supernatural.

The first foreigners to arrive in the area were Arab traders in the 1840s. From about 1850 the first Europeans began to arrive. John Speke reached Buganda in 1860 and was the first European to locate the source of the Nile (see box, page 582).

The late 19th century was a period of instability in much of Uganda, and there were wars on a surprisingly large scale. In 1888 the British East Africa Company was given the royal charter and their control over the area was consolidated by a treaty with the Kabaka of Buganda (the central and most prominent kingdom) in 1891. However the Company found administering the territory too much for it to manage, and in 1894 the British Government took over responsibility and Buganda was declared a Protectorate. Similar status was given to Bunyoro, Toro and Ankole in 1896. During the following years the boundaries of the country were finalized, with a section of Uganda being transferred to Kenya as late as 1912.

Buganda Agreement of 1900

The so-called 'Buganda Question' goes back to the signing in 1900 of the Uganda Agreement (at this time, and until about 1906 the British referred to the District of Buganda as Uganda) which proved to be a watershed in the history of Buganda and, indeed, the whole of Uganda. It formalized the association between the British and the Buganda that had developed since Speke's arrival in 1862.

One of the most important aspects of the Agreement was that it secured a remarkably privileged position for Buganda in comparison with its neighbours. The constitutional relationship between the Protectorate Government and the Government of the Kingdom of Buganda was set out at some length, and it emphasized Buganda's political identity while assuring it a greater measure of internal autonomy than the other districts enjoyed. Some of the other districts had their own agreements, but none were as comprehensive or as favourable as that accorded the Bugands.

The Agreement led to important changes in land tenure. It won over the majority of the chiefs by giving them land grants known as *mailo*, and in doing so it recognized that land was a marketable commodity. The land not given to the Kabaka and chiefs became Crown land to be used for the benefit of the Kingdom. The Agreement thus created a landed class. It also gave, for the first time, recognition to the notion of indirect rule through the chiefs. The colonialists needed local allies to help them administer with the minimum expenditure, and to produce an economic surplus that could pay for the administration. In time the interests of the chiefs and the Government became more closely interwoven. The chiefs collected regular salaries and promoted government policies, and in the public's mind they began to be associated with the Protectorate administration.

The benefit of the Agreement was in addition to the natural advantages that Buganda already had with fertile soils, regular rainfall, and a location on the shore of Lake Victoria which ensured good transport links. Missionary activity in the area, stimulated by competition between the Protestant and Catholics led to a greater concentration of hospitals, schools and other educational facilities. Britain encouraged the production of cotton, the major cash crop in the south, while parts of the remaining areas were discouraged from growing cash crops and were instead developed as a labour reserve. This served to accentuate further the differences between Buganda and the rest of the Protectorate, with the south producing cash crops and the north providing migrant labour. In keeping with this division, the north also provided soldiers to the army throughout the colonial period. Buganda's farmers benefited greatly from high coffee prices after the war and in the early 1950s industrial and commercial development were concentrated in the south generally and in Buganda with its locational and educational advantages, in particular.

The period of British rule in Uganda saw dramatic changes in the politics and economy of the country. Most of the wars and disputes were brought under control and the peace which grew up became known as Pax Britanica. The country was divided into Districts which were headed by a District Commissioner, and the Districts into Counties (*saza*), Sub-counties (*gombolola*), Parishes (*miruka*) and Sub-Parishes (*bukungu* or *batongole*). A system of indirect rule was developed, with local people used at all these levels. In cases where a system of government was already in place the incumbents were used, but where this was absent other Ugandans – usually Baganda – were brought in. This meant that in many parts of Uganda in the early years the British Administration the British controlled large areas of Uganda through appointed Baganda chiefs.

While the south of the country developed into an agriculturally productive area producing, in particular cotton and coffee, the north and southwest developed mainly as a labour pool. Migration into the southern and central region became crucial to maintaining the high production in these areas. There was also a great deal of migration from outside Uganda to the central region. This was mainly from what was then known as Ruanda Urundi (later to be Rwanda and Burundi) but was also from Tanganikya and the Congo. Migration was not just to government jobs on large scale, such as the building of the railway and the army, but also to work for individual cotton and coffee farmers in Buganda. There were some large-scale European-owned farms and plantations in Uganda, but they were never as extensive as in Kenya and it was always planned that Uganda should be developed primarily for Africans. Thus, during the Depression of the late 1920s and early 1930s, the Uganda Colonial Government was not prepared to give the Europeans financial support to get them through the difficult times. Many went bust and left the country. A number of the plantations were later bought up by Asians and were developed into the sugar plantations that can be seen on the road from the Kenya border to Kampala.

The Christian missions arrived in Uganda early and their impact was enormous. Islam was also introduced into Uganda but never made the same impact. The first schools and hospitals were all mission-run, the Catholic and Protestants tried desperately to win the most converts, and the key was to provide superior education. The two Christian faiths divided the country up between their different groups so that, for example the White Fathers went to Southern Uganda, the Mill Hill Fathers to Eastern Uganda and the Verona Fathers to the north. The Church Mission Society (CMS) are to be found across most of the country and their influence was very great.

Countries under colonial rule have usually achieved independence when a growing nationalist movement has been successful both in mobilizing a large section of the population and in extracting concessions from the colonial power. In Uganda however, it has been said that it was not nationalism that produced independence but instead it was the imminence of independence that produced nationalist parties. It was taken for granted that independence would be granted at some stage and instead concern was concentrated on the position and role that Buganda would take in an independent country. The Baganda did not wish for their role to be diminished after independence. By the same token, the rest of the country had no wish to be dominated by the Baganda.

The issue of Baganda separatism came to a head when Sir Andrew Cohen was appointed governor in 1952, and was determined to push Uganda as quickly as possible along the road to self-government. A vital principle underlying his policies was that Uganda must develop as a unitary state in which no part of the country should dominate any other. Thus a strong central Government was required, in which all districts, including Buganda, would be represented on an equal footing. This challenged the privileged position that the Buganda had enjoyed since 1900.

Kabaka Crisis of 1953-55

The crisis of 1953-55 was sparked off by a chance remark in London by Sir Oliver Lyttleton, the Colonial Secretary, about the possibility of introducing a federal system in East Africa embracing the three British territories of Kenya, Uganda and Tanganyika. This was very unpopular with all Ugandans as it was feared the federation would be dominated by the Europeans in Kenya. In a wider union the Baganda were even more fearful that they would be unable to safeguard their privileged position. Cohen responded to Lyttleton's remarks by giving public reassurances in the Legislative Council that there would be no imposition of a federation against public wishes. The Kabaka, Mutesa II, accepted these reassurances but took the opportunity to ask for the affairs of Buganda to be transferred from the Colonial Office to the Foreign Office, which would be a clear indication that Baganda was not merely just another colony, but had a more privileged position being a protected state whose monarch had invited British protection. He also asked for a timetable for Independence to be drawn up.

The Kabaka then went a step further and rejected the policy of a unitary state and asked for the separation of Buganda from the rest of the country. Cohen demanded assurances in line with the 1900 Agreement that the Kabaka would not publicly oppose the government's policies for Uganda's development. However the Kabaka refused, pleading that he first needed to consult the *Lukiko*, the Buganda council of elders. On 30 November 1953 Cohen signed a declaration withdrawing Britain's recognition from Mutesa as Native ruler in Buganda, deported the Kabaka by air to Britain and declared a State of Emergency. Troops were deployed around Kampala but there was no outbreak of violence.

Following the Kabaka Crisis discussions got underway to attempt to resolve the situation which led to the Namirembe Conference of July-September 1954. In October 1955 the Kabaka returned to Uganda and signed the Buganda Agreement of 1955 – the outcome of the Conference. The Agreement declared that Buganda should continue to be an integral part of the Protectorate of Uganda, and recommended that the *Lukiko* should agree to elected Baganda participation in the Legislative Council, a step which, fearful of being submerged, it had consistently rejected. The Kabaka in theory returned as a constitutional monarch stripped of political power, but in reality the crisis had served to unite the various clans of the Baganda firmly behind the Kabaka, and thereby increased his political influence.

The crisis had a number of major effects. Firstly the question of federation with the rest of East Africa was ruled out. Secondly, the Buganda continued to have a special position and virtual internal self-government. Thirdly, the Kabaka's personal power and popularity increased. Fourthly a statement in the House of Commons was made that Uganda would be developed primarily as an African country, with proper safeguards for minorities. Fifthly, non-Baganda members of the Legislative Council adopted an increasingly nationalist attitude and began to question the special treatment accorded to the Buganda, sowing the seeds of confrontation. And finally, now that independence in Uganda was clearly just a matter of time the major question turned to who would hold the power after independence, and what would be the Buganda's and the Kabaka's role.

From the mid-1950s the first political parties were formed. They were the Democratic Party (DP), led by Benedicto Kiwanuka, with particular support amongst Catholics. They wanted a unitary state after independence and wanted to limit the powers of the Baganda – so initially the party did not find much support in Buganda. The Uganda National Congress (UNC) was more nationally-based and wanted greater African control of the economy in a federal independent state. In 1958 a splinter group broke off from the UNC and formed the Uganda People's Congress (UPC), led by Milton Obote. A political party called Kabaka Yekka (KY) – 'The King Alone' – also formed, representing the interests of the Baganda.

The immediate run-up to independence was one of non-cooperation by the Baganda who feared losing their political identity as part of a unitary state and became increasingly hostile towards the Protectorate Government. They refused to proceed with elections for Buganda's Legislative Councillors until Buganda's role in a future central government and the role of the Kabaka had been decided. On the 31 December 1960 the Baganda declared themselves independent however this was a meaningless gesture as they did not have the power to make independence a reality.

In 1961 an inquiry was set up to look into the question of the relationship of the various parts of Uganda with the centre. It recognized that Buganda enjoyed what was virtually a federal relationship with the rest of the Protectorate, and recommended that this should continue. Uganda should therefore become a single democratic state with a strong central government, with which Buganda would have a federal relationship.

In 1961 the first elections were held – the two main parties being UPC and DP. The Baganda boycotted the election so that only three percent of the Buganda electorate voted, allowing the DP to make a clean sweep in Buganda. Overall UPC won a majority of votes but DP's success in Buganda gave them the majority of the seats. Obote, as leader of the UPC opposition, and the Kabaka were both anxious to eject the DP from power in the 1962 elections, and so Obote agreed to support Buganda's demands – particularly for indirect elections to the National Assembly – in return for Buganda's return to the centre and acceptance of a single central government. Thus Buganda participated in the Constitutional Conference in London in September 1961.

At this conference the structure of the future government was agreed and the date of full independence was set for 9 October 1962. Buganda obtained virtually everything that it had demanded. There would be a federal relationship with the centre, and the constitution would define all matters concerning the Kabakaship and traditional institutions. This opened the way for the Baganda to participate once again in central government which they did through the Kabaka Yekka party, formed in 1961. They made an alliance with the UPC and the February 1962 elections in Buganda were really a fight between KY and DP, and KY won 65 of the 68 seats. The KY victory determined the composition of the new government formed after the national, pre-independence, elections in April 1962. Obote's UPC won a comfortable victory over DP outside Buganda, and within it the KY-UPC alliance ensured a majority of seats for the alliance. In May 1962 Obote was sworn in as Prime Minister of the UPC-KY government and the Kabaka's role was that of constitutional monarch. On 9 October 1962, the day Uganda became an independent nation, Obote spoke of the joy felt by all in Uganda at the achievement of Uganda's independence, and particularly as this had been reached in an atmosphere of peace and goodwill. He went on to speak of the need for a unity of purpose, mutual understanding and respect, and a resolve to place country above tribe, party and self.

Independence: Obote I

However, the coalition between UPC and KY was fragile and by 1964 enough KY and DP members had crossed the floor to join the UPC so that the alliance was no longer necessary and Obote dismissed KY from the government.

In February 1966 Obote suspended the constitution, deposed the president and transferred all executive powers to himself. Shortly afterwards an interim constitution was imposed that the parliament had neither read or debated, which withdrew regional autonomy, and introduced an executive presidency – which Obote assumed, thus becoming Head of State with absolute power. This became known as the pigeon-hole constitution because MPs were told to vote on it before they were allowed to read it – it was placed in their pigeon holes for them to read afterwards. When the Baganda demanded the restoration of their autonomy, troops led by second-in-command of the army, Col Idi Amin, seized the Kabaka's palace. The Kabaka fled to Britain, where he died in exile in a Bermondsey council flat – a sad end for a man who had spent much of his time at Cambridge travelling down to the engineering works in Derby to supervise the carving of ivory from elephants he had shot to make the switches on the dashboard of his Rolls Royce.

The late 1960s saw the beginning of the years of repression for which Uganda was later to became notorious. Detentions and armed repression became increasingly common. A 'Move to the Left' was introduced which redistributed resources by way of nationalization and increased central power. However, Obote, who had used the army to prop up his own régime, was to be ousted by that same army under the command of Amin. The takeover occurred in January 1971 while Obote was out of the country at a Commonwealth Conference. Amin declared himself the new head of state and promised that there would be a return to civilian government within five years. This however was not to be. It is worth remembering that Amin was initially greeted with widespread support amongst the Ugandan population, particularly the Baganda, as well as in the Western world.

Amin

Not long into his régime, however, Amin suspended all political activity and most civil rights. The National Assembly was dissolved and Amin ruled the country by capricious decree. In August 1972 Amin announced the expulsion of all non-citizen Asians. The directive was later expanded to all Asians, although under great pressure Amin backtracked on this latter point. However in the atmosphere that had been established, all but a handful of the 75,000 Asians left the country. Most went to Britain, while many others went to Canada and the States. 25 years on the Asians in Britain have shown their entrepreneurial skills, work ethic and are held up as model immigrants. Britain cut off diplomatic relations and imposed a trade embargo. By the end of the year most other Western countries had followed suit. The businesses that had been owned by Asians were Africanized, that is, given to various cronies of Amin. The expulsion of Asians and policy of Africanization was popular with the majority of the Ugandan population. Many had resented the success of Asian businesses and this seemed to be the time to make things fairer. However many businesses collapsed and the sudden and dramatic loss of technical skills brought other enterprises to a standstill. Amin attempted to gain the popularity of the Baganda by returning the body of the Kabaka for burial in the Kisubi tombs outside Kampala. The administration under Amin was propped up by military aid from the Soviet Union and Libya. Meanwhile the infrastructure – water supply, schools, hospitals, roads – collapsed, and many former cash-crop producers returned to subsistence production in an effort to survive. Unexplained disappearances increased, particularly among the Acholi and Langi people. There was conflict within the army.

In 1978, in an attempt to detract attention from the internal turmoil, Amin launched an attack on Tanzania. The Kagera Salient in southwest Uganda has, since the drawing of international boundaries, been rather an problematic area. Just to the west of Lake Victoria the international boundary is a straight line following the 10 latitude. However the Kagera River forms a loop to the south of this. There is, therefore, an area of land which is part of Tanzania, but because of the river, has more contact with Uganda. One of the most important agreements that the Organization of African Unity (OAU) reached soon after its formation was that, however unfair or illogical, the international boundaries drawn by the colonial powers, they should not be disputed. Amin's claim to the Kagera salient was clearly in breach of this. Amin's undisciplined troops were no match for the Tanzanian army and the 1979 war led to massive destruction, as the army fled north pillaging and destroying as it went. Amin fled and went into exile, first in Libya, and later in Saudi Arabia. His excellency, self-styled Field Marshall and Life President of Uganda, Amin awaits the call to return once the 'misunderstanding' which led to his overthrow is cleared up. At his villa in Jeddah, Amin remains convinced that his people still love him. It is believed that the money he took with him from Uganda has gone, but the Saudi government grants him an allowance.

Following the war, the Tanzanian army remained in Uganda to maintain the peace. Meanwhile on the political front the Tanzanians arranged the Moshi Conference in March 1979. At this conference Dr Lule (who had formerly been Vice Chancellor of Makerere) was chosen to be the leader of the National Consultative Committee of the Uganda National Liberation Front which together with a military commission undertook the interim rule of Uganda. In April, Lule was sworn in as president. He was not, however, to last long and in June, was voted out of office by the 30 strong National Consultative Committee. In his place was put Binaisa, the former Attorney General. His length of office was to be only a year and in May 1980 the UNLF's military commission took over. This was headed by Paulo Mwanga and was supported by Museveni as vice-chairman. Elections were set for December 1980 and were contested by four political parties. The major two were UPC (headed by Obote) and DP (headed by Paul Ssemogerere), a newer party the Uganda Patriotic Movement (UPM), headed by Museveni, and the Conservative Party which was largely a Buganda-based party derived from Kabaka Yekka.

Obote II This election for which Uganda had such high hopes is widely believed to have been fixed – crowds had gathered in the streets of Kampala as the first results came out and word was that the DP had won. However Mwanga announced that no further results of the election could be released before they had been approved by him. Needless to say, when the results were finally published – announcing a UPC victory – there was widespread belief that the results had been falsified. The truth of the election result will probably never be known – but in the end the UPC had a majority of 20 seats, Obote was proclaimed President with Mwanga as Vice-President. The election of the new government did not, however, bring peace and stability to the country. The policies that the UPC put forward were such as to attract World Bank and IMF sponsored economic reconstruction, but rebuilding the country was not to be easy. On the security side the situation in many parts of the country deteriorated still further.

The dissatisfaction that resulted from the doubts over the elections led to a number of groups going into the bush from where they carried out a guerrilla war. These included the National Resistance Army (NRA) led by Museveni who were based largely in the southern part of the country. The NRA was the most organized and it grew from a small collection of fighters into a powerful army. The atrocities perpetrated by the government in what became known as the Luwero Triangle, an area to the north of Kampala were an attempt to rid the NRA of civilian supporters. Large numbers of people displaced by these atrocities joined up with the NRA, including children orphaned by the civil war.

Meanwhile there was also trouble within the UNLA – it was an ethnic division within the army, which was largely made up of Acholi and Langi, that was to lead to another change in leadership. This was led by the two Okello's (Tito and Basilio – not related) and occurred in July 1985. Obote fled to Kenya and from there to Zambia and Tito Okello took over as president. The NRA did not join Okello but remained fighting and within a few months had taken over Fort Portal and Kasese in the west of the country. By the end of the year the NRA was within a few miles of Kampala. There were efforts at negotiation at a conference held in Nairobi and in late December a peace treaty was signed. However, just three weeks after the signing, Museveni's troops advanced on Kampala.

Okello's troops fled north, Museveni was sworn in as the President and formed a broad-based government with ministries being filled by members of all the main political factions. However, in the north fighting continued. By the late 1980s under an amnesty offered to the rebels, almost 30,000 of them had surrendered.

Museveni

Uganda

Museveni, however, has not been without his critics. An Amnesty International report published in late 1991 accused the NRA of torturing and summarily executing prisoners during the operations against the rebels in the north. The criticism most commonly aimed at Museveni, particularly by the Western donors, is his apparent avoidance of democratic elections. When he first came to power political parties were suspended and it was announced that there would be no elections for three years. In October 1989 the NRM extended the government's term of office to a further five years from January 1990, when their mandate was due to run out. Museveni argued that the time was not ready for political parties and that a new constitution had to be drawn up before elections could take place. In March 1990 the ban on political party activities was extended for five years. A new constitution was adopted in 1995, and Museveni was elected president in 1996.

Museveni has allowed the Kabaka (King) of Buganda to return to the country and to be crowned in a highly publicized ceremony in 1993 (see box, page 565). This was obviously immensely popular with the Baganda, although the government insists that his role will be purely cultural and ceremonial without any political function. Whether the Baganda will settle for this remains to be seen.

The Asian community have been encouraged to return, and the property they relinquished on their departure has been restored. The Asians have been cautious, but they are once again filling positions in retailing, distribution and provision of skilled services.

People

The largest group in Uganda are the Baganda, with 16 percent of the total. Other main groups are the Soga with eight percent; the Nkole with eight percent; the Teso with eight percent; the Kiga with seven percent; the Lango with six percent; the Gisu with five percent; the Acholi with four percent and the Alur with four percent. The Ik are a small group of remote mountain people who inhabit a chain of volcanic mountains in the northeast of the country between the Timu forest bordering Kenya and Kidepo Valley National Park. In all, there are 14 groups with more than one percent of the population. Prior to their expulsion in 1972 the Asians comprised about two percent of the total.

Modern Uganda

Politics   Although Museveni has remained in power since 1986, and brought political stability and economic recovery to the country, Uganda's appalling record makes him wary of a return to a multiparty political system. No new political structures appear to have emerged, and the parties waiting in the wings are based on the old groupings that fought the initial pre-independence election. Given that they failed on two occasions before, Museveni has little confidence that they would succeed now. In addition there is the restoration of the Kabaka and the possible re-emergence of pressure for the separation of Buganda. If boxed into a corner by the international community (and Uganda is the only country in the region not committed to a multiparty system) it is thought Museveni will launch his own party incorporating key figures from other political groupings.

Museveni has continued to argue that multi-party democracy is not suited to Uganda which needs instead what he calls "no party democracy" or a "movement" system with representatives of the main factions involved in government.

A significant event in 1994 was the setting up of the Constituent Assembly. As a result, the country's political system changed significantly to try to ensure greater representation of the people in political affairs and to decentralize certain elements of power. Each district has more decision-making ability on how to spend income raised locally through taxation. This will be good for areas where a cash economy is well established and taxation is possible, but far harder in subsistence areas where revenue is likely to be low.

A cabinet reshuffle in November 1994, including the appointment of a woman, Dr Specioza Wandira Kazibwe to the vice-presidency, has ensured he is surrounded by anti-multi-party and pro-NRM decentralization people. Most political commentators agree that the reshuffle was an astute move as it removed some political confrontational elements and increased public confidence.

In 1995 the Constituent Assembly endorsed a further five years of the current 'movement' system. The question of a change to a multiparty system is to be settled by a referendum in 2000. Political parties will be allowed to campaign in the run-up to the referendum.

In May 1996, Presidential elections took place, the two main candidates being Museveni and Paul Ssemogerere. Ssemogerere is an experienced politician who ran with DP and UPC support (although the elections were formally non-party), and who served as a Deputy Prime Minister in Museveni's government before resigning in 1995.

In a reasonable high turn-out (73 percent), Museveni received 76 percent and Ssemogerere 22 percent. The election was favourably viewed by observers, and only minor irregularities were reported. The result of the Presidential election would appear to settle the multi-party issue for the present.

In 1998 a Land Act was passed which proposes to transfer ownership to tenants of 12 years standing. This is expected to have a major impact in Buganda areas, proving popular with tenants, but raising opposition from the Buganda land-owning elite.

Meanwhile the Lord's Resistance Army (LRA) appears to have gained in strength in the north. Previously it operated from Sudan, but now it is thought to have bases in Uganda. In 1996, convoys have been attacked while Gulu and surrounding areas have been harassed.

Two other rebel groups operate in the northwest, the West Nile Bank Front (WNBF) and the Uganda National Rescue Front (UNRF), but a history of antagonism based on ethnic allegiance has prevented them forming a common cause with the LRA.

The international community would like to see a negotiated settlement, and given the small size of the LRA, thought to be less than a thousand, such a settlement should not prove costly to the government. Over 20 percent of government expenditure is thought to go on the war in the north.

Uganda has given support to the rebel SPLA in Sudan, which is pressing for secession from the Islamic government in the north. This is a retaliation for Sudan allowing the LRA to operate from bases inside its borders, while also encouraging the SPLA to regard the LRA as its enemies. This strategy gambles on the SPLA having success either militarily or in a political settlement, and both of the outcomes seem some way off at present.

Museveni appears to have relaxed his opposition to negotiations with the LRA, and there are rumours of talks with Sudan.

It had been hoped that the success of Laurent Kabila in overthrowing Zaire's Mobutu would prevent rebels using RD Congo (formerly Zaire) as a refuge. In the event, eastern RD Congo has been dogged by pockets of rebel activity, lacking any political focus, but which are difficult to flush out of the mountainous terrain which they occupy.

This has escalated into a serious conflict with around 15,000 Ugandan troops and 5,000 from Rwanda supporting rebel groups campaigning to overthrow Kabila. Forces from Zimbabwe, Namibia, Angola and Mozambique are backing Kabila. Any resolution of the confrontation appears deadlocked, both militarily and politically. The situation has improved with a ceasefire agreement between Kabila and Museveni.

There is now also rebel activity in the southwest of the country, around Kasese. A series of bomb attacks on buses and two serious assaults on Kasese have displaced some 70,000 people. It is thought that the groups forming the Allied Democratic Forces (ADF) are opportunistic rather than idealistic, and number only around 500 activists. Material support is said to come from Libya, Iran and the United Arab Emirates, and that the ADF has a strong Islamic element.

Although the rebel activity has no prospect of overthrowing the Museveni government, it has closed two parks, put areas off limits for tourists, proved expensive for the government and made life a misery for local people in the affected areas.

In March 1999, eight tourists and four rangers were killed by Rwandan Hutu rebels in the Bwindi Impenetrable Forest National Park. This episode set gorilla-tracking tourism back, and Museveni has responded by promising improved security.

Economics

Economic strategy has fluctuated with Obote initially pledged to pursue a socialist development path, followed by the chaos of the Amin years which included the expulsion of the skilled Asian community. The restored Obote régime relied on market forces, but lack of security prevented any substantial progress. Museveni spent a while considering development options, but is now committed the government to an IMF-supported market-oriented strategy.

Economic structure

The population in 1999 was estimated at 21.6 million. The uplands in the east and west form the most densely populated areas, whereas the west has low population densities. The average population density is 92 persons per square kilometre, and this is well above the Africa average. Urban population, at 12 percent of the total is low. Turmoil in recent years has led many to flee the towns to survive by subsistence production in the countryside. As urban employment opportunities have expanded only slowly, most people have been reluctant to return. The population growth rate at 3.2 percent a year is high despite the impact of AIDS.

GDP in 1999 was US$7.2bn, and in terms of economic size it is a medium sized economy among the East African group. Income estimated by the exchange rate conversion method was US$333 per head, placing Uganda firmly in the low-income category. Estimated by purchasing power of the currency it is rather higher, at US$1,613 per head, but again this indicates low-income status.

Agriculture is the largest sector, providing over half of GDP, and it is even more important in that it provides the livelihood of around 86 percent of the population. Industry is small, generating 12 percent of GDP, but incomes are high in this sector, as it comprises only four percent of total employment. Similarly with services which contribute 35 percent of GDP, but make up only 10 percent of employment.

Most expenditure, as to be expected in a low income economy, is in private consumption. Investment is slightly higher than the African average and is supported by donor contributions to rehabilitation of infastructure. Government spending is low, and reflects limited ability to raise revenue and to administer and monitor spending.

Uganda

Exports make a very small contribution at 12 percent of GDP, although this probably underestimates export activity as the main crop, coffee, is easy to smuggle out through neighbouring states, where prices are often higher. Exports are 61 percent coffee, with gold eight percent, fish six percent and maize three percent. Import dependence is 21 percent of GDP, and this level can only be sustained, in view of modest earnings from exports, by aid from the donor community. Imports are mostly machinery and transport equipment (46 percent) manufactures (38 percent) and fuel (six percent).

Economic performance

Given the state of the economy following the Amin period and its aftermath, Uganda has made an excellent recovery. GDP growth has averaged around six percent a year 1995-9 and living standards have risen by three percent a year.

It is the resurgence of the industrial and services sectors, boosted by the return of the Asian community, that has spear-headed the performance. Agriculture has kept pace with population growth at 3.8 percent a year, but industry has expanded at 11 percent a year, while services have grown at 8.2 percent.

Export growth has been good with volumes growing at four percent a year.

In recent years, the inflation has come under control, and in 1997-9 it has averaged about four percent a year.

Aid is clearly very important and it comprises almost a fifth of total income. Without this support, the level of imports could not be sustained, and essential agricultural inputs of machinery and fuel would fall and economic progress would be impossible to maintain. Debt service is under control and accounts for 20 percent of export earnings.

Recent economic developments

In May of 1987 President Museveni appeared to end the period of indecision over Uganda's economic strategy when agreement was reached on a programme with the IMF on a return to a market-based economic strategy. The Kampala Stock Exchange opened for business in January 1988.

A privatization programme is under way, with 78 enterprises sold out of a total of 148. Progress has been slow as it has proved difficult to value assets and confirm trading records to present to potential buyers.

Recently the Uganda Commercial Bank has been sold to a Malaysian bank, Uganda Spinning Mills to a Belgian company and Kasese Cobalt to a Canadian, Australian and French consortium.

Uganda Airways has been absorbed into Alliance Airways, run from South Africa and including Air Tanzania, with twice-weekly flights to London. Cotton and coffee trading have been liberalized and private traders are now operating. Other developments include a US$250m industrial park 15 kilometres east of Kampala, financed from Egypt, and plans for three new breweries.

As inflation has been brought under control so the exchange rate has stabilized and there is currently an annual depreciation of around nine percent.

Tourism is recovering, with 160,000 visitors in 1997, almost 50 percent more than anticipated but this has been set back by the killing of tourists in the Bwindi gorilla park in March 1999.

With improving security, and the resolution of Uganda's economic strategy, there has been further increases in aid commitments and substantial promises of new funds, mostly in infrastructure, health and education.

Economic outlook

Future prospects depend on maintaining political stability and internal security. The problems in the north, the southwest and the hostile groups operating from R D Congo have dented Uganda's image. If these problems can be brought under control, the greater confidence will be and international business will be encouraged to expand investment. As things stand, Uganda can expect to enjoy rising living standards, and this modest pace of improvement will accelerate if tourism and mining can be restored to the levels of the 1960s.

King's College, Budo

Elementary education became widely established in England in the 1870s, and by the 1890s, similar provision was being made throughout Buganda. For a select few it was considered desirable to provide some secondary education where the discipline of work and games in a boarding school would prepare pupils to take their place in administrative and industrial life.

King's College was built in 1907 on the Coronation Hill of the Buganda Monarchy (see Box, page 565), to serve all the communities in Uganda. There were four houses, England, South Africa, Australia and Turkey. Members of Turkey House asked that it be changed to Canada House as being more fitting with the notion of Empire. The school motto is Cecil Rhodes' dying words 'So little done – so much to do'.

The routine was strict in regular boarding school tradition, with an emphasis on English and mathematics, a Christian daily assembly and daily games from 1600-1800, mainly soccer, cricket and athletics. The first African to play international cricket, Prince George Muwanda, learned the game at Budo (see Box, page 98). Budo is famous for having established a splendid school spirit. At the Gold Jubilee in 1957 there were four Ugandan kings, all old boys, present at the ceremonies.

Uganda

Social conditions

Adult literacy is about 38 percent, below the African average. In former times literacy rates were better, but have been adversely affected by the disruption of the Amin years and the aftermath. Primary and secondary enrolments have slipped in recent years. The priority is basic education, however, and numbers attending primary school are better than in Africa generally. Tertiary education enrolment is low. In common with much of Africa, the main responsibility for further education is being directed away from government provision and financing, and several new, private universities have been commissioned.

Life expectancy is low at 42 years, and is the result of poor medical facilities, particularly in the rural areas. Infant mortality rates are among the highest in the world and are more than ten times the rates in the high income western countries. About a quarter of children under five are malnourished.

Access of females to primary education in comparison to that of males is inferior by about 14 percent. The disparity is much greater in secondary education, with only 60 percent as many females as males enrolled. There is a high participation of women in work outside the home, caused by the heavy reliance on subsistence production and demands on women to contribute to household farm production. The burden on women is increased by high fertility rates and low access to contraception.

Environment

Economic collapse invariably has an adverse effect on afforestation in low-income countries. There is increased demand for land and woodfuel for cooking, and in Uganda the forested area has been diminishing by about one percent a year.

Fresh water supplies are plentiful with adequate rainfall, resulting from the high altitude and location by Lake Victoria. Low industrial output means annual water usage per head is low, and only 0.3 percent of renewable freshwater supplies are used.

Ethiopia

6

Ethiopia is a large country both in terms of population and geographical area. It experienced no protracted period of colonial rule, although the country was occupied by the Italians for six years from 1935. It has recently emerged from a disastrous period under a military régime, 1974-91, which followed the fall of Haile Selassie. Visits to many parts of the country were not possible and permits, issued by an infuriatingly obstructive and inefficient bureaucracy, were required for travel outside the capital. Happily this is now all in the past, but the legacy is that tourist facilities have been neglected. Travellers seeing the countryside (virtually unvisited for two decades), people, culture, wildlife and historical sites for the first time are astonished by the richness and diversity. Prices have risen– do not be surprised if some of the rates quoted have been revised upwards quite sharply. Heavy rains in 1997/98 associated with the 'El Niño' phenomenon have disrupted transport and communication links and repairs are still being made.

In May 1998 relations with Eritrea deteriorated seriously as a result of a border dispute. There have been bombing raids, the borders between the two countries are closed and it is uncertain as to when they will reopen. Tourists are advised against visiting areas near the border with Eritrea until this dispute is resolved.

Exchange Rate (September 1999) Birr 8 = US$1

Ethiopia

Essentials

Planning your trip

Where to go Ethiopia has a unique atmosphere. The people have a distinctive appearance, partly like their neighbours in the Middle East and partly like the rest of Africa. However they are a strongly Christian people, and the influence of the church is considerable. Ethiopia has its own written language, Amharic, and traditions in literature, dress, dance and music that have flourished in the relative isolation provided by their mountainous territory.

Major attractions are the ancient cities of Gondar, Axum, and Harar, and these have all retained the atmosphere of their historical backgrounds. There are some extraordinary churches hewn from rock in Lalibela. This circuit is becoming popular with visitors and there are daily flights between the cities.

Colourful spectacles are provided by Ethiopia's festivals, some going on for several days (see box, page 680).

Ethiopia has some fine wildlife, and all the major animals except for rhinoceros are present in the selection of relatively small but delightful parks scattered across the country. The birds are a particular attraction.

The capital city, Addis Ababa, is friendly, and attractively located on a hilly site. It has a strong diplomatic community and the UN Economic Commission for Africa, and the Organization of African Unity have their headquarters there.

Ethiopia is bounded to the west by Sudan, to the south by Kenya and to the east and southeast by Somalia and Djibouti. Eritrea, which gained formal independence from Ethiopia in May 1993 lies to the north, and Ethiopia is now land-locked. The country is divided into 12 self-governing regions and two chartered cities – Addis Ababa and Harar.

The names of places and people are spelt in a variety of ways reflecting periods of French, Italian and British influence in translating the Amaharic characters into a European equivalent. The phonetic sound of a word is sometimes the clearest guide.

When to go It is best to avoid the rainy season from June to September. The hot and dry months are April and May. However, if you do travel in the rainy season the countryside is very green, and the temperature is lower.

Before you travel

Getting in **Visas** Visas are required by all visitors (with the exception of Kenyan nationals and citizens of Djibouti), and should be obtained before departure through an Ethiopian Embassy, see page 671. Tourist visas are usually valid for 30 days. Normal cost US$68, US$70 for a business visa, you may need to present a yellow fever certificate plus one photograph. It is possible to get a visa extended at the Immigration Office, opposite Post Office on Churchill Ave in Addis Ababa. An extension costs US$18 for one month. The extension should be requested within two days of expiry of original visa, but this does not appear to be rigidly enforced. **NB** If you are planning to visit Eritrea or Djibouti, you will require a multiple-entry visa (only available for Business Visas).

A **transit** visa for 72 hours can be granted on arrival. Transit visas will only be issued if the person holds confirmed onward booking and an entry visa for the destination country. Can be extended for up to seven days. You will be required to surrender your passport, and it costs around US$50.

Business visas for one month can usually be obtained by an Ethiopian contact.

Journalists must obtain a permit from the Ministry of Information, PO Box 1020 Addis Ababa, T111124, and this can take up to three months to be granted.

Ethiopian embassies and consultates

Austria, Freidrich Schmidt Platz 3/3, 1080 Vienna, Austria, T4028410, F4029413.
Belgium, B-1040 Brussels, T7333929/4869/9818, F7321816.
Canada, Suite 208, 112 Kent St, Ottawa.
China, No 3 Xiu Shui Nan Jie, Jian Gue Nen Wai, Beijing.
Cote d'Ivoire, Immeuble Nour Al Hayat, 4 eme Etage, PB 3712 Abidjian 01.
Egypt, 3 Ibrim Osman St Mohandessin Cairo, T3477805, F3477902.
France, 35 Ave Charles Floquet, 75007 Paris, T47838395, Tx43065214.
Germany, Brentanostrasse 1, D-5300, Bonn 1, T233041/42/43, F233045.
India, 7/50 G Satya Marg, Chanakyapuri, New Delhi 11021.
Iran, 772 North Pasdaran Ave 19547, PO Box 19575/544 Sahebgharanie, Tehran, T283217/282312, F289441, Tx226621.
Israel, 69 Bograshov St Tel Aviv 63429, T5250383, F5250428.
Italy, Via Andrea Vesalio, 16-18, 00161 Rome,

T4402602/4403653, F4403676, Tx614414.
Japan, 1-14-15 Midorigaoka, Meguro-ku, Tokyo 152, T7181003/5, F7180978, TxJ28402.
Korea (North), PO Box 55, Pyongyang.
Nigeria, PO Box 2488 Marina, Lagos, T613198, F615055.
Saudi Arabia, PO Box 459, Jeddah 21411, T5250383, F5250428.
Sweden, Ostemalmsgatan 34, PO Box 26116, 10041 Stockholm.
Switzerland, 56 Rue de Moillebeau, PO Box 204, 1211 Geneva 19.
Uganda, nr Uganda Museum on Kira Rd, T241325, visas for Ethiopia cost US$63 and are issued in 24 hours.
UK, 17 Princes Gate, London, SW7 1PZ, T0171-5897212.
United States, 2134 Kalorama Rd Northwest, Washington DC 20008, T2342281, F3287950.
Zimbabwe, PO Box 2745 Harare, T725823/720259.
Overseas representation in Ethiopia See under Addis Ababa, see page 691.

Customs Under the Mengistu régime, there were comprehensive restrictions. These are now in the process of being relaxed, and some of the limitations listed below may no longer apply. *Ethiopian Customs Office*, PO Box 4838 Addis Ababa, T153100.

Duty free allowance of 200 cigarettes, 50 cigars, 250 gms tobacco, 0.5 litres of spirits or two bottles of perfume, equipment for personal use. All duty-free goods must be declared. Souvenirs for export are limited to a value of around US$250 per person. Any specialized film, recording or video equipment requires a special permit from Ministry for Informantion and National Guidance (PO Box 1020 Addis Ababa, T121011).

Export of any antiquities requires a permit from the Antiquities Department of the National Museum (PO Box 76 Addis Ababa, T117150) for which there is a small charge of US$0.20 (see page 744). Sporting firearms require a permit from Wildlife Conservation Department (PO Box 386 Addis Ababa, T444417). Export of any wildlife items requires a permit from Wildlife Conservation Department (PO Box 386 Addis Ababa, T444417).

Export and import of books, cassettes and records may require a permit from the Censorship Department (PO Box 1364 Addis Ababa, T115704).

Vaccinations A yellow fever innoculation certificate is compulsory. Vaccination against cholera is only required if the visitor is coming from an affected area, but it is wise to have the vaccination in any case.

Money **Currency** The currency is the Birr. 100 cents = 1 Birr. Denominations: 1, 5, 10, 25, and 50 cent coins; 1, 5, 10, 50 and 100 Birr notes. New bills are in circulation since December 1997 – the old notes are now invalid. Bear this in mind if changing money on the black market, where rates are only three percent better.

The value of the currency was held fixed at Birr 2.07 = US$1 from 1973 to October 1992, and in this period there was a black market in foreign exchange. The devaluation in 1992 set the exchange rate at Birr 5 = US$1. The exchange rate is now set by foreign currency auctions. There is a black market, offering around three to five percent more than the official rate.

Ethiopia

The Commercial Bank of Ethiopia (state-owned – all banks were nationalized in 1975) offers foreign exchange facilites, and is represented in all the major towns. The Commercial Bank of Ethiopia will exchange US$, Canadian $, Australian $, Swiss franc, French franc, Deutch mark, Italian lira and sterling in every big town, but the service is slow. In Addis hours are 0800 to 1400 Monday to Friday, and 0900 to 1200 on Saturday. Out of Addis the banks tend to have a prolonged lunch break.

The larger hotels and the government-owned hotels operate *Bureau d'Exchange*, and some, such as the Hilton in Addis Ababa offer a 24-hour service.

It is possible to save money on internal air fares by paying in Birr – you will need to lodge an official currency exchange receipt from a bank with the airline. However, you may be required to pay for your internal flights in US$ cash.

A currency declaration form has to be completed on arrival and surrendered on departure. In principle you can change Birr back into US$ on departure provided that you can show from your currency exchange receipts that you have spent US$30 a day. The Ethiopian authorities tend to be much stricter with the currency declaration form than other African countries. Keep bank receipts as they are often tallied. A student discount is given in many places on production of a valid student card. Validation of the student card is required – see page 690.

It can be a major problem obtaining cash in Ethiopia. Hotels offer only limited supplies and are often reluctant to provide the important exchange stamp on your form. Take sufficient supplies of US dollars rather than relying on travellers' cheques.

Credit cards The large hotels and the main airlines (including *Ethiopian Airlines*) will accept cards. Outside Addis Ababa cards are not accepted.

Tourist information *Ethiopian Tourism Commission*, Ras Mekonin Ave, PO Box 2183, Addis Ababa, T447470, provides information for tourists, and promotes tourism overseas. *Ethiopian Airways* offices are situated in 54 cities around the world. Invariably they have a staff member who takes responsibility for providing tourist information, and is a reliable source for information on any recent changes in visa regulations, health requirements etc.

Travel and tour agents *National Tour Operation* is the state-owned tourist organization. Main office near *Ghion Hotel* on Ras Mekonin Ave, PO Box 5709, T512955, F517688. Branch in *Hilton Hotel*. Five regional offices, including one in Dire Dawa. It organizes a sightseeing around Addis Ababa; excursions from Addis Ababa; vistis to Omo, Gambela, Bahar Dar, Gondar, Lalibela, Harar; hiking tours; hunting safaris; fishing; birdwatching. There are many new private travel and tour firms, that have set up since 1991, see page 692.

Getting there

Air The national carrier is *Ethiopian Airlines*. It is one of the most efficient airlines in Africa. It has offices in 54 cities around the world. In Addis Ababa, it has three offices in City centre. Near National Theatre on Churchill Ave, T447000. *Addis Ababa Hilton*, T158400. Tx21104. Menelik Ave. In Piazza at southern end of Eden St.

In the Horn of Africa region, Ethiopian Airways flies twice a week to **Djibouti** from Addis Ababa (Tuesday and Thursday) and the fare is US$306 return. There are no flights currently to Somalia or Eritrea.

NB That flights to Djibouti and Asmara can be included in special round-trip tickets taking in destinations in Ethiopia other than Addis Ababa.

Ethiopian Airlines international flights: *Europe*: Athens, Berlin, Frankfurt, London, Moscow, and Rome. *Asia*: Beijing and Bombay. *Middle East*: Abu Dhabi, Aden, Dubai, Jeddah, Sanaa. *Africa*: Abidjian, Asmara, Cairo, Djibouti, Harare, Kinshasa, Johannesburg, Lagos and Nairobi. Return flights Nairobi/Addis cost US$300.

Ethiopian Airlines offers half day accommodation, lunch, free airport transfer when connecting flights are inconvenient.

Other carriers The following airlines have flights to and from their capitals and Addis Ababa. *Aeroflot*, PO Box 7018, Addis Ababa. T1573. *Alitalia*, PO Box 3240, Addis Ababa. T154640. *Alyemda*, PO Box 40461, Addis Ababa. T441049. *Kenya Airways*, PO Box 3381, Addis Ababa. T443018. *Lufthansa*, PO Box 2484, Addis Ababa. T155961. *Yemenia*, PO Box 107, Addis Ababa. T445076. The following airlines have offices in Addis Ababa. *Air France*, T159044. *Air Tanzania Corporation*, T157533. Air Egypt also flies from Europe via Cairo to Addis Ababa and Asmara.

Airport on Bole Rd accessed by minibus from Piazza (destination Bole) and cost US$0.50. On arrival it is necessary to walk for one kilometre toward the city to catch a minibus. Taxi to and from airport is about US$8. Airport tax on departure US$20.

Specialist agencies Special excursion fares for fixed dates of departure and return (around US$900 return London/Addis Ababa in high season in July, August and December; otherwise low season US$730) can be arranged through: *World Express*, 29 Great Pulteney St, Room 202, London W1R 3DD, T0171-4372955/0171-4341897, F0171-7342550. *Willesden Travel Service* (WTS), 5 Walm Lane London NW2 5SJ, T0181-4517778, F0181-4514727. *Ericommerce*, Robin House, 2A Iverson Rd, London NW6 2HE, T0171-3727242, F0171-6246716. See also general section, page 28.

A 782 kilometre railway connects Addis with Djibouti on the Red Sea. It is primarily a freight **Train** service, but passengers are taken. Unfortunately, recently there have been incidents when passengers have been held up by bandits on this journey. Check the situation locally before booking. The stretch of line running through the Awash National Park affords stunning views, making what can be an uncomfortable trip more than worthwhile.

The trains from Addis Ababa leave daily at around 0700 and 1930, arriving in Djibouti approximately 24 hours later. Booking is at the railway station at the southern end of Churchill Rd. It is necessary to make a reservation as the train is often full. The fare is US$60 first class (a sleeper on the overnight train); US$30 second class; US$16 third class. Djibouti-Ethiopian Railroad Company, Addis Ababa, T447250.

In principle it should now be possible for non-Africans to enter Ethiopia overland. However, it **Road** is a lengthy journey, taking up to six days. Vehicles must travel in convoys, and this may incur a further delay. It is very difficult to make the journey during the rainy season. The main routes are from Kenya, crossing at Moyale (three days hiring a lift from a truck to Moyale, two days Moyale to Addis Ababa); from Malakal in Sudan to Gambela; from Eritrea on the routes from Asmara to Adwa, and Assab to Debaysima; from Djibouti to Galafi; and from Hargeisa in Somalia to Jijiga.

The routes from Sudan and Somalia are not really feasible as a result of restrictions and turmoil in these two countries. The route from Kenya is becoming easier and Djibouti (two days by bus). The political tension in 1998 between Ethiopia and Eritrea led to the closure of the border. A peace plan has been agreed and the situation is expected to improve.

Since Eritrea became Independent in 1993, Ethiopia has become land locked. Access by sea is **Sea** through Massawa and Assab in Eritrea, or through the port at Djibouti.

In the period when the rains make the river Baro navigable (June-September) it should be **River** possible to enter by boat from Khartoum to Gambela. The current political situation in the south of Sudan makes this impossible.

Ethiopia

Touching down

Business contacts *Addis Ababa Chamber of Commerce*, PO Box 2458 Addis Ababa, T448240. **Ministry of Foreign Trade**, PO Box 2559 Addis Ababa, T151066.

Electricity *220 volts, 50 cycles AC. A variety of sockets are to be found around the country, and an adaptor is desirable.*

Hours of business *0800-1200 and 1300-1600.*

IDD *251. Equal tones with long pauses* means it is ringing; equal tones with equal pauses means engaged.

Official time *Three hours later than GMT. Local people use a 12 hour clock, which starts at 0600. Thus 0800 is 'hour two of the day'. At 1800 the night clock begins. Thus 0400 is 'hour ten of the night'.*

Weights and measures *Metric weights and measures are in use in the main towns and cities. In country areas, customs vary.*

Touching down

Airport information The main airport is Bole International Airport, some five kilometres southeast of the city. There is a departure tax of US$20 only payable in US$. When entering Ethiopia you have to declare your foreign currency on a blue form. Any amount of money exchanged at a bank is registered on this form. When you leave Ethiopia it must be handed in. However, they do not appear to be checked and travellers occasionally 'lose' them without apparent dire consequences.

Transport to town A taxi from Bole Airport to town is around US$8. A minibus is around US$1. Ethiopian Airlines operate a free shuttle bus to town.

Bureaucracy There are several occasions (for example when arriving at the airport, and when cashing travellers' cheques) when you will be asked for a telephone number. It will facilitate things if you have a hotel number you can give.

Rules, customs & etiquette **Conduct** It is customary for men to wear suits for business occasions, particulary when visiting government offices. Women would normally be expected to dress neatly on such occasions – it is regarded as a mark of respect for the persons you are meeting as much as anything else.

Visitors are invariably offered a cup of tea or coffee, and it is a friendly gesture to accept.

When entering a church or mosque, it is necessary for shoes to be removed. Women are not normally allowed to enter mosques unless there is a special prayer room for women.

When photographing local people, religious ceremonies or festivals, it is courteous to ask permission first.

Safety Ethiopia is a safe country, and it is possible to walk around with confidence although it is sensible to take taxis after dark. An exeption can be Addis Ababa, especially at night in the Mercato area. It is wise to keep a close eye on belongings – there are pickpockets and sneak thieves in operation.

Recently there have been incidents in Eastern Ethiopia and on the train to Djibouti where foreign travellers have been attacked and robbed with some fatalities. The British Embassy in Addis has advised against travel to Eastern Ethiopia. Caution is urged before using the train which has been targetted by bandits (1997). Recent travellers have reported that bars have been fitted to the train windows, improving security. Check before you depart (see Embassies, page 691).

Although there are no restrictions on photographing tourist sites, military installations, airports, bridges, civil engineering works, government buildings, military personnel and political gatherings should not be photographed. These rules have been more rigidly applied since the outbreak of hostilities between Ethiopia and Eritrea.

Photographs of museums, art works, churches and mosques will often require permission.

Accommodation sting

A couple travelling to Addis Ababa City centre from the Airport will invariably be asked by the driver if they are married. If they are not, the driver warns that they won't be able to stay in the same room in one of the large state-owned Hotels – it is against the law. Even a married couple will need to show some documentary evidence, and this can be a problem – many passports do not show marital status. This puritanical attitude comes as something of a surprise seeing that Ethiopia takes pride in tracing its origins to an episode of casual adultery and group sex (see box, page 739).

However, the driver explains that he can fix things. The couple just need to stay in a private guest-house where the restrictions do not apply. A farrago of a search then ensues with the driver clocking up unnecessary distance as unsavoury shacks round the outskirts are successively rejected. Sometimes the driver will persuade the couple to pay in advance for an unseen room which is turned down, but alas the money cannot be returned.

The final outcome is that the driver demands an exorbitant fare and the couple are stuck in an overpriced, miserable dive, miles from anywhere. See page 686 for comfortable, central, civilized

Beggars The beggars are a big nuisance almost everywhere in Ethiopia. In almost all the towns including Addis Ababa small children crowd around shouting "You, you", "Give" and "Money". However tolerant you are to start with, it eventually becomes a source of irritation. See page 29 for a constructive alternative to encouraging this practice.

Where to stay

Until the demise of Mengistu, tourists were officially only allowed to stay in the large hotels owned by the state and run by **Ethiopian Hotels and Spas Corporation (EHC)**. These hotels were grouped into 5 regional chains, each with a flagship hotel in Addis Ababa. The **Ghion Hotels** cover the north and the historic towns of Godor and Axum. The **Ras Hotels** are in the east and include Dire Dawa and Harar. **Ethiopia Hotels** cover the west and in the south are the **Wabi Shabelle Hotels**. The **Filwoha Hotels** specialize in resorts and spas, with no regional concentration. It is difficult to recommend any hotel which charges fewer than 20 Birr a night. Generally speaking these hotels will be dirty, many of them squalid. The sheets on the bed may be clean, but the blankets will not, and you may well share your bed with bedbugs (if you are suspicious, give yourself a dusting over with insecticide powder before you retire). The communal washing and toilet facilities are probably unspeakable, and water and electricity absent. There is really nothing to be gained by staying in this kind of place when the sums of money involved are, by western standards, so small. There are very few exceptions to this rule and they will be mentioned where appropriate. If it is at all possible go for a room with its own bathroom and toilet, as these are a lot cleaner. In this context you will find a pair of flip flops are invaluable, as there will be bathroom floors you would rather not have to tread on, and the flip flops supplied look very doubtful.

There has been pressure to privatize these hotel chains, and in principle the government is in agreement with this policy, but as yet there has been little actual implementation. The **Hilton Hotel** in Addis Ababa is the one major hotel that has remained independent. The recently opened **Sheraton Addis**, is also independent.

Plenty of middle range (B & C), privately-owned hotels have opened in the last few years, and they represent the best value at present.

There are smaller establishments all over the country which serve the needs of ordinary Ethiopians. They are very simple, but cheap, and the proprietors are invariably very welcoming to visitors. These vary in price and standard, but they all charge 'farangi' prices. This is the annoying practice of charging foreigners twice or more the rate paid by Ethiopians. This is, apparently, quite legal, and, although the sums of money involved are small, it is the principle that is irritating, and it is a particular source of annoyance if you are travelling with Ethiopians. Some private hotels also try this ploy – you should offer to pay the local price, and

Hotels
See inside front cover for details of price codes

Ethiopia

threaten to go elsewhere if you are charged more. Two men or women sharing a room are invariably charged more than a couple. See Sleeping classification, page 31.

Getting around

Air The national carrier is *Ethiopian Airlines*. In Addis Ababa, it has three offices in City centre: near National Theatre on Churchill Ave, T01-517000, F01-611474; Addis Ababa Hilton, T158400, Tx21104. Menelik Ave; in Piazza at southern end of Eden St.

There are daily flights to Bahar Dar, Gondar, Axum, Lalibela and Dire Dawa. Special round-trips arranged – there is no cost saving, but the flights are always busy and booking the tour will avoid delays. Thus the Historic Route (Bahar Dar, Gondar, Axum and Lalibela) is US$167, and these cities as well as Dire Dawa (for Harar) is US$267. Asmara and Djibouti can be included in these round trips. A word of warning: sometimes internal flights are cancelled without warning. The fleet is probably too small to replace aircraft taken out of circulation for maintenance. Frequently internal flights do not offer refreshments. When delays occur due to cancellations, the situation is made worse by how difficult it is to ascertain when alternate flights will be laid on by Ethiopian Airlines. This leads to great frustration for travellers. Allow extra time for almost inevitable delays when planning your trip.

When travelling north use the EA office at Gondar to book/confirm onward flights – it has computers. There's nothing computerized in either Axum or Lalibela.

Flights to many of the northern towns have been suspended because of the border conflict.

Train There is one train daily in each direction along the line from Addis Ababa to Djibouti, see page 690.

Road There are asphalt roads in Ethiopia, mostly linking Addis with the regional capitals. However, the instability of the Mengistu period has led to some of these asphalt roads being in poor repair, and in the rainy season (June-September) there will be delays. Elsewhere, roads are mostly unsealed. Bus and minibus transport is available on all main routes. As a rough guide, road transport costs around US$0.05 per kilometre.

Outside Addis Ababa, bus conductors may try to overcharge for your luggage if it has to go on the roof. It should not be more than 25 percent of the fare, but check with other travellers. Recent travellers have indicated that the charge is US$0.75 a piece (that is a backpack).

Ethiopia air routes

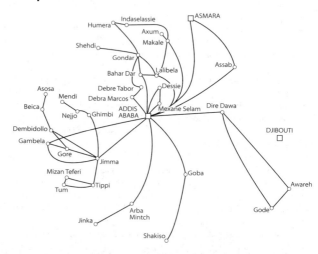

Amharic Qwerty

An alphabet of 236 characters presented a challenge in adapting the typewriter to Amharic. The problem was solved by allocating two characters to each key, and a further six keys for the vowel suffixes.

Many of these original machines can still be seen in use in offices throughout Ethiopia. The first Amaharic typewiter is on display in the National Museum in Addis Ababa.

Long distance buses in Ethiopia have the drawback that they rarely display a timetable. The bus stations usually open at 0600, by which time many people will have gathered by the gate. The government buses tend in general to be in better condition than the private buses. Aim to catch the early bus. There may be later buses but it's impossible to estimate their departure time. Sometimes tickets are sold in advance. Other times you may pay at the bus station or on the bus. Again it is difficult to predict and information is very hard to collate. Having obtained your ticket, you join the scramble for seats – the front seats are more comfortable as the roads are bad. You have to put your luggage on the roof, where it gets covered by canvas. The bus leaves when it's full up. The whole loading whole procedure can take up to one and a half hours. Richer people hire someone to buy a ticket and reserve a seat, switching a few minutes before departure. Bus journeys are a good way to meet interesting Ethiopians.

You do not require a carnet if driving into Ethiopia. A temporary import licence costs US$7.

Car hire Car hire can be arranged through the **National Tour Operation**. Main office near *Ghion Hotel* on Ras Mekonin Ave (PO Box 5709, T152955). Branch in *Hilton Hotel*. 5 regional offices, including one in Dire Dawa.

Keeping in touch

Language The official language is *Amharic*. It has its own unique alphabet, and a wide and extensive vocabulary. There are about 200 other local languages and dialects.

English is widely spoken, and is the language of instruction in secondary schools and at the University. French, Italian and Arabic are also spoken.

Postal services Post offices open 0800-1600. Mail is delivered only to PO box numbers. **Poste restante** available at all post offices, no charge.

Telephone services Telecommunications everywhere are very good, even from small towns. A deposit of around US$25 is usually required.

Media **Cinemas** Most large towns will have cinemas, often open-air.

Newspapers *Ethiopian Herald* is published three times a week in English, is government-owned, and covers only domestic issues. The *Monitor* is also published three times a week in English, but carries some international news. *Addis Tribune* is a weekly in English, with a section *Tribune d'Addis* in French. There is also an English language quarterly, *Yekatit. Yezareyitu* is a weekly paper in Amharic, *Al Ahem* is a weekly Arabic newspaper, and *Berissa* is a weekly Oromo paper.

Radio Radio Ethiopia has a National Service and an International (External) Service. There are broadcasts in six Ethiopian languages each day. Broadcasts are in Arabic 1700-1800, English 1800-1900 and French 2000-2100.

BBC World Service can be received in Ethiopia if you have a radio with short waveband reception. See guide, page 33.

Ethiopia

Languages of Ethiopia

Amharic *is widely spoken*. Oromifaa *is the language of the Oromo who live in central and southern Ethiopia. Tigrigna is the language of the Tigrayans in the north, and it is also spoken in Eritrea.*

Amharic Basics

Thank you	Amesegenalehu
Excuse me	Yekirta
How are you?	Tenastilign
Goodbye	Dehnahanu
Yes	Ow
No	Aydellem
How much?	Sintinu
Water	Wiha
Coffee	Buna
Tea	Shai
Toilet	Shintibait

Oromifaa Basics

Thank you Galtoomi	
Excuse me	Dhiifama
How are you?	Akkam Jirtuu
Goodbye	Negaa-ti
Yes	Heya
No	Miti
How much?	Meega
Water	Bishaan
Coffee	Buna
Tea	Shaaye
Toilet	Mana Fincaani

Other useful words and phrases:

Ishee   The nearest English equivalent is the modern meaning of the word "cheers". That is, it can be anything from a greeting, to a farewell via a word of thanks or agreement.

Yellem   Literally means "there is none", but is quite a useful negative.

Chigger yellem	*No problem*

Tigrinya Basics

Thank you	Yekin yelly
Excuse me	Yekireta
How are you?	Kamelekhum
Goodbye	Dehankunu
Yes	Uwe
No	Aykonnen
How much?	Kindey
Water	Maji
Coffee	Bun
Tea	Shahi
Toilet	Shintibait

Television   There is one television channel, which broadcasts in colour, 1900-2300 on Monday to Friday and on Sunday, and 1800-2400 on Saturday. About a third of the programmes are in English and two-thirds are in local languages, mostly Amharic. The service can only be received in Addis Ababa.

Food and drink

Food   In Addis western type food can be found, but if you eat in the smaller places and when you go out of town, you will normally be offered Ethiopian dishes. They are very palatable, even if they do get monotonous after a while.

The carbohydrate staple is called *injera*, and is made from wheat barley or maize, often mixed. It is said that the best *injera* is made from *teff*, a grain of fine grass seed grown in the highlands. In appearance it is grey, thin, flat and spongy. In simple restaurants it is spread flat on a large tin plate and various spicy sauces served with it. In more sophisticated places it will be rolled up like a carpet.

The spicy sauces are known by the general term *wat*, and come in two basic forms:
Kai wat   red and peppery – pieces of meat in a sauce.
Alicha wat   yellowish with meat, slightly greasy.

Other versions of the red and peppery *wat* include:
Duro fanta   pronounced 'Door-raw' and includes egg.
Spestini   with potatoes.
Duro wat   with chicken.

Ethiopia

Kifto wat with minced meat – the meat can be raw or cooked, and you should specify which you want – the uncooked version is risky.

Misto wat includes both *kai* and *alicha*, and is not too peppery.

Misaire wat is meatless and consists of a variety of vegetables such as lentils and spinach, usually only available on Wednesday and Friday, because these are the fasting days of the Ethiopian Church, and *misaire wat* is considered to be a 'fasting food', rather like fish in the western world. (Spaghetti, a legacy of the Italian occupation, another fasting food.)

Terps wat roasted pieces of meat with green peppers and chilli.

Secundo a treat, not always available, and consists of a great variety of meat and vegetables.

All these are served with either *injera* or bread *(dahbo)*. Sometimes the only food available will be *tibs*. This consists of small pieces of fried meat in a rather watery gravy and again served with *injera* or sometimes bread. Vegetables are rarely available, and, though there are salads these, like all uncooked food, are much better avoided. Whatever you eat you will be expected to use your fingers. All restaurants have somewhere where you can wash your hands, though the facilities are often less than clean.

Among Ethiopians chewing *chat* – sometimes called ghat/qat is widespread as a social event, and groups of men are frequently seen sitting around tables talking and chewing. It is a mild stimulant and somewhat addictive, and is grown, especially in the east around Harar, as a cash crop. The green leaves are sold at the roadside in bunches, usually wrapped up in a sack. See Restaurant classification, page 31.

Drink *Tella* is the local beer and *tej* a local type of mead. A local liqueur is *araki*. In the south there is a local beer made from sorghum or millet, called *chaka*. Coffee is served black in small cups, so, though delicious, is not thirst quenching. Tea is served in bigger cups, also with no milk, and varies enormously from the very refreshing tea with added spices such as cinnamon, to a tea bag hung over the edge of the cup. Both tea and coffee are apparently boiled during the making, so would seem to be safe to drink. Coco cola, and fanta are widely available. The local bottled spring water comes in two types. In most of the country it is called *Ambo*, but in the east it is *Babille*. These are the names of the places where it is bottled. There is a subtle difference in the taste of the two varieties, but both are unbeatable if you have a raging thirst, and seem to be safe to drink. The most widely available bottled beer is called *Bedele*, but in the east it is *Harar beera*. There are also draught beers available in many places.

Much is made in tourist guides about the Coffee Ceremony, but there is nothing very ceremonial about it. It consists of a young woman roasting the beans over a charcoal fire, then grinding them in a mortar and making the coffee in a special coffee pot, which is heated over charcoal. This is usually done sitting on the floor and sometimes a stick of incense is burnt at the same time. This is a social occasion in much the same way that tea drinking is in England. The **Hilton Hotel** presents a coffee ceremony each week (but see box, page 745).

Holidays and festivals

New Year's Day (Julian Calendar) 1 January
Genna (Ethiopian Christmas: birth of Christ) 7 January
Timkat (Ethiopian Epiphany: baptism of Christ) 19 January
Adwa Day (commemorates the victory by Menelik II over Italy in 1896) 2 March
Patriots' Day (celebrates end of Italian occupation in 1941) 6 April
International Labour Day 1 May
Ethiopian Good Friday May (variable)
Fasika (Ethiopian Easter Sunday) May (variable)
Idd al Fitr (end of month of fasting for Ramadan) May (variable)
Idd al Adha August (variable)
Buhe (Ethiopian Halloween) 21 August
Enkutatash (Ethiopian New Year) 11 September
Popular Revolution Day 12 September

Festivals

Celebrations in Ethiopia are great and colourful events, mostly religious, and frequently take place over several days, providing wonderful pageants.

Timkat – Feast of the Epiphany, 19 January

This is an extremely colourful three-day festival commemorating Christ's baptism. The night before, priests take the Tabot (which symbolizes the Ark of the Covenant containing the Ten Commandments) from each Church. Concealed by an ornamental cloth, it is taken to a tent, close to a consecrated pool or stream, accompanied by much ringing of bells, blowing of trumpets and the burning of incense. In Addis Ababa many tents are pitched at Jan Meda, to the northeast of the city centre. At 0200 there is a Mass, and crowds attend, with picnics lit by oil lamps. At dawn the priest extinguishes a candle burning on a pole set in a nearby river using a ceremonial cross. Some of the congregation leap into the river. The Tabots are then taken back to the Churches in procession, accompanied by horsemen, while the festivities continue.

Buhe – 21 August

Bands of small boys call at each house, singing and jostling until they are given some fresh dough (buhe), that is being prepared for baking. In the evening, bonfires are lit outside each home.

Enkutatash – New Year, 11 September

This festival celebrates both the New Year and the Feast of John the Baptist. At the end of the long rains the season is Spring, and the Highlands become covered in wild flowers. Children dressed in new clothes dance through the villages, distributing garlands and tiny paintings. In the evening every house lights a bonfire and there is singing and dancing. In Amharic, enku means jewels, and it is as though the country is bejewelled by the flowers of spring.

Maskal – Finding of the True Cross, 27 September

Legend has it that the cross upon which Christ was crucified was discovered in the year 326 by Empress Helen, Mother of Constantine the Great. Unable to find the Holy Sepulchre, she prayed for help and was directed by the smoke of an incense burner to where the cross was buried.

In the Middle Ages, the Patriarch of Alexandria gave the Ethiopian Emperor Dawit half of the True Cross in return for the protection afforded to the Coptic Christians. A fragment of the True Cross is reputed to be held at the Gishen Marien monastery, which is about 70 kilometres to the northwest of Dessie. Maskal means `cross' in Amharic.

On the day of the festival, bright yellow Maskal daisies are tied to fronds, and piled high in town squares. Colourful processions carrying burning torches converge on to the square, where the brands are thrown onto the pyre. The bonfire burns and the celebrations continue until dawn. In Addis Ababa, the celebrations take place in Maskal Square, to the southeast of the City centre.

Kullubi – Feast of St Gabriel, 28 December

St Gabriel is the Patron Saint who guards over homes and churches. There is a huge pilgrimage to St Gabriel's Church on Kulubi hill, which is on the route from Addis Ababa eastwards, about 70 kilometres before Dire Dawa. Many pilgrims carry heavy burdens as a penance, children are brought to be baptized, and offerings are made to be distributed to the poor.

Maskal (Finding of the True Cross) 27 September
Maulid (Birth of Prophet Mohammad) November (variable)
Kullubi (Feast of St Gabriel) 28 December

Calendar Ethiopia uses the Julian calendar, named after Julius Caeser, which is seven years and eight months behind the Gregorian (European) calendar – a result of differences of opinion over Christ's exact date of birth. The Julian calendar consists of 12 months of 30 days and a 13th month of five or six days. Hence the Ethiopians claim that they enjoy 13 months of sunshine.

Ethiopia

Health

Yellow fever inoculation is compulsory. It is wise to have a cholera vaccination even though it is only compulsory if the visitor is coming from an infected area. Inoculation against typhoid and hepatitis are strongly recommended. **Staying healthy**

Anti-malaria tablets and general anti-mosquito measures, see page 41, are strongly recommended for visitors to the low-lying areas outside the capital. Addis Ababa is above the mosquito zone.

Acclimatization to the altitude normally takes about three days. Visitors with heart conditions or high blood pressure should take the precaution of seeking medical advice before they arrive.

Swimming in lakes that have still water sometimes carries the risk of billharzia – it is necessary to check locally. The alkaline lakes at Debre Zeit and Langano are safe.

In Addis Ababa, tap water is safe to drink. Many people will, however, try to avoid even the smallest risk of a stomach upset by drinking only boiled, sterilized or bottled water. Tap water should not be drunk outside Addis Ababa although some travellers report no problems. **Water**

For further advice see the section on Health, see page 35.

Further reading

Marcus, HG (1975) *The Life and Times of Menelick II*, Oxford: Clarendon Press. A thorough account of the career of the extraordinary emperor who defeated the Italians and created modern Ethiopia. **History**

Haile Selassie, I (1975) *My Life and Ethiopia's Progress: the Autobiography of Emperor Haile Selassie*, Oxford: OUP. The man who ruled Ethiopia for 48 years, and whose demise brought to an end a dynasty reputedly stretching back to Solomon and Sheba.

Marcus, HG (1994) *A History of Ethiopia*, Berkeley: University of California.

Ofcansky, TP and Berry, L (Eds, 1993) *Ethiopia: A Country Study*, Washington DC: US Govt Publications.

Marsden-Smedley, P (1990) *A Far Country: Travels in Ethiopia*, London: Arrow Books. An account of travels undertaken by an Ethiopia enthusiast in 1988 when the restrictions imposed by the Mengistu régime on tourists were a source of considerable frustration. **Travellers' Tales**

Murphy, D (1968) *In Ethiopia with a Mule*. A mule-trek from Massawa to Addis Ababa, with good observations on local history, culture and customs.

Waugh, E (1932) *Black Mischief*, London: Chapman & Hall. Based on material gathered by Waugh when he went to Addis Ababa in 1930 to report on the coronation of Haile Selassie for *The Times* newspaper. **Fiction**

Briggs, P (1996), *Guide to Ethiopia*, Bradt Publications, UK. **Guide books**

Spectrum Guide to Ethiopia (1996), Camerapix Publications, International Nairobi. Includes a lot of photographs.

Also recommended is the *Bartholomew Map "Sudan, Ethiopia, North East Africa"* (1993).

Ethiopia

Addis Ababa

9°2'N 38°42'E
Population: 2 million
Altitude: 2,400m
Phone code: 1
Colour map 1, grid C3

Addis Ababa (the name means 'new flower') is of fairly recent origin – Menelik II founded the city in 1887 (also spelt Addis Abeba). Situated in the foothills of the Entoto mountains and standing 2,400 metres above sea level (the third highest capital in the world), the city has a population of about two million. Before moving to the present site of Addis Ababa, Menelik had established temporary capitals at six different locations – caused by exhausting the fuelwood at each of these sites. Addis itself was in danger of being abandoned until the introduction of fast-growing eucalyptus trees from Australia provided the city with a regular source of fuel.

In and outs

Getting there Bole International Airport is 5 kilometres from the city centre and is undergoing major extensions, with a new International Passenger Terminal Building under construction. *Ethiopian Airlines* run a free shuttle bus into town. Taxis and 'contract taxis' to and from the airport are run by the National Tour Operation. On a shared basis the fare is about US$8. A minibus ride is about US$0.50, and leave city from Piazza area, from airport you need to walk about 1 kilometre toward city. The 2 main bus stations in Addis are the Autobus Terra near Mercato, and the smaller terminal on Ras Mekonin Ave near the railway station. All National buses, with the exception of buses to Nazret and Debre Zeyit, leave from the Autobus Terra. Buses to Nazret and Debre Zeyit depart from the terminal in Ras Mekonin Ave.

Getting around The first thing to note about Addis Ababa is that very few streets have names, and if they do, they may not be known by the names on the map. The exception to this is Churchill Avenue which is the main thoroughfare and shopping street in Addis. If you try to find your way by using many of the other street names as marked on the maps, people will not understand you. It is far better to navigate by using such landmarks as the Post Office *(posta bet)*, Abiot (also known as Meskal), the station *(la gare)* and areas like Piazza and Mercato, which are shopping areas. Some roads have one name on the map and another in general use. For example Africa Avenue on the map is universally known as Bole Road, and Ras Biru Avenue as Debre Zeit Road. These generally used names tell you where the road is going to, and you will come across other examples.

Public transport in Addis is easy as there is a large and efficient network of blue and white minibuses which cover the whole town. It takes a little time to tune in to the system, as you need to be able to recognize the destinations shouted out by the conductors. They are so cheap that it is often simpler to take several buses if you are going on a long or complicated journey and change buses at the large road junctions. The fares are US¢ 5, US¢ 10 or US¢ 15 depending on distance travelled. The one thing to remember is don't travel in the evening rush hour, as you will have great difficulty in elbowing your way onto the bus.

Safety is becoming an increasing concern in Addis. A number of tourists have been attacked and robbed in the Merkato area. Be careful walking after dark, especially in

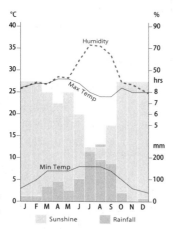

*Climate:
Addis Ababa*

St Yared

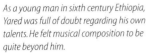

As a young man in sixth century Ethiopia, Yared was full of doubt regarding his own talents. He felt musical composition to be quite beyond him.

One day, as he sat despondently below a tree, he saw a caterpillar struggling to climb up it. Three times it fell, but on the fourth attempt it reached one of the branches and began to spin a cocoon. Inspired, Yared buckled down to his studies and went on to compose almost all of Ethiopia's religious music.

A painting of St Yared is to be seen in St Georges Cathedral in Addis Ababa.

poorly lit areas. Persistent beggars, including children, may follow you for quite a long way asking for money.

Public lavatories Access to lavatories can be a problem in downtown Addis. Some hotels, such as the *Ras* keep their washrooms locked, and claim they are out of order (which they may well be). The *Hilton* has lavatories you can use, but it is a little away from the centre. The *Harambee Hotel* are the most accommodating in the central area. Take care wearing sandals as there is human excrement on many of the pavements of Addis.

The city is now large and sprawling, displaying little evidence of planning. Bounded by mountains to the north, Addis is spreading south, and industrial and residential suburbs are expanding rapidly.

Addis Ababa is an important administrative centre not only for Ethiopia but for the whole of Africa. The headquarters of the UN Economic Commission for Africa was established here in 1958. In 1963 the city hosted the African Heads of State Conference at which the charter of the Organization of African Unity (OAU) was signed by 30 independent African nations, and Addis Ababa was subsequently chosen as the site of the OAU's secretariat.

When going into many buildings such as government offices and sometimes banks, you will be asked if you have a camera, and your bag may be searched. If you do have a camera it will be taken away from you and you will be given a token with which to claim it back.

Sights

Africa Hall is on Menelik II Ave – an imposing symbol of African independence and optimism, perhaps now looking a little jaded. It houses the headquarters of the UN Economic Commission for Africa. The huge stained glass windows depict the suffering of the people of Africa. Just to the west of the Africa Hall are the **Filwoha Springs** (now a murky pool) which prompted Queen Taytu to persuade her husband to establish his new capital at Addis Ababa. The thermal waters are now diverted to an adjacent bathing complex. Also next to the Africa Hall lies the huge **Maskal** (also spelt **Meskal**) **Square**, previously known as **Abiot (Revolution) Square** – a natural amphitheatre where rallies were held every September to mark the 1974 revolution. Portraits of Marx, Engels, Lenin and Comrade Mengistu used to adorn the square.

At the other (north) end of Churchill Rd, the city's main commercial boulevard, behind the dominant city hall, lies the **St George Cathedral** (Giorgis Cathedral). Built in 1896 in the traditional octagonal shape to commemorate Ethiopia's victory over the Italians at the Battle of Adwa, the cathedral houses the work of Afewerk Tekle, the renowned Ethiopian artist responsible for the stained glass windows of the Africa Hall. ■ *Cathedral opens 0800-0900 and 1200-1400.* There is a small museum in the compound which includes some rifles used in the Battle of Adwa, a survey of church architecture in Ethiopia, and exhibits from Haile Selassie and his

Ethiopia

family. ■ *Guide, English speaking, with entrance of US$1.50. 0800-1230.* Nearby are the **Menelik Mausoleum** and the **Trinity Cathedral**, built in 1911 and 1941 to serve as the tombs of emperors and princes. The Trinity Cathedral was built to commemorate Ethiopia's liberation from five years of Italian occupation. Haile Selassie's **Grand Palace** is just to the east of Churchill Ave at the end of Colsen St. The Emperor had a second residence, Juilee Palace, on Menelik Ave, just north of the *Ghion Hotel.*

Addis Ababa

To Organisation of African Unity & Carrera Lodge Hotel

The **National Museum**, quite small, is located at Han St Kilo crossroads, just north of St Mary's Church.

Take a minibus to Arat Kilo, which is the name of a roundabout with a tall clock tower in the middle, quite near the Piazza. The Museum is a short walk from there past the German Cultural Centre and a rather fine church. From the outside the Museum looks a little unkempt. But inside it is well kept and the entrance fee is only US$1.75, which includes the services of a guide. The guides vary a bit in their command of English and in their knowledge. The best are excellent. Other than a few

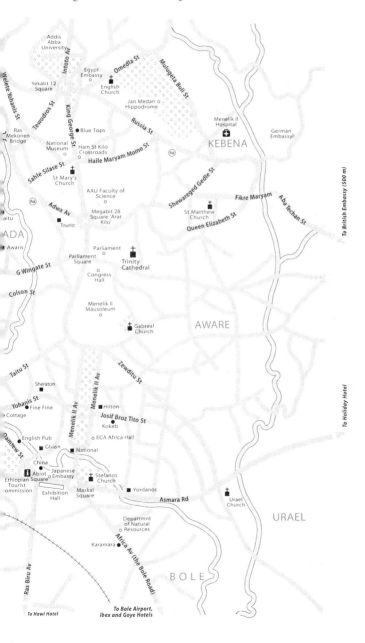

notices on the walls next to each exhibit, the guides are the only source of information, so a good guide is really necessary. The exhibits are very varied, and include 'Lucy', the female fossil skeleton found in northeast Ethiopia in 1974, believed to be about three and a half million years old, the oldest known Ethiopian and one of our earliest ancestors. She is known as 'Dinkenesh' in Amharic, meaning 'you are beautiful'. The museum has an extensive collection of artefacts, some predating the Axumite civilization of Tigre. There is a large collection of female stone statues, thought to be fertility symbols and believed to be 2,500 years old. There is also a collection of modern imperial robes. It also includes a selection of the more than 200 designs of crosses found in Ethiopia. Many of these are decorative, but some have uses such as the one with a small spoon at the end, which was used for cleaning the wax from ears. No photos allowed. ■ *0830-1230 and 1330-1730.*

Just five minutes walk from the museum are the **Lion Cages**, US$1.50, probably the only place in Ethiopia to see the Abyssinian lion (males have a dark mane). The lions are kept in depressingly small cages and the keepers appear to enjoy taunting the animals.

Further north lies **Addis Ababa University**. Another **Museum** is part of the campus and it is quite extensive, and well maintained.

The **Merçato** covers a vast area of western Addis Ababa. It is one of the largest markets in Africa and offers a dazzling array of colours, aromas, costumes, produce and jewellery. Groups of pickpockets operate in this area.

Entoto, the mountain range which rises to the north of Addis, is easily accessible from the city. This is where Menelik started his first capital, and the **Church of Entoto Mariam** where he was crowned can still be visited. Reaching the top of the Entonto plateau stunning views unfold away to the north and the Blue Nile Gorge. At the top of the hill is the **Church of Entonto Raguel** which was previously at the centre of the old capital of Entoto.

Essentials

Sleeping
■ *on map page 684*
Price codes:
on inside front cover

NB The *Ghion, Ethiopia, Wabe Shebelle, Africa, Harambee, Ras* and *National* hotels are all government owned, and there may be restrictions on unmarried couples sharing rooms (see box on page 675). Government hotels can be booked through the NTO or the head office of the hotel chain. The Ghion Group manages the Ghion, the Taitu and the National hotels T513222, F515381. The Ras Group manages the Ras, Nile and the Africa hotels, T517060, F517533. The Wabe Shebelle Group manages the Wabe Shebelle and the Maskal Flower Hotels, T517187. The Ethiopian Group manages the Harambee, Ethiopia and Tourist hotels, T517400. *Buffet de la Gare* is easily the best value in town. Hotel staff are not used to foreign tourists, and this is reflected in their attitude, which though usually friendly, is less professional and welcoming, and the standard of English is rather basic.

A+ *Addis Ababa Hilton*, very central on Menelik Ave, T518400, F510064, Tx21104. Luxury accommodation with comprehensive business and recreation facilities, a/c, swimming pool (warm water from thermal spring), tennis, restaurants, bars, jacuzzi, sauna, massage, bookshop, gift shop, tours office, pharmacy, pleasant gardens. **A+** *Sheraton Addis*, very central on Yohanis St, PO Box 6002, Woreda 14, Kebele 24, Addis Ababa, T517138, F514029, reservations T517138. Pleasantly designed, low-elevation buildings. Recently opened luxury hotel set in landscaped gardens. Banquet and conference facilities.

B *Africa*, Dejazmach Wolde Mikael St, T517060/447385. Bar, restaurants, mosaic of Ethiopian folklore on wall of one function room. **B** *Aros*, Belai Zeleke St. **B** *Carrera Lodge*, Roosevelt St, to southeast of centre, PO Box 6273, T755144, F754499. **B** *Ethiopia*, Yohannes Ave, near Churchill Rd, T517400/447400, Tx21072. Located in business and commercial district. Restaurant, coffee bar, souvenir shop, function rooms. **B** *Ghion*, very central on Menelik Ave, close to Revolution Square, T513222/443170, Tx21112. Bungalows and appartments, swimming pool (Olympic size, natural hot-spring water), function rooms, tours office, gift shop, restaurants, bars, extensive gardens, the Saba Rooms have ceiling paintings of the Queen of Sheba legend. **B** *Guenet*, Beyene Merid St, T518125, older style. **B** *Harambee*, Taitu St, T517400/154000/154327/154226/154457, Tx21072. Souvenir shop, Magala Lounge is decorated in the style of the old city of Harar. **B** *Ibex*, Bole Rd, T654400. New, comfortable hotel, bar, restaurant, special buffets on Tuesday, Thursday, Saturday. **B** *National*, Menelik Ave, T513222/155166, Tx21112. Some scope for self-catering in rooms with kitchenettes, bar, restaurant. **B** *Blue Nile*, Ras Mekonin Ave, T517060. **B** *Ras*, Churchill Rd, T517060/447060, Tx21485. Just north of railway station, very popular, one of the oldest hotels in Addis, restaurants, bar, gardens. **B** *Wabe Shebelle*, Ras Abebe Aragay St, T515187/447187/90.

C *Awaris*, near Piazza. Restaurant. **C** *Axum*, Asmara Rd, PO Box 40318, T188832. Restaurant, bar, s/c, hot water. **C** *Balu*, near Piazza. Good value, clean. **C** *Buffet de la Gare*, near station, PO Box 2381, T517888/517125, F515959. Excellent value, ideal location, bungalow style, first rate restaurant. All highly recommended. **C** *Central Shoa*, Asmara Rd north side. Shower, restaurant. **C** *Goye*, Old Airport Rd, T710987. New hotel, a little away from the centre, sauna and massage. **C** *Maskal Flower Hotel*, adjacent to the Debre Zeit Road, T517187. Central, good value. **C** *Taitu*, near Piazza, T513222. Built by Menelik II's wife, and is the oldest hotel in Addis. Part of it was destroyed by fire recently and it may be closed for rebuilding for some time. **C** *Tourist*, near Grand Palace and Trinity Cathederal. Popular, restaurant.

D *Filwoha Hotel*, T511404. Good value, sited near the hot springs. **D** *Fin-Fin Hotel*, opposite the Filwoha Hotel at the hot springs. similar standard but has greater charm. **D** *Hawi*, Debre Zeit Rd, south of the city centre. Smart, modern, well run. **D** *Holiday Hotel*, Asmara Rd, near the Plaza Hotel. Clean rooms, spacious and spotless bathroom, serve delicious western food, friendly and helpful staff, sited close to a minibus stop, excellent value. **D** *Plaza*, Asmara Rd. S/c, hot water. **D** *Yordanos Hotel*, Asmara Rd, 10 minutes walk from Maskal Square, T515711, F516655, PO Box 1647. Clean and friendly hotel, has about 30 rooms, no a/c, ensuite bathrooms, hot water/shower and flushing toilets, satellite TV bar, restaurant, laundry and post facilities, not too noisy. Excellent value. Recommended.

E *Baro*, Muniyem St, east of Churchill Ave, Piazza area. Small bar and restaurant, patio, internet access/fax, hot water, not very clean, some rooms have squat toilets and private bathrooms, you can organize a four-wheel drive to Omo NP from here. **E** *Bel Air Hotel*, on a side road off Queen Elizabeth St, near Ras Ambas Hotel. Clean, own bathroom, hot shower, safe parking, camping possible. **E** *Deborah Hotel*, nice clean hotel, water supply intermittent, some rooms have a toilet and shower. **E** *Debre Damo*, Asmara Rd. Hot showers. Recommended. **E** *Park Hotel*, near *Deborah*. Simple and cheap. **E** *Tropical Hotel*, close to National Bank, T512180. Basic clean and safe. **E** *Wutma Hotel*, Muniyem St, east of Churchill Ave, Piazza area, PO Box 9919, T125360, near the *Baro Hotel*. Basic facilities, cheap, hot water, quiet, clean, good restaurant. Luggage storage lockers available. Bathrooms swampy.

Along Fatiwrari Hable Giyorgis St, near the bus station, there are many basic hotels for less than US$3 a night, some do not have showers. Many bars also have cheap rooms at the back

4 *Abiata Restaurant*, Wabe Shebelle Hotel, Ras Abebe Aragay St, T447187/90, International cuisine. **4** *Addis Ababa Restaurant*, Weatherall St. Traditional Ethiopian food, in a circular dining room (*tukul*), once the home of Queen Zauditu, an excellent variety of *wat*, see page 678, is on offer and food is eaten the local way – without knives and forks. **4** *Addis Tsegenet*, Wabe Shebelle Hotel, Ras Abebe Aragay St, T447187/90. Roof-top location, on 11th floor, splendid views. **4** *Casino Restaurant*, Ghion Hotel, Menelik Ave, T443170, Tx21112. International cuisine. **4** *China Bar*, off Ras Mekonin Ave. Wide variety of Chinese dishes, well decorated in Oriental style. **4** *Finfine Hotel*, Atse Yohanness Ave, near the *Hilton Hotel*. Ethiopian cuisine, leather stools and mats in one dining area, previously the home of a *Ras* (nobleman) who used Greek craftsmen to decorate and carve the wooden interior. **4** *Ghion Restaurant*, Ghion Hotel, Menelik Ave, T443170, Tx21112. International cuisine. **4** *Harrar Grill*, Addis

Eating
● *on map*
Price codes:
on inside front cover
HABESHA
(BOLE RD)

Ethiopia

Ababa Hilton, Menelik Ave, T158400, Tx21104. French cuisine. **4** *Jacaranda*, *Addis Ababa Hilton*, Menelik Ave, T158400, Tx21104. Italian and Mexican food, overlooks pool and gardens. **4** *Lombardia*, on Ras Abebe Aregay Ave, T150791. Italian food. **4** *Ras Hotel*, Churchill Rd, T447060, Tx21485. 2nd floor restaurant with International cuisine, buffet on Saturday, live band on Friday and Saturday. **4** *Unity House*, *Ghion Hotel*, Menelik Ave, T443170, Tx21112. Stands in gardens with bar and terrace, *Flambé* nights on Friday and Saturday.

3 *Africa Hotel*, Dejazmach Wolde Mikael St, T447385. Basement of hotel has a restaurant in traditional style, with thatched roof, serving Ethiopian food, there is also a restaurant with international cuisine. **3** *Blue Tops*, oppoite National Museum on King George St, north of centre. Stylishly designed with blue tented awnings, reasonable value food, tables with local grains, under the glass tops. **3** *Castelli's*, T111058, in Piazza area close to Ethiopian Airways. Local paintings of 18th and 19th century, high standard, need to book at weekends. **3** *China Bar & Restaurant*, Desta Damtew Ave. **3** *Cottage Restaurant & Pub*, near the *Harambee Hotel* on Desta Demtew Ave. Offers Swiss food, and Swiss chalet-style decor. **3** *English Pub*, off Desta Demtew Ave. International food, darts. **3** *Ethiopia Restaurant*, *Ethiopia Hotel*, Atse Yohannes Ave, near Churchill Rd, T447400. *Flambé* night with live band on Saturday, buffet with Ethiopian dishes on Thursday. **3** *Fanfan Tavern*, *Harambee Hotel*, Tito St, T154000/154327/154226/154457, Tx21072. 2nd floor barbecue grill, traditional *masho* bead lamps, murals on walls. **3** *Garden Snack Bars*, *Wabe Shebelle Hotel*, Ras Abebe Aragay St, T447187/90. 3 traditional circular *tukuls*, one serving traditional Ethiopian food. **3** *Gazebo*, *Addis Ababa Hilton*, T158400, Tx21104. Café beside the pool, barbecues and snacks. **3** *Harar Restaurant*, *Harambee Hotel*, Tito St, T154000/154327/154226/154457, Tx21072. Decorated in style of old city of Harar, international cuisine. **3** *International Hotel*, Menelik Ave, T155166, Tx21112. Ground floor restaurant overlooking gardens to the rear, international cuisine. **3** *Kaffa House*, *Addis Ababa Hilton*, Menelik Ave, T158400, Tx21104. Coffee shop with reasonably extensive menu. **3** *Karamara Restaurant*, on Africa Ave, between Revolution Square and Bole Rd. Rondavel style, entertainment from strolling singers and musicians, Ethiopian cuisine. **3** *La Tavern Grill*, off Debre Zeit Rd, T162179. International food, good for children, with playground in the garden, *Al Fresco* barbecues on Saturday. **3** *Lalibela*, Ras Desta Ave, T158734. International cuisine, elaborate decor based on the rock-hewn churches. **3** *Oroscope Pizzeria*, off Churchill Rd. Serves international food as well as pizza, its chicken soup is especially recommended. **3** *Pizzeria Ristorante de Goiton*, near the Piazza and *Awaris Hotel*. Good, friendly and reasonably priced. **3** *Shala Bar*, *Wabe Shebelle Hotel*, Ras Abebe Aragay St, T447187/90. American food. **3** *Villa Verde*, off Churchill Rd. Italian cuisine. **3** *Wutma*, PO Box 9919, Muniyem St, T125360. Huge salads, Ethiopian and Italian dishes, also offers a minibus and taxi service.

2 *Ambassador Cinema*, on Desta Damtew St. Contains a small restaurant offering good value food. **2** *Arada Restaurant*, in Piazza (above Ethiopian office). Serves Western and Ethiopian food, bar serves European beers, good friendly service. **2** *Bole*, on Africa Rd. Only open until 1900. **2** *Enrico* off Churchill Rd. Coffee, pastries, ice cream. **2** *Four Corners Armenian Restaurant*, Desta Damtew Ave, near Revolution Square. Good value. **2** *Hard Luck Cafe*, hamburgers and western food, also sells T shirts (à la Hard Rock Cafe) for US$10. **2** *Hong Kong Chinese Restaurant*, Churchill Rd, near St Saviour Cathedral. **2** *Kokeb Restaurant*, Menelik II Ave, near Africa Hall. Display of jewellery and horse-riding equipment, on 10th floor of apartment block. International and Ethiopian food, good views from terrace. **2** *Kunama*, *Africa Hotel*, Dejazmach Wolde Mikael St, T447385. Terrace snack bar. **2** *Kyriazis Patisserie*, Piazza area, near Ethiopian Airways. **2** *Peacock Restaurant*, Bole Rd. Convenience food. **2** *Pool Café*, *Ghion Hotel*, Menelik Ave, T443170, Tx21112. Barbecues and pizzas, draught beer. **2** *Ras Restaurant*, Mexico Square, T444182. International and Ethiopian food, modern decor, good value. **2** *Rendez Vous*, Abiot Square, off Ras Mekonin Ave. Barbecues on central grill. **2** *Sangam*, Bole Rd. Indian cuisine. **2** *Soul Kid Pastry Shop*, Piazza near the Ethiopian Tourist Board shop. **2** *Tukul*, *Ghion Hotel*, Menelik Ave, T443170, Tx21112. Snack bar. **1** *G K Restaurant*, Ghandi St. Has good pizzas and salads. **1** *Rosteceria*, Ghandi St (next door). Has good lasagna.

Snack bars Cheap snack bars are clustered around the Piazza and offer local food. **1** *Kili Snack*. **1** *Port Bar*. **1** *Star Café*.

Cinema Mainly American, Indian and Arabic films. *Ambassador Theatre*, near National Theatre and *Harambee Hotel* on Atse Yohannes Ave. *Cinema Ethiopia*, near Piazza. *Addis Katama* in Merkato. *Agar Fikhr* (Patriotic Association), close to Piazza. Shows films on an occasional basis. *National Theatre* on Churchill Rd, and *City Hall*, at the north end of Churchill Rd also show films from time to time. See *Ethiopian Herald* for programmes. **Entertainment**

Theatre: traditional dance, music and classical western plays (Shakespeare is very popular, and has been translated into Amharic) at the *National Theatre* on Churchill Rd near the Ethiopia Hotel, and at *City Hall*, at the north end of Churchill Rd. National Theatre has regular traditional dance and music 1600-1800 on Thursday. *Agar Fikhr* (Patriotic Association), close to Piazza. Traditional dance and music 1600 Tuesday. See *Ethiopian Herald* for programmes. *Haifas*, Bole Rd. Occasional bands and dancers.

Nightclubs Inveterate nightlifers are advised to hire a taxi by the hour (US$4) and to tour the dives. *Concord Nightclub* on Concord Ave. Very popular. *3M Club* at *Carrera Lodge Hotel*, on Roosevelt St to the southwest of the centre. Live bands at weekends. *Ghion Nightclub*, T443170, Tx21112, very central on Menelik Ave, close to Revolution Square. Live music, features Roha, a celebrated Ethiopian band. *Ras Hotel*, Churchill Rd, T447060, Tx21485. Just north of railway station, regular discos. *Shala Bar*, *Wabe Shebelle Hotel*, Ras Abebe Aragay St, T447187/90. From 2200, live band, Friday and Saturday only. *Stars Nightclub*, another popular venue. *The Tunnel*, on Churchill north of *Ras Hotel*. No T-shirts or tennis shoes allowed. *Memo*, just off Africa Ave (Bole Rd) near *Flamingo Bar*. Every night, good grill and bar outside, quite popular.

Sport (participant) Bowling: at Emboy Mesk in Debre Zeit Rd. Also *Guenet Hotel*. **Canoeing**: archery at Jan Meda. Northeast of the City centre off Mulugetsa St. Call the race track at Jan Meda (T112540) for information. **Gym**: at Arat Kilo to the north of the city, going northeast from the Piazza along Adwa Ave. **Horse riding**: at a site near the Victory Department Store along the old Airport Rd. **Rafting**: International River Grade 2, but can reach 4 at high water flows in September on the River Omo. Contact Adrift, Wessex House, 127 High St, Hungerford, Berkshire, RG17 0DL, T01488-684509, F01488-685055, SafariDrive@compuserve.com/raft@adrift.co.uk, www.adrift.co.uk or USA c/o Bio Bio Expeditions Worldwide, PO Box 2028, Truckee, California 96160, T1-800-2467238, F1-916-5826865, H20marc@aol.com . 3 trips available – the Upper Omo, the Lower Omo and the African Queen which is a combination of both. **Sauna**: available at the *Hilton* hotel and the *New Filowcha* hotel, opposite the *Fanfan Tavern*, Tito St. US$2. Message service not recommended. **Swimming**: at *Ghion Hotel*, US$2 (Olympic-size pool) and at *Hilton Hotel*, US$4. **Tennis**: at *Ghion Hotel*, *Hilton Hotel*, *Guenet Hotel*, *Taitu Hotel*.

Sport (spectator) Horse racing: at Jan Meda, T112540. Northeast of the City centre off Mulugetsa St. **Soccer**: at Addis Ababa Stadium on Ras Desta Damtew Ave. There are games on most Thursday evenings and on Saturday and Sunday. See *Ethiopian Herald* for programmes.

The high quality shopping area is along *Churchill Ave*. A useful supermarket is opposite the *Ras Hotel* on Churchill Ave. The main hotels all have a variety of shops. The area for bargains is *Merkato*, the main market of the city to the west (it is about 1 kilometre from Churchill Ave, access is easy by taxi). Merkato has food, household items, imported goods and traditionally made craftwork. There are some covered sections, the Adrash market halls, which contain the imported goods and the traditional items. The other local shopping area is the *Piazza*, at the north end of Churchill Rd, to the west. The jewellery, gold and silverware is mainly concentrated here, as well as flower shops, ceramics and leather goods. **Shopping**

Still mineral water only available in Addis, stock up if needed for contact lens soaking.

Bookshops *The Africa Bookshop*, Adwa Ave. Has a large collection of second hand non-fiction books. There is also a bookshop by the *German Cultural Institute*, midway from the *National Museum* to Arat Kilo. It stocks a reasonable collection of non-fiction books about Ethiopia. There are also a couple of bookstalls in the *Piazza* area.

Curios & crafts The *Hilton Hotel* and the *Ghion Hotel* both have shops selling traditionally made and antique items. The *Ethiopian Tourist Trading Corporation* (ETTC) has shops at Bole Airport, and in the Tourist Commission building in Abiot Square off Ras Mekonin Ave. *Haile Selassie Alemayehu*, on Churchill Rd has a large selection, fixed prices, better value than either the *Hilton* shop or Bole Airport shop. *Churchill Rd* has many small shops and stalls selling these items. *Ethiopian Crafts and Antiques*, close to the Ras Hotel on Churchill Rd has a good selection of high quality craftwork. There are also craft items in *Merkato*, the large market to the west of the City centre, and jewelry and leather goods in the *Piazza*, off the north end of Churchill Ave. *Addis Ababa City Gold* and the *Silversmith Co-operative Society* are particularly good sources for jewelry in the Piazza.

Hairdressers Salons at *Hilton* and *Filwoha hotels*.

Newspapers Foreign newspapers (*International Herald Tribune, Times, Washington Post*) available at airport, *Hilton* and British Council Library.

Student Card verification, which enables entry to the National Parks at a reduced rate, needs to be validated at the *Ethiopian Wildlife Authority*, Desta Damtew St, near the *Ghion Hotel*.

Transport **Local Bus**: for bus journeys to the regions it is necessary to buy a ticket the day before departure. The bus station ticket office opens at 0800, and to be certain of booking you should arrive by 0700. There is a secondary market in booked tickets at around double the face value. Arrive for departure by 0600. There is an extra charge for a big luggage pack.

Red and yellow *ambasa* (lion) buses operate within the city, stopping at every red and yellow marking. There is a flat fare per person for a one-way trip. Minibuses (*wi yi yit*) are also available, running on set routes. The blue/white minibuses are called 'taxis', while the blue/white cars (usually Fiats) are known as 'contract taxis'. The former have a flat rate of around US$0.15. For the contract taxis you'll have to agree a price before departure. It usually costs US$1.50 within the city centre between tourist sites. **Taxi**: cream coloured NTO (National Tour Operator) taxis operate at Bole International Airport costing between US$1.50-3 if you go directly to the drivers outside the airport. Brand new yellow Hyundi taxis cost the most at US$3, but are worth it. Taxis also operate from outside all the major hotels. There is also a minibus service from the airport. The minibus can be found in the airport car parking area or 600 metres away on the road towards town. Also, the private taxi service operates in the smaller blue and white cars along set routes, often on a vehicle-sharing basis.

Air The national carrier **Ethiopian Airways** connects with many European destinations and with 23 African cities. In addition there are direct flights by **Alitalia, Aeroflot, Alyemda, Lufthansa, Interflug, Yemenia** and **Kenya Airways**. Internal flights with *Ethiopian Airlines* are efficient and cheap. Friendly helpful staff. The round trip by Air (Addis – Bahar Dar – Lalibela – Gondar – Addis) costs US$160 with sectors like Lalibela to Gondar costing just US$30 – so low, that they must be expected to rise. Airport taxes US$20 international, US$1.50 national. Internal flights to the northern towns have been suspended due to the border conflict.

Train A 782 kilometre railway connects Addis with Djibouti on the Red Sea. Recently however there have been incidents where travellers have been attacked by bandits on this train, check the situation locally before booking. The trains from Addis Ababa leave daily at around 0700 and 1930, arriving in Djibouti approximately 24 hours later. The main stop is at Dire Dawa, a bit over half way. Booking is at the railway station at the southern end of Churchill Rd. It is necessary to make a reservation as the train is often full. The fare to Djibouti is US$58 1st class (a sleeper on the overnight train); US$37 2nd class; US$19 3rd class. Djibouti-Ethiopian Railroad Company, T447250. Addis/Dire Dawa departure is at 1630 arriving at 1200 the following day – daily service. Prices 1st class US$11, 2nd class US$7, 3rd class US$3.50. Even when you reserve your seat you may still have to 'fight' to get the allocated place.

Road Buses to and from the regions are frequent. However the roads are in poor condition, so allow for extra journey time, for example 1 hour to Debre Zeit and 1½ hours to Harar. The main bus terminal is at Merkato, while a second bus station near the railway station on Ras Mekonin Ave, has frequent services to nearby destinations such as Debre Zeit, Mojo and Nazret.

Airline offices *Aeroflot*, PO Box 7018, T1573. *Air Djibouti*, T157322. *Air France*, T519044. *Air* **Directory**
Tanzania Corporation, T157533. *Alitalia*, PO Box 3240, T154640. *Alyemda*, PO Box 40461, T441049.
Ethiopian Airlines has 3 offices in City centre, near National Theatre on Churchill Ave (use this office for internal flights, which have to be paid for in US$ cash), T447000. The head office is at the airport T512222/612222, F611474. *Addis Ababa Hilton*, Menelik Ave, T158400, Tx21104 and in Piazza at southern end of Eden St. *Egyptair* is on Churchill Ave. *Kenya Airways*, PO Box 3381, T443018.
Lufthansa, PO Box 2484, New Insurance Building, Churchill St/Ras Mekonin Ave, F515666, F512988.
Saudi Airways which is located next door to the Ambassador Theatre, T517746. *Yemenia*, PO Box 1079, T445076. Sending unaccompanied air freight from Addis is cheap – eg 30 kg Addis/London using Lufthansa US$80 (1997).

Banks *Commercial Bank of Ethiopia*, at airport. *National Bank of Ethiopia*, Churchill Rd. *Commercial Bank of Ethiopia*, Churchill Rd.

Communications Post Office: main Post Office on Churchill Ave near Adua Square, open 0800-1600.
Telephone: calls can be made through the *Telecommunications Head Office* opposite *Holy Saviour Church*. Telex, telegram and fax (US$6 a page to Europe) services are also available from here, and from the main Post Office on Churchill Rd. Collect (reverse charge) calls can be made. Most of the larger hotels have telex and telegram facilities.

Embassies & Consulates *Algeria*, PO Box 5740, T7113000, F712586, Tx21302. *Argentina*, Tx21172.
Austria, PO Box 1219, T712144, F712140, Tx21060. *Belgium*, Fikre Mariam Rd, T611813, F613636.
Bulgaria, PO Box 987, T612971, Tx21450. *Burundi*, PO Box 3641, T651300, Tx21069. *Cameroon*, Bole Rd, PO Box 1026, Tx21121. *Canada*, African Solidarity Insurance Building, 6th Flr, Churchill Ave, PO Box 1130, T713022/511100, F710333/512818, Tx21053. *Chad*, T611819, Tx21419. *China*, PO Box 5643, Tx21145. *Congo*, PO Box 5571, T154331, Tx21406. *Cote d'Ivoire*, PO Box 3668, T711213, Tx21061. *Cuba*, Jimma Rd, PO Box 5623, T202010, Tx21306. *Czech Republic*, PO Box 3108, T516132, F513471, Tx21021.
Djibouti, PO Box 1022, T613006/613200, F612504, Tx21317. *Egypt*, PO Box 1611, T553077, F552722.
Equatorial Guinea, PO Box 246. *Eritrean Embassy*, PO Box 2571, T512940/512844, F514951/514911, on the southwest corner of Ras Mekonin Ave/Ras Biru Ave. Visas for Eritrea cost US$25 and are issued in 24 hrs. *Finland*, Tedla Dest Building, Bole Rd, PO Box 1017, T513900, Tx21259. *France*, PO Box 1464, T550066, F511180/551793, Tx21040. *Gabon*, PO Box 1256, F181075, Tx21208. *Germany*, PO Box 660, T550433, F551311, Tx21015. *Ghana*, PO Box 3173, T711402, F712511. *Greece*, PO Box 1168, T449712.
Guinea, PO Box 1190, T449712. *Holy See*, PO Box 588, T712100, Tx21815. *Hungary*, Abattoirs Rd, PO Box 1213, T651850, Tx21176. *India*, PO Box 528, T552100, F552521, Tx21148. *Indonesia*, Mekanisa Rd, PO Box 1004, T202104, Tx21264. *Iran*, Jimma Rd, PO Box 1144, T200369, Tx21118. *Ireland*, PO Box 9585, T613361. *Israel*, PO Box 1266, Addis Ababa, T251-1-610999, F610608/612456. *Italy*, PO Box 1105, T551565, F550218, Tx21342. *Jamaica*, National House Africa Ave, PO Box 5633, T613656, Tx21137. *Japan*, Finfine Building, Revolution Square, PO Box 5650, T511088, F511350, Tx21108. *Kenya*, Fikre Mariam Rd, PO Box 3301, T610033/610303, F611433, Tx21103. *Korea Democratic People's Republic*, PO Box 2378. *Korea Republic*, Jimma Rd, PO Box 2047, T444490, Tx21140. *Liberia*, PO Box 3116, T513655, Tx21083. *Libya*, PO Box 5728, Tx21214. *Malawi*, PO Box 2316, T712440, F710494, Tx21087. *Mexico*, Tsige Mariam Building, Churchill Rd, PO Box 2962, T443456, Tx21141. *Netherlands*, PO Box 1241, T711100, F711577, Tx21049. *Niger*, Debrezenit Rd, PO Box 5791, T651175, Tx21284.
Nigeria, PO Box 1019, T120644, Tx21028. *Poland*, Bole Rd, PO Box 1123, T610197, Tx21185. *Romania*, Africa Ave, PO Box 2478, T181191, Tx21168. *Russia*, PO Box 1500, T611828/552061, F613795, Tx21534.
Rwanda, PO Box 5618, T610300, F610411, Tx21199. *Saudi Arabia*, PO Box 1104, T448010, Tx21194.
Senegal, Africa Ave, PO Box 2581, T611376, Tx21027. *Sierra Leone*, PO Box 5619, T710033, Tx21144.

Ethiopia

Slovakia, PO Box 3108, T516152, F513471, Tx21021. *Spain*, Entoto St, PO Box 2312, T550222, Tx21107. *Sudan*, PO Box 1110, T516477, F518141, Tx21293. *Sweden*, PO Box 1029, T516699, F515830, Tx21039. *Switzerland*, Jimma Rd, PO Box 1106, T710577/711107, F712805/712177, Tx21123. *Tanzania*, PO Box 1077, T44064, Tx21268. *Tunisia*, PO Box 10069. *Turkey*, PO Box 1506, T612321, Tx21257. *Uganda*, PO Box 5644, T513088, F514355, Tx21143. *UK*, Fikre Miriam St, PO Box 858, T612354, F610588, Tx21299. *USA*, Entoto St, PO Box 1014, T551002/550666, F551166, Tx21282. *Venezuela*, Debre Ziet Rd, PO Box 5584, T654790, Tx21102. *Vietnam*, PO Box 1288. *Yemen*, PO Box 664, T21346. *Yugoslavia*, PO Box 1342, T517804. Tx21233. *RD Congo*, Makinisa Rd, PO Box 2723, T20485, Tx21043. *Zambia*, PO Box 1090, T711302, Tx21065. *Zimbabwe*, PO Box 5624, T183872, Tx21351.

Hospitals & medical services Hospitals: *Black Lion Hospital* on Churchill Rd behind Tiglachin monument, modern, good casualty department. *Ethio-Swedish Clinic*, T449933. **Pharmacies:** City Council runs a number of inexpensive public pharmacies. There is one next to the National Tour Operation head office, near *Ghion Hotel* off Menelik Ave, on Ras Dista Deneten St. It stocks some imported medicines. Also pharmacy in *Hilton Hotel*.

Tour companies & travel agents The travel business has opened up dramatically since the collapse of the Mengistu régime. In addition to the state-owned National Tour Operation, there are many private tour and travel agencies offering their services. *Alfa Travels*, PO Box 4263, T511177. *Al-Tad Travels*, PO Box 1223, T513755, F515244, Tx21981. *Distance Travel Agency*, PO Box 70186, T151715, F515963. *Eastern Travel and Tourist Agency*, PO Box 1136, T511574, F511468. *East West Travel Agency*, PO Box 2020, T204245/46, F513977. *Ethio-Adam International Tour and Travel*, PO Box 3543, T518003, F510947. *Ethiopian Rift Valley Safaris*, PO Box 3658, T551127, F550298, organize fly-down safaris to the Omo Valley. Very experienced company with a river base camp and a permanent on-site 4WD. Can arrange game drives, river rafting and walking safaris. *Forship Travel Agency*, PO Box 30754, T552159, Tx21634. *Four Season Travel Agency*, PO Box 2856, T613121, F613616. *Experience Ethiopia Travel*, (EET), PO Box 9354 Churchill Ave close to the National Theatre, T152336, F519982. Recommended reputable company. Well informed about less well visited parts of the country. *Galaxi*

Rock of truth

In the 14th century, a recluse, Gabre Manfus, is said to have lived for 363 years, much of that time among his friends, the creatures of the wild on Mount Zaquella. He become Ethiopia's patron saint of animals.

On the feast of Gabre Manfus, lovers travel to Mount Zaquella. High on the mountain is a split rock. As they pass through the cleft, they know that if their love is untrue, the rock will close and crush them. Scores of followers of Gabre Manfus, hermits in flowing yellow robes, continue to live on the mountain, existing on the fruits of the forest and sleeping in caves.

A painting of Gabre Manfus, surrounded by a lion, a leopard and a raven, is in St Georges Cathedral in Addis Ababa.

Travel Services, PO Box 8309, T510875, F511236. *Gebre Admasu Travel*, PO Box 7611, T513890, F513890. *Globe Travels*, PO Box 5603, T510437, Tx21305. *Host Ethiopia Travel*, PO Box 5944, T157878, Tx21274. *Itco Tourist and Travel Agency*, PO Box 1048, T516311, F512382, Tx21131. *Kaleb Travel Agency*, PO Box 3541, T515704, F513977. *Lalibela Travel Agency*, PO Box 2590, T514403. *Luxor Travel Agency*, PO Box 30714, T515730, F517422. *Nile Touring Co*, PO Box 4090, T518238, F518238. *No 9 Tour & Travel Agency*, PO Box 26847, T129254, F553832, Tx551787, ninett@telecom.net.et. *Peers Tours and Travel Agency*, PO Box 3545, T515140, F513177. *Prime Tours*, PO Box 8542, T515529, F515099. *Safeway Travel and Tours*, PO Box 8449, T511600, F511800. *Selam International Travel and Tourist Agency*, PO Box 30208, T117444, F513950. *Sheba Travel Agency*, PO Box 3422, T513032. *Skyline Travel Agency*, PO Box 50146, T756656, F754688. *Solast Travel Agency*, PO Box 26847, T513423, F551233. *Telul Travel Agency*, PO Box 5576, T514342, F512826. *Travel Ethiopia*, PO Box 9438, T510168, F510200, travelethiopia@telecom.net.et. *Union of Nations Travel Agency*, PO Box 5261, T519550, F519550. *Yumo International Agency*, PO Box 5698, T518878, F513451.

Tourist offices *Ethiopian Tourist Commission*, on the corner of Desta Damtew St/Abiot Square, PO Box 5709, T152955. Branch in Addis Ababa *Hilton*, T158400, Tx21104, Menelik Ave. Open daily, have an excellent free brochure about Lalibela and the Simeon Mts not available in Lalibela. However, these booklets are sometimes out of print. *The Department of Natural Resources*, just off Africa Ave (the road towards Bole). Sells a range of information sheets and maps for many of the national parks, for just a nominal charge. *The Ethiopian Wildlife Society*, T517200, Rm 235 during working hours. They organize monthly visits to historical sites within easy reach of Addis Ababa.

Excursions within reach of Addis Ababa

A garden on the Debre Zeit road southeast of Addis Ababa. Get a minibus from Abiot and get off opposite a large cemetery on your left. The entrance to Bihere Tsige is off to the right and about a 15 minute walk from the bus stop – follow the tarmac. During the week it is very quiet and only the gardeners will be there. It is a marvellous place for an introduction to Ethiopian birds and several of the endemic species are present. At the weekend it is a popular place for weddings.

Bihere Tsige

An hour's journey south of Addis brings you to Debre Zeit, meaning Mount of Olives in Amharic, still known as Bishoftu by the local Oromo people, a busy commercial centre tangled under a canopy of bougainvillea, flame trees and jacarandas. Around town there are two-wheeled horse-drawn taxis called *garis*. The town is encircled by five crater lakes, characteristic of the East African Rift Valley. The principal lake, Hora, is used for watersports and is home to a stunning array of bird life. Lake Hora is two kilometres from town – follow the signposts to the *Hora Ras Hotel*, from where you can walk to the lake shore. There is also a footpath that follows the crater rim around the lake. Nearby Lake Chalaklaka is shallow and home to flamingoes. Within a five kilometre radius of Lake Hora are the other lakes – Bobogaya, Green Kuriftu and Bishoftu. The most dramatic lake, Bishoftu, is a short walk off the main highway – a sheer wall plunging down to the dark green surface. Green Lake is particularly good for birds, including flamingoes.

**Debre Zeit &
Crater Lakes**
Colour map 1, grid C3

Ethiopia

Sleeping **B** *Hora Ras Hotel*, perched on the rim of the crater beside Lake Hora, provides excellent views. **C** *Bishoftu Hotel*, near town centre, behind petrol station, fine views over Bishoftu Lake. Good value and recommended. **E** *Tourist Hotel*, close to bus stand in town.

Eating **2** *Warka Restaurant*, set in gardens with oleander and hibiscus, is a good place for a meal. It gets its name from a huge and magnificent Ficus tree, which is called Warka in Amharic. It is almost next door to the *AFH (Airforce Hotel)* and near the Telecom tower.

Transport It can be difficult to get a place on a bus going south or east as they are usually full coming from Addis Ababa. Take a bus to Mojo, where a connection can be made.

Mount Zaquella Known to local people as Mount Zuq'alla/Ziquala, this is an excursion off the main highway from Debre Zeit rises 600 metres above the plain. An ancient monastery stands on the crater rim looking down at the lake. The monastery was built in honour of Abuna Gebremenfes Kidus, or 'Abo', a hermit who lived in the vicinity for many years and reputedly made the area holy. He is regarded as a saint and is honoured every year by large crowds on the 5th of Tikemt and Megabit (October and March). The water of the lake is regarded as being holy. It is a stiff two and a half hour climb to the top, but majestic views looking south and east down the rift valley, the valley lakes glinting away in the distance, are the reward. Alternatively, it is possible to hire a local taxi to drive up. A little way beyond Debre Zeit, past the small transit town of Mojo (one petrol station, two hotels) the road crosses the Awash River. Here the hot blue waters of thermal springs gush up from the molten interior of the rift and merge with the silty waters of the Awash. Lurking crocodiles prey on the fish here, and further downstream there's a hippo pool. On through the bustling cattle town of Nazareth to the spa town of Sodere – two hours' drive from Addis and a favourite week-end resort. Here, the volcanic mineral springs constantly replenish swimming pools with clear blue, warm water. Giant shade trees cast a cool canopy around the pools and baboons, hippos and crocodiles can be seen when walking along the river bank. **Sleeping** **B** *Sodere Filwoha Resort*.

Mangasha to Ambo The Mangasha park lies only 35 kilometres west of Addis Ababa; a mountain forest sanctuary for birds and animals, and the climb through the forest to the beautiful crater valley of Wachacha is popular. The church of Debre Tsion at Addis Alem is worth a visit, and then on to Hagere Heywot (or Ambo), 125 kilometres west of Addis Ababa on the same road. The spas here are good for swimming and 26 kilometres away along a dirt track is the beautiful volcanic crater lake of Wonchi. South of Hagere Heywot (variously spelt Hagere Hiywet) is the Gefersa reservoir, a lake formed by damming the River Gefersa, which means buffalo in the local Orominya language. The reservoir, which supplies Addis Ababa, has a varied bird population of both indigenous birds and pelicans, cormorants and Egyptian geese. The peaks of two extinct volcanoes can be seen from here – Mangasha (Managasha) and Wechacha (Wonchi/Wenchi). The mountains can be reached by following a 15 kilometre winding dirt road. The mountain slopes are covered with juniper forests and are host to the black and white Colobus monkeys and the timid Menelik's bush buck and klipspringer. **Sleeping** **B** *Ras Hotel*, located at Ambo.

Blue Nile Gorge
Colour map 1, grid B2

90 minutes north from Addis a turning leads down to the ancient 13th century monastery of **Debre Libanos**, perched on the edge of a 700 metres gorge. Not long after Debre Libanos is the Blue Nile Gorge. This river begins its journey far to the north at Lake Tana, finally carving its way through a gorge that must be one of the most remarkable and breathtaking phenomena on Earth. A mile wide and almost as deep, the road winds down over 1,000 metres, a journey of over 45 minutes in a car, and at times the road actually leaps away from the side of the gorge, supported by Italian-built stanchions. A single span bridge crosses the river at the bottom before the

ascent again on the other side. Alternatively, it is possible to walk down. It is forbidden to take photos of the bridge.

The gorge is easy to access by bus from Addis Ababa, fare about US$1.50, journey time 12 hours. If necessary, it is possible to stay at the village of Dejen just north of the gorge. **C** *Tisale Hotel*, just at the entrance to Dejen. Good restaurant, keep a tame dik-dik as a pet, that likes to eat Enjera. **E** *Lake Tana Hotel* near the petrol station. Simple but satisfactory.

Ethiopia

West to Gambela

*The Nilotic peoples – Anuak and Nuer – who inhabit the lowlands around Gambela
are quite unique, as is the surrounding vegetation, landscape and climate. The western
section of the central plateau comes to an abrupt end in the province of Lullabor,
around the picturesque town of Gore, and from here the land falls away to the Nilotic
lowlands.*

Descending from the highlands, where it is forced between steep-sided gorges, the
river Baro loses momentum as it reaches the plain, spreading out to a broad river
bed. Here, the Anuak settlements are interspersed between mango and banana
plantations, while further downstream the vast grassland plains begin.

The southwest corner of Ethiopia is geographically part of the lowlands of Sudan,
and has a very different feel to it compared to the rest of Ethiopia. It is much more the
stereotypical Africa with hot and humid weather, drums at night and fireflies flickering
in the grass. The scenery too, is different. The road down the escarpment is very dramatic with passes through rugged mountains, and, when the forest stops the landscape becomes bare and harsh looking. The hills gradually flatten out into rolling
plains of tall elephant grass and occasionally swamps and forests. The people are of
Nuer or Anuak stock and look very different from the highlanders. There are also
many refugees from Sudan who have settled in the area. You will find no begging children here. Indeed the children are more likely to run away and hide at the sight of you.

The road from Addis to Jimma passes across the high plateau. The scenery is
pleasant, if not special. Look out for Wattled Cranes *(Bugeranus carunculatus)* as
you go through the Tefki marshes about one hour from Addis Ababa. The vegetation changes slowly, especially after you have crossed the spectacular Gibe River
gorge. The Jimma side of this gorge is much more like central Africa, with its red soil
and banana plantations. There are two banana-like plants to be seen. As well as the
ordinary banana plant the so-called false banana is also grown. This is superficially

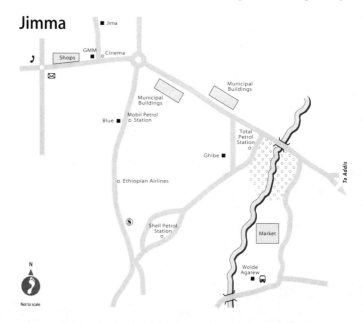

Jimma

very like the true banana, but the leaves are longer, broader and grow more upright. The leaves of the true banana curve downwards, and of course, produce the well known fruit. The false banana does not produce fruit, but the root and part of the stem are cooked and eaten. Along this western road you may notice a green leaf being spread out on the tarmac verges to dry. This is *gesho (Rhamnus prinoides)*, which is used in brewing the local beer.

Jimma (also spelt Jima) is a pleasant, fairly large town, the biggest in western Ethiopia, approximately 350 kilometres from Addis Ababa, which is sufficiently high to have a cool climate. This is the coffee growing region of Ethiopia and the villages along the road from Jimma to Gambela sell coffee beans and honey, which can be obtained quite cheaply. **Sleeping D** *Wolde Agarew Hotel*, behind the bus station, has murals on the front wall. This three-storey building gives no indication of being a hotel but is probably the best of the budgets in Jimma. Clean and has hot water, also a restaurant and bar. **E** *Blue Hotel*, blue-painted anonymous hotel opposite the Mobil petrol station is said to be the best value in town, and it therefore fills up early, is a bit run down with off-hand staff, it does not have a proper restaurant, but the cafe downstairs is good for breakfast and snacks, and here the staff are very pleasant; **E** *GMH Hotel*, has a bar at ground level with first floor lounges overlooking the bar area. Rooms are run down, there is a choice of s/c bathrooms or communal showers.

Jimma
7°40'N 36°47'E
Phone code: 7
Colour map 1, grid C2

Bonga

Ethiopia

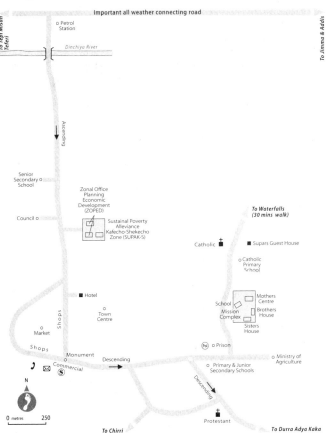

The usual price difference between residents and tourists is enforced here.

Ethiopian Airlines T07-11207/07-110030 operate a service to Jimma.

Bonga
Colour map 1, grid C2

A small town which straggles across a grassy hill top in the middle of the Bonga Forest with about 15,000 inhabitants. This lush green area of Ethiopia is in stark contrast to the arid image of Ethiopia. It rains almost every day apart from during the dry season, November to February. The forest is well worth exploring and is very reminiscent of the forests in central Africa. This area is the original home of coffee, and wild plants can be seen growing in the forest undergrowth. Bonga is not really a place to choose to spend the night as it does not have much tourist accommodation, and it is better to go on to Matu. The town contains a Post and Telecommunications office next to the Commercial Bank. In the same area there are shops and a market. Bonga also has a Zoped-Susaks (aid offices) compound, primary and secondary schools and a prison. Bonga also has both Orthodox and Norwegian-Protestant churches.
Sleeping E *Police Station Hotel*, a non-descript hotel run by a pleasant and obliging woman. The annexe is new and therefore still quite clean, with fresh paint. This is a two-building-hotel compound, separated by a small sand path.

The stretch of road from Bonga to Matu goes through Misan Teferi and Tepi. It is almost unbroken forest, with a switch back ride up and down the sides of steep, forested valleys. It is said to be a sensitive area and there are several police checkpoints, but they all seem fairly relaxed. Recent travellers report seeing no police checkpoints on recent trips.

Between Bonga and Matu there are several small villages, all of which have hotels, but none can be recommended.

From Bonga on the way to Adya Kaka-Durra on the right side of the road, there is a marvellous walk descending to a natural bridge, over a tributary of the Dynchiya River. The walk takes approximately 45 minutes. A local guide is needed to take you on to an orthodox church (which is on the left side of the main road). This walk takes you through a cool green valley inhabited by monkeys.

Misan Tefari

The best bet looks to be the **E** *Aden Hotel*, next to the town football field.

After Misan Tefari, the road changes direction, going northwest to the small town of Tepi and then north through **Goré** and on to **Matu**.

Matu
8°16'N 35°34'E
Colour map 1, grid C2

Variously spelt Mattuu, Matuu, Mettu or Metu is the capital of the province of Illubabor. The variation in the spelling of the name reflects the difficulty in agreeing a phonetic approximation of the Cushitic pronunciation. Matu has a rapidly growing population, currently estimated to number over 20,000. On Monday, Thursday and Saturday, there is a good outdoor market in town, to the right of the telecom building if coming from Gore. **E** *Hotel Biftu Gada* has good basic facilities and an attached restaurant. The **E** *Lusii Hotel* is a gem. Here you get a genuinely clean room with hot shower. The restaurant in this hotel is expensive and the food indifferent, but in town there are a number of reasonable cafés. **E** *Hotel Salaam* is also recommended. The restaurant is good, serving excellent Arosto and Tibs, with indoor

Matu

To Yayu & Bedele

Total Petrol Station

Lusii Hotel

Shops and Cafés

Telecom Tower

Telecom Building

Mobil Petrol Station

Football Field

N

Not to scale

To Gore

and outdoor seating. Prices are similar to those charged at *Lusii Hotel*. This is a particularly good one which serves delicious bread and honey for breakfast. *Restaurant Franca* is recommended. A family concern where the sons speak excellent English. Best place to eat in Matu, with a large variety of Ethiopian dishes, omelettes, salads and wonderful bread. *Restaurant Mangoo* is also recommended and is popular with residents.

Travelling southwest to **Gore** (25 kilometres) is possible by bus or taxi, where there are several hotels. There is also a flight from Addis to Gore on Thursday and Sunday, with the Thursday flights more reliable. Returning to Addis by air from Gore is fraught with difficulties, as the aircraft goes to Gambela first and give preference to the passengers bookings there. Reconfirming the flight from Gore to Addis requires great patience and persistance. The air fare (round trip) is about US$100. The bus trip costs US$6, takes two days, with an overnight stop in Jimma and is a more reliable form of transport.

Gambela

Located about 600 kilometres from Addis Ababa, Gambela has a strange history. From 1902 until it was captured by the Italians in the Second World War, it was administered by the British, the only part of Ethiopia to be so governed. The reason for this is that the British opened a port there on the wide and navigable Baro River, which during four months of the rainy season is navigable and provides direct access to the sea Nile through Khartoum. Ethiopian coffee was exported via this route, up to 1940. Now, alas, the port has fallen into disrepair, though remains of the warehouses and jetty can be seen. At its peak, up to 40 ships would be in dock at any one time.

8°14'N 34°38'E
Colour map 1, grid C1

Gambela (sometimes spelt Gambella) gives access to the **Gambela National Park**. The undulating plains of high Sudanese grass offer excellent opportunities for wilderness exploration. All the elements of African safari are found here, including elephants, lions, crocodiles and 100 kilograms Nile perch.

Beyond Gambela towards the Sudanese border, the Anuak cultivators give way to the nomadic Nuer. These pastoralists herd their long-horned cattle into huge camps when they stop for the night.

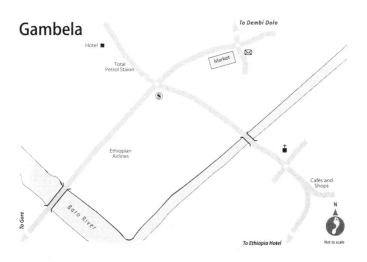

Gambela

Proverbs of Ethiopia

To lie about a far country is easy.
When you eat crow, call it pigeon.
One stone is enough against fifty clay pots.
You cannot build a house for last winter.
A good man earns more than his wages.
Even if you know many things, do not argue
with the judge.
The fool and a rich man can say what they
please.

Small boys and smoke disappear
mysteriously.
When a wise man is foolish it is a big matter.
One who proposes an exchange knows which
is the better.
After the hyena passes, the dog barks.
A hearty eater is not in love.
Who hits the father, hits the son.
Do not try to taste honey if you see it on a
thorn.

Sleeping & eating **C** *Ethiopia*, the only tourist class hotel, it is government-owned, well-kept gardens and a pleasant, shady verandah, welcoming staff. There is a restaurant and bar. It is now also possible to stay in local guest houses round the market area and the docks. Accommodation is a bit of a lottery in these establishments. There are many small eating places in these areas as well.

Transport **Air** There are 4 flights a week by **Ethiopian Airlines**, T07-510099, from Addis Ababa (Monday, Thursday, Friday, Sunday), and the fare is around US$125 return. **Road Bus** leave from the bus stand on Addis Katema St, just to the west of Merkato in Addis Ababa, the fare is around US$18 one-way, and the journey takes at least about 2 days, longer in the rainy season.

Returning to Addis Ababa on the northern loop via **Dembi Dolo** and **Gimbi** will lead on to **Nek'emte**, the capital of Welega province. It is a pretty town set among forests. The Museum has a very large collection of Oromo artefacts, including woodcarvings, leatherwork and basketware. Due south of Nek'emte is the small town of **Bedele** which connects to Matu, and has Ethiopia's newest brewery.

Transport **Road Bus** links to Addis Ababa via Bako. The scenery between Nek'emte and Hagere Heywot is dramatic, passing through forests and moorland and the highland area just before Guder. See page 694 for sights close to Hagere Heywot.

Ethiopia

East to Djibouti

Addis
Ababa

Following the Assab highway east, 225 kilometres from the capital is the spectacular **Awash National Park** *– the oldest game reserve in Ethiopia. The headquarters of the park are found near the dramatic Awash falls. One of the most beautiful areas is the Kudu valley which takes its name from the large antelopes which inhabit it. Other game includes oryx, Soemmerrings gazelle, wild pig, the tiny dik-dik antelope, zebra, hippos and big cats such as leopard and cheetah. Over 400 species of bird are found within the 700 square kilometres park.*

Another feature is the extensive area of hot springs found to the north of the park – an oasis surrounded by tall green trees amidst the dry desert scrub. The superheated water emerges into translucent turquoise pools, quickly cooling to temperatures which are ideal for swimming.

Metahara

Metahara is near Awash NP and also near Fantelle, a still occasionally active volcano. Nearby Lake Beseke is a good spot for bird watching and exploring the extraordinary volcanic larva fields. Metahara has large sugar plantations on the edge of the town. **Sleeping E** *Ergoshaa Hotel*, near the Shell petrol station, charges 20 Birr a night for a room with its own cold water shower, it is a new hotel and, therefore, at the moment fairly clean, though that may change in the near future.

The small town of **Awash** lies outside the National Park boundary, approximately 30 kilometres past Metahara. Behind the station there is a wonderful view of the Awash Gorge. **Sleeping E** *Buffet D'Auche Hotel*, pleasant French building built to service the railway, lots of faded charm, restaurant attached.

Beyond the entrance to Awash NP the tarmac ends and the road continues eastwards across the Rift Valley as a fairly good dirt road, which is very dusty in the dry weather. Towards Harar it climbs up into the eastern highlands and the landscape changes, as do the birds and plants. The acacia of the Rift changes to prickly pear, which becomes the dominant plant. The camels give way to donkeys and sorghum is more apparent as you climb.

Kulubi

Located about 200 kilometres from Awash, 10 kilometres from the junction with the road running between Harar and Dire Dawa. St Gabriel's Church is on a hilltop and is the scene of an annual pilgrimage. It is here that there was said to be divine intervention during the Italian invasion, and even today, miracles are said to occur there.

Ethiopia

Dire Dawa

Roughly half way on the Addis Ababa – Djibouti railway is Dire Dawa. It is 517 kilometres east of Addis and with a population of 98,000 has existed for less than a century. The main reason for its expansion is its position on the road and railway. The climate here is warm and dry and the atmosphere is relaxed. The market place is full of camel-herding Oromos, Somalis and Afars. The caves, just outside town, contain prehistoric rock paintings.

9°35'N 41°45'E
Phone code: 5
Colour map 1, grid B4

A popular arrangement is to take a train to Dire Dawa from Addis Ababa, and the bus back. The bus and train take different routes, with the bus trip particularly attractive through the **Arba Guga** mountains.

Dire Dawa is most useful as a point from which to explore the ancient city of **Harar**, only 54 kilometres away – a spectacular journey up the escarpment of the rift valley. The road passes lakes Adele and Alemaya, and in these rich farmlands, some of Ethiopia's finest coffee is cultivated. The local narcotic, *khat*, is also widespread here.

Recently there have been a number of attacks on travellers with some fatalities. The British Embassy in Addis has advised against travel to Eastern Ethiopia – check with your Embassy (see page 691). Caution is also urged before using the train which has been targetted by bandits.

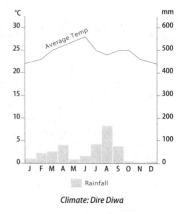

Climate: Dire Diwa

Sleeping **B** *Ras*, Government-owned, a/c, swimming pool, bar; restaurant, good standard. **C** *Karamara*, bar, restaurant, reasonably comfortable. **C** *Olympic*, bar, restaurant, adequate. **D** *Mekkonen*, pleasant terrace. **E** *Continental*, close to train station/shared bathrooms. **E** *Lyos*, basic but cheap. **E** *Tedrost*, simple, reasonable and inexpensive.

There are some cheaper local guesthouses round the station and market place. There are many small eating places in these areas as well.

Entertainment **Cinemas** There are 2 open-air cinemas in the town.

Transport **Air** Ethiopian Airways, PO Box 176, T05-111147/05-11369/05-112546/05-113317 flies daily to Dire Dawa. The cost is around US$100 return. If you are visiting other cities, there are special round-trip fares, see page 676. Taxi between Dire Dawa airport and Dire Dawa bus station costs US$1.50.

Train The trains from Addis Ababa leave daily at around 0700 and 1930, arriving in Dire Dawa approximately 12 hours later. The departure times can vary, so it is best to check locally. Journey times also vary considerably, and may be twice the time advised at Addis. Booking at the railway station at the southern end of Churchill Rd. It is necessary to make a reservation as the train is often full. The fare is US$32 1st class (a sleeper on the overnight train); US$15 2nd class; US$8 3rd class.

Road Buses leave from the bus stand on Addis Katema St, just to the west of Merkato in Addis Ababa, the fare is around US$15 one-way, and the journey takes a day, longer in the rainy season, with a stop at **Nazret**, where **C** *Plaza Hotel*, is a new hotel – "poshest place in town". **E** *Bekele Mola Hotel*, excellent value, hot showers. **E** *Canal Hotel*, clean, cold en-suite shower/bathroom. **E** *Hotel Warka*, convenient and good value.

Harar

9°20'N 42°8'E
Population: 62,000
Phone code: 5
Colour map 1, grid C4

Harar (sometimes spelt Harer), is a walled city which is the provincial capital of Harergé, stands on the eastern wall of the great rift valley and is the provincial capital of Ethiopia's largest administrative region, Hararghe. The city's lofty situation gives wonderful views of the surrounding country – the vast Danakil desert to the north, the fertile Harar mountains to the east and the cattle-rich Ogaden plains to the south.

Harar was a fiercely religious city from the early days of Islamic expansion into the Horn of Africa when it was a 'forbidden city', that is, closed to visitors, until 1887 when Menelik restored central rule. It was from here that Ahmed Gragn launched his attack on the Christian highlands in 1527, and Harar, with its 99 mosques is considered to be the fourth most holy city in Islam after Mecca, Medina and the Dome of the Rock in Jerusalem. The crowning glory is the 16th century Grand Mosque, with its beautiful twin towers and slender minaret.

In the town centre there is a church – Medhane Alem, built at the end of the 19th century which contains excellent examples of traditional religious art. Just around the corner a few metres away is the **Community Museum**, with displays relating to the way of life in earlier times. ■ *US$0.50.* On the road to the Erer Gate lies the 16th century domed tomb of Emir Nur and the al-Jami Mosque which reputedly dates from the 13th century. Women are not permitted inside the mosque.

The setting is thrilling. Medieval walls tightly embrace the ancient city, its bustling and vivid market place regarded as one of the most colourful in all Ethiopia. The market activity is great, in several parts of the old city and just ouside Shoa Gate. The afternoons are frequently even busier because the Droma traders take some time to reach the city from the surrounding countryside. The twisting alleys and flat roofed buildings are little changed from when the town was visited in the 19th century by the British explorer **Sir Richard Burton**. Off the road from the Sauga Gate to the main market lies Ras Mekonin's house, where Haile Selassie spent most of his childhood.

Next to Ras Mekonin is what is known locally as Rambo's house, reputed to be where the French poet **Rimbaud** stayed in Harar. It is two storied, with an Oriental appearance with unusual architectural features, including a frescoed ceiling reputedly painted by the poet. ■ *US$0.50.* The whole town is surrounded by soaring mountains and is fanned by cool, bracing air. The Ahmar Mountains around Harar produce some of the best coffee in Ethiopia.

Harar had a long trading history with the Middle East and India. It used to have a slave market, supplying slaves from all over East Africa, and also supplied eunuchs to harems in Arabia. The women of Harar are said to be the most beautiful in Africa.

Harar gate has three blank, whitewashed squares at the top entrance. These previously had portraits of Marx, Lenin and Engels until 1991.

One of the city's peculiarities is the so-called **Hyena Men**, who make their living by collecting offal and bones to feed to the wild hyenas outside the walls. The snarling creatures come out of the darkness just after sunset to take food from their benefactor's hands. If you go to watch there is a charge. Get a group together and expect to pay about US$22 for one to four people. This includes the taxi fare and a guide. It is very easy to walk there yourself. There is a well established group about 100 metres outside the Fallana Gate of the old city. It starts at about 1900 finishing at 2000, although most tourists find 15-20 minutes viewing is sufficient. Be aware that some locals have set up as rival 'hyena men' enticing a couple of hyenas to take their offerings. The famed hyena man is said to feed a group of up to 20 hyenas close to the Erer gate, where there is a desolate spot with a white tomb overgrown by a large tree. The show starts at 2000 and lasts up to one and a half hours.

Harar is famed for its silversmiths, and there are beautiful necklaces, bracelets and chains to be found in the market. The basketry is also impressive. There are two colourful markets in Harar, the Christian and the Muslim, which are separated from one another.

Local guides can be hired to help discover all the secrets of the town. A reasonable price is US$5 for a two to three hour tour.

French used to be more commonly spoken than English but this has changed. The locals call foreigners "Farengo", said to be a corruption of the word "French". Being on the former frontline of the war with Somalia over the Ogaden, there used to be many Cuban soldiers stationed here, so in the

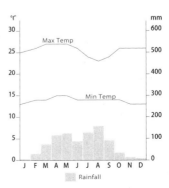

Climate: Harar

Ethiopia

late 1970s to early 1980s foreigners were called "Cuba Cuba". The locally brewed Harar beer is cheap (US$0.30) and recommended. Three different beers are brewed, one traditional, one stout and an alcohol-free malt drink.

However, recently foreign travellers have been attacked and some killed in Eastern Ethiopia. The British Embassy in Addis has advised against travelling to Harar – it is wise to check before departing (see Embassies, page 691).

Just outside Harar to the southeast is the **Valley of Marvels**. A minibus goes to **Babille Village** (also spelt Babile) (45 minutes, nice drive). From there you can pick up sparse transport to **Dakota**, five kilometres past Babille. This area to the west contains noteworthy rock formations including the remarkable Balancing Rock. Dakata is difficult to find, there is no village, no signs, no trails and no vendors. It is on the Babille – Jijiga road, which is served by an occasional bus. Alternatively, you can hire private transport from Babille – Dakata – Babille. A minibus would cost US$7.

Just outside Harar to the southeast is the **Valley of Marvels**. A minibus goes to **Babilk Village** (also spelt Babile), 45 minutes, nice drive. From there you can pick up sparse transport to **Dakata**, five kilometres past Babille. This area to the west contains noteworthy rock formations including the remarkable Balancing Rock. Dakata is difficult to find, there is no village, no signs, no trails and no vendors. It is on the Babille-Jijiga road, which is served by an occasional bus. Alternatively, you can hire private transport from Babille-Dakata-Babille. A minibus would cost US$7.

Babille Elephant Sanctuary is close by (see page 735).

Sleeping **C** *Ras*, outside the Old Town, one of the better establishments in this government-owned chain, bar, restaurant, food quite good, 15 minute walk from the Old City.

E *Academy*, main square near church. Bucket shower, squat toilets. **E** *Belayneh Hotel*, a new hotel next to the Bus Station near the Old City. Clean. Recommended. **E** *Mobil Station*, on left-hand side road into Harar from the north, an unmarked hotel next to the petrol station. Reasonably clean and own shower. **E** *Thewodras Hotel*, small bedrooms with private bathroom, friendly, clean, good restaurant, one English-speaking staff member, information on the hyena man has been unreliable in the past.

There are some small private guest houses, bars and eating places much to be recommended on grounds of atmosphere, near Feres Magala, the old horse market.

Transport Taxi within Harar (shared) US$0.15. A shared taxi or a seat in a minibus costs around US$2 from Dire Dawa and takes 1-2 hours. Minibus between Dire Dawa and Harar US$0.75. Abandoned tanks litter the roadside. Dire Dawa can be reached by train road or air, see page 690.

Harar

South: Rift Valley Lakes and Bale Mountains

The East African Rift Valley displays some of the most dramatic scenery in the world. The valley's passage through Ethiopia is marked by a string of lakes, seven in all, which dot the valley floor and are home to a fine array of flora and fauna.

Travelling southeast from Addis for 13 kilometres lies the town of **Akaki Beseka**, which is dominated by an extinct volcano Mount Zaquella (see page 694). Following along the same road 50 kilometres from Addis Ababa is the small town of **Debre Zeit**, known by the local Oromo people as Bishoftu. It is surrounded by five crater lakes (see page 693). Further south is the small town of **Nazret** (sometimes spelt Nazareth), a favoured weekend resort by residents of the capital. 20 kilometres southeast of Nazret is the resort of **Sodere** (or Sodore) which has volcanic springs which surface on the banks of the Awash River. Driving south on the main highway towards Awasa, just after Mojo a bridge spans the river Awash. At the Koka dam birds wade in the shallows, and the first lake reached is **Lake Ziway**, 160 kilometres from Addis Ababa. This is the most northern of the Rift Valley lakes of Ethiopia, 26 kilometres long and 18 kilometres wide this is the largest of the valley lakes, dotted with islands and fringed with fig trees. Birds to be seen here include black egret pelicans, marabou, ibises, herons and storks, black headed orioles, jacanas and the handsome African fish eagle. To the north, the Mekli River flows in to replenish the lake's waters, creating a wide bay where hippos gather. The island of **Tullo Guddo** is situated on Lake Ziway, clearly visible from the shoreline. According to

legend the Ark of the Covenant was taken to Tullo Guddo for safe-keeping in the ninth century by refugee priests from Axum. Most Zay people only visit the islands for religious ceremonies. An active monastery Debre Zion lies on the highest peak. **E** *Bekele Mola Hotel*, north of Lake Ziway at Langano. It is sited near the lake behind the Agip Garage. There is reasonable food available. *Wabe Shebele Hotel (Restaurant)* has better food than the *Bekele Mola*. However, there is no public transport for the 15 kilometres journey.

If you take the secondary road, going southwest via Sebeta and Butajira on the road that links Addis to Ziway, it is worth visiting **Tiya** archaeological site where there are engraved stelae. The stones are believed to mark mass graves, possibly of soldiers. There are about 40 stelae, mostly upright, up to two metres in height. ■ *US$1.50*. There are some local restaurants. Tiya is about 30 kilometres south of Melka Awash, and the stelae field is about 500 metres out ot town to the east, near the telecommunications signpost.

Ethiopia

Ethiopia

Rastafarians

The mixture of embattled Christianity in an unconquered independent African has for long been an appealing image to black people in the Caribbean, and as early as 1784 the Ethiopian Baptist Church was established in Jamaica. The defeat of the Italians at Adowa in 1896 by Emperor Menelik II was a particularly inspiring event.

The Rastafarian movement was founded by Leonard Howell, a Jamaican who had travelled to West Africa and fought with the Ashanti against the British. The focus was Ras Tafari, the eldest son of Ras Makonnen, Duke of Harar, who in 1930 became Emperor Haile Selassie of Ethiopia.

Now back in Kingston, Leonard interpreted the Book of Revelations to prophesize the advent of Haile Selassie, and sold pictures of the Emperor as passports to Ethiopia. At a rally in 1933 he announced the six principles of the Rastafarian: black supremacy; hatred of whites; revenge on the whites; the overthrow of the constitution of Jamaica; the goal of a return to Africa; the recognition of Haile Selassie as the Supreme Being and the only ruler of black people. Howell was arrested and jailed. On his release he set up the Ethiopian Salvation Society in the hills in a community called Pinnacle, where he lived with his 13 wives. His followers cultivated bananas and ganja (marijuana), and grew their hair into dreadlocks, symbolizing defiance of white authority. Pinnacle was raided periodically and the community broken up, only for it to reform again later. In 1960, Howell died in Kingston Mental Hospital.

In **Godeti** there is a wonderful view of the Awash River from the bridge. The Awash River gorge has a series of three waterfalls, with deep swirling base pools. It is no longer possible to visit the **Melka Kuntumé** archaeological site near Godeti. 25 kilometres south of Butajira, there is another stelae field at **Silje** with intricately carved stones. Silje is on the road to Hosaina and also has a beautiful crater lake.

Lake Langano

Colour map 1, grid C3 Before you reach the lake, there are the ruins of an old fortress, towering over the village of Adami Tulu. Langano itself is a very popular resort – 210 kilometres from the capital and set against the beautiful Arsi mountains. There is a wide choice of hotel and camping accommodation and the lake is good for swimming and watersports.

Sleeping **A** *Langano Resorts*, on shores of lake, pleasing location, has bungalows which accommodate 4 persons costing between US$35-US$50, bar, restaurant. **B** *Bekele Mola*, on Lake Langano. **D** *Ghike Guest House*, self-catering, on the shores of nearby Lake Shala, close to the Ghike hot spring. **Camping** Available at *Bekele Mola Hotel* and at 2 sites on nearby Lake Shala, just south of the park HQ at Dole.

Lakes Abyata and Shala

Colour map 1, grid C3 Not far from Langano, situated in the heart of the Rift Valley National Park (sometimes called the Abyata or Abijata – Shala or Shalla National Park), are lakes Abyata and Shala. Abyata is a bird paradise. A soda lake, it has vast expanses of white shoreline and its surface is a carpet of pink flamingoes. Also resident are fish eagles, herons, cormorants and storks, spoonbills and ibises and numerous species of duck. During the Northern winter, the lake becomes home to thousands of migrant European birds. Shala is a pristine wilderness, surrounded by an aura of almost primeval splendour. It is also an important breeding ground for the birds and is well known for its colony of great white pelicans. ■ *US$7 per person, US$1.50 per car.*

There is a very good road between Shashamene and Arba Minch, much better than the Addis – Shashamene road. After Arba Minch there are no good roads, making travel almost impossible in the rainy season.

Beyond the town of **Shashamene** E *Bekele Mola Hotel*, good basic hotel, restaurant. E *Hotel Keenyaa*, comfortable, water but no showers. E *Hotel Zariaayi Darasi*, pleasant rooms, water but no showers, there is a beautiful wooded valley of ancient indigenous trees. In the valley is a lodge at **Wendo Gennet** (or Genet), 20 kilometres south of Shashamene, with natural hot springs. There are two pools for swimming, the shallower one is known as 'Haile Selassie' who was of modest stature. There are changing cabins and showers. ■ *US$0.50. Entrance free if staying at the Wabe Shebelle Group Hotel, you're allowed to camp in the grounds, hot pools open until 2100.* To the southeast of Shashamene the scenery is magnificent even before you reach Bale Mountain National Park. The town of **Goba** is the largest in this area and has good facilities and is an excellent base to explore this area. 20 kilometres west of Shashamene near the village of **Aje**, where you take the road to the right, is **Lake Chitu** (not signposted). Hot springs and flamingoes are found in this beautiful and peaceful place. Just north of Shashamene is **Jamaica**, a community of Rastafarians from the Caribbean (see Box, page 706). Close by to the southwest is **Lake Awasa**, generally considered the most beautiful of the valley lakes. A gentle chain of mountains and a low plateau surround the waters, opening to a wide bay in the south. The local fish is a speciality. The small town of **Awasa** is on the main north/south route from Kenya. There is a raised footpath which begins about one kilometre north of the *Wabe Shebelle* hotel, which follows the lake shore south and is the best way of exploring the area.

Sleeping B *Awasa Resort*, on lake, excellent location but very run down. B *Wabe Shebelle*, close to Wendo Gennet. Good restaurant, overpriced, poor maintenance. There is a **Tourist Office** close to the hotel entrance, with helpful staff. D *Koko*, on main road next to Awesh Bank. Good value, hot water all day. E *Kobeb Hotel*, clean, quiet, with s/c rooms. E *Unique Park*, Awasa, near the lake. Clean and cheap.

Eating *Pinna Pastry and Restaurant*, Awasa in the high street, PO Box 52, Awasa, T201231. Good food and juices, brand new 2-storey café, efficient service.

Dila Small town on the main north/south route from Kenya. E *Audinet*, cheap basic accommodation, has a popular bar, ask local directions. The bus northwards (including Addis Ababa) leaves from the bus station at around 0600. Journey to Addis takes 10 hours, cost US$3.50, passes through beautiful countryside.

Lakes Abaya and Chamo

The two southernmost lakes of the chain, Abaya and Chamo, are quite remote and demand a trip of several days. There is, however, rich wildlife, lush vegetation and hordes of hippos and crocodiles. One spot on the western shores of lake Chamo is referred to locally as 'crocodile market' because of the many crocodiles that congregate there. Boat trips on Lake Chamo cost US$43, taking two hours for five people. **Necht Sar** (also spelt Nechichar and Necleser) National Park encompasses the eastern shores of these lakes – a sanctuary for Swaynes hartebeest, an endangered animal unique to Ethiopia. The roads are difficult to drive on during the rainy season. Zebras, baboons, crocodiles, turtles and a great variety of birdlife are easy to spot. ■ *US$7 per person and US$1.50 per car.*

On the bluff between the two lakes is the town of **Arba Minch**, a good base from which to explore the area. To see the 'Crocodile Market' you have to rent a boat. This can be arranged at Bekele Mola. The boat costs US$50 and takes approximately two hours for the round trip. It is recommended that you get a list of the local market days for the area whilst in Arba Minch.

6°30'N 37°50'E
Colour map 1, grid C3

Ethiopia

Sleeping **D** *Bekele Mola* (or Molla), this is stylish and pleasantly located with good views of both lakes from the restaurant terrace, though a little delapidated, boat trips can be organized from here. **E** *Abaya*, located in Arba Minch town, good value and often full. Serves excellent fish – Asa cutlet, reported to be better prepared, tastier than elsewhere in Arba Minch. **E** *Zawuke Hotel*, very simple hotel, mosquito nets, not very clean. *Roza's Restaurant* in the same street as the Abay is also recommended for its Asa Kutilet – fish fried in batter with a hot spicy dip. Roza's also cook a range of good cheap local foods. **Camping** Available at a pleasant site in the Netch Sar National Park, on the Kulfi River.

Transport **Air** Ethiopian Airlines flies to Arba Minch on Thursday and Saturday. The fare is around US$70 return. **Road** **Bus** buses run regularly from Addis Ababa to Arba Minch. **Car hire** is available. A four-wheel drive costs US$100-US$200 per day. Trucks go at 0500 from the Agip petrol station at Roza's (Shecha end of town), sun protection is advisable. **Konso** has a great market, with very friendly people. Slaughtering is observed with the blood being drunk out of pumpkins. Trucks go from there (plenty of accommodation at around US$3 a room, no water. **E** *Saint Mery Hotel* is the most acceptable and vast new extension is under construction) to **Kayaffer** and **Jinka**. You can also camp at the Norwegian Mission. You can fly to Jinka from Addis 3 times a week, cost US$50. Jinka's airport is the soccer field. **Jinka** a town which is about 200 kilometres by road from Arba Minch, is the gateway to the Omo area. The drive takes about 8 hours, passing through the town of Konso and the Woita River Valley. Here you may see crocodiles and baboons. Onwards transport from Jinka is limited to hitching. The Natural Resources office in Jinka can recommend safe camping areas.

From Jinka you can go down to **Dimeka**, where on market days you can see the **Hamar** people, only partly dressed with very interesting hair styles and goat skins. They are very friendly, in marked contrast to the **Mursi**. The Mursi are famous for the clay lip plates and ear lobe decorations of the women. The menfolk cut deep incisions in their arms to show how many of the enemy they have killed. The Mursi have a reputation of being very aggressive and caution is advisable in their company.

Omo National Park

6°25'N 36°10'E
Colour map 2, grid B3

Further to the southeast is the remote and little visited Omo National Park. Virtually free from human habitation, except along the banks of the river Omo, this is the largest park in the country – 3,450 square kilometres – an area of true wilderness. Zebra, oryx, elephants, buffalo, giraffes, lions, leopards and cheetahs roam this park in huge numbers. The valley is also rich in fossils, the latest hominid remains to be discovered date back over four million years. Access to the park can be made by bus through Arba Minch, Konso and Jinka. Places to stay in Jinka are **E** *Arit*, **E** *Omo*, **E** *Amaluk*, all having restaurants but no hot water.

White water rafting An American company, *Sobek*, (named after the crocodile god of the Nile) runs trips each year by raft on the **Omo River**. The season is September and October when the river is in flood from the June-September rains. The expeditions commence where the Gibe Bridge on the Addis Ababa to Jimma road crosses the Omo, and finish in the Omo National Park (see main map page 730). The trip covers 600 kilometres of river and takes three weeks. The rapids are brisk (rated at three to four), but not as violent as some in Africa. The party returns to Addis Ababa by air from a local strip. *Sobek* also run one and two-day trips on the **Awash River** east of Addis Ababa. Contact *Ethiopia Experience*, PO Box 9354, Addis Ababa, T519291, F519982. *Adrift* also organize rafting trips on the

Awasa

Boat hire

Unique Park

Kobeb

Pinna

Lake Awasa

upper and lower reaches of the River Omo. Prices can be negotiated as all-in packages from the UK or USA or locally for just the river run. Local river run costs for the Upper Omo are US$400, the Lower Omo US$400 or the African Queen US$450 for the combined trip. See page 689 for details of how to contact Adrift. Guided trips to the Omo region are better arranged as an organized safari. *Ethiopian Rift Valley Safaris* PO Box 3658, Addis Ababa, T551127, F550298 are expensive but well recommended. This company has a permanent camp on the banks of the Omo River, and has many years of experience in this region.

Air There are flights to Arba Minch. T06-810649.

Transport

Road Bus there are regular buses running along this route from Addis Ababa, going via Jinka. Four-wheel drive Landcruisers can be hired US$200 a day from *Bob Travel*, Jinka, although travellers have reported that it is possible to hire a battered four-wheel drive locally for US$100 per day.

Small town 30 kilometres before Dila on road to Addis Ababa, has new hotel (unnamed), clean, friendly, hot showers, bar, restaurant and safe parking.

Virga Chefe

Moyale

Southern town adjacent to the Kenyan border on the National north/south road. Border crossings have been simplified since Immigration and Customs now share a building, provided you have a visa. All money must be declared on entry and receipts have to be shown on exit. Petrol and diesel available here.

3°30'N 39°0'E
Colour map 2, grid B4

Ethiopia

Kenyan side of the border closes at 1600. The Ethiopian border is closed all day Sunday, and public and religious holidays.

The bus going north to Addis Ababa leaves at around 0500, so it is not possible to leave Moyale by bus on the day of entry. The bus northwards leaves from *Brothers Hotel* courtyard.

D *Port Hotel*, close to border checkpoint. Clean, self-contained rooms. **D** *Ysosadoyo Borena Moyale Hotel*, T93, close to the border checkpoint, located on the main road north to Addis Ababa, opposite the commercial bank and petrol station. Good value, friendly, clean, hot showers, good restaurant and safe parking. Well recommended. **E** *Abraham Hotel*, close to the bus station, on the main road. Basic, reasonable, standard. **E** *Brothers Hotel*, on the main road. Clean single rooms, showers and toilets en-suite in some of the rooms. **E** *Tewodros Hotel*, clean s/c rooms, has bar and restaurant, friendly. The disadvantage is that it is a long walk along the main road, 1500 metres uphill from the border crossing.

Sleeping

The bus journey to Addis Ababa takes 2 days from Moyale which is now served by a new sealed tarmac road. On the first day it goes to Dila for an overnight stop – journey time 11 hours, cost US$5. Alternatively some buses stop overnight at Shashamene US$6 Moyale-Shashamene. The bus leaves the bus station at 0600, you need to arrive no later than 0500.

Transport

Addis
Ababa

North to Tigray

*The area to the north of Ethiopia contains some of the most most interesting historical sites, including the ancients cities of **Gondar** and **Axum** as well as the site of the extraordinary **rock-hewn churches** at Lalibela. Lake Tana has the spectacular **Tisissat Falls** on the Blue Nile, and between Gondar and Axum is the **Simien National Park**. Addis Ababa is in the geographical centre of the country and roads connect it to all the regions. The roads to the north, the historic route, lead to the marvels of Ethiopia's heritage. Two roads branch out from Addis, the road to Gondar going due north to Fiche and then continuing northwesterly through Debre Markos to Bahir Dar, Gondar, Debark and on to Axum. The other road to the north travels initially in a northeasterly direction to Debre Birhan, Debra Sina and then due north to Dessie/Dese, Weldiya, Makale and northwards to Adigrat. The historic route is a circuit using both these roads.*

Fiche & Debre Libanos The northern route leads to the beginning of the great gorges of the Blue Nile. **Fiche**, 103 kilometres north of Addis Ababa, is an unremarkable town, but is of interest to travellers because it is the closest town, 15 kilometres north, to the important religious centre comprised of the church and monastery of **Debre Libanos**. The monastery was established by the 13th century Ethiopian saint Abuna Tekle Haimanot. The church was built in the 1950s, adjacent to the monastery, and from the mountain wells above it a number of springs bubble out. These springs are believed to have miraculous curative properties, and people travel from all over Ethiopia to bathe in them.

Sleeping D *The Alem Hotel*, on the main Debre Markos Rd, just north of the junction. Probably the best hotel in this area. The owner is very helpful and informative about buses/vehicles heading north. There are also several small hotels in Fiche itself, 3 kilometres away to the east.

After returning to the main road, and driving on a rocky track on the opposite side there is a 16th century bridge known as the '**Portuguese Bridge'**, which is still in use by the local people.

Continuing on the main road leads to the **Blue Nile Gorge**, one kilometre deep, with stunning scenery. The road was built by the Italians, supported by several viaducts and is an amazing engineering feat, absolutely terrifying at times. At the bottom there is a modern bridge spanning the Blue Nile.

Dejen Dejen a small town north of the gorge has cheap hotels and is close enough to enable you to explore the area. However this option is less attractive because of the persistent hassling of tourists by the local vociferous youths.

A few kilometres north of Dejan the road divides into the direct route to Bahir Dar and the more circuitous route to the same destination via the regional capital of Gojam, **Debre Markos**. It has a pleasantly laid out town centre, and has a more comfortable climate associated with its altitude. Debre Markos makes a convenient break on the long bus journey between Addis and Bahar Dar. **E** *Abah Hotel*, clean comfortable hotel, hot showers. **E** *Mari Zenib Hotel* has large upstairs rooms, cold showers. **E** *Tourist Hotel* close to the bus stop offers reasonable basic accommodation.

Ethiopia

Bahar Dar

Travelling north about 300 kilometres from the Blue Nile Gorge you come to the town of Bahar Dar, sometimes spelt Bahir Dar, population 54,000, situated at the southern end of **Lake Tana** (3,700 square kilometres). The Tana area is the traditional homelands of the Christian Amhara people, whose language was the national dialect of Ethiopia for many years. The southeast corner of the lake is the source of the Blue Nile. Hippos and crocodiles are often visible from the bridge which spans the river. Lake Tana contains many islands which house very old churches and monasteries, containing religious frescoes and artefacts. Many of the churches are closed to women. This exclusion is said to date from the ninth century when an evil Jewish/Falasha Queen Judit reigned over the Axumite Kingdom. Boat trips to visit the three monasteries Debre, Naryam and Pake take half a day and cost US$25, with a US$2 entry fee to the monasteries. A feature of Lake Tana is the papyrus tankwa (boats) that can be seen on the shore. They are made from papyrus leaves bound together, and have been in use since time immemorial. These papyrus boats resemble the boats of Ancient Egypt. Bahar Dar is the centre from which to explore the spectacular **Tisissat Falls** – more frequently called Tis Abay by the locals – the largest waterfall on the Blue Nile River – which drains the lake just to the north. The falls are 30 kilometres south of the town and are reached on foot from the nearby village Tis Abay, 'Smoke of the Nile'. There are excellent views if you continue walking 20 minutes past the main viewpoint, then cross a small river which takes you to the base

11°37'N 37°10'E
Colour map 1, grid B2

Ethiopia

Bahar Dar

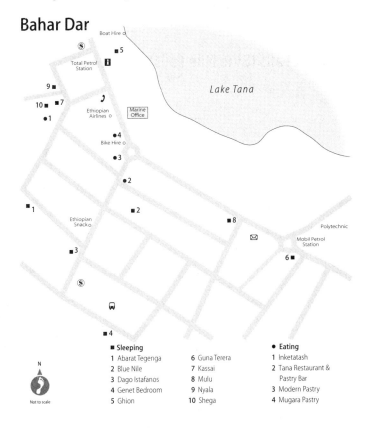

Lake Tana

■ Sleeping
1 Abarat Tegenga	6 Guna Terera
2 Blue Nile	7 Kassai
3 Dago Istafanos	8 Mulu
4 Genet Bedroom	9 Nyala
5 Ghion	10 Shega

● Eating
1 Inketatash
2 Tana Restaurant & Pastry Bar
3 Modern Pastry
4 Mugara Pastry

N

Not to scale

on the right side of the falls. There are great rainbows in the morning but the site is wet and muddy. Visitors will be offered trips to the falls by car, with guides, or in a papyrus boat, all of which are quite expensive compared with the local bus from Bahar Dar. The public bus leaves every morning at about 0600 from the station, but may also leave later at 0900, 1200 or 1500 or whenever it 'fills up'. It has the great advantage of being cheap, US$0.40. It takes about an hour to get to the drop-off village, where you buy an entrance ticket. A guide costs US$1. Any number of young boys will offer to guide you there, but are not really necessary. However these boys are very persistent and can be a nuisance – if you don't want one make this clear, if you do fix the price at the start. The most direct route, a 30 minute walk, is to proceed to the end of the village, turning right 50 metres before the gate to the power station. Then take the path to the left toward the river, over the old Portuguese 17th century bridge, reputedly built from lime, eggs and milk. Turn left after the bridge; there are two viewpoints opposite the falls which offer a dramatic panorama. It is possible to follow the path all around so that you arrive at the bottom of the falls, where there is a pool you can swim in, or you can shower in the spray. Everywhere you walk you are standing in your own rainbow! An alternative route involves a boat crossing for US$1 per person. Falls best in September after the heavy rains. ■ *Entrance to falls is US$2.50, US$1 student concession. Check the return times for the bus before setting off as it fills up quickly. You are advised to allow a full day to view the Tisissat Falls because of the vagaries of the transport links. If you wish to do the trip in half a day take the 0600 bus to the falls and the 1100 bus back to Bahar Dar. Alternatively, hire a bicycle to get to the Falls.*

In Bahar Dar is **St George's Church**. In the church compound is a two-storey building constructed by Pero Paes (see box below, page 714).

Tisissat Falls (Blue Nile Falls)

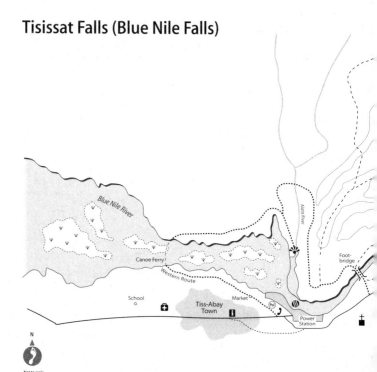

The monastery of **Dek Stefanos** at Bahar Dar holds a priceless collection of icons and manuscripts and houses the mummified remains of a number of Ethiopian emperors. There are monasteries on many of the numerous islands which dot the southern end of the lake, most dating from the 14th century. The most accessible from Bahar Dar are **Kebran Gabriel** (still forbidden to women) and **Ura Kidanemereth** on the Zegie peninsula which is famous for its frescoes which women are permitted to visit.

Boats to islands to see the monasteries vary between US$23 and US$35 per person in a government boat. It is cheaper to rent a private boat – haggle with the owner. Expect to pay 150-200 Birr for the trip (US$23-31). A trip to the closest island, which has a (non-famous) monastery will cost about US$12. The entrance fees to the monasteries are about US$2.50. Allow plenty of time to cope with the vagaries of local time keeping. **Haile Selassie Palace** is located 10 kilometres from Bahar Dar, with good views of Lake Tana. The Palace is currently closed to visitors, but can be viewed from the outside. It is possible to hire bicycles at US$1.50 per hour – ask at hotel, or see map. Taxi will cost approximately US$8. There is a steep hill on the approach to the Palace, but you gain on the return bike trip.

Every Saturday there is a busy market near the bus station. There's lots to buy including 'shammas', rugs, jewellery, honey. There are many other bars and brothels in the vicinity.

A *Tana*, on shores of lake. Good standard, pleasant location, excellent food.

Sleeping

Ethiopia

B-D *Ghion*, town centre, 5 minutes from market and pier. Camping available at US$6 per tent, including the use of one of the hotel bathrooms. Safe car and bike parking. Has an excellent restaurant overlooking the lake. Nice grounds right on Lake Tana shore. Flexible prices, open to negotiation, rooms a bit shabby. Ghion Hotel arranges boat trips to 3 monasteries Kebran, Gabriel and one in the Blue Nile Delta for US$11 per person. Good chance of seeing hippos, especially at dusk when they come up out of the water to graze.

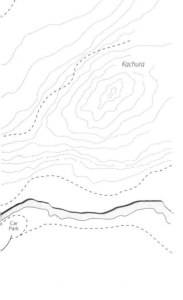

E *The Aksum*, located just past the Telecommunications Office and roundabout on the main street. Has squat toilets, cold showers and a restaurant/bar. **E** *Blue Nile Springs Hotel*, on the Gondar Rd next to a petrol station approximately 1 kilometre past the *Tana Hotel*. Attractive grounds, lake views but no access, large comfortable self-contained rooms, no restaurant, hot water. **E** *Dago Istafanos Hotel*, near the bus station. Rooms with private showers, excellent value, very popular, no mosquito nets, intermittent water supply. **E** *Genet*, behind bus stand. Often full, shared bathrooms, clean and friendly. **E** *Mulu Hotel*, not well maintained, rooms grubby, toilets dirty, plumbing unreliable, shared shower, central situation on the corner of the main road. **E** *Pension Betel*, basic, clean and cheap, will provide a bucket of hot water. **E** *Tekla Hotel*, next street to the Commercial Bank of Ethiopia (under construction). Has a pleasant central courtyard, hot water, very basic toilets. **E** *Zenbaba*, main street. Shared bathroom.

Kachura

Car Park

········ Footpath to the falls

Source of the Blue Nile

The first European to visit the source of the Blue Nile was a Spanish Jesuit, Pero Paes in 1618. He was part of an expedition seeking to convert Ethiopia to Catholicism, and was travelling with Emperor Susneyos. Two springs at Gish 130 kilometres south of Lake Tana were identified as the start of the great river. They come together to form a stream Tinash Abbay (Little Nile) which flows into Lake Tana.

A Portuguese Jesuit, Jeronimo Lobo visited the springs shortly after and gave a description of Tisissat Falls ('Smokefire Falls'). He also described the single arch bridge at Alata over the Blue Nile (the Abbay), which was commissioned by Emperor Susneyos, and constructed by an Indian mason, Abdel Kerim.

The explorer who did most to publicize the Blue Nile and its origin was James Bruce, a Scotsman, who landed a Massawa 1769.

After an extensive expedition he reached the source springs a year later. He also visited Tisissat Falls, and disputed Lobo's observation that it was possible to walk behind the cascading water. James Bruce become known for his exploits as 'Bruce of Abyssinia' and his exploits are described in his five-volume Travels to Discover the Source of the Nile written in 1770. In it he describes the Tisissat Falls: "The River had been considerably increased by the rains, and fell in one sheet of water, without any interval, about half an English mile in breadth, with a force and noise that was truly terrible, and which stunned and made me, for a time, perfectly dizzy. A thick fume or haze, covered the fall all around, and hung over the course of the stream both above and below. It was one of the most magnificent, stupendous sights in creation."

There are several cheap hotels in Bahar Dar near the bus station (**E** grade), cheap food, from cafés or street vendors, can also be bought in this area. It is almost impossible to change money at the weekend as bank receipts are needed for the authorities.

Eating **3** *Inkutatash Restaurant*, located behind the Telecom Building. Slightly more expensive than the other restaurants, generous portions. Excellent fish for US$1.50.

1 *Bamboo*, next to the *Mulu Hotel*. Very cheap, does excellent fish cutlet. **1** *The Central Snack and Pastry Bar*, next to the bus station, T201782/200214. Managed by Said, serves good juices, cakes and eggs, spicy egg sills recommended for breakfast. **1** *Ethiopian Snack*. Recommended for breakfast and lunch. **1** *Tama Restaurant and Pastry Bar*, cheap tasty local foods. **1** *Zambara Restaurant*, best fish cutlet in town, fish curry (spicy), njera with meat, friendly and reasonably priced, ask any of the local boy guides to bring you here.

Transport **Air** Ethiopian Airways, T08-200020/08-200948 flies daily to Bahar Dar. The cost is around US$75 return. Departure tax US$1. If you are visiting other cities, there are special round-trip fares, see page 676. Taxi from airport is around US$6.

Road The bus station opens at 0600. Watch your bag – in the scramble to get a seat travellers' property has been stolen. It may be worth hiring a kid to run on board to claim a seat (1-2 birr tip) while you supervise your luggage being loaded on top of the bus. Route is via Debre Markos and the whole journey is 400 kilometres. Travel is difficult in June-September when the rains are heavy. It is realistic to allow 2 days for the journey there, with a stop in Debre Markos or Dejen, where **E** *Lake Tana*, near the petrol station, is an acceptable stopover, and allows a visit to the Blue Nile Gorge (see page 694). There are regular buses running along this route, fare US$6 from Addis Ababa. An alternative route from Addis is on the Mota Rd which is 35 kilometres shorter, allowing you to visit the Tisissat Falls before reaching Bahar Dar. **Bike hire**: US$0.75 to US$2 per hour, depending on your bartering skills, from in front of the Ghion Hotel. Rough road to Haile Selassie Palace but worth it. Allow 1 hour each way for the ride.

....

A leper in the scales of justice

Balaya Sab was a cannibal, whose lifetime sustenance comprised 69 souls. One day, however, out seeking a snack, he came across a leper. Considering the item well past its sell-by date, Balaya Sab declined him as a repast, gave him some water, and carried on foraging.

When Balaya Sab died, things did not look to promising as St George stacked up the 69 two-footed take-aways in one pan of the scales of justice. But when the Virgin Mary tossed the spared leper, to whom Balaya Sab had extended the merest morsel of kindness in the form of a sup of water, into the other pan, such was the power of human kindness in the final reckoning that it outweighed the 69 sins and Balaya Sab was allowed to enter paradise.

There is a fresco of Balaya Sab in the Church of Debra Kota Mariam on Dek Island in Lake Tana.

....

Gondar

Gondar is 2,200 metres above sea level. The name is variously spelt Gondar, Gonder and Gondor. 50 kilometres north of Lake Tana, 500 kilometres north of Addis Ababa and nestling in the foothills of Simien mountains is the ancient city of Gondar, population 64,000, undoubtedly one of the most thrilling experiences that Ethiopia has to offer with its churches, castles and mountain scenery. Gondar was the capital of Ethiopia from the rise of Fasilades (1632-35) to the fall of Tewodros (1855-68), a status that is reflected in the many castles and palaces which grace the city. At first site the architecture seems to reflect Moorish-European influence, and indeed, the presence of the Portuguese in the 16th century may have influenced the design of some of the fortresses. But closer inspection reveals a continuity with the Axumite tradition. The city's main imperial precinct, known as the **Royal Enclosure**, covers an area of 7.6 hectares and contains five castles, raised walkways and connecting tunnels surrounded by high stone walls. The oldest of these is the **Castle of Fasilades**. Built of stone in the mid-17th century it reflects a number of influences, Axumite, Portuguese and Indian. The walls downstairs are decorated with a symbol which resembles the Star of David, later to become the Royal Ethiopian emblem. The upper storey offers panoramic views and Lake Tana is visible on a clear day. The castle has been having renovation work carried out recently, and has been temporarily closed to visitors. Fasilades' grandson, Iyasu the Great, who was considered one of Gondar's greatest leaders, built his own fantastic castle and decorated it with ivory, gold and precious stones. An earthquake in the early 19th century caused damage, a problem compounded by British bombing during the Second World War of the wartime Italian headquarters based in the Royal Enclosures. ■ *Entrance to the Royal Enclosure and the Bath of Fasilades (bring your ticket with you) is US$9. No student discount. Video recorder charge US$11.50.*

Other than the castles there is the **Palace of Ras Beit**, built in the 18th century as a private residence of the the famous king maker, Ras Mikael Sehul – and in continuous occupation ever since. Two kilometres distance away is the impressive **Bath of Fasilades**. The sunken pool is still in use for the Timkat Festival in January. Overlooking the pool there is a two-storey building, which is believed to have been Fasilades' second residence.

12°39'N 37°30'E
Altitude: 2,200 metres
Phone code: 8
Colour map 1, grid B2

Ethiopia

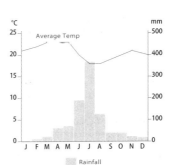

Climate: Gondar

The **Church of Debre Birhan Selassie** stands on raised ground to the northeast of the city. Built during the reign of Iyasu the Great, it is well preserved, its ceiling and interior walls being beautifully decorated with colourful religious paintings by the 17th century artist Haile Meskel. Reputed to be the most famous church ceiling in Ethiopia. No flash photos are allowed. You are permitted to photograph it using a tripod and fast film. ■ *US$2.50, US$1.50 student concession, guide recommended to enhance the visit to this church built in 1682. Go early while prayers are being recited. The priests are very welcoming.*

Quouquaim Church. Outside the city in the direction of the airport, this lovely church is situated on a hill. Great views. Very nice walk. ■ *US$3.*

Many Ethiopians claim that Gondar is the most famous place for the Timkat Festival (see box on page 680).

Excursions **Falasha Village** Four kilometres north from the centre on the Debark Rd. Almost all Falash (Ethiopian Jews) residents have been airlifted to Israel now, but this village prides itself on being the centre of Ethiopian Jewry. There are reports that only three Falasha individuals remain in all Ethiopia. The village contains three former synagogues, which are used for other purposes now. Small figurines of King Soloman and Queen of Sheba are on sale. Taxi to Falasha and back costs US$4.50.

Sleeping
Overall it is fairly basic.

B *Goha*, c/o Ethiopian Hotels and Spaas Corporation (EHC), PO Box 1263, Addis Ababa, T0811-0364, Tx21112, fine location on rise on the edge of town. Good standard food. Probably the best accommodation in town. **C** *Quara*, close to centre of town, in the Piazza.

D *Fagera Hotel*, basic, originally built by one of Mussolini's fascists as a villa, spacious rooms. **D** *Misrak Pension*, Woreda 1, Kebeale 2, No 217, PO Box 391, T8110069. Very clean, nice garden, quiet, just a 5-minute walk from the Post Office. Recommended. **D** *Nile Hotel*, close to the Ethiopia Hotel. Has constant hot water, a good restaurant and a pleasant terrace bar. **D** *Tarara Hotel*, Italian built, spacious gardens adjacent to the Imperial precinct. Friendly helpful staff, good laundry service.

E *Abba Jelli Hotel*, clean, good value with views of the castles. **E** *Ethiopia*, erratic water supply, but close by is a public shower with hot water and soap, popular with travellers. **E** *Fasilades*, on the airport road. Clean and friendly, safe parking for vehicles and a good restaurant. **E** *Patrice Lumumba*, close to the piazza/telecommunications bldg (near the *Misrak*), the sign is in Amharic. You can barter over the price of the hotel, restaurant attached. **E** *Yimam*, good value and with a restaurant next door. Also has safe parking facility for vehicles. There are many other **E** grade range hotels in the vicinity of the piazza/telecom buildings.

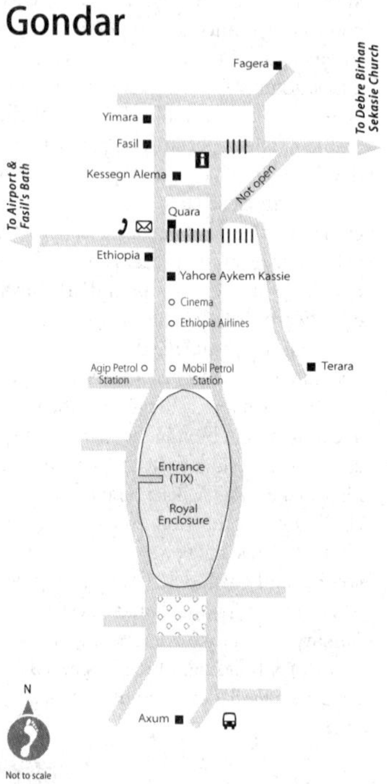

Eating *Quara Hotel*, government run hotel with restaurant. Good value. *Tele Club*, next to the stairs of the Post Office – coffee, bread, excellent breakfasts. *Ethiopia Café*, charming, old fashioned, ground floor of hotel, packed all day, excellent coffee. There are many other cheap cafés in the city centre. Many of the cheap hotels also offer food.

Gondar

Map labels: To Airport & Fasil's Bath, Fagera, To Debre Birhan Sekasie Church, Yimara, Fasil, Not open, Kessegn Alema, Quara, Ethiopia, Yahore Aykem Kassie, Cinema, Ethiopia Airlines, Agip Petrol Station, Mobil Petrol Station, Terara, Entrance (TIX), Royal Enclosure, N, Axum, Not to scale

The legend of Gondar

Archangel Raguel revealed to Emperor Lebna Dengel in a dream that Ethiopia would be blessed with a sacred capital, and that the name of the location would begin with the letter 'G'.

Nothing daunted, successive Emperors began and worked their way doggedly down a list of places with names beginning with the designated consonant, dragging their entourage of 50,000 or so courtiers and

camp-followers from site to site. Here and there they started some tentative civic construction, but never managed to establish anything that endured. Until, that is, Emperor Fasilades, hunting in the mid-17th century, stood to drink at a lake. As he raised his eyes, he saw a holy man rise out of the waters. Fasilades was advised that he was in the paradise of Ezra and Enoch, and he was commanded to build his capital right there, at Gondar.

There is a great pastry shop across the street from the Post Office near the *Quara Hotel*. **The Mintaub**, a small restaurant tucked away behind the palaces. Recommended.

Fresh fruit is mainly available in Gondar in the mornings. However fruit is virtually unavailable in Debark.

Air Ethiopian Airways, PO Box 130, T08-110129, flies daily to Gondar. The cost is around US$100 return. If you are visiting other cities, there are special round-trip excursions, see page 676. Airport is 17 kilometres from town and a taxi is around US$6. A shared taxi from the airport costs around US$3 per person. Alternatively, from town to the airport take a taxi or minibus until Azezo, US$0.30, then a horse taxi for the last seven kilometres. You are recommended to book/confirm onward flights at the Ethiopian Airlines office in Gondar because the office has computers – there's nothing computerized in either Axum or Lalibela.   **Transport**

Road Route from Addis is via Bahar Dar and the whole journey is 600 kilometres. Travel is difficult in June-September when the rains are heavy. It is realistic to allow 3 days for the journey there, with stops in Debre Markos or Dejen and Bahar Dar. There are regular buses running along this route. From Bahar Dar the journey takes 5 hours and costs US$2. There is now a direct bus service between Gondar and Shire (Inda Silase) leaving at 0630 from both Gondar and Shire. However if the bus fills up before the planned departure time, it leaves, so arrive by at least 0530. The journey takes about 11 hours and there is a stop at Debark (4 hours from Gondar).

Bank There is a bank which will change money in Gondar.   **Directory**

Debark and Simien Mountains

North of Gondar are the **Simien Mountains**, designated by UNESCO as a world heritage site. The jagged peaks of this volcanic range are so young that erosion has not yet softened their outline. The highest peak in Ethiopia and the fourth highest in Africa, **Ras Deshen**, stands adjacent to the 225 square kilometres park. In this spectacular setting are to be found the Waliba ibex, the Simien red fox, and the Gelada baboon – three animals unique to Ethiopia. A trek in the Simiens is highly recommended. The National Park offers a range of mountain trekking which can be handled by any reasonably fit walker, who doesn't mind camping. The mountain huts were destroyed during the 1980s in the war, and although they are being rebuilt, their use is restricted to park employees only. No electricity or running water but memorable scenery. Guided one or two day trips to look at the Simien Mountains can be arranged at the very helpful NTO office in Gondar.

However, it is preferable to allow five to eight days for a more extensive trek. The nearest town is **Debark**, which is 100 kilometres north and three to four hours by bus from Gondar through attractive rolling hills. At the Parks Office, guides, armed scout, mules/pack horse and a horseman can be arranged. You have to bring your own food and camping gear and allow extra for the guide, scouts and porters who frequently run out of supplies by day three. Expect to feed them despite what you are told beforehand by them or at the office. The daily hikes are about six hours a day, returning to your camp at around 1400. There is a road to Sankaber, and all the way to Chenek Camp. In the afternoon you can explore the surroundings on your own – spotting the huge Lammergeyer Vultures with a wing span of two and a half to three metres, and Gelada baboons. The landscape is dramatic. The hike is easy and the horse/mule can carry your packs. It gets windy and chilly at night. Camps are at 4,000 metres or so. Excellent views from Mietgogo Peak. You are unlikely to spot the Simien red fox.

Sleeping **E** *Simien Park Hotel*, basic communal hot shower (only hot water available in Debark). **E** *Simien Hotel*, bad communal toilets – hole in the ground. Definitely down market from the Simien Park Hotel.

For those short of time and unable to do a 2-4 day trek to the Simien Mountains, just 5 kilometres from Debark is Lamalimu Camp which is on the edge of the escarpment within the Simien NP. Hire a ranger, a guide and a mule at the National Park Office. Highly recommended trip, which offers the opportunity to see the wildlife too.

The road goes to Chenek Camp and extends another 100 kilometres further east. The 4 day trek (see page 734) trail crosses the road, but only occasionally follows it.

The children en route usually ask for pens or sweets. The further you get from Debark the less frequent are these requests.

Travelling north, **Debark** is separated from **Adi Arkay** by a spectacular switch-back road built by the Italians. The descent is over 1,000 metres at the Wolkefit Pass. The **Simien Mts National Park**, a world heritage site, lies to the right of the road. **Shire** (Inda Silase) is the next town north after Adi Arkay. It is in Tigre province and is an attractive town. The name of the district is Shire, and the town is actually named **Inda Silase**. However, it is widely referred to as **Shire**. The best accommodation is the **E** *Africa Hotel* at the eastern end of the town, close to where the Axum bus drops its passengers. **E** *Tekaze Hotel* behind the Mobil garage. Also recommended and serves excellent food. **Air** Ethiopian Airways, T03-440224.

Debark

To Axum & the Falasha Village

To Sankaber

o Market

Simien ■ ✉

■ Simien Park

N

National Park office o

0 metres 250

To Gondar

Axum

14°5'N 38°40'E
Colour map 1, grid B2

A further 365 kilometres northeast of Gondar lies the town of Axum (also spelt Aksum), site of Ethiopia's oldest city. Axum dates back some 2,000 years to when it was the hub of the Axumite Empire. The Queen of Sheba made it her capital 1000 years before Christ. The Ethiopian Orthodox Church was founded here in the fourth century and Axum remains the holiest city of the Ethiopian Orthodox Church. All that remains now of its past glories are the huge granite stele (pillars), some fallen and some still perpendicular. Made of single blocks of granite, the tallest stood over 33 metres high – the largest monolith in the world. The biggest now standing is 23 metres. The carving is deep and precise, showing beams and windows. It reflects a style of building still employed at Hadramaut in southern Yemen. ■ *US$7 to the* compound or to take photographs (even outside the fence). However, it is possible to see the stelea free of charge through the perimeter fencing. Free photographs can be taken if you climb the mountain next to the Yeha Hotel.

Also of interest is the 16th century **Church of St Mary of Zion**, closed at present for restoration work. Supposedly the repository of the original Ark of the Covenent (a sacred gold-covered chest from Old Testament times), St Mary's is the holiest Christian sanctuary in Ethiopia. Ethiopians believe that St Mary of Zion houses the Ark of the Covenant, containing the tablets on which Moses wrote the Ten Commandments. Menelik is reputed to have brought it to Axum, along with 12,000 Jewish children. The story is impossible to verify. However, the Chapel is constantly guarded by monks, and not even the President has sufficient authority to investigate further. ■ *US$10. The attached monastery is closed on Sunday and only the museum with the crown jewels can be visited US$3.*

Other historical sites include the **Grave of King Kaleb** and the **Grave of King Gabre** (as one traveller reports 'not worth a visit', 'it's pitch-black and the guide just knocks on some hollow coffin and says "so-and-so is buried there"'), the reputed **Bath of the Queen of Sheba** (variously described as "Resembles a concrete-walled reservoir with green water, in which little children swim or local women do their washing" – and "not awe-inspiring" by recent travellers), a **Museum**, and the ruins of the vast **Royal Palace**, over which the road to Gondar now passes. About three kilometres out of town to the north lie the remains known as the **Palace of Sheba**. Recent excavations indicate that they date from seventh century, rather than over 2000 years ago. The entrance stairs and floor plan are intact and the Palace had over

Ethiopia

Axum

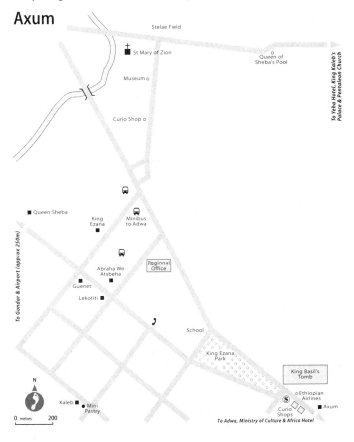

Stelae Field

✝■ St Mary of Zion

○ Queen of Sheba's Pool

Museum ○

To Yeha Hotel, King Kaleb's Palace & Pentaleon Church

Curio Shop ○

🚏

■ Queen Sheba

King Ezana ■

🚏 Minibus to Adwa

To Gondar & Airport (approx 250m)

🚏

Abraha We Atsbeha ■

Regional Office

Guenet ■

Lekotiti ■

♪

School

King Ezana Park

King Basil's Tomb

N

○ Ethiopian Airlines

Kaleb ■ ● Mini Pastry

Ⓢ

◇◇ ■ Axum

Curio Shops

0 metres 200

To Adwa, Ministry of Culture & Africa Hotel

50 rooms. ■ *To visit all the attractions and take photographs costs US$8.50, excluding the church. The entrance ticket to the sights of Axum allows only one entry to each site but visits may take place over several days. It is **essential** to bring your own torch to view the tombs.*

To reach **King Kaleb's Palace** start from the square in front of the main stelae field, facing the stelae. Follow the asphalted road to your right. After a few hundred metres you reach Queen Sheba's Pool (cemented over). Follow the road uphill, leaving the stelae field behind you. After one and a half kilometres the ruins of Kaleb are to be found at the right hand side of an intersection. When leaving the ruins, follow the path to your right. After a pleasant walk of a few kilometres through fields and grasslands, you will reach **Pentaleon**, US$2, located at the top of a hill called Debre Katin. Women are not allowed to enter the church, but they can go into the grounds and see the book and the cross. It is a lovely setting. It's a very pleasant walk and offers an escape from the "you – money" cat-calls of enthusiastic locals.

The road from Axum to Makale passes through spectacular desert to **Alamata** – an Italian-built road of fierce Alpine switchbacks requiring three, five or seven point turns by the bus, which faces out over the void as it negotiates the bends. Dirt road, which is being regraded, descends over 1,000 metres. (Just north of **Debark** the **Wolkefit Pass** to **Adi Arkay** is another spectacular example of Italian road engineering of similar dimensions, with a 1,000 metres descent.) Ethiopians talk of these two passes with equal admiration for the Italian engineers. It is worth travelling these sections for the experience.

Sleeping **B** *Yeha*, T750605. Part of the government run Ghion chain. Offers a student discount, very beautiful hotel, overlooks the stelea and the Dome of the Church of St Mary of Zion, good bar, restaurant and lounge. **C** *Axum*, c/o Ethiopian Hotels and Spaas Corporation (EHC), PO Box 1263, Addis Ababa, T152700, Tx21112. Basic food only.

D *Africa*, close to bus stand. 14 hot showers, clean, safe parking for cars and motorcycles, basic restaurant.

E *Amir Pension*, located near the market. Cheap hotel run by a Saudi woman. **E** *Bazen Hotel*, close to the market. Has showers. **E** *Ethiopia*, centrally located near the market. Cheap. **E** *Ghenet*, clean and comfortable, restaurant. **E** *Kaleb*, some rooms with own bath, hot water available for short periods only, restaurant. **E** *Mona Lisa*, cheap, basic hotel near the market and *Ghenet Hotel*. **E** *Queen Sheba*, close to market. Basic and friendly, restaurant. **E** *Tourist Bar*, cheap, basic, on the airport road. Some of the hotel names are only written in Amharic so ask one of the local boys to direct you!

Eating The *Bazen*, *Kaleb*, *Ghenet* and *Africa* hotels all have a bar and restaurant. There are also plenty of basic 1-star cafés in town. The *Mini Pastry* next door to the Kaleb Hotel serves very good coffee, fruit juices as well as cakes. In addition the scrambled eggs for breakfast are recommended. It has a charming courtyard.

Transport **Air** Ethiopian Airways, T03-750226/750300, daily flights from Addis Ababa. The airport is located very close to town, within walking distance. The cost is around US$150 return. If you are visiting other cities, there are special round-trip excursions, see page 676.

Road Route from Addis is via Bahar Dar and Gondar and the whole journey is 1,100 kilometres. Good sealed road to Adigrat. Access is difficult June-September when the rains are heavy. It is realistic to allow at 4 days for the journey there, with stops in Debre Markos, Bahar Dar and Gondar. There are regular buses running along this route. From Gondar the journey takes a full day and costs US$3.50. It is sometimes necessary to change buses at Shire (sometimes marked as Inda Silase). The bus stand in Axum is right in the centre next to the Big Tree. There are 2 buses daily to Asmara, one leaves at 0800, the journey is 170 kilometres and costs US$4, takes 5 hours. It is best to purchase a ticket in advance. At weekends take a bus to

Adwa the night before and make a connection. Journey takes 12 hours. Ensure you have a valid Eritrean visa. It is possible to hire bikes to visit nearby sights. If travelling into Eritrea the Rama border post, which is about 1 hour's drive from Axum, opens at 0900. Recent travellers have reported no difficulties with the crossing. The 120 kilometre journey between Axum and Adigrat takes 4 hours by bus. However, there are many places of interest en route, including the ancient ruins at Yeha, the tableland monastery of Debre Damo (see page 721) and the town of Adwa. There are frequent minibuses between Axum and Adwa. Close to Adigrat the road climbs up to over 3,000 metres, offering a view of the highest peak, Alegua, at 3,291 metres, and overlooks the Hista River gorge offering spectacular views of the terraced slopes and cliffs.

Tour companies & travel agents The *Galaxy Tours* office is based at the *Yeha Hotel*, and the **Directory**
Experience Ethiopia Tours office is based at the *Axum Hotel*.

Just south of the Axum to Yeha road is the site of the famous **Battle of Adwa** (some- **Adwa**
times spelt Adowa), where, in 1896 Menelik II defeated the Italians (see page 741). The town of Adwa contains the handsome **Church of Medhane Alem**.

About 28 kilometres northeast of Axum, Yeha is an ancient town thought to contain **Yeha**
Ethiopia's oldest buildings. Yeha is five kilometres off the main road to the north, marked by a faded white signpost. These include a rectangular stone **Temple**, esti-mated to date from around 700 BC, located on a small hill with a mountain behind. The temple is 20 metres by 15 metres and 10 metres high, made of large dressed stone blocks, some up to three metres long. The roof (probably supported by tim-ber) and west wall are missing. There is a small stele (stone pillar) nearby, and the temple is in a compound surrounded by a more recent stone wall interspersed with gate-houses at intervals. ■ *US$4*.

Close by is the **Church of Abba Afse**, named after one of the nine saints who came to Ethiopia from Syria in the fifth century. The present church dates from the middle ages, and replaced the original church on the site. It is notable for a set of stone ibex heads which possibly came from the original building, set into the front wall. The ibex was a sacred animal in pre-Christian southern Arabia.

Adjacent to the church is an *Iqa-bet*, a two-storey stone storage building, which contains religious artefacts. There are some stone blocks with raised inscriptions in *Sabbaean*, the ancient language of southern Arabia; religious robes and fine silk umbrellas; illustrated manuscripts; drums; rattles with metal discs (*sistra*); and wooden objects (*meqwomeya*) rather like shooting-sticks on which the priests sit during long services.

There is a sixth century monastery called **Debre Damo** in the small town of **Bizet**, a farming settlement, which lies on the road between Axum and Adigrat. To get to this monastery, which is situated at the top of a small tableland, you have to use a chain to scale a 20-30 metres rockface, spectacular views; this climb excludes the less agile tourist. **NB** Women are prohibited to visit this monastery. There are buses from Axum to Adigrat, leaving at 0600 daily. Bizet is approximately 70 kilometres from Axum – the bus fare is US$2 and the journey takes approximately three hours. Alter-natively take the bus to Adwa and change there for the bus to Adigrat, and get off at Bizet, journey time four to five hours. Debre Damo is about 12 to 15 kilometres from Bizet. Take the Axum road, and after approximately one hour you see a sign for Debre Damo. 400 metres from the sign turn right on the path. Next to a stone build-ing you come on to a road. Follow this for about half an hour. When descending from a small hill there are some white buildings and a shed – take the path to the right, (white building on your left). Follow this path over a small hill. Cross the river in the valley and keep on the path up the mountain (tableland). Climb the tableland, traverse it, going slightly around it to reach the chain. (See sketch). Make sure that you carry sufficient water with you prior to setting off. It is difficult to get back to

Axum the same day because public transport is not available in the afternoon. Lorries may be hitchhiked but are slow. Taxi to Adwa will cost about US$12. ■ *Entry to the Debra Damo monastery costs US$4.* **Sleeping** **E** *Axum Hotel*, in the village, clean and basic.

Adigrat
14°20'N 39°26'E
Colour map 1, grid A3

Adigrat lies at the T junction of the Axum/Adigrat and Makale/Asmara roads. It is the second largest town in the Tigre region, wonderfully sited in the mountains and is a good base from which to explore the rock-hewn churches of this region. There is a busy market which sells honey from the Alitena area. Chirkos Church, adjacent to the market is ornately decorated with paintings depicting angels. The church has a balcony which offers splendid views over the town. Close to the stadium is an imposing Catholic Church claimed to resemble a Florentine church. There are several rock-hewn churches in the vicinity of Adigrat. **Sleeping** **E** *Ethiopia Hotel*, near the Shell garage. Hot communal shower, restaurant. **E** *Modern Hotel* close to the Total garage. Very good value, restaurant attached. Tholoh (vegetarian dish) recommended. **E** *Pension*, close to the bus station. Clean basic rooms.

Axum to Lalibela

Travelling east from Axum, some 25 kilometres to **Adwa**, is the beginning of an area of rock-hewn churches centred on Dugem (sometimes spelt Degum or Dugum). There are believed to be over 100 rock-hewn churches in the Tigre region. The rock-hewn churches of the Tigre region are believed to pre-date those at Lalibela. The churches in Tigre were mostly carved into the cliff face, whereas at Lalibela, many of the churches are below ground level. The greatest concentration is in the **Gheralta** region. There are a cluster of over 30 rock-hewn churches in the Gheralta region, southwest of **Hawzen**, which is a small town 22 kilometres west of the Adigrat-Makale road. Take the side road that branches from Sinkata, 60 kilometres south of Adigrat. Hawzen has a tiny rock-hewn church, **Hwazen Tekla Haymanot**, which is enveloped by a more modern building. It is believed to be one of the oldest rock-hewn churches in Tigray.

Hawzen has two basic hotels. The main clusters of rock-hewn churches are around the villages of **Megab** and **Dugem**. Dugem is 22 kilometres from Hawzen and Megab is 13 kilometres. There is no public transport. Access is via a four-wheel drive vehicle or alternatively you can hike there. The best day to try to hitch a ride is

Debre Damo Monastery access from Bizet
not to scale

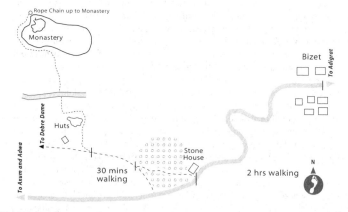

Wednesday, which is market day in Hawzen. Between Hawzen, Megab and Dugem the landscape is relatively flat. The walk to Dugem from Hawzen would take about six hours, but to visit the churches involves a steep climb. Using a guide is recommended, can be arranged at Hawzen. Further details can be obtained from the Tigre Tourist Bureau, PO Box 124, Mekele, T03400769, who have a free leaflet "Tigre: The Open Air Museum", which includes a sketch map of the location of some of the churches on the back of it. ■ *The entry fee to the churches is usually US$3.50 each with a few of the churches charging much more.*

15 kilometres southeast of Dugem, going towards Wukro is **Abraha Atsbeha**, the most celebrated cruciform shaped church in the Tigre region, the site of an annual pilgrimage on 14th October. From Abraha Atsbeha to Wukro is a further 25 kilometres. Approximately 20 kilometres north of Wukro, close to the village of Negash on the main Adigrat/Makale road is the most easily accessed group of rock-hewn churches called the **Takatisfi cluster**. They lie approximately two kilometres to the east of the main road. There are three churches in close proximity to each other. The best known is **Medhane Alem Adi Kasho**, one of the oldest in the region.

Wukro (sometimes spelt Wik'ro) is a large town on the Adigrat-Makale road and contains an impressive rock-hewn church **Wukro Chirkos**. This is to be found 500 metres out of town on the east. It is one of the most impressive of the rock-hewn churches and is one of the most accessible. Recommended. **Sleeping** E *Selam Pension*, basic hotel, cold showers. E *Fasika Hotel*, clean, communal hot showers.

Continuing south, down the eastern flanks of the Simien mountains, you will pass through **Makale**, the regional capital of Tigray. Here is the **Palace of Emperor Yohannes IV**, built by an Italian architect, Giacomo Naretti in 1886. It has turrets and battlements, but the Emperor is reported never to have inspected the fortifications as he refused to climb any stairs. Makale (sometimes spelt Mek'ele or Makalle) has an interesting TPLF monument which dominates the town. A miniature Eiffel Tower of marble cased concrete, it rises 55 metres from the town's central hill. It is topped with a wheel of industry beneath a gold sphere, and is surrounded by 20 large bronze statues depicting the misery of the war – very movingly portrayed. The war is still a big emotive issue in Tigray, discussed with a mixture of pride and sadness. The main market day is Monday when local traders sell salt, brought by camel from the

Ethiopia

Gheralta

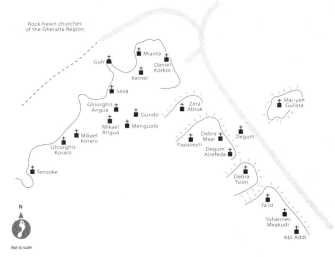

Rock-hewn churches
of the Gheralta Region

Mianta
Guh
Daniel
Korkor
Kemer
Sella
Zera
Abruk
Ghiorghis
Angua
Mariyon
Gulista
Gundo
Mikael
Angua
Menguolo
Debra
Maar
Papaseyti
Degum
Mikael
Koraro
Degum
Airefeda
Ghiorghis
Koraro
Tensoke
Debra
Tsion
Ya'id
N
Yohannes
Meakudi
Not to scale
Abi Addi

Danakil desert. The staff at the Mekele Tigre Tourist Bureau, T400769, are very helpful and well informed about local historical sites. **Sleeping D** *Abraha Castle Hotel* (Ghion chain) overlooks the town from a hill. Good restaurant. **E** *National Hotel* below the Abraha Castle Hotel is a cheaper alternative, with hot water, s/c. **Air** Ethiopia Airlines offer a service to Makale T03-400055/03-404052. Continuing south past Lake Ashangé there is a track to the west at K'obo to the famous rock-hewn churches of Lalibela, high-up, at an altitude of 2,600 metres. The **rock-hewn churches** here, are set in rugged, awe-inspiring scenery.

Lalibela

12°2'N 39°2'E
Colour map 1, grid B3

Lalibela (a listed World Heritage Site – UNESCO) was built as the capital of a local king following the fall of Axum, and it became the centre of religious authority in Ethiopia. The churches were sculpted out of the rock in the 12th century, standing completely free from the surrounding stone. They are tended by priests who guard their precious artistic and religious treasures and each contains extravagant murals, crosses and manuscripts. According to legend, in the 12th century Prince Lalibela, of the Zagwe Dynasty, was drugged by his brother the King, who feared he would be overthrown. During his drugged sleep angels brought him to heaven, where God instructed him to return home and build churches of a unique style. His brother later abdicated and Lalibela was crowned King. He gathered an army of craftsmen, who carved out the cliff face at Roha fashioning 11 churches. Legend has it that local people believed that the churches were completed so quickly because angels carried on the work at night.

There is a double church and the famous cross-shaped **Bieta Giorgis**, in the group, all linked by narrow paths and tunnels. The entrance for 11 churches is about US$17 (excludes the monasteries outside the town). Official guides who have been trained are quite knowledgeable, charge from US$7 to US$17. Ask to see their certificate. Make sure their English is good before hiring one. Unofficial guides (usually boys) ask much less, as little as US$5 and often speak much better English. Some of the official guides have been reported to charge tourists exorbitant amounts for their services and for entry charges. (There have been recent steep price increases in Ethiopia, payable at the priest's office, and the churches will be unlocked for you to look inside – however, it is possible to view the churches from outside for free.) There are six churches to the north and five churches to the south of the Jordan River. Many of the churches are being renovated at present and are surrounded by scaffolding. It is recommended to use a guide otherwise you risk missing a lot as much is virtually hidden. The full tour takes three to four hours, and you need to start before 1600. If you wish to use an English-speaking guide, make sure you fix the price in advance. Tours of Lalibela begin at the eastern cluster of churches. From the *Seven Olives Hotel* walk down the hill. The ticket is valid to see the churches over several days. **Bieta Medhane Alem** is located at the eastern end of this cluster of churches, and is the largest rock-hewn church in the world, almost 800 square metres in area. The interior is reminiscent of a cathedral. From the courtyard outside a tunnel leads to another courtyard which has another three churches. The most imposing of these is **Bieta Maryam** dedicated to the Virgin Mary. It is much more ornately decorated than Bieta Medhane Alem, with carvings of the Star of David and the Lalibela Cross.

Lalibela

A third courtyard grants access to another two churches, where the remains of the King of Lalibela are rumoured to be buried.

The western cluster of churches includes the cruciform shaped **Bieta Giorgis**, which has been excavated to below the ground level, including a sunken courtyard, all encompassed by steep vertical walls. **Bieta Abba Libanos** is built around a cave in a vertical cliff face. The back and sides of the church have been carved to separate them from the cliff face but the roof is still part of the original rock. Legend has it that this church was built by King Lalibela's wife, with the help of angels. It is connected by a tunnel to a chapel, **Bieta Lehem**, reputedly used by the King. **Bieta Mercurios** is a cave church but the interior has partially collapsed. The entrance was renovated in the 1980s.

There are several possible day excursions: to **Inrahanna Kristos**, a church in a cave on Mount Abuna Josef; to the monastery and church visible on the mountain above Lalibela. Guides will advise, but again, fix a price first. If you are fit it is possible to visit other rock-hewn monasteries at a fraction of the cost of the 11 well-known churches including **Bieta Giorgis**.

Asheton Monastery has very friendly priests and is an approximate two hour hike up steep, rocky paths, with wet, slippery sections. It takes approximately 55 minutes to reach a lush plateau, with quiet villages. The next 30 minutes takes you through wet farmland and the last 30 minutes is a climb up a steep mountain. It's very envigorating with fabulous views. The trails are unmarked and a guide would be helpful. The further you can get without one, the cheaper it will be. Expect to pay a guide about US$3 for the round trip. Children often prove to be excellent guides. The views are fantastic. This hike is prohibitive for most people, but remains a cheap, viable alternative for fit travellers, entrance fee US$3. It is possible to combine the walk to Asheton Monastry with a trip to Na'akuto La'ab – a monastery which appears glued to a rock. It is seven kilometres from Lalibela and four kilometres from Asheton Monastery. There is a small steep footpath between the two monasteries.

The town is relatively inaccessible during the rainy season (June-September) and the best time to visit is during *Timkat* (Epiphany) in January (see box, page 680).

The persistent nagging from young children, wishing to act as your guide around the churches can be very irritating. The children are very reluctant to take no for an answer. Try saying "Alfalegum" meaning "I don't want to" emphatically when accosted, or more politely "tenaestelin" ("good day"). Alternatively keep quiet, this deters even the most persistant – would be guide eventually.

Flies are terribly annoying in and around Lalibela. Insect repellent helps a little. The town is very dusty in dry seasons. No taxis or buses in town. Area is very hilly. There are lots of beggars.

Timkat celebrations (see box page 680) in Lalibela attract a lot of tourists, but it is still not commercialized. Make air and hotel reservations in advance. It starts at 1600 on 18th January at the various churches, then a converging procession winds along the main road to a field across the Roha Hotel (two kilometres walk). There are prayers and celebrations at this site throughout the night. On 19th January the major part of the celebration is held from 0900 to 1400. There is a very colourful procession back to the churches, which is very photogenic. However, professional photographers jostle intrusively to get the best shots. On 20 January a smaller celebration is held in honour of St Michael.

Locals say that Lalibela is the most famous place for Genna (the Eastern Orthodox Christmas, 7 January) and Gondar for Timkat.

On Saturdays there is a local market which attracts hundreds of people. It sells little in the way of tourist tat as it caters for the local people.

Ethiopia

Sleeping & eating

There is a very limited choice if shopping for foodstuffs. Little fresh bread or fruit available.

C *Roha*, part of the government run Ghion chain. Cold showers, unreliable water supply, best hotel location for Timkat, rock-hewn toilets, basic. Roha's disadvantage is that it is sited approximately 2 kilometres from the town centre. Food is recommended, but you need to order in advance. **C** *Seven Olives*, at top of village. Will change travellers' cheques and issue receipts, has been known to run out of cash, hot showers, indifferent service, the restaurant serves good western food. Good location for seeing churches and hiking to Asheton Monastery. The NTO office and *Ethiopian Airlines* office are on site. Camping available in the grounds but is expensive. **C** *Hotel Asheton*, clean and cheap, central, near the *Seven Olives Hotel* (300 metres). Recommended. Nice courtyard, restaurant, haggle over prices which tend to be variable. Restaurant serves good French food, nice atmosphere. Safe parking for cars and motorcycles. Camping possible. **C** *Lal Hotel*, at the edge of the village offers adequate accommodation. Water use restricted to limited hours but management will turn on the supply on request. Third best hotel in town. Pleasant open-air restaurant.

E *Helen*, located just past the Roha on the main road. Cheap, reasonable. **E** *Kademt*, near the square where *Seven Olives* faces. Very cheap and basic. **E** *Lasta*, basic, communal showers. **E** *Hotel Private Roha*, at market entrance at bottom of village. Privately owned and popular, disgusting communal toilet, good beds, only one communal shower.

Transport

Air **Ethiopian Airways**, T000246 via operator, flies daily to Lalibela. There is a new airport under construction and a second runway has recently been built (unmade) which has improved access during the rainy season. There is now a metal terminal shed for passengers. The cost from Addis Ababa is around US$100 return. If you are visiting other cities, there are special round-trip fares, see page 676. The airport is some distance away (12 kilometres) up a steep hill to town. A government-owned bus runs into town and charges US$4, leaving town at 0800. Travellers have reported that it is much cheaper to try to organize a private vehicle, certainly for the return journey. As there are very few private cars, the chances of hitching a ride are slim. Another transport option is an NTO four-wheel drive vehicle – cost US$12 for the round trip. Reconfirm your onward flight the day before. Ethiopian Airlines is located next to *Seven Olives Hotel*, up a long flight of steps.

Road No petrol station. Diesel available in the Shell shop. Access is not easy overland – for a long while Lalibela was in the zone affected by the fighting in Tigray. The route is via Dessie, which is 300 kilometres to the northeast from Addis Ababa. Lalibela is a further 200 kilometres from Dessie. A new road has recently been built from Addis, reducing the route by 200 kilometres and has greatly reduced Lalibela's remoteness. Access is still difficult June-September when the rains are heavy. It is realistic to allow at least 2 days for the journey there from Addis Ababa. The first leg to Dessie takes 12 hours and costs US$4. Fill up with petrol before leaving by car/bike as there is sometimes no fuel until Debre Tabot.

Bus Leaving Lalibela by public bus is a time-consuming journey. The bus leaves at 0600 and reaches Weldiya at 1300. However by this time the buses to other cities have left, so it is worth trying to hitch a lift to Weldiya, but bear in mind that the official line is that private trucks are forbidden to compete with the government bus.

Weldiya

11°50'N 39°34'E
Colour map 1, grid B3

Weldiya is a pleasant little town with lush vegetation situated amongst pretty rolling hills, and nice terrace cafés lining the busy piazza, worth a visit. The market is held on Tuesdays. However, this is also a serious famine area. Average families can produce only three to six months food supply and have to rely on aid. Weldiya is the centre of the aid agencies (FAO, SCF UK, Médicins Sans Frontiers etc). **D** *Hotel Lal*, T367. Nice rooms, hot water, good restaurant. **E** *Kidane*, is close to bus stand, but toilets and shower are poor. **E** *Lala Hotel*, near the roundabout, clean, hot shower, safe parking for cars and motorcycles. Good restaurant and meeting place in the evening for locals. There are several other small places of a similar standard locally.

There is now a relatively expensive government bus from Weldiya to Lalibela US$3. This bus fills from 0600 but doesn't leave till 1100, once the Dessie bus has arrived and off-loaded passengers. It takes six to seven hours, arriving in Lalibela at 1730-1800. Excellent views, with mountain passes at altitudes of 3,000 metres. The bus trip from Weldiya to Makale takes around 10 hours. Buses to Asmara leave Makale at 0400 and 0500 and reach the Eritrean border at about 1100 and Asmara at 1700.

Dessie
11° 5' N, 39° 40' E
Phone code: 3
Colour map 1, grid B3

Dessie (sometimes spelt Desé) is a beautiful, old, mainly Muslim town, situated picturesquely in a steep valley. Dessie is the capital town of the Welo region. 30 kilometres north of Dessie is **Lake Hayk Hayk** situated in verdant rolling hills and bordered by papyrus beds. Birds abound. From the town of Hayk take the side road which runs parallel to the main road – the mosque should be on your right side. Take the right fork when the road bifurcates, and at the second junction the right fork will bring you to the lake shore close to a disused snack bar. The left fork will bring you to Hayk Istafanos, a small monastery which lies on a small, wooded peninsula, thought to date from the 13th century. **Sleeping C** *Ambarass Hotel* on the Dessie-Weldiya road, T112820. Good value, very clean, hot showers, good restaurant and nice nightclub, closes at midnight. **E** *Fasika*, about 200 metres from the bus stand. Clean, restaurant. Several other small places. From Dessie to Weldiya, the bus leaves at 0600, and takes four to five hours.

Air Ethiopia Airlines, T03-112571.

Kembolcha

A small town about 18 kilometres southwest of Dessie where the road divides to Addis Ababa and Djibouti or Assab. **E** *Wien Hotel* on the main road. Showers, clean, friendly, safe parking. From Kembolcha to Debre Birhan is 250 kilometres. There is plenty of traffic on this major road, with long haul buses and private transport.

Debre Birhan

Debre Birhan, 133 kilometres northeast of Addis Ababa, is a very pleasant highland town, noticeably cooler than the capital, and perched on the edge of the escarpment with magnificent views across the plains below. It grew in medieval times when power shifted south from Axum to Lalibela initially and later to Debre Birhan. It was said to have been founded by Emperor Zara Yagob who was influenced by a mysterious light that appeared at his campsite. Debre Birhan means 'the place of light' and the Emperor built a church and a palace there. The palace was destroyed a long time ago but the church, Debre Birhan Selassie church, is still standing. It contains a painting, claimed to be of Halley's comet at the beginning of the 20th century. 42 kilometres from Debre Birhan to the east is the small town of **Ankober**, which was the capital until the late 19th century of the Shoan kings, Sahle Selassie and Hailemelekot, and the early years of Menelik II. The remains of the fort are outside the town on a hillside. If you go through Debre Burhan to the end of the town take the right turning which leads to the edge of the escarpment. This is a good place to stay if you want to see that elusive bird the Ankober Serin *(Serinus ankoberensis)*. The Ankober Serin can be found along the escarpment north of Ankober, and although Ankober town is the nearest to this area, it is to be avoided as a place to stay. At the bottom of this escarpment, which is reached by an amazing road with breathtaking views, lives the Yellow-throated Serin *(Serinus*

9°41'N 39°31'E
Colour map 1, grid B2

Debre Birhan

Helen
Tsiqedera
To Dessie
Agip Petrol Station
Cafes and Shops
Shell Petrol Station
Green
Total Petrol Station
N
To Addis Ababa
Not to scale

Ethiopia

flavigula), yet another extremely localized Ethiopian endemic bird. Other endemics can be seen in this general area, too. Lammergeyers *(Gypaetus barbatus)* sail along the top of the escarpment where you will get good views. Troops of gelada baboons may also be spotted.

Sleeping   E *Helen Hotel*, said to be the best in town, but is regularly booked up by lunch time. **E** *Green Hotel*, an anonymous hotel here which is an exception to the rule of not spending less than 20 Birr a night, it is in a side street and is painted green, clean room, own shower, hot water, the restaurant serves Ethiopian food and does an especially good *tibs*.

Air   Ethiopia Airlines Dessie, T03-112571.

National Parks and Sanctuaries

The parks are well run with helpful staff who try hard to make visitors welcome. All the major African animals are present, with the exception of rhinoceros. Awash, Abyatta-Shala, Nechisar, Simien Mountains, Harar Elephant Sanctuary and Bale Mountains are readily accessible from Addis Ababa. Bale Mountains offers horse trekking, which is a splendid way to tour the park.

Tours are available and there is a wide variety of operators, as well as the state-owned service, see page 672. Until 1991 there were daunting restrictions on visitors, and the tourist sector is only now beginning to get back to normal.

Awash National Park

The park is located 225 kilometres east of Addis Ababa off the highway to Assab (now part of Eritrea). It stretches about 30 kilometres from east to west and a little less from north to south. The terrain is covered with grassland and acacia woodland. The central feature is the Fantalle volcano, now dormant. A track leads part of the way up the volcano, and it is possible to climb the rest of the way to the crater edge. There are hot-springs in deep, clear, blue pools at Filwoha in the north. The area also contains unusual rock formation in the shape of blisters. The Awash River Gorge runs along the southern edge of the park and there is a spectacular waterfall near the

11°45'N 41°5'E
Colour map 1, grid C3

Ethiopia

Awash National Park

Ethiopian national parks and reserves

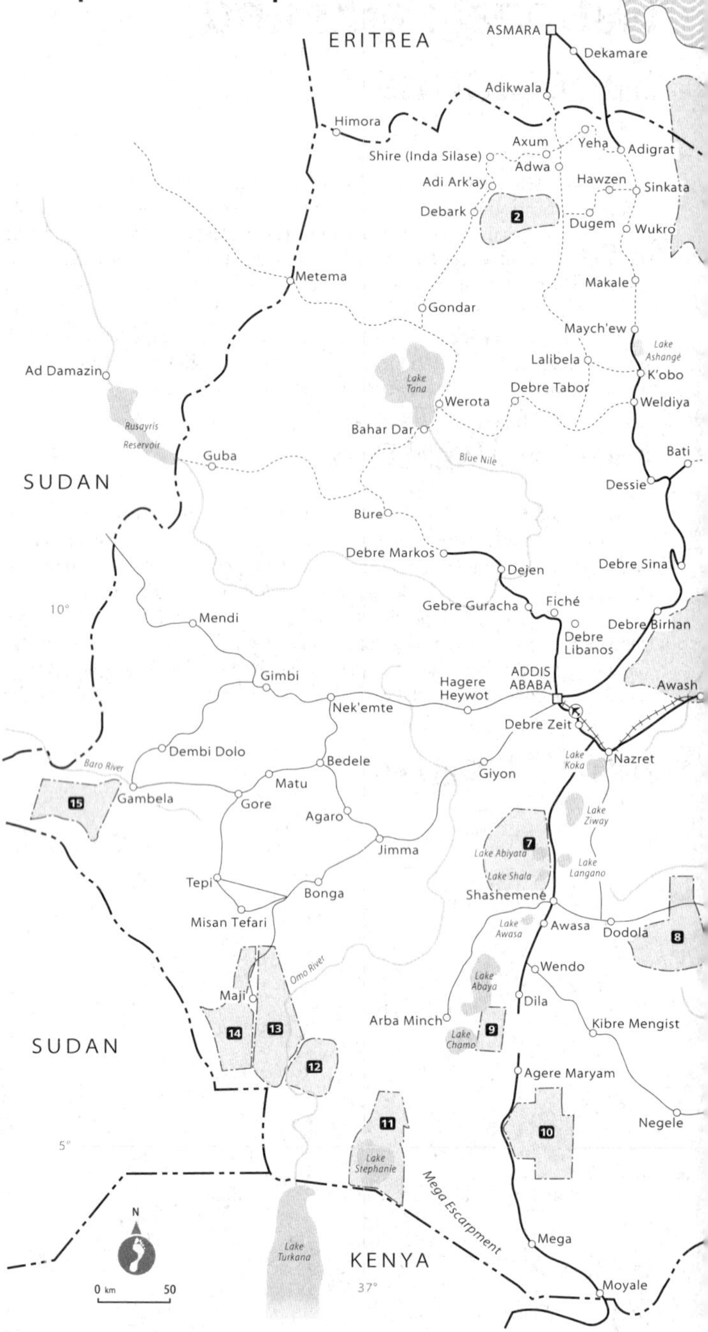

National Parks & Game Reserves

1 Denakil Depression
2 Simien Mountains NP

3 Langwe Rassa NP
4 Yangudi Rassa Reserve
5 Awash NP

6 Harar Wildlife Sanctuary
7 Rift Valley NP
8 Bale Mountains NP

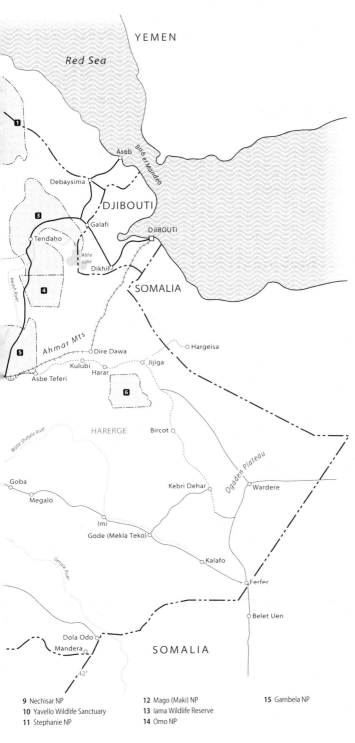

9 Nechisar NP

10 Yavello Wildlife Sanctuary

11 Stephanie NP

12 Mago (Maki) NP

13 Iama Wildlife Reserve

14 Omo NP

15 Gambela NP

park headquarters. Although the river is substantial in the park, it does not reach the sea, and peters out in the Danakil Depression on the border with Djibouti where the water evaporates off in a series of lakes.

The main African wildlife of the plains are present with the exception of rhinos, giraffe and buffalo although the animals are sparse compared with parks in Kenya. The main species to be seen are oryx and reedbuck and less frequently leopard, bush-buck, hippo, Soemmerring's gazelle, caracal, colubus and green monkeys, Anubis and Hamadryas baboons, klipspringer, Grevy's Zebra, cheetah, greater and lesser kudu, ardvaarks, and bat-eared foxes. Over 400 species of bird are present.

Sleeping   C *Kereyou Lodge*, c/o Ethiopian Hotels and Spas Corporation (EHC), PO Box 1263, Addis Ababa, T152700, Tx21112, located on the Awash River on the southern boundary of the park. It is a group of caravans, but reasonably comfortable. **Camping** Available at 6 sites, a couple of which are just outside the park boundary.

Transport   Regular buses and minibuses from Addis Ababa along the route through Debre Zeit to Awash.

Bale Mountains National Park

6°20'N 41°30'E
Colour map 1, grid C3

The Bale mountains park is 400 kilometres southwest of Addis Ababa, to the east of the the town of Shashamene on the highway that runs south to the Kenyan border. It is about 60 kilometres from east to west and 80 kilometres from north to south. The terrain is juniper and heather moorlands in the foothills, with woodland in the higher reaches. There are many swift-flowing streams, and the climate is alpine. **Garba Guracha** ('black lake') has particularly attractive surroundings. Several of the peaks are over 4,000 metres, the highest being **Mount Tullu Deemtu** ('red mountain') at 4,377 metres.

The main feature of the park is that it houses three of the species unique to Ethiopia, the Simien red fox (also found in the Simien Mountains), Menelik's bushbuck, and the Mountain Nyala. Other wildlife includes leopards, black servals, lions, black and white colubus monkeys, olive baboons, grivet, and Sykes monkeys. There are several endemic rodents, including the giant mole rat, which burrows leaving heaps of debris on the surface. The streams contain rainbow and brown trout introduced from Kenya. The giant lobelia, growing up to five metres in height is a form of vegetation unique to the park. Over 200 bird species are to be found, including the bearded vulture.

Entrance to the park is US$8 for 48 hours; camping fee is US$3.50 for 48 hours; horse, mule or donkey (for riding or carrying luggage) US$1.50 per day; guide US$5 per day. It is best to schedule six days for a thorough tour. Stock up on provisions at Shashamene as Dinsha (also known as Dinshoo) has limited supplies. From Dinsha it is easy to go to the **Hot Springs**. Ask at the bus station, half hour bus trip, fare US$0.25, and a 15 minute walk at the other end. Entrance fee US$0.50.

Sleeping   B *Goba Ras*, c/o Ethiopian Hotels and Spaas Corporation (EHC), PO Box 1263, Addis Ababa, T152700, Tx21112, just east of the park. C *Bekele Mola*, c/o EHC above, in Robe, 15 kilometres north of Goba. D *Swedish Guest House*, at Dinsha, self-catering, comfortable and popular. **Camping** At 2 sites near the park HQ at Dinsha, and at a site to the south of the escarpment at Katcha on the road from Goba to Mena, which runs through the park.

Transport   **Air** Goba is among **Ethiopian Airlines** list of destinations, but not included in the current schedules. It is understood that they will put down at the airstrip at Goba if required. There are 6 flights a week (not Thursday) on this route. **Road Bus**: from Addis Ababa to Shashamene by bus. Then bus to Goba, disembarking at Dinsha (US$2.50).

Rift Valley National Park

The park is in the chain of seven lakes which run from Debre Zeit south toward Lake Turkana in Kenya. For description of the Lakes that are not parks, see page 706. *7°N, 38°E Colour map 1, grid B3*

    The park is about 200 kilometres south of Addis Ababa, and consists of two lakes, just to the west of Lake Langano. They are particularly attractive stretches of water, and they are very different in character to each other. The main interest stems from the the extensive bird life that the lakes attract, with over 400 species recorded. **Senkello Swayne's Hartebeest Sanctuary** is close to the park, and is administered by the staff. It contains about 2,000 of these hartebeest, which are endemic to Ethiopia.

    Lake Abyatta is the more northern of the two, and is about 20 kilometres across. It is shallow and surrounded by grass-covered shores and acacia woodland. The water is alkaline, and among the birds attracted to feed on the algae are greater and lesser flamingoes and white pelicans, white-necked cormorants, herons, storks, spoonbills, ibises, ducks, gulls and terns. Surrounding woodland contains trogons, turacos and weaver birds. In the northern hemisphere winter, the lake is host to migratory ducks and waders from Europe and Asia. There are a few mammals on the shores, including Grant's gazelle, warthog and oribi.

    Lake Shala is deep, 260 metres at maximum, and it is surrounded by black peaks and cliffs. There are two lots of hot springs on the margins of the lake. One, Ghike, is close to the park HQ at Dole, and the other is further round the lake on the southern shore. The lake is particularly famous for its colony of great white pelicans, (about 15,000 pairs), ibises, Abdimi's storks, and the white-necked cormorant.

    Details of sleeping and transport are to be found under Lake Langano which is adjoining, see page 706.

Nechisar National Park

South of Shashamene, 500 kilometres from Addis Ababa on the Rift Valley road, this park lies on the eastern shores of Lake Abaya and Lake Chamo. There are some hot springs in the southeast corner. The lakes are surrounded by heavy vegetation, and the waters contain Nile perch, tigerfish, hippos and crocodiles. In the park itself are Swayne's hartebeest (one of the species unique to Ethiopia), Guenther's dikdik, greater kudu, Burchell's zebra and olive baboons. Arba Minch is the nearest main town, and the park headquarters are nearby. *6°N, 37°E Colour map 1, grid C2*

    Details of sleeping and transport are to be found under Arba Minch, see page 707.

Simien Mountains National Park

The park is 100 kilometres to the north of Gondar, off the road to Axum. The park was generally inaccessible up to 1991 as a result of the fighting in the north, but it is now possible to visit again. It is another World Heritage Site (UNESCO) and well worth visiting. *13°N, 38°E Colour map 1, grid B2*

    It is a rocky massif which slopes down to grasslands. The slopes are cut by gorges, some over 1,000 metres deep, with fast-flowing streams. The highest peak in Ethiopia is just to the southeast of the park, outside the NP, Mount Ras Deshen (sometimes spelt Dashen) at 4,620 metres, and it is the fourth highest mountain in Africa.

    Three of Ethiopia's endemic mammals are found here, the Walia ibex, the Simien red fox, and the Gelada baboon. Also present are Hamadryas baboon, the klipsringer and the bushbuck. Birds include the lammergeyer (the 'bonebreaker', a spectacular vulture with a wingspan of two and a half to three metres which drops the bones of animals killed by other predators onto rocks, to consume the marrow), the Auger buzzard, Verreaux's eagle, kestrel and Lanner falcon. In the Simien

Ethiopia

Mountains near Gich are found the Muslim descendants of Ahmed the Left Handed, a 16th century Muslim rebel from southeast Ethiopia. He mounted a murderous campaign to wipe out the Christians in this region and was killed by Portuguese-backed forces in 1543.

Entrance charge for 48 hours US$8, campsite charge for 48 hours US$3, ranger/guard per day US$3, mule per day US$1.50, guide per day US$8.50. It is expected to give a tip, if the trip was good, on the basis of two day's pay, that is guide US$17, ranger/guard US$6, muleteer US$3. The **Parks Office**, about ten minutes walk from the Simien Hotel, is a green, corrugated iron building set back off the left hand side of the road at the beginning of Debark, coming from Gondar. Faded sign on road. You can hire transport for US$60 one way from Debark to Sankaber which is 37 kilometres by road, but only 23 kilometres on the unsealed trail which utilizes short cuts. An armed ranger/guard is compulsory and the park rules also stipulate that all visitors must use a guide from the National Parks Office. The guides are not National Park employees but are an organized group of trained guides, who speak English, and take tourists into the park on a rotational basis. The guides all receive training from the tourist office in Gondar, and provide an excellent service. It is difficult to see much in less than four days. **Suggested Route of four-day walk: Day 1 Sankaber**, 23 kilometres on trail from Debark 2,600 metres to Sankaber 3,200 metres (six hours) wonderful scenery and villages not visible from the road. **Day 2** 21 kilometres to next camp **Gich** (also spelt Geech) 3,600 metres with two long uphill climbs (five hours) short side trip to 500 metres high waterfall. **Day 3** six kilometres to **Miet Gogo** (3,926 metres) on edge of escarpment, great views and Saha, which also has magnificent views especially in the afternoon light. Then back 21 kilometres to Sankaber. **Day 4** 23 kilometres back to Debark. The mountain huts were destroyed in the 1980 war, and although they are being rebuilt, their use is restricted to park employees only. At Gich Camp it is sometimes possible to buy a goat for US$10 – usually your team will prepare it for you in return for a share of the spoils. To climb Mount Ras Deshen requires eight days. In the park it is occasionally possible to stay with villagers (US$3 per night) or hire a tent from a guide. It is recommended that you hire a cook if you can. Suggested rate US$4 a day, plus US$10 to go to market to buy four days supply of food – a well worth while investment. Stoves and tents can be hired for the walk – ask your guide. Debark has a large market, with a reasonable range of supplies. More choice is on offer in Gondar or Axum. Because of deforestation it is not recommended to cook over an open fire. Stoves can be hired – ask at the National Parks office. It can be cold because of the altitude, and you will require warm clothing. Water needs to be boiled for 20 minutes or use purifying tablets.

Sleeping & transport Nearest town is Debark which is 3-4 hours by bus from Gondar, costing US$1.50. Alternatively, a taxi from Gondar to Debark will cost US$60 to US$70, taking approximately 2 hours. If you wish to return by taxi, make arrangements with the driver to be collected, as there are no taxis for hire in Debark. **E *Simien Park Hotel***, on main road between bus stop and National Park Office. New, excellent, cheap, good local food, hot showers – bucket. **E *Simien***, restaurant, and several other small places. Otherwise, see Axum, which is about 250 kilometres – 2 days travel by bus (change at **Inda Silase**, also known as **Shire**) or Gondar (100 kilometres) .

Gambela National Park

8° N, 34° E
Colour map 1, grid C1

This park is 600 kilometres west of Addis Ababa on the river Baro. It is not particularly easy to access. The terrain is undulating grassland. In the river are to be found huge Nile perch, up to 100 kilograms, crocodiles and hippos. Other wildlife includes buffalo, giraffe, waterbuck, Roan antelope, zebra, bushbuck, Abyssinian reedbuck, warthog, hartebeest, lion and elephant.

Unfortunately, there are very few animals to be seen in the Park, but the birds are many and varied. The olive baboon and the local race of the vervet, with its white whiskers, are very common, as is the black and white colobus monkey. Other than these monkeys, the commonest animal would seem to be the hyaena, which you will hear 'whooping' around Gambela town every night.

Details of sleeping and transport are to be found under Gambela, the nearby town, see page 700.

Omo and Mago National Parks

6° N, 36° E
Colour map 2, grid B2

These parks are located either side of the Omo River in the southwest of Ethiopia, 700 kilometres from Addis Ababa. Access is via the highway that runs through Jimma. There is negligible human habitation in the parks, and they are particularly abundant in wildlife, including oryx, Burchell's zebra, Lelwel's hartebeest, buffalo, giraffe, waterbuck, kudu, lion, leopard and cheetah.

The area has proved a rich source of early hominid remains, and in 1982 skeletons were found which are thought to be over four million years old.

White water rafting on the River Omo is possible – see pages 689 or 708.

**Sleeping &
transport**

It is possible to charter a plane to visit Omo and Mago through NTO, see page 693. **Camping** There are several sites, but negligible facilities, and all equipment and provisions need to be taken.

Yangudi Rassa National Park

11° N, 41° E
Colour map 1, grid B4

About 500 kilometres from Addis Ababa on the road to Djibouti and Assab. It was primarily established to preserve a population of Somali wild ass. There are only a few other animals in the park, mainly Grevy's zebra, greater and lesser kudu, gerenuk and cheetah. Nearest reliable accommodation is at Awash, about 200 kilometres away, see page 732.

Stephanie National Park

4° 40' N, 36° 50' E
Colour map 2, grid B2

This new park surrounds Lake Chew Bahir (also known as Lake Stephanie) on the southern border with Kenya. The lake is seasonal, and for much of the year is marshland. There is a rich variety of bird-life, with black-tailed godwits and spotted redshanks to be seen. Nearest reasonable accommodation is at Arba Minch, 150 kilometres away, see page 707. There are 4 flights a week by **Ethiopian Airlines** to Jinka, which is very close, on Tuesday, Wednesday, Saturday and Sunday. The fare is around US$150 return.

Harar (Babille) Elephant Sanctuary

9° N, 42° 30' E
Colour map 1, grid B4

Located just southeast of the city of Harar, a large area devoted to a sub-species of elephant only found in Ethiopia. The park is not particularly well developed, and it is not easy to sight the elephants.

However, birds are numerous, including the rare Salvadori Seedeater (*serinus xantholaema*), only sighted a dozen times altogether, the last being in 1989. There are few visitors.

See nearby Harar for accommodation and trnasport, page 704.

Ethiopia

Yavello Sanctuary

South of Addis Ababa, about 600 kilometres distant, and to the east of the road to Kenya. The area is mainly to preserve four endemic bird species: Stresemann's bush crow, the Sidamo lark, the white-tailed swallow and Prince Ruspoli's turaco. The sanctuary also contains lesser and greater kudu, gerenuk, Grevy's zebra, beisa oryx, dikdik and giraffe.

There are some small hotels in nearby Yavello town. There are flights to Arba Minch, about 150 kilometres distance, page 707.

Background

The land

Elevations range from 4,000 metres above sea level to 100 metres below, the highest point **Geography**
in the country being Ras Dashan in the Simien mountain range, which rises to a height of
4,620 metres northeast of Lake Tana. The southern part of Ethiopia is bisected by the East
African Rift Valley, 40-60 kilometres wide, the valley floor scattered with lakes. North of
Addis, the western wall of the valley runs parallel to the Red Sea coast, creating a wide
plain between the escarpment and the coastline. Further north, this plain narrows until the
foothills of the escarpment run right down to the sea. To the west of the rift system, the
gently dipping plateau runs down into Sudan, drained by the tributaries of the Nile which
have scarred deep canyons in the land. This part of the country is seriously denuded of
top-soil, much of it having washed away to collect on the flood plains of Egypt.

The eastern wall of the rift valley runs due east from Addis, forming a steep escarpment
which rises abruptly to over 1,000 metres, commanding wide views over the Afar plains to
the north. Ethiopia lies between latitude 3° and 18° north and longitude 33° 48° east.

The dominant feature of the country's topography is the high Central Plateau, generally
between 2,000-3,000 metres, and it is here that the majority of the population is
concentrated. This plateau contains a number of river systems, the most significant of
which is the Blue Nile (*Abbay*). The most fertile part of Ethiopia lies to the extreme south.
Agricultural potential here is rich, and parts of the Sidamo Highlands, with rolling grassland
and wooded hills are in complete contrast to the image of Ethiopia as unrelentingly dry
and arid.

The vegetation of the plateau is dominated by mountain grassland and settled
agriculture. Population pressure has forced farmers into areas which are very marginal in
rainfall and soil quality, particularly along the eastern escarpment, and this has exacerbated
the drought and famine conditions which have characterized parts of Ethiopia since 1973.
Coniferous forests have now largely disappeared from the highlands, although in the
south, lower elevations and higher temperatures have produced broad-leaved forests
which, largely due to their inaccessibility, have not yet been subjected to extensive
commercial exploitation.

The lowlands, depending on the amount of rainfall, have dry zone vegetation, ranging
from limited areas of desert to thorn scrub and savannah.

Ethiopia's climate is determined by altitude and proximity to the Indian Ocean. **Climate**
Considerable variations in temperature are reflected in the traditional climate zone
divisions: *dega*, the temperate plateau, *kolla*, hot lowlands, and the intermediate frost
free zone of the *woina dega*. Average annual temperatures vary over these zones from
16° to 26°C.

Rainfall varies considerably. In most parts of the central highlands the average is well
over 1,000 millimetres per year, while the drier lowlands receive less than 500
millimetres. There are two principal seasons; rainy from June to October and relatively
dry for the rest of the year, although some regions experience short April rains as well
(the *belg*). The country is extremely vulnerable to drought conditions, particularly in the
low lying pastoral areas and along the eastern escarpment, where there is heavy
dependence on the *belg* rains. A further set of rains (the *meher*) in October, November
and December allow a second harvest.

Ethiopia

Luigi Balugani

Luigi Balugani was born in Lucca in northern Italy in 1737 and he studied draughtsmanship and architecture at the Accademia Clementina in Bologna. In 1761 he met James Bruce in Rome and was recruited to make drawings for Bruce's impending African expedition. He made over 300 drawings of flora and fauna which were *used, but not acknowledged, in Bruce's* Travels to Discover the Source of the Nile.

When Bruce and Balugani returned to Gondar, having found the source, Balugani fell ill with fever and died. He is buried there at the Church of St Rafael. In 1991 the illustrations that Balugani made were published in a volume Drawings of African Plants.

Flora and fauna

Mammals The wildlife of Ethiopia has suffered considerably in the last few decades and visitors should not expect to see the same abundance of animals that can be seen in the other East African Parks. Various species of antelope are fairly widespread, if not numerous, in many of the Game Parks, and dikdik, oribi, reedbuck, bushbuck and greater and lesser kudu can all be seen. Outside of the Game Parks two monkeys are quite common: the black and white colobus and the vervet. Compared with the animals of East Africa, both these monkeys occur in a slightly different form in Ethiopia. The colobus *(Colobus abyssinicus)*, usually known as the guereza, has a large and conspicuous white mantle extending downwards from the shoulders. The vervet *(Cercopithicus aethiops)* has very long and noticeable white whiskers. Baboons are also common. The olive baboon *(Papio anubis)* is usually known as the anubis in Ethiopia, where it is the commonest baboon. The endemic gelada baboon *(Papio gelada)* is often seen in parties in wild and rocky places (a species is said to be endemic to a certain place when it occurs in that place only, and nowhere else). The male gelada is an impressively large animal with a well-developed mane and bare red patches on its chest. Occasionally smaller mammals such as the abyssinian hare *(Lepus habessinicus)* and some species of ground squirrel can be observed from the road. At night jackals are quite often seen, as is the spotted hyaena *(Crocuta crocuta)*, though this latter is more often heard. Hyaenas are often seen dead on the highways. It is a scavenger, and, especially on the edge of towns and villages, its eerie whooping is a characteristic sound of the Ethiopian night.

Birds Although the animals in Ethiopia may not be as numerous as those elsewhere in East Africa, this is more than compensated for by the wonderful birdlife. There are more than 20 endemic species in Ethiopia and many of them can be seen around Addis Ababa. Furthermore, they are often large or colourful and common.

Other endemics seen here include the white-billed starling *(Onychognathus albirostris)*, wattled ibis *(Bostrychia caranculata)*, white-collared pigeon *(Columba albitorques)*, black-winged lovebird *(Agapornis taranta)*, thick-billed raven *(Corvus crassirostris)*, abyssinian longclaw *(Macronyx flavicollis)* and flocks of the black-headed siskin *(Serinus nigriceps)*.

Crops Chickpeas are grown near Addis in small untidy looking fields. They have a pretty blue flower and the peas are sold at the roadside still attached to the plant. Linseed, with its blue flower, is also a commonly grown crop. Teff, the staple grain crop of Ethiopia, grows in small fields and looks just like a rather straggly grass.

King Solomon, the Queen of Sheba & the Lion of Judah Dynasty

On the last day of the visit of the Queen of Sheba to King Solomon in Jerusalem, the King asked if the Queen would spend the night in his room. She consented, but took his invitation literally, making it a condition that Solomon should not force his attentions upon her. Taken aback, Solomon sought to save his dignity by demanding that the Queen, in her turn, should respect both his person and his property. An agreement was struck and deviously, the King ordered a grand banquet of ten courses, all highly spiced and salted. They settled for the night in separate beds, a vessel of water between them. A little peeved, the King made do with a maid from the Queen's entourage, and the son she subsequently bore became the first King in the Zagne Dynasty in Ethiopia.

During the night, the Queen became thirsty, and drank some water from the vessel the King had placed between the beds. This allowed Solomon, somewhat ungallantly, to claim that the Queen had broken the agreement, and that she must now replace the maid in his bed. The child of this union was Menelik I, the first Ethiopian King of the line that was to stretch down the centuries.

During the course of this modestly productive night, Solomon had a disturbing dream. He saw a glittering sun rise over Israel and then shift to shine on Axum. A second sun arose, illuminating all the world but casting its rays with special brilliance on Italy and Ethiopia.

The first sun is interpreted as the Ark of the Covenant, taken by Menelik I from the Temple in Jerusalem to St Mary's Church in Axum, where it is concealed in a secret chamber.

The second sun represented the teachings of Christ. In 330 AD a Syrian ship sailing up the Red Sea was boarded, and all but two boys from the crew were slain. The two were taken to the Imperial court at Axum where one, Frumentius, so impressed with his wisdom that a few years later he ruled for a while in place of Ezana, the young Regent. When Ezana became Emperor, Frumentius went to Alexandria where he was consecrated as the first Bishop of Axum. On his return to Ethiopia, he spread the word of Christ throughout the land.

This legend is recorded from oral sources in the 14th century in Kebra Nagast, the Ethiopian Book of the Glory of the Kings. The work was commissioned by St Tekla Haimanot, who pursued holy devotions for 27 years in a cave at Debre Libanos.

Ethiopia

History

Fossil remains discovered at a site on the Lower Awash River in northeast Ethiopia in 1974 by US palaeontologist Donald Johanson and named 'Lucy' have been identified as the earliest example of an upright walking hominid. Dated at three and a half million years old, these remains constitute our oldest known ancestors, and many now consider this region of Ethiopia to be the true cradle of mankind. A more recent find in early 1999 of a previously unidentified animal, dated two and a half million years old, is speculated to be the 'missing link'. The skull of a new hominid species, named Australopithecus garhi with a brain capacity of 450 cc, as compared to 1400 cc of modern man, was discovered near the small village of Bouri, northeast of Addis Ababa. Three independent discoveries were made in the vicinity of Bouri of a skull, and the arm and leg bones of a second individual, believed to have belonged to the same species and to have lived during the same period. Close to these huminoid remains were the bones of antelopes, horses and other animals, which showed clear evidence of having been cut with stone tools. Some of the animal bony remains had curved incision marks on them and the ends of the long bones had been crushed or broken off to enable the marrow to be extracted. This is the first evidence that stone tools were used for butchering. Anthropologists have theorized that eating fat rich marrow enabled the dramatic increase in brain size. However, other scientists have theorized that the discovery of how to cook root vegetables to provide a source of disgestible carbohydrates would have been of greater significance.

Cradle of mankind

👉 *Harrison Smith and the Sword of Honour*

In 1884 the British found themselves with several garrisons surrounded by hostile Dervishes in eastern Sudan. They entered into a three-sided treaty with Egypt, and Emperor Yohannes IV of Ethiopia, agreeing to mutual support. Yohannes promptly met his side of the bargain, dispatching his commander Ras Alula to relieve the beleaguered garrisons.

Yohannes was less than impressed with the British sense of honour, when, a mere 18 months later, they did nothing to prevent the Italians occupying Massawa.

The British government sought to make amends by sending a naval officer, Francis Harrison Smith, with a letter from Queen Victoria and a Sword of Honour for the Emperor.

Harrison Smith docked at Massawa in 1886 and travelled via Asmara down to Yohannes' camp near Lake Ashange. The letter and the sword were accepted graciously, but, alas, did nothing to protect Yohannes who was slain at the battle of Metemma in 1889.

The early history of Ethiopia begins with the glorious but still only partly understood Axumite Kingdom, which grew up around Axum in the north highlands in the third century BC and endured until the 10th century AD. The achivements of this early civilization are recorded today in the ruins of the old Axumite cities and towns, reservoirs, dams, temples and stone stele (pillars) on which are recorded fragments of the history of the empire and dynasty. Legend records that Cush, son of Ham and grandson of Noah, came to Ethiopia from Mesopotamia (now Iraq). Other stories claim that Menelik I, the child born to the union of King Solomon and the Queen of Sheba (see box, page 739), settled in Axum, bringing with him the Ark of the Covenant from the Temple in Jerusulem and establishing a dynasty which ruled – with only brief interruptions – until the fall of Haile Selassie in 1974.

Ethiopia's historical importance stemmed partly from its favourable location and terrain. Lying on the edge of the Graeco-Roman world it was linked to both by the Red Sea and the Nile. Kinship, trade and culture also tied it strongly to the Persian Empire. Axumite commerce was based largely on the export of gold and ivory and trade links reached as far as Ceylon, although the strongest links were with Egypt and Greece.

Christianity reached Axum in the fourth century AD, during the reign of the Conqueror King Ezana. He was converted by a young Syrian named Frumentius who was shipwrecked off Adulis and who subsequently became the first Bishop of Axum (see box, page 739). Early coins from Ezana's reign show the traditionally worshipped symbols of the sun and moon, while later coins bear the sign of the cross.

The Axumite Empire reached its zenith in the sixth century when King Kaleb crossed the Red Sea to conquer parts of Saudi Arabia. However, the rise of Islam in the seventh century drove the Axumites back onto home territory and as Islam asserted itself in East Africa, the Ethiopian Christians became increasingly isolated.

Middle Ages The Axumite Kingdom, denied the trade routes which were its lifeblood, declined during the 10th century, after which the balance of political and religious power shifted south to Lasta and the new Zagwe Dynasty. Its most important ruler was King Lalibela, renowned for the rock-hewn churches which he built at the capital which was later to bear his name.

The Zagwe were in turn overthrown in the late 12th century by Yekuno Amlak, who claimed descent from the rulers of Axum and thus restored the Solomonic Dynasty. This was a period of rule by chiefs and warlords who collected taxes and made war on each other, but who would submit themselves to the king of their province and through him to the King of Kings.

In 1531, as the Ottoman Empire began to expand, General Ibn Ibrahim, or Gragn (the left handed), led a Muslim army into the Ethiopian Highlands. Emperor Labna Dengal appealed to Portugal for military assistance, which duly arrived in the form of Christopher de Gama (son of the explorer Vasco) and 400 men, and defeat was avoided. Subsequently, in 1571, the Pope sent the first of several Jesuit missions to Ethiopia in an attempt to introduce Roman Catholicism, but little headway was made and the Jesuits were banished in the mid-17th century.

The monarchy of Gondar, which had become an important political and commercial centre in the early 17th century, lost its authority in the 18th century when the feudal lords became independent of central control. A hundred years of near anarchy ensued, giving way eventually to major attempts at reunification in the second half of the 19th century, moves which were given greater urgency as first France and England and then Italy began to cast covetous eyes on Ethiopia. The main work of unification was left to Menelik II, an enterprising, vigorous and imaginative young king from Shoa, who guided Ethiopia through the maelstrom of Europe's scramble for Africa. Menelik reigned as King of Shoa from 1865-89 and as Emperor of Ethiopia from that year until his death in 1913.

By fraudulent misrepresentation of the Treaty of Wuchale, which Italy concluded with Menelik, Italy laid claim to Ethiopia as its protectorate – a claim supported by Britain and France as they shared out the rest of eastern Africa between themselves. However, at the Battle of Adwa, on 1 March 1896, Menelik's forces routed the Italians, thus preserving Ethiopia's independence throughout the colonial era. Menelik established most of Ethiopia's present frontiers. He also founded Addis Ababa and was a great modernizer, setting up schools and banks, a railway and a postal system.

Italy still continued to have designs on Ethiopia, and although it became a member of the League of Nations after the First World War, this did not prevent Mussolini from overrunning the country in 1936. Italian forces remained in occupation for five years, despite pleas to the international community from the young emperor, Haile Selassie. Italy was forced out of Ethiopia by guerrilla and Allied forces during the Second World War and the country resumed its status as an independent nation. However, unrest continued in the north. After 11 years of British administration, Eritrea was federated to Ethiopia in 1952, but when in 1962 the federation was dissolved and the province was annexed by Haile Selassie, guerrilla warfare broke out. Eritrea had not been part of Ethiopia for several hundred years, and the subsequent struggle for independence was to dominate Ethiopian history until the early 1990s.

Haile Selassie

Haile Selassie had established himself as a national hero during the campaigns against the Italians and had become a respected African statesman. He concentrated on international affairs, securing Addis Ababa as the headquarters of the Organization for African Unity (OAU) and the UN Economic Commission for Africa. A close ally of the US, he ensured that Ethiopia was a major recipient of US aid in the 1950s and 1960s. However, Haile Selassie governed Ethiopia like a medieval fiefdom, unable to understand or respond to the agricultural stagnation, inequitable distribution of land and general lack of development. The continuing cost of revolt in Eritrea and drought and famine in Wollo 1972-74, with the death of 200,000 people, contrasted starkly with the accumulation of wealth by the nobility and the church. This caused a mass outbreak of resentment and on 12 September 1974, against a background of strikes, student demonstrations and army mutiny, Haile Selassie was deposed. The monarchy was abolished the following year. The former emperor died in his palace, under armed guard, several months later. Haile Selassie's son, Crown Prince Asfa Wossen, lives in exile in London.

Civil war & revolution

The imperial régime was replaced by a provisional military administrative council, known as the Dergue, which saw itself as the vanguard of the Ethiopian Revolution. It began to implement a programme of socialist, revolutionary reforms – nationalizing companies, implementing literacy campaigns and setting up over 30,000 locally elected associations. After two years of infighting within the Dergue, Lt-col Mengistu Haile Miriam emerged at the head of the dictatorship – executing his rivals within the régime and launching an urban terror campaign against the Ethiopian People's Revolutionary Party, which argued for the immediate creation of civilian government and supported the Eritrean struggle. Tens of thousands were killed or tortured as Mengistu wiped out the opposition and imposed his own vision of Marxism-Leninism.

Military disarray in Addis prompted the Eritreans to step up their campaign, and in 1977 Somalia began encroaching into southeastern Ethiopia. The Dergue may well have collapsed at this time but for the intervention of the USSR and Cuba who re-equipped and trained the Ethiopian army. With this new weaponry and some 16,000 Cuban troops the army went back on the offensive, repulsing Somalia from occupied Ogaden and rolling back the gains which the rival Eritrean People's Liberation Front (EPLF, predominantly Christian) and the Eritrean Liberation Front (ELF, predominantly Muslim) had made in Eritrea. The EPLF dug in around the remote northern town of Nacfa and over several years continued to inflict heavy losses on the Ethiopian army. In 1982 the EPLF, in alliance with the Tirayan People's Liberation Front (TPLF), drove the ELF into Sudan where they disarmed and fragmented.

Mengistu was never able to achieve widespread support, largely due to his failure to solve the nationality problem, of which the stuggle in Eritrea was the most obvious symptom. The revolution had raised expectations of regional autonomy among various nationalities such as the Oromos in the south and the Tigrayans in the north. The Oromo Liberation Front (OLF), advocating self-determination for Oromia and respect for its language and culture, gained support during the early 1980s from the rural base in the region which had benefited from reforms implemented in 1975. But the most serious threat came from the TPLF established in 1975 to struggle for Tigrayan self-determination, receiving arms and training from the EPLF.

Mengistu's political and military responses to the nationalist movements were inadequate and the country was further weakened by the catastrophic famine of 1984-85. The international community's response to the disaster was slow, partly because of Ethiopia's close links with the Soviet Union and when help did arrive, conflict ensured that many of the worst-hit rebel areas, especially in Tigray, were denied relief. The government's own relief measures consisted largely of an unpopular resettlement programme, in which 600,000 people were moved into the south and west of the country. At the same time the TPLF moved 200,000 Tigrayans into the Sudan.

The military situation deteriorated for Mengistu after 1988. While the EPLF continued to make gains in Eritrea, the TPLF now controlled all of Tigray and began to push south to Addis under the flag of the Ethiopian People's Revolutionary Democratic Front (EPRDF). Disillusionment grew in the army and Mengistu's refusal to seek a political solution was increasingly seen as a liability. By February 1990 the EPLF had captured the Red Sea port of Massawa, cutting off supply lines to the Ethiopian Army in Eritrea, and Mengistu was forced to make concessions. He abandoned Ethiopian socialism, invited opposition groups to participate in a unity party and built free market principles into economic planning. But this was insufficient and problems began to mount. The fall in the world price of coffee added to economic hardships, and with the collapse of the Eastern European régimes, Ethiopia lost most of its overseas alliances. As the opposition forces closed in on Addis Ababa in February 1991, Mengistu fled to Zimbabwe. On 28 May the EPRDF entered the capital and subsequently established an interim government.

A four-year transition period allowed the formulation of a new constitution. The first elections, in May 1995, for national and regional representatives, were won comfortably by the EPRDF.

Relations with Eritrea have been affected by the introduction of a new currency by Ethiopia's neighbour. This has complicated cross-border trade and made Ethiopia aware of the implications of the independence of Eritrea in making Ethiopia land-locked. The border between the two countries is disputed, and in June 1998 this erupted into armed conflict and bombing raids, with all borders closed.

Culture

There has never been a full census carried out in Ethiopia, but the population is esti- **People**
mated at about 56 million, with 85 percent working on the land. The central plateau
is characterized by settled cultivation of cereals and pulses, while nomadic lifestyles
persist at the desert margins.

There are over 80 languages and dialects. In Tigray region, around Axum, the
Semitic language Tigrinya is spoken, while the heartland of Ethiopia is the home of
Amharic, the official language. To the south and east are the Cushitic speaking peo-
ples, the Oromos, Afars and Somalis. Ethiopia's Nilotic peoples, the Nuer and the
Anuak are found to the far south and west. Living close to the border with Sudan the
Nuer and the Anuak are related to the people of southern Sudan. The Nuer are
mainly a cattle-herding tribe, while the Anuak are fishermen living by the Baro River
and adjacent swamplands. There Nilo, the Hamitic language, differs totally from the
Semitic and Cushitic languages used in the rest of Ethiopia. The Falasha, living
around Gondar, are linked to Ethiopia's early ties to Judaic Palestine, and thousands
of Falasha were airlifted out of the country by Israel during the 1984-85 famine.
Amharas and Tigrays are predominantly Orthodox Christian while Oromos, the
largest ethnic group in the country, are more mixed, with communities following
Christian, Muslim and traditional religions.

Arts and crafts

Jewellery is particularly fine, forged mostly from silver in a characteristic style,
sometimes with amber decoration. Bracelets, necklaces, rings and pendants are all
made.

Weaving traditional cloth, mostly from cotton, but sometimes from wool. Decoration is often by delicate embroidery, or in the rural areas by sewing on cowrie shells.

Leatherwork, hides and skins. Sheepskin capes are a speciality. Traditional curing
of leather involves sun-drying the skin and then treating it with clotted milk and linseed oil.

Pottery is made without use of a wheel by coiling ribbons of clay. Decoration is
sometimes effected by smoking the clay, and polishing with a stone after open-pit
firing. There are good examples of the large disc-shaped *injera* cooking plates, coffee
pots and water carriers of varying sizes.

Horn is carved and polished to make drinking vessels, boxes and ornaments. Horn
is fashioned into vessels by heating it until it is malleable.

Basketwork includes both woven items, and pieces made by coiling bundles of
fibres. As well as containers, basketry techniques can be used to make brushes,
brooms and umbrellas.

Woodcarving products are furniture, particularly three-legged stools and coffee
tables. Vases, ashtrays and candle-sticks and musical instuments are also made.

It is often possible to watch craftsmen at work in co-operatives. Contact the Handicrafts and Small-scale Industries Development Agency near the Wabe Shebelle
Hotel, T448809.

Ethiopia

☞ *Wax and gold*

In fashioning a gold figure, the first step is to make a wax model, which is then covered with wet clay. A small hole in the clay allows the wax to run out when the clay is fired. Molten gold is poured through the hole into the cast, and when it sets, the mould is broken to reveal the figure.

In Ethiopian poetry, and in verses sung by minstrels, at the initial level there is a story, pleasing in itself. But this is an allegory for something more valuable and profound. Puns and double meanings are features of this structure. The imagery for the two levels of meaning is sammena wark, wax and gold.

NB If you purchase a souvenir that is particularly old or rare, you will need to get a clearance from the National Museum in Addis Ababa (see page 685) before it can be exported. There is a small charge (US$0.20). You should always ensure you get a receipt for an antique item, and can produce it if challenged. Some travellers have been harassed, and even spent time in jail for antiquities offences, so do take care.

Modern Ethiopia

Politics

With the overthrow of the Dergue régime, the EPRDF (see pages 741 and 742 for full names of political groups) drew up a national charter which allowed for the creation of an 87 seat council of representatives, representing some 32 political organizations and with the EPRDF occupying 32 of the seats. New internal boundaries were created, reflecting ethnicity and political power. Large powerful and concentrated groups (Tigray and Oromo) appeared to gain fertile areas and relinquish desert while weaker and dispersed groups (Amhara and Gurage) lost good land.

The intention is to allow Ethiopia's main ethnic groups to have self-determination within a federal structure. The EPRDF has found it difficult to maintain cohesion as there are now over 100 political groups based mostly on ethnic affiliations. The OLF and some other minor groups decided not to participate in the elections in 1992, and also withdrew from the government. An attempt by the OLF to revive guerrilla resistance has provided cause for concern, though not serious. The OLF is split into several factions which limits its effectiveness.

The EPRDF dominated the 1992 elections, winning 890 out of 978 seats in Addis Ababa, and 81 out of 84 in the regions. Elections were postponed in two areas, it is said because the EPRDF had not got itself well enough organized.

By 1991, the EPLF had established a provisional government in Eritrea. In the process, more than 100,000 non-Eritreans were deported to Tigray. A referendum in April 1993 endorsed separation from Ethiopia, Eritrea became an independent state and joined the UN.

The new constitution was finally adopted at the end of 1994. It has a federal framework based on nine regions. There are three legislative levels: regional state councils and a bi-cameral Federal Assembly. The chief executive is the Prime Minister, chosen by the elected Council of Peoples Representatives, one of the houses of the Federal Assembly. The President is to have a largely ceremonial role.

The first elections, in 1995, under the new system resulted in an overwhelming victory for the EPRDF – however, the polls were boycotted by the main opposition groups. The Prime Minister is Meles Zenawi who was President in the transitional administration. The President is an Oromo, Negaso Gidada. The new constitution has reorganized the administration, and there are now nine regions and the metropolitan council of Addis Ababa. Most of the regions have a strong ethnic identity, raising the possibility of future tensions.

Coffee ceremony sting

It is not unusual for a visitor to Addis Ababa to be approached in the street by a young man who will present himself as a student at the University, wishing to chat as a way of improving his English. After the usual inconsequential pleasantries he will mention that the University students have a club nearby, and will invite the visitor there to observe the coffee ceremony.

One such `club' is in a bungalow off Bole Road. The arrivals are seated on sofas in a lounge, and are joined by a girl in traditional dress who will begin roasting the coffee beans. The visitor is served a soft drink.

The matron who is in charge of the club joins the guest together with a couple of girls who explain that they are University students. The visitor is a little puzzled that the girl who says she is studying Economics claims never to have heard of supply and demand analysis, let alone macroeconomics and Maynard Keynes. As the coffee is being prepared, one of the girls will ask if they might be invited to have a drink as well. It seems churlish to refuse, but instead of soft drinks, a well-worn cognac bottle is produced and its contents generously distributed to the girls and the matron.

The coffee is finally brewed and drunk. The cognac is finished and the visitor declines an invitation to purchase another, asks for the bill. It is about US$10 for the coffee ceremony, US$50 for the bottle of cognac and US$5 for the soft drinks. Invariably the visitor pays. Closer examination of the cognac reveals it to be a local Martini, costing US$2 a bottle.

On leaving, it is suggested that the visitor might, for a suitably extravagant sum, like to have sex with one or both of the girls in a rear room of the bungalow. So they were University students, after all.

Ethiopia's border with Somalia continues to present problems. The Somali *Al-Ihihad* militia has been involved in cross-border terrorist activity, and there have been clashes with Ethiopian government forces including hot pursuit into Somalia.

In November 1997 Eritrea introduced its own currency, the Nakfa, replacing the Ethiopian Birr which had previously been in use. This complicated trade relations, particularly goods in transit now that Ethiopia is land-locked. Ethiopia retaliated by insisting that all transactions be undertaken in hard currency, a problem for Eritrea which has limited foreign currency reserves.

Relations with Eritrea have been exacerbated by a dispute over the 1,500 kilometre border between the two countries. Eritrea is claiming the territory marked by the Italian colonisers. These borders were ammended when Eritrea was annexed by Ethiopia in 1962 and five small zones were allocated to Ethiopian provinces. Eritrea is claiming the old Italian borders, and both sides have made efforts to occupy the disputed areas, all of no economic significance.

In May 1998 there were a series of air strikes and bombing raids on the airport in Asmara by the Ethiopians and on the airport and town of Makele by the Eritreans.

It is not clear which side initiated the armed conflict, how it will be resolved or when the closed borders will re-open. The dispute is utterly unnecessary and has aptly been described as 'two bald men fighting over a comb'.

After a lull in late 1988, when diplomatic intiatives to end the dispute were in progress, fighting resumed in the early part of 1999. The conflict is disastrous – transport links have been broken, both sides have expelled citizens and seized assets with around 400,000 now displaced. Agriculture has been disrupted, and the war effort has absorbed resources and increased government expenditure, thereby undermining structural reforms of the economy.

Economics

The economy was badly affected by the repressive bureaucracy, capricious government interference and civil conflicts of the Mengistu period of 1974-91. Desperate shortages, decaying infrastructure and famine were the order of the day. In the past eight years, however, with firm commitment to a market economy, Ethiopia has made an excellent recovery.

Economic & social structure
The size of the population has been revised downward in recent years, and it is now estimated at around 61.1 million for 1999. This still, however, makes Ethiopia the most populous country in Africa, with the exception of Nigeria. The low level of development is reflected in the low level of urbanization, with only 13 percent living in the towns. Ethiopia is more densely populated than most of Africa – in fact the number of persons per square kilometre is more than double the Africa average. As with most other countries in Africa, the population is growing fairly rapidly at 2.7 percent a year, and this rate implies an extra one and a half million persons each year.

Measured by production of output, the economy, with a GDP of US$5,694m in 1998 is about average in size compared with the rest of Africa. However, the large population means that living standards are very low. Both methods of converting GDP to US$ indicate that Ethiopia is one of the two or three poorest countries in the world. The exchange rate method gives GDP per head of US$100, and purchasing power parity US$450.

Low living standards lead to an emphasis on agriculture, mostly in small family farms, producing output for household consumption, and agriculture generates 55 percent of GDP. Industry is very modest at 12 percent of GDP, as are services at 33 percent.

Most expenditure is on consumption, at 81 percent of GDP, while investment has improved to 16 percent. The government sector, hampered by inability to raise revenue, and the dislocation following the collapse of the Mengistu régime, undertakes a low proportion of overall spending (12 percent). Aid is equivalent to 23 percent of GDP, and this is above the African average.

Exports are low at only 15 percent of GDP, and comprise mostly coffee (44 percent) and hides and skins (13 percent). Ethiopia is the third largest coffee exporter in Africa after Uganda and Côte d'Ivoire. Imports are 26 percent of GDP, and are at this level as a result of aid receipts. The main imports are foodstuffs (23 percent), vehicles (13 percent), machinery (12 percent) and fuels (10 percent).

Economic performance
The growth rate of the economy was negative for much of the 1980s, and the period was one of falling living standards. However, since the collapse of the Mengistu government there has been some improvement, and the economy since 1991 has grown faster than population, resulting in significant recovery in living standards.

Poor performance was experienced in agriculture, in particular in the 1980s, with output growing at only 0.3 percent a year, while the population was growing at 2.7 percent. Production in this sector was not helped by government policies which relocated rural populations, and the situation was compounded by the droughts in the middle of the decade. Industry and services appeared to grow a little faster, but in fact this was a reflection of government emphasis on military expediture, bolstered by foreign support.

Export volumes declined as the economy was run down. Import volumes declined as well, but not as fast as exports, and were supported by aid and other receipts from outside. Heavy reliance on coffee and hides and skin makes Ethiopia very vulnerable to changes in world prices, and the terms of trade have declined by about a quarter since 1987, compounding Ethiopia's problems, such that 25 percent more needs to be exported to purchase the same volume of imports.

Inflation was very modest at three percent a year, 1980-92. Performance slipped in 1995 to above 10 percent a year, but is now below five percent.

The pro-Soviet leanings of Mengistu meant that Ethiopia did not accumulate external debt to any great degree in relation to the size of the economy, and debt service payments are a manageable 14 percent of export earnings.

Lion of Judah's Lions

The Emperor Haile Selassie kept his own pride of lions at his palace in Addis Ababa. A lion would accompany him, on a lead, when official visitors were received. When touring Europe in 1924, Haile Selassie took six lions with him, giving four to the French and two to King George V.

Recent economic developments

In the face of evidence of a downward spiral in the economy, the later period of the Mengistu régime saw some belated efforts at economic reform. Private traders were allowed in the agricultural sector and prices to small farmers rose.

After 1991 the new EPRDF government, supported by the IMF and the World Bank, committed itself to a more thorough-going reform in its Economic Relief and Rehabilitation Programme (ERRP). Prices have been decontrolled, private traders allowed in most markets, and moves have been made to privatize state-owned enterprises. 175 state-owned enterprises have been sold, but most of these are small. There are another 114 to be privatized, but progress is slow. The programme is due to be completed by 2001. The financial sector is still mostly state-owned, and private banks are not envisaged until 2002.

The civil service is being restructured and retrenchment is anticipated. Tariff reforms are making the economy more open, and the average level of customs duties is under 30 percent.

The currency was devalued in October 1992 and foreign currency auctions are now used to set the exchange rate. These reforms appear to have been a significant factor in the economic recovery of the past six years. However, the mainstay of the economy, the agricultural sector, is still very vulnerable to the vagaries of the weather. Despite favourable harvests in 1991 and 1992, food aid needs were still considerable. Poor harvests in 1993/4 and again in 1997/8 continued to threaten Ethiopia's food security, although the 1998/9 grain harvest has been good. The commissioning of a new sugar refinery in 1997 should enable Ethiopia to become a major sugar exporter.

The border dispute with Eritrea that erupted in May 1998 can be expected to curtail trade. In addition there are the disruptive effects of the 'El Niño' flooding which have hit agriculture, transport and communications over the past year.

Mining is waiting on commitment by foreign investors. The Lega Dembi deposits southwest of Addis Ababa, with current output of gold of three tonnes a year and 500 tonnes deposits, has been privatized and sold to a Saudi-Ethiopian consortium.

Tourism is expanding rapidly with 136,000 tourists, up from 117,000 a year ago. Ethiopian Airlines continues to be a success in the services sector, posting profits of US$30m in the last financial year. Russia is expected to cancel most of its outstanding debt. Together with the 1997 reduction of debt under the 'Naples Terms', Ethiopia's external debt has become much more manageable. Servicing of the debt, which absorbed 45 percent of export earnings in 1997, now accounts for only 15 percent.

The election successes of the EPRDF strengthened the commitment to the reform programme and the market economy. The emphasis is on privatization, joint ventures and foreign investment.

Economic outlook In the long-term, the economy can be expected to show continuing recovery, although agricultural output will remain heavily dependent on the weather.

There are considerable deposits of minerals in Ethiopia, all of which are only partially exploited. At last the international mining houses appear to be confident Ethiopia's political future is stable, and that the government is going to persevere with the economic reforms. Foreign investment in mining will be a big boost to the economy.

Short-term prospects depend crucially on a quick end to the dispute with Eritrea.

Social conditions

Adult literacy is estimated at 35 percent, and this is poor even by African standards. Only 23 percent of children in the appropriate age groups go to primary school, a very poor enrolment rate, and about a third of the African average. Secondary enrolments do not compare quite so unfavourable, but with 12 percent going to secondary school, there is hardly any education at this level for children outside the urban areas. Tertiary education levels are also low.

Life expectancy is 49 years. Almost half of children under five are malnourished. Infant mortality rates are among the highest in the world. Availability of doctors is a little better than in Africa generally, but they are almost all concentrated in the urban areas, and medical provision in the rural areas is woeful.

Primary education and secondary education both have lower enrolments for women. The disparity is less great at the secondary level, but again it must be remembered that secondary education is really only available in the towns, where there is a more enlightened attitude to the educational needs of females.

As with everywhere in Africa, there is pressure on women to help support their families by working outside the home, mostly by contributing to agricultural production, and two-thirds of women are so engaged. The burdens on women are compounded by an average fertility rate of almost seven births per woman, with only four percent of women using contraceptives.

Environment

The forested area is about 13 percent of the total land area. Economic collapse invariably has an adverse effect on afforestation in low-income countries. There is increased demand for land and woodfuel for cooking, and in Ethiopia the forested area has been diminishing by 0.3 percent a year.

Domestic water usage is very low at six cubic metres per person a year, and industrial and agricultural is comparatively low as well. As a result, Ethiopia puts little general strain on its renewable supplies of fresh water, utilizing only two percent of the total availability.

750

Eritrea

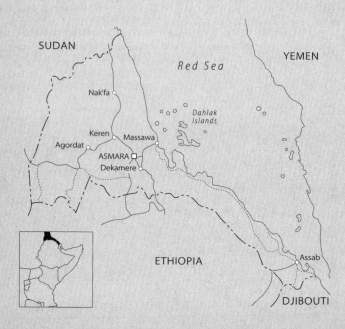

SUDAN

Red Sea

YEMEN

Nak'fa

Dahlak
Islands

Keren

Agordat

Massawa

ASMARA □

Dekamere

ETHIOPIA

Assab

DJIBOUTI

After 30 years of war, Eritrea achieved effective independence from Ethiopia in 1991 and this was formally declared on 24 May 1993. Since then, the country has concentrated on achieving some degree of political stability, as well as reintegrating thousands of demobilized soldiers, men and women, back into economic activity. There has thus been little time to devote to promoting tourism, given other more pressing national priorities. However, this does not in any way mean that visitors are not welcome – Eritrea is a friendly and relaxed country to visit, where you are soon made to feel at home. It has a great deal to offer – from Asmara, the capital, with its array of bars and cafes in wide, palm-lined streets, to the beautiful mountain scenery, miles of unspoilt white sandy beaches along the coast, the coral reefs and aquatic life at Dahlak Islands, and a number of historical sites dating back to the Axumite Kingdom. The emergence of Eritrea as an independent, self-reliant, working state is a testament to the resolution of the people of Eritrea and their considerable organizational skills. Their currency, introduced in November 1997 to replace the Ethiopian Birr, is named after the remote mountain retreat of Nakfa, the symbol of resistance to Ethiopian occupation, where the rebels survived 10 years of shelling from the Ethiopian army. To reach Nakfa takes 10 hours in a 4WD from the capital, over rough mountain terrain – a journey of just over 200 kilometres.

In June 1998 a border dispute with Ethiopia led to armed conflict and bombing raids. The borders are closed, and it is uncertain as to when they will be re-opened.

The heavy 'El Niño' rains in 1997/98 have disrupted transport and communications.

Eritrea

Essentials

Before you travel

When to go The main rainy season in the hinterland is July and August, the coast has rain in December to February, but the showers are short, and the rest of the day will be sunny. However if you do travel in the rainy season, the country is wonderfully green, the temperature is cooler and there are less tourists.

Visas A visa is required by anyone wishing to enter Eritrea. Visas are available from Eritrean embassies around the world and they cost about US$60 in European cities and are usually obtainable within 24-48 hours. If there is no embassy in your country, you may be able to get one from Addis Ababa in Ethiopia but this service has been disrupted due to the current political situation. A one-month, single entry visa costs US$25 in Addis Ababa. A transit entry visa costs US$15. If travelling by motorbike a carnet is not required, but you need to get a temporary import licence which costs US$14. You may be asked to provide proof of a return ticket or your next destination when applying for a visa. The dispute with Sudan (see page 776) has made it difficult to get a visa in Sudan. The border with Sudan is reported open, but it is essential to have a valid visa.

Vaccinations You will need a Yellow Fever vaccination certificate.

Money **Currency** Since November 1997 the unit of currency is the Eritrean Nakfa. In April 1998 the exchange rate is Nakfa 7.30 = US$1.

You will be best advised to get money exchanged in the capital, Asmara, as banking facilities in other parts of the country can be hard to find. Branches of the Commercial Bank of Eritrea are quick and efficient. The best currency to carry is the US dollar, though the English pound, the Italian lire, German mark and Japanese yen are alright. You may have problems having any other currencies recognized. You should bring some cash, but the majority of your money should be in travellers' cheques.

There is a modest black market at only marginally enhanced rates above the official rate.

Credit cards Major cards are sometimes taken by large hotels in Asmara and Ethiopian Airways. Not generally acceptable outside Asmara.

Getting there

Air The international carriers to Eritrea are Egyptair, Yemen Airways, Saudi Airlines and Lufthansa. Eritrean Airlines operates flights to Middle Eastern countries and internally. Since the border dispute of 1998 Ethiopian Airlines no longer fly to Eritrea. Lufthansa operates two flights weekly to Asmara via Frankfurt.

Taxis to town cost US$5, buses operate from 0600 every half an hour costing US$0.10, departure tax of US$12 - payable only in US$.

Road It is not possible to get into Eritrea from Ethiopia by road at present due to the border dispute. The two routes are: from Addis Ababa to Asmara via Adigrat, or from Addis Ababa to Assab and then north along the coast. There is no regular public transport operating on this route. There has been a programme of road building with excellent new roads from the border (Adigrat/Ethiopia) to Asmara, from Asmara to Massawa and from Asmara to Keren. From Keren to Barentu a road is under construction, aiming for completion in 1999 although the road building schedule has slipped due to the hostilities.

Eritrea embassies and consulates

Several Etritrean Embassies and Consulates have been set up recently and include:
Australia, 26 Guilfoyle St, Yarralumla, ACT Canberra 2600, T6-2823489, F6-2825233.
Belgium, 382 Ave Louise, 1050 Bruxelles, T2-5349563, F2-5393928.
Canada (consulate), ERRA in Canada IN, PO Box 2038 STND, Ottawa, Ontario KIP 5W3, T613-234-2181, F613-234-6123.
China, Ta Yuan Ran Gong Lou, 1-4-2, No 4 South Liang Maho Rd, Chao Yang District, Beijing PRC, T1-5326534/1-5326535, F1-5326532.
Djibouti, PO Box 1944, Djibouti, T355187/354961, F351831.
Egypt, PO Box 2624, 87 Shahab St, Al Muhandesein, Cairo, T3030516, F3030517.
Ethiopia, PO Box 2571, Addis Ababa, T514302/512692, F514911.
Germany, Markt Str 8, 50968, Köln, T221-373016, F221-3404128. **Italy**, Via Ferrucio 44/2, 00185 Rome, T06-70497908/06-70497924, F06-70497940.

Kenya, PO Box 38651, New Woumin House, 4th floor, West lanols, Nairobi, T443164, F443165.
Saudi Arabia, Ahmed Lary St, PO Box 770, Jeddah, T6612263, F6612014.
Sudan, PO Box 8129, Khartoum, T73165/74175, F24911452256.
Sweden, Ostermalmsgatan 34, Box 26068, 100 41 Stockholm, T08201470, F08206606.
UAE, PO Box 2597, Abu Dhabi, T2331838/2326355/T2346451.
UK (consulate) 96 White Lion St, London N1 9PF, T0171-7130096, F0171-7130161.
USA, 910 17th St, NW Ste 400, Washington DC 20006, T202-4291991, F202-4299004.
Yemen, PO Box 11040, T209422, F009671/214088.
In other places information can be obtained from Ethiopian Embassies (see page 691).

Overseas representation in Eritrea All the diplomatic representation is in Asmara (see page 762).

It is also possible to enter the country from Djibouti to Assab, though the route from Assab to Asmara is particularly uncomfortable and long (1,100 kilometres). If you do choose to go overland, be sure you have received an exit stamp at the border crossing. From Sudan the border crossing is between Kassala and Teseney, the distance between the two towns being 70 kilometres. The border crossing takes a full day to complete, with both the Eritrean and Sudanese formalities protracted by the current dispute (see page 776).

Rail Work has begun to repair the rail link between Asmara and Massawa destroyed in the protracted fighting. 42 kilometres have been restored plus two steam trains.

Sea There are two important ports in Eritrea: Massawa and Assab. Massawa is currently operational, though in disrepair, and many cargo ships dock here from other countries along the Red Sea. Every two weeks there is a cargo boat to Jeddah (Saudi Arabia), Port Sudan (Sudan) and Suez (Egypt). Fare to Suez US$115. You may be able to get dhows to Assab on the Djibouti, Ethiopian, Eritrean border in the south.

Touching down

Tourist information The new tourist office is to be set up in Post Office Square, just to the north of Independence Ave.

Travel & tour agents The main carrier into Eritrea used to be *Ethiopian Airways*, with offices situated in 54 cities around the world. In Asmara, the Ethiopian Airlines Office is on Liberation Ave, between the Catholic Cathedral and the Imperio Cinema. Invariably they have a staff member who takes responsibility for providing tourism information, and will cover developments in Eritrea, providing a reliable source for information on any recent changes in visa regulations, health requirements etc. This service has been suspended due to the 1998 border dispute.

Touching down

Hours of business *0800 to 1200 and 1400 to 1600. Banks and Ethiopian Airlines close for lunch at 1100.*

Official time *The Ethiopian timekeeping practice of using the 12-hour clock, starting at 0600 is no longer in use. Eritrea now uses the standard 24-hour clock, three hours ahead of GMT.*

IDD *291. Equal tones with long pauses means that it is ringing; short equal tones with equal pauses means engaged.*

Voltage *Both 110 and 220 volts. A variety of sockets are to be found around the country. It is advisable to bring an adaptor.*

Weights and measures *Metric weights and measures are in use in the main towns and cities. In country areas, customs vary.*

Ericommerce, Robin House, 2A Iverson Road, London, NW6 2HE, T0171-3727242, F0171-6246716, provide an up-to-date Eritrean travel information service.

As tourism develops, guided tours of the major cities and sights organized before departure from Europe/USA are becoming available. One UK company **Silk Steps** organizes a seven day itinerary by road that includes a visit to Asmara, Keren and Massawa, from where it is possible to visit the Great Rift Valley, costing US$450 (excluding flights to/from Eritrea). **Silk Steps Ltd**, PO Box 24, Bristol BS16 6JY, T0117-9402800, F0117-9406900, Info@silksteps.co.uk, www.silksteps.co.uk.

Rules, customs & etiquette

Conduct It is expected that dress will be sober for formal occasions, particularly when visiting government offices – it is regarded as a mark of respect for the persons you are meeting as much as anything else.

Visitors are often offered a cup of tea or coffee, and it is considered a friendly gesture to accept.

When entering a church or mosque, it is necessary for shoes to be removed. Women are not normally allowed to enter mosques unless there is a special prayer room set aside for them.

Photographs of museums, art works, churches and mosques will often require permission. When photographing local people, religious ceremonies or festivals, it is courteous to ask permission first, and a small fee might be requested.

Religion The country is fairly equally divided between Muslims and orthodox Christians, though there are some Roman Catholic and Protestant communities.

Safety Eritrea is a very safe country, and it is possible to walk about with confidence in the cities and towns even after dark. It is sensible to keep a close eye on belongings.

Although there are no restrictions on photography, military installations, airports, bridges, civil engineering works, government buildings, and military personnel should not be photographed. However changes may be made to take photos of ancient sites and buildings.

Where to stay

Sleeping The only place you are likely to find reasonable quality accommodation is in the capital, Asmara, as most facilities around the rest of the country were either destroyed during the war or have fallen into disrepair. However, you will be able to find modest places to stay in most towns.

Government hotels usually require payment in US dollars, while private hotels accept birr. It is advisable to ask whether the price is inclusive of 10% sales tax and another 10 percent service charge.

Camping is possible particularly on the coast, although there are no official campsites in the country as yet. See sleeping classification, page 31.

Tigrinya

Tigrinya is the most widely spoken local language. It has a complicated alphabet, and there is no widely accepted transliteration of the phonetic language into the Roman alphabet. For those wanting to go further, Edward Paice Guide to Eritrea *Chalfont St Peter: Bradt* contains a wider selection of words and phrases (although transliterated slightly differently).

Tigrinya Basics

Please	Bedja
Thank you	Yekanielay
Hello	Salam
Goodbye	Salamat
Yes	Uway

No	No
Good	Tsebook
Bad	Hmark
How much?	Kenday
Where is?	Abay
Why?	Nementaree
Water	Maee
Room	Koosaree
One	Harde
Two	Kilte
Three	Seleste
Four	Arbarte
Five	Hamushte
Ten	Arsete
Hundred	Meti
Thousand	Shek

Getting around

Air Air Eritrea operates an internal service between Assab and Asmara every Tuesday, leaving Asmara at 0800, returning later in the evening. Asmara airport, T181891, can provide passenger air arrival and departure information.

Train The railway between Massawa, Asmara, Keren and Agordat was dismantled during the war. A stretch of the track from Massawa inland is being reopened.

Road Eritrea's transport infrastructure was severely damaged as a result of the war though the government is putting much of its financial and manpower resources into redeveloping the road system. There has been a huge road building programme during the past few years, and there are now excellent new roads from Adigrat/Ethiopia to Asmara, from Asmara to Massawa and from Asmara to Keren. From Keren to Barentu a new road is being built, scheduled for completion in 1999.

Otherwise there are few sealed roads and they are invariably in a bad state of repair. The way north is rough and difficult from Asmara up towards Sudan through the arid hills of Afabet and Nakfa.

There are daily buses between most of the smaller towns, morning and afternoon buses between Asmara and Massawa and between Asmara and Keren.

Car hire Hiring a car as a means of exploring Eritrea is not a cheap option, although this may change as the country begins to receive more visitors. If you only plan to travel from Asmara to Keren and other major towns, you can hire a vehicle for about US$50 a day. If you want to go to other areas, you will need a four-wheel drive vehicle, which can be hired for about US$80 a day, plus mileage.

It is possible to hire chauffeur driven cars from Asmara (see page 762).

Keeping in touch

Language Arabic and Tigrinya are both commonly spoken.

Media **Newspapers** *Hadas Eritrea* is published twice a week in Tigrinya and Arabic by the transitional government of Eritrea. There is also an English-language weekly paper first produced in 1994, called *Eritrea Profile*. At the moment it's only available in Asmara.

Television and radio *Voice of the Broad Masses of Eritrea* is a government-controlled radio station broadcasting in Arabic, Tigrinya, Afar and Kunama. *ERI-TV* was established in 1992 by the government and began broadcasting in 1993 to provide educational and technical information for the purpose of national reconstruction. Transmissions are limited to Asmara and are broadcast in Arabic and Tigrinya.

BBC World Service can be received in Eritrea with a radio that has short waveband reception.

Food and drink

Italian food has been absorbed into traditional Eritrean eating habits in the hotels and a standard menu will have pasta followed by a meat or fish course and ice cream or fruit. Traditional Eritrean food is the large pancake made of fermented batter called *injera* which is served with a variety of meat or vegetable sauces. *Zigini* is the local name for Eritrean stew, which you will find in many places. Local cheeses, particularly those made from goats' milk, are well worth trying. Sweet black tea is the staple drink, which you may be offered at times as a gesture of welcome.

You will be able to find most forms of alcohol – beer, whisky, wine – though they are expensive as they have to be imported. It is well worth trying Asmara lager (previously known as Melotti) a local beer or the spirit *araki*, a colourless aniseed drink both of which are available in most bars around the country. There are also quite reasonable Eritrean and Ethiopian wines.

The water is supposed to be safe to drink, though this very much depends on your constitution. Local bottled spring water is available throughout the country. See restaurant guide, page 31.

Holidays and festivals

As yet no official set of holidays and festivals has been declared. The following are days that will be observed by at least some sections of the Eritrean community:

New Year's Day 1 January
Genna (Ethiopian Christmas – Birth of Christ) Julian Calendar 7 January
Timket (Ethiopian Epiphany – Baptism of Christ) 19 January[2]
Women's Day 8 March
International Labour Day 1 May
Liberation Day 24 May
Ethiopian Good Friday May (variable)
Fasika (Ethiopian Easter Sunday) May (variable)[2]
Idd al Fitr (End of month of fasting for Ramadan) May (variable)[1]
Martyrs' Day 20 June
Id Al Adha Araja Summer[1]
Start of Armed Struggle 1 September
Id Mawlid-el-Nabi (Prophets Birthday) Late Summer[1]
Engutatsh (Ethiopian New Year) 11 September
Maskel (Finding of the True Cross) 27 September[2]

[1] Date determined by lunar cycle
[2] Indicates an Orthodox holiday

Calendar When Eritrea was part of Ethiopia it used the Julian calendar, named after Julius Caesar, which is seven years and eight months behind the Gregorian (European) calendar – a result of differences of opinion over Christ's exact date of birth. The Julian calender consists of 12 months of 30 days and a 13th month of five or six days. The Gregorian calendar is now officially used.

Health

Yellow fever inoculation is compulsory. It is wise to have a cholera vaccination even though it **Staying** is only compulsory if the visitor is coming from an infected area. However the vaccine **healthy** certificate is not always checked on arrival. Inoculation against typhoid and hepatitis are strongly recommended.

Anti malaria tablets and general anti-mosquito measures are strongly recommended.

Although the water is said to be safe to drink, many people will try to avoid even the smallest risk of a stomach upset by drinking only boiled, sterilized or bottled water.

For further advice see the section on Health, page 35.

Further reading

Parkyns, M (1868) *Life in Abyssinia* London: John Murray. An account of travels from Massawa west to Khartoum, which began in 1843, and took six years.

Tonkin, T (1972) *Ethiopia With Love*, London: Hodder and Stoughton. Contains descriptions of Massawa and Asmara during the time of Haile Selassie, with some excellent line drawings which evocatively capture the atmosphere of Eritrea.

Connell, D (1993) *Against All Odds* New Jersey: Red Sea Press. An account of the last 16 years of Eritrea's struggle for liberation, written by a journalist who travelled with the guerrilla armies. An insight into some of the characters and communities who fought for their freedom.

Paice, E (1994) *Guide to Eritrea* Chalfort St Peter: Bradt. Good specialized guide, quite excellent photographs, and clearly written by an enthusiast.

Murphy, D (1968) *In Ethiopia with a Mule*. A mule-trek from Massawa to Addis Ababa, with good observations on local history, culture and customs.

Eritrea

Asmara

Asmara (also spelt Asmera) is the capital city in the centre of Eritrea set on the eastern edge of the high plateau with a population of around 350,000. The name, meaning 'Forest of Flowers', is indicative of its feel – it is as friendly and relaxed as any small town, with an easy-going pace of life. Unlike most capital cities, its streets are clean and safe to stroll around, day or night. As it is about 2,300 metres above sea level, the temperature is comfortable, an average of 17°C. Rainfall is approximately 500 millimetres per year, and comes mostly in June and July. Prior to the Italian occupation from 1889, Asmara was a small village and the home of Ras Alula the then governor of the region. Before independence, it was the second largest city in Ethiopia.

15°19'N 38°55'E
Colour map 1, grid A2

There are surprisingly few signs that this city has been at war for over 20 years in that, except for the obvious neglect of buildings, there are few bullet scars or signs of bomb damage. However, Asmara was occupied by the Ethiopian Dergue and a legacy of this era is the prison at Mariam Gimbi where members of the Ethiopian army tortured EPLF sympathizers. The prison is now The Ministry of Water Supply and access to the public is prohibited. Also, there are hundreds of captured tanks and armoured vehicles waiting to be disposed of at Kagnew Station, a US communications centre in the time of the Emperor, now a military base on the edge of town, and home to the EPLF.

Sights

It is easy to get around Asmara on foot, and you will be rewarded with evidence of the city's diverse heritage. The main market is a popular place to visit with its abundance of fruit, vegetables, spices and crafts and bustling atmosphere. During the Italian occupation of Asmara, the market area was the 'native' quarter of town. The main boulevard, Independence Avenue which runs through the centre of Asmara, is a pleasant palm-lined street with a number of open-air cafés that reflect a style of life established during the Italian period. If you want to soak up the atmosphere of Asmara, then this is the place to find it – sampling the bars, cafés and patisseries along the Avenue.

The old **Imperial Palace** in neoclassical style, is at the western end of Liberation Avenue, and is surrounded by pleasant gardens. The Palace, now known as the **National Museum**, provides a useful introduction to Eritrea's history. There are scrolls in the ancient language, Ge'ez, and a particularly interesting ethnographic section demonstrating some of the traditions and customs of the nine tribes of Eritrean people. There are also archaeological and war sections, the latter with a collection of weaponry, and illustrates the Eritrean struggle for independence. ■ *0800-1100 and 1500-1700 daily. However recent travellers have reported that the National Museum is currently closed (1997). US$0.30.*

The imposing **Catholic Cathedral**, red brick with a distinctive narrow gothic bell-tower, designed by an Italian architect Scanavini, and built in 1922, lies about half way along Liberation

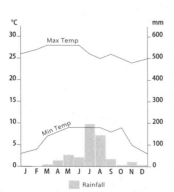

Climate: Asmara

Rainfall

Eritrea

Avenue. The Cathedral, a Capuchin monastery, a nunnery and a primary school are in the same compound and are open to visitors. **St Mariam's (Mary's) Coptic Cathedral** was built in 1917 in a combination of Ethiopian and Italian styles. It has a brightly coloured mosaic front and a bell tower at each side. There is a traditional stone bell to the left of the main entrance. The open area in front of the Cathedral is packed for religious festivals. The tower is a good landmark if you lose your bearings in the town. Other religious buildings are the **Kidane Mehret Orthodox Church** about a kilometre north of Liberation Avenue, whose dome and minaret tower over the market; and the **Al Qurafi al Rashidin Mosque**, designed by an Italian and built in 1937, at the eastern end of Liberation Avenue. The **Forto Baldissera**, an old Italian fort in the western part of the city, one kilometre from the town centre, offers good views from the hill as entrance to the fort is prohibited. Unfortunately this view has recently been blighted by a new office block, built in the middle of the ruins.

On the outskirts of Asmara en route to Massawa, lies the **English War Cemetery**, dating from the time of the conquest in 1941. Nearby there is also a sacred Hindu burial ground, resting place for Indian soldiers who served alongside the British at the time.

The Muslim quarter is situated behind the *Keren Hotel*. It contains spice markets, fabric shops, silversmiths and several mosques.

Essentials

Recent street name changes include 1) **Liberation Ave** formerly Independence Ave and National Ave; 2) **Victory St** formerly Empress Menem Ave; 3) **Martyr's Ave** formerly Ave Queen Elizabeth II.

Eritrea

Asmara

Sleeping

There are many small, privately owned pensions of good standard in the lower price ranges.

B *Ambasoira*, 32 Dejatch Hailu St, T113222. The best hotel in town and also the most modern. **B** *Nyala*, Martyrs Ave, T123111. Slightly further out of town and is a high-rise building, restaurant serves national dishes, from a series of small tents – it's certainly different. **B** *Selam*, past the National Museum, T127244, F120662. Conference centre, recently refurbished, business hotel, restaurant. **B** *Hamasien*, 30 Dejatch Hailu St, T110233. Similar to *Keren* in that it also was built in the colonial era and has a certain charm after its recent refurbishment, it is next to the *Ambasoira*.

C *Ambassador*, 36 Liberation Ave, T126544. Is the most centrally placed and is another high-rise, it is in the process of being refurbished and upgraded. Accepts all major credit cards. **C** *Bologna Hotel* T119360. New wing under construction. Advised to avoid the rooms above the restaurant, music and street noise until late, accepts all major credit cards. **C** *Expo*, T181967, 5 minutes out of the centre of town, in Tiravolo district (head down Martyrs' Ave, take the turning on the right at the Clothing Factory), a taxi should cost about US$2. This is a reasonable standard private hotel, with an Italian restaurant and shady terrace. **C** *Keren*, formerly the *Albergo Italia*, 7 Victory St, T120740, is a few blocks from Liberation Ave. This hotel was built in the colonial era in 1899 and its interior of decorative urns and chandeliers reflects this, though it has gone to seed a bit.

D *Legese*, T125054. Good central location, this is a popular place and is good value, has its own restaurant. **D** *White*, T122844. Clean and central, popular meeting place for travellers, currently closed for repairs.

E *Africa House*, short walk from Liberty Ave. Villa with gardens. **E** *Capri*, located north of Liberation Ave, close to Ethiopian Airlines. Shared bathrooms, large, comfortable rooms, very good value. **E** *Lion*, T126700, also in the Tiravolo district (for directions see *Expo Hotel* above). Popular with locals as well as tourists, mainly because it serves tasty food at cheap prices. **E** *Green Island Pension*, central. Close to Cathedral, friendly, basic. **E** *Pension Lalibela*, near the roundabout at the end of Liberation Ave, near the petrol station. Safe parking for motorbikes, clean, hot showers. **E** *Oasis Pension*, just off Liberation Ave near the Impero Cinema. Cold bucket showers available. **E** *Impero Pension*, next door to the cinema. Basic, cheap pension. **E** *Pensione St Georg*, close to Ethiopian Airlines, just north of Liberation Ave. Shared bathrooms. **E** *Red Sea Hotel*, on a side turning off Liberation Ave near the roundabout. Clean basic facilities. **E** *Tsegareda Pension* to the rear of the Impero Cinema block. Very clean, friendly and quiet. Facilities for washing/drying clothes on the rooftop. **E** *Victory* or *Vittoria*, opposite Cathedral on Liberation Ave. Shared bathrooms, hot water.

Eating

Most hotels have their own restaurant, but the menus tend to be standard and a little unimaginative. Most restaurants are quite cheap, meals are unlikely to cost more than US$5 for supper. There is a great variety of cafés and bars, offering light meals and snacks, which are usually good value. 'Restaurants' tend to serve traditional dishes like *augera*. 'Snack bars' serve non-traditional food which is cheap and often authentically Eritrean for example *fatta* is like pizza except there is no crust. 'Cafés' serve tea, coffee, cappucino and Italian pastries, and sometimes fruit juices.

4 *Cherhi*, north of Menelik I St. Chinese, good but not cheap, located in a tall, rather curiously-designed building situated at probably the highest point in Asmara, affording very impressive 360° views of the city.

3 *San Giorgio*, Liberation Ave. Italian cuisine, reasonable standard.

2 *Asmara*, Liberation Ave, near Post Office. Serve *injira* and other Eritrean food as well as most of the popular Italian dishes, gets busy at lunch time. **2** *Bar Vittoria*, near the British Council Library. An old café but offers excellent delicacies, in interesting surrounds. **2** *Bereket Fast Food* opposite the *Imperio Cinema*. Popular venue offering good local food. **2** *Bologna Hotel Restaurant*, reasonable choice of dishes. **2** *Café Alba*, serves a good breakfast and is run by an Italian family in a street running parallel to Liberation Ave, it also serves pizza and Italian pastries. **2** *Caravelle Bar and Restaurant*, Italian place serving good food, worth a visit for the weird and wonderful decor. **2** *Castello*, another good Italian restaurant. **2** *Expo Hotel*, the restaurant is very popular. **2** *Napoli Pizza*, 4 roads west of the Cathedral, just above Liberation Ave. Very good pizza, exremely popular among travellers. **2** *Pizzeria Eritrea*, Gamela St, north of Liberation Ave. **2** *Sudan Brothers'*, on a street behind the *Ambassador Hotel*. Offers a good range of Sudanese and Eritrean dishes.

1 *Bar Royal*, previously called *Café Royal*, Liberation Ave. Popular street café with seats outside, a/c, smoking prohibited near the Cathedral. **1** *Cathedral Bar* on the main road opposite the cathedral has excellent fruit juices. **1** *Geneth Bar*, Haramat St. Good bar, very popular in the evenings. **1** *Hollywood Stars Bar*, across from Napoli Pizzeria. Music non-stop. **1** *Impero Bar*, on Liberation Ave, 2 streets east of Cathedral. Good ice cream (next door to cinema). The **1** *Italian Club* offers a comfortable respite serving lunch. **1** *Modern Snack Bar*, 2 roads west of the Cathedral. Serves light local dishes like *silsi, fool* and burgers. **1** *Portico Snack*, Liberation Ave, a few streets west of the Catholic Cathedral. Offers milkshakes, burgers, fries etc, popular with good atmosphere, also has seats outside on the pavement. **1** *Rino*, corner Ali Osman St and Liberation Ave. Good value, main dishes. **1** *Sesen Pastry*, described as having the best pastries in the Horn of Africa.

The Hard Rock Cafe has closed and now functions as the *The Ambassador Hotel* bar.

Some of the hotels organize evening entertainment. The Italian community have set up a **Entertainment** club at *Casa d'Italiano*, off Liberation Ave which apart from being an interesting place to visit can be a useful source of advice about how to get around the country, what to visit etc. *Caravelle* not far from the *Nyala Hotel* has a disco on Friday and Saturday nights, 1100-0500, entrance fee US$5.50. The *Mocambo Club*, off Liberation Ave has live music each week. The other main disco is at the *Junior Club*. Entrance is about US$7. Venues are well advertised in hotels and shops, so check these for newly-opened clubs.

Discotheques *Patamata's Night Club*, next to Impero Cinema, Liberation Ave. Open Wednesday, Friday and Saturday nights from 1130 to 0500, entry cost US$4.50 but free entry up to midnight, popular with Eritreans who have lived abroad, Afro-American rap included. *Delux Disco*, Massawa Rd, near the glass factory in Debezito section of town in the east end. Popular with teenagers on summer school holidays, closed during term time. *Lagetto Disco*, also in the east end of town. Open Friday and Saturday nights. *Sembel Huts*, on the road to the airport. Very popular disco, entry US$7. *National Theatre Association*, across the street from Impero Cinema, Liberation Ave. Has a bar which has a Friday/Saturday night disco, extremely popular.

Bookshops there is a good bookshop on the corner of Liberation Ave and Martyrs Ave **Shopping** called the *City Book Store*, contains many socio-politico historical books written in English about Fritrea. Next door to the Cathedral there is a Catholic bookshop named *Friendship Bookstore*.

Curios and crafts lack of tourists means there are few places specializing in curios and crafts. However, textiles, ceramics, woodwork, silverware and basketry are available in Asmara's main market. Some of Eritrea's religious artefacts are very attractive and you will see a few shops around town specializing in old and new Abyssinian Christian objects including distinctive Coptic crosses. Haile Gebrehiwat at the end of Ras Mangesha St near the *Keren Hotel* has craftwork and curios of a high standard.

Newspapers *Eritrea Profile*, is a weekend newspaper published both in Tigrinya and English.

Eritrea

Transport **Local Bus**: buses are a cheap and reasonably reliable way of travelling, but not if you're on a tight schedule. They usually load with passengers between 0700 and 0900, and leave when they are full. The main bus station is near the market and there are fairly frequent buses. **Massawa** takes 5 hours and costs US$2 (morning and afternoon departures); **Keren**, 3 hours, US$1.50 (morning and afternoon departures); **Axum**, there are no longer direct buses from Asmara to Axum because of the separate currencies. However it is easy to catch transport at the border to Adigrat; **Assab**, 10 days, US$15. Most journeys only take a few hours' along reasonable roads. There are also minibuses/taxis available from the bus depot. **Car hire** it is possible to rent chauffeur driven vehicles, either Fiat cars, Land Rovers or minibuses from Africa Garage at 29 Ras Wole Butul, T111755. **Taxis** to town from the airport cost US$4-5, there is a bus service which starts at 0600, every half an hour costing US$0.10.

Air The daily flight between Asmara and Addis Ababa costing about US$100 one-way has been suspended since the 1998 border dispute started. Asmara is the international airport in Eritrea, so all incoming flights arrive here. There is a US$12 departure tax, not payable in Nakfa.

Road There is a road from Asmara to Addis Ababa, Ethiopia but it is in bad condition and the journey can take 5 days. Road access between Ethiopia and Eritrea has been suspended since the 1998 hostilities. However, major road building and repair works are being carried out at present so the situation is expected to improve. It is also possible to reach Asmara from Assab on the Ethiopian border in the south but again the road is not good and the journey is exhausting.

Directory **Airline offices** *Ethiopian Airlines*, Liberation Ave, between the Cathedral and *Imperio Cinema*, 0800-1100 and 1300-1600, open 7 days a week. *Eritrean Air*, 89 Liberty Ave Asmara, T115500, flies from Asmara to Assab. *Saudi Airlines*, 97 Liberty Ave Asmara, T120166/120153 and *Egypt Air*, T125501/125500 (Egyptair) all have offices on Liberation Ave. *Lufthansa*, T182707.

Banks The main branch of the *National Bank of Eritrea* is on Liberation Ave where money can be exchanged. It was established in 1992. The main hotels will also change money. The newly established *Commercial Bank* on National Ave, also changes money, hours 0800-1100 and from 1400-1600, black market rate is only marginally more than the official rate.

Communications Post Office: the post office is just off the main street, Liberation Ave. Since telephone and fax numbers are likely to change as the service expands the Directory Enquiries number T97 could prove useful. Opposite the Tsegareda Pension (behind the Impero Cinema) there is an Import/Export company where you can email and receive faxes (T/F291-1-126667).

Embassies, high commissions & consulates *China*, PO Box 204, 6 Arbagugu St, Asmara, T116988, F1572123 (satelite). *Djibouti*, Andinnet St, towards airport, PO Box 678 Asmara, T182189, F181001. *Egypt*, 5 Deg Affwok St, Asmara, T123603/124935, F123294. *Ethiopia*, Franklin Roosevelt St, T116144. Visas same price here as elsewhere. *German Embassy* is on the airport road, 20 minutes walk from the centre. *Israel*, Deg Fecrem Ariam St, T120137, F120187. *Italy*, 45 Shemelis Habte St, Asmara, T120774, F121115. *Lufthansa*, T182707. *Sudan*, PO Box 371, Deg Fecrem Ariam St, Asmara, T124176, F120287. *UK*, PO Box 5584, 54 Emperor Yohannes Ave, Asmara, T120145, F120104. *USA*, PO Box 211, Franklin Roosevelt St, T123720/123410, F127584. *Yemen*, PO Box 5566, 5 Lt Tesfalidet Idris St, T110208/118962, F118962.

Libraries *British Council*, Rogu T Mariam St, off Liberation Ave. Has good selection of books and newspapers. There is a US Information Service with a library in town, and an Alliance Française. The Lufthansa office has a supply of free German newspapers.

Places of worship The Orthodox Church is *Kidane Mehret*, near the main market. There is a Catholic church about half way along the central boulevard, Liberation Ave. Has an English language mass on Sat evenings at 1800. A number of mosques are scattered throughout the city.

Tourist offices The Ministry of Tourism, PO Box 1010, Asmara, T120073/123941, F126949 is on 3rd floor of the building in Liberty Ave which houses the Eritrean Shipping and Transit Agency, east of the Ethiopian Airlines office. The Eritrean Tour Service (ETS), PO Box 889, is located at 61 Liberty Ave,

Asmara, T124999, F126366. The ETS can arrange sightseeing tours of Asmara, trips to Massawa and car hire services. Another useful source of information, particularly about conditions outside Asmara can be from the numerous international development agencies which have set up in the capital such as UNDP, which is on the Airport Rd.

Useful services Public toilets: access to lavatories can be a problem in Asmara. However, there are some public toilets very close to the *Ethiopian Airlines* office.

Asmara environs

Dekamere (also spelt Dek émháre) was once a beautiful small town to the southeast of Asmara developed by the Italians in their style. It is set in a fertile region which produced the best wine in the country. Unfortunately today it is almost destroyed as for some time it straddled the frontline of the war.

Dekamere
15°6'N 39°0'E
Colour map 1, grid A2

Although the town itself has little to recommend it except as a reminder of past glories, the surrounding countryside is spectacular and often a route for cycling races, a truly colonial inheritance. Travel west to Sudan is possible, but you must ensure you have a valid visa (see page 752 and page 753). The road from Dekamere through the hills of **Adi Keyeh** is particularly lovely. Along the route you can see the start of the rebuilding process underway in Eritrea with irrigation schemes in operation nurturing nurseries and market gardens. There are some small guest houses and cafés near the market. Regular buses run from the bus stand near the market in Asmara.

Overlooked by a seemingly impregnable fortress, which still bristles with Ethiopian army cannon, the town itself boasts stylish public buildings and a Romanesque Catholic church. Today, Keren's community is largely Muslim. The pace is relaxed – here, you are more likely to see camels than cars.

Keren
15°45'N 38°28'E
Colour map 1, grid A2

Eritrea

Keren is situated high up on a plateau in the midst of impressive mountain scenery, 105 kilometres west of Asmara. It is a potentially productive agricultural area, with fertile soils and a temperate climate. The Eritreans controlled Keren briefly in 1977-78, but much of the town was destroyed by the Ethiopian army upon recapture.

The Sahel open-air park is a lovely place to visit. You can get a refreshing fruit juice here (mango and guava amongst others), as well as grilled and barbecued meats. Other places of interest are **St Mariam Dearit**, a shrine built into a baobab tree, a 20-30 minute walk out of town, with no shade on the way, past the Italian cemetery. Women wait outside to perform the coffee ceremony (which can take up to three hours) – the belief is that wishes are granted if the ceremony is performed there with a traveller or a foreigner. At **Liberation Park**, down by the Ciuf-Ciufit River, is the wood market, where camels unload timber brought from surrounding areas.

Keren has a British associaton. In 1941 at the height of the war in East Africa, Keren was the scene of some of the fiercest fighting between the Allies and Mussolini's troops. More than 1000 soldiers were killed, and on the ouskirts of the town lies the British war cemetery, immaculately maintained by an elderly Eritrean. 400 British soldiers are buried here.

Across the town, the Italian cemetery for soldiers who were killed in the same battle, is likewise beautifully maintained.

Monday is market day. Not only do the merchants bring their goods in on camels but there is also a camel market, where you can buy a ruminant with a three-chambered stomach for US$300. Vaccination is an additional US$0.50. A saddle is advisable. The market is past the Italian cemetery – follow the early morning crowd.

100 metres from the main roundabout down in the riverbed is where the wood selling market is to be found. Camels are used to transport the wood to and from the market.

Thief-seekers

In traditional areas of Eritrea, if someone discovers he has had possessions stolen, he will hire the services of a *lieba shai*. This is a boy thief-seeker, trained for the purpose and retained by a local elder. The thief-seeker fasts for a night, takes a draught of drugged milk, and smokes a pipe containing some special herbs. This potent cocktail on an empty stomach, causes the boy to collapse, and the elder intones over the inert form until he recovers and reels away, sometimes in quite a frenzy. The elder follows, holding onto a sash round the boy's waist. Care is taken to avoid water, which will break the spell. The boy leads the elder to the stolen articles, and identifies the thief by breathing in great gasps, kneeing the culprit, and grasping him by the neck. The thief-seeker is then given beer and bread to make him vomit and throw off the effects of the drugs.

A wrong-doer can thwart the thief-seeker by drenching himself in water, which makes him proof against the charm. Another ploy is to make as if to jump off a precipice, which the thief-seeker will copy unless the elder can manage to haul him back in time.

Sons of poor families are chosen to be thief-seekers and are trained by being drugged and set to find previously hidden goods. The powers disappear with the onset of puberty, but there are long-term effects such as 'weakness in the head', ex-thief-seekers have reputations as 'drunkards and ravers', and alcohol induces wild staring eyes, a vacant expression and physical weakness.

Sleeping C *Keren*, the best of the basic accommodation available (rooms vary, so ask to see a few), located near the fruit and vegetable market, the Keren has a roof terrace with good views over the town, the bar is a popular drinking place in the early evening, the restaurant serves reasonable food, mostly Italian. **E** *Barka*, a Muslim hotel, with just 10 rooms. **E** *Eritrea*, Union Ave. A small hotel with a bar which tends to get quite noisy in the evening. **E** *Sicilian*, next door to the *Eritrea*. Reportedly the oldest hotel in Keren, range of rooms, friendly, clean and comfortable. Bucket showers, safe parking for motorcycles.

Eating There are a number of restaurants around the market area, behind the **Keren Hotel**. There is a reasonable choice of cafés – look for those with shade, bougainvillaea, and a menu which includes Egyptian/Sudanese stewed beans. In Sahel Park street vendors serve grilled and barbecued food. The park is a 10 minute walk from the main plaza.

Transport There are morning and afternoon buses to Asmara. The road between Keren and Asmara is sealed and in good condition.

Nakfa Capital of Sahel province, Nakfa (sometimes spelt Nacfa) is about 150 kilometres
16°40'N 38°32'E north of Keren. It holds a special significance for Eritreans, being home to the EPLF
Colour map 1, grid A2 during the war. As a result, it was very heavily damaged with only a mosque surviving. It is planned to rebuild the town and reconstruction is already under way, but facilities are still very basic. Many young people doing their national service opt to spend part of it rebuilding Nakfa, planting trees to revive the blighted landscape. Despite an altitude of 2,700 metres some windchill and impoverished soil, the government plans to turn Nakfa into a regional centre. Most of the hotels or guest houses are made of corrugated iron, some without shower or toilet. If you are interested in military history the trenches of Denden merit a visit – one hour's climb to the peak, which overlooks the Ethiopian frontline 500 metres away. 20 kilometres to the north of Nakfa is the Tsabra underground hospital, built into the mountainside, affording it protection during the lengthy conflict.

Kerora in the far north of Sahel province has cave paintings. However access is difficult until the road is rebuilt.

Agordat Also spelt Akordat, this is 75 kilometres further west from Keren, and is a town of
15°30'N 37°40'E 24,000 in the Western Lowlands. It is at the western termination of the railway from
Colour map 1, grid A2

The railway

The line was built by the Italians and it was the first railway to be constructed in East Africa. The work began on the 95 centimetre gauge track from Massawa in 1887, and it reached its present point of termination, Agordat, 280 kilometres inland, in 1928. Market towns sprung up around the various stations along the route, and it was vital to communications and the economy. It was envisaged that the line would eventually be extended west to Khartoum.

It is a very considerable engineering feat, considering the difficult terrain and the fact that it climbs to a high point of 2,128 metres a few kilometres before the gentle descent into Asmara. There are 65 bridges and 30 tunnels, the longest being 320 metres, with most tunnels having to be bored through solid rock. The crossing at the Obel River is a fourteen arch bridge, and there are viaducts before Nesfit, and just after Devil's Doors, the highest point on the line, where the track runs along the edge of a precipice. Between Mai Atal and Damas the gradient is so steep that trains have to be split and each half hauled up separately.

At its peak in 1965 the railway carried 446,000 passengers and 200,000 tonnes of freight. There was a daily service hauled by diesel locomotives between Asmara and the coast, and trains ran on alternate days from Asmara up-country to Agordat. It ceased operation during the war but is now being restored.

Massawa. The town can experience high temperatures, and sandstorms known as *haboob*. It is located on the river Barca, and the area is famous for its banana plantations. The main hotel, the **D** *Savoy*, near the railway station is now very run-down, but there are new hotels being built, complete with nightclubs and swimming pools. There are some small guest houses and basic cafés in the railway station area. A new open-air market complex is also under construction. There are regular buses from outside the railway station to Keren.

Further southwest of Agordat is **Barentu**, the provincial capital of Gash Setit. The government **D** *Rest House*, high up on the hill overlooking the town, is the best place to stay. There's usually a pleasant breeze, and it is quieter than other places in the town. The **D** *Asmara Hotel* has a good restaurant.

Asmara to Massawa

The journey down from Asmara to Massawa on the coast is a stunning one. The descent of about 2,500 metres will take about three hours by car, or five hours if you take a bus.

Alternatively, you can easily do the 120 kilometres from Asmara to Massawa on a bicycle, since it is all downhill for six hours! Going back you put it on the roof of the bus, or pay US$1 for someone to do so on your behalf. *Olympia* bicycles in Asmara rent out mountain bikes for US$5 per day. Olympia can be found by going down Liberation Avenue to Martyr's Avenue, over the first roundabout, and turn right between Nacja House and the Fiat garage. Olympia are 200 metres down that road on your left. There is an early viewpoint, about 10 kilometres out of Asmara, at the Bar Durfo, which is well worth a short stop.

The first town you pass on the winding road to Massawa is **Nefasit**, with the **Debre Bizen Monastery** situated high up above the town. The monastery was built in 1361 and was home to a Coptic religious community. Today, there are over 100 monks there. The tomb of its founder, Abuna Filipos, is in the grounds. It is a two-hour climb up to Debre Bizen from Nefasit, which if you decide to do you will be suitably rewarded with views of the sea and Dahlak Islands in one direction, and mountains in the other. There is one drawback though, in that women are not allowed to visit. And men need to have obtained permission to visit in advance, from the Coptic Church in Asmara. It houses a collection of ancient manuscripts in Ge'ez and nearby there is a large round church.

Another 10 kilometres on, you come to **Embatcala**, a pleasant town set amidst lush green hillsides, and dominated by a large church. Moving on a further 15 kilometres, there is another pretty town called **Ghinda**, a place which used to be popular with Italians. Buses from Asmara to the coast usually stopover at Ghinda for lunch. There are a few hotels and restaurants in the town centre.

The next town on the journey is **Dongollo**, famous for its production of bottled mineral water. As you approach Massawa, about 10 kilometres before the town centre, you will find the **EPLF Martyrs' Cemetery**, and the **Italian Cemetery** situated a few kilometres away.

Massawa and the Coast

Massawa was heavily damaged during Eritrea's struggle for independence. But it has managed to retain some of its atmosphere, and is likely to be of some significance to tourists as it is the gateway to the islands – Taulud and Port Island.

Massawa

Massawa (also spelt Mitsiwa) consists of two islands and two peninsulas and used to be the headquarters of the Ethiopian navy. It is 120 kilometres from Asmara, and has a population of about 20,000. It can get extremely hot, up to 40°C June to August with little difference between day and night-time temperatures. The monsoon rains are December to February. The earliest signs of settlement here were when the Turks occupied the island port in the 16th century. By around 1850 the Egyptians took control only to be ousted by the Italians under a special arrangement in 1885. Unfortunately today there is very little to see of its rich and varied history as it was fought over by both sides during the war and was devastated by the fighting. Haile Selassie's palace, the colonial residences, the mosque, the waterfront and all major hotels were destroyed. At one time the yacht club, and the nearby beaches and islands were popular places for weekends and vacations for the residents of Asmara. A famous craft of Massawa was the manufacture of mother- of- pearl buttons.

15°35'N 39°25E
Colour map 1, grid A3

Massawa is now Eritrea's main port and access to the rest of the world and is being rehabilitated. The dockyard is back in operation and handling an impressive tonnage of merchandise. An arrangement between Eritrea and Ethiopia has meant Ethiopian trade still comes via Massawa. Much of Massawa is dilapidated, although most of the hotels have now been repaired.

Scuba diving is said to be among the best in the Red Sea, and offshore from Dahlak Islands the coral gardens are beautiful. Dahlak Kabir is the largest island and on the south side there is an ancient necropolis. The gravestones have inscriptions with Kufic characters. Close by are famous water collecting cisterns cut out of the coral. These were mentioned in the writings of English travellers in the 19th century, James Bruce and Henry Salt, described as one of the wonders of the ancient world. There are some yacht trips to the islands in the *Nobile* for US$20, arranged through the Dahlak Hotel. The islands were once an Ethiopian military base upon which the Israelis have built an airstrip.

About 15 minutes out of Massawa to the south there is a hotel-restaurant on the sea front offering swimming and sunbathing on the white sands. There are also beach facilities a few kilometres to the north of the city at Goragusm (minibus US$1, taxi US$4) and some modest hotels.

Fishing along this part of the Red Sea is said to be particularly good as it has never seriously been exploited. The area is rich in tuna, barracuda, dolphin and mero.

South of Massawa is **Danakil** which lies 116 metres below sea level and is one of the hottest and most inhospitable places on earth with temperatures reaching up to 50°C. Danakil lies in the stretch of desert called **Denkalia**, the land of the Afar tribespeople. This is not easy travelling territory, as it consists mainly of volcanic rock and mountain.

B *Dahlak*, T552818. Rooms with a/c, good restaurant, bar, best hotel in Massawa, near the port. **B** *Gugasam*, north of Massawa is a beach hotel with rooms, or 2 bedroomed cottages on offer, plus sitting room and bathroom. Each room has a/c and is comfortable. The hotel has an indooor restaurant and the management have an incomprehensible rule that you are not permitted to eat outside. Unfortunately the beach views are uninspiring with a cement

Sleeping

Eritrea

factory being one of the main features. The beach has no shade and is dirty. There is a dearth of water activities, with no available dinghies, water skiing etc. The hotel gets livelier at the weekend when Asmara residents come down to the coast.

C *Central*, located on the waterfront. Recently refitted, has its own restaurant, with terrace, rooms have a/c. **C** *Corallo*, T552406, close to *Dahlak Hotel*. Small, basic place on the waterfront on Taulud Island, some rooms are self-contained with shower and a/c.

D *Savoya*, clean but drab.

E *Massawa*, small place with only 10 rooms, own restaurant, on Port Island. **E** *Hotel Ghenet*, on the second peninsula. Communal toilets/showers, reliable water supply, clean, some rooms have fans, outdoor sleeping allowed US$1.50 per night, safe parking for motorcycles. **E** *Yussef Hotel*, close to *Hotel Ghenet*. Cheap basic hotel.

Eating   Most of the reasonable places to eat are along the harbour front selling simple meals of fish at reasonable prices. Alternatively, most of the hotels will have a restaurant.

2 *Adulis Sea Food Restaurant*, Port Island. Good food at a reasonable price. **2** *Dahlak Hotel*, good standard and reasonably priced. **2** *Eritrea*, located on Port Island, across from the *Massawa Hotel*. Lively place, serving tasty food, serves excellent fresh fish, generous portions. **2** *Selam*, past *Adulis Sea Food Restaurant* at the Mosque Square, turn right and it is on the next corner. Unbeatable fish for US$2. Highly recommended.

Beaches   It is difficult to get to the beaches without a car, but there is an appealing trolley-train which goes from Massawa to the northern beach areas, cost US$0.10. Trips to **Green Island** can be arranged by Dolphin. Their boat is moored at the Dahlak, but it is better to arrange the trip the day before at the Dolphin's Club.

Transport   **Road**   The 120 kilometres road from Asmara to Massawa takes you through breathtaking scenery down from the hills to the Red Sea. Regular buses run from the bus depot near the market in Asmara. There are two departures a day, in the morning and the afternoon. A taxi from Massawa to Asmara takes about 3/4 hours and costs approximately US$45.

Sea   Boat: there are cargo boats which carry passengers which go to Port Sudan, Jeddah and Suez every 2 weeks. Fare to Suez US$115.

If you plan to go to Jeddah by ship, go to the shipping Agent's office behind the immigration building at the port (unmarked). Ask for the ship Alra sheet; costs: US$80 per person, US$100 for a motorcycle and US$300 for a car, plus US$10 for the paperwork. Only the cost of the passenger ticket is payable in Nakfa, the remainder is payable in US dollars. You have to pay on board in dollars for the vehicle. In addition you have to give the captain a US$150 deposit per person for a hotel in Jeddah, and US$75 for each person if you are in transit to Suez by ship. If you are in transit overland to Jordan, you do not have to give a deposit. However, you will have to pay US$30 in cash for the paperwork, which takes hours. It is not permitted to drive your vehicle in the harbour area, a port employee will do it for you. Allow plenty of time to process the paperwork. The cost of any damage to your vehicle whilst being driven by the port employee is likely to be borne by you, as reported by a recent traveller.

Any surplus Nakfa cannot be changed into other currencies at the bank. Small quantities of Nakfa can be used up on board the ship. A black market operates in Massawa to redress this problem. World cruising yachts frequently dock at Massawa, following the winds and escaping the monsoons. You can easily get a lift in the right season, paying little or nothing in return for helping out on the boat.

Rail The railway from Asmara to Massawa, destroyed in the independence struggle, is being rebuilt. The workers, many now grandfathers, who built the original railroad in the 1930s have taught their grandsons to lay reforged rails back towards Asmara. Metal detritus of war has been used to make the rails. 42 kilometres of track has been laid in the past 2 years and two 1938 Italian steam engines have been restored to working order.

Assab

Assab (also spelt Aseb) used to be Ethiopia's main port for its arms supplies during the war. It is a large, modern port, with an oil refinery built by the former Soviet Union. Assab is close to the border with Djibouti, and is best reached by air from Asmara or Addis Ababa, or by road from Addis.

13°0'N 42°40'E
Colour map 1, grid B4

The town centre is divided into two main parts – Assab Kebir and Assab Seghir (big and little Assab respectively). There are some pleasant uncrowded beaches. The town has a few hotels and restaurants, as well as a bank, post office, and even an open-air cinema.

The weather is hot from June to September, usually 40°C. Even though there is a sea breeze, the temperature at night rarely falls below 20°C. For the rest of the year, the climate is more moderate.

A *The Port Club*, located down by the beach, T661114. Rooms are clean, with hot water and a/c. **B** *Agip Motel*. Rather uninspired, but a reasonable standard and good restaurant. **C** *Albergo Assab*. Old colonial-style, bar, restaurant, some rooms a/c. **D** *Nino's*, near the petrol station in town. **E** *Asmara*, on the opposite corner to the petrol station. This is a small place with communal showers.

Sleeping

4 *The Port Club*, wide-ranging menu, from seafood to hamburgers, in pleasant surroundings. **2** *Aurora*, down by the port. Good reputation for Italian dishes.

Eating

Air All *Ethiopian Airways* services are suspended. *Air Eritrea* operates a weekly air service between Asmara and Assab on Tuesdays. **Road** The distance between Asmara and Assab is considerable (1,100 kilometres), the roads are in poor shape and transport is very meagre. **Bus**: there were regular buses from Addis Ababa, 750 kilometres away, but these services have been suspended during the current conflict.

Transport

Eritrea

South of Asmara

The southern highlands are the most densely populated region of Eritrea. From Asmara, there are two main routes heading south for Ethiopia.

The first of these takes you through a number of villages, **Zigib**, 20 kilometres south of the capital, in the forefront of **Mount Ad Hannes** (2,850 metres). A further 30 kilometres away, you pass through **Afelba**, notable for its two churches, Coptic and Catholic.

Adi Qayeh, also spelt Adik'eyih, is the provincial capital, and from here you can visit significant historical sites, such as **Toconda** and **Qohaito**. The plain of Qohaito, also known as Cohaito (Coloe in ancient times), lies 12 kilometres south of Adi Qayeh, measuring 15 kilometres by two and a half to three kilometres. There are precipitous descents on either side and looking to the south affords views of the highest peak in Eritrea, Mount Ambasoira, 3,000 metres. The descent can be made on foot or by camel for maximum impact. The ancient ruins of Qohaito, some dating to pre-Axumite times, King Saba's palace and several stellae are about 10 kilometres from the main road. Safra's dam, with its lengthy inscription in the ancient religious language of Ge'ez is nearby. Ge'ez is believed to be akin to the Sabaean language brought to the area from Southern Arabia. The Ethiopian influence gained ascendancy over the structure and the result was the Ge'ez language, which is the ancestor of several of the modern languages of Ethiopia. Safra's dam with its protruding headers and overall construction is reminiscent of the great dam at Marib in the Yemen.

Qohaito was believed to be an important staging post between Axum and Adulis, the ancient Axumite port. There are quite a few places to stay at Adi Qayeh, some more basic than others. There are rock paintings at 25 locations in the area around Adi Qayeh.

Continuing onto **Senafe** (2,400 metres), this is the last town on the Eritrean side of the border, the crossing being about 25 kilometres further. The remains of the ancient Axumite city of Metara (also spelt Matara) can be seen about one and a half kilometres southwest of the town of Senafe. The area has beautiful scenery and the ruins are known as 'Zala Kaleb' (the ruins of King Kaleb) by the local people. There is a legend that the Emperor of Axum marched with his army to wreak vengeance on Metara's townspeople for their ill-treatment of a Tsadqan (saint). On seeing the approaching army the townsfolk fled. The king ordered a tunnel to be dug, and later destroyed the population of Belew Kalew. Two tunnel entrances in the towns can still be seen but the distance from Axum to Metara is approximately 100 kilometres so the accuracy of the legend cannot be verified.

A five metre stela stands beside the road at Metara, and at the top there is an inscription of a disc and a crescent dated to the third century. At eye level there is a four line inscription in Ge'ez. Recent excavations nearby by the Ethiopian Institute of Archaeology to the west of the stela have identified the remains of four edifices. These walls with alternating projecting and receding steps are in the classical Axumite architectural tradition. Excavations have also revealed evidence of earlier civilizations. In 1963 a bronze vase was found containing a remarkable group of gold objet d'art including two crosses, one of which had been gem encrusted. The bronze vase is on display at the Archaeological Museum in Addis Ababa.

To the south of Senafe is the village of **Hamm** and the monastery of **Debre Libanos** which is the oldest monastery in Eritrea (not to be confused with the 13th century monastery near the Blue Nile Gorge with the same name). The monastery lies in a steep valley, which takes about one to one and a half hours to descend and one and a half to two hours to ascend. You need to be both fit and sure footed to visit this monastery, which is believed to date from the sixth century. The villagers from Hamm will be happy to act as guides to reach it. Nearby are a number of mummified bodies, believed to date from the fourth century. Further archaeological excavations are being carried out in this area.

The second route to the border takes you via **Adi Ugri**, provincial capital of Seraye. The most notable building in Adi Ugri is the enormous Roman Catholic Cathedral school. East of it is the very large Coptic church of St Ghiorgis (George). Again, there are a number of hotels to choose from if you are planning to stay overnight, the **E** *Semhar* is probably the best. The only other town of any significant size before the border is **Adi Qala**, also spelt Adikwala, where the plateau ends. The border crossing is at Ghundet, by the river Mareb, whose level dictates whether you can cross or not.

Further west of Agordat is **Barentu**, the provincial capital of Gash Setit province. **Sleeping & eating E** *Govt Rest House*, up on the hill overlooking the town. Pleasant breeze, and relatively quiet place to stay. **2** *Hotel Asmara*, restaurant serves good pasta dishes.

National Parks

An unfortunate casualty of the recent war was the protection of flora and fauna. However, given the diversity of environments in Eritrea and the fact that it is so unspoilt, there is great potential for the country to develop national parks. The decades of fighting scared the elephants away, but recent reports indicate that six elephants have been sighted since the country gained independence. Prior to the war there were Reserves near Tessenei in the west; just to the northeast of Keren; and in the north on the border with Sudan. The information given here is based on the only park established before the split with Ethiopia.

Dahlak (also spelt Dahalac) Marine National Park

The Dahlak Islands lie between 15 and 110 kilometres from the Massawa coast scattered over an area of approximately 15,500 square kilometres. There are some 200 islands in all though not all are inhabited and many are barren. Although some were used as a military base by the Ethiopian army and the military base is still there, the waters provide a fascinating place to visit. The shallow waters and coral gardens house a great diversity of marine life including the barracuda and the manta ray and the less common dugong (nicknamed the sea cow). On the islands themselves you may be able to spot soot falcons, the brown booby, spoonbill, osprey and a number of other birds and gazelle graze amongst the acacias. To visit the park, enquire at the Department of Protocol at the *Ambasoira Hotel* in Asmara or at the Department of Tourism when it begins operation in the Post Office square.

15°50'N 40°10'E
Colour map 1, grid A3

Eritrea

Eritrea's national parks & reserves

Background

The land

Geography Eritrea is 121,320 square kilometres in area, being narrow in the south and broadening out in the north. It is situated in the Horn of Africa bordered by Sudan to the west and north and Ethiopia and Djibouti to the south. It lies between 12° and 18° latitude north, and 36° and 44° longitude east. There are about 1,000 kilometres of the country bordering onto the Red Sea opposite Saudi Arabia and Yemen. Its territory includes the Dahlak Islands which were formally used as a military base by the Ethiopians.

Eritrea consists of 10 provinces which cover its four main geographical regions. The first runs from Djibouti upwards and is little more than a long strip of desert. The central and northern part of the country – covering about 30 percent of the land mass – is made up of highlands and is an extension of the Ethiopian highlands, at an average height of 1,500 metres (Asmara, the capital, is in this area). It is in this region that most cultivation takes place. Much of the coniferous forest that used to cover the hillsides has been cleared either for fuelwood or land and as a consequence, soil erosion is becoming an increasingly severe problem. West of the highlands spreading into Sudan lies the potentially fertile lowlands which are mainly flat. The fourth region is in the far north and comprises rugged hills which give way to lowlands going down to the coastal plain to the east where only pastoralism is possible. In 1995, the National Assembly approved a proposal to reorganize Eritrea into six administrative regions or zones.

Eritrea's natural resources are to some extent still untapped. In prehistoric times there was evidence of iron ore, gold and copper ore being mined and it remains to be seen if these are still exploitable assets. Off the coast, some seepages of oil and offshore natural gas have been recorded and exploration for these resources is currently under way.

Climate Given the diverse geographical make-up of the country, there are a number of different types of climate. The higher plateaus expect an average temperature of 18°C with an annual rainfall of around 500 millimetres while the coast's average temperature is 30°C with rainfall of less than 200 millimetres each year. In coastal areas, the months from June to September can be extremely hot, at times reaching 50°C. The main rainy season throughout the country is between June and September and there are short rains between October and March along the northern coastal region, though these are unpredictable. December is generally the coolest month.

History

Eritrea's history is a long and splendid one. During the third and fourth centuries AD, it was part of the kingdom of Axum which spread from Meroe in Sudan right across the Red Sea to Yemen. The capital of Axum was in the highlands of Tigray (now a province in Ethiopia), and the main port was at Adulis which is now called Zula in Eritrea. This kingdom was based on trade across the Red Sea and was founded by Semetic people originally from Arabia. Christianity was the predominant faith of Axum introduced through contact with traders throughout the region.

By the sixth century AD the Persian Empire expanded and with it went the expansion of Islam. In 710 AD Muslims destroyed Adulis and the ancient kingdom of Axum declined until it was reduced to a small Christian enclave. For the next few centuries, the region settled into being a remote, isolated community only re-emerging by the early 16th century as Abyssinia. The Abyssinian Kingdom covered the Ethiopian and Eritrean highlands ruled by kings and peopled by Christian Tigrinyans and remaining fairly isolated.

The community had little or no contact with the lowlands of the region which was home to predominantly Muslim communities.

This period in Eritrea's history is highly contentious. The Ethiopians claimed Eritrea had been an integral part of historic Ethiopia but though there are some common practices and religious beliefs between Eritreans and Ethiopia, these ties do not extend throughout Ethiopia. In fact, large parts of Eritrea, it would seem, were linked to other empires. The Ottoman Empire and Egypt had relations with the north and east part of the country, and various Sudanic Empires to the west and northwest have had their influence.

19th century expansion

Abyssinia was subject to the expansionism of the Egyptians and some European powers (French, Italian, and British). In the early part of the century, Ali Pasha invaded Sudan and gradually pushed on the Western Lowlands of present-day Eritrea. By mid-century, European interest in the area was also increasing. The British had a consulate in Massawa, and the French already had a presence. Italian missionaries were established in Keren.

Emperor Tewodros II, who ruled Abyssinia from 1855-68, also had to deal with rebel forces in Tigray and Shoa, who chose Ras Kassa as their ruler. Tewodros was defeated in 1868 after the British General Sir Robert Napier had landed in Zula to release the Consul and other prisoners held by the Emperor. After Tewodros's defeat, Ras Kassa was crowned Emperor Yohannes IV in 1872. Yohannes's forces won a significant battle against the Egyptians at Gura in 1875. From this victory, Yohannes's foremost General, Ras Alula, became governor of the province of Hamasien, and prince of Eritrea.

Italian influence

The first Italian mission in Abyssinia was at Adua in 1840, under Father Giuseppe Sapeto. He was the vehicle through which the Italian government bought up pieces of land near Assab, initially on behalf of the national Rubattino Shipping Company. But as the European 'Scramble for Africa' gathered pace, the Italian government took over the land in 1882 and began to administer it directly. They also ousted the Egyptians from Massawa on the coast. However, expansion further inland soon led to clashes with Emperor Yohannes. In 1887, Ras Alula's forces inflicted a heavy defeat on the Italians at Dogali, forcing them to retreat.

This was a significant victory for Yohannes, who was also facing a number of other threats on different fronts at the same time – not only the Italians, but the Dervishes, and Menelik, an increasingly disloyal general. Yohannes was eventually killed after being captured in battle against the Dervishes at Gallabat. Following his death, Ras Alula withdrew to Tigray. This allowed Menelik to be named Yohannes's successor in 1889 with substantial Italian backing, instead of the natural heir, Ras Mangasha.

The Italians then moved rapidly, taking Keren in July 1889 and Asmara one month later. Menelik had signed the Treaty of Uccialli with the Italians the same year, detailing the areas each controlled. Just four years later, Menelik renounced the treaty over a dispute arising from further Italian expansionist attempts. After more military clashes and in the face of sizeable Italian reinforcements, Menelik signed a peace treaty. Italy then began establishing colonial rule in the areas it controlled.

Colonial rule

The Italians initially used a system of indirect rule through local chiefs at the beginning of the 20th century. The first decade or so concentrated on expropriation of land from indigenous owners. The colonial power also embarked on the construction of the railway from Massawa to Asmara in 1909. Fascist rule in the 1920s and the spirit of 'Pax Italiana' gave a significant boost to the number of Italians in Eritrea, adding further to loss of land by the local population.

In 1935, Italy succeeded in over-running Abyssinia, and decreed that Eritrea, Italian Somaliland and Abyssinia were to be known as Italian East Africa. The development of regional transport links at this time round Asmara, Assab and Addis produced a rapid but short-lived economic boom.

However, there began to be clashes between Italian and British forces in 1940. Under General Platt, the British captured Agordat in 1941, taking Keren and Asmara later the same year. As Britain did not have the capacity to take over the full running of the territory, they left some Italian officials in place. One of the most significant changes under the British was the lifting of the colour bar which the Italians had operated. Eritreans could now legally be employed as civil servants. In 1944, with changing fortunes in the Second World War, Britain withdrew resources from Eritrea. The post-war years and economic recession led to comparatively high levels of urban unemployment and unrest.

Ethiopian rule When the British withdrew, the fate of Eritrea was left in the balance. It was known that the British favoured partition – the north and west of Eritrea to Sudan, the rest to Ethiopia, which suited Haile Selassie. After initial presentations on the possible future of Eritrea, in 1949 the UN established a Commission of Enquiry with the task of finding out what Eritreans wanted for their own future. For a number of reasons, countries represented on the Commission could not agree on recommendations, but went along with the view that the Christian majority in Eritrea favoured unity with Ethiopia.

At the same time, Ethiopia had been strengthening its ties with the United States, even sending troops to fight with the Americans in the Korean War in 1950. In December that year, the UN finally declared Eritrea an autonomous unit federated to Ethiopia. Haile Selassie saw to it that the first three governors of the federated unit were related to him. In 1959, Tigrinya and Arabic were forbidden as teaching languages, and replaced with Amharic. Student protests and boycotts ensued, but were repressed.

For the next 40 years, Eritrea's plight was virtually ignored by the international community. Frustration at the lack of room for political manoeuvre finally resulted in the launch of an armed struggle, in 1961. Ethiopia formally annexed Eritrea in 1962.

The Eritrean Liberation Movement, one of the earliest opposition groupings, was formed mainly by exiles in Sudan. The founder members were all Muslims, but they gained some support from the Christian population too. However this group came into conflict with the Eritrean Liberation Front (ELF) based in Cairo. The latter, consisting of old leaders of the pro-independence opposition in the 1940s, gained more support from Eritreans despite being less well organized.

In 1965 the ELF restructured its forces into four command zones, adding a fifth zone, known as the 'Christian zone', one year later. The fifth zone covered the province of Hamasien, including Asmara.

There followed a period of bitter and destructive faction fighting, out of which resulted a coalition in 1972, comprising the Eritrean Liberation Force (another ELF) and the People's Liberation Front (PLF). At the start, they were only 500 strong. The three movements also clashed. In October 1974, the ELF fought the ELF-PLF while they were both launching an attack on Asmara. After some negotiations, they fought together in a second attack in January 1975. Later that year, the PLF's leader entered into an alliance with the other ELF, although his forces did not support him. The fighters of the ELF-PLF coalition then renamed themselves as the EPLF. The different groups continued to clash for the next decade.

Despite these internal problems, the Eritrean guerrilla forces (estimated to number 20,000) managed to win considerable victories against the occupying Ethiopians. They were close to final victory in early 1978, but had not planned on the Soviet Union's crucial intervention in the form of military aid for Mengistu's régime in Ethiopia.

The EPLF and ELF forces withdrew to the north. The EPLF held its first congress in 1977, and from that time on their ranks were strengthened by ELF fighters who had defected. By the end of the 1970s, the ELF was no longer a viable fighting force.

Through most of the war, Ethiopia occupied the southern part of Eritrea. The EPLF had to settle in the inhospitable northern hills towards the Sudanese border. These hills became a safe haven for the families of soldiers and the orphans and disabled. Consequently, much of the region around Afabet and Nakfa in Sahel province became home to makeshift homes, schools, orphanages, hospitals, factories, printers, bakeries etc in an attempt to live life as normally as possible under extraordinary conditions. Most structures were built either into the ground or in caves to avoid being bombed by Ethiopian jets. The steep narrow areas were chosen as they were the hardest for the jets to negotiate.

Shamma

🖝

This is the dress worn widely in both Ethiopia and Eritrea by both men and women. It is made from handwoven cotten, and is very delicate in texture. Two pieces, one being about one metre square, and the other two metres by one metre, make up the garment. The borders of the fabric are decorated with bright borders, sometimes with linen and silk interleaved in the weave. The larger piece is wrapped round to make a dress, with the border making up the hemline. The smaller piece is used as a scarf or to make a hood over the head.

The Ethiopian army under Haile Mariam Mengistu (an army officer who deposed Haile Selassie in 1974) intensified the war against Eritrea, but it was easily defeated in 1991 after Mengistu fell from power.

The war had a devastating effect on Eritrea. Around 60,000 people lost their lives, there are an estimated 50,000 children with no parents and 60,000 people who have been left handicapped. However, there is now great optimism with people pulling together to rebuild the country. The 100,000 strong army (without pay) is helping with reconstruction and Eritreans who fled the during the fighting are returning with their skills.

In May 1993, Eritrea separated from Ethiopia and became an independent sovereign state.

Tension with Ethiopia increased with the introduction of Ethiopia's own currency, the Nakfa, in November 1997, and erupted, in June 1998 in territorial disputes, armed conflict, bombing raids and closed borders.

People

In 1984, the Ethiopian census put the population of Eritrea at 2.7 million, though years of war have affected this figure. Around 60,000 people are said to have been killed and at least 750,000 fled the country into neighbouring Sudan and Ethiopia. There is even a strong Eritrean community in the UK. With a natural rate of population increase at three percent a year, this will leave the population currently at around 2.6 million, though some estimates put the population at over 3.8 million.

Eritrea was a creation of the colonial era whose boundaries were drawn up in the late 19th century with little consideration for the customs and cultures of different groups of people, consequently the country is home to nine different ethnic groups. There are two main groups, the Tigrinya making up about 50 percent of the population, and the Tigre who account for a further 34 percent of Eritreans. The two groups are closely associated, the language of both groups having originated from the ancient Ethiopian language of Ge'ez. The Tigrinya are mainly Christians (Orthodox or Roman Catholic) who live in the high plateau of the country. They have much in common with their neighbouring highlanders in the Tigray province of Ethiopia having similar language, faith and customs. The majority of Tigrinya are agriculturalists cultivating *tef* (a local type of grain), maize, wheat, millet and barley as well as a variety of different vegetables. Some people also herd animals as a supplementary form of income.

The Tigre are Muslims who live in the Western Lowlands, the northern hills and the coastal regions of the country. Their way of life is primarily as nomadic pastoralists. This group is made up of many different clans including the Beni Amer, the largest clan who have historical ties with the Beja of Sudan.

Eritrea's other Muslim peoples include the Danakil herdsmen who live in the desert regions in the south and who are closely associated with the Afar in Djibouti. There are also the Rashayda of Arabic origin and the Tukrir who are originally from Nigeria. The Tukrir set off from Nigeria on a pilgrimage to Mecca but came to Eritrea and decided to settle there. The smaller ethnic groups include the Afar, the Bilen, Hedareb, the Kunama, the Nara (or Baria), the Rashaida and the Saho.

Eritrea

Arabic and Tigrinya are the two working languages. Arabic is widely spoken throughout the coastal areas of the country reflecting Eritrea's long trade associations with countries across the Red Sea.

Modern Eritrea

Politics

The Eritrean Liberation Movement was founded in 1958 to liberate Eritrea from Ethiopian rule. It was succeeded by the Eritrean Liberation Front (ELF) in 1961. Clashes of ideology soon developed between its members who were from both the Christian highlands and the Muslim eastern lowland towns. A group left the ELF to set up what became known as the Eritrean People's Liberation Front (EPLF). Between 1972-1974 a civil war developed. By the early 1980s the different factions came together to form a disciplined political and military organization.

Throughout the 1970s and 1980s new recruits joined the EPLF as Ethiopian forces terrorized resistance groups. By 1978 the EPLF had retreated into the hillsides of northern Eritrea with thousands of young supporters, both male and female. From then on, the EPLF steadily pushed back Ethiopian forces, capturing military equipment in the process. As they grew in numbers and military strength, so they turned from a guerilla force into a regular army. In 1990 the EPLF captured the strategically important port of Massawa, and they entered Asmara, now the capital of Eritrea, in 1991.

At a conference held in London in 1991 the Ethiopian People's Revolutionary Democratic Front (EPRDF), who were now in control of Ethiopia having ousted Mengistu and were sympathetic to Eritrean nationalist aspirations, accepted the EPLF as the provisional government of Eritrea. So began the long process towards independence and international legitimation of Eritrea as a country in its own right.

In April 1993 a referendum was held in which 1,102,410 Eritreans voted; 99.8 percent endorsed national independence and on 28 May Eritrea became the 182nd member of the UN. Thus it is now eligible to receive international aid to help reconstruct and develop its shattered economy. The Head of State is Isaias Afewerki, formerly secretary-general of the EPLF. The government is in the process of establishing a constitution based on a pluralist political system. Since establishing a provisional government in 1991, Eritrea has been a stable and peaceful political entity, with all political groups represented in the transitional government.

A new constitution was adopted in May 1997, with a 150 seat transitional National Assembly, with 75 seats allocated to the People's Front for Democracy and Justice (PFDJ), formerly the EPRDF. 60 seats are to be filled by members of the Constituent Assembly, and 15 by Eritreans resident overseas. Tigrinya and Arabic are working languages, but there will be no official language. English is the language of instruction in secondary schools.

Regional relations, however, have not been so smooth. In particular, relations with neighbouring Sudan have become strained. Eritrea severed diplomatic ties with Sudan in December 1994, in response to allegations that the Sudanese government was backing the 'Eritrean Islamic Jihad', a rebel grouping which has been trying to destabilize the country. A number of minor incidents had been reported in the Western Lowlands region.

Sudan for its part, accuses Eritrea of supporting a Sudanese opposition group in exile in Asmara. It seems clear that Eritrea is prepared to support Sudanese rebels fighting the National Islamic Front government in Khartoum. Complicating the issue are the 300,000 Eritrea refugees in Somalia. Eritrea is pressing for their return, which is being obstructed by Sudan, partly motivated by a desire to continue to benefit from the aid directed to the support of the refugees.

Eritrea has accused Sudan of an assassination plot, and it is reported that Libya is attempting to mediate.

There has also been a dispute with Yemen over the uninhabited Zaquar-Hanish islands situated due north of Assab in the Red Sea. It has been agreed that the dispute will now go to international arbitration. The islands are thought to have a strategic importance, and there is always the issue of any off-shore minerals.

An unusual gift

When contemplating matrimony, it is the practice of the Afar, formerly known as the Danakil, to acquire an extra set of male genitals to present to their betrothed.

The most serious development has been the dispute with Ethiopia. The introduction in November 1997 of the Nakfa to replace the Ethiopian Birr, previously in use, has added complications to cross border trade. Ethiopia retaliated by demanding that all transactions be settled in hard currency, a problem for Eritrea which has limited foreign exchange reserves. More than anything, this has brought home to Ethiopia the implications of being landlocked now that Eritrea is independent.

The Italians established a border with the then Abyssinia when they colonized Eritrea after 1885. However, when Ethiopia annexed Eritrea in 1962, five small areas were reallocated from Eritrea to Ethiopian provinces. Eritrea wants the Italian borders recognized, and both sides have made efforts to occupy the disputed zone. Armed raids took place in June 1998 and Ethiopia has bombed the airport at Asmara, while Eritrea has bombed the airport and civilian areas in Makale. After a lull in late 1998 when diplomatic initiatives were being pursued, fighting broke out again in early 1999. Ethiopia has expelled citizens of Eritrean descent and seized their assets. Eritrea has done likewise. The loss of Eritrean income from goods in transit to Ethiopia through the port of Assab has been considerable.

It is uncertain how the issue will be resolved, or when the borders will re-open.

The disputed zones are without any economic significance, and the dispute has aptly been described as "two bald men fighting over a comb".

Economics

As Eritrea is such a new nation, data is very sparse, and it will be a while before the necessary surveys are undertaken to give a more complete picture of economic life and performance.

Even such basic statistics as the level of population are not reliable – there were 2.7 million people enumerated in the most recent Ethiopian census in 1984, but it is not clear what the overall impact of war has been. Many hundreds of thousands of people fled from Ethiopia; on the other hand the natural rate of population increase has been around 3.1 percent a year, and refugees have begun to return since 1991. Estimates suggest around 3.9 million in 1998. Urbanization at 10 percent is low by African standards, but this again has been affected by the war, with people fleeing the towns and reverting to subsistence production in the countryside. The population growth rate of 3.1 percent reflects only the natural rate – it is to be expected that the actual population growth will be boosted by the return of refugees. Population density at 30 persons per square kilometres is close to the African and regional average, but needs to be assessed in the light of much of the southern coastal strip being arid.

The economy with GDP estimated at US$860mn in 1999 is small, with most activity being subsistence agriculture on small-scale family farms. Levels of income are modest, reflecting the struggle for existence that the war has brought about.

Exports totalled US$95mn in 1996 and comprised food (30 percent), minerals (35 percent) and manufactures (30 percent).

Imports were US$514mn, and the gap between this and export receipts is covered by tourism earnings, aid, and investment by Eritrean expatriates. Imports comprised food (22 percent), fuel (eight percent), machinery and transport equipment (36 percent).

Almost all the labour force is involved in agriculture in one form or another, as growing food has been the key to survival. The issue of land is being dealt with by the new Land Proclamation, which will come into effect from 1996 onwards. This invests land ownership rights in the government, allowing for land to be allocated to Eritrean nationals for the span of their lifetime. The same land can also be passed on to their children.

Eritrea's future prospects are reasonably promising and the most recent estimates suggest that the economy expanded at about seven percent a year in 1996 and 1997, although this has slowed as a result of the disruption caused by the Ethiopian war to about five percent a year. The government is keen to encourage foreign investment, and there are inflows of capital from Eritreans overseas. Eritrea is in the enviable position of not being saddled with a massive external debt to service.

The government is committed to a market economy. By early 1997 nine privatizations had taken place, comprising mostly small enterprises in furniture, timber, hotels and the like. A further 37 privatizations are being contemplated. Telecommunications and Eritrean Airlines are the most substantial of the planned privatizations.

International help is quite generous, and at US$50 per head, aid receipts are above the African average. Saudi Arabia has funded a US$35m electricity project. The Chinese are constructing a US$10m pharmaceutical factory. Several companies have taken up licences to prospect for minerals, mainly gold, copper and potash in the south and southwest highlands. Rift Resources of Canada is reported to have discovered gold at Adi Meshela. A US company is engaged on a US$29m oil exploration exercise. At Mount Adid, an extinct volcano about 100 kilometres southwest of Massawa, there is a geothermal project to generate electricity. At present, all Eritrea's power comes from diesel generators.

There were some 200,000 arrivals in 1995, of which half are thought to be tourists and the other half returning Eritreans. Hotels are being refurbished and there is a US$300m casino project for the Dahlak Islands.

An independent currency, the Nakfa was introduced in November 1997, and has hampered trade with Ethiopia who have insisted on payments being settled in hard currency. The territorial dispute that erupted in June 1998 led to a cessation of trade with Ethiopia, and this will be an impediment to economic progress as well as a colossal waste of resources.

A further problem is that the heavy 'El Niño' rains in 1997/98 which disrupted agriculture, transport and communications.

Over the past few years the government has asked all but six Aid providers to leave, including all religious organizations and Oxfam. This reflects President Issaias Afewerki's aim to avoid external reliance.

Djibouti

8

Djibouti

Djibouti is a small country sandwiched between Eritrea, Ethiopia and Somalia consisting of little more than a port at the southern entrance to the Red Sea. Its importance increased dramatically during both the Gulf War and the UN intervention in Somalia when it acted as a base for allied troops. The capital, Djibouti houses over half the population of the country acting as an international transit port and refuelling centre. Although some people visit the country for its desert scenery, interesting sea life and fine white sand beaches, most people are simply passing through to other countries in the area.

Exchange rate (September 1999) Dfr 172 = US$1

Essentials

Before you travel

When to go From June to August when the humidity is at its lowest.

Getting in **Visas** All people entering Djibouti require visas except French nationals. French nationals only need a visa if intending to stay for more than 3 months. Visas are easily obtainable from Djibouti or French embassies around the world and are valid for 10 days. They can be renewed at the airport if necessary.

A transit visa can be obtained on arrival at the airport for nationals of Belgium, Denmark, Finland, Germany, Italy, Japan, Luxembourg, Netherlands, Norway, Sweden, UK and US. In order to get a transit visa you must have an onward ticket, if you do not, you will be forced to buy one before being granted a transit visa.

Vaccinations International certificates of vaccination against yellow fever and cholera are required. It is wise to protect against malaria.

Tourist information Tourist Information is available from Djibouti City at *L'Office de Developpement du Tourism*, Place Menelik, BP 1938, T352800, F356322, Tx5938.

Travel and tour agents *Djibouti Tours*, Av General de Gaulle, T353022.

Money **Currency** The currency is the Djibouti Franc divided into 100 centimes. In September 1999 the exchange rate stood at US$1 = 172 Dfr. Any amount of local or foreign currency may be taken into or out of the country. US dollars and French francs are widely accepted, and welcomed by the authorities. There are no money changing facilities at the airport.

Credit cards All major cards accepted by large hotels, restaurants and travel agents.

Getting there

If you intend to travel between Djibouti, Ethiopia or Somalia, it is best to check on access before making your travel plans.

Air All flights go to the capital city and flight information is on page 787.

Train The Djibouti-Ethiopian railway provides regular services from Addis Ababa and Dire Dawa to the capital. It is a long slow journey, but comfortable with sleeping accommodation available in first class carriages, see page 787. Recently this train has been targetted by bandits. Please check the situation locally before booking.

Road There is a sealed road from Addis Ababa to Djibouti. Buses go from Djibouti to Assab in Eritrea, but it is an awkward journey through Tadjoura and Obock, and the roads are poor from Obock on. There are normally road links with Somalia, with a mixture of bus and lorry transport to Hargeisa and Berbera. However, the current political situation will need to stabilize before this route becomes possible again.

Djibouti embassies

There are very few Djibouti embassies: in Paris (France), New York (US), Cairo (Egypt), Djedda (Saudi Arabia), Addis Ababa (Ethiopia) and Mogadishu (Somalia). Visas can be obtained from French embassies in other parts of the world.

All overseas embassies and consulates are based in the capital city. For list see section under Djibouti city, see page 788.

Hours of business *Banking hours are from Monday-Saturday 0700-1200.*
Official time *Three hours ahead of GMT.*
Language *French and Arabic are the official languages, and Afar and Somali are spoken locally. Some English is spoken in the capital.*
IDD *253; there are no area codes. Equal tones with long pauses means it is ringing; equal tones with equal pauses means engaged.*

The importance of Djibouti as a port means many cargo ships dock here. In principle it should **Sea** be possible to travel by boat from Marseille and Aden, although the political disturbances in Aden in 1994 rule this possibility out for the present. Djibouti has many dhows and it is possible to get to Berbera, Sudan, Karachi, Aden and the Persian Gulf this way. It is also possible to reach Djibouti by dhow from Al Mokha in North Yemen, it takes about 16 hours and you are even able to take a car or motorcycle with you.

Where to stay

There are a number of first class hotels in the capital all of which are air conditioned and have **Hotels** restaurants, but they are expensive. There are also some cheaper hotels without a/c in the African quarter of town. In other parts of the country, accommodation for tourists or travellers is scanty. See hotel classifications, page 31.

Food and drink

There are restaurants to suit all tastes in both the capital and the main seaside resort of Arta with French, Vietnamese, Chinese and Arab cuisine. In other parts of the country simple local food (grills, stews and rice) are available. See restaurant classifications, page 31.

Getting around

There are domestic flights on Air Djibouti to Tadjoura and Obock each day. It is possible to **Air** charter a plane, (see details under Djibouti City, page 787).

The railway between Djibouti and Ethiopia makes stops in Djibouti at Hol Hol, Daasbiyo and **Train** Ali-Sabieh.

Public transport is limited. Hiring a car is a good option for travelling around the country by **Road** road. Over two-thirds of the roads are not surfaced, and half are only usable by lorries or four-wheel drive vehicles. There are now roads linking the capital, Djibouti City with both the north and south of the country, and the road to the Ethiopian frontier is bitumen-surfaced.

It is possible to hire cars in Djibouti City (see under car hire section, page 786). **Car Hire**

Keeping in touch

There is only one local paper, *La Nation* which is published weekly. There are also *L'Atout*, a **Newspapers** twice yearly paper published by the Centre National de la Promotion Culturelle et Artistique, and the *Carrefour Africain* published fortnightly by the Roman Catholic mission.

Broadcasting is state controlled and operated from Djibouti City. There are programmes in **Television &** French, Afar, Somali and Arabic. Radio transmission is 24 hours and television 7 hours daily. **radio** Djibouti is also a member of the Arab Satellite Communication Organisation which transmits both radio and television programmes.

BBC World Service can be received in Djibouti if you have a radio with short waveband reception. See guide, page 33.

Djibouti

Holidays and festivals

New Year 2 February
Lailat al-Miraji February[1]
Labour Day 1 May
Eid al-Fitr April[1]
National Day 27 June
Eid al-Adha July[1]
Assumption Day 15 August
Muslim New Year July[1]
Al-Ashura August[1]
Prophet's Birthday October[1]
All Saints Day 1 November
Christmas Day 25 December

[1] These dates marking Muslim holidays are approximate as they depend on the lunar year.

Health Remember to protect against malaria. It may be wise to take protections against prickly heat. Clothing should be light and cotton; avoid synthetic fabrics. See general Health section, page 35. It is quite safe to drink tap water.

Further reading

General Thompson, V and Adloff, R (1968) *Djibouti and the Horn of Africa*, London: OUP. Thorough coverage of historical, political and economic issues prior to independence.

Travellers' Tales Waugh, E (1931) *Remote People*, London: Duckworth. Includes Waughs's impressions of Djibouti on the way to Addis Ababa in 1930, and on the way back.

Djibouti

Djibouti City

The city lies on a peninsula separating the Gulf of Tadjoura from the Gulf of Aden at the 11° 30' N, 43° 5' E
mouth of the Red Sea. More than half the population of the country live in Djibouti. The Colour map 1, grid B4
city is the centre of economic activity in the country as well as the administrative, politi-
cal and legal centre. In recent years it has become of strategic importance to the UN and
allied forces, firstly in the Gulf War and later as a base from which to go into Somalia.
The city has an Arab flavour to it both in terms of its architecture and its culture. It is an
expensive place to visit not geared to the needs of budget travellers.

There is a colourful and interesting market in the centre of town near the mosque **Sights**
which retains elements of African, European and Arab culture. Just outside Djibouti
(about 5 kilometres) there are pleasant walks in the **Ambouli palm grove**. There are
good beaches at **Dorale** (12 kilometres) and **Khor Ambado** (15 kilometres) though
you will need a four-wheel drive to reach the latter.

There are relatively few cheap places to stay in Djibouti, and they are all situated in the Afri- **Sleeping**
can quarter of town.

A+ *Djibouti Sheraton*, Plateau du Serpent, PO Box 1924, T35 04 05, F35 58 92, Tlx 5912.
Casino, discotheque, tennis, beach with watersports, , a/c, pool, restaurant, bars, pleasant
gardens.

Djibouti city

A *Continental*, Place Menelik, PO Box 675,
T35 01 46. A/c, bars, restaurant. **A** *La Siesta*,
Plateau du Serpent, PO Box 508, T35 14 92.
A/c, bars, restaurant. **A** *Hotel Residence
Europe*, Place Menelik, PO Box 83, T35 50 60.
A/c, bars, restaurant. **A** *Plein Ciel*, Blvd
Bonheure, PO Box 1869, T35 38 41. Pleasant
location on west edge of commercial area,
close to shore, a/c, bars, restaurant.

B *Djibouti Palace*, Ave General de Gaulle,
PO Box 166, T35 09 82. Eastern side of commercial centre, overlooks railway line and
bay. **B** *Relais*. Close to the airport.

C *Bienvenue*, Blvd du Bender, on the south
edge of the commercial centre. **C** *Doraleh*,
10 kilometres outside the city. **C** *Hotel de
France*, Blvd de Gaulle, T351843). Close to
the Assemblé Nationale. Large clean rooms
wiht fans, a/c and TV.

Restaurants in the hotels tend to be expen- **Eating**
sive, but serve good European style food.

4 *Chez Mamma Elena*. High quality Italian
food. **4** *Hanoi*. French influenced Chinese
and Vietnamese cuisine. **4** *Restaurant Le
Kintz*. French cuisine, high standard.

Waugh in Djibouti

In 1930 the novelist Evelyn Waugh went from Djibouti to Addis Ababa by train. He was travelling to report on the coronation of Haile Selassie for The Times newspaper.

His first sight of the low coastline of French Somaliland, as Djibouti then was, came at dawn from the deck of the French steamship Azay le Rideau from Marseille. A haggard couple in evening dress were dancing to a wind-up gramophone. Sleep was impossible as the retinue of the Egyption delegation barked orders, dragging around numerous tin trunks of luggage and the massive crates which contained the Egyptian gift to the Emperor, a suite of bedroom furniture.

It began to rain. Exhausted, the dancing couple slunk off to bed. Small boys hung around the deck, shivering and offering to dive for coins. Bags of coal were being hauled aboard over planks from barges. Ashore, they found the next train, in three days' time, was reserved in its entirety for the Duke of Gloucester. The next, in a further three days, was allocated to Prince Udine.

Waugh, and a traveller morbidly obsessed by the impossibility of staying healthy in the tropics, repaired to the Hotel des Arcades. Run by a handsome Frenchwoman it had a fading stucco façade, a few first floor bedrooms at the back facing onto a broad verandah, and hot water. In the courtyard a black monkey sat in a lemon-tree.

After lunch the rain subsided and Waugh toured the town in a one-horse cab churning through pools of steaming mud. The 'elegant and smiling boulevards' of the guidebook proved to be mere stretches of waste land between blocks of decaying buildings. A shower of stucco and bricks fell about them from one of the structures and a clutch of Indian clerks and Greek traders scampered into the street. It was an earthquake that they had not noticed due to the jolting of the cab.

The local people struck Waugh as a race of exceptional beauty, slender and tall, with delicate features and wide-set eyes. Most wore a strip of rag round the waist and a few coils of copper wire on their wrists and ankles. Heads shaven or dyed with yellow ochre. Half-a -dozen harlots besieged the cab. Naked children splashed through the mud screeching for money. Some warriors with spears spat contemptuously as they passed. At the edge of town, Waugh viewed the local dwellings which he likened to inverted birds' nests of mud, twigs, grass, rags and flattened tins with one low hole through which a man might crawl on his belly.

On returning to the hotel the travellers learned that places had been secured for them on a special train leaving that evening. Cheered up, Waugh bought a French novel with a lurid cover, some cheroots and changed some bank-notes for Marie Therese silver thalers, the massive coins minted in Vienna and the principle currency in Ethiopia. As darkness fell they chuffed and creaked slowly out of what Waugh described as "the intolerable desolation of French Somaliland – a country of dust and boulders, utterly devoid of any sign of life".

3 *Chez Therese*. Local Ethiopian food. **3** *Mickey*. High quality Italian food. **3** *Restaurant Palmier en Zinc*. Sound French fare. **3** *Vietnam*. Chinese and Vietnamese cuisine, friendly atmosphere.

There are a number of local restaurants serving cheap Arab and local dishes, some good ones are near the market past the Place Mahamoud Harbi.

Shopping   **Curios & crafts**: a good place to buy souvenirs is around the Place Menelik though they are expensive.

Transport   **Local** Taxis are widely available in the city and from the airport. Tariffs increase by 50 percent at night. **Car hire**: it is possible to hire a car in Djibouti from **Hertz**, T352651 or from the airport, T352513. **Stophi**, T352494 rents out four-wheel drive vehicles for trips into the interior of the country. It is advisable to take plenty of water and petrol on any expedition off the beaten track.

Air Air France has daily flights between **Paris** and Djibouti. **Ethiopian Airways** flies twice a week between Djibouti and **Addis Ababa** (Tuesday and Thursday) and the fare is US$306 return. There are no flights currently to Somalia or to Asmara, Eritrea. **Air Djibouti**, T35 26 51, flies daily to **Tadjoura** and **Obock**. As there is no bus service from the airport to the city which is 5 kilometres south of the centre, you will need to get a taxi. There are no left luggage facilities at the airport.

Train A 782 kilometre railway connects Djibouti with Addis Ababa on the Red Sea. Recently (1997) however there have been incidents where travellers have been attacked by bandits on this train. Check the situation locally before booking. The trains leave daily at around 0700 and 1930, arriving in Addis approximately 24 hours later. Stops at Ali-Sabieh before the Ethiopian border and at Dire Dawa and Aouache in Ethiopia before going on to Addis Ababa. It is a long slow journey, but comfortable, with sleeping accommodation available in first class carriages. Booking is at the railway station at the north end of Blvd de la Republique. It is

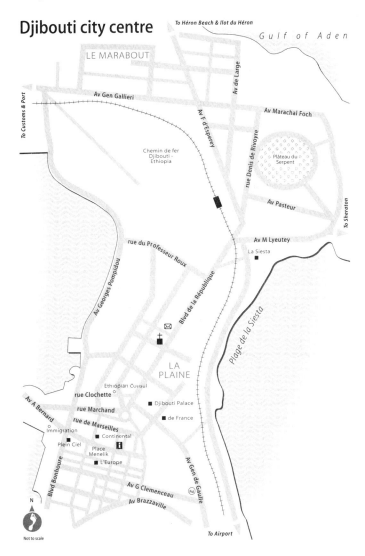

Djibouti city centre

To Héron Beach & Ilot du Héron

Gulf of Aden

LE MARABOUT

Av de Large

To Customs & Port

Av Gen Gallieri

Av Marachal Foch

Av F. d'Esperey

Chemin de fer
Djibouti -
Ethiopia

rue Denis de Rivoyre

Plateau du
Serpent

Av Pasteur

To Sheraton

rue du Professeur Roux

Av M Lyeutey

La Siesta

Av Georges Pompidou

Blvd de la République

Plage de la Siesta

rue Clochette

LA
PLAINE

Ethiopian Consul

Av A Bernard

rue Marchand

Djibouti Palace

rue de Marseilles

de France

Immigration

Continental

Plein Ciel

Place
Menelik

L'Europe

Blvd Bonhoure

Av G Clemenceau

Av Gen de Gaulle

Av Brazzaville

N

Not to scale

To Airport

Djibouti

necessary to make a reservation as the train is often full. The fare to Addis Ababa is US$60 1st class (a sleeper on the overnight train); US$30 2nd class; US$16 3rd class. Djibouti-Ethiopian Railroad Company, T447250.

Road The best roads are between Djibouti and Ethiopia especially the road towards Assab or west into Ethiopia via Dikhil. Most other roads are rough but passable throughout the year. There is a good tarmac road between Addis Ababa in Ethiopia and Djibouti.

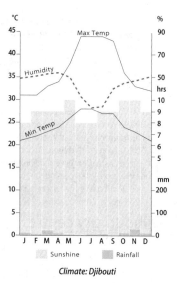

Climate: Djibouti

Directory **Airline offices** International: A number of international airlines operate to Djibouti; Air France, Air Madagascar, Yemen Airways, Al Yemda, Ethiopian Airlines, and Somali Airways. All these airlines have offices on Rue de Marseilles. **Charter: There is a small private airline from which it is possible to charter a plane. Contact the Aero Club at the airport.**

Banks & money changers There are several Bureaux de Change in the Place Menelik. The main banks are: *Banque de Djibouti et de Moyen Orient*, BP 2471. *Banque Indosuez*, Place Lagarde, PO Box 88, T353016. *Banque pour le Commerce et l'Industrie*, Place Lagarde, T350857. *British Bank of the Middle East*, Place Lagarde, T353291.

Communications Post Office: Main post office on Blvd de la Republique.

Embassies and consulates Belgium*, T350960 ; China, T352246; Egypt, BP 1989, T351231; Ethiopia, BP 230, T350718; France, 45 Blvd du Marechal Foch, BP 2039, T352503/350718; Germany*, T350507; India*, T350219; Iraq, BP 1983, T353469; Italy*, T351162; Libya, BP 2073, T353339; Netherlands*, T352022; Norway*, T352351; Oman, BP 1996, T350852; Russia, BP 1913, T352051; Saudi Arabia, BP 1921, T351645; Somalia Blvd del Republique, BP 549, T353521; Sudan*, T351483; Sweden, T352022; Yemen Arab Republic, BP 194, T352975; USA, Villa Plateau du Serpent, Blvd Marechal Joffre, BP 185, T353995/353849.

Places of worship Almost the entire population is Muslim, consequently there are a number of mosques throughout the city. There is a Roman Catholic Church on Blvd de la Republique, as well as a Greek Orthodox church and a Protestant church.

Tour companies & travel agents *Djibouti Tours*, Blvd de Gaulle, T353022.

Tourist offices L'Office de Developement du Tourism, Place Menelik, BP 1938, T353790. For railway information go to Plateau-du-Serpent T350353. For information on ferries to Obock and Tadjoura, Societé du Bac le Goubet, T352351.

Useful addresses Police: Ave General de Gaulle

Djibouti

Outside Djibouti

There are a number of places which are interesting to visit around the country. **Arta** is a small summer resort used by the expatriates, situated in the mountains overlooking the Gulf of Tadjoura. It is about 40 kilometres outside Djibouti on a sealed road. There is a good restaurant there which is part of a hotel school.

100 kilometres southwest of Djibouti is **Lake Assal**. At 153 kilometres below sea level this dead lake is encircled by mountains and makes an interesting though somewhat eerie place to visit. The cold dead waters of the lake are surrounded by a crystal bank of salt and startlingly white gypsum. There are hot springs nearby. The road to the lake is only passable using a four-wheel drive vehicle.

Lake Abbe near the Ethiopian border in the southwest corner of the country is the home of flocks of flamingoes, ibis and pelicans. This lake has an unearthly moonlike appearance as it is surrounded with jagged needles of rock. This lake is near the town of **Dikhil**, an attractive small town perched on a rocky outcrop. The area around the town is home to many gazelle, antelope, hyenas, jackals and camels.

The mountain town of **Ali-Sabieh** makes an interesting excursion from Djibouti for those with a four-wheel drive vehicle. This is an Issa town which has a large flourishing market. It is a major stop for the train between Addis Ababa and Djibouti.

The **Gulf of Tadjoura** to the north of Djibouti is a haven for those interested in aquatic life. It is possible to go skin diving, spear fishing or to do some underwater photography here as the area offers a wide variety of flora and fauna including many species of fish and different types of coral. The best time for these activities is between September and May when the waters of the Red Sea are at their clearest. The picturesque town of **Tadjoura** is worth a visit for its beautiful mountain setting. The **Goda Mountains** just behind the town have a wealth of rare plants and there is a fossilized forest which has been created into a national park.

Djibouti

Background

The land

Geography   The country covers an area of 21,783 square kilometres, most of which is volcanic rock-strewn desert wastes with occasional patches of arable land and spectacular salt lakes. It lies at 12° latitude north and 43° longitude east. The physical core consists of a triangular depression which is part of the East African rift system and is made up of a complex pattern of volcanic plateau, sunken plains and lakes (most of which are salty). Much of the territory is below sea level – millions of years ago this area was ocean floor but submarine volcanic activity caused rock and lava formations to develop into what is there today. There are vast deposits of salt around the country which are mined, mainly by the Afar, and used throughout the region.

Vegetation in the country is spartan and seasonal and comprises mainly grasses, thorn trees and scattered palms. The only part of the country with continuous annual vegetation is the upper part of the basaltic range, north of the Gulf of Tadjourah where the altitude reaches more than 1,200 metres above sea level. The poor quality of the soil and the arid climate prevents any large-scale crop production.

Climate   The climate is tropical with high temperatures and humidity during the monsoon season. Average rainfall is less than 125 mm per annum, and temperatures can reach as high as 45°C. The country is particularly parched between June and August when temperatures are at their highest, and the dusty *khamsin* blows from the desert. It is cooler between October and April with occasional light rains.

History

Earliest times   The area known as Djibouti was only sparsely populated by nomadic peoples, mainly the Afars and the Issas (see Culture and Life, page 791) who used it as grazing land, until the French became interested in its strategic value in 1859.

Colonial period   The initial interest by the French in the area was to counteract the British trading presence in Aden on the other side of the Babel-Mandeb Straits stimulated by the desire of both countries to control the entrance to the Red Sea. In 1862 they established themselves in Obock on the coast and drew up a treaty with Afar leaders, the Sultans of Obock and Tadjourah, to legitimize their acquisition of the coastal region in the north. In 1888 the construction of Djibouti began. Treaties in 1884, 1885 and 1896 with the Afars, the Issas and Emperor Menelik of Ethiopia eventually led to the establishment of the boundaries of French Somaliland (later to be known as Djibouti). The establishment of the boundaries was made without any consideration to the ethnic links, language, trading patterns or even traditional grazing rights of the Afar or Issa people. The problems caused by these issues continue to dominate politics.

In a treaty in 1897, the French made an agreement with Emperor Menelik which designated Djibouti as the `official outlet of Ethiopian commerce' and led to the building of a railway from Djibouti to Addis Ababa which would act as the major trade route into Ethiopia. The railway was completed in 1915 and from this point on, the port of Djibouti and the trade route has become the mainstay of the Djibouti economy. The railway is of vital strategic and commercial importance to Ethiopia and it is for this reason that Ethiopia is hostile to the idea of a merger between Somalia and Djibouti.

The French had habitually supported the Issas in the region but the anti-colonial demonstrations, which started as early as 1949 by the Somalis and Issas, eventually meant that in the 1960's the French switched their support to the Afar, with their strong Ethiopian links, in order to counter Somali government claims to the territory. This also served to strengthen Emperor Haile Selassie in Ethiopia, who was seen as an ally. As a result of the switch of allegiance, the French placed the Afar, Ali Aref and his Afar colleagues in control of the local government council, displacing the previous Issa administration.

In 1967 a referendum was held to determine if the people of Djibouti wished to remain a colony of France. Electoral manipulation condoned by the French meant the country remained a French overseas territory with the Afar dominating local politics. The vote was achieved by arresting opposition leaders and by the massive expulsion of Somalis, many of whom went on to join the Somali Coast Liberation Front. In 1973 the Afar still dominated local politics and reaffirmed Djibouti's links with France but by the mid 1970's Issa opposition to Afar rule grew, culminating in an assasination attempt on the Afar leader, Ali Aref in 1975.

International pressure from the Arab League and the OAU, local unrest and the increasingly turbulent situation in the horn of Africa eventually led to the French withdrawing from Djibouti in 1976. An independent referendum was held in which a predominantly Issa assembly was elected headed by Hassan Ghouled, leader of the Ligue Populaire Africaine pour l'Independance (LPAI).

Independence

Self-determination did not bring harmony to the former colony and tensions between the Afar and Issa have been a feature of the last 15 years.

In 1981 the Rassemblement Populaire Pour le Progrès (RPP) was declared the sole legal political party.

Hostilities broke out in the late 1980's after Aden Robleh Abwalleh, a former cabinet minister was expelled from the party for opposing Hassan Ghouled and the existing regime. Abwalleh fled the country and formed a new opposition party, the Mouvement National Djiboutien pour l'Instauration de la Démocratie (MNDID). Inter-tribal hostilities erupted in Djibouti city in 1989 and in the Afar town of Tadjourah. Security forces subsequently arrested several hundred people, some of whom were deported. From 1990-2 a number of opposition parties were formed to press for political reform. Among these was the Front Pour la Restauration de l'Unité et de la Democratie (FRUD), an Afar-based group committed to armed conflict. FRUD suffered a set-back from a determined government assault in July 1993, and has now retreated to the mountains in the north. FRUD has been further weakened by an internal split, and the government has begun negotiations with one of the factions. As a result of the conflict, approximately 15,000 Afars have fled to Ethiopia.

A new constitution was drawn up in 1992 and a multi-party system has been introduced. Ghouled was re-elected as president of the country and many opposition leaders have been released from custody. In the 1999 elections, President Ghouled stood down, and his successor as leader of the ruling party, Ismael Omar Guellah was elected President with an emphatic majority over a combined opposition candidate.

Djibouti still has close links with France and over 3,500 French troops remain on its territory.

Djibouti

Culture

The population of the country is thought to be around 500,000 though seasonal migrations of the nomadic peoples who make up about half the population of the country make any accurate figures hard to estimate.

The indigenous population of Djibouti is evenly divided between the Issa who are of Somali origin and mainly occupy the south part of the country, and the Afar who live in the north part of the country. Both the Afar and the Issa are Muslim Cushitic-speaking peoples with a nomadic culture and close cultural affinities despite frequent rivalry. Both groups spill across the artificial boundaries of Djibouti into neighbouring Somalia and Ethiopia. There are also many refugees, about 30,000, who have fled into the country as a result of various wars in neighbouring Ethiopia, Ogaden and Somalia. Expatriates, mostly French, make up the rest of the population and are mainly in government employment or are members of the armed forces.

Religion   Largely Sunni Muslim (96 percent) though there are a small number of Christians (4 percent).

Modern Djibouti

Politics

Since independence, politics in Djibouti have been heavily influenced by events in the neighbouring countries of Somalia and Ethiopia reflecting the sympathies of the Issa to Somalia and Afar to Ethiopia. In 1977, just after independence, tension between the two groups was considerable over the Ogaden war between Ethiopia and Somalia (Somalia were trying to recapture the region which had strong ethnic links with its people), with the Issa supporting Somalian interests. President Hassan Ghouled used the initial Somali successes in the Ogaden war as an opportunity to remove Afars from key posts in the administration and security forces. As a result, Ethiopia reduced its trading activities through Djibouti which had negative effects on the country's economy.

The Ethiopian victory in the Ogaden war (won with Russian and Cuban support) highlighted the importance of Djibouti's links with that country and led to President Ghouled to try to reach a compromise between the interests of the Issa and the Afar. Thus, the majority of Afar prisoners were released and any Afar who had been removed from office was reinstated into the civil service and security forces. Also, efforts were made to develop the north Afar region of the territory.

A further source of political and economic discontent has been the substantial flow of refugees from the Eritrean and Ogaden conflicts in Ethiopia into Djibouti since the early 1980's. The United Nations High Commission for Refugees (UNHCR) has begun a programme to repatriate Ethiopian refugees, said to number about 35,000, but has only had limited success. This problem has been exacerbated by the number of immigrants flooding in from Somalia – by 1993 these were estimated to number 120,000. Djibouti has attempted to tighten its border controls and the checking of identity papers, but has not really succeeded in materially stemming the flow. The high influx of peoples not only places an economic burden on the country, but is also a source of insecurity as it damages the balance between the Issa and Afar.

Djibouti's geographical position, and limited natural resource base, has meant that good relations with its neighbours are essential. Since 1985, Djibouti has developed agreements with Ethiopia and Somalia for closer co-operation in transport, communication and trade. It has played an important role in developing diplomatic relations between Ethiopia and Somalia, firstly by promoting the creation of the Intergovernmental Authority on Drought and Development with a permanent secretariat in Djibouti, and secondly by bringing heads of state of the two countries to meet and agree to re-establish diplomatic relations and withdraw troops from their common borders.

In recent years the dissatisfaction among the Afars at their marginalization has led to the formation of the Front Pour la Restauration de l'Unité et Democratic (FRUD) which has pursued a policy of armed conflict against the government.

At the election in 1991, the RPP gained all 65 seats in the Assembly. The main opposition, Parti pour le Renouveau Démocratique (PRD) polled 28 percent of the popular vote. Two other parties have been recognized, Groupe pour la Démocratie de la République (GDR), and Parti National Democratique (PND). The constitution, drawn up with French advice, allows only four parties.

The White Train and the Black Arrow

Emperor Menelik II, the architect of modern Ethiopia, conceived the idea of a rail line from Djibouti to Addis Ababa. A pair of European engineers formed the Compagnie Imperiale des Chemins de Fer Ethiopiens, and bolstered by the Franco-Ethiopian Treaty of 1897, French financiers backed the project. Construction started the same year.

The terrain was difficult, mostly desert and mountains, and Addis Ababa is 2.5 kilometres higher than Djibouti. Avoiding the most obstructive features added another 150 kilometres to the line on its way up to the Ethiopian capital. Local labour was supremely uninterested in joining the work-camps building the line, and most of the labourers and all the skilled craftsmen were imported for the job. The nomads along the route gleefully took the iron rails, pins and fittings to fashion into spears, bracelets and necklaces. They grumbled about their cattle being killed by the locomotives, so the company agreed to compensate them for every animal lost. This was the signal for the pastoralists to round up every sick, halt and lame beast in the horn of Africa and lay fodder for them on the tracks.

By 1900, the line had got to Dire Dawa, and a watering post and repair workshops were established there. The traffic was limited on this stretch, and the company went bankrupt in 1907. A new company with loans guaranteed by the French governent was formed in 1908, and a single line of one metre gauge, 748 kilometres long, finally reached Addis Ababa in 1917.

Two trains departed in each direction each day, and stopped at 32 stations along the line. Passengers were taken in the White Train which travelled only in the day and took two and a half days to make the whole journey. Freight went by the Black Arrow which took five days, at an average speed of under seven kilometres per hour.

Having a virtual monopoly of transport up to the capital of the Mountain Kingdom enabled the line to charge high rates, and the company was reported to be the most profitable in the entire history of railways. This was particularly the case in the period 1936-8 when the Italians were obliged to ship vast quantities of men and munitions up to Addis Ababa in their effort to subdue the country. So stung were the Italians by the charges that they built a road from Addis to the port of Assab in Eritrea (which they controlled), and imported 400 trucks to haul freight. So good was this road that the winner of the motorcycle race staged in 1938 to inaugurate the route won at an average speed of 85 kilometres per hour. Competition from the road heralded the end of the highly profitable era for the line.

When the British captured Ethiopia from the Italians in 1941, they ran the line until 1946, when ownership was restored to the original French company. In 1959, the Ethiopian government took half ownership of the railway, by which time diesel locomotives had cut the travel time up to Addis to 24 hours.

A determined assault by government forces in 1993, reduced FRUD to carrying on its activities by cross-border raids. However, the army increased in size from 3,000 troops in 1991 to 18,000 by 1994. The government would like to demobilize half these troops, and is looking to raise US$15 million from the donor community to make severance payments of US$1,500 per head.

A peace initiative in 1994 succeeded with one faction in FRUD, and two FRUD members were given cabinet posts. The other wing of FRUD, led fom Paris by former prime minister Ahmed Dini, continues the armed struggle.

In the elections in December 1997, the alliance between RPP and FRUD won all 65 seats in the National Assembly.

In the April 1999 elections, the nephew of President Ghouled, Ismael Omar Guelleh, took over as leader of RPP. PND and PRD formed the Opposition Djiboutienne Unifiée to fight for the Presidency with Moussa Ahmed Idriss, a former RPP deputy as candidate. Guelleh took 74 percent of the vote, and with RPP holding all the seats in the assembly, will lead a strong government.

The border dispute conflict that erupted between Ethiopia and Eritrea in 1998 has led to Djibouti breaking diplomatic relations with Eritrea. As Djibouti has gained enormously from the re-routing of Ethiopian freight through its port, it is hard to see this as anything other than cynical opportunism. The presence of French troops, however, continues to maintain stability, and Djibouti City remains secure.

Economics

Economic data is sparse for Djibouti. Nevertheless, such information as is available is presented and gives a reasonable overall picture of economic conditions in the territory.

Economic structure Estimates for 1999 suggest a population of 662,000. It is thought that over 100,000 of these are refugees from Somalia, but it is difficult to be certain as to the exact numbers. There is a density of 27 persons to the square kilometre, and although this is not greatly different from elsewhere in Africa, it has to be viewed in the context of Djibouti's arid terrain. Population growth is 2.9 percent a year is quite high, and kept at this level by regular influxes of refugees from troubled neighbouring states. About half of the population live in the town of Djibouti which has a population of over 300,000.

GDP in 1993 was estimated at US$284 million. The level of income per head, converting local currency to US$ using exchange rates, is estimated at US$442, and Djibouti is classified as a lower middle income country.

The economy relies heavily on the port facilities it provides, and this is reflected in the structure of the economy with agriculture providing only 3 percent of GDP, industry 21 percent and services 76 percent.

The demand structure of the economy indicates that private consumption represents 71 percent of GDP. Gross domestic investment absorbed 12 percent of GDP. Government consumption was 38 percent.

The openness of the economy resulting from small size and specilized activities is reflected in 35 percent of GDP being generated by exports. Apart from the export of port services, there are exports of livestock, hides and skins to Somalia, Yemen, Saudi Arabia and Ethiopia. Expenditure on imports is equivalent to 68 percent of GDP. The gap is mainly covered by foreign assistance with France the main benefactor. In fact aid, at US$250 per head is many times greater than the Africa average of US$36.

Overall, Djibouti has a small economy with high urbanization at 86 percent. The economy depends heavily on the supply of port services, levels of government expenditure appear high, and there is a substantial deficit on the current account of the balance of payments.

Economic performance GDP is estimated to have fallen at 1.5 percent a year 1993-98 and GDP per head will have declined at 4.4 percent a year. The record for GDP per head growth is poor, and this is mostly due to the influx of refugees leading to such a large increase in the population allied until recently to stagnant demand for port services from Ethiopia. Living standards are estimated to have fallen by 20 percent during the 1991-4 civil war, and unemployment rose to 50 percent.

However, since the border dispute between Ethiopia and Eritrea erupted in 1998, Ethiopia has ceased using the Eritrean ports of Massawa and Assab, and has routed all its freight through Djibouti. This has been an enormous boost for Djibouti, with freight handling in some months more than ten times the normal level.

Inflation is low, and is running at under 5 percent a year. The exchange rate has been reasonably steady around DFr180 = US$1 in recent years.

External debt is around US$280 million, and debt service is quite manageable, taking up only 5.2 percent of export earnings.

The completion of a new container terminal in 1984, at a cost of US$142 million, is expected to be the country's major source of revenue up to the end of the 1990's. Customs-free port facilities are offered for storage and freight in transit. Traffic with Ethiopia fell after the 1977-8 Ogaden war, and Djibouti hoped to increase trans-shipment traffic to other regional ports to compensate for this loss. However, results have been disappointing. Port up-grading has continued, and tonnage handled almost doubled in 1990 as a result of the Gulf War. France provided US$8 million for further dock modernization and management improvement. With economic improvement in Ethiopia this has led to a doubling of port traffic since 1996.

Recent economic developments

Parastatal organizations have accumulated arrears, with the airport US$2.8 million behind with payments to creditors on a US$22 million upgrading programme. 19 parastatals in all, including water, electricity and the airport are scheduled for privatisation. Air Djibouti with an accumulated deficit of US$4 million has been liquidated but reformed under the private ownership of middle-east business interests.

Two geothermal drillings of a 4-well US$16.6 million drilling programme have not yielded water of high enough temperature in the Hanle Gaggade region to make them commercially viable, but later drillings in the Goubet-Lac-Assal region appear more promising. It is hoped that the wells could meet Djibouti's electricity needs, and the programme is being funded by the International Development Association of the World Bank, Italy, the African Development Bank, the OPEC Fund for International Development and the UN Development Programme.

Construction of an US$800 million petroleum refinery began in 1990, and was expected to come on-stream in 1994. This may now be delayed because of disturbances caused by FRUD's activities.

A major source of income is the use of Djibouti by the French as their main overseas military base. With 3,200 troops stationed in the port, the military community is more than 6,000, and contributes an estimated US$53 to the economy. The number of troops is to be cut by a fifth, and this will have a marked effect in depressing local incomes.

It is assumed that Djibouti's stability will remain good, with continuing French support and military presence. The activities of FRUD are containable, and the government will hope support for the remaining FRUD faction still fighting on will diminish in the new multiparty setting. In the long-term, Djibouti's outlook is particularly sensitive to the strength of economic recovery in Ethiopia, and progress in the Somaliland Republic. Recent expansion of the economy in Ethiopia and the dispute with Eritrea has caused a massive increase in port traffic. This seems likely to boost the economy at least until the dispute is resolved. The coming years should see steady economic growth, although the refugee problem will continue to hamper improvements in living standards until the Somali situation is resolved.

Economic outlook

Djibouti

Social conditions

Adult literacy at 19 percent is very poor, well below the average for Africa, and well out of line with Djibouti's middle-income status. Primary and secondary enrolments are also low and and below the Africa averages. There is little tertiary education in Djibouti, and most students have to seek higher education places overseas.

Life expectancy is 49 years, and infant mortality is high, both of these being worse than for Africa generally. Availability of doctors is very good, however almost ten times better than the rest of Africa. Clearly there is good provision for the elite, and very poor provision for others. Nutrition provision is adequate to meet minimum requirements.

Females have significantly less access to both primary and secondary education compared with males, and Djibouti is less egalitarian in this respect than the rest of Africa. On average women bear 6.6 children, and this presents a formidable challenge in providing adequate nutrition, shelter and clothing in the poorer families.

Environment

Djibouti has negligible forest area, but what little exists is being maintained.

Despite being very arid, the population uses only 2 percent of renewable freshwater resources each year. This is because per capita utilization, at 30 cubic metres per person a year, is well below the African average of 120 cubic metres per person. Low utilisation, in turn, results from the small size of the agriculture sector and low demand for water for irrigation.

Footnotes

9

Footnotes

Shorts

Significant pieces on and about East Africa

Footnotes

Footnotes

Advertisers

Footnotes

Index

Note: grid references to the colour maps are shown in italics after place names.
So 'Arusha M3A4' can be found on Map 3, square B2.

Footnotes

Maps

Footnotes

Complete listing

Latin America
Argentina Handbook 1st
1 900949 10 5 £11.99
Bolivia Handbook 1st
1 900949 09 1 £11.99
Bolivia Handbook 2nd
1 900949 49 0 £12.99
Brazil Handbook 1st
0 900751 84 3 £12.99
Brazil Handbook 2nd
1 900949 50 4 £13.99
Caribbean Islands Handbook 2000
1 900949 40 7 £14.99
Chile Handbook 2nd
1 900949 28 8 £11.99
Colombia Handbook 1st
1 900949 11 3 £10.99
Cuba Handbook 1st
1 900949 12 1 £10.99
Cuba Handbook 2nd
1 900949 54 7 £10.99
Ecuador & Galápagos Handbook 2nd
1 900949 29 6 £11.99
Mexico Handbook 1st
1 900949 53 9 £13.99
Mexico & Central America Handbook 2000
1 900949 39 3 £15.99
Peru Handbook 2nd
1 900949 31 8 £11.99
South American Handbook 2000
1 900949 38 5 £19.99
Venezuela Handbook 1st
1 900949 13 X £10.99
Venezuela Handbook 2nd
1 900949 58 X £11.99

Africa
East Africa Handbook 2000
1 900949 42 3 £14.99
Morocco Handbook 2nd
1 900949 35 0 £11.99
Namibia Handbook 2nd
1 900949 30 X £10.99
South Africa Handbook 2000
1 900949 43 1 £14.99
Tunisia Handbook 2nd
1 900949 34 2 £10.99
Zimbabwe Handbook 1st
0 900751 93 2 £11.99

Wexas
Traveller's Handbook
0 905802 08 X £14.99
Traveller's Healthbook
0 905802 09 8 £9.99

Asia
Cambodia Handbook 2nd
1 900949 47 4 £9.99
Goa Handbook 1st
1 900949 17 2 £9.99
Goa Handbook 2nd
1 900949 45 8 £9.99
India Handbook 2000
1 900949 41 5 £15.99
Indonesia Handbook 2nd
1 900949 15 6 £14.99
Indonesia Handbook 3rd
1 900949 51 2 £15.99
Laos Handbook 2nd
1 900949 46 6 £9.99
Malaysia & Singapore Handbook 2nd
1 900949 16 4 £12.99
Malaysia Handbook 3rd
1 900949 52 0 £12.99
Myanmar (Burma) Handbook 1st
0 900751 87 8 £9.99
Nepal Handbook 2nd
1 900949 44 X £11.99
Pakistan Handbook 2nd
1 900949 37 7 £12.99
Singapore Handbook 1st
1 900949 19 9 £9.99
Sri Lanka Handbook 2nd
1 900949 18 0 £11.99
Sumatra Handbook 1st
1 900949 59 8 £9.99
Thailand Handbook 2nd
1 900949 32 6 £12.99
Tibet Handbook 2nd
1 900949 33 4 £12.99
Vietnam Handbook 2nd
1 900949 36 9 £10.99

Europe
Andalucía Handbook 2nd
1 900949 27 X £9.99
Ireland Handbook 1st
1 900949 55 5 £11.99
Scotland Handbook 1st
1 900949 56 3 £10.99

Middle East
Egypt Handbook 2nd
1 900949 20 2 £12.99
Israel Handbook 2nd
1 900949 48 2 £12.99
Jordan, Syria & Lebanon Handbook 1st
1 900949 14 8 £12.99

Sales & distribution

Footprint Handbooks
6 Riverside Court
Lower Bristol Road
Bath BA2 3DZ England
T 01225 469141
F 01225 469461
E Mail info@
footprintbooks.com

Australia
Peribo Pty
58 Beaumont Road
Mt Kuring-Gai
NSW 2080
T 02 9457 0011
F 02 9457 0022

Austria
Freytag-Berndt Artaria
Kohlmarkt 9
A-1010 Wien
T 01 533 2094
F 01 533 8685

Reiseladen
Dominikanerbastei 4
A-1010 Wien
T 0222 513 8936
F 0222 513 893619

Belgium
Craenen BVBA
Mechelsesteenweg 633
B-3020 Herent
T 016 23 90 90
F 016 23 97 11

Canada
Ulysses Travel Publications
4176 rue Saint-Denis
Montréal
Québec H2W 2M5
T 514 843 9882
F 514 843 9448

Caribbean
Kingston Publishers
10, LOJ Industrial Complex
7 Norman Road
Kingston CSO
Jamaica
T 001876 928 8898
F 001876 928 5719

Europe
Bill Bailey
16 Devon Square
Newton Abbott
Devon TQ12 2HR. UK
T 01626 331079
F 01626 331080

Denmark
Kilroy Travel
Skindergade 28
DK-1159 Copenhagen K
T 33 11 00 44
F 33 32 32 69

Nordisk Korthandel
Studiestraede 26-30 B
DK-1455 Copenhagen K
T 3338 2638
F 3338 2648

Scanvik Books
Esplanaden 8B
DK-1263 Copenhagen K
T 33 12 77 66
F 33 91 28 82

Finland
Akateeminen Kirjakauppa
Keskuskatu 1
FIN-00100 Helsinki
T 09 12141
F 09 121 4441

Suomalainen Kirjakauppa
Koivuvaarankuja 2
01640 Vantaa 64
F 08 52 78 88

France
L'Astrolabe
46 rue de Provence
F-75009 Paris 9e
T 1 42 85 42 95
F 1 45 75 92 51

VILO Diffusion
25 rue Ginoux
F-75015 Paris
T 01 45 77 08 05
F 01 45 79 97 15

Germany
GeoCenter ILH
Schockenriedstrasse 44
D-70565 Stuttgart
T 0711 781 94610
F 0711 781 94654

Brettschneider
Fernreisebedarf
Feldkirchnerstrasse 2
D-85551 Heimstetten
T 089 990 20330
F 089 990 20331

Geobuch Gmbh
Rosental 6
D-80331 München
T 089 265030
F 089 263713

Gleumes
Hohenstaufenring 47-51
D-50674 Köln
T 0221 215650

Globetrotter Ausrustungen
Wiesendamm 1
D-22305 Hamburg
F 040 679 66183

Dr Götze
Bleichenbrücke 9
D-2000 Hamburg 1
T 040 3031 1009-0

Hugendubel Buchhandlung
Nymphenburgerstrasse 25
D-80335 München
T 089 238 9412
F 089 550 1853

Kiepert Buchhandlung
Hardenbergstrasse 4-5
D-10623 Berlin 12
T 030 311880

Greece
GC Eleftheroudakis
17 Panepistemiou
Athens 105 64
T 01 331 4180-83
F 01 323 9821

India
Roli Books
M-75 GK II Market
New Delhi 110048
T (011) 646 0886
F (011) 646 7185

Israel
Geographical Tours
8 Tverya Street
Tel Aviv 63144
T 03 528 4113
F 03 629 9905

Italy
Librimport
Via Biondelli 9
I-20141 Milano
T 02 8950 1422
F 02 8950 2811

Kenya
Textbook Centre
Kijabe Street
PO Box 47540
Nairobi
T 2 330340
F 2 225779

Netherlands
Nilsson & Lamm bv
Postbus 195
Pampuslaan 212
N-1380 AD Weesp
T 0294 494949
F 0294 494455

Norway
Schibsteds Forlag A/S
Akersgata 32 - 5th Floor
Postboks 1178 Sentrum
N-0107 Oslo
T 22 86 30 00
F 22 42 54 92

Tanum
PO Box 1177 Sentrum
N-0107 Oslo 1
T 22 41 11 00
F 22 33 32 75

Olaf Norlis
Universitetsgt 24
N-1062 Oslo
T 22 00 43 00

Pakistan
Pak-American Commercial
Zaib-un Nisa Street
Saddar
PO Box 7359
Karachi
T 21 566 0418
F 21 568 3611

South Africa
Faradawn CC
PO Box 1903
Saxonwold 2132
T 011 885 1787
F 011 885 1829

South America
Humphrys Roberts
Associates
Caixa Postal 801-0
Ag. Jardim da Gloria
06700-970 Cotia SP
Brazil
T 011 492 4496
F 011 492 6896

Southeast Asia
APA Publications
38 Joo Koon Road
Singapore 628990
T 865 1600
F 861 6438

Spain
Altaïr
Balmes 69
08007 Barcelona
T 93 3233062
F 93 4512559

Bookworld España
Pje Las Palmeras 25
29670 San Pedro Alcántara
Málaga
T 95 278 6366
F 95 278 6452

Libros de Viaje
C/Serrano no 41
28001 Madrid
T 01 91 577 9899
F 01 91 577 5756

Sweden
Hedengrens Bokhandel
PO Box 5509
S-11485 Stockholm
T 8 6115132

Kart Centrum
Vasagatan 16
S-11120 Stockholm
T 8 111699

Lantmateriet Kartbutiken
Kungsgatan 74
S-11122 Stockholm
T 08 202 303
F 08 202 711

Switzerland
Artou
8 rue de Rive
CH-1204 Geneva
T 022 311 4544
F 022 781 3456

Office du Livre OLF SA
ZI 3, Corminboeuf
CH-1701 Fribourg
T 026 467 5111
F 026 467 5466

Schweizer Buchzentrum
Postfach
CH-4601 Olten
T 062 209 2525
F 062 209 2627

Travel Bookshop
Rindermarkt 20
Postfach 216
CH-8001 Zürich
T 01 252 3883
F 01 252 3832

USA
NTC/ Contemporary
4255 West Touhy Avenue
Lincolnwood
Illinois 60646-1975
T 847 679 5500
F 847 679 2494

Will you help us?

We try as hard as we can to make each Footprint Handbook as up-to-date and accurate as possible but, of course, things always change. Many people write to us - with corrections, new information, or simply comments.

If you want to let us know about an experience or adventure - hair-raising or mundane, good or bad, exciting or boring or simply something rather special - we would be delighted to hear from you. Please give us as precise information as possible, quoting the edition number (you'll find it on the front cover) and page number of the Handbook you are using.

Your help will be greatly appreciated, especially by other travellers. In return we will send you details about our special guidebook offer.

Write to Elizabeth Taylor
Footprint Handbooks
6 Riverside Court
Lower Bristol Road
Bath
BA2 3DZ
England
or email info@footprintbooks.com

EXPLORE A CONTINENT
WITH KENYA AIRWAYS

It's not just Kenya
when you fly
with Kenya Airways!

From our Nairobi base,
we serve 20 points across
Africa, as well as The
Seychelles - giving you
the choice of top cities
such as Johannesburg,
classic safari gateways
like Harare or popular
beach destinations such
as Mombasa.

Transferring in Nairobi is
convenient and quick,
with Kenya Airways'
dedicated transit lounge
providing additional
comfort.

With an eigth-times-a
week service from
London-Heathrow to
Nairobi, no-one knows
Africa like us.
So explore a continent
with Kenya Airways ...
the airline for Africa.

Tel: 01784 888222   www.kenyaairways.co.uk

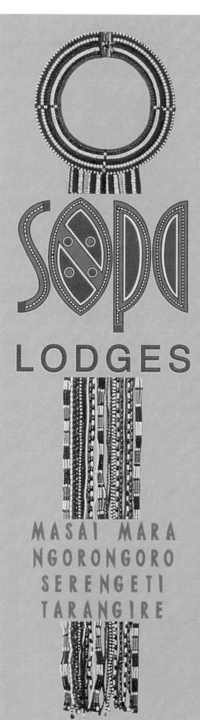

There are many elements which go towards making an unforgettable safari holiday - magnificent wildlife in the parks, staggeringly beautiful scenery, friendly people and safari lodges designed with modern day comfort in mind. Add the extra special ingredient - Sopa Hospitality and discover true safari magic.

All-suite, luxury safari lodges located in the best game parks of East Africa.

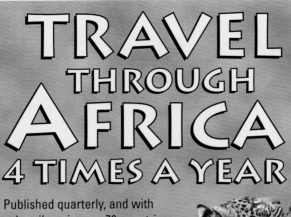

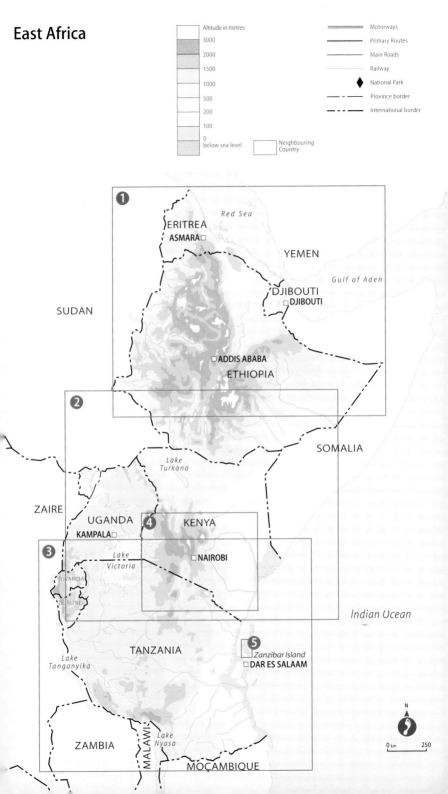

East Africa

Altitude in metres

3000
2000
1500
1000
500
200
100
0
below sea level

Neighbouring Country

Motorways
Primary Routes
Main Roads
Railway
National Park
Province border
International border

1

Red Sea

ERITREA
ASMARA □

YEMEN

Gulf of Aden

SUDAN

DJIBOUTI
□ DJIBOUTI

□ ADDIS ABABA
ETHIOPIA

2

SOMALIA

Lake Turkana

ZAIRE

UGANDA
KAMPALA □

4 KENYA

3

Lake Victoria

□ NAIROBI

RWANDA

BURUNDI

Indian Ocean

TANZANIA

5 Zanzibar Island
□ DAR ES SALAAM

Lake Tanganyika

Lake Nyasa

N

ZAMBIA

MALAWI

MOÇAMBIQUE

0 km   250

YEMEN

N

0 km   80

Ed

Beylul

Assab

Gulf of Aden

Debaysima

Moulhoule

DJIBOUTI

Bab el Mandeb

Balho

Randa

Obock

Galafi

Gulf of
Tadjoura

DJIBOUTI

Yoboki

Ali-Sabieh

Abhe Lake

Dikhil

angudi Rassa
National Park

Aysha

SOMALIA

Ahmar Mts

Dire Dawa

Kulubi

Harar

Jijiga

Asbe Teferi

Harar Wildlife
Sanctuary

Degeh Bur

Domo

Bircot

Megalo

Imí

Shilabo

Wabe Shebele River

Kelafo

4

5

6

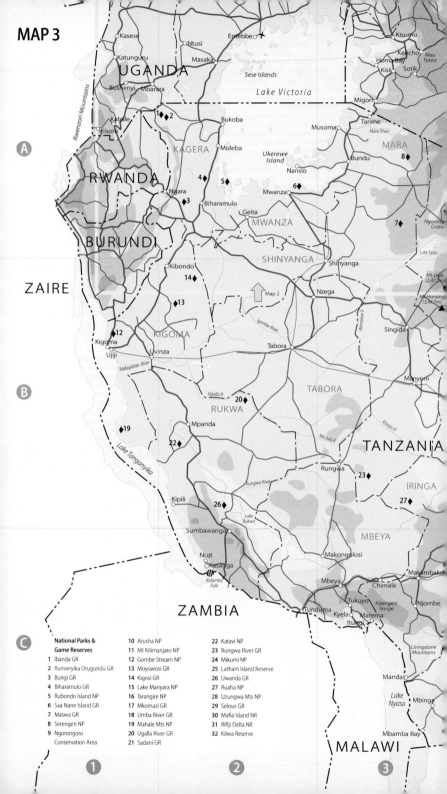

MAP 3

UGANDA

Kasese · Ntusi · Entebbe · Kisumu

Katunguru · Masaka · Kelicho · Mau Forest

Homa Bay · Kisii · Sotik

Rwenzori Mountains

Bushenyi · Mbarara

Sese Islands

Lake Victoria

Migori

Kabale · 1 ◆ 2 · Bukoba · Musoma · Tarime · Mara River

Kisoro

RWANDA

KAGERA · Muleba · Ukerewe Island · Nansio · Bundu · **MARA** · 8 ◆

Ngara · 4 ◆ · 5 ◆ · Ngorongoro Crater · 7 ◆

3 ◆ · Biharamulo · Geita · Mwanza · 6 ◆

MWANZA · Lake Eyasi

BURUNDI

ZAIRE

Kibondo · **SHINYANGA** · Shinyanga · Mt Lega (2,417m)

14 ◆ · Nzega · Mt Hanang (3,417m)

13 ◆ · Map 2 · Igombe River · Singida

KIGOMA · Tabora

12 ◆ · Kigoma · Uvinza

Ujiji · Malagarasi River

BURUNDI

Ugalla R · **RUKWA** · 20 ◆ · **TABORA** · Manyoni

19 ◆ · Mpanda · Nkululu R · Kizigo R

22 ◆ · **TANZANIA**

Rungwa River · Rungwa · 23 ◆ · **IRINGA**

Kipili · 26 ◆ · Lake Rukwa · 27 ◆

Lake Tanganyika

Sumbawanga · **MBEYA**

Nuzi · Kasanga · Makongolosi · Makambako

Kalamba Falls · Mbeya · Chimala · Njombe

Tukuyu · Kipengere Range

ZAMBIA · Tunduma · Kyela · Matema · Livingstone Mountains

Itungi

Manda

Lake Nyasa · Mbinga

Mbamba Bay

MALAWI

National Parks & Game Reserves

1 Ibanda GR	10 Arusha NP	22 Katavi NP
2 Rumanyika Orugundu GR	11 Mt Kilimanjaro NP	23 Rungwa River GR
3 Burigi GR	12 Gombe Stream NP	24 Mikumi NP
4 Biharamulo GR	13 Moyowosi GR	25 Latham Island Reserve
5 Rubondo Island NP	14 Kigosi GR	26 Uwanda GR
6 Saa Nane Island GR	15 Lake Manyara NP	27 Ruaha NP
7 Maswa GR	16 Tarangire NP	28 Uzungwa Mts NP
8 Serengeti NP	17 Mkomazi GR	29 Selous GR
9 Ngorongoro Conservation Area	18 Umba River GR	30 Mafia Island NR
	19 Mahale Mts NP	31 Rifiji Delta NR
	20 Ugalla River GR	32 Kilwa Reserve
	21 Sadani GR	

1 · 2 · 3

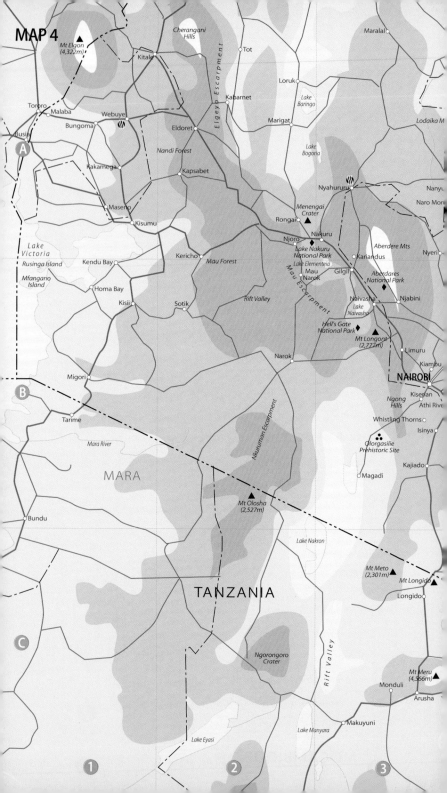

MAP 5 Zanzibar Island

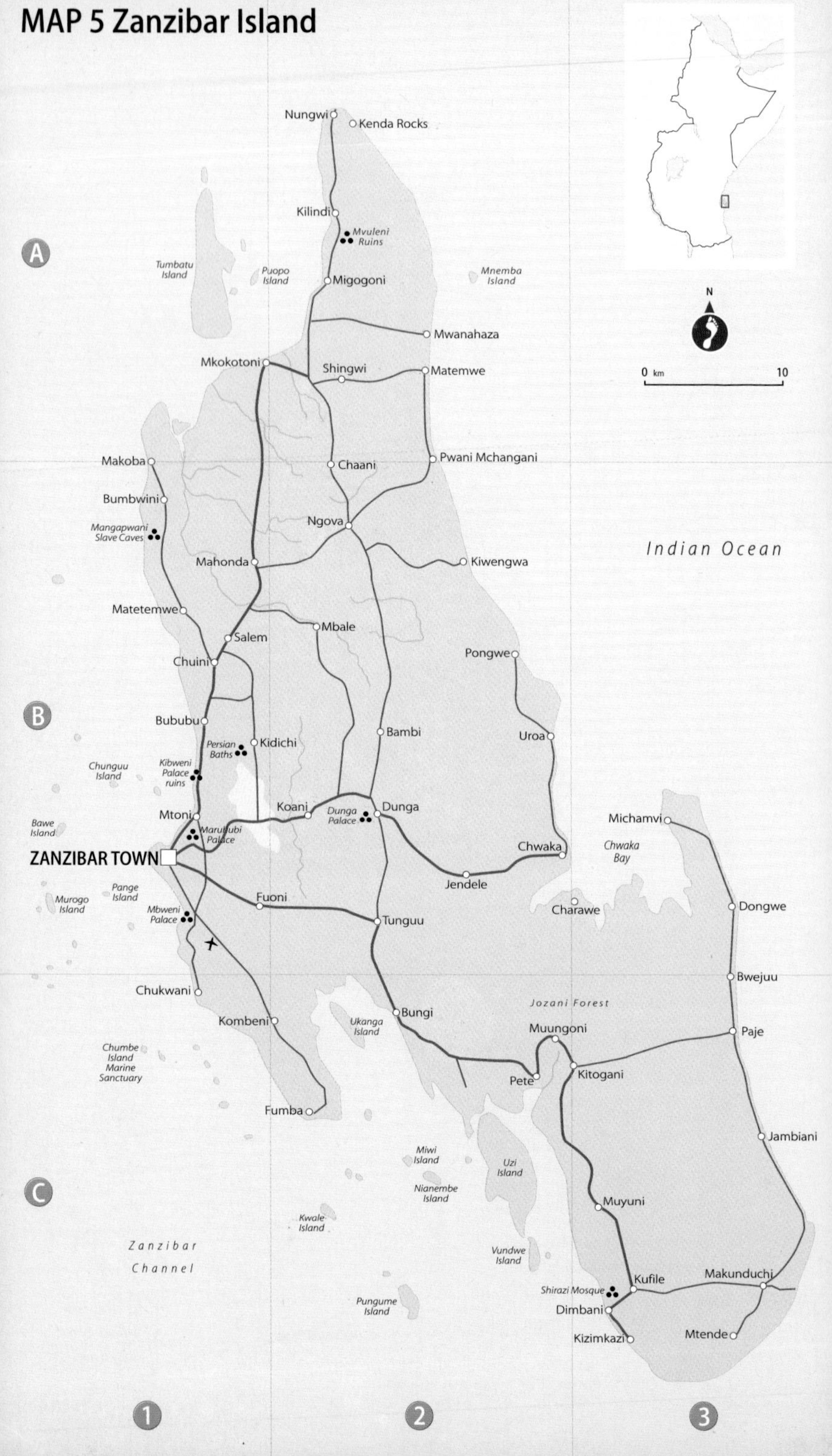

Nungwi
Kenda Rocks

Kilindi
Mvuleni Ruins

A

Tumbatu Island
Puopo Island
Migogoni
Mnemba Island

Mwanahaza

Mkokotoni
Shingwi
Matemwe

Makoba
Chaani
Pwani Mchangani

Bumbwini
Ngova

Mangapwani Slave Caves
Mahonda
Kiwengwa

Indian Ocean

Matetemwe
Salem
Mbale
Pongwe

Chuini

B

Bububu
Persian Baths
Kidichi

Chunguu Island
Kibweni Palace ruins
Bambi
Uroa

Bawe Island
Mtoni
Koani
Dunga Palace
Dunga

Marahubi Palace
Chwaka

Michamvi

ZANZIBAR TOWN
Chwaka Bay

Murogo Island
Pange Island
Fuoni
Jendele
Charawe
Dongwe

Mbweni Palace
Tunguu

Chukwani
Bwejuu

Chumbe Island Marine Sanctuary
Kombeni
Ukanga Island
Bungi
Jozani Forest
Muungoni
Paje

Fumba
Pete
Kitogani

Miwi Island
Uzi Island
Jambiani

Nianembe Island

C

Kwale Island
Vundwe Island

Zanzibar Channel
Muyuni

Shirazi Mosque
Kufile
Makunduchi

Pungume Island
Dimbani
Kizimkazi
Mtende

1
2
3

N

0 km 10

Paradies Safaris offers you the opportunity for your dream holiday in Africa's unique wildlife paradise. The company is under owner-management of German biologist Ms. Keil. She has lived in Arusha, Tanzania for the last 15 years and the company's experience and reliability is what you need to make your own safari dream come true. For tailor-made guided tours, walking safaris, Mount Meru and Kilimanjaro climbs and beach holidays on Zanzibar please contact Ms. Keil on Mobitel **00255-811-510334** (she'll ring you back) or send an email to

paradies91@twiga.com

Phone: 00255-811- 510334   Fax: 00255-57-8002 or 8220

PO Box 2632, Arusha, Tanzania

What the papers say

"I carried the South American Handbook in my bag from Cape Horn to Cartagena and consulted it every night for two and a half months. And I wouldn't do that for anything else except my hip flask."

Michael Palin

"Footprint's India Handbook told me everything from the history of the region to where to get the best curry."

Jennie Bond, BBC correspondent

"Of all the main guidebook series this is genuinely the only one we have never received a complaint about."

The Bookseller

"All in all, the Footprint Handbook series is the best thing that has happened to travel guidebooks in years. They are different and take you off the beaten track away from all the others clutching the competitors' guidebooks."

The Business Times, Singapore

Kenya & Tanzania during their trip from Cape Town to Mombasa; but the garland this year adorns the neck of **Caroline Feune** of Delemont, Switzerland, who sent an amazing amount of information, beautifully laid out, with many corrections of our maps, all gathered from her travels through Tanzania, Zanzibar, Kenya, and Ethiopia. Lengthy contributions were received from: **Mike Appleton** of Worthing, Surrey on Tanzania and Zanzibar; **John R. Jones** of London about Tanzania; **Praveen Moman** of Volcanoes Tours, London; **Peter MacDougall** of Essex, UK Representative for Tanganyika Wildlife Safari; **Kay Loffler** of Pinneberg, Germany with Tanzanian information; **Richard Potez** of Sussex, UK for an account of his Tanzanian trip; **Manfred Heine Dusseldor** of Germany covering Tanzania; **Fabian Velezgonalez** of Nairobi Kenya about the Mzizi Cultural Centre; **Warren Moorman** of Colchester, UK who advised us about the increased costs of Balloon Safaris and updated us about accommodation in the Serengeti National Park; **James Moss-Gibbons** of Reading UK with information about Kenya and Tanzania; **Dr K. Deggeller** of TS Roden, The Netherlands who sent us useful updates about Uganda; **Dr J.D. Renton** of Oxford, UK with helpful data about Uganda; **David Foster** of Oxford, UK with advice about cashing TCs and updated information reflecting his Uganda trip; **Miss T. Thomas** of Devon, UK with sketch maps of Addis Ababa and Kisumu; **Emma Sadler** of Southampton who updated us on Rwanda.

Other very useful information came from: **Rolf Lattmann** of Zurich about internet facilities in Dar es Salaam; **Elizabeth Dossett & Carole Tiernan** on safari operators; **Emily Headings** updating price changes in Kenya; **Leonardo Borella** about Watamu; **Mundia Kama**u with infomation on Canyon Gym in Nairobi; **Mark Boekstein** of South Africa who has contributed to previous editions; **Bunyonyi Overland Camp** in Uganda; **Alfred Moser** about Mbuyu Sarari Park in the Selous Game Reserve; **Masaru Yamada** on Tanzanian Game Park fees; **Fi Morley** with notes on Uganda; **Andre Hesselback** of Sweden; **Drew Conroy** of Maine, USA for the information about infrequently visited parts of Northern Tanzania; **Whistling Thorns** in Kenya; **Carolyn Postgate** about Rwanda; **Pascal & Stephanie** on travelling in Uganda; **Ryan Snider** of Cybersafaris Naroibi, Kenya; **Annabel Falcon** of Kampala, Uganda about Gorilla Conservation; **Joerg Andre** with information gathered during his trip to Tanzania; **Shamil Idriss** of Bujumbura in Burundi for his Kenyan information; **Ephrem Mefret-ab**, Head of Information, Ethiopian Embassy, London; **Mr Moindi**, Kenya National Tourist Commission, London; the **Tanzania Trade Centre**, London; **Devota Karamaga** of the Tanzania Tourist Board in Dar-es-Salaam, with thanks for the comprehensive information forwarded to assist us in the update; **Alex** at the Uganda High Commission, London; **Richard Shepherd** of Colchester Essex about Uganda and Kenya; **Mr Harrison** on internal African flights; **Mrs M.W. Good** of Surrey about her early experiences in Kenya; **Ingvar Andersson** of Jarfalla, Sweden recounting his Kilimanjaro experience; **Sue Lawrence-Brown** of Bamburi, Kenya with information about her trip to Tanga; **Tatiana Rosak** of San Francisco, USA on problems with encountered with tour operators; **Marina Josephs** of London about Zanzibar; **Tilde Rye Anderson & Dan Olesen** about Bagamoya and Dar es Salaam; **Iradex** of London, UK; **Ineke Jongerius** of Fort Portal, Uganda; **Samuel Muller** of Stadtsteinach, Germany about accommodation in Mbale, **John Walker** of Weybridge, UK who pointed out some corrections; **Joseph Clavan** of Philadephia, USA over his Safari experience; **Mr & Mrs D.C. Sweeting** of Ipswich, UK for the information about Kikambala; **Moneib** of Touch the Wild Safari, Malindi, Kenya; **Marie Louise Boley** of Whistling Thorns, Kenya; **S.M. Marriott** of Lewa Wildlife Conservancy, Isiolo, Kenya; **Danny Norris** of London on bicycle trips through Ethiopia; **Cam McLeay & Philippa Smith** of Adrift UK; **Kumuka** of London; **Abercrombie & Kent** of London; **Remco van der Voort & Natalia Bezakova** of Utrecht, Netherlands with entries for the Forbidden Handbook; **Baziro Christine** of Sophie's Motel, Entebbe, Uganda.

Acknowledgements

Contributor

Margaret Carswell (Wildlife text) was born on a tea garden in Assam, India, and she spent her early childhood there. From school under the shadow of Mount Everest to the Sussex countryside, these rural surroundings meant that an interest in natural history was inculcated at an early age. During nearly 20 years spent working in a hospital in Uganda she pursued this interest in natural history, and has written papers on Ugandan birds. In other incarnations she has presented a music programme on American radio, worked as a chambermaid and crewed on a cross-Channel Dutch barge.

We thank **Dr David Snashall** for his contribution to the health section. David has practised medicine in Africa in southern Tanzania. He is currently Senior Lecturer in Occupational Health at the United Medical Schools of Guy's & St Thomas' Hospitals in London and is Chief Medical Officer of the British Foreign and Commonwealth Office.

Acknowledgements

Many thanks to my friend and colleague, **Luta Maliyamkono.** He has made it possible for me to visit Africa more times than I ever imagined possible, and we have had a lot of good fun together.

A large number of people have continued to contribute to this book. The excellence of their work is apparent from the finished product. Initial background material came from **Susan Murrell, Grace Carswell** and **Dan Collison.**

For the current edition, your Editor has visited Southwest Uganda and updated the route from Kampala to Kisovo. My wife **Angela** has once again carried the heat and burden of updating including the incorporation of comments from travellers. My son **Jack** observed with some glee that there was "no chance of meeting the book deadline this year as no doubt you will be following your Kenyan friends round the country in the Cricket World Cup".

We are always thrilled when you write in to say nice things about the book, make constructive criticisms and provide information to improve it and keep it up-to-date. This year there were fifty percent more than the usual number of contributors producing first-rate, extensive information well over and above the normal call: **Guenther Schaefer** of Herbertingen, Germany sent us comprehensive notes and corrections about Kenya, Uganda, Ethiopia, Eritrea and Tanzania; **Leigh-Anne Murray** of East Sussex, UK with lots of helpful points on Tanzania; **Thomas Schweiger** of Brussels, Belgium made many useful suggestions about ways to improve the Handbook, much information about Uganda and Tanzania and a diary record of an usually wet journey through Northern Kenya to Moyale; **Anett Drechsler & Henrik Gross** of Kabale, Uganda sent extensive information about Kenya and Uganda including map corrections; **Iain Jackson** of Edinburgh, Scotland provided information about Kenya, Djibouti but mostly about Ethiopia, including lots of good points about muddled information and typos on the Northern circuit; **K.N.G. Nienhuys** of Maastricht, Netherland, after an extended stay in Tanzania sent us lots of excellent information about cycling, villages and towns off the beaten track and the excellent schemes organised by SNV, a Dutch NGO; **Soren Kjeldgaard** of Copenhagen, Denmark provided copious notes about Ethiopia, including an excellent map of how to reach Debre Damo Monastery; **Mila Bianchi & Reto Maurer** of Vacalle, Switzerland sent extensive information about their trip through several East African countries which they visited during their African safari; **Flo Beaumon** of Seattle provided thorough notes collected during her four month trip through Tanzania, Uganda and Ethiopia; **Peter Faulkner & Ruth Taylor** contributed a large amount of information gathered from their travels in